CONTENTS

INTRODUCTION

This is a dictionary based on spoken Japanese, in two parts:
Japanese–English and English–Japanese. It aims to be of immediate use to the beginning student of Japanese who wants to
know the meaning of an expression he has just heard or who
seeks to express himself in ordinary, everyday situations. This
is the place to look for the words to help you get a plumber,
staples for your stapler, or sushi without the horseradish. It will
also help you when you are groping for the appropriate form
of a Japanese verb; here, too, you will find just which different
verbs may converge in a given form, such as **itte** [行って, 要っ
て, 言って], which can mean "going," "needing," or "saying."
This dictionary cannot take the place of a textbook or a reference
grammar, but it can remind you of the important points made by
those books.

If you are primarily interested in reading and writing
Japanese, you will need other tools, but certain features of
this work will be useful to you in unexpected ways. Japanese
sentences can be written using only kana—all hiragana or all
katakana or a mixture of the two. However, the result is often
hard to read because the Japanese do not traditionally use any
device to separate words, such as the spaces we use in English.
Japanese sentences written in romanized form (in any system)
are easier to read because the spaces make the words stand out
individually. Also, judiciously placed hyphens make the structure of compound words more accessible to the eye.

The Japanese normally write their sentences in a mixed script
by using kanji (Chinese characters) for the more salient words,
especially nouns, and hiragana as a kind of neutral background,
appropriate for grammatical endings, particles, and the like.
They also use kana as a kind of fallback, when they are uncertain
or ignorant of the appropriate kanji. By using katakana for modern foreign words and other oddities, and also kanji for the words

bají *n* バッジ badge
báka *n* ばか・バカ・馬鹿 fool, idiot
　báka na *adj* ばかな foolish, stupid
　baká-ni-shimásu *v* ばかにします
　makes a fool of (*a person*)
　baka-bakashíi, baka-rashíi *adj* ばか
　ばかしい absurd, foolish (= **baka-**
　rashíi ばからしい)
　baka-bánashi *n* ばか話 nonsense; idle
　talk; hot air, bull (= **muda-bánashi**
　無駄話)
　báka-me *adj* ばかめ damn (fool) idiot
　baka-shō´jiki (na) *adj* ばか正直(な)
　gullible
...bákari, ...bákkari *suffix* ...ばかり,
　...ばっかり only, just (= **dake** だけ); ~
　de/ja naku ...mo ...ばかりで/じゃな
　く...も not only ..., but also
bakazu-o-fumimásu (fumu) *v* 場数を
　踏みます(踏む) gets a lot of practical
　experience
bakégaku *n* 化学・化け学 chemistry
　(= **kágaku** 化学)
bake-móno *n* 化け物 monster, ghost
　(= **obáke** お化け・おばけ, **yōkai henge**
　妖怪変化)
baken *n* 馬券 betting ticket
baketsu *n* バケツ bucket
bakkin *n* 罰金 fine, penalty
bákku *n* バック back: ~ **shimásu** バック
　します moves back/backward
　bakku-áppu *n* バックアップ backup,
　support
　bakku-mírā *n* バックミラー rearview
　mirror
bákku, baggu *n* バック, バッグ bag
bakuchi *n* 博打 gambling
bakudai (na) *adj* ばくだい(な)
　immense, vast, huge, enormous
bakudan *n* 爆弾 bomb
bákufu *n* 幕府 (*the time of*) the shogunate
　government
bakugeki *n* 爆撃 bombing: ~ **shimásu**
　爆撃します bombs it
　bakugéki-ki *n* 爆撃機 bomber
bakuhatsu *n* 爆発 explosion, bursting
bakuteria *n* バクテリア bacteria
bakuzen (to) *adv* 漠然(と) vaguely,
　obscurely
bámen *n* 場面 scene (= **shiin** シーン)

ban *n* 晩 [BOOKISH] evening, night:
　(**hitó-ban** 一晩 one night, **futá-ban**
　二晩 two nights; **íku-ban** 幾晩 some
　nights, how many nights?; **kon-ban**
　今晩 tonight; **mai-ban** 毎晩 every
　night
　ban-góhan, ban-meshi *n* 晩ご飯,晩飯
　evening meal (*dinner/supper*) (=
　yūshoku 夕食)
bán *n* 番 guard, watch
　ban-ken *n* 番犬 watchdog
　ban-nín *n* 番人 watchman
...-ban *suffix* ...番 number: **ichí-ban**
　一番 number one, **nán-ban** 何番 what
　number?
　ban-chi *n* 番地 address (*house number*):
　nan-bánchi 何番地 what house/lot
　number?
　ban-gō´ *n* 番号 number (*assigned*)
　...-banmé (no) *suffix, adj* ...番目
　(の) [numeral] -th
　...-ban-sen *suffix* ...番線 track
　number ... (*train station*): **nan-bansen**
　何番線 what (number) track?
bānā *n* バーナー burner
bánana *n* バナナ banana
ban-cha *n* 番茶 coarse green tea
bando *n* バンド **1.** strap, band (*watch-
　band, etc.*); belt **2.** band (*music*)
bane (-jíkake) *n* ばね(仕掛け) spring
　(*device*)
bangarō´ *n* バンガロー bungalow
ban-gasa *n* 番傘 oilpaper umbrella
bangumi *n* 番組 program (*TV, etc.*)
Bánkoku *n* バンコク Bangkok
bánkoku *n* 万国 international; all the
　world
　bánkoku-hakurankai, banpaku *n* 万国
　博覧会,万博 international exposition
bánira *n* バニラ vanilla
bannō *n* 万能 versatility, ability to do
　anything
bansō *n* 伴奏 musical accompaniment
bansōko, bansōkō *n* 絆創膏 adhesive
　plaster/tape
banzái *interj* 万歳 hurray!
bara *n* バラ・薔薇 rose (*flower*)
bára (de) *adv* ばら(で) loose,
　separately
barabara (ní) *adv* ばらばら(に)

separate, in pieces: ~ **ni narimásu** ばらばらになります scatters, into pieces

baransu n バランス balance: ~ **o torimásu** バランスをとります redress the balance

barashimásu, barásu v ばらします, ばらす **1.** exposes (*a secret*) **2.** takes it apart, disassembles **3.** kills, shoots (*to death*)

báre n バレエ ballet

barē(bō´ru) n バレー(ボール) volleyball

baremásu, baréru v ばれます, ばれる [INFORMAL] surfaces, is disclosed, is discovered

barenai v ばれない = **baremasén** ばれません (is not disclosed/discovered)

barentáindē n バレンタインデー Valentine's Day

bareriina n バレリーナ ballerina

barikan n バリカン clippers (*barber's*)

bariki n 馬力 horsepower

baromē´tā n バロメーター barometer

barukónii n バルコニー balcony

basho n 場所 **1.** place **2.** a (*two-week*) sumo tournament

bassári adv ばっさり fast and furious, drastically, without hesitation

basshi n 抜歯 pulling out a tooth/teeth

basshimásu, bassuru v 罰します, 罰する punishes

básu n バス bus

basu-téi n バス停 bus stop

basu-gáido n バスガイド bus tour guide

basu-rū´mu n bath, bathroom (= **furo** 風呂)

basu-tsuki バス付き with bath

basue n 場末 suburb (*outskirts*)

basukétto n バスケット **1.** basket **2.** basketball

basukétto bō´ru n バスケットボール basketball, basketball game

básuto n バスト bust

báta n バター butter

batafurai n バタフライ butterfly (*swimming*)

batakusai adj バタ臭い has a Western air

batán (to) adv ばたん(と) with a bang, with a thud

batā-rō´ru n バターロール (butter) roll (*bread*)

bāten(dā) n バーテン(ダー) bartender

batomínton n バトミントン badminton (= **badominton** バドミントン)

baton n バトン baton

baton tatchi n バトンタッチ passing the torch, having someone take over

bátsu n ばつ cross (= X *"wrong"*)

bátsu n 罰 retribution, punishment (= **bachí** 罰)

batta n バッタ grasshopper

báttā n バッター batter (*baseball*)

battári adv ばったり unexpectedly

battén n ばってん X (*"wrong"*), a black mark

batterii n バッテリー battery

battingu n バッティング batting (*baseball*)

bátto n バット bat (*baseball*)

baundo n バウンド bound

bawai, baai n 場合 situation, case, circumstance, occasion

bázā n バザー bazaar

bebiishíttā n ベビー・シッター baby sitter

béddo, bétto n ベッド,ベット bed

beddo-táun n ベット・タウン bedroom community, suburb

Bei n 米 America(*n*): **hoku-bei** 北米 North America: **nan-bei** 南米 South America: **nich-bei** 日米 Japan and America; **ō-bei** 欧米 Europe and America

Béi-koku n 米国 America (= **Amerika** アメリカ)

Bei-koku-jin n 米国人 American (= **Amerika-jin** アメリカ人)

beiju n 米寿 (*auspicious, happy event*) eighty-eighth birthday

beikingu-páudā n ベイキング・パウダー baking powder

... béki *suffix* ...べき: **...-suru ~ desu** するべきです should do, ought to do [BOOKISH]

bekkan n 別館 annex (*building*)

bekkō n ベッコウ・鼈甲 tortoise shell

bekkyo n 別居 separate living: ~ **shimásu** 別居します lives apart; separately

made up of elements borrowed many years ago from China, a writer can make words stand out from the background in a way that partly makes up for the absence of spaces between them.

Unfortunately, the use of kanji tempts the writer into relying entirely on the eye, forgetting that texts might be read over the telephone or listened to in the dark. For this reason, words confusing to the ear should be avoided. As a result, written Japanese today is an artificial and unstandardized medium of communication, varying in complexity with each writer and every text. If you ask ten Japanese to write out a typical long sentence read aloud from a magazine or newspaper, you will probably find you have eight to ten different versions. Many writers feel free to create new words and abbreviations based solely on the meanings associated with the kanji, and with total disregard to whether the result is meaningful to the ear.

Yet all of that is a superstructure imposed on the basic language which underlies the written text, and the basic language: Spoken Japanese. That is why it is necessary to approach the written language from a good knowledge of the sentence structure and vocabulary of the spoken language.

GUIDE TO SYMBOLS

A fall of pitch occurs after the marked syllable (denoted by the mark ´). When the accent is on the last, the syllable's fall in pitch is sometimes not apparent unless another word follows it.

    áme 雨   rain
    ashí 足[脚]   foot, leg
    (vowels: **á**, **é**, **í**, **ó**, **ú**; long vowels: **ā´**, **ē´**, **ō´**, **ū´**)

Long vowels **ā**, **ē**, **ō**, and **ū**: Vowels with macrons (a horizontal bar above the letter) are pronounced twice as long as regular vowels.

Examples:		*Meaning*
byōdō (na)	平等（な）	equal
kyūka	休暇	vacation, furlough
pēji	ページ・頁	page

Sounds: The following have suppressed vowels.

Examples:		*Meaning*
i, u		(These vowels are suppressed.)
h̲i̲to	人	person, man, fellow, people
sukḭ-ma	隙間	crack; opening; opportunity

Note: A fuller explanation of the symbols shown above can be found in the Pronunciation.

PRONUNCIATON

In this dictionary, because we are dealing with the spoken language, the words are given in romanized form, based on the Hepburn romanization, which is traditionally favored by foreigners, with a few additional marks to help with the pronunciation. If at first the marks bother you, just disregard them; later you will probably find the notations useful as a reminder of what you have heard.

Japanese phrases are accompanied by little tunes that help the hearer know what words a phrase contains. The tunes consist of a limited number of patterns of higher and lower pitch; each phrase has an inherent pattern. For example, the following common tune is rather monotonous: the pitch is slightly lower on the first syllable, then rises and stays on a plateau for the rest of the word or phrase:

kono kodomo wa nakanai   'this child does not cry'

この 子ども は 泣かない

Yokohama e iku   'goes to Yokohama'
横浜 へ 行く

A less common tune starts high and immediately falls, staying down till the end:

áme des<u>u</u>   雨 です   'it's rain'

Méguro e mo iku 目黒 へ も 行く 'goes to Meguro too'

Other tunes rise to a plateau and then fall at some point before the end:

A**ká**saka   赤坂   'Akasaka'

I**kebú**kuro   池袋   'Ikebukuro'

ya**sumimá**shita   休みました   'rested'

When the accent, i.e., a fall of pitch, is on the last syllable, you sometimes cannot hear it unless another word, such as a particle, is attached:

ha**na (ga akai)**   鼻(が 赤い)   'the nose (is red)'

ha**ná (ga akai)**   花(が 赤い)   'the flower (is red)'

When the change of pitch is within a long syllable, you will probably notice a rise or fall within the syllable, as shown by these place names:

Ōsaka 大阪 = o^{osaka}　　　　　　Kyōto 京都 = ^{kyó}oto

Ryūkū 琉球 = ryu^{ukyú}u

Taitō-ku 台東区 = ta^{itó}oku

When a word has more than one accent mark that means the word has variant forms. Some people may say it with the fall at one of the syllables, others at a different syllable. When an accent mark appears in parentheses, the word is often phrased with the preceding word, which carries an accent. That accounts for the difference between **hírō shimásu** [披露します] 'performs, announces, etc.' and **riyō shimásu** [利用します] 'presumes, uses, etc.'. The accent of a particular word, especially a verb form, may change in certain contexts, as explained in the section on Grammar; the changes often involve an accent acquired or lost on the last syllable of the form. A compound word has an inherent tune that follows rules somewhat independent of those of the component elements.

Japanese speakers often reduce the short vowels **i** and **u** in certain words by devoicing (whispering) them or even suppressing them completely. The vowel reductions are a surface phenomenon, a kind of last-minute touch when you are about to speak your sentence, and they are ignored by the traditional writing system and most transcriptions. But there are many subtleties to the rules that call for **i** and **u** instead of **i** or **u**, and they often involve word boundaries and other grammatical factors. It isn't just a matter of "whisper **i** and **u** when used between voiceless consonants (**p, t, k, f, s, h**)," though that is a good rule. You can have more than one whispered vowel in a word (**kikimáshita** [聞きました] 'I heard it') but not in successive syllables (**kikitai** [聞きたい] 'I want to hear it'). Usually it is the first of two susceptible syllables that are whispered, but not always. Syllables beginning with (**p, t, k**) are more resistant than those that begin with the affricates (**ch** and **ts**). And, syllables beginning with these affricates are more resistant than syllables that begin with fricatives (**f, h, s, sh**), in **rekishi̱-ka** [歴史家] 'historian' (from **rekishi** [歴史] 'history'). In the foregoing fricatives, it is the second of the susceptible syllables that is whispered.

Another general rule is that **i** and **u** are unvoiced at the end of a word that has an inherent accent when that word ends a phrase or sentence. That is why we write all the polite non-past forms as **...másu̱** [...ます].

The vowel will remain voiceless before a voiceless consonant (**dekimásu̱ ka** [できますか] 'Can you do it?') but usually will get voiced before a voiced consonant (**dekimásu ga** [できますが] 'I can, but'). For nouns, however, and for verb forms other than **...másu̱** [...ます], we have not marked as voiceless such cases of final **...i** and **...u**, because so often they are followed by particles or other elements that begin with a voiced consonant. For example, by itself **gásu̱** [ガス] 'gas' is pronounced **gásu̱** (and **dásu̱** [出す] 'puts it out' is pronounced **dásu̱**) but the second syllable will be voiced in the more common phrases that you hear, such as **gásu o tsu̱kéte kudasai** [ガスをつけて下さい] 'turn on the gas.'

When **shimásu̱** [します] 'does' is attached to a noun that ends in a reducible syllable, we write the voiceless vowel: **insatsu̱** [印刷] 'printing' that becomes **insatsu̱ shimásu̱** [印刷します] 'prints it'. (This dictionary does not always call your attention to regular situations that will bring back the voicing, as in **insatsu shi̱te** [印刷して] 'printing it'.) At the beginning of a word (**kusá** [草] 'grass') or in the middle (**enpi̱tsu** [えんぴつ] 'pencil'), an unvoiced vowel remains unvoiced except when the syllables are recited, sounded out, or sung.

The first letter represents a nasal syllable that takes its color from the sounds around it, so that when positioned before a sound made with the lips (**m, b, p**) it sounds like a long **m**.

Before **f**, however, and in all other situations, when the syllable contains the letter **n**, then that 'pamphlet' is pronounced **pánfu-rétto** [パンフレット].

Many Japanese pronounced **fu** as **hu**. The syllable **hi** is often spoken as a palatal fricative (like German *ich*), and you may notice that quite a few speakers make it sound just like **shi**, especially when the i is devoiced; if your ears hear **shito**, be aware that it is very likely just a variant of **hito** [人] 'person.' The lips are not much rounded for the Japanese vowel **u** and are totally disengaged in the syllables **su** and **tsu**, for which the tongue is moved quite far forward, so that the **u** sound is somewhere between **i** and **u**.

We have not shown the distinction between the two kinds of **g** that are used by many speakers because the present-day situation is in flux and the distinction, which carries little semantic weight, is missing in many parts of the country. The prestige pronunciation, however, favors a "softened" form of **...g...** when it is felt to be internal to a word, or begins a particle, as in **... ga** [...が]. The softened form is pronounced through the nose, like the **ng** at the end of English 'sing.' Some speakers use a murmured version of **...g...**, a voiced fricative, instead of the nasal.

The long vowels **ō** and **ū** are written with a macron in virtually all cases, though they are functionally equivalent to double vowels, **oo** and **uu** and are often so transcribed. The long vowels **ā** and **ē** are similar, but except in foreignisms, most cases of long **ē** are written as **ei**, following the practice of the hiragana orthography, which takes into account the fact that in some areas people pronounce **ei** as a diphthong, as once was true everywhere.

The long vowels are written in katakana with a bar (a dash) after the syllable; in hiragana they are written as double vowels **oo**, **uu**, **ii**, **ee**, **aa**, but for historical reasons most often the long **ō** is written **ou**. That is why when you use romanization to type your input for a Japanese word processor you have to write **ho u**

GRAMMAR

ho u to produce the hiragana string that can be converted into the
kanji deemed appropriate for the word **hōhō** [方法] 'method.'
(But you input **Ōsaka** [大阪] as **o o sa ka** because the first element of that name, the **ō** of **ōkíi** [大きい] 'big,' happens to be
one of the handful of common exceptions.) We write the word
for 'beer' as **bíiru** [ビール] instead of putting a long mark over
a single **i** both for esthetic reasons and for linguistic consider-
ations: most cases of long **i** consist of two grammatically different elements, as in the many adjectives that end in **...i-i** or, less
obviously, such nouns as **chíi** [地位] 'position.'

GRAMMAR

This dictionary differs from other dictionaries in a number of
ways. The verb forms are cited primarily in the normal polite
form (**...másu** [...ます]), for that is what the beginning student
will most often hear and practice using at the end of sentences.
Other common forms are also given, such as the plain nonpast (**...u** [...う] or **...ru** [...る]) and the gerund (**...te** [...て]
or **...de** [...で]). The nonpast forms, whether plain or polite,
refer to general, repeated, or future situations ('does' or 'will
do'); they are also used for situations that started in the past
but continue on into the present, such as 'I have been staying here since the day before yesterday' (**ototói kara koko ni
imásu** [おとといからここにいます]), or that have a result
that lasts, such as 'I have gotten married' (**kekkon shite imásu**
[結婚しています]), another way to say 'I am married.'

The past forms ('did') are easily made: for the polite past,
change **...másu** [...ます] to **...máshita** [...ました], and for the
plain, take the gerund and change its final **e** to **a**, with the result
being **...ta** [...た] or **...da** [...だ]. The plain nonpast form for the
[NOUN] **désu** [です] 'it is [a matter of]' is **...dá** [...だ], but that
is replaced by **... no** [...の] or **... na** [...な] when the expression

xi

modifies a following noun. The choice of **... no** [...の] or **... na** [...な] depends on a number of factors that are described in grammars and textbooks. This dictionary gives the appropriate form in parentheses in many cases. The polite past of the [NOUN] **désu** [です] is **... déshita** [...でした], the plain past is **... dátta** [...だった] (even when the nonpast would change to **na** [な] or **no** [の]), and the gerund is **... dé** [...で]). The form **... ni** [...に], in addition to its many uses as a particle ('to,' 'at,' 'for'), also functions as a form of **... désu** [...です], the infinitive in the meaning 'so as to be,' as in **jōzu ni narimáshita né** [上手になりましたね] 'has gotten good at it.'

The infinitive form of verbs (**...i** or **...e**) in spoken Japanese is mainly used to form compounds, and many nouns are derived from infinitives by a change of accent, e.g., **yasumí** [休み] 'vacation' or 'work break' from **yasúmi** [休み] 'to rest'). The common nouns and infinitives derived in this manner are included in the Japanese-English section of this dictionary. The polite negative nonpast forms of verbs are made by changing **...másu** [...ます] to **...masén** [...ません] and the past to **...masén deshita** [...ませんでした]. They are run together as if they are one word; the plain nonpast forms end in **...nai** [...ない] and the plain past forms end in **...nakatta** [...なかった]. The negative gerund is **...´náide** [...ないで], as in **Isogánaide kudasai** [急がないで] 'Don't go so fast,' but before **... mo** [...も] or **... wa** [...は], it is usually **...´ nákute** [...なくて], as in **Isogánakute wa damé desu** [急がなくてはだめです] 'You've got to go fast' and **Tabénakute mo íi desu** [食べなくてもいいです] 'We don't have to eat.' In the English-Japanese section, the citation form for verbs is the English infinitive ('to do' minus the 'to ...'), whereas most Japanese-English dictionaries use the plain nonpast as a citation form; do not confuse that with the English infinitive. This dictionary gives most English translations as third-person singular ('does'), but Japanese verbs nonspecific with reference to person.

Adjectives are cited in the plain forms **-i** [－い] (**samui** [寒い] 'it's cold') for they are often used before a noun, where the plain form is most common. The polite forms appropriate at the end of a sentence end in **...´-i desu** (**samúi desu** [寒いです] 'it's cold'). The plain past is made by replacing **-i** [－い] with **-kátta** [－かった] (**samukátta** [寒かった] 'it was cold'), and the polite past, with **-kátta desu** [－かったです] (**samukátta desu** [寒かったです] 'it was cold'). (Do not confuse **-´i desu** [－いです] and **-kátta desu** [－かったです] with the [NOUN] **désu** [（名詞）です], for which the past is [NOUN] **déshita** [（名詞）でした].) The infinitive ('so as to be') ends in **-ku** [－く], as in **sámuku narimáshita** [寒くなりました] 'it turned cold.' There are many adverbs derived from the adjective infinitive, such as **háyaku** [速く, 早く] 'quickly' or 'early.' And the **-ku** [－く] combines with **arimasén** [ありません] (plain form **nái** [ない]) to make the negative: **sámuku arimasén** [寒くありません] 'it isn't cold,' **sámuku nái hí ni wa** [寒くない日には] 'on days that are not cold.' The past of the negative is **-ku arimasén deshita** [－くありませんでした] (plain past **-ku nákatta** [－くなかった]). The gerund of the adjective ('being ...' or 'is ... and') ends in **-kute** [－くて], and the negative gerund, as in **-ku nákute** [－くなくて].

But many Japanese words that translate as English adjectives belong to a different class of words and are treated more like nouns. For that reason they are sometimes called 'adjectival nouns' or 'nominal adjectives,' but you may want to think of them simply as '**na** words,' since they attach the word **na** ('that/who is ...') when they modify a following noun: **heyá ga shízuka desu** [部屋が静かです] 'the room is quiet,' **shízuka na heyá desu** [静かな部屋です] 'it is a quiet room.' As with nouns, the nonpast form of **na** words is **... désu** [...です] (plain form **dá** [だ] or nothing, but replaced by **no** [の] or **na** [な] before a noun), and the past is **... déshita** [...でした] (plain form

... dátta [...でした]). The negative is **... ja arimasén** [...じゃ
ありません] (plain form **... ja nái** [...じゃない]), the negative
past is **... ja arimasén deshita** [...じゃありませんでした]
(plain form **...ja nákatta** [...じゃなかった]); all are usually
run together with the preceding word to make one long phrase.
The gerund is **... dé** [...で], as in **heyá ga shízuka de kírei desu**
[部屋が静かできれいです] 'the rooms are quiet and clean,'
and **kírei de shízuka na heyá** [きれいで静かな部屋] 'rooms
that are quiet and clean.' The infinitive **... ni** [...に] means 'so
as to be ...' as in **shízuka ni narimáshita** [静かになりまし
た] 'became quiet' or '...ly' as in **shízuka ni asonde imásu**
[静かに遊んでいます] 'is playing quietly.'

In a similar manner, Japanese nouns are often followed by
some form of **... désu** [...です] (often called the "copula"),
replacing a more specific predicate. When the predicate is a
verb or an adjective, the role of the noun is marked by a particle. Because the particles go on the end of the noun, they
are sometimes called "postpositions," a kind of mirror image
of English prepositions: **Kyō´to kara Nára e ikimáshita**
[京都から奈良へ行きました] 'I went from Kyoto to Nara.'
English subjects and objects are usually unmarked except by
word order, but since that is not the case in Japanese, particles
mark the subject and object: **Dáre ga náni o shimásu ka** [誰が
何をしますか] 'Who does what?', **Nani o dáre ga shimásu ka**
[何を誰がしますか] 'Just who does what?'

There is often little semantic need for such marking, for
you can usually tell subjects and objects from the context: it is
usually people who act and things that are acted upon. So if the
particles **... ga** [...が] and **... o** [...を] are omitted, as is required
when you attach **... mo** [...も] 'also ..., even ...' or **... wa** [...は]
'as for ...', you usually still know who is doing what: **Watashi
mo kikimáshita** [私も聞きました] 'I, too, heard it [as did oth-
ers],' **Sore mo kikimáshita** [それも聞きました] 'I heard that
too [as well as other things].'

For many nouns in spoken Japanese, it is quite common to attach a personalizing prefix **o-** [お-], which conveys a vague sense of 'that important thing.' The prefix is also used to make honorific or humble verb forms, with reference to the subject of a sentence. **O-tégami** [お手紙] often means 'your letter,' but does not tell us whether the reference is the letter you have written, or a letter that has been written *to you*; and it can mean just 'the letter' or 'letters,' said with a personalizing touch much appreciated by women and children. Another prefix **go-** [ご-] (**go-ryōshin** [ご両親] 'your parents') attaches to certain nouns (mostly of Chinese origin).

Although these personalized forms are ignored by most dictionaries, we have included many of them, because they are often irregular in accentuation or in some other way. Do not try to use the prefixes **o-** [お-] and **go-** [ご-] with new nouns unless you find the forms in this dictionary or hear them from a Japanese speaker. Honorific and humble verb forms, however, can be made up rather freely, though for certain common verbs they are replaced by euphemisms or unrelated forms; for example, **osshaimásu** [おっしゃいます] 'deigns to say' as the honorific of **iimásu** [言います] 'says.'

KANJI & KANA

Japanese kanji and kana characters have been introduced into the original dictionary and can be found immediately after the romanized forms of the entries. The most contemporary renderings of kanji have been used, including the 2,136 characters from the *jōyō* kanji [常用漢字] list. As it is unreasonable to attempt to convert all romanized words into kanji, kanji is provided only when it is commonly used by the Japanese. In some cases, the kana representation appears before the kanji, and in other cases, after. This means that in the former case kana is most commonly used but at times kanji may be preferable because it conveys the precise meaning of the original word. In the latter case this means that the word is usually written in kanji but kana may sometimes be substituted when the kanji is perceived as too difficult or too long to write.

Other dictionaries provide difficult kanji that are rarely used by native Japanese, but we have chosen to avoid this and focus on contemporary usage. It is possible to write "lemon" in kanji, for example, with the kanji 檸檬, but the katakana form レモン is much preferred.

Every effort has been made to reflect common usage of kanji and kana; thus the ordering of the kanji and kana that follows the romanization is based on frequency of usage. Centered dots mean "or," so "appearance" **yōsu** 様子・ようす indicates that 様子 is more frequently used but ようす is also an acceptable representation for "appearance." Kanji is of course important to clarify the exact meaning of the word; as the Japanese language contains many homonyms there is a certain amount of vagueness in the usage of kana, especially out of context.

In general, romanized words are not hyphenated unless the hyphen represents a morpheme boundary within a compound word. In addition, in this dictionary we have provided kanji and kana renderings for all forms of the romanized words offered, including constituent parts of words that are abbreviated by a hyphen or substituted by a swung dash. Although this takes up extra space, it will facilitate understanding of the exact forms of the relevant word.

A

ā ああ **1.** *adv* like that, that way **2.** *interj* oh; yes **3.** *interj* hello (*on encountering someone*)

á *interj* あっ oh!

abakimásu, abaku *v* 暴きます, 暴く discloses

abaremásu, abareru *v* 暴れます, 暴れる rages, storms, rampages

abare-mono *n* 暴れ者 ruffian, rough-neck, wild person

abekobe *n* あべこべ upside down

abimásu, abiru *v* 浴びます, 浴びる bathes oneself in; douses, showers

abisemásu, abiseru *v* 浴びせます, 浴びせる pours on, showers

abuku *n* あぶく bubble

abuku-zéni *n* あぶく銭 easy money

abunai *adj* 危ない dangerous (= **kiken (na)** 危険(な))

abunakkashii *adj* 危なっかしい is insecure, unsteady

abunōmaru *n* アブノーマル abnormal

abura *n* 油 oil, grease

abura o urimásu 油を売ります [IDIOM] shoots the breeze

abura *n* 脂 fat (= **shibō** 脂肪)

aburá(á)ge *n* 油揚げ deep-fried bean curd

aburakkói *adj* 油っこい・脂っこい oily, greasy, fatty

aburimásu, abúru *v* 炙ります, 炙る grills

āchi(-gata) *n* アーチ(形) arch

ācherii *n* アーチェリー archery

achí-kochi *adv* あちこち here and there (= **achíra-kóchira** あちらこちら)

achira *pron* あちら **1.** that one (of two) over there, the other one (over there) **2.** over there, yonder **3.** he/him, she/her, they/them

achira-gawa *n* あちら側 that (his/her/their) side, other side

ada *n* あだ・仇 [BOOKISH] disservice, foe: ~ **o uchimásu** 仇を討ちます avenges, revenges (= **kataki** 仇)

adana *n* あだ名 nickname (= **aishō** 愛称)

adaputā *n* アダプター (electrical) adapter

adéyaka *adj* 艶やか gorgeous, fascinatingly elegant

adobáisu *n* アドバイス advice

adokenai *adj* あどけない innocent, childlike

adoresu *n* アドレス address

mēru-adoresu メールアドレス e-mail address

adoribu *n* アドリブ ad-lib

áeba *v* 合えば (if it fits) → **aimásu** 合います

áeba *v* 会えば (if one meets) → **aimásu** 会います

aegimásu, aégu *v* 喘ぎます, 喘ぐ gasps, pants (for breath)

aéide *v* 喘いで → **aegimásu** 喘ぎます

aemásu, aéru *v* 和えます, 和える dresses (vegetables, etc.)

aemásu, aéru *v* 会えます, 会える can meet

aé-mono *n* 和え物 vegetables mixed with a dressing

áen *n* アエン・亜鉛 zinc

aénai *v* 会えない = **aemasén** 会えません (cannot meet)

aénai *v* 和えない = **aemasén** 和えません (not dress …)

aenai *adj* 敢えない tragic, sad: **aénaku mo** 敢えなくも tragically enough

aéreba *v* 会えれば (if one can meet) → **aemásu** 会えます

aéreba *v* 和えれば (if one dresses …) → **aemásu** 和えます

áete *v* 敢えて dare (to do): ~ **… (shimásu)** 敢えて…(します) dares (*to do*)

afuremásu, afuréru *v* 溢れます, 溢れる overflows

Afurika *n* アフリカ Africa

Afurika-jin *n* アフリカ人 an African

afutā-sābisu *n* アフターサービス service (*maintenance and repair*), servicing

afutā shēbu lōshon *n* アフターシェーブローション aftershave (*lotion*)

agakimásu, agaku *v* 足掻きます, 足掻く struggles

agaméru *v* 崇める worships, adores

agarí *n* 上がり **1.** rise **2.** income **3.** *n, adj* finishing, (*resulting*) finish

agarimásu, agaru *v* 上がります, 上がる **1.** goes up, rises **2.** feels self-conscious, nervous; gets stage fright

agari-guchi, agari-kuchi *n* 上り口 the entrance (= **iriguchi** 入り口)

...-ágari (no) *adj* ...上がり(の) fresh from ..., right after ...: **yami-ágari no** 病み上がりの just out of sickbed; **ame-ágari no** 雨上がりの right after the rain

agatte *v* 上がって → **agarimásu** 上がります

age-ashi *n* 揚げ足 fault finding

ageku *n* 挙句 negative outcome ageku no hate 挙句の果て in the end

agemásu, agerú *v* **1.** あげます, あげる gives **2.** ...**-te agerú** ...てあげる does someone's favor

agemásu, agerú *v* 上げます, 上げる raises up

agemásu, agerú *v* 揚げます, 揚げる fries; raises

agenai *v* あげない = **agemasén** あげません (not give)

agenai *v* 上げない = **agemasén** 上げません (not raise)

agenai *v* 揚げない = **agemasén** 揚げません (not fry)

age(ra)remásu, age(ra)rerú *v* あげ(ら)れます, あげ(ら)れる can give

age(ra)remásu, age(ra)rerú *v* 上げ(ら)れます, 上げ(ら)れる can raise

age(ra)remásu, age(ra)rerú *v* 揚げ(ら)れます, 揚げ(ら)れる can fry

agereba *v* あげれば (if one gives) → **agemásu** あげます

agereba *v* 上げれば (if one raises) → **agemásu** 上げます

agereba *v* 揚げれば (if one fries) → **agemásu** 揚げます

age ro 上げろ [IMPERATIVE] (raise up!) → **agemásu** 上げます

ageyō *v* あげよう = **agemashō** あげましょう (I'll give it (to you).)

ago *n* あご・顎 jaw, chin ago-hige あごひげ beard, goatee, (chin-)whiskers

agura *n* あぐら sitting cross-legged

áhen *n* アヘン・阿片 opium

ahiru *n* アヒル duck (*tame*)

aho, ahō *n* あほ(う)・阿呆 fool

ái *n* 愛 love (= **aijō** 愛情): **ai-shimásu** 愛します loves

ái-bu *n* 愛撫 caress: ~ **shimásu** 愛撫します caresses

ai-chaku *n* 愛着 affection

ai-doku *n* 愛読 reading with pleasure: ~ **shimásu** 愛読します likes to read

ai-jin *n* 愛人 mistress

ai-jō *n* 愛情 affection, love (= **ai** 愛)

ai-ken *n* 愛犬 one's (pet) dog

ai-sha *n* 愛車 one's beloved vehicle

ái *n* 藍 Japanese indigo plant ái zome *n* 藍染め Japanese indigo dye

aiaigasa *n* あいあい傘 sharing an umbrella

aibiki *n* 逢引 secret rendezvous

aibō *n* 相棒 partner

aida *n, prep, adv* 間 interval, space, between; while

aidagara *n* 間柄 relationship (*between people*)

aidéa *n* アイデア idea

áidoru *n* アイドル idol

aigo *n* 愛護 [BOOKISH] protection

ai-hanshimásu, ai-hansuru *v* 相反します, 相反する conflicts

aiirenai *adj* 相容れない exclusive, incompatible, irreconcilable

aí-kagi *n* 合鍵 duplicate key

aikawarazu *adv* 相変わらず as usual/ever/always

aikí-dō *n* 合気道 aikido

áiko *n* あいこ (**o-aikó** おあいこ) tie (*in sports, games*), stalemate

aikō-ka *n* 愛好家 lover (*devotee of ...*)

aikoku-shin *n* 愛国心 patriotism

aikotoba *n* 合い言葉 password, shibboleth (*INFORMAL talk*)

aikyō *n* 愛嬌[愛敬] charm, attractiveness: ~ **ga arimásu** 愛嬌[愛敬]があります is nice, attractive, charming

aima *n* 合間 spare time

aimai (na) *adj* 曖昧(な) vague

aimasu, áu *v* 会います, 会う: **... ni aimasu** ...に会います meets; sees

aimasu, áu *v* 合います, 合う matches with: **kuchi ni ~** 口に合います suits one's taste; (**...ni) ma ni ~** (...に) 間に

2

合います is in time (for …)

…-aimasu, -au/áu …合います, 合う [VERB INFINITIVE +] (to) each other

aimátte adv あいまって combined

ainiku adv あいにく unfortunately

ainiku (na) adj あいにく(な) regrettable

ainorí n 相乗り ride together

airáin n アイライン eyeliner

airashii adj 愛らしい lovely, sweet

airon n アイロン iron(ing)

Airurándo n アイルランド Ireland

ai-sánai v 愛さない = **ai-shimasén** 愛しません (not love)

áisatsu n 挨拶, [HONORIFIC] **go-áisatsu** ご挨拶 greeting: **(…) ni ~ shimásu** (…)に挨拶します greets

aishádō n アイシャドー eye shadow

ai-shimásu, ai-súru v 愛します, 愛する loves (= **ai-su** 愛す)

ái-shite v 愛して → **ai-shimásu** 愛します

aishō n 愛称 nickname

aishō n 相性 compatibility, congeniality: **~ ga/no íi** 相性が/のいい congenial, compatible

aisó, aisō n あいそ(う)・愛想 **1. ~ ga/no íi** あいそ(う)[愛想]が/のいい is amiable, sociable, agreeable **2. o-aiso, o-aisō** お愛想 (restaurant) bill, check; incense

aisu… prefix アイス… iced…

aisu-hókkē n アイスホッケー ice hockey

aisu-kōhii n アイスコーヒー iced coffee

aisu-kuríimu n アイスクリーム ice cream

aisu-kyándii n アイスキャンディー popsicle

aisu-sukēto n アイススケート ice skating, ice skates

aisu-tii n アイスティー iced tea

aite v 開いて → **akimásu** 開きます

aite n 相手 (**o-aite** お相手) the other fellow; companion, partner; opponent

aite imásu (iru) v 開いています(いる) is open

aite imásu (iru) v 空いています(いる) vacant, empty

aitii (IT) n IT (アイティー) information technology (computer)

aitō n 哀悼 condolence: mourning

aitsu pron あいつ that guy, that creep; **aitsú-ra** pron あいつら those damn ones

aitsúide adv 相次いで one after another

āiu adj ああいう … that kind/sort of … (= **anna** あんな, **āyū** ああゆう)

aiuchí n 相打ち hitting/killing each other at the same time

aiúeo n あいうえお the Japanese syllabary

áizu n 合図 signal, sign: **~ shimásu/ o okurimásu** 合図します/を送ります makes a sign, cues, prompts

aizúchi n 相槌: **~ o uchimásu** 相槌を打ちます gives responses to make the conversation go smoothly

aji n 味 taste; flavor, seasoning: **~ ga shimásu** 味がします it tastes (has flavor) **~ ga usuidesu** 味が薄いです is bland: **~ o oboemásu** 味を覚えます acquires a taste for: **~ o shimemásu** 味をしめます gets a taste of success

áji n アジ・鯵 horse mackerel, saurel

Ájia n アジア Asia

Ajiá-jin n アジア人 an Asian

ajike-nái adj 味気ない insipid, flat

ajísai n アジサイ hydrangea

ajiwaemásu, ajiwaéru v 味わえます, 味わえる can taste it

ajiwaimásu, ajiwáu v 味わいます, 味わう tastes it

áka n 赤 red (color)

aka-bō n 赤帽 redcap, porter

áka-chan n 赤ちゃん・あかちゃん baby

aká-gai n 赤貝 ark shell, blood(y) clam

aka-go n 赤子 [BOOKISH] baby

akai adj 赤い red: **akaku narimásu** 赤くなります turns red, blushes

aka-jí n 赤字 red letters; deficit figures: **~ ni narimásu** 赤字になります goes/ gets in the red

aka-mi n 赤身 lean (meat/fish); unfatty (red) tuna

akan-bo, akan-bō n 赤んぼ, 赤ん坊 → **áka-chan** 赤ちゃん・あかちゃん

aka-shíngo n 赤信号 red light (signal)

aká n あか・垢 dirt, grime

akádemii n アカデミー academy

akademíkku n アカデミック academic

aka-gane n あかがね・銅 copper

akanai v 開かない = **akimasén** 開きません (not open)

áka-no-tanin n 赤の他人 complete/ total stranger [IN NEGATIVE SENSE]

3

akaramemásu, akarameru v 赤らめ ます, 赤らめる blushes

akarasama (na/ni) *adj, adv* あからさま (な/に) frank(ly), plain(ly), open(ly) [IN NEGATIVE SENSE]

akari *n* 明かり light, lamp

akarui *adj* 明るい bright, light, clear, gay, cheerful

akarumi *n* 明るみ: ~ **ni demásu** 明るみ に出ます surfaces, comes to light, is brought to light

akéba *v* 開けば (if it comes open)

ākēdo *n* アーケード arcade, roofed passageway, shopping arcade

akegata *n, adv* 明け方 daybreak, dawn

akemáshite o-medetō (gozaimásu [HONORIFIC]) *interj* 明けましておめで とう(ございます) Happy New Year!

akemásu, akeru v 開けます, 開ける opens it

akemásu, akeru v 空けます, 空ける leaves empty, vacates

akemásu, akeru v 明けます, 明ける it opens up, (*the day/year*) begins: **yo ga ~** 夜が明けます (it/dawn) breaks

akenai *v* 開けない = **akemasén** 開けま せん (not open it)

ake(ra)remásu, ake(ra)reru v 開け (ら)れます, 開け(ら)れる can open it

akeréba *v* 開ければ (if one opens it) → **akemásu** 開けます

ake ro *v* 開けろ [IMPERATIVE] (open it!) → **akemásu** 開けます

akete *v* 明けて → **akemásu** 明けます

akeyō *v* 開けよう = **akemashō** 開けま しょう (let's open it!)

áki *n* 秋 autumn, fall

　aki-same *n* 秋雨 autumn rain

akí- *prefix* 空き empty, vacant

　aki-bako *n* 空き箱 empty box

　aki-beya *n* 空き部屋 empty room

　aki-bin *n* 空き瓶 empty bottle

　aki-chi *n* 空き地 vacant lot (*land*)

　aki-kan *n* 空き缶 empty can

　aki-shitsu *n* 空き室 empty room/office

　aki-ya *n* 空き家 vacant/empty house

　aki-su *n* あき巣・空き巣 sneak thief

akimásu, akíru v 飽きます, 飽きる wearies (*gets tired*) of; gets enough of

akimásu, aku v 開きます, 開く opens,

comes open

akimásu, aku v 空きます, 空く gets empty/vacant

akínai *v* 飽きない = **akimasén** 飽きま せん (not weary of)

akinaimásu, akinau v 商います, 商う blushes

akíraka *adj* 明らか clear (*evident*): ~ **ni shimásu** 明らかにします makes it public, reveals, explains

akirame *n* 諦め resignation, acceptance: ~ **ga warui** 諦めが悪い not knowing when to give up

akiramemásu, akiraméru v 諦めます, 諦める: **... o ~** ...を諦めます gives up (*on*), resigns oneself to

akiremásu, akireru v 呆れます, 呆れ る gets amazed; gets disgusted

akirete *v* 呆れて → **akiremásu** 呆れ ます

akíru *v* 飽きる = **akimásu** 飽きます (wearies of)

ákite *v* 飽きて → **akimásu** 飽きます

akka *n* 悪化 worsening: ~ **shimásu** 悪化 します grows worse, worsens

akkan *n* 圧巻 overwhelming

akke-nái *adj* あっけない not long enough: ~ **ketsumatsu** あっけない結末 disappointing ending: **akkenaku makeru** あっけなく負ける is beaten too easily

akke ni toraremásu (torareru) v 呆気 に取られます(取られる) is stunned

akkerakán (to) *adv* あっけらかん(と) looks unconcerned

akogaremásu, akogaréru v 憧れます, 憧れる adores, admires; longs for, yearns for

akogi (ná) *adj* あこぎ(な) cruel and heartless

akú v 開く = **akimásu** 開きます (it opens)

áku *n* 悪 an evil

　aku-bun *n* 悪文 poor writing

　aku-fū *n* 悪風 bad custom, bad practice, a vice

　aku-heki *n* 悪癖 [BOOKISH] bad habit

　aku-hō *n* 悪法 bad law

　aku-hyō *n* 悪評 criticism (*unfavorable*)

　áku-i *n* 悪意 ill will, malice

aku-jōken *n* 悪条件 bad/unfavorable/adverse condition

aku-júnkan *n* 悪循環 vicious circle

áku-ma *n* 悪魔 devil, Satan

áku-mu *n* 悪夢 nightmare

aku-nin *n* 悪人 an evil person

aku-ratsu (na) *adj* 悪辣（な）unscrupulous, foul, nasty, mean

aku-sei *n* 悪政 [BOOKISH] bad government

aku-sei no *adj* 悪性の malignant

aku-sen *n* 悪銭: [IDIOM] **~ mi ni tsukazu** 悪銭身につかず Ill got, ill spent./Easy come, Easy go.

aku-shitsu (ná) *adj* 悪質（な）malignant, pernicious, vicious

aku-shū *n* 悪臭 stink, smell: **o hana-chimásu** 悪臭を放ちます smells out;

aku-shū *n* 悪習 abuse, bad habit: **~ ni somarimásu** 悪習に染まります gets into bad habits

aku-shumí *n* 悪趣味 bad/poor taste

aku-toku *n* 悪徳 vice: **akutoku-gyō-sha** 悪徳業者 dishonest business person

aku-zei *n* 悪税 unreasonable tax

akú *n* アク・灰汁 scum, lye: **~ o torimásu** 灰汁を取ります removes the scum: **~ga tsuyoi** 灰汁が強い is self-involved

akuaríumu *n* アクアリウム aquarium

akubí *n* 欠伸 yawn(ing): **~ (o) shimásu** 欠伸（を）します yawns

akurobátto *n* アクロバット acrobat, acrobatics

akúryoku *n* 握力 grasping power

ákuseku *adv* あくせく laboriously, (working) hard, drudging (away)

akusen-kutō *n* 悪戦苦闘 fight desperately

ákusento *n* アクセント accent

ákuseru *n* アクセル gas pedal, accelerator: **~ o fumimásu** アクセルを踏みます steps on the gas

ákusesari(i) *n* アクセサリ（ー）an accessory

akushon *n* アクション action

akushon-eiga *n* アクション映画 an action film

ákushu *n* 握手 handshake: **~ shimásu** 握手します shakes hands

ákuta *n* 芥 dirt, rubbish

amá *n* アマ・亜麻 flax plant, linen

amá iro (no) *adj* 亜麻色（の）flaxen,

linen, towheaded

amá *n* 尼 nun

áma *n* 海女 woman sea diver, a pearl diver

ama-... *prefix* 雨

amá-do *n* 雨戸 rain shutters

ama-gasa *n* 雨傘 umbrella (= **kasa** 傘)

amá-gutsu *n* 雨靴 rain shoes, galoshes

amá(chuá) *n* アマ（チュア）an amateur

amaemásu, amaéru *v* 甘えます, 甘える presumes on someone's goodwill, acts like a baby

amanógawa *n* あまのがわ・天の川 the Milky Way

amai *adj* 甘い sweet; lenient, permissive

amaku mimásu (míru) *v* 甘くみます（みる）underestimates

amari *n* 余り remainder, surplus; leftover

amari *adv* あまり [+ NEGATIVE verb] not very, not much, not many (= **anmari** あんまり): **~ arimasen/nai** あまりありません/ない There are not so many. I/We have not much.

amarimásu, amáru *v* 余ります, 余る is left over, remains, is in excess, is too much/many

amarí(ni) *adv* あまり（に）too, too much, very

amatō *n* 甘党 have a sweet (tooth)

amátte *v* 余って → amarimásu 余ります

amayakashimásu, amayakásu *v* 甘やかします, 甘やかす pampers, babies

amé *n* アメ・飴 candy (= **kyandi(i)** キャンディ（ー）)

áme *n* 雨 rain: **ama-yadori shimásu** 雨宿りします takes shelter from the rain

amē´ba *n* アメーバ amoeba

Amerika *n* アメリカ America, U.S.(A.) = **Amerika Gasshū´koku** アメリカ合衆国 United States of America

Ameriká-jin *n* アメリカ人 an American

amí *n* 網 net

amí-do *n* 網戸 screen door

amimásu, ámu *v* 編みます, 編む knits, braids

amí-mono *n* 編み物 knitting, knitted goods

ā mondo *n* アーモンド almond

án *n* 案 **1.** proposal, suggestion, idea

(= **kangae** 考え, **teian** 提案) **2.** plan
(= **keikaku** 計画, **kikaku** 企画)

án *n* あん・餡 bean jam/paste
án-ko *n* あんこ・餡子 bean jam/paste;
an-man *n* アンマン steamed bun
stuffed with bean jam

aná *n* 穴 hole; slot
ana-go *n* アナゴ conger eel
ana-guma *n* アナグマ・穴熊 badger

anáta *pron* あなた you
anatá-tachi, anatá-gáta *pron* あなた
達, あなた方 you (all)
anatá-jishin *pron* あなた自身 yourself
anáta(-tachi) no *pron* あなた(達)の
your(s)

anaúnsā *n* アナウンサー announcer
anáunsu *n* アナウンス announcement
andárain *n* アンダーライン underline
andāshátsu *n* アンダーシャツ undershirt
andon *n* 行灯 traditional night-light
anadorimásu, anadoru *v* 侮ります,
侮る not think much of
ándo *n* 安堵 relief: ~ **shimásu** 安堵し
ます feels relief
áne *n* 姉 older sister (= (**o-)nē´-san** (お)
姉さん)
ángai *adv* 案外 **1.** unexpectedly (much)
2. contrary to expectations
ángai (na) *adj* 案外(な) unexpected
angō *n* 暗号 secret code
anguru *n* アングル angle (= **kakudo**
角度), viewpoint
áni *n* 兄 elder brother (= (**o-)nii´-san**
(お)兄さん)
anime, animēshon *n* アニメ, アニメー
ション animation, animaed cartoon
anji *n* 暗示 a hint: ~ **shimásu** 暗示します
hints, suggests
jiko-anji *n* 自己暗示 autosuggestion
ánkā *n* アンカー anchor
ankēto *n* アンケート questionnaire
anki *n* 暗記 memorizing: ~ **shimásu**
暗記します memorizes; **ankí shite**
暗記して by/from memory
ankōru *n* アンコール encore
anma *n* 按摩 masseur/masseuse
(= **massá´ji** マッサージ)
anmari *adv* あんまり too much, overly;
[+ NEGATIVE] not (very) much
anmoku-no-ryōkai *n* 暗黙の了解 an

unspoken agreement
anna... *adj* あんな… that kind of…:
anna ni あんなに to that extent
annái *n* 案内, [HONORIFIC] **go-annai**
ご案内 guidance, information: (**go-)~**
shimásu (ご)案内します guides, leads,
ushers
annai-jó *n* 案内所 information desk
annái-nin *n* 案内人 guide (*person*),
usher (= **annai-gákari** 案内係)
annái-shó *n* 案内書 guide(book)
anó *adj* あの that (over there; *known to
you and me*)
anó-hito *pron* あの人 he/him, she/her:
anó-hito-tachi あの人達 they/them
anó-ko *pron* あの子 she/her, he/him
ano-yo *n* あの世 the next world,
another world
ano, anō *interj* あの, あのう (*with
nervous diffidence*) well, uh …
ano né *interj* あのね (*mostly children
or female*) well, listen, you know
anpáia *n* アンパイア umpire
anpán *n* アンパン sweet roll with bean
jam inside
anpéa *n* アンペア ampere
anpo *n* 安保 Security: **Nichibei Anzen
Hoshō Jōyaku** 日米安全保障条約 the
U.S.-Japan Security Treaty
anpu *n* アンプ amplifier
anpuru *n* アンプル ampule
anraku *n* 安楽 comfort
anraku (na) *adj* 安楽(な) comfortable,
easy
anraku shi *n* 安楽死 mercy killing,
euthanasia
ansei *n* 安静 rest: ~ **ni shimásu** 安静に
します keeps/lies quiet
anshín *n* 安心 peace of mind; relief;
security; confidence, trust: ~ **shimásu**
安心します not worry, relaxes (one's
anxieties), is relieved (of worry)
anshitsu *n* 暗室 darkroom
anshō *n* 暗唱 recitation from memory:
~ **shimásu** 暗唱します recites
ánta *pron* あんた [INFORMAL] (rude or
rough) you (= **anáta** あなた [FORMAL])
antei *n* 安定 stability: ~ **shimásu** 安定し
ます stabilizes
antena *n* アンテナ antenna, aerial

ánzan *n* 安産 safe/easy delivery

anzan kigan *n* 安産祈願 wishing someone a safe delivery

anzán *n* 暗算 mental calculation: ~ **shimásu** 暗算します calculates mentally

anzen (na) *adj* 安全(な) safe (*harm-proof*)

anzén-pin *n* 安全ピン safety pin

anzimásu, anjiru (anzuru) *v* 案じます、案じる(案ずる) worries, concerns: [IDIOM] **anzuru yori umu ga yasushi** 案ずるより産むがやすし easier than one thinks

anzu *n* アンズ・杏 apricot

áo *n* 青 blue, green (*color*)

aói *adj* 青い blue, green, pale

ao-jáshin *n* 青写真 blueprint

ao-mi *n* 青味 blueness

ao-mushi *n* 青虫 green caterpillar

ao-nísai *n* 青二才 immature [IN NEGATIVE SENSE]

ao-shíngō *n* 青信号 green light (*signal*)

ao-suji *n* 青筋 **ao-suji o tateru** 青筋を立てる bursts a blood vessel

ao-zóra *n* 青空 blue sky

aō *v* 会おう = **aimashō** 会いましょう (let's meet!)

aogimásu, aógu *v* 扇ぎます、扇ぐ fans; fans oneself

aogimásu, aógu *v* 仰ぎます、仰ぐ looks up at/to; respects (= **miageru** 見上げる)

aóide *v* 扇いで・仰いで → **aogimásu** 扇ぎます・仰ぎます

aomuké *n* 仰向け facing upward

aorimásu, aóru *v* 煽ります、煽る fans; stirs up, incites

aótte *v* 煽って → **aorimásu** 煽ります

ao-zamemásu, aozameru *v* 青ざめます、青ざめる pales, is pale

apā́to *n* アパート apartment (*house*)

appaku *n* 圧迫 pressure; oppression; suppression: ~ **shimásu** 圧迫します puts pressure on; oppresses, suppresses

appáre あっぱれ **1.** *interj* Bravo! **2.** *adj* admirable

áppu *n* アップ raising, up

appu-dḗto *n* アップデート update

appu-gurḗdo *n* アップグレード upgrade

appu-rṓdo *n* アップロード upload

appu-áppu *adj* あっぷあっぷ grasping for breath: ~ **shimásu** あっぷあっぷします bobs up and down

appurú-pai *n* アップルパイ apple pie

apurṓchi *n* アプローチ approach: ~ **shimásu** アプローチします approaches

ára *interj* あら (*female*) oh!! (*shows surprise, amazement*): **árá-mā** あらまあ (*female*) Oh, dear!

ará *n* あら・粗 fault

ará sagashi *n* あら捜し nitpicking: ~ **shimásu** あら捜しします tries to find fault with

ara-suji *n* あらすじ summary, outline, synopsis (= **gaiyō** 概要, **yōyaku** 要約)

Arabia, Árabu *n* アラビア, アラブ an Arab

Arabia-go *n* アラビア語 Arabic; Arabia-jin, Arabú-jin *n* アラビア人、アラブ人 an Arab

Arabia no *adj* アラビアの Arabian

araemásu, araeru *v* 洗えます、洗える can wash

araí *adj* 荒い rough, coarse

ara-ara-shii *adj* 荒々しい rude, wild, rough

ara-ryōji *n* 荒療治 take drastic measures [steps]

araí *adj* 粗い rough, not smooth, coarse

araimásu, arau *v* 洗います、洗う washes

arakajime *adv* あらかじめ in advance (= **maemotte** 前もって)

arakáruto *n* アラカルト a la carte (*item*)

araō *v* 洗おう = **araimashō** 洗いましょう (let's wash it!)

arare *n* あられ・霰 hail (= **hyṓ** ひょう [雹])

arare *n* あられ rice-cracker cubes

árashi *n* 嵐 storm

arashimásu, arásu *v* 荒らします、荒らす devastates, damages, ruins

arasoí *n* 争い contention, struggle; strife, disturbance, war

arasoimásu, arasóu *v* 争います、争う contends for; argues, quarrels

arasótte *v* 争って → **arasoimásu** 争います

aratamarimásu, aratamáru *v* 改まります、改まる to be changed, to be replaced by something new

aratamemásu, arataméru *v* 改めます、改める changes, alters, corrects

aratámete *adv* 改めて anew; again

arawaremásu, arawaréru v 現れます、現れる appears, shows up, comes out

arawashimásu, arawásu v 現します、現す shows, reveals

arawashimásu, arawásu v 表します、表す expresses (= hyōgen shimásu 表現します)

arawashimásu, arawásu v 著します、著す publishes, writes

arayúru adj あらゆる all, every (= subete no すべての)

aré pron あれ that one (over there; known to you and me)

aré-ra pron あれら those, they/them

aré interj あれ! Dear! (surprise)

áreba v あれば (if there be) → arimásu あります

aremásu, areru v 荒れます、荒れる goes to ruin, falls to waste, gets dilapidated; gets rough/wild; rages

aremoyō (no) adj 荒れ模様(の) stormy, inclement (weather)

arenai v 荒れない = aremasén 荒れません (not get rough)

areréba v 荒れれば (if it rages; if ...) → aremásu 荒れます

arérugii n アレルギー allergy: kafun-arérugii 花粉アレルギー hay fever (= kafunshō 花粉症)

arete v 荒れて → aremásu 荒れます

arí n アリ・蟻 ant

ári v あり → arimásu あります

ariári (to) adv ありあり(と) vividly

ariawase n ありあわせ on hand

aribai n アリバイ alibi

arifúreta adj ありふれた very common, commonplace

arigachi adj ありがち common, typical [IN NEGATIVE SENSE]

arigatai adj ありがたい appreciated, welcome; grateful: arigata meiwaku ありがた迷惑 unwanted favor, misplaced favor

arígatō (gozaimásu [HONORIFIC]) ありがとう(ございます) Thank you (very much)

árika n 在り処 whereabouts (= yukue 行方)

arikitari adj ありきたり commonplace, so typical [IN NEGATIVE SENSE]

arimáshita, atta v ありました、あった there was, we had; it was (located)

arimásu, aru v あります、ある there is, we've got; it is (located)

arí mo shinai adj ありもしない nor is there, there even/also isn't, nonexistent

arinomama (ni/de) adv ありのまま (に/で) as is, without exaggeration

ari-sama n ありさま condition, state; scene, sight

ari-sō(-na) adj ありそう(な) likely; ~ mo nái ありそうもない unlikely

áritoarayúru adj ありとあらゆる every single, all kinds/sorts of

arí wa/ya shinai v ありは/やしない = arimasén ありません = nái ない (is not)

arō´ v あろう [LITERARY] = áru darō´ あるだろう = áru deshō あるでしょう (probably is)

áru ... adj ある certain ...、some ... áru-hi ある日 a one/certain day

áru v ある = arimásu あります (there is, it is (located))

arubáito n アルバイト side job, side-line, part-time job (= baito バイト)

arufabétto n アルファベット alphabet

árugamama n あるがまま as is, for what it is

arúite v 歩いて → arukimásu 歩きます

arúi-wa conj 或いは or else; possibly

arukimásu, arúku v 歩きます、歩く walks

arukō v 歩こう = arukimashó 歩きましょう (let's walk!)

arukōru n アルコール alcohol

arumínium n アルミニウム aluminum

áruto n アルト alto

arya v ありゃ [INFORMAL] = are wa あれは (as for that)

asá n 麻 flax, linen

ása n, adv 朝 morning

ása-ban (ni) n, adv 朝晩(に) morning and night/evening

asa-yake n 朝焼け a red glow in the morning sky

asá-gao n アサガオ・朝顔 morning glory (flower)

asa-góhan n 朝ご飯 breakfast (= [BOOKISH] chōshoku 朝食、(mostly male) asa-meshi 朝飯)

ása-hi n 朝日 morning sun, rising sun
asá-meshi-máe n 朝飯前 a cinch
asái adj 浅い shallow
asá-haka (na) adj 浅はか(な) shallow
asa-gurói adj 浅黒い swarthy, dark-colored, bistered
asa-se n 浅瀬 shallows
Asakusa n 浅草 Asakusa
asari n アサリ・浅蜊 short-necked clam
asátsuki n アサツキ・浅葱 scallion, green onion; chives
asátte n,adv あさって・明後日 the day after tomorrow
áse n 汗 sweat: ~ ga demásu 汗が出ます, ~ o kakimásu 汗をかきます sweats
hiya-áse 冷や汗 cold sweat
Asean n アセアン ASEAN
asemásu, aséru v 褪せます, 褪せる fades
asénai v 褪せない = asemásén 褪せません (not fade)
aseránai v 焦らない = aserimásén 焦りません (not feel rushed)
aserimásu, aséru v 焦ります, 焦る feels rushed/pressed
aséru v 褪せる = asemásu 褪せます (fades)
aséru v 焦る = aserimásu 焦ります (feels rushed/pressed)
ásete v 褪せて → asemásu 褪せます
asétte v 焦って → aserimásu 焦ります
áshi n アシ・葦 leed
ashi-áto n 足跡 footprint
ashi-dai n 足台 footstool (= ashinosé-dai 足乗せ台)
ashi-de mátoi n 足手まとい a drag (on)
ashí-kubi n 足首 ankle
ashi-móto n 足もと・足元: ~ ni ki o tsukéte 足元に気を付けて Watch your step!
ashi-dome saremásu (sareru) v 足止めされます(される) is strained, is stuck
ashi-ga-demásu (-deru) v 足が出ます (出る) runs over the budget
ashí-o-araimásu (-arau) v 足を洗います(洗う) washes one's hands of, drops one's beads, cuts one's ties with
ashí-o-nobashimásu (-nobasu) v 足を伸ばします(伸ばす) goes a little farther
ashirai n あしらい treatment, hospitality, service, arrangement

ashiraimásu, ashiráu v あしらいます, あしらう handles, manages, deals with; receives (a guest): hana de ~ 鼻であしらいます turns up one's nose at (a person)
ashirawánai v あしらわない = ashirai-masén あしらいません (not arrange)
ashita n,adv あした・明日 tomorrow: [IDIOM] ~ wa ~ no kaze ga fuku 明日は明日の風が吹く Tomorrow is another day. (= asu あす・明日)
asobi n 遊び fun, amusement; a game, play; a visit
asobi hanbun (de) adv 遊び半分(で) half-seriously
asobimásu, asobu v 遊びます, 遊ぶ has fun, plays; visits
asoko, asuko pron あそこ, あすこ (that place) over there; that place (known to you and me)
assári adv あっさり simple/simply, plain(ly); easy/easily; frank(ly), without apparent difficulty: assári (to) shíta + [NOUN] ... あっさり(と)した... simple, plain, light, easy; frank
assén n あっせん・斡旋 1. mediation; good offices, help (= sewá 世話): ... no ~ de ... の斡旋で through the good offices of ..., with the help of ... 2. recommendation (= suisen 推薦)
asshō n 圧勝 win an overwhelming: ~ shimásu 圧勝します wins an overwhelming victory
asshuku n 圧縮 compression: ~ shimásu 圧縮します compresses
asu n,adv あす・明日 tomorrow (= ashíta あした・明日)
asufáruto n アスファルト asphalt
asupara(gásu) n アスパラ(ガス) asparagus
asupirin n アスピリン aspirin
asurechikku-kúrabu n アスレチッククラブ athletic club
āsu-sen n アース線 ground wire
asutarísuku n アスタリスク asterisk (such as "*") (= hoshi-jírushi 星印)
asutorinzen n アストリンゼン astringent
ataemásu, ataeru v 与えます, 与える gives, provides, grants

9

átafuta *n* あたふた: **~ shimásu** あたふ たします gets flustere°d/confused (= **awatemásu** 慌てます)

ataisuru 値する **1.** *v* = **atai shimásu** 値します (deserves) **2.** *adj* deserved

átakamo *adv* あたかも as if

átákku *n* アタック attack, strenuous effort

atama *n* 頭 head
  atama-kín *n* 頭金 down payment, up-front money; deposit
  atama-wari (no/de) *adj, adv* 頭割り (の/で) per head
  atama-ni-kimásu (kuru) *v* 頭にきます (くる) gets mad at, be angly with
  atama-o-kakaemásu (kakaeru) *v* 頭を抱えます(抱える) tears one's hair (out), holds one's head in one's hands
  atama-o-tsukaimásu (tsukau) *v* 頭を使います(使う) uses one's head/mind

ataranaí *v* 当たらない = **atarimásén** 当たりません (not hit, is not correct)

atarashíí *adj* 新しい new; fresh
  atarashi-gariya *n* 新しがり屋 novelty hunter

ataráshiku *adv* 新しく newly, freshly

atarazu-sawarazu *adj, adv* 当たらず さわらず innocuous (= **atarisawari no nai** 当たりさわりのない)

ataréba *v* 当たれば (if it hits, if it's cor-rect) → **atarimásu** 当たります

atari 当たり **1.** *n* a hit **2.** *adj* good luck, lucky
  ataridokoro *adj* 当たり所: **~ ga warui** 当たり所が悪い hitting in a vital spot
  atari-doshi *n* 当たり年 lucky year
  atari-hazure *adj* 当たり外れ unpredictable, risky
  atari-kuji *n* 当たりくじ winning number
  atari-yaku *n* 当たり役 a hit in the role

átari *n* 辺り neighborhood: **kono ~ de/ wa** この辺りで/は around here

atarichirashimásu, atarichirasu *v* 当たり散らします, 当たり散らす takes out one's spite on everybody

atarimae (no) *adj* 当たり前(の) natu-ral, reasonable, proper; suitable

atarimásu, ataru *v* 当たります, 当たる hits, faces, applies; is correct

atashi *pron* あたし (*mostly children or female*) I/me (= **wata(ku)shi** わた(く) し・私)

atasshu-kē su *n* アタッシュケース attache case, briefcase

atatakái *adj* 暖かい warm (*air temperature*)

atatakái *adj* 温かい warm (*liquid, heart, etc.*)

atatakáku *adv* 暖かく・温かく warmly, kindly

atatamarimásu, atatamáru *v* 暖まり ます・温まります, 暖まる・温まる warms up

atatememásu, atataméru *v* 温めます, 温める warms it up, heats

atatte *v* 当たって → **atarimásu** 当た ります

atchi *pron* あっち [INFORMAL] = **achira** あちら (*the other one, over there*)

ate *n* 当て **1.** reliance, trust **2.** anticipa-tion, expectation (= **kitai** 期待) **3.** goal, object (= **mokuteki** 目的) **4.** clue, trace (= **tegákari** 手掛かり)

…-ate (nó) *suffix, adj* …宛て(の) addressed to …
  ate-na *n* 宛(て)名 address

ate-hamarimásu, ate-hamáru *v* 当て はまります, 当てはまる fits, conforms

ate-hamemásu, ate-haméru *v* 当て はめます, 当てはめる applies, adapts, conforms, fits it (*to*): **… ni ate-hámete** …に当てはめて in conformity/ accordance with …

atekosuri *n* 当てこすり a snide remark

atemásu, ateru *v* 当てます, 当てる guesses; hits; designates; touches

atenai *v* 当てない = **atemásén** 当てま せん (not guess)

ate(ra)remásu, ate(ra)reru *v* 当て(ら) れます, 当て(ら)れる can guess/hit/…

ate ro 当てろ [IMPERATIVE] (hit!) → **atemásu** 当てます

ateuma *n* 当て馬 dodge

ā´tisuto *n* アーティスト/アーチスト artist (= **geijutsu-ka** 芸術家)

áto (de/ni) *prep, adv* 後(で/に) after(wards), later (= **nochi ni** 後に): **áto no …** 後の…the remaining …; **… shita áto de …** した後で … after doing
  ato-máwashi *n* 後回し: **~ ni shimásu** 後回しにします postpones, leaves something until later (= **ato ni mawasu**

ato-(に回す)

ató-aji *n* 後味 aftertaste: **~ ga warui** 後味が悪い leaves a bad aftertaste

ato-kátazuke *n* 後片付け cleanup

áto-no-matsurí *n* 後の祭(り) The damage is done.

ato-módori *n* 後戻り retreat, back tracking: **~ shimásu** 後戻りします retreats, turns back

ato-saki *n* 後先 consequence

ato-shímatsu *n* 後始末: **~ o shimásu** 後始末をします deals with the aftermath, picks up the pieces

áto *n* 跡 mark, track, trace

ató-tsugi *n* 跡継ぎ successor

ā́to *n* アート art

atorakushon *n* アトラクション attraction, side entertainment

atorie *n* アトリエ studio, workshop, atelier

atsuatsu (no) *adj* アツアツ(の) lovey-dovey

atsuatsu (no) *adj* 熱々(の) piping hot

atsubottai *adj* 厚ぼったい thick (= **(bu)atsui** (ぶ)厚い)

atsui *adj* 厚い thick (= **atsubottai** 厚ぼったい)

atsu-zoko *n* 厚底 heavy-bottom (*things*)

atsúi *adj* 暑い hot (*air*)

atsúi *adj* 熱い hot: **atsuku shimásu** 熱くします makes it hot

atsukamashíi *adj* 厚かましい impudent (= **zūzúshui** ずうずうしい)

atsukaimásu, atsukau *v* 扱います, 扱う deals with

atsumarimásu, atsumáru *v* 集まります, 集まる meets, assembles

atsumemásu, atsuméru *v* 集めます, 集める collects, gathers, accumulates

atsúryoku *n* 圧力 pressure

atsusa *n* 厚さ thickness

átsusa *n* 暑さ heat, warmth (*air temperature*)

átsusa *n* 熱さ heat, warmth (= **netsu** 熱)

átta *v* あった = **arimáshita** ありました (there was, we had; it was (*located*))

átta *v* 会った = **aimáshita** 会いました (met, saw (*a person*))

attakái *adj* 暖かい warm (*air temperature*) (= **atatakái** 暖かい)

attakái *adj* 温かい warm (*liquid, heart, etc.*) (= **atatakái** 温かい)

at(a)tememásu, at(a)taméru *v* 温めます, 温める warms it up, heats

átte *v* あって → **arimásu** あります

átte *v* 会って → **aimásu** 会います

atto-hṓmu (na) *adj* アットホーム (な) homelike atmosphere, homely

atto-mā́ku *n* アットマーク at mark (such as "@")

attō-shimásu (suru) *v* 圧倒します (する) overwhelms

attō-teki na *adj* 圧倒的な overwhelming

áu *v* 合う = **aimásu** 合います (matches with)

áu *v* 会う = **aimásu** 会います (meets; sees)

áuto *n* アウト out (*baseball*)

auto-kṓsu アウトコース outer lane/track

auto-putto アウトプット output

auto-rain アウトライン outline

awa *n* 泡 bubble; foam

áwa *n* アワ・粟 millet

áwabi *n* アワビ・鮑 abalone

awánai *v* 合わない = **aimasén** 合いません (not match with)

awánai *v* 会わない = **aimasén** 会いません (not meet; not see)

áware (na) *adj* 哀れ(な) pity, pitiful

awase *n* 袷・あわせ = a lined garment

awasemásu, awaséru *v* 合わせます, 合わせる puts together, combines

awásete *adj* **1.** *adv* all together **2.** *v* → **awasemásu** 合わせます

awatadashii *adj* 慌ただしい hurried, flustered, confused

awatemásu, awateru *v* 慌てます, 慌てる gets flustered/confused (= **atafuta shimásu** あたふたします)

awate-mono *n* 慌て者 a person easily flustered; a scatterbrain (= **awatenbō** あわてん坊)

ayabumimásu, ayabumu *v* 危ぶみます, 危ぶむ doubts

ayafuya (na) *adj* あやふや(な) indecisive

ayamari *n* 誤り error, mistake

ayamari *n* 謝り apology

ayamarimásu, ayamáru *v* 誤ります, 誤る errs, makes a mistake

ayamarimásu, ayamáru v 謝ります、謝る apologizes

ayamátte v 誤って・謝って → **ayamarimásu** 誤ります・謝ります

ayashii adj 怪しい questionable, suspicious, shady; unreliable; weird

ayashimásu, ayasu v あやします、あやす lulls

ayatóri n あやとり cat's cradle

ayatsurimásu, ayatsúru v 操ります、操る manipulates

ayauku adv 危うく (something undesirable) about to happen; critically

āyū adj ああゆう ... that kind/sort of ... (= **áiu** あいう, **anna** あんな)

áyu n アユ・鮎 (= **ái** アイ・鮎) sweetfish, river trout

aza n 痣 bruise

azakeri n あざけり・嘲り mockery (= **keibetsu** 軽蔑)

azakerimásu, azakeru v あざけり[嘲

り]ます, あざける・嘲る mocks, scorns

azárashi n アザラシ seal (animal)

azawarai n あざ[嘲]笑い mockery, sneer, scornful laugh (= **chōshō** 嘲笑, **reishō** 冷笑)

azawaraimásu, azawarau v あざ[嘲]笑います, あざ[嘲]笑う mocks, sneers

azáyaka (na) adj 鮮やか(な) bright, vivid

azen-to-shimásu (-suru) v 唖然とします is dumbfounded, is speechless

azukari-jo-sho n 預かり所 check room

azukarimásu, azukáru v 預かります、預かる takes in trust, keeps, holds

azukemásu, azukéru v 預けます、預ける gives in trust, entrusts; checks; deposits

azukeraremásu, azukeraréru v 預けられます、預けられる can give in trust

azukí n アズキ・小豆 red beans

B

...-ba conj ...ば [EMPHATIC] (if) indeed: **... nára(ba)** ...なら(ば) if; **... dáttara(ba)** ...だったら(ば); **...-káttara(ba)** ...かったら(ば) if/when it is (or was); **...-tára (ba)** ...たら(ば) if/when it does (or did)

ba n 場 1. place (for something) (= **basho** 場所) 2. occasion, time (= **baai, bawai** 場合) 3. scene (= **bamen** 場面)

bā́ n バー bar (for drinking)

baai, bawai n 場合 situation, case, circumstance, occasion: **no ~ ...** の場合 if

baba-núki n ばば抜き old maid (card game)

bābékyū n バーベキュー barbecue

bā́bon n バーボン bourbon

bachí n 罰 retribution, punishment (= **batsu** 罰)

ba-chígai (na/no) adj 場違い(な/の) out of place; not from the right/best place

bā́gen n バーゲン bargain sale

bái n 倍 double: **~ ni narimásu** 倍になります(なる) it doubles; **~ ni shimásu** 倍にします doubles it

bai-ritsu n 倍率 magnification, magnifying power

...-bai suffix ...倍 ...times, ...-fold

bai-... prefix 売... selling

bái-bai n 売買 buying and selling

bai-meikōi n 売名行為 [BOOKISH] publicity seeking, publicity stunt

bai-shun n 売春 prostitution: **baishún-fu** 売春婦 prostitute; whore

bai-ten n 売店 booth, kiosk, stand (selling things)

Báiburu n バイブル Bible (= **seisho** 聖書)

báidoku n 梅毒 [BOOKISH] syphilis

baikin n ばい菌 germ

báikingu n バイキング smorgasbord ("Viking")

báiku n バイク motorbike: **báiku-bin** n バイク便 motorcycle courier

baindā n バインダー binder

baiorin n バイオリン violin

baio-tekunórojii n バイオテクノロジー biotechnology

baipasu n バイパス bypass

baíríngaru n バイリンガル bilingual

baishṓ-kin n 賠償金 indemnity, reparation

baiyā n バイヤー buyer (professional)

12

bē´kon *n* ベーコン bacon

bén *n* 弁 valve

bén *n* 便 1. convenience (= **béngi** 便宜): **~ ga íí** 便がいい convenient (= **bénri (na)** 便利(な)) 2. feces
  bén-jo *n* 便所 toilet
  bén-ki *n* 便器 bedpan
  bén-pi *n* 便秘 constipation
  dai-bén *n* 大便 excrement, faces, stool
  shō/shon-bén *n* 小便 urine, pee

…-bén *suffix* …遍 = **…-hén, ...-pén** 遍 (*counts times or occasions*)

bénchi *n* ベンチ bench

béngi *n* 便宜 convenience, accommodation (= **bén** 便): **~ o hakarimásu** 便宜を図ります does someone a favor

bengóshi *n* 弁護士 lawyer

béni *n* 紅 rouge (= **kuchi-beni** 口紅)

benkai *n* 弁解 [BOOKISH] justification (= **iiwake** 言い訳): **~ suruna!** 弁解するな! Don't give excuses!

benkyō *n* 勉強 study, (*mental*) work; cutting a price: **~ shimásu** 勉強します studies; cuts the price
  benkyō-ka *n* 勉強家 a studious person, a good student

bénri (na) *adj* 便利(な) handy, convenient

benri-ya *n* 便利屋 handyman (*or his shop*)

benron *n* 弁論 debate, speech, rhetoric
  benron-taikai *n* 弁論大会 speech contest

benshō *n* 弁償 compensation: **~ shimásu** 弁償します recompenses

bentō *n* 弁当 (**o-bentō** お弁当) box lunch

berabō (ni) *adv* べらぼう(に) astonishingly, considerably, extremely

beranda *n* ベランダ veranda

béru *n* ベル bell, doorbell

Berurín *n* ベルリン Berlin

beruto *n* ベルト belt (= **bando** バンド)
  anzen-béruto *n* 安全ベルト safety belt

bessó´ *n* 別荘 villa, vacation house

bēsu *n* ベース 1. base, basis 2. base (*baseball*) 3. = **bēsu gitā** ベースギター bass guitar

bēsu áppu *n* ベースアップ upping/raising the base pay; a pay raise

bēsubōru *n* ベースボール baseball

(= **yakyū** 野球)

bésuto *n* ベスト best
  besuto-tén *n* ベストテン best ten
  besuto-serā´ *n* ベストセラー best seller

beteran *n* ベテラン veteran, expert
  beteran-kyōshi *n* ベテラン教師 an experienced teacher

betsu (na/no) *adj* 別(な/の) separate, special, particular
  betsu-betsu (na/no) *adj* 別々(な/の) separate, individual
  betsu (no) *adj* 別(の) other; extra
  betsu-ryō´kin *n* 別料金 extra (*charge*), separate bill

betsu (ni) *adv* 別(に) 1. [+ NEGATIVE] not particularly 2. **… tó wa ~ ni (shite)** …とは別に(して) quite apart/separately from …

bétto *n* ベット bed (= **béddo** ベッド)

bia-hō´ru *n* ビアホール beer hall

bíichi *n* ビーチ beach

biifu sutēki *n* ビーフステーキ beefsteak

bíiru *n* ビール beer: **biirú-bin** ビール瓶 beer bottle: **kan-bíiru** 缶ビール canned beer: **nama-bíiru** 生ビール draft beer

bíito *n* ビート beet

bijin *n* 美人 beautiful woman, a beauty

bíjinesu *n* ビジネス business
  bíjinesu-hoteru *n* ビジネスホテル economy hotel
  bíjinesu-man *n* ビジネスマン businessperson (= **kaisha-in** 会社員)

bijón *n* ビジョン vision

bijutsu *n* 美術 art
  bijútsú-kan 美術館 *n* art museum (*art gallery*)

bikkúri-shimásu (-suru) *v* びっくりします(する) gets startled, gets a surprise (= **odorokimásu** 驚きます)

bimyō (na) *adj* 微妙(な) delicate, subtle, fine, nice

bín *n* 瓶 bottle; jar
  bin-bíiru *n* 瓶ビール bottled beer
  ka-bin *n* 花瓶 vase

…´-bin *suffix* 便 flight (number) …

bínbō (na) *adj* 貧乏(な) poor (*needy*)

biní(i)ru *n* ビニ(ー)ル vinyl, polyvinyl; plastic

15

bini(i)rú-bukuro n ビニ(一)ル袋 plastic bag

binkan (na) adj 敏感(な) sensitive

binsen n 便箋 (letter-)writing paper, stationery

bínta n びんた slapping (a person's face): ~ **o harimásu/shimásu** びんたを 張ります/します slaps

birá n びら leaflet, handbill, pamphlet

bíri (no) adj びり(の) the last, the tail end, the rear: ~ **ni narimásu** びりにな ります finishes last

biródo n ビロード velvet

bíru n ビル building

Bíruma n ビルマ Burma (Myanmar)

bisai (na) adj 微細(な) minute, detailed, fine

bishonure n びしょ濡れ soddenness

bisshíri adv びっしり cramped; packed

bisshóri adv びっしょり completely soaked: **ase** ~ 汗びっしょり is all sweaty; ~ **nuremásu** びっしょり濡れ ます gets soaking wet through

bisukétto n ビスケット crackers

bitámin n ビタミン vitamin(s) bitámin-zai ビタミン剤 vitamin pills

bitoku n 美徳 virtue

bíwa n ビワ・枇杷 loquat (fruit)

bíwa n 琵琶 lute (musical instrument)

biya-hō´ru n ビヤホール beer hall (= **bia hō´ru** ビアホール)

biyō´in n 美容院 beauty parlor

bíza n ビザ visa (= **sashō** 査証)

bō n 棒 pole (rod); stick, club (= **bō-kire** 棒きれ, **bōkkíre** 棒つっきれ) tetsu-bō n 鉄棒 (iron) bar

bóchi n 墓地 cemetery, graveyard

bōchō shimásu (suru) v 膨脹します (する) swells, expands

bōchū´zai n 防虫剤 insecticide; mothballs

bōdai (na) adj 膨大(な) enormous, gigantic, massive

bōdō n 暴動 riot

bōei n 防衛 defense (= **bōgyo** 防御)

Bōei-shō n 防衛省 Ministry of Defense (DA)

bōeki n 貿易 commerce, trade: ~ **shimásu** 貿易します conducts foreign trade

bōeki-shōsha/gaisha n 貿易商社/会 社 trader, trading company

bōenkyō n 望遠鏡 telescope

bōfū n 暴風 storm, gale, hurricane

bōfú-zai n 防腐剤 antiseptic (substance), preservative

bōhan-béru n 防犯ベル burglar alarm

bōhatéi n 防波堤 breakwater

bōi n ボーイ (bell)boy, waiter

bōi-furéndo n ボーイフレンド boyfriend (= **káre(-shi)** 彼(氏))

boikótto n ボイコット boycott

boin n 拇印 thumbprint

boin n 母音 vowel

bóirā n ボイラー boiler

bóisukáuto n ボーイスカウト boy scout

bōkaru n ボーカル vocalist

bōken n 冒険 adventure bōken-ka n 冒険家 adventurer

bóki n 簿記 bookkeeping

bō-kire, bōkkíre n 棒きれ, 棒つっきれ pole (rod); stick, club (= **bō** 棒)

bokkusu n ボックス bokkusu-seki n ボックス席 booth (in a tavern etc.) denwa-bókkusu n 電話ボックス phone booth

bókoku n 母国 mother country, home-land

bóku pron 僕 (male) I/me bóku-ra, bóku-táchi pron 僕ら, 僕た ち we/us

bokuchiku n 牧畜 stockbreeding

bokujō n 牧場 ranch

bókushi n 牧師 (Christian) minister, preacher, pastor, priest; Reverend

bókushingu n ボクシング boxing

bokusō n 牧草 meadow grass

bon n 盆 (**o-bon** お盆) tray

Bón n 盆 (**O-bón** お盆) the Bon Festival (Buddhist All Saints Day)

…-bon suffix …本 book, volume, text **…´-bon** (…´-hon,…´-pon) suffix …本 (counts long objects): → **nán-bon** 何本 (how many ~)

bō´nasu n ボーナス (wage) bonus

bonchí n 盆地 basin

bóndo n ボンド bond

bōnén-kai n 忘年会 year-end party

bonnétto *n* ボンネット (car-) hood, bonnet

bonsai *n* 盆栽 dwarf trees (in pots)

bon'yári-shimásu (suru) *v* ぼんやりします(する) is absent-minded, daydreams

bonyū *n* 母乳 breast milk

bora *n* ボラ gray mullet

boróntia *n* ボランティア volunteer

bōrei *n* 亡霊 ghost (*commonly lacks legs and feet*) (= **yūrei** 幽霊)

bōringu *n* ボーリング bowling

bóro *n* ぼろ rag

bōru *n* ボール ball

bōru-gami *n* ボール紙 cardboard

bōru-pen *n* ボールペン ballpoint pen

boruto *n* ボルト **1.** bolt (*of nut and bolt*) **2.** volt (*electricity*)

bō´ryoku *n* 暴力 violence (*brute force*)
  bōryoku-dan *n* 暴力団 mob, gangbanger

boryūmu *n* ボリューム volume

bō-san *n* 坊さん (**obō-sán** お坊さん) Buddhist monk (= **bō´zu** 坊主)

bósei *n* 母性 maternity

bōseki *n* 紡績 [BOOKISH] spinning
  bōseki-kō´jō *n* 紡績工場 spinning mill

bōshi *n* 帽子 hat

boshikátei *n* 母子家庭 family without a father

boshū *n* 募集 recruitment: ~ **shimásu** 募集します recruits, collects

bōsōzoku *n* 暴走族 motorcycle gang

bōsui (no) *adj* 防水(の) waterproof

bótan *n* ボタン button

bótan *n* ボタン・牡丹 tree peony

bótchan *n* 坊ちゃん (little) boy, (your) son (= **bō´ya** 坊や)

bō´to *n* ボート boat

bōtō *n* 冒頭 opening, at [in] the beginning

bōtoku *n* 冒とく sacrilege, violence; blasphemy

bótsubotsu *adv* ぼつぼつ **1.** *adv* (= **sórosoro** そろそろ) little by little, gradually; (*leave*) before long **2.** *n* (*with*) dots, spots, bumps

bottō-shimásu (-suru) *v* 没頭します devotes oneself, buries oneself in

bō´ya *n* 坊や (little) boy

boyakimásu, boyáku *v* ぼやきます,

ぼやく grumbles, complains

bōzen *adj* 茫然 stunned: ~ **to shita kao** 茫然とした顔 dazed-looking: ~ **to shimásu** 茫然とします is struck dumb with amazement.

bōzu *n* 坊主 Buddhist monk or priest
  bōzu-atama *n* 坊主頭 shaven head

bú *n* 部 (*suffix* ...'**-bu** ...部) part, division, section

bú-bun *n* 部分 part, portion

bu-chō *n* 部長 department/division/ section head, manager

bu-gáisha *n* 部外者 outsider

bu-hín *n* 部品 parts

bú-ka *n* 部下 a subordinate

bu-mon *n* 部門 sector

eigyō-bu *n* 営業部 business/sales department

...'**-bú** *suffix* ...部 (*performance*) **hiru-no-bú** 昼の部 matinee; **yóru-no-bú** 夜の部 evening performance

...'**-bu** *suffix* ...分 (1-9) percent: **sán-wari sán-bu** 三割三分 = **sánjū san-pāsénto** 33パーセント 33 percent

...'**-bu** *suffix* ...部 copies (*of a book*); **ichí-bu** 一部 one copy

buai *n* 歩合 commission
  buai-sei *n* 歩合制 commission system

bu-áisō (na) *adj* 無愛想(な) unsociable, blunt, brusque, curt

buatsui *adj* 分厚い thick (= **atsubottai** 厚ぼったい)

buchimásu, butsu *v* ぶちます, ぶつ hits (= **tatakimásu** 叩きます)

bu-chō´hō *n* 不調法 a gaffe, a blunder: ~ **o shimásu** 不調法をします makes a blunder
  bu-chō´hō-monó *n* 不調法者 abstainer
  bu-chō´hō (na) *adj* 不調法(な) awkward, clumsy, impolite

Budda *n* 仏陀 Buddha

budō *n* ブドウ・葡萄 grapes
  budō-shu *n* ブドウ酒 wine

búdō *n* 武道 martial arts (= **bújutsu** 武術)

bu-énryo (na) *adj* 不遠慮(な) frank, unreserved, forward, pushy, rude

búffe *n* ビュッフェ buffet

búgaku *n* 舞楽 traditional court dances and music

būingu n ブーイング booing

buji (ni) adv 無事(に) safely (without incident)

bujoku n 侮辱 insult(ing)

bújutsu n 武術 martial arts (= **búdō** 武道)

búki n 武器 weapon, arms

bu-kimi (na) adj 不気味(な) ghastly, eerie

bu-kíryō (na) adj 不器量(な) homely, ugly

bu-kíyō (na) adj 不器用(な) clumsy

bukká n 物価 commodity prices

bukkirábō (na) adj ぶっきらぼう(な) blunt, brusque, curt

bukku n ブック book

   bukku-fea n ブックフェア book fair

Búkkyō n 仏教 Buddhism

bū´mu n ブーム boom (fad)

bún n 文 sentence, text (= **búnshō** 文章)

   bun-bō-gu n 文房具, **bunpō´-gu** 文房具 stationery supplies: **bunbōgu-ya** 文房具屋 stationery shop

   bun-chin n 文鎮 paperweight

   bún-gaku n 文学 literature

   bún-go n 文語 literary language/word: **bungo-teki (na)** 文語的(な) literary

   bún-ka n 文化 culture, civilization; **Bunka-no-hí** 文化の日 Culture Day (3 November); **bunká-sai** 文化祭 cultural festival

   bun-ko(-bon) n 文庫(本) pocketbook

   bun-ken n 文献 literary document: **bunken-mokuroku** 文献目録 bibliography

   bun-mei n 文明 civilization

   bun-pō n 文法 grammar

   bún-raku n 文楽 puppet play (traditional)

   bún-shō n 文章 (written) sentence

bún-... prefix 分... part, portion, share; state, status

   bun-ben n 分娩 childbirth delivery: **bunben-shitsu** 分娩室 labor room

   bun-dóki n 分度器 protractor

   bun-jō n 分譲 sale in lots, lotting out: **bunjō-manshon** 分譲マンション condominium

   bun-kai n 分解 breakup (material)

   bun-katsu n 分割 dividing, splitting

   bun-pu n 分布 distribution

   bun-retsu n 分裂 breakup (countries, human relationship)

   bun-rúi n 分類 classification: ~ **shimásu** 分類します classifies, divides into (types/groups)

   bun-seki n 分析 analysis

   bún-shi n 分子 molecule, numerator

   bun-tan n 分担 (taking) partial charge; allotment, share: ~ **shimásu** 分担します takes partial charge of, shares in; pays/does one's share

...-bun suffix ...分 numeral -th

   yon-bun no ichí 4分の1 one-fourth

   han-bun (no) n 半分(の) half

búppō n 仏法 the teachings of Buddhism

búrabura adv ぶらぶら idly dangling, idling, hang around: ~ **shimásu** ぶらぶらします loafs (around); swings (one's leg back and forth)

buraindo n ブラインド window shade: ~ **o oroshimásu** ブラインドを下ろします pulls the blind down

burá(jā) n ブラ(ジャー) bra(ssiere)

Burajiru n ブラジル Brazil

burakku n ブラック black coffee (= **burakku-kō´hii** ブラックコーヒー)

   burakku-bókkusu n ブラックボックス black box

   burakku-kō´hii n ブラックコーヒー black coffee

   burakku-rísuto n ブラックリスト black list

   burakku-yū´moa n ブラックユーモア black humor

buránch n ブランチ brunch

burandē n ブランデー brandy

burando n ブランド brand

buránketto n ブランケット blanket

buránko n ブランコ a swing (in a park, etc.)

burári (to) v ぶらり(と) drops by (at), calls over

burasagarimásu, burasagaru v ぶら下がります, ぶら下がる hangs (down)

burasagemásu, burasageru v ぶら下げます, ぶら下げる hangs (down), suspends

búrashi n ブラシ brush

   ha-burashi n 歯ブラシ toothbrush

buratsukimásu, buratsuku v ぶらつきます, ぶらつく hangs around, wonders, strolls around

buraun-kán n ブラウン管 TV tube

buráusu n ブラウス blouse

burauza n ブラウザ browser (*computer*)

buréi n 無礼 discourtesy
buréi na *adj* 無礼な impolite, rude

burēkā n ブレーカー circuit breaker (box): **~ ga ochimásu** ブレーカーが落ちます The breakers trip.

burē´ki n ブレーキ brake: **~ o kakemásu** ブレーキをかけます puts on the brake

buréza n ブレザー blazer

búri n ブリ・鰤 yellowtail (*fish*): cf. **hamachi** ハマチ, **inada** イナダ

buríifu n ブリーフ brief(s)

buriifu-kē´su n ブリーフケース briefcase

búrijji n ブリッジ bridge (*card game*)

buriki n ブリキ tin

burō´chi n ブローチ brooch

burōdobando n ブロードバンド broadband (*computer*)

burogu n ブログ blog, weblog (= **weburogu** ウェブログ)

burōkā n ブローカー agent, broker

burókkori(i) n ブロッコリ(ー) broccoli

buronzu n ブロンズ bronze

burū (na) *adj* ブルー(な) feeling blue, mood dip (= **yūtsu** 憂鬱)

burudóggu n ブルドッグ bulldog

burudō´za n ブルドーザー bulldozer

burujoa n ブルジョア bourgeois

burūsu n ブルース blues (*music*)

bu-sáhō n 無[不]作法 a social gaffe, a faux pas
bu-sáhō na *adj* 無[不]作法な rude, blunt

bu-sata n 無沙汰 neglecting to write/visit (= **go-busata** ご無沙汰): **go-busata shiteimásu** ご無沙汰しています It's been a long time./ I'm sorry I haven't written in so long. [HONORIFIC]

búshi n 武士 Japanese warrior, samurai (= **samurai** さむらい・侍)

bushí-dō n 武士道 Bushido, the way of the samurai

búsho n 部署 department (*in the office*)

bushō (na) *adj* 無[不]精(な) lazy; slovenly
bushō-hige n 無精ひげ a three-day beard, a five-o'clock shadow
bushō-mono n 無精者 sluggard

búshu n 部首 radical (*Chinese character*): **búshu-kensaku** 部首検索 index by radical

...-búsoku n ...不足 shortage (= **fusoku** 不足): **ne-busoku** 寝不足 not enough sleep

busshitsu n 物質 matter, substance
busshitsu-teki (na) *adj* 物質的(な) material

busshoku n 物色 looking around for: **~ shimásu** 物色します looks/shops around for, seeks

bussō´(na) *adj* 物騒(な) troubled, unsafe, dangerous

búsu n ぶす ugly female

butá n ブタ・豚 pig
buta-niku n 豚肉・ブタニク pork

bútai n 舞台 stage

bútai n 部隊 troops, unit, outfit

butchō-zura n 仏頂面 a sullen face

bútikku n ブティック boutique

Butsu n 仏 Buddha (= **budda** 仏陀)
butsu-dan n 仏壇 household altar (*Buddhist*)
Butsu-zō n 仏像 Buddha (*statue*)

bútsubutsu iimásu (iu) v ぶつぶつ言います(言う) complains (*muttering way, grumbling way*) [+ NEGATIVE]

butsukarimásu, butsukaru v ぶつかります, ぶつかる collides with, runs into

butsukemásu, butsukeru v ぶつけます, ぶつける hits

bútsuri n 物理, **butsurígaku** 物理学 physics: **butsurigákú-sha** 物理学者 physicist

buttai n 物体 thing, matter, object, body, material body

búzā n ブザー buzzer

byákudan n ビャクダン・白壇 sandalwood

byō´ n 秒 a second (*of time*)
byō´-yomi n 秒読み countdown
byō-shin n 秒針 second hand/pointer

byō´... *prefix* 病... sickness, patients

19

byō-in *n* 病院 hospital; clinic, doctor's office, health service: **kyūkyū-byōin** 救急病院 emergency hospital

byō-ki (no) *adj* 病気(の) sick, ill; sickness, illness: **byōki-gachi (na)** 病気がち(な) sickly, unhealthy

byō-nin *n* 病人 an invalid, a patient

byō-reki *n* 病歴 medical history

byō-shin *n* 病身 sick body

byō-tō *n* 病棟 hospital ward

byō´ *n* 鋲 a tack; a thumbtack (= **gabyō** 画鋲)

byōbu *n* 屏風 screen *(folding)*

byōdō (na) *adj* 平等(な) equal

byōsha *n* 描写 depiction, description: ~ **shimásu** 描写します describes

C

cha *n* 茶 (**o-chá** お茶) tea, green tea

cha-bán-geki *n* 茶番劇 farce, burlesque

cha-bín *n* 茶瓶 teapot

cha-gará *n* 茶殻 tea leaves

cha-gashí *n* 茶菓子 (**o-chagashí** お茶菓子) tea cake

cha-iro (no) *adj* 茶色(の) brown

cha-me *n* 茶目 (**o-cháme (na)** お茶目(な)) mischievous, playful [IN POSITIVE SENSE], elfish, kidder

cha-no-má *n* 茶の間 (**o-cha-no-má** お茶の間) *(Japanese style)* living room

cha-nomi-tómodachi *n* 茶飲み友達 coffee-drinking companion, crony

cha-sají *n* 茶匙 teaspoon

cha-wán *n* 茶碗 (**o-cháwan** お茶碗) rice bowl; tea cup *(for tea ceremony)*

cha-wán-mushi *n* 茶碗むし steamed egg hotchpotch in a teacup *(made from broth and egg)*

cha-zuké *n* 茶漬け (**o-chazuké** お茶漬け) a bowl of rice with hot tea

...cha *suffix* ...ちゃ = ...-téwa ...ては (doing/being, if one does/be)

cháchi (na) *adj* ちゃち(な) [INFORMAL] petty, flimsy, cheap

chā´han *n* チャーハン・炒飯 *(Chinese)* fried rice

cháimu *n* チャイム chime

chairudo-shíito *n* チャイルドシート child seat

chājí *n* チャージ charge

chakkō *n* 着工 starting

chákku *n* チャック zipper

... cháku *suffix* ...着 arriving at (TIME/PLACE)

chakuchaku (to) *adv* 着々(と) steadily

chakuchí *n* 着地 landing on: ~ **shimásu** 着地します lands on

chakufukú *n* 着服 [BOOKISH] embezzlement: ~ **shimásu** 着服します have one's fingers in the till, embezzles

chakugán *n* 着眼 [BOOKISH] attention: ~ **shimásu** 着眼します turns one's attention

chakugán-ten *n* 着眼点 viewpoint

chakujítsu (na) *adj* 着実(な) steady, constant

chakunan *n* 嫡男 [BOOKISH] heir, eldest son

chakurikú *n* 着陸 *(from sky or wide water area)* landing, touching ground: ~ **shimásu** 着陸します lands on the ground

chakuséki *n* 着席 taking a seat: ~ **shimásu** 着席します takes a seat

chakushi *n* 嫡子 [BOOKISH] heir

chakushoku *n* 着色 colo(ring), stain

chákushu *n* 着手 [BOOKISH] begin, start

chakusō *n* 着想 [BOOKISH] conception, idea, inspiration: ~ **shimásu** 着想します conceives, comes by

chakusúi *n* 着水 landing on water, splashing down: ~ **shimásu** 着水します lands on water, splashes down

chā´mingu *n* チャーミング charming, attractive

...(-) chan *suffix* ...ちゃん [INFORMAL] *(mostly attached to children's or girls' names)* (= **san** さん)

chanbará *n* ちゃんばら sword battle *(historical period drama)*

chánnerú *n* チャンネル channel (TV)

chánpion *n* チャンピオン champion

chánpon n ちゃんぽん mixing (one's drinks/foods, etc.)

chánsu n チャンス chance

chantó adv ちゃんと safe(ly) (*without incident*), firmly, securely
chantó shita adj ちゃんとした proper, secure

chárachara shita adj ちゃらちゃら した [INFORMAL] showy [IN NEGATIVE SENSE]

charénji n チャレンジ challenge

cháritii n チャリティー charity

cháshū n チャーシュー (*Chinese*) roast pork
chāshū-men n チャーシュー麺 Chinese noodles with sliced roast pork

chātā n チャーター charter
chātā-bin n チャーター便 chartered flight, charter service
chātā′-ki n チャーター機 chartered plane

chatto n チャット chatting, chat (*internet*)

chékku n チェック check (*look-over*); (*bank*) (= **kogitte** 小切手); (*pattern*)
chekku-áuto n チェックアウト check-out
chekkú-in n チェックイン check-in

Chéko n チェコ Czech
Cheko-go n チェコ語 Czech (*language*)
Cheko-jín n チェコ人 a Czech

chē′n n チェーン chain, snow chain

chéro n チェロ cello

chi n 血 blood: **~ ga demásu** 血が出ます bleeds
chi-bashítta adj 血走った bloodshot
chi-dome n 血止め styptic pencil
chi-daraké adj 血だらけ bloody
chi-manakó n 血眼 n bloodshot eyes: **~ ni nátte** 血眼になって with bloodshot eyes
chi-namagusái adj 血生臭い bloody
chi-sují n 血筋 lineage, genealogy

chi n 地 ground, earth, land
chi-chū′ n 地中 underground
chi-chū′-kai n 地中海 the Mediterranean
chi-hei-sén n 地平線 horizon
chi-hō′ n 地方, **chí-iki** 地域 area,

district, region, province: **~ no** 地方の local

chi-jō′ n 地上 above ground, on the ground

chí-ka n 地下 underground: **chiká-shitsu** 地下室 basement: **chiká-tetsu** 地下鉄 subway

chi-kai n 地階 basement

chi-kakú n 地殻 (*geology*) the earth's crust

chí-ku n 地区 section, sector (*area*)

chi-méi n 地名 the name of a place/land

chi-shitsú n 地質 the geology (*of a place*): **chishitsú-gaku** 地質学 geology

chi-sō n 地層 (*geology*) stratum

chi-tai n 地帯 zone: **anzen-chitái** 安全地帯 safety zone

chí-zu n 地図 map

chián n 治安 law and order, security, public order

chiaríídā n チアリーダー cheerleader

Chibetto n チベット Tibet
Chibetto-go n チベット語 Tibetan (*language*)
Chibetto-jín n チベット人 a Tibetan

chíbi n ちび [INFORMAL] midget
chibi-kko n ちびっ子 (tiny) tot

chibu n 恥部 **1.** private parts, pubic area **2.** source of embarrassment

chíbusa n 乳房 (woman's) breasts

chíchi (oya) n 父(親) father

chíchi n 乳 mother's milk; breasts and nipples
chi(chi)-bánare n 乳離れ past the breast, is weaned, become independent

chidorí-ashi n 千鳥足 swaying gait: **~ de arukimásu** 千鳥足で歩きます walks drunkenly

chié n 知恵 wisdom
chié-okure (no) n, adj 知恵遅れ(の) mentally retarded

chién n 遅延 [BOOKISH] delay
chién-shōmeisho n 遅延証明書 train delay certificate

chífusu n チフス typhus, typhoid (*fever*)

chigái n 違い difference, discrepancy

chigaimásu, chigau v 違います, 違う is different; is wrong; is not like that

chigatté v 違って → **chigaimásu** 違います

chigirimásu, chigiru v 千切ります, 千切る tears into pieces

chigúhagú (na) adj ちぐはぐ(な), ill-assorted, mismatched

chihō (-shō´) n 痴呆(症) (medical) dementia

chíi n 地位 rank, position, status

chíifu n チーフ chief

chíimu n チーム team
chiimuwāku n チームワーク teamwork

chiisái, chíisa na adj 小さい, 小さな little, small

chíitā n チーター cheetah

chiizu n チーズ cheese
chiizu-kēki n チーズケーキ cheese-cake

chíji n 知事 governor

chijimárimásu, chijimaru v 縮まります, 縮まる shrinks, shortens

chijimemásu, chijimeru v 縮めます, 縮める shortens (it)

chijimimásu, chijimu v 縮みます, 縮む (it) shrinks

chijin n 知人 [BOOKISH] acquaintance

chijiremásu, chijireru v 縮れます, 縮れる becomes curly

chijoku n 恥辱 disgrace, shame

chiká goro n, adv 近頃 lately, recently

chikái n 誓い vow, pledge, oath

chikái adj 近い near, close by: ~ **uchí ni** 近いうちに in the near future

chikaimásu, chikáu v 誓います, 誓う swears, vows, pledges

chíkaku adj, adv 近く close, near-by

chikakú n 知覚 perception

chiká-michi n 近道 short cut

chikán n 痴漢 (sexual) molester, groper

chikará n 力 power, strength; ability (= **nō-ryoku** 能力); effort (= **doryoku** 努力): o-chi-kara お力 influence (= **eikyōryoku** 影響力)

chika-yorimásu, chika-yoru 近寄ります, 近寄る approaches, draws/comes near

chika-zukemásu, chika-zukéru v 近付けます, 近付ける lets one approach, brings close; associates (keeps company) with; can approach it

chika-zukimásu, chika-zúku v 近付きます, 近付く (= **chika-yorimásu, chika-yoru** 近寄ります, 近寄る)

chíketto n チケット ticket (= **kippu** 切符)

chikén n 知見 knowledge, learning, information

chíkin n チキン chicken

chikokú n 遅刻 late: ~ **shimásu** 遅刻します is late (for)

chíkubi n 乳首 nipple, teat

chíkuchiku-shimásu (suru) v ちくちくします(する) pricks, prickles, tickles

chikuón-ki n 畜音機 phonograph

chikúrimásu, chikuru v チクります, チクる tells, snitches on, informs on

chikuseki n 蓄積 accumulation, store

chikushō, chikishō 畜生, ちきしょう 1. interj Damn! (curse) 2. n beast(s)

chikuwá n チクワ broiled fish cake

chikyū´ n 地球 the Earth
chikyū-gi n 地球儀 globe

chímachima adv ちまちま small and neatly arranged; frugally; unadventurous (person)

chimatá n 巷 public: ~ **no uwasa dewa…** 巷のうわさでは… People say that…

chiméikizu n 致命傷 vital wound, fatal injury

chiméiteki (na) adj 致命的(な) fatal, capital, mortal, deadly

chimitsú adj 緻密 close, minute, elaborate: ~ **na keikaku** 緻密な計画 careful planning

chinatsu n 鎮圧 suppression: ~ **shimásu** 鎮圧します suppresses

chinbotsu n 沈没 sinking: ~ **shimásu** 沈没します sinks

chínchin n ちんちん (o-chínchin おちんちん) penis [baby, informal talk]

chinden n 沈殿 deposition, settling: ~ **shimásu** 沈殿します is deposited, settles out

chíngin n 賃金 wage

chinjutsú n 陳述 statement, parol: ~ **shimásu** 陳述します makes a statement

chinka n 沈下 sinkage, subsidence: ~ **shimásu** 沈下します subsides, settles down

chínmi n 珍味 delicacy, bonne bouche

chinmoku n 沈黙 silence: **~ shimásu** 沈黙します stops talking

chínō n 知能 intelligence
chinō-shisū n 知能指数 intelligence quotient

chinomígo n 乳飲み子 an infant, nursling

chínpira n ちんぴら・チンピラ a punk; hoodlum; juvenile delinquent

chinretsu n 陳列 exhibition, display: **~ shimásu** 陳列します exhibits, puts on display

chinseizai n 鎮静剤 sedative, tranquilizer

chinshaku n 賃借 letting and hiring, rental: **~ shimásu** 賃借します rents

chíntai n 賃貸 lease, rental, rented apartment

chíppu n チップ tip (money)

chiranai v 散りらない = **chirimasén** 散りません (not scatter)

chirári-to-mimásu (miru) v ちらりと見ます(見る) glances

chira(ka)shimásu, chira(ka)su v 散ら(か)します, 散ら(か)す scatters, strews

chirashí n チラシ leaflet

chirashi-zushi n ちらし寿司[鮨] sushi rice covered with fish tidbits

chiratsuki n ちらつき flicker

chiréba v 散れば (if they disperse/scatter/fall about) → **chirimásu** 散ります

chirí n 塵 dust (on ground, floor, etc.)
chiri-tóri n ちり[塵]取り dustpan

chíri n 地理 the geography, the lay of the land
chiri-gaku n 地理学 (the study/science of) geography
chiri-jō (no) adj 地理上(の) geographical
chiri-teki (na) adj 地理的(な) geographical

chiri-gamí, chiri-kami, chiri-shi n ちり紙 tissues (Kleenex) (= **tisshu(pēpā)** ティッシュ(ペーパー))

chirimásu, chiru v 散ります, 散る disperses, scatters, falls about

chiryō n 治療 treatment (medical): **~ shimásu** 治療します treats, cures

chísei n 知性 intellect, intelligence, mind, mentality

chishiteki (na) adj 致死的(な) death-dealing

chisetsú n 稚拙 childish

chíshiki n 知識 knowledge
chishikí-jin n 知識人 intellectual(s)

Chishimá n 千島, **Chishíma-réttō** 千島列島 the Kurile Islands

chishíryō n 致死量 overdose

chísso n チッソ・窒素 nitrogen

chissokú n 窒息 suffocation

chisui n 治水 flood control

chitchái adj ちっちゃい [INFORMAL] little (= **chiisái** 小さい)

chi(sei)teki (na) adj 知(性)的(な) intelligent, intellectual

chitsu n 膣 vagina

chítsujo n 秩序 order, discipline, system

chitté v 散って → **chirimásu** 散ります

chittó-mo adv ちっとも [INFORMAL], [+ NEGATIVE verb] not a bit, not in the least

chō n 腸 intestines

chō n チョウ・蝶 butterfly (= **chō´chō** チョウチョ(ウ)・蝶々)
chō-músubi n 蝶結び bow (of a ribbon)
chō-nékutai n 蝶ネクタイ bow tie

(…-)chō´ suffix (…)丁 block (or block area) of a city: **(…-) chō-mé** (…)丁目 (…-th) block (of city)

(…-)chō´ suffix (…)長 head, chief, leader

(…-)chō´ suffix (…)兆 trillion

chóbo n ちょぼ a dot

chōbó n 帳簿 (account) book
chōbo-gákari n 帳簿係 book-keeper

chōchín n 提灯 lantern

chó´chō n 町長 town mayor

chōdai-shimásu (suru) v ちょうだい[頂戴]します(する) I (humbly) receive/accept

…chōdái interj …ちょうだい [INFORMAL] **1.** Please **2.** Give me… (= **kudasai** ください・下さい)

chōdo adj ちょうど exactly, just

chōgō n 調合 preparation: **~ shimásu** 調合します prepares, compounds

chō´hō (na)

chō´hō (na) *adj* 重宝(な) useful, convenient, valued: ~ **shimásu** 重宝します appreciates, values, cherishes

chō´ji *n* 丁子 cloves

chō´jo *n* 長女 eldest daughter

chojō´ *n* 頂上 top, summit, peak

chō´ka *n* 超過 [BOOKISH] excess: ~ **shimásu** 超過します exceeds, goes/runs over

chōkán *n* 朝刊 morning paper

chō´kan *n* 長官 chief (*head*)

chō´ki *n* 長期 long period, long range

chokín *n* 貯金 deposit, savings: ~ **shimásu** 貯金します deposits (*money*), saves

chokin-bako *n* 貯金箱 saving box

chokkán *n* 直感 intuition

chokkí *n* チョッキ vest

chóko *n* ちょこ (**o-chóko** おちょこ) saké cup

chōkoku *n* 彫刻 carving, engraving: ~ **shimásu** 彫刻します carves, engraves

choko(rē´to) *n* チョコ(レート) chocolate

chō´ku *n* チョーク chalk

chokuryū´ *n* 直流 DC, direct current

chokusén *n* 直線 straight line

chokusetsu *n, adv* 直接 direct(ly)

chō-kyóri *n* 長距離 long distance

chō´mi *n* 調味 seasoning (*food*)

chōmi-ryō *n* 調味料 spice

chō´nán *n* 長男 eldest son

chōryū *n* 潮流 current, tide; trend

chō´sa *n* 調査 examination, inquiry, investigation, research, survey: ~ **shimásu** 調査します examines, inquires, investigates, researches, surveys

chosáku-ken *n* 著作権 copyright

chōséi *n* 調整 adjustment: ~ **shimásu** 調整します adjusts (= **chōsetsú** 調節)

chōsen *n* 挑戦 challenge

chōsen-sha *n* 挑戦者 challenger

Chō´sén *n* 朝鮮 → **Kita Chōsén, Kankoku**

chōsetsú *n* 調節 → **chōséi** 調整

chósha *n* 著者 writer, author

chōshí *n* 調子 tune; condition; trend; ~ **ni norimásu** 調子に乗ります, ~ **ga demásu** 調子が出ます gets into the swing of things: ~ **ga ii/warui** 調子がいい/悪い is in good/bad condition

chósho *n* 著書 one's book

chō´sho *n* 長所 strong point, merit, advantage

chōshokú *n* 朝食 morning meal, breakfast (= **asa-gohan** 朝ご飯)

chōshu *n* 聴取 listening in: ~ **shimásu** 聴取します listens in

chōshu-sha *n* 聴取者 (*radio*) listener

chōshū *n* 聴衆 audience

chōshū *n* 徴収 [BOOKISH] collection (*of taxes, etc.*), levying: ~ **shimásu** 徴収します collects, levies

chosúi-chi *n* 貯水池 reservoir

chō´ten *n* 頂点 climax, peak, high-point

chō-tsúgai *n* 蝶つがい hinge

chótto *adv* ちょっと just a little; just a minute; somewhat

chottóshitá *adj* … ちょっとした… slight, trivial; quite a …, a decent …

chōwá *n* 調和 harmony, agreement: … **to ~ shimásu** …と調和します is in harmony (*agrees*) with

chū *n* 注 annotation, note

chū *adj* 中 middle; medium

chū´-bu *n* 中部 middle (*part*)

chū-gákkō *n* 中学校 middle school (*junior high school*)

chū-gáku-sei *n* 中学生 junior high school student

chū-gatá (no) *n* 中型(の) medium-size (*model*)

chū-gén *n* 中元 (**o-chūgén** お中元) midsummer gift

chū´-i *n* 中尉 1st lieutenant; lieutenant junior grade (j.g.)

chū´-jō *n* 中将 (*army*) lieutenant general; (*navy*) vice admiral

chū-jún *n* 中旬 the middle of (*month*)

chū-kán *n* 中間 middle: … (**no) chū-kán** … (の) 中間 beween …: **chūkán-shiken** 中間試験 intermediate exam: **chūkán-kanríshoku** 中間管理職 mid-level executive, middle management

chū-kán *n* 中巻 middle volume (*of a set of three*)

chū-nen *n* 中年 middle age, **chū-nen (no)** 中年(の) middle-aged (*person*)

chū-níkai *n* 中二階 mezzanine (*floor*)

chū-sa *n* 中佐 lieutenant colonel; (*navy*) commander

chū´-sei *n* 中世 medieval times, the Middle Ages

chū-shō-kígyō *n* 中小企業 medium-sized and small companies

Chū´-tō *n* 中東 the Middle East

chū-toró *n* 中とろ・中トロ medium-fat (pink) tuna

chū-za *n* 中座 excusing oneself, leaving in the middle: **~ shimásu** 中座 します excuses oneself

...-chū *suffix* 中 **1. ... chū (ni)** ...中(に) during, while, within (*time*) **2. ... chū (no)** ...中(の) in course ...of, under (*doing*)

kōji-chū *n* 工事中 under construction

chū´bu *n* チューブ tube

chū´cho *n* ちゅうちょ・躊躇 [BOOKISH] hesitation: **~ shimásu** ちゅうちょ[躊躇]します hesitates

chū´doku *n* 中毒 addiction, poisoning

arukōru-chū´doku アルコール中毒 (= **aruchū** アル中) alcohol addiction

shoku-chū´doku 食中毒 food poisoning

Chū´goku *n* 中国 China

Chūgokú-jin *n* 中国人 a Chinese

Chūgokú-go *n* 中国語 Chinese (*language*)

Chūgoku-chíhō *n* 中国地方 the Chugoku area of Japan (*Okayama, Hiroshima, Yamaguchi, Shimane, Tottori Prefectures*)

chū-hai *n* 酎ハイ a *shōchū* highball

chū´i *n* 注意 attention; note, notice, reminder: **~ shimásu** 注意します pays attention; is careful of; advises, warns

chūi-bukái *adj* 注意深い careful

chūingámu *n* チューインガム chewing gum

chūjitsu (na) *adj* 忠実(な) faithful

chū´ka *n, adj* 中華 Chinese..., Chinese food

chū´ka-gai *n* 中華街 Chinatown

chū´ka-ryō´ri(-ten) *n* 中華料理(店) Chinese cooking (restaurant)

chūkái *n* 仲介 mediation: **~ shimásu** 仲介します goes between

chūkai-gyōsha *n* 仲介業者 broker, intermediary agent

chūko (no) *adj* 中古(の) secondhand

chūkó-hin *n* 中古品 secondhand goods

chūkó-sha *n* 中古車 used car

chūkokú *n* 忠告 advice: **~ shimásu** 忠告します advises

chūmoku *n* 注目 attention, notice: **~ shimásu** 注目します pays attention

chūmon *n* 注文 an order

chūō´ *n* 中央 the center

chūō no *adj* 中央の central

Chūō-sen *n* 中央線 the (JR) Chuo Line

chūritsú *n* 中立 neutral(ity)

chūséi *n* 忠誠 loyalty, fidelity, allegiance: **~ o chikaimásu** 忠誠を誓います pledges one's loyalty

chūséi *adj* 中性 neutral

chūsén *n* 抽選 lottery, drawing

chūshá *n* 駐車 parking

chūsha-jō *n* 駐車場 parking lot/garage

chūsha-kinshi *n* 駐車禁止 No Parking

chūshá *n* 注射 injection: **yobō-chūsha** 予防注射 preventive injection

chūshá-ki *n* 注射器 syringe (*for injections*)

chūshí *n* 中止 suspension (*abeyance*): **~ shimásu** 中止します suspends, stops (*in the midst*)

chūshín *n* 中心 center, heart, middle

chūshin no *adj* 中心の central

chūshin-chi *n* 中心地 central area

chūshō *n* 中傷 slander

chūshokú *n* 昼食 lunch (= **hiru-góhan** 昼ご飯, **ranchi** ランチ)

chūshō-teki (na) *adj* 抽象的(な) abstract

chūsū (shinkei) *n* 中枢(神経) nerve center

chūsúi-ki *n* 注水器 douche, syringe (*for water*)

chūto (de) *adv* 中途(で) on the way, halfway (= **tochū (de)** 途中(で))

chūto-hanpa (na) *adj* 中途半端(な) half-done, incomplete

chūyō *n* 中庸 [BOOKISH] moderation: **~ o emásu** 中庸を得ます exercises moderation

chūzái *n*, 駐在 residence, presence: **~ shimásu** 駐在します resides

chūzái-in *n* 駐在員 resident officer

chūzái-táishi *n* 駐在大使 ambassador

chūzetsu *n* 中絶 abortion: **chūzetsu-shujutsu o ukemásu** 中絶手術を受けます undergoes an abortion

D

... da *suffix* …だ: → **... -ta** た

... dá *v* …だ = **... désu** …です is; it is

dabingu *n* ダビング dubbing: **~ shimásu** ダビングします dubs

daboku-shō *n* 打撲傷 bruise

dabudabu (no) *adj* だぶだぶ(の) baggy, loose, full, voluminous: **~ no fuku** だぶだぶの服 voluminous dress

daburimásu, dabúru *v* ダブります, ダブる gets doubled, overlaps, repeats, is repeated (by mistake)

dáburu *n* ダブル **1.** = **dabururū´mu** ダブルルーム a double (*room*) **2.** double(-size) drink **3.** double-breasted suit **4.** = **dáburusu** ダブルス (*tennis*) doubles

daburu-béddo *n* ダブルベッド double bed

dabútte *v* ダブって → **daburimásu** ダブります

dachin *n* 駄賃 (**o-dachin** お駄賃) reward, tip

dada *n* 駄々 fretful: **~ o konemásu** 駄々をこねます is fretful, acts like a baby: **dada-kko** 駄々っ子 fretful/unreason-able/spoiled child

dadappiroi *adj* だだっ広い rambling, too spacious

daeki *n* 唾液 saliva

daen *n* 楕円 ellipse, oval

dága *conj* だが [BOOKISH] but (= **shi-kashi** しかし)

dageki *n* 打撃 blow, shock: **dageki o ataemásu** 打撃を与えます hits, delivers a blow

daha *n* 打破 defeat

dái- *prefix* 第 [+ number] number …; (= **...-banmé**…番目) [numeral]-th; (*separate word except when attached to a single-unit numeral*)

dái-go *adj* 第五 number five; (= **go-banmé** 五番目) fifth

dái-hachi *adj* 第八 number eight; (= **hachi-banmé** 八番目) eighth

dái-ichi *adj* 第一 number one; (= **ichi-banmé** 一番目) first: **dái-ichi no** 第一の (the) first; **dái-ichi ni** 第一に first (of all)

dái-jū *adj* 第十 number ten; (= **jūban-mé** 十番目) tenth

dai-ku *adj* 第九 (= **dái-kyū** 第九) number nine; (= **kyū-banmé** 九番目) ninth

dái-nana *adj* 第七 number seven; (= **nana-banmé** 七番目) seventh

dái-ni *adj* 第二 number two; (= **ni-banmé** 二番目) second: **Dái-ni-ji Sekaitaisen** 第二次世界大戦 World War II

dái-roku *adj* 第六 number six; (= **roku-banmé** 六番目) sixth: **dái-rokkan** 第六感 six sense

dái-san *adj* 第三 number three; (= **sanbanmé** 三番目) third: **dái-san-sha** 第三者 third party

dái-yon *adj* 第四 number four; (= **yonbanmé** 四番目) fourth

dái *n* 題 **1.** title (= **daimei** 題名) **2.** topic, theme (= **daimokú** 題目)

dai 代 **1.** *n* (**o-dai** お代) charge (*fee*), bill: **takushii-dai** タクシー代 taxi fare **2.** [numeral]-**dai** …age, generation: **nijū´-dai** 20代 twenties; **nanajū-nen-dai** 70年代 70's (seventies); **ni-dai(me)** 2代目 The Second, junior (*family*)

...´-dai *suffix* …台 (*counts mounted machines, vehicles*)

daibā *n* ダイバー diver

daiben *n* 大便 defecation, feces: **~ o shimásu** 大便をします defecates

daiben *n* 代弁: **~ shimásu** 代弁します speaks for another

daibingu *n* ダイビング dive: **~ shimásu** ダイビングします dives

daibu *adv* 大分 quite, very, much

dai-búbun *n* 大部分 the majority

daibutsu *n* 大仏 giant statue of Buddha

daidái *n* ダイダイ・橙 bitter orange daidái-iro 橙色 (*color*) orange

dáidai *adj, adv* 代々 generation after generation, for generations

daidokoro *n* 台所 kitchen (= **kitchin** キッチン)

daidokoro-dō'gu n 台所道具 kitchen utensils

daietto n ダイエット diet

daifuku (mochi) n 大福 (もち) soft rice cake stuffed with sweet bean jam

daigaku n 大学 college, university
daigakú-in n 大学院 graduate school: **daigakuín-sei** 大学院生 graduate student
daigakú-kōnai n 大学構内 campus (= **daigaku-kyanpasu** 大学キャンパス)
daigaku-sei n 大学生 college student, undergrad(uate)

daigiin n 代議員 deputy

daigishi n 代議士 Diet member

daigomi n 醍醐味 relish, whole point

daihitsu n 代筆 ghost-writing: **~ shimásu** 代筆します write for someone

daihon n 台本 script (= **kyakuhon** 脚本)

daihyō n 代表 representative
daihyō-sha n 代表者 a representative (person)
daihyō-teki (na) adj 代表的 (な) representative, typical, model

daiji n 大事 a matter of importance; **~ o torimásu** 大事をとります plays it safe: **(o-)karada o (o-)daiji ni ...** (お)体を(お)大事に... take good care of yourself
daijí (na) adj 大事 (な) important, precious (= **taisetsu (na)** 大切 (な))

daijin n 大臣 minister (cabinet)

dai-jō'bu adj 大丈夫 OK, all right; safe (and sound); no need to worry, no problem: **~ desu** 大丈夫です It's all right.

daikei n 台形 trapezoid

dáikichi n 大吉 very good luck, excellent luck

daikin n 代金 the price/charge, the bill: **~ hjikikae (de)** 代金引換え (で), **daibiki (de)** 代引き (で) C.O.D., collect (on delivery)

daikō n 代行 acting as agent
daikō'-sha n 代行者 agent (= **dairi-nin** 代理人)

daikō n 代講 substitute class/teacher

daikoku-bashira n 大黒柱 pillar, breadwinner: **ikka no ~** 一家の大黒柱 the supporter of a family

daikon n 大根 giant white radish
daikon-óroshi n 大根おろし grated radish

dáiku n 大工 carpenter

daikyū n 代休 compensation day, substitute holiday

daiméishi n 代名詞 pronoun

daimoku n 題目 (**o-daimoku** お題目) topic (= **dái** 題)

daimyō' n 大名 (**o-daimyō** お大名) feudal lord

dainamaito n ダイナマイト dynamite

dainamikku n ダイナミック dynamic

dainashi n 台無し ruin, spoil: **~ ni shimásu** 台無しにします ruins, spoils

dainingu-kitchin (DK) n ダイニングキッチン (DK) a combined dining room-kitchen, an eat-in kitchen

dainingu-rūmu n ダイニングルーム dining room

daí (no) ... ** adj 大 (の) ..., **dai-... 大... big, great
dai-kibo (na) adj 大規模 (な) large scale
dai-kirai (na) adj 大嫌い (な) loathing, aversion
dái-suki (na) adj 大好き (な) favorite, greatly liked
dai-tasū n 大多数 large number; majority

dairi n 代理 commission, agent, agency
dairi-bo n 代理母 surrogate mother
dairí-nin n 代理人 agency
dairí-ten n 代理店 agency

dairiseki n 大理石 marble (stone)

daishi n 台紙 mount, board (art)

dai-shō n 大小 size

dai-shō n 代償 price, compensation

dái-sū n 代数 algebra, literal arithmetic

daitai adv 大体 in general, on the whole, approximately, almost (= **oyoso** およそ)

daitán (na) adj 大胆 (な) bold

daite v 抱いて → **dakimásu** 抱きます

daitōryō n 大統領 president (of a nation)

dáiya n 1. ダイヤ schedule (train) **2. = daiya(móndo)** ダイヤ (モンド) diamond

daiyaku n 代役 substitute, alternate

daiyaru n ダイヤル dial

daiyō n 代用 substitution: ~ **shimásu** 代用します substitutes

daiza n 台座 [BOOKISH] pedestal, seat

daizai n 題材 material, subject matter

dáizu n 大豆・ダイズ soy beans

dajare n 駄洒落 pun, equivoque

... -**daka** ...高 **1.** quantity, volume; sum **2.** higher by ...: **hyakuén-daka** 百円高 100 yen up

dakanai v 抱かない = **dakimásen** 抱きません (not hug)

dákara (sa) conj だから(さ) and so; therefore; that's why

... **daké** suffix ...だけ only, just: ... (**-ta**) **daké de** ...(た)だけで just from (having done it)

dakemásu, dakeru v 抱けます, 抱ける can hug, can hold in the arms

dakenai v 抱けない = **dakemásén** 抱けません (cannot hug)

dakete 抱けて → **dakemásu** 抱けます

dakimásu, daku v 抱きます, 抱く holds in the arms

daki-shimemásu v 抱き締めます → **dakimásu** 抱きます

dakyō n 妥協 compromise

daku v 抱く = **dakimásu** 抱きます (holds in the arms)

damarimásu, damáru v 黙ります, 黙る is/becomes silent; shuts up

damashimásu, damásu v 騙します, 騙す deceives, cheats

damátte v 黙って → **damarimásu** 黙ります

damé (na) adj 駄目(な) no good, no use, won't; bad, broken, malfunctioning; don't!: ~ **ni narimásu** 駄目になります gets ruined, spoiled; ~ **ni shimásu** 駄目にします ruins it, spoils it

dámu n ダム dam

dán n 段 **1.** step(s); grade, order **2.** (page) column; scene, act **3.** (...**dán** ... 段) case, event

dan-bō´ru n ダンボール・段ボール corrugated cardboard

dan-chō no omoi n 断腸の思い heartbreaking grief

dan-dán adv 段々 gradually

dan-kai n 段階 grade, rank, stage (of a process)

dan-raku n 段落 paragraph

dan-tei n 断定 decision, conclusion: ~ **shimásu** 断定します decides

dan-zoku-teki (na) adj 断続的(な) intermittent

dan n 団 group, party, team

dan-chi n 団地 housing development

dan-chō n 団長 leader, head

dango n 団子 (**o-dango** お団子) dumpling

dan-tai n 団体 organization, group

dan n 壇 platform: **dan-jō ni agarimásu** 壇上に上がります steps onto the platform

dan n 談 conversation, talk

dan-shō n 談笑 chatting: ~ **shimásu** 談笑します has a pleasant chat

dan-wa n 談話 [BOOKISH] conversation: **danwa-shitsu** 談話室 common room

dan-... prefix 男... male

dán-jo n 男女 male and female: **dánjo-kyōgaku** 男女共学 coeducation; **dánjo-byōdō** 男女平等 sexual equality

dan-kon n 男根 penis

dan-sei n 男性 male

dán-shi n 男子 boy: **dánshi-gakusei/seito** 男子学生/生徒 schoolboy

dan-shō n 男娼 male prostitute

dan-shoku n 男色 male homosexual love

dan-son johi n 男尊女卑 male chauvinism

danatsu n 弾圧 suppression: ~ **shimásu** 弾圧します clamps down

danbō n 暖房 heating (of room, house)

danbō-sō´chi n 暖房装置 heating device, radiator

danbō-sétsubi n 暖房設備 heating (equipment)

dangan n 弾丸 [BOOKISH] bullet

dani n ダニ mite, tick

danna n 旦那 **1.** my husband **2. danna-san/-sama** 旦那さん/様 (your/someone else's) husband **3.** master (of a shop, etc.)

danpingu n ダンピング dumping

danryoku n 弾力 elastic force

dansu n ダンス dance

dan'yaku n 弾薬 ammunition, powder and ball

-darake suffix ...だらけ full of..., covered with...

28

daradara (to) *adj* だらだら(と)
lengthy: ~ **(to) sugoshimásu** だらだら
(と)過ごします slobs about

daraku *n* 堕落 corruption: ~ **shimásu**
堕落します corrupts

darari-to *adv* だらりと loosely, lollingly

darashinai *adj* だらしない slovenly,
loose

dáre *pron* 誰 who: **dáre no** 誰の whose;
dáre dé mo 誰でも anybody (at all),
everybody

dáre-dare *pron* 誰々 someone or other, so-and-so, what's-his/her-name

dáre ka *pron* 誰か somebody, someone

dáre mo *adv* 誰も (not) anybody;
[+ NEGATIVE verb] nobody

dáre-sore *pron* 誰それ someone or
other, so-and-so, what's-his/her-name

...daró *suffix* ...だろう probably,
probably (it) is; I think; don't you
think? (= **...deshō´** ...でしょう)

dasai *adj* ダサい frumpish, unstylish

dasánai *v* 出さない = **dashimasén**
出しません (not put out; not ...)

dáseba *v* 出せば (if one puts out; if ...)
→ **dashimásu** 出します

dasei *n* 惰性 inertia, (force of) habit

daseki *n* 打席 trip to the plate, at-bat

dasha *n* 打者 a batter/hitter

dashí *n* だし soup stock, broth: **dashí-
no-moto** だしの素 instant bouillon

dashimásu, dásu *v* 出します, 出す
puts out; serves (food/drink); produces;
pays, spends; mails; begins

dashimono *n* 出し物 play, act, show

dashin *n* 打診 (medical examination
by) percussion, tapping; sounding a
person out

dashinuke (ni) *adv* 出し抜け(に)
abruptly

dashinukimásu, dashinuku *v* 出し抜
きます, 出し抜く outwits, gets the
better of

dasoku *n* 蛇足 icing on the cake

dassen *n* 脱線 derailment: ~ **shimásu**
脱線します is derailed; gets off the
track, gets sidetracked

dasshí-men *n* 脱脂綿 absorbent cotton

dasshí-nyū *n* 脱脂乳 skim milk

dasshū´-zai *n* 脱臭剤 deodorant

(personal) (= **deodoranto** デオドラント)

dassō *n* 脱走 escape, desertion

dā´su *n* ダース dozen: **ichi-dā´su** 1ダー
ス one dozen

datai *n* 堕胎 abortion: ~ **shimásu** 堕胎
します has an abortion

daten *n* 打点 run batted in, RBI

datō *n* 打倒 overthrow, defeat

datō *n* 妥当 appropriate, reasonable

datsumō´-zai *n* 脱毛剤 depilatory

datsuraku *n* 脱落 omission, dropout

datsuryoku *n* 脱力 faintness, lassitude

...dátta *v* ...だった was; it was (= **...
déshita** ... でした)

dattai *n* 脱退 withdrawal: ~ **shimásu** 脱
退します withdraws

...dáttara *conj* ...だったら if/when it
is (or was)

...dáttari (shimásu/desu) *suffix* ...だ
ったり(します/です) being represent-
atively/sometimes/alternately ...

dátte *conj* だって but; however, even
so, though (= **démo** でも)

...dátte *suffix* ...だって even being ...;
... or something (= **...démo** ... でも)

de *n* 出 **1.** a person's origins (family,
birthplace, school); (... **no de** ...の出)
born in/of ..., a graduate of ... **2.** (out)
flow **3.** emergence, appearance

...de *particle* ...で → **...-te** ...て

...dé *suffix* ...で (happening) at, in, on;
with, by (means of), through

...dé *conj* ...で is/was and; being, its
being; with (its being) [COPULA GERUND]

...de arimásu *v* ...であります = **...
désu** ...です is; it is

...de gozaimashō´ *v* ...でございまし
ょう = **...deshō´** ...でしょう probably
is; I think it is (, sir/ma'am)

...de gozaimásu *v* ...でございます
[DEFERENTIAL] = **...desu** ...です is; it is
(sir/ma'am)

...de orimásu *v* ...でおります
[DEFERENTIAL/HUMBLE] (I/we) stay/
keep (go on) being: **...de imásu** ...でい
ます stays/keeps (goes on) being

deaikeisaito *n* 出会い系サイト online
dating website (Internet)

de-aimásu, de-áu *v* 出会います, 出
会う: **... ni ~** ...に出会います encoun-

29

ters, meets, happens to see/meet, runs/
bumps into

de-átte v 出会って → **de-aimásu**
出会います

de-awánai v 出会わない = **de-aimásén**
出会いません (not encounter)

déguchi n 出口 exit, outlet

deiríguchi n 出入り口 gate(way),
doorway

dekake ro v 出掛けろ [IMPERATIVE] (go
out!) → **dekakemásu** 出掛けます

dekakemásu, dekakeru v 出掛けま
す, 出掛ける starts off/out, goes out,
departs

dekiai n 溺愛 blind love: ~ **shimásu**
溺愛します loves blindly

dekiai (no) adj 出来合い(の) ready-
made

dekígoto n 出来事 happening, accident

dekimásu, dekíru v 出来ます, 出来
る can (do), is possible, produced,
done, finished, through, ready

dekí-mónó, o-déki n できもの, おでき
swelling, sore, boil, pimple

dekínai v 出来ない impossible = **dekimasén** 出来ません (cannot)

dekíru v 出来る = **dekimásu** 出来ます
(can (do))

dekíru-dake adv できるだけ as much
as possible

dek(k)ai adj で(っ)かい [INFORMAL]
big (= **ōkii** 大きい)

dékki n デッキ deck

dekoboko (no) adj でこぼこ(の)
bump(y), rough (road, etc.); uneven

déma n デマ false rumor

demae n 出前 catering, food delivered
to order, restaurant delivery (service/
person)

demásu, déru v 出ます, 出る goes/
comes out, emerges, appears; is
served; leaves, starts

démo conj でも but, however, even
so, though

démo n デモ demonstration

... **démo** suffix ...でも even/also
(being) ..., even if it be; ...or something

demokurashii n デモクラシー democracy

de-mukaemásu, de-mukaéru v 出迎

えます, 出迎える meets, greets, welcomes

dénai v 出ない = **demasén** 出ません
(not go/come out; ...)

denbu n でんぶ sweet cooked ground
fish

denbu n 臀部 [BOOKISH] buttock, hips
[medical]

denbun n 伝聞 hearsay

denbun n 電文 telegram, telegraphic
message

dénchi n 電池 battery

denchō n 電柱 telephone/light pole

dendō n 伝道 conduction
　dendō-tai n 伝導体 conductor
　dendō-sha n 伝道者 a missionary

déndō n 電動 electric operation,
electric-powered
　déndō-isu n 電動椅子 electric-
powered wheelchair

dengaku n 田楽 assorted boiled foods
(= **o-dén** おでん)

dengon n 伝言 message (= **messēji**
メッセージ)

denki n 伝記 biography

dénki n 電気 electricity, power; lights
　denki-sutándo n 電気スタンド desk/
floor lamp
　denki-sutō'bu n 電気ストーブ electric
heater
　denki-yō'hin n 電気用品 = **denki-kígu**
電気器具 electrical appliances
　denki-kámisori n 電気かみそり
electric shaver
　denki-kónro n 電気コンロ hot plate
　denki-sōjíki n 電気掃除機 vacuum
cleaner
　denki-ya (san) n 電気屋(さん) electrician

denkyū n 電球 light bulb

denmāku n デンマーク Denmark

dénpa n 電波 electric wave, radiowave

denpō n 電報 telegram, telegraph: ~
o uchimásu 電報を打ちます sends a
telegram

denpun n でんぷん starch (for cooking)
　denpún-shitsu (no) n (adj) でんぷん
質(の) starch(y)

denpyō n 伝票 check (restaurant bill)

denrai n 伝来 [BOOKISH] introduction,

30

import: **senzo ~ (no)** 先祖伝来（の） descendant, patrimonial

denrei n 伝令 [BOOKISH] orderly, herald

dénryoku n 電力 electric power
denryoku-gáisha n 電力会社 power company

denryū n 電流 electric current

densen n 電線 electric wire, power line

densen n 伝染 contagion
densen-byō n 伝染病 contagious/ communicable disease, epidemic

densetsu n 伝説 tradition (legend): ~ ni narimásu 伝説になります passes into legend

dénsha n 電車 (electric) train, streetcar

dénshi (no) adj 電子（の） electron(ic)
denshi-manē n 電子マネー electronic money, cyberbuck (internet)
dénshi-renji n 電子レンジ microwave
denshi-shoseki n 電子書籍 computer book, digital book, e-book, electronic book (internet)

densho-bato n 伝書鳩 carrier pigeon

dentatsu n 伝達 conveyance, transmission

dentō n 電灯 lamp, light, flashlight

dentō n 伝統 tradition
dentō-teki (na) adj 伝統的（な） traditional

denwa n 電話 telephone (call): ~ ni demásu 電話に出ます answers the phone; ~ o kakemásu/shimásu 電話を かけます/します makes a phone call
denwa-bángō n 電話番号 telephone number
denwa-bókkusu n 電話ボックス phone booth
denwa-chō n 電話帳 telephone book/ directory
denwa-kōkánshu n 電話交換手 telephone operator
denwa-sen n 電話線 phone line, telephone wire(s)

deodoranto n デオドラント deodorant

depáto n デパート department store

déppa n 出っ歯 bucktooth

déreba v 出れば (if one goes/comes out; if …) → **demásu** 出ます

dé ro v 出ろ [IMPERATIVE] (go out!) → **demásu** 出ます

déru v 出る = **demásu** 出ます (goes out, comes out, leaves, starts, attends, appears, graduates from)

deshí n 弟子 (**o-deshi** お弟子) apprentice, disciple

… déshita v …でした was; it was;
…-masén deshita …ませんでした didn't

… deshō v …でしょう probably, probably (it) is; I think; don't you think?

… desu, dá v …です, だ is, has been (and still is), will be; it is

déta v 出た = **demáshita** 出ました (emerged; graduated from)

dē´ta n データ data

detarame n でたらめ nonsense
detarame na adj でたらめな irresponsible, unreliable

detchiagemásu, detchiagéru v でっ ちあげます, でっちあげる fake

déte v 出て **1.** → **demásu** 出ます [GERUND] **2.** ~ kimásu 出て来ます comes out; ~ ikimásu 出て行きます goes out

dē´to n デート date (time; engagement)

dé wa conj では well then; in that case; and so; and now (= **ja** じゃ)

… dé wa suffix では (with) its being, it is and; if it be: ~ arimasén (~ nái) …ではありません（ではない）= **ja arimasén (ja nái)** じゃありません（じ ゃない） it is not

dezáin n デザイン design

dezáinā n デザイナー designer

dezā´to n デザート dessert

dii-kē´ n ディーケー (= **DK**) → **dainingu-kítchin** ダイニングキッチン

disukáunto n ディスカウント discount

do n 度 degree; moderation; ~ **o sugoshimásu/koshimásu** 度を過ごし ます/越します goes too far, goes to excess

do-… prefix ど… exactly, really
do-mannaka n ど真ん中 dead center
do-konjō n ど根性 a lot of guts

…-dó suffix …度 **1.** times (occasions) **2.** degrees

dō´ adj どう how, why; (in) what (way)
Dō´-shimáshita ka. どうしましたか. What happened? What did you do?

Dō´-itashimashite. どういたしまして. You're welcome.

dō´ *n* 銅 copper (= **aka-gane** あかがね・銅)

dō-ka *n* 銅貨 coin (*brass or copper*)

dō-sei (no) *adj* 銅製(の) made of copper

dō-zan *n* 銅山 copper mine

dō-zō *n* 銅像 statue (*bronze*)

dō´ *n* 胴 torso (= **dōtai** 胴体)

dō-age *n* 胴上げ tossing person in(*to*) the air in celebration

dō´-... *prefix* 同... the same ...

dō-gaku *n* 同額 a like amount, the same amount (of money)

dō-gi-go *n* 同義語 = **dōi-go** 同義語 synonym

dō-gyō *n* 同業 same trade: **dōgyō-sha** 同業者 professional brother/brethren

dō-hō *n* 同胞 brother(s)/sister(s) with same mother, (fellow) countryman

dō-i-tai *n* 同位体 isotope

dō-itsu (no) *adj* 同一(の) same: **dōitsu-shi shimásu** 同一視します identifies

dō´-ji *n* 同時 **1. dō´-ji (no)** 同時(の) simultaneous: **dōji-tsū´yaku** 同時通訳 simultaneous translation **2. ... to dō´-ji ni** ...と同時に at the same time as ...; while ..., on the other hand **3.** at a (single) time, at one time

dō-jidai (ni) *adv* 同時代(に) (*in*) the same age/era

dō´-jidai (no) *adj* 同時代(の) contemporaneous, same generation

dō-jō *n* 同情 sympathy, compassion: **(... ni) ~ shimásu** (...に)同情します sympathizes (with ...)

dō-ka *n* 同化 elaboration, assimilation: **~ shimásu** 同化します assimilates

dō-kaku *n* 同格 apposition, coordination, equal rank: **~ desu** 同格です is equal

dō-kan *n* 同感 same sentiment, empathy

dō´-ki *n* 同期 the same period

dō´-kí (-sei) *n* 同期(生) classmates who joined the school in the same year (= **dōkyū´-sei** 同級生), employees who joined the company in the same year

dō-koku-jin *n* 同国人 fellow countryman/countrymen

dō-kyū´-sei *n* 同級生 classmate

dō-ryō *n* 同僚 colleague

dō-sedai *n* 同世代 one's fellow generation

dō´-sedai (no) *adj* 同世代(の) same generation

dō-sei (no) *adj* 同性(の) person of the same sex: **dōseí-ai (no)** 同性愛(の) homosexual

dō-sei (no) *adj* 同姓(の) having the same name: **dōsei-dòmei (no)** 同姓同名 (の) person with the same family and given name

dō-shitsú *n* 同室 same room: **dōshitsú-sha** 同室者 roommate: **~ ni narimásu** 同室になります shares a room

dō-zai (no) *adj* 同罪(の) being equally guilty

dóa *n* ドア door

doa-nobu *n* ドアノブ door knob

doai *n* 度合い degree, level, rate: **~ o mashimásu** 度合いを増します compounds

do-bin *n* 土瓶 teapot

dobu *n* どぶ・溝 gutter

dōbutsu *n* 動物 animal

dōbutsu-en *n* 動物園 zoo

dōbutsú-gaku *n* 動物学 zoology

dóchira *pron* どちら which one (*of the two*) = **dotchi** どっち; [DEFERENTIAL] where (= **dóko** どこ), who (= **dáre** 誰)

dóchira dé mo *adv* どちらでも either one of the two; [+ NEGATIVE verb] neither one of the two

dochíra-gawa *n* どちら側 which one

dóchira ka *adj, adv* どちらか one of the two

dochira mo *adv* どちらも [+ NEGATIVE verb] neither one; both

dóchira sama *n* どちら様 [DEFERENTIAL] who (are you)

dō dé mo *adv* どうでも anyhow (at all)

dōfū shimásu (suru) *v* 同封します(する) encloses (*in envelope*)

dōga *n* 動画 animation, moving image

dōgan *n* 童顔 childlike face

dōgan no hito *n* 童顔の人 childlike faced person

dogeza n 土下座 kneeling on the ground: **~ shite ayamarimásu** 土下座して謝ります falls on one's knees to ask for pardon

dōgi n 道義 moral principle

dogitsui adj どぎつい [INFORMAL] gaudy

dogitsui iro n どぎつい色 loud color

dogitsui hyōgen n どぎつい表現 shocking expression

dōgu n 道具 tool

dōgú-bako n 道具箱 tool box

dohyō n 土俵 sumo-wrestling ring: **~ ni agarimásu** 土俵に上がります steps onto the sumo ring

dōi n 同意 agreement, approval: **~ shimásu** 同意します agrees, concurs, consents

dōin n 動員 mobilization, recruitment

doite v どいて → **dokimásu** どきます

dóitsu pron どいつ which damn one

Dóitsu n ドイツ Germany

Doitsu-go n ドイツ語 German language

Doitsú-jin n ドイツ人 a German

Doitsu-kei n ドイツ系 of German ancestry

dō-iu ... adj どういう... what kind/sort of...

doji n どじ goof (= **hema** へま) boob

dō-jimásu, dō-jíru v 動じます, 動じる gets agitated, upset

dō-jinai = (...-témo) dō-jimasén (...ても)動じません (is unfazed (by))

dojji bōru n ドッジボール dodge ball

dojō n ドジョウ loach, mudfish

dojō n 土壌 [BOOKISH] soil borne

dō·jō n 道場 martial arts hall

dō'ka interj どうか please: **~ onegai desukara** どうかお願いですから for God's *[Christ's, Heaven's, Pete's]* sake

dō'ka suffix どうか: **~ shiteimásu** どうかしています something wrong with, crazy, mad

... dō'ka suffix ...どうか: **... ka ~ ...**か どうか (whether ...) or not

dokanai v 退かない = **dokimasén** 退きません (not get out of the way)

doke v 退け [IMPERATIVE] (get out of the way!) → **dokimásu** 退きます

dóki n 土器 earthenware: **Jomon-dóki** 縄文土器 Jomon ware

dōki n 動機 motivation, motive

dōki n 動悸 beat, pulse: **~ ga shimásu** 動悸がします palpitates

dókidoki shimásu (suru) v どきどきします(する) one's heart throbs (beats, flutters)

dokimásu, doku v 退きます, 退く gets out of the way

dókku n ドック dock

dóko pron どこ where, what part/place; **~ e ikimásu ka?** どこへ行きますか Where *(to what place)* are you going? **~ kara kimáshita ka?** どこから来ましたか Where did you come from?

dóko-dé-mo adv どこでも anywhere (at all)

dóko-doko pron どこどこ somewhere or other, such-and-such a place (= **dóko-soko** どこそこ)

dóko ka n, adv どこか somewhere

dóko made adv どこまで where to; how far

doko mo adv どこも [+ NEGATIVE verb/adj] nowhere

dōkoku n 慟哭 [BOOKISH] crying out with grief

...-dókoroka adv ...どころか = **sore-dókoroka** それどころか rather, on the contrary

dokú n 毒 (= **dokú-butsu** 毒物) poison

doku-késhi n 毒消し antidote

doku-mi n 毒見 tasting food/drink before offering it to the others: **dokumi-yaku** 毒見役 food taster:

dokudan n 独断 dogma

dokudan-teki (na/ni) adj, adv 独断的 (な/に) dogmatic(ally)

dokudan-jō n 独壇場 [BOOKISH] monopoly

dokudoku nagaremásu (nagareru) v どくどく流れます(流れる) gurgles

dokudokushii adj 毒々しい gaudy, virulent

dokugaku n 独学 self-study: **~ shimásu** 独学します studies by oneself

dokuhaku n 独白 monologue

dokuritsu n 独立 independence: **~ shimásu** 独立します will stands on one's own two feet; **dokuritsu-shita …** 独立した … independent

dokuryoku (de) *adj* 独力(で) by oneself

dokusái-sha *n* 独裁者 dictator, absolute ruler

dókusha *n* 読者 reader (*person*)

dokushin *n* 独身 single, bachelor

dokushin-sha *n* 独身者 single

dokushin-ryō *n* 独身寮 dormitory for singles

dokusho *n* 読書 reading books: ~ **no aki** 読書の秋 autumn reading

dokusō *n* 独走 leaving all the other runners far behind: ~ **shimásu** 独走します is far ahead of others

dokusō *n* 独奏 solo performance: ~ **shimásu** 独奏します plays a solo

dokusō-sei *n* 独創性 originality: ~ **ni kakeru/toboshii** 独創性に欠ける/乏しい unoriginal

dokutā kōsu *n* ドクターコース doctoral program

dokutā sutoppu *n* ドクターストップ doctor's order to stop

dokutoku (no/na) *adj* 独特(の/な) characteristic, peculiar, unique

dō´kutsu *n* 洞窟 cave

dokuzetsu *n* 毒舌 a barbed/spiteful tongue

dokuzetsu-ka *n* 毒舌家 person with a poisonous/sharp tongue

dokyumentarii dorama *n* ドキュメンタリー・ドラマ infotainment (*documentary film*)

…´-dómo 共 (*makes humble plurals*): **watakushi-dómo** わたくし[私]ども we/us

domein-mei (nēmu) *n* ドメイン名 (ネーム) domain-name (*internet*)

dō´mo どうも **1.** *interj* thank you **2.** *interj* excuse me **3.** *adj* somehow

dōmō (na) *adj* 獰猛(な) fierce, savage

domorimásu, domoru *v* どもります, どもる stammers, stutters

dón どん・ドン boom, bam (*sound*)

…-don ...丼 → **donburi** どんぶり[丼] (→ ten-don 天丼, una-don うな丼, katsu-don カツ丼)

donarimásu, donáru *v* 怒鳴ります, 怒鳴る shouts, yells

dónaritsukemásu, dónaritsukeru *v* 怒鳴りつけます, 怒鳴りつける chews out

dónata *pron* どなた [DEFERENTIAL] who (= **dáre** 誰)

donburi *n* どんぶり・丼 large rice bowl

donburi/don-mono *n* 丼もの a bowl of rice with some kind of topping

dóndon *adv* どんどん one right after another, in large numbers

do-nichi *n* 土日 Saturday and Sunday

dō´ni ka *adv* どうにか somehow: ~ **shimásu** どうにかします manages to do

Donmai *interj* ドンマイ Don't worry., Never mind.

dónna *adj* …どんな… what kind of…:

dónna ni どんなに to what extent, how much

dóno … *adj* どの… which … (*of more than two*)

dono-gurai/kurai *adv* どの位 how many/much/far/long

dónsu *n* どんす・緞子 damask

donyori (to shita) *adj* どんより(とした) dull, gray, somber

dorafuto *n* ドラフト draft

doraggu *n* ドラッグ drug

doraggu sutoa *n* ドラッグストア drugstore

doraibā *n* ドライバー driver

doraibu *n* ドライブ drive

doraibu-in *n* ドライブイン roadside restaurant

doraibu-surū *n* ドライブスルー drive-through (*restaurant*)

dorai-kuríiníngu *n* ドライクリーニング dry cleaning

dorái (na) *adj* ドライ(な) dry; modern, sophisticated, unsentimental

doraiyā *n* ドライヤー dryer, drier

dōrákú *n* 道楽 **1.** dissipation **2.** (**o-dōrákú** お道楽) pastime, hobby

dóre *pron* どれ which one (*of more than two*): ~ **ka** どれか some/any one of them; ~ **dé mo** どれでも whichever/ any of them; ~ **mo** どれも (not) any of them; **dóre-gurai/kurai** どれ位 how many/much/far/long (= **dono-gurai/ kurai** どの位)

dorei *n* 奴隷 slave

dóresu *n* ドレス dress, frock

dōrí *n* 道理 reason (*what is sensible*)

...-dōrí ...通り avenue; just as (*according with*): **jikan-dōrí (ni)** 時間通り(に) on time ...

dóriru *n* ドリル drill (*tool; practice*)

doró *n* 泥 mud; muck (*filth, dirt*) **doro-dárake/mamire (no)** *adj* 泥だらけ/まみれ(の) muddy

dō′ro *n* 道路 road **dōro-hyō′shiki** 道路標識 road sign

dorobō *n* 泥棒 thief, robber, burglar

dóru *n* ドル dollar **dóru-bako** *n* ドル箱 cash cow, gold mine, moneymaker

dóryoku *n* 努力 effort: **~ shimásu** 努力します makes an effort, tries (*hard*), endeavors, strives

dō′sa *n* 動作 (body) movements, gestures

dosamawari *n* どさ回り road show: **~ o shimásu** どさ回りをします goes on the road, goes on a tour

dō′san *n* 動産 [BOOKISH] movable property

dosanko *n* 道産子 native people/horses born in Hokkaido

dōsei *n* 同棲 living together (*for unmarried couple*)

dosha *n* 土砂 earth and sand **dosha-buri** *n* 土砂降り torrential downpour

dōshi *n* 動詞 verb

...dō′shi *suffix* ...同士: **otoko-dō′shi no yakusoku** 男同士の約束 promise between man and man: **onna-dō′shi no oshaberi** 女同士のおしゃべり girl talk, woman-to-woman chat

dō′shi *n* 同志 fellow ..., comrade

dōshin *n* 童心 juvenile mind: **~ ni kaerimásu** 童心に返ります retrieves one's childish innocence

dō′-shite *adv* どうして why; how: **~ mo** どうしても one way or another, some how or other

dosō *n* 土葬 burial under the earth

dōsō′-kai *n* 同窓会 alumni association; class reunion

dossari *adv* どっさり all of a heap: **~ ataemásu** どっさり与えます showers on: **~ aru** a pile of

dotabata *adv* どたばた noisily: **~ shimásu** どたばたします makes a noise, romps about

dotanba (de) *adv* 土壇場(で) (*at*) the last moment

dótchi *pron* どっち = **dóchira** どちら which one (*of the two*)

dote *n* 土手 dike

dōtei *n* 童貞 virgin (*male*)

dotera *n* どてら padded bathrobe (= **tanzen** 丹前)

dōtoku *n* 道徳 morals, morality **dōtoku-teki (na)** *adj* 道徳的(な) moral

dótto *adv* どっと suddenly, with a rush

dōwa *n* 童話 fairy tale

dōyō (no) *adj* 同様(の) the same

dōyō′ *n* 動揺 [BOOKISH] agitation, unrest: **~ shimásu** 動揺します is agitated (*nervous*)

dōyō′ *n* 童謡 (*traditional*) children's song

Doyō′(bi) *n* 土曜(日) Saturday

doyomeki *n* どよめき clamor, hubbub

doyomekimásu, doyomaku *v* どよめきます、どよめく rings, (*a crowd of people*) makes a ruckus

dō′yū ("iu") ... *adj* どうゆう(いう)... what kind/sort of... (= **dónna ...** どんな ...)

dō′zo *interj* どうぞ **1.** please **2.** here it is

dy... → **j...**

dz... → **z...**

E

é *n* 絵 picture, painting, drawing
e-hágaki *n* 絵葉書 picture postcard
e-hón *n* 絵本 picture book

e *n* 柄 handle

e (-sá) *n* え（さ）・餌 bait
e-zuke *n* 餌付け: **~ o shimásu** 餌付け
をします feeds

e *interj* えっ eh?, what?

ē *interj* ええ yes

… e *particle* …へ to (*a place*); [replaces **… ni** …に *before* **… no …** …の…] to (*a person*)

ea-kon *n* エアコン air conditioning/
conditioner

eaméru *n* エアメール airmail

earain *n* エアライン airline

earobíkusu *n* エアロビクス aerobics

eatáminaru *n* エアターミナル air
terminal

eba-míruku *n* エバミルク evaporated
milk

ebi *n* エビ・海老 shrimp: **kurumá-
ebi** 車エビ prawn; **isé-ebi** 伊勢エビ
lobster; **shibá-ebi** 芝エビ tiny shrimp
ebi-fúrai *n* エビフライ shrimp fried in
bread crumbs
ebi-ten *n* エビ天 batter-fried shrimp

ē-bii-shíi *n* エービーシー・ABC
alphabet (ABC)

echikétto *n* エチケット etiquette

eda *n* 枝 branch
eda-ge *n* 枝毛 outgrowth of hair, hair
with split ends
eda-mame *n* 枝豆 green soy beans (*to
be boiled, podded and eaten as appetizers*)

efutiipii (FTP) *n* FTP File Transfer
Protocol, FTP (*computer*)

egáite *v* 描いて → **egakimásu** 描き
ます

egakimásu, egáku *v* 描きます、描く
draws (a picture)

egao *n* 笑顔 smiling face

ei-… *prefix* 英… **1.** English **2.** great
ei-bun *n* 英文 English text
ei-chi *n* 英知 wisdom
ei-dan *n* 英断 wise decision

eiei-jiten *n* 英英辞典 English-English
dictionary

Ei-go *n* 英語 English (*language*)

ei-kaiwa *n* 英会話 English conversation: **eikaiwa-gakkō** 英会話学校
English conversation school

ei-ki *n* 英気 vigor, energy

Ei-koku *n* 英国 Great Britain, the
United Kingdom (U.K.) = **Igirisu** イギ
リス England: **Eikoku-jin** 英国人 a
British person = **Igirisu jin** イギリス人
an English person

ei-wa *n, adj* 英和 English-Japanese:
eiwa-jíten 英和辞典 English-Japanese
dictionary

ei-yaku *n* 英訳 English translation:
~ shimásu 英訳します translates into
English

ei-yū *n* 英雄 hero, heroine

eien (no) *adj* 永遠(の) eternal, permanent
eien ni *adv* 永遠に eternally, permanently (= **eikyū (ni)** 永久(に))

eíga *n* 映画 movie, film
eigá-kan *n* 映画館 movie theater
eiga-haiyū *n* 映画俳優 movie actor/
actress
eiga-sutā *n* 映画スター movie star

eiga *n* 栄華 prosperity: **~ o kiwamemásu** 栄華を極めます is at the height
of its prosperity

eigō *n* 永劫 [BOOKISH] eon: **mirai-eigō**
未来永劫 eon

eigyō *n* 営業 (*running a*) business:
~ shimásu 営業します do business;
opens
eigyō-chū *n* 営業中 (we're) open
eigyō-jikan *n* 営業時間 business
hours, operating hours

eikaku *n* 鋭角 acute angle

eikan *n* 栄冠 crown, aureole

eiki *n* 鋭気 spirit

eikō *n* 栄光 glory, honor

eikyō *n* 影響 influence: **~ o ataemásu** 影
響を与えます influences; **~ o ukemásu**
影響を受けます receives an influence

eikyū (ni) *adv* 永久(に) eternally,

permanently, forever (= **eien (ni)** 永遠
(に))
eisei *n* 衛生 hygiene, health, sanitation
eisei-teki (na) *adj* 衛生的(な) sanitary
eisei *n* 衛星 satellite: **jinkō-éisei** 人工衛
星 artificial satellite
eisei chūkei *n* 衛星中継 satellite transmission
eishá-ki *n* 映写機 movie projector
éito *n* エイト eight; 8-oared racing boat
eiyō *n* 栄養 nutrition, nourishment
eizō *n* 映像 picture, image
eizoku *n* 永続 permanence
éizu *n* エイズ AIDS
éki *n* 駅 railroad station
eki-ben 駅弁 box lunches sold at railroad stations
eki-chō *n* 駅長 stationmaster
ekisu *n* エキス extract
ekitai *n* 液体 liquid
ekkusu-sen *n* エックス[X]線 X-ray
(= **rentogen** レントゲン)
ékubo *n* えくぼ dimple
ekurea *n* エクレア éclair
emásu, éru *v* 得ます, 得る [BOOKISH]
gets; can do
én *n* 円 circle (= **maru** 丸): **én-gurafu**
円グラフ pie chart: **én-taku** 円卓
round table
en-kei *n* 円形 circle: **enkei-datsumōshō**
円形脱毛症 *alopecia areata* (loss of hair)
en-shū *n* 円周 circumference: **enshū-
ritsu** 円周率 circle ratio, pi
én *n* 円, ...**-en** ...円 yen (¥): **én-daka
/-yasu** 円高/安 high /low value of the
yen: **endate** 円建て yen basis
énai *v* 得ない = **emasén** 得ません (not
get; cannot)
enbō *n* 遠望 distant view
enchō *n* 延長 extension: ~ **shimásu** 延
長します extends, lengthens, prolongs
enchō-kō'do 延長コード extension cord
endan *n* 縁談 marriage proposal
endan *n* 演壇 lecture platform
éndō (-mame) *n* エンドウ(豆) peas
enen (to) *adv* 延々(と) endlessly
enérúgii *n* エネルギー energy
enérugísshu (na) *adj* エネルギッシュ
(な) energetic
engan *n* 沿岸 the coast

engawa *n* 縁側 (*wooden*) veranda,
porch (*in traditional Japanese house*)
engei *n* 園芸 gardening
engei-jō *n* 演芸場 vaudeville (*theater*)
engeki *n* 演劇 drama, play
engeki-jin *n* 演劇人 theater people
engeru-keisū *n* エンゲル係数 Engel's
coefficient
engi *n* 縁起 **1.** omen, luck **2.** (*historical*)
origin: ~ **ga/no yoi** 縁起が/の良い
is of good omen, lucky: ~ **o katsugimásu** 縁起をかつぎます believes in
omens, superstitious
éngi *n* 演技 performance; acting
engí-sha *n* 演技者, **én-ja** 演者 performer
engo *n* 援護 support
engun *n* 援軍 rescue forces, support
arms, reinforcement
engumi *n* 縁組み marriage, match
énjin *n* エンジン engine (*of automobile*): ~ **ga kakarimásu** エンジン
がかかります the engine starts; ~ **o
kakemásu** エンジンをかけます starts
the engine
enjínia *n* エンジニア engineer, specialist
enjimasu, enjiru *v* 演じます, 演じる
plays, acts, performs
énjo *n* 援助 support (*aid*), backing
enjói *n* エンジョイ: ~ **shimásu** エンジ
ョイします enjoys
enjuku *n* 円熟 [BOOKISH] fully maturing: ~ **shimásu** 円熟します mellows
enka *n* 演歌 sad and melancholic
Japanese songs (*ballad*)
enkai *n* 宴会 party, banquet: ~ **o
hirakimásu** 宴会を開きます holds a
party
enkaku *n* 沿革 [BOOKISH] history
enkaku *n* 遠隔 [BOOKISH] remoteness
enkaku-sōsa *n* 遠隔操作 remote
handling
enkei *n* 遠景 distant landscape
enki *n* 延期 postponement: ~ **shimásu**
延期します postpones
enkinkan *n* 遠近感 perspective
enkyori *n* 遠距離 long distance
enkyori-ren'ai *n* 遠距離恋愛 long-
distance love affair

enman (na) *adj* 円満（な）satisfactory

enmei *n* 延命 life extension
  enmei-chiryō *n* 延命治療 life-sustaining treatment

enmoku *n* 演目 program

enmusubi *n* 縁結び matchmaking:
  enmusubi-no-kami 縁結びの神 the god of marriage

énnichi *n* 縁日 a temple fair (*festival*)

ennō *n* 延納 [BOOKISH] delayed payment

enokí-dake/take *n* エノキダケ・榎茸 straw mushrooms

enpitsu *n* 鉛筆 pencil
  enpitsu-kezuri *n* 鉛筆削り pencil sharpener

enro *n* 遠路 from a long distance: ~ **harubaru** 遠路はるばる all the way

enryo *n* 遠慮 (**go-enryo** ご遠慮) reticence, social reserve, shyness: ~ **ga nái** 遠慮がない frank: ~ **shimásu** 遠慮 します hesitates, holds back, is shy; **Go-enryo náku.** ご遠慮なく. Don't be shy/reticent.: ~ **shite okimásu** 遠慮して おきます takes a rain check, declines for now

enshi *n* 遠視 farsightedness (*presbyopia*)

enshutsu *n* 演出 production, staging (*play, movie*): ~ **shimásu** 演出します produces, stages

énso *n* 塩素 chlorine

ensō *n* 演奏 performance (*musical instrument*): ~ **shimásu** 演奏します performs, plays
  ensō´-kai *n* 演奏会 concert

ensoku *n* 遠足 picnic, outing: ~ **ni ikimásu** 遠足に行きます goes on an excursion

entai *n* 延滞 arrear (*overdues*): ~ **shimásu** 延滞します being overdue
  entai-ryōkin *n* 延滞料金 deferred premium

entátei(n)mento *n* エンターテイ（ン）メント entertainment

enten *n* 炎天 [BOOKISH] scorching sun/ weather: **enten-ka de** 炎天下で under a blazing sun

entotsu *n* 煙突 chimney, smokestack

enyō (no) *adj* 遠洋（の）pelagic, ocean

enzetsu *n* 演説 address, speech (*public*)

épuron *n* エプロン apron

erā *n* エラー error
  erā-messēji *n* エラーメッセージ error message

erabanai *v* 選ばない = **erabimasén** 選びません (not choose/elect/select)

erabeba *v* 選べば (if one chooses/ selects/elects) → **erabimásu** 選びます

erabimásu, erábu *v* 選びます, 選ぶ chooses, selects, elects

erái *adj* 偉い **1.** great, grand, superior (*person*) **2.** terrible, awful (= **hidoi** ひどい・酷い)

éreba *v* 得れば (if one gets) → **emásu** 得ます

erebé´tā *n* エレベーター elevator

ereganto (na) *adj* エレガント（な）elegant (= **yūga (na)** 優雅（な））

erí *n* えり・襟 collar (*of closing/ clothes*): ~ **o tadashimásu** 襟を正します straightens oneself

éro-hon *n* エロ本 pornography book

éru *v* 得る = **emásu** 得ます (gets)

ese-… *adj* えせ… pseudo-… (= **nise** にせ・偽[贋])

essē *n* エッセー essay

esu-efu *n* SF science fiction

esukarē´tā *n* エスカレーター escalator

etai-no-shirenai *adj* 得体の知れない strange, as deep as a well

étchi (na) *adj* エッチ（な）dirty-minded: ~ **na hanashí** エッチな話 a dirty (*an off-color*) story

éte *v* 得て → **emásu** 得ます

éte-shite *adv* 得てして usually: ~ **... shimásu** 得てして... します is apt to do it

ē-to *interj* えーと／ええと well now, uh, let me see

ézu (ni) *v* 得ず（に）= **énai de** 得ないで (not getting; unable) → **emásu** 得ます

F

fáiawōru *n* ファイアウォール firewall (*internet security*)

fáibā *n* ファイバー fiber

fáindā *n* ファインダー finder

fáiringu *n* ファイリング filing: ~ **shimásu** ファイリングします files

fáiru *n* ファイル file

fáito *n* ファイト fight

fákkusu *n* ファックス fax, facsimile (= **fakushimiri** ファクシミリ)

fámikon *n* ファミコン Nintendo Entertainment System

fán *n* ファン fan (*enthusiast*); **yakyū-fan** 野球ファン baseball fan

fan-kurabu *n* ファンクラブ fan club

fan-retā *n* ファンレター fan letter

fánkushon *n* ファンクション function

fánshii *n* ファンシー fancy

fántajii *n* ファンタジー fantasy

fáshisuto *n* ファシスト fascist

fásshon *n* ファッション fashion

fásunā *n* ファスナー zipper

fāsuto-fūdo *n* ファーストフード fast food

fāsuto-nēmu *n* ファーストネーム first name

fáuru *n* ファウル foul

feisu bukku *n* フェイスブック Facebook (*internet*)

fiibā *n* フィーバー: ~ **shimásu** フィーバーします becomes fevered

Firípin *n* フィリピン Philippines

fírumu, fuirumu *n* フィルム、フイルム film

fírutā *n* フィルター filter

fisshingu *n* フィッシング phishing (*fraud*)

fō´ku *n* フォーク fork

fu *n* フ・麩 pieces of dried wheat gluten

fu- *prefix* フ un-, non-
fu-an (na) *adj* 不安(な) uneasy, anxious
fú-ben (na) *adj* 不便(な) inconvenient, unhandy
fu-chū´i *n* 不注意 carelessness: **fuchū'i (na)** 不注意(な) careless
fu-dō´toku *n* 不道徳 immorality: **fudō'toku (na)** 不道徳(な) immoral

fugō´kaku *n* 不合格 failure: **fugō'kaku (no)** 不合格(の) unqualified, failed

fu-kánō (na) *adj* 不可能(な) impossible

fú-kai (na) *adj* 不快(な) unpleasant, displeasing, displeased (= **fu-yúkai (na)** 不愉快(な))

fu-kéiki *n* 不景気 depression, recession, hard times (= **fukyō** 不況)

fu-kísoku (na) *adj* 不規則(な) irregular

fu-kō´ *n* 不幸 misfortune: **fukō na** 不幸な unfortunate, unlucky: **fukō ni (mo)** 不幸に(も) unfortunately

fu-kō´hei (na) *adj* 不公平(な) unfair

fu-kyō *n* 不況 business slump, depression (= **fukeiki** 不景気)

fú-jiyū (na) *adj* 不自由(な) inconvenient, restricted; needy; weak

fu-jō (no/na) *n* 不浄(の/な) unclean, unhygienic (= **fuketsu (na)** 不潔(な))

fu-man(zoku) *n* 不満(足) discontent: **fuman (na)** 不満(な) discontented, dissatisfied, unhappy (= **fuhei** 不平): ~ **na kao** 不満な顔 discontented face

fu-mei (no) *adj* 不明(の) unknown, obscure: **yukue-fumei (no)** 行方不明(の) disappearance, missing

fú-ri (na) *adj* 不利(な) unfavorable

fu-rin *n* 不倫 adultery

fu-ryō (no) *adj* 不良(の) bad, no good

fu-senmei (na) *adj* 不鮮明(な) obscure, unclear

fu-shin *n* 不審 doubt, suspicion: **fushimu (na)** 不審(な) doubtful, suspicious

fu-shinnin *v* 不信任 no-confidence

fu-shi (no) *adj* 不死(の), **fujimi no** 不死身の immortal(ity): **fujimi no hito** 不死身の人 immortal person

fu-shízen (na) *adj* 不自然(な) unnatural

fu-shō´ji *n* 不祥事 scandal: ~ **o okoshimásu** 不祥事を起こします disgraces

fu-soku *n* 不足 shortage, insufficiency: ~ **shimásu** 不足します runs short

fu-tegiwa *n* 不手際 mismanagement

fu-tei (no) *adj* 不定(の) unfixed, uncertain, indefinite, undecided: **futeiki (no)** 不定期(の) irregular

fu-tei (na) *adj* 不貞 (な) unfaithful (to her husband): **~ o hatarakimásu** 不貞を働きます cheats on her husband

fu-teki (na) *adj* 不敵 (な) bold, lawless: **daitan-futeki (na)** 大胆不敵 (な) fearless

fu-tekinin (na) *adj* 不適任 (な) unfit: **futekinin-sha** 不適任者 misfit

fu-tekiō (na) *adj* 不適応 (な) maladjustment (*maladaptive*)

fu-tekisetsu (na) *adj* 不適切 (な) irrelevance, inappropriate: **~ na hatsugen** 不適切な発言 inappropriate remark(s)

fu-tekitō (na) *adj* 不適当 (な) inadequate, unsuitable

fu-tokui (na/no) *adj* 不得意 (な/の) poor/weak at

fu-tokutei (no) *adj* 不特定 (の) indefinite: **futokutei-tasū (no hito)** 不特定多数 (の人) general public

fu-tō (na) *adj* 不当 (な) unfair, unjustified; unreasonable

fu-tōshiki *n* 不等式 inequality

fu-tōeki *n* 不凍液 antifreeze

fu-tōitsu *n* 不統一 disunity

fu-tōkō *n* 不登校 non-attendance at school, truancy: **futōkō-ji** 不登校児 truant student

fu-tsuriai *n* 不釣合い imbalance

fu-un (na) *adj* 不運 (な) unfortunate

fu-yō (no) *adj* 不要 (の) unnecessary

fu-yō (no) *adj* 不用 (の) useless, disused

fu-yúkai (na) *adj* 不愉快 (な) unpleasant, displeasing: **~ ni shimásu** 不愉快にします displeases, offends

fu-zai *n* 不在 absence: **fuzai-tōhyō** 不在投票 absentee vote

fú *n*, *suffix* 府, **…´-fu** … 府 an urban prefecture: **Kyōto-fu** 京都府 Kyoto Prefecture, **Ōsaka-fu** 大阪府 Osaka Prefecture

fū´ *n* 封 sealing: **… no ~ o shimásu** … の封をします seals a letter

… fū´ *suffix* … 風, **…-fū** … 風 air; way, fashion, manner; style

fúbo *n* 父母 father and mother, one's parents (= **ryōshin** 両親)

fúbuki *n* 吹雪 snowstorm

fuchí *n* 縁 edge, rim, frame

fuda *n* 札 label, tag, card, check: **o-fuda** お札 talisman (*of a shrine*)

fúdan *adv* 普段 usually, ordinarily

fúdan (no) *adj* 普段 (の) usual, everyday, ordinary

fudán-gí *n* 普段着 everyday clothes

fude *n* 筆 writing/painting brush

fude-bako *n* 筆箱 pencil box/case

fudoki, fūdoki *n* 風土記 topography, records of the culture and geography of a province

fudō-myōō *n* 不動明王 [BOOKISH] Cetaka, Acala (*Buddhism*)

fudō (no) *adj* 不動 (の) [BOOKISH] steadfast: **~ no chii** 不動の地位 an impregnable position

fudō´san *n* 不動産 real estate

fue *n* 笛 whistle; flute

fuemásu, fuéru *v* 増えます, 増える multiplies; grows in quantity/number, gets bigger, swells, increases, expands

fuenai *v* 増えない = **fuemasén** 増えません (not grow/increase)

fuéreba *v* 増えれば (if they grow, …) → **fuemásu** 増えます

fúe ro *v* 増えろ [IMPERATIVE] (grow!) → **fuemásu** 増えます

fúete *v* 増えて → **fuemásu** 増えます

fū´fu *n* 夫婦 husband and wife, (*married*) couple

fúgú *n* フグ・河豚 blowfish, puffer

fú-gú *n* (*discriminatory term*) 不具 cripple

fui (ni) *adv* 不意 (に) suddenly

fuji *n* フジ・藤 wisteria

fujin *n* 婦人 lady, woman (**go-fujin** ご婦人 [HONORIFIC])

fujin *n* 夫人 wife: **-fujin** -夫人 Mrs. …

Fuji (-san) *n* 富士 (山) Mount Fuji, Fujiyama

fujo *n* 婦女 [BOOKISH] lady, woman (= **fujin** 婦人): **fujo-bōkō** 婦女暴行 sexual assault

fujo *n* 扶助 aid, support: **fujo-kin** 扶助金 benefits

fuká *n* フカ big shark (*used in western Japan*) (→ **same** サメ・鮫)

fukái *adj* 深い deep: **fukáku** 深く deeply

fukanai *v* 拭かない = **fukimasén** 拭きません (not wipe)

f̲ukánai ν 葺かない = **f̲ukimasén** 葺き
ません (not roof)

f̲ukánai ν 吹かない = **f̲ukimasén** 吹き
ません (not blow)

f̲ukása n 深さ depth

f̲ukashimás̲u, f̲ukás̲u ν 蒸かします、
蒸かす steams (*food*)

f̲ukashimás̲u, f̲ukás̲u ν 吹かします、
吹かす smokes

f̲ukashimás̲u, f̲ukás̲u ν 吹かします、
吹かす: énjin o ~ エンジンを吹かしま
す、吹かす races the engine

f̲ukashimás̲u, f̲ukás̲u ν 更かします、
更かす: yó o ~ 夜を更かします、更か
す stays up late

f̲uké ν ふけ dandruff

f̲uké ν 拭け [IMPERATIVE] (wipe it!) →
f̲ukimás̲u 拭きます

f̲úke ν 吹け [IMPERATIVE] (blow!) →
f̲ukimás̲u 吹きます

f̲ukéba ν 拭けば (if one wipes/roofs) →
f̲ukimás̲u 拭きます

f̲úkeba ν 吹けば (if it blows) →
f̲ukimás̲u 吹きます

fū´kei n 風景 scenery, landscape
fūkei-ga n 風景画 landscape
painting(s)/picture(s)

f̲ukemás̲u, fukeru ν 拭けます、拭ける
can wipe

f̲ukemás̲u, f̲ukéru ν 更けます、更ける
to get late: yo ga ~ 夜が更けます、更ける
(*the night*) grows late

f̲ukemás̲u, f̲ukéru ν 老けます、老ける
gets old, ages

f̲ukemás̲u, f̲ukéru ν 吹けます、吹ける
can blow

f̲ukenai ν 拭けない = **f̲ukemasén** 拭け
ません (cannot wipe)

f̲ukénai ν 更けない = **f̲ukemasén** 更け
ません (not grow late)

f̲ukénai ν 老けない = **f̲ukemasén** 老け
ません (not age)

f̲ukénai ν 吹けない = **f̲ukemasén** 吹け
ません (cannot blow)

f̲ukereba ν 拭ければ (if it can wipe) →
f̲ukemás̲u 拭けます

f̲ukéreba ν 更ければ (if it grows late)
→ f̲ukemás̲u 更けます

f̲ukéreba ν 吹ければ (if one can blow)
→ f̲ukemás̲u 吹けます

f̲ukete ν 拭けて → f̲ukemás̲u 拭けます

f̲ukéte ν 更けて・老けて・吹けて →
f̲ukemás̲u 更けます・老けます・吹
けます

fuketsu (na) adj 不潔(な) unclean,
dirty, filthy

fuki n フキ・蕗 bog rhubarb

f̲ukimás̲u, f̲uku ν 拭きます、拭く
wipes

f̲ukimás̲u, fúku ν 葺きます、葺く covers
with (a roof)

f̲ukimás̲u, fúku ν 吹きます、吹く blows

fukín n 布きん washcloth, dishcloth

fukín n 付近 vicinity

f̲ukkakemás̲u, f̲ukkakéru ν ふっかけ
ます、ふっかける overcharges

f̲uku ν 拭く = **f̲ukimás̲u** 拭きます
(wipes)

f̲ukú n 服 clothes, suit, dress uniform

f̲úku ν 吹く = **f̲ukimás̲u** 吹きます
(blows; plays (*instrument*))

f̲úku ν 葺く = **f̲ukimás̲u** 葺きます (covers with (*a roof*))

fuku n 福 happiness (= kōfuku 幸福,
shiawase 幸せ, saiwai 幸い)

fuku-biki n 福引 lottery; raffle

fuku no kami n 福の神 god of wealth

fuku- prefix 副- vice-, assistant-

fuku-shachō n 副社長 vice-president
(*of a company*)

fuku-daitō´ryō n 副大統領 vice-
president (*of a nation*)

fukú-sayō n 副作用 side/after-effect

fuku- n 複 double

fuku-sei n 複製 replica, reproduction,
reprint: ~ **shimás̲u** 複製します reproduces, reprints

fuku-sha n 複写 reproduction, copy:
~ **shimás̲u** 複写します copies (*reproduces*) it

fuku-sū n 複数 plural

fukugō-go n 複合語 compound (*word*)

fukúme ν 含め [IMPERATIVE] (include!,
hold in the mouth!) → f̲ukumimás̲u
含みます

fukumemás̲u, fukuméru ν 含めます、
含める includes, adds

fukumimás̲u, f̲ukúmu ν 含みます、
含む holds in the mouth; contains

fukuramashimás̲u, f̲ukuramás̲u ν

41

膨らまします, 膨らます bulges,
inflates

fukurami *n* 膨らみ bulge

fukuramimásu, fukuramu *v* 膨らみま
す, 膨らむ swells up, bulges

fukuremásu, fukureru *v* 膨れます, 膨
れる swells up; pouts, sulks

fukuró *n* 袋 bag, sack

fukurō *n* フクロウ・梟 owl

fukushi *n* 副詞 adverb

fukúshi *n* 福祉 welfare

fukushi-séisaku *n* 福祉政策 welfare
policy

fukushi-shísetsu *n* 福祉施設 welfare
facility

fukushū *n* 復習 review (*study*): ~
shimásu 復習します(する) reviews
(*study*)

fukushū *n* 復讐 revenge, vengeance:
~ shimásu 復讐します(する) takes
revenge, revenges

fukusō *n* 服装 dress, clothes, costume

fukuzatsu (na) *adj* 複雑(な)
complicated: ~ na shinkyō 複雑な心境
mixed feelings; ~ na tachiba 複雑な立
場 complicated situation

fukyū *n* 普及 diffusion, popularization:
~ shimásu 普及します gets diffused
(*spread, popularized*)

fumanai *v* 踏まない = fumimasén 踏み
ません (not tread)

fumé *v* 踏め [IMPERATIVE] (tread it!) →
fumimásu 踏みます

fuméba *v* 踏めば (if one treads) →
fumimásu 踏みます

fumemásu, fumeru *v* 踏めます, 踏め
る can tread

fū´mí *n* 風味 flavor

fumi-komimásu, fumi-kómu *v* 踏み込
みます, 踏み込む **1.** steps into/on
2. trespasses (*on*); raids

fumimásu, fumu *v* 踏みます, 踏む
steps on, treads

fumotó *n* 麓 foot (*of a mountain*)

fún *n* 糞 feces, dung

…´-fun *suffix* …分 minute(s)

fúna *n* フナ・鮒 crucian carp

funá-... *prefix* 船... ship, vessel

funá-bin *n* 船便 sea mail

funa-ni *n* 船荷 ship cargo

funá-nori *n* 船乗り sailor

funá-yoi *n* 船酔い seasick(ness): ~
shimásu 船酔いします gets seasick

funbari *n* 踏ん張り effort: funbari-
másu 踏ん張ります hold on, stand firm

funbetsu *n* 分別 discretion, sense: ~ ga
tsukimásu 分別がつきます cuts a tooth

funde *v* 踏んで → fumimásu 踏みます

fundoshi *n* ふんどし・褌 loincloth,
breechcloth

fúne *n* 船[舟] boat, ship

fungai *n* 憤慨 [BOOKISH] indignation,
resentment; ~ shimásu 憤慨します gets
indignant, resents

fun'íki *n* 雰囲気 atmosphere (*of a place*),
mood, aura, air: ~ no yoi 雰囲気の良い
with a good/nice atmosphere

funka *n* 噴火 eruption: funká-kō 噴火
口 crater; ~ shimásu 噴火します erupts

funmatsu *n* 粉末 powder: ~ ni shimásu
粉末にします powders

funpatsu *n* 奮発: ~ shimásu 奮発します
puts a lot of effort, spoils oneself

funshitsu *n* 紛失 loss

funsō *n* 扮装 disguise: ~ shimásu 扮装
します is costumed, makes up

funsō *n* 紛争 conflict, dispute
funsō-chiiki *n* 紛争地域 disputed area,
conflict-affected region

funsui *n* 噴水 fountain

funtō *n* 奮闘 struggle

funuke *n* 腑抜け coward

furafura shimásu (suru) *adv* ふらふ
らします(する) swims

furai-pan *n* フライパン frying pan

furamenko *n* フラメンコ flamenco

furanai *v* 振らない = furimasén 振りま
せん (not wave)

furánai *v* 降らない = furimasén 降りま
せん (not precipitate)

Furansu *n* フランス France
Furansu-go *n* フランス語 French
(*language*)
Furansú-jin *n* フランス人 a French

furaremásu, furareru *v* 振られます,
振られる be rejected by, get dumped,
get the ax

furari (to) *adv* ふらり(と) aimlessly: ~
to tachiyorimásu ふらりと立ち寄りま
す drops in

furasuko *n* フラスコ flask

furatsukimásu, furatsuku *v* ふらつき
ます, ふらつく staggers, sways

furé *v* 振れ [IMPERATIVE] (wave it!) →
furimásu 振ります

furéba *v* 振れば (if one waves it) →
furimásu 振ります

fúreba *v* 降れば (if it rains/snows) →
furimásu 降ります

furemásu, fureru *v* 触れます, 触れる
1. touches (= **sawarimásu** 触ります)
2. contacts with; touches upon
3. mentions, refers to

furemásu, fureru *v* 振れます, 振れる
can wave it, can shake it

furete *v* 触れて・振れて → **furemásu**
触れます・振れます

furí *n* 振り manner, pretense, air; fake:
neta ~ 寝た振り a fox's sleep

furí *n* 降り rain/snow, downpour: **ame-
fúri** 雨降り rainy

furi-gana *n* ふりがな・フリガナ
readings marked (*for Chinese characters*)

furi-kae *n* 振(り)替(え) transfer (*of
funds*)

　furikae-yókin *n* 振替預金 transfer
　deposit

　furikae-kō´za *n* 振替口座 a transfer
　account

　furikae-kyū´jitsu *n* 振替休日
　compensating/substitute holiday

furi-kaemásu, furi-kaeru *v* 振(り)替
えます, 振(り)替える transfers it

furi-kaerimásu, furi-kaéru *v* 振り返
ります, 振り返る looks back (= **furi-
mukimásu** 振り向きます)

furi-kake *n* ふりかけ flavor sprinkles
(*to top rice*)

furi-kakemásu, furi-kakéru *v* 振り掛
けます, 振り掛ける sprinkles it

furimásu, furu *v* 振ります, 振る
1. waves, shakes, swings **2.** wags it

furimásu, furu *v* 降ります, 降る falls,
it precipitates (*rains, snows*)

furi-mukimásu, furi-múku *v* 振り向き
ます, 振り向く looks back

furin *n* 風鈴 wind-chimes

furisodé *n* 振り袖 long-sleeved kimono

furo *n* 風呂 (**o-fúro** お風呂) bath: **~ ni
hairimásu** 風呂に入ります takes a bath

furo-bá *n* 風呂場 (**o-furoba** お風呂場)
bathroom

furo-shiki *n* 風呂敷 a cloth wrapper

furonto *n* フロント front desk

　furonto-garasu *n* フロントガラス
　automobile windshield

furō´-sha *n* 浮浪者 homeless person

furu *v* 振る = **furimásu** 振ります
(waves, shakes, swings, etc.)

fúru *v* 降る = **furimásu** 降ります (falls)
(rains, snows)

furuemásu, furueru *v* 震えます, 震え
る it shakes

furui *n* ふるい sieve, sifter

furúi *adj* 古い old (*not new*), stale (*not
fresh*); secondhand, used

furumai *n* 振る舞い behavior
(*deportment*): **furumaimásu** 振る舞い
ます behaves

**furui(okoshi)masu, furui(okosu),
furu-u** *v* 奮い(起こし)ます, 奮い
(起こす), 奮う summons: **yúki o
furuiokoshite/furutte**……**勇気を奮い
起こして/奮って** …with gathering up
of one's courage

furū´to *n* フルート flute

furútsu *n* フルーツ fruit: **furútsu-párā**
フルーツパーラー soda fountain

fū´ryū (na) *adj* 風流(な) elegant

fúsá *n* 房 bunch (*cluster*)

fusagarimásu, fusagaru *v* 塞がりま
す, 塞がる gets blocked (off), clogged/
stopped up, gets occupied, booked up

fusagimásu, fusagu *v* 塞ぎます, 塞ぐ
stops up, closes, blocks

fusái *n* 夫妻 Mr. and Mrs.; husband and
wife (= **fūfu** 夫婦)

fusaide *v* 塞いで → **fusagimásu** 塞ぎ
ます

fusawashíi *adj* 相応しい suitable,
worthy; becoming: **fusawáshiku** 相応
しく suitably

fusegimásu, fuségu *v* 防ぎます, 防ぐ
prevents; defends, protects

fuséide *v* 防いで → **fusegimásu** 防げ
ます

fusemásu, fuséru *v* 伏せます, 伏せ
る covers (up), conceals; lays it face
down: **mi o ~** 身を伏せます gets down,
crouches (*so as not to be seen*): **mé o ~**

目を伏せさせます lowers one's eyes: **fuse-ji** 伏せ字 turned letter(s)

fūsen *n* 風船 balloon: **kami-fūsen** 紙風船 paper balloon

fūsen-gámu *n* 風船ガム bubble gum

fushi *n* 節 **1.** joint **2.** knot, knob **3.** tune **4.** point (*in a statement*)

fushi-me *n* 節目 turning point

fushigi (na) *adj* 不思議(な) strange, mysterious; wonderful; suspicious

fushin *n* 普請 building (*construction*), repairs

fu-shínsetsu (na) *adj* 不親切(な) unkind

fushō *n* 負傷 injury

fusso *n* フッ素 fluorine

fusumá *n* 襖 opaque sliding panel/door

futa *n* 蓋 lid, cover

futa-... *adj* 二... two: **futá-ban** 二晩 two nights: **futá-kumi** 二組 two pairs (*of*)

futago *n* 双子 twins

futamatá (no) *adj* 二又[叉](の) forked, bifurcate(d): **futamata-sokétto** 二又[叉]ソケット two-way socket, double plug

futarí *n* 二人・ふたり (**o-futari** お二人) two persons

futa-sén *n* 二千・2,000, two thousand (= **ni-sén** 二千・2,000)

futatsú *n* 二つ・2つ・ふたつ two (*pieces, small objects*) (= **ní-ko** 二個); two years old (= **ní-sai** 二歳[才])

futatsú-mi(t)tsu *n* 二つ三つ two or three

futebuteshii *adj* ふてぶてしい impudent, audacious: **~ taido** ふてぶてしい態度 surly attitude

futekusareta *adj* ふてくされた pouty: **futekusaremásu** ふてくされます has the sulks, gets sulky

futene *n* ふて寝 going to bed in a huff, staying in bed sulking

futo *adv* ふと unexpectedly; by chance, suddenly: **~ ki ga tsukimásu** ふと気がつきます comes to a sudden realization

futō *n* 埠頭 pier, wharf, quay

fūtō *n* 封筒 envelope: **henshin-yō fūtō** 返信用封筒 return-mail envelope

futodoki (na) *adj* 不届き(な) outrageous

futō-fukutsu (na/no) *adj* 不撓不屈 (な/の) indomitable, unyielding

futoi *adj* 太い fat, thick (and round)

futoji *n* 太字 boldface

futokoro *n* 懐 bosom, finance: **~ ga atatakai/samui (sabishii)** 懐が暖かい/寒い(さびしい) has a heavy/light purse: **~ ga fukai** 懐が深い is magnanimous, has deep insight

futomomo *n* 太腿 thigh

futon *n* 布団 (**o-futón** お布団) padded quilt, futon: **~ o hoshimásu** 布団を干します airs out futons

futorimásu, futóru *v* 太ります, 太る gets fat: **futótte imásu** 太っています is fat

futsū *n, adv* 普通 ordinar(il)y, usual(ly), regular(ly), typical(ly), normal(ly): **futsū-dénsha** 普通電車 local (*non-express*) train

futsū *n* 不通 disconnect

futsubun *n* 仏文 French literature

futsufutsu (to) *adv* ふつふつ(と) gradually: **~ to wakideru** ふつふつ湧き出る bubbling

futsuka *n* 二日・2日・ふつか **1.** 2nd day (of month) **2.** two days: **futsuka-kan** 二日間 for two days

futsuka-yoi *n* 二日酔い hangover

futsū-yókin *n* 普通預金 (*ordinary*) savings account

futten *n* 沸点 boiling point

futtō *n* 沸騰 boiling: **~ shimásu** 沸騰します boils

futto bōru *n* フットボール American football

futto wāku *n* フットワーク footwork: **~ ga karui** フットワークが軽い light on one's feet

fuyáse *v* 増やせ [IMPERATIVE] (increase it!) → **fuyashimásu** 増やします

fuyáseba *v* 増やせば (if it increases) → **fuyashimásu** 増やします

fuyashimásu, fuyásu *v* 増やします, 増やす increases it/them

fuyō *n* 扶養 support, keeping

fuyō-kazoku *n* 扶養家族 dependent family/relatives

fuyō-teate *n* 扶養手当 family allowance

fuyú *n* 冬 winter: **fuyu-gomori** 冬ごもり winter confinement

fuyu-fuku *n* 冬服 winter clothes

fuyu-yásumi *n* 冬休み winter break/
vacation

fuzakemásu, fuzakeru *v* ふざけます,
ふざける fool around, kid around

fuzei *n* 風情 taste, appearance, look: ~
no aru 風情のある tasteful

fuzoku *n* 付属・附属 attachment,
belonging, accessory

fuzokú-hin *n* 付属品 attachments,
accessories

fuzoroi *n* 不揃い irregularity: **fuzoroi na**
不揃いな irregular

G

ga *n* ガ・蛾 moth

ga *n* 我 oneself, ego, atman: ~ **ga tsuyoi**
我が強い egotistic; ~ **o tōshimásu** 我を
通します has one's own way

...ga *...particle ...が* marks subject (who
does, what is), but marks also object of:
... ga arimásu ...があります (has what);
... ga dekimásu ...が出来ます (can do
what)

... ga *conj* ...が but (= **shikashi** しかし);
and

...´-ga *suffix ...*画 painting, picture

gabugabu *adv* ガブガブ: ~ **nomi-másu**
ガブガブ飲みます gulps

gabyō *n* 画鋲 thumbtack

gachō *n* ガチョウ・鵞鳥 goose

gādeningu *n* ガーデニング gardening

gādoman *n* ガードマン guard

gādorēru *n* ガードレール guardrail

gādoru *n* ガードル girdle

gāgā *adv* ガーガー quack, croak

gágaku *n* 雅楽 [BOOKISH] music
traditional to the imperial court

gái *n* 害 damage, harm, injury

gai-... *prefix* 外... external, foreign:
gái-bu *n* 外部 the outside, the exterior:
gáibu (no) 外部(の) external

gai-jin *n* 外人 = **gaikokú-jin** 外国人
foreigner

gai-kan *n* 外観 external appearance,
external looks

gai-ken *n* 外見 appearance

gai-kō *n* 外交 diplomacy, diplomatic
relations: **gaikō´kan** 外交官 diplomat(-
ic officer); **gaikō-teki (na)** 外交的(な)
diplomatic

gai-koku *n* 外国 foreign countries
(= **ikoku** 異国): **gaikoku-go** 外国語
foreign language(s); **gaikokú-jin** 外国
人 foreigner; **gaikoku-kawase** 外国為

替 foreign currency operations

gai-men *n* 外面 the outside, the exterior:
gaimen (no) 外面(の) external

gai-sen *n* 外線 outside line/extension
(*phone*)

gai-shoku *n* 外食 eating out: ~ **shimásu**
外食します eats out

gai-shutsu *n* 外出 going out: ~ **shimásu**
外出します goes out (= **dekakemásu**
出掛けます); **gaishutsu-chū désu** 外出
中です is out

gai-tō *n* 外套 coat, overcoat

gai-sha *n* 外車 foreign car

gai-yō *n* 外洋 high sea

...´-gai *prefix ...*外 outside (*of*): **senmon-
gai (no)** 専門外(の) unprofessional

...-gai *suffix ...*貝 (*name of*) shell:
hotate-gai ホタテガイ・帆立貝 scallop

gáido *n* ガイド guide

gáidoku *n* 害毒 [BOOKISH] evil, harm,
bad influence on society

gaikan *n* 概観 survey, bird's-eye view

gaikotsu *n* 骸骨 skeleton

Gaimú-shō *n* 外務省 Ministry of
Foreign Affairs of Japan (MOFA)

gáinen *n* 概念 concept

gairo *n* 街路 broad street(s) in the town

gáisan *n* 概算 approximate calculation

...-gáisha *n* ...会社 = **kaisha** 会社
company

gaitame *n* 外為 = **gaikoku-kawase** 外国
為替 foreign currency operations

gaitō *n* 街頭 street, wayside

gaitō *n* 街灯 street lamp

gaiyō *n* 概要 outline, summary

gaka *n* 画家 painter, artist

...-gákari *...*係 attendant (*in charge*)

gake *n* 崖 cliff

gakí *n* 餓鬼 [BOOKISH] hungry/begging
ghost; ガキ・がき・餓鬼 brat

45

gakka *n* 学科 subject (*school*): **gakka-shiken** 学科試験 examinations in academic subjects

gakkai *n* 学会 scholarly society, association: **gakkai-shi** 学会誌 academic journal

gakkári shimásu (suru) *v* がっかりします(する) is disappointed, discouraged

gakki *n* 学期 term (*of school*); semester

gakki *n* 楽器 musical instrument

gakkō *n* 学校 school → **shōgakkō** 小学校, **chūgákkō** 中学校

gakkyū *n* 学級 class/grade in school

gaku *n* 学 learning, study, science: ...-**gaku** ...学 ...-ology

gaku-bu *n* 学部 department

gaku-chō *n* 学長 president of a school (*college/university*)

gaku-dō *n* 学童 school child(ren): **gakudō-hoiku** 学童保育 after-school care for children

gaku-en *n* 学園 academy

gaku-gei *n* 学芸 liberal arts: **gakugei-in** 学芸員 museum attendant

gaku-gyo *n* 学業 schoolwork, academic work

gaku-ha *n* 学派 school of thought

gaku-hi *n* 学費 academic fees: ~ **o kasegímásu** 学費を稼ぎます earns academic fees

gáku-i *n* 学位 academic degree: **gakui-rónbun** 学位論文 dissertation

gakú-mon *n* 学問 knowledge, learning, education

ga-kunen *n* 学年 school year

ga-kureki *n* 学歴 educational background

gaku-ryoku *n* 学力 academic ability

gaku-sei *n* 学生 student: **gakuséi-fuku** 学生服 school uniform; **gakuséi-shō** 学生証 student identification card

gaku-sha *n* 学者 scholar

gáku-shi *n* 学士 bachelor's degree: **gakushi-rónbun** 学士論文 senior essay

gaku-shū *n* 学習 study, learning: ~ **shimásu** 学習します studies, learns (*a basic subject*)

gakushū́-sha *n* 学習者 the student of a subject (*in general*): **Eigo-gakushū́-sha**

英語学習者 the student of English

gáku *n* 額 amount, sum

gaku-buchi *n* 額縁 frame (*of picture*)

gakudan *n* 楽団 band (*of musicians*)

gakufu *n* 楽譜 musical score

gamaguchi *n* がま口 purse, wallet, pocketbook (= **saifu** 財布)

gáman *n* 我慢 patience, perseverance: ~ **shimásu** 我慢します puts up with, stands, tolerates, perseveres; ~ **deki-masén** 我慢できません cannot stand it; **gaman-zuyói** 我慢強い is patient

gamen *n* 画面 screen (*of TV, computer*)

gámu *n* ガム (chewing) gum

gán *n* がん・癌 cancer, carcinoma

gán *n* ガン・雁 wild goose

gāna *n* ガーナ Ghana

ganbarimásu, ganbáru *n, interj* 頑張ります, 頑張る stands firm, bears up, hangs in there; tries hard

gānetto *n* ガーネット garnet

gani-mata (no) *adj* がに股(の) bowlegged

ganjitsu, gantan *n* 元日, 元旦 New Year's day, first day of the year

gánko (na) *adj* 頑固(な) stubborn

gánnen *n* 元年 the first year of an era; Year One

gánrai *adv* 元来 originally, primarily

gánsho *n* 願書 application

gantan *n* 元旦 = **ganjitsu** 元日 (New Year's day, first day of the year)

gan'yaku *n* 丸薬 pill (= **jōzai** 錠剤)

gappei *n* 合併 merger, combination, union: ~ **shimásu** 合併します (they) merge, unite, combine

gara *n* 柄 pattern

garagara *n* がらがら・ガラガラ rattle

gáragára *adv* がらがら・ガラガラ rattling (*noise*)

garakuta *n* がらくた junk

garasu *n* ガラス glass (*the substance*)

garasú-bin *n* ガラス瓶 glass jar/bottle

gárḗji *n* ガレージ garage

gári *n* ガリ pickled ginger slices (= **amazu-shṓga** 甘酢生姜[ショウガ])

gáru-furéndo *n* ガールフレンド girlfriend (= **kánojo** 彼女)

gasorin *n* ガソリン gasoline: **gasorin-sutándo** ガソリンスタンド gas(oline)/

service station

gassō *n* 合奏 concert: ~ **shimásu** 合奏
します plays in concert

gásu *n* ガス (*natural*) gas
  gasú-dai *n* ガス代 gas bill
  gasú-kónro *n* ガスこんろ (*gas*) stove
  gasú-rénji *n* ガスレンジ gas range

…-gata …型 type, model; size

…gáta …方 [HONORIFIC PLURAL]
esteemed (*persons*)

gā´ta *n* ガーター garter

gata ga kiteimásu (kiteiru) *v* がたが
来ています, がたが来ている gets old
and rickety

gátagata shimásu (suru) *v* がたがた
します(する) clatters, rattles

gatchi *n* 合致 accordance: ~ **shimásu**
合致します corresponds

gatchiri-shita *adj* がっちりした well-
built

…-gatsu …月 (*name of*) month of the
year

gatten *n* 合点 consent, understanding

-gawa *n* 側 side: **hidari-gawa** 左側 the
left side, **migi-gawa** 右側 the right side,
mukō-gawa 向こう側 the other side

gāze *n* ガーゼ gauze

gazō *n* 画像 image

gé´tā *n* 下 = **ge-kan** 下巻 last volume (*of a
set of 2 or 3*)

gedoku-zai *n* 解毒剤 antidote (= **doku-
késhí** 毒消し)

gehín (na) *adj* 下品(な) vulgar

géi *n* 芸 arts, accomplishments; tricks
  gei-mei *n* 芸名 screen/stage name
  gei-nō *n* 芸能 performance arts:
    geinō´-jin 芸能人 entertainer(s)
  gei-sha *n* 芸者 geisha

géi *n* ゲイ gay: **gei-bā** ゲイバー gay bar

geigō *n* 迎合 assentation: ~ **shimásu**
迎合します caters to one's feelings/
opinions/wishes

geijutsu *n* 芸術 art(s)
  geijutsu-ka *n* 芸術家 artist

geiyu *n* 鯨油 whale oil

gejun *n* 下旬 late part/end of a month

geka *n* 外科 surgery (*as a medical
specialty*)
  geká-i *n* 外科医 surgeon
  geka-shujutsu *n* 外科手術 surgical

operation

géki *n* 劇 play, drama

gékido *n* 激怒 furious anger: ~ **shimásu**
激怒します gets mad

geki-ga *n* 劇画 [BOOKISH] graphic novel

gekijō *n* 劇場 theater

gekiron *n* 激論 [BOOKISH] violent
controversy

gekkei *n* 月経 menstruation (= **seiri**
生理)

gekkéi-ju *n* ゲッケイジュ・月桂樹
laurel

gekkyū *n* 月給 monthly salary

geko *n* 下戸 non-drinker

gekokujō *n* 下克上 forcible displace-
ment of a superior by one's inferior

gē´mu *n* ゲーム game

gén *n* 弦 string
  gen-gakki *n* 弦楽器 string
  instrument(s)

gén(-) … *prefix* 現 … present (*time*),
current

gen-ba *n* 現場 site

gén-dai *n* 現代 the present: **géndai
(no)** 現代(の), **gendai-teki (na)** 現代的
(な) modern, up-to-date

gen-eki (no-hito) *n* 現役(の人)
(*person who is on*) active service

gen-jitsu *n* 現実 actuality, reality:
genjitsu (no) 現実(の) actual, real;
genjitsu-teki (na) 現実的(な) realistic

gen-jō *n* 現状 the present conditions/
state, the status quo

gen-jū´sho *n* 現住所 current address

gen-kín *n* 現金 ready money; **genkin-
kákitome** 現金書留 cash envelope
(*registered mail*)

gen-kōhan (no) *adj* 現行犯(の) red-
handed

gén-zai *n, adv* 現在 the present (*time*);
at present, now: **génzai (no)** 現在(の)
current, present

géndo *n* 限度 limit: **saidai/saikō-
gén(do)** 最大/最高限(度) the
maximum/highest (degree); **saishō/
saité-gen(do)** 最小/最低限(度) the
minimum/lowest (degree)

genetsu-zai *n* 解熱剤 antipyretic agent

géngo *n* 言語 language: **gengó-gaku**
言語学 linguistics

gengō n 元号 era name
gen'in n 原因 cause, origin, root
genjū (na) adj 厳重(な) strict: ~ **na keibi** 厳重な警備 very strict guard
génkan n 玄関 entrance (hall), porch
génki n 元気 (**o-génki** お元気) energy, vigor, pep: **génki (na)** 元気(な) well, healthy, cheerful, vigorous; ~ **ga ii** 元気がいい cheerful; ~ **ga nai** 元気がない cheerlessly: **O-genki desu ka.** お元気ですか. How are you?
genko n 拳固 = **genkotsu** 拳骨 fist
genkō n 言行 sayings and doings: **genkō-itchi** 言行一致 behavior consonant with one's words
genkō n 原稿 manuscript: ~ **o shiage-másu** 原稿を仕上げます finishes one's article
genkō-yōshi n 原稿用紙 squared paper, manuscript paper
genkoku n 原告 suitor, accuser
genkyū shimásu (suru) v 言及します (する) [BOOKISH] refers to …, mentions … (= **(… ni) furemásu** (…に)触れます)
génmai n 玄米 unpolished rice
genmai-cha n 玄米茶 Genmaicha, brown rice tea
genmitsu (na) adj 厳密(な) strict
genryō´ n 原料 (*raw*) materials, basic ingredient
gensaku n 原作 the original (*writing*)
gensan (no) adj 原産(の) (*plants and animals*) native to: **gensan-chi** 原産地 place of origin
génshi n 原子 atom
genshi-bákudan n 原子爆弾 atomic bomb
genshi-ryoku n 原子力 atomic energy
génshi (no) adj 原始(の) primitive
genshō n 現象 phenomenon
genshō n 減少 decrease
gensoku n 原則 a basic principle, a rule: ~ **to shite** 原則として as a (*general*) rule
gentei shimásu (suru) v 限定します (する) limits, restricts
genzō shimásu (suru) v 現像します (する) develops (*film*)
geppu n 月賦 monthly installments/

payments: **geppu-barai** 月賦払い monthly payments
géppu n げっぷ belch: ~ **o shimásu** げっぷをします belches, burps
geragera ν げらげら[ゲラゲラ]: ~ **waraimásu** げらげら[ゲラゲラ] 笑います laughs with great guffaws
geretsu adj 下劣 rude, abusive, mean
geri n 下痢 diarrhea
geri-dome n 下痢止め anti-diarrhetic
geshi n 夏至 summer solstice
geshuku n 下宿 lodgings, room (and board): ~ **shimásu** 下宿します rooms, boards, lodges
geshuku-ya n 下宿屋 rooming house
gessori-shimasu (suru) ν げっそり します(する) loses a lot of weight (= **gessori-yasemasu** げっそりやせます)
gés-súi-kin n 月水金 Monday-Wednesday-Friday
gesui n 下水 sewage, (*kitchen*) drain
gesui-dame n 下水溜め cesspool
gesui-shorijō n 下水処理場 sewage treatment plant
gesui-dō n 下水道 sewage system
getá n 下駄 wooden clogs (*shoes*)
geta-bako n 下駄箱 shoe box (*at entryway*)
…-getsu *suffix* …月 month
getsumatsu n 月末 the end of a month
getsumen n 月面 surface of the moon
Getsuyó´(bi) n 月曜(日) Monday
gezai n 下剤 laxative
gi-… *prefix* 偽… pseudo-…
gi-shō n 偽証 false testimony
gi-zen n 偽善 hypocrisy
gi-… *prefix* 義 = **giri (no)** 義理の …-in-law
gi-bo n 義母 = **girí no haha** 義理の母 mother-in-law
gí-fu n 義父 = **girí no chichi** 義理の父 father-in-law
gíchō n 議長 chairperson
gífuto n ギフト gift (= **okurimono** 贈り物)
gíin n 議員 member of parliament: **Kokkai-giin** 国会議員 member of a national legislature
giji-dō n 議事堂: **kokkai giji-dō** 国会議事堂 Diet building

gíjutsu *n* 技術 technique
gijutu-sha *n* 技術者 technician, engineer

gíkai *n* 議会 parliament, assembly, congress; (*the Japanese*) Diet (= **kokkai** 国会)

gikochinái *adj* ぎこちない awkward, clumsy

gimon *n* 疑問 question, doubt
gimón-fu *n* 疑問符 question mark

gímu *n* 義務 duty, obligation
gimu-kyōˊiku *n* 義務教育 compulsory education

gín *n* 銀 silver
gin-gami *n* 銀紙 silver paper
gin-iro (no) *adj* 銀色(の) silver (*color*)
gin-ka *n* 銀貨 silver coin
gin-sekai *n* 銀世界 snowy world

Gínga *n* 銀河 the Milky Way

ginjō *n* 吟醸 produce from the use of selected ingredient(s): **ginjō-shu** 吟醸酒 quality sake brewed from the finest rice

ginkō *n* 銀行 bank
ginkōˊ-in *n* 銀行員 bank clerk

ginmi *n* 吟味 investigation: **~ shimásu** 吟味します examines

ginnán *n* ギンナン・銀杏 gingko nuts

ginyūshijin *n* 吟遊詩人 minstrel

girei *n* 儀礼 courtesy

girí *n* 義理 (**o-gíri** お義理) obligation, sense of obligation, honor: **girí no ...** 義理の... -in-law

Gírish(i)a *n* ギリシャ・ギリシア Greece
Girish(i)a-go ギリシャ・ギリシア語 Greek (*language*)
Girish(i)a-jin ギリシャ・ギリシア人 Greek (*people*)

gíron *n* 議論 discussion

giryo *n* 技量 skills, abilities

gisei *n* 犠牲 a sacrifice: **... o ~ ni shimásu** ...を犠牲にします makes a sacrifice/scapegoat of ...; **~ ni narimásu** 犠牲になります falls a victim, is sacrificed
gisé-sha *n* 犠牲者 victim

gíshi *n* 技師 engineer

gíshiki *n* 儀式 ceremony, ritual

gíta *n* ギター guitar

gítcho (no) *adj* (*discriminatory term*) ぎっちょ(の) left-handed (*person*) (= **hidari-kiki (no)** 左利き(の))

giwaku *n* 疑惑 doubt, suspicion

gí(y)a *n* ギア・ギヤ gearshift

gizō *n* 偽造 forgery

gó *n* 碁 the board game Go (= **ígo** 囲碁): **go-ban** 碁盤 a Go board

gó *n* 五・5 five
go-ban *n* 五番 number five
go-banmé (no) *adj* 五番目 fifth
go-dai *n* 五台 five machines/vehicles
go-dó *n* 五度 five times (= **go-kai** 五回)
gó-do *n* 五度 five degrees
gó-hiki *n* 五匹 five (*fishes/bugs, small animals*)
go-hon *n* 五本 five (*pencils/bottles, long things*)
go-kái *n* 五回 five times
go-kai *n* 五階 five floors/stories; fifth floor
go-ko *n* 五個 five (*pieces, small objects*)
go-mai *n* 五枚 five sheets (*flat things*)
go-nen *n* 五年 the year 5: **go nén-kan** 五年間 (*for*) five years
go-nín *n* 五人 five people
gó-sai *n* 五歳 five years old (= **itsutsu** 五つ)
gó-satsu *n* 五冊 five copies (*books, magazines*)
go-tō *n* 五頭 five (*horses/oxen, large animals*)
gó-wa *n* 五羽 five (*birds, rabbits*)

go-... *prefix* ご・御... honorific (*personalizing*) *prefix* (*cf.* **o-** お・御)
go-chisō *n* ご馳走・ご馳走 treat (*of food*): **~ shimásu** ごちそうします provides a treat; **gochisō-sama** (**deshita**). ごちそうさま(でした). Thank you for the treat
go-fujō *n* 御不浄 [HONORIFIC] toilet, rest room, lavatory (= **tóire** トイレ)
go-jibun *n* ご自分 you, yourself [HONORIFIC]
go-jísei *n* ご時世 the times [HONORIFIC] → **jísei** 時世
go-kazoku *n* ご家族 (*your/someone else's*) family [HONORIFIC] → **kázoku** 家族
go-kigen *n* ご機嫌 mood, feeling: **~**

ikága desu ka ご機嫌いかがですか. How are you (feeling)?: **Go-kigen yō´** ごきげんよう. Good-bye./Hello. [HONORIFIC] → **kigen** 機嫌

go-méiwaku *n* ご迷惑 trouble, bother [HONORIFIC] → **méiwaku** 迷惑

go-mottomo *interj* ごもっとも You're absolutely right.

go-ón *n* ご恩 (*your/someone else's*) kindness, my obligation to you [HONORIFIC] → **ón** 恩

go-riyaku *n* ご利益 divine help/grace

go-ryō´shin *n* ご両親 (*your/someone else's*) parents [HONORIFIC] → **oyago-san** 親御さん) → **ryō´shin** 両親

go-shinpai *n* ご心配 [HONORIFIC] : ~ **naku** ご心配なく Don't worry about it. → **shinpai** 心配

go-shínsetsu *n* ご親切 (*your/someone else's*) kindness [HONORIFIC] : ~ **ni dōmo arigató (gozaimásu)** ご親切にどうもありがとう(ございます) Thank you very much for your kindness. → **shínsetsu** 親切

go-shújin *n* ご主人 (*your/someone else's*) husband [HONORIFIC] → **shújin** 主人

go-téinei (na) *adj* ご丁寧(な) polite; careful [HONORIFIC] → **téinei** 丁寧

go-tsugō *n* ご都合 convenience [HONORIFIC] : ~ **ga yoroshikereba** … ご都合がよろしければ… If you are available …: ~ **wa iikaga desuka** ご都合はいかがですか Is it convenient for you? → **tsugō** 都合

go-yō´ *n* ご用 (*your/someone else's*) business [HONORIFIC] → **yō´** 用

gó-zen *n* ご膳 low meal table, dining tray (= **o-zen** お膳); meal (= **o-shokuji** お食事) [HONORIFIC]

go-zónji *v* ご存知: ~ **désu ka?** ご存知ですか? Do you know? [HONORIFIC] (= **shitte(i)másu ka?** 知って(い)ますか?); **zónji(age)másén** ご存知(あげ)ません don't know [HONORIFIC] (= **shiri-masén** 知りません)

go-... *prefix* ご・誤... wrong
go-hō *n* 誤報 false report
go-shin *n* 誤診 wrong diagnosis
go-yō *n* 誤用 inappropriate use

go-kai *n* 誤解 misunderstanding: ~ **shimásu** 誤解します misunderstands

go-... *prefix* 語... language; word(s)
go-chō *n* 語調 tone of talk, intonation
gó-gaku *n* 語学 (*foreign*) language learning
go-gen *n* 語源 etymology
gó-i *n* 語彙 vocabulary (*item*)
go-ró *n* 語呂 sound harmony: **goró awase** 語呂合わせ pun

-go *suffix* 後 after, later, since: **sono-go** その後 after that, since then

...-go *suffix* ...語 (*name of*) language; word(s): **Nihon-go** 日本語 the Japanese (*language*)

-gō *suffix* 号: **...-gatsugō** ...月号 (*magazine issues*); **...-gōshitsu** ...号室 (*room numbers*)

gobō *n* ゴボウ・牛蒡 burdock (*root*)

go-busata *n* ご無沙汰: ~ **shite orimásu** ご無沙汰しております I have been neglectful (*in keeping in touch with you*).

gochagocha (shita) *adj* ごちゃごちゃ (した) messy, jumble

gochamaze *adj* ごちゃ混ぜ jumble (= **gotamaze** ごたまぜ)

gōdō *n* 合同 combination, union, fusion; congruence: **gōdō no** 合同の combined, united, joint

gofuku *n* 呉服 yard/dry goods; (*traditional Japanese clothing*) kimono: **gofuku-ya** 呉服屋 dry goods store; kimono shop

Gó-gatsu *n* 五月・5 月 May

gógo *n* 午後 afternoon, p.m.

góhan *n* ご飯 (*cooked*) rice; meal, dinner (= **shokuji** 食事); food

go-hyakú *n* 五百・500 five hundred

gō´i *n* 合意 agreement

gōin (na) *adj* 強引(な) forcible, highhanded: **gōin ni** 強引に forcibly, highhandedly

go-ishi *n* 碁石 a Go stone (*piece*)

go-jū´ *n* 五十・fifty 50

go-jū´on *n* 五十音 the Japanese *kana* syllabary

gó´ka (na) *adj* 豪華(な) luxurious, deluxe: ~ **na shokuji** 豪華な食事 delicious cuisine

gōkai (na) *adj* 豪快(な) dynamic

gō´ka-kenran *adj* 豪華絢爛 absolutely gorgeous

gōkaku *n* 合格 passing (*an exam*): **(shiken ni) ~ shimásu** (試験に)合格します passes (*an exam*)

gōkan *n* 強姦 rape

gōkei *n* 合計 total (*sum*): **~ shimásu** 合計します totals (up)

goke (-san) *n* 後家(さん) widow

gokiburi *n* ゴキブリ cockroach

góku *adv* 極 very, exceedingly

gōkyū *n* 号泣 crying bitterly, crying out: **~ shimásu** 号泣します wails

goma *n* ゴマ・胡麻 sesame (*seeds*): **~ o surimásu** ゴマをすります grinds sesame; flatters

goma-súri *n* ごますり flattery

gomakashimásu, gomakásu *v* ごまかします、ごまかす deceives, cheats, misrepresents; **tsurisen o ~** 釣り銭をごまかします shortchanges

go-mán *n* 五万・50,000 fifty thousand

gōman (na) *adj* 傲慢(な) haughty, arrogant

gomen *interj* ごめん: **Gomen nasái.** ごめんなさい. Excuse me. (= **sumimásen** すみません); **Gomen kudasái.** ごめん下さい. Hello, anybody home?

gomí *n* ゴミ trash, rubbish, garbage, house refuse, (*house*) dust

gomí-bako *n* ゴミ箱 trash box, garbage can, dustbin

gomi-búkuro *n* ゴミ袋 garbage bag

gomi-suteba *n* ゴミ捨て場 garbage dump

gomí-ya *n* ゴミ屋 trash/garbage collector, ashmen (= **gomi kaishū gyō-sha** ゴミ回収業者)

gomoku *n* 五目 variety of ingredients

gomoku-chāhan *n* 五目チャーハン Chinese fried rice with a variety of ingredients

gomoku-nárabe *n* 五目並べ gobang (a simplified version of the game Go)

gomoku-sóba *n* 五目そば Chinese noodles with a variety of ingredients

gómu *n* ゴム rubber: **wa-gomu** 輪ゴム rubber band

gomú-naga(gutsu) *n* ゴム長(靴) rubber boots

gondora *n* ゴンドラ gondola(s)

gonge *n* 権化 incarnation, embodiment: **... no gonge ...**の権化 ... personified

gongodōdan (na) *adj* 言語道断(な) egregious

goraku *n* 娯楽 entertainment, recreation, amusement

goraku-shisetsu *n* 娯楽施設 amusement facility

goran *v* ご覧: **~ ni narimásu** ご覧になります [HONORIFIC] (you) see; **~ kuda-sai** ご覧下さい Please look/see. → **miru** 見る

góri *n* 合理 accordance with reason: **góri-teki (na)** 合理的(な) rational, reasonable, sensible

gōrí-ka *n* 合理化 rationalization (*making it reasonable*); streamlining: **~ shimásu** 合理化します makes it reasonable, rationalizes

gorin *n* 五輪 Olympics

gorira *n* ゴリラ gorilla

... góro (ni) *suffix, adv* ...ごろ[頃](に) (*at*) about (*a time*)

goro-ne *n* ごろ寝 sacking out: **~ shimásu** ごろ寝します sacks out

gorotsuki *n* ごろつき cheap hoodlum(s)

gō´ru *n* ゴール goal (*sports*): **gō´ru kiipā** ゴールキーパー goalkeeper

gōruden-uíiku/wíiku *n* ゴールデンウイーク／ウィーク Golden Week holidays (29 April – 5 May)

górufā *n* ゴルファー golfer

górufu *n* ゴルフ golf

gorufu-jō *n* ゴルフ場 golf course

gōryū *n* 合流 merger, confluence: **~ shimásu** 合流します merges, joins

gōryū-ten *n* 合流点 confluence

gōsain *n* ゴーサイン go sign, green light

go-sén *n* 五千・5,000 five thousand

... -gō´sha *suffix* ...号車 train or car number ...: **nan-gō´sha** 何号車 what (number) car

go-shín *n* 護身 self-defense: **goshin-jutyu** 護身術 art of self-defense

gósho *n* 御所 imperial palace (*in Kyoto*)

gotaku *n* ごたく cant: **~ o narabemásu** ごたくを並べます talks a load of garbage

gotamaze *n* ごたまぜ jumble (= **gocha-maze** ごちゃ混ぜ)

gōtō *n* 強盗 robber; robbery: **gōtō-jiken** 強盗事件 robbery

... **gótoku** *suffix*, *adv* ...ごとく: [LITERARY] ... **no gótoku** ...のごとく= ... **no yō´ (ni)** ... のよう(に) like

... **goto** *suffix*, *adv* ...ごと: every ..., each ...: **koto áru ~ (ni)** こと あるごと(に) every chance one gets

gō´u *n* 豪雨 heavy rain, (*torrential*) downpour: **shūchū-gō´u** 集中豪雨 local downpour, local heavy rain

gozá *n* ござ (*thin floor mat*) straw mat

gozaimásu *v* ございます [DEFEREN-TIAL] = **arimásu** あります there is, we've got; it is (located)

gózen *n* 午前 morning, a.m.

gu *n* 具 ingredients, fillings

gu *n* 愚 stupidity: ~ **no kotchō** 愚の骨頂 ultimate silliness

gu-chi *n* 愚痴 complaint, gripe: ~ **o koboshimásu** 愚痴をこぼします complains, gripes

...**-guchi** *suffix* ...口: **mado-guchi** 窓口 window, wicket: **deiri-guchi** 出入り口 doorway, gateway

gugen (ka) *n* 具現(化) realization

gū´gū *adv* グーグー snoring (away), Zzz

gūhatsu teki (na/ni) *adj*, *adv* 偶発的 (な/に) accidental(ly)

guigui (to) *adv* グイグイ(と) strongly: ~ **hipparimás<u>u</u>** グイグイ引っ張ります keeps pulling strongly

gui(t)to *adv* グイ(ッ)と with a jerk

gún *n* 軍 army, troops
  gún-dan *n* 軍団 corps
  gun-jin *n* 軍人 soldier, military person
  gun-kan *n* 軍艦 warship
  gun-puku *n* 軍服 military uniform
  gún-tai *n* 軍隊 troops, army; (*armed*) service (*forces*)

gún *n* 郡 county

gunshū *n* 群衆 crowd

gúrabu *n* グラブ → **gúrōbu** グローブ

gurafu *n* グラフ graph

... **gúrai** *suffix* ...位・ぐらい about (*an amount*; *the same extent as*); at least

gúramu *suffix* *n* グラム gram(s)

gúrasu *n* グラス glass (*drinking, glass, the container*)

gura(u)ndo *n* グラ(ウ)ンド playground

gurē´ (no) *adj* グレー(の) gray

gurēpufurū´tsu *n* グレープフルーツ grapefruit

guríin (no) *adj* グリーン(の) green: **guríin-sha** グリーン車 the Green Car (*first-class seats*)

gúrōbu *n* グローブ (*baseball, boxing*) glove (= **gúrabu** グラブ)

guruguru (to) *adv* ぐるぐる(と) round and round

gurume *n* グルメ gourmet

gurū´pu *n* グループ group

gussúri *adv* ぐっすり (*sleeping*) soundly

gutai-rei *n* 具体例 specific example

gutai-teki (na) *adj* 具体的(な) con-crete, substantial, tangible, material

gūtara (mono) *n* ぐうたら(者) lazybones, drone

gú(i)t (-to) *adv* グ(イ)ッ(と) with a jerk: **gúitto nomimás<u>u</u>** グイッと飲みま す gulps down a drink

gūwa *n* 寓話 allegory, fable

gūzen (no) *adj* 偶然(の) accidental, fortuitous: **gūzen ni** 偶然に by chance, accidentally

gūzō *n* 偶像 idol

gúzu *n* ぐず dullard

gúzuguzu *adj* ぐずぐず unready

gúzuguzu iimás<u>u</u> (iu/yū) *v* ぐずぐず 言います(言う) complains, grumbles

gúzuguzu shimás<u>u</u> (suru) *v* ぐずぐず します(する) delays, dawdles

gyaku (no/ni) *adj*, *adv* 逆(の/に) opposite, contrary, backwards

gyakutai shimás<u>u</u> (suru) *v* 虐待しま す(する) mistreats

gyáppu *n* ギャップ gap

gyo- *prefix* 御 → **go-** ご・御

gyō´ *n* **1.** 行 line (*of words*); line of the kana chart: **gyōkan** 行間 line space **2.** 行 ascetic practices, meditation (= **shugyō** 修行)

gyō´ *n* 業 line of work (= **shokúgyō** 職業)

gyōchū *n* ぎょう虫 pinworm

gyōfu *n* 漁夫 fisherman

gyōgi *n* 行儀 behavior, manners: **~ ga ii/warui** 行儀がいい/悪い well/bad mannered

gyógyō *n* 漁業 fishing (*business*)

gyōgyōshii *adj* 仰々しい pompous

gyō´ji *n* 行事 ceremony, event

gyōkai *n* 業界 industry, world: **gyōkai-shi** 業界紙 trade paper: **gyōkai-yōgo** 業界用語 industry jargon

gyōko *n* 凝固 [BOOKISH] coagulation

gyomin *n* 漁民 fisherperson

gyōmu *n* 業務 business, work: **gyōmu-jikan** 業務時間 business hours

gyorori (to) *v* ぎょろり(と): **~ to niramimasu** ぎょろりと睨みます[に

らみます] goggles, glares

gyorui *n* 魚類 fishes

gyōsei *n* 行政 administration (*of government*): **gyōsei kikan** 行政機関 administrative agency

gyōseki *n* 業績 achievements: **~ o agemásu** 業績を上げます improves performance

gyosha *n* 御者 coachman/coachmen

gyotto shimasu (suru) *v* ぎょっとします(する) is startled

gyōza *n* ギョウザ・餃子 *chiao-tze* (*jiaozi*)

gyūgyūzume *adj* ぎゅうぎゅう詰め jam-packed

gyūniku *n* 牛肉 beef

gyūnyū *n* 牛乳 (cow's) milk: **gyūnyū-ya** 牛乳屋 dairy (*shop*)

H

ha *n* 葉 leaf (= **happa** 葉っぱ): **ko-no-ha** 木の葉 leave(s) of trees: **ochi-ba** 落ち葉 fallen leave(s)

ha-maki *n* 葉巻 cigar

há *n* 歯 tooth

ha-búrashi *n* 歯ブラシ tooth brush

há-guki *n* 歯茎 gum (*teethridge*)

ha-isha *n* 歯医者 dentist

ha-ita *n* 歯痛 toothache (= **shitsū** 歯痛)

ha-mígaki *n* 歯磨き brushing of teeth: **hamígaki-ko** 歯磨き粉 dentifrice, toothpaste (= **neri hamígaki** 練り歯磨き): **~ (o) shimásu** 歯磨き(を)します brushes one's teeth

há *n* 刃 edge (*of knife*), blade (*of razor*)

ha *interj* は [DEFERENTIAL] yes

hā *interj* はあ **1.** aha **2.** phew

haba *n* 幅 width

habamemásu, habaméru *v* 阻めます, 阻める can prevent/thwart

habamimásu, habámu *v* 阻みます, 阻む prevents, thwarts

habánde *v* 阻んで → **habamimásu** 阻みます

habatsu *n* 派閥 faction, clique

hā´bu *n* ハーブ herb(s)

habúite *v* 省いて → **habukimásu** 省きます

habukimásu, habúku *v* 省きます, 省く cuts out, reduces, saves, omits

hachi *n* ハチ・蜂 bee (= **mitsú-bachi** 蜜蜂)

hachi-mitsu *n* ハチミツ・蜂蜜 honey

hachí *n* 鉢 (**o-hachi** お鉢) bowl, basin, pot, rice bucket/tub

hachí-mono *n* 鉢物 potted plant (= **hachi-ué** 鉢植え)

hachí *n* 八・8 eight

hachí-dó *n* 八度 eight times (= **hachi-kái, hak-kái** 八回, **hap-pen** 八編)

hachí-do *n* 八度 eight degrees

hachi-hon, háp-pon *n* 八本 eight (*pencils/bottles, long objects*)

hachí-ko, hák-ko *n* 八個 eight pieces (*small objects*) (= **yáttsu** 八つ)

hachí-mai *n* 八枚 eight sheets (*flat things*)

hachí-wa, háp-pa *n* 八羽 eight (*birds, rabbits*)

Hachí-gatsu *n* 八月 August

hachi-mán *n* 八万・80,000 eighty thousand

hachūrui *n* ハ虫類・爬虫類 reptile

háda *n* 肌 skin: **hada-iro** 肌色 flesh color

hada-gí *n* 肌着 underwear

hadaka (no) *adj* 裸・はだか（の） naked

hadashi *n* 裸足 barefoot

hadé (na) *adj* 派手（な）gaudy, showy, flashy, bright, loud (*color*)

hādowéa *n* ハードウェア (*computer*) hardware

hae *n* ハエ・蝿 (house)fly: **hae-tataki** ハエ叩き fly flap

háeba *v* 這えば (if one crawls) → **haimásu** 這います

haemásu, haéru *v* 生えます, 生える (*tooth, hair, mold, …*) grows

hagaki *n* はがき・葉書 (**o-hágaki** お葉書) postcard

hagane *n* ハガネ・鋼 steel

hagashimásu, hagasu *v* 剥がします, 剥がす peels off, tears off

háge *n* 禿 bald spot, baldness: **hagete imásu** 禿げ[はげ]ています is bald

hagemashimásu, hagemásu *v* 励まします 励ます encourages

hagemásu, hagéru *v* 剥げます, 剥げる it peels off

hagemásu, hagéru *v* 禿[はげ]ます, 禿げる・はげる gets/goes bald

hagemímásu, hagému *v* 励みます, 励む works hard

hagéru *v* 剥げる = **hagemásu** 剥げます (it peels off)

hagéru *v* 禿げる・はげる = **hagemásu** 禿げ[はげ]ます (it goes bald)

hageshíí *adj* 激しい violent, severe, fierce, acute

hágete *v* 禿げて・はげて → **hagemásu** 禿げ[はげ]ます

hágeta *v* 禿げた・はげた = **hagemá-shita** 禿げ[はげ]ました (…bald)

hagimásu, hágu *v* 剥ぎます, 剥ぐ peels off

hagó-íta *n* 羽子板 battledore

ha-gúruma *n* 歯車 cog (*wheel*), gear

háha, haha-oya *n* 母, 母親 mother (= **oká´-san** お母さん)

hahen *n* 破片 broken piece(s)

hai *n* 灰 ashes: **hai-zara** 灰皿 ash tray

hai *n* 肺 lungs

    hai-byō *n* 肺病 tuberculosis, TB (= **kekkaku** 結核)

    hai-en *n* 肺炎 pneumonia: **~ ni nari-másu** 肺炎になります gets pneumonia

hai-gan *n* 肺がん lung cancer

hái *interj* **1.** はい yes (= **ē** ええ (*mostly female*)) **2.** here you are!

…´-hai *suffix* …杯 cupful(s), bowlful(s)

haiboku *n* 敗北 defeat, loss

haibōru *n* ハイボール highball

haibun *n* 配分 distribution (= **bunpai** 分配): **~ shimásu** 配分します distributes

haichi *n* 配置 layout, allocation, location, placement, setup: **~ shimásu** 配置します puts in position

haifu *n* 配布 distribution, circulation: **~ shimásu** 配布します distributes, circulates

haigo *n* 背後 rear, backside

haigō *n* 配合 composition: **haigō-zai** 配合剤 compounding agent

haigūsha *n* 配偶者 spouse

haigyō *n* 廃業 end of a business: **~ shimásu** 廃業します closes a business

haihiiru *n* ハイヒール high-heeled shoes

hai-iro (no) *adj* 灰色（の）gray

haijin *n* 俳人 *haiku* poet

haijin *n* 廃人 cripple, wreck

háijo *n* 排除 removal, elimination, exclusion: **~ shimásu** 排除します removes, eliminates, excludes

haikan *n* 配管 piping: **~ shimásu** 配管します lays a pipe

haikan *n* 廃刊: **~ ni narimásu** 廃刊になります discontinues the publication

haikan *n* 拝観 admission: **~ shimásu** 拝観します [HUMBLE] has the honor of seeing

haikan-ryō *n* 拝観料 admission fee

haikara (na) *adj* ハイカラ（な）fashionable, high-class

haikei *n* 背景 background, BG

háikei *n* 拝啓 [BOOKISH] Dear Sir/Madam (*in a letter*)

haiken *n* 拝見: **~ shimásu** 拝見します [HUMBLE] I/We (will) look at/see (= **mimasu** 見ます)

haiki *n* 排気 exhaust

    haiki-gásu *n* 排気ガス exhaust (*fumes*)

    haikí-sen *n* 排気扇 exhaust fan

haiki *n* 廃棄 disposal, abolition, rejection: **~ shimásu** 廃棄します scraps: **haiki-butsu** 廃棄物 waste(s)

háikíngu n ハイキング hike, hiking: ~
o shimásu ハイキングをします hikes

háiku n 俳句 *haiku* (short (17-syllable)
poem)

haikyo n 廃墟 ruin: ~ to narimásu 廃墟
となります ruins

haikyū n 配給 rationing: ~ shimásu 配
給します rations

haimásu, háu n 這います, 這う crawls

háire v 入れ [IMPERATIVE] (enter!) →
hairimásu 入ります

hairemásu, hairéru v 入れます, 入れ
る can enter

hairimásu, háiru v 入ります, 入る
enters: **furo ni ~** 風呂に入ります takes
a bath; **háitte imásu** 入っています is
inside

hairyo n 配慮 consideration: ~ shimásu
配慮します considers; **go-hairyo
(itadaki) arigató-gozaimasu** ご配慮(い
ただき)ありがとうございます Thank
you all for your help and support.

haishaku-shimásu (suru) v 拝借しま
す(する) [HUMBLE] (I) borrow (= **kari-
masu** 借ります)

haishi n 廃止 abolition: ~ shimásu 廃止
します abolishes

haishinkōi n 背信行為 [BOOKISH]
treachery

haisui n 排水 drainage
  haisui-ponpu n 排水ポンプ drainage
  pump

haita n 排他 [BOOKISH] exclusion
  haita-teki (na) adj 排他的(な)
  exclusive
  haita-shugi n 排他主義 exclusivism

haitatsu n 配達 delivery: ~ shimásu 配
達します delivers

haite v 履いて → hakimásu 履きます
(wears, puts on)

háite v 吐いて → hakimásu 吐きます

haitōkin n 配当金 dividends, annuity

háiyā n ハイヤー limousine for hire

haiyū n 俳優 actor (= **yaku-sha** 役者),
actress (= **joyū** 女優)

haji(-kko) n 端(っこ) → hashi 端

hají n 恥 shame: embarrassment: ~ o
kakimásu 恥をかきます disgraces/
embarrasses oneself

hajikemásu, hajikéru v はじけます,

はじける it pops, snaps

hajikí n はじき (**o-hájiki** おはじき)
marbles

hajikimásu, hajíku v はじきます, はじ
く snaps it, repels it (*water, ...*)

hajimari v 始まり beginning, start

hajimarimásu, hajimaru v 始まりま
す, 始まる it begins (*starts*)

hajimásu, hajiru v 恥ます, 恥じる
feels shame, feels embarrassed

hajime n 初め the beginning; in the
beginning: **hajime no** 初めの the first
…; **hajime wa** 初めは at first

hajime v 始め [IMPERATIVE] (start!) →
hajimemásu 始めます

Hajimemáshite. interj 初めまして
How do you do? (*on being introduced*)

hajimemásu, hajimeru v 始めます, 始
める begins (starts) it

hajimeraremásu, hajimerareru v 始
められます, 始められる can begin it

hajimete n 始めて → hajimemásu
始めます

hajímete adv はじめて・初めて for
the first time

haká n 墓 (**o-haka** お墓) grave (*tomb*):
(o)haka-mairi (お)墓参り visiting
one's grave
  haka-bá n 墓場 graveyard, cemetery

hakadorimásu, hakaréru v はか
どります, はかどる makes good
progress: **shigoto ga ~** 仕事がはかど
ります gets ahead with one's work

hakai n 破壊 destruction, demolition:
~ shimásu 破壊します destroys,
demolishes

hakaku (no) adj 破格(の) unprecedented: ~ no nedan 破格の値段 rock-
bottom price, bargain price

hakama n 袴 traditional Japanese skirt-
like trousers for male

hakanai v 履かない = **hakimasén** 履き
ません (not wear)

hakanái adj 儚い fleeting, transitory

hakánai v 吐かない = **hakimasén** 吐き
ません (not vomit)

hakánai v 掃かない = **hakimasén** 掃き
ません (not sweep)

hakaraimásu, hakarau v 計らいます,
計らう arrange

hakáre ν 測れ・量れ [IMPERATIVE] (measure it!) → **hakarimásu** 測ります・量ります

hakaremásu, hakaréru ν 測れます, 測れる can measure

hakaremásu, hakaréru ν 量れます, 量れる can weigh

hakarí n 秤 (*weighting/weight*) scales

hakarigóto n 謀 plot, trick, scheme

hakarimásu, hakáru ν 測ります, 測る measures

hakarimásu, hakáru ν 量ります, 量る weighs

hakarimásu, hakáru ν 図り[謀り]ます, 図[謀]る plans, designs; plots

hákase n 博士 doctor (Ph.D.) (= **haku-shi** 博士): **hakase-rónbun** 博士論文 doctoral dissertation

hakátte ν 測って・量って・図って → **hakarimásu** 測ります・量ります・図ります

haké ν 履け [IMPERATIVE] (wear it!) → **hakemásu** 履きます

haké n 刷毛 brush

haké ν 捌け drainage, draining: **~ ga íi désu** 捌けがいいです it drains/sells well

háke ν 掃け [IMPERATIVE] (sweep!) → **hakimásu** 掃きます

háke ν 吐け [IMPERATIVE] (vomit!; spill it out!) → **hakimásu** 吐きます

hakéba ν 履けば (if one wears) → **hakimásu** 履きます

hákeba ν 吐けば (if one vomits) → **hakimásu** 吐きます

hákeba ν 掃けば (if one sweeps) → **hakimásu** 掃きます

haké-kuchi/-guchi n 捌け口 outlet (*for water/emotion/goods*)

hakemásu, hakeru ν 履きます, 履ける can wear (*footwear, pants, skirt, socks*)

hakemásu, hakéru ν 捌けます, 捌ける it drains off; it sells (well)

hakemásu, hakéru ν 吐けます, 吐ける can vomit/spill out

hakemásu, hakéru ν 掃けます, 掃ける can sweep

haken n 派遣 dispatch: **~ shimásu** 派遣します sends, dispatches; **jinzai-haken** 人材派遣 temporary staffing

hakeréba ν 履ければ (if one can wear) → **hakemásu** 履けます

hakéreba ν 捌ければ (if it drains off) → **hakemásu** 捌けます

hakéreba ν 吐ければ (if one can vomit) → **hakemásu** 吐けます

hakéreba ν 掃ければ (if one can sweep) → **hakemásu** 掃けます

hakete ν 履けて → **hakemásu** 履けます

hákete ν 吐けて・掃けて → **hakemásu** 吐けます・掃けます

haki ν 履き → **hakimásu** 履きます

háki n 覇気 ambition (*energetic spirit*): **~ ga arimásu** 覇気があります is full of spirit

háki ν 吐き・掃き → **hakimásu** 吐きます・掃きます

hakihaki (to) adj はきはき(と) lively, briskly: **~ to hanashimásu** はきはきと話します talks clearly and briskly

haki-ké n 吐き気 nausea: **~ ga shimásu/o moyōshimásu** 吐き気がします/を催します feels nauseated/queasy

hakimásu, haku ν 履きます, 履く wears (*on feet or legs*), puts/slips on (*shoes, socks, pants*)

hakimásu, háku ν 吐きます, 吐く **1.** vomits **2.** spits out

hakimásu, háku ν 掃きます, 掃く sweeps

hakimono n 履物 footwear

hakka n ハッカ peppermint (= **pepā-minto** ペパーミント)

hakkā n ハッカー hacker, hack (*computer*)

hak-kái, hachi-kái n 八回 eight times

hakken n 発見 discovery: **~ shimásu** 発見します discovers

hakketsu-byō n 白血病 leukemia

hakkí n 発揮 exertion: **~ shimásu** 発揮します exerts

hakkíri adv はっきり plainly, clearly, distinctly, exactly: **~ (to) shimásu** はっきり(と)します becomes clear

hakkō n 発行 publication: **hakkōsha** 発行者 publisher: **~ shimásu** 発行します publishes, issues

hakkō n 発光 light emission: **~ shimásu** 発光します emits light

hakkō *n* 発酵 ferment: **~ shimás<u>u</u>** 発酵
します ferments

hakkutsu *n* 発掘 exhumation: **~ shi-
más<u>u</u>** 発掘します digs up, excavates

hakkyō *n* 発狂 derangement: **~ shimás<u>u</u>**
発狂します becomes insane

hako *n* 箱 box, case, chest, container

hakobimás<u>u</u>, hakobu *v* 運びます, 運
ぶ carries, conveys

hakonde *v* 運んで → **hakobimás<u>u</u>**
運びます

haku *v* 履く = **hakimás<u>u</u>** 履きます
(wears, puts/slips on)

haku *v* 吐く = **hakimás<u>u</u>** 吐きます
(vomits; spits out)

haku *v* 掃く = **hakimás<u>u</u>** 掃きます
(sweeps)

haku-... *prefix* 白... white
haku-chō *n* ハクチョウ・白鳥 swan:
hakuchō-za 白鳥座 Cygnus
háku-i *n* 白衣 white coat: **~ no tenshi**
白衣の天使 nurse, angel (*not to
literally mean, "angel in white"*)
haku-jin *n* 白人 Caucasian
hakú-mai *n* 白米 polished rice
haku-shi *n* 白紙 blank sheet of paper:
~ ni modoshimás<u>u</u> 白紙に戻します
withdraws, takes back
haku-sho *n* 白書 white paper

...-haku *suffix* ...泊, **...-paku** ...泊
(*counts nights of lodging*)

hakuai *n* 博愛 humanitarianism:
hakuai-shugi 博愛主義 philanthropism

hakubúts<u>u</u>-kan *n* 博物館 museum

haku<u>chū</u>mu *n* 白昼夢 daydreaming: **~
o mimás<u>u</u>** 白昼夢を見ます is spaced out

hakugai *n* 迫害 persecution: **~ o uke-
más<u>u</u>** 迫害を受けます suffers from
persecution

hakujaku (na) *adj* 薄弱(な) weak,
tenuity: **ishi-hakujaku** 意志薄弱 weak
will

hákujō *n* 白状 confession: **~ shimás<u>u</u>**
白状します confesses

hakujō (na) *adj* 薄情(な) [BOOKISH]
unfeeling, heartless, cruel: **hakujō na
hito** 薄情な人, **hakujō-mono** 薄情者
heartless person

hakurai (no) *adj* 舶来(の) imported
hakurai-hin *n* 舶来品 imported goods

hakurán-kai *n* 博覧会 exhibition,
exposition

hakuryoku *n* 迫力 punch, power: **~ ga
arimás<u>u</u>** 迫力があります is powerful

hakusái *n* ハクサイ・白菜 Chinese
cabbage

hakushi *n* 博士 doctor (Ph.D.) (=
hakase 博士): **hakushi-katei** 博士課程
doctoral course

hákushu *n* 拍手 clapping: **~ shimás<u>u</u>**
拍手します claps one's hands

hamá *n* 浜 beach

hama-be *n* 浜辺 seabeach, seashore

hamachi *n* ハマチ・魚 young yellowtail (*cf.* **búri** ブリ・鰤, **inada** イナダ)

hamáguri *n* ハマグリ・蛤 clam

hamé *n* はめ plight, fix (*one gets into*)

hamemás<u>u</u>, hameru *v* はめます, は
める wears (on fingers, hands (*ring,
gloves, etc.*))

hame(ra)remás<u>u</u>, hame(ra)reru *v* は
め(ら)れます, はめ(ら)れる can wear
(*on fingers, hands*)

hametsu *n* 破滅 ruin

hamidashimás<u>u</u>, hamidasu *v* はみ出
します, はみ出す protrudes, runs off
the edge, sticks out, goes over

há-mono *n* 刃物 cutlery, knives

hámu *n* ハム ham: **hamu-éggu** ハムエ
ッグ ham and eggs; **hamu-sándo** ハム
サンド ham sandwich

hán *n* 半 half (= **hanbún** 半分): **han-...**
半... half a ...; **...-hán** ... 半 and a half

hán *n* 判 a "chop" = a seal (*to stamp
name*) (= **hankó** 判こ)

hana *n* 鼻 (**o-hana** お鼻) nose; trunk
(*of elephant*)
hana-ji *n* 鼻血 nosebleed: **~ ga de-más<u>u</u>**
鼻血が出ます gets a nosebleed
hana-mizú *n* 鼻水 snivel, nasal mucus:
~ ga demás<u>u</u> 鼻水が出ます has a runny
nose

hana *n* はな nasal mucus, snivel (=
hana-mizú 鼻水): **~ o kamimás<u>u</u>** はな
をかみます blows one's nose

haná *n* 花 (**o-hana** お花) flower; flower
arrangement
hana-mí *n* 花見 (**o-hanami** お花見)
cherry blossom viewing: **(o-)~ o shi-
más<u>u</u>** (お)花見をします goes to see

the cherry blossom

haná-tába *n* 花束 bouquet

hana-wa *n* 花輪 wreath (*of flower*)

haná-ya *n* 花屋 florist, flower shop

hána *n* はな・端 beginning, outset; edge

hána-bi *n* 花火 fireworks: **hababí-taikai** 花火大会 big exhibition of fireworks

haná-fuda *n* 花札 (*the game of*) flower cards (= **hana-gáruta** 花がるた)

hanágata *n* 花形 a star (*in a theatrical production*): **hanágata-senshu** 花形選手 star player

hanahada *adv* はなはだ extremely

haná-michi *n* 花道 the runway to the stage (in Kabuki)

hana-múko *n* 花婿 bridegroom

hanao *n* 鼻緒 thong (on *geta*)

hanaremásu, hanaréru *v* 離れます, 離れる separates, becomes distant, leaves

hanasánai *v* 話さない = **hanashi-masén** 話しません (not speak)

hanasánai *v* 放さない = **hanashi-masén** 放しません (not release)

hanasánai *v* 離さない = **hanashi-masén** 離しません (not separate something)

hanáseba *v* 話せば (if one speaks) → **hanasemásu** 話せます

hanáseba *v* 放せば (if one releases) → **hanasemásu** 放せます

hanáseba *v* 離せば (if one separates something) → **hanasemásu** 離せます

hanasemásu, hanaséru *v* 話せます, 話せる can speak

hanasénai *v* 話せない = **hanasemasén** 話せません (cannot speak)

hanasénai *v* 放せない = **hanasemasén** 放せません (cannot release)

hanasénai *v* 離せない = **hanase-masén** 離せません (cannot separate something)

hanashí *n* 話 talk, story, tale, speech, conversation; something to talk about: **~ o shimásu** 話をします talks, speaks

hanashi-ái *n* 話し合い conference, discussion, negotiation

hanashi-aimásu, hanashi-áu *v* 話し合います, 話し合う talk together, dis-

cuss, confer, negotiate

hanashi-ka *n* 噺家 (comic) storyteller (= **rakugo-ka** 落語家)

hanashimásu, hanásu *v* 話します, 話す speaks, talks

hanashimásu, hanásu *v* 放します, 放す release, lets loose/go, sets free

hanashimásu, hanásu *v* 離します, 離す separates (*something*) from, parts with; detaches, disconnects

hanáyaka (na) *adj* 華やか(な) colorful, showy, gorgeous, glorious, bright

haná-yome *n* 花嫁 bride

hanbā´gā *n* ハンバーガー a hamburger

hanbā´gu *n* ハンバーグ hamburger (meat)

hanbai *n* 販売 sale: **~ shimásu** 販売します deals in, sells

hanbái-ki *n* 販売機 vending machine

hanbái-daka *n* 販売高 sales volume

hanbai-moto *n* 販売元 sales agency

hanbai-in *n* 販売員 salesperson

hanbai-nin *n* 販売人 seller, dealer

hanbái-ten *n* 販売店 sales outlet

hanbai-sokushin *n* 販売促進 sales promotion (= **hansoku** 販促)

hanbai-kakaku *n* 販売価格 selling price

hanbei (no) *adj* 反米(の) anti-American

hanbún *n* 半分 half

hándán *n* 判断 judgment: **~ shimásu** 判断します judges, gives judgment

handō *n* 反動 reaction, repercussion

handō-teki (na) *adj* 反動的(な) reactionary

handobággu, handobákku *n* ハンドバッグ, ハンドバック handbag, pocketbook

handoru *n* ハンドル steering wheel; handle

hane *n* 羽 feather

hane *n* 羽根 wing; shuttlecock

hané-tsuki *n* 羽根つき battledore and shuttlecock (*a kind of badminton*)

hanei *n* 反映 reflection: **~ shimásu** 反映します is reflected

hanei *n* 繁栄 prosperity: **~ shimásu** 繁栄します gains prosperity

hanemásu, hanéru *v* 跳ねます, 跳ねる jumps, splashes

hanga *n* 版画 woodblock print

hángā *n* ハンガー hanger

hangaku *n* 半額 half price

hangyaku *n* 反逆 rebellion: ~ **shimásu** 反逆します rebels
hangyáku-sha 反逆者 rebel

hanhan *n* 半々 half-and-half

hán'i *n* 範囲 scope, range, limits: (**... no**) **han'í-gai/-nai** (…の)範囲外/内 beyond/within the limits (of …)

hanigo *n* 反意語 antonym

hanikamimásu, hanikámu *v* はにかみます, はにかむ acts shy, is bashful: **hanikami-ya** はにかみ屋 shy

hánji *n* 判事 judge

hánjō *n* 繁盛 prosperity: **shōbai-hanjō** 商売繁盛 flourishing business, boom of business

hánkachi *n* ハンカチ handkerchief

hankagai *n* 繁華街 downtown area, shopping and amusement districts

hankan *n* 反感 antipathy: ~ **o kaimásu** 反感を買います provokes one's antipathy

hankei *n* 半径 radius

hanketsu *n* 判決 judgment: ~ **o kuda-shimásu** 判決を下します adjudges, gives sentence

hanki *n* 半期 half of the business year

hankō *n* はんこ・判子 a "chop" (*signature seal, name stamp*) (= **han** 判, **in** 印, **inkan** 印鑑)

hankō *n* 反抗 opposition, resistance: **... ni ~ shimásu** …に反抗します opposes, resists (= **hanpatsu** 反発)

hankō *n* 犯行 crime, perpetration: **hankō-genba** 犯行現場 scene of a crime: **hankō-seimei** 犯行声明 criminal declaration

hankyō *n* 反響 echo: **hankyō-on** 反響音 acoustic echo

hankyōran *n* 半狂乱 frantic, partial insanity: ~ **ni narimásu** 半狂乱になります becomes frantic

hankyū *n* 半休 half day off: ~ **o torimásu** 半休を取ります takes a half day off

hankyū *n* 半球 hemisphere

hánmā *n* ハンマー hammer

hanmei *n* 判明 coming-out: ~ **shimásu** 判明します comes out, turns out

hanmen *n* 反面 on the other hand: **hanmen-kyōshi** 反面教師 person who serves as an example of how not to be

hanmen (no) *adj* 半面(の) half-faced

han-nichi *n* 半日 half a day, a half-day

hannichi (no) *adj* 反日(の) anti-Japanese

hánnin *n* 犯人 a criminal, culprit

hannō *n* 反応 reaction, response: ~ **shimásu** 反応します reacts

hanpa *n* 半端 half: **hanpa-mono** 半端物 oddments → **chūto hanpa (na)** 中途半端(な)

hanpatsu *n* 反発 **1.** repelling **2.** repulsion **3.** resistance (= **hankō** 反抗): ~ **shimásu** 反発します repels; rebounds; resists

hanpén *n* ハンペン・はんぺん boiled fish cake

hanran *n* 反乱 revolt: ~ **o okosu** 反乱を起こす revolts, rebels

hanran *n* 氾濫 overflowing: ~ **shimásu** 氾濫します overflows, floods

hanrei *n* 凡例 explanatory notes (*on how to use a reference work*)

hanryo *n* 伴侶 companion: **shōgai no ~** 生涯の伴侶 spouse (*literally, "lifetime companion"*)

hánsa (na) *adj* 煩瑣(な) troublesome, complicated

hansei *n* 反省 reflection, thinking-over: ~ **shimásu** 反省します reflects (*on*), ponders

hansen (no) *adj* 反戦(の) antiwar: **hansen-katsudō** 反戦活動 antiwar activity

hansen-byō *n* ハンセン病 Hansen's disease, leprosy

hansha *n* 反射 reflection: ~ **shimásu** 反射します reflects

hánshi *n* 半紙 rice paper (*stationery*)

han-shimásu (-súru) *v* 反します is contrary (*to*), goes against, opposes: **... ni hánshite** …に反して contrary to, against, in contrast with

hanshū *n* 半周 semicircle

hansode *n* 半そで・半袖 half sleeves

hansoku *n* 反則 foul

hansoku *n* 販促 sales promotion: **hansoku-tsūru** 販促ツール sales promotion tool (= **hanbai-sokushin** 販売促進)

hantai n 反対 opposite, contrary, reverse (= **gyaku** 逆): **hantai-gawa** 反対側 opposite side; **hantai-go** 反対語 antonym; **hantai ni** 反対に vice versa: ~ **shimásu** 反対します opposes

hantén n 半纏 *happi* coat (= **happi** はっぴ・法被)

hantō n 半島, ...**-hántō** ...半島 peninsula: **Izu-hántō** 伊豆半島 Izu Peninsula

han-toshí n 半年 half a year

han-tsukí n 半月 half a month

han'yake (no) adj 半焼け(の) medium-rare (*meat*), half-done (= **nama-yake (no)** 生焼け(の))

hanzai n 犯罪 crime: ~ **o okashimásu** 犯罪を犯します commits a crime

hanzatsu (na) adj 煩雑(な) troublesome, complicated

hanzubon n 半ズボン short-pants

haori n 羽織 (**o-háori** お羽織) traditional Japanese coat

hap- n 八・8 eight
hap-pén n 八遍 eight times (= **hachí-kai** 八回, **hachí-do** 八度)
háp-pa, hachí-wa n 八羽 eight (*birds, rabbits*)
hap-piki n 八匹 eight (*fishes/bugs, small animals*)
háp-pon, hachi-hon n 八本 eight (*pencils/bottles, long objects*)
háp-pun n 八分 eight minutes

happa n 葉っぱ leaf (= **ha** 葉)

happi n 法被 *happi* coat (= **hantén** 半纏)

hap-pyakú n 八百・800 eight hundred

happyō n 発表 announcement, publication; (*research*) paper: ~ **shimásu** 発表します announces, publishes

hā´pu n ハープ harp (*Western*)

hará n 腹 1. belly, stomach (= **o-naka** お腹): ~ **ga herimásu** 腹が減ります gets hungry; ~ **ga itamimásu** 腹が痛みます one's stomach aches 2. mind, heart: ~ **ga tachimásu** 腹が立ちます, ~ **o tatemásu** 腹を立てます gets angry; ~ **ga kurói** 腹が黒い black-hearted; ~ **o kimemásu** 腹を決めます makes up one's mind

hára, hárappa n 原, 原っぱ field

haradatashíi adj 腹立たしい aggravating, vexatious

haráe v 払え [IMPERATIVE] (pay!) → **haraimásu** 払います

haráeba v 払えば (if one pays; if ...) → **haraimásu** 払います

haraemásu, haraéru v 払えます, 払える 1. can pay 2. can brush aside, can shake out

harahara adv はらはら: ~ **shimásu** はらはらします gets anxious, is scared; ~ **sasemásu** はらはらさせます scares

haraimásu, haráu v 払います, 払う 1. pays 2. brushes aside, shakes out

harai-modoshi n 払い戻し a refund

harai-modoshimásu, harai-modósu v 払い戻します, 払い戻す refunds

hará-maki n 腹巻き stomach band

haranai v 貼らない = **harimásén** 貼りません (not paste it)

haranai v 張らない = **harimásén** 張りません (not spread/stretch it)

harátte v 払って → **haraimásu** 払います

haráu v 払う = **haraimásu** 払います (pays; brushes aside, shakes out)

harawánai v 払わない = **haraimásén** 払いません (not pay; not ...)

harawáta n 腸 intestines

hare n 腫れ swelling: **me no** ~ 目の腫れ a bag (= **(me no) kuma** (目の)くま)

haré v 貼れ [IMPERATIVE] (paste it!) → **harimásu** 貼ります

haré v 張れ [IMPERATIVE] (spread it!) → **harimásu** 張ります

haré n 晴れ fair (clear) weather

haréba v 貼れば (if one pastes it) → **harimásu** 貼ります

haréba v 張れば (if one spreads/stretches it) → **harimásu** 張ります

haremásu, hareru v 腫れます, 腫れる swells up

haremásu, hareru v 貼れます, 貼れる can paste

haremásu, hareru v 張れます; 張れる can spread/stretch it

haremásu, haréru v 晴れます, 晴れる (*weather*) clears up: **hárete imásu** 晴れています is clear/fair/sunny

hare-mono *n* 腫れ物 swelling, boil (*on skin*)

haréréba *v* 腫れれば (if it swells) → **haremásu** 腫れます

haréreba *v* 晴れれば (if it clears up) → **haremásu** 晴れます

haretsu *n* 破裂 bursting: **~ shimásu** 破裂します bursts

hari-gami *n* 貼り紙 poster

hári *n* 針 needle, pin; needlework; hand (*of clock*); a staple (*of stapler*)
　hari-gane *n* 針金 wire
　hari-shígoto *n* 針仕事 needlework (*of all types*)

hári *n* 鍼 acupuncture

harimásu, haru *v* 貼ります, 貼る sticks on, pastes

harimásu, haru *v* 張ります, 張る spreads/stretches it

haru *v* 貼る = **harimásu** 貼ります

haru *v* 張る = **harimásu** 張ります

háru *n* 春 spring (*season*)
　haru-same *n* 春雨 bean-flour threads; spring rain
　haru-yásumi *n* 春休み spring break/ vacation

harubaru *adv* はるばる all the way

háruka (ni) *adv* 遥か(に) far (off); long ago; by far
　háruka na *adj* 遥か(な) distant, far

haru-maki *n* 春巻 Chinese egg rolls, spring rolls

hasamarimásu, hasamáru *v* 挟まります, 挟まる gets caught (*in*) between, becomes sandwiched (*in*) between

hasáme *v* 挟め [IMPERATIVE] (insert!) → **hasamimásu** 挟みます

hasamemásu, hasaméru *v* 挟めます, 挟める can insert (*put between*)

hasamí *n* はさみ・鋏 scissors, clippers

hasamí *n* はさみ・螯 pincer(s), claw (*of crab*)

hasamimásu, hasámu *v* 挟みます, 挟む inserts, puts between

hasan *n* 破産 bankruptcy: **~ shimásu** 破産します goes bankrupt

hashi, haji *n* 端 edge, end (= **hashi-kko, hajikko** 端っこ)

hashí *n* 橋 bridge

háshi *n* 箸 (**o-háshi** お箸) chopsticks: **~ o tsukaimásu** 箸を使います uses chopsticks
　hashí-óki *n* 箸置き chopstick rest

hashigo *n* 梯子 ladder, stairs: **hashigó-zake** はしご酒 bar hopping

hashika *n* はしか measles

hashira *n* 柱 pillar, post

hashíre *v* 走れ [IMPERATIVE] (run!) → **hashirimásu** 走ります

hashiremásu, hashiréru *v* 走れます, 走れる can run

hashirimásu, hashíru *v* 走ります, 走る runs

hashitanai *adj* はしたない in bad taste, shameful

hashítte *v* 走って → **hashirimásu** 走ります

hason *n* 破損 damage

hassan *n* 発散 emanation, transpiration: **~ shimásu** 発散します gives out, emanates, exhales; **sutoresu ~** ストレス発散 stress release

hás-satsu *n* 八冊 eight copies (*books, magazines*)

hassei *n* 発生 outbreak, occurrence, origin, birth, growth: **~ shimásu** 発生します breaks out, occurs, appears, grows

has-sén *n* 八千・8,000 eight thousand

hassha *n* 発車 departure: **~ shimásu** 発車します departs

hasshin *n* 発進 (*vehicle etc.*) starts: **~ sasemásu** 発進させます moves (*car*)

hasshin *n* 発信 transmission: **~ shimásu** 発信します sends, transmits

hasshin *n* 発疹 (*skin*) rash

hasu *n* ハス・蓮 lotus

hasu (no) *adj* 斜(の) oblique, slanting: **hasu ni** 斜に・はすに obliquely (= **naname (ni)** 斜(に))

hata *n* 端 **1.** the side: **(… no) hata de** (…の)端で off to the side (*of*) **2.** the outside; **~ kara** 端から from the outside, to an outsider

hatá *n* 旗 flag

hatá *n* 機 loom

hátachi *n* 二十歳 20 years old

hatáite *v* はたいて → **hatakimásu** はたきます

hatake *n* 畑 field (*dry*): **~ o tagayashi-másu** 畑を耕します cultivates one's patch

hatáke *v* はたけ (= **tatake** 叩け) [IMPERATIVE] (slap/dust it!) → **hataki-másu** はたきます

hatakemásu, hatakéru *v* はたけます, はたける can slap; can dust

hatakí *n* はたき duster

hatakimásu, hatáku *v* はたきます, はたく slap, beat; dust (= **tatakimásu** 叩きます)

hatan *n* 破綻 bankruptcy, failure, collapse: **~ shimásu** 破綻します falls, collapses

hatarakemásu, hatarakeru *v* 働けます, 働ける can work

hataraki *n* 働き work(ing), activity, operation, function; achievement; ability

hatarakimásu, hataraku *v* 働きます, 働く works, labors; commits (*a crime*)

hataraki-mono *n* 働き者 hard worker

hatasemásu, hataséru *v* 果たせます, 果たせる can accomplish

hatashimásu, hatásu *v* 果たします,果たす accomplishes: **yakusoku o ~** 約束を果たします fulfills a promise

háto *n* ハト・鳩 pigeon, dove

hato-ba *n* 波止場 pier, wharf, quay (= **futō** 埠頭)

hatsu (no) *adj* 初 (の) first

hatsuan *n* 発案 design idea

hatsubai *n* 発売 sale, release: **~ shimásu** 発売します sells hatsubai-bi *n* 発売日 sells/release date

hatsudén-ki *n* 発電機 generator

hatsudō'-ki *n* 発動機 motor

hatsuiku *n* 発育 growth: **~ ga yoi/ii** 発育が良い/いい is well grown

hatsuka *n* 二十日 20 days; 20th of the month: **hatsuka-mé** 二十日 the 20th day; **hatsuka-nézumi** 二十日ネズミ [鼠] mouse

hatsukoi *n* 初恋 first love

hatsumei *n* 発明 invention: **~ shimásu** 発明します invents

… hátsu (no) *suffix* …発 (の) departing at/from (*time/place*); dispatched from/at (*place/time*)

hatsuon *n* 発音 pronunciation: **~ shimásu** 発音します pronounces

hattatsu *n* 発達 development: **~ shimásu** 発達します it develops

hatte *v* 貼って・張って・ → **hari-másu** 貼ります・張ります

hátte *v* 這って ~ = **haimásu** 這います

hatte imásu (iru) *v* 張っています(いる) is tense, taut

hátte imásu (iru) *v* 這っています(いる) is crawling

hatten *n* 発展 development, expansion, growth: **~ shimásu** 発展します develops, expands, grows hatten-tojō'koku 発展途上国 developing nation

hát-tō *n* 八頭 eight (*horses/oxen, large animals*)

hatto (shite) *adv* はっと (して) with a sudden start (*of surprise*)

Háwai *n* ハワイ Hawaii

hawánai *v* 這わない = **haimasén** 這いません (not crawl)

hayái *adj* 速い fast, quick

hayái *adj* 早い early, soon

háyaku *adv* 速く (*so as to be*) fast

háyaku *adv* 早く (*so as to be*) early, soon: **háyaku-tomo** 早くとも at the earliest

hayamé ni *adv* 早めに early (*in good time*)

hayarimásu, hayáru *v* 流行ります, 流行る gets popular, comes into fashion, spreads; (*disease*) spreads rapidly

hayari (no) *adj* 流行り (の) fashionable, popular

háyasa *n* 速さ speed

hayashi ráisu *n* ハヤシライス beef hash over rice

hayashí *n* 林 grove

hayashí *n* 囃し (**o-hayashi** お囃し) Japanese instrument accompaniment

hayashimásu, hayásu *v* 生やします, 生やす grows it (*hair, teeth*); lets it grow (*sprout*)

hayashimásu, hayásu *v* 囃します, 囃す (*musically*) accompanies

hayátte *v* 流行って → **hayarimásu** 流行ります

háze *n* ハゼ・沙魚 goby (*fish*)

... hazu désu *v* ...はずです presumably; ought to, should

... hazu ga/wa arimasén (nái) *v* ... は ずが/はありません（ない）there is no reason to expect/think that ...

hazukashíi *adj* 恥ずかしい ashamed; embarrassed, shy; shameful, disgraceful

hazumi *n* 弾み impetus, momentum; impulse; chance

hazumimásu, hazumu *v* 弾みます, 弾 む bounces (back)

hazuremásu, hazureru *v* 外れます, 外れる gets disconnected, comes off; misses, fails

hazushimásu, hazusu *v* 外します, 外す disconnects, takes off, undoes, unfastens; misses: **séki o ~** 席を外しま す leaves one's seat

hé *n* 屁 flatulence, fart (= **onara** おなら): **~ o hirimásu/shimásu** 屁をひります/ します flatulates, farts

hē *interj* へえ oh, really, wow

hébi *n* ヘビ・蛇 snake

hechima *n* ヘチマ・糸瓜 sponge gourd, luffa (loofah)

hedatarimásu, hedatáru *v* 隔たりま す, 隔たる is distant, is estranged

hedatemásu, hedatéru *v* 隔てます, 隔 てる estranges them, separates them, gets them apart

heddoráito *n* ヘッドライト headlight(s)

hédo *n* 反吐 vomit

hei *n* 塀 wall, fence

hei *n* 兵 soldier (= **heishi** 兵士)
  hei-eki *n* 兵役 military service: **~ ni tsukimásu** 兵役につきます serves in the army
  hei-ki *n* 兵器 weapon, arms
  hei-ryoku *n* 兵力 military force
  héi-sha *n* 兵舎 barracks
  hei-shi *n* 兵士 soldier (= **hei** 兵)
  hei-tai *n* 兵隊 soldier (boy), rank:
    heitai-ari 兵隊アリ soldier ant

heibon (na) *adj* 平凡（な）commonplace, conventional, ordinary

heichi *n* 平地 flat land (= **heiya** 平野) plain

heijitsu *n* 平日 weekday

heijō (ni) *adv* 平常（に）usually, ordinarily, generally

heijō-shin *n* one's senses/mind: **~ o tamochimásu** 平常心を保ちます keeps one's cool/calm

heika *n* 陛下 majesty, Your Majesty.

heikai *n* 閉会 closing a meeting: **heikai-shiki** 閉会式 closing ceremony

heikin *n* 平均 average, on the average: **heikin-nenrei** 平均年令 average age; **heikin-jumyō** 平均寿命 average life span (*lifetime*); **heikin-ten** 平均点 average score

heiki (na) *adj* 平気（な）calm, composed, cool, unperturbed, unfazed: **heiki de** 平気で calmly

heikō *n* 平行 parallel, parallelism: **~ o tadorimásu** 平行線をたどります remains as far apart as ever

heikō-shimásu (suru) *v* 閉口します （する）is annoyed, is overwhelmed, gets stuck

heimen *n* 平面 flat surface: **heimen-zu** 平面図 two-dimensional diagram

heimin *n* 平民 common person: **heimin-kaikyū** 平民階級 commons

heisa *n* 閉鎖 closing: **kōjō-heisa** 工場閉 鎖 factory closure

heiten *n* 閉店 closing a store: **~ shimásu** 閉店します closes a store

heiwa *n* 平和 peace; **~ ni narimásu** 平和になります becomes peace; **~ na kuni** 平和の国 peaceful nation
  haiwa na *adj* 平和な peaceful

heiya *n* 平野 plain (*flat land*)

heizen (to) *adv* 平然（と）without embarrassment: **~ to shiteimásu** 平然と しています remains unruffled

hekichi *n* 僻地 remote area (= **henpi na tochi** 辺ぴな土地)

hekieki-shimásu (suru) *v* 辟易します （する）is disgusted

hekiga *n* 壁画 wall painting

hekomimásu, hekomu *v* へこみます, へこむ gets hollow, depressed, dents: **hekonde imásu** へこんでいます is dented, depressed

héma *n* へま [INFORMAL] bungle, goof: **~ (o) shimásu** へま（を）します goofs up

hemásu, héru *v* 経ます, 経る passes (by), elapses

... **hen** *suffix* ...辺 vicinity, nearby, neighborhood (= **chikaku** 近く)

...-**hén** *suffix* ...遍 (*counts times*) (= **do** 度, **kai** 回)

henai *v* 経ない = **hemasén** 経ません (not pass)

hen'átsu-ki *n* 変圧器 voltage converter, transformer

henji *n* 返事 (**o-henji** お返事) answer, reply, response

hénka *n* 変化 change: **... ni ~ shimásu** ...に変化します it changes into ...

henkaku *n* 変革 innovative changes: **~ shimásu** 変革します changes, transforms

henkan *n* 変換 conversion: **~ shimásu** 変換します converts, replaces, changes, transforms

henkán-ki *n* 変換器 converter

henkan-kíi *n* 変換キー the *kana-to-kanji* conversion key (*on a Japanese computer*)

henkan *n* 返還 return

henken *n* 偏見 prejudice

henkin *n* 返金 refund (*[note] tax refund* = **kanpu** 還付)

hén (na) *adj* 変(な) strange, odd, peculiar, funny, queer

henpi (na) *adj* 辺ぴ(な) odd, off the beaten path: **~ na tochi** 辺ぴな土地 odd parts (= **hekichi** 僻地)

hensei *n* 編成 organization: **~ shimásu** 編成します organizes

henshin *n* 返信 reply, return mail: **~ shimásu** 返信します replies

henshin *n* 変身 transformation: **~ shimásu** 変身します transforms

henshū *n* 編集 editing: **~ shimásu** 編集します edits

henshū-chō *n* 編集長 editor in chief

henshū-sha *n* 編集者 editor

hensoku-rébā *n* 変速レバー gear-shift

hentō *n* 返答 [BOOKISH] = **henjí** 返事: **~ shimásu** 返答します answers, replies, responses

heranai *v* 減らない = **herimasén** 減りません (not decrease)

herashimásu, herasu *v* 減らします, 減らす decreases it, cuts it down

heréba *v* 減れば (if it decreases) →

herimásu 減ります

heri *n* 減り a decrease

herí *n* 縁 border, edge, rim (= **fuchi** 縁)

herikoputā *n* ヘリコプター helicopter

herikudarimásu, herikudaru *v* へりくだります, へりくだる is modest, abases oneself

herikutsu *n* 屁理屈 sophistry, quiddity (*using clever arguments to support something that is not true*): **~ o iimásu** 屁理屈を言います quibbles

herimásu, heru *v* 減ります, 減る decreases, dwindles, goes down

heripōto *n* ヘリポート heliport

heroin *n* ヘロイン heroin

herumetto *n* ヘルメット helmet

herunia *n* ヘルニア hernia

hérupā *n* ヘルパー helper

hérupesu *n* ヘルペス herpes

hérupu *n* ヘルプ help: **herupu-kinō** ヘルプ機能 (*computer*) help function

heso *n* へそ (**o-heso** おへそ) navel, bellybutton

hesokuri *n* へそくり・ヘソクリ pin money tucked/hidden away

hetá (na) *adj* 下手(な); unskillful, inept, clumsy, poor, bad, inexpert: **~ o suru to** へたをすると if you are unlucky, if you are not careful

héta *v* 経た = **hemáshita** 経ました (passed)

hetakuso (na) *adj* 下手くそ(な) → **hetá (na)** 下手(な)

hetarikomimásu, hetarikomu *v* へたり込みます, へたり込む collapses, sinks down, slumps

héte *v* 経て → **hemásu** 経ます: **... o héte** ...を経て by way of (*through, via*) ...

hetoheto *adj* へとへと is dead, is beaten: **~ ni narimásu** へとへとになります is fagged out, is dead tired

hetta *v* 減った = **herimáshita** 減りました (decreased)

hette *v* 減って → **herimásu** 減ります

heyá *n* 部屋 (**o-heya** お部屋) room

hi *n* 日 day

hí-bi *n* 日々 every day: **~ no seikatsu**

日々の生活 daily life

hi-goro *adv* 日頃 usually

hí-goto (ni) *adv* 日毎(に) day by day

hi-nichi *n* 日にち (fixed) day; number of days

hi-zuke *n* 日付 date (*of month*): **hizuke-henkōsen** 日付変更線 change-of-day line, dateline

hi (ohi-sama) *n* 日(お日様) sun (= **taiyō** 太陽): **~ no hikari** 日の光 sunshine (= **níkkō** 日光)

hi-atarí *n* 日当たり exposure to the sun, sunniness: **~ ga íi** 日当たりがいい is sunny

hi-gása *n* 日傘 parasol (*umbrella*)

hi-gure *n* 日暮れ sunset (*time*); the dark

hi-kage *n* 日陰 shadow (*from sunlight*)

hi-nata *n* 日なた sunshine: **hinata-bókko** 日なたぼっこ sunbathing, basking (*in the sun*)

hi-no-de *n* 日の出 sunrise

hi-no-iri *n* 日の入り sunset

hi-yake *n* 日焼け sunburn: **~ o shimásu** 日焼けをします gets a sunburn

hi-yoke *n* 日よけ sunshade, blind, awning (= **hi-ói** 日覆い)

hi-yori *n* 日和 weather (conditions)

hi-yorimi *n* 日和見 waiting policy: **hiyorimi-shugi** 日和見主義 time-serving

hí *n* 火 fire

hí-bachi *n* 火鉢 hibachi, charcoal brazier

hi-bana *n* 火花 spark: **~ o chirashimásu** 火花を散らします gives off sparks

hi-bashi *n* 火箸 tongs (*for fire*)

…´-hi *suffix* …費 expense

hibí *n* ひび crack (*fine*): **~ ga dekimásu** ひびができます crazes

hibíite *v* 響いて → **hibikimásu** 響きます

hibikí *n* 響き echo

hibikimásu, hibíku *v* 響きます, 響く echoes, resounds

Hibiya *n* 日比谷 Hibiya: **Hibiya-Kō´en** 日比谷公園 Hibiya Park

hibō *n* 誹謗 [BOOKISH] slander: **~ shimásu** 誹謗します defames

hibō-chūshō 誹謗中傷 mental abuse

hichíriki *n* ひちりき an oboe-like reed instrument (in *gagaku*)

hidari *n* 左 left: **hidari-dónari** 左隣り next (door) on the left; **hidari-kíki/-giki (no)** 左利き(の) left-handed (*person*); **hidari-máwari (ni)** 左回り(に) counterclockwise

hidari-gawa *n* 左側 left side

hidói *adj* ひどい severe, terrible, unreasonable, vicious, bitter, awful: **hidoi-kao** ひどい顔 face like a dropped pie

hídoku *adv* ひどく hard, cruelly, terribly: **~ obiemásu** ひどく脅[怯え]ます has one's heart in one's mouth

hie *n* 冷え chill: **híe-shō** 冷え性 feeling of cold, excessive sensitivity to cold

hieta *adj* 冷えた cold

hiemásu, hiéru *v* 冷えます, 冷える gets cold

hiéreba *v* 冷えれば (if it gets cold) → **hiemásu** 冷えます

hiéte *v* 冷えて → **hiemásu** 冷えます

hífu *n* 皮膚 skin

higái *n* 被害 damage, injury, casualty: **higái-chi** 被害地 stricken area; **higái-sha** 被害者 victim (= **gaisha** 該者)

higashí *n* 東 east: **higashí-guchi** 東口 the east exit/entrance; **higashí-káigan** 東海岸 east coast

hige *n* ひげ・髭 beard; mustache (= **kuchí-hige** 口ひげ): **~ o hayashimásu** ひげを生やします grows a beard/mustache; **~ o sorimásu** ひげを剃ります shaves

hige *n* ひげ・ヒゲ whiskers

hígeki *n* 悲劇 tragedy

híhan *n* 批判 judgment, criticism: **~ shimásu** 批判します judges, criticizes

hihán-sha *n* 批判者 critic, judge

hihán-teki (na) *adj* 批判的(な) critical

hihyō *n* 批評 criticism, review: **~ shimásu** 批評します reviews, critiques

hihyō-ka *n* 批評家 critic, reviewer

híiki *n* ひいき illegitimate favor, patronage: **~ shimásu** ひいきします shows preference/partiality

hiita *v* 引いた = **hikimáshita** 引きました (pulled)

híita *n* ヒーター heater

hiite *v* 引いて → **hikimásu** 引きます

hijí *n* 肘 elbow: **~ o harimásu** 肘を張り

ます bends out one's elbows: **hiji-kake-isu** 肘掛け椅子 armchair

hijō n 非常, **hijōji** 非常時 emergency: **hijō-buré'ki** 非常ブレーキ emergency brake; **hijō-dénwa** 非常電話 emergency phone; **hijō-guchi** 非常口 emergency exit; **hijō-kaidan** 非常階段 emergency stairs

hijō na adj 非常 (な) unusual, extreme

hijō ni adv 非常 (に) extremely

hikaemásu, hikaeru v 控えます, 控える refrains, withholds

hikaemé (na) adj 控え目 (な) modest

hikaku n 比較 comparison: ~ **shimásu** 比較します compares

hikaku-teki (ni) adv 比較的 (に) relatively, comparatively

hikan n 悲観 pessimism: ~ **shimásu** 悲観します is pessimistic

hikan-teki (na) adj 悲観的 (な) pessimistic

hikanai v 引かない = **hikimasén** 引きません (not pull)

hikaremásu, hikareru v 引かれます, 引かれる gets pulled (out), gets drawn/dragged/tugged/subtracted

hikaremásu, hikareru v 轢かれます, 轢かれる gets run over

hikaremásu, hikareru v 挽かれます, 挽かれる gets sawed

hikaremásu, hikareru v 弾かれます, 弾かれる gets played

hikaremásu, hikareru v ひかれます, ひかれる gets ground

hikaremásu, hikareru v 惹かれます, 惹かれる get attracted (to)

hikaremásu, hikareru v 光れます, 光れる can glow/shine

hikarí 光 1. n light 2. v → **hikari-másu** 光ります

hikari-kēburu n 光ケーブル optical cable (internet)

hikarimásu, hikáru v 光ります, 光る it shines, glows

hike v 引け [IMPERATIVE] (pull!) → **hikimásu** 引きます

hikéba v 引けば (if one pulls) → **hikimásu** 引きます

hikemásu, hikeru v 引けます, 引ける can pull

hikéreba v 引ければ (if one can pull) → **hikemásu** 引けます

hiketsu n 秘訣 [BOOKISH] secret, formula: **seikō no** ~ 成功の秘訣 key to success

hiki- v 引き ("pull", "influence")

...-hiki (-ppiki) ...匹 (counts small animals, fish, insects (bugs))

hiki-age n 引き上げ refloating; rise/hike (in price, wage, fee)

hiki-age n 引き揚げ evacuation, repatriation; salvage

hiki-agemásu, hiki-agéru v 引き上げます, 引き上げる pulls up; refloats; raises (price, wage, fee)

hiki-agemásu, hiki-agéru v 引き揚げます, 引き揚げる withdraws, leaves; evacuates, gets repatriated

hikiagé-sha n 引 (き) 揚げ者 evacuee, repatriate

hikidashi n 引き出し drawer

hikidashimásu, hikidasu v 引き出します, 引き出す pulls/draws out; withdraws

hikigane n 引き金 trigger

hiki-haraimásu, hiki-haráu v 引き払います, 引き払う checks out (of hotel)

hikiimásu, hikiíru v 率います, 率いる leads, commands

hikiíte v 率いて → **hikiimásu** 率います

hiki-kaemásu, hiki-káeru v 引き換えます, 引き換える exchanges, converts

hiki-kaeshimásu, hiki-káesu v 引き返します, 引き返す turns back, returns

hikimásu, hiku v 引きます, 引く pulls (out); draws; drags, tugs; attracts; subtracts; deducts; looks up a word (in dictionary)

hikimásu, hiku v 轢きます, 轢く runs over (a person)

hikimásu, hiku v 挽きます, 挽く saws

hikimásu, hiku v 弾きます, 弾く plays (a instrument)

hikimásu, hiku v 挽きます, 挽く grinds (into powder)

hikimásu, hiku v 退きます, 退く retires

hikinige n ひき [轢き] 逃げ hit and run

hiki-niku n 挽き肉 chopped/minced/ground meat

híki-torimásu, hiki-tóru 引き取ります、引き取る **1.** takes over, looks after, receives **2. íki o** — 息を引き取ります takes/draws one's last breath, dies

hiki-tsugimásu, hiki-tsúgu v 引き継ぎます、引き継ぐ takes over for, succeeds (*in a projection*)

hiki-ukemásu, hiki-ukéru v 引き受けます、引き受ける undertakes, takes charge of, takes responsibility for; guarantees: **tegata o** — 手形を引き受けます accepts a bill (*of payment*)

hiki-wake n 引き分け tie, draw
hiki-wakemásu 引き分けます、hiki-wakeru 引き分ける draws apart; plays to a draw

hiki-zan n 引き算 subtraction: **~ (o) shimásu** 引き算（を）します subtracts

hiki-zurimásu, hiki-zuru v 引きずります、引きずる drags

hik-kakimásu, hik-káku v 引っ掻きます、引っ掻く scratches it

hikken n 必見 must-see

hikki n 筆記 writing down: **~ shimásu** 筆記します takes notes
hikki-tai n 筆記体 running hand, script
hikki-yōgu n 筆記用具 writing instrument

hikkoshi n 引っ越し moving (*house*)
hikkoshi-ya n 引っ越し屋 (house) mover
hikkoshi-torákku n 引っ越しトラック mover's van

hikkoshimásu, hikkósu v 引っ越します、引っ越す moves (*house*)

hikkuri-kaerimásu, hikkuri-káeru v 引っくり返ります、引っくり返る it tips (*over*); it upsets

hikkuri-kaeshimásu, hikkuri-káesu v 引っくり返します、引っくり返す upsets (*overturns*) it

hikō n 飛行 flying (*a plane*): **~ shimásu** 飛行します flies (*a plane*)
hikō-jō n 飛行場 airport (= **kū-kō** 空港)
hikō´-ki n 飛行機 airplane: **~ ni nori-másu** 飛行機に乗ります gets on a plane
hikō-yoi n 飛行酔い airsick(ness)

hikō v 引こう = **hikimashō** 引きましょう (let's pull!)

hi-kō´shiki (no) adj 非公式（の）unofficial, informal

hiku v 引く = **hikimásu** 引きます (pulls (out), etc.)

hikúi adj 低い low, short

hikyō´ (na) adj 卑怯（な）cowardly

hima n 暇 time; leisure, spare time:
hima-tsubushi 暇つぶし time killing
hima na adj 暇（な）at leisure, unoccupied, not busy, free (*of business*); slow (*business*)

híme n 姫 (**ohíme-sama** お姫様) princess

himei n 悲鳴 a scream: **~ o agemásu** 悲鳴を上げます screams out

himitsu (no) adj 秘密（の）secret

himo n ひも string, cord, tape, strap

himokawa(-údon) n ひもかわ（うどん）long thin udon

hin n 品 elegance, refinement, dignity:
~ ga arimásu 品があります has class

hinagata n ひな形 form; pattern; shape

hina-mátsuri n ひな祭(り) the Dolls Festival, the Girl's Festival (*3 March*)

hínan n 非難 blame, reproach

hínan n 避難 taking refuge
hinán-sha n 避難者 refugee

hina-níngyō n ひな人形 (*festival*) dolls

hinerimásu, hinéru v 捻ります、捻る twists; turns

hinétte v 捻って → **hinerimásu** 捻ります

hiniku n 皮肉 sarcasm: **~ o iimásu** 皮肉を言います makes sarcastic remarks
hiniku na adj 皮肉（な）sarcastic, cynical

hinin n 避妊 contraception: **~ shimásu** 避妊します prevents pregnancy
hinín-gu n 避妊具 contraceptive (*device*) (= **kondómu** コンドーム)
hinín-yaku n 避妊薬 contraceptive drug/pill

hinkon n 貧困 poverty, necessity

hinoki n ヒノキ・檜・桧 cypress
hinoki-butai n 檜舞台 the stage of a major (*first-class, leading*) theater

hinshi n 品詞 part of speech

hinshi n 瀕死 moribundity, near death:
hinshi no 瀕死 moribund

hinshitsu n 品質 quality: **~ o hoshō shimásu** 品質を保証します guarantees the quality: **hinshitsu-hoshō** 品質保証 quality guarantee, warranty

hinshuku-o-kaimásu (kau) n ひんしゅくを買います(買う) invites frowns of disgust, is frowned upon

hínto n ヒント hint, reminder: **~ o ataemásu** ヒントを与えます gives a hint

hipparimásu, hippáru v 引っ張ります, 引っ張る pulls, drags, tugs (at)

hira-ayamari n 平謝り humble apology: **~ ni ayamarimásu** 平謝りに謝ります makes a humble apology

hirágáná n ひらがな・平仮名 hiragana (the roundish Japanese letters)

hiráite v 開いて → **hirakimásu** 開きます

hiraki n 開き open and dried fish

hirakí-do n 開き戸 hinged door

hirakimásu, hiráku v 開きます, 開く opens up; has/holds (a party)

hirame n ヒラメ・平目 flounder

hiramekimásu, hirameku v ひらめきます, ひらめく flashes on

hiraoyogi n 平泳ぎ breaststroke

hira (shain) n 平(社員) rank-and-file employee

hiratai adj 平たい flat (= **tiara na** 平らな): **hiratai-hana** 平たい鼻 flat nose

hirataku adv 平たく flat: **~ iu to/ieba** 平たく言うと/言えば put simply

hire n ヒレ・鰭 fin

hire n ヒレ fillet (of pork, etc.)

hirefushimásu, hirefusu v ひれ伏します, ひれ伏す grovels, falls on one's face

hirei n 比例 proportion: **~ shimásu** 比例します is proportionate

híró-bá n 広場 a square, a place, (public) an open space

hiroe v 拾え [IMPERATIVE] (pick it up!) → **hiroimásu** 拾います

hiroemásu, hiroeru v 拾えます, 拾える can pick it up

hirogarimásu, hirogaru v 広がります, 広がる it spreads, widens

hirogemásu, hirogeru v 広げます, 広げる spreads/widens it

hirói adj 広い wide, broad; big (room, etc.)

hiroimásu, hirou v 拾います, 拾う picks it up

hiroku adv 広く wide, widely

hiromarimásu, hiromáru v 広まります, 広まる it spreads, gets diffused

hiromemásu, hiroméru v 広めます, 広める spreads/diffuses it

hírosa n 広さ width

Hiroshima n 広島 Hiroshima

hirō n 披露 presentation

hirō-en n 披露宴 reception, wedding banquet (engagement, wedding, etc.)

hirō-kai n 披露会 reception (engagement, wedding, etc.)

hirō-shimásu (suru) v 披露します (する) announces (wedding, etc.)

hirotte v 拾って → **hiroimásu** 拾います

hirowanai v 拾わない = **hiroimasén** 拾いません (not pick up)

hirú n 昼 (**o-híru** お昼) daytime, noon: **~ kara** 昼から afternoon; **~ no bú** 昼の部 matinee

hiru-góhan n 昼ご飯 (**o-hiru-góhan** お昼ご飯) noon meal, lunch (= **hiru-meshi** 昼飯)

hiru-má n 昼間 daytime

hiru-ne n 昼寝 nap: **~ (o) shimásu** 昼寝（を）します takes a nap

hiru-súgí n 昼過ぎ afternoon

híru n ヒル・蛭 leech

hisashi-buri (ni) adv 久しぶり（に）after a long time (of absence)

hishaku n 柄杓 scoop, ladle

hishó n 秘書 secretary (private)

hí´ssha n 筆者 the writer/author (= **chosha** 著者)

hisúi n ヒスイ・翡翠 jade

hitai n 額 forehead, brow

hitchaku n 必着 must-reach: **ni-gatsu muika ~** 2月6日必着 due NLT (not later than) February 6

hitei n 否定 denial: **~ shimásu** 否定します denies

hito, **… hitó** …人 person, man, fellow, people; someone, somebody

hitó-bito n 人々 people (in general) (= **hitó-tachi** 人達)

hito-gara n 人柄 character, personality

hito-góroshi n 人殺し murder

hito-… prefix 一… one, a

hito-ánshin n ひと安心 a relief (from

worry) → **anshín** 安心

hitó-ban *n* 一晩 one night: **~ tomari-másu** 一晩泊まります stays overnight

hito-gomi *n* ひとごみ・人込み crowd: **~ o sakemásu** 人込みを避けます avoids crowded places

hito-hako *n* 一箱 one boxful

hitó-iki *n* 一息 a breath: **hitó-iki de** 一息で with a gulp: **~ iremásu/tsukimásu** 一息入れます/つきます catches one's breath

hitó-kátamari *n* ひと固まり・一塊 one lump/loaf: **hitó-kátamari no** 一塊 の a pat of

hitó-kire *n* 一切れ (one) piece (*a cut*): **hitó-kire no** 一切れの a piece of

hito-koto *n* 一言 a word: **~ de iu to** 一言で言うと put simply

hito-kuchi *n* 一口 one mouthful; one bite; one drink, sip: **~ de iuto** 一口で言うと in a word

hito-kumi *n* 一組 a set (*collection*); a couple, a pair

hitó-maki *n* 一巻き one (*roll, bolt of cloth*)

hitó-mori *n* 一盛り scoop (*one scoopful*)

hitó-nemuri *n* 一眠り a nap: **~ shimásu** 一眠りします takes a nap → **nemurimásu** 眠ります

hitó-oyogi *n* ひと泳ぎ a swim: **~ shimásu** ひと泳ぎします takes a swim → **oyogimásu** 泳ぎます

hitó-ri *n* 一人 (**o-hitó-ri** お一人) one person; (**hitó-ri de** ひとりで・独りで) alone; (**hitori-bótchi (no)** ひとりぼっち（の）lonely; **hitori-mónó** 独り者 single (*unmarried*) person

hitó-saji *n* 一匙 one spoonful: **hitósaji no** 一匙の one spoonful of

hito-shibai *n* 一芝居 playing a trick, acting: **~ uchimásu** 一芝居打ちます plays a trick on, puts on an act → **shibai** 芝居

hito-shigoto *n* 一仕事 bout of work: **~ shimásu** 一仕事します works → **shigoto** 仕事 (**o-shígoto** お仕事)

hito-suji *n* 一筋 shaft: **~ no hikari** 一筋 の光 a ray of light

hitó-tsu *n* ひとつ・一つ one (= **ík-ko**

一個) : one year old (= **ís-sai** 一歳); one and the same

hitó-yama *n* 一山 one heap/bunch: **~ atemásu** 一山当てます strikes oil

hitómazu (wa) *adv* ひとまず（は）for a while; for the time being

hitori-de ni *adv* ひとりでに spontaneously, automatically, by/of itself

hitori-goto *n* 独り言 talking to oneself: **~ o iimásu** 独り言を言います says to oneself

hitosashiyubi *n* 人差し指 forefinger, index finger

hitoshíi *adj* 等しい equal, identical

hitsugi *n* 棺 coffin

hitsuji *n* ヒツジ・羊 sheep

Hitsuji-doshi *n* 未年 year of the Sheep

hitsujuhin *n* 必需品 necessity article: **seikatsu-hitsujuhin** 生活必需品 daily necessaries, commodities

hitsuyō *n* 必要 necessity, need: **... suru ~ ga arimásu** ...する必要があります needs to...: **... ga ~ desu** ...が必要です needs...

hitsuyō na 必要な *adj* necessary, essential

hitteki *n* 匹敵 comparison: **~ shimásu** 匹敵します is comparable

hittó *n* ヒット a hit (*baseball*): **~ shimásu** ヒットします hits

hittó-kyoku *n* ヒット曲 hit song

híya *n* 冷や (**o-híya** お冷や) cold water

hiya-múgi *n* 冷や麦・ひやむぎ chilled wheat-flour noodles (*cf.* **só'men** そうめん)

hiyashimásu, hiyásu *v* 冷やします, 冷やす cools it off, refrigerates, chills: **atama o** ~ 頭を冷やします cools one's head

hiya-yákko *n* 冷ややっこ cooled bean curd (*tōfu*)

híyō *n* 費用 cost, expense: **~ ga kaka-rimásu** 費用がかかります costs

hiyowa *n* ひ弱 weak: **~ na kodomo** ひ弱な子供 frail child

hiza *n* 膝 knee, lap

hizamazukimásu, hizamazuku *v* ひざまずきます, ひざまずく falls on one's knees, kneels down

hizume *n* 蹄 hoof

hó *n* 帆 sail

hō *interj* ほお? oh?

hō *n* 法 law (= **hōritsu** 法律); rule (= **hōsoku** 法則); method (= **hōhō** 方法)

hō *n* ほお・頬 cheek (= **hoho** ほほ・頬, **hoppéta** ほっぺた)

... **hō** ... *n* ... 方 alternative, the one (*of two*) that ...: ~ **ga íi desu** ... 方がいいです ... is better

hōbi *n* 褒美 (**go-hō´bi** ご褒美 [HONORIFIC]) prize, reward

hóbo *adj* ほぼ nearly; roughly

hobo *n* 保母 nursery teacher

hō´bō *n*, *adv* 方々 everywhere, all over: ~ **kara** 方々から from various quarters

hōchi *n* 放置 neglect: **hōchi-jitensha** 放置自転車 illegally-parked bicycle

hóchikisu *n* ホチキス stapler: ~ **no hari** ホチキスの針 strip of staples

hochō *n* 歩調 pace: ~ **o awasemásu** 歩調を合わせます keeps step

hōchō *n* 包丁 knife (*big*); cleaver (= **nikukiri-bō´chō** 肉切り包丁)

hochōki *n* 補聴器 hearing aids: ~ **o tsukemásu** 補聴器をつけます wears a hearing aid

hōdan *n* 砲弾 bombshell

...**-hōdai** *suffix* 放題 can...as much as: **tabe-hōdai** 食べ放題 all-you-can-eat; **nomi-hōdai** 飲み放題 all-you-can-drink: **shitai-hōdai** したい放題 does whatever one feel like doing

hōden *n* 放電 electric(al) discharge

(...) **hodo** *suffix* (...)程・ほど extent; limits; moderation; approximate time; about (*as much as*), (not) so much as: the more ... the more

hodō *n* 歩道 walk(way), sidewalk: **hodō-kyō** 歩道橋 crossover bridge

hōdō *n* 報道 news report: ~ **shimásu** 報道します reports

hodóite *v* 解いて → **hodokimásu** 解きます

hodóke *v* 解け [IMPERATIVE] (undo/untie it!) → **hodokimásu** 解きます

hodokemásu, hodokéru *v* 解けます, 解ける **1.** can undo, can untie **2.** comes loose, comes undone

hodokimásu, hodóku *v* 解きます, 解く undoes, unties

hodokóshi *v* 施し charity: ~ **o ukemásu** 施しを受けます accepts charity

hodokóshimásu, hodokósu 施します, 施す gives charity

hoemásu, hoéru *v* 吠えます, 吠える (dog) barks

hoeraremásu, hoeraréru *v* 吠えられます, 吠えられる can bark; is barked

hō´fu (na) *adj* 豊富(な) rich: ~ **na keiken** 豊富な経験 abundant experience

hō´gai (na) *adj* 法外(な) exorbitant, inordinate, excessive, unreasonable: ~ **na kingaku/nedan** 法外な金額/値段 unreasonable price

hōgaku *n* 方角 direction, one's bearings

hōgaku *n* 邦楽 Japanese music

hō´gaku (-bu) *n* 法学(部) (*science/study of*) law; School of Law

hōgan *n* 包含 inclusion, comprehension

hōgan *n* 砲丸 cannonball: **hōgan-nage senshu** 砲丸投げ選手 shot-putter

hógaraka (na) *adj* 朗らか(な) bright, sunny; cheerful

hogei *n* 捕鯨 whaling

hōgén *n* 方言 dialect

hógo *n* 保護 protection: ~ **shimásu** 保護します protects, safeguards, shields hogo-sha 保護者 guardian

hoguremásu, hoguréru *v* 解れます, 解れる it loosens

hoho *n* ほほ・頬 cheek (= **hō** ほお・頬, **hoppéta** ほっぺた)

hōhō *n* 方法 method, process

hohoemashii *adj* 微笑ましい heart-warming, pleasant

hohoemi *n* 微笑み smile

hohoemimásu, hohoému *v* 微笑みます, 微笑む smiles

hoikú-en *n* 保育園 nursery school, pre-kindergarten

hoippu kuriimu *n* ホイップクリーム whipping cream

hōji *n* 法事 mass (*Buddhist*), Buddhist memorial service

hōjin *n* 法人 corporation hōjin-zei *n* 法人税 corporation tax

hójo *n* 補助 help, assistance hojo-kin *n* 補助金 grant: **hojokin-seido** 補助金制度 bounty system

hoka *n* ほか・外・他 other, in addition

70

to, other than (= **ta** 他): **hoka no** 他の other, another

hoken n 保険 insurance: **…ni ~ o kake-másu** …に保険をかけます insures
  hoken-gáisha n 保険会社 insurance company
  kenkō-hoken n 健康保険 health insurance
  hoken-ryō n 保険料 insurance fee

hoken n 保健 healthcare, preservation of health: **sekai-hoken-kikō** 世界保健機関 World Health Organization (WHO)

hōken n 封建 feudal(ism)
  hōken-jídai n 封建時代 feudal period
  hōken-séido n 封建制度 feudal system

hoketsu n 補欠 substitute, alternate
  hoketsu-senshu n 補欠選手 benchwarmer

hō´ki n 放棄 abandonment: **~ shimásu** 放棄します gives up, abandons

hō´ki n 箒 broom: **~ de hakimásu** 箒で掃きます sweeps with a broom
  hōki-boshi n 箒星 comet

Hokkáidō n 北海道 Hokkaido

hókkē n ホッケー hockey

hókku n ホック hook (snap): **~ de tomemásu** ホックでとめます hooks up

Hokkyoku n 北極 North Pole, Arctic
  Hokkyoku-guma n ホッキョクグマ・北極グマ polar bear, white bear (= **shiro-kuma** 白熊)
  Hokkyoku-sei n 北極星 North Star
  Hokkyoku-ken n 北極圏 Arctic Circle

hōkō n 方向 direction

hōkoku n 報告 report
  hōkoku-sho n 報告書 report, statement

hokora n 祠 small shrine

hokorashii adj 誇らしい is proud

hokoremásu, hokoréru v 誇れます, 誇れる can brag

hokori n 埃 dust (in the air): **~ o haraimásu** 埃を払います brushes dust off

hokorí n 誇り pride, boast

hokorimásu, hokóru v 誇ります, 誇る brags about/of

hokōsha n 歩行者 pedestrian: **hokōsha-tengoku** 歩行者天国 area of streets temporarily closed to vehicular traffic, pedestrian mall

hoku-… prefix 北… north (= **kita no…** 北の…)

Hoku-Bei n 北米 = **Kita-Ámerika** 北アメリカ North America

hóku-bu n 北部 the north, the northern part

hóku-i n 北緯 north latitude

Hoku-ō n 北欧 Northern Europe

hoku-sei n 北西 northwest

hoku-tō n 北東 northeast

hoku-yō n 北洋 northern sea

Hoku-riku-chíhō n 北陸地方 the Hokuriku area of Japan (Toyama, Ishikawa, Fukui prefectures)

hokuro n 黒子 mole (on skin)

hokosoemimásu, hokusoemu v ほくそ笑みます, ほくそ笑む chuckles, snickers to oneself

hokyō n 補強 reinforcement, corroboration: **~ shimásu** 補強します reinforces, corroborates

hokyū n 補給 supply: **~ shimásu** 補給します supplies

hōkyū n 俸給 [BOOKISH] pay, wages, salary (= **kyūryō** 給与, **o-kyūryō** お給料)

homé n 褒め: **o-homé ni azukarimasu** お褒めにあずかります is praised [HONORIFIC]

home-kótoba n 褒め言葉 compliment, word of praise

homemásu, homéru v 褒めます, 褒める praises, admires

hōmén n 方面, **…-hō´men** …方面 direction, quarter, district

hómo (no) adj ホモ(の) homosexual

hōmon n 訪問 visit, call: **~ shimásu** 訪問します visits, calls on

homosapiensu n ホモサピエンス Homo sapiens

hō´mu n ホーム 1. platform (at station) 2. home

hōmu-dórama n ホームドラマ soap opera

hōmuresu n ホームレス homeless: **~ ni narimásu** ホームレスになります becomes homeless

hōmushikku n ホームシック homesick: **~ ni narimásu** ホームシックになります gets homesick

Hōmu-shō n 法務省 Ministry of Justice

hōmu-sutei n ホームステイ homestay:
~ **shimásu** ホームステイします does
homestay

hón n 本 book

  hón-bako n 本箱 bookcase

  hón-dana n 本棚 bookshelf

  hón-tate n 本立て bookends

  hón-ya n 本屋 bookshop (= **shoten** 書店)

hon-... prefix 本... main; chief; this;
the; the present; real

  hon-ba n 本場 original place, area of
production: ~ **no** 本場の authentic

  hon-ban n 本番 real part, real thing

  hón-bu n 本部 central office, headquarters (= **hón-sha** 本社)

  hon-dai n 本題 main issue: ~ **ni hairimásu** 本題に入ります comes to the
main issue

  hon-dō n 本道 the main route

  hon-mono n 本物 the real thing: **hon-
mono no** 本物の genuine: ~ **no aji** 本物
の味 authentic flavor

  hon-ne n 本音 true (*inner*) feeling,
real intention (= **hon-shin** 本心): ~ **ga
demásu** 本音が出ます says the truth

  hon-nin n 本人 (*the person*) himself/
herself/myself, principal: **honnin-
kakunin** 本人確認 identifying

  hón-rai adv 本来 originally, from the
start

  hon-ron n 本論 main discussion/ issue

  hón-seki n 本籍 permanent residence

  hon-shin n 本心 true (*inner*) feeling,
real intention (= **honne** 本音)

  hon-ten n 本店 head office, main store

...´-hon (...´-**pon**, ...´-**bon**) suffix ...本
(*counts long objects*)

hónbun n 本分 one's duty

honé n 骨 bone: ~ **o orimásu** 骨を折り
ます takes (great) pains, goes to much
trouble; ~ **ga oremásu** 骨が折れます
requires much effort, is hard/difficult

  hone-gúmi n 骨組み framework

  hone-óri n 骨折り (**o-honeori** お骨折り
[HONORIFIC]) effort

hongoshi-o-iremásu (ireru) v 本腰を
入れます (入れる) gets down to
seriously

honki (no/de) adj, adv 本気(の/で)
serious(ly), (*in*) earnest: ~ **ni shimásu**

本気にします takes it seriously

Hónkón n ホンコン・香港 Hong Kong

honmatsu-tentō n 本末転倒 putting
the cart before the horse

honmei n 本命 the favorite: **honmei no**
本命の main, real; favorite

honmō n 本望 one's long-cherished
ambition: ~ **o togemásu** 本望を遂げま
す realizes one's heart's desire

honno ... adj ほんの ...just a (little),
only a, a mere/slight ...: ~ **sukoshi/
chotto** ほんの少し/ちょっと ... just a
little; just a minute

honō n 炎 flame

honomekashimásu, honomekásu v
仄めかします, 仄めかす hints

Honóruru n ホノルル Honolulu

hon-ryō n 本領 one's element/sphere:
~ **o hakki shimásu** 本領を発揮します
show oneself at one's best

Hónshū n 本州 Honshu

hontō (no), honto (no) adj 本当(の),
ほんと(の) true, real, genuine: ~ **no
koto** 本当の事 truth; ~ **ni** 本当に really,
truly, indeed, absolutely

hon'yaku n 翻訳 translation: ~ **shimásu**
翻訳します translates

  hon'yáku´-sha(ka) n 翻訳者(家)
translator

hoppéta n ほっぺた cheek (= **hō, hoho**
ほお・ほほ・頬)

hoppō n 北方 the north

hóra n ホラ・法螺 1. trumpet-shell
(= **horá-gai** 法螺貝) 2. exaggeration,
bragging, bull (= **uso** 嘘): ~ **o fukimásu** ほらを吹きます brags, talks big

hóra interj ほら! Look!, Here!, There!,
You see!

horā n ホラー horror

  horā-eiga n ホラー映画 horror movie

hora-ana n ほら穴 cave (= **dōkutsu**
洞窟)

horá-gai n 法螺貝 trumpet-shell

horánai v 掘らない = **horimasén** 掘り
ません (not dig)

hóre v 掘れ [IMPERATIVE] (dig!) →
horimásu 掘ります

hóreba v 掘れば (if one digs) →
horimásu 掘ります

hōrei n 法令 law, act

horemásu, horeru v 惚れます、惚れ
る: **... ni hore(komi)másu** ...に惚れ(込
み)ます falls in love (with)

horemásu, horéru 掘れます、掘れる
can dig

horenai v 惚れない = **horemasén** 惚れ
ません (not fall in love)

horénai v 掘れない = **horemasén** 掘れ
ません (cannot dig)

hōrénsō n ホウレンソウ・ほうれん草
spinach

horete v 惚れて → **horemásu** 惚れ
ます

hórete v 掘れて → **horemásu** 掘れ
ます

hori n 掘 ditch, moat
    hori-wari n 掘(り)割り canal

horidashi-mono n 掘り出し物 a
bargain, a real find, lucky find

horimásu, hóru v 掘ります、掘る digs,
carves; excavates

horimásu, hóru v 彫ります、彫る carves

horí-mónó n 彫物 a carving, tattoo

hōritsu n 法律 law (legal system)
    hōritsu-ka n 法律家 jurist

hōrō n 放浪 wandering: **~ shimásu** 放浪
します wanders, strolls

horobimásu, horobíru v 滅びます、滅
びる perishes

horoboshimásu, horobósu v 滅ぼし
ます、滅ぼす destroys

hōrókú n 焙烙 [BOOKISH] earthenware
pan

hóru v 掘る = **horimásu** 掘ります(digs)

hóru v 彫る = **horimásu** 彫ります
(carves)

hórun n ホルン horn (music)

hōsaku n 方策 measures, policy

hōsaku n 豊作 abundant/rich harvest

hosánai v 干さない = **hoshimasén** 干し
ません (not dry it)

hóseba v 干せば (if one dries it) →
hoshimásu 干します

hōseki n 宝石 jewel, gem
    hōseki-shō n 宝石商 jeweler
    hōseki-bako n 宝石箱 jewel box

hosemásu, hóseru v 干せます、干せる
can dry it

hosénai v 干せない = **hosemasén** 干せ
ません (cannot dry it)

hósete v 干せて → **hosemásu** 干せ
ます

hōshanō n 放射能 radioactivity

hōshasen n 放射線 (nuclear) radiation

hoshi n 星 star
    hoshi-jírushi n 星印 star (symbol),
    asterisk (*)
    hoshi-uranai n 星占い astrology
    hoshi-zora n 星空 starry sky

hōshi n 奉仕 service: **~ shimásu** 奉仕し
ます serves, gives one's service
    hōshi-katsudō n 奉仕活動 voluntary
    service, voluntary activity

hōshi n 胞子 spore(s)

hoshigarimásu, hoshigáru v 欲しが
ります、欲しがる wants it

hoshíi v 欲しい is desired/desirable;
desires, wants, would like, wishes

hoshimásu, hósu v 干します、干す
dries it; airs it

hōshin n 方針 policy, course (of action),
aim (direction)

hōshin n 疱疹 (medical) herpes

hōshin n 放心 absent-mindedness:
hōshin-jōtai 放心状態 is lost in
abstraction

hóshi (ta) adj 干し(た) dried
    hoshi-búdo n 干しブドウ raisin(s)
    hoshí-gaki n 干し柿 dried persimmons
    hoshi-kusa n 干(し)草 hay, dried plant

hóshite v 干して → **hoshimásu** 干し
ます

hoshō n 保証 guarantee, warranty:
hoshō´-sho 保証書 letter of guarantee

hoshō n 補償 compensating: **~ shimásu**
補償します compensates
    hoshō´-kin n 補償金 compensation
    (money), indemnity

hōshoku n 飽食 full feeding: **~ no jidai**
飽食の時代 age of plenty

hōshoku-hin n 宝飾品 jewelry goods

hóshu n 保守 maintenance, upkeep:
~ shimásu 保守します maintains,
preserves
    hoshu-ha n 保守派 conservative wing
    hoshu-teki (na) adj 保守的(な)
    conservative: **~ na kangae** 保守的な考
    え conservative thinking/view

hóshu n 捕手 catcher

hōshū n 報酬 reward: **~ o emásu** 報酬

を得ます gets a reward

hōshutsu *n* 放出 emission: **~ shimásu** 放出します emits

hōsō *n* 放送 broadcasting: **hōsō'-kyoku** 放送局 broadcasting station: **~ shimásu** 放送します broadcasts

hōsō *n* 包装 packing, wrapping: **~ shimásu** 包装します packs, wraps hōsō'-butsu *n* 包装物 package, packet: **kogata (no)** ~ 小型(の)包装物 small packet hōsō'-shi *n* 包装紙 package, wrapper

hosói *adj* 細い slender; narrow; thin

hōsoku *n* 法則 rule(s), law(s)

hosomichi *n* 細道 lane, path

hosonagái *adj* 細長い long and slender/narrow

hossa *n* 発作 attack, seizure: **shinzō-hossa** 心臓発作 heart attack

hósu *v* 干す = **hoshimásu** 干します (dries it)

hō'su *n* ホース hose

hósutesu *n* ホステス hostess

hósuto *n* ホスト host

hōtai *n* 包帯 bandage: **~ o makimásu** 包帯を巻きます applies a bandage

hotaru *n* ホタル・蛍 lightning bug, firefly: **Hotaru no hikari**「ほたるの光」"Auld Lang Syne"

hotaté-gai *n* ホタテガイ・帆立貝 scallop(s)

hōtei *n* 法廷 law court

hōteishiki *n* 方程式 equation

hōten *n* 法典 code law

hóteru *n* ホテル hotel: **ichiryū-hoteru** 一流ホテル first-class hotel

hōtō *n* 放蕩 [BOOKISH] debauchery: **hōtō-musuko** 放蕩息子 prodigal son

hotobashiru *v* ほとばしる gush

Hotoke(-sámá) *n* 仏(様) Buddha (= **budda** 仏陀)

hotóndo *adv* ほとんど almost (*all*), nearly; almost all the time; [+ NEGATIVE verb] hardly (*ever*), seldom

hototógisu *n* ホトトギス・時鳥・不如帰 (little) cuckoo

hottan *n* 発端 beginning, onset: **koto no ~** 事の発端 It all starts (with…)

hotte/hótte oku *v* ほって/放っておく leaves alone, let alone: **Hōtte oite/**

hottoite! 放っておいて/放っといて! Leave me alone!

hotto doggu *n* ホットドッグ hot dog

hotto kēki *n* ホットケーキ pancake

hótto (na) *adj* ホット(な) hot: **~ na wadai** ホットな話題 hot topic

hotto purēto *n* ホットプレート hot plate, grill

hotto rain *n* ホットライン hotline

hóttó-shimásu (-suru) *v* ほっとします(する) breathes a sigh of relief

hōwa *n* 飽和 saturation, impregnation **hōwa-jōtai** *adj* 飽和状態 saturated state

hoyō *n* 保養 rest, recuperation: **me no ~** 目の保養 feast for the eyes

hu... ふ...・フ... → **fu...**

hyak-kái *n* 百回 a hundred times

hyakka-jíten *n* 百科事典 encyclopedia

hyakká-ten *n* 百貨店 department store (= **depáto** デパート)

hyakú *n* 百・100 hundred hyakú-do *n* 百度 **1.** a hundred times (= **hyak-kái** 百回) **2.** a hundred degrees hyakú-doru *n* 百ドル a hundred dollars hyaku en-dama *n* 百円玉 hundred yen coin hyaku-mán *n* 百万・1,000,000 one million hyakú-nen *n* 百年 100 years; a century (= **hyaku nén-kan** 百年間) hyaku-nichi-seki *n* 百日咳 pertussis (*cough*)

hyappatsu-hyakuchū *n* 百発百中 hitting the mark ten times out of ten

hyō *n* 表 table, schedule, list: **~ ni shimásu** 表にします lists

hyō' *n* ヒョウ・豹 leopard

hyō' *n* ひょう・雹 hail (= **arare** あられ・霰)

hyō *n* 票 vote: **~ o tōjiru** 票を投じる votes, casts a vote

hyōban *n* 評判 reputation, fame: **hyōban no** 評判の famous, popular: **~ ga ii** 評判がいい money is on: **~ ga warui** 評判が悪い have a bad reputation

hyōdai *n* 表題・標題 title (*of book, article, e-mail...*)

hyō'ga *n* 氷河 glacier: **hyō'ga-ki** 氷河期 ice age

hyōgen *n* 表現 expression (words): ~ **shimásu** 表現します expresses

hyōgo *n* 標語 slogan; motto

Hyō′go *n* 兵庫 Hyogo

hyōgu-ya *n* 表具屋 picture-framer

hyōhen *n* 豹変: ~ **shimásu** 豹変します changes one's spots completely

hyōhyō to *adv* ひょうひょうと aloof from the world: ~ **shiteimásu** ひょうひょうとしています is free as the wind

hyōjō′ *n* 表情 expression (*on face*): ~ **o yawaragemásu** 表情を和らげます softens one's expression

hyōjun *n* 標準 standard **hyōjun-go** *n* 標準語 standard Japanese (*language*)

hyō′ka *n* 評価 grade, opinion, appraisal

hyōkín (na) *adj* ひょうきん（な）funny, comical: **hyōkin-mono** ひょうきん者 a ham

hyokkori *adv* ひょっこり by chance, accidentally: **arawaremásu** ひょっこり現れます appears unexpectedly

hyokohyoko *adv* ひょこひょこ lightly

hyōmén *n* 表面 surface: **hyōmen-chōryoku** *n* 表面張力 surface tension

hyōri *n* 表裏 two faces: **hyōri-ittai** 表裏一体 two sides of the same coin

hyōron *n* 評論 criticism, comment(ary): ~ **shimásu** 評論します criticizes, reviews

hyōron-ka *n* 評論家 critic, commentator, reviewer;

hyōryū *n* 漂流 drift

hyōshi′ *n* 表紙 cover (*book, magazine, etc.*)

hyōshiki *n* 標識 sign, mark(er): **kōtsū-hyō′shiki** 交通標識 traffic sign; **dōro-hyō′shiki** 道路標識 road sign

hyōshinuke *n* 拍子抜け: ~ **shimásu** 拍子抜けします suddenly feels it is pointless

hyōshō *n* 表彰 official commendation: **hyōshō-jō** 表彰状 certificate of commendation: **hyōshō-shiki** 表彰式 awarding ceremony

hyōtán *n* 瓢箪 gourd: ~ **kara koma** 瓢箪から駒 produces an unexpected dividend

hyōten *n* 評点 evaluation score, grade

hyōten *n* 氷点 freezing point

hyótto-shite *adv* ひょっとして by any chance, maybe, possibly, could be. (= **hyotto-shitára** ひょっとしたら, **hyotto-suru to** ひょっとすると)

hyō′zan *n* 氷山 iceberg: **hyō′zan no ikkaku** 氷山の一角 tip of the iceberg

hyū′zu *n* ヒューズ fuse: ~ **ga tobi-másu** ヒューズがとびます blows out

I

i *n* 胃 = **i-búkuro** 胃袋 stomach **i-búkuro** *n* 胃袋 [BOOKISH] stomach **i-chō** *n* 胃腸 [BOOKISH] stomach and intestines **i-gan** *n* 胃癌 (*medical*) stomach cancer **i-káiyō** *n* 胃潰瘍 (*medical*) (*gastric*) ulcer

i-... *prefix* 医... medicine, medical, doctoring **i-gaku** *n* 医学 medicine, medical science/studies: **igaku-sei** 医学生 medical student; **í-gaku-bu** 医学部 medical department **i-sha** *n* 医者 (**o-isha(-san/sama)** お医者 (さん/様)) doctor, physician

...-i *suffix* ...医 doctor, (= **senmón-i** 専門医) medical specialist

...-i *suffix* ...位 rank, grade

ian *n* 慰安 consolation, comfort; recreation

ibarimásu, ibáru *v* 威張ります, 威張る is/acts important, haughty; swaggers

ibiki *n* いびき snore: ~ **o kakimásu** いびきをかきます snores

ibo *n* 異母 different mother: **ibo-kyōdai** 異母兄弟 half brother(s), half sister(s)

ibuningu-doresu *n* イブニングドレス evening dress

ibushimásu, ibusu *v* いぶします, いぶす smokes, fumigates, fumes

ibutsu *n* 異物 [BOOKISH] exogenous material, foreign body

ibutsu n 遺物 relics, artifact
icha ν いちゃ [INFORMAL] = **ité wa** いては
ichí n 一 ・ 1 one (**ik-, íp-**): **ichí ka bachi ka** 一か八か all or nothing
ichí-ban (no) adj 一番 (の) number one; first
ichí-banme (no) adj 一番目 (の) first
ichí-bu n 一部 a part, portion; a copy (of a book)
ichí-byō n 一秒 a second (1/60 minute)
ichí-dai n 一台 one (machine, vehicle)
ichi-danraku n 一段落 one stage: ~ **shimásu** 一段落します completes one stage
ichí-dó n 一度 one time (= **ik-kái** 一回, **íp-pen** 一遍)
ichí-do n 一度 one degree
ichi-en n 一円 one yen
ichí-go n 一語 one word
ichí-ji n 一時 1. one o'clock 2. **ichí-ji (no)** 一時 (の) at one-time, once, temporary: **ichiji-shinogi** 一時しのぎ makeshift
ichi-jitsú n 一日 one day; someday (= **aru hi** ある日, **ichi-nichi** 一日)
ichí-mai n 一枚 a sheet; one sheet (flat things): **ichimai-uwate** 一枚上手 is a cut above
ichi-mán n 一万 ・ 10,000 ten thousand
ichí-mei n 一名 [BOOKISH] one person (= **hitóri** 一人)
ichí-nen n 一年 the year 1; one year (= **ichi nén-kan** 一年間): **ichi nén-sei** 一年生 first-year student, freshman
ichi-nichí n 一日 one day: **ichi nichi-jū** 一日中 all day long
ichí-wa n 一羽 one (bird, rabbit)
ichí-wari n 一割 ten percent
ichí n 位置 position, location, situation
íchí(bá) n 市 (場) market, marketplace: **boro-ichi** ぼろ [ボロ] 市 rag fair
ichi-ban n 一番 most: ~ **íi/warui** 一番いい/悪い best/worst
ichibu-shijū n 一部始終 all the details: ~ **o katarimásu** 一部始終を語ります tells the whole story
ichidō n 一同 all (who are concerned/ present)
ichi-gatsú n 一月 ・ 1 月 January (= **Shōgatsú** 正月)

ichigo n いちご ・ イチゴ ・ 苺 strawberry
ichigo-ichie n 一期一会 [IDIOM] once in a lifetime chance
ichii n いちい ・ イチイ yew
ichi-ichi adv いちいち one by one, each time
ichí-in n 一員 a member
ichí-in n 一因 a cause
ichíjiku n イチジク ・ 無花果 fig
ichijirushíi adj 著しい [BOOKISH] conspicuous, prominent, remarkable
ichijirúshiku adv 著しく [BOOKISH] conspicuously, prominently, remarkably, strikingly
ichiji-teki (na) adj 一時的 (な) temporary
ichi-mi n 一味 accomplice
ichiō adv 一応 ・ いちおう as far as it goes, just in case, tentatively
ichi-rei n 一例 an example: ~ **o agemásu** 一例を挙げます takes an example
ichiryū (no) adj 一流 (の) first-rate, topflight, elite, superb
ichō n イチョウ ・ 銀杏 gingko (tree)
idai (na) adj 偉大 (な) great: ~ **na hito/jinbutsu** 偉大な人/人物 great person
iden n 遺伝 heredity
iden-shi n 遺伝子 gene
ideorogii n イデオロギー ideology
í(do) n 井 (戸) a well
ído n 緯度 latitude
ie interj いえ (= **iie** いいえ) no
ié ν 言え [IMPERATIVE] (say it!) → **iimásu** 言います
ié n 家 a house, a home
iéba ν 言えば = **iya** 言や (if one says) → **iimásu** 言います
ie-dé n 家出 running away from home: ~ **shimásu** 家出します runs away
iede-nin n 家出人 a runaway
iemásu, ieru ν 言えます, 言える can say/tell
iemásu, iéru ν 癒えます, 癒える heals
Ierō-pēji n イエローページ Yellow Pages
Iesu (Kirisuto) n イエス (キリスト) Jesus Christ
íga n 衣蛾 clothes moth
igai (na) adj 意外 (な) unexpected: ~

na ketsumatsu 意外な結末 unexpected ending

ígai ni *adv* 意外(に) unexpectedly

(…) ígai *suffix* (…)以外 outside (of …), except (*for*) …

igen *n* 威厳 dignity: **~ o tamochimásu** 威厳を保ちます keep one's dignity

ígi *n* 意義 [BOOKISH] significance, sense, meaning: **~ no aru** 意義のある meaningful

ígi *n* 異議 [BOOKISH] objection: (*in the court*) **ígi ari** 異議あり! Objection!

Igirisu *n* イギリス England (= **Eikoku** 英国)

Igirisú-jin *n* イギリス人 an English person

ígo *n* 囲碁 the board game *Go* (= **gó** 碁)

(…) ígo *suffix* (…)以後 afterward, from … on (= (…) **ikō** (…)以降)

igokochi *n* 居心地 feeling of staying: **~ ga ii** 居心地がいい feels comfortable while staying: **~ ga warui** 居心地が悪い feels ill at ease

iguana *n* イグアナ iguana

igyō *n* 偉業: **~ o nashi-togemásu** 偉業を成し遂げます accomplishes a great achievement

ihan *n* 違反 violation, offense: **kōtsū-ihan** 交通違反 traffic violation: (… ni) **~ shimásu** (…に)違反します violates, offends (*against*) …

íi *adj* いい good; OK, right, correct (= **yoi** 良い); [NEGATIVE] **yóku arimasén** 良くありません; [PAST] **yókatta desu** 良かったです

ii-hito いい人 **1.** a good person **2.** sweetheart, lover

ii-arawashimásu, ii-arawásu *v* 言い表(わ)します, 言い表(わ)す expresses, puts into words

iie *interj* いいえ no

ii-kaemasu, ii-káeru *v* 言い換えます, 言い換える rephrases, puts/says it another way

ii-kagen (na) *adj* いい加減(な) random, perfunctory; vague, haphazard

ii-kata *n* 言い方 way of saying/telling/putting it, expression

iímasén *v* 言いません = **iwanai** 言わない not say

iimáshita *v* 言いました = **itta** 言った said

iimásu, iu/yū *v* 言います, 言う(ゆう) says, tells; expresses

íin *n* 委員 committee member(s)

iin-kai *n* 委員会 committee

ii-tai *n* 言いたい wants to say: **~ kotó** 言いたいこと[事] what one wants to say; **~ hō'dai** 言いたい放題 says whatever one wants/feels

ii-tsukemásu, ii-tsukéru *v* 言い付けます, 言い付ける commands, orders; tells on, tattles on (= **tsugeguchi-shimásu** 告げ口します)

ii-wake *n* 言い訳 explanation, excuse

íji *n* 意地 temper, disposition: **~ ga warúi** 意地が悪い, **iji-waru** 意地悪 ill-tempered, mean(-spirited)

íji *n* 維持 maintenance, upkeep, support: **~ shimásu** 維持します maintains, supports

ijí-hi *n* 維持費 upkeep (*expense*)

ijime *n* いじめ teasing, torment

ijimek-ko *n* いじめっ子 bully

ijimemásu, ijimeru *v* いじめます, いじめる teases, torments

ijō *n* 異状/異常 something unusual/wrong (*the matter*), abnormality: **ijō-kisho** 異常気象 abnormal climate

ijo na *adj* 異常(な) abnormal; unusual; remarkable

(…) ijō *n*, *suffix* (…)以上 above, over, upwards of; the above; that's it! (*end of message/speech*) = thank you (*for your attention*): **~ desu** 以上です That's all.

ijū *n* 移住 emigration, immigration: **~ shimásu** 移住します emigrates, immigrates

ijū-sha *n* 移住者 emigrant, immigrant (= **imin** 移民)

ika *n* イカ cuttlefish, squid

ika-sumi *n* イカ墨 squid ink

(…) íka *n*, *suffix* (…)以下 below (…), less than …: **~ no tōri desu** 以下の通りです as (*described*) below, as follows

ikada *n* 筏 raft

ikága *adv* いかが how (about it)? [DEFERENTIAL] (= **dō´** どう): **chōshi wa ~ desuka?** 調子はいかがですか? How's it going?

ikagawashíi *adj* いかがわしい suspicious, questionable, shady

ika-hodo *adj* いかほど how many? (= **íkura** いく[幾]ら); how ...? (= **dono-gurai (-kurai)** どの位)

ikan *n* 遺憾 regret: ~ **nágara ...** 遺憾ながら ... I regret that ..., Unfortunately ...

ikanai *v* 行かない = **ikimasén** 行きません (not go)

ikaremásu, ikareru *v* 行かれます, 行かれる **1.** can go (= **ikemásu** 行けます) **2.** [PASSIVE] have them go (*to one's distress*); [HONORIFIC] goes (= **irasshaimásu** いらっしゃいます)

ikari *n* 錨 anchor

ikari *n* 怒り anger: ~ **o shizumemásu** 怒りを静めます calms the anger

ikasemásu, ikaseru *v* 行かせます, 行かせる sends (*a person*); lets (*a person*) go

ikashimásu, ikásu *v* 生かします, 生かす **1.** lets/makes it live, brings life to; keeps it alive **2.** makes the most of, makes good use of

iké *v* 行け [IMPERATIVE] (go!) → **ikimásu** 行きます

iké *n* 池 pond

ikéba *v* 行けば (if one goes) → **ikimásu** 行きます

ikébana *n* 生け花 [活花] flower arrangement

ikégaki *n* 生(け)垣 hedge

ikemasén, ikenai *v* いけません, いけない **1.** it won't do; you mustn't; don't **2.** (*that's*) too

ikemasén, ikenai *v* 行けません, 行けない (= **ikaremasén** 行かれません, **ikarenai** 行かれない) cannot go

ikemasén, ikenai *v* 生[活]けません, 生[活]けない not arrange (*flowers*)

ikemásu, ikeru *v* 行けます, 行ける (= **ikaremásu** 行かれます, **ikareru** 行かれる) can go

ikemásu, ikéru *v* 生[活]けます, 生[活]ける arranges (*flowers*)

íken *n* 意見 opinion, idea: **go-íken** ご意見 (*your/someone else's*) opinion [HONORIFIC]

íken *n* 違憲 constitutional violation

ikenai *v* いけない = **ikemasén** いけません (it it won't do; you mustn't; don't)

ikenai *v* 行けない = **ikemasén** 行けません (cannot go)

ikénai *v* 生[活]けない = **ikemasén** 生[活]けません (not arrange flowers)

ike(ra)remásu, ike(ra)réru *v* 生[活]け(ら)れます, 生[活]け(ら)れる can arrange (*flowers*)

ikéreba *v* 生[活]ければ (if one arranges flowers) → **ikemásu** 生[活]けます

ikete *v* 行けて → **ikemásu** 行けます

íkete *v* 生[活]けて → **ikemásu** 生[活]けます

iki (na) *adj* 粋(な) smart, stylish

íki *n* 息 breath: ~ **o shimásu** 息をします breathes

iki-gire *n* 息切れ shortness of breath

iki-gurushii *adj* 息苦しい stuffy

...-iki (no) *suffix* ...行き(の) bound for ...

ikidōrí *n* 憤り indignation, resentment

ikidōrimásu, ikidṓru *v* 憤ります, 憤る gets indignant, resents

ikigai *n* 生き甲斐 something to live for: ~ **o kanjimásu** 生き甲斐を感じます feels one's life is worth living, feels alive

ikimásu, iku *v* 行きます, 行く goes

ikimásu, ikíru *v* 生きます, 生きる lives

ikímono *n* 生き物 living thing(s), animal(s), creature(s)

ikínai *v* 生きない = **ikimasén** 生きません (not live)

ikíoi *n* 勢い energy: ~ **yóku** 勢いよく energetically

ikíreba 生きれば (if one lives) → **ikimásu** 生きます

ikíru *v* 生きる = **ikimásu** 生きます (lives)

ikísatsu *n* いきさつ details, circumstances, complexities; complications

iki-tai *v* 行きたい wants to go

iki-tai *v* 生きたい wants to live

íkite *v* 生きて → **ikimásu** 生きます (lives): ~ **imásu** 生きています is alive

iki-yasúi *adj* 行きやすい accessible, easy to get to

iki-zumarimásu, iki-zumáru *v* 行き詰まります, 行き詰まる gets bogged down

ik- *n* 一 one

ik-kai *n* 一階 one floor/story; first floor, ground floor

ik-kai (no) *n, adj* 一回(の) one time, once (= **ichi-dó** 一度)

ik-ken *n* 一軒 one house/building (*counter for buildings*)

ik-ken *n* 一件 one case/matter: **ikken-rakuchaku** 一件落着 The case is closed.

ik-ko *n* 一個 one (*piece, small object*) (= **hitótsu** ひとつ・一つ)

ik-ko *n* 一戸 a house, a household: **ik-ko-date** 一戸建て detached house

ik-kyoku *n* 一曲 a piece of music, a song, a tune

ik-kyoku *n* 一局 a game ((i)go (*the board game Go*) and/or shōgi (*Japanese chess*)): **(i-)go/shōgi o uchimásu** (囲)碁/将棋を一局打ちます plays a game of *(i)go/shōgi*

ikkansei *n* 一貫性 consistency

ík-ki ni *adv* 一気に with a gulp, with a dash, with a burst

ik-kō *n* 一考 consideration: ~ **shimásu** 一考します considers

ik-kō (ni)... *adv* 一向(に)... [+ NEGATIVE] not at all, never: ~ **ni kamaimasen** 一向に構いません I don't mind at all.

ik-kyo-ryōtoku *n* 一挙両得 [IDIOM] Kill two birds with one stone. (= **is-seki-nichō** 一石二鳥)

ik-kyū *n* 一級 first class

ikō´ *v* 行こう = **ikimashō´** 行きましょう (let's go!)

ikó´ *v* 憩う = **ikoimásu** 憩います (rests and relaxes)

ikō *n* 意向 one's mind, inclination, intention; one's views

(...) **íkō** *suffix* (...)以降 afterward, from ... on (= (...) **ígo** (...)以後)

ikoi *n* 憩い rest and relaxation: ~ **no ba(sho)** 憩いの場(所) recreation area: **ikoimásu** 憩います rests and relaxes

ikoku *n* 異国 foreign countries

ikoku-jōcho (no) *adj* 異国情緒(の) exotic

ikon *n* 遺恨 grudge

ikotsu *n* 遺骨 remains (*of person*)

iku *v* 行く = **ikimásu** 行きます (goes)

íku-... *prefix* いく・幾 ... = **nán-...**

何... how many ...

ikudōon (ni) *adv* 異口同音(に) unanimously

ikuji *n* 育児 child care: **ikuji-kyūka** 育児休暇 child-care leave

ikuji-nashi *n* 意気地なし coward, chicken; ~ **(no/ga) nai** 意気地(の/が)ない is a coward, cowardly

ikura *n* イクラ salmon roe (*caviar*)

íkura *n* いくら (**o-ikura** おいくら) how much: **O-ikura desu ka?** おいくらですか? How much is it?; ~ **ka** いくらか some, a little; **ikura mo** いくらも ever so much, [+ NEGATIVE] not very much; ~ **de mo** いくらでも a lot, as much as you like

ikusa *n* 戦 war (= **sensō** 戦争)

ikusei *n* 育成 fosterage, nourishment: ~ **shimásu** 育成します fosters, nourishes

íkutsu *n* いくつ (**o-ikutsu** おいくつ) how many; how old: **O-ikutsu desu ka?** おいくつですか? "How old are you?" *or* "How many do you want?"; ~ **ka** いくつか several, a number of; ~ **mo** いくつも ever so many, [+ NEGATIVE] not very many; ~ **de mo** いくつでも as many as you like

imá *n* 居間 living room (*Western-style*)

íma *n* 今 now, this time: ~ **wa** 今は at present; ~ **no tokoró wa** 今のところは for the time being, so far; ~ **goro wa** 今ごろは about this time

ima-máde *adv* 今まで until now, up to the present (*time*)

íma-ni *adv* 今に before long, soon, by and by, presently: **íma-ni mo** 今にも at any moment

ima-sara *adv* 今さら at this point

ima-da ni *adv* 未だに still (= **mada** まだ)

imásu, iru *v* います、いる is, stays

imásu, íru *v* 射ます、射る shoots

imē´ji *n* イメージ (*psychological/social*) image (= **gazō** 画像): ~ **torēningu** イメージトレーニング image training

iimēru *n* Eメール e-mail (= **mēru** メール)

ími *n* 意味 meaning: **... to iu ~ desu** ...という意味です, **... o ~ shimásu** ...を意味します it means ...

imin *n* 移民 immigrant(s)/emigrant(s)

imó *n* イモ・芋 (**o-imo** お芋) yam; potato

imó *n* いも dork, country bumpkin (= **inaka-mono** 田舎者)

í mo/ya shinai *v* いも/やしない stay/be; not even/also stay or be

imōtó *n* 妹 younger sister: **imóto-san** 妹さん (your) younger sister

inabíkari *n* 稲光 lightning

inada *n* イナダ baby yellowtail (*cf.* **hamachi** はまち・ハマチ, **buri** ブリ・鰤)

inai *v* いない = **imasén** いません (not stay)

(…) **ínai** *suffix* (…)以内 within

inaka *n* 田舎 country(side); one's home area (*hometown*): **inaka no** 田舎の rural; **inaka-mono** 田舎者 country bumpkin (= **imó** いも)

inarí-zushi *n* いなり鮨[寿司] sushi in a bag of *aburage* (fried bean-curd) (= **o-inari san** お稲荷さん)

inázuma *n* イナズマ・稲妻 lightning

inbō *n* 陰謀 [BOOKISH] dark plot(s), intrigue(s)

(…-)**inchi** *suffix* (…)インチ inch(es)

ínchiki (na) *adj* いんちき(な) fake, fraud(ulent)

inchō *n* 院長 hospital head/director

Indian *n* インディアン (*American*) Indian, native American

Indo *n* インド India

Indó-jin *n* インド人 Indian (*from India*)

Indonéshia *n* インドネシア Indonesia

Indoneshia-go *n* インドネシア語 Indonesian (*language*)

Indoneshiá-jin *n* インドネシア人 an Indonesian

íne *n* 稲 rice plant: **ine-kari** 稲刈り harvesting rice

inemúri-shimásu (suru) *v* 居眠りします(する) dozes off

infomēshon *n* インフォメーション information

infure *n* インフレ inflation

infuruénza *n* インフルエンザ flu, influenza

íngen, ingénmame *n* インゲン・い

んげん, インゲンマメ・いんげん豆 kidney beans, French beans

ín(kan) *n* 印(鑑) [BOOKISH] seal, stamp (= **hán** 判, **hankó** 判子)

inkei *n* 陰茎 penis [FORMAL, MEDICAL TERM] (= **chínchin** ちんちん, **o-chín-chin** おちんちん)

inki (na) *adj* 陰気(な) gloomy, glum

ínku, ínki *n* インク, インキ ink

ínku-jetto *n* インクジェット ink jet: **ínku-jetto purintā** インクジェットプリンター inkjet printer

ínochi *n* 命 one's life (= **séimei** 生命)

inorí *n* 祈り (**o-inori** お祈り) prayer

inorimásu, inóru *v* 祈ります, 祈る prays; wishes for, hopes for

inpo *n* インポ sexual impotence

inreki *n* 陰暦 lunar calendar

inryoku *n* 引力 attractive force, gravity

inryō-sui *n* 飲料水 drinking water (= **inyō-sui** 飲用水)

insatsu *n* 印刷 printing: **insatsú-butsu** 印刷物 printed matter; ~ **shimásu** 印刷します prints

inshi *n* 印紙 revenue stamp (= **shūnyū-ínshi** 収入印紙)

inshō *n* 印象 impression

inshō-teki (na) *adj* 印象的(な) impressive

inshoku *n* 飲食 drinking and eating

inshoku-ten *n* 飲食店 restaurant(s) (= **resutoran** レストラン)

inshu *n* 飲酒 drinking: **inshu-unten** 飲酒運転 driving after drinking

insū-bunkai *n* 因数分解 factorization

insutanto *n* インスタント instant: **insutanto kōhii** インスタントコーヒー instant coffee: **insutanto rāmen** インスタントラーメン instant noodles

insutorakutā *n* インストラクター instructor

insutōru *n* インストール install (*on computer*)

intabyū *n* インタビュー interview: **intabyū-kiji** インタビュー記事 interview article

intāchenji *n* インターチェンジ highway interchange(s)

intāhai *n* インターハイ interscholastic athletic meet

intāhon n インターホン intercom

intai n 引退 retirement: ~ shimásu 引退
します retires

intān n インターン intern

intānashonaru n インターナショナル
international

intānetto n インターネット Internet

intānetto-kafe n インターネットカフ
ェ Internet cafe (= netto-kafe ネットカ
フェ)

intānetto-tsūhan n インターネット通
販 (= netto-tsūhan ネット通販) online
shopping, Internet shopping

intān-shippu n インターンシップ
internship

interi n インテリ intellectual; highbrow

interia n インテリア interior (accessory)

inú n イヌ・犬 dog: inú-goya 犬小屋
kennel

Inu-doshi n 戌年 year of the Dog

in'yō n 引用 quoting, quotation: ~
shimásu 引用します quotes

in'yō n 陰陽 yin and yang

inyō-sui n 飲用水 drinking water
(= inryō-sui 飲料水)

inzei n 印税 royalties (from one's
book(s))

iō v 言おう = iimashō 言いましょう
(let's say it!)

ip- n 一 one

íp-pai n 一杯 a cupful, a glassful; a
drink

ip-paku n 一泊 one night's lodging/
stay: ippaku-futsuka 一泊二日 two-
day one-night (trip)

ip-pén n 一遍 one time (= ichi-dó
一度, ik-kái 一回)

ip-pikí n 一匹 one (fish/bug, small
animal): ippiki-ōkami 一匹狼 lone wolf

ip-pon n 一本 one (pencil/bottle, long
thing), a point

íp-pun n 一分 one minute

ippai n いっぱい fully, full of; many,
much, lots (= takusan たくさん): ippai
(no) いっぱい(の) full, filled

-ippai suffix いっぱい whole, entire:
konshū-ippai 今週いっぱい all this
week, whole week

ippan (no) adj 一般(の) general,
overall

ippan-teki (na/ni) adj, adv 一般的
(な/に) general, in general

ippin-ryō´ri n 一品料理 à la carte dishes

ippō´ n 一方 1. one side 2. mō ~ (de
wa) もう一方(では) the other side, on
the other hand; but, meanwhile

ippō-tsū´kō n 一方通行 one-way
(traffic, argument)

irai n 依頼 request; dependence, reliance; trust, commission: ~ shimásu
依頼します requests, asks for,
depends/relies (on); entrusts, commissions

(…) írai suffix, conj (…)以来 (ever)
since…

iranai v 要らない = irimasén 要りませ
ん (not need)

iránai v 炒らない = irimasén 炒りませ
ん (not roast)

iraremásu, irareru v いられます, いら
れる can stay/be

iráshite v いらして = irasshátte いらっ
しゃって → irasshaimásu いらっし
ゃいます

irasshái interj いらっしゃい =
irasshaimáse いらっしゃいませ
[IMPERATIVE] (Welcome!)

irasshaimásu, irassháru v いらっ
しゃいます, いらっしゃる [HONORIFIC]
1. comes (= kimásu 来ます) 2. goes (=
ikimásu 行きます) 3. stays, is
(= imásu います)

irásuto n イラスト illustration

iréba v いれば (if one be/stays) →
imásu います

iréba v 要れば (if one needs/wants) →
irimásu 要ります

íre ba v 炒れば (if one roasts) →
irimásu 炒ります

íre ba v 射れば (if one shoots) →
ímásu 射ます

iremásu, ireru v 入れます, 入れる puts
in, lets in, admits; includes: o-cha o ~
お茶を入れます makes tea; denwa o ~
電話を入れます puts in a call

ire-ba n 入れ歯 false teeth: sō-ireba 総
入れ歯 full denture

ire-mono n 入れ物 container

ire-zumi n 入れ墨・刺青 tattoo
(= tatū タトゥー)

iremásu, iréru v 炒れます, 炒れる can roast

iremásu, iréru v 射れます, 射れる can shoot (*arrow*)

irenai v 入れない = **iremasén** 入れません (not put/let in)

irénai v 炒れない = **iremasén** 炒れません (cannot roast)

irénai v 射れない = **iremasén** 射れません (cannot shoot)

ireréba v 入れれば (if one puts/lets in) → **iremásu** 入れます

iréreba v 炒れれば (if one can roast) → **iremásu** 炒れます

iréreba v 射れれば (if one can shoot) → **iremásu** 射れます

ire ró v 入れろ [IMPERATIVE] (put it in!) → **iremásu** 入れます

ireta v 入れた = **iremáshita** 入れました (put/let in)

íreta v 炒れた = **iremáshita** 炒れました (could roast)

íreta v 射れた = **iremáshita** 射れました (could shoot an arrow)

irete v 入れて → **iremásu** 入れます

írete v 炒れて・射れて → **iremásu** 炒れます・射れます

ireyó v 入れよう = **iremashó** 入れましょう (let's put it in!)

iriguchi, irikuchi n 入口 entrance

irimásu, iru v 要ります, 要る is necessary; needs, wants

irimásu, íru v 炒ります, 炒る roasts

iri-támago n 炒り卵 scrambled eggs

iri-yō (na) adj 入り用(な) needed (= **nyūyō (na)** 入り用(な))

iró n 色 color; sex

 iro-ai n 色合い tone (*coloring*)

 iró-gami n 色紙 colored paper

i ró v いろ [IMPERATIVE] (stay!) → **imásu**

í ro v 射ろ [IMPERATIVE] (shoot!) → **imásu**

iroiro (no/na) adj いろいろ(の/な) various

ironna ... adj いろんな... various

iroppói adj 色っぽい erotic

iru v いる = **imásu** います (is, stays)

iru v 要る = **irimásu** 要ります (needs)

íru v 炒る = **irimásu** 炒ります (roasts)

íru v 射る = **imásu** 射ます (shoots an arrow)

is- n 一 one

 ís-sai n 一歳 one year old (= **hitótsu** 一つ)

 is-satsú n 一冊 one book (*magazine*)

 is-sén n 一千・1,000 one thousand (= **sén** 千)

isé-ebi n 伊勢エビ[海老] lobster

isei n 異性 (*person of*) the opposite sex

isei (ga/no) adj 威勢(が/の)いい spirited, buckish

iseki n 遺跡 remains

iseki n 移籍 [BOOKISH] transfer: ~ **shimásu** 移籍します transfers

isharyō n 慰謝料 compensation/damages for mental suffering

ishí n 石 stone, rock: **ishi-atama** 石頭 stubborn, hardhead

íshi n 意志 will, intention: **ishi ga yowai** 意志が弱い, **ishi-hakujaku** 意志薄弱 having no willpower

íshiki n 意識 consciousness: ~ **o ushinaimásu** 意識を失います loses consciousness, passes out; ~ **fumei (no)** 意識不明(の) unconscious

íshindenshin (de) adv 以心伝心(で) (by) telepathy

ísho n 遺書 will

íshō n 衣装 costume

íshoku n 移植 transplantation: **shinzō-ishoku** 心臓移植 cardiac transplantation

ishokujū n 衣食住 food, clothing and shelter

isogashíi adj 忙しい busy: **shigoto ga** ~ 仕事が忙しい is busy at work

isogí n 急ぎ haste

 isogí no adj 急ぎの hasty, hurried, urgent

isogimásu, isógu v 急ぎます, 急ぐ hurries, rushes

isóida v 急いだ = **isogimáshita** 急ぎました (hurried, rushed)

isóide adv 急いで in a hurry → **isogimásu** 急ぎます

isōrō n 居候 freeloader: ~ **shimásu** 居候します freeloads

íssái adj, adv 一切 all, everything, without exception: ~ **kankei arimasen**

一切関係ありません It's not my business at all.

issakú- 一昨-: **issakú-ban/-ya** 一昨晩/夜 night before last (= **ototói no ban/yoru** 一昨日の晩/夜); **issakú-jitsu** 一昨日 day before yesterday (= **ototói** 一昨日); **issakú-nen** 一昨年 year before last (= **ototóshi** 一昨年)

ís-sei *n* 一世 **1.** first generation: **nikkei-issei** 日系一世 *Issei*, first-generation Japanese immigrants **2.** ... the First: **Erizabesu-issei** エリザベス一世 Elizabeth I

is-sei *n* 一世 one generation: **~ ichidai (no)** 一世一代(の) once in a lifetime: **~ o fūbi shimásu** 一世を風靡します takes the world by storm

is-sei (ni) *adv* 一斉(に) all together

is-seki-nichō *n* 一石二鳥 [IDIOM] Kill two birds with one stone. (= **ikkyo-ryōtoku** 一挙両得)

is-setsú *n* 一節 passage (*of text*)

isshō *n* 一生 one's whole life

ís-shō *n* 一升 1.8 liters: **isshō´-bin** 一升瓶 a 1.8-liter bottle (*of saké*)

isshō-kénmei (ni) *adv* 一生懸命(に) desperately; very hard

issho (ni) *adv* 一緒(に) together

ís-shu *n* 一種 a kind, a sort

isshun *n* 一瞬 a moment: **~ no dekigoto** 一瞬の出来事 moment event/ happening

isso *adv* いっそ rather, preferably

issō *adv* 一層 all the more..., still/ much more ...: **issō íi** 一層いい still better

issō *n* 一掃 sweep, cleanup: **~ shimásu** 一掃します sweeps・cleans up

isu *n* いす・イス・椅子 chair

Isuraeru *n* イスラエル Israel
　Isuraeru-jin *n* イスラエル人 Israeli

Isuramu-kyō *n* イスラム教 Islam (= **kaikyō** 回教)
　Isuramu-kyōto *n* イスラム教徒 Muslim, Moslem

íta *n* 板 board, plank
　ita-choko *n* 板チョコ chocolate bar

itachi *n* イタチ weasel: **itachi-gokko** イタチごっこ vicious circle

itadaite *v* いただいて・頂いて =

itadakímáshite いただきまして・頂きまして → **itadakimásu** いただきます・頂きます

itadaki *n* 頂 peak, summit (= **chōjō´** 頂上)

itadakimásu, itadaku *v* いただきます, いただく (*I/we humbly*) receive, eat, drink

itade *n* 痛手 damage: **~ o ukemásu** 痛手を受けます gets damage(s)

i-tai いたい wants to stay

itái *adj* 痛い painful, hurting, sore

itamae *n* 板前 chef (*of Japanese food*)

itamemásu, itaméru *v* 痛めます, 痛める hurts, injures: **kokóro o ~** 心を痛めます worries (*oneself*), grieves

itamemásu, itaméru *v* 傷めます, 傷める damages, spoils it

itamemásu, itaméru *v* 炒めます, 炒める (pan-)fries, sautés: **itame-mono** 炒め物 stir-fry

itamé ro *v* 痛めろ [IMPERATIVE] (hurt it!) → **itamemásu** 痛めます

itamé ro *v* 傷めろ [IMPERATIVE] (injure it!) → **itamemásu** 傷めます

itamé ro *v* 炒めろ [IMPERATIVE] (fries it!) → **itamemásu** 炒めます

itamí *n* 痛み an ache, a pain

itamí *n* 傷み damage

itamimásu, itámu *v* 痛みます, 痛む it aches

itamimásu, itámu *v* 傷みます, 傷む it spoils, rots

itarimásu, itáru *v* 至ります, 至る arrives (*at*), reaches (*to*), goes/comes (*to*)

Itaria *n* イタリア Italy
　Itaria-go *n* イタリア語 Italian (*language*)
　Itariá-jin *n* イタリア人 an Italian

itashimásu, itásu *v* 致します, 致す [HUMBLE/DEFERENTIAL] do(es) (= **shimásu** します)

itatte *adv* 至って extremely

itátte *v* 至って → **itarimásu** 至ります

itazura *n* いたずら mischief, prank: **itazura-denwa** いたずら電話 prank call: **~ (o) shimásu** いたずら・悪戯 (を)します gets into mischief, plays a trick itazurá-kko _n_ いたずらっ子 naughty child

itazura ni _adv_ いたずらに in vain, for nothing

itchi _n_ 一致 agreement, consensus: (**… to) itchi-shimásu** (…と)一致します agrees/accords (_with_)

ité _v_ いて → **imásu** います

ite-za _n_ 射手座 Sagittarius

íto _n_ 糸 thread, yarn, string: **tako-ito** 凧糸 kite string

itó-maki _n_ 糸巻き spool; reel

íto _n_ 意図 intention, plan, purpose: **ito-shite** 意図して intentionally, on purpose (= **ito-teki ni** 意図的に)

ito-teki ni _adv_ 意図的に on purpose (= **íto-shite** 意図して)

itóko _n_ いとこ・従兄弟・従姉妹 cousin: (**o-)itoko-san** (お)いとこさん (_your/someone else's_) cousin

itomá _n_ 暇 (**o-itoma** お暇) **1.** leave-taking: **o-itoma (ita)shimásu** お暇 (致)します I will take my leave. **2.** free time (= **hima** 暇); leave of absence

itoshíi _adj_ 愛しい dear (_beloved_)

ítsu _n, adv_ いつ when

ítsu dé mo _adv_ いつでも any time (_at all_): **~ daijóbu desu** いつでも大丈夫です Any time would be fine (_with me_).

itsu-goro _n_ いつ頃 about when

itsuká _n_ 五日 five days; fifth day (_of month_)

ítsu-ka _adv_ いつか sometime

ítsu kara _adv_ いつから since when, how long

itsukushimi _n_ 慈しみ tender love (= **jiai** 慈愛): **itsukushimásu** 慈しみます loves tenderly

ítsu made _adv_ いつまで until when, how long

ítsu made mo _adv_ いつまでも forever

ítsu made ni _adv_ いつまでに by when

ítsu-mo _adv_ いつも always, usually: **ítsu-mo no** いつもの usual

ítsu-no-ma-ni (ka) _adv_ いつの間]に (か) before one knows it

itsútsu _n_ 五つ five pieces (_small objects_) (= **gó-ko** 五個); five years old (= **gó-sai** 五歳)

itsuwári _n_ 偽り falsehood, lie (= **uso** 嘘)

itta _v_ 行った (went)→ **ikimásu** 行きます

itta _v_ 言った (said) → **iimásu** 言います

itta _v_ 炒った (fried) → **irimásu** 炒ります

ítta _v_ 射った (shot) → **ímasu** 射ます

ittai … _adv_ 一体 … on earth, … ever … !: **~ dōshitandesuka?** 一体どうしたんですか? What on earth happened

ittai-ka _n_ 一体化 unification: **~ shimásu** 一体化します unites

itte _v_ 行って → **ikimásu** 行きます

itte _v_ 言って → **iimasu** 言います

itte _v_ 要って・入って → **irimásu** 要ります・入ります

ítte _v_ 炒って → **irimásu** 炒ります

ítte _v_ 射って → **ímasu** 射ます

ittei (no) _adj_ 一定(の) fixed, settled, definite

Itte(i)rasshái _interj_ いって(い)らっしゃい, **Itte(i)rasshaímáse** [HONORIFIC] いって(い)らしゃいませ Good-bye! (_said to those departing home_)

Itte kimásu, Itte mairimásu _interj_ 行ってきます/参ります。 Good-bye! (_said to those staying home_)

it-tō´(no) _n, adj_ 一等(の) first, first class

it-tō _n_ 一頭 one (_horse/ox, large animal_)

it-tsui _n_ 一対 a pair

iu _v_ 言う = **yū** ゆう = **iimásu** 言います (says, tells; expresses)

iwá _n_ 岩 rock, crag

iwa-ba _n_ 岩場 rocky stretch

íwa ba _conj_ いわば so to speak

iwái 祝い **1.** _n_ (**o-iwai** お祝い) celebration **2.** _v_ → **iwaimásu** 祝います

iwaimásu, iwáu _v_ 祝います, 祝う celebrates

iwanai _v_ 言わない = **iimasén** 言いません (not say)

iwashi _n_ イワシ・鰯 sardine

iwátte _v_ 祝って → **iwaimásu** 祝います

iwawánai _v_ 祝わない = **iwaimasén** 祝いません (not celebrate)

iwáyúru _adj_ いわゆる [BOOKISH] so-called, what is known as

iya _interj_ いや (_usually male_) no, nope

iyá (na) _adj_ 嫌(な) unpleasant; disliked; disagreeable; disgusting, nasty

iya-garimásu, iya-gáru v 嫌がります、嫌がる dislikes, hates
íyaringu n イヤリング earring
iyashii adj 卑しい lowly, vulgar
í ya shinai v いやしない = **ínai** いない (not stay)
í ya shinai v 射やしない = **ínai** 射ない (not shoot)
iyō v いよう = **imashō´** いましょう (let's stay!)
iyó-iyo adv いよいよ **1.** at last, finally **2.** more and more **3.** surely

iza adv いざ when it comes to (actually do so): **~ to iu toki** いざという時 in a pinch, in the worst case
(...)ízen suffix (...)以前 before, up until ..., ago
izumi n 泉 fountain, spring
izure adv いずれ some other time; someday: **~ wakarudeshō** いずれ分かるでしょう You will see soon.; **~ mata aimashō** いずれまた会いましょう Let's meet up again sometime.

J

ja interj, adv じゃ、**jā´** じゃあ [INFORMAL] well, well then; in that case; (well) now (= **déwa** では)
...ja suffix ...じゃ [INFORMAL] = **...dé wa** ...では
　...ja arimasen v じゃありません = **...ja nái** じゃない it is not; it is not a case of
　...ja nákereba suffix, v ...じゃなければ = **...ja nái to** ...じゃないと unless it be: **~ narimasén** ...じゃなければなりません must (has to) be
　...ja náku(te) suffix, v ...じゃなく(て) (it) is not and/but; without being
　...ja nákute mo suffix, v ...じゃなくても even if it not be: **~ íi desu** ...じゃなくてもいいです it need not be
　...ja nákute wa suffix, v じゃなくては = **...ja nákya** ...じゃなきゃ not being, without being; unless it be
ja n 蛇 snake: **~ no michi wa hebi** 蛇の道は蛇 Set a thief to catch a thief.
jaaku (na) adj [BOOKISH] 邪悪(な) evil
jabu n ジャブ jab
jagā n ジャガー jaguar
jagaimo n じゃがいも・ジャガイモ (Irish) potato
jaguchi n 蛇口 faucet, tap
jajauma n じゃじゃ馬 shrew
jāji n ジャージ jersey
jákétto n ジャケット jacket
jakén (na/ni) adj, adv 邪険(な/に) blunt(ly)
jakkan (no) adj 若干(の) some

(amount of), several
jakku n ジャック jack
jakō n ジャコウ・麝香 civet, musk: **jakō-neko** ジャコウネコ musk cat: **jakō-nezumi** ジャコウネズミ (house) musk shrew
jakuhai (mono) n [BOOKISH] 若輩(者) young and inexperienced person
jakunen-sha n [BOOKISH] 若年者 the young, a youth (= **wakamono** 若者)
jakusha n 弱者 the weak (person)
jakuten n 弱点 weak point
jama n 邪魔 (**o-jama** お邪魔) disturbance, hindrance, obstacle: **jama (na)** 邪魔(な) intrusive, bothersome; **~ ni narimásu** 邪魔になります、**~ o shimásu** 邪魔をします gets in the way, becomes a bother
Jamaika n ジャマイカ Jamaica
jámu n ジャム jam (to eat)
jānarisuto n ジャーナリスト journalist
jānarizumu n ジャーナリズム journalism
jānaru n ジャーナル journal
janbo n ジャンボ jumbo: **janbo-jetto-ki** ジャンボジェット機 jumbo jet aircraft
jánguru n ジャングル jungle: **janguru-jímu** ジャングルジム jungle gym
janku-fūdo n ジャンクフード junk food
jánpā n ジャンパー windbreaker (jacket)
jánpu n ジャンプ jump: **~ shimásu** ジャンプします jumps

janru

JAPANESE–ENGLISH

janru n ジャンル genre
jarajara adj ジャラジャラ jangling sound
jara-shimásu, jara-su v じゃらしま
す、じゃらす plays with
jari n 砂利 gravel, pebbles
Járu n ジャル JAL (*Japan Airlines*)
jashin n [BOOKISH] 邪心 wicked heart
jashin n [BOOKISH] 邪神 false god(s)
Jawa n ジャワ Java
jazu n ジャズ jazz
Jei áru, Jē áru n ジェイアール、ジェー
アール, JR (*Japan Railway*)
jettó-ki n ジェット機 jet (*plane*)
ji n 痔 hemorrhoids
jí n 字 moji 文字 a letter (*symbol*):
kanji 漢字 a Chinese character
jí n 地 land, ground; texture; fabric
ji-... *prefix* 自... self; one's own
ji-bun n 自分 oneself; myself; alone:
jibun-katte/gatte (na) 自分勝手 (な)
selfish; **jibun de** 自分で by oneself, in
person; **jibun no** 自分の (*one's*) own;
go-jibun ご自分 yourself; **jibun-jishin**
n 自分自身 time (= **jishin** 自身)
ji-ga n 自我 ego
ji-ko n 自己 (one)self
ji-sei n 自制 self-control
ji-shin n 自信 self-confidence/-assur-
ance: ~ **o mótte ... (shimásu**) 自信を
持って...(します) (does it) with
confidence
ji-taku n 自宅 one's home/residence:
jitaku-taiki 自宅待機 home standby
...-ji *suffix* ...時 o'clock
...-ji *suffix* ...寺 temple (*name*):
Kinkaku-ji 金閣寺
jiai n [BOOKISH] 慈愛 tender love (=
itsukushimi 慈しみ)
jibikí n 字引き dictionary (= **jísho** 辞書)
jíbun n 時分 time
jidai n 時代 age, period, era, time,
...-jidai ...時代 period: **Edo-jidai** 江戸
時代 the Edo period; **jidai-mono** 時代
物 antique (= **kottó-hin** 骨董品)
jídō n 児童 child (*elementary school
student*) (= **seito** 生徒)
jidō n 自動 automatic
jidō-doa n 自動ドア auto(matic) door
jidō-hanbaiki n 自動販売機 vending
machine

jidō-sha n 自動車 automobile (=
kuruma 車)
jidō-teki (na/ni) adj 自動的 (な/に)
automatic; adv automatically
jidō-shi n 自動詞 intransitive verb
Jiei-tai n 自衛隊 the Self-Defense Forces
jigoku n 地獄 hell
jigyō n 事業 enterprise, business,
undertaking
jíi n 自慰 masturbation (= **onanii** オナ
ニー)
jii-pan n ジーパン blue jeans (= **jiinzu**
ジーンズ)
jíjitsu n 事実 fact, truth: ~ **o mitomemásu** 事実を認めます admits the fact
jijō n 事情 circumstances; conditions: ~
o nomikomimásu 事情を飲み込みます
understands the situation
jikan n 時間 (**o-jíkan** お時間) time;
hour(s): ~ **ga kakarimásu** 時間がかか
ります it takes time; **jikan-dō ri (no/
ni)** 時間通り (の/に) on time: ~ **ni rūzu
(na)** 時間にルーズ (な) unpunctual
...-jikan *suffix* ...時間 time; hour(s):
eigyō-jikan 営業時間 business hours;
kinmu-jikan 勤務時間 working hours
jikan-hyō n 時間表 timetable, schedule
(= **jikoku-hyō** 時刻表)
jika ni adv 直に directly; personally
(= **chokusetsu (ni)** 直接 (に))
jikan-wari (hyō) n 時間割 (表) school
time schedule (*table*)
jíken n 事件 happening, incident, event,
affair, case: ~ **o kaiketsu shimásu** 事件
を解決します solves a case/cases
jíki n 時期 time; season: **jiki-shōsō (na)**
時期尚早 (な) prematurity (premature)
jíki n 時機 opportune time, opportunity,
chance
jíki n 磁器 porcelain → **tō ki** 陶器
jíki (no) n 磁気 (の) magnetic: ~ **o
obiteiru...** 磁気を帯びている... mag-
netize ...
jiki (ni) adv 直 (に) soon; immediately
jikka n 実家 one's parent's home
jikken n 実験 experiment: ~ **shimásu**
実験します experiments
jikkō n 実行 performance; practice;
realization, running: ~ **shimásu** 実行し
ます runs; practices

86

jíko *n* 事故 accident

jíkoku *n* 時刻 time (*specified*)

jikoku-hyō *n* 時刻表 time schedule, timetable (= **jikan-hyō** 時間表)

jikú *n* 軸 axis, axle: **chi-jiku** 地軸 earth axis: **jiten-jiku** 自転軸 (*planet's*) rotational axis

jiman *n* 自慢 pride, boast: ~ **shimásu** 自慢します boasts, brags about

jímen *n* 地面 ground (*surface*)

jimí (na) *adj* 地味(な) plain, sober

jímu *n* 事務 business, office work

jimu-in *n* 事務員 office clerk

jimu-sho *n* 事務所 office

jímu *n* ジム gym(nasium)

...´-jín *suffix* ...人 person

jínbutsu *n* 人物 personage

jindō *n* 人道 **1.** humanity: **jindō-shugisha** 人道主義者 humanitarian **2.** walkway, pedestrian path

jingū´ *n* 神宮 (large) Shinto shrine

jinin *n* 人員 personnel

jínja *n* 神社 Shinto shrine

jínji *n* 人事 personnel/human affairs

jinji-ka *n* 人事課 personnel (section)

jínjō *adj* 尋常 [BOOKISH] usual, normal (= **futsū** 普通): **jinjō-de nai** 尋常でない unusual, abnormal

jinken *n* 人権 human rights

jinkō *n* 人口 population

jinkō (no) *adj* 人工(の) artificial

jinríki-sha *n* 人力車 ricksha

jinrui *n* 人類 human beings, the human race: **jinrúi-gaku** 人類学 anthropology

jinsei *n* 人生 (*one's*) life

jinshin-jiko *n* 人身事故 (traffic) accident of injury and/or death

jinshu *n* 人種 race (*peoples*): ~ **sabetsu** 人種差別 racial discrimination: ~ **no rutsubo** 人種のるつぼ melting pot

ji-nushi *n* 地主 landowner

jinzō *n* 腎臓 kidneys

jinzō (no) *adj* 人造(の) artificial, imitation, false (*man-made*): **jinzō-ningen** 人造人間 artificial human

jíppā *n* ジッパー zipper

jira-shimásu, jira-su *v* じらします、じらす irritates someone, tantalizes

jírojiro mimásu (míru) *v* じろじろ見ます(見る) stares at

jísa *n* 時差 difference in time: **jisa-boke** 時差ぼけ jet lag; **jisa-shukkin** 時差出勤 staggered work hours

jisan shimásu (suru) *v* 持参します (する) brings along, takes along

jisatsu *n* 自殺 suicide: ~ **shimásu** 自殺します commits suicide

jisei *n* 時勢 (*the trend of*) the times

jisei *n* 時世 (**go-jísei** ご時世) the times

jísetsu *n* 時節 season; (*appropriate*) time, occasion, opportunity

jíshaku *n* 磁石 magnet

jishin *n* 地震 earthquake

jishin *n* 磁針 magnetic needle: **hōi-jishin** 方位磁針 compass

-jishin *n* 自身 oneself; myself (= **jibun-jishin** 自分自身): **kare-jishin** 彼自身 himself

jísho *n* 辞書 dictionary

jishoku *n* 辞職 resignation (*from a position*): ~ **shimásu** 辞職します resigns

jísoku *n* 時速 (*per hour*) speed

jissai *n*, *adv* 実際 actual conditions, reality; in practice; in fact, really

ji-súberi *n* 地滑り landslide

jítai *n* 事態 situation, state of affairs

jítai *n*, *adv* 自体 **1.** the thing itself **2.** originally

jítai *n* 辞退: ~ **shimásu** 辞退します declines, refuses

jitchi *n* 実地 actuality, (*putting to*) practice: **jitchi (no)** 実地(の) practical, actual

jiten *n* 辞典 dictionary (= **jísho** 辞書): **kokugo-jiten** 国語辞典 Japanese dictionary: **eiwa-jiten** 英和辞典 English-Japanese dictionary

jiten *n* 事典 dictionary, subject book: **hyakka-jíten** 百科事典 encyclopedia: **jinmei-jiten** 人名事典 personal names dictionary

jitén-sha *n* 自転車 bicycle: **jitensha-ya** 自転車屋 bicycle shop/dealer

jitsú *n* 実 truth: **jitsú ni** 実に truly, really, indeed; **jitsú no** 実の true, real; **jitsú wa** 実は to tell the truth, actually, in fact

jitsu-butsu *n* 実物 the real thing; the actual person: **jitsubutsu-saizu** 実物サイズ actual size, original size jitsu-ryoku n 実力 (real) strength, ability, proficiency; force, power

jitsu-yō n 実用 practical use/application, utility: **jitsuyō-teki na** 実用的な practical

jitsugyō n 実業 business, enterprise: **jitsugyō-ka** 実業家 businessperson, businessman

jitto adv じっと intently, steadily, fixedly (*staring*); quietly: ~ **shiteimásu** じっとしています holds still

jiyū´ n 自由 freedom, liberty: **jiyū´ (na)** 自由(な) free; fluent, at ease; **jiyū´ ni** 自由に freely; fluently; **jiyū´-gyō** 自由業 freelancing, freelance work; **jiyū´-seki** 自由席 unreserved seat

jizen n 慈善 charity

jō´ n 錠 **1.** (= **jō-mae** 錠前) lock **2.** (= **jōzai** 錠剤) pill

jō adj, n 上 **1.** (= **jōtō (na)** 上等(な)) deluxe **2.** (= **jō-kan** 上巻) first volume (*of a set of 2 or 3*)

...´-jō suffix ...畳 (*counts room sizes by tatami mat*): **hachí-jō (ma)** 八畳(間) eight tatami mats (room)

...´-jō suffix ...城 castle (*name*): 大阪城 the Osaka-jō castle

jōbu (na) adj 丈夫(な) sturdy, firm, healthy; safe (= **daijōbu** 大丈夫)

jochō n 助長 promotion, furtherance: ~ **shimásu** 助長します promotes, encourages, fosters, foments

jochū n 女中 maid-servant

jōdán n 冗談 joke: ~ **hanbun (ni)** 冗談半分(に) half in jest

jōei n 上映 showing (*movie*)

jōen n 上演 performance: ~ **shimásu** 上演します performs

jo-gákusei, joshi gákusei n 女学生, 女子学生 female student

jōge n 上下 top and bottom, high and row, up and down

jōgi n 定規 ruler (*to measure with*)

jogingu n ジョギング jog(ging): ~ **(o) shimásu** ジョギング(を)します jogs

jō´go n 漏斗 funnel

jōhín (na) adj 上品(な) elegant, refined

jōhō n 情報 information

jōkén n 条件 condition, stipulation, provision, term

jō´ki n 蒸気 steam, vapor

jokki n ジョッキ jug, (*beer*) mug

jōkyaku n 乗客 passenger

jōkyō n 状況・情況 situation, circumstances, state of affairs

jōkyū n 上級 high/upper class: **jōkyū-kōsu** 上級コース advanced course

jō-mae n 錠前 lock (= **kagi** 鍵)

jomei n 除名 excision, excommu-nication: ~ **shimásu** 除名します expels, excommunicates

jomei n 助命 sparing the life/lives (= **kyūmei** 救命): ~ **shimásu** 助命します spares

jōmén n 上面 top (*top side*)

jōmuin n 乗務員 crew: **kyakushitsu** ~ 客室乗務員 (*airplane*) flight attendant

jōnetsu-teki (na) adj 情熱的(な) passionate

joō´ n 女王 queen

jōriku n 上陸 disembarking, landing: ~ **shimásu** 上陸します lands, disembarks, comes ashore

jōro n じょうろ・ジョウロ watering can

jōryū (no) adj 上流(の) classy, upper; upstream

jōryū´-sui n 蒸留水 distilled water

josei n 女性 woman, female: **josei-go** 女性語 women's language (*terms*) (= **onna kotoba** 女言葉)

joseikin n 助成金 grant

joseki n 除籍 removal from register, expulsion (*from a school/university*): ~ **shimásu** 除籍します removes someone from the register

josetsu n 除雪: ~ **shimásu** 除雪します removes the snow

jōsha n 乗車 getting into a car, getting on a train/bus, boarding: ~ **shimásu** 乗車します boards

jōshá-ken n 乗車券 passenger ticket

joshi n 助詞 particle (*auxiliary word*)

jóshi n 女子 girl, woman: **joshi-dáisei** 女子大生 woman college student; **joshi-kō´sei** 女子高生 female (*senior*) high school student

jōshiki n 常識 common sense

joshō n 序章 introduction section (*book*)

joshu n 助手 helper, assistant

josō *n* 助走 running up: **~ shimásu** 助走
します runs up

josō *n* 除草 weeding: **~ shimásu** 除草し
ます eradicates weeds

josō *n* 女装 drag

josō *n* 序奏 (*music*) introduction

jōsui-chi *n* 浄水池 reservoir

jotai *n* 除隊 discharge: **~ shimásu** 除隊
します discharges

jōtai *n* 状態 condition, situation, state,
circumstances

jōtō (no) *adj* 上等（の）the best, first-
rate, deluxe

joya *n* 除夜 New Year's Eve: **joya no
kane** 除夜の鐘 the bells on New Year's
Eve

jōyaku *n* 条約 treaty, agreement:
Washinton-jōyaku ワシントン条約
Washington Convention

jōyō *n* 常用 common use: **jōyō-kanji**
常用漢字 Chinese characters in
common use

jōyōˊ-sha *n* 乗用車 passenger car

jōyōˊ-sha *n* 常用者 addict

joyū *n* 女優 actress

jōzai *n* 錠剤 pill, tablet

jōzō-sho *n* 醸造所 brewery

jōzú (na) *adj* 上手（な）skilled, clever,
good at

jū *n* 銃 gun: **jū-sei** 銃声 gunshot(s)

jūˊ *n* 十・10 ten (**juk-, jup-, jut-**)

jū-bai *n* 十倍 ten times, tenfold

jū-banme (no) *adj* 十番目（の）tenth

jūˊ-do *n* 十度 ten times (= **júk-kai**
十回); ten degrees

jū-en-dama *n* 十円玉 ten-yen coin

jūˊ-go *n* 十五・15 fifteen

jū-hachí *n* 十八・18 eighteen

jū-ichí *n* 十一・11 eleven

jūˊ-ji *n* 十時・10時 ten o'clock

juk-kai *n* 十階 ten floors/stories; tenth
floor

júk-kai *n* 十回 ten times (= **jūˊ-do** 十度)

júk-ko *n* 十個 ten (*pieces, small objects*)

jūˊ-ku, jū-kyūˊ *n* 十九・19 nineteen

jū-mán *n* 十万・100,000 a hundred
thousand

jū-nána *n* 十七・17 seventeen

jū-ní *n* 十二・12 twelve

jū-óku *n* 十億・10億 a thousand

million; (*U.S.*) a billion

júp-pa *n* 十羽 ten (*birds*)

júp-pon *n* 十本 ten (*pencils/bottles,
long things*)

júp-pun *n* 十分 10 minutes

jū-rokú *n* 十六・16 sixteen

jūˊ-san *n* 十三・13 thirteen

jū-shi *n* 十四・14 fourteen (= **jū-yon**
十四)

jut-tō *n* 十頭 ten (*horses/oxen, large
animals*)

jū-yok-ka *n* 十四日 14 days; 14th day
(*of month*)

jūˊyo-nin *n* 十四人 14 people

...-jū *suffix* ...じゅう・中 throughout
the (*entire*)...: **ichi-nen-jū** 一年中
throughout the year: **sekai-jū** 世界中
all over the world

jūatsu *n* 重圧 pressure

jūbako *n* 重箱 nested boxes

jūbún (na) *adj* 十分［充分］（な）
enough, sufficient

jūdai (na) *adj* 重大（な）serious (*heavy,
grave*); important: **jūdái-ji** 重大事 a
matter of importance

jūˊdō *n* 柔道 judo, jujitsu (*an art of
weaponless defense*): **jūdōˊgí** 柔道着
judo outfit/suit

Jū-gatsu *n* 十月・10月 October

jūgeki *n* 銃撃 gunfight

jūgun *n* 従軍 serving in an army: **~
shimásu** 従軍します serves in an army

júgyō *n* 授業 class instruction,
classroom teaching: **jugyō-jíkan** 授業
時間 school/teaching hours; **~ o okonaimásu** 授業を行います teaches (*class*);
~ o ukemásu 授業を受けます attends
a class

jūgyō *n* 従業 employment: **~ shimásu**
従業します is employed

jūgyō-in *n* 従業員 employee

jūi *n* 獣医 veterinary

Jū-ichi-gatsu *n* 十一月・11月
November

jūˊji *n* 十字 a cross (*symbol*)

jūji-ka *n* 十字架 a cross (*wooden*)

jūji-ro *n* 十字路 crossroad(s)

jūˊji *n* 従事 engaging in (*an activity*): **...
ni ~ shimásu** ...に従事します engages
in ...

jūkinzoku *n* 重金属 heavy metal

jūketsu *n* 充血 congestion: **me ga ~ shimásu** 目が充血します gets red eyes

júku *n* 塾 a cram/tutoring school

jūku bokkusu *n* ジュークボックス jukebox

jukudoku *n* 熟読 reading thoroughly: **~ shimásu** 熟読します reads thoroughly

jukugo *n* 熟語 idiomatic expression

jukukō, jukkō *n* 熟考 serious thought: **~ shimásu** 熟考します considers carefully (= **jukuryo** 熟慮)

jukunen *n* 熟年 mature age

jukuryo *n* 熟慮 → **jukukō, jukkō** 熟考

jukushimásu, jukúsú *v* 熟します, 熟す ripens, gets ripe

jukusui *n* 熟睡 sound sleep: **~ shimásu** 熟睡します falls fast asleep

jukutatsu *n* 熟達 mastery: **~ shimásu** 熟達します gets in practice

Júkyō *n* 儒教 Confucianism

jukyu *n* 需給 supply and demand

jūmin *n* 住民 resident: **jūmin hyō** 住民票 residence certificate

jun *n* 順 order: **jun(ban) ni** 順(番)に in order

jún (na) *adj* 純(な) pure

junban *n* 順番 (place in) order, turn

júnbi *n* 準備 preparation(s), arrangements

junchō (na) *adj* 順調(な) smooth(ly going)

Jū-ni-gatsú *n* 十二月・12月 December

jun-jimásu, jun-jiru *v* [BOOKISH] 準じます, 準じる applies correspond-ingly (*to*); is made to accord (*with*)

júnjo *n* 順序 order, sequence

junkan *n* 循環 circulation; cycle: **~ shimásu** 循環します circulates

jun-kyō´ju *n* 准教授 associate professor

júnsa *n* 巡査 policeman, patrolman (= **omawari-san** お巡りさん)

junsui (na) *adj* 純粋(な) pure

jūō *n* 縦横 vertical and horizontal

jūō-mujin (ni) *adv* 縦横無尽(に) freely

jū´rai (wa) *adv* 従来(は) traditionally, previously: **jū´rai (no)** 従来(の) traditional, accustomed, customary

jūryō´ *n* 重量 weight: **jūryō-age** 重量挙げ weight-lifting

juryō´-shō *n* 受領証 receipt

jū´sho *n* 住所 residence, address

jushō *n* 受賞 winning an award: **~ shimásu** 受賞します wins

jushō´-sha *n* 受賞者 winner, awardee

jū´su *n* ジュース juice: **orenji-jūsu** オレンジジュース orange juice

jūtai *n* 渋滞 congestion: **~ shite imásu** 渋滞しています is congested (*backed up*)

jūtaku *n* 住宅 residence, house

jū´tan *n* じゅうたん・絨毯 rug, carpet (= **kā´petto** カーペット)

júyo *n* 授与 awarding, conferring: **~ shimásu** 授与します awards

jūyō (na) *adj* 重要(な) important

juzú *n* 数珠 beads: **~ tsunagi** 数珠つな[繋]ぎ bunching

K

ka *n* カ・蚊 mosquito: **ka-tori senkō** 蚊取り線香 mosquito coil

   ka-ya *n* 蚊帳・かや mosquito net: **~ no soto** 蚊帳の外 out of scheme

ka *n* 可 pass

ká *n* 課, **...´-ka** ...課 section, division; lesson: **Sōmu-ka** 総務課 General Affairs Division: **Jinji-ka** 人事課 Human Resources Division: **dai ik-ka** 第1課 Lesson 1

ká *n* 科 **1.** family (*biological taxonomy*) **2.** department: (*university*) **Eibun-ka** 英文科 Department of English Language & Literature, **Kokubun-ka** 国文科 Department of Japanese Language and Literature: (*hospital*) **Ge-ka** 外科 surgery, **Nai-ka** 内科 internal medicine

ka-... *prefix* 仮... temporary (*tentative*)

... ka *conj* ...か or; (*the question*) whether

...-ka *suffix* ...化 ...-ization: **-ka shimásu** ...化します ...-izes

kaba *n* カバ・河馬 hippopotamus

kabā n カバー cover, covering: **bukku-kabā** ブックカバー book cover; **kabā-retā** カバーレター cover letter (= **sōfu-jō** 送付状)

kabaimásu, kabau v 庇います, 庇う protects, defends

kaban n かばん・カバン・鞄 briefcase, bag

kabayaki n 蒲焼き broiled eel

kabe n 壁 wall: **kabe-gami** 壁紙 wallpaper

kabi n カビ mold, mildew: ~ **ga haete imásu** カビが生えています is moldy

kabin n 花瓶・かびん flower vase

kabocha n カボチャ pumpkin

kabu n 株 stock (*in a company*): **kabu-shiki-shijō** 株式市場 stock market

kabu n カブ・蕪 = **kabura** カブラ・蕪 turnip

kā'bu n カーブ curve (*road*)

kabuki n 歌舞伎 a traditional style of Japanese theater: **kabuki-za** 歌舞伎座 the Kabuki theater (*building*)

kaburimásu, kabúru v 被ります, 被る puts on (*to wear a hat, etc. on one's head/shoulders*)

kabushiki-gáisha n 株式会社 joint-stock corporation

kabútte v 被って → **kaburimásu** 被ります

káchi n 価値 value: ~ **ga arimásu** 価値があります is worth

kachí n 勝ち victory, win

kachimásu, kátsu v 勝ちます, 勝つ wins

ka-chō n 課長 section manager

kadai n 課題 **1.** problem, difficult matter (= **mondai** 問題) **2.** assignment, homework, task **3.** subject, theme (= **daimoku** 題目)

kádan n 花壇 flower bed

kádan n 下段 [BOOKISH] lower stand

kádan (na) n 果断 (な) [BOOKISH] decisive

kādigan n カーディガン cardigan

kádo n 角 (*outside*) corner, street corner

kádo n 過度 excessiveness: **kádo ni** 過度に excessively: **kádo no** 過度の extreme

kadō n 稼動 [BOOKISH] operating: ~

shimásu 稼動します operates

kadō n 華道 flower arrangement (= **ikebana** 生け花): ~ **kyōshitsu** 華道教室 flower arrangement class(es)

kādo n カード card: **messēji-kādo** メッセージカード message card

kaé v 買え [IMPERATIVE] (buy it!) → **kaimásu** 買います

káe v 飼え [IMPERATIVE] (raise it!) → **kaimásu** 飼います

kaéba v 買えば (if one buys) → **kaimásu** 買います

káeba v 飼えば (if one raises) → **kaimásu** 飼います

kaede n カエデ・楓 maple

kaemásu, kaeru v 変えます, 変える changes it

kaemásu, kaeru v 換え[替え]ます, 換える[替える] exchanges, replaces

kaemásu, kaeru v 買えます, 買える can buy

kaemásu, káeru v 飼えます 飼える can raise

kaenai v 変えない = **kaemasén** 変えません (not change it)

kaenai v 換え[替え]ない = **kaemasén** 換え[替え]ません (not exchange)

kaenai v 買えない = **kaemasén** 買えません (cannot buy)

káenai v 飼えない = **kaemasén** 飼えません (cannot raise)

kaeránai v 帰らない = **kaerimasén** 帰りません (not go home)

kae(ra)remásu, kae(ra)reru v 変え(ら)れます, 変え(ら)れる can change it

kae(ra)renai v 変え(ら)れない = **kae(ra)remasén** 変え(ら)れません (cannot change)

káere v 帰れ [IMPERATIVE] (go home!) → **kaerimásu** 帰ります

kaeréba v 変えれば (if one changes it) → **kaemásu** 変えます

kaeréba v 換え[替え]れば (if one exchanges) → **kaemásu** 換え[替え]ます

kaeréba v 買えれば (if one can buy) → **kaemásu** 買えます

káereba v 飼えれば (if one can raise) → **kaemásu** 飼えます

káereba v 帰れば (if one goes home) → **kaerimásu** 帰ります

kaeremásu, kaeréru v 帰れます, 帰れる can go home, can return

kaerénai v 帰れない = **kaeremásén** 帰れません (cannot go home)

kaerí n 帰り (the) return

kaerimásu, káeru v 帰ります, 帰る goes home, goes back, returns, leaves

kaerō´ v 帰ろう = **kaerimashó´** 帰りましょう (let's go home!)

kaeru n カエル・蛙 frog: **hiki-gaeru** ヒキガエル toad

kaeru v 変える = **kaemásu** 変えます (changes it)

kaeru v 換える[替える] = **kaemásu** 換え[替え]ます (exchanges, replaces)

kaeru v 買える = **kaemásu** 買えます (can buy)

káeru v 飼える = **kaemásu** 飼えます (can raise)

káeru v 帰る = **kaerimásu** 帰ります (goes home)

kaesánai v 返さない = **kaesímasen** 返しません (not returns it)

káeseba v 返せば (if one returns it) → **kaeshimásu** 返します

kaeshimásu, káesu v 返します, 返す returns it

káeshite v 返して → **kaeshimásu** 返します

kaete v 変えて・換え[替え]て・買えて → **kaemásu** 変えます・換え[替え]ます・買えます

káete v 飼えて → **kaemásu** 飼えます

káette adv 却って contrary to expectations

káette v 帰って → **kaerimásu** 帰ります

kaeyō´ v 変えよう = **kaemashō** 変えましょう (let's change it!)

kafún n 花粉 pollen: **kafún-shō** 花粉症 hay fever

káfusu n カフス cuff: **kafusu-botan** カフスボタン cuff links

kagai n 課外 extracurricular: **kagai-katsudō** 課外活動 extracurricular activity

kágaku n 科学 = **sáiensu** サイエンス science: **kagaku-teki (na)** 科学的(な) scientific

kagáku-sha n 科学者 scientist

kágaku n 化学 = **bake-gaku** 化け学・化学 chemistry: **kagaku-séihin** 化学製品 chemicals, **kagaku-yakuhin** 化学薬品 pharmaceuticals

kagáku-sha n 化学者 chemist

kagamí n 鏡 mirror: **te-kagami** 手鏡 hand mirror

kagamimásu, kagamu v 屈みます, 屈む bends over

kaganai v 嗅がない = **kagimásén** 嗅ぎません (not smell it)

kagayakimásu, kagayáku v 輝きます, 輝く shines, gleams, glitters

kagé v 嗅げ [IMPERATIVE] (smell it!) → **kagimásu** 嗅ぎます

káge n 影 shadow: **hito-kage** 人影 human figure: **kage-bō´shi** 影法師 shadow (of a person)

káge n 陰 shade: **ko-kage** 木陰 shade of trees

kagéba v 嗅げば (if one smells it) → **kagimásu** 嗅ぎます

kágeki n 歌劇 opera

kageki (na) adj 過激(な) excessive, extreme, radical: **kagekí-ha** 過激派 the radicals, the extremists

kagemásu, kageru v 嗅げます, 嗅げる can smell it

kagen n 加減 **1. o-kagen** お加減 (state of) one's health (= **guai** 具合)
2. allowance (= **tekagen** 手加減)
3. degree, extent (= **teido** 程度):
yu-kagen 湯加減 hot water temperature
4. adjustment, moderation (= **chōsei** 調整) (= **ii-kagen** いい加減): ~ **shimásu** 加減します adjusts, moderates, makes allowance for

kagenai v 嗅げない = **kagemásén** 嗅げません (cannot smell it)

...-ká-getsu suffix ...か月・ヶ月・カ月・箇月 (counts months): **ikka-getsu (kan)** 1か月 (間) (for) one month

kagí n 鈎 hook: **kagi-tsume** 鈎つめ claw: **kagi-kakko** かぎ括弧 Japanese quotation marks (「」)

kagí n カギ・鍵 key: **(... no) ~ ga kakarimásu** (…の)鍵がかかります it locks, **(... no) ~ o kakemásu** (…の)鍵をかけます locks it kagi-ana n 鍵穴 keyhole

kagimásu, kagu v か嗅ぎます, 嗅ぐ smells it

kágiri n 限り limit

kagirimasén, kagiranai v 限りません, 限らない not necessarily, not always

kagirimásu, kagíru v 限ります, 限る limits (delimits) it: ... ni ~ ...に限ります there is nothing like (so good as, better than) ...

kagitte v 限って: ... ni ~ ...に限って it is best to ...

kago n かご・籠 basket, (bird) cage: tori-kago 鳥かご birdcage

kagō n カイ ごう = kagimashō´ 嗅ぎましょう (let's smell it!)

kagu v 嗅ぐ = kagimásu 嗅ぎます (smells it)

kágu n 家具 furniture

kagú-ya n 家具屋 furniture store

kágura n 神楽 Shinto music and dances

kái n カイ・貝 shellfish: kai-gara 貝殻 shell (of shellfish)

... kai? interj ...かい? [INFORMAL] = desu ka? ですか? (yes-or-no question)

...-kái suffix ...階 (counts floors/stories)

...-kái suffix ...回 (counts times/occasions)

...-kai suffix ...会 society, association, club; social gathering, party, meeting: (o-)tanjō´bi-kai (お)誕生日会 birthday party: nomi-kai 飲み会 drinking party: en-kai 宴会 party, banquet

...-kai suffix ...海 (name of) sea: Karibu-kai カリブ海 Caribbean Sea: Nihon-kai 日本海 Japan Sea

kaibatsu n 海抜 above sea level

kaibō n 解剖 autopsy: kaibō-gaku 解剖学 anatomy

kaibutsu n 怪物 monster (= bake-móno 化け物, obáke お化け, mónsutā モンスター)

kaichō n 会長 chairperson

kaichū (no) adj 懐中(の) pocket(able): kaichū-déntō 懐中電灯 flashlight

kaichū (de/no) adv, adj 海中(で/の) in the sea, under the sea

kaichū n 回虫 (intestinal) worms

kaida v 嗅いだ = kagimáshita 嗅ぎました (smelled)

kaidan n 階段 stairs, stairway

kaidan n 会談 [BOOKISH] (official) meeting: shunō-kaidan 首脳会談 summit (= samitto サミット)

kaidan n 怪談 ghost story, scary story

kaidame n 買いだめ hoarding: ~ shimásu 買いだめします hoards (= kaioki 買い置き)

kaide v 嗅いで → kagimásu 嗅ぎます

kaidō n 会堂 an auditorium

kaidō n 街道 main road/avenue

kaien n 開演 starting a performance: kaien-chū 開演中 during the performance; kaien-jíkan 開演時間 curtain time: ~ shimásu 開演します starts (performance)

kaifuku n 回復 recovery, recuperation: ~ shimásu 回復します recovers, recuperates

káiga n 絵画 painting, picture

káigai n 海外 overseas, abroad: kaigai-ryokō 海外旅行 overseas travel

kaigan n 海岸 seashore, coast, beach: kaigan-sen 海岸線 shoreline, coastline

kai-gara n 貝殻 shell (of shellfish)

káigi n 会議 meeting, conference (= míitingu ミーティング): kaigi-chū 会議中 in conference, in a meeting; kaigí-shitsu 会議室 conference room

káigun n 海軍 navy: kaigun-kichi 海軍基地 navy base

kaigyō n 開業 opening a business: ~ shimásu 開業します opens a business

kaihatsu n 開発 development: ~ shimásu 開発します develops kenkyū-kaihatsu n 研究開発 research and development, R&D

kalheilai n 海兵隊 Marine Corps

kaihi n 会費 membership fee, dues: nen-kaihi 年会費 annual membership fee

kaihō n 解放 liberation: ~ shimásu 解放します liberates

kaihō n 開放 open: ~ shimásu 開放します opens, leaves open (windows, doors, etc.)

kai-in n 会員 member: kaiin-sei (no) 会員制(の) membership system, members-only

kaijō n 開場 opening (of place/event): ~

shimásu 開場します opens; **kaijō-jíkan** 開場時間 opening time

kaijō n 会場 hall

kaijō (de/no) adv, adj 海上(で/の) on the sea (surface)

kaijū n 怪獣 monster

kaika n 開花 flowering; ~ **shimásu** 開花します blooms

kaika n 階下 downstairs

kaikaku n 改革 [BOOKISH] reformation, reinvention

kaikan n 会館 a public hall, a building

kaikan n 開館 [BOOKISH] opening (a hall): ~ **shimásu** 開館します opens (a hall)

kaikan n 快感 [BOOKISH] pleasure, pleasant feeling

kaikei n 会計 **1. o-kaikei** お会計 accounts; bill, check (= **o-kanjō** お勘定): **o-kaikei/o-kanjō onegai shimásu** お会計/お勘定お願いします Check please **2.** accountant (= **kaikei-gákari** 会計係, **kaikéi-shi** 会計士)

kaiken n 会見 [BOOKISH] interview: **kisha-kaiken** 記者会見 press conference

kaiketsu n 解決 solution, settlement; ~ **shimásu** 解決します solves, settles

kaiki n 回帰 [BOOKISH] revolution, recurrence, retouring: **kita (minami)-kaiki-sen** 北(南)回帰線 the Tropic of Cancer (Capricorn): ~ **shimásu** 回帰します returns

kaíko n 解雇 [BOOKISH] dismissal (from employment), discharge: ~ **shimásu** 解雇します dismisses, discharges, fires, disemploys

káiko n 蚕 (**o-káiko** お蚕) silkworm

kaikyaku n 開脚 legs spread (exercise): ~ **shimásu** 開脚します has one's legs spread, spreads one's legs wide apart

kaikyo n 快挙 remarkable/wonderful achievement, great accomplishment

kaikyō n 海峡 strait(s)

kaikyō n 回教 Islam (= **Isuramu-kyō** イスラム教)

kaikyū n 階級 class, rank: **chūryū-kaikyū** 中流階級 the middle class

kaimásu, kau v 買います, 買う buys

kaimásu, káu v 飼います, 飼う raises, keeps (pets, farm animals, etc.)

kaimen n 海綿 sponge

kai-mono n 買い物 shopping

kaioki n 買い置き **1.** things bought in for the future, hoarded things **2.** hoarding (= **kaidame** 買いだめ); ~ **shimásu** 買い置きします hoards

kaiō-sei n 海王星 Neptune

kairaku n 快楽 pleasure: **kairaku-shugi-sha** 快楽主義者 an Epicurean

kairi n 解離 [BOOKISH] disaggregation, dissociation; ~ **shimásu** 解離します disassociate, dissociates

kairi n 海里 nautical mile

kairyō n 改良 [BOOKISH] improvement, modification: ~ **shimásu** 改良します improves, modifies

kairyū n 海流 ocean current

kaisai n 開催 [BOOKISH] holding, opening (an event); ~ **shimásu** 開催します holds, opens

kaisan shimásu (suru) v 解散します (する) breaks up, disperses

kaisatsu n 改札 ticket examining: **kaisatsú-guchi** 改札口 (ticket) wicket

kaisei n 改正 [BOOKISH] revision

kaisei n 快晴 clear and fine weather

kaiseki (ryōri) n 懐石(料理) an assortment of elegant Japanese foods, Japanese foods in season

kaisetsu n 解説 explanation, comment: ~ **shimásu** 解説します explains, comments; **nyū'su ~** ニュース解説 news commentary

kaisétsu-sha n 解説者 commentator

kaisha n 会社 company, business concern; "the office" (= **kígyō** 企業): **kaishá-in** 会社員 company employee (= **sha-in** 社員, **sararii-man** サラリーマン)

káishaku n 解釈 [BOOKISH] interpretation, explanation, exposition: ~ **shimásu** 解釈します construes, interprets, explains, expounds

kaisho n 楷書 block-style letter (of Japanese): **kaisho-tai** 楷書体 printed style/square of writing Chinese characters

kaisō n 海藻・海草 seaweed

kaisō n 回送 (**kaisō-chū** 回送中) **1.** forwarding (mail matter, letter, etc.) **2.** deadhead (an empty car, etc.):

~ shimásu 回送します forwards, deadheads; **kaisó-sha** 回送車 a car out of service, an off-duty taxi; **kaisō-ressha** 回送列車 deadhead train

kaisō *n* 回想: recollection: **~ shimásu** 回想します recollects

kaisō shiin *n* 回想シーン retrospective scene:

kaisū *n* 回数 the number of times
kaisū´-ken *n* 回数券 ticket book (*for commuting*), coupon ticket

kaisui *n* 海水 seawater
kaisui-yoku *n* 海水浴 sea bathing: **~ o shimásu** 海水浴をします has a bath in the sea

kai-te *n* 買い手 buyer

kaite *v* 欠いて → **kakimásu** 欠きます
káite *v* 書いて → **kakimásu** 書きます

kaitei *n* 改訂 revision (*of documents, books, etc.*): **kaitei-ban** 改訂版 revised version: **~ shimásu** 改訂します revises

kaitei *n* 海底 bottom of the sea

kaiteki (na) *adj* 快適(な) comfortable, peasant

kaiten *n* 回転 revolution, rotation: **~ shimásu** 回転します revolves, rotates

kaiten *n* 開店 opening a shop (*for the first time or for the day*): **~ shimásu** 開店します opens shop/business

kaitō *n* 解答 answer: **~ shimásu** 解答します answers it

kaitō *n* 回答 reply: **~ shimásu** 回答します replies it

kai-torimásu, kai-tóru *v* 買い取ります, 買い取る buys up

kaiun *n* 開運 fotune, good-luck

kaiwa *n* 会話 conversation: **~ shimásu** 会話します has a conversation

kaizen *n* 改善 [BOOKISH] improvement: **~ shimásu** 改善します improves

kaizoku *n* 海賊 pirate: **kaizoku-ban** 海賊版 pirated edition

káji *n* 火事 a fire (*accidental*): **~ ga okorimásu** 火事が起こります Fire breaks out.: **Káji da!** 火事だ! Fire!

káji *n* 舵 helm: **~ o torimásu** 舵をとります takes the helm, steers

káji *n* 家事 housework: **kaji-tetsudai** 家事手伝い housework helper

kájiki *n* カジキ swordfish

kajiránai *v* かじらない = **kajirimásen** かじりません (not gnaw)

kajirimásu, kajíru *v* かじります, かじる gnaws, nibbles

kajitte *v* かじって → **kajirimásu** かじります

kajō *n* 過剰 glut, surplus, excess: **kajō (no)** 過剰(の) superfluous, surplus: **kajō (ni)** 過剰(に) excessively: **kajō-hannō** 過剰反応 overreaction, overresponse

kakaemásu, kakaéru *v* 抱えます, 抱える **1.** holds in one's arms: **atama o ~ 頭** 頭を抱えます tears one's hair out **2.** keeps, retains, has; employs **3.** has family to support of (*child(ren), sick person(s), etc.*) **4.** has a problem(s): **shakkin o kakaete imásu** 借金を抱えています has debts: **shigoto o kakaete imásu** 仕事を抱えています has works

kakaku *n* 価格 price (= **nedan** 値段): **kakaku-kyōsō** 価格競争 price competition

kakanai *v* 欠かない = **kakimásen** 欠きません (not lack)

kakánai *v* 書かない = **kakimásen** 書きません (not write)

kakan (ni) *adv* 果敢(に) boldly, decisively: **ni tatakaimásu** 果敢に戦います fights with valor

kakaránai *v* 掛からない = **kakari-másen** 掛かりません (not hang)

kákari *n* 係 = **kakarí-in** 係員 attendant (*in charge*)

kakarimásu, kakáru *v* 掛かります, 掛かる **1.** it hangs **2.** it takes, requires **3.** it weighs **4.** it begins, (*engine*) starts

kakarimásu, kakáru *v* 架かります, 架かる is built

kakashi *n* カカシ・案山子 scarecrow

kakato *n* 踵 heel: **~ no takai kutsu** 踵の高い靴 high-heeled shoes (= **haihiiru** ハイヒール)

kakátta *v* 掛かった = **kakarimáshita** 掛かりました (it hung; it took; required; it weighed; it began; (*engine*) started)

kakátte *v* 掛かって → **kakarimásu** 掛かります

kake *n* 欠け lacking, a lack, wane

kaké *n* 掛け credit

kaké *n* 賭け bet, wager: **kaké-ya** 賭け屋 bookie

káke *v* 書け [IMPERATIVE] (write it!) → **kakimásu** 書きます

kake-ashi *n* 駆け足 running

kakéba *v* 欠けば (if it lacks) → **kakimásu** 欠きます

kákeba *v* 書けば (if one writes) → **kakimásu** 書きます

kake-búton *n* 掛け布団 overquilt, top quilt

kakegoe *n* 掛け声 shout of encouragement: **~ o kakemásu** 掛け声をかけます shouts encouragement

kaké (goto) *n* 賭け（事）gambling; a bet: **~ (o shi)másu** 賭（をし）ます bets, makes a bet

kakehiki *n* 駆け引き tactics, bargaining: **~ ga umai** 駆け引きが上手い is good at bargaining

kakei *n* 家計 household budget: **kakei-bo** 家計簿 housekeeping book: **o sasaemásu** 家計を支えます supports a household

kakei *n* 家系 one's family line: **kakei-zu** 家系図 a family tree (= keizu 系図)

kakéji *n* 掛け字 = **kaké-jiku** 掛け軸, **kaké-mono** 掛け物 scroll (*hanging*)

kakemásu, kakéru *v* 欠けます, 掛ける hangs it; multiplies; begins it: ... **ni denwa o ~** ...に電話を掛けます telephones; **énjin o ~** エンジンを掛けます starts (engine)

kakemásu, kakéru *v* 欠けます, かける・欠ける lacks it, needs

kakemásu, kakéru *v* 賭けます, 賭ける bets

kakemásu, kakéru *v* 駆けます・駆ける runs, gallops (*human, animal*)

kakemásu, kakéru *v* 書けます, 書ける can write

kaké-mono *n* 掛け物 scroll (*hanging*) (= **kaké-jiku** 掛け軸)

kakenai *v* 欠けない = **kakemásen** 欠けません (not lack it)

kakenai *v* 掛けない = **kakemásen** 掛けません (not hang)

kakenai *v* 賭けない = **kakemásen** 賭けません (not bet)

kakénai *v* 駆けない = **kakemásen** 駆け

ません (not run)

kakénai *v* 書けない = **kakemásen** 書けません (cannot write)

kakera *n* カケラ・欠片 fragment

kake(ra)remásu, kake(ra)reru *v* 掛け（ら）れます, 掛け（ら）れる can hang it, can telephone

kakeréba *v* 欠ければ (if one lacks it) → **kakemásu** 欠けます

kakéreba *v* 掛ければ (if one hangs) → **kakemásu** 掛けます

kakéreba *v* 賭ければ (if one bets) → **kakemásu** 賭けます

kakéreba *v* 駆ければ (if one runs) → **kakemásu** 駆けます

kakéreba *v* 書ければ (if one can write) → **kakemásu** 書けます

kaketa *v* 欠けた = **kakemáshita** 欠けました (lacked it)

káketa *v* 掛けた = **kakemáshita** 掛けました (hung)

káketa *v* 賭けた = **kakemáshita** 賭けました (bet)

káketa *v* 駆けた = **kakemáshita** 駆けました (ran)

káketa *v* 書けた = **kakemáshita** 書けました (was able to write)

kakete *v* 欠けて → **kakemásu** 欠けます

kákete *v* 掛けて・賭けて・駆けて → **kakemásu** 掛けます・賭けます・駆けます

kákete *v* かけて: **... ni kákete** ...にかけて (*extending*) through, with respect to, as regards

kake-uri *n* 掛け売り credit sales (= **uri-kake** 売り掛け)

kakeyō´ *v* 掛けよう = **kakemashō** 掛けましょう (let's hang it!)

kaké-zan *n* 掛け算 multiplication

kaki *n* カキ・柿 (*fruits*) persimmon

kaki *n* カキ・牡蠣 oyster

káki *n* 下記 the following: **~ no tōri** 下記の通り as follows, as below

káki *n* 花器 flower vase

káki *n* 夏期 summer (*period/term*): **kaki-kyūkā** 夏季休暇 summer holiday: **kaki-kōshū** 夏季講習 summer school

kaki *n* 火気 [BOOKISH] fire, flame: **Kaki-genkin** 火気厳禁 No Fire, Flammables

kakiage *n* かき揚げ a tangle of tidbits fried as *tempura*, fritters

kaki-atsumemásu, kaki-atsuméru *v* かき集めます, かき集める rakes (them up)

kaki-iremásu, kaki-iréru *v* 書き入れます, 書き入れる fills in (*information*)

kaki-kaemásu, kaki-káeru *v* 書き換えます, 書き換える rewrites

kaki-kata *n* 書き方 way of writing; spelling

kakimásu, káku *v* 欠きます, 欠く it lacks, it is lacking/wanting

kakimásu, káku *v* 書きます, 書く writes

kakimásu, káku *v* 描きます, 描く paints, draws: **e o ~** 絵を描きます draws a picture (= **egakimásu** 描きます)

kakimásu, káku *v* 掻きます, 掻く scratches

kaki-mawashimásu, kaki-mawasu *v* かき回します, かき回す stirs

kaki-naoshimásu, kaki-naósu *v* 書き直します, 書き直す rewrites

kakíne *n* かき根・垣根 fence

kakitome (yūbin) *n* 書留 (郵便) registered mail

kakitori *n* 書き取り dictation: **kakítorimásu** 書き取ります dictates

kakki *n* 活気 liveliness, activity

kakko *n* 括弧 parenthesis, square bracket, brace

kakkō *n* **1.** 格好 shape, form, appearance: **~ ga íi** 格好がいい = **kakkō ii** かっこいい shapely, cool, stylish; **~ ga waruí** 格好が悪い = **kakko warui** かっこ悪い unsuitable **2. kakkō (na/no)** 格好 (な/の) suitable, moderate, reasonable (*price*)

kákkō *n* カッコウ cuckoo

káko *n* 過去 the past
  kako-kei *n* 過去形 the past tense
  kako-kanryō *n* 過去完了 the past perfect: **kako kanryō-kei** 過去完了形 the past perfect tense

kakō *n* 加工 processing (*industrially treating*): **~ shimásu** 加工します processes

kakō *n* 下降 [BOOKISH] descent: **~ shimásu** 下降します descends, declines

kakō *n* 河口 estuary

kakō *n* 火口 crater (= **kurḗtā** クレーター)

kakō *v* 書こう = **kakimashō** 書きましょう (let's write it!)

kakō´-gan *n* 花崗岩 granite

kakoku (na) *adj* 過酷 (な) [BOOKISH] too severe, harsh

...-kákoku *suffix* ...か国・ヶ国・カ国 (*counts countries*)

kakomi *n* 囲み an enclosure, a box: **kakomi-kiji** 囲み記事 column, boxed article(s) (= **koramu** コラム)

kakomimásu, kakomu *v* 囲みます, 囲む surrounds (= **tori-kakomimásu** 取り囲みます)

kakon *n* 禍根 the source of trouble, the root of evil: **~ o nokoshimásu** 禍根を残します creates potential problem(s) in the future

káku *n* 角 corner: **san-kaku(kei)/san-kakkei** 三角 (形) triangle: **shikakú(kei) /shikakkei** 四角 (形) square

káku (do) *n* 角 (度) angle (= **anguru** アングル): **chok-kaku** 直角 right angle: **eikakú** 鋭角 acute angle

káku *n* 核 core, heart, stone: **chū-kaku** 中核 (*central*) core
  kaku-heiki *n* 核兵器 nuclear weapon
  káku (no) *n* 核 (の) nucleus, nuclear: **genshi-kaku** 原子核 atomic nucleus

káku *v* 欠く = **kakimásu** 欠きます (it lacks)

káku *v* 書く = **kakimásu** 書きます (writes)

káku *v* 描く = **kakimásu** 描きます (draws)

káku *v* 掻く = **kakimásu** 掻きます (scratches)

káku(-) *prefix* 各... each, every
  kakú-eki *n* 各駅 every station: **kakuekí-téisha/ressha** 各駅停車/列車 local train (*which stops at every station*)
  kaku-ron *n* 各論 each detail: **~ ni hairimásu** 各論に入ります gets down into specifics

...káku *suffix* ... 覚 sense (*five senses*): **shi-kaku** 視覚 sense of sight: **chō-kaku** 聴覚 sense of hearing: **mi-kaku** 味覚 sense of taste: **shū-kaku** 嗅覚 sense of smell: **shok-kaku** 触覚 sense of touch

kakū (no) adj 架空(の) imaginary:
~ no jinbutsu 架空の人物 fictional
character

kakudai n 拡大 enlargement: ~ shimásu
拡大します enlarges

kakudan (ni/no) adv, adj 格段(に/の)
remarkably, remarkable: kakudan
no shinpo 格段の進歩 remarkable
progress

kakugen n 格言 maxim, wise saying

kakugo n 覚悟 resolution, resignation,
premeditation: ~ shimásu 覚悟します,
~ o kimemásu 覚悟を決めます is
resolved (to do), is prepared for, is
resigned to

kakuheki n 隔壁 [BOOKISH] division
wall, partition

kakuho n 確保 securement, saving: ~
shimásu 確保します secures, saves

kakujitsu n 確実 certainly kakujitsu
(na) 確実(な) certain, reliable,
authentic (= tashika na 確かな)

kakumaimasu, kakumau v 匿います,
匿う harbors, shelters: hannin o ~ 犯人
を匿います harbors a criminal

kakumaku n 角膜 cornea

kakumaku n 隔膜 diaphragm

kakumei n 革命 revolution (political,
etc.)

kakunin n 確認 confirmation: ~
shimásu 確認します confirms

kakuran n かく乱 disturbance: ~
shimásu かく乱します disturbs

kakurega n 隠れ家 asylum, shelter,
refuge

kakuremásu, kakuréru v 隠れます, 隠
れる hides: kakurenbo, kakurenbō か
くれんぼ, 隠れん坊 hide-and-seek

kakuri n 隔離 [BOOKISH] isolation: ~
shimásu 隔離します isolates
kakuri-byō'tō´ 隔離病棟 isolation ward

kakuritsu n 確立 establishment: ~
shimásu 確立します establishes

kakuritsu n 確率 probability: kōsui-
kakuritsu 降水確率 probability of rain

kakusei n 覚醒 [BOOKISH] awakening,
emergence, arousal: ~ shimásu 覚醒し
ます awakes
kakusei-zai n 覚醒剤 stimulant drug

kakuséi-ki n 拡声器 loudspeaker

kakushimásu, kakúsú v 隠します, 隠
す hides (something)

kakushin n 核心 core, heart (= káku
核): ~ ni furemásu 核心に触れます
touches the core of…

kakutei n 確定 determination, fixedness,
settlement: ~ shimásu 確定します
determines, fixes, settles
kakutei-shinkoku 確定申告 final
income tax return

kákuteru n カクテル cocktail: kaku-
teru-bā カクテルバー cocktail bar:
kakuteru-pātii カクテルパーティ
cocktail party

kakutō n 格闘 fight: ~ shimásu 格闘し
ます fights
kakutō-gi n 格闘技 martial art

kakutō n 確答 [BOOKISH] definite
answer: ~ shimásu 確答します
answers definitely

kakutoku n 獲得 [BOOKISH] acquisition,
gain: ~ shimásu 獲得します acquires,
gains; winning (medal/trophy)

kakuyasu n 格安 bargain, discounted:
kakuyasu-kōkúken 格安航空券
discounted airline ticket

kakuzai n 角材 block of wood

kakuzuke n 格付け rating, grading: ~
shimásu 格付けします rates, grades

kakyū (no) adj 下級(の) low-class:
kakyūsei 下級生 underclassman

kamá n かま・窯 oven, kiln

kamá n かま・釜 (Japanese style)
kettle, iron pot, cauldron, boiler
kama-meshi n 釜飯 (cooked) rice
(with chicken, crab, or shrimp) served
in a clay pot

káma n 鎌 sickle

kamaboko n かまぼこ・カマボコ
steamed fish cake

kamachí n 框 frame, rail

kamachi n カマチ cachema

kamado n かまど (Japanese
traditional) kitchen range, stove; oven

kamaimasén, kamawánai v 構いませ
ん, 構わない it makes no difference;
never mind; not to bother, it's o.k.

kamakiri n カマキリ praying mantis

kamánai v 噛まない = kamimasén 噛
みません (not chew/bite)

kamasú _v_ カマス barracuda, saury-pike

kamé _n_ 瓶 jar (_with large mouth_)

káme _n_ カメ・亀 tortoise, turtle

káme _v_ 噛め [IMPERATIVE] (chew!) → **kamimásu** 噛みます

kámeba _v_ 噛めば (if one chews it) → **kamimásu** 噛みます

kamei _n_ 仮名žを an assumed name; a temporary/tentative name

kamei _n_ 加盟 affiliation: ~ **shimásu** 加盟します affiliates

kamei _n_ 家名 family name

kamemásu, kaméru _v_ 噛めます, 噛める can chew/bite

kamen _n_ 仮面 mask (= **másuku** マスク)

kaménai _v_ 噛めない = **kamemasén** 噛めません (cannot chew/bite)

kámera _n_ カメラ camera: **dejitaru-kamera** デジタルカメラ digital camera: **bideo-kamera** ビデオカメラ video camera

kaméreba _v_ 噛めれば (if one can chew/bite) → **kamemásu** 噛めます

kamí _n_ 紙 paper
  kami-básami _n_ 紙ばさみ file folder; file; paperclip
  kami-búkuro _n_ 紙袋 paper bag
  kami-hikōki _n_ 紙飛行機 paper airplane
  kami-kúzu _n_ 紙くず wastepaper
  kami-yásuri _n_ 紙やすり sandpaper

kámi _n_ 神 **1.** God, gods (= **kámi-sama** 神様) **2.** divinity (= **shinsei** 神性)
  kami-dana _n_ 神棚 household altar (_Shinto_)
  kámi-sama _n_ 神様 God, gods, Dear Lord

kamimásu, kamu _v_ かみます, かむ: **hana o ~** 鼻をかみます blows one's nose

kamimásu, kámu _v_ 噛みます, 噛む chews, bites: **gamu o ~** ガムを噛みます chews gum

kaminári _n_ かみなり・カミナリ・雷 thunder, thunderstorm: **~ ga narimásu** 雷が鳴ります it thunders

kamí (no ke) _n_ 髪(の毛) hair (_on head_): **~ (no ke) o araimásu** 髪(の毛)を洗います shampoos

kami-san _n_ かみさん [INFORMAL] my wife

kamisóri _n_ 剃刀 razor: **~ no ha** 剃刀の刃 razor blade

kami-tsukimásu, kami-tsuku _v_ 噛みつきます, 噛みつく bites

kámo _n_ カモ・鴨 wild duck

kámo _n_ かも・カモ dupe, sucker

kamó´ _v_ 噛もう = **kamimashō** 噛みましょう (let's chew/bite it!)

kamoku _n_ 科目 subject, course (_in school_): **hisshū-kamoku** 必修科目 required course/subject

Kamome _n_ カモメ・鴎 seagull

... kámo (shiremasén) _suffix_, _v_ ...かも(しれません) = **kámo shirenai** かもしれない maybe ..., perhaps ...

kamu _v_ かむ = **kamimásu** かみます (blows one's nose)

kámu _v_ 噛む = **kamimásu** 噛みます (chews, bites)

kán _n_ 缶 can → **kan-zúmé (no ...)** 缶詰(の...)
  kan-biiru 缶ビール canned beer: kan-kírí 缶切り can opener

kán _n_ 燗 (**o-kan** お燗) heating rice wine: **(o-)kan o tsukémasu/shimásu** (お)燗をつけます/します warms the saké

kán _n_ 管 tube, pipe, duct: **suidō-kan** 水道管 water pipe: **kek-kan** 血管 blood vessel

kán _n_ 巻 volume (_books, tapes_): **(dai) ik-kan** (第)一巻 vol. 1

...´- kan _suffix_ ...間 for the interval of; between

...´- kan _suffix_ ...感 feeling, sense: **go-kan** 五感 five senses: **dai-rok-kan** 第六感 sixth sense: **shok-kan** 触感 tactile (_sensation_): **shok-kan** 食感 food texture

kana _n_ かな kana (_Japanese syllabic writing_) → **furi-gana** ふりがな・フリガナ

...ka na/ne _interj_ ...かな/かね I wonder/whether (= **deshō ka** でしょうか)

Kánada _n_ カナダ Canada
  Kanadá-jin _n_ カナダ人 a Canadian

kánai _n_ 家内 **1.** my wife **2.** one's family: **kanai-anzen** 家内安全 well-being/safety of one's family: **kanai-kōgyō** 家内工業 cottage industry

kanaimásu, kanáu *v* 適います、適
　う accords/agrees (*with*): **dōri ni ~** 道
　理にかないます it stands to reason;
　mokuteki ni ~ 目的にかないます it
　serves the purpose
kanaimásu, kanáu *v* 敵います、敵う is
　a match (*for*), matches, is equal (*to*)
kanaimásu, kanáu *v* 叶います、叶う
　(= **dekimásu** できます) is accom-
　plished, attained, achieved, realized:
　yume/negai ga ~ 夢/願いが叶います
　a dream/wish comes true
kanamono *n* 金物 hardware: **kanamo-
　no-ya** 金物屋 hardware store
kanarazu *adv* 必ず for sure; necessity;
　inevitably
kánari *adv* かなり fairly, rather
kanaria *n* カナリア canary
kanashii *adj* 悲しい sad
kanashimi *n* 悲しみ sadness·
kanashimimásu, kanashimu *v* 悲し
　みます、悲しむ to be sad
kanazuchi *n* かなづち・カナヅチ・
　金槌 **1.** hammer **2.** a person who can-
　not swim
kanban *n* 看板 **1.** signboard, sign
　2. (*diner, pub*) closing time
　kanban-musume *n* 看板娘 beautiful
　lady who attracts customers/customers
　kanban-yakusha *n* 看板役者 star actor
kanbasu *n* カンバス canvas (= **kyán-
　basu** キャンバス)
kanbatsu *n* かんばつ・干ばつ drought
　(= **hideri** ひでり・日照り)
kanben *interj* 勘弁: **~ shitekudasai** 勘弁
　して下さい Please give me a break
kanben (na) *n, adj* 簡便(な) conven-
　ience, convenient, simple and easy
kanbi *n* 完備 full equipment: **~ shitei-
　másu** 完備しています is fully equipped
kanbi (na) *adj* 甘美(な) sweet,
　luscious, dulcet: **~ na merodii** 甘美な
　メロディー dulcet melody
kanbu *n* 患部 [BOOKISH] diseased part,
　affected area
kanbu *n* 幹部 [BOOKISH] executive
kanbun *n* 漢文 Chinese classics
kanbutsu *n* 乾物 dry food
kanbō *n* 感冒 [BOOKISH] common cold:
　ryūkōsei-kanbō 流行性感冒 influenza

　(= **infuruénza** インフルエンザ)
kanbō *n* 官房 [BOOKISH] Secretariat:
　naikaku kanbō-chōkan 内閣官房長官
　Chief Cabinet Secretary
kanbō *n* 監房 [BOOKISH] ward, jail cell
kanbojia *n* カンボジア Cambodia
　Kanbojia-go *n* カンボジア語
　Cambodian (*language*)
　Kanbojia-jin *n* カンボジア人 a
　Cambodian
kanboku *n* 潅[灌]木 bush
kanbotsu *n* 陥没 [BOOKISH] cave-in,
　subsidence, sinking: **~ shimásu** 陥没し
　ます subsides, caves
kanbyō *n* 看病 nursing: **~ shimásu** 看病
　します nurses
kanchi *n* 感知 appreciation, sense: **~
　shimásu** 感知します senses
kanchi *n* 完治 complete cure: **~
　shimásu** 完治します cures completely
kanchō *n* 浣腸 enema
kánchō *n* 艦長 captain (*of warship*)
kánchō *n* 官庁 government office
kanchō *n* 干潮 ebb, low tide
kandai (na) *adj* 寛大(な) generous,
　lenient: **~ na shochi** 寛大な処置 lenient
　judgment: **~ na hito** 寛大な人 broad-
　minded person
kandán-kei *n* 寒暖計 (*room*) thermo-
　meter
kande *v* かんで → (**hana o**) **kami-
　másu** (鼻を)かみます (blows nose)
kánde *v* 噛んで → **kamimásu** 噛みま
　す (chews, bites)
kandō *n* 感動 (strong) emotion, (deep)
　feeling: **~ shimásu** 感動します is
　impressed
kane *n* 金 **1.** money (= **o-kane** お金)
　2. metal (= **kinzoku** 金属)
kane *n* 鐘 large bell (*of church, temple,
　etc.*): **joya no ~** 除夜の鐘 the bells on
　New Year's Eve
… ka ne *interj* …かね [INFORMAL]
　(*mostly male*) = **… ka ne/na** …かね/か
　な (I wonder/whether)
kane-bako *n* 金箱 **1.** cashbox, money
　box (= **zeni-bako** 銭箱) **2.** patron, gold
　mine, moneymaker, cash cow
　(= **doru-bako** ドル箱)
kanemásu, kanéru *v* 兼ねます、

兼ねる combines, unites; dually/ concurrently serves as

kanemóchí (no) adj 金持ち（の）rich (wealthy)

kan'en n 肝炎 hepatitis

kānēshon n カーネーション carnation(s)

kanetsu 加熱 heat, heating: ~ **shimásu** 加熱します heats
kanetsu-ki 加熱器 heater

kangáe n 考え thought, idea, opinion

kangaemásu, kangáeru v 考えます, 考える thinks, considers

kangaeraremásu, kangaeraréru v 考えられます, 考えられる can think; it is thought

kangei n 歓迎 welcome (= **kantai** 歓待): ~ **shimásu** 歓迎します welcomes
kangei-kai n 歓迎会 reception (welcome party)

kangeki n 感激 (strong) emotion (feeling): ~ **shimásu** 感激します is touched; (= **kandō** 感動)

kango n 漢語 Chinese word/vocabulary (in Japanese)

kángo n 看護 nursing (a patient): ~ **shimásu** 看護します nurses
kangó-shi n 看護師 a nurse (= **kangó-fu** 看護婦)

kani n カニ・蟹 crab

kānibaru n カーニバル carnival

kanja n 患者 (medical) patient

kanji n 漢字 a Chinese character (symbol), kanji

kanji n 感じ feeling (= **kankaku** 感覚): **konna (sonna/anna) -kanji (de/no)** こんな（そんな/あんな）感じ（で/の）like this (that)

kan-jimásu, kan-jiru v 感じます, 感じる feels

kanjō n 感情 emotion

kanjō n 環状 [BOOKISH] loop (shape): **kanjō (no)** 環状（の）ring-shaped, circular; **kanjō-sen** 環状線 loop/belt line

kanjō´ n 勘定 **o-kanjó** お勘定 (= **o-kaikei** お会計) bill, check, account: **o-kanjō onegai shimásu** お勘定お願いします Check please
kanjō-gákari 勘定係 cashier

kankaku n 感覚 sense, sensibility, feeling, sensation

kankaku n 間隔 space, interval (of time, space)

kankei n 関係 connection, relationship, interest, concern, relevance: **... no kankéi-sha** ...の関係者 the people/ authorities concerned with ...

kánki n 換気 ventilation: **kankí-sen** 換気扇 ventilator: **kanki-só´chi** 換気装置 ventilation system

kankō n 観光 sightseeing, tour: **kankō-básu** 観光バス sightseeing bus
kankó´-kyaku n 観光客 tourist, sightseer

Kánkoku n 韓国 South Korea
Kankoku-go n 韓国語 Korean (language)
Kankokú-jin n 韓国人 a Korean

kankyaku n 観客 audience, spectator

kankyō n 環境 environment: **kankyō-osen** 環境汚染 environmental pollution; **kankyō-hogo** 環境保護 environmental protection

Kankyō-shō n 環境省 Ministry of the Environment (MOE)

kanmatsu n 巻末 end of a book

kanmi n 甘味 sweetness: **kanmi-ryó** 甘味料 sweetening

kanna n かんな・カンナ plane (tool)

kannai n 館内 inside the building: **kannai-hōsō** 館内放送 announcements in the building: **kannai-tsuā** 館内ツアー guided tour of the building

kannen n 観念 **1.** idea (Platonism) (= **idea** イデア) **2.** concept, conception **3.** giving up **4.** meditation (Buddhism): ~ **shimásu** 観念します gives up, meditates

kannin n 堪忍 [BOOKISH] patience: ~ **shimásu** 堪忍します is patient and forgives; ~ **shitekudasai** 堪忍して下さい Please forgive me.

kanningu n カンニング (during examination, test, etc.) cheating: ~ **shimásu** カンニングします cheats
kanningu-pēpā n カンニングペーパー crib note

kannō n 感応 [BOOKISH] response, participation: ~ **shimásu** 感応します sympathizes

kannō teki (na) adj 官能的（な） sensual, erotic

kannúki n かんぬき bolt (of door)

kánnushi n 神主 priest (Shinto)

káno-jo pron 彼女 she/her; girlfriend, mistress

kanō (na) adj 可能(な) possible: **kanō-sei** 可能性 possibility

kanpa n カンパ fund-raising campaign (comes from the Russian "kampaniya"): **~ shimásu** カンパします contributes to the fundraising campaign

kanpai n 乾杯 a toast, "bottoms up": **~ shimásu** 乾杯します toasts: **Kanpai!** 乾杯 Cheers!

kanpai n 完敗 complete defeat: **~ shimásu** 完敗します is completely beaten

kanpán n 甲板 deck (of ship)

kanpan n 乾パン hardtack

kanpeki (na) adj 完璧(な) perfectness, perfect

kanpi n 官費 government expense, government expenditure

kanpō n 官報 gazette

kanpō (yaku) n 漢方(薬) Chinese medicine

kanpu n 還付 refund: **kanpu-kin** 還付金 tax refund

kanpū n 寒風 cold wind

kanpū n 完封 shut-out: **kanpū-jiai** 完封試合 shutout game

kanpuku n 感服 → **kanshin** 関心

kanpyṓ n カンピョウ dried gourd strips, dried ground shavings

kanrán-seki n 観覧席 grandstand (seats)

kanren n 関連 relevance (= **kankei** 関係): **(… ni) ~ shimásu** (…に)関連します is relevant (to), is connected (with)

kánri n 管理 control (= **kontorōru** コントロール)

kanri-nin n 管理人 custodian, janitor, manager, landlord (rental manager)

kanri-sha n 管理者 administrator

kanroku n 貫禄 presence (= **igen** 威厳): **~ ga arimásu** 貫禄があります has a presence

kansai-chihō n 関西地方 The Kansai area of Japan (Kyoto, Osaka, Kobe, Nara, Shiga, Hyogo, Wakayama prefecture etc.)

kansatsu n 観察 watching, observation

kansatsú-sha n 観察者 observer

kansatsu n 監察 [BOOKISH] inspection

kansatsú-kan n 監察官 inspector

kansatsu n 鑑札 [BOOKISH] license (tag)

kansatsu shimásu (suru) v 観察します(する) observes, watches

kansatsu shimásu (suru) v 監察します(する) inspects

kansei n 完成 completion, perfection: **~ shimásu** 完成します completes, perfects

kansetsu n 関節 joint (of two bones): **(shu)shi-kansetsu** (手)指関節 knuckle: **soku-kansetsu** 足関節 ankle (= **ashikubi** 足首): **kansetsu-en** 関節炎 arthritis

kansetsu (no) adj 間接(の) indirect: **kansetsu-kisu** 間接キス indirect kiss

kansetsu(-teki) ni adj 間接(的)に indirectly

kánsha n 感謝 thanks, gratitude: **~ shimásu** 感謝します appreciates, thanks

kansha-sai n 感謝祭 Thanksgiving

kan-shimásu (-súru) v 関します(する) relates (to), concerns, is connected (with): **… ni kánshite** …に関して concerning, with respect to …

kanshin n 関心 concern, interest (= **kyōmi** 興味): **~ ga arimásu** 関心があります is interested in

kanshin n 感心 admiration (= **kanpuku** 感服, **kantan** 感嘆): **~ shimásu** 感心します admires, is impressed

kanshō n 干渉 interference, meddling: **~ shimásu** 干渉します interferes; **~ shinai de kudasai** 干渉しないで下さい Please stay away from me.

kanshō n 鑑賞 [BOOKISH] appreciation (art, work, music)

kanshō n 観賞 [BOOKISH] admiration, enjoyment: **kanshō-shokubutsu** 観賞植物 ornamental plant

kansoku n 観測 observation; opinion (= **íken** 意見): **hoshi no ~** 星の観測 observation of the stars: **~ shimásu** 観測します observes

kansō n 感想 impression: **dokusho kansō-bun** 読書感想文 book report (at school)

kansō n 乾燥 dryness: **~ shimásu** 乾

燥します dries (*something*), It is dry weather.

kansō-ki *n* 乾燥機 dryer (*washing machine*)

kansōgei-kai *n* 歓送迎会 welcome and farewell party

kantai *n* 歓待 [BOOKISH] welcome (= **kangei** 歓迎): **~ shimásu** 歓待します welcomes

kantan *n* 感嘆 → **kanshin** 関心

kantan (na) *adj* 簡単(な) easy, simple, brief

kantei *n* 鑑定 [BOOKISH] judgment: **~ shimásu** 鑑定します judges, authenticates

kantei *n* 官邸 [BOOKISH] official residence: **shushō-kantei** 首相官邸 official residence of the prime minister

kanten *n* カンテン・寒天 gelatin from *tengusa* seaweed

kantō-chihō *n* 関東地方 the Kantō area of Japan (*Tokyō, Chiba, Saitama, Kanagawa, Ibaraki, Tochigi, Gunma, Yamanashi prefecture*) → **shutó-ken** 首都圏

kantoku *n* 監督 supervision; supervisor, overseer, manager, director: **~ shimásu** 監督します supervises, oversees, manages (*a team*), directs (*a film*) eiga-kantoku *n* 映画監督 film director

kantō´shi *n* 間投詞 interjection

kanzei *n* 関税 customs duty (*tariff*)

kanzen *n* 完全 perfection, completeness: **kanzen na...** 完全な... perfect...: **kanzen ni** 完全に completely

kanzō *n* 肝臓 liver

kan-zúme (no ...) *adj* 缶詰(の...) **1.** canned (*food*), can, tin **2.** confine oneself

kao *n* 顔 face; looks, a look: **... (no) o shite imásu ...** (の)顔をしています has/wears an expression of ...

kao-iro *n* 顔色 complexion: **~ o ukagaimásu** 顔色をうかがいます watches a person's reactions

kaō *v* 買おう = **kaimashō** 買いましょう (let's buy it!)

kaō *v* 飼おう = **kaimashō** 飼いましょう (let's raise it!)

kaomoji *n* 顔文字 Emoticon

kaori *n* 香(り) fragrance, incense (= **kō´** 香): **kaorimásu** 香ります is fragrant

kā´pétto *n* カーペット carpet (= **jū´tan** じゅうたん・絨毯)

kappa *n* かっぱ・カッパ・河童 **1.** water imp **2.** (*sushi bar term*) cucumber (= **kyū´ri** キュウリ・胡瓜): **kappa-maki** かっぱ巻き seaweed-rolled sushi with cucumber in the center

kapparaimásu, kapparáu *v* かっぱらいます、かっぱらう [INFORMAL] swipes, steals, shoplifts

kappatsu (na) *adj* 活発(な) active, lively

kappō *n* 割烹 Japanese restaurant, Japanese cuisine: **kappō-gi** 割烹着 Japanese-style apron

káppu *n* カップ a cup (*with handle*): **kōhii-káppu** コーヒーカップ coffee cup: **magu-káppu** マグカップ mug

káppuru *n* カップル a couple (*of lovers*)

kápuseru *n* カプセル capsule: **kapuseru-hoteru** カプセルホテル capsule hotel

kara *n* 殻 shell, crust: **monuke no ~** もぬけのから[殻] completely empty (= **karappo (no)** 空っぽ(の))

kara (no) *adj* から[空](の) empty: **karappo (no)** から[空]っぽ(の) completely empty (= **monuke no kara** もぬけのから[殻])

... kará *prep, conj* ...から **1.** from..., since... (*time, space*): **... kara, ... máde** ...から...まで from ... to ... **2.** because...

kárā *n* カラー collar (= **eri** 襟)

kárā *n* カラー color (= **iro** 色)

karada *n* 体・身体 body; one's health: **~ ni ki o tsukete (kudasai)** (身)体に気をつけて(下さい) Please take care of yourself.

karái *adj* 辛い **1.** spicy, hot, peppery, pungent **2.** salty (= **shio-karai** 塩辛い; **shoppai** しょっぱい)

karakaimásu, karakáu *v* からかいます、からかう teases, pokes fun at

kara-kása *n* 唐傘 (*oil-paper*) umbrella

karanai *v* 刈らない = **karimásén** 刈りません (not mow)

karaoke n カラオケ karaoke

karashi n カラシ・芥子 mustard (= **masutādo** マスタード)

karasu n カラス・烏 crow

karate n カラテ・空手 karate (*weaponless self-defense*): **karaté-gí** 空手着 karate outfit/suit

káre *pron* 彼 he/him

káre-ra *pron* 彼ら they/them

káre n 彼 boyfriend (*lover*) (= **kare-shi** 彼氏)

karē n カレー curry: **karē-ráisu** カレーライス rice with curry

karéba v 刈れば (if one mows) → **karimásu** 刈ります

kárei n カレイ flatfish, turbot

karemásu, kareru v 枯れます, 枯れる withers: **karete imásu** 枯れています is withered

karemásu, kareru v 刈れます, 刈れる can mow/cut

karenai v 枯れない = **karemasén** 枯れません (not wither)

karéndā n カレンダー calendar (= **koyomí** 暦)

karéréba v 枯れれば (if it withers) → **karemásu** 枯れます

káre-shi n 彼氏 boyfriend (*lover*) (= **káre** 彼)

karete v 枯れて・刈れて → **karemásu** 枯れます・刈れます

kari (no) *adj* 仮(の) temporary, tentative: **kari-zumai** 仮住まい temporary residence

kári n 狩り hunting: **~ o shimásu** 狩りをします hunts

kari n 借り borrowing: **~ ga arimásu** 借りがあります I owe you. **karí-chin** n 借り賃 rent (*charge*) kari-te n 借り手 the borrower/renter, the lessee, the tenant

karimásu, karu v 刈ります, 刈る mows, cuts

karimásu, káru v 狩ります, 狩る hunts

karimásu, kariru v 借ります, 借りる borrows/rents it (from …)

karinai v 借りない = **karimasén** 借りません (not borrow)

kari(ra)remásu, kari(ra)reru v 借り(ら)れます, 借り(ら)れる can borrow

karite v 借りて → **karimásu** 借ります

kariyō v 借りよう = **karimashō´** 借りましょう (let's borrow/rent it!)

karō´ v 刈ろう = **karimashō´** 刈りましょう (let's mow!)

karō n 過労 overfatigue: **karō-shi** 過労死 death from overwork

karu v 刈る = **karimásu** 刈ります (mows, cuts)

kāru n カール curl

karui *adj* 軽い light (*of weight*)

karuishi n 軽石 pumice

Karukatta n カルカッタ Calcutta (Kolkata)

kása n 傘・かさ umbrella: **kasa-tate** 傘立て umbrella stand

kása n 笠 bamboo hat; (*mushroom*) cap

kasá n 嵩 bulk

kasabarimásu, kasabaru v かさばります, かさばる is bulky, takes up much space

kasai n 火災 fire (*accidental*) (= **káji** 火事): **kasai-kéihō** 火災警報 fire alarm, **kasai-hōchíki** 火災報知器 fire alarm (*device*), fire bell

kasanai v 貸さない = **kashimasén** 貸しません (not lend)

kasanarimásu, kasanaru v 重なります, 重なる they pile up

kasanemásu, kasaneru v 重ねます, 重ねる piles them up, puts one on top of another

kase n かせ shackles: **te-kase** 手かせ handcuffs: **ashi-kase** 足かせ fetters: **~ o hazushimásu** かせを外します unshackles

kase v 貸せ [IMPERATIVE] (lend it!) → **kashimásu** 貸します

kaséba v 貸せば (if one lends) → **kasimásu** 貸します

kasegimásu, kaségu v 稼ぎます, 稼ぐ earns, works for (*money*)

kasei n 火星 Mars

kaséi-jin n 火星人 a Martian

kaséide v 稼いで → **kasegimásu** 稼ぎます

kaséi-fu n 家政婦 housekeeper, hired maid

kaseki n 化石 fossil(s)

kasemásu, kaseru v 貸せます, 貸せる can lend

kasen *n* 下線 underline: ~ o hikimásu 下線を引きます draws an underline

kasen *n* 化繊 [BOOKISH] synthetic fiber

kasenai *v* 貸せない = kasemasén 貸せません (cannot lend)

kasetto (tēpu) *n* カセット(テープ) cassette (tape)

káshi *n* 歌詞 lyrics

káshi *n* 菓子 (o-káshi お菓子) cakes, sweets, pastry, candy: wa-gáshi 和菓子 Japanese-style confection; yō-gáshi 洋菓子 Western-style confection

kashí-ya *n* 菓子屋 candy store, confectionary; confectioner

kashikiri (no) *adj* 貸切り(の) chartered (= chātā チャーター)

kashikói *adj* 賢い wise

kashikomarimáshita かしこまりました. I understand and will comply (with your request). [HONORIFIC]

kashí-ma *n* 貸間 rooms for rent; rented/rental room(s)

kashimásu, kasu *v* 貸します, 貸す lends; rents (it out to)

kashirá *n* 頭 (o-kashira お頭) head; chief, leader

... káshira *interj* ...かしら (*mostly female*) I wonder/whether

kashi-te *n* 貸し手 the lender/landlord

kashite *v* 貸して → kashimásu 貸します

kashitsu *n* 過失 mistakes, errors, faults: kashitsu-sekinin 過失責任 negligence liability

kashi-ya *n* 貸家 house for rent; rented/rental house

...-kásho *suffix* ...か所・箇所・個所 (*counter for places, installations, institutions*)

kashoku-shō *n* 過食症 bulimia nervosa

kashu *n* 歌手 singer: ryūkō-kashu 流行歌手 pop singer

kasō *n* 仮装 disguise: kasō-pátii 仮装パーティ costume party: kasō-ishō 仮装衣装 costume (= kosuchūmu コスチューム)

kasō *n* 火葬 cremation

kasō *n* 仮想 [BOOKISH] virtual, imaginary: kasō-kūkan 仮想空間 virtual space

kasō *n* 下層 [BOOKISH] lower layer:

kasō-kaikyū 下層階級 lower class society

kasō´ *v* 貸そう = kashimashō 貸しましょう (let's lend it!)

kasoku *n* 加速 acceleration: ~ shimásu 加速します accelerates

kasoku-pédaru 加速ペダル gas pedal (= akuseru アクセル)

kāsoru *n* カーソル cursor (*on the computer screen, etc.*)

kasu *v* 貸す = kashimásu 貸します (lends)

kásu *n* かす[滓] 1. sediment, dregs, grounds 2. waste, scum, mud, trash, rags, scrap, junk (= kúzu くず[屑]: moe-kasu 燃えかす cinders: ningen/seken no kásu 人間/世間のかす the scum of the earth 3. particles: tabe-kasu 食べかす food particles

kásu *n* かす[糟・粕] lees: sake-kasu 酒粕 sake lees

kásuka (na/ni) *adj, adv* かすか・微か (な/に) faint(ly), dim(ly), slight(ly)

kasumemásu, kasumeru *v* 掠めます, 掠める skims, grazes

kasume-torimásu, kasume-toru *v* 掠め取ります, 掠め取る skims off; robs (*it of ...*), cheats (*one out of ...*) (= kasumemásu 掠めます)

kasumi *n* かすみ・霞 haze, mist

kasumimásu, kasumu *v* 霞みます, 霞む gets dim, hazy, misty

kasurimásu, kasuru *v* かすります, かする grazes

kasutanetto *n* カスタネット castanet(s)

kasutera *n* カステラ Japanese sponge cake, Castella

kata *n* 型 1. form, shape, size, mold, pattern: ~ ni hamemásu 型にはめます stereotypes: ō-gata 大型 large-size 2. type, model: ketsueki-gata 血液型 blood type

káta *n* 肩 shoulder(s)

kata-gaki *n* 肩書き (*business/position*) title

...-kata *suffix* ...方 manner of doing, way: yari-kata やり方 method, process (= hōhō 方法): kangae-kata 考え方 one's way of thinking, one's point of view

... katá n ...方 (o-kata お方) (honored) person: ano-kata あの方 that person, anata-gata あなた方 you people

kata-... prefix 片... one (of a pair) (= katáhō 片方): kata-ashi 片足 one leg/foot: kata-gawa 片側 one side

katá-hō n 片方, katáppō 片っぽう, katáppo 片っぽ one of a pair; the other one (of a pair)

kata-koto n 片言 imperfect language, limited language: ~ de hanashimásu 片言で話します speaks broken language (does not speak fluently)

kata-michi n 片道 one-way: katamichi-kíppu 片道切符 one way ticket

katachi n 形 form, shape

katadoru adj かたど[象・模]る imitated, copied, modeled, symbolized (= shōchō 象徴)

... katá-gata suffix ...方々 (honored) persons (= ... katá-tachi ...方達)

katagi (na) adj 堅気 (な) respectable, steady, honest

katai adj 固い hard; tight; firm; strict

katai adj 硬い hard, stiff; stilted upright

katai adj 堅い hard; solid; sound; reliable; serious; formal

katákána n カタカナ・片かな・片仮名 katakana (the squarish Japanese letters)

katakúríko n 片栗粉 potato starch

katamari n 固まり・塊 lump, clot, mass; loaf (of bread)

katamarimásu, katamaru v 固まります, 固まる it hardens, congeals, clots, (mud) cakes

katamemásu, katameru v 固めます, 固める hardens it, congeals it; strengthens it

katamuki n 傾き slant; inclination, tendency

katamukimásu, katamúku v 傾きます, 傾く leans (to one side), slants

katána n 刀 sword

katánai adj 勝たない = kachimasén 勝ちません (not win)

katáppo n 片っぽ one of a pair; the other one (of a pair) (= katáhō 片方)

katarimásu v 語ります, kataru 語る relates, tells

... katá-tachi n ...方達 (honored) persons

katáwa n 片輪 (discriminatory term) cripple

kata-yorimásu, kata-yóru v 片寄り[偏り]ます, 片寄る[偏る] leans (to one side); is partial (to)

kata-zukemásu, kata-zukéru v 片付けます, 片付ける puts in order, straightens up, tidies, cleans up

kata-zukimásu, kata-zúku v 片付きます, 片付く it gets tidy (put in order)

káte v 勝て [IMPERATIVE] (win!) → kachimásu 勝ちます

káteba v 勝てば (if one wins) → kachimásu 勝ちます

katei n 仮定 hypothesis, supposition: ~ shimásu 仮定します supposes, presumes

katei n 課程 process (course, stage)

katei n 家庭 home, household

katei-yō'gu/yō'hin n 家庭用具/用品 home appliances

katemásu, katéru v 勝てます, 勝てる can win

kā'ten n カーテン curtain, drapes: kāten-róddo カーテンロッド curtain rod: kāten-rēru カーテンレール curtain rail: shawā-kāten シャワーカーテン shower curtain

katénai v 勝てない = katemasén 勝てません (cannot win)

katō' v 勝とう = kachimashō' 勝ちましょう (let's win!)

kātorijji n カートリッジ cartridge: inku-kātorijji インクカートリッジ ink cartridge

Katoríkku n カトリック Catholic

kátsu v 勝つ = kachimásu 勝ちます (wins)

kátsu n カツ a Japanese "cutlet" (fried in deep fat): ton-katsu 豚カツ・トンカツ pork cutlet

katsu-don n カツ丼 a bowl of rice with sliced pork cutlet on top

katsudō n 活動 action, activity, movement: ~ shimásu 活動します acts, moves into action

katsugimásu, katsúgu v 担ぎます, 担ぐ carries on shoulders

katsúide v 担いで → katsugimásu 担ぎます

katsuji *n* 活字 movable type: **~ ni shi-másu** 活字にします prints, is in print

katsuo *n* カツオ・鰹 bonito: **katsuo-bushi** カツオ[鰹]節 a dried bonito fish

katsura *n* かつら・カツラ wig

kátsute *adv* かつて at one time, formerly

katsuyaku *n* 活躍 activity: **~ shimásu** 活躍します is active

katta *v* 買った・飼った = **kaimáshita** 買いました・飼いました (bought; raised)

katta *v* 刈った = **karimáshita** 刈りました (mowed)

kátta *v* 勝った = **kachimáshita** 勝ちました (won)

…-kátta *v* …かった : [ADJECTIVE] **-kátta (desu)** …かった(です) was …

katte *n* 勝手 kitchen
  katte-dó'gu *n* 勝手道具 kitchen utensils
  kátte-guchi *n* 勝手口 kitchen door, back door

katte (na/ni) *adj, adv* 勝手(な/に) selfish(ly), as one wishes

katte *v* 買って → **kaimásu** 買います

katte *v* 刈って → **karimásu** 刈ります

kátte *v* 勝って → **kachimásu** 勝ちます

kau *v* 買う = **kaimásu** 買います (buys)

káu *v* 飼う = **kaimásu** 飼います (raises pets, farm animals, etc.)

kaunserā *n* カウンセラー counselor

kauntā *n* カウンター counter

kawá *n* 川 river

kawá *n* 河 big river

kawá *n* 皮・革 skin; leather; (*tree*) bark; crust: **kawa-seihin** 革製品 leather goods

kawai-garimásu, kawai-gáru *v* かわいがり[可愛がり]ます, かわいがる・可愛がる treats with affection, loves (*children, pets, etc.*)

kawaíi *adj* かわいい・可愛い cute, lovable, darling (= **kawairashíi** かわいらしい・可愛らしい)

kawai-sō´(na) *adj* かわいそう(な) pitiful, poor

kawáite *v* 乾いて → **kawakimásu** 乾きます

kawakashimásu, kawakásu *v* 乾かします, 乾かす dries it (out)

kawakimásu, kawáku *v* 乾きます, 乾く gets dry

kawakimásu, kawáku *v* 渇きます, 渇く: **nodo ga ~** のどが渇きます gets thirsty

kawanai *v* 買わない = **kaimasén** 買いません (not buy)

kawánai *v* 飼わない = **kaimasén** 飼いません (not raise)

kawara *n* 瓦 tile: **kawara-buki (no)** 瓦ぶき(の) tile-roofed

kawaranai *adj* 変わらない = **kawari-masén** 変わりません (not change)

kawari *n* 変わり (**o-kawari** お変わり) change (*in health*): **o-kawari ari-masénka.** お変わりありませんか。 Is everything all right? (*greeting*)

kawari *n* 代わり **1.** substitute: **… no kawari ni** … の代わりに instead of **2. o-káwari** おかわり a second helping (*usually of rice*): **okawari-jiyū (desu)** おかわり自由(です) has free refills

kawarimásu, kawaru *v* 変わります, 変わる: (**… ni) kawarimásu** (…に)変わります it changes (into…)

kawarimásu, kawaru *v* 代わります, 代わる: (**… ni) kawarimásu** (…に)代わります it takes the place (*of …*)

kawaru-gáwaru *adv* 代わる代わる・かわるがわる alternately

kawase *n* 為替 a money order: **kawase-rēto** 為替レート currency exchange rates

kawatta *v* 変わった = **kawarimáshita** 変わりました (changed; unusual, novel)

kawatte *v* 変わって → **kawarimásu** 変わります: **kawatte imásu** 変わっています is unusual, novel

kayaku *n* 火薬 gunpowder

Kayō´(bi) *n* 火曜(日) Tuesday

kayoi *adj* 通い: **kayoi (no)** 通い(の) commuting, live-out (help)

kayoimásu, kayou *v* 通います, 通う commutes, goes back and forth, goes (regularly)

kayowanai *v* 通わない = **kayoimasén** 通いません (not commute)

kayu *n* 粥・かゆ (**o-kayu** お粥) rice gruel, porridge

kayúi *adj* 痒い itchy

kázan *n* 火山 volcano: **kazán-bai** 火山灰 volcanic ash

kazari *n* 飾り = **kazari-mono** 飾り物 ornament, decoration

kazarimásu, kazaru *v* 飾ります, 飾る decorates

kazari-mono *n* 飾り物 ornament, decoration

kaze *n* 風 wind: ~ **ga tsuyói** 風が強い is windy

kaze *n* かぜ・カゼ・風邪 a cold: ~ **o hikimásu** かぜをひきます catches (a) cold

kaze-gúsuri *n* かぜ薬・風邪薬 medicine for colds

kazoe-kirenai *adj* 数え切れない countless, innumerable

kazoemásu, kazoéru *v* 数えます, 数える counts

kazoeraremásu, kazoeraréru *v* 数えられます, 数えられる can count

kazoé ro *v* 数えろ [IMPERATIVE] (count!) → **kazoemásu** 数えます

kázoku *n* 家族 family: **kazoku-omoi no** 家族思いの family-minded (*person*)

kázu *n* 数 number

kazu no ko *n* カズノコ・数の子 herring roe

ke *n* 毛 hair; wool; feathers

...-ke *suffix* ...家 (*name of certain*) clan, family: **Suzuki-ke** 鈴木家 Suzuki family

kē´buru *n* ケーブル cable: **kēburú-kā** ケーブルカー cable car: **kēburú-terebi** ケーブルテレビ cable TV

kecháppu *n* ケチャップ ketchup

kéchi (na) *adj* けち(な) stingy, miser

kéchinbō, kéchinbo *n* けちん坊, けちんぼ stingy person, skinflint, miser

kedamono *n* けだもの・ケダモノ・獣, **kemono** けもの・ケモノ・獣 animal; beast

kédo *conj* けど [INFORMAL] though, but = **kéredo (-mo)** けれど(も) [FORMAL] however, though, but

kegá *n* けが・ケガ・怪我 (**o-kéga** お怪我) injury, mishap: ~ **o shimásu** 怪我を

します gets hurt; ~ **o sasemásu** 怪我をさせます injures (*someone*)

ke-gawa *n* 毛皮 fur: **ke-gawa-no-kōto** 毛皮のコート fur coat

kéi *n* 刑 (*criminal*) sentence

...-kei *suffix* ...系 **1.** type, model: **dō-kei-shoku** 同系色 similar color **2.** of ...ancestry: **kei-zu** 系図 genealogy, family tree (= **kakei-zu** 家系図)

keiba *n* 競馬 horse racing/race **keiba-jō** 競馬場 racetrack

keibetsu *n* 軽蔑 contempt, despising: ~ **shimásu** 軽蔑します despises

kéibi *n* 警備 security: ~ **shimásu** 警備します guards **keibi-in** *n* 警備員 security guard

keiei *n* 経営 management, operation: ~ **shimásu** 経営します runs a business **keiéi-sha** *n* 経営者 manager, operator, proprietor

keigo *n* 敬語 honorific (*word*): ~ **o tsukaimásu** 敬語を使います uses honorific words

keihin *n* 景品 [BOOKISH] giveaway

keihō *n* 警報 alarm, alert, warning

keiji *n* 繋辞 [BOOKISH] copula, (*grammar term*) link

kéiji *n* 刑事 (*police*) detective

keiji *n* 掲示 bulletin: ~ **shimásu** 掲示します posts **keiji-ban** *n* 掲示板 bulletin board

kéijō *n* 形状 geometry

keika *n* 経過 course (*of time*), progress, development: ~ **shimásu** 経過します (*time*) passes, elapses, expires

keikai *n* 警戒 [BOOKISH] vigilance, watch, guard; warning, caution: ~ **shimásu** 警戒します guards against, watches out (*for ...*), warns, cautions

keikaku *n* 計画 plan, scheme, program, project (= **puran** プラン): (**... no**) ~ **o tatemásu** (...の)計画を立てます = (**...**) ~ **shimásu** (...を)計画します plans

keikan *n* 警官 [BOOKISH] policeman, (police) officer (= **keisatsu-kan** 警察官): **keikan-tai** 警官隊 a contingent of policemen

keiken *n* 経験 experience: ~ **shimásu** 経験します experiences, undergoes shokumu-keiken *n* 職務経験 job experience

keiki *n* 景気 business conditions, prosperity, boom: **keiki-taisaku** 景気対策 economy-boosting measure(s): **~ ga ii** 景気がいい Business is good.

kéiki *n* 契機 [BOOKISH] opportunity

kéiki *n* 刑期 prison term: **~ o oemásu** 刑期を終えます serves out one's sentence

kei(ryō)ki *n* 計(量)器 meter (*device*)

kéiko *n* 稽古 (**o-kéiko** お稽古) exercise, practice, drill (= **naraigoto** 習い事)

keikō *n* 傾向 [BOOKISH] tendency, trend

keikō *n* 経口 [BOOKISH] oral: **keikō-hinínyaku** 経口避妊薬 oral contraceptive (= **piru** ピル)

keikoku *n* 警告 [BOOKISH] warning: **keikoku-hyōji** 警告表示 alarm display: **~ shimásu** 警告します warns

keikō-tō *n* 蛍光灯 fluorescent light

keimú-sho *n* 刑務所 jail, prison

keireki *n* 経歴 [BOOKISH] career (*history*)

keirin *n* 競輪 [BOOKISH] bicycle race: **keirin-jō** 競輪場 bicycle racetrack

keirō *n* 敬老 respect for the aged Keirō-no-hí *n* 敬老の日 Respect-for-the-Aged Day (*Third Monday of September*)

keiryaku *n* 計略 [BOOKISH] plot, scheme, trick, strategy: **~ o nerimásu** 計略を練ります engineers a plot

keiryō-kappu *n* 計量カップ measuring cup

keisan *n* 計算 calculation, computation: **~ shimásu** 計算します calculates, computes

keisán-ki *n* 計算機 calculator

keisatsu *n* 警察 police: **keisatsu-shó** 警察署 police station; **keisatsu-kan** 警察官 policeman, (police) officer (= **keikan** 警官)

keishiki *n* 形式 form, formality

keishoku *n* 軽食 snack, light foods

keisotsu (na) *adj* 軽率(な) hasty, rash

keitai *n* 形態 pattern, shape

keitai **1.** *adj* 携帯 portable **2.** *n* 携帯 cell-phone, mobile (tele)phone (= **keitai-denwa** 携帯電話) **3.** *v* ~ **shimásu** 携帯します carries, takes along

keitai-denwa *n* 携帯電話 cell-phone, mobile (tele)phone (= **keitai** 携帯)

keiteki *n* 警笛 [BOOKISH] horn (*of car*) (= **kuráku-shon** クラクション)

keito *n* 毛糸 wool; yarn: **~ no tama** 毛糸の玉, **keito-dama** 毛糸玉 ball of wool/yarn

keiyaku *n* 契約 contract, agreement: **~ shimásu** 契約します, **~ o kawashimásu** 契約を交わします contracts, signs (*up*)

keiyaku-sho *n* 契約書 contract sheet

keiyó´shi *n* 形容詞 adjective

… kéiyu (de/no) *adv*, *adj* …経由(で/の) by (*way of*) …, via …: **keiyu-bin** 経由便 indirect flight

kéizai *n* 経済 economics, finance

keizai-gaku *n* 経済学 (*science of*) economics

keizai-teki (na) *adj* 経済的(な) economical

Keizai-Sangyō-shō *n* 経済産業省 Ministry of Economy, Trade and Industry (METI)

kē´ki *n* ケーキ cake: (**ichigo no**) **shōto-kēki** (イチゴ[苺])のショートケーキ sponge cake (with strawberry and whipped cream) (*very popular shortcake arranged for Japanese*)

kekka *n* 結果 result, effect; as a result (*consequence*)

kekkaku *n* 結核 tuberculosis

kekkan *n* 欠陥 defect, deficiency

kekkan *n* 血管 blood vessel

kekkō *n* 欠航 cancelled flight; "flight cancelled"

kékkō (na) *adj* 結構(な) **1.** splendid, excellent **2.** fairly well; enough: **Kékkō desu** 結構です No, thank you.

kekkon *n* 結婚 marriage (= **konin** 婚姻): **(… to) ~ shimásu** (…と)結婚します marries

kekkón-shiki *n* 結婚式 wedding

kekkyokú *n*, *adv* 結局 after all, in the long run

kemono *n* けもの・ケモノ・獣 = **kedamono** けだもの・ケダモノ・獣 (*animal; beast*)

kemúi, kemutai *adj* 煙い、煙たい smoky

kemuri n 煙 smoke

kemushi n ケムシ・毛虫 caterpillar

kén n 県 a Japanese prefecture (*like a state*), …´-ken …県: **Chiba´-ken** 千葉県 Chiba prefecture

kén n 剣 (*double-edged*) sword

…´-ken suffix …軒 (*counts houses, small buildings and shops*)

…´-ken suffix …券 ticket: **nyūjō-ken** 入場券 admission ticket

kenbái-ki n 券売機 ticket vending machine

kenbi-kyō n 顕微鏡 microscope

kenbutsu n 見物 sightseeing: **~ shimásu** 見物します sees the sights

kenbutsu-nin n 見物人 bystander

kénchi n 見地 [BOOKISH] viewpoint

kenchiku n 建築 construction; architecture

kenchiku-ka n 建築家 architect

kénchō n 県庁 the prefectural government (office)

kéndō n 剣道 the art of fencing (*with bamboo swords*)

ken'etsu n 検閲 [BOOKISH] censor(ship)

kengaku n 見学 study by observation, field study/trip/work

kénji n 検事 (*public*) prosecutor

kenjū n 拳銃 pistol

kenka n けんか・喧嘩 quarrel, argument: **~ shimásu** けんか[喧嘩]します quarrels, argues

kenkō n 健康 health: **kenkō-shókuhin** 健康食品 health food(s); **kenkō-hoken** 健康保険 health insurance; **kenkō-shindan** 健康診断 health check, medical examination

kenkō (na) adj 健康(な) healthy

Kenkoku̱-kínen-no-hi n 建国記念の日 National Foundation Day (*11 February*)

kenkyo (na) adj 謙虚(な) humble (*modest*)

kenkyū n 研究 research, study: **~ shimásu** 研究します studies, researches

kenkyū-jo n 研究所 research institute, laboratory

kenmei (na) adj 賢明(な) wise

kénpō n 憲法 constitution: **Kenpō-kinénbi** 憲法記念日 Constitution (Memorial) Day (*3 May*)

kénri n 権利 right (*privilege*)

kenri-kin n 権利金 "key money" (*to obtain rental lease*)

kenritsu (no) adj 県立(の) prefectural

kenryoku n 権力 power, authority: **kenryoku-sha** 権力者 person of power

kénsa n 検査 inspection, examination, check-up, test: **~ shimásu** 検査します inspects, checks, tests

kensatsu n 検札 [BOOKISH] ticket examining (*on board*): **~ shimásu** 検札します examines tickets

kensetsu n 建設 construction (*work*) (*building*)

kenshō n 検証 [BOOKISH] vertification

kentō n 拳闘 boxing (= **bókushingu** ボクシング)

kentō´ n 見当 aim; direction; estimate, guess: **~ ga tsukimásu** 見当がつきます gets a rough idea (*of it*): **~ o tsukemásu** 見当をつけます makes a guess, takes aim

kentō n 検討: **~ shimásu** 検討します examines it, investigates it

…-kéntō suffix …見当 approximately, about, approximately

ken'yaku n 倹約 economy, thrift, economizing: **~ shimásu** 倹約します economizes on, saves

kénzan n 剣山 a frog (*pinholder*) for flowers

ke-orimono n 毛織物 woolen goods

keránai v 蹴らない = **kerimasén** 蹴りません (not kick)

kéreba v 蹴れば (if one kicks) → **kerimásu** 蹴ります

kéredo (-mo) conj けれど(も) however, though, but

keremásu, keréru v 蹴れます, 蹴れる can kick

kerénai v 蹴れない = **keremasén** 蹴れません (cannot kick)

kérete v 蹴れて → **keremásu** 蹴れます

kéri n けり: **~ o tsukemásu** けりをつけます winds up

kerimásu, kéru v 蹴ります, 蹴る kicks

kerō´ v 蹴ろう = **kerimashō´** 蹴りましょう (let's kick!)

ké ro v 蹴ろ [IMPERATIVE] (kick!)

[IRREGULAR IMPERATIVE of **kerimásu** 蹴ります]

kéru v 蹴る = **kerimásu** 蹴ります (kicks)

késa n, adv 今朝 this morning

kesanai v 消さない = **keshimasén** 消しません (not extinguish)

kese v 消せ [IMPERATIVE] (turn it off!, put it out!) → **keshimásu** 消します

keséba v 消せば (if one extinguishes) → **keshimásu** 消します

kesemásu, keseru v 消せます, 消せる can extinguish

kesenai v 消せない = **kesemasén** 消せません (cannot extinguish)

kesete v 消せて → **kesemásu** 消せます

keshi-gomu n 消しゴム (*rubber*) eraser

keshi-in n 消印 cancellation mark/stamp

késhiki n 景色 scenery, view

keshimásu, kesu v 消します, 消す extinguishes, puts out; turns off; expunges, erases, deletes

keshite v 消して → **keshimásu** 消します

keshō n 化粧 (o-**keshō** お化粧) cosmetics, make-up
keshō-hin n 化粧品 cosmetics
keshō-shitsu n 化粧室 restroom, bathroom, toilet, lounge

kesō v 消そう = **keshimashō´** 消しましょう (let's extinguish it!)

kessaku n 傑作 masterpiece

kessan n 決算 settling accounts

kesseki n 欠席 absence (*from school, work*): ~ **shimásu** 欠席します is absent
kesséki-sha n 欠席者 absentee

kesshin n 決心 determination, resolve: (... **shiyō to**) ~ **shimásu** (... しようと) 決心します resolves (*to do*)

kesshite adv 決して [+ NEGATIVE] never

kesshō n 決勝 finals, title match: **jun-kesshō** 準決勝 semifinals

kesu v 消す = **keshimásu** 消します (puts out; turns off; erases)

kē´su n ケース case (*a particular instance*): **kēsu-bai-kē´su** ケースバイケース case by case; case (*container*)

keta n けた・ケタ・桁 1. (*cross*) beam, girder 2. abacus rod, (*numerical*) column

ketsu n 1. けつ・尻 (= **o-ketsu, o-shiri** お尻 [POLITE FORM]) buttock 2. けつ the tail end, the last (*bottom*) (= **shiri** しり・尻)

ketsuatsu n 血圧 blood pressure; ~ **ga takái/hikúi** 血圧が高い/低い has high/low blood pressure: ~ **o hakarimásu** 血圧を計ります takes one's blood pressure
ketsuatsu-kei n 血圧計 blood-pressure gauge; sphygmomanometer

ketsúeki n 血液 blood

ketsumatsu n 結末 outcome

ketsuron n 結論 conclusion: ~ **to shite** 結論として in conclusion: ~ **o dashimásu** 結論を出します concludes

kétta v 蹴った = **kerimáshita** 蹴りました (kicked)

kétte v 蹴って → **kerimásu** 蹴ります

kettei n 決定 determination, decision: ~ **shimásu** 決定します decides, determines (*to do*)

kettén n 欠点 flaw, defect, short-coming

kétte shimaimásu v 蹴ってしまいます = **kerimásu** 蹴ります (kicks)

kewashíi adj 険しい steep, precipitous; severe

kezuremásu, kezureru v 削れます, 削れる can sharpen

kezurimásu, kezuru v 削ります, 削る sharpens, shaves

ki n 気 spirit; feeling; mind, heart
ki (ga) adv 気(が): ~ **ga mijikái** 気が短い is impatient; ~ **ga omoi** 気が重い is depressed; ~ **ga tachimásu** 気が立ちます gets excited; ~ **ga tsukimásu** 気が付きます comes to one's senses
ki ni adj 気に: ~ **irimásu** 気に入ります appeals to one, is pleasing; (... **ga**) ~ **narimásu** (...が)気になります worries (*one*); (... **o**) ~ **shimásu** (...を) 気にします worries about ..., minds; ... **suru** ~ **narimásu** ...する気になります gets in the mood (*to do*)
ki o adv 気を: ~ **tsukemásu** 気を付けます (is) careful; ~ **ushinaimásu** 気を失います loses consciousness, faints

111

ki n 木 tree; wood

kibarashi n 気晴らし diversion, refresh (= **kibun tenkan** 気分転換)

kiben n 詭弁 sophistry

kibishíi adj 厳しい strict, severe

kibō n 希望 hope: ~ **shimásu** 希望します hopes, aspires
kibō´-sha n 希望者 candidate, applicant

kíbun n 気分 feeling, mood: **kíbun-tenkan** 気分転換 diversion, refresh (= **kibarashi** 気晴らし)

kibutori n 着太り looking fatter in clothes: ~ **shimásu** 着太りしますis looked fatter in clothes

kíchi n 基地 military base

kíchi n 機知 wit

ki-chigái (no) adj 気違い(の) mad, insane

kichín-to adv きちんと punctually; precisely; neat(ly)

kichō n 記帳 [BOOKISH] registration (*at hotel, etc.*): ~ **shimásu** 記帳します checks in, registers

kichō´ n 機長 captain (*of an airplane*)

kichō (na) adj 貴重(な) valuable
kichō-hin n 貴重品 valuables

kichō´men (na) adj 几帳面(な) meticulous, particular; punctual

kidate-no/ga-yoi adj 気立ての/が良い good-natured

kido n 木戸 entrance gate, wicket

kídoairaku n 喜怒哀楽 emotions, delight, anger, sorrow and pleasure

kidorimásu, kidoru v 気取ります, 気取る puts on airs: **kidotte imásu** 気取っています, **kidotta ...** 気取った... affected, stuck-up

kiemásu, kieru v 消えます, 消える is extinguished, goes out; fades, vanishes

kigae n 着替え a change of clothing

kigaemásu, kigáeru v 着替えます, 着替える changes (*clothes*) [*newer form of*]

kigaru (na) adj 気軽(な) lighthearted, casual

kígeki n 喜劇 comedy

kigen n 機嫌 (*state of*) health, mood: ~ **ga íi** 機嫌がいい cheerful; ~ **ga warúi** 機嫌が悪い unhappy, moody →

go-kigen ご機嫌 [HONORIFIC]

kígen n 期限 term, period; deadline

kígen n 起源 origin

kigō n 記号 sign, mark, symbol

kígu n 器具 implement, fixture, apparatus

kígyō n 企業 company, business concern; "the office" (= **kaisha** 会社)

kihon n 基本 basis, foundation:
kihon-teki (na) 基本的(な) basic, fundamental

kíi n キー key: (*computer*) **kiibōdo** キーボード keyboard

kiiro (no) adj 黄色(の) = **kiiroi** 黄色い yellow

kiita v 聞いた = **kikimáshita** 聞きました (listened, heard; obeyed; asked)

kiite v 聞いて → **kikimásu** 聞きます

kí-ito n 生糸 raw silk

kiji n キジ・雉 pheasant

kiji n 記事 article, news item, piece, write-up: **shinbun-kiji** 新聞記事 newspaper article

kiji n 生地 cloth material, fabric

kíjitsu n 期日 [BOOKISH] appointed day; deadline

kijun n 基準 [BOOKISH] basis, standard

kikai n 機会 chance, opportunity, occasion

kíkai n 機械 machine, machinery, instrument: **kikai-teki (na)** 機械的(な) mechanical

kikai n 器械 instrument: **kikai-taisō** 器械体操 (*apparatus*) gymnastics

kikai (na) adj 奇怪(な) mysterious, strange

kikaku n 企画 plan(ning), project:
Kikaku-bu 企画部 planning department: ~ **shimásu** 企画します plans

kikaku n 規格 norm, standard
kikaku-ka n 規格化 standardization: ~ **shimásu** 規格化します standardizes

kikan n 期間 term, period

kíkan n 機関 engine; instrument; agency, activity, organization: **kikan-jū** 機関銃 machine gun; **kinyū-kikán** 金融機関 financial institution

kikán (no) adj 季刊(の) quarterly:
kikán-shi 季刊誌 a quarterly

kikanai v 聞かない = **kikimasén** 聞きません (not listen, not ask)

kikasemásu, kikaseru v 聞かせます、聞かせる lets someone hear, tells someone (*a story*); reads (*someone a book*); reasons with (*a child*)

kike v 聞け [IMPERATIVE] (listen!) → **kikimásu** 聞きます

kikéba v 聞けば (if one listens, …) → **kikimásu** 聞きます

kikemásu, kikeru v 聞けます、聞ける can listen/hear, can ask

kiken n 危険 danger, peril: **kiken (na)** 危険(な) dangerous (= **abunaí** 危ない)

kiken n 棄権 abstention: ~ **shimásu** 棄権します abstains

kikenai v 聞けない = **kikemasén** 聞けません (cannot listen/hear/ask)

kikete v 聞けて → **kikemásu** 聞けます

kíki n 危機 crisis, critical moment, emergency

kiki-ashi n 利き足 stronger leg

kikimásu, kiku v 聞きます、聞く listens, hears; obeys; asks

kikimásu, kiku v 効きます、効く takes effect, is effective, works

kiki-me n 効き目 effect (*effectiveness*) (= **kōyō** 効用, **kōnō** 効能): ~ **ga arimásu** 効き目があります is effective

kiki-te n 聞き手 hearer, listener

kiki-ude n 利き腕 stronger hand: **migi-kiki** 右利き right-hander(s): **hidari-kiki** 左利き left-hander(s)

kikkake n きっかけ opportunity, occasion

kikkari adj きっかり exactly, just (= **chōdo** ちょうど・丁度)

kikō n 気候 climate

kikō n 機構 system, organisation, structure: **kokusai-kīkō** 国際機構 international organization

kikō n 紀行 [BOOKISH] travel: **kikō-bun** 紀行文 travel notes

kikō n 寄稿 [BOOKISH] contribution: **kikō-kiji** 寄稿記事 contributed article

kikō n 奇行 one's eccentricity: **kikō-heki** 奇行癖 eccentric habit

kikő v 聞こう = **kikimashő** 聞きましょう (let's listen/ask!)

kikoemásu, kikoeru v 聞こえます、聞こえる can hear; is heard

kikoenai v 聞こえない = **kikoemasén**

聞こえません (not hear)

kikoku n 帰国 returning to one's country (Japan): ~ **shimásu** 帰国します returns from abroad

kikoku-shíjo n 帰国子女 returnees

kikú v 聞く = **kikimásu** 聞きます (listens, hears; obeys; asks)

kikú v 聴く = **kikimásu** 聴きます (listens to music, etc.)

kikú v 訊く・聞く = **kikimásu** 訊[聞]きます (asks)

kikú v 効く = **kikimásu** 効きます (takes effect, is effective, works)

kikú n キク・菊 chrysanthemum

ki-kúrage n 木くらげ・キクラゲ・木耳 tree-ears (*an edible fungus*)

kikyū n 気球 balloon: **netsu-kikyū** 熱気球 hot-air balloon

kimae ga íi adj 気前がいい generous

kimagure n 気まぐれ fickle, easy to change one's mood

kimari n 決まり rule; settlement, arrangement; order; regulatio*n*

kimari ga warúi adj きまりが悪い is/feels embarrassed

kimarimásu, kimaru v 決まります、決まる is settled, is arranged

kimásu, kiru v 着ます、着る wears

kimásu, kúru v 来ます、来る comes

kimé n きめ[木目・肌理] 1. grain, texture 2. smooth (*human skin*) 3. fine: **kime-komakai** きめ細かい、**kime-komayaka (na)** きめ細やか(な) meticulous, attentiveness (*attentive*), tender (= **komayaka (na)** こま[細・濃]やか(な))

kimemásu, kimeru v 決めます、決める settles, arranges, decides

kimi n 君・きみ you [*familiar*] Kimi-ga-yo 君が代 national anthem of Japan

kimi n 黄身 yolk (*of egg*)

kimí n 気味 feeling, sensation: ~ **ga warúi** 気味が悪い nervous, apprehensive, weird (*feeling*)

kimídori (iro) n 黄緑(色) yellowish green (color)

kimijika n 気短 short-tempered person (= **tanki** 短気)

kimó n きも[肝・胆] 1. liver 2. guts,

courage, pluck: **kimo-dameshi** 肝試し test of courage: **kimo-ga-futoi** 肝[胆]が太い brave, gritty

kimochi n 気持ち feeling, sensation: **~ ga íi** 気持ちがいい it feels good, is comfortable; **~ ga warúi** 気持ちが悪い is uncomfortable, is feeling bad/unwell

ki-mono n 着物 clothes; a (*Japanese*) kimono

ki-músume n 生娘 virgin (*female*), green girl

ki-muzukashíi n 気難しい fussy, difficult (*person*)

kímyō (na) adj 奇妙(な) strange, peculiar

kín n 金 gold: **kin-ka** 金貨 gold coin

-kin suffix 金 money: **shikin** 資金 fund, capital: **shikíkin** 敷金 security deposit (*for rental*): **shakkín** 借金 debt

kínai n 機内 on a plane: **kinai-shoku** 機内食 airplane meal

kinai v 着ない = **kimasén** 着ません (not wear)

kínako n きな粉[黄な粉] soybean meal/flour: **kinako-mochi** きな粉餅 rice cake powdered with soybean

kinben (na) adj 勤勉(な) industrious, hardworking, diligent

kinchō n 緊張 strain, tension: **~ shite imásu** 緊張しています is tense

kinen n 記念 commemoration; **kinen-kítte** 記念切手 commemorative stamp

kinen-hin n 記念品 souvenir

kin'en n 禁煙 smoking prohibited, no smoking: **kin'én-sha** 禁煙車 no(n)-smoking car

kinénbi n 記念日 anniversary

kingaku n 金額 amount (*of money*)

kingan (no) adj 近眼(の) near-sighted, shortsighted, myopic

kingyo n 金魚 goldfish: **kingyo-bachi** 金魚鉢 bowl for goldfish(es)

kiníine n キニーネ quinine

ki-nikúi v 着にくい uncomfortable (*to wear*)

kin-iro (no) adj 金色(の) gold (color), golden

kin-jimásu, kin-jiru v 禁じます, 禁じる forbids, prohibits

kínjo n 近所 neighborhood, vicinity

kinkán n キンカン・金柑 kumquat

kinki-chihō n 近畿地方 the Kinki area of Japan (*Osaka, Hyōgo, Kyōto, Shiga, Nara prefectures*)

kínko n 金庫 safe (*strongbox*), (*small*) cash box

kinkyū n 緊急 [BOOKISH] urgency, emergency; **kinkyū na** 緊急な urgent, critical

kinmákie n 金蒔絵 gold lacquer

kínmu n 勤務 duty, service, work: **~ shimásu** 勤務します works, is on duty

kinmú-saki n 勤務先 place of work/employment

kínniku n 筋肉 muscle: **kinniku-tsū** 筋肉痛 muscular pain, myalgia

kinō´ n, adv きのう・昨日 yesterday

kinō n 機能 function

ki-no-dókú na adj 気の毒な pitiful, pitiable

kino káge n 木の陰 shade of trees (= **ko-kage** 木陰)

kino kawá n 木の皮 bark (*of tree*)

kínoko n キノコ・茸 mushroom

kí-no-me n 木の芽 **1.** tree sprout **2.** pepper sprout

kí-no-mi n 木の実 nuts, tree produce (*nuts, fruits, berries*)

kinō´ no ban n きのう[昨日]の晩 last night

kinpaku shimásu (suru) adv 緊迫します(する) tense

kinpatsu (no) adj 金髪(の) blond

kinpira n キンピラ・きんぴら・金平 fried burdock root and carrot strips served cold

Kinrō-kánsha no hí n 勤労感謝の日 Labor Thanksgiving Day (23 November)

kínryoku n 筋力 muscle (*power*)

kinshi n 禁止 prohibition, ban: **~ shimásu** 禁止します prohibits, bans

kinshi n 近視 = **kingan** 近眼 (near-sighted)

kintamá n [INFORMAL] 金玉 testicle(s)

kínu n 絹 silk

Kin'yō´(bi) n 金曜(日) Friday

kinyū n 記入: **~ shimásu** 記入します fills in

kin'yū n 金融 finance: **kin'yū-shíjō** 金融市場 the money market

kínzoku n 金属 metal

kioku n 記憶 memory: **kiokúryoku** 記憶力 memory (*capacity*), retentiveness

kíppári (to) adv きっぱり（と）definitely, firmly, flatly

kippu n 切符 ticket: **kippu-úriba** 切符売り場 ticket office

kirai (na) adj 嫌い（な）disliked

kiraku (na) adj 気楽（な）carefree, comfortable; easygoing

kiránai v 切らない = **kirimasén** 切りません (not cut)

ki(ra)remásu, ki(ra)reru v 着（ら）れます, 着（ら）れる can wear

kirasánai v 切らさない = **kirashimasén** 切らしません (not exhaust)

kirashimásu, kírásu v 切らします, 切らす exhausts the supply of, runs out of: **shibiré o** ～ しびれを切らします loses patience; **... o kiráshite imásu** ... を切らしています is out of ...

kiráshite v 切らして → **kirashimásu** 切らします

kiré v きれ・切れ a piece, a cut (*of cloth*)

kíre v 切れ [IMPERATIVE] (cut it!, ...) → **kirimásu** 切ります

kíreba v 着れば (if one wears) → **kimásu** 着ます

kíreba v 切れば (if one cuts) → **kimásu** 切ります

kírei (na) adj きれい[綺麗]（な）pretty; clean; neat, tidy; nice (-looking), attractive: ～ **ni shimásu** きれいにします cleans/tidies up

kiremasén, kirénai v 切れません, 切れない cannot cut; cannot run out; cannot break (off)

ki(ra)remásu, ki(ra)reru v 着（ら）れます, 着（ら）れる can wear

kiremásu, kiréru v 切れます, 切れる **1.** can cut; cuts (*well*) **2.** runs out **3.** breaks (off)

kire-mé n 切れ目 a gap, a break, a pause

kirénai v 切れない **1.** dull(-edged), blunt **2.** = **kiremasén** 切れません (cannot cut; not run out; not break)

kiréreba v 切れれば (if one can cut; ...) → **kiremásu** 切れます

kírete v 切れて → **kiremásu** 切れます

kiri n 霧 fog, mist: ～ **ga fukái/koi** 霧が深い/濃い is foggy

kiri n 桐 paulownia (*tree or wood*)

kiri n 錐 a hole-punch, an awl, a drill

kirí n きり end; limit ～ **ga nai** きりがない endless, no limit (*no boundary*)

kiri-kabu n 切り株 (*tree*) stump

kirimásu, kíru v 切ります, 切る cuts; cuts off, disconnects; hangs up (*phone*)

kirinuki n 切り抜き clipping (*from newspaper, etc.*)

kirisame n 霧雨 drizzle

Kirisuto n キリスト Christ

Kirisuto-kyō n キリスト教 Christianity

kiritsu n 規律 discipline

kíro n キロ **1.** kilogram **2.** kilometer **3.** kilowatt **4.** kiloliter

kiró' v 切ろう = **kirimashō** 切りましょう (let's cut it!)

kiroku n 記録 (*historic*) record: **shin-kíroku** 新記録 a new record (*an event*)

kiru v 着る = **kimásu** 着ます (wears)

kíru v 切る = **kimásu** 切ります (cuts)

kíryō n 器量 personal appearance; looks; ability

kisaku (na) adj 気さく（な）not put on airs

kisen n 汽船 steamship

kisen n 貴賤 [BOOKISH] rank

kisétsu n 季節 season: **kisetsu-fū** 季節風 seasonal wind

kishá n 汽車 (*non-electric/steam*) train

kishá n 記者 = **shinbun-kíshá** 新聞記者 newspaper reporter, journalist

kishí n 岸 shore, bank

kishi-men n きしめん long thin udon (= **himo-kawa(-údon)** ひもかわ（うどん））

kishitsu n 気質 temperament

kishō n 気象 weather: **kishō-dai** 気象台 weather observatory

kishúkúsha n 寄宿舎 dormitory; boarding house

kisó n 基礎 base, foundation (*base*)

kisoimásu, kisóu v 競います, 競う competes, vies: **... o kisótte** ... を競って competing (*in competition*) for ...

kisóku n 規則 rule, regulation

kissa-ten n 喫茶店 a tearoom, a coffee house, a café

kísu n キス kiss

kísu n キス・鱚 sillago (fish)

kita ν 着た = **kimáshita** 着ました (wore)
kitá ν 来た = **kimáshita** 来ました (came)
kita n 北 north: **kita-guchi** 北口 the north exit/entrance; **kita-yori (no kaze)** 北寄り (の風) northerly (wind)
Kita-Ámerika n 北アメリカ North America
Kita-Chōsen n 北朝鮮 North Korea
kita-yori adj 北寄り northerly: ~ **no kaze** 北寄りの風 northerly wind
kitaemásu, kitaéru ν 鍛えます, 鍛える forges, tempers; drills, disciplines
kitai n 期待 expectation: ~ **shimásu** 期待します expects, anticipates
kitai n 気体 vapor, a gas
ki-tai ν 着たい wants to wear: **ki-taku arimasén** 着たくありません doesn't want to wear
ki-tái ν 来たい wants to come: **ki-táku arimasén** 来たくありません doesn't want to come
kitaku n 帰宅 returning home: ~ **shimásu** 帰宅します returns home
kitanái adj 汚い dirty; untidy, messy
kite ν 着て: **kíte-ikimásu/kimásu** 着ていきます/きます wears it there/here → **kimásu** 着ます
kité ν 来て → **kimásu** 来ます
kitei n 規定 [BOOKISH] regulation, rule, stipulation: **kítei no …** 規定の… regular, stipulated, compulsory: ~ **shimásu** 規定します prescribes, stipulates, requires
kiteki n 汽笛 whistle (steam)
kiten n 機転 wit: ~ **no kiku** 機転の利く quick-witted
kitsuen n 喫煙 smoking: ~ **shimásu** 喫煙します smokes
kitsuén-sha n 喫煙者 smoker
kitsuén-shitsu(/-seki) n 喫煙室(/席) smoking room (area/zone/seat)
kitsúi adj きつい 1. tight: **sukejūru ga** ~ スケジュールがきつい (one's) schedule is tight; **uesuto ga** ~ ウエストがきつい is tight in the waist 2. severe, hard, strict (character)
kitsune n キツネ・狐 fox
kittá ν 切った = **kirimáshita** 切りました (cut)
kitte n 切手 (postage) stamp: **kitte-chō**

切手帳 stamp album
kítte ν 切って → **kirimásu** 切ります
kítto adv きっと surely, doubtless, no doubt, undoubtedly
kiwa n 際 brink, edge
kiwadói adj 際どい delicate, dangerous, ticklish
kiwamarimásu, kiwamáru ν 極まります, 極まる comes to an end; gets carried to extremes
kiwamemásu, kiwaméru ν 極めます, 極める carries to extremes
kiwamemásu, kiwaméru ν 究めます, 究める investigates thoroughly
kiwámete adv 極めて extremely
kiyase adj 着やせ looking thinner in clothes: ~ **shimásu** 着やせします is looked thinner in clothes
kiyo ν 着よう = **kimashō** 着ましょう (let's wear)
kíyō (na) adj 器用 (な) skillful, nimble, clever
kíyū n 杞憂 groundless fear
kizamimásu, kizamu ν 刻みます, 刻む chops fine; carves, engraves; notches, nicks
kizashi n 兆し sign(s), symptom(s), hint(s), indication(s), omen(s)
kizu n きず・傷・疵・瑕 wound; scratch, crack, blemish; fault, defect
kizu (ni) ν 着ず (に) = **kináide** 着ないで (not wearing)
kizu-ato n 傷跡 scar
ki-zúite ν 気付いて → **kizukimásu** 気付きます
ki-zúkai n 気遣い anxiety, concern, worry, care (= **hairyo** 配慮, **kokoro-kubari** 心配り)
ki-zukaimásu, ki-zukáu ν 気遣います, 気遣うis anxious/worried about, is concerned over
ki-zukátte ν 気遣って → **ki-zukai-másu** 気遣います
ki-zukimásu, ki-zúku ν 気付きます, 気付く notices
ki-zukimásu, ki-zúku ν 築きます, 築く builds it
kizu-tsukemásu, kizu-tsukéru ν 傷つけます, 傷つける wounds, injures, damages

kizu-tsukimásu, kizu-tsúku v 傷つきます, 傷つく gets wounded, injured, damaged

ko n 子 child (= (*person*) **kodomo** 子供)

ko n 仔 child (*animals in particular*) (→ **ko-néko** 仔猫, **ko-inu** 仔犬, **ko-buta** 仔豚)

kó, koná n 粉 flour

ko-... *prefix* 小… little…, small…: **ko-bako** 小箱 small box

...'-ko *suffix* …個 (*counts small objects*)

...'-ko *suffix* …湖 Lake…: **Biwa-ko** びわ[ビワ・琵琶]湖 Lake Biwa

kō *adv* こう (**kó´** こう + [PARTICLE], **kō´désu** こうです) this way, like this

kō´ n 香 (**o-kō** お香) incense: **o-kō o takimásu** お香を焚きます burns incense (*in a temple, before the memorial tablet of the deceased, etc.*)

kō-... *prefix* 高… high…: **kō-kétsú-atsu** 高血圧 high blood pressure

...'-kō *suffix* …港 port (*of …*): **Kōbé-kō** 神戸港 the port of Kobe

...'-kō *suffix* …校 school, branch (*school*); counter for schools

kōbá, kōjō n 工場 factory, plant

kobamimásu, kobamu v 拒みます, 拒む refuses, rejects; opposes, resists

kóban n 小判 Japanese old coins made of gold (*Edo period*): **koban-zame** コバンザメ・小判鮫 remora (*fish*)

kōban n 交番 police box

kobanashi n 小話 anecdote

kobánde v 拒んで → **kobamimásu** 拒みます

kobaruto n コバルト cobalt: **kobaruto-iro** コバルト色, **kobaruto-burū** コバルトブルー cobalt blue

Kōbe n 神戸 Kobe; **Kōbé-Eki** 神戸駅 Kobe Station

kobito n 小人 dwarf

koboremásu, koboréru v こぼれます, こぼれる it spills

koboshimásu, kobósu v こぼします, こぼす spills it: **guchi o ~** 愚痴をこぼします grumbles, complains

kobú n こぶ・瘤 bump, knob, swelling, lump, hump

kobú-cha n 昆布茶 hot water with dried sea tangle (*drink*)

kó-bun n 子分 henchman, subordinate, follower

kobune n 小舟 small boat

kobura n コブラ cobra

kobushi n こぶし・拳 fist (= **nigiri-kobushi** 握り拳)

ko-buta n 子豚・仔豚 piglet(s), little pig(s)

kōbutsu n 好物 favorite (*food/drink*)

kōcha n 紅茶 (black/red) tea

kóchi n コチ flathead (*fish*)

kō´chi n コーチ coach (*sports*)

kochira *pron* こちら **1.** this one (*of two*) **2.** here, this way **3.** I/me, we/us: **kochira kóso** こちらこそ (*it is used that I should be expressing the apology/gratitude.*)

kochira-gawa n こちら側 this/my/our side

kochō n 誇張 [BOOKISH] exaggeration: **~ shimásu** 誇張します exaggerates

kōchō n 校長 principal/head of a school (*elementary school, junior/senior high school*)

kōchō (na) *adj* 好調(な) satisfactory, favorable, in a good condition: **~ na suberidashi/sutāto** 好調な滑り出し/スタート flying start, good start

kódai n 古代 ancient times: **kódai no** 古代の ancient: **kodai-iseki** 古代遺跡 ancient monument(s)

ko-dakara n 子宝 child(ren): **~ ni megumaremásu** 子宝に恵まれます is blessed with child, has a baby

kodama n こだま echo (= **yama-biko** やまびこ)

kōdan n 公団 public corporation

kōdan n 講壇 [BOOKISH] lecture platform

kodō n 鼓動 heartbeat, pulse

kō´do n コード **1.** (*electricity*) cord **2.** code

kó´do n 高度 high degree, altitude

kōdō n 公道 highway

kōdō n 行動 action, behavior

kōdō n 講堂 public (*lecture*) hall, auditorium

kodoku n 孤独 loneliness

kodomo n 子供 child (= **ko** 子): **kodomó-tachi** 子供たち[達] children; **Kodomo-no-hí** こどもの日 Children's

Day (*5 May*); ~ **no koro** 子供の頃 one's early years

kóe *n* 声 voice; cry: ~ **o dáshite** 声を出して aloud, out loud

koeda *n* 小枝 twig

koemásu, koeru *v* 超[越]えます, 超[越]える crosses (*a height, an obstacle*) = **(koshimásu** 超[越]します, **kosu** 超[越]す)

koemásu, koéru *v* 肥えます, 肥える gets fat (= **futorimásu** 太ります)

kōen *n* 公園 public park

kōen *n* 講演 [BOOKISH] lecture, speech

kōen *n* 後援 [BOOKISH] support, backing

koenai *v* 超[越]えない = **koemasén** 超[越]えません (not cross)

koénai *v* 肥えない = **koemasén** 肥えません (not get fat)

koeraremásu, koerareru *v* 超[越]えられます, 超[越]えられる can cross

koe ro *v* 超えろ [IMPERATIVE] (cross it!) → **koemásu** 超えます

koeru *v* 越える = **koemásu** 越えます (crosses)

koeru *v* 超える = **koemásu** 超えます (crosses)

koeru... *adj* 超える: **o koeru ...** (を)超える... over..., more than... (*people, country, money, temperature, etc.*)

koéru *v* 肥える = **koemásu** 肥えます (gets fat)

koete *v* 超[越]えて → **koemásu** 超[越]えます

kóete *v* 肥えて → **koemásu** 肥えます

kōfuku *n* 幸福 happiness: **kōfuku (na)** 幸福(な) happy

kōfuku *n* 降伏 surrender: ~ **shimásu** 降伏します surrenders

kōfun *n* 興奮 excitement: ~ **shiteimásu** 興奮しています is excited

kōgai *n* 公害 (*environmental*) pollution

kōgai *n* 郊外 suburbs, suburbia

kōgaku *n* 工学 engineering

kōgaku-shin *n* 向学心 desire to learn

kogan *n* 湖岸 [BOOKISH] lakeshore

kōgan *n* 睾丸 testicle(s) [FORMAL]

kōgan *n* 紅顔 peaches and cream, rosy, fresh face (*of young man*)

kōgan *n* 厚顔 [BOOKISH] impudence: **kōgan-muchi (no)** 厚顔無恥(の)

impudent and shameless

kogánai *v* 漕がない = **kogimasén** 漕ぎません (not row)

kōgan-zai *n* 抗がん剤 anticancer drug

kogashimásu, kogásu *v* 焦がします, 焦がす scorches it

kogata (no) *adj* 小型(の) small-size (*model*)

koge *n* 焦げ scorch

kóge *v* 漕げ [IMPERATIVE] (row!) → **kogimásu** 漕ぎます

kógeba *v* 漕げば (if one rows) → **kogimásu** 漕ぎます

kōgeki *n* 攻撃 attack: ~ **shimásu** 攻撃します attacks

kogemásu, kogéru *v* 焦げます, 焦げる gets scorched/burned

kogemásu, kogéru *v* 漕げます, 漕げる can row

kogénai *v* 焦げない = **kogemasén** 焦げません (not get scorched)

kogénai *v* 漕げない = **kogemasén** 漕げません (cannot row)

kogéreba *v* 焦げれば (if it gets scorched) → **kogemásu** 焦げます

kogéreba *v* 漕げれば (if one can row) → **kogemásu** 漕げます

kógeta *adj* 焦げた scorched, burnt, overcooked

kógete *v* 焦げて → **kogemásu** 焦げます

kógete *v* 漕げて → **kogemásu** 漕げます

kō´gi *n* 講義 lecture

kō´gí *n* 抗議 protest: ~ **shimásu** 抗議します protests

kogimásu, kógu *v* 漕ぎます, 漕ぐ rows (*a boat*)

kogítte *n* 小切手 (*bank*) check

kogō *v* 漕ごう = **kogimashō´** 漕ぎましょう (let's row!)

kōgo *n* 口語 spoken language, colloquial (*word*): **kōgo-teki (na)** 口語的(な) colloquial

kogoe *n* 小声 low voice, whisper

Kōgō´(-sama) *n* 皇后(様) the Empress: **Kōgō-héika** 皇后陛下 Her Majesty the Empress

kogoto *n* 小言 (**o-kógoto** お小言) scolding, complaint

kógu *v* 漕ぐ = **kogimásu** 漕ぎます (rows a boat)

kōˊgyo *n* 工業 industry

kohada *n* コハダ shad

kōhai *n* 後輩 one's junior (*colleague, fellow student*)

kohaku *n* コハク・琥珀 amber, succinite: **kohaku-iro** コハク色・琥珀色 amber (*color*)

kohan *n* 湖畔 [BOOKISH] lakeside

kōhei (na) *adj* 公平(な) fair, impartial

kōhii *n* コーヒー coffee: **kōhii-jáwan/-káppu** コーヒー茶碗/カップ coffee cup; **kōhii-pótto** コーヒーポット coffee pot; **kōhii-ten** コーヒー店 coffee shop/house (= **kissaten** 喫茶店)

ko-hítsuji *n* 小羊・子羊 lamb, small sheep: **mayoeru ~** 迷える子羊 The Lost Sheep

kōhyō *n* 好評 favorable criticism

kói *n* 請い・乞い request (= **tanomí** 頼み)

kói *n* コイ・鯉 carp (*fish*)

kói *n* 恋 love (*affair*), romance: **~ ni ochimásu** 恋に落ちます falls in love

kói (no) *adj* 故意(の) deliberate; **kói ni** 故意に deliberately

kói *adj* 濃い deep (*color*), strong (*coffee, tea, taste*), well saturated

kói *v* 来い [IMPERATIVE] (come!) → **kimásu** 来ます

kōˊi *n* 好意・厚意 [BOOKISH] goodwill, favor: **~ o misemásu** 好意を見せます does a favor

kōˊi *n* 行為 act, deed; behavior

koibito *n* 恋人 sweetheart, lover, boyfriend/girlfriend

kóida *v* 漕いだ = **kogimáshita** 漕ぎました (rowed)

koide *v* 漕いで → **kogimásu** 漕ぎます

kóin *n* コイン coin: **koin-rókkā** コインロッカー coin locker

kōin *n* 工員 factory worker

koi-nóbori *n* コイ[鯉]のぼり carp streamers (*for Children's Day (5 May)*)

ko-inu *n* 小犬・子犬・仔犬 puppy/puppies, small dog(s)

koiru *n* コイル coil

koishi *n* 小石 pebble(s)

koitsu *n* こいつ this damn one: **koitsu-ra** こいつら these damn ones

kóji *n* 孤児 orphan: **kóji-in** 孤児院 orphanage

kōˊji *n* 工事 construction work: **kōji-chū** 工事中 under construction

kojiki *n* こじき・乞食 beggar

Kojiki *n* 古事記 "Kojiki, the Records of Ancient Matters"

kójin *n* 個人 an individual

kojin-teki (na) *adj* 個人的(な) individual, personal: **~ iken** 個人的(な)意見 personal opinion

kojiremásu, kojiréru *v* こじれます, こじれる gets twisted, complicated, entangled; (*illness*) worsens

kōjitsu *n* 口実 excuse, pretext

kojō (de/no) *adv, adj* 湖上(で/の) on the lake (*surface*)

kojō *n* 古城 old castle

kōjōˊ *n* 工場 factory, plant (= **kōbá** 工場)

kōjyutsu *n* 口述 dictation

kōjyutsu (no) *adj* 後述(の) after-mentioned

kōˊka *n* 効果 effect: **hiyō-kōka** 費用効果 cost effect

kōˊka *n* 硬貨 coin

kōˊka *n* 高価 high price: **kōˊka (na) ...** 高価(な) ... expensive ... (= **takai** 高い)

kōˊkai *n* 航海 voyage: **~ shimásu** 航海します makes a voyage, sails, navigates

kōˊkai *n* 後悔 regret

kōkai (no) *adj* 公開(の) open to the public, open, public: **~ shimásu** 公開します opens it to the public, discloses; **eiga no ~** 映画の公開 movie release

kokáin *n* コカイン cocaine

kokan *n* 股間 [BOOKISH] between the legs: **kokan-setsu** 股関節 hip joint

kōkan *n* 交換 exchange: **~ shimásu** 交換します exchanges, trades; **meishi-kōkan** 名刺交換 exchanging business cards; **purezento-kōkan** プレゼント交換 exchanging gifts

kōkan-ryūgakusei *n* 交換留学生 exchange student;

kōkan-shinkei *n* 交感神経 sympathetic nerve: **fuku-kōkan-shinkei** 副交感神経 parasympathetic nerve

kōkán-shu n 交換手 operator (= **operēta⁻** オペレーター): **denwa-kōkan-shu** 電話交換手 telephone operator

kōkatsu (na) adj 狡猾(な) sly

koké n 苔 moss

koké n こけ foolishness, a fool: **~ ni saremásu** こけにされます gets trashed

kō-kéiki n 好景気 prosperity, good business conditions

kō-ki n 好機 [BOOKISH] (favorable) opportunity, chance, occasion

kō-ki n 後期 the latter period

kō-ki n 後記 afterword, postscript (= **ato-gaki** 後書き): **henshū-kōki** 編集後記 editor's postscript

kō-kí (shin) n 好奇(心) curiosity, inquisitiveness

kō-kíatsu n 高気圧 high (barometric) pressure

kókka n 国家 nation

kokkai n 国会 assembly, parliament, congress, Diet (= **gikai** 議会)

kokkei (na) adj こっけい[滑稽](な) amusing, funny

kokki n 国旗 national flag

kokkō n 国交 diplomatic relations

kókku (-san) n コック(さん) cook, chef

kokkyō n 国境 border (of country)

koko pron ここ here, this place

kō-kō n 高校 senior high school

kókóa n ココア cocoa

kōkoku n 広告 advertisement

kókóna(t)tsu n ココナ(ッ)ツ coconut (= **yashi no mi** ヤシの実): **kokonáttu-miruku** ココナッツミルク coconut milk

kokonoka n 九日 nine days; the 9th day (of month)

kokónotsu n 九つ nine; nine years old (= **kyūsai** 九歳)

kokóro n 心 mind, heart, spirit, feeling: **~ kara (no)** 心から(の) heart-felt, sincere

kokoro-atari n 心当たり idea

kokoro-bosói adj 心細い lonely

kokoro-kubari n 心配り concern, care (= **hairyo** 配慮, **ki-zúkai** 気遣い)

kokoromi n 試み trial, attempt, test

kokoromimásu, kokoromíru v 試みます, 試みる tries, attempts, tests

kokoro-mochi n 心持ち feelings, spirit, mood

kokorozashi n 志 1. mind; intention; purpose 2. ambition, hope 3. good-will, kindness; gift

kokorozashimásu, kokorozásu v 志します, 志す sets one's mind

kokoro-zuke n 心付け tip, gratuity (= **chippu** チップ)

kokoro-zuyói adj 心強い heartening, encouraging: **~ sonzai** 心強い存在 dependable person: **~ kotoba** 心強い言葉 encouraging words

kōkō´-sei n 高校生 (senior) high-school student: **joshi/danshi kosei** 女子/男子高生 high-school girl/boy

...´-koku suffix ...国 1. (name of certain) country: **Bei-koku** 米国 America (= **Amerika** アメリカ America, U.S.(A.), **Amerika-Gasshū´-koku** アメリカ合衆国 United States of America): **Ei-koku** 英国 Great Britain, the United Kingdom (U.K.) (= **Igirisu** イギリス): **Chū´-goku** 中国 China (= **Chūkajinmin-kyōwá-koku** 中華人民共和国): **Nihón-koku** 日本国 Japan (= **Nihón, Nippón** 日本) 2. **koku-...** 国...national, state

kokuban n 黒板 blackboard: **kokubán-keshi** 黒板消し, **kokubán-fuki** 黒板拭き blackboard eraser

kōkū-bin n 航空便 = **kōkū-yū´bin** 航空郵便 airmail

kokubō n 国防 national defense

kokudō n 国道 highway

Kokudo-Kōtsū-shō n 国土交通省 Ministry of Land, Infrastructure, Transport and Tourism (MLIT)

kōkū-gáisha n 航空会社 airline company

kokujin n 黒人 black people, Afro-American

kokumin n 国民 a people, a nation; national(s), citizen(s)

kokúmotsu n 穀物 grain (cereal)

kokúnai (no) adj 国内(の) internal, domestic, inland

kokuritsu (-) adj 国立 national,

government-established: **kokuritsu-toshokan** 国立図書館 national library: **kokuritsu-daigaku** 国立大学 national university

kokúrui *n* 穀類 cereal(s), grain

kokusai *n* 国際: **kokusai-dénwa** 国際電話 international phone call; **kokusai-teki (na)** 国際的(な) international (= **intānashonaru (na)** インターナショナル(な))

Kokusai-réngō *n* 国際連合 United Nations

kokusan (no) *adj* 国産(の) domestic(ally) made, made in Japan: **kokusan-hin** 国産品 domestic product: **kokusan-sha** 国産車 domestic car

kokuseki *n* 国籍 nationality

kōkū-shōkan *n* 航空書簡 air letter

kōkyo *n* 皇居 palace (*in Tokyo*); the Imperial Palace

kókyō *n* 故郷 hometown, birth-place (= **furusato** ふるさと)

kōkyō (no) *adj* 公共(の) public: **kōkyō-no-ba** 公共の場 public area

kōkyō-ryō´kin *n* 公共料金 utility bills/charges

kokyū *n* 呼吸 respiration, breathing

kōkyū (na) *adj* 高級(な) high-class/grade, high-ranking; fancy: **kōkyū-hin** 高級品 fancy goods

kóma *n* こま・コマ・独楽 a toy top: **koma-máwashi** 独楽回し top-spinning

komakái *adj* 細かい **1.** fine, small **2.** detailed, exact **3.** thrifty **4.** small (*change*): **komakakú shimásu** 細かくします cashes it into smaller bills/coins

koma-mono *n* 小間物 notions, haberdashery, dime-store goods

komamónó-ya *n* 小間物屋 dime store, haberdasher

koma-nezumi *n* コマネズミ・独楽鼠 (*Japanese*) dancing mouse

komarasemásu, komaraséru *v* 困らせます, 困らせる bothers, causes inconvenience; embarrasses

komarimásu, komáru *v* 困ります, 困る gets perplexed, embarrassed, troubled; is at a loss; is in need: **komátta-kotó** 困った事 predicament, mess, plight

komāsharu *n* コマーシャル commercial (*message*) (= **shiiému** シーエム): **terebi-komāsharu** テレビコマーシャル TV commercial

komayaka (na) *adj* こま[細]やか(な) meticulous, attentive, tender: **~ na aijō** 細やかな愛情 tender love: **(kime-) ~ na** (きめ)細やかな detailed; fine, mild; kind

komé *n* コメ・米 (**o-kome** お米) rice (*hulled, uncooked*)
komé-ya *n* 米屋 (**o-komeya** お米屋) rice dealer/store

kómeba *v* 込めば・混めば (if it gets crowded) → **komimásu** 込み[混み]ます

komemásu, koméru *v* 込めます, 込める includes

koméreba *v* 込めれば (if one includes) → **komemásu** 込めます

kómete *v* 込めて → **komemásu** 込めます

komichi *n* 小道 path, lane

komi-itta *v* 込み入った complicated, intricate (*situation, subject*)

komimásu, kómu *v* 込み[混み]ます, 込む・混む gets crowded

kōmin *n* 公民 citizen, civilian (= **shímin** 市民)

kōmoku *n* 項目 item: (**nyūryoku**) **hissu-kōmoku** (入力)必須項目 mandatory field(s)

kómon *n* 顧問 [BOOKISH] consultant, adviser: **komon-bengoshi** 顧問弁護士 a legal adviser

kōmon *n* 校門 school gate

kōmon *n* 肛門 anus

komórí *n* 子守, 子守り babysitter: **komori-uta** 子守歌[唄] lullaby, cradle song

kō´mori *n* コウモリ bat (*flying mammal*)
kōmori-gása *n* こうもり[コウモリ]傘 umbrella (*black, cloth umbrella often used by males in Japan*)

komúgi *n* 小麦 wheat: **komúgi-ko** 小麦粉 wheat flour

kōmū-in *n* 公務員 government worker/employee, official

kōmurimásu, kōmúru *v* 被ります,

被る sustains, suffers, incurs (*unfair treatment, tribulation*): **songai o ~** 損害を被ります suffers a loss

kón *n* 紺 = **kon-iro** 紺色 (dark blue)

koná *n* 粉 powder; flour
kona-gona *n* 粉々: **~ shimásu** 粉々にします pulverize
kona-gúsuri *n* 粉薬 powdered medicine
kona-míruku *n* 粉ミルク powdered milk, dry milk

kónai *v* 来ない = **kimasén** 来ません (does not come)

kō´nai *n* 構内 campus: **kō´nai (no)** 構内(の) intramural

konaidá *adv* こないだ [INFORMAL] → kono-aidá この間

kónakatta *v* 来なかった = **kimasén deshita** 来ませんでした (didn't come)

konashimásu, konasu *v* こなします, こなす **1.** powders; digests **2.** (ful)fills, manages (*to do it*): **chūmon o ~** 注文をこなします fills an order

kónban *n* 今晩 tonight: **Konban wa** こんばんは Good evening.

konbini(-ensu sutoá) *n* コンビニ(エンススストアー) convenience store

konbō *n* 棍棒 [BOOKISH] club, bludgeon

kónbu *n* コンブ・昆布 kelp (*a kind of seaweed*)

konchū *n* 昆虫 insect

kondate *n* 献立 [BOOKISH] menu (= **ményū** メニュー)

kónde *v* 込んで・混んで → komimásu 込みます・混みます: **kónde-imásu** 混んでいます is crowded

kóndo *n, adv* 今度 this time; next

kondō´mu *n* コンドーム condom

kóne *n* コネ connection, "pull": **~ o tsukemásu** コネを付けます establishes a connection, gets pull (*with a person*)

ko-néko *n* 小猫・子猫・仔猫 kitten(s), small cat(s)

konekutā *n* コネクター connector

kongan *n* 懇願 [BOOKISH] entreaty: **~ shimásu** 懇願します begs, implores, requests

kongari yakimásu (yaku) *v* こんがり焼きます(焼く) bakes/toasts/roasts/grills/sunburns until a beautiful brown

kongetsu *n* 今月 this month

kongō´-seki *n* 金剛石 [BOOKISH] diamond (= **daiya(mondo)** ダイヤ(モンド))

kongo (wa) *adv* 今後(は) from now on, in the future

kon'i (na/ni) *adj, adv* 懇意(な/に) friendly, close, intimate: **... to ~ ni shite imásu** ...と懇意にしています is very intimate with ...

konin *n* 婚姻 marriage (= **kekkon** 結婚): **konin-todoke** 婚姻届 marriage notification

kōnin (no) *adj* 公認(の) authorized, certified: **kōnin-kaikéishi** 公認会計士 certified public accountant (CPA), chartered accountant

kon (iro) *n* 紺(色) dark blue

konkai *n, adv* 今回 this time

konkan *n* 根幹 [BOOKISH] basis, foundation

konki *n* 根気 [BOOKISH] patience: **~ ga iru shigoto** 根気がいる仕事 work which requires patience

konki *n* 婚期 [BOOKISH] marriageable age: **~ o nogasu** 婚期を逃す is past marriageable age

konkurabe *n* 根比べ waiting game, endurance contest

konkuríito *n* コンクリート concrete (*cement*)

konkū´ru *n* コンクール prize contest, prize competition (= **konpe** コンペ)

kónkyo *n* 根拠 basis, grounds, authority, evidence: **konkyo-chi** 根拠地 base, home ground: **~ no nai uwasa** 根拠のない噂 groundless rumor

konkyū *n* 困窮 [BOOKISH] poverty: **~ shite imásu** 困窮しています is in poverty, is in financial difficulties

konna ... *adj* こんな... such as, this kind of: **konna ni** こんなに to this extent, this much

kónnan *n* 困難 [BOOKISH] difficulty, trouble, hardship
kónnan (na) *adj* 困難(な) difficult

Konnichi wa *interj* こんにちは Good afternoon; Hello!

konnyákú *n* コンニャク devil's-tongue root made into gelatin

kono... *adj* この... this ..., these...

122

kono-aidá *adv* この間 the other day, a while ago, lately (= konaidá こないだ)

kono-goro *adv* この頃 recently (= chíká goro 近頃, saikin 最近)

kono-máe (no)... *adj* この前(の)... the last...

kono-tsúgi *n* この次 next time (= jikai 次回 [BOOKISH])

kōnō *n* 効能 effect (*effectiveness*) (= kōyō 効用, kiki-me 効き目): ~ ga arimásu 効能があります is effective

kónome, kí-no-me *n* 木の芽 **1.** tree sprout **2.** Japanese pepper sprout

konomi *n* 好み (o-konomi お好み) liking, taste: konomí no ... 好みの... that one likes, that is to oné's taste/liking, favorite ...: ~ no taipu 好みのタイプ one's type: o-konomi-yaki お好み焼き seasoned pancake

konomimásu, konómu *v* 好みます, 好む likes, is fond of, prefers

konónde *v* 好んで → konomimásu 好みます

kónpasu *n* コンパス compass (*for drafting*)

konpe *n* コンペ prize competition, prize contest (= konkū´ru コンクール)

konpon *n* 根本 [BOOKISH] foundation, basis: konpon-teki (na) 根本的(な) fundamental, basic

konpyū´ta *n* コンピュータ computer

konran *n* 混乱 mess (*disorder*), confusion, jumble: ~ shimásu 混乱します gets confused

kónro *n* コンロ stove (*portable cooking*)

konsárutanto *n* コンサルタント consultant: keiei-konsarutanto 経営コンサルタント management consultant: konsarutanto-gaisha コンサルタント会社 consultant company

konseki *n* 痕跡 [BOOKISH] trace, mark, vestige (= áto 跡): ~ o nokoshimásu 痕跡を残します leaves a mark

kónsénto *n* コンセント **1.** (*electricity*) outlet, (*light*) plug: ~ ni tsunagimásu コンセントにつなぎます plugs in **2.** consent: infōmudo-konsento インフォームド・コンセント informed consent

konshín-kai *n* 懇親会 reception, get-together party

konshū *n* 今週 this week

konsome *n* コンソメ thin Western soup, consomme

kōn-sutáchi *n* コーンスターチ cornstarch

kontákuto *n* コンタクト = kontakuto-rénzu コンタクトレンズ contact lenses

kónténa *n* コンテナ container (*for transporting goods*)

kóntesuto *n* コンテスト contest

kón'ya *n* 今夜 tonight

kon'yaku *n* 婚約 engagement (*to be married*): konyaku-yubiwa 婚約指輪 engagement ring (= engéji ringu エンゲージリング): (... to) ~ shite imásu (...と) 婚約しています is engaged (to ...)

kon'yoku *n* 混浴 (*hot springs*) mixed bathing

kónzatsu *n* 混雑 jam, congestion: ~ shiteimásu 混雑しています is crowded

kópii *n* コピー copy (*photocopy*) (= fukusha 複写)

koppu *n* コップ a glass, a cup

kōra *n* コウラ・甲羅 shell (*of tortoise, etc.*)

kó'ra *n* コーラ cola

koraemásu, koráéru *v* 堪えます, 堪える **1.** stands, bears **2.** controls, restrains, represses

kōran *n* コーラン Koran, Quran

koramu *n* コラム column, boxed article(s) (= kakomi-kiji 囲み記事)

koranai *v* 凝らない = korimásén 凝りません (not get engrossed/absorbed (*in*); not get stiff)

kōranai *v* 凍らない = kōrimasén 凍りません (not freeze)

ko(ra)remásu, ko(ra)réru *v* 来(ら)れます, 来(ら)れる **1.** can come **2.** [PASSIVE] has them come (*to one's distress*); [HONORIFIC] comes (= ira-sshaimásu いらっしゃいます)

ko(ra)rénai *v* 来(ら)れない = ko(ra)remasén 来(ら)れません (cannot come)

ko(ra)réru *v* 来(ら)れる = ko(ra)remásu 来(ら)れます (can come)

kōrasemásu, kōraseru *v* 凍らせます, 凍らせる freezes it

kō´rasu n コーラス chorus, choir

kore pron これ this one: ~ **kara** これから from now on; ~ **to iu/yū** …これという/ゆう… specific, particular

kóreba v 凝れば (if one gets engrossed; if it gets stiff) → **korimásu** 凝ります

koréra (no) adj これら(の) these (things, matters, etc.)

kórera n コレラ cholera: **korera-kin** コレラ菌 Vibrio cholerae

korí n 凝り stiffness, hardening: **káta-korí** 肩こり a stiff shoulder

kōri n 氷 ice: **kaki-gōri** かき氷 shaved ice (eaten with syrup)

kō´ri/kóri n 行李 wicker trunk

korimásu, kóru v 凝ります, 凝る
1. gets engrossed/absorbed (in)
2. (shoulder) gets stiff

korimásu, koriru v 懲ります, 懲りる learns a lesson from one's failure

kōrimásu, kōru v 凍ります, 凍る it freezes

kōritsu (no) adj 公立(の) public, municipal, prefectural

kōritsu n 効率 efficiency: **kōritsu-teki na** 効率的な efficient: **kōritsuka** 効率化 streamlining (= **gōrika** 合理化)

…koro suffix 頃 (at that) time, (at) about (a time), occasion (= … **góro (ni)** …頃(に) (at) about (a time)): **ano-koro (wa)** あの頃(は) (at) that time, then, (in) those days (= **tō´ji (wa)** 当時(は), **sono-koro (wa)** その頃(は)): **kodomo no ~** 子供の頃 (in) one's childhood

koroai n 頃合い suitable time: (**sorosoro**) ~ **desu** (そろそろ)頃合いです It's (about) time to…

korobimásu, korobu v 転びます, 転ぶ falls down, tumbles

korogarimásu, korogaru v 転がります, 転がる it rolls, tumbles

korogashimásu, korogasu v 転がします, 転がす rolls it

korosaremásu, korosareru v 殺されます, 殺される gets killed

koroshimásu, korosu v 殺します, 殺す kills

kóru v 凝る = **korimásu** 凝ります (gets engrossed/absorbed (in); (shoulder)

gets stiff)

kōru v 凍る = **kōrimásu** 凍ります (it freezes)

Korukata n コルカタ Kolkata (former Calcutta)

kóruku n コルク = **korukú-sen** コルク栓 cork

korukú-nuki n コルク抜き corkscrew

kō´ryo n 考慮 consideration, reflection, thought: ~ **shimásu** 考慮します considers; ~ **ni iremásu** 考慮に入れます takes into consideration/account

kō´ryō´ n 香料 spice (= **supaisu** スパイス)

koryōrí-ya n 小料理屋 small traditional Japanese restaurant

kōryū n 交流 1. AC (alternating current) 2. ~ **shimásu** 交流します exchanges, interchanges

kósa n 濃さ strength (of saturation), deepness (of color)

kosaemásu, kosaeru v こさえます, こさえる = **koshiraemásu** こしらえます makes, concocts

kōsai n 交際 social relations, company, association (= **kōyū** 交遊): **kōsai-hi** 交際費 an expense account: ~ **shimásu** 交際します associates, keeps company

ko-saji n 小さじ teaspoon (= **tii-supūn** ティースプーン)

kōsaku shimásu (suru) v 工作します (する) 1. builds 2. handcrafts

kosame n 小雨 light rain, drizzle

kōsan n 降参 surrender: ~ **shimásu** 降参します surrenders, You've got me!; gives up, goes down (= **Máitta** 参った)

kosanai v 越さない = **koshimasén** 越しません, etc. (not go over; not …)

kosasemásu, kosaséru v 来させます, 来させる has/lets one come

kosasénai v 来させない = **kosasemásén** 来させません (not have/let one come)

kosásete v 来させて = **kosasemásu** 来させます

kōsa-ten n 交差点 an intersection (of streets), a crossing

kose v 越せ [IMPERATIVE] (exceed it!) → **koshimásu** 越します

kosé v 漉せ [IMPERATIVE] (strain it!) → **koshimásu** 漉します

koséba v 越せば (if it exceeds; if …)
→ koshimásu 越します

kosei n 個性 individuality, character,
personality: kosei-teki 個性的 unique
(= yuniiku ユニーク): ~ o nobashimásu
個性を伸ばします develops
individuality: kosei-yutaka 個性豊か
has a very distinctive personality

kōsei n 構成 constitution, construction,
composition

kōsei n 更正 reclamation, reformation

kōsei n 更生 revival, reformation;
regeneration, rehabilitation: hikō-
shōnen no ~ 非行少年の更生
rehabilitation of juvenile delinquents

kōsei n 公正 impartiality
kōsei na 公正(な) adj impartial, fair

kōsei n 校正 proofreading: ~ shimásu
校正します proofreads
kōsei-sha, kōsei-gakari n 校正者, 校
正係 proofreader

kōsei-bússhitsu n 抗生物資 anti-
biotic(s): ~ o tōyoshimásu 抗生物質を
投与します administers

Kōsei-Rōdō-shō n 厚生労働省
Ministry of Health, Labor and Welfare

kōsei shimásu (suru) v 構成します
(する) constitutes

kōsei shimásu (suru) v 更生します
(する) reforms, starts a new life

kōsei shimásu (suru) v 校正します
(する) proofreads

koseki n 戸籍 family register: koseki-
tōhon 戸籍謄本 full copy of one's
family register: koseki-shōhon 戸籍抄
本 abstract of one's family register

kosemásu, koseru v 越せます, 越せ
る can go over; can move (house)

kosemásu, koseru v 漉せます, 漉せ
る can filter/strain it

kōsen n 光線 ray, beam (of light), light

kosenai v 越せない = kosemásén 越せ
ません (cannot go over; cannot move
(house))

kosete v 越せて → kosemásu 越せ
ます

kōsha n 後者 the latter

kōsha n 校舎 school-house

koshi n 腰 loin, hip, lower part of back
koshi-káké n 腰掛け seat, chair, bench

(= isu いす・椅子)

koshi-maki n 腰巻き loincloth;
petticoat

koshi -no-kubire n 腰のくびれ waist
(= uesuto ウエスト)

koshi v 越し → koshimásu 越します

kō´shi n 講師 instructor(s), lecturer(s)

Kōshi n 孔子 Confucius

koshi-káke n 腰掛け seat, chair (= isu
椅子)

koshi-kakemásu, koshi-kakéru v 腰
掛けます, 腰掛ける sits down

koshimásu, kosu v 越します・越す
goes/runs over, goes across; moves
house (= hikkoshimásu 引っ越します)

koshimásu, kosu v 超します, 超す
goes/runs over (= chō´ka shimásu
超過します, ō´bā shimásu オーバーし
ます); exceeds: do o ~ 度を超します
goes too far

koshimásu, kosu v 漉します, 漉す
filters/strains it

kōshin n 行進 march(ing)

kōshin n 更新 renewal, update

kōshin shimásu (suru) v 行進します
(する) marches

kōshin shimásu (suru) v 更新します
(する) renews, updates (a contract,
website, etc.)

koshiraemásu, koshiraeru v 拵えま
す, 拵える makes, concocts

koshite v 越して → koshimásu
越します

koshite v 漉して → koshimásu
漉します

kosho n 古書 old book(s), antique
book(s); secondhand book(s) (= furu-
hon 古本)

koshō n 故障 1. breakdown, something
wrong: ~ shimásu 故障します it breaks
down (gets inoperative) 2. hindrance

koshō´ n コショウ・胡椒 pepper

koshō n 呼称 appellation, name

koshō n 小姓 foot page

koshō n 交渉 negotiations

kōshoku (na) adj 好色(な) erotic;
lecherous: kōshoku-kan 好色漢 lecher

kōshū n 公衆 the public, the masses:
kōshū-dénwa 公衆電話 public
telephone

kōshū no adj 公衆の public

kōshū(kai) n 講習 (会) lecture class, course (*not regular classes in school*)

... **kóso** (*masa-ni*) adv ...こそ (まさに) precisely, exactly, just; certainly, really → **mása-ni** まさに・正に: **kore-koso** これこそ This is precisely/exactly/just the thing: **kare-koso** 彼こそ he is truly

kosó´ v 越そう = **koshimashō´** 越しましょう (let's go over)

kosó´ v 漉そう = **koshimashō´** 漉しましょう (let's filter!)

kōsō no adj 高層 (の) highrise: **kōsō-bíru** 高層ビル high-rise building, skyscraper

kosuku n 高速 [BOOKISH] high speed: **kōsoku-dō´ro** 高速道路 expressway, freeway; **kōsoku-gí(y)a** 高速ギア[ギヤ] high gear

kossetsu n 骨折 bone fracture: ~ **shimásu** 骨折します fractures

kossóri (to) adv こっそり (と) secretly, sneakily, sneakingly, on the sly

kosu v 越す = **koshimásu** 越します (goes/runs over, goes across, moves house)

kosu v 漉す = **koshimásu** 漉します (filters/strains it)

kosu v 超す = **koshimásu** 超します (goes/runs over)

kōsu n コース **1.** course; (*traffic, swim*) lane **2.** a set series of chef's choices, a set meal: **mein-kōsu** メインコース main course: **osusume (no)** ~ お勧め(の)コース recommended course

kosuchūmu n コスチューム costume (= **kasō** 仮装)

kōsui n 香水 perfume

kosupure n コスプレ cosplay

kosurimásu, kosúru v 擦ります, 擦る rubs, scrapes

kosu´tté v 擦って → **kosurimásu** 擦ります

kotáé n 答 (え) an answer, reply, response (= **kaitō** 回答, **henji** 返事 (**o-henji** お返事), **hentō** 返答)

kotáé n 応え a response, an answer (= **henji** 返事 (**o-henji** お返事), **hentō** 返答, **ōtō** 応答) (= → **tegótae** 手応え)

kotaemásu, kotáéru v 答えます, 答える answers

kotaemásu, kotáéru v 応えます, 応える responds, responds to, meets: **kitai/yōbō ni** ~ 期待/要望に応えます meets one's expectations/request

kotaé ro 答えろ [IMPERATIVE] (answer!) → **kotaemásu** 答えます

kotai n 固体 a solid

kōtai n 交替 alternation: ~ **shimásu** 交替します alternates, shifts (*with*)

Kōtáishi n 皇太子, **Kōtáishi-sama** 皇太子さま the Crown Prince **Kōtáishi-hi** n 皇太子妃 the Crown Princess

kōtaku n 光沢 luster, gloss, sheen: ~ **ga arimásu** 光沢があります lustrous, glossy, shiny

kotatsu n こたつ (**o-kóta** おこた) traditional quilt-covered heating arrangement (*foot warmer*)

kotchí pron こっち → **kochira** こちら

kotei n 固定 fixation: ~ **shimásu** 固定します fixes, fastens, stabilizes

kōtei n 校庭 school grounds

kōtei n 肯定 affirmation: ~ **shimásu** 肯定します affirms

kōtei n 皇帝 emperor: **Rōma-kōtei** ローマ皇帝 Roman emperor

kōtei n 工程 process, progress: **seisaku-kōtei** 製作工程 process for forming: **sagyō-kōtei** 作業工程 working process: **kōtei-kanrihyō** 工程管理表 process management timetable

kotēji n コテージ cottage

koteki-tai n 鼓笛隊 drum and fife band

koten n 古典 classic work (*literature, art, etc.*) (= **kurashikku** クラシック): **koten-ongaku** 古典音楽 classic music: **koten-bungaku** 古典文学 classic literature: **koten-teki na** 古典的な classical

koten n 個展 private exhibition: ~ **o hirakimásu** 個展を開きます holds a private exhibition

kotesaki n 小手先: ~ **de gomakashimásu** 小手先でごまかします uses cheap tricks

kote-shirabe (ni) adv 小手調べ(に) (*for*) a trial, (*for*) practice

126

kōtetsu *n* 鋼鉄 steel (= **suchiiru** スチ ール)

kotó *n* こと・事 thing, matter; fact; words, sentence; case, circumstance, happening; experience

kóto *n* 琴 (**o-kóto** お琴) Japanese harp
koto-ji *n* 琴柱 the bridges on a Japanese harp

kóto *n* 古都 ancient capital

kō'to *n* コート **1.** coat: **~ o haorimásu** コートを羽織ります puts on one's coat **2.** (*athletic*) court: **tenisu-kō'to** テニスコート tennis court

kotō *n* 孤島 [BOOKISH] solitary island

kotobá *n* 言葉 (**o-kotoba** お言葉) **1.** word, words; sentence (*spoken*); remark **2.** speech **3.** language (= **gengo** 言語) **3. o-kotoba** お言葉: **~ ni amaete…** お言葉に甘えて… I will accept your kind offer; **~ desu ga…** お言葉ですが… not to split hairs, but…; **~ o kaesu yō desu ga…** お言葉を返すようですが… I don't mean to contradict you, but…

kōtō-gákkō *n* 高等学校 = **kōkō** 高校 high school: **kōtō-gákkō no séito** 高等学校の生徒 (**kōkō'-sei** 高校生) high-school student

kotogara *n* 事柄 [BOOKISH] affair, matter (= **kotó** こと・事)

kotonarimásu, kotonáru *v* 異なります, 異なる is different, differs: **kotonátte imásu** 異なっています is different; **kotonátta …** 異なった… different

kóto-ni *adv* ことに・殊に **1.** especially (= **tóku-ni** 特に) **2.** [+ NEGATIVE] less likely **3.** moreover, what is more

koto (no) *adj* 口頭(の) oral, verbal.
kōtō-shímon 口頭試問 oral examination

ko-tori *n* 小鳥 small bird

kotosara *adv* ことさら particularly

kotoshi *n* 今年 this year

kototarimásu, kototariru *v* 事足ります, 事足りる suffices, is enough: **… to ie ba ~** …と言えば事足ります suffice to say that …

kotawári *n* 断り refusal; notice, warning; permission: **~ mo náku** 断りもなく without notice/permission/leave

kotowarimásu, kotowáru *v* 断ります, 断る **1.** refuses, declines, begs off **2.** makes excuses **3.** gives notice **4.** dismisses, lays off, fires

kotowaza *n* ことわざ・諺 proverb(s)

kotozuké, kotozute *n* 言付け, 言づて a message (*for someone*) (= **méssēji** メッセージ)

kotsú *n* こつ[コツ] knack, trick, tip

kotsū *n* 交通 traffic, transportation; communication(s): **kotsū-hyō'shiki** 交通標識 traffic signs; **kotsū-jū'tai** 交通渋滞 traffic jam; **kotsū-shíngō** 交通信号 traffic signal(s)

kotsuban *n* 骨盤 pelvis

kotsubu *n* 小粒 small grain

kō-tsugō *n* 好都合 (*convenience*) expediency

kotsūjū'tai *n* traffic jam 交通渋滞; **~ de no iraira** 交通渋滞でのイライラ road rage

kotsúzui *n* 骨髄 bone marrow

ko-tsuzumi *n* 小鼓 small hourglass-shaped drum

kótta *v* 凝った = **korimáshita** 凝りました (got stiff)

kótta *v* 凍った = **kōrimáshita** 凍りました (it froze)

kótte *v* 凝って → **korimásu** 凝ります

kótte *v* 凍って → **kōrimásu** 凍ります: **~ imásu** 凍っています is frozen

kottō'-hin *n* 骨董品 curios, antiques

kotton *n* コットン cotton (= **mén** 綿, **momen** 木綿)

kōun *n* 幸運 good fortune

ko-uri *n* 小売り retail: **~ shimásu** 小売りします retails, sells retail

kouri-gyō *n* 小売業 retail business

kouri-ten *n* 小売店 retail store, retailer

kowagari *n* 怖[恐]がり a coward (= **okubyō-monó** 臆病者): **kowagari-másu** 怖[恐]がります fears, takes flight, is afraid

kowái *adj* こわい・怖[恐]い is afraid; frightful; terrific

kowairo *n* 声色 **1.** tone of voice (= **kowane** 声音) **2.** impersonation: **~ o tsukaimásu** 声色を使います impersonates

kowane *n* 声音 tone of voice (= **kowairo** 声色)

kowaremásu, kowaréru v 壊れます、壊れる it breaks/smashes

kowaremono n こわれ物 fragile (*article*): **kowaremono-chū´i** こわれ物注意 Handle With Care

koware-yasúi *adj* 壊れやすい fragile, easily broken, breakable

kowashimásu, kowásu v 壊します、壊す breaks/smashes it, destroys: **kuruma o ~** 車を壊します wrecks a car; **karada o ~** 体をこわします ruins one's health, **o-naka o ~** おなかをこわします develops stomach trouble; **(hito no) kíbun o ~** (人の)気分をこわします spoils a person's mood, makes a person feel bad

koya n 小屋 hut, shed, cabin

kōya n 荒野 wild land, wilderness

kōyaku n 公約 (*public*) pledge
kōyaku-sū n 公約数 common factor

koyama n 小山 hill

koyō n 雇用 [BOOKISH] employment (*hiring*): **koyō-keiyakusho** 雇用契約書 employment agreement

koyó´ v 来よう = **kimashō´** 来ましょう (let's come!)

kōyō n 紅葉 red leaves

kōyō n 効用 effect (*effectiveness*) (= **kiki-me** 効き目, **kōnō** 効能): **~ ga arimásu** 効用があります is effective

kōyō (no) *adj* 公用(の) official: **kōyō-go** 公用語 official language

koyomí n 暦 calendar (= **karénda** カレンダー)

kōyu n 香油 balm

kōyu n 鉱油 mineral oil

kōyū n 交友 companion, friend(s)

kōyū n 交遊 social relations, company, association (= **kōsai** 交際): **~ shimásu** 交遊します associates, keeps company

kō yū (iu) ... *adj* こうゆう(いう)... this kind/sort of ..., such ... (= **konna** こんな)

koyú (no) *adj* 固有(の) characteristic

kōza n 口座 an account: **ginkō-kóza** 銀行口座 bank account: **~ o hirakimásu** 口座を開きます opens an account

kō´zan n 鉱山 a mine

kō´zan n 高山 high mountain

ko-zara n 小皿 saucer

kōzen (no/to) *adj, adv* 公然(の/と) open(ly), public(ly)

ko-zeni n 小銭 small change, coins

kozō´ n 小僧 young monk

kōzō´ n 構造 structure, makeup, organization

kōzu n 構図 (*picture*) composition

kózuchi n 小槌 a small hammer: **uchide-no-kozuchi** 打ち出の小槌 lucky mallet, magical mallet

kozue n 梢 treetop

kōzui n 洪水 flood: **~ ga okorimásu** 洪水が起こります floods

kózukai n 小使い janitor, custodian; attendant; servant

kózukai n 小遣い (**o-kózukai** お小遣い) pin money, pocket money

kózu (ni) *adv* 来ず(に) = **kónai de** 来ないで (not coming)

kozútsumi n 小包 package, parcel

kú n 九 nine (= **kyū** 九)

kú n 句 phrase

kú n 区, ...´**-ku** ...区 **1.** a ward (*in a city*) (→ **ku-yákusho** 区役所): **Tōkyō nijūsan-ku** 東京23区 twenty-three wards of Tokyo, the special 23 wards which make up the core and the most populous part of Tokyo (**Adachi-ku** 足立区, **Arawkawa-ku** 荒川区, **Bunkyo-ku** 文京区, **Chiyoda-ku** 千代田区, **Chuo-ku** 中央区, **Edogawa-ku** 江戸川区, **Itabashi-ku** 板橋区, **Katsushika-ku** 葛飾区, **Kita-ku** 北区, **Koto-ku** 江東区, **Meguro-ku** 目黒区, **Minato-ku** 港区, **Nakano-ku** 中野区, **Nerima-ku** 練馬区, **Ota-ku** 大田区, **Setagaya-ku** 世田谷区, **Shibuya-ku** 渋谷区, **Shinjuku-ku** 新宿区, **Shinagawa-ku** 品川区, **Suginami-ku** 杉並区, **Sumida-ku** 墨田区, **Taito-ku** 台東区, **Toshima-ku** 豊島区) **2.** zone (= **kúiki** 区域)

ku-yákusho n 区役所 ward office

kū´ v 食う (VULGAR FORM *of* eats, bites *used mainly by males*) = **kuimásu** 食います (eats, bites) (POLITE FORM **tabemásu** 食べます)

kubarimásu, kubáru v 配ります、配る distributes, allots; deals (*cards*)

kúbetsu n 区別 difference, differentiation; discrimination: **~**

shimásu 区別します differentiates, discriminates

kubi n 首 neck: **~ ni shimásu** 首にします fires, lays off, disemploys; **kubi-kázari** 首飾り necklace

kubi-wa n 首輪 (*dog*) collar

kubire n くびれ neck (*of a bottle*), constricted place, waist

kubomi n くぼみ・窪み hollow, dent, depression

kuchi n 口 **1.** mouth: **kuchi (kará) no** 口（から）の oral **2.** words, speech: **~ o hasamu** 口をはさむ interrupt **3.** entrance; hole, opening, slot **4.** cork, stopper **5.** job opening

kuchi-beni n 口紅 lipstick

kuchi-bue n 口笛 whistling (*with one's lips*): **~ o fukimásu** 口笛を吹きます whistles

kuchi-génka n 口げんか[喧嘩] argument

kuchi-hige n 口ひげ・口髭 mustache

kuchi-komi n 口コミ word of mouth: **~ de hiromarimásu** 口コミで広まります spreads by word of mouth

kuchibiru n 唇 lip

kuchimásu, kuchiru v 朽ちます, 朽ちる rots, decays

kúchite v 朽ちて → kuchimásu 朽ちます

kúda n 管 pipe, rube

kudáita v 砕いた = kudakimáshita 砕きました (broke it)

kudáite v 砕いて → kudakimásu 砕きます

kudáke v 砕け [IMPERATIVE] (break it!) → kudakimásu 砕きます

kudakemásu, kudakéru v 砕けます, 砕ける **1.** it breaks, smashes, crumbles **2.** can break it

kudákete v 砕けて → kudakemásu 砕けます

kudakimásu, kudáku v 砕きます, 砕く breaks it, smashes it, crumbles it

kudámono n 果物 fruit: **kudamónó-ya** 果物屋 fruit market

kudari n 下り descent; outbound (*from Tokyo*), the down train

kudarimásu, kudaru v 下ります, 下る comes/goes down, descends; falls, drops

kudasái v 下さい give; (**shite kudasái** して下さい) please (do) [IMPERATIVE of **kudasáru** 下さる = kudasaimásu 下さいます]

kudasaimáshite v 下さいまして = kudasátte 下さって → kudasaimásu 下さいます

kudasaimásu, kudasáru v 下さいます, 下さる gives (*he/she to you, you to me*); does as a favor (*he/she for you, you for me*), kindly (*does*)

kudasátta, kudasútta v 下さった, 下すった = kudasaimáshita 下さいました (gave (me))

kudasátte, kudasútte v 下さって, 下すって → kudasaimásu 下さいます

kudashi n 下し: **mushi-kúdashi** 虫下し a vermifuge

kudatta v 下った = kudarimáshita 下りました (went down)

kudatte v 下って → kudarimásu 下ります

kudói adj くどい **1.** long-winded, dull **2.** thick, greasy

kúe v 食え [IMPERATIVE] (eat!) → kuimásu 食います

kúeba v 食えば (if one eats) → kuimásu 食います

kuemásu, kuéru v 食えます, 食える can eat (*polite form* **taberaremásu** 食べられます)

kuéreba v 食えれば (if one can eat) → kuemásu 食えます

kufū n 工夫 device, scheme, idea, invention, artifice, ingenuity: **~ (o kora-)shimásu** 工夫（を凝ら）します schemes, contrives

kūfuku (no) adj 空腹(の) hungry

Kú-gatsu n 九月・9月 September

kugi n 釘 nail, peg

kugi-nuki n 釘抜き claw hammer

kugiri n 区切り punctuation; **kugiri-másu** 区切ります divides

kūgun n 空軍 air force: **kūgun-kíchi** 空軍基地 air base

kugurimásu, kuguru v 潜ります, 潜る passes under

kūhaku n 空白 a blank (*space*) (= **kūsho** 空所, **supésu** スペース)

kúi n 杭 post, stake, pile: [IDIOM] **deru**

~ wa utareru 出る杭は打たれる A tall tree catches much wind.

kuichigai n 食い違い discrepancy

kúiki n 区域 zone

kuimásu, kū´ v 食います, 食う eats (*inelegant*) (= **tabemásu** 食べます)

kúi-shínbō (na) adj 食いしん坊(な) glutton(ous); greedy

kujaku n クジャク・孔雀 peacock

kúji n くじ・クジ a lot (*in a lottery*) (= **takara-kuji** 宝くじ)

kujíite v 挫いて → **kujikimásu** 挫きます

kujikemásu, kujikéru v 挫けます, 挫ける (*a plan*) gets frustrated: **ashí ga ~** 足が挫けます gets a sprained ankle; **ki ga ~** 気が挫けます gets disheartened, discouraged

kujikimásu, kujíku v 挫きます, 挫く 1. sprains: **ashí o ~** 足を挫きます sprains an ankle 2. frustrates (*a plan*); **ki o ~** 気を挫きます disheartens, discourages

kujira n クジラ・鯨 whale

kujō n 苦情 complaint: **~ o iu/yū** 苦情を言う complains

kūkan n 空間 space

kukí n 茎 stalk, stem

kū´ki n 空気 air

kūkō n 空港 airport

kúma n クマ・熊 bear (*animal*)

kumade n 熊手 rake

kumanai v 汲まない = **kumimasén** 汲みません (not scoop)

kúmanai v 組まない = **kumimasén** 組みません (not braid)

kuméba v 汲めば (if one scoops) → **kumimásu** 汲みます

kúmeba v 組めば (if one braids) → **kumimásu** 組みます

kumí n 組 a set, suit, pack; a class, band, company

kumiai n 組合 association, guild, union: **rōdō-kumiai** 労働組合 (labor) union

kumi-awase n 組み合わせ assortment, mixture

kumi-awasemásu, kumi-awaseru v 組み合わせます, 組み合わせる combines, puts together, teams them up

kumimásu, kumu v 汲みます, 汲む 1. scoops, draws, ladles 2. considers,

sympathizes (= **dōjō shimásu** 同情します)

kumimásu, kúmu v 組みます, 組む braids; assembles, sets up, puts together; folds (*arms*), clasps (*hands*), crosses (*legs*); teams up (*with*)

kumi-tate n 組み立て structure, setup, makeup, organization, framework

kumi-tatemásu, kumi-tateru v 組み立てます, 組み立てる sets up, organizes; assembles, puts together

kúmo n 雲 cloud: **kumo-gakure** 雲隠れ disappearing, dropping out of sight

kúmo n クモ・蜘蛛 spider

kumó´ v 汲もう = **kumimashō** 汲みましょう (let's scoop!)

kumó´ v 組もう = **kumimashō** 組みましょう (let's braid!)

kúmo no su n クモ[蜘蛛]の巣 spider-web, cobweb (= **kúmo no íto** クモ[蜘蛛]の糸 spider threads

kumori n 曇り cloudy weather

kumorimásu, kumóru v 曇ります, 曇る gets cloudy: **kumótte imásu** 曇っています is cloudy

… kun suffix …君 [INFORMAL] (*mostly attached to one's junior's or boys' names*) (= **san** さん [FORMAL])

kunda v 汲んだ = **kumimáshita** 汲みました (scooped)

kúnda v 組んだ = **kumimáshita** 組みました (braided)

kunde v 汲んで → **kumimásu** 汲みます

kúnde v 組んで → **kumimásu** 組みます

kuni n 国 (**o-kuni** お国) 1. country, nation: **kuni no** 国の national, state, government 2. native place, home area

kúnren n 訓練 training, drill: **~ shimásu** 訓練します trains, drills

kuō´ v 食おう = **kuimashō** 食いましょう (let's eat!) (= **tabemashō** 食べましょう)

kurá n 鞍 saddle

kurá n 倉・蔵 warehouse, storeroom (*storehouse*), cellar, godown

kū´rā n クーラー air conditioner

kurabemásu, kuraberu v 比べます・較べます, 比べる・較べる compares, contrasts

kúrabu *n* クラブ club (*group; card suit*); (*golf*)club: **kurabu katsudō** クラブ活動 club activities

kurage *n* クラゲ jellyfish

kurai *n* 位 grade, rank

kurai *adj* 暗い dark, gloomy; dim (*light*)

... kúrai *suffix* ...くらい・位 = **... gúrai** ...ぐらい・位 (about; (*an amount*); at least)

kurákkā *n* クラッカー crackers

kurákushon *n* クラクション klaxon, horn (*of car*)

kurashikku *n* クラシック classic (= **koten** 古典)

kurashimásu, kurasu *v* 暮らします, 暮らす lives, gets by; makes a living

kúrasu *n* クラス class (*group*)

kurátchi *n* クラッチ clutch (*of car*): **kuratchi-pédaru** クラッチペダル clutch pedal

kure *n* 暮れ the dark; the end of the year: **kure no** 暮れの year-end

kure *v* くれ [IMPERATIVE] (*gives; does as a favor*) (gimme!)

kúreba *v* 来れば (if one comes) → **kimásu** 来ます

kurejitto-kā'do *n* クレジットカード credit card

kuremásu, kureru *v* くれます, くれる gives (*to me/us; he to you*): **shite** ~ してくれます does as a favor (*for me/us; he for you*)

kuremásu, kureru *v* 暮れます, 暮れる: **hi ga ~** 日が暮れます it gets dark

kurē'n *n* クレーン crane (*machine*)

kurenai *v* くれない = **kuremasén** くれません (not give)

kureréba *v* くれれば (if one gives) → **kuremásu** くれます

kureréba *v* 暮れれば (if it gets dark) → **kuremásu** 暮れます

kurētā *n* クレーター crater (= **kakō** 火口)

kurete *v* くれて・暮れて → **kuremásu** くれます・暮れます

kurí *n* 栗 chestnut

kuríimu *n* クリーム cream

kuríiningu *n* クリーニング cleaning: **kuriiningu-ya** クリーニング屋 (*dry*) cleaner(s); laundry

kuri-kaeshimásu, kiri-kaesu *v* 繰り返します, 繰り返す repeats

kuríppu *n* クリップ clip

Kurísúmasu *n* クリスマス Christmas

kúro (no) *adj* 黒(の) black
kuro-bíiru *n* 黒ビール black beer
kuró-i *adj* 黒い black (= **kúro (no)** 黒(の))
kuro-pan *n* 黒パン brown bread

kúrō *n* 苦労 difficulties, hardships: **Go-kúrō-sama (deshita).** ご苦労様 (でした). Thank you for the hard work./Thank you for your trouble. You did good work for me.(*usually to person in a lower position than yours*) (→ **O-tsukare-sama (déshita)** お疲れ様(でした).)

kurō'ku *n* クローク cloakroom, check room

kúrō'to *n* 玄人 expert, professional

kúru *v* 来る = **kimásu** 来ます (comes)

kuruimásu, kuru'u *v* 狂います, 狂う gets warped; gets out of order: **ki ga ~** 気が狂います goes mad (*insane*)

kuruma *n* 車 car; taxi; vehicle, (*hand*) cart (= **jidó'-sha** 自動車)

kurumá-ebi *n* 車エビ[海老] prawn, jumbo shrimp

kurumi *n* クルミ・胡桃 walnut; nut

kurushíi *adj* 苦しい painful; hard; heavy

kurushimemásu, kurushiméru *v* 苦しめます, 苦しめる afflicts, pains, distresses, embarrasses

kurushimí *n* 苦しみ affliction, agony, suffering, distress

kurushimimásu, kurushímu *v* 苦しみます, 苦しむ suffers; gets afflicted/distressed/embarrassed

kusá *n* 草 grass

kusái *adj* 臭い smelly, stinking; fishy, questionable

kusari *n* 鎖 chain

kusarimásu, kusáru *v* 腐ります, 腐る goes bad, rots, decays, spoils, sours: **kusátte imásu** 腐っています is spoiled/rotten

kusé *n* 癖・くせ a (*bad*) habit, a quirk

kūsha *n* 空車 vacant car, "(taxi) available"

ku̱shámi *n* くしゃみ a sneeze

kushí *n* くし・櫛 a comb

kushí *n* 串 a skewer, a spit

kūsho *n* 空所 a blank (*space*) (= **kūhaku** 空白)

kusó *n* くそ・クソ・糞 dung, excrement, feces

kūsō *n* 空想 fantasy

kusugurimásu, kusuguru *v* くすぐります, くすぐる tickles

kusuguttai *adj* くすぐったい ticklish

kusuri *n* 薬 medicine, drug: **kusuri-ya (san)** 薬屋 (さん) drugstore; druggist

kutabarimásu, kutabáru *v* くたばります, くたばる gets to die

kutabiremásu, kutabiréru *v* くたびれます, くたびれる gets tired

kutakuta, kuttakuta *adj* くたくた, くったくた dead tired, utterly exhausted

...-kutatte ... *suffix, conj* くたって even being ... (= **...-kute mo** ... くても)

...-kute *suffix, conj* ...くて is and (*also/so*)

kutsú *n* 靴・クツ shoes

kutsu-béra *n* 靴べら[ベラ] shoehorn

kutsú-himo *n* 靴ひも shoelace

kutsu-mígaki *n* 靴磨き shoeshine

kutsu-náoshi *n* 靴直し shoe-repair person/shop

kutsú-shita *n* 靴下・くつ下 socks, stockings

kutsú-ya *n* 靴屋 shoe shop/store

kutsu-zoko *n* 靴底 shoe sole

kutsu-zure *n* 靴ずれ a foot sore (*from shoe rubbing*)

kutsurogimásu, kutsurógu *v* くつろぎます, くつろぐ relaxes, gets comfortable

kútta *v* 食った = **kuimáshita** 食いました (ate) (= **tabemáshita** 食べました)

...-kútte *v* 食って → **kuimásu** 食います

...-kútte *suffix, conj* ...くって = **...-kute** ...くて: **nemu-kútte** 眠くって, **nemukute** 眠くて sleepy

kúttsukimású, kuttsúku *v* くっつきます, くっつく sticks to

kuwa *n* くわ・鍬 hoe

kúwa *n* クワ・桑 mulberry

kuwadate *n* 企て plan, attempt, undertaking

kuwadatemásu, kuwadatéru *v* 企てます, 企てる plans, attempts, undertakes

kuwaemásu, kuwaeru *v* 加えます, 加える adds (*on*); imposes

kuwánai *v* 食わない = **kuimasén** 食いません (not eat) (POLITE FORM **tabenai** 食べない)

kuwasemásu, kuwaséru *v* 食わせます, 食わせる feeds (POLITE FORM **tabesasemasu** 食べさせます)

kuwashíi *adj* 詳しい detailed, exact: (... **ni ~** ...に詳しい) is knowledgeable (about ...), is well versed (in ...); **~ kotó** 詳しい事 details; **kuwáshiku** 詳しく in detail

kuyamimásu, kuyamu *v* 悔やみます, 悔やむ regrets

kuyashíi *adj* 悔しい humiliating, mortifying, vexatious

kuzu (mono) *n* くず[クズ](物) waste, scum, mud, trash, rags, scrap, junk (= **gomi** ごみ・ゴミ, **kásu** かす・滓)

kuzu-híroi *n* くず拾い ragpicker

kuzú-kago *n* くずかご wastebasket

kúzu *n* クズ・葛 arrowroot: **kuzu-yu** 葛湯 arrowroot gruel

kuzu-ko *n* 葛粉 powdered arrowroot

kuzuremásu, kuzuréru *v* 崩れます, 崩れる it crumbles, breaks (down); (*weather*) deteriorates

kuzushimásu, kuzúsu *v* 崩します, 崩す **1.** cashes, changes, breaks (*into small money*) **2.** breaks it down, demolishes **3.** writes (*a character*) in cursive style

kyábarē *n* キャバレー cabaret, night club

kyábetsu *n* キャベツ cabbage

kyaburétā *n* キャブレター carburetor

kyaku *n* 客 visitor, guest, company; customer (= **o-kyaku-sámá** お客様 [HONORIFIC])

kyaku-ma *n* 客間 guest room

kyaku-sha *n* 客車 (*railroad*) passenger car, coach

kyánbasu *n* キャンバス canvas (= **kanbasu** カンバス)

kyándii, kyándē *n* キャンディ, キャンデー candy (= **ame** アメ・飴)

kyánpasu *n* キャンパス campus

kyánpu *n* キャンプ camp(ing): ~ **o shimásu** キャンプをします camps

kyánseru *n* キャンセル cancellation: ~ **shimásu** キャンセルします cancels

kyáppu *n* キャップ cap (*of a pen*)

kyáputen *n* キャプテン captain

kyarameru *n* キャラメル caramel

kyā *interj* きゃー・キャー: **kyā(t)-to sakebimásu** きゃー(っ)[キャー(ッ)]と叫びます screams

kyō´ *n* 今日・きょう today

kyō´ (no miyako) *n* 京(の都) Kyoto (= **Kyō´to** 京都)

...-kyō *n* ...教 (*name of*) religion: **Kirisuto-kyō** キリスト教 Christianity; **Isuramu-kyō** イスラム教 Islam (= **kaikyō** 回教); **Buk-kyō** 仏教 Buddhism

kyōbai *n* 競売 [BOOKISH] auction (= **ōkushon** オークション)

kyōchō *n* 強調 [BOOKISH] emphasis: ~ **shimásu** 強調します emphasizes

kyodai (na) *adj* 巨大(な) huge

kyō´dai (-shimai) *n* 兄弟(姉妹) brothers and/or sisters; brother; sister

kyōdan *n* 教壇 [BOOKISH] platform, pulpit: ~ **ni tachimásu** 教壇に立ちます teaches at school

kyōdan *n* 凶弾 [BOOKISH] bullet (*of assassin, etc.*): ~ **ni taoremásu** 凶弾に倒れます is shot to death (*by an assassin, etc.*)

kyōdan *n* 教団 [BOOKISH] religious organization

kyōdō *n* 共同 union, cooperation, joint (*activity*): **kyōdō-seikatsu** 共同生活 living together, living with others

kyōdō *n* 協同 cooperation: **kyōdō-kumiai** 協同組合 cooperative association (= **seikatsu-kyōdō-kumiai** 生活協同組合, **seikyō** 生協)

kyō´fu *n* 恐怖 [BOOKISH] fear, terror

kyōgeki *n* 京劇 classic Chinese pantomime/opera

kyōgen *n* 狂言 traditional Noh farce

kyō´gi *n* 協議 conference, discussion

kyō´gi *n* 競技 (*athletic*) game, match, contest, (*game*) event

kyōgi-jō *n* 競技場 stadium

kyōhan(sha) *n* 共犯(者) accomplice

kyōhi *n* 拒否 refusal, rejection, veto (= **kyozetsu** 拒絶): ~ **shimásu** 拒否します refuses, rejects, vetoes

kyōiku *n* 教育 education: ~ **o ukemásu** 教育を受けます gets an education

kyōin *n* 教員 [BOOKISH] teacher

kyojin *n* 巨人 giant (*person*): **Kyójin(-gun)** 巨人(軍) the Giants [*baseball team*]

kyōju *n* 教授 professor: **daigaku-kyōju** 大学教授 university professor

kyoju *n* 居住 [BOOKISH] residency: **kyojū-sha** 居住者 a resident: **kyojū-chi** 居住地 residence (*location*), address (= **jūsho** 住所)

kyóka *n* 許可 permit, permission: **kyoka-sho** 許可証 permit (*card*)

kyōkai *n* 教会 church

kyōkai *n* 協会 society, association

kyōkai *n* 境界 border (*of district, etc.*)

kyōká-sho *n* 教科書 text(book)

kyōki *n* 凶器 [BOOKISH] lethal weapon

kyōki *n* 狂気 [BOOKISH] insanity, madness, lunacy: ~ **no sata** 狂気の沙汰 absolutely crazy

kyōki *n* 驚喜 [BOOKISH] amazement and gladness: ~ **shimásu** 驚喜します is amazed and glad

kyokō *n* 虚構 [BOOKISH] fabrication, fiction (= **fikushon** フィクション): ~ **no sekai** 虚構の世界 imaginary world

kyōkō *n* 強行 forcing: **kyōkō-toppa** 強行突破 forcing/bulldozing one's way through: **kyōko-saiketsu** 強行採決 railroading

kyóku *n* 局, **...´-kyoku** ...局 office, bureau, station: **terebi-kyoku** テレビ局 TV station

kyokuba *n* 曲馬 horseback stunts: **kyokubá-dan** 曲馬団 circus (= **sā´kasu** サーカス)

kyokugei *n* 曲芸 acrobat, acrobatics (= **akurobátto** アクロバット): **kyokugei-shi** 曲芸師 acrobat, stunt performer

kyokugen *n* 極限 [BOOKISH] limit: **kyokugen-jōtai** 極限状態 extreme situation, ultimate state

kyōkun *n* 教訓 lesson, teaching, moral: ~ **ni narimásu** 教訓になります learns one's lesson

kyokután (na) *adj* 極端(な) extreme: **kyokután ni** 極端に extremely

Kyokutō *n* 極東 Far East

kyōkyū *n* 供給 supply(ing), provision: **~ shimásu** 供給します supplies; **juyō to kyōkyū** 需要と供給 supply and demand (= **jukyū** 需給)

kyō´mí *n* 興味 interest (*pleasure*): **kyōmi-bukái** 興味深い interesting

kyónen *n* 去年 last year

kyóri *n* 距離 distance

kyōryoku *n* 協力 cooperation: **kyōryo-ku shimásu** 協力します cooperates

kyōryoku (na) *adj* 強力(な) strong, powerful

Kyō-ryō´ri *n* 京料理 Kyoto-style cooking/dishes

Kyōsan-shúgi *n* 共産主義 Communism: **Kyōsan shugí-sha** 共産主義者 a Communist: **Kyōsan (shugí)-koku** 共産(主義)国 communist country

kyō´shi *n* 教師 teacher, instructor, tutor: **katei-kyōshi** 家庭教師 home tutor

kyōshitsu *n* 教室 classroom

kyōshoku *n* 教職 teaching profession: **~ ni tsukimásu** 教職に就きます becomes a teacher

kyōshuku shimásu (suru) *v* 恐縮します(する) [HONORIFIC] **1.** feels grateful/obliged/ashamed: **ohome ni azukari kyōshuku desu** お褒めにあずかり恐縮です I am very grateful for your compliment.; **2.** feels sorry/ashamed: **taihen kyōshuku desuga...** 大変恐縮ですが... I am very sorry, but...

kyoshoku-shō *n* 拒食症 anorexia

kyōsō *n* 競争 competition, rivalry, contest, race: **~ shimásu** 競争します competes

kyōsō-áite *n* 競争相手 competitor

kyōson, kyōzon *n* 共存 [BOOKISH] coexistence: **~ shimásu** 共存します coexists

kyōten *n* 経典 **1.** sutra (*Buddhist scripture*) (= **o-kyō** お経) **2.** religious text, sacred scripture

Kyō´to *n* 京都 Kyoto (= **kyō´ (no) miyako**) 京(の都)); **Kyōtó-Eki** 京都駅 Kyoto Station; **Kyotó-jin** 京都人 Kyotoite

kyōtsū (no) *adj* 共通(の) common, general

kyōyo *n* 供与 grant, allowance: **~ shimásu** 供与します grants it

kyōyō (no) *adj* 共用(の) for common use, for public use

kyōyō *n* 教養 culture, education, refinement: **~ no nai** 教養のない uneducated, uncultivated

kyōyō *n* 強要 [BOOKISH] forcing: **~ shimásu** 強要します forces, compels

kyōzai *n* 教材 teaching materials

kyozetsu *n* 拒絶 [BOOKISH] refusal, rejection, veto (= **kyóhi** 拒否): **~ shimásu** 拒絶します refuses, rejects, vetoes

kyū *n* 灸・きゅう (**o-kyū** お灸) moxibustion (*burning moxa on the skin*)

kyū *n* 急 crisis, emergency, danger: **kyū (na)** 急(な) sudden; urgent; precipitous, steep: **~ na (o-)shirase/renraku** 急な(お)知らせ/連絡 short notice; **kyū ni** 急に suddenly (= **totsuzen** 突然)

kyū-byō *n* 急病 sudden illness

kyū-kō *n* 急行 express (*train, etc.*): **kyūkō´-ken** 急行券 express ticket

kyū-ryū *n* 急流 (*river*) rapids

kyū-sei (no) *adj* 急性(の) acute (*sudden*): **kyūsei-shikkan** 急性疾患 acute disease

kyū-shi *n* 急死 sudden death

kyū-yō *n* 急用 urgent business

kyū´ *n* 級 class, grade

kyū´ *n* 九・9 nine (= **kú** 九・9)

kyū-banmé *n* 九番目 ninth

kyū´-dai *n* 九台 nine (*machines, vehicles*)

kyū´-do *n* 九度 nine degrees; nine times (= **kyū´-kái** 九回, **kyū´-hén** 九遍)

kyū´-hyaku *n* 九百・900 nine hundred

kyū´-hon *n* 九本 nine (*pencils/bottles, long things*)

kyū-jū *n* 九十・90 ninety

kyū-kai *n* 九階 nine floors/stories, ninth floor

kyū-ko *n* 九個 nine pieces (*small objects*) (= **kokonotsu** 九つ)

kyū´-kái *n* 九回 nine times (= **kyū´-do** 九度, **kyū´-hén** 九遍)

kyū´-mai n 九枚 nine sheets (*flat things*)
kyū-mán n 九万・90,000 ninety thousand
kyū´-satsu n 九冊 nine copies (*books, magazines*)
kyū-sén n 九千・9,000 nine thousand
kyū´-tō n 九頭 nine (*horses/oxen, large animals*)
kyū´-wa n 九羽 nine (*birds, rabbits*)
kyū´(-) *prefix* 旧... ... old
kyūden n 宮殿 palace
kyū´dō n 弓道 (*the traditional art of*) archery (= kyū´jutsu 弓術)
kyūji n 給仕 waiter/waitress, steward, attendant, factotum
kyūjin n 求人 job offer(s)
kyūjitsu n 休日 day off, holiday
kyū´jo n 救助 rescue, relief: kyūjo-tai 救助隊 rescue party/team: ~ shimásu 救助します rescues
kyūjō n 球場 ball park, (*baseball*) stadium (= yakyū-jō 野球場)
kyūka n 休暇 vacation, furlough: ~ o torimásu 休暇を取ります takes day(s) off
kyūkei n 休憩 rest, recess, break: ~ shimásu 休憩します takes a rest, takes a break
kyūkéi-shitsu n 休憩室 lounge (*room*), break room
kyūkon n 求婚 proposal of marriage (= puropōzu プロポーズ)
kyū´kutsu (na) *adj* 窮屈(な) constrained, uncomfortable

kyūkyū (no) *adj* 救急(の) for emergencies
kyūkyū-bako n 救急箱 first-aid kit
kyūkyū-chiryō shitsu 救急治療室 emergency room, ER
kyūkyū´-sha n 救急車 ambulance
kyū´ri n キュウリ・胡瓜 cucumber
kyū´ryō n 給料 (o-kyū´ryō お給料) salary, pay (= sárarii サラリー, kyū´yo 給与)
kyūryō´-bi 給料日 payday
kyūseishu n 救世主 Savior
kyūshi n 休止 pause
kyūshi-kigō 休止記号 breath mark
kyūsho n 急所 jugular (*vein*)
kyūshoku (katsudō) n 求職(活動) job hunting, seeking employment
kyūshoku n 休職 leave of absence from work
kyūshoku n 給食 school lunch
Kyū´shū-chihō n 九州地方 The Kyushu area of Japan (*Fukuoka, Saga, Nagasaki, Kumamoto, Miyazaki, Kagoshima, Ōita prefectures*)
kyūsu n きゅうす・急須 teapot
kyūtei n 宮廷 (*imperial/royal*) court
Kyū-yaku seisho n 旧約聖書 the Old Testament
kyū´yo n 給与 allowance, grant, compensation, salary (= sárarii サラリー, kyū´ryō 給料): kyūyo-meisai (sho) 給与明細書 pay slip
kyūyō n 休養 rest: ~ shimásu 休養します rests

M

ma n 間 1. room; space (*available*) 2. time, interval; (= hima 暇) leisure: ~ o okimásu 間を置きます gives a pause: ...ni ~ ni aimásu ...に間に合います is in time (*for ...*)
ma... *prefix* 真... mid..., very...
ma-fuyu n 真冬 midwinter
ma-hiru n 真昼 midday
ma-kká (na) *adj* 真っ赤(な) crimson, deep red: ~ ni narimásu 真っ赤になります crimsons, flushes deeply
ma-kkúro (na) *adj* 真っ黒(な) jet

black: ~ ni narimásu 真っ黒になります turns to a deep black
ma-natsu n 真夏 midsummer
ma-yónaka n 真夜中 midnight
ma-n-mae (ni/de) *adv* 真ん前(に/で) right in front
ma-n-maru (no/na) *adj* 真ん丸(の/な) perfectly round
ma-n-naka n 真ん中 the very middle, center (= chūshin 中心, sentā センター): ma-n-naka no 真ん中の central, middle

ma-ssáka-sama (ni) *adj* 真っ逆さま (に) head over heels

ma-sshíro (na) *adj* 真っ白(な) snow white

ma-ssúgu (na) *adj* 真っ直ぐ(な) straight

mā´ まあ *interj* **1.** oh well; I should say; perhaps, I guess **2.** dear me! (*mostly female*); good heavens/grief!

ma-bátaki *n* 瞬き wink(ing), blink(ing)

mabayui *adj* 眩い [BOOKISH] dazzling, glaring (= **mabushíi** 眩しい)

māburu *n* マーブル marble

mabushíi *adj* 眩しい dazzling, glaring (= **mabayui** 眩い)

mábuta *n* まぶた・瞼 eyelid

macchi *n* マッチ match

machí *n* 町・街 town, city: **machí no** 町の local (→ **chō´chō** 町長)

māchi *n* マーチ march

máchi *v* 待ち → **machimásu** 待ちます [INFINITIVE]

machi-ái-shitsu *n* 待合室 waiting room

machi-awasemásu, machi-awaseru *v* 待ち合わせます, 待ち合わせる makes an appointment

machibuse *n* 待ち伏せ ambush

machidōshíi *adj* 待ち遠しい long awaited; waiting for a long time

machigáe *n* 間違え, **machigái** 間違い mistake, error (= **misu** ミス, **erā** エラー)

machigaemásu, machigáeru *v* 間違えます, 間違える mistakes

machigaenai *v* 間違えない = **machigae-masén** 間違えません (not mistaken)

machigaimásu, machigáu *v* 間違います, 間違う is mistaken, is wrong, is in error

machigátta *adj* 間違った wrong (*mistaken*)

machigáu *v* 間違う = **machigaimásu** 間違います (is mistaken)

machigawanai *v* 間違わない = **machi-gaenai** 間違えない = **machigaemasén** 間違えません (not mistaken)

machimásu, mátsu *v* 待ちます, 待つ waits for, awaits, expects, anticipates

máchinē *n* マチネー matinee

máda *adv* まだ **1.** (not) yet [+ NEGATIVE verb] **2.** still (*to be*)

madara *n* 斑 spots, speckles: **madara no** 斑の spotted: **madara-moyō** 斑模様 patchy pattern

...máde *suffix, conj* ...まで (*all the way*) to, till, until

... máde ni *suffix, conj* ...までに by, no later than, before (*it gets to be time*)

... máde ni wa *suffix, conj* ...までには by ... at the latest

mádo *n* 窓 window

mado-gárasu *n* 窓ガラス windowpane

madó-guchi *n* 窓口 window (*opening*), wicket

mado-waku *n* 窓枠 (*window*) sash

madoimasu, madou *v* 惑います, 惑う gets dazed

maekagami *n* 前屈み leaning forward: **~ ni narimásu** 前屈みになります leans forward

mae-mótte *adv* 前もって (*in*) advance (*beforehand*)

mae-muki (no) *adj* 前向き(の) **1.** far-sighted (*forward-looking*) **2.** positive, constructive, affirmative: **~ na kangae** 前向きな考え positive thinking (= **pojitibu shinkingu** ポジティブシンキング); **mae-muki ni** 前向きに facing front; positively

máe (ni) *adv* 前(に) front; in front of; before, ago: **máe no** 前の previous, former; **suru ~ ni** する前に before doing; **daibu ~ kara** だいぶ前から for quite a long time (*now*)

maeoki *n* 前置き introduction (= **into-rodakushon** イントロダクション)

maeuri *n* 前売り advanced sale: **maeuri-ken** 前売り券 advanced-sale ticket

mafurā *n* マフラー muffler, scarf

mafia *n* マフィア Mafia

mafin *n* マフィン muffin

magao *n* 真顔 serious/earnest/sober/conscientious/honest look (*on one's face*) (= **majime na kao** 真面目な顔, **shinken na kao** 真剣な顔)

magari *n* 曲がり a curve, a bend: **heso-magari** へそ曲がり perverse person: **magari-kado** 曲がり角 street corner

magari *n* 間借り renting a room

magari-nin *n* 間借り人 tenant (*of apartment, room*)

magarimásu, magaru v 曲がります、曲がる **1.** turns, goes around **2.** it bends, curves

māgarin n マーガリン margarine

magaru v 曲がる = **magarimásu** 曲がります (turns, curves)

magemásu, mageru v 曲げます、曲げる **1.** bends it, curves it

magiremásu, magiréru v 紛れます、紛れる: **... ni ...** …に紛れます gets distracted (by …); gets confused (with …), gets mixed up (with)

... mágiwa (ni/de) suffix, adv …間際 (に/で) just before …, right on the brink of (when) …

magó n 孫 grandchild: **o-mago-san** お孫さん (your/someone else's) grandchild

magó-no-te n 孫の手 back-scratcher

magó n 馬子 a packhorse driver: [IDIOM] **~ ni mo ishō** 馬子にも衣装 Clothes make the man.

magokoro n 真心 sincerity: **~ o komete** 真心を込めて sincerely

magure (atari) n まぐれ(当たり) fluke, (dumb/good) luck, accident, fortuity (= **gúzen** 偶然)

maguro n マグロ・鮪 tuna

magusa n まぐさ[秣・馬草] hay

máhi n マヒ・麻痺 paralysis

mahō´ n 魔法 magic

mahō´-bin n 魔法瓶[びん・ビン] vacuum/thermos bottle

mai n 舞 (Japanese) dance: **~ o maimásu** 舞を舞います dances

mai-... prefix 毎… each, every

mai-asa n, adv 毎朝 every morning

mai-ban n, adv 毎晩 every night

mai-do n, adv 毎度 every time: **~ arígatō gozaimásu** 毎度ありがとうございます。We appreciate your (continuing) patronage.

mai-getsu, mai-tsuki n, adv 毎月 every month: **mai-getsu/-tsuki no** 毎月の monthly

mai-kai n, adv 毎回 every time, each time

mai-nen, mai-toshi n, adv 毎年 every year: **mai-nen/-toshi no** 毎年の annual, yearly

mái-nichi n, adv 毎日 every day; all the time: **mái-nichi no** 毎日の daily; **~ no yō´ni** 毎日のように almost everyday

mai-shū n, adv 毎週 every week: **mái-shū no** 毎週の weekly

mai-yo n, adv 毎夜 every night (= **mai-ban** 毎晩)

...´-mai suffix …枚 (counts flat things)

máigo n 迷子 a lost child: **~ ni narimásu** 迷子になります a child becomes lost

mai-hōmu n マイホーム owned house, one's house and home

mainasu n マイナス less (minus); a minus, a disadvantage

mairimáshita, máitta v 参りました、参った You've got me!; gives up, goes down (= **kōsan** 降参)

mairimásu, máiru v 参ります、参る [HUMBLE] **1.** I come/go **2.** visits, calls on

maisō n 埋葬 burial: **~ shimásu** 埋葬します buries the body

maite v 巻いて → **makimásu** 巻きます

máite v 蒔いて → **makimásu** 蒔きます

májan n マージャン・麻雀 mahjong: **mājan-ya** マージャン[麻雀]屋 mahjong parlor

majime (na) adj 真面目(な) serious, earnest, sober, conscientious, honest

májin n マージン margin

majinai n まじない・呪い **1.** charm (= **o-majinai** おまじない) **2.** curse (= **noroi** のろい・呪い) **3.** spell, magic, incantation (= **jujutsu** 呪術)

majinai-shi n まじない[呪い]師 witch doctor

majirimásu, majíru v 混じります、混じる it mixes (with)

majiwarimásu, majiwáru v 交わります、交わる associates with

majo n 魔女 witch

makanai v 巻かない = **makimasén** 巻きません (not roll it up)

makánai v 蒔かない = **makimasén** 蒔きません (not sow)

makasemásu, makaséru v 任せます、任せる entrusts with

makashimásu, makasu v 負かします、負かす defeats

137

make *n* 負け defeat, loss

make *v* 巻け [IMPERATIVE] (roll it up!)
→ **makimásu** 巻きます

máke *v* 蒔け [IMPERATIVE] (sow!) →
makimásu 蒔きます

makéba *v* 巻けば (if one rolls it up) →
makimásu 巻きます

makéba *v* 蒔けば (if one sows) →
makimásu 蒔きます

makemásu, makeru *v* 負けます,負け
る loses, is defeated; comes down on
the price; is inferior

makemásu, makeru *v* 巻けます, 巻け
る can roll it up

makemásu, makéru *v* 蒔けます, 蒔け
る can sow (*seed*)

makenai *v* 負けない = **makemasén**
負けません (not lose)

makenai *v* 巻けない = **makemasén**
巻けません (cannot roll it up)

makénai *v* 蒔けない = **makemasén**
蒔けません (cannot sow)

make ro *v* 負けろ [IMPERATIVE] (lose!)
→ **makemásu** 負けます

mākétto *n* マーケット market (= **shijō**
市場)

maki *n* 薪 firewood

maki *n* 巻き **1.** a roll; a volume
2. (...-**maki** ...巻き) a bolt (*of cloth*)

makimásu, maku *v* 巻きます, 巻く
rolls up; winds; wraps

maki-mono *n* 巻き物 scroll

maki-tábako *n* 巻きタバコ cigarette(s)

makimásu, máku *v* 蒔きます, 蒔く
sows (*seed*)

maki-e *n* 蒔(き)絵 raised lacquer

makō *v* 巻こう = **makimashō'** 巻きま
しょう (let's roll it up!)

makō' *v* 蒔こう = **makimashō** 蒔きま
しょう (let's sow!)

makoto (no) *adj* 誠[真]まこと(の)
sincere; faithful; true; genuine (= **honto
(no), hontō (no)**): **makoto ni**
誠[真]に sincerely

maku *v* 巻く = **makimásu** 巻きます
(rolls up)

makú *n* 幕 (*stage*) curtain; (*play*) act: ~
ga agarimásu/akimásu 幕が上がりま
す/開きます the curtain goes up

máku *v* 蒔く = **makimásu** 蒔きます

maku ai *n* 幕間 intermission (*between
acts*)

makunóuchi *n* 幕の内 a riceball
lunch(box)

mákura *n* まくら・マクラ・枕 pillow

mama *n* ママ **1.** (*baby talk*) mommy,
mom (= **kā-chan** 母ちゃん) **2.** hostess
(*in a bar, etc.*)

mama-... *prefix* まま[継]... step

mama-chichi *n* まま[継]父 stepfather

mama-haha *n* まま[継]母 stepmother

mama-ko *n* まま[継]子 stepchild

mā-mā *adj, adv* まあまあ (just) so-so,
not bad

... mamá (*de/no*) *suffix, adv, adj*
...まま(で/の) intact, untouched/
undisturbed: **sono ~ de** そのままで just
as it is/was, **tátta ~ de** 立ったままで
without sitting down, with standing

mamé *n* マメ・豆 bean(s)

mamé *n* まめ blister

mame (na) *adj* まめ(な) diligent/
dedicated (*person*)

mame (ni) *adv* まめ(に) often,
frequently

ma-mó-naku *adv* 間もなく soon,
before long, shortly

mamorimásu, mamóru *v* 守ります,
守る defends, protects, guards

mán *n* 万 ten thousand 10,000

man-bai *n* 万倍 ten-thousandfold
(*10,000 times doubled*)

man(-) ... *prefix* 満... fully ...

man-chō *n* 満潮 high tide

man-getsu *n* 満月 full moon

man'-in *n* 満員 full (*of people*)

man-jō-icchi *n* 満場一致 unanimous
(*agreement*)

man-men *n* 満面 the whole face: **~ no
emi/egao** 満面の笑み/笑顔 big smile:
tokui ~ desu 得意満面です is proud as
a peacock, is in triumph

man-pai *adj* 満杯 is filled: **yoyaku ga
~ desu** 予約が満杯です is fully booked

man-puku *n, v* 満腹 full stomach

man-rui *n* 満塁 (*baseball*) with the
bases loaded: **~ hōmuran** 満塁ホーム
ラン a grand slam

man-tan *n* 満タン: **~ ni shimásu** 満タ
ンにします fills the tank, fills it up

man-ten *n* 満点 perfect score

man-ten *n* 満天 the whole sky

manabimásu, manabu *v* 学びます, 学ぶ learns, studies

manaíta *n* まな板 chopping board (*for cooking*)

manande *v* 学んで → manabimásu 学びます

manazashi *n* 眼差し a look in one's eyes: **yasashii ~** 優しい眼差し gentle look in one's eyes: **utagai no ~** 疑いの眼差し suspicious look in one's eyes

manbiki *n* 万引き shoplifting, shoplifter

manbyō *n* 万病 all kinds of disease: [IDIOM] **kaze wa ~ no moto** 風邪は万病のもと A cold often leads to all kinds of disease.

mane *n* 真似 imitation, mimicry; **… no ~ o shimásu** …の真似をします imitates, mimics (= manemásu 真似ます)

maneíte *v* 招いて → manekimásu 招きます

mánē´ja *n* マネージャー manager

manekimásu, manéku *v* 招きます, 招く invites

manekin *n* マネキン mannequin

manekineko *n* 招き猫 beckoning cat

manemásu, maneru *v* 真似ます, 真似る imitates

manga *n* マンガ・漫画 cartoon, comics, manga: **manga-bon** マンガ[漫画]本 comic book: **manga-kissa** マンガ[漫画]喫茶 manga cafe

manhattan *n* マンハッタン Manhattan

manhōru *n* マンホール manhole

ma-ni-aimásu, ma-ni-áu *v* 間に合います, 間に合う: **… ni ~** …に間に合います is in time (*for …*); **ma-ni-aimasén** 間に合いません arrives too late (*for …*), misses (*the train/bus/plane*)

ma-ni-awase *v* 間に合わせ make-shift

ma-ni-awasemásu, ma-ni-awaséru *v* 間に合わせます, 間に合わせる: **… de ~** …で間に合わせます makes do (*with …*)

mán'ichi *n* 万一 = **mán ga ichi** 万が一 if by any chance

Mánira *n* マニラ Manila

manjū´ *n* 饅頭 a steamed bun stuffed with ground pork (= **niku-man** 肉まん)

or sweet bean paste (= **anman** あんまん)

manmosu *n* マンモス mammoth

mannén-hitsu *n* 万年筆 fountain pen

manneri(zumu) *n* マンネリ（ズム） mannerism

manpokei *n* 万歩計 pedometer

mánshon *n* マンション a luxury apartment (*house*)

mánto *n* マント cloak

mantohihi *n* マントヒヒ hamadryas

mantora *n* マントラ mantra: **~ o tonaemásu** マントラを唱えます chants mantra

mantsūman *n* マンツーマン one-to-one, one-on-one

manugare[manukare]másu, manugareru [manukaréru] *v* まぬがれ[まぬかれ]ます・免れます, まぬがれる[まぬかれる]・免れる escapes from, is exempt from, avoids

Manyōshū *n* 万葉集 the Man'yoshu, Collection of Ten Thousand Leaves

manzái *n* 漫才 cross-talk comedy: **~ konbi** 漫才コンビ a comic duo

mánzoku (na) *adj* 満足（な） satisfactory: **(… de) ~ shimásu** …（で）満足します is satisfied/contented (*with …*)

marason *n* マラソン jog(ging); (= **marason-kyō´sō** マラソン競争) marathon

maré (na) *adj* 稀（な） rare, infrequent: **maré ni** 稀に rarely

Marē hantō *n* マレー半島 Malay Peninsula

Marēshia *n* マレーシア Malaysia

Marēshia-jin *n* マレーシア人 a Malaysian

Marēshia-go *n* マレーシア語 Bahasa Malaysia (*language*)

mari *n* まり・マリ・鞠 ball, (*Japanese*) **temari** ball

marine *n* マリネ marinade

marifana *n* マリファナ marijuana

maru *n* 丸・まる circle, ring; zero

maru(-) … *prefix* 丸・まる … fully, whole…

maru-anki *n* 丸暗記 rote learning

maru-utsushi *n* 丸写し copying entirely

maru-yaki *n* 丸焼き roast whole

maru-yake n 丸焼け being completely burned (*by fire, etc.*)

maru de *adj* まるで **1.** completely [+ NEGATIVE]: ~ **chigau/kotonaru** まるで違う／異なる quite different **2.** ~ **...no yō (na)** まるで...のよう（な）as if: ~ **kodomo no yō (na)** まるで子供のよう（な）just like a child

marui *adj* 丸い round

maru ku *adv* 丸く roundly: ~ **shimásu** 丸くします makes ... round; **me o ~ shimásu** 目を丸くします(*with*) wide eyes; **se(naka) o ~ shimásu** 背（中）を丸くします hunches up

maruta n 丸太 log

másaka まさか **1.** *adv* ~ **...dewa nai (desu) yo ne?** まさか...ではない（です）よね? Don't tell me that... **2.** *interj* no kidding!; you don't say! impossible!

masanai *v* 増さない = **mashimasén** 増しません (not increase)

mása-ni *adv* まさに exactly, just; certainly, really

masarimásu, masáru *v* 勝ります, 勝る surpasses, is superior

masatsu *n* まさつ・摩擦 friction: ~ **shimásu** 摩擦します rubs (= **kosurimásu, kosuru**, 擦ります, 擦る)

...-máse ...ませ [IMPERATIVE of polite auxiliary] → ...-**másu** ...ます

maséba *v* 増せば (if increased) → **mashimásu** 増します

...-masén *suffix*, *v* ...ません does not: **...masén deshita** ...ませんでした did not

mashi *n* 増し an increase; a surcharge

mashimásu, masu *v* 増します, 増す increases, raises, swells

...-máshite *suffix* ...まして [GERUND of polite auxiliary]

mashumaro *n* マシュマロ marshmallow

massá´ji *n* マッサージ massage: **massá´ji´-shi** マッサージ師 masseur

massatsu *n* 抹殺 [BOOKISH]: ~ **shimásu** 抹殺します eliminates, murders, kills

masshurūmu *n* マッシュルーム mushroom

masu *v* 増す = **mashimásu** 増します (increases)

masú *n* マス・鱒 trout

másu *n* 升 a small measuring box (*from which saké can be drunk*)

...-másu *suffix*, *v* ...ます [INFINITIVE of polite auxiliary]

masu-komi *n* マスコミ mass communication (*media*)

masukotto *n* マスコット mascot

másuku *n* マスク mask (= **kamen** 仮面)

másu-masu *adv* 益々 more and more, increasingly

masutádo *n* マスタード mustard (= **karashi** カラシ・芥子)

masuto *n* マスト mast

matá *conj*, *prep* また・又 again; moreover; **Mata dō´zo** またどうぞ Please (*come, etc.*) again.

matá *n* 股 crotch, groin

máta *conj* また・又 and also/another/more (= **... mo máta** ...もまた)

matagarimásu, matagáru *v* 跨がります, 跨がる: **... ni ~** ...に跨がります straddles, sits astride, mounts, rides; stretches/extends over, spans

matáge *v* 跨げ [IMPERATIVE] (stride over it!) → **matagimásu** 跨ぎます

matagemásu, matagéru *v* 跨げます, 跨げる can stride over

matagimásu, matágu *v* 跨ぎます, 跨ぐ strides over

mataide *v* 跨いで → **matagimásu** 跨ぎます

matánai *v* 待たない = **machimasén** 待ちません (not wait for)

matátaki *n* 瞬き blink(ing)

matátakímásu, matátaku 瞬きます, 瞬く blinks

matá-wa *conj* または・又は or, or else, on the other hand; also; and/or

matcha *n* 抹茶 powdered green tea (*for tea ceremony*)

mátchi *n* マッチ match(es) (*for fire*)

matchí-bako *n* マッチ箱 matchbox

máte *v* 待て [IMPERATIVE] (wait!) → **machimásu** 待ちます

matemásu, matéru *v* 待てます, 待てる can wait

mato *n* 的 target, aim (= **tágetto** ターゲット)

matō´ *v* 待とう = **machimashō** 待ちましょう (let's wait!)

matomarimásu, matomaru ν まとまります、まとまる is settled, arranged, finished

matomemásu, matomeru ν まとめます、まとめる settles, arranges, finishes

mátsu n マツ・松 pine tree (= mátsu-no-kí 松の木)

mátsu ν 待つ = machimásu 待ちます (waits)

matsuba-zúe n 松葉杖 crutch(es)

mátsuge n まつげ・睫(毛) eyelash(es)

matsuri n 祭り (o-matsuri お祭り) festival

matsutake n マツタケ・松茸 a kind of mushroom (thumb-shaped)

matsu-yani n 松脂 pine resin

mattaku adv 全く quite, completely, exactly (= zenzen 全然): mattaku no 全くの perfect

mátte ν 待って → machimásu 待ちます: ~ imásu 待っています is (or will be) waiting/awaiting

mátto n マット mat

mawari n 周り: (... no) mawari (ni/no) (...の) 周り(に/の) around ...

mawari... prefix 回り... revolving..., rotating...

mawari-butai n 回り舞台 revolving stage

mawari-dōro n 回り灯ろう・回り灯籠 revolving lantern

mawari-kaidan n 回り階段 spiral stairway

mawari-michi n 回り道 detour

mawari-kudoi adj 回りくどい round-about

mawarimásu, mawaru ν 周ります、周る goes around

mawarimásu, mawaru ν 回ります、回る turns, revolves, circulates, rotates (= kaitenshimásu 回転します)

mawashi n 回し sumo wrestler's belt (loincloth)

mawashimásu, mawasu ν 回します 回す turns it around, passes it around, circulates it

mawata n 真綿 floss silk

mayaku n 麻薬 narcotic(s), dope (= kusuri クスリ・薬, yaku ヤク・薬, yakubutsu 薬物)

mayoimásu, mayóu ν 迷います、迷う gets lost; gets perplexed

mayonēzu n マヨネーズ mayonnaise

mayótte ν 迷って → mayoimásu 迷います

máyu n 眉 eyebrow(s) (= máyuge 眉毛)

máyu n マユ・繭 cocoon

mazarimásu, mazáru ν 混ざります、混ざる it mixes

mazemásu, mazéru ν 混ぜます、混ぜる mixes it

mazénai ν 混ぜない = mazemasén 混ぜません (not mix it)

máze ro ν 混ぜろ [IMPERATIVE] (mix it!) → mazemásu 混ぜます

mazeyō´ ν 混ぜよう = mazemashō´ 混ぜましょう (let's mix it!)

mázu adv まず first of all, before anything else (= saisho (ni) 最初(に), hajime (ni) 初め(に))

mázu adv まず perhaps, nearly

mazúi adj 不味い untasty, bad-tasting

mazúi adj 1. まずい poor, awkward 2. inadvisable 3. ugly

mazushíi adj 貧しい poor (needy)

mé n 目 eye

mé n 芽 bud

...-me interj ...め・奴 [deprecates people] (fool) ...: baka-me ばかめ・馬鹿め damn (fool) idiot

...-mé suffix ...目 [NUMERAL] -th: itsutsu-mé 五つ目 fifth

méate n 目当て a guide (for the eye); aim

mechamecha adj めちゃめちゃ・目茶目茶 in pieces, all confused, in disorder (= mechakucha めちゃくちゃ・目茶苦茶): ~ ni shimásu めちゃめちゃにします ruins, upsets, messes up

medachimásu, medátsu ν 目立ちます、目立つ stands out, becomes conspicuous

medama-yaki n 目玉焼き fried egg(s)

medarisuto n メダリスト medalist

medaru n メダル medal

medátta ... ν 目立った... outstanding, conspicuous → medachimásu 目立ちます

medátte adv 目立って outstandingly, conspicuously: ~ imásu 目立っています is outstanding, conspicuous → medachimásu 目立ちます

medetái *adj* めでたい **1.** happy (*events*), matter for congratulation **2.** = **o-medetái** おめでたい simple-minded, optimistic; idiot

médo *n* 針孔 the eye of a needle

médo *n* 目処 aim (= **méate** 目当て)

mēdo *n* メード = **meido** メイド maid

megabaito *n* メガバイト megabyte (MB)

megakemásu, megakéru *v* 目掛けます, 目掛ける aims at: ... **o megákete** ...を目掛けて (aiming) at, (going) toward

mégane *n* メガネ・眼鏡 (*eye*) glasses: ~ **o kakemásu** メガネ[眼鏡]を掛けます puts on (*wears*) glasses

megumaremásu, megumareru *v* 恵まれます, 恵まれる gets blessed: ... **ni megumárete imásu** ...に恵まれています is blessed with ...

megumi *n* 恵み blessing, mercy, charity

megumimásu, megumu *v* 恵みます, 恵む blesses with, gives mercifully (*in charity*)

megunde *v* 恵んで → **megumimásu** 恵みます

megurimásu, meguru *v* 巡ります, 巡る centers on, surrounds, concerns

me-gúsuri *n* 目薬・眼薬 eye lotion, eye drops

megutte *v* 巡って → **megurimásu** 巡ります: ... **o megutte** ...を巡って centering on, surrounding, concerning

méi *n* 姪 = **meikko** 姪っ子 niece

...´**-mei** *suffix* ...名 (*counts people*) [BOOKISH] (= ...**-nin** ...人): **ichí-mei** 一名 one person

meibo *n* 名簿 list (*catalog*) of names, directory, register, roll

méibutsu *n* 名物 a local specialty, a special attraction, a famous product

méigo-san *n* 姪御さん (*your*) niece

meihaku (na) *adj* 明白 (な) clear, obvious, explicit: **meihaku ni** 明白に clearly, obviously, explicitly

mei-jimásu, mei-jiru *v* 命じます, 命じる commands; appoints, nominates, orders

meijín *n* 名人 expert

mei-jite *v* 命じて → **mei-jimásu** 命じます

meimon (no) *adj* 名門 (の) distinguished: ~ **no de** 名門の出 person who comes from a very distinguished family: **meimon-kō** 名門校 distinguished school

meirei *n* 命令 order, command

meiro *n* 迷路 labyrinth, maze

mé-isha *n* 目・眼医者 eye doctor, oculist

meishi *n* 名刺 business card, calling card, visiting card, name card: **meishí-ire** 名刺入れ card case

meishi *n* 名詞 noun

meisho *n* 名所 famous place: **kankō-meisho** 観光名所 famous sightseeing spot

méiwaku *n* 迷惑 (**go-méiwaku** ご迷惑) trouble, bother, nuisance: **méiwaku na** 迷惑な troublesome: (... **ni**) (**go-**)~ **o kakemásu** (...に) (ご) 迷惑をかけます causes (*one*) trouble

meiwaku-mēru *n* 迷惑メール e-mail spam, junk mail (= **supamu-mēru** スパムメール)

méiyo *n* 名誉 prestige, honor, glory

mē´kā *n* メーカー maker, manufacturer

mekaké *n* 妾 (**omekake-san** お妾さん) mistress, concubine

me-kákushi *n* 目隠し a blindfold

mekata *n* 目方 weight

me-kyábetsu *n* 芽キャベツ Brussels sprouts

mēkyáppu *n* メーキャップ makeup

mémo *n* メモ note, memo(-randum): **memo-chō** *n* メモ帳 note pad, tablet

memorii *n* メモリー (*computer*) memory (= **yōryō** 容量): ~ **ga tarinai** メモリーが足りない runs out of memory

men *n* 面 **1.** mask **2.** face, front **3.** surface (= **hyōmén** 表面)

mén *n* 綿 cotton (= **momen** 木綿, **kotton** コットン)

mén-bō *n* 綿棒 cotton swab

mén *n* めん・麺 (**mén-rui** めん類・麺類) noodles

ménbā *n* メンバー member

mendō *n* 面倒 trouble, bother, nuisance: **mendō na** 面倒な bothersome (= **mendō-kusái** 面倒臭い)

mendori *n* メンドリ hen

menjō´ *n* 免状 license; diploma

menkai *n* 面会 interview, meeting (= **intabyū** インタビュー): **menkai-nin** 面会人 visitor: ~ **shimásu** 面会します interviews, meets

ménkyo(-sho) *n* 免許(証) driver's license (= **unten ménkyo(-sho)** 運転免許(証)); license, permit (= **menkyó-jō** 免許状)

ménseki *n* 面積 area

mentenansu *n* メンテナンス maintenance

ményū *n* メニュー menu (= **kondate** 献立)

menzei (no) *adj* 免税(の) tax-free/-exempt: **menzei-hin** 免税品 tax-free goods

mērā *n* メーラー (= **mēru sofuto** メールソフト, **mēru kuraianto** メールクライアント) mailer (*computer*)

merii gō rando *n* メリーゴーランド merry-go-round

meriyasu *n* メリヤス knitted goods

merodii *n* メロディー melody

méron *n* メロン melon

mēru *n* メール e-mail (= **ii mēru** Eメール): **mēru-bokkusu** メールボックス e-mail box

mesánai *v* 召さない = **meshimasén** 召しません (do not wear/eat/drink/catch cold) → **meshimásu** 召します

meshí *n* 飯 cooked rice; a meal

meshiagarimásu, meshiagaru *v* 召し上がります, 召し上がる [HONORIFIC] eats; drinks

meshí-bitsu *n* めしびつ・飯櫃 rice bucket/tub (= **o-hitsu** お櫃, **o-hachi** お鉢)

meshimásu, mésu *v* 召します, 召す [*in* FORMAL SPEECH *can replace such verbs as* **kimásu** 着ます (*wears*), **tabemásu** 食べます (*eats*), **nomimasu** 飲みます (*drinks*), **(kaze o) hikimásu** (風邪を)ひきます (*catches cold*), *etc., that involves the body*]

meshitá (no) *adj* 目下(の) inferior (*in status/rank/age*)

meshi-tsúkai *n* 召し使い servant

méssēji *n* メッセージ message (= **kotozuke** 言付け)

mesú *n* 雌・メス female animal: *... no* **mesú** ...の雌・メス female...

mesu *n* メス surgeon's knife

mētā *n* メーター meter (*device*)

mētoru *n* メートル meter(s) (*of length*)

mé-tsuki *n* 目付き a look (*in one's eye*): ~ **ga/no warui** 目付きが/の悪い has evil eyes

métta (na) *adj* 滅多(な) reckless, rash

métta (ni) *adv* 滅多(に) [+ NEGATIVE verb] seldom: ~ **ni nakimasen** 滅多に泣きません rarely cries

meue (no) *n* 目上(の) superior (*in status/rank/age*)

meushi *n* 雌牛 cow

me-yaní *n* 目やに matter (*gum, mucus*) from the eye

meyásu *n* 目安 **1.** a standard **2.** guide; aim (= **méate** 目当て)

mezamashi (dokei) *n* 目覚まし(時計) alarm clock

mezamemásu, mezaméru *v* 目覚めます, 目覚める awake

mezashimásu, mezásu *v* 目指します, 目指す heads for (*a destination*): *... o* **mezáshite** ...を目指して heading for, aiming at

mezurashíí *adj* 珍しい rare, uncommon, novel, curious, unusual, unexpected (*but welcome*)

mezuráshiku *adv* 珍しく unusually

mi *n* 実 **1.** fruit (= **furūtsu** フルーツ) **2.** nut (= **nattsu** ナッツ)

mi... *prefix* 未... un-...

mi-chi (no) *adj* 未知(の) unknown: ~ **no sekai** 未知の世界 unknown world

mi-hakken (no) *adj* 未発見(の) undiscovered

mi-hattatsu (no) *adj* 未発達(の) undeveloped

mi-kaihatsu (no) *adj* 未開発(の) undeveloped

mi-kaiketsu (no) *adj* 未解決(の) unsolved: ~ **no mondai** 未解決の問題 unsolved problem

mi-kai (no) *adj* 未開(の) wild, uncultivated

mi-kakunin (no) *adj* 未確認(の) unidentified, unconfirmed: **mikakunin-hikōbuttai** 未確認飛行物体 unidentified flying object (UFO) (= **yūfō** ユーフォー)

mi-kon (no) *adj* 未婚(の) unmarried:
~ no haha 未婚の母 unmarried mother

mi-shō (no) *adj* 未詳(の) [BOOKISH]
unknown: sakusha-mishō 作者未詳
unknown author

mi-zō (no) *adj* 未曾有(の) [BOOKISH]
unprecedented, unheard-of, unparalleled

mi *n* 身 body

mi ni amarimásu (amaru) *v* 身に余
ります(余る): mi ni amaru kōei desu
身に余る光栄です It is an undeserved
honor.

mi ni oboe ga arimasen (nai) *v* 身に
覚えがありません(ない) I am
innocent. / I know nothing about it.

mi ni shimimásu (shimiru) *v* 身に染み
ます(染みる): mi ni shimimashita 身に
染みました 1. It sank deeply into my
mind. / It went to my heart. 2. pierces
one's body: samusa ga ~ 寒さが身に染
みます The cold pierced me.

mi ni tsukemásu (tsukeru) *v* 身につ
けます(つける) 1. wears, puts on:
akusesari(i) o ~ アクセサリ(一)を身に
つけます wears an accessory 2. learns,
acquires: nintairyoku o ~ 忍耐力を身に
つけます learns to be patient

mi ni tsumasaremásu (tsumasareru)
v 身につまされる(つまされる)
hits close to home, feels deeply,
sympathizes deeply

mi no okiba ga arimasen (nai) *v* 身の
置き場がありません(ない) There is
no place to be/go.

mi o hikimásu (hiku) *v* 身を引きます
(引く) 1. retires 2. recedes, stands
down, backs off

mi o iremásu (ireru) *v* 身を入れます
(入れる) puts oneself

mi o kiru (yō na/yō ni) *adj* 身を切る
(ような/ように) cutting: ~ yō ni
tsumetai kaze 身を切るように冷たい
風 biting cold wind: mi o kirareru yō
na omoi 身を切られるような思い as if
cut to the heart

mi o ko(na) ni shite hatarakimásu
(hataraku) *v* 身を粉にして働きます
(働く) works hard, sweats one's guts
out

mi o makasemásu (makaseru) *v* 身を

任せます(任せる) surrenders oneself
(= mi o yudanemásu 身をゆだねます):
unmei ni ~ 運命に身を任せます
accepts one's fate

mi o tatemásu (tateru) *v* 身を立てま
す(立てる) establishes oneself (as…),
makes a career

mi o yudanemásu (yudaneru) *v* 身
をゆだねます(ゆだねる) surrenders
oneself (= mi o makasemásu 身を任せ
ます): unmei ni mi o ~ 運命に身をゆだ
ねます accepts one's fate

miai *n* 見合い (*broker-arranged*) meeting of prospective bride and groom:
miai-kékkon 見合い結婚 an arranged
marriage

mibō´-jin *n* 未亡人 widow

míbun *n* 身分 social standing: mibun-
shōmei-sho 身分証明書 identification
card (*driver's license, insurance card,
student identification card, alien
registration card, etc.*)

míburi *n* 身振り gesture, movement
(= jesuchā ジェスチャー)

michi *n* 道 1. way, path: ikiru ~ 生き
る道 the way to live 2. street, road (=
dōro 道路): ~ ga kondeimásu 道が混
んでいます There is traffic congestion
on the road.

michi-bata *n* 道端 wayside, roadside
(= robō 路傍)

michi-jun *n* 道順 the way, the route (*on
the road*) (= junro 順路): ... made no ~ o
tazunemásu ...までの道順を尋ねます
asks the way to ...

michi-zure *n* 道連れ travelling
companion, fellow traveler

michibikimásu, michibíku *v* 導きま
す, 導く leads, guides

michimásu, michíru *v* 満ちます, 満ち
る gets complete, full: michite imásu
満ちています is complete, full

midaré *n* 乱れ disorder, messiness:
kami no ~ 髪の乱れ messy hair

midaremásu, midaréru *v* 乱れます,
乱れる gets disturbed, disordered

midashi *n* 見出し 1. heading, caption,
headline 2. a dictionary entry; a head-
word (= midashigo 見出し語)
3. contents (= mokuji 目次), index (=

sakuin 索引), title (= **hyōdai** 標題・表題)

midashimásu, midásu v 乱します、乱す throws into disorder, upsets, disturbs

mídori (no) adj 緑(の) green: **midori-iro** 緑色 green color: **mídori-no-madóguchi** みどりの窓口 the Green Window (for JR train tickets)

Mi-doshi n 巳年 year of the Snake

mié n 見栄 show, display; (dramatic) pose: **mie-ppari** 見栄っぱり a show-off: **~ o harimásu** 見栄を張ります shows off, puts on air, tries to make oneself look good

miemásu, miéru v 見えます、見える 1. is visible, can be seen 2. appears; shows up, comes 3. seems

miénai v 見えない = **miemasén** 見えません is invisible, cannot be seen, does not appear: **~ narimásu** 見えなくなります vanishes (from sight)

míete v 見えて → **miemásu** 見えます

migaite v 磨いて → **migakimásu** 磨きます

migakimásu, migaku 磨きます、磨く polishes, shines

migara n 身柄: **~ no kōsoku** 身柄の拘束 custody

migi n 右 right (not left)

migi-ashi n 右足 right leg/foot

migi-dónari n 右隣り next on the right

migi-kiki (no) adj 右利き(の) right-handed

migi-máwari (ni) adv 右回り(に) clockwise

migi-te n 右手 right hand

migi-ude n 右腕 right arm

mígoto (na) adj 見事(な) splendid, admirable, beautiful

migurushíi adj 見苦しい unseemly, unsightly

mí-hako n 三箱 three boxfuls

mihon n 見本 1. a sample (= **sanpuru** サンプル, **shikyōhin** 試供品) 2. model, example (= **mohan** 模範, **tehon** 手本 (= **o-tehon**お手本))

mii-hā´ n ミーハー lowbrow person

míira n ミイラ mummy

miī´tingu n ミーティング meeting, conference (= **káigi** 会議)

miitobōru n ミートボール meatball

mijikái adj 短い short (not long); brief

mijíkaku adv 短く briefly, short mijíkaku shimásu (suru) v 短くします(する) shortens

mijitaku n 身支度 dressing oneself: **~ shimásu** 身支度します dresses

Mikado n 帝 (Japanese) the mikado

mikagé-ishi n 御影石 granite

mikake n 見かけ・見掛け 1. appearance 2. outward appearance: **mikake wa** 見掛けは outwardly, seemingly

mikaku n 味覚 sense of taste

míkan n ミカン・蜜柑 tangerine, mandarin (orange)

mikata n 味方 friend), accomplice, supporter, side: **~no ~ ni tsukimásu** ...の味方につきます takes sides with...

mi-kátá n 見方 a viewpoint: **...no ~ o kaemásu** ...の見方を変えます changes one's viewpoint: **~ ni yotte (wa)** 見方によって(は) in a way

mikazuki n 三日月 crescent (moon): **mikazuki-gata** 三日月形 crescent shape

mike n 三毛 calico: **mike-neko** 三毛猫 tortoiseshell cat, calico cat

míki n 幹 trunk (of tree)

míki n 神酒 (**o-miki** 御神酒) saké offered to the gods

míkisā n ミキサー blender

mikka n 三日 three days; 3rd day (of month)

miko n 巫女 shrine maiden

mikomi n 見込み 1. promise, hope 2. outlook, expectation 3. opinion, view

mikoshi n おみこし・御輿 (**o-míkoshi** お御輿) portable shrine (for festival parades)

mikoshi n 見越し forethought

mikoshimásu, mikosu v 見越します、見越す allows, foresees

mikuji n みくじ・神籤 (**o-mikuji** おみくじ) written fortune

mimai n 見舞い (**o-mimai** お見舞い) a visit (of solicitude): **mimái-kyaku** 見舞い客 visitor

... míman suffix ...未満 less than, below (a quantity, an age)

mimásu, míru v 見ます, 見る sees, looks, watches; tries doing

mimí n 耳 ear: **~ ga tōi** 耳が遠い is hard of hearing

mimi-kaki n 耳かき earpick

mimi-kázari n 耳飾り earring

mimiuchi n 耳打ち whisper(ing): **~ shimásu** 耳打ちします whispers

mimoto n 身元 one's identity: **~ fumei no** 身元不明の unidentified

mínai v 見ない = **mimasén** 見ません (not see)

minami n 南 south: **minami-guchi** 南口 the south exit/entrance; **minami-yori (no)** 南寄り(の) southerly

Minami-Amérika n 南アメリカ South America

mi-naraimásu, mi-narau v 見習います, 見習う follows (learns from) the example of

miná-san, mina-sama n 皆さん, 皆様 you all, everybody; (you) ladies and gentlemen

minato n 港 port: **minato-machi** 港町 port town

mine n 峰 peak, summit

mineraru-wōtā n ミネラルウォーター mineral water

mingei(-hin) n 民芸(品) folkcraft

mí ni-... prefix, v 見に...: **~ iku** 見に行く [goes] to see

minikúi adj 醜い ugly

mini-sukāto n ミニスカート miniskirt

minkan (no) adj 民間(の) civil(ian), private (non-government)

mi(n)ná n み(ん)な・皆 everybody, all; everything, all, completely (= **zénbu** 全部): **~ de** み(ん)なで・皆で altogether

míno n ミノ・蓑 straw raincoat

míno-mushi n ミノムシ・蓑虫 bagworm

minori n 実り crop, harvest

minorimásu, minóru v 実ります, 実る bears fruit; ripens

minoshirokin n 身代金 ransom

mi-no-take n 身の丈 **1.** one's height (= **mitake** 身丈) **2.** one's condition: **~ ni atta** 身の丈にあった within one's income

mi-no-ue n 身の上 one's station in life (= **misora** 身空): **minoue-banashi** 身の上話 one's life story: **minoue-sōdan (ran)** 身の上相談(欄) personal-advice (column)

minshū n 民衆 the masses, the people (= **shomin** 庶民, **taishū** 大衆)

minshúku n 民宿 bed and breakfast (B&B), family inn, hostelry,

minshu-shúgi n 民主主義 democracy

minto n ミント mint

min'yō n 民謡 folk song, ballad (= **fōku songu** フォークソング)

mínzoku n 民族 race

mioboe n 見覚え recognition: **~ ga arimásu** 見覚えがあります recognizes

mi-okurimásu, mi-okuru v 見送ります, 見送る sees (them) off

miomo n 身重 pregnant female (= **ninpu** 妊婦)

mírai n 未来 future

míreba v 見れば (if one sees) → **mimásu** 見ます

mirin n ミリン・味醂 sweet rice wine (for cooking)

míru v 見る = **mimásu** 見ます (sees)

mirú-gai n ミルガイ・みる貝 surf clam, geoduck

míruku n ミルク milk (= **gyūnyū** 牛乳): **miruku-sē'ki** ミルクセーキ milkshake

miryoku n 魅力 charm (attraction): **miryoku-teki (na)** adj 魅力的(な) charming

mísa n ミサ (Catholic) mass

misago n ミサゴ osprey

misairu n ミサイル missile

misakai-nai/naku adj, adv 見境ない/なく indiscriminate(ly)

misaki n 岬 cape, promontory, headland

misao n 操 chastity

mise n 店 (**o-mise** お店) store, shop (= **sutoa** ストア)

mise-kake (no) adj 見せかけ(の) sham, make-believe, pretend(ed)

misemásu, miséru v 見せます, 見せる shows

mise-mónó n 見せ物 show, exhibition, exhibit

misénai v 見せない = **misemasén** 見せません (not show)

míse ro v 見せろ [IMPERATIVE] (show it!) → **misemásu** 見せます

misete v 見せて → **misemásu** 見せます

míshin n ミシン sewing machine

mishō (no) adj 実生(の) seedling

miso n 味噌 (**o-míso** お味噌) (fermented) bean paste 2. **o-míso** お味噌 → **misokkasu** みそっかす

misogi n 禊 purification

misoji n みそじ・三十路 thirty years old

misoka n 晦日 last day of month (→ **ō-mísoka** 大晦日)

misokkasu n みそっかす 1. *miso* strainings 2. good for nothing 3. child who is considered to be immature (*while playing, etc.*) (= **o-míso** お味噌)

misoppa n 味噌っ歯 decayed tooth

misora n 身空 oneself, one's station in life (= **mi no ue** 身の上): **wakai ~ de...** 若い身空で... ...at such a young age

miso-shíru n 味噌汁 (**omiso-shíru** お味噌汁) soup seasoned with *miso*, *miso* soup

missetsu (na) adj 密接(な) thick, dense; close, intimate

misu n 御簾 bamboo blind

mísu n ミス miss, mistake

míta v 見た = **mimáshita** 見ました (saw)

mi-tái v 見たい wants to see

... mítai desu ...みたいです (= **... no yṓdesu/(da, na, de, ni)** ...の様です(/だ、な、で、に)) seems/looks (like)

mitake n 身丈 1. total length of garment 2. one's height (= **mi-no-take** 身の丈) 3. one's situation

mitama n 御霊 [HONORIFIC] departed soul (= **rei** 霊)

mitame n 見た目 physical appearance

mitashimásu, mitásu v 満たします, 満たす fills up, satisfies

mitate n 見立て 1. diagnosis, selection: **isha no ~** 医者の見立て doctor's opinion 2. choosing clothes

míte v 見て → **mimásu** 見ます

mitei n 未定 to be determined: **shōsai wa ~ desu** 詳細は未定です The details are not yet fixed.

mitomemásu, mitomeru v 認めます, 認める recognizes, acknowledges, admits

mitorimásu, mitoru v 看取ります, 看取る 1. cares for the sick, nurses (= **kanbyō shimásu** 看病します) 2. attends to someone on his/her deathbed

mitorizu n 見取り図 blueprint, sketch

mitōshi n 見通し prospect, outlook

mikoshi 見越し forethought

mítsu n 三つ = **mittsú** 三つ (*three*)
mitsu-ba n 三ツ葉 trefoil leaves; honewort (*stone parsley*): **mitsuba no kurōbā** 三つ葉のクローバー three-leaf clover

mítsu n ミツ・蜜 honey
mitsú-bachi n ミツバチ・蜜蜂 (honey-)bee

mitsugo n 三つ子 triplets

mitsukarimásu, mitsukaru v 見つかります, 見つかる is found, discovered; it turns up

mitsukemásu, mitsukeru v 見つけます, 見つける finds, discovers

mi-tsumemásu, mi-tsumeru v 見つめます, 見つめる gazes at, stares at

mi-tsumori n 見積もり an estimate

mi-tsumorimásu, mi-tsumóru v 見積もります, 見積もる estimates, rates

mitsurin n 密林 jungle

mitsurō n 蜜蝋 beeswax

mitsuyu n 密輸 smuggling

mittsú n 三つ three; three years old (= **san-sai** 三歳): **mittsu-mé** 三つ目 third

mittsū n 密通 adultery, intrigue

miuchi n 身内 family, close relatives and close friends

miugoki n, v 身動き [(usually) +NEGATIVE] moving oneself: **~ ga toremasen** 身動きがとれません 1. is stuck on (*a packed train*) 2. is tied up (*with busy work*)

mi-ukemásu, mi-ukéru v 見受けます, 見受ける observes, happens to see; appears (*to be*)

mi-wakemásu, mi-wakéru v 見分けます, 見分ける discriminates, distinguishes

miwaku n 魅惑 [BOOKISH] enchantment

miwaku teki (na) *adj* 魅惑的（な） enchanting

miya *n* 宮 **1. o-miya** お宮 Shinto shrine **2.** prince, princess

miyage *n* 土産 (**o-miyage** おみやげ・お土産, **o-míya** おみや) = **miyage-mono** みやげ物 souvenir: **miyage mono-ya** みやげ物屋 gift shop

miyako *n* 都 capital city

mi-yasúi *adj* 見やすい clear (*easy to see*)

miyó´ *v* 見よう = **mimashō** 見ましょう (let's look!)

miyori *n* 身寄り relatives: ~ **no nai** 身寄りのない has no relatives (*to rely on*)

mizo *n* 溝 drain, ditch, gutter

mizoochi *n* 鳩尾 pit of the stomach

mizore *n* みぞれ・霙 sleet

mizu *n* 水 (**o-mizu** お水) (*not hot*) water: **tsumetai** ~ 冷たい水 cold water: **nurui** ~ ぬるい水 lukewarm water

　mizu-búkure *n* 水膨れ blister

　mizu-búsoku *n* 水不足 water shortage

　mizu-déppō *n* 水鉄砲 water pistol

　mizu-fūsen *n* 水風船 water balloon

　mizu-gi *n* 水着 swim suit, bathing suit

　mizu-iro *n* 水色 light blue

　mizu-kíri *n* 水切り colander

　mizu-kusa *n* 水草 waterweed

　mizu-mushi *n* 水虫 athlete's foot

　mizu-sáshi *n* 水差し water pitcher

　mizu-taki *n* 水炊き chicken, bean curd, etc., boiled into hot broth

　mizu-tama moyō *n* 水玉模様 polka dot (*design*)

　mizu-wari *n* 水割り (*highball of*) whisky and water

mizú´mi *n* 湖 lake

mo *n* 喪 mourning: ~ **ni fukushimásu** 喪に服します mourns (*the passing*)

… mo *suffix, prep* …も too, also, even; (*not*)… either/even; indeed; number **mo** も [+ NEGATIVE] not even (*so much as*), [+ AFFIRMATIVE] as many/much as, all of

… mo … mo *conj* …も…も both … and …; [+ NEGATIVE] neither … nor …

mō´ *adv* もう already; now: **mō´ súgu** もうすぐ right away

mō *adj* もう more; (*not*) … any more: ~ **hitóri** もう一人 another (*one more*) person; ~ **hitótsu** もう一つ another,

one more, the other one; ~ **ichi-dó/ík-kai** もう一度／一回 one more time, again; ~ **sukóshi** もう少し (a bit) more

mochi *n* 餅 rice cake

mochi-agemásu, mochi-agéru *v* 持ち上げます, 持ち上げる lifts

mochi-awase *n* 持ち合わせ **1.** what is on hand (*in stock*): ~ **no** …の持ち合わせの stock of … **2.** cash on hand

mochi-awasemásu, mochi-awaséru *v* 持ち合わせます, 持ち合わせる has on hand (*in stock*)

mochiba *n* 持ち場 one's post of duty

mochi-gome *n* もち米 glutinous rice

mochiimásu, mochíiru *v* 用います, 用いる uses (= **tsukaimásu** 使います)

mochimásu, mótsu *v* 持ちます, 持つ has, holds, carries; it lasts

mochi-mono *n* 持ち物 **1.** belongings **2.** what to bring

mochí-nushi *n* 持ち主 owner

mochíron *adv* もちろん of course, certainly

mōchō *n* 盲腸 appendix

mōchō´(-en) *n* 盲腸（炎）appendicitis

mōchū *n* 喪中 mourning period

modemu *n* モデム modem

moderu *n* モデル model

mōdō-ken *n* 盲導犬 seeing-eye dog

modorimásu, modóru *v* 戻ります, 戻る goes back, returns, reverts

modoshimásu, modósu *v* 戻します, 戻す **1.** vomits **2.** sends back, returns

moegara *n* 燃え殻 cinder(s)

moemásu, moeru *v* 燃えます, 燃える (*fire*) burns

mō´fu *n* 毛布 blanket

mōfuku *n* 喪服 mourning dress

mogi *n* 模擬 imitation

mogi-shiken *n* 模擬試験 trial test, mock examination

mogura *n* モグラ・土竜 a mole (*rodent*)

moguri *n* 潜り diving; a diver

mogurimásu, mogúru *v* 潜ります, 潜る dives (*under*); gets into (*bed*); goes under(ground)

mohan *n* 模範 model, pattern, example (= **mihon** 見本, **tehon** 手本 (**o-tehon** お手本)): ~ **o shimeshimásu** 模範を示します gives an example mohan-sei *n* 模範生 model student

mohan-kaitō *n* 模範解答 model answers

mohan-shū *n* 模範囚 model prisoner

mohaya *adv* もはや [+ NEGATIVE verb] no longer

móji *n* 文字 letter, character, writing: **ō-moji** 大文字 capital/upper-case letter: **ko-moji** 小文字 small/lower-case letter: (*computer*) **zenkaku-moji** 全角文字 double-byte character: **hankaku-moji** 半角文字 one-byte character

moji-ban *n* 文字盤 dial window

moji-dōri *adv* 文字どおり literally

mójin *n* 盲人 blind person

mōkarimásu, mōkáru *v* 儲かります, 儲かる is profitable, it makes money

mokei *n* 模型 model, mold (= **moderu** モデル)

mokei-hikōki *n* 模型飛行機 model airplane

mokei-jidōsha *n* 模型自動車 model car

mōkemásu, mōkéru *v* 儲けます, 儲ける makes money, profits

mōkemásu, mōkéru *v* 設けます, 設ける prepares, sets up

Mō´ko *n* 蒙古 Mongolia (= **mongoru** モンゴル): **Mōko-jin** 蒙古人 an Mongolian: **Mōko-han** 蒙古斑 Mongolian blue spot

mokugeki *n* 目撃 witness: **~ shimásu** 目撃します witnesses

mokugeki-sha *n* 目撃者 a witness, an eyewitness

mokuhan (-ga) *n* 木版(画) wood-block print

mokuhyō *n* 目標 target, goal (= **tāgetto** ターゲット, **gōru** ゴール)

Mokusei *n* 木星 Jupiter

mokusei (no) *adj* 木製(の) made of wood

mokusō *n* 黙想 meditation (= **meditēshon** メディテーション)

mokután *n* 木炭 charcoal (= **sumi** 炭)

mokuteki *n* 目的 aim, objective, purpose, end, goal (= **nerai** 狙い, **mato**

的, **mokuhyō** 目標): **~ no tame ni (wa) shudan o erabimasen** 目的のために (は)手段を選びません uses any trick to achieve one's ends

mokutekí-chi *n* 目的地 destination, goal: **~ ni (tadori-)tsukimásu** 目的地 に(辿り)着きます arrives at one's destination

mokuteki-go *n* 目的語 (*grammar*) object

mokutō *n* 黙祷 silent prayer: **~ o sasagemásu** 黙祷を捧げます offers silent prayer

Mokuyō´(bi) *n* 木曜(日) Thursday

mokuyoku *n* 沐浴 bathing, washing oneself (*to clean*)

mokuzai *n* 木材 wood

mokuzen (no) *adj* 目前(の) immediate (= **me-no-mae** 目の前): **~ no rieki** 目前 の利益 immediate advantage

momanai *v* 揉まない = **momimasén** 揉みません (not rub)

mome *v* 揉め [IMPERATIVE] (massage it!) → **momimásu** 揉みます

moméba *v* 揉めば (if one massages) → **momimásu** 揉みます

mome-goto *n* 揉め事 discord, tiff, trouble: **~ o okoshimásu** 揉め事を起こ します causes troubles

momemásu, momeru *v* 揉めます, 揉め る **1.** is in discord/trouble: **ki ga ~** 気 が揉めます feels uneasy/troubled **2.** can massage (*rub with both hands*)

momen *n* 木綿 cotton (= **men** 綿, **kot-ton** コットン)

momete *v* 揉めて → **momemásu** 揉めます

momi *n* もみ・籾 unhulled rice

mómi *n* モミ: **~ no ki** モミの木 fir tree

momigara *n* もみ殻 chaff

mómiji *n* モミジ・紅葉 **1.** maple **2.** autumn leaves

momimásu, momu *v* 揉みます, 揉む massages, rubs with both hands

momo *n* モモ・桃 peach

mómo *n* 股 thigh

momō´ *v* 揉もう = **monimáshō** 揉みま しょう (let's massage it!)

momohiki *n* 股引き longjohns; drawers (= **zubón-shita** ズボン下)

momo-iro (no) adj 桃色(の) pink, rosy: ~ **no hada** 桃色の肌 pink skin

món n 紋 family crest (= **monshō** 紋章)

món n 門 gate (= **gēto** ゲート)

món-ban n 門番 gatekeeper, watchman, guard, porter (= **mon'ei** 門衛)

mon-ei n 門衛 gatekeeper, watchman, guard, porter (= **monban** 門番)

mon-gen n 門限 curfew

Monbu-Kagaku-daijin n 文部科学大臣 Minister of Education, Culture, Sports, Science and Technology

Monbú-Kagaku-shō n 文部科学省 Ministry of Education, Culture, Sports, Science and Technology (MEXT)

mondai n 問題 **1.** question, topic, subject, exercise: ~ **ni naránai** 問題にならない unimportant **2.** problem, issue, trouble (= **toraburu** トラブル)

monde v 揉んで → **momimásu** 揉みます

mongái-kan n 門外漢 outsider, non-specialist, layman

Mongoru n モンゴル Mongolia (= **mōko** 蒙古)

Mongoru-jin n モンゴル人 a Mongolian

Mongoru-go n モンゴル語 Mongolian (language)

mónku n 文句 **1.** phrase: **utai-monku** 謳い文句 a motto, catchphrase, slogan: **odoshi-monku** 脅し文句 threatening words **2.** complaint (= **fuhei** 不平, **fufuku** 不服, **kujō** 苦情): ~ **no tsukeyō ga arimasen** 文句のつけようがありません is perfect

monó n 物 thing, object, article, something, stuff

...mono suffix ... もの ... shita monó/ món desu ...したもの/ものです used to do(= ... **món**... もん)

monó n 者 person, fellow [BOOKISH] (= **hito** 人)

monogátari n 物語 tale, legend

monógoto n 物事 things, everything

monohoshisō (na/ni) adj, adv 物欲しそう(な/に) wistful(ly)

monohoshi-zuna (-zao) n 物干し綱 (竿) clothesline (laundry pole)

monomane n ものまね・物真似

mimic(ry), impersonation: ~ **o shimásu** ものまねをします mimics, impersonates

mono-óboe n 物覚え memory: ~ **ga ii (warui)** 物覚えがいい(悪い) is quick (slow) to learn (= **nomikomi ga hayai (osoi)** のみ込みが早い(遅い))

mono-óki n 物置き shed (store-house)

monoraru n モノラル monaural sound

monorē´ru n モノレール monorail

monorōgu n モノローグ monologue (= **dokuhaku** 独白)

monosashi n 物差し ruler (foot rule); measure; criterion

mono-sugói adj 物凄い terrible, awesome

mono-súgóku adv 物凄く terribly, extremely

monózuki (na) adj 物好き(な) curious, inquisitive

monshō n 紋章 family crest

Monsirochō n モンシロチョウ cabbage butterfly

moppara adv 専ら principally, chiefly

móppu n モップ mop

moraimásu, morau v もらいます, もらう receives, gets; has someone do it

mō´ra shimásu (suru) v 網羅します (する) includes, comprises, covers (all): **mō´ra shita ...** 網羅した... exhaustive, complete

morashimásu, morásu v 漏らします, 漏らす lets leak; reveals

moratta v もらった = **moraimáshita** もらいました (got)

moratte v もらって → **moraimásu** もらいます

morawanai v もらわない = **morai-masén** もらいません (not get)

more v 盛れ [IMPERATIVE] (heap it up!) → **morimásu** 盛ります

moremásu, moréru v 漏れます, 漏れる leaks out; is omitted; it leaks (= **morimásu** 漏ります)

mori n 森 woods, forest

morimásu, moru v 盛ります, 盛る heaps/piles it up

mori-bana n 盛り花 a flower arrangement

morimásu, móru v 漏ります, 漏る it leaks

morói *adj* もろい・脆い brittle, frail

morote *n* もろて・諸手 both hands: **~ o agete** 諸手を挙げて wholeheartedly

morotomo *n* もろとも together [BOOKISH]: **shinaba ~** 死なばもろとも go to the grave together

mó'ru *n* モール braid

moruhíne *n* モルヒネ morphine

morutaru *n* モルタル (*material*) mortar

móshi (*... shitára*) *conj* もし (…したら) if, perchance

mó'shi-agemásu, mó'shi-agéru *v* 申し上げます, 申し上げる [HUMBLE] **1.** I say (= **mōshi-agemásu** 申し上げます) **2.** I humbly do (= **itashimásu** 致します)

móshi-de *n* 申し出 proposal, offer; report, application, claim
mōshi-demásu, mōshi-déru *v* 申し出ます, 申し出る proposes, offers; reports, applies for, claims

móshi-ire *n* 申し入れ (*public*) proposal, offering
mōshi-iremásu, mōshi-iréru *v* 申し入れます, 申し入れる (*publicly*) proposes, offers

moshi-ka-shitara (-suru to) *adv* もしかしたら(すると) perhaps

móshi-komi *n* 申し込み application; reservation, subscription; proposal, offer
mōshi-komimásu, mōshi-kómu *v* 申し込みます, 申し込む applies; reserves, subscribes; proposes, offers
mōshikomí-sha *n* 申し込み者・申込者 applicant
mōshikomi-yōshi *n* 申込用紙 application form

móshimásu, mō'su *v* 申します, 申す [HUMBLE] **1.** I say (= **mōshi-agemásu** 申し上げます) **2. ... to ~** I am, this is (= **désu** です)

móshi-moshi! *interj* もしもし! hello! hey! say there! (*on the phone*)

mó'shitate *n* 申し立て statement, testimony, allegation: **igi-mōshitate** 異議申し立て formal objection

mō'shi-wake *n* 申し訳 excuse: **~ arimasén/gozaimasén** 申し訳ありません/ございません I am very sorry.

mó'shon *n* モーション motion; sexual overture, pass: **... ni ~ o kakemásu** …にモーションをかけます makes a pass at, makes eyes at

Mosukuwa *n* モスクワ Moscow

mō'tā *n* モーター motor
mōtā-bōto *n* モーターボート motor-boat

motánai *v* 持たない = **mochimasén** 持ちません (not have; not last)

motaremásu, motaréru *v* もたれます, もたれる: **(... ni) motaremásu** (…に)もたれます leans (*against ...*)

motasemásu, motaséru *v* 持たせます, 持たせる lets one have, provides (*one with*), gives

móte *v* 持て [IMPERATIVE] (hold it!) → **mochimásu** 持ちます

móteba *v* 持てば (if one has; if it lasts) → **mochimásu** 持ちます

motemásu, motéru *v* 持てます, 持てる **1.** is popular, well-liked **2.** can hold

motenashi *n* もてなし hospitality

mōteru *n* モーテル motel

motó *n* 元・本 origin, source; cause (*of an effect*)

motó *n* 下 (*at the*) foot (*of*), under

...-moto *suffix* …元 the source of an activity: **shuppan-moto** 出版元 the publisher(s); **hanbai-moto** 販売元 sales agency; **seizō-moto** 製造元 the maker(s); **oroshi-moto** 卸元 the wholesaler

motó (no) *adj* 元(の) former, earlier, original: **~ kara** 元から from the beginning, always, all along

motó' mochimashō 持ちましょう (let's hold it!)

motomemásu, motoméru *v* 求めます, 求める **1.** wants, looks for **2.** asks for, demands **3.** buys, gets

motomoto *n* 元々 from the start, originally; by nature, naturally: **...-témo ~ désu ...** ても元々です is no worse off even if ..., it will do no harm to ...

móto wa *adv* 元は originally; earlier, before (= **motomoto wa** 元々は)

mótó-yori *adv* もともより from the beginning; by nature

motozukimásu, motozúku *v* 基づきます, 基づく is based on; conforms to

mótsu v 持つ = **mochimás<u>u</u>** 持ちます (has, holds, carries)

motsuré n もつれ tangle, entanglement; complications

motsuremás<u>u</u>, motsureru v もつれます, もつれる gets entangled/complicated: **shitá ga ~** 舌がもつれます lisps

mottai-nái adj もったいない 1. undeserving 2. wasteful

motte v 盛って → **morimás<u>u</u>** 盛ります

motte v 持って = **mótte** 持って (holding) [*before verbs of movement*]

mótte v 漏って → **morimás<u>u</u>** 漏ります

mótte v 持って → **mochimás<u>u</u>** 持ちます [*but* **motte** 持って *before verbs of movement*]

motte ikimás<u>u</u> (iku) v 持って行きます(行く) takes, carries; brings (*to you, there*)

mótte imás<u>u</u> (iru) v 持っています(いる) has, holds, owns, possesses

motte itte v 持って行って taking it: **~ kudasái** 持って行って下さい please take it with you

motte kimás<u>u</u> (kúru) v 持って来ます(来る) brings (*to me, here*)

mottékite v 持って来て bringing it: **~ kudasái** 持って来て下さい please bring it here

motte kói v 持って来い [IMPERATIVE] (bring it here!) → **motte kimás<u>u</u>** 持って来ます

motte-kói (no) adj もってこい(の) most desirable, ideal; just the thing/ticket (= **... ni chōdo yoi ...** にちょうど良い, **uttetsuke no** うってつけ(の))

mótto adv もっと more, still more; longer, further: **~ íi** もっといい better; **~ warúi** もっと悪い worse; **~ takus<u>á</u>n** もったくさん lots more; **~ saki (ni)** もっと先(に) further

móttomo adv, conj もっとも 1. indeed, of course 2. but, however, to be sure

móttomo adv 最も most; exceedingly

móya n もや・靄 mist, haze

moyashi n モヤシ bean sprouts

moyō n 模様 pattern, design (→ **shima-moyō** 縞模様) (= **dezain** デザイン)

moyōshimás<u>u</u>, moyō´su v 催します, 催す holds/gives (*an event*); feels

mozaiku n モザイク mosaic

mozō n 模造 imitation

mozō-hin n 模造品 imitation products

mu... prefix 無... un-, without..., ...less

mu-bō (na) adj 無謀(な) reckless

mu-chákuriku (no) adj 無着陸(の) non-stop (flight)

mú-cha (na) adj 無茶(な) unreasonable; reckless; disorderly

mú-chi n 無知 ignorance: **múchi (na)** adj 無知(な) ignorant

mu-dan (de) adj 無断(で) without notice, without permission

mu-ími (na) adj 無意味(な) meaningless

mu-íshiki (no/na) adj 無意識(の/な) unconscious, involuntary

mú-jaki (na) adj 無邪気(な) naive, innocent, unsophisticated

mú-ji (no) adj 無地(の) solid-color

mu-jirushi (no) adj 無印(の) unmarked, unbranded

mu-jō´ken (no) adj 無条件(の) unconditional: **~ de** 無条件で unconditionally

mu-jō (na) adj 無情(な) heartless, unfeeling

mu-kánkaku (na) adj 無感覚(な) numb

mu-kánkei (na) adj 無関係(の/な): **... to mukánkei ...** と無関係(の/な) unrelated (*unconnected, irrelevant*) to ...

mu-kánshin (no/na) adj 無関心(の/な): **... ni ~ ...** に無関心(の/な) indifferent to ..., unconcerned with ...

mu-kidō (no) adj 無軌道(の) reckless, trackless

mu-kigen (no/ni) adj, adv 無期限(の/に) indefinite(ly)

mu-kimei (no) adj 無記名(の) unsigned, unregistered

mu-kō (no/na) adj 無効(の/な) invalid (*not valid*), null

mu-sékinin (na) adj 無責任(な) irresponsible

mu-shoku (no) adj 無職(の) jobless: **~ no otoko** 無職の男 jobless man

mu-shoku (no) *adj* 無色(の) achroma, colorless(ness): **mushoku-tōmei** 無色透明 colorless and transparent

mu-teki *n* 無敵 invincibility, too strong to have as rival: **tenka-muteki** 天下無敵 having no rival in the world

mu-tón-chaku/-jaku (na) *adj* 無頓着/無自覚(な) careless

mú-yō (no) *adj* 無用(の) unnecessary; useless; having no business

mú-zai (no) *adj* 無罪(の) innocent, not guilty

mu-zō´sa (na) *adj* 無造作(な) easy, effortless: **mu-zō´sa ni** 無造作に easily, readily; casually, carelessly

múchi *n* 鞭 a whip: **~ de uchimásu** 鞭で打ちます whips

muchū *n* 夢中 trance, ecstasy: **... ni ~ ni narimásu** …に夢中になります gets entranced with (*engrossed in*) ...

muda-bánashi *n* 無駄話 idle talk, hot air, bull: **~ o shimásu** 無駄話をします shoots the bull

muda (na) *adj* 無駄(な) futile, no good, wasteful; useless: **muda-ashi** 無駄足 fool's errand

muda (ni) *adj* 無駄(に) in vain: **~ ni shimásu** 無駄にします wastes

muda-zúkai *n* 無駄使い extravagance, waste

múgi *n* 麦 wheat, barley

mugi-wara *n* 麦わら straw

mugói *adj* むごい cruel, brutal

muika *n* 六日 six days; the 6th day (*of month*): **muika-mé** 六日目 the 6th day

muite *v* 向いて・剥いて → mukimásu 向きます・剥きます

mujun *n* 矛盾 inconsistency, contradiction: **~ shi(te) (i)másu** 矛盾し(てい)ます is inconsistent, contradictory

mukade *n* ムカデ・百足 centipede

mukae *n* 迎え a welcome

mukaemásu, mukaeru *v* 迎えます, 迎える meets; welcomes; invites

mukai *n* 向かい: **mukai-gawa** 向かい側 an opposite side; **mukai-atte** 向かいあって face to face

mukai-kaze *n* 向かい風 headwind

mukaimásu, mukau *v* 向かいます, 向かう: **... ni mukaimásu** …に向かいます opposes; heads for

múkamuka shimásu *v* むかむか[ムカムカ]します is queasy, feels nauseated

mukanai *v* 向かない = **mukimasén** 向きません (not face)

mukashi *n* 昔 long (time) ago; ancient days

mukashi no *adj* 昔の ancient, old(-en)

mukashi-bánashi *n* 昔話 legend; folk tale

mukashi kará no *adj* 昔からの old (*from way back*)

mukatte *v* 向かって → **mukaimásu** 向かいます

muke *v* 向け・剥け [IMPERATIVE] (turn!; pare!) → **mukemásu** 向けます・剥けます

mukéba *v* 向けば (if one faces) → **mukimásu** 向きます

mukemásu, mukeru *v* 向けます, 向ける turns (*one's face/eyes/attention to*), directs/points it (*at*)

mukemásu, mukeru *v* 剥けます, 剥ける can skin, can pare

...-muke (no) *suffix, adj* …向け(の) (*bound/intended*) for ...: **kazoku-muke (no)** 家族向け(の) for family

mukete *v* 向けて・剥けて → **mukemásu** 向けます・剥けます

mukimásu, muku *v* 向きます, 向く faces

mukimásu, muku *v* 剥きます, 剥く: **kawá o ~** 皮を剥きます skins, pares, peels

...-muki (no) *suffix, adj* …向き(の) facing; (*suitable*) for ...

múko *n* 婿 son-in-law; bridegroom (= **o-muko-san** お婿さん)

mukō *prep, adv* 向こう beyond; across the way, over there: **mukō no** 向こうの opposite, facing

mukō-gawa *n* 向こう側 the other side/party, the opposite side

mukō´-mizu (na) *adj* 向こう見ず(な) reckless, rash: **mukō´-mizu ni** 向こう見ずに recklessly

mukō´ *v* 向こう = **mukimashō** 向きましょう (let's face it!)

mukúi *n* 報い bad karma; good karma:

... (no) mukúi o ukemásu ...(の)報い を受けます pays a price (for)

mukuimásu, mukuíru v 報います, 報 いる [BOOKISH] repays; compensates

mukuínai v 報いない = **mukuimasén** 報いません (not repay/compensate)

mukúite v 報いて → **mukuímásu** 報います

mumei (no) adj 無名(の) nameless, anonymous; obscure

munashii adj 空しい・虚しい empty; futile, in vain

muné n 胸 **1.** chest, breast **2.** heart, mind

muné n 旨 gist, purport, intent, effect

muné n 棟 ridge (of roof)

murá n 村 village: **mura-bito, mura no hito** 村人, 村の人 village people: **mura-hachibu** 村八分 ostracism

muragarimásu, muragáru v 群がり ます, 群がる they flock/throng together

murásaki n **1.** murásaki (no) 紫(の) purple **2.** 紫 soy sauce (= **shōyu** しょうゆ・醤油)

muré n 群れ group, throng, flock

múri 1. n 無理 strain, (undue) force: ~ **(o) shimásu** 無理(を)します overdoes, overworks, forces oneself **2. múri na** 無理な unreasonable, forced; violent; overdoing; (over-)demanding

muri mo arimasen (nai) v 無理もあり ません(ない) no wonder

múri ni sasemásu (saseru) v 無理に させます(させる) forces one (to do)

múri ni shimásu v 無理にします strains, forces; overdoes (it); demands too much

múri wa nái adj 無理はない = **múri wa arimasén** 無理はありません: **... no mo arimasén** ...のもありません it is no wonder that...

muriyari adv 無理矢理 forcibly

muryō (no) adj 無料(の) free of charge: **muryō-chū´shajō** 無料駐車場 free parking

musánai v 蒸さない = **mushimasén** 蒸しません (not steam)

musen n 無線 radio; wireless

musen-ran n 無線 LAN wireless LAN, Wi-Fi (computer)

mushi n ムシ・虫 insect, bug; moth; worm: ~ **no iki** 虫の息 breathing faintly, being at death's door

mushi-kúdashi 虫下し vermifuge

mushi-megane n 虫眼鏡 magnifying glass

mushi-yoke n 虫よけ insect repellent; mothballs

mushi-yoké-ami n 虫よけ網 window screen (= **amido** 網戸)

mushi n 無視 neglect, ignorance

múshi shimásu (suru) v 無視します (する) ignores, neglects, disregards

mushi-atsúi adj 蒸し暑い muggy, close, sultry, humid

mushi-ba n 虫歯 decayed tooth

mushimásu, músu v 蒸します, 蒸す steams it; is sultry, humid

mushí-mono n 蒸し物 steamed foods

múshiro adv むしろ rather; preferably

múshite v 蒸して → **mushimásu** 蒸します

musō n 夢想 dream, imagination: ~ **shimásu** 夢想します dreams, imagines

musō-ka n 夢想家 dreamer

musubi n むすび (**o-músubi** おむすび) riceball (= **onigiri** おにぎり)

musubi v 結び → **musubimásu** 結び ます: **musubi-me** 結び目 knot

musubimásu, musubu v 結びます, 結 ぶ ties, ties up: **nékutai o** ~ ネクタイを 結びます wears a tie

musuko n 息子 son: **musuko-san** 息子 さん (your/someone else's) son

musume n 娘 daughter; girl: **musume-san** 娘さん (your/someone else's) daughter, lady

musū´ (no) adj 無数(の) innumerable, countless

musunde v 結んで → **musubimásu** 結びます

mutsukashii, muzukashii adj 難しい hard, difficult

muttsú n 六つ・6つ six (= **rok-ko** 6 個); six years old (= **roku-sai** 六歳)

múyami (ni) adv 無闇(に) recklessly; indiscriminately; immoderately

múzumuzu suru adj むずむずする itchy, crawly, creepy

myakú n 脈, **myakuhaku** 脈拍 pulse:

~ o hakarimásu 脈を計ります checks one's pulse (rate)

myō... *prefix* 明... tomorrow...

myō´-ban *n, adv* 明晩 tomorrow night (= **asu/asita no ban/yoru** 明日の晩/夜)

myō-chō *n, adv* 明朝 [BOOKISH] tomorrow morning (= **asu/ashita no asa** 明日の朝)

myō-gó-nichi *n, adv* 明後日 [BOOKISH] day after tomorrow (= **asatte** あさっ

て・明後日)

myō´-nichi *n, adv* 明日 tomorrow (= **ashita, asu** 明日)

myōga *n* ミョウガ・茗荷 Japanese ginger (buds)

myō ji, miyoji *n* 名字・苗字 family name [*as written*] (= **sei** 姓)

myō´(na) *adj* 妙(な) strange, queer, wondrous

myūjikaru *n* ミュージカル musical

N

n´ ("un") *n* ん(うん) uh-huh, yeah [INFORMAL] (= **hai** はい [FORMAL])

n´ ("ūn") *n* んー(うーん) hmm, well, lessee

...´n ... *suffix* ...ん... = **...´no ...**
...の...: **...´n desu (da)** ...んです(だ) it's that ...

na *n* 名 name (= **namae** 名前)

na bakari (no) *adj* 名ばかり(の) nominal

na-dakái *adj* 名高い famous (= **yūmei** 有名)

na-fuda *n* 名札 name plate/tag; dog tag

na no aru *adj* 名のある famous

na no tōtta *adj* 名の通った well-known

na o nasu *v* 名を成す becomes famous

na o nokoshimásu (nokosu) *v* 名を残します, 残す earns one's place

ná *n* 菜 greens, vegetables; rape (= **náppa** 菜っ葉)

...´ ná/nā´ *interj* ...な/なあ (*usually male*) = **...´ né/nē´** ...ね/ねえ (*female*) isn't it, don't you think/ agree

nábe *n* 鍋 (**o-nábe** お鍋) **1.** pan, pot **2.** food cooked and served in a pan (= **nabé-mono** 鍋物)

nabé-mono *n* 鍋物 food cooked and served in a pan

nabigētā *n* ナビゲーター navigator

nadamemásu, nadaméru *v* 宥めます, 宥める soothes, pacifies

nadare *n* 雪崩 avalanche; snowslide (= **yuki-nádare** 雪なだれ)

nademásu, nadéru *v* 撫でます, 撫でる strokes, smooths, pats, pets

nadé ro *v* 撫でろ [IMPERATIVE] (stroke!, pet!) → **nademásu** 撫でます

... nádo *suffix* ...など・等 and so forth/on, and what-not, and the like

náe *n* 苗 seedling: **nae-doko** 苗床 seed-bed

náeba *v* なえば (if one twists it) → **naimásu** ないます

naemásu, naéru *v* 萎えます, 萎える droops, withers

naemásu, naéru *v* なえます, なえる can twist it (*into a rope*)

naénai *v* 萎えない = **naemasén** 萎えません (not droop)

naénai *v* なえない = **naemasén** なえません (cannot twist it)

naéreba *v* 萎えれば (if it droops) → **naemásu** 萎えます

naéreba *v* なえれば (if one can twist it) → **naemásu** なえます

nafutarin *n* ナフタリン (*naphthalene*) mothballs

naga-... *prefix* 長... long

naga-chōba *n* 長丁場 [BOOKISH] time-consuming: **~ no shigoto** 長丁場の仕事 time-consuming work

naga-gutsu *n* 長靴 boots

naga-iki *n* 長生き longevity, long life (= **chōju** 長寿)

naga-isu *n* 長椅子 couch

naga-negi *n* 長ネギ[葱] leek (*the regular* **négi** ネギ・葱, *as contrasted* *with* **tama-négi** タマネギ・玉葱 round onion)

naga-sode *n* 長袖 long sleeves, long-sleeved garment

naga-yu *n* 長湯: **~ o shimásu** 長湯をします takes a long bath

nagái *adj* 長い long

nagaku *adv* 長く long

nagamé *n* 眺め view, scenery

nagamemásu, nagaméru *v* 眺めます、眺める gazes/stares at, views

... (-)nágara *suffix, adv* ...ながら while (*during/although*)

nagaré *n* 流れ a stream, a flow

nagare-sagyō *n* 流れ作業 assembly line

nagare-zu *n* 流れ図 flow chart

nagaré-boshi *n* 流れ星 shooting star

nagaré-dama *n* 流れ弾 stray bullet

nagaremásu, nagaréru *v* 流れます、流れる flows

nagárénai *v* 流れない = **nagaremásén** 流れません (not flow)

nagárete *v* 流れて → **nagaremásu** 流れます

nágasa *n* 長さ length

Nagásaki *n* 長崎 Nagasaki: **Nagasáki-ken** 長崎県 Nagasaki Prefecture; **Nagasáki-shi** 長崎市 Nagasaki City

nagasánai *v* 流さない = **nagashimásén** 流しません (not let flow)

nagashí *n* 流し kitchen sink

nagashimásu, nagásu *v* 流します、流す lets it flow, washes away

naga(t)tarashii *n* 長(っ)たらしい [IN NEGATIVE SENSE] lengthy, tedious

naga-ya *n* 長屋 tenement house

nage-ire *v* 投げ入れ a flower arrangement (*in a tall vase*)

nagéite *v* 嘆いて → **nagekimásu** 嘆きます

nagekánai *v* 嘆かない = **nagekimásén** 嘆きません (not grieve)

nagekí *n* 嘆き grief, lamentation

nagekimásu, nagéku *v* 嘆きます、嘆く grieves, weeps, moans, laments

nagemásu, nagéru *v* 投げます、投げる throws

nagénai *v* 投げない = **nagemásén** 投げません (not throw)

nagé ro *v* 投げろ [IMPERATIVE] (throw!) → **nagemásu** 投げます

nágete *v* 投げて → **nagemásu** 投げます

nageyō *v* 投げよう = **nagemashō´** 投げましょう (let's throw it!)

nagisa *n* なぎさ・渚 water's edge, beach, shore

nagori *n* 名残 traces, remains, remnant: **nagorioshii** 名残惜しい hates to leave

nagurimásu, nagúru *v* 殴ります、殴る knocks, beats, strikes

nagusame *n* 慰め comfort, consolation

nagusamemásu, nagusaméru *v* 慰めます、慰める comforts, consoles

nagusami *n* 慰み amusement, entertainment

nagútte *v* 殴って → **nagurimásu** 殴ります

nái *v* ない = **arimásén** ありません (there is no ..., lacks, has no ...)

nai-... *prefix* 内... within, in(-side), inner, internal

nái-bu (no) *adj* 内部(の) internal

naibu-kokuhatsu *n* 内部告発 exposuring from within, whistle-blowing: **naibu-kokuhatsusha** 内部告発者 a whistleblower

nái-chi *n* 内地 inside the country

nai-en (no) *adj* 内縁(の) common-law: **~ no otto/tsuma** 内縁の夫/妻 common-law husband/wife

nai-fuku *n* 内服: **~ shimásu** 内服します takes one's medicine orally: **naifuku-yaku** 内服薬 oral medicine

nai-jō *n* 内情 internal affairs (= **naibu jijō** 内部事情): **~ ni tsújita** 内情に通じた privy

nai-ju *n* 内需 domestic demand

nai-ka *n* 内科 internal medicine

nai-men *n* 内面 inner face, interior surface

nai-mitsu (no) *adj* 内密(の) confidential, secret, private [FORMAL]

Nai-mō´ko, Nai-mongoru (jichi-ku) *n* 内蒙古, 内モンゴル(自治区) Inner Mongolia (= **Uchi-mō´ko, Uchi-mongoru (jichi-ku)** 内蒙古, 内モンゴル(自治区))

nai-ran *n* 内乱 civil strife

nai-riku *n* 内陸 inland

nai-sen *n* 内線 extension (*phone line, inside*)

nai-sen *n* 内戦 civil war, internal fighting

nai-shin *n* 内心 **1.** (*one's*) thoughts in mind **2.** inner center (*not outer center*)

nai-shin *n* 内診 **1.** internal examination (*gynecology*) **2.** medical examination by a doctor at home (= **takushin** 宅診)

nai-shukketsu *n* 内出血 internal bleeding

nai-tei *n* 内偵 [BOOKISH] secret investigation: ~ **shimásu** 内偵します investigates secretly

nai-teki (na) *adj* 内的(な) internal: ~ **shō'ko** 内的証拠 internal evidence

nai-ya *n* 内野 infield, baseball diamond

nai-zō *n* 内臓 internal organs

...´-nai *suffix* ...内 within, in(side) (→ **kanai** 家内, **shánai (no)** 社内(の), **kokúnai (no)** 国内(の), **kō'nai** 構内)

naichingēru *n* ナイチンゲール nightingale

...-náide *suffix, adv* ...ないで not [do] but instead, without [do]ing → **shin-áide** しないで

náifu *n* ナイフ knife

náigai *n* 内外 **1.** inside and out **2.** home and abroad (= **kokunaigai** 国内外)

...-náigai *suffix* ...内外 approximately: **senen-naigai** 千円内外 approximately 1,000 yen

Naijeria *n* ナイジェリア Nigeria Naijeria-jin *n* ナイジェリア人 a Nigerian

naiji *n* 内示 unofficial announcement (*in office*)

náikaku *n* 内閣 a government cabinet: **naikaku-sōridaijin** 内閣総理大臣 prime minister

naimásu, náu *v* ないます, なう twists (*into a rope*)

náin *n* ナイン nine; baseball team

náiron *n* ナイロン nylon

... náishi ... *conj* ...ないし... [BOOKISH] **1.** and/or (= **mátáwa** または・又は) **2.** from ... to ... = **...kara...máde** ...から...まで

naishin (sho) *n* 内申(書) (*one's*) school record

naishó (no) *adj* 内緒・内証(の) confidential, secret, private: ~ **no hanashí** 内緒の話, **naisho-bánashi** 内緒話 a private talk

naita *v* 泣いた = **nakimáshita** 泣きました (cried)

náitā *n* ナイター night game (*of baseball*)

naite *v* 泣いて → **nakimásu** 泣きます

naitei *n* 内定 unofficial decision, informal appointment: ~ **(no) torikeshi** 内定(の)取り消し withdrawal of a job offer

naiyō *n* 内容 contents

náka *n, prep* 中 inside; **... no náka de/ni** ...の中で/に in ...

naka-darumi *n* 中だるみ slump (= **suranpu** スランプ)

naká-mi *n* 中身・中味 contents

naka-niwa *n* 中庭 courtyard

naka-yubi *n* 中指 middle finger

náka *n* 仲 relations, terms (*between people*); **(... to) náka ga íi** (...と)仲がいい is on good terms (with ...); ~ **tagai** 仲違い discord

naka-dachí *n* 仲立ち go-between, intermediary: **nakadachí-nin** 仲立ち人 broker

naká-gai *n* 仲買 broker

naka-má *n* 仲間 (**o-nakama** お仲間) friend, pal, companion

nakabá *n* 半ば middle: **kokorozashi-nakabá de** 志半ばで without fulfilling one's ambition

nakanai *v* 泣かない = **nakimásén** 泣きません (not cry)

nakanaka *adv* なかなか extremely, very (*long, hard, bad, etc.*), more than one might expect

nákatta *v* なかった = **arimasén deshita** ありませんでした (was not, did not have)

...-nákatta *suffix, v* ...なかった = **...masén deshita** ...ませんでした (did not)

nákattara *v* なかったら if/when there isn't/we don't; unless there is (we have)

...-nákattara *suffix, v* ...なかったら if/

when one doesn't; unless one does

nákattari *v* なかったり sometimes/alternately there isn't (*we don't have*)

...**-nákattari (shimásu)** *suffix, v* なかったり(します) sometimes/alternately does not do

nake´ *v* 泣け [IMPERATIVE] (cry!) → **nakimásu** 泣きます

nakéba *v* 泣けば (if one cries) → **nakimásu** 泣きます

nakemásu, nakeru 泣けます, 泣ける can cry

nakeréba *v* 泣ければ (if one can cry) → **nakemásu** 泣けます

nákereba *v* なければ (unless there is, unless one has)

...**-nákereba** *suffix, v* ...なければ unless one does: ~ **narimasén** ...なければなりません has to/must do

náki ... *prefix, adj* なき... [LITERARY] = **nái ...** ない... (lacking, nonexistent)

náki ... *prefix, adj* 亡き... [LITERARY] = **nái ...** ない... (deceased): **íma wa náki ...** 今は亡き... the late ...

naki-gara *n* 亡骸 [BOOKISH] corpse

nakimásu, naku 泣きます, 泣く weeps; cries

naki-dokoro *n* 泣きどころ Achilles' heel = **jakuten** 弱点, **kyūsho** 急所

naki-goe *n* 泣き声 cry, sob (*of person*)

naki-goto *n* 泣き言 complaining: ~ **o iimásu** 泣き言を言います complains

naki-mushi *n* 泣き虫 crybaby

nakimásu, naku *v* 鳴きます, 鳴く makes an animal sound

naki-goe *n* 鳴き声 chirp, song, chirping (*of animals, birds, insects, etc*)

nakō *v* 泣こう = **nakimashō´** 泣きましょう (let's cry!)

nakō´do *n* 仲人 go-between (*matchmaker*)

naku *v* 泣く = **nakimásu** 泣きます (weeps; cries)

náku *v* なく so that there isn't any (*we don't have any*); there not being; without

(...-)**nákucha** *suffix, v* (...)なくちゃ = (...-) **nákute wa** (...)なくては

...**-naku (narimásu)** *suffix, v* ...なく(なります) (*gets*) so that one doesn't do

(= ...**-nai yō´ni (narimásu)** ...ないように(なります))

naku-narimásu, naku-naru *v* 亡くなります, 亡くなる dies; gets lost

naku-narimásu, naku-naru *v* なくなります, なくなる vanishes (*from existence*)

nakusanai *v* なくさない = **nakushimasén** なくしません (not lose)

nakushimásu, nakusu *v* なくします, なくす loses

nákute *adj* なくて without, lacking → **nái** ない = **arimasén** ありません

...**-nákute mo** *suffix, v* ...なくても even not doing, even if one does not do; **shinákute mo íi** しなくてもいい need not do

...**-nákute wa** *suffix, v* ...なくては not doing, if one does not do; **shinákute wa ikemasén** しなくてはいけません must (*ought to*) do

náma *adj, n* 生 **1. náma (no/de)** 生(の/で) raw, uncooked, fresh **2.** (= **nama-bíiru** 生ビール) draft beer

nama-chūkei *n* 生中継 live coverage (= **jikkyō-chūkei** 実況中継)

nama-gomi *n* 生ごみ garbage (*kitchen waste*)

nama-gusái *adj* 生臭い fishy(-smelling)

nama-henji *n* 生返事 half-hearted reply

nama-hōsō *n* 生放送 live program, live broadcast

nama-kuríimu *n* 生クリーム (*fresh*) cream

nama-yake (no) *adj* 生焼け(の) rare (*little cooked*), underdone (= **han'yake (no)** 半焼け(の))

namae *n* 名前 (**o-namae** お名前) name (= **shimei** 氏名, **seimei** 姓名)

namaiki (na) *adj* 生意気(な) impertinent

namakemásu, namakéru *v* 怠けます, 怠ける idles, is lazy

namake-mono *n* 怠け者 lazy (*person*)

namari *n* ナマリ・鉛 lead (*metal*)

namarí *n* なまり・訛り dialect, accent (= **hōgen** 方言)

namarimásu, namaru *v* 鈍ります, 鈍る **1.** becomes rusty: **hōchō ga ~** 包丁

が鈍ります a kitchen knife gets dull
2. becomes weak (*one's body part*)
namasu *n* ナマス・鱠 raw fish tidbits
with vegetables in vinegar
namazu *n* ナマズ・鯰 catfish
namé ro *v* なめろ [IMPERATIVE] (lick it!)
→ **namemásu** なめます
namemásu, naméru *v* なめます, なめ
る licks, tastes
naméraka (na) *adj* なめらか(な)
smooth
namí *n* 波 wave
nami-nori *n* 波乗り surfing
námida *n* 涙 tear (*in eye*): **namida-me**
涙目 teary eyes: **namida-moroi** 涙もろ
い easily moved to tears
namiki *n* 並木 row of trees: **namiki-**
michi 並木道 tree-lined road, tree-lined
street
nami (no) *adj* 並(の) ordinary, common,
average, regular
nán *n* ナン nan bread
nán *n* 何 (*before* **d, t, n**) = **náni** 何 what
nán-... *prefix* 何... how many ...: **nán**
[COUNTER **ka**] **(no...)** 何 [COUNTER か]
(の...) a number (of ...)
nán-ba 何羽 how many (*birds, rabbits*)
(= **nan-wa** 何羽)
nan-bai 何倍 how many times (*doubled*)
nán-bai 何杯 how many cupfuls
nán-ban 何番 what number
nán-bén 何遍 how many times
nán-biki 何匹 how many (*fishes/bugs,*
small animals)
nán-bon 何本 how many (*pencils/bot-*
tles, long objects)
nán-byaku 何百 how many hundreds
nán-dai 何台 how many (*machines,*
vehicles)
nán-do 何度 how many times
nan-gai/-kai *n* 何階 how many floors/
stories; what (number) floor
nán-gatsu 何月 what month
nán-gen 何軒 how many (*buildings,*
shops, houses...)
nán-ji 何時 what time; **nan-jíkan** 何時
間 how many hours
nan-kágetsu 何か月 how many months
nán-kai 何回 how many times
nan-kai/-gai 何階 what floor; **nankai/**

gai-date 何階建て how many stories/
floors
nan-kákoku 何か国 how many countries
nan-kákokugo 何か国語 how many
languages
nan-kásho 何か所 how many places
nán-ko 何個 how many (*piece(s);*
small object(s))
nán-mai 何枚 how many (*flat thing(s)*)
nán-mán 何万 how many tens of thou-
sands
nán-nen 何年 what year; how many
years
nán-nichi 何日 what day (*of the*
month); how many days
nán-nin 何人 how many people
nán-paku 何泊 how many nights
nán-pun 何分 how many minutes
nán-sai 何歳 how (*many years*) old
nán-satsu 何冊 how many copies
(*books, magazines*)
nán-seki 何隻 how many boats
nán-shoku 何食 how many meals
nán-sō 何艘 how many ships
nán-tō 何頭 how many (*large animals*)
nan-yō'bi 何曜日 what day (*of the*
week)
nán-zoku/-soku 何足 how many pairs
(*of footwear*)
nan-... *prefix* 南...south (= **minami**
no... 南の...)
Nan-bei *n* 南米 = **Minami-Ámerika** 南
アメリカ South America
nán-boku *n* 南北 north and south
nán-bu *n* 南部 the south, the southern
part
nán-i *n* 南緯 the south latitude
nan-ka *n* 南下 going south: ~ **shimásu**
南下します goes southward
nan-kyoku *n* 南極 South Pole
nan-sei *n* 南西 southwest
nan-tō *n* 南東 southeast
nan-pō *n* 南方 the south, south
direction
nan-... *prefix* 難...difficult, tough
nan-gi *n* 難儀 difficulty, suffering,
trouble [BOOKISH]
nan-ido *n* 難易度 difficulty level
nan-kan *n* 難関 difficulty, obstacle,

159

challenge: **nankan-kō** 難関校 school which is difficult to enter

nan-kyoku *n* 難局 difficult situation

nan-min *n* 難民 refugee

nanpa-sen *n* 難破船 shipwreck

nan-zan *n* 難産 difficult delivery

nan-... *prefix* 軟...soft, weak, mild

nan-jaku *adj* 軟弱 [BOOKISH] weak, soft, flaccid [IN NEGATIVE SENSE]: **~ na karada** 軟弱な体 weak body

nan-kin *n* 軟禁 [BOOKISH] house arrest: **~ shimásu** 軟禁します confines (*someone*) (*somewhere*)

nan-kyū *n* 軟球 a rubber ball (*not hard ball*)

nan-sui *n* 軟水 soft water

nána *n* 七・7 seven

naná-do *n* 七度 **1.** seven degrees **2.** seven times

naná-hén *n* 七遍 seven times

naná-kai *n* 七階 seven floors/stories, seventh floor

naná-kái *n* 七回 seven times

nana-korobi ya oki 七転び八起き [IDIOM] Have nine lives.

naná-mei *n* 七名 [BOOKISH] seven people (= **shichí-nin, naná-nin** 七人)

naná-nen *n* 七年 the year 7; **nana nén-kan** 七年間 seven years

naná-nin *n* 七人 → naná-mei 七名

naná-satsu *n* 七冊 seven copies (*books, magazines*)

naná-hyaku *n* 七百・700 seven hundred

naná-jū *n* 七十・70 seventy

nana-mán *n* 七万・70,000 seventy thousand

nana-sén *n* 七千・7,000 seven thousand

naná-tsu *n* 七つ・7つ seven, seven years old (= **nana-sai** 七歳); **nanatsu-mé** 七つ目 seventh

naname (no/ni) *adj, adv* 斜め (の/に) aslant, oblique, diagonal

nánbā *n* ナンバー = **nanbā puré'to** ナンバープレート (*car*) license plate

nán-da-i *interj* 何だい what is it (= **nán desu ka** 何ですか)

nán-de-mo *adv* 何でも whatever it may be, anything (at all), everything

... **nán desu (da, de)** *suffix, v* ...なんです(だ, で) it's that it is ...

nándo *n* 納戸 back room, closet

náni *n* 何 what: **náni (ga/o) ...-témo** 何(が/を) ...ても whatever

nani-go 何語 what language

nani-iro 何色 what color

naní-jin 何人 what nationality

nanibun *adv* 何分 anyway, anyhow

nanige-nái *adj* 何気ない casual

náni ka *n* 何か something, anything

nani mo *adv* 何も [+ NEGATIVE] nothing, (not) anything

náninani *n* 何々 something or other, so-and-so, what's-it(s-name)

náni-shiro *adv* 何しろ after all

náni yori *adv* 何より than what: **~ mo** 何よりも more than anything

nánji *pron* 汝 [BOOKISH] thou

... **nánka** *suffix* ...なんか and so forth/on, and what-not; the likes of

Nankín-mame *n* 南京豆・ナンキンマメ peanut(s) (= **rak-kasei** 落花生, **piina(t)tsu** ピーナ(ッ)ツ)

nankō *n* 軟膏 ointment

nankō *n* 難航 rough sailing: **~ shimásu** 難航します has a rough passage

nankuse *n* 難癖 cavil

nan-nára *conj* 何なら if you like, you don't mind; if you don't want to

nan ni mo *adv* 何にも [EMPHATIC] → nani mo 何も

nan ni mo *adv* 何にも (= **nán no ... ní mo** 何の ...にも [+ NEGATIVE] not to/for/at anything

nán no *adj* 何の what (*kind of*); of what

nanoka *n* 七日 seven days; the 7th day (*of month*)

... **ná no ni** *conj* ...なのに in spite of its being ..., despite that it is ...

nanpa *n* 難破 shipwreck

nanpa *n* ナンパ: **~ shimásu** ナンパします picks up (*a girl*)

nán-rá ka no ... *adj* 何らかの... some

nán-ra (no) ... *adj* 何ら (の)... [+ NEGATIVE] not any, not in any way

nán to ... *conj* 何と ... with what, what and ... ; (*saying/thinking/meaning*) what

nán to itté mo *adv* 何と言っても eventually, come what may

nán to ka shite *adv* 何とかして by some means (*or other*), somehow or other

nan to mo *adv* 何とも [+ NEGATIVE] nothing (at all), not … at all

nán to shitémo *adv* 何としても inevitably; at any cost

náo *adv* 尚 still more; moreover

naorimásu, naóru *v* 直ります, 直る is righted, fixed, repaired, improves

naorimásu, naóru *v* 治ります, 治る is cured, gets well, recovers, improves

nao-sara *adv* 尚更 all the more, still more

naóse 直せ [IMPERATIVE] (fix it!) → naoshimásu 直します

naoshí *v* 直し mending, repair(ing), correcting, correction

naoshimásu, naósu *v* 直します, 直す
1. makes it right, corrects, repairs, mends, fixes, alters, improves it
2. [INFINITIVE +] does it over (*and better*), re-does it

naoshimásu, naósu *v* 治します, 治す cures it

naótte 直って・治って → naorimásu 直ります・治ります

náppa *n* 菜っ葉 greens, vegetables; rape (*plant*)

nápukin *n* ナプキン 1. napkin
2. sanitary pad (= seiriyō nápukin 生理用ナプキン)

nára *n* ナラ・楢 Japanese oak

… nára *conj* …なら, **… ～ ba** …ならば if it be, provided it is [NEGATIVE **… ja nákereba** … じゃなければ]; [VERB]-**ru/-ta nára** る/たなら, [ADJECTIVE]-**i/-i-katta nára** い/かったなら if (it be a matter of) …

narabe *v* 並べ [IMPERATIVE] (line up!) → narabimásu 並びます

narabemásu, naraberu *v* 並べます, 並べる arranges, lines them up

narabe ro *v* 並べろ [IMPERATIVE] (line them up!) → narabemásu 並べます

narabi *n* 並び row (*line*)

narabimásu, narabu *v* 並びます, 並ぶ they line up, arrange themselves

naráe *v* 習え [IMPERATIVE] (learn it!) → naraimásu 習います

naraemásu, naraéru *v* 習えます, 習え る can learn

naraigoto *n* 習い事 culture lesson(s)

naraimásu, naráu *v* 習います, 習う learns

naraku *n* 奈落 hell (= jigoku 地獄): **～ no soko** 奈落の底 the abyss of despair

naranai *v* 鳴らない = narimasén 鳴り ません (not sound)

naránai *v* ならない = narimasén なり ません (not become)

narande *v* 並んで → narabimásu 並びます: **～ imásu** 並んでいます are in a row, are lined up

narase *v* 鳴らせ [IMPERATIVE] (sound!) → narashimásu 鳴らします

narasemásu, naraseru *v* 鳴らせます, 鳴らせる can sound

narasenai *v* 鳴らせない = narase-masén 鳴らせません (cannot sound)

narashimásu, narasu *v* 鳴らします, 鳴らす sounds, rings it

narashimásu, narasu *v* 均します, 均 す smooths, averages

narashimásu, narasu *v* 馴らします, 馴らす domesticates, tames

narátta *v* 習った = naraimáshita 習い ました (learned)

narátte *v* 習って → naraimásu 習い ます

naráu *v* 習う = naraimásu 習います (learns)

narawánai *v* 習わない = naraimasén 習いません (not learn)

narazumono *n* ならず者 rogue, vaga-bond (= gorotsuki ごろつき, buraikan 無頼漢, hōtō-mono 放蕩者)

náre *v* 鳴れ [IMPERATIVE] (sound!) → narimásu 鳴ります

náre *v* なれ [IMPERATIVE] (become!, get to be!) → narimásu なります

naréba *v* 鳴れば (if it sounds) → narimásu 鳴ります

naréba *v* なれば (if it becomes) → narimásu なります

naremásu, naréru *v* 慣れます, 慣れる: **… ni ～** …に慣れます gets used to

naremásu, naréru *v* 馴れます, 馴れる:

161

... ni naremásu ...に馴れます grows familiar with

naremásu, naréru v なれます, なれる can become

narénai v 慣れない = **naremasén** 慣れません(not get used to)

narenareshii adj 馴れ馴れしい too friendly, overly familiar

narēshon n ナレーション narration

naresome n 馴れ初め the thing which brought man and woman (*lovers*) together

nari n なり・形 (**o-nári** おなり) form; personal appearance

narikin n 成金 nouveau riche

narimásu, náru v なります, なる becomes, gets to be, turns into; is done, completed; amounts to be ...; [HONORIFIC] **o-nari ni ~** おなりになります, **... ni** ([ADJECTIVE]-**ku**) **~** ...に (...く) なります gets so it is ..., gets to be ..., turns into ... **~ suru kotó ni ~** ...する事になります it gets arranged/decided to (do) ...

narimásu, naru v 鳴ります, 鳴る it sounds, rings

narimono iri (de) adv 鳴り物入り (で) with a fanfare

nariyuki v 成り行き process, course, development; result: **~ o mimásu** 成り行きを見ます watches how things develop (turn out)

narō' v なろう = **narimashō** なりましょう (let's become ...!)

naru-beku ... adv なるべく... as ... as possible

naru-hodo interj なるほど I see; quite so; you are so right; how true

narushisuto n ナルシスト narcissist

nasái v なさい [IMPERATIVE] (please do it!) → **nasaimásu** なさいます

nasaimásu, nasáru v なさいます, なさる (*someone honored*) does

násake n 情け (**o-násake** お情け) affection, feeling, tenderness, compassion, sympathy

nasake-nái adj 情けない wretched, miserable; shameful

nasánai v 成さない = **nashimasén** 成しません (not achieve)

nasátta v なさった = **nasaimáshita** なさいました (did)

nasátte v なさって → **nasaimásu** なさいます

nashí n ナシ・梨 pear

náshi v なし [LITERARY] = **nái** ない (= **arimasén** ありません) (there is no ..., lacks, has no ...)

nashimásu, násu v 成します, 成す achieves, forms, does

... náshi ni suffix, prep, adv ...なしに = **... ga náku(te)** ...がなく(て) without, lacking, not having

násu n ナス[茄子・茄], **násubi** なすび eggplant

násu v 成す = **nashimásu** 成します (achieves, forms, does)

nasátta v なさった = **nasátta** なさった = **nasaimáshita** なさいました (did)

nasútte v なすって = **nasátte** なすって

nata n なた・鉈 hatches

natsú n 夏 summer

natsukashii adj 懐かしい dear (*dearly remembered*), good old, nostalgic

natsume n ナツメ・棗 date (*fruit*)

natsu-mikan n 夏ミカン・夏蜜柑 Japanese grapefruit (*pomelo*)

natsu-yásumi n 夏休み summer vacation/holiday

natta v 鳴った = **narimáshita** 鳴りました (it sounded)

nátta v なった = **narimáshita** なりました (became)

nátta v なった = **naimáshita** ないました (twisted it)

natte v 鳴って → **narimásu** 鳴ります

nátte v なって → **narimásu** なります (becomes ...)

nattō' n ナットウ・納豆 fermented soy beans

nattoku n 納得 understanding, compliance, assent; (**... o**) **~ shimásu** (...を)納得します gets persuaded/convinced (*of* ...), complies with; (**... o**) **~ sasemásu** (...を)納得させます persuades/convinces one (*of* ...)

náttsu n ナッツ nuts

náu v なう = **naimásu** ないます (twists it)

nawá n 縄 rope, cord

nawabari *n* 縄張り one's territory:
nawabari-arasoi 縄張り争い territorial
fight

nawánai *v* なわない = **naimasén** ない
ません (not twist it)

naya *n* 納屋 barn, shed

nayamí *n* 悩み suffering, distress,
torment

nayamimásu, nayamu *v* 悩みます, 悩
む suffers

nayánde *v* 悩んで → **nayamimásu**
悩みます

nayonayo (shita) *adj* なよなよ(した)
wishy-washy, weedy [IN NEGATIVE
SENSE]

náze *adv* なぜ・何故 why: ~ **ka to iu
to** …なぜかと言うと … the reason is
that …

nazo *n* 謎 riddle, mystery
nazo-nazo *n* なぞなぞ riddle (*game*)
nazuke-oya *n* 名付け親 godparent

nazukemásu, nazukéru *v* 名付けます,
名付ける names, dubs

nazuké ro *v* 名付けろ [IMPERATIVE]
(name it!) → **nazukemásu** 名付け
ます

nazúkete *v* 名付けて → **nazukemásu**
名付けます

…´n desu (da) *suffix*, *v* …んです(だ)
it's that …

ne *n* 音 (= **otó** 音) sound: **suzu no ~** 鈴
の音 bell jingles: **mushi no ~** 虫の音
insects chirping

ne o agemásu (ageru) *v* 音を上げま
す(上げる) gives up

ne *n* 値 (= **nedan** 値段) price: ~ **ga takái**
値が高い is expensive

ne-age *n* 値上げ price rise; raising the
cost

ne-biki *n* 値引き discount (*of price*)

ne-dan *n* 値段 (**o-nédan** お値段) price

ne *n* 根 1. root (= **nekko** 根っこ): **ki no
ne(kko)** 木の根(っこ) root of a tree 2.
cause (= **kongen** 根源) 3. one's nature:
~ **wa yasashii** 根は優しい basically
gentle, kind at heart

ne-hori ha-hori *adv* 根掘り葉掘り: ~
kikaremásu 根掘り葉掘り聞かれます
is questioned about every detail

ne *n* 寝 (= **nemuri** 眠り) sleep(ing)

ne-búsoku *n* 寝不足 having not
enough sleep: ~ **desu** 寝不足です
didn't get enough sleep

ne-isu *n* 寝椅子 couch, lounge (*chair*)

ne-maki *n* 寝巻き pajamas

… né/nē *interj* …ね/ねえ (*mostly
female*) isn't it, don't you think/agree

nébaneba shimásu (suru) *v* ねばねば
します(する) is sticky

nebarí *n* 粘り stickiness: **nebari-zuyoi**
粘り強い persevering: **nebarímásu**
粘ります hangs on

necha *v* 寝ちゃ = **neté wa** 寝ては:
nechaimásu 寝ちゃいます = **nete
shimaimásu** 寝てしまいます →
nemásu 寝ます

nechigaemásu, nechigaeru *v* 寝違
えます, 寝違える gets a crick in one's
neck (*while sleeping*)

nechiketto *n* ネチケット netiquette
(*comes from network + etiquette*)

nechizun *n* ネチズン netizen (=
netto(wāku)-shimin ネット(ワーク)市
民) (*comes from network + citizen*)

Ne-doshi *n* 子年 year of the Rat

negái *n* 願い a request

negaimásu, negáu *v* 願います, 願う
asks for, requests, begs

négi *n* ネギ・葱 onion (*green*)

neiro *n* 音色 (*sound*) tone

néji *n* ねじ・ネジ screw

neji-máwashi *n* ねじ回し screw-driver

nejiránai *v* ねじらない = **nejirimasén**
ねじりません (not twist)

nejirimásu, nejiru *v* ねじります, ねじ
る twists

nejítte *v* ねじって → **nejirimásu**
ねじります

nekashimásu, nekasu *v* 寝かします,
寝かす puts to bed/sleep; lays it on its side

nekki *n* 熱気 1. hot air 2. air of excitement, fever 3. fever, pyrexia

nékkuresu *n* ネックレス necklace

nekkyō *n* 熱狂 enthusiasm: ~ **shimásu**
熱狂します gets excited

néko *n* ネコ・猫 cat
néko baba *n* 猫ばば: ~ **shimásu** 猫ば
ばします embezzles
néko-jita *n* 猫舌 [IDIOM] the one whose
tongue is very sensitive to heat

163

néko kawaigari *n* 猫かわいがり: ~ **shimásu** 猫かわいがりします dotes on

néko mo shakushi mo *adv* 猫も杓子も [IDIOM] anything or anybody (*without distinction*)

néko nade-goe (de) *n* 猫なで声 [IDIOM] in a wheedling tone of voice

néko ni katsuobushi *n* 猫に鰹節 [IDIOM] Like trusting a wolf to watch over sheep

néko ni koban *n* 猫に小判 [IDIOM] Casting pearls before swine. (= **buta ni shinju** 豚に真珠)

néko no te mo karitai *v* 猫の手も借りたい [IDIOM] busy as a bee (*not to literally mean, "I am so busy that I would even welcome the help of a cat."*)

néko o kaburu *v* 猫をかぶる [IDIOM] pretends to be innocent/nice

néko-ze *n* 猫背 [IDIOM] slouch, slight stoop, rounded back (*like that of cat*)

nékutai *n* ネクタイ necktie: ~ **o musubimásu** ネクタイを結びます puts on (*wears*) a necktie

nemásu, neru *v* 寝ます、寝る goes to bed, lies down, sleeps

ne-motó *n* 根元 (*the part*) near the root, the base (*of a tree*)

nemui *adj* 眠い sleepy

nemuri *n* 眠り sleep(ing)

nemurimásu, nemuru *v* 眠ります、眠る sleeps

nemutte *v* 眠って → **nemurimásu** 眠ります

nén *n* 年 year

nén-... *prefix* 年... yearly, annual
nén-do *n* 年度 year period, fiscal year: **kon-nendo** 今年度 this fiscal year: **rai-nendo** 来年度 next fiscal year

nen-kan (no) *adj* 年間(の) for a year; annual: **nenkan-kōsuiryō** 年間降水量 annual rainfall: **nenkan-uriage (-daka)** 年間売上(高) annual sales: **nenkan-shotoku** 年間所得 annual income

nen-kan *n* 年鑑 yearbook, almanac

nen-kan (no) *adj* 年刊(の) (*paper publication*): **nenkan-hōkokusho** 年刊報告書 annual report

nen-matsu *n* 年末 the end of the year: **nenmatsu-nenshi kyūka** 年末年始休暇 year-end and New Year's day holidays

nen-pō *n* 年俸 annual salary

nen-ri *n* 年利 annual interest

nen-shi *n* 年始 New Year's day

nen-shō *n* 年商 annual turnover

nén *n* 念 sense, feeling; desire; caution, care, attention; (...) **ni tamé (ni)** 念のため(に) to make sure, just in case, just to be sure, as a precaution; (... **ni**) ~ **o iremásu** (...に)念を入れます pays attention (to ...), is careful (*of/about* ...), ~ **o oshimásu** 念を押します double-checks

nén-... *prefix* 年... age
nen-chō(-sha) *n* 年長(者) one's senior

nen-pai(-sha) *n* 年配[年輩](者) the elderly, middle-aged person

nen-rei *n* 年齢 (*one's*) age [BOOKISH] (= **toshí** 年・歳・齢)

nen-shō (-sha) *n* 年少(者) young person, one's junior

nen-... *prefix* 粘... sticky
nen-chaku-té'pu *n* 粘着テープ adhesive tape

nén-do *n* 粘土 clay

nenai *v* 寝ない = **nemasén** 寝ません (not go to bed)

nengá *n* 年賀 New Year's greetings: ~ **ni ikimasu** 年賀に行きます makes a New Year's call/visit

nengá-hágaki *n* 年賀葉書 a New Year greeting postcard

nengá-jō *n* 年賀状 New Year's card

nengan *n* 念願 desire: ~ **ga kanaimásu** 念願が叶います (*one's*) dream/wish has come true

nengáppi *n* 年月日 date (*year/month/day*) (→ **seinen-gáppi** 生年月日)

nenki *n* 年季 one's term of service: ~ **no haitta** 年季の入った seasoned, experienced

nenkin *n* 年金 pension: **kōsei-nenkin** 厚生年金 employee pension; **kojin-nenkin hoken** 個人年金保険 individual annuity insurance

nenryō *n* 燃料 fuel: **nenryō-tanku** 燃料タンク fuel tank

nenshō *n* 燃焼 combustion: ~ **shimásu** 燃焼します burns

nenza n 捻挫 sprain: **~ shimásu** 捻挫します sprains one's ankle

neon n ネオン **1.** neon **2.** neon sign

Nepáru n ネパール Nepal
Nepáru-go n ネパール語 Nepalese (*language*)
Nepáru-jin n ネパール人 a Nepalese

neppū n 熱風 hot wind

nerae v 狙え [IMPERATIVE] (aim!) → **neraimásu** 狙います

neraemásu, neraeu v 狙えます, 狙える can aim

nerai n 狙い aim, object; idea, intention, what one is driving at

neraimásu, nerau v 狙います, 狙う aims at, watches for, seeks

neránai v 練らない = **nerimasén** 練りません (not knead)

neraremásu, nerareru v 寝られます, 寝られる can go to bed, can lie down, can sleep

nerarereba v 寝られれば (if one can sleep) → **neraremásu** 寝られます

nerarete v 寝られて → **neraremásu** 寝られます

neratte v 狙って → **neraimásu** 狙います

nerawanai v 狙わない = **neraimásén** 狙いません (not aim at)

nére v 練れ [IMPERATIVE] (knead!) → **nerimásu** 練ります

neréba v 寝れば (if one goes to bed) → **nemásu** 寝ます

néreba v 練れば (if one kneads) → **nerimásu** 練ります

neremásu, nereru v 寝れます 寝れる = **neraremásu** 寝られます (can go to bed, can sleep)

neremásu, neréru v 練れます, 練れる can knead; can drill, train

neréreba v 練れれば (if one can knead) → **neremásu** 練れます

neréreba v 練れれば (if one can knead) → **neremásu** 練れます

nerete v 寝れて = **nerarete** 寝られて (can go to bed, can sleep)

neri-hamigaki v 練り歯磨き toothpaste (= **hamigaki-ko** 歯磨き粉)

nerí-kó n 練り粉 dough

nerimásu, néru v 練ります, 練る

kneads; drills, trains

ne ro 寝ろ [IMPERATIVE] (sleep!) → **nemásu** 寝ます

nerō´ v 練ろう = **nerimashō´** 練りましょう (let's knead it!)

neru v 寝る = **nemásu** 寝ます (goes to bed, lies down, sleeps)

néru n ネル = **furanneru** フランネル flannel

néru v 練る = **nerimásu** 練ります (kneads; drills, trains)

nē´-san n 姉さん (**o-né´-san** お姉さん) older sister; Miss!; Waitress!

nes-shimásu, nes-suru v 熱します, 熱する **1.** gets hot, gets excited **2.** heats it, warms it

nésshin (na) adj 熱心 (な) enthusiastic
nésshin ni adv 熱心に enthusiastically

neta v 寝た = **nemáshita** 寝ました (went to bed; slept)

netamashíi adj 妬ましい envious; enviable

netamimásu, netámu v 妬みます, 妬む envies

nete v 寝て → **nemásu** 寝ます

netsú n **1.** 熱 fever **2.** o-nétsu お熱 heat
netsu-ben n 熱弁 passionate speech: **~ o furuimásu** 熱弁を振るいます makes a passionate speech
netsu-bō n 熱望 ambition (*hope*): **~ shimásu** 熱望します is eager, eagerly desires

nétta v 練った = **nerimáshita** 練りました (kneaded)

nettai (-chí´hō´) n 熱帯 (地方) tropic(s): **nettai-urin** 熱帯雨林 tropical rainforest: **nettai-kíkō** 熱帯気候 tropical climate; **nettai-shokubutsu** 熱帯植物 tropical plant

nétte v 練って → **nerimásu** 練ります

netto n ネット **1.** net **2.** network **3.** the Net (= **intánetto** インターネット)
netto-bukku n ネットブック netbook (*computer*)
netto-ginkō n ネット銀行 on-line bank
netto-kafe n ネットカフェ Internet café, Net café (= **intánetto-kafe** インターネットカフェ)

netto-ōkushon n ネット・オークション online auction (= **onrain ōkushon** オンライン・オークション)

netto-sāfin n ネットサーフィン net surfing

netto-tsūhan n ネット通販 online shopping, Internet shopping (= **intānetto tsūhan** インターネット通販)

nettō n 熱湯 boiling water

netto-wāku n ネットワーク network

netto(wāku)-shimin ネットワーク（ワーク）市民 netizen (= **nechizun** ネチズン)

neuchi n 値打ち value, worth: ~ **ga arimásu** 値打ちがあります is worth

neyō v 寝よう = **nemashō´** 寝ましょう (let's go to bed!)

nezumi n ネズミ・鼠 mouse, rat

nezumi-iro (no) adj ネズミ色(の) gray

nezumí-tori n ネズミ捕り[取り] mousetrap

ní n 荷 **1.** load **2.** burden (= **nímotsu** 荷物, **o-nímotsu** お荷物)
ni-zúkuri n 荷造り packing

ní n 二・2 two

ni bai n 二倍 twice (double)

ni-banmé (no) adj 二番目(の) second

ní dai n 二台 two (machines, vehicles)

ní dó n 二度 two times, twice; **nido-mé** 二度目 the second time

ni do n 二度 two degrees (temperature)

ni fun n 二分 two minutes

ní-gō (san) n 二号(さん) mistress, concubine

ní hai n 二杯 two cupfuls

ni hén n 二遍 two times

ní hon n 二本 two (pencils/bottles, long objects)

ni kai n 二階 second floor; upstairs

ni kái n 二回 two times; **nikai-mé** 二回目 the second time

ní ken n 二軒 two buildings

ní ko n 二個 two pieces (small objects)

ní mai n 二枚 two sheets (flat things)

ni-mán n 二万・20,000 twenty thousand

ní-mei n 二名 [BOOKISH] = **futarí** 二人・ふたり two people

ní-nen n 二年 the year 2; = **ninén-kan** 二年間 two years; = **ninén-sei** 二年生 second-year student, sophomore

ní-sai n 二歳 two years old (= **futatsu** ふたつ)

ní satsu n 二冊 two copies (books, magazines)

ní-wa n 二羽 two (birds, rabbits)

... ni (´) particle ...に **1.** to/for (a person) **2.** at/in (a place), at (a time) **3.** (= **... é** ...へ) to (a place) **4.** as, so as to be, (turns/makes) into being, being

ni-aimásu, ni-áu v 似合います, 似合う: **... ni ni-aimásu**...に似合います is becoming (to), suits

nia misu n ニアミス near miss

nibúi adj 鈍い dull, blunt

Nichi-... prefix 日..., **...-Nichi** ...日 Japan(ese), **Nichi-Ei** 日英 Japanese-English, **Ei-Nichi** 英日 English-Japanese...

...-nichi suffix ...日 day (counts/names days)

nichi-botsu n 日没 sunset (time of sunset)

Nichiyō´(-bi) n 日曜(日) Sunday
Nichiyō´-daiku n 日曜大工 Sunday carpenter, do-it-yourself

Nichiyō-hin(-ten) n 日用品(店) grocery (store); houseware (store)

niemásu, nieru v 煮えます, 煮える it boils, it cooks

niete v 煮えて → **niemásu** 煮えます

ní-fuda n 荷札 (baggage/package) tag

nigái adj 苦い bitter, wry: ~ **kōhii** 苦いコーヒー bitter coffee; ~ **keiken** 苦い経験 bitter experience; **niga-warai** 苦笑い bitter smile, wry smile

nigaoe n 似顔絵 portrait

nigashimásu, nigásu v 逃がします, 逃がす turns loose; lets one get away, lets it slip away

nigate adj 苦手 (thing, person, etc.,) which is not one's cup of tea: **nigate na** 苦手な which one is not good at

Ni-gatsú n 二月・2月 February

nigemásu, nigéru v 逃げます, 逃げる runs away, escapes, flees

nigé ro v 逃げろ [IMPERATIVE] (run away!) → **nigemásu** 逃げます

nígeta v 逃げた = **nigemáshita** 逃げました (fled)

nígete v 逃げて → **nigemásu** 逃げます

nigirimás̲u, nigiru v 握ります, 握る grasps, grips, clutches

nigiri-meshi n 握り飯 riceball (= **o-nígiri** おにぎり)

nigiri-zushi n にぎり[握り]寿司 sushi hand-packed into small balls (*as traditional in Tokyo*)

nigitte v 握って → **nigirimás̲u** 握ります

nigíyaka (na) adj にぎやか・賑やか(な) merry, bustling: **~ na tōri** 賑やかな通り busy street; **~ na fun'iki** 賑やかな雰囲気 lively atmosphere; **~ na hito** 賑やかな人 cheerful person

nigorimás̲u, nigóru v 濁ります, 濁る **1.** gets muddy **2.** (*a voiceless sound*) becomes voiced (k > g, f/h > b, ch/sh > j, s > z, t/ts > z)

Nihón n 日本 Japan (= **Nippón** 日本, **Nihón-koku** 日本国)

Nihon-fū n 日本風 Japanese style

Nihon-ga n 日本画 Japanese-style painting

Nihon-ginkō n 日本銀行 Bank of Japan (= **nichi-gin** 日銀)

Nihon-go n 日本語 Japanese (*language/word*)

Nihon-jín n 日本人 a Japanese

Nihon-kai n 日本海 the Sea of Japan

Nihon-ma n 日本間 Japanese-style room

Nihon-ryōri n 日本料理 Japanese cuisine

Nihon-sei n 日本製 made in Japan

Nihon-shu n 日本酒 saké (*rice wine*) (= **sake** 酒)

Nihon-teien n 日本庭園 Japanese traditional garden

ni-hyakú n 二百 200 two hundred

níi-san n 兄さん (**o-níi-san** お兄さん) older brother

niji n 虹 rainbow: **niji-iro** 虹色 rainbow colors

ni-jū n 二重 double, duplicate

nijū-nábe n 二重鍋 double boiler

nijū-ago n 二重あご[顎] double chin

nijū-jinkaku n 二重人格 double personality, split personality

ní-jū n 二十・20 twenty: **nijū-yokka** 二十四日 24 days, 24th day (*of month*); **nijū-banmé** 二十番目 20th

nijús̲-sai n 二十歳 20 years old (= **hátachi** 二十歳・はたち)

nikawa n にかわ・膠 glue: **nikawa-nabe** にかわ鍋 glue pot

ni-kayoimás̲u, ni-kayóu v 似通います, 似通う **... ni/to ~** ...に/と似通います closely resembles

Nikei (no) adj 日系(の) (*of*) Japanese ancestry; **Nikkéi-jin** 日系人 person of Japanese ancestry

níkibi n にきび pimple

níkki, níkkei n にっき, にっけい・肉桂 cinnamon

nikki n 日記 (*private*) diary

níkkō n 日光 sunshine; **Nikkō** 日光 Nikko (*place*) (= **hi no hikari** 日の光)

nikkō-yoku n 日光浴 sun bathing

nikkyū n 日給 daily wage

nikochin n ニコチン nicotine

nikomi n 煮込み stew (*food*): **nikomi-udon** 煮込みうどん stew with Udon (*Japanese wheat noodle*)

níkoniko adj にこにこ smiling: **~ shimás̲u** にこにこします smiles

nikú n 肉 (**o-níku** お肉) meat

niku-dángo n 肉団子 Chinese meatballs

niku-gyū n 肉牛 beef cattle

niku-kiri-bō̄chō n 肉切り包丁 butcher/carving knife, meat cleaver

niku-man n 肉まん steamed bun stuffed with ground pork

nikú-ya n 肉屋 butcher (shop)

nikú n **1.** 肉 (**o-níku** お肉) **2.** flesh (= **nikutai** 肉体)

niku-sei n 肉声 natural voice (*without a microphone, etc.*)

niku-shoku (dōbutsu) n 肉食(動物) carnivore

niku-shu n 肉腫 sarcoma

niku-tai n 肉体 body

niku-yoku n 肉欲 sexual desire

niku-zuki no ii n 肉付きのいい plump, fleshy

nikúi adj 憎い hateful

...nikúi suffix ...にくい・難い (... **shi-nikúi** ...しにくい) hard, difficult (*to do*)

nikumimás̲u, nikúmu v 憎みます, 憎む hates, detests

nikúnde v 憎んで → **nikumimásu** 憎みます

nikushin n 肉親 blood relative

nikuzure n 荷崩れ cargo shifting

nikuzure n 煮崩れ breaking up while boiling/cooking (*fishes, potatoes, etc.*)

nimásu, niru v 似ます、似る resembles

nimásu, niru v 煮ます、煮る boils, cooks

... -ní mo *suffix* ...にも also (*even*) at/in, to, as

ni-mono n 煮物 boiled foods

nímotsu n 荷物 (**o-nímotsu** お荷物) 1. baggage 2. load

...(')-nin *suffix* ...人 person, people; **yo-nín** 四人 four people

ninác v 担え [IMPERATIVE] (carry it!) → **ninaimásu** 担います

ninái *adj* 似ない = **nimasén** 似ません (not resemble)

ninái *adj* 煮ない = **nimasén** 煮ません (not boil/cook it)

ninaimásu, nináu v 担います、担う carries on shoulders

ninátte v 担って → **ninaimásu** 担います

ninawánai v 担わない = **ninaimásén** 担いません (not carry)

ninchi n 認知 [BOOKISH] 1. recognition, acknowledgment 2. affiliation

ningen n 人間 human being (= **hito** 人)

ningyo n 人魚 mermaid

ningyō n 人形 (**o-ningyō** お人形) doll

ningyō-shíbai n 人形芝居 puppet show

ningyō-tsukai n 人形使い puppeteer

nini n 任意 [BOOKISH] option

nínja n 忍者 a master of stealth, Ninja

ninjin n ニンジン・人参 carrot

ninjō n 人情 human nature, human feelings, warm-heartedness: **ninjō-mi no aru** 人情味のある human, warm-hearted; **giri to ~** 義理と~ duty and sympathy

nínjutsu n 忍術 the art of stealth

ninka n 認可 [BOOKISH] permission

ninki n 人気 popularity: **~ ga arimásu** 人気があります is popular

ninki n 任期 (*one's*) term, term of office: **~ o tsutomemásu** 任期を務めます serves one's term

...-ninmae *suffix* ...人前 (*counts portions*)

ninmei n 任命 [BOOKISH] appointment: **~ shimásu** 任命します appoints

ninmu n 任務 duty, assignment, task, mission: **~ o hatashimásu** 任務を果たします accomplishes one's errand

ninniku n ニンニク・大蒜 garlic

ninpu n 妊婦 pregnant woman

ninpu n 人夫 [BOOKISH] laborer

ninshiki n 認識 [BOOKISH] awareness, recognition

ninshin n 妊娠 pregnancy: **~ shite imásu** 妊娠しています is pregnant

ninshin-chū' zetsu n 妊娠中絶 abortion

ninshō n 認証 certification

ninshō daimeishi n 人称代名詞 personal pronoun

ninsō n 人相 looks, facial features

nintai n 忍耐 endurance

nintai-ryoku n 忍耐力 ability to be patient

nínzū n 人数 number of people; population (= **jinkō** 人口)

niō dachi n 仁王立ち: **~ ni narimásu** 仁王立ちになります stands firm with one's feet set apart (*like two Deva Kings stone statue*)

niói n 臭い・匂い a smell; (**...no**)**-ga shimásu** (...の)臭い[匂い]がします it smells (of ...)

nioimásu, nióu v 臭います・匂います, 臭う・匂う it smells, is fragrant

niótte v 臭って・匂って → **nioimásu** 臭います・匂います

Nippón n 日本 = **Nihón(-koku)** 日本(国) Japan

nirá n ニラ a leek; a green onion

niramimásu, nirámu v 睨みます、睨む glares, stares

niránde v 睨んで → **niramimásu** 睨みます

níre n ニレ・楡 yew (*tree*)

niréba v 似れば (if it resembles) → **nimásu** 似ます

niréba v 煮れば (if one boils/cooks it) → **nimásu** 煮ます

ni ro v 煮ろ [IMPERATIVE] (boil it!) → **nimásu** 煮ます

niru v 似る = **nimásu** 似ます (resembles)

168

niru v 煮る = **nimásu** 煮ます (boils, cooks)

ní-san (no) adj 二、三 (の) two or three …

ní-sei n 二世 second generation (Japanese emigrant); … the Second

nisemásu, niseru v 似せます、似せる imitates, copies; counterfeits (money), forges (a document, signature)

ni-sén n 二千・2,000 two thousand

nise (no) adj にせ・偽 (の) false, phony, fake, imitation

nise-mono n 偽物・にせもの a fake, an imitation; a forgery

nise-satsu n 偽札・贋札・にせ札 counterfeit bill (currency)

nishi n 西 west: **nishi-guchi** 西口 the west exit/entrance; **nishi-yori (no kaze)** 西寄り (の風) westerly (wind) nishi-káigan n 西海岸 west coast

níshiki n 錦 brocade

nishime n 煮しめ (**o-níshime** お煮しめ) boiled fish and vegetables

níshin n ニシン・鰊 herring

nishoku-tsuki (no) adj 二食付き (の) with two meals incuded

nisshi n 日誌 diary, journal (of business, nursing, etc.): **gyōmu-nisshi** 業務日誌 business diary; **kango-nisshi** 看護日誌 nurse's daily record

nissū´ n 日数 the number of days

nísu n ニス = **wánisu** ワニス varnish

nita … adj 似た…similar (= **nite iru** 似ている…) → **nimásu** 似ます

nita v 煮た = **nimáshita** 煮ました (boiled)

nite v 似て・煮て → **nimásu** 似ます・煮ます

… ní te particle …にて [LITERARY] = … de …で (at; …)

nité ya shinai v 似てやしない, **nité wa inai** 似てはいない = **nicha inai** 似ちゃいない = **nitemasen, nite(i-)nai** 似てません, (似て) (い) ない (not resemble)

ni-tō (no) adj 二等 (の) second class; **nitō´-shō** 二等賞 the second prize

nittei n 日程 schedule, program, itinerary

niwa n 庭 (**o-niwa** お庭) garden

… níwa suffix, prep, conj …には to; at/in; as

níwaka (no/ni) adj, adv にわか (の/に) sudden(ly), unexpected(ly);

nikawa-áme にわか雨 sudden shower

niwatori n ニワトリ・鶏 chicken

niyō v 煮よう = **nimashō´** 煮ましょう (let's boil it!)

n´n interj んん 1. "un-un" (うんうん) huh-uh, uh-uh 2. "u-un" (ううん) nope

nó n 野 field (dry) (= **nó-hara** 野原)

no-… prefix 野… wild
nó-bana n 野花 [BOOKISH] wildflower
nó-gusa n 野草 [BOOKISH] wild grass
no-usagi n 野ウサギ・野兎 wild rabbit

…´no suffix …の 1. the one/time/place that; (= **hitó** 人, **monó** 物, **tokí** 時, **tokoró** 所) 2. the (specific) act/fact of … (cf. **kotó** 事) 3. which/that is … (→ **désu** です, **dá** だ, **na** な)

nō n 脳 brain: **dai-nō** 大脳 cerebrum: **shōnō** 小脳 cerebellum: **kan-nō** 間脳 diencephalon
nō-miso n 脳みそ・脳味噌 [INFORMAL] brain (= **nō** 脳)

nō´ n 能 1. ability (= **nōryoku** 能力, **sainō** 才能): [IDIOM] ~ **aru taka wa tsume wo kakusu** 能ある鷹は爪を隠す Who knows most speaks least. 2. o-nō お能 Noh (Japanese classical theater) (→ **nō-men** 能面)

nō-… prefix 農… farming, agriculture
nō-chi n 農地 farm land
nō´-gyō n 農業 agriculture, farming
nō-jō´ n 農場 farm
nō´-ka n 農家 farm house/family; farmer
nō-min n 農民 the farmers

nobashimásu, nobásu v 伸ばします, 伸ばす extends (lengthens, stretches, deters) it

nobashimásu, nobásu v 延ばします, 延ばす prolongs

nobé ro v 述べろ [IMPERATIVE] (tell it!) → **nobemásu** 述べます

nobemásu, nobéru v 述べます, 述べる tells, relates

nobimásu, nobíru v 伸びます, 伸びる it extends, reaches; it spreads

nobori n 上り inbound (to Tokyo), the up train

noborimásu, noboru v 登ります, 登る climbs

noborimásu, noboru v 上ります, 上る goes up

noborimásu, noboru v 昇ります, 昇る rises: **hi ga noborimásu** 日が昇ります the sun rises

nóbu n ノブ knob: **doa-nobu** ドアノブ door knob

nochi n のち・後: **nochi-hodo** のちほど[程] later (= **áto (de)** あと・後(で))

nódo n のど・喉 throat: **~ ga kawaki-máshita** のどが渇きました is thirsty

nō'do n 濃度 density, thick (*liquid*), concentration: **nisankatanso-nōdo** 二酸化炭素濃度 carbon dioxide concentration

nódoka (na) adj のどか(な) tranquil, peaceful, quiet, calm

nōdō-tai n 能動態 the active voice (*not the passive voice*)

nó-hara n 野原 field

noite v 退いて → **nokimásu** 退きます

noirōze n ノイローゼ neurosis

nó-juku n 野宿 rough sleeping: **~ shimásu** 野宿します sleeps rough

nokanai v 退かない = **nokimasén** 退きません (not get out of the way)

noke ro v 退けろ [IMPERATIVE] (omit it!); (get out of the way!) → **nokimásu** 退きます

nokemásu, nokeru v 退けます, 退ける removes; omits

nokenai v 退けない = **nokemasén** 退けません (not remove/omit)

nokete v 退けて → **nokemásu** 退けます

noki n 軒 eaves

nokimásu, noku v 退きます, 退く gets out of the way

nókku shimásu (suru) v ノックします (する) knocks (*on door*)

nokogíri n のこぎり・鋸 a saw (*tool*)

nōkō (na) adj 濃厚(な) thick, rich, dense, passionate: **nōkō na aji** 濃厚な味 rich taste; **~ na kisu** 濃厚なキス passionate kiss

nokorí n 残り the rest, the remainder, what is left, the leftover
  nokori-bi n 残り火 embers
  nokori-ga n 残り香 lingering scent
  nokori-monó n 残り物 leftovers,

remains, leavings: [IDIOM] **~ niwa fuku ga aru** 残り物には福がある Last but not least.

nokorimásu, nokóru v 残ります, 残る remains, is left behind/over

nokoshimásu, nokósu v 残します, 残す leaves behind/over

nománai v 飲まない = **nomimasén** 飲みません (not drink)

nóme v 飲め [IMPERATIVE] (drink it!) → **nomimásu** 飲みます

nómeba v 飲めば → **nomimásu** 飲みます

nomemásu, noméru v 飲めます, 飲める can drink; is (very) drinkable

nō-men n 能面 mask (*Noh drama*)

noménai v 飲めない = **nomemasén** 飲めません (cannot drink)

noméreba v 飲めれば (if one can drink) → **nomemásu** 飲めます

nómete v 飲めて → **nomemásu** 飲めて

nomí n ノミ・蚤 flea

nómi n ノミ・鑿 chisel

...nómi suffix, adj ...のみ (= **... daké** ...だけ) only

nomi-komimásu, nomi-komu v 飲み込みます, 飲み込む swallows (*ingests*)

nomimásu, nómu v 飲みます, 飲む drinks; smokes; takes (*medicine*)
  nomi-kai n 飲み会 drinking party
  nomí-mizu n 飲み水 drinking water
  nomí-mono n 飲み物 beverage, something to drink, refreshments
  nomí-ya n 飲み屋 tavern, neighborhood bar

nomō´ v 飲もう = **nomimashō´** 飲みましょう (let's drink!)

nonbē, nonbei n 飲兵衛・呑兵衛, のんべい [INFORMAL] a heavy drinker

nonbiri adj のんびり easy, leisurely: **nonbiri ya** のんびり屋 happy-go-lucky person (= **nonki** のん気[呑気]): **~ shimásu** のんびりします relaxes

nónda v 飲んだ = **nomimáshita** 飲みました (drank)

nónde v 飲んで → **nomimásu** 飲みます

non-fikushon n ノンフィクション nonfiction

nónja v 飲んじゃ = **nónde wa** 飲んでは: ~ **damé (desu)** 飲んじゃだめ(です) don't drink it!

nónki (na) adj のん気[呑気](な) easygoing, happy-go-lucky, carefree

nonoshirimás<u>u</u>, nonoshíru v 罵ります、罵る reviles, abuses, swears at, curses

nonoshi´tte v 罵って → **nonoshirimás<u>u</u>** 罵ります

non-sumōkā n ノンスモーカー non-smoker

nosutarujia n ノスタルジア nostalgia

nore v 乗れ [IMPERATIVE] (aboard!) → **norimás<u>u</u>** 乗ります

noremás<u>u</u>, noreru v 乗れます、乗れる can ride/board

noren n のれん・暖簾 shop curtain; credit: ~ **o oroshimás<u>u</u>** 暖簾を下ろします closes down one's store

nori n ノリ・海苔 seaweed (green)
norí-maki n のり[海苔]巻き sushi rice in a seaweed roll

norí n のり・糊 paste; starch

nori-kaemás<u>u</u>, nori-káeru v 乗り換えます、乗り換える changes (vehicles)

norimás<u>u</u>, noru v 乗ります、乗る gets aboard, rides; is carried
nori-ba n 乗り場 boarding place; platform (at station); taxi stand; bus stop
nori-kae n 乗り換え change, transfer (of vehicle)
nori-komi n 乗り込み drive-in
nori-mono n 乗(り)物 vehicle

Nōrin-Suisan-shō n 農林水産省 Ministry of Agriculture, Forestry and Fisheries of Japan (MAFF)

nōritsu n 能率 efficiency

norō´ v 乗ろう = **norimasho** 乗りましょう (let's get aboard!)

norói n 呪い a curse

norói adj 呪のろい [INFORMAL] slow, dull, sluggish

noroimás<u>u</u>, noróu v 呪います、呪う curses, utters a curse

noronoro adv のろのろ slowly, sluggishly: ~ **unten** のろのろ運転 driving slowly: ~ **arukimás<u>u</u>** のろのろ歩きます slouches along

norótte v 呪って → **noroimás<u>u</u>** 呪います

noru v 乗る = **norimás<u>u</u>** 乗ります (gets aboard, rides; is carried)

noruma n ノルマ norm, quota: ~ **o tasseishimás<u>u</u>** ノルマを達成します achieves one's quota

nō´ryoku n 能力 ability (= **nō** 能, **sainō** 才能)

nose ro v 乗せろ [IMPERATIVE] (load/carry it!) → **nosemás<u>u</u>** 乗せます

nosemás<u>u</u>, noseru v 乗せます、乗せる loads, puts aboard, ships, carries

nosemás<u>u</u>, noseru v 載せます、載せる publishes (in book, magazine, etc.), posts (an article, etc.)

nosete v 乗せて・載せて → **nosemás<u>u</u>** 乗せます・載せます

nōshuku n 濃縮 [BOOKISH] concentration (of liquid or air)

noten (de/no) adv, adj 野天(で/の) outdoors: **noten-búro** 野天風呂 outdoor bath (= **roten-búro** 露天風呂)

nōtenki (na) adj 能天気(な) happy-go-lucky, easy, optimistic (person)

nō´to n ノート = **nōtobúkku** ノートブック notebook

notta v 乗った = **norimásh<u>i</u>ta** 乗りました (got aboard)

notte v 乗って → **norimás<u>u</u>** 乗ります

nottóri n 乗っ取り → **nottorimás<u>u</u>** 乗っ取ります
nottorí-han n 乗っ取り犯 hijacker
nottori-jíken n 乗っ取り事件 a hijacking; (illegal) takeover, seizure

nottorimás<u>u</u>, nottóru v 乗っ取ります、乗っ取る hijacks; (illegally) takes over, seizes

nottótte v 乗っ取って → **nottorimás<u>u</u>** 乗っ取ります

noyama n 野山 fields and mountains

nōzei n 納税 payment of taxes: ~ **shimás<u>u</u>** 納税します pays one's taxes

nozoite v 除いて → **nozokimás<u>u</u>** 除きます

nozoke´ v 覗け [IMPERATIVE] (peek!) → **nozokimás<u>u</u>** 覗きます

nozokemás<u>u</u>, nozokeru v 覗けます、覗ける can peek/peep at

nozokemás<u>u</u>, nozokeru v 除けます、除ける can remove; can omit

nozokimás<u>u</u>, nozoku v 覗きます、覗く

peeks/peeps at

nozoki-ana *n* のぞき[覗き]穴 peep-hole

nozoki-ya *n* のぞき[覗き]屋 peeping Tom

nozokimásu, nozoku *v* 除きます, 除く eliminates, removes; omits

nozokō *v* 覗こう・除こう = **nozoki-mashō** のぞ覗きましょう; 除きましょう (let's peek!; let's remove/omit it!)

nozomashii *adj* 望ましい desirable, welcome

nozomi *n* 望み a desire; a hope, an expectation

nozomimásu, nozomu *v* 望みます, 望む desires, looks to, hopes for

nozomimásu, nozomu *v* 臨みます, 臨む [BOOKISH] looks out on

nozonde *v* 望んで・臨んで → **nozomimásu** 望みます・臨みます

nū´ *v* 縫う = **nuimásu** 縫います (sews)

nū´do *n* ヌード a nude

núe *v* 縫え [IMPERATIVE] (sow it!) → **nuemásu** 縫えます

núeba *v* 縫えば (if one sews) → **nuemásu** 縫えます

nuemásu, nuéru *v* 縫えます, 縫える can sew

nuénai *v* 縫えない = **nuemásen** 縫えません (cannot sew)

nugánai *v* 脱がない = **nugimásen** 脱ぎません (not take it off)

núge *v* 脱げ [IMPERATIVE] (take it off!) → **nugimásu** 脱ぎます

nugemásu, nugéru *v* 脱げます, 脱げる **1.** it slips/comes off **2.** can take it off

nugénai *v* 脱げない = **nugemásen** 脱げません (not slip off; cannot take it off)

núgeta *v* 脱げた = **nugemáshita** 脱げました (it slipped; could take it off)

núgete *v* 脱げて → **nugemásu** 脱げます

nugimásu, núgu *v* 脱ぎます, 脱ぐ takes off (*clothes, shoes*)

nugō *v* 脱ごう = **nugimashō´** 脱ぎましょう (let's take it off!)

nuguemásu, nuguéru *v* 拭えます, 拭える can wipe it away

nuguénai *v* 拭えない = **nuguemásen** 拭えません (cannot wipe it away)

nuguimásu, nuguu´ *v* 拭います, 拭う wipes it away

nugútta *v* 拭った = **nuguimáshita** 拭いました

nugútte *v* 拭って → **nuguimásu** 拭います

nuguwánai *v* 拭わない = **nuguimásen** 拭いません (not wipe it away)

núi *v* 縫い → **nuimásu** 縫います

núida *v* 脱いだ = **nugimáshita** 脱ぎました (took it off)

núide *v* 脱いで → **nugimásu** 脱ぎます

nuigurumi *n* 縫い包み stuffed toy

nuimásu, nuu´ *v* 縫います, 縫う sews
núi-bari *n* 縫い針 sewing needle
nui-mé *n* 縫い目 seam

nuita *v* 抜いた = **nukimáshita** 抜きました (uncorked/removed it)

nuite *v* 抜いて → **nukimásu** 抜きます

nukashimásu, nukasu *v* 抜かします, 抜かす skips, leaves out

nuke´ *v* 抜け [IMPERATIVE] (uncork/remove it!) → **nukimásu** 抜きます

nukemásu, nukeru *v* 抜けます, 抜ける comes off; escapes; is omitted
nuke-ana *n* 抜け穴 **1.** passage which allows one to go through **2.** passage to run away **3.** loophole

nukete *v* 抜けて → **nukemásu** 抜けます

...-nuki (de/no) *suffix, adj, adv* ...抜き (で/の) without (*omitting*)

nukimásu, nuku *v* 抜きます, 抜く uncorks; removes; surpasses; selects
nuki-ashi (sashiashi)(de) 抜き足 (差し足) (で) stealthily, on tiptoe
nuki-uchi *n* 抜き打ち (*test, inspection, etc.,*) without notice: **nukiuchi-tesuto** 抜き打ちテスト popquiz: **nukiuchi-kensa** 抜き打ち検査 surprise inspection

nukō *v* 抜こう = **nukimashō** 抜きましょう (let's uncork/ remove it!)

numá *n* 沼 pond: **numa-chi** 沼地 swamp, marsh

nuno *n* 布 cloth: **nuno-ji** 布地 fabric

nuranai *v* 塗らない = **nurimásen** 塗りません (not paint it)

nurashimásu, nurasu *v* 濡らします, 濡らす wets, dampens

nuré v 塗れ [IMPERATIVE] (paint it!) →
nurimásu 塗ります

nuréba v 塗れば (if one paints it) →
nurimásu 塗れば

nure-ginu n 濡れ衣 false accusation

nuremásu, nureru v 濡れます, 濡れる
gets wet, damp; **nurete imásu** 濡れてい
ます is wet

nuremásu, nureru v 塗れます, 塗れる
can paint it

nurenai v 濡れない = **nuremasén** 濡れ
ません (not get wet)

nurenai v 塗れない = **nuremasén** 塗れ
ません (cannot paint it)

nureréba v 濡れれば (if it gets wet) →
nuremásu 濡れます

nureréba v 塗れれば (if one can paint
it) → nuremásu 塗れます

nurete v 濡れて・塗れて →
nuremásu 濡れます・塗れます

nuri n 塗り lacquer, varnish, painting

nuri-kaemásu, nuri-káeru v 塗り替え
ます, 塗り替える repaints

nurimásu, nuru v 塗ります, 塗る
lacquers, paints, varnishes, stains;
(*butter*) spreads

nuri-gúsuri n 塗り薬 ointment

nuri-mono n 塗り物 lacquerware

nurō´ v 塗ろう = **nurimashō** 塗りまし
ょう (let's paint it!)

nuru v 塗る = **nurimásu** 塗ります (paints)

nurúi adj ぬるい・温い lukewarm,
tepid

nushi n 主 master, owner (= **aruji** 主)

nusumí n 盗み theft

nusumimásu, nusúmu v 盗みます, 盗
む steals, swipes, robs, rips off

nutta v 塗った = **nurimáshita** 塗りまし
た (painted)

nútta v 縫った = **nuimáshita** 縫いまし
た (sewed)

nutte v 塗って → **nurimásu** 塗ります

nútte v 縫って → **nuimásu** 縫います

nuwánai v 縫わない = **nuimasén** 縫い
ません (not sew)

núya v 縫や → **núeba** 縫えば

nyō n 尿 [BOOKISH] urine, urinating (=
shíkko しっこ, **o-shíkko** おしっこ)

nyō´bō, nyó´bo n 女房 my wife

nyū... prefix 入... entering

nyū-en n 入園 entering a kinder-
garten/nursery: ~ **shimásu** 入園します
enrolls (*in kindergarten/nursery*);
nyūen-shiki 入園式 entrance ceremony

nyū-gaku n 入学 admission to a
school, entering a school; **nyūgaku-
shiken** 入学試験, **nyū-shi** 入試
entrance exam; **nyūgaku-shiki** 入学式
school entrance ceremony: ~ **shimásu**
入学します enrolls (*in school*)

nyū-in n 入院 entering a hospital,
hospital admission: ~ **shimásu** 入院し
ます enters a hospital: **nyūinshite
imásu** 入院しています is in a hospital

nyū-jō n 入場 admission (*to a place*):
~ **shimásu** 入場します is admitted,
enters; **nyūjō´-ken** 入場券 admission
ticket, platform (*non-passenger*) ticket;
nyūjō´-ryō 入場料 admission fee

nyū-ka n 入荷 arrival (*of goods*)(*in
shop, market, etc.*): ~ **shimásu** 入荷し
ます receives (*goods*)

nyū-kai n 入会 admission to an
association: **nyūkai-kin** 入会金
admission fee: ~ **shimásu** 入会します
becomes a member

nyū-koku n 入国 entering a country;
immigration: ~ **shimásu** 入国します
enters a country; **nyūkoku kanri-kyoku**
入国管理局 Immigration Bureau of
Japan

nyū-kyo n 入居 moving into an apartment: **nyūkyó-sha** 入居者 tenant,
resident (*of an apartment*)

nyū-seki n 入籍 registering one's
marriage: ~ **shimáshita** 入籍しました
We officially got married.

nyū-sen n 入選 winning a prize: ~
shimásu 入選します wins a prize

nyū-sha n 入社 entering (*joining*)
a company: ~ **shimásu** 入社します
enters a company: **nyūsha-shikén** 入社
試験 employment selection exam

nyū-shitsu n 入室 entering a room

nyū-yoku n 入浴 bath, taking a bath: ~
shimásu 入浴します takes a bath

nyūbai n 入梅 the rainy season (*in
Japan*) (= **tsuyu** 梅雨)

nyūdō-gumo n 入道雲 thunderhead,
cumulonimbus cloud

nyū-eki

nyū-eki *n* 乳液 1. latex 2. milky lotion, milky liquid (*cosmetic*)

nyū-gan *n* 乳がん・乳癌 breast cancer

nyū-gyū *n* 乳牛 dairy cattle

nyū-inryō *n* 乳飲料 milk beverage

nyū-ji *n* 乳児 infant

Nyūjiirándo *n* ニュージーランド New Zealand; **Nyūjiirandó-jin** ニュージーランド人 a New Zealander

nyūnen (na/ni) *adj, adv* 入念(な/に) careful(ly)

nyūsan-kin *n* 乳酸菌 lactobacillus (*a type of bacteria*)

nyū-seihin *n* 乳製品 foods made from milk (*butter, cheese, etc.*)

nyūshō *n* 入賞 winning a prize: **nyū-sho-sha** 入賞者 a prizewinner; ~ **shimásu** 入賞します wins a prize

nyū´su *n* ニュース news: **nyūsu-bangumi** ニュース番組 news program: **nyūsu-kyasutā** ニュースキャスター newscaster

nyū´toraru *n* ニュートラル neutral (*gear*): **(gía o) ~ ni iremásu** (ギアを)ニュートラルに入れます shifts the gear into neutral

Nyūyō´ku *n* ニューヨーク New York

nyūyō (na) *adj* 入用(な) necessary, needed

O

ó *n* 尾 = **shippó** しっぽ・尻尾 tail

ó *n* 緒 = **hanao** 鼻緒 thong, strap

o- *prefix* お・御 [HONORIFIC] (personalizing): "your" or "that important thing"

o-aiso *n* おあいそ・お愛想, **o-aisō** おあいそう・お愛想 1. compliment, flattery (= **aiso** 愛想) 2. **o-aiso** おあいそ (*restaurant*) bill, check

o-azuke *interj* お預け Wait! (*training one's dog*)

o-báke *n* お化け・おばけ ghost, monster

o-bā´-san *n* おばあさん・お祖母さん grandmother (*family*) (= **bā-san** ばあさん, **obā-chan** おばあちゃん, **só-bo** 祖母)

o-bā´-san *n* おばあさん・お婆さん (*not relative*) old lady/woman (= **bā-san** ばあさん, **obā-chan** おばあちゃん)

o-bentō *n* お弁当 box lunch (= **bentō** 弁当): **(o-)bentō-bako** (お)弁当箱 lunch box

o-bon *n* お盆 tray (= **bon** 盆, **torei** トレイ)

O-bón *n* お盆 the Bon Festival (*Buddhist All Saints Day*) (= **Bon** 盆)

o-bō-san *n* お坊さん Buddhist monk (= **bō-san** 坊さん)

o-cha *n* お茶 Japanese green tea; the tea ceremony (= **cha** 茶)

o-chóko *n* おちょこ saké cup

o-chūgen *n* お中元 midyear present, summer gift

o-daiji ni *interj* お大事に: **(dōzo) ~ (shitekudasai)!** (どうぞ)お大事に(して下さい)! (*Please*) take care of yourself!

o-fúro *n* お風呂 bath (= **furo** 風呂)

o-hachi *n* お鉢 rice bucket/tub (= **hachi** 鉢) (= **o-hitsu** お櫃・おひつ, **meshi-bitsu** 飯びつ)

o-hana *n* お花 flower (= **hana** 花); flower arrangement

o-hana *n* お鼻 nose (= **hana** 鼻)

o-háshi *n* お箸 chopsticks (= **hashi** 箸)

o-hima *n* お暇 (*your*) spare time, free time (= **hima** 暇)

o-hína sama *n* おひな[雛]様 (*Dolls Festival*) dolls

o-hi-sama *n* お日様 sun (*baby talk*)

o-hitáshi *n* お浸し boiled greens (*usually spinach, served cold with seasoning*)

o-híya *n* お冷や cold water

o-ikura (désu ka) おいくら(ですか) What's the bill/tab/price? How much is this? (= **ikura (désu ka)** いくら(ですか))

o-ikutsu (désu ka) おいくつ(ですか) How old (*are you*)? (= **ikutsu (désu ka)** いくつ(ですか))

o-isha (san) *n* お医者（さん）doctor (= **isha** 医者)

o-itoko-san *n* おいとこ［従兄弟］さん (*your/someone else's*) cousin (= **itoko** いとこ・従兄弟)

o-itoma *n* お暇 leave-taking, farewell: **O-itoma (ita-)shimásu** お暇（致）します I will take my leave.

o-iwai *n* お祝い celebration (= **iwai** 祝い)

o-jama *n* お邪魔 (= **jama** 邪魔): **O-jama shimáshi̱ta.** お邪魔しました. Excuse me for having interrupted/bothered you

o-jigi *n* お辞儀: ~ **o shimásu** お辞儀をします bows

o-jíi-san *n* おじいさん・祖父さん grandfather (*family*) (= **jii-san** じいさん・祖父さん, **ojii-chan** おじいちゃん)

o-jíi-san *n* おじいさん・お爺さん (*not relative*) old (gentle-)man (= **jii-san** じいさん・爺さん, **ojii-chan** おじいちゃん)

o-jū′ *n* お重 nested boxes; picnic boxes (= **jūbako** 重箱)

O-kaeri nasái! *interj* お帰りなさい! Welcome back!

o-kane *n* お金 money (= **kane** 金)

o-kan *n* お燗 heating sake (= **kán** 燗)

o-ká′-san *n* お母さん mother [FORMAL] (= **kā′san** 母さん・かあさん, **ofukuro** お袋)

o-káshi *n* お菓子 confections, sweets, pastry, candy, cakes, cookies, biscuits (= **kashi** 菓子) (→ **wa-gáshi** 和菓子, **yō-gáshi** 洋菓子)

o-kawari *n* お変わり change (*in health*): ~ **arimasénka.** お変わりありませんか。Is everything all right? (*greeting*) (= **kawari** 変わり)

o-káwari *n* おかわり・お代わり a second helping (*usually of rice*)

o-kayu *n* お粥・おかゆ gruel (*rice*) (= **kayu** 粥)

o-kazari *n* お飾り **1.** decorations and/or offerings to the gods and Buddha **2.** New Year's decorations **3.** mere figurehead (= **kazari** 飾り)

o-kéiko (goto) *n* お稽古（ごと）practice (*artistic*) (= **kéiko** 稽古, **naraigoto** 習い事)

o-kome *n* お米 (**kome** 米) rice (*hulled, uncooked*)

o-ko-san *n* お子さん (*your/someone else's*) child (= **ko(domo)** 子(供))

o-kyaku(-san/-sámá) *n* お客(さん/様) visitor; customer, patron (= **kyaku** 客)

o-kyō *n* お経 sutra (*Buddhist scripture*) (= **kyō** 経)

o-kyū *n* お灸 moxibustion (= **kyū** 灸)

o-matsuri *n* お祭り festival (= **matsuri** 祭り)

o-me ni kakarimásu (kararu) *n* お目にかかります(かかる): **hajimete ~ ni ~** おはじめてお目にかかります I meet/see you first time; **o-me ni kakemásu** お目にかけます I show it to you

o-meshi ni narimásu (náru) *v* お召しになります(なる) [HONORIFIC] **1.** wears **2.** buys **3.** invites **4.** kaze o ~ 風邪をお召しになります catches a cold

o-miya *n* お宮 shrine (*Shinto shrine*)

o-miyage *n* おみやげ・お土産, **o-míya** おみや (*baby talk*) gift, present (*as souvenir*) (= **miyage** みやげ)

o-múko-san *n* お婿さん (*your/someone else's*) son-in-law; bridegroom (= **muko** 婿)

o-negai *n* お願い favor (*requested*), request (= **negai** 願い): ~ **shimásu** お願いします please

o-né′-san *n* お姉さん older sister (= **nē′-san** 姉さん, **ane** 姉, **aneki** 姉貴)

o-níkai *n* お二階 upstairs (= **nikai** 二階)

o níi san *n* お兄さん older brother (= **níi-san** 兄さん, **ani** 兄, **aniki** 兄貴)

o-nō *n* お能 Noh (*Japanese classical theater*) (= **nō′** 能)

o-rei *n* お礼 an acknowledgment, a thank-you, a present (*of appreciation*) (= **rei** 礼); **(… ni) ~ o iimásu** (…に) お礼を言います thanks

o-sáji *n* お匙 spoon (= **sájí** さじ・匙)

o-sake *n* お酒 saké (*Japanese rice wine*); liquor (= **sake** 酒)

o-saki ni *adv* お先に Excuse me for going first: **dō′zo ~** どうぞお先に, ~

dō´zo お先にどうぞ Please go first; ~ **shitsúrei shimásu** お先に失礼します Excuse me for being the first to leave

o-séchi *n* おせち・お節 a season; a festival: **osechi-ryó´ri** おせち料理 festival cookery (*for New Year's*)

o-seibo *n* お歳暮 year-end present, winter gift

o-seji *n* お世辞・おせじ compliment, flattery; ~ **o iimásu** お世辞を言います pays compliments, flatters

o-sénbei *n* お煎餅 rice crackers (= **sénbei** せんべい・煎餅)

o-séwa *n* お世話 care, assistance, help (= **sewá** 世話) (→ **o-sewa-sama** お世話様)

o-shirase *n* お知らせ report, notice, information (= **shirase** 知らせ)

o-shiri *n* お尻 buttock, hip (= **shiri** 尻)

o-shiro *n* お城 castle (= **shiro** 城)

O-shōgatsu *n* お正月 New Year; January (= **Shōgatsu** 正月)

o-soba *n* おそば・お側 near, close(-by), (be)side (= **sóba** 側)

o-soba *n* おそば・お蕎麦 buck-wheat (noodles) (= **sóba** そば・蕎麦)

o-sobaya *n* おそば[蕎麦]屋 noodle shop (= **sobá-ya** そば[蕎麦]屋)

o-sōshiki *n* お葬式 funeral (= **sōshiki** 葬式)

o-su *n* お酢 vinegar (= **sú** 酢)

o-sumō-san *n* お相撲さん sumo wrestler (= **sumō** 相撲, **rikishi** 力士)

o-súshi *n* お寿司・お鮨 (*rice seasoned with sweetend vinegar with raw fish*)

o-sushi-ya *n* お寿司[お鮨]屋 = **sushí-ya** すし[寿司・鮨]屋 sushi bar

o-témae *n* お点前 tea ceremony procedures (= **temae** 点前)

o-ténki *n* お天気 **1.** weather (= **ténki** 天気) **2.** fair weather

o-tera *n* お寺 Buddhist temple (= **tera** 寺)

o-tō´-san *n* お父さん・おとうさん father (= **tō´san** 父さん・とうさん, **oyaji** 親父)

o-toshi *n* お年・お歳・(*your/someone else's*) age (= **toshi** 年・歳)

ó-tsuki-sama *n* お月さま・お月様

moon (= **tsukí** 月)

o-tsúmami *n* おつまみ appetizer (with drinks); finger food (= **tsumami** つまみ)

o-tsuri *n* おつり・お釣り change (*money returned*) (= **tsuri** つり・釣り)

o-tsutome *n* お勤め・お務め job, work(ing); duty, role (= **tsutome** 勤め・務め)

o-ukagai *n* お伺い visit; inquiry, consultation (= **ukagai** 伺い)

o-yakusho *n* お役所 government office (= **yakusho** 役所)

o-yakusoku *n* お約束 promise, agreement, appointment, engagement, date, commitment (= **yakusoku** 約束)

o-yásai *n* お野菜 vegetables (= **yasai** 野菜)

o-yasumi *n* お休み rest; holiday; recess; time off (= **yasumí** 休み, **kyūka** 休暇 [FORMAL])

o-yu *n* お湯 hot water (= **yu** 湯): ~ **o wakashimásu** お湯を沸かします boils water

o-yome-san *n* お嫁さん (*your/someone else's*) bride (= **yome** 嫁)

o-zen *n* お膳 dining tray (= **zen** 膳)

o-zōni *n* お雑煮 rice cakes boiled with vegetables (*eaten as New Year's soup*) (= **zōni** 雑煮)

... o ...を *particle*: marks direct object (*gets what, loves whom*) or path traversed (*goes through/along where, using what path*)

ō´ *n* 王, **ō-sama** 王様 king

ō-chō *n* 王朝 royal dynasty

ō-dō *n* 王道 royal road

ō-hi *n* 王妃 queen

ō-i keishō *n* 王位継承 succession to the throne

ō-ja *n* 王者 **1.** king **2.** champion: **sekai ōja** 世界王者 world champion **3.** ruler (= **hasha** 覇者)

ō-ji (-sama) *n* 王子(様) prince

ō-jo (-sama) *n* 王女(様) princess

ō-kan *n* 王冠 **1.** crown **2.** bottle cap

ō-koku *n* 王国 kingdom

ō-sama *n* 王様 king

ō-shitsu *n* 王室 royal family

ō-... *prefix* 大... big, great

176

ō-áme *n* 大雨 heavy rain

ō-buri *n* 大降り a downfall, heavy rain and/or snow

ō-buri *n* 大振り big swing

ō-buroshiki *n* 大風呂敷 very large square wrapping cloth: [IDIOM] **~ o hirogeru** 大風呂敷を広げる talks big, blows one's horn

ō-dáiko *n* 大太鼓 large drum

ō-dō´ri *n* 大通り main street, avenue

ō-fúbuki *n* 大吹雪 blizzard

ō-gara (na) *adj* 大柄 (な) **1.** big, large (body, build) **2.** big, large patterns

ō-gata *n* 大型 large-size (*model*)

ō-gesa (na) *adj* おおげさ[大袈裟] (な) exaggerated

ō´-góe (de) *adv* 大声 (で) in a loud voice

ō-gosho *n* 大御所 leading figure, prominent figure: **bundan no ~** 文壇の大御所 prominent figure in the literary world: **seikai no ~** 政界の大御所 a political bigwig

ō-hiroma *n* 大広間 great hall

ō-isogi (no/de) *adj, adv* 大急ぎ (の/で) (*in*) a great rush, a big hurry

ō-kaze *n* 大風 strong wind

ō´-mízú *n* 大水 flood (= **kōzui** 洪水)

ō-moji *n* 大文字 capital letter

ō-mono *n* 大物 a big shot

ō-mori *n* 大盛 (り) large helping/serving: **~ de onegai shimásu** 大盛りでお願いします A large helping of it, please.

ō-mugi *n* オオムギ・大麦 barley

ō-ótoko *n* 大男 a giant of a man, big man

ō-saji *n* 大匙・大さじ tablespoon

ō-sáwagi *n* 大騒ぎ fuss, disturbance: **~ shimásu** 大騒ぎします makes a fuss

ō-sōji *n* 大掃除 great cleaning: **nenmatsu no ~** 年末の大掃除 year-end cleaning

ō-uridashi *n* 大売り出し big sale

ō-yasu-uri *n* 大安売り special bargain sale

ō-yórokobi (de) *adv* 大喜び (で) with great delight

ō-yuki *n* 大雪 heavy snow

ō-zúmō *n* 大相撲 a grand sumo

tournament; an exciting match

ō-zora *n* 大空 big sky

oashisu *n* オアシス oasis

ō´bā *n* オーバー overcoat, (top) coat

ōbā(-kōto) *n* オーバー（コート）overcoat

ō´bā (na) *adj* オーバー（な）exaggerated, over(ly), too much

oba(-san) *n* おば[叔母]（さん）aunt (*younger sister of father or mother*) (= **oba-chan** おば[叔母]ちゃん)

oba(-san) *n* おば[伯母]（さん）aunt (*older sister of father or mother*) (= **oba-chan** おば[伯母]ちゃん)

oba(-san) *n* おば[小母]さん (*not relative*) lady, woman (*middle-aged*) (= **oba-chan** おばちゃん)

ō´bā shimásu (suru) *n* オーバーします（する）goes over, goes past: **jikan ga ~** 時間がオーバーします runs overtime

Ōbei *n* 欧米 Europe and America: **Ōbei-shokoku** 欧米諸国 the various countries of Europe and America

obekka *n* おべっか flattery

óbi *n* 帯 girdle, sash, belt, (*Japanese*) obi

ōbii *n* オービー・OB **1.** (*abbreviation for the word "old boy"*) male graduate, alumnus **2.** (*abbreviation for the word "out of bounds"*) OB (*golf*)

obi-jō (no) *adj* 帯状 (の) belt(-like), a narrow strip (*of*)

obitadashii *adj* おびただしい a great number of, immense, tremendous

ōbō (na) *adj* 横暴 (な) high-handed, tyrannical

obóe *n* 覚え memory; consciousness

oboe-gaki *n* 覚 (え) 書 (き) memo(-randum), note (= **bibōroku** 備忘録)

oboemásu, obóeru *v* 覚えます、覚える remembers, keeps in mind; learns

oboko (-músume) *n* おぼこ（娘）virgin (*female*)

oboremásu, oboreru *v* 溺れます、溺れる drowns

ō´bo shimásu (suru) *v* 応募します（する）applies

obuimásu, obú *v* 負ぶいます、負ぶう carries on one's back (= **seoimásu, shoimásu** 背負います)

ōbun *n* オーブン oven

oburāto *n* オブラート wafer paper

obutsu *n* 汚物 dirt

obútte *v* 負ぶって → **obuimásu** 負ぶっています

obuwánai *v* 負ぶわない= **obuimasén** 負ぶいません (not carry)

ōchaku *n; adj* 横着(な) lazy: ~ **na taido** 横着な態度 lazy attitude

ochi *n* 落ち **1.** omission, lack: **te-ochi** 手落ち oversight **2.** punch line **3.** the end, the result

ochimásu, ochíru *v* 落ちます, 落ちる falls, drops; is omitted; fails; is inferior

óchi-ba *n* 落ち葉 fallen leaves

óchite *v* 落ちて → **ochimásu** 落ちます

ochi-tsuite 落ち着いて **1.** *adv* calmly **2.** *v* calm down!: ~ **kudasai** 落ち着いて下さい Please calm down.

ochi-tsukanai *v* 落ち着かない= **ochi-tsukimasén** 落ち着きません is restless

ochi-tsuki *n* 落ち着き: ~ **ga aru/nai** 落ち着きがある/ない is calm/restless

ochi-tsukimásu, ochi-tsuku *v* 落ち着きます, 落ち着く calms down, keeps cool, settles down, relaxes

ōdāmeido *n* オーダーメイド made-to-order: **ōd´āmeido (no)** オーダーメイド(の) custom-made

ōdan *n* 黄疸 (*medical*) jaundice

ōdan *n* 横断 crossing, going across, intersecting: **ōdan-hodō** 横断歩道 pedestrian crossing

odatemásu, odateru *v* おだてます, おだてる coaxes

odáyaka (na) *adj* 穏やか(な) quiet, calm, peaceful, gentle; moderate

odéko *n* おでこ forehead (= **hitai** 額)

odén *n* おでん assorted boiled foods (*Japanese hot pot*)

ōdio *n* オーディオ audio: **ōdio-mania** オーディオマニア audiophile, audio nut

ōdishon *n* オーディション audition

odokashimásu, odokasu *v* 脅かします, 脅かす threatens

odoranai *v* 踊らない = **odorimasén** 踊りません (not dance)

odoré *v* 踊れ [IMPERATIVE] (dance!) → **odorimásu** 踊ります

odoremásu, odoreru *v* 踊れます, 踊れる can dance

odori *n* 踊り dance, dancing

odorimásu, odoru *v* 踊ります, 踊る dances

odoróite *v* 驚いて → **odorokimásu** 驚きます

odorokashimásu, odorokásu *v* 驚かします, 驚かす surprises, scares, astonishes

odorokimásu, odoróku *v* 驚きます, 驚く is surprised, astonished

odoshi *n* 脅し threat

odoshimásu, odosu *v* 脅します, 脅す threatens

odotte *v* 踊って → **odorimásu** 踊ります

oé *v* 追え [IMPERATIVE] (chase it!) → **oimásu** 追います

óe *v* 負え [IMPERATIVE] (carry it (*on your back*)!) → **oimásu** 負います

ō´e *v* 覆え [IMPERATIVE] (cover it!) → **ōimásu** 覆います

oéba *v* 追えば (if one chases) → **oimásu** 追います

óeba *v* 負えば (if one carries) → **oimásu** 負います

ō´éba *v* 覆えば (if one covers) → **ōimásu** 覆います

oemásu, oeru *v* 終えます, 終える ends it, finishes, completes

oemásu, oeru *v* 追えます, 追える can chase, can pursue

oemásu, oeru *v* 負えます, 負える can carry on one's back

ōemásu, ōéru *v* 覆えます, 覆える can cover

ōen *n* 応援 help, assistance; cheering for; support: ~ **shimásu** 応援します helps, assists; cheers for; supports

ōen-dan *n* 応援団 cheering party

oeréba *v* 終えれば・追えれば (if one ends it; if one can chase) → **oemásu** 終えます; 追えます

oeréba *v* 負えれば (if one can carry) → **oemásu** 負えます

ōeréba *v* 覆えれば (if one can cover) → **ōemásu** 覆えます

oé ro *v* 終えろ [IMPERATIVE] (end it!) → **oemásu** 終えます

ōeru *n* OL, オーエル office lady

oeta *v* 終えた・追えた = **oemáshita** 終えました; 追えました (ended it; could chase)

oeta *v* 負えた = **oemáshita** 負えました (could carry)

ō´eta *v* 覆えた = **ōemáshita** 覆えました (could cover)

oete *v* 終えて・追えて・負えて → **oemásu** 終えます; 追えます; 負えます

ō´ete *v* 覆えて → **ōemásu** 覆えます

oetsu *n* 嗚咽 sobbing

ofisu *n* オフィス office

ōfuku *n* 往復 round trip: ~ **shimásu** 往復します goes and returns

ōfuku-kippu 往復切符 round-trip ticket:

ofukuro *n* おふくろ・お袋 (*familiar, usually male*) (= **okā´-san** お母さん・おかあさん) my mother; **ofukuro-san** お袋さん (*your/someone else's*) mother

ofureko (no) *adj* オフレコ(の) off the record

ofu-shiizun *n* オフシーズン off season (= **kansanki** 閑散期)

ogakuzu *n* おが屑 sawdust

ogamimásu, ogámu *v* 拝みます, 拝む worships, looks at with respect

ogánde *v* 拝んで → **ogamimásu** 拝みます

ōganikku (no) *adj* オーガニック(の) organic (= **yūki** 有機)

ogawa *n* 小川 brook, stream

ógi *n* オギ・荻 a reed

ōgi *n* 扇 a folding fan

oginái *n* 補い supplement

oginaimásu, ogináu *v* 補います, 補う completes; complements; makes good, makes up for

ōgon *n* 黄金 gold (= **kin** 金)

ogorimásu, ogoru *v* 驕ります, 驕る is extravagant

ogorimásu, ogoru *v* 奢ります, 奢る treats (*pays the bill*)

ogotte *v* おごって → **ogorimásu** おごります

ohako *n* おはこ・十八番 one's hobby; one's "thing", specialty, (*favorite*) trick

O-hayō (gozaimásu) *interj* おはよう (ございます) Good morning!

ōhei *n* 横柄 arrogance (= **gōman** 傲慢・ごうまん): ~ **na taido** 横柄な態度 insolence

Ohōtsuku-kai *n* オホーツク海 Sea of Okhotsk

oi *n* 甥 nephew

oi-go-san *n* 甥御さん (*your/someone else's*) nephew

oi-kko *n* 甥っ子 nephew (= **oi** 甥)

ói *interj* おい hey! (*mostly male, very* INFORMAL)

ō´i *adj* 多い many, numerous; lots

ō´ku *adv* 多く a lot of, many

oide *interj* おいで Come! (*training one's dog, etc.*)

oide (ni narimásu) *v* おいで(になります) = **irasshaimásu** いらっしゃいます [HONORIFIC] **1.** comes **2.** goes **3.** is, stays

oi-kakemásu, oi-kakéru *v* 追い掛けます, 追い掛ける chases

oi-koshimásu, oi-kósu *v* 追い越します, 追い越す (*overtakes and*) passes

oi-kaze *n* 追い風 tail wind

oi-koshi *n* 追い越し Passing: **oi-koshi kinshi** 追い越し禁止 No Passing: **oi-koshi shasen** 追い越し車線 passing line

oimásu, ou *v* 負います, 負う carries on one's back

oimásu, oiru *v* 老います, 老いる grows old

ōimásu, oou´, ōu´ *v* 覆います, 覆う covers, shields

ōin *n* 押韻 [BOOKISH] rhyme (= **in** 韻)

ōin *n* 押印 [BOOKISH] putting one's seal: ~ **shimásu** 押印します seals

oi ni *adv* おおいに・大いに very, greatly (= **hijō ni** 非常に, **totemo** とても)

óiru *n* オイル oil (*for car engine*)

oishii *adj* おいしい・美味しい tasty, nice, delicious, yummy (= **umai** うま[旨・美味]い)

oishisō *adj* おいしそう looks tasty/nice/delicious/yummy (= **umasō** うま[旨・美味]そう)

179

oisoreto *adj* おいおそれと [(*usually*) + NEGATIVE verb] easily, quickly

oita *v* 置いた = **okimáshita** 置きました (put) [**...-te óita** ...て置いた]

oitachi *n* 生い立ち (*one's*) personal history

oitára *v* 置いたら (if/when one puts) [**...-te óitara** ...て置いたら] → **okimásu** 置きます

oitári *v* 置いたり (sometimes putting) [**...-te óitari** ...て置いたり] → **okimásu** 置きます

oite *v* 置いて (puts) [**...-te óite** ...て置いて] → **okimásu** 置きます

oite おいて: **... ni oite** ... において [BOOKISH] = **... de** ...で (at/in)

oi-tsukimásu, oi-tsukú *v* 追い付きます, 追い付く (**... ni ...**に) catches up (*with*), overtakes

ōjii *n* OG, オージー (*abbreviation for the word "old girl"*) female graduate, alumna

ō-jimásu, ō-jiru *v* 応じます, 応じる responds (*to*), accedes (*to*), complies (*with*)

ōji (-sama) *n* 皇子(様) emperor's son

oji (-san) *n* おじ[叔父](さん) uncle (*younger brother of father or mother*) (= **oji-chan** おじ[叔父]ちゃん)

oji (-san) *n* おじ[伯父](さん) uncle (*older brother of father or mother*) (= **oji-chan** おじ[伯父]ちゃん)

oji (-san) *n* おじ[小父]さん (*not relative*) (gentle) man, (*middle-aged*) man (= **oji-chan** おじちゃん)

ō-jite *v* 応じて → **ō-jimásu** 応じます; **... ni ~** ...に応じて in accordance/ compliance with ...

ojoku *n* 汚辱 disgrace, shame, scandal

ōjo (-sama) *n* 皇女(様) emperor's daughter

ojō-san *n* お嬢さん a young lady; (*your/someone else's*) daughter; Miss

oka *n* 丘 hill

oka *n* 陸 dry land

okabu *n* お株 = **ohako** おはこ・十八番 (specialty, habit)

okage *n* おかげ・お蔭・お陰; **... no ~ de** ...のおかげ[お蔭・お陰]で thanks to ...

okage-sama (de) おかげさま(で) thanks to your solicitude; thank you (*I'm very well* or *it's going very nicely*)

ōkakumaku *n* 横隔膜 diaphragm

okáme *n* おかめ moon faced/ugly woman

okámi *n* 御上・お上 the authorities, the government

okámi *n* おかみ・女将 = **okami-san** おかみ[女将]さん landlady; married woman, (*your/someone else's*) wife (= **oku-san/sama** 奥さん/様)

ō´kami *n* オオカミ・狼 wolf

okanai *v* 置かない = **okimasén** 置きません (not put)

o-kara *n* オカラ bean-curd lees

ōkare sukunakare *adv* 多かれ少なかれ more or less

okaruto *n* オカルト occult: **okaruto-eiga** オカルト映画 occult film(s)

okasánai *v* 犯さない = **okasimasén** 犯しません・ (not violate)

okasánai *v* 侵さない = **okasimasén** 侵しません (not invade)

okasánai *v* 冒さない = **okasimasén** 冒しません (not brave/attack)

okashíi *adj* おかしい, **okáshi na (...)** おかしな(...) **1.** amusing, funny **2.** strange, peculiar, queer

okashimásu, okásu *v* 犯します, 犯す commits, perpetrates; violates

okashimásu, okásu *v* 侵します, 侵す encroaches upon, invades

okashimásu, okásu *v* 冒します, 冒す braves; attacks

ōkata *adv* おおかた・大方 **1.** for the most part **2.** probably

okazu *n* おかず main/side dish (*to go with the rice*)

oké *v* 置け [IMPERATIVE] (put it!) → **okimásu** 置きます

oke *n* 桶 tub, wooden bucket: **furo-oke** 風呂桶 bathtub: **kan-oke** 棺桶 coffin [INFORMAL] (= **hitsugi** 棺 [FORMAL])

ōkē *n* オーケー okay, ok

okéba *v* 置けば (if one puts) → **okimásu** 置きます

okemásu, okeru *v* 置けます, 置ける can put

okenai *v* 置けない = **okemasén** 置けま

せん (cannot put)

okeréba v 置ければ (if one can put) →
okemásu 置けます

ōkesutora n オーケストラ orchestra

oki n 沖 offshore, offing

　oki-ba n 置き場 a place (*to put something*)

　oki-miyage n 置き土産 keepsake,
　parting present/gift (= **senbetsu** 餞別)

　oki-mono n 置き物 ornament; bric-a-
　brac

　oki-tegami n 置き手紙 letter/note left
　behind

ō-kíi adj 大きい big, large; loud (= **ō'ki
na** 大きな)

ō'-kiku adv 大きく greatly, much(ly),
loudly; so as to be big/loud: **~ nái
(arimasén)** 大きくない (ありません)
small, modest

ō-ki (na) adj 大き (な) big, great

okimásu, oku v 置きます, 置く puts
(*aside*), places, sets, lays; **shite ~**
して置きます does for later, does for now (*for
the time being*)

okimásu, okíru v 起きます, 起きる
gets up; arises

okina n 翁 old man,

okínai v 起きない = **okimasén** 起きま
せん (not get up; not arise)

o-ki-ni-iri n お気に入り favorite;
bookmarks (*web browser*)

okiraremásu, okiraréru v 起きられま
す, 起きられる can get up

okíreba v 起きれば (if one gets up; if it
arises) → **okimásu** 起きます

okí ro v 起きろ [IMPERATIVE] (get up!)
→ **okimásu** 起きます

okíru v 起きる = **okimásu** 起きます
(gets up; arises)

ōkisa n 大きさ size (= **saizu** サイズ)

ókita v 起きた = **okimáshita** 起きまし
た (got up)

okite n 掟 law, rule, regulation: **~ o
mamorimásu/yaburimásu** 掟を守りま
す/破ります observes/breaks a rule

ókite v 起きて → **okimásu** 起きます

okiwasuréru v 置き忘れる forgets

okiyō' v 起きよう = **okimashō'** 起きま
しょう (let's get up!)

okkochimásu, okkochíru v 落っこち
ます, 落っこちる falls

okkū (na) adj 億劫 (な) troublesome,
bothersome

okō v 置こう = **okimashō'** 置きましょ
う (let's put it!)

ōkō (suru) adj 横行 (する) rampant

okonai n 行い act(ion), deed, conduct:
higoro no ~ 日ごろの行い daily
behavior

okonaimásu, okonau v 行います, 行
う acts, does, carries out, performs

okonatte v 行 (な) って →
okonaimásu 行 (な) います

okonawanai v 行 (な) わない = **oko-
naimásén** 行 (な) いません (not act)

okonomi-yaki n お好み焼き seasoned
pancake

okorí n 起こり origin, source,
beginning: **koto no ~ (wa)...** 事の起こ
り (は)... it happened because..., it
started like this...

okorí n おこり ague, the shakes

okorimásu, okóru v 起こります, 起こ
る happens, occurs, arises

okorimásu, okóru v 興ります, 興る
starts; prospers; rises

okorimásu, okóru v 怒ります, 怒る
gets mad/angry

okoshimásu, okósu v 起こします,
起こす raises; establishes; gets a
person up, rouses

okoshimásu, okósu v 興します, 興す
gives rise to, brings about

okotarimásu, okotaru v 怠ります, 怠
る neglects, shirks; is lazy about

okótta v 起こった = **okorimáshita** 起こ
りました (happened)

okótta v 怒った = **okorimáshita** 怒りま
した (got mad)

okótte v 起こって・怒って →
okorimásu 起こります・怒ります

oku v 置く = **okimásu** 置きます (put)

óku n 億 a hundred million: **oku-man
chōja** 億万長者 a billionaire

óku n 奥 the back or inside part

　óku-ba n 奥歯 back tooth

oku-... prefix 屋... house, roof

　oku-gai (no/de) adj, adv 屋外 (の/で)
　outdoor(s), outside

　oku-jō (no/de) adj, adv 屋上 (の/で)
　on the roof(top), rooftop floor

oku-nai (no/de) *adj, adv* 屋内(の/で) indoor(s), inside, interior(ly)

ō´ku 多く **1.** *n* a lot, for the most part **2.** *adv* mostly

okubi *n* おくび belch

okubyō´ *n* 臆病 cowardice: **okubyō´(na)** 臆病(な) cowardly, timid; **okubyō-monó** 臆病者 a coward (= **kowagari** 怖[恐]がり)

okuranai *v* 送らない = **okurimasén** 送りません (not send)

okure *n* 1. 後れ a lag: **~ o torimásu** 後れ を取ります falls behind, gets defeated

okure *v* 送れ [IMPERATIVE] (send it!) → **okurimásu** 送ります

o-kure *v* おくれ [HONORIFIC INFINITIVE of **kudasái** 下さい, *used as a command*] please give (*it to me*)

okuremásu, okureru *v* 遅れます, 遅れ る is late, gets delayed; lags, falls behind; runs late

okuremásu, okureru *v* 送れます, 送れ る can send; can spend (*time*)

okuremásu, okureru *v* 贈れます, 贈れ る can present/award

okurenai *v* 遅れない = **okuremasén** 遅れません (is not late)

okurenai *v* 送れない = **okuremasén** 送れません (cannot send)

okurete *v* 遅れて・送れて → **okuremásu** 遅れます・送れます

okurimásu, okuru *v* 送ります, 送る sends; sees a person off; spends (*time*)

okurimásu, okuru *v* 贈ります, 贈る presents, awards

okuri-mono *n* 贈り物 gift, present

okurō´ *v* 送ろう = **okurimashō** 送りま しょう (let's send it!)

óku-san/-sama *n* 奥さん/様 (*your/ someone else's*) wife; lady, Madam

okusoku *n* 憶測 guess

okutte *v* 送って・贈って → **okurimásu** 送ります・贈ります

ō-kyu *n* 応急 emergency

ōkyū-shochi *n* 応急処置 first aid (= **ōkyū-téate** 応急手当て)

ōkyū-sochi *n* 応急措置 emergency measure

ōkyū-téate *n* 応急手当て first aid (= **ōkyū-shochi** 応急処置)

okuyami *n* お悔やみ condolences

O-machidō-sama déshita *interj* お待 ちどうさまでした。Thank you for waiting. (*at restaurant, etc.*)

omae *pron* お前 (*mostly male; familiar or rude*) you

omake *n* おまけ extra, bonus, premium: **omake ni** おまけに to boot, in addition

o-mamori *n* お守り amulet, charm, good-luck piece

omaru *n* おまる bedpan; chamber-pot

O-matase (ita)shimashita *interj* お 待たせ(致)しました。Sorry to have made you wait.

omáwari (-san) *n* お巡り(さん)・おま わり(さん) policeman, (*police*) officer

ō-medama o kuimásu (kū) *v* 大目玉を 食います(食う) gets severely scolded, gets it in the neck

omedeta *n* おめでた blessed event (*pregnancy, childbirth, marriage, etc.*)

o-medetō (gozaimásu) *interj* おめで とう(ございます) congratulations: **akemáshite o-medetō (gozaimásu)** 明け ましておめでとう(ございます) Happy New Year!

omei *n* 汚名 disgrace

ōme ni mimásu (miru) *v* 大目に見ます (見る) overlooks (= **minogashimásu** 見逃します): **(dōka) ōme ni mitekudasai** (どうか)大目に見て下 さい Please give me a break.

o-mi- *prefix* おみ (*for a few words*) = **o-** お・御 [HONORIFIC]

o-mi-ki *n* 御神酒 saké offered to the gods (= **miki** 神酒)

o-mí-koshi *n* お神輿 portable shrine (= **mikoshi** 神輿)

o-mi-kuji *n* おみくじ fortune (*written*)

ō-mísoka *n* 大晦日 last day of year; New Year's eve

omo-... *prefix* 面... face

omo-naga (na/no) *adj* 面長(な/の) long-faced

...(na) omo-mochi *suffix, n* ...(な) 面持ち look on one's face: **fuan na/ kinchō no ~** 不安な/緊張の面持ち a worried/nervous look on one's face

omo-yatsure *n* 面やつれ drawn and haggard face (*due to worry and/or*

182

illness) (= **omo-yase** 面瘦せ)

omócha n おもちゃ・オモチャ・玩具 toy

omóe v 思え [IMPERATIVE] (think!) → **omoimásu** 思います

omóeba v 思えば = **omóya** 思や (if one thinks) → **omoimásu** 思います

omoemásu, omóeru v 思えます, 思える 1. can think 2. = **omowaremásu** 思われます (is thought)

omoi adj 重い heavy; grave, serious; important

omói n 思い thought, idea; feeling, mind, heart; desire, will

omoi-dashimásu, omoi-dásu v 思い 出します, 思い出す remembers, recalls

omoide n 思い出 memory (a recollection)

omoigakénai v 思いがけない unexpected, surprising

omoimásu, omóu v 思います, 思う thinks, feels

omomuki n 趣 1. taste, flavor 2. atmosphere, air 3. circumstance, contents 4. condition

omoya n 母屋 main building/house

omoi-yari n おもいやり consideration (being kind), solicitude

ómo (na) adj 主(な) principal, main: **ómo ni** 主に mainly

omo-ni n 重荷 burden (on one's mind)

omosa n 重さ weight

omoshi n 重し a weight (object)

omoshirói adj おもしろい・面白い interesting, pleasant, amusing, funny

omoté n 表 front (side), surface, outer side/surface

omote-dōri n 表通り main street

omote-mon n 表門 (front) gate

omote-muki (no/wa) adj, adv 表向き (の/は) ostensible (ostensibly), on the surface, official(ly)

omótta v 思った = **omoimáshita** 思い ました (thought)

omótte v 思って → **omoimásu** 思い ます

omóu v 思う = **omoimásu** 思います (thinks)

omowánai v 思わない = **omoimasén** 思いません (not think)

omowánu ... adj 思わぬ...; unexpected, unanticipated

omowaremásu, omowaréru v 思わ れます, 思われる is thought; seems, appears

omowasemásu, omowaséru v 思わせます, 思わせる reminds one of, makes one think of

omóya v 思や → **omóeba** 思えば

ōmu n オウム・鸚鵡 parrot

omunibasu n オムニバス omnibus: **omunibasu-eiga** オムニバス映画 omnibus film/movie

omu-ráisu n オムライス omelet wrapped around rice

omuretsu n オムレツ omelet

omútsu n おむつ diapers

on n 音 sound; pronunciation

on-kyō n 音響 sound: **onkyō-kōka** 音響効果 sound effect

on-pa n 音波 sound wave

on-ritsu n 音律 rhythm

on-ryō n 音量 sound volume: **~ o agete/sagete kudasai** 音量を上げて/下 げて下さい Please turn up/down the volume.

on-sa n 音叉 tuning fork

on-setsu n 音節 syllable

on-tei n 音程 musical interval

on-yomi n 音読み Chinese reading of kanji/Chinese character in Japanese

on- prefix 御 (for a few words) = **o-** お・御 [HONORIFIC]: **on-rei mōshiagemásu** 御礼申し上げます Thank you for ...

...on-chū n ...御中 [HONORIFIC] Messrs. (on envelope); Dear (letter)

on-sha n 御社 (letter) (your) good self, your esteemed institution/ organization

on-zōshi n 御曹司/御曹子 scion; son of a noble/distinguished family

ón n 恩, **go-ón** ご恩 obligation; kindness: **kono ~ wa isshō wasuremasen** この(ご)恩は一生忘れません I will never forget what you have done for me/your kindness.

on-gaeshi n 恩返し returning the favour/repaying the favour

on-jin n 恩人 benefactor: **inochi no ~**

命の恩人 person to whom one owes his/her life

ón ni kimásu, ón ni kiru v 恩に着ます, 恩に着る I appreciate it. I am deeply grateful.

ón ni kisemásu, ón ni kiseru v 恩に着せます, 恩に着せる emphasizes the favor one has done: **on-kisegamashii** 恩着せがましい condescending, patronizing

on-shi n 恩師 former teacher

ōnā n オーナー owner

onaji (...) adj 同じ (...) the same (...): **onaji yō´ (na)** 同じよう (な) alike, similar

o-naka n お腹 stomach: **~ ga sukimáshita** おなかがすきました is hungry; **~ no guai ga warúi** おなかの具合いが悪い has an upset stomach; **~ o kowashimásu** おなかを壊します develops stomach trouble

onanii n オナニー masturbation (= **jíi** 自慰)

onara n おなら flatulence, fart

ónbu shimásu (suru) v おんぶします (する) carries baby on back; rides on back

óndo n 温度 temperature; **ondo-kei** 温度計 thermometer

ondori n オンドリ・雄鶏 rooster

ōnetsu-byō n 黄熱病 (medical) yellow fever

óngaku n 音楽 music

ongak(u)-ka n 音楽家 musician

ongák(u)-kai n 音楽会 concert

oní n 鬼 1. demon, devil, ogre: [IDIOM] **~ ni kanabō** 鬼に金棒 A good condition makes the strong much stronger.; [IDIOM] **~ no me nimo namida** 鬼の目にも涙 Even the hardest heart will sometimes be moved to pity. 2. cruel person 3. **shigoto no ~** 仕事の鬼 a workaholic

oní-baba n 鬼婆 hag

oní-gokko n 鬼ごっこ tag (child game)

onkei n 恩恵 favor

onná n 女, **~ no hitó/katá** 女の人/方 woman, female; **~ no kyō´dai** 女のきょうだい sister(s) (= **shímai** 姉妹)

onna-gata n 女形, **oyáma** おやま・女形 female impersonator (in Kabuki)

onna-gokoro n 女心 woman's heart

onna-jotai n 女所帯 all female household

onna-kotoba n 女言葉 woman's language

onna-mono n 女物 women's wear

onná-no-ko n 女の子 girl (= **joshi** 女子)

onna-shújin n 女主人 hostess

onna-tárashi n 女たらし womanizer, Don Juan, Casanova, lady-killer, seducer

onna-yu n 女湯 women's (section of the) bath

óno n 斧 ax, hatchet

onóono adj 各々・おのおの each, respectively, severally: **onóono no** 各々の respective

onore n おのれ self [BOOKISH]

onozukara adv 自ずから automatically, spontaneously

onparēdo n オンパレード on parade, succession

onrain n オンライン online

onrain ōkushon n オンライン・オークション (= **netto ōkushon** ネット・オークション) online auction

onrain gēmu n オンラインゲーム online game (internet)

onrain shōsetsu n オンライン小説 online story

onrain tsūhan saito n オンライン通販サイト (= **onrain shoppu** オンラインショップ, **netto shoppu** ネットショップ) online shopping site

onryō n 怨霊 vengeful ghost/spirit

onsen n 温泉 hot spring; spa: **onsen-ryokō** 温泉旅行 hot spring trip: **onsen-ryōhō** 温泉療法 spa treatment: **onsen-ryokan** 温泉旅館 Japanese inn and hot-spring

onshin n 音信 contact, news: **~ futsū** 音信不通です is out of contact, lost touch with

onshitsu n 温室 greenhouse

onsui n 温水 warm water

onwa adj 温和 1. mild, moderate (climate) 2. gentle, quiet, calm and peaceful person

on za rokku n オンザロック on the rocks (whiskey, etc.)

oō ν 追おう = **oimashō´** 追いましょう (let's chase!)

oō´ ν 負おう = **oimashō´** 負いましょう (let's carry it!)

oou´, ōu´ ν 覆おう = **ōimashō´** 覆いましょう (let's cover it!)

opekku n オペック Organization of Petroleum Exporting Countries, OPEC

ópera n オペラ opera

óppai n おっぱい (= **(o-)chichí** (お) 乳 (*baby talk, slang*) breast; milk (= **chíbusa, nyūbō** 乳房)

ō´pun n オープン open: **ō´pun shimásu** オープンします (*a shop, an event*) opens
ō´pun na *adj* オープンな open, candid

ōra n オーラ aura: **ōra ga arimásu** オーラがあります has radiance

ōrai n 往来 traffic; communication; thoroughfare

ō´rai n オーライ "all right, OK", (*all clear, go ahead*)

ōraka (na) *adj* おおらか(な) generous, big-hearted, easygoing: **~ na seikaku** おおらかな性格 generous personality

oránai ν おらない = **orimasén** おりません (not stay)

oránai ν 折らない = **orimasén** 折りません (not break/fold/bend)

oránai ν 織らない = **orimasén** 織りません (not weave)

Oranda n オランダ Holland; (= **Oranda no** オランダの) Dutch
Oranda-go n オランダ語 Dutch (*language*)
Orandá-jin n オランダ人 a Dutch

ore *pron* おれ・俺 (*male, unrefined*) I/me

ore ν 折れ [IMPERATIVE] (break/fold/bend it!) → **orimásu** 折ります

óre ν 織れ [IMPERATIVE] (weave it!) → **orimásu** 織ります

óreba ν 居れば (if one be/stays) → **orimásu** 居ります

óreba ν 折れば (if one breaks it) → **orimásu** 折ります

óreba ν 織れば (if one weaves) → **orimásu** 織ります

oremásu, oréru ν 折れます, 折れる
1. it breaks; it folds **2.** can break/fold/bend it

oremásu, oréru ν 織れます, 織れる can weave it

orénai ν 折れない = **oremasén** 折れません (not break/fold; cannot break it)

orénai ν 織れない = **oremasén** 織れません (cannot weave it)

orénji n オレンジ orange
orenji-jú´sú n オレンジジュース orange juice/drink

oréreba ν 折れれば (if it breaks; if one can break it) → **oremásu** 折れます

oréreba ν 織れれば (if one can weave it) → **oremásu** 織れます

oresen-gurafu n 折れ線グラフ line graph

órete ν 折れて・織れて → **oremásu** 折れます・織れます

ori n おり・澱 dregs, sediment

orí n 檻 cage; jail

orí n 折 time, occasion

orientēringu n オリエンテーリング orienteering

orientēshon n オリエンテーション orientation

orígami n おりがみ・折り紙 paper-folding (art)

oríibu n オリーブ olive
oriibu-yu/-oiru オリーブ油/オイル olive oil

orimásu, óru ν 居ります, 居る [DEFERENTIAL/HUMBLE] is, stays (= **imásu** 居ます, **iru** 居る)

orimásu, óru ν 折ります, 折る breaks (*folds, bends*) it
ori-mé n 折り目 fold, crease, pleat

orimásu, óru ν 織ります, 織る weaves it
ori-mono n 織物 cloth, textile, fabric

orimásu, oríru ν トリます, トりる goes down

orimásu, oríru ν 降ります, 降りる gets down, gets off (*a ship/plane*), gets out (*of a car*)
ori-mono n おりもの vaginal discharge

orínai ν 下りない = **orimasén** 下りません (not go down)

orínai ν 降りない = **orimasén** 降りません (not get down)

oriraremásu, orirareéru ν 下り[降り] られます, 下り[降り]られる can get down

orirárereba v 下り[降り]られれば (if one can get down) → **oriraremásu** 下り[降り]られます

orirárete v 下り[降り]られて → **oriraremásu** 下りられます・降りられます

oríreba v 下りれば (if it go down) → **orimásu** 下ります

oríreba v 降りれば[下り]れば (if one gets down) → **orimásu** 降り[下り]ます

orí ro v 下りろ [IMPERATIVE] (get down!) → **orimásu** 下ります

órita v 下りた = **orimáshita** 下りました (went down)

órita v 降りた = **orimáshita** 降りました (got down)

ori-tatamimásu, ori-tatamu v 折り畳みます, 折り畳む folds up

oríte v 下りて・降りて → **orimásu** 下ります・降ります

oriyṓ v 降りよう = **orimashṓ** 降りましょう (let's get down)

orṓ v 折ろう = **orimashṓ** 折りましょう (let's break/fold/bend it!)

orṓ v 織ろう = **orimashṓ** 織りましょう (let's weave it!)

óroka adj 愚か [BOOKISH] foolish (= **baka na** 馬鹿な)

órora n オーロラ aurora

orosánai v 下ろさない = **oroshimasén** 下ろしません (not lower)

orosánai v 降ろさない = **oroshimasén** 降ろしません (not drop off)

oróse v 下ろせ [IMPERATIVE] (lower it!) → **oroshimásu** 下ろします

oroshí v おろし **1.** a grater (= **oroshí-gane** おろし金) **2.** (something) grated: **daikon-óroshi** 大根おろし grated radish

oroshimásu, orósu v 下ろします, 下ろす takes down, lowers; unloads; invests; **yokin o ~** 預金を下ろします withdraws (deposited money)

oroshimásu, orósu v 降ろします, 降ろす lets one off (a ship/plane), drops off (from a car), lets out (of a car)

oroshimásu, orósu v 堕ろします, 堕ろす aborts, has an abortion

óroshí (no/de) adj, adv 卸(の/で) wholesale

oroshi-uri n 卸し売り (selling)

wholesale: ~ shimásu 卸し売りします sells wholesale, wholesales

orosṓ v 下ろそう = **oroshimashṓ** 下ろしましょう (let's take it down/drop off!)

óru v 居る = **orimásu** 居ります (is, stays)

óru v 折る = **orimásu** 折ります (breaks (folds, bends) it)

óru v 織る = **orimásu** 織ります (weaves it)

ōrudo misu n オールドミス old maid, spinster

orugōru n オルゴール music box

ōru maitii adj オールマイティ almighty **1.** the ace of spades (card game) **2.** all-around (= **zennō** 全能)

ōru-naito adj オールナイト all-night (= **shūya** 終夜); all-night show (= **~ kōgyō** オールナイト興行); **~ eigyō** オールナイト営業 Open all night

ōryō n 横領 embezzlement

osaemásu, osáeru v 押さえます, 押さえる represses; covers; holds

osaemásu, osáeru v 抑えます, 抑える controls, restrains

Ōsaka n 大阪 Osaka
Ōsaka-Eki n 大阪駅 Osaka Station
Ōsaká-jin n 大阪人 an Osakan

osamarimásu, osamáru v 収まります, 収まる gets reaped (collected, brought in)

osamarimásu, osamáru v 納まります, 納まる is paid

osamarimásu, osamáru v 治まります, 治まる settles (down/in)

osamemásu, osaméru v 収め[納め]ます, 収め[納め]る reaps, harvests, collects; gets; finishes

osamemásu, osaméru v 納めます, 納める pays (tax, premium, etc.)

osamemásu, osaméru v 治める governs; pacifies

o-san n お産 childbirth (= **shussan** 出産)

osanái adj 幼い infant(ile), very young; childish, green (inexperienced)

osanai v 押さない = **oshimasén** 押しません (not push)

o-san shimásu (suru) v お産します (する) gives birth to (= **shussan**

186

shimásu (suru) 出産します（する））

osarai *n* おさらい [INFORMAL] review
(= **fukushū** 復習 [FORMAL]): **~ shimásu**
おさらいします reviews

osé *v* 押せ [IMPERATIVE] (push!) →
oshimásu 押します

oséba *v* 押せば (if one pushes) →
oshimásu 押します

o-sékkai *n* お節介 meddling: **~ o
yakimásu** お節介を焼きます meddles;
o-sékkai (na) お節介（な）meddlesome

osen *n* 汚染 [BOOKISH] contamination,
pollution

ōsen *n* 応戦 fighting back: **~ shimásu**
応戦します fights back

o-sewa-sama お世話様 (*thank you for*)
your help/attention

osháberi *n* おしゃべり chatter-box,
gossip

osháburi *n* おしゃぶり teething ring,
pacifier

o-sháre *n* おしゃれ・お洒落 dandy: **~
na hito** おしゃれな人 fancy dresser

oshi *n* おし・唖 a (deaf-)mute

oshibana *n* 押し花 pressed dried flower

o-shíbori *n* おしぼり damp hand-towel

oshie ro *v* 教えろ [IMPERATIVE]
(teach!) → **oshiemásu** 教えます

oshiego *n* 教え子 a student (*of a
teacher's*)

oshiemásu, oshieru *v* 教えます、教え
る teaches, shows, tells, informs

oshieta *v* 教えた = **oshiemáshita** 教え
ました (taught, told)

oshiete *v* 教えて → **oshiemásu** 教え
ます

oshieyō *v* 教えよう = **oshiemashō´** 教え
ましょう (let's teach!)

oshíi *adj* 惜しい regrettable; precious

ōshii *adj* 雄々しい manly, manful,
brave, strong (*not feminine or sissy*)

oshi-ire *n* 押し入れ (*traditional
Japanese*) closet, cupboard

o-shimai *n* おしまい the end (*baby
talk*) (= **owari** 終わり)

oshimásu, osu *v* 押します、押す *v*
pushes, presses (*on*)

oshíme *n* おしめ diapers

oshin *n* 往診 house call: **~ shimásu**
往診します makes a house call

o-shinko *n* おしんこ・お新香 radish
(etc.) pickles

oshiroi *n* おしろい・白粉 face powder

oshite *v* 押して → **oshimásu** 押し
ます

oshitsukémásu, oshitsukéru *v* 押し
付けます、押し付ける pushes, presses;
intrudes

oshiuri *n* 押し売り high-pressure
selling; a high-pressure salesman:
shinsetsu no ~ 親切の押し売り
unwelcome kindness, **~ shimásu** 押し
売りします pressures someone to buy

oshí-zushi *n* 押し鮨 sushi rice and
marinated fish pressed in squarish
molds (*Osaka style*)

ōshoku jinshu *n* 黄色人種 Mongoloid,
Asians

oshō (-san) *n* 和尚（さん）Buddhist priest

Ō´shū *n* 欧州 Europe (= **Yōróppa** ヨー
ロッパ）

osō *v* 押そう = **oshimashō´** 押しましょ
う (let's push!)

osoi *adj* 遅い late; slow

osóimásu, osou *v* 襲います、襲う
attacks, assaults; strikes, hits

osokare hayakare *adv* 遅かれ早かれ
sooner or later

osoku *adv* 遅く late; slow: **osóku-tomo**
遅くとも at the latest

o-sómatsu-sama *interj* お粗末さま
Please excuse the poor fare (*reply to
gochisō-sama* ごちそうさま)

osóraku *adv* おそらく・恐らく
probably, maybe, possibly

osoré *n* 恐れ fear

osóre-irimásu *v* 恐れ入ります
1. excuse me **2.** thank you

osoremásu, osoréru *v* 恐れます、恐
れる fears

osoroshíi *adj* 恐ろしい fearful,
dreadful, awful, terrible, horrible (=
kowái 怖い・恐い）

osoróshiku *adv* 恐ろしく terribly

osowarimásu, osowaru *v* 教わりま
す、教わる is taught, studies, learns

osowatte *v* 教わって →
osowarimásu 教わります

osshái *v* おっしゃい [IMPERATIVE] (say
it!) → **osshaimásu** おっしゃいます

187

osshaimásu, ossháru ν おっしゃい
ます, おっしゃる (*someone honored*)
says; is called

osshátta ν おっしゃった = **osshaimá-
shita** おっしゃいました (said)

osshátte ν おっしゃって →
osshaimásu おっしゃいます

osu ν 押す = **oshimásu** 押します

osú n 雄・オス male animal; **... no osú**
…の雄 a he-… (→ **o-ushi** 雄牛)

osui n 汚水 sewage

osui-dame n 汚水溜め cesspool

ōsuji n 大筋 outline

Ōsutorária n オーストラリア
Australia
Ōsutoráriá-jin n オーストラリア人
an Australian

Ōsutoria n オーストリア Austria
Ōsutoriá-jin n オーストリア人
an Austrian

o-suwari *interj* お座り Sit! (*training
one's dog*)

otafukukaze n おたふく風邪 mumps

o-tagai (no) *adj* お互い(の) mutual,
reciprocal: **o-tagai (ni)** お互い(に)
mutually, reciprocally

otamajakushi n オタマジャクシ
tadpole

o-taku n お宅 your house; you
o-taku no *pron* お宅の your, yours

ó-te *interj* お手 Give me your paw!
Shake hands! (*training one's dog*)

o-teage n お手上げ giving up

o-teárai n お手洗い washroom, toilet,
restroom

o-témae n お手前 prowess, skill, ability

o-tenba n お転婆 tomboy

o-ténto-sama n おてんとさま・お天
道さま the sun (= **táiyō** 太陽)

o-tétsudai (-san) n お手伝い(さん)
(*household*) helper, maid(-servant)

otó n 音 sound, noise: **~ ga shimásu**
音がします it makes a noise, there is
a noise

ōtō n 応答 reply, response, answer: **~
shimásu** 応答します replies, responds,
answers
shitsugi-ōtō n 質疑応答 questions and
answers

ōtóbai n オートバイ motorcycle

otokó n 男 = **no hitó/katá** 男の人/方
man, male, boy; **~ no kyō´dai** 男の兄弟
brother(s)

otoko-gokoro n 男心 man's heart

otoko-jotai n 男所帯 all male household

otoko-kotoba n 男言葉 man's
language

otoko-mono n 男物 menswear

otokó-no-ko n 男の子 boy (= **danshi**
男子)

otoko-tárashi n 男たらし seductress,
man-eater, a Cleopatra

otoko-yámome n 男やもめ widower

otoko-yu n 男湯 men's (*section of the*)
bath

ōtokuchū´ru n オートクチュール
haute couture, high fashion

o-tokui (-san) n お得意(さん) good
customer(s), regular customer(s)

otome n 乙女 **1.** (*young*) girl, lady
2. maiden, virgin: **urawakaki ~** うら若
き乙女 young maiden

o-tómo shimásu (suru) ν お伴します
(する) (*will*) accompany (you)

otona n 大人・おとな adult

otonashíi *adj* おとなしい gentle, well-
behaved

otonáshiku *adv* おとなしく gently

otori n おとり・囮 decoy; lure

otoroemásu, otoróéru ν 衰えます, 衰
える declines, fades, grows weak

otóru *adj* 劣る is inferior, worse, weak,
poor (= **ototta** 劣った)

otosánai ν 落とさない = **otoshimasén**
落としません (not drop it)

otóse ν 落とせ [IMPERATIVE] (drop it!)
→ **otoshimásu** 落とします

otóseba ν 落とせば (if one drops it)
→ **otoshimásu** 落とします

otoshi-dama n お年玉 money given as
a New Year's gift

otoshimásu, otósu ν 落とします, 落
とす drops; omits

otoshimono n 落とし物 lost, dropped
things

otoshi-támago n 落とし卵 poached
eggs (= **pōchido-eggu** ポーチドエッグ)

otóshite ν 落として → **otoshimásu**
落とします

otótó *n* 弟 younger brother: **otóto-san** 弟さん (*your/someone else's*) younger brother

otótói *n* おととい・一昨日 day before yesterday

otótoshi *n* おととし・一昨年 year before last

ótótsu *n* 凹凸 unevenness, bump (= **dekoboko** でこぼこ・凸凹)

O-tsukare-sama (déshita) *interj* お疲れ様(でした). You did good work (*today, at the end of a project, etc.*) (*One of the frequently used phrases as a parting expression after work, when leaving the office or greeting to the person who is leaving*), You must be weary (*tired, exhausted*). (→ **Go-kúrō-sama (deshita)**. ご苦労様(でした).

otsu (na) *adj* おつ[乙](な) chic, stylish

otta *v* 追った = **oimáshita** 追いました (chased)

otta *v* 負った = **oimáshita** 負いました (carried on back)

ótta *v* 織った = **orimáshita** 織りました (wove)

ótta *v* 折った = **orimáshita** 折りました (broke)

ótta *v* 居った = **orimáshita** 居りました (stayed)

ōtta *v* 覆った = **ōimáshita** 覆いました (covered)

otte *v* 追って・負って → **oimásu** 追います・負います

ótte *v* 織って・折って・居って → **orimásu** 織ります; 折ります; 居ります

ōtte *v* 覆って → **ōimásu** 覆います

otto *n* 夫 (*my*) husband

ototta *adj* 劣った is inferior, worse, weak, poor (= **otoru** 劣る)

ou *v* 追う = **oimásu** 追います (chases, pursues)

ou *v* 負う = **oimásu** 負います (carries on one's back)

ōu *v* 覆う = **ōimásu** 覆います (covers, shields)

o-ushi *n* 雄牛 bull, ox

o-úsu *n* お薄 light green tea (*tea-ceremony*) (= **usu-cha** 薄茶)

o-wakare *n* お別れ parting, farewell (= **wakaré** 別れ)

owanai *v* 追わない = **oimásen** 追いません (not chase)

owanai *v* 負わない = **oimásen** 負いません (not carry on back)

ōwanai *v* 覆わない = **ōimásen** 覆いません (not cover)

owaranai *v* 終わらない = **owari-masén** 終わりません (cannot end)

oware *v* 終われ [IMPERATIVE] (end it!) → **owarimásu** 終わります

owareba *v* 終われば (if (it) ends) → **owaremásu** 終われます

owaremásu, owareru *v* 終われます, 終われる can end it

owaremásu, owareru *v* 追われます, 追われる gets chased

owari *n* 終わり the end: ~ **no ...** 終わりの... the last, final; ~ **no nai** 終わりのない endless

owarimásu, owaru *v* 終わります, 終わる it ends; ends it

owarō´ *v* 終わろう = **owarimashō´** 終わりましょう (let's end it!)

owatta *v* 終わった = **owarimáshita** 終わりました (ended)

owatte *v* 終わって → **owarimásu** 終わります

oyá *n* 親 parent

oya-baka *n* 親ばか[馬鹿] doting parent(s)

oya-fukō *n* 親不幸 unfilial behavior, unfilial child

oya-go-san *n* 親御さん (*your/someone else's*) parent (= **goryōshin** ご両親)

oya-ji *n* 親父 (*familiar, usually male*) (= (**o-**)**tō´-san** お父さん・おとうさん) my father: **oyaji-san** 親父さん (*your/someone else's*) father

óya-ko *n* 親子 parent and child

oya-ko-dónburi/don *n* 親子丼 rice topped with chicken and onions cooked in beaten eggs *or* rice topped with salmon and salmon roe

oya-kōkō *n* 親孝行 filial piety (*honoring one's parents*)

oya-masari *n* 親勝り talent surpassing that of one's parent(s)

oya-moto *n* 親元 (*one's*) parent's home

oya-shirazu *n* 親知らず wisdom tooth

oya-yuzuri *n* 親譲り something like
constitution, character, property, etc.
which is inherited from one's parents

Oya *interj* おや Gee whiz! I say! How
(a)bout that!; **Oya mā!** おやまあ good
heavens

óyaoya *interj* おやおや Dear dear!,
Oh dear.

óyá-bun *n* 親分 boss, ringleader, chief

ōyake (no/ni) *adj, adv* 公(の/に)
public(ly), open(ly), official(ly)

óyama *n* おやま・女形 female impersonator (of **Kabuki**) (= **onna-gata** 女形)

ō´ya (-san) *n* 大家(さん) landlord

O-yasumi nasái *interj* おやすみなさい.
Good night.

o-yátsu *n* おやつ snacks, sweets (*for
mid-afternoon*)

oya-yubi *n* 親指 thumb

ōyō *n* 応用 application, putting to use:
~ shimásu 応用します applies it, puts
it to use

ōyō (na) *adj* 鷹揚(な) easygoing: ~ na
taido 鷹揚な態度 generous attitude

oyobanai *v* およばない = **oyobimasén**
およびません (not reach)

óyobi *prep* および and (*also*) (= **to** と)

oyobimásu, oyobu *v* およびます、お
よぶ reaches, extends to, equals

oyóge *v* 泳げ [IMPERATIVE] (swim!) →
oyogimásu 泳ぎます

oyogemásu, oyogéru *v* 泳げます、泳
げる can swim

oyógete *v* 泳げて → oyogemásu
泳げます

oyogí *n* 泳ぎ swimming

oyogimásu, oyógu *v* 泳ぎます、泳ぐ
swims

oyogō *n* 泳ごう = **oyogimashō´** 泳ぎま
しょう (let's swim!)

oyóida *v* 泳いだ = **oyogimáshita** 泳ぎ
ました (swam)

oyóide *v* 泳いで → oyogimásu 泳ぎ
ます

oyonda *v* およんだ = **oyobimáshita**
およびました (reached)

oyonde *v* およんで → oyobimásu
およびます

oyoso (no) *adj* およそ(の) about,
roughly

ōzáppa (na) *adj* おおざっぱ(な) rough

ōzéi *n* 大勢 large crowd, throng: **ōzéi
de** 大勢で in large numbers (= **takusan
(no)** たくさん(の))

ōzéi no *adj* 大勢の many

ō´-zeki *n* 大関 champion sumo wrestler

ozon *n* オゾン ozone: **ozon-sō** オゾン層
ozone layer

ō-zume *n* 大詰め ending: ~ o mukaemásu 大詰めを迎えます is/will be in
the final stage/phase

P

pachinko *n* パチンコ pinball (*machine*):
pachinko-ya パチンコ屋 pachinko parlor

pái *n* パイ pie

pái *n* パイ・ぱい・牌 a mahjong tile

paináppuru *n* パイナップル pineapple

páipu *n* パイプ pipe; cigarette holder

pairótto *n* パイロット pilot

pajama *n* パジャマ pajamas (= **nemaki**
寝巻き)

pākingu *n* パーキング parking (=
chūsha-jō 駐車場)

pakkēji *n* パッケージ package

...-paku *suffix* ...泊: **ip-paku** 一泊 one
night's lodging/stay → ...-haku ...泊

pāma *n* パーマ permanent wave

pán *n* パン bread: **kashi-pan** 菓子パン
sweet bun: **shoku-pan** 食パン loaf of
bread, pain de mie, sandwich loaf:
pan-kēki パンケーキ pancake

pan-kó *n* パン粉 1. bread crumbs
2. bread flour

pan-kúzu *n* パンくず (*bread*) crumbs

pán-ya *n* パン屋 1. bakeshop, bakery
2. baker

pánda *n* パンダ panda

pánfu (rétto) *n* パンフ(レット) pamphlet, brochure (= **shō-sasshi** 小冊子)

pánikku *n* パニック panic

panikuru *v* パニくる [INFORMAL] gets
panicky

panku n パンク puncture, blowout: **taiya ga ~ shimásu** タイヤがパンクします gets a flat tire

pánku n パンク punk: **panku rokku** パンクロック punk rock, punk music

pansuto n パンスト panty hose

pántaron n パンタロン (*women's*) slacks, pantaloons

pántii n パンティー underwear for ladies (*panties*)

pántsu n パンツ underwear (*underpants*); slacks, pants

papa n パパ (*baby talk*) daddy, dad (= **(o-)tō-chan** (お)父ちゃん)

parashūto n パラシュート parachute

Pári n パリ Paris

paripari (no) adj ぱりぱり (の) crisp; first-rate

pāsénto n パーセント percent

paso-kon n パソコン personal computer

pásu n パス pass(ing); **~ shimásu** パスします passes (*an exam*) (= **gōkaku shimásu** 合格します)

pasupō'to n パスポート passport

patá'n n パターン pattern

pā'tii n パーティー party: **hōmu-pātii** ホームパーティ house party

patokā n パトカー patrol/police car

pātonā n パートナー partner

patoron n パトロン patron

pāto(taimu) n パート（タイム）part-time work

pázuru n パズル puzzle: **jigusō-pazuru** ジグソーパズル jigsaw puzzle

pedaru n ペダル pedal: **jitensha no ~** 自転車のペダル bicycle pedal

pēji n ページ・頁 page

Pékin n ペキン・北京 Beijing, Peking

pén n ペン pen

...-pén suffix ...遍 = **...-hén** ...遍 (*counts times*)

pénchi n ペンチ pliers, pincers

péndanto n ペンダント pendant

penki n ペンキ paint; **(... ni) ~ o nuri-másu** (...に)ペンキを塗ります paints penki-ya n ペンキ屋 painter (*house-painter*)

pénshon n ペンション pension (*small hotel, lodge, inn, etc.*)

perapera adj, adv ぺらぺら・ペラペラ fluent(ly) (= **ryūchō** 流暢): **nihongo ga ~ desu** 日本語がぺらぺらです speaks Japanese fluently

péten n ペテン fraud (= **sagi** 詐欺, **ikasama** いかさま): **peten-shi** ペテン師 swindler (= **sagi-shi** 詐欺師, **ikasama-shi** いかさま師)

pétto n ペット pet: **~ o katte imásu** ペットを飼っています has a pet/pets

piano n ピアノ piano: **gurando-piano** グランドピアノ grand piano

píiman n ピーマン green bell pepper: **aka-piiman** 赤ピーマン red bell pepper

píinát(t)su n ピーナッ（ッ）ツ peanut(s)

pikápika (no) adj ピカピカ (の) flashing, glittering: **~ shimásu** ピカピカします flashes

píkunikku n ピクニック picnic

pín n ピン pin (*for hair*)

pínchi n ピンチ pinch (= **kiki** 危機): **~ ni ochiirimásu** ピンチに陥ります gets in a pinch

pínku adj ピンク pink: **pinku-iro** ピンク色 pink color (= **momo-iro** 桃色)

pinsétto n ピンセット tweezers (*originally came from a French word "pincette"*)

pin (to) adv ぴん（と）(*stretched*) taut: **~ to kimásu** ぴんと来ます hits home with one, comes home to one

pinto n ピント focus (= **shōten** 焦点): pin-boke ピンぼけ out-of-focus

piramíddo n ピラミッド pyramid

pisutoru n ピストル revolver, pistol

pittári adv ぴったり exactly, perfectly, closely; just right

píza n ピザ pizza

póchi, pótsu n ぽち, ぽつ a dot

pokétto n ポケット pocket

pomā'do n ポマード pomade, hair oil

ponbiki n ぽん引き a pimp

póndo n ポンド pound (*weight or money*)

pónpu n ポンプ pump

pónsu, ponzú n ポン酢 juice of bitter orange

poppukōn n ポップコーン popcorn

poppusu n ポップス pops, popular music

pori(-) *n, prefix* ポリ poly(ethylene); plastic

pori-búkuro *n* ポリ袋 (*plastic*) bag

póruno *n* ポルノ pornography; **poruno-éiga** ポルノ映画 a porno film

pósuto *n* ポスト mail box

pō´ta *n* ポーター porter

potá´ju *n* ポタージュ potage, thick Western soup

pótéto *n* ポテト potato

pótto *n* ポット pot

púragu *n* プラグ (*electric*) outlet, plug

puramómoderu *n* プラモデル plastic model

púran *n* プラン plan (= **keikaku** 計画, **kikaku** 企画): ~ **o tatemásu** プランを立てます makes a plan

puranetariúmu *n* プラネタリウム planetarium

purásuchíkku *n* プラスチック plastic(s)

puratto-hōmu *n* プラットホーム (*station*) platform

purehabu-jūtaku *n* プレハブ住宅 prefabricated house

purei-gáido *n* プレイガイド a "Play Guide" theater ticket agency

purézento *n* プレゼント present, gift

púrin *n* プリン a small custard; crème brûlée

purínta *n* プリンター printer

purinto *n* プリント printing, printout, printed matter (= **insatsú** 印刷)
purinto auto プリントアウト printing, printout (= **insatsú-butsu** 印刷物)

púro *n* プロ pro(-fessional)

purogurámā *n* プログラマー programmer

purogúramu *n* プログラム program

púropan *n* プロパン propane; **puropan-gásu** プロパンガス propane gas

puro-resu *n* プロレス professional wrestling

pū´ru *n* プール **1.** swimming pool **2.** motor pool, parking lot

pusshúhon *n* プッシュホン touch-tone telephone

R

...´-ra *suffix* ...ら and others (= **nado** など・等); all of

rabel *n* ラベル label

rábo *n* ラボ lab (= laboratory)

rágubii *n* ラグビー rugby

rai-... *prefix* 来... **1.** next **2.** coming
rái-getsu *n, adv* 来月 next month
rai-nen *n, adv* 来年 next year
rai-se *n* 来世 afterlife, next life
rai-shū *n, adv* 来週 next week
rai-hō *n* 来訪 [BOOKISH] a visit: **raihō-sha** 来訪者 a visitor
rai-kyaku *n* 来客 guest, caller, visitor, company

raibaru *n* ライバル rival

raifurú-jū *n* ライフル銃 rifle

ráimu *n* ライム lime (*fruit*)

raion *n* ライオン lion

ráisensu *n* ライセンス license, permit

ráisu *n* ライス rice (*served on plate*)

raitā *n* ライター **1.** lighter (*cigarette*) **2.** writer (*professional*)

ráiu *n* 雷雨 [BOOKISH] thunderstorm

rajié´tā *n* ラジエーター radiator (*car*)

rájio *n* ラジオ radio: **rájio-bangumi** ラジオ番組 radio program

rakétto *n* ラケット racket: **tenisu-raketto** テニスラケット tennis racket

rakkan *n* 楽観 optimism ~ **shimásu** 楽観します takes a favorable view (*of events, conditions, etc.*)
rakkan-teki (na) *adj* 楽観的(な) optimistic

rakú *adj* 楽 **1.** comfort (= **anraku** 安楽): **Dō´zo ~ ni shitekudasai** どうぞ楽にして下さい Please make yourself comfortable/at home.
rakú (na) *adj* 楽(な) **1.** comfortable; **2.** easy (= **kantan** 簡単, **yasashii** やさしい[易しい])

rakuda *n* ラクダ camel

rakudai *n* 落第 [BOOKISH] failure (*in a test*): ~ **shimásu** 落第します fails

rakuen *n* 楽園 paradise: **chijō no ~** 地上

の楽園 earthly paradise

rakugaki *n* 落書き scribbling; doodling

rakugo *n* 落語 (*traditional Japanese*) comic storytelling: **rakugo-ka** 落語家 a comic storyteller

rā´men *n* ラーメン Chinese noodles (*in broth*)

ramune *n* ラムネ lemon soda

rán *n* ラン・蘭 orchid

rán *n* 欄 column, field: **nyūryoku-ran** 入力欄 entry field

rán *n* 乱 disturbance; war

ranbō *n* 乱暴 violence, outrage

　ranbō (na) *adj* 乱暴(な) violent, wild, rough, disorderly

ránchi *n* ランチ **1.** lunch **2.** launch (*boat*)

　ranchi-sā´bisu *n* ランチサービス special lunch, a luncheon special

randóseru *n* ランドセル knapsack for elementary school children

ranma *n* らんま・欄間 transom window

ranningu *n* ランニング running

ránpu *n* ランプ **1.** lamp **2.** ramp

rappa *n* ラッパ trumpet, bugle

… rashíi *suffix, adj* …らしい (*seems*) like, apparent, seems to be

rashinban *n* 羅針盤 compass (*for directions*)

rasshu-áwā *n* ラッシュアワー rush hour

ratai (no) *adj* 裸体(の) nude (= **nūdo (no)** ヌード(の)): **ratai-ga** 裸体画 a nude (*picture*)

Raten-go *n* ラテン語 Latin (*language*)

réa *n* レア rare (*beef*)

rébā *n* レバー **1.** liver (*to eat*) **2.** lever

régyurā *n* レギュラー regular

rei *n* 礼 **1.** thanks, gift (= **o-rei** お礼) **2.** remuneration, reward, fee (= **sharei** 謝礼)

　rei-kin *n* 礼金 "thank-you money" (*to obtain rental*)

réi *n* 礼 **1.** greeting **2.** bow (= **o-jigi** お辞儀)

　rei-gí *n* 礼儀 courtesy, etiquette; **reigi-tadashíi** 礼儀正しい polite

　rei-hai *n* 礼拝 worship

réi *n* 零・0 zero

　réi-ji *n* 零時・0時 zero o'clock, twelve o'clock

réi *n* 例: **zenrei** 前例 precedent; **ichi-rei** 一例 example; **réi no …** 例の… the… in question, the said … ; the usual/customary …

　rei-gai *n* 例外 exception (*to the rule*)

reibō *n* 冷房 air conditioning

reinkō´to *n* レインコート raincoat

reisei (na) *adj* 冷静(な) calm, cool, composed

reishō *n* 冷笑 sneer, scoff (= **chōshō** 嘲笑)

reitō *n* 冷凍 freezing: **reitō-ko** 冷凍庫 freezer: **~ shimásu** 冷凍します freezes

　reitō-shokuhin *n* 冷凍食品 frozen food

reizō´ko *n* 冷蔵庫 refrigerator, icebox

réjā *n* レジャー leisure, recreation: **rejā-shisetsu** レジャー施設 leisure facilities: **rejā-yōhin** レジャー用品 leisure goods

réji *n* レジ cashier; checkout counter

rekishi *n* 歴史 history: **rekishi-teki (na)** 歴史的(な) historical

　rekishi-ka *n* 歴史家 historian

rékkā *n* レッカー, **rekkā´-sha** レッカー車 wrecker (*tow truck*)

rekō´do *n* レコード a record (*phonograph*)

rekurié´shon *n* レクリエーション recreation

rémon *n* レモン lemon: **remóntii** レモンティー tea with a slice of lemon

　remonē´do *n* レモネード lemonade

ren'ai *n* 恋愛 love: **ren'ai-kánkei** 恋愛関係 a love affair; **ren'ai-kékkon** 恋愛結婚 a love marriage

rénchi *n* レンチ wrench

renchū, renjū *n* 連中 crowd, clique

rénga *n* レンガ・煉瓦 brick

rengō *n* 連合 union, alliance, Allied: **rengō´-koku** 連合国 the Allies; **rengō´-gun** 連合軍 the Allied Forces

rénji *n* レンジ cooking stove, kitchen range; **denshi-rénji** 電子レンジ microwave oven

renkon *n* レンコン・蓮根 lotus root

renmei *n* 連盟 union, federation

rennyū *n* 練乳 condensed milk

renraku *n* 連絡 connection, liaison; relevance; **(… to) ~ shimásu** (…と)連絡します gets in touch (*with*), contacts renraku-saki *n* 連絡先 address of contact

renshū *n* 練習 training, practice, drill: ~ shimásu 練習します trains, practices

rentákā´ *n* レンタカー rental car

rentogen *n* レントゲン, rentogen-sen レントゲン線 X-ray: ~ o torimásu レントゲンを撮ります takes an X-ray

renzoku *n* 連続 continuity; series: ~ satsujin 連続殺人 serial murder

rénzu *n* レンズ lens; kontakuto-rénzu コンタクトレンズ contact lens

repó'to *n* レポート report (= hōkoku (-sho) 報告(書))

rē´sā *n* レーサー racing driver

resépushon *n* レセプション a reception

reshíito *n* レシート receipt

ressha *n* 列車 a train; ressha-jíko 列車事故 train accident/wreck

réssun *n* レッスン lesson

rē´su *n* レース **1.** lace: ~ no kāten レースのカーテン lace curtain **2.** race: rēsu-jō レース場 racetracks

resukyū-tai *n* レスキュー隊 rescue team (= kyūjo-tai 救助隊)

résuringu *n* レスリング wrestling

résutoran *n* レストラン restaurant: famirii-resutoran ファミリーレストラン family restaurant

rétasu *n* レタス lettuce

rétsu *n* 列 row, line; queue

retteru *n* レッテル label

rettō *n* 列島, ...-réttō ...列島 archipelago, chain of islands

rí *n* 利 advantage, profit, interest

ríbon *n* リボン ribbon: ribon-musubi リボン結び ribbon-tie

ríeki *n* 利益 benefit, advantage, profit

rihabiri *n* リハビリ rehabilitation: rihabiri-chiryō リハビリ治療 rehabilitation treatment

rihā´saru *n* リハーサル rehearsal

rihatsu *n* 理髪 [BOOKISH] haircut(ting): ~ shimásu 理髪します gets/gives a haircut

rihátsú-ten *n* 理髪店 barbershop

ríidā *n* リーダー leader

ríido shimásu (suru) *v* リードします (する) leads

ríka *n* 理科 science

ríkai *n* 理解 [BOOKISH] understanding, comprehension: ~ shimásu 理解します understands, comprehends

rikai-ryoku *n* 理解力 comprehension (ability)

rikon *n* 離婚 divorce; (... to) ~ shimásu (...と)離婚します gets divorced (from ...), divorces

rikō (na) *adj* 利口(な) clever, sharp, smart, intelligent: rikō ni *adv* 利口に cleverly

riku (chi) *n* 陸(地) land, dry land

rikúgun *n* 陸軍 army

rikutsu *n* 理屈 reason, argument: he-rikutsu へ理屈 quibble [IN NEGATIVE SENSE]

rimokon *n* リモコン remote control: terebi no ~ テレビのリモコン TV remote control

rín *n* スズ・鈴 a bell, a doorbell (= beru ベル)

suzu-mushi *n* スズムシ・鈴虫 bell cricket

ringo *n* リンゴ apple

rinji (no) *adj* 臨時(の) [BOOKISH] extraordinary, special, temporary: rinji-nyūsu 臨時ニュース irregular/special news: rinji-shūnyū 臨時収入 extra income

rínki-ōhen (ni) *adv* 臨機応変(に) depending on the time and situation, on a case-by-case basis, flexibly

rinneru *n* リンネル linen

rínri *n* 倫理 ethics: seimei-rinri 生命倫理 bioethics: kigyō-rinri 企業倫理 corporate ethics

rippa (na) *adj* 立派(な) splendid, admirable, excellent, great: rippa ni *adv* 立派に admirably, splendidly, well

rireki *n* 履歴 a history, a record, rireki-sho 履歴書 one's personal history, career summary

ririku *n* 離陸 [BOOKISH] take-off (plane); ~ shimásu 離陸します takes off

ríron *n* 理論 theory: sōtaisei-riron 相対性理論 theory of relativity

ríshi *n* 利子 interest (on money) (= risoku 利息)

risō *n* 理想 an ideal: risō-teki (na) 理想的(な) ideal

194

risoku *n* 利息 interest (*on money*) (= **rishi** 利子)

rísu *n* リス squirrel

rísuto *n* リスト list

rítsu *n* 率 **1.** rate, proportion; average **2.** a cut, a percentage

rittai *n* 立体 solid; 3-D: **rittai-kyō** 立体鏡 stereoscope: **rittai-chūshajō** 立体駐車場 multi-story parking garage

rittoru *n* リットル liter(s)

riyō *n* 利用 use, utilization: ~ **shimásu** 利用します utilizes, makes use of **riyō-sha** 利用者 user

riyū *n* 理由 reason, cause, grounds; ... **to iu ~ de ...** という理由で for the reason that ...

rizaya *n* 利ざや margin

rízumu *n* リズム rhythm

ro *n* 炉 furnace

... **ro (yo)** *interj* ...ろ(よ) [*eastern Japan*] = ... **yo** ...よ (IMPERATIVE of ...**i**-...い and ... **e**-...え verb stems)

rō-... *prefix* 老... old (*not young*) **rō-gan (no)** *adj* 老眼(の) presbyopic **rō-jin** *n* 老人 old person **rō-nen** *n* 老年 old age

rō *n* ろう・蝋 wax; beeswax (= **mitsurō** 蜜蝋)

róba *n* ロバ donkey

róbii *n* ロビー lobby

róddo *n* ロッド rod (*curtain, etc.*)

rōdō *n* 労働 labor: **rōdō-kúmiai** 労働組合 labor union; **rōdō´-sha** 労働者 worker, laborer

rōdo-shō´ *n* ロードショー road-show attraction, first-run movie

rōgoku *n* 牢獄 jail

rōhi *n* 浪費 [BOOKISH] extravagance (= **muda-zúkai** 無駄使い): ~ **shimásu** 浪費します wastes

róji *n* 路地 alley

rōka *n* 廊下 passage(way), corridor

rō´karu (na) *adj* ローカル(な) local

rokétto *n* ロケット rocket

rok-... *prefix* 六... ・6 six **rok-kái** *n* 六回 six times **rók-kai** *n* 六階 sixth floor, six stories **rók-ko** *n* 六個 six pieces (*small objects*)

rókkā *n* ロッカー locker

rókku *n* ロック rock, rock'n'roll (*music*)

rokú- *n* 六・6 six **roku-banme (no)** *adj* 六番目(の) sixth **rokú-dai** *n* 六台 six (*machines, vehicles*) **rokú-dó** *n* 六度 six times (= **rok-kái** 六回) **roku-do** 六度 six degrees **roku-jū** *n* 六十・60 sixty **roku-mai** *n* 六枚 six sheets (*flat things*) **roku-mán** *n* 六万・60,000 sixty thousand **rokú-mei** *n* 六名 six people (= **rokú-nin** 六人) **rokú-sai** *n* 六歳 six years old (= **muttsu** 六つ) **rokú-satsú** *n* 六冊 six copies (*books, magazines*) **roku-sén** *n* 六千・6,000 six thousand

rokuga *n* 録画 recording (*video*): ~ **shimásu** 録画します records (*video*)

Roku-gatsú *n* 六月・6月 June

rokuon *n* 録音 recording (*sound*): ~ **shimásu** 録音します records (*sound*)

rokuro *n* ろくろ potter's wheel

Rō´ma *n* ローマ Rome

rōma-ji *n* ローマ字 romanization, Latin letters

rómansu *n* ロマンス romance, love affair: **romansu-shōsetsu** ロマンス小説 romance novel

romen-densha *n* 路面電車 streetcar

rón *n* 論 argument, discussion; treatise; theory **ron-bun** *n* 論文 treatise; essay; **gakui rónbun** 学位論文 dissertation, thesis

Róndon *n* ロンドン London

rōnin *n* 浪人 **1.** an unemployed samurai **2.** a student between schools **3.** a man without a job

ron-jimásu, ron-jiru *v* 論じます, 論じる discusses, argues, debates

rónri *n* 論理 logic; **ronri-teki (na)** 論理的(な) logical

ronsō *n* 論争 controversy, dispute, argument, debate, discussion

rop-... *prefix* 六... ・6... six **rop-pai** *n* 六杯 six cupfuls **rop-pén** *n* 六遍 six times (= **rok-kái** 六回, **rokú-dó** 六度) **róp-pon** *n* 六本 six (*long objects*) **róp-pun** *n* 六分 six minutes

rop-pyakú n 六百 · 600 six hundred

rō´pu n ロープ rope

rō´rā n ローラー roller; **rōra sukē´to**
ローラースケート roller-skates/skating

rōru-pan n ロールパン roll: **batā-rō´ru**
バターロール (butter) roll

Rosanzérusu n ロサンゼルス Los
Angeles (= **Rosu** ロス)

rosen n 路線 (bus, train) route

Roshia n ロシア Russia; **Roshia-go**
ロシア語 Russian (language); **Roshiá-
jin** ロシア人 a Russian

rōsóku n ろうそく candle (= **kyan-doru**
キャンドル)

rō´suto n ロースト roast; **rōsuto bíifu/
chíkin** ローストビーフ/チキン roast
beef/chicken

rō´tarii n ロータリー traffic circle,
rotary

rō´to n ろうと・漏斗 [BOOKISH] funnel
(= **jō´go** じょうご)

...´-rui suffix ...類 kinds, (different)
species of ...

dō-rui n 同類 same kind

shin-rui n 親類 kindred, relative

shu-rui n 種類 kind, variety: **arayuru
~ (no)** あらゆる種類 (の) various kinds
(of)

jin-rui n 人類 humankind

honyū-rui n 哺乳類 mammal (class)

rui-... prefix 類... similar ...

rui-ji n 類似 resemblance, similarity;
analogy; **... ni/to ~ shimásu** ...に/と類
似します resembles, is similar to

rui-(gi)go n 類(義)語 synonym (=
dōgigo 同義語): **rui-(gi)go-jiten** 類(義)
語辞典 synonym dictionary, thesaurus

ruiseki n 累積 [BOOKISH] accumulation:
~ shimásu 累積します accumulates;
ruiseki-akaji 累積赤字 accumulated
deficit; **ruiseki-saimu** 累積債務
accumulating debts

rūmu-sā´bisu n ルームサービス room
service (at hotel, etc.)

rū´ru n ルール rule

rúsu (no) adj 留守 (の) absent, away
from home

rusu-ban n 留守番 (**o-rúsu-ban** お留守
番) someone to take care of the house
in one's absence

rusu-ban-denwa n 留守番電話
answering machine

ryaku (-go) n 略(語) abbreviation

ryakusánai v 略さない = **ryakushi-
masén** 略しません (not abbreviate)

ryakushimásu, ryakusú v 略します,
略す abbreviates, shortens; omits

ryo... prefix 旅... =

ryo-kaku n 旅客 = **ryokyaku** 旅客
(traveler, passenger)

ryo-kan n 旅館 inn (traditional)

ryo-ken n 旅券 passport (= **pasupōto**
パスポート)

ryo-kō n 旅行 travel, trip: **~ shimásu**
旅行します travels, makes a trip

ryo-kō-gaisha n 旅行会社 travel
agency

ryo-kō´-sha n 旅行者 traveler;
ryokō(sha)-yō kogítte 旅行(者)用小
切手 traveler's check (= **toraberázu-
chekku** トラベラーズチェック)

ryo-kyaku n 旅客 traveler, passenger

ryō´ n 猟 hunting (as sport): **~ o
shimásu** 猟をします hunts

ryō´-shi n 猟師 hunter (= **hantā** ハン
ター)

ryō´ n 漁 fishing (as sport): **~ o shimásu**
漁をします fishes

ryō´-shi n 漁師 fisherman

ryō´ n 寮 dormitory, boarding house:
gakusei-ryō 学生寮 student dormitory:
dokushin-ryō 独身寮 dormitory for
singles

ryō´ n 陵 mound, mausoleum

ryō´ n 領 territory

ryō´-chi n 領地 territory (= **ryō´do**
領土): **sen-ryō chi** 占領地 occupied
territory

ryō´-do n 領土 territory, domain:
ryōdo-ken 領土権 territorial rights:
ryōdo-funsō 領土紛争, **ryōdo-arasoi**
領土争い territorial dispute

ryō´ n 量 quantity, volume

ryō-... prefix 両 ... both

ryō-gawa n 両側 both sides

ryō-hō´ n, adv 両方 both

ryō-mén n 両面 both sides/directions:
ryōmen-kopii 両面コピー two-sided
copy

ryō´-shin n 両親 (both) parents

ryō-te *n* 両手 both hands

...-**ryō** *suffix* ...料 fee, charge: **nyūjō-ryō** 入場料 admission fee: **haikan-ryō** 拝観料 admission fee (*for temple, etc.*): **isha-ryō** 慰謝料 consolation money, palimony

ryōgae *n* 両替 money exchange/changing: ~ **shimásu** 両替します changes (*money*)

ryōgaé-ki *n* 両替機 money-changing machine, money-changer

ryō´ji *n* 領事 consul

ryōji-kan *n* 領事館 consulate

ryōkai shimásu (suru) *v* 了解します (する) consents, understands [FORMAL]

ryō´kin *n* 料金 fee, charge, fare, rate

ryō-kin-jo *n* 料金所 tollgate

ryōkō *n* 良好 good [BOOKISH]: **seiseki-ryōkō** 成績良好 good record/achievement (*at school, in office, etc.*): **gyōseki-ryōkō** 業績良好 good business performance

ryoku-cha *n* 緑茶 green tea

ryō´ri *n* 料理 cooking: ~ **(o) shimásu** 料理(を)します cooks/prepares it

ryōri-nin *n* 料理人 cook

ryōri-ya *n* 料理屋 a restaurant (= **ryōri-ten** 料理店, **kappō** 割烹, **resutoran** レストラン)

ryōshiki *n* 良識 good/common sense

ryō´shin *n* 良心 conscience; **ryōshin-teki (na)** 良心的(な) conscientious:

~ **no kashaku** 良心の呵責 remorse of conscience

ryōshū-sho *n* 領収書 receipt (= **reshíito** レシート)

ryū´ *n* 竜・龍 dragon

ryūchi *n* 留置 custody: **ryūchi-jō** 留置場 detention house: ~ **shimásu** 留置します keeps someone in custody, locks up

ryū´chō (na) *adj* 流暢(な) [BOOKISH] fluent (= **perapera** ぺらぺら・ペラペラ [INFORMAL])

ryūgaku *n* 留学 studying abroad: ~ **shimásu** 留学します studies abroad

ryūgaku-sei *n* 留学生 foreign student(s)

ryúkku, ryukkusákku *n* リュック, リュックサック knapsack

ryūkō *n* 流行 popularity, vogue, fashion, trend: ~ **shimásu** 流行します becomes popular, becomes fashionable

ryūkō (no) *adj* 流行(の) fashionable

Ryūkyū´ *n* 琉球 the Ryukyu (*Okinawa, etc.*): **Ryūkyū-rettō** 琉球列島, **Ryōkyū-shotō** 琉球諸島 Ryukyu Islands

ryūtsū *n* 流通 circulation, distribution: **ryūtsū-sentā** 流通センター distribution center: **ryūtsū-kosuto** 流通コスト distribution cost: ~ **shimásu** 流通します circulates

ryū´zan *n* 流産 miscarriage: ~ **shimásu** 流産します miscarries

S

sa *n* 差 difference, discrepancy (= **sai** 差異・差違, **chigai** 違い)

...-sa *suffix* ...さ ...ness (*abstract noun formed from an adjective*)

sā´ *interj* さあ well; come on; let me see

saba *n* サバ・鯖 mackerel

sābā *n* サーバー (*computer*) server

sabaku *n* 砂漠 desert

sábetsu *n* 差別 discrimination: ~ **shimásu** 差別します discriminates

jinshu-sabetsu *n* 人種差別 racial discrimination

sabetsu-yōgo *n* 差別用語 discriminatory words

sabi *n* さび・サビ・錆 rust

sabimásu, sabíru *v* 錆びます, 錆びる it rusts

sabínai *adj* 錆びない rustproof

sabishíi *adj* 寂しい・淋しい lonely: **anata ni aenakute (totemo) ~ desu.** あなたに会えなくて(とても)さびしいです I miss you so much.

sā´bisu *n* サービス 1. service: **sābisú-ryō** サービス料 service charge, cover charge: **sābisu-seishin** サービス精神 spirit of good service 2. free (*as part of the service*): **sābisu-zangyō** サービス残業 unpaid overtime 3. service (*games*) (= **sābu** サーブ)

sā´bisu-eria *n* サービスエリア

1. service area (*tennis court, etc.*)
2. coverage **3.** highway service area

sábite ν 錆びて → **sabimásu** 錆びます

saborimásu, sabóru ν サボります、サボる loafs, skives (*on the job*); cuts class, plays hookey, stays away

saboten n サボテン cactus

sabótte ν サボって → **saborimásu** サボります

sābu n サーブ serve (*games*) (= **sābisu** サービス)

sáchi raito n サーチライト searchlight

sadamarimásu, sadamáru ν 定まります、定まる is settled, fixed

sadamemásu, sadaméru ν 定めます、定める settles it, fixes it

sadisuto n サディスト sadist

sadizumu n サディズム sadism

sádo n サド **1.** sadist **2.** sadism

sádō n 茶道 tea ceremony

sádō n 作動 [BOOKISH] operation (*of machine*): ~ **shimásu** 作動します operates, works

sāfā n サーファー surfer, surfrider

safaia n サファイア sapphire

sāfin n サーフィン surfing, surfriding

sagaku n 差額 the difference (*in price*), the balance

sagan n 砂岩 sandstone

sagan n 左岸 left bank

sagarimásu, sagáru ν 下がります、下がる it hangs down; goes down

sagashimásu, sagasu ν 探します、探す looks/hunts for something/someone one wants: **shoku-sagashi** 職探し looking/hunting for a job: **takara-sagashi** 宝探し looking/hunting for treasure: **shakuya-sagashi** 借家探し looking/hunting for a house for rent

sagashimásu, sagasu ν 捜します、捜す searches for a missing person/thing (= **sōsaku** 捜索)

sagashite ν 探して・捜して → **sagashimásu** 探します・捜します

sagátte ν 下がって → **sagarimásu** 下がります

sagemásu, sagéru ν さげます・下げます、さげる・下げる hangs it, lowers it, brings it down, clears from the table

sagemásu, sagéru ν 提げます、提げる carries (*dangling from hand*)

sagé ro ν 下げろ [IMPERATIVE] (lower it!, bring it down!, clear from the table!) → **sagemásu** 下げます

ságete ν 下げて・提げて → **sagemásu** 下げます・提げます

sagi n サギ・鷺 heron

sági n 詐欺・サギ fraud: **sagi-shi** 詐欺師 a fraud

sagurimásu, saguru ν 探ります、探る gropes

sagútte ν 探って → **sagurimásu** 探ります

ságyō n 作業 **1.** work (*commonly physical labor*) 農作業 agricultural work: **sagyō-fuku** 作業服 work clothes: **sagyō-in** 作業員 laborer **2.** operations: **sagyō-jikan** 作業時間 working hours: **sagyō-kōtei** 作業工程 working process

sáhō n 作法 manners, etiquette: **gyōgi-sahō** 行儀作法 manners and behaviors

sai n 菜 (**o-sai** お菜) side dish (*to go with the rice*) (= **okazu** おかず、**fuku-shoku(-butsu)** 副食(物))

sái n 妻 (*my*) wife: **ryōsai-kenbo** 良妻賢母 a good wife and wise mother: **gusai** 愚妻 [HUMBLE] a dumb wife **sai-shi** 妻子 wife and child(ren)

sái n 差異・差違 [BOOKISH] difference (= **chigai** 違い、**sa** 差)

sái n 才 talent, ability: **ta-sai na** 多才な multi-talented

…-sai *suffix* …歳・才 years of age: **nijús-sai** 二十歳[才] = **hátachi** 二十歳・はたち twenty years old, 20; **sánjús-sai** 三十歳[才] = **sánjū** 三十 thirty years old, 30

(…-)sái n (…)際 time, occasion: **kono-sai** この際 on this occasion: **kinkyū no ~** 緊急の際 in case of emergency

sái-shite *conj* 際して: **… ni ~** …に際して on the occasion of, at the time of, when, in case of

sai- *… prefix* 再… re- (*doing*) **sai-gen** n 再現 reappearance: ~ **shimásu** 再現します reappears

sai-hakkō n 再発行 reissue: ~ **shimásu** 再発行します reissues

sai-hōsō n 再放送 rebroadcasting: ~

shimásu 再放送します rebroadcasts
sai-kai *n* 再開 resuming, restarting: ~
shimásu 再開します resumes, restarts
sai-kai *n* 再会 meeting again: ~
shimásu 再会します meets again
sai-kákunin *n* 再確認 reconfirmation:
~ **shimásu** 再確認します reconfirms
sai-kentō *n* 再検討 review: ~ **shimásu**
再検討します reviews
sai-kō *n* 再考 reconsideration: ~
shimásu 再考します reconsiders
sai-kon *n* 再婚 remarriage: ~ **shimásu**
再婚します marries again
sai-nyúʻkoku *n* 再入国 reentry (*into
the country*): **sai-nyūkoku-kyokashō**
再入国許可証 reentry permission
sai-sei *n* 再生 reproduction, playback:
saisei-botan 再生ボタン play button:
saisei-shi 再生紙 recycled paper: ~
shimásu 再生します reproduces, plays
sai-shiken *n* 再試験 makeup exam
(= **tsuishi (-ken)** 追試(験))
sai-… *prefix* 最…the most
sai-ai (no) *adj* 最愛(の) one's beloved:
~ **no tsuma** 最愛の妻 one's dear wife
sai-aku (no) *adj* 最悪(の) the worst: **~ no
jitai** 最悪の事態 worst-case scenario
sái-chū *n* 最中 midst (= **chū**… 中. . .):
shokuji no ~ 食事の最中 while eating
sai-dai (no) *adj* 最大(の) the largest,
the most, the greatest: ~ **no buki** 最大
の武器 the strongest weapon: **saidai-
kōyakusū** 最大公約数 the greatest
common divisor (GCD)
sai-dai-gén (no) *adj* 最大限(の)
maximal, maximum, utmost: **~ no chūi
o haraimásu** 最大限の注意を払います
pays the utmost attention
sái-go (no) *adj* 最後(の) last, final:
~ no bansan 最後の晩餐 Last Supper:
saigo-tsūchō 最後通牒 ultimatum (=
saigo-tsūkoku 最後通告)
sai-jō (no) *adj* 最上(の) best, highest,
topmost: **saijō-kai** 最上階 the top floor:
saijō-i 最上位 top-level (*position,
rank, etc.*)
sai-kai *n* 最下位 last place (*position,
rank, etc.*)
sai-kō (no) *adj* 最高(の) the highest,
the best, tops; maximal, maximum,

awesome: **~ no kibun** 最高の気分 great
feeling, wonderful feeling: **shijō-saikō-
kiroku** 史上最高記録 all-time high
record
sai-ryō (no) *adj* 最良(の) the best: **sai-
ryō no saku** 最良の策 the best policy
sai-shin (no) *adj* 最新(の) newest,
up-to-date
sai-sho *adv* 最初 the very beginning,
the outset (= **hajime** 初め): **~ no** 最初
の…the first …
sai-shō (no) *adj* 最小(の) smallest:
saishō-gén (-do) 最小限(度) the
minimum (degree)
sai-shō (no) *adj* 最少(の) least,
minimal, minimum: **saishō-nenrei**
最少年齢 minimum age
sai-shū (no) *adj* 最終(の) final, the
very end (*last*): **saishū-ban** 最終版
final version: **~ densha** 最終電車 the
last train (= **shūden** 終電)
sai-tei (no) *adj* 最低(の) lowest, worst,
bottom(most); minimum: **saitei-gen(do)**
最低限(度) the minimum (degree),
lowest limit: **saitei-chingin** 最低賃金
the minimum wage
sai-zen *n* 最善 the best; one's best/
utmost (= **besuto** ベスト): **~ o tsukushimásu** 最善を尽くします I'll give it
my best shot.
saibai *n* 栽培 cultivation: ~ **shimásu**
栽培します cultivates
sáiban *n* 裁判 trial: ~ **shimásu** 裁判し
ます judges
saibán-kan *n* 裁判官 judge
saiban-shó *n* 裁判所 court
sabun *n* 差分 difference; **sabun-hō**
差分法 finite difference method:
sabun-hōteishiki 差分方程式
difference equation
sáidā *n* サイダー (*fizzy lemon*) soda
(*originally came from "cider"*) (=
tansan-inryō 炭酸飲料): soda water
(= **tansan-sui** 炭酸水, **sōdā-sui** ソーダ
一水)
saidan *n* 祭壇 altar
saidan *n* 裁断 **1.** judgment: **~ o
kudashimásu** 裁断を下します passes
judgment **2.** cutting (*paper, cloth, etc.*):
~ shimásu 裁断します cuts out

saido-burḗki *n* サイドブレーキ handbrake

saido-raito *n* サイドライト side light

sai-en *n* 菜園 vegetable garden

sáiensu *n* サイエンス science (= **kagaku** 科学)

saifu *n* 財布 (**o-saifu** お財布), purse, wallet

saigai *n* 災害 disaster: **shizen-saigai** 自然災害 natural disaster

sai-getsu *n* 歳月 years, time

saigi *n* 祭儀 rituals

saigishin *n* 猜疑心 suspicion: ~ **ga tsuyoi** 猜疑心が強い is very suspicious

saihō *n* 裁縫 sewing: **saihō-dōgu** 裁縫道具 sewing set

saijitsu *n* 祭日 → **shukujitsu** 祝日

saiken *n* 債券 bond (*debenture*): **saiken-shijō** 債券市場 bond market

saikin *n* 細菌 germ: **saikin-gaku** 細菌学 bacteriology

saikin *adv* 最近 recently, lately: **saikin no** 最近の recent

saikóro *n* さいころ・サイコロ dice, a die (= **sai** さい・さ・賽): ~ **o furimásu** サイ(コロ)を振ります throws a dice

saikú *n* 細工 work(manship), handiwork (= **te-záiku** 手細工), ware(s): ~ **shimásu** 細工します uses tricks

saikuringu *n* サイクリング cycling (*by bicycle*)

saikuru *n* サイクル cycle (= **shūki** 周期)

saikutsu *n* 採掘 mining, digging: ~ **shimásu** 採掘します mines

saimin *n* 催眠 hypnogenesis, hypnosis: **saimin-jutsu** 催眠術 hypnotism

saimu *n* 債務 [BOOKISH] debt: ~ **o oimásu** 債務を負います has debts

sáin *n* サイン **1.** signature (= **shomei** 署名) **2.** autograph **3.** sign (= **aizu** 合図, **angō** 暗号, **kigō** 記号)

sainán *n* 災難 calamity, disaster: **sainan-yoke** 災難除け charm against evil; ~ **ni aimásu** 災難に遭います has a disaster

sáinō *n* 才能 talent, ability (= **nō** 能, **nōryoku** 能力)

sainyū *n* 歳入 annual revenue (*of government, local public organization, etc.*)

sáiren *n* サイレン siren (*sound*): ~ **o narashimásu** サイレンを鳴らします sounds a siren

sairen-sā *n* サイレンサー silencer (*gun*)

saisan *n* 採算 profit: ~ **ga toremásu** 採算が取れます pays, is profitable

saisan *adv* 再三 [BOOKISH] many times, repeatedly (= **nando mo** 何度も): ~ **itte imásu** 再三言っています has told over and over

saisén *n* さい銭・賽銭 (**o-saisen** お賽銭) money offering (*at a shrine*); **saisén-bako** 賽銭箱 offering box

saishin (no) *adj* 細心(の) careful: ~ **no chūi** 細心の注意 close attention

saishokú-shugi-sha *n* 菜食主義者 vegetarian (= **bejitarian** ベジタリアン): **kanzen-saishoku-shugisha** 完全菜食主義者 vegan

saishū *n* 採集 collection, picking and gathering (*as specimen, data, etc.*) (= **korekushon** コレクション): ~ **shimásu** 採集します collects, picks and gathers; **konchū-saishū** 昆虫採集 insect collecting

saisoku *n* 催促 reminding someone, urging (= **tokusoku** 督促): ~ **shimásu** 催促します; **saisoku-jō** 催促状 a reminder; reminds, urges

saita *v* 咲いた = **sakimáshita** 咲きました (bloomed)

saíta *v* 裂いた = **sakimáshita** 裂きました (split it)

saite *v* 咲いて → **sakimásu** 咲きます

saíte *v* 裂いて → **sakimásu** 裂きます

saiten *n* 祭典 **1.** festival **2.** extravaganza

saiten *n* 採点 rating, grading, marking: ~ **shimásu** 採点します grades, marks

saiwai *n* 幸い **1.** *n* happiness (= **kōfuku** 幸福, **shiawase** 幸せ・しあわせ): **fukō-chū no** ~ 不幸中の幸い is lucky it wasn't worse **2.** *adv* fortunately

saiyō *n* 採用 employment, adoption: ~ **shimásu** 採用します employs, adopts

sáizu *n* サイズ size (= **ōkisa** 大きさ)

sájí *n* さじ・サジ・匙 spoon (= **supūn** スプーン)

saji-kagen *n* さじ[匙]加減 **1.** prescription **2.** allowance (= **te-kagen** 手加減)

3. consideration (= **hairyo** 配慮)

saji o nagemásu (nageru) v 匙を投げます（投げる）gives up (*not to literally mean, "throw a spoon"*)

saká n 坂 hill, slope: **saka-michi** 坂道 sloping road

saka-... *prefix* 酒... *drinking*

saka-bā n 酒場 bar/pub (*for drinking*) (= **izakaya** 居酒屋, **bā** バー, **pabu** パブ)

saka-ya n 酒屋 liquor shop

saka-mori n 酒盛(り) drinking party (= **enkai** 宴会)

sakaemásu, sakáeru v 栄えます, 栄える thrives, flourishes, prospers

sakái n 境 boundary, border: **sakai-me** 境目 boundary line

sakan (na) *adj* 盛ん（な) flourishing, prosperous; splendid, vigorous, lively

sakana n 魚 (**o-sakana**お魚) fish

sakáná-tsuri n 魚釣り fishing (*as sport*)

sakana-ya n 魚屋 fish dealer/market

sakana n 肴 (**o-sakana** お肴) **1.** appetizers to go with drinks (= (**o-)tsumami** おつまみ) **2.** interesting story to add to the fun with drinks

sakanai v 咲かない = **sakimasén** 咲きません (not bloom)

sakánai v 裂かない = **sakimasén** 裂きません (not split)

sakanoborimásu, sakanobóru v 遡り[溯り]ます, 遡る[溯る]: ... ni ~ ...に遡り[溯り]ます goes against (*the stream*), goes upstream; goes back (*in time*) to

sakaraimásu, sakaráu v 逆らいます, 逆らう: ... ni ~ ...に逆らいます acts contrary to, defies, opposes, contradicts

sakari n 盛り prime: ~ **no tsuita neko** 盛りのついた猫 cat in heat

sakari-ba n 盛り場 downtown area (= **hanka-gai** 繁華街)

sakasa(ma) (no/ni) *adj, adv* 逆さ（ま）(の/に) upside down

sā´kasu n サーカス circus

sakazukí n 杯 saké cup (= **choko** ちょこ (**o-choko** おちょこ))

sake n 酒 (**o-sake** お酒) **1.** saké (*Japanese rice wine*) **2.** alcoholic drinks

sáke n サケ・鮭 salmon (= **sháke** シャケ・鮭)

sakéba v 咲けば (if it blooms) → **sakimásu** 咲きます

sákeba v 裂けば (if one splits/tears it) → **sakimásu** 裂きます

sakebimásu, sakébu v 叫びます, 叫ぶ cries out, shouts

sakemásu, sakéru v 避けます, 避ける avoids

sakemásu, sakéru v 裂けます, 裂ける **1.** it splits, it tears **2.** can split/tear it

sakénai v 避けない = **sakemasén** 避けません (not avoid)

sakénai v 裂けない = **sakemasén** 裂けません (not split; cannot split/tear it)

sakénda v 叫んだ = **sakebimáshita** 叫びました (shouted)

sakénde v 叫んで → **sakebimásu** 叫びます

sakeraremásu, sakeraréru v 避けられます, 避けられる **1.** is avoided **2.** can avoid

sáketa v 避けた = **sakemáshita** 避けました (avoided)

sáketa v 裂けた = **sakemáshita** 裂けました (it tore)

sákete v 避けて・裂けて → **sakemásu** 避けます・裂けます

sakeyō´ v 避けよう = **sakemashō´** 避けましょう (let's avoid it!)

saki n, adv 先 (**o-saki** お先) **1.** front; future; ahead; first (*ahead of others*); **kono** ~ この先 ahead of here; → **o-saki ni** お先に **2.** point, tip **3.** address, destination

saki-gake n 先駆け pioneer, forerunner, lead (= **senku-sha** 先駆者, **paionia** パイオニア)

saki-iki, sakiyuki n 先行き prospect, future, outlook: ~ **wa akarui desu** 先行きは明るいです has a bright future

saki-hodo 先程 [BOOKISH] a little while ago (= **sakki** さっき)

sakimásu, saku v 咲きます, 咲く blooms, blossoms

sakimásu, sáku v 裂きます, 裂く splits it; tears it

sakin n 砂金 gold dust

sákka n 作家 writer (*novelist, etc.*): **joryū-sakka** 女流作家 a woman writer

sákkā n サッカー soccer: **sakkā-senshu**

サッカー選手 soccer player (*professional*): **sakkā-bōru** サッカーボール soccer ball

sakkaku *n* 錯覚 illusion: **me no ~** 目の錯覚 optical illusion

sákki *adv* さっき [INFORMAL] a little while ago (= **saki-hodo** 先程 [FORMAL])

sakkin *n* 殺菌 sterilization (= **mekkin** 滅菌): **sakkin-kōka** 殺菌効果 antiseptic effect: **sakkin-zai** 殺菌剤 germicide

sákku *n* サック **1.** sack, case **2.** → **kondō´mu** コンドーム

sakkusu *n* サックス saxophone (= **sakusofōn** サクソフォーン)

sakkyoku *n* 作曲 music composition: ~ **shimásu** 作曲します writes music **sakkyoku-ka** 作曲家 a musical composer

sakō´ ν 裂こう = **sakimashō´** 裂きましょう (let's split/tear it!)

sakoku *n* 鎖国 national isolation

sakotsu *n* 鎖骨 collarbone

saku ν 咲く = **sakimás̲u** 咲きます (blooms)

sáku ν 裂く = **sakimás̲u** 裂きます (splits/tears it)

saku *n* 柵 fence

saku-…, saki-… *prefix* 昨… last

sakú-ban *n, adv* 昨晩 [BOOKISH] last night (= **kinō no yoru/ban** 昨日の夜/晩)

saku-jitsu *n, adv* 昨日 [BOOKISH] yesterday (= **kinō** 昨日)

saku-nen *n, adv* 昨年 [BOOKISH] last year (= **kyonen** 去年)

saki-ototoi *n, adv* さきおととい・一昨々日 [BOOKISH] three days ago (= **mikka mae** 三日前)

saki-ótotoshi *n, adv* さきおととし・一昨々年 [BOOKISH] three years ago (= **sannen mae** 三年前)

sakubun *n* 作文 writing a composition (*a theme*): **~ o kakimás̲u** 作文を書きます writes a composition

sakuga *n* 作画 **1.** drawing a picture (= **byōga** 描画) **2.** taking a photograph

sakugen *n* 削減 cut, reduction: ~ **shimás̲u** 削減します reduces; **kosuto-sakugen** コスト削減 cost reduction; **jin'in-sakugen** 人員削減 head-count reduction

saku̲hin *n* 作品 a work (*of literature or*

art): **geijutsu-sakuhin** 芸術作品 a work of art: **bungaku-sakuhin** 文学作品 a literary work

sakuin *n* 索引 index (= **indekkusu** インデックス)

sakui-teki *adj* 作為的 intentional (= **ito-teki** 意図的)

sakumotsu *n* 作物 **1.** crops **2.** a piece of work (= **sakubutsu** 作物, **sakuhin** 作品)

sakura *n* 桜・サクラ cherry tree: **~ no haná** 桜の花 cherry blossoms: **sakura-mochi** 桜餅 rice cake with bean paste wrapped in a cherry leaf (*Japanese cakes/sweets*)

sakuranbo *n* サクランボ・桜ん坊・桜桃 cherry

saku(ryaku) *n* 策(略) plot (= **kōryaku** 攻略): **sakuryaku-ka** 策略家 plotter (= **sakushi** 策士)

saku-shi *n* 策士 plotter (= **sakuryaku-ka** 策略家)

sakusen *n* 作戦 tactics: **~ o tatemás̲u** 作戦を立てます plans one's tactics

sakusha *n* 作者 author (= **chosha** 著者)

sakushi *n* 作詞 writing the lyrics: **sakushi-ka** 作詞家 songwriter

sakushu *n* 搾取 [BOOKISH] exploitation: **~ shimás̲u** 搾取します exploits; **~ saremás̲u** 搾取されます is exploited

sakusofōn *n* サクソフォーン saxophone (= **sakkusu** サックス)

sakusō(shita) *adj* 錯綜(した) complicated and intricated (= **kōsaku (shita)** 交錯(した)): **~ shimás̲u** 錯綜します gets entangled; **~ jōhō** 錯綜した情報 entangled information

sakyū *n* 砂丘 sand dune: **Tottori-sakyū** 鳥取砂丘 Tottori sand dune

… (-)sama *suffix* …様・さま [HONORIFIC] = **… (-)san** …さん Mr., Ms., Mrs., Miss

samatagemás̲u, samatagéru ν 妨げます, 妨げる obstructs, hinders

samayoimás̲u, samayóu ν 彷徨います, 彷徨う wanders about

samáza ma (na/no) *adj* 様々(な/の) diverse, all kinds of

same *n* サメ・鮫 shark (= **fuká** フカ)

samemás̲u, saméru ν 覚めます, 覚め

る wakes up, comes to one's senses

samemásu, saméru v 冷めます, 冷める gets cold, cools off

samemásu, saméru v 褪めます, 褪める it fades, loses color

saménai v 覚めない = **samemasén** 覚めません (not wake up, not come to one's senses)

saménai v 冷めない = **samemasén** 冷めません (not get cold, not cool off)

saménai v 褪めない = **samemasén** 褪めません (not fade, not lose color)

samitto n サミット summit (*conference*) (= **shunō-kaidan** 首脳会談)

sá-mo nákereba conj さもなければ [BOOKISH] otherwise (= **sa-mo nakuba** さもなくば)

samue n 作務衣 traditional craftsman's outfit of long sleeve jacket tied at right side and matching loose trousers; also popular as leisure clothes

samúi adj 寒い cold (*air temperature*), chilly

samuke n 寒気 chill, rigor (= **okan** 悪寒): **~ ga shimásu** 寒気がします feels a chill

samurai n サムライ・侍 samurai (*Japanese warrior*) (= **bushi** 武士)

san n 酸 **1.** acid **2.** sour taste: **san-mi** 酸味 sour taste, sour flavor (= **suppai aji** 酸っぱい味)

san(...) n, prefix 三・3 (...) three (, tri-...)

sán-ba n 三羽 three (*birds, rabbits*)

san-bai adj 三倍 triple

sán-bai n 三杯 three glassfuls

san-banmé n 三番目 third

sán-bén n 三遍 three times

sán-biki n 三匹 three (*fishes/bugs, small animals*)

sán-bon n 三本 three (*pencils/bottles, long objects*)

sán-byaku n 三百・300 three hundred

sán-dó n 三度 **1.** three times (= **san-kai** 三回); **sando-mé** 三度目 the third time **2.** three degrees

san-gai n 三階 three floors/stories; third floor

san-gánichi n 三が日 the first three days of the New Year

sán-gen n 三軒 three buildings/houses

sán-ji n 三時 three o'clock: **~ no oyatsu** 三時のおやつ snacks, sweets for tea time at three o'clock (= **oyatsu** おやつ)

san-jū n 三重 triplicity: **san-jū-sō** 三重奏 **trio** (= **torio** トリオ) (*musical instruments, piano, violin, cello, etc.*): **piano-sanjūsō-kyoku** ピアノ三重奏曲 piano trio

sán-jū n 三十・30 thirty

sán-kái n 三回 three times (= **san-do** 度); **san kai-mé** 三回目 the third time

san-kyaku n 三脚 tripod (stand): **ninin-sankyaku** 二人三脚 **1.** three-legged race (*on field day, etc.*) **2.** cooperating with singleness of purpose

sán-mai n 三枚 three sheets (*flat things*): **sán-mai-me** 三枚目 a cutup

sán-mei n 三名 [BOOKISH] three people (= **sannín** 三人)

san-nen n 三年 the year 3; **san nén-kan** 三年間 three years; **san nén-sei** 三年生 third-year student, junior

san-nín n 三人 three people (= **sen mei** 三名): **san-nin-shō** 三人称 third person

san-pai n 三拝 [HUMBLE] bowing three times, bowing several times

san-paku n 三泊 three night's lodging: **san-paku-yokka** 三泊四日 four days three nights (*tour, etc.*)

sán-pun n 三分 three minutes

sán-sai n 三歳 three years old (= **mittsu** 三つ)

san-san-ku-do (no sakazuki) n 三三九度 (の杯) three-times-three exchange of nuptial cups

sán-satsu n 三冊 three (*books, magazines, etc.*)

sán-sei n 三世 third generation (*of emigrant Japanese*); ... the Third

san-shi-... n 三、四 = **san-yo(n)-...** three or four

sán-shoku n 三食 three meals

sán-tō n 三頭 three (*horses/oxen, large animals*)

sán-tō n 三等 third class: **san-tō-shō** 三等賞 third prize

san-yo(m/n)- n 三、四 = **san-shi-...** three or four: **san yon-bai** 三、四倍

three or four times as much: **sanyo-banmé** 三、四番目 third or fourth: **sanyo-jíkan** 三、四時間 3–4 hours, **sán-yokka** 三、四日 three or four days: **sanyo-nín** 三、四人 3–4 people: **sanyo-ninmae** 三、四人前 3–4 servings
san-zén *n* 三千 3,000 three thousand
sán-zoku/-soku *n* 三足 three pairs (*of footwear*)

sán *n* 酸 acid
san-sei *n* 酸性 acidity: **sansei-u** 酸性雨 acid rain

... (-) **san** …さん Mr., Ms., Mrs., Miss (= … (-) **sama** …様・さま)

...´-**san**, -´**zan** …山 (*name of certain*) mountain: **Fuji-san** 富士山 Mt. Fuji: **Takao-zan** 高尾山 Mt. Takao

san-... *prefix* 山… mountain
san-myaku *n* 山脈 mountain range: **Arupusu-sanmyaku** アルプス山脈 Alps (*range*)
san-chō *n* 山頂 mountaintop
san-gaku-chitai *n* 山岳地帯 mountainous region
san-puku *n* 山腹 sidehill
san-sai *n* 山菜 edible wild plants
san-zoku *n* 山賊 bandit

sanba *n* サンバ samba
sanba *n* 産婆 (**osanba-san** お産婆さん) midwife (= **josanpu** 助産婦)
sanbashi *n* 桟橋 pier
sanbi *n* 賛美 admiration, worship: **sanbi-ka** 賛美歌 hymn (= **sei-ka** 聖歌, **san-ka** 賛歌)
sanbun *n* 散文 prose: **sanbun-shi** 散文詩 prose poem
sanbutsu *n* 産物 product, produce; fruit, outcome
sánchi *n* 産地 home (*of a product/crop*)
sandan-jū *n* 散弾銃 shotgun (= **shotto-gan** ショットガン)
sandaru *n* サンダル sandal
...-**sándo** *suffix* …サンド sandwich (= **sandoítchi** サンドイッチ): **tsuna-sándo** ツナサンド tuna-fish sandwich: **tamago-sando** タマゴ[卵]サンド egg sandwich: **yasai-sando** 野菜サンド vegetable sandwich: **katsu-sando** カツサンド cutlet sandwich
sandō *n* 参道 approach to a shrine;

omote-sándō 表参道 main road to a shrine

sandō *n* 賛同 approval, support, (= **sansei** 賛成): ~ **shimásu** 賛同します agrees, approves
sandoítchi *n* サンドイッチ sandwich
sandopē´pā *n* サンド・ペーパー sandpaper
Sanfuranshísuko *n* サンフランシスコ San Francisco
Sán-gatsu *n* 三月・3月 March
sangi-in *n* 参議院 House of Councilors (= **san-in** 参院): **sangi-in-senkyo** 参議院選挙 House of Councilors' election
sángo *n* サンゴ・珊瑚 coral
sango-shō *n* サンゴ[珊瑚]礁 coral reef
sangurasu *n* サングラス sunglasses
sangyō *n* 産業 industry: **sangyō-kakumei** 産業革命 industrial revolution: **sābisu-sangyō** サービス産業 service industry
sánji *n* 賛辞 [BOOKISH] praise, compliment (= **home-kotoba** 褒め[誉め]言葉): ~ **o okurimásu** 賛辞を送ります compliments
sanka *n* 賛歌 [BOOKISH] hymn (= **sanbi-ka** 賛美歌, **sei-ka** 聖歌)
sanka *n* 傘下 [BOOKISH] under the umbrella: **sanka-kigyō** 傘下企業 affiliated enterprise: ~ **ni hairimásu** 傘下に入ります comes under the umbrella
sanka *n* 参加 participation; (... **ni**) ~ **shimásu** (…に)参加します participates (*in*), joins
sanká-sha *n* 参加者 participant
sánkan *n* 参観 [HUMBLE] one's visiting: **jugyō-sankan-bi** 授業参観日 open school day: **jugyō o ~ shimásu** 授業を参観します visits to observe one's child during a class
sánkaku *n* 三角 triangle: **sankaku-kei**, **sankak-kei** 三角形 triangular shape: **sankaku-kankei** 三角関係 a love triangle
sanke-zukimásu, sanke-zuku *v* 産気づきます, 産気づく goes into labor
sankō *n* 参考 reference (= **sanshō** 参照): **sankō-(to-)sho** 参考(図)書

204

reference book: **gakushū-sankōsho** 学習参考書 study-aid book: **~ ni shimásu** 参考にします refers

sanma n サンマ・秋刀魚 mackerel pike

sanmon n 山門 temple gate

sanpatsu n 散髪・さんぱつ haircut: **~ shimásu** 散髪します gets/gives a haircut

sanpatsu-ya n 散髪屋 barber(shop)

sanpo n 散歩 a walk, a stroll: **~ shimásu** 散歩します takes a walk

sanpuru n サンプル sample (= **mihon** 見本, **shikyō-hin** 試供品)

sanretsu n 参列 presence: **~ shimásu** 参列します is present

sanrín-sha n 三輪車 tricycle

sansei n 賛成 approval, support (= **sandō** 賛同): **~ shimásu** 賛成します agrees, approves

sansei n 参政 participation in government: **sansei-ken** 参政権 political suffrage

sanshō n サンショウ・山椒 Japanese pepper (mild)

sanshō n 参照 reference (= **sankō** 参考): **~ shimásu** 参照します refers

sánso n 酸素 oxygen: **sanso-masuku** 酸素マスク oxygen mask: **kassei-sanso** 活性酸素 active oxygen

sansū n 算数 (elementary school) arithmetic, calculation (= **keisan** 計算), mathematics (= **sūgaku** 数学)

santora n サントラ sound track (= **saundo-torakku** サウンド・トラック)

saó n さお・竿・棹 pole, rod

sapōʹtā n サポーター jockstrap, (athletic) supporter

sappári adv さっぱり [+ NEGATIVE verb] not at all: **~ wakarimasen** さっぱり分かりません I have no idea.

sappári-shita adj さっぱりした clean, fresh; frank: **sappári-shita aji** さっぱりした味 plain taste, lightly seasoned (food)

sappūkei (na) adj 殺風景(な) (looks) bare, bleak: **~ na niwa** 殺風景な庭 a bleak garden

sara n 皿 (**o-sara** お皿) plate, dish; saucer; ashtray

sara-arai-ki n 皿洗い機 dishwasher

sarabureddo n サラブレッド 1. thoroughbred 2. blue blood

sárada n サラダ salad

sarái-... prefix 再来...... after next

sarái-getsu adv 再来月 [BOOKISH] month after next (= **nikagetsu-go** 二ヵ月後)

sarai-nen adv 再来年 [BOOKISH] year after next (= **ni nen-go** 二年後)

sarai-shū adv 再来週 [BOOKISH] week after next (= **ni shūkan-go** 二週間後)

sára-ni adv 更に anew; (some) more; further

sárarii n サラリー salary (= **kyūʹyo** 給与)

sararii-man n サラリーマン salaried man, company employee (= **kaishá-in** 会社員, **sha-in** 社員)

sarashimásu, sarasu v 晒します・曝します, 晒す・曝す 1. exposes: **kiken ni mi o ~** 危険に身をさらし[晒し・曝し]ます exposes oneself to danger 2. bleaches: **nuno o ~** 布をさらし[晒し]ます bleaches cloth 3. dries under the sun: **hi ni ~** 日にさらし[晒し]ます dries it in the sun 4. reveals: **haji o ~** 恥をさらし[晒し・曝し]ます brings disgrace on oneself

saremásu, sareru v されます, され る 1. has it done to one (unwantedly) 2. is done; **hakai ~** 破壊されます is destroyed 3. [HONORIFIC] = **nasaimásu** なさいます

sarimásu, sáru v 去ります, 去る leaves, goes away; removes it

sāroin n サーロイン sirloin: **sāroin-sutēki** サーロイン・ステーキ sirloin steak

sáru v 去る 1. = **sarimásu** 去ります 2. [+ DATE] last ..., most recent, (past day) of this month

sáru n サル・猿 (**o-saru** おサル・お猿) monkey

Saru-doshi n 申年 year of the Monkey

sasa n ササ・笹 bamboo grass: **~ no ha** 笹の葉 bamboo leaf

sasaé n 支え a support, a prop

sasaemásu, sasaeru v 支えます, 支える supports, props (up)

sasanai v 指さない = **sashimasén** 指しません (not point to)

sasanai *v* 刺さない = **sashimasén** 刺し
ません (not stab)

sásai (na) *adj* 些細 (な) petty, trifling,
trivial, not a big deal at all (= **toruni-
tarinai** 取るに足りない): ~ **na mondai**
些細な問題 minor problem: ~ **na chigai**
些細な違い slight difference

sasáyaka (na) *adj* ささやか(な) small
(-scale), petty: ~ **na pātii** ささやかなパ
ーティ little party: ~ **na okurimono**
ささやかな贈り物 modest gift

sasayakí *n* 囁き a whisper, murmur:
sasayaki-goe 囁き声 whispery voice

sasayakimásu, sasayáku *v* 囁きます,
囁く whispers

sase ro *v* させろ [IMPERATIVE] (let
them do it!) → **sasemásu** させます

sáse *v* 刺せ [IMPERATIVE] (stab!) →
sashimásu 刺します

sáseba *v* 指せば (if one points to) →
sashimásu 指します

sáseba *v* 刺せば (if one stabs) →
sashimásu 刺します

sasemásu, saseru *v* させます, させる
makes/has/lets one do

sasemásu, saséru *v* 指せます, 指せる
can point to

sasemásu, saséru *v* 刺せます, 刺せる
can stab

sasenai *v* させない = **sasemasén** させ
ません (not make/have/let one do)

sasénai *v* 指せない = **sasemasén** 指せ
ません (cannot point to)

sasénai *v* 刺せない = **sasemasén** 刺せ
ません (cannot stab)

saseréba *v* させれば (if one makes/has/
lets them do) → **sasemásu** させます

saséreba *v* 指せれば (if one can point
to) → **sasemásu** 指せます

saséreba *v* 刺せれば (if one can stab)
→ **sasemásu** 刺せます

sasete *v* させて → **sasemásu** させ
ます

sásete *v* 指せて → **sasemásu** 指せ
ます

sásete *v* 刺せて → **sasemásu** 刺せ
ます

saseyō *v* させよう = **sasemashō** させ
ましょう (let's make/let them do it!)

sashi-agemásu, sashi-ageru *v* 差し

上げます, 差し上げる [HUMBLE/
DEFERENTIAL] presents, give (*I give
you, you give them*); holds up

sashidegamashii *adj* 差し出がましい
officious

sashidéguchi *n* 差し出口 uncalled-for
remark; ~ **o hasamimásu** 差し出口をは
さみます interrupts

sashi-e *n* 挿絵 illustration (*of book,
newspaper, magazine, etc.*)

sashi-komi *n* 差(し)込み plug outlet
(*electricity outlet*) (= **sashikomi-guchi**
差(し)込み口)

sashi-komimásu, sashi-komu *v*
差(し)込みます, 差し込む inserts

sashimásu, sásu *v* 指します, 指す
points to, indicates

sashimásu, sásu *v* 差します, 差す
holds (*umbrella*)

sashimásu, sásu *v* 刺します, 刺す
stabs, stings

sashimí *n* 刺身・さしみ (**o-sashimi**
お刺身) sliced raw fish

sashitsukae *n* 差し支え・さしつかえ
1. hindrance, impediment **2.** previous
appointment/engagement

sáshizu *n* 指図 directions, instructions,
a command (= **shirei** 指令, **shiji** 指示):
~ **shimásu** 指図します directs, instructs,
commands

sashō *n* 査証 [BOOKISH] visa (= **bíza**
ビザ): **nyūkoku-sashō** 入国査証
an entry visa

sashō *n* 詐称 [BOOKISH] false
statement: ~ **shimásu** 詐称します
makes a false statement; **nenrei-sashō**
年齢詐称 false statement of one's age;
gakureki-sashō 学歴詐称 false statement of one's educational background;
mibun-sashō 身分詐称 false statement
of one's status

sasō´ *v* 刺そう = **sashimashō´** 刺しまし
ょう (let's stab!)

sasoi *n* 誘い invitation; temptation

sasoimásu, sasou *v* 誘います, 誘う
invites; tempts

sasoō *v* 誘おう = **sasoimashō** 誘いまし
ょう (let's invite/tempt them!)

sasotte *v* 誘って → **sasoimásu** 誘い
ます

sasou v 誘う = **sasoimásu** 誘います (invites; tempts)

sasowanai v 誘わない = **sasoimasén** 誘いません (not invite/tempt)

sásshi, sásshu n サッシ、サッシュ sash (*window sash*)

sásshi n 冊子 brochure shō-sasshi n 小冊子 pamphlet, brochure (= **pánfu(rétto)** パンフ (レット))

sas-shi n 察し conjecture, guess; perception, understanding; sympathy: **~ ga tsukimásu** 察しがつきます perceives, guesses (*correctly*); **o-sasshi no tōri** お察しの通り as you have surmised

sas-shinásu, sas-suru v 察します、察する perceives, understands; conjectures, guesses; sympathizes

sas-shite v 察して → **sas-shimásu** 察します

sassoku adv 早速 at once, right away, promptly, immediately: **sassokú (no)** 早速 (の) immediate, prompt

sásu v 指す = **sashimásu** 指します (points to, indicates)

sásu v 差す = **sashimásu** 差します (holds (*umbrella*))

sásu v 刺す = **sashimásu** 刺します (stabs, stings)

sasuga adv さすが: **sasuga (ni)** さすが (に) as we might expect, indeed

sasupendā n サスペンダー suspender **1.** galluses (= **zubon-tsuri** ズボンつり) **2.** garter

sasupensu n サスペンス suspense: **sasupensu-eiga** サスペンス映画 suspense film

sátá n 沙汰 (**go-sáta** ご沙汰) [BOOKISH] message; command; affair

satchū-zai n 殺虫剤 insecticide

sá-te interj さて well now/then, and now/then, as to the matter at hand

satei n 査定 assessment (*to decide the rank, salary, etc.*): **satei-gaku** 査定額 assessed value

sáten n サテン satin

saten n 茶店 café (= **kissaten** 喫茶店)

sato n 里 **1.** village **2.** hometown (= **furusato** ふるさと・故郷, **kokyō** 故郷): **o-sato** お里 one's origin,

upbringing **3.** countryside

sato-oya n 里親 foster parent

sato-gaeri n 里帰り goes home (*to see one's parent(s)*)

satoˊ n 砂糖・サトウ (**o-sató** お砂糖) sugar

satori n 悟り enlightenment

satorimásu, satóru v 悟ります、悟る realizes (*comprehends*)

satsu n 札 (**o-satsu** お札) folding money, currency bill/note satsu-iré n 札入れ billfold, wallet (= **saifu** 財布) satsu-taba n 札束 a roll/wad of (currency) bills

…-satsú suffix …冊 copy (*counts books, magazines*)

…-satsú suffix …札 (currency) bill

satsuei n 撮影 shooting a film, filming, taking a photograph: **satsuei-jo** 撮影所 studio (= **sutajio** スタジオ)

satsujin n 殺人 murder: **satsujin-jiken** 殺人事件 murder case

Satsumá-age n さつま [薩摩] 揚げ deep-fried fish cake

Satsuma-imo n さつま [薩摩] 芋・サツマイモ sweet potato

Saujiarabia n サウジアラビア Saudi Arabia

Saujiarabia-jin n サウジアラビア人 a Saudi Arabian

sauna n サウナ steam bath (originally came from Finnish term "sauna")

saundo n サウンド sound (= **oto** 音, **onkyō** 音響) saundo-efekuto n サウンド・エフェクト sound effect (= **onkyō-kōka** 音響効果) saundo-sukēpu n サウンドスケープ soundscape (= **oto (no) fūkei** 音 (の) 風景, **onkei** 音景) saundo-torakku n サウンド・トラック sound track (= **santora** サントラ)

sawagashíi adj 騒がしい boisterous, noisy

sáwagi n 騒ぎ **1.** noise (*boisterous*), clamor **2.** unrest, disturbance, tumult, strife; riot (= **sōdō** 騒動)

sawagimásu, sawágu v 騒ぎます、騒ぐ makes lots of noise, clamors

sawáide *v* 騒いで → **sawagimásu** 騒ぎます

sawara *n* サワラ・鰆 mackerel

sawarimásu, sawaru *v* 触ります、触る touches

sawatte *v* 触って → **sawarimásu** 触ります

sawáyaka (na) *adj* さわやか(な)・爽やか(な) refreshing, bracing; fluent

sáya *n* サヤ・莢 sheath, pod: **saya-endō** サヤエンドウ・さやえんどう podded pea: **saya-ingen** サヤインゲン・さやいんげん French bean

sayonára, sayōnára *interj* さよなら、さようなら good-bye (= **baibai** バイバイ [INFORMAL])

sáyori *n* サヨリ halfbeak (*fish*)

sáyū *n* 左右 right and left: **zengo-sayū** 前後左右 left to right, back and forth

sázae *n* サザエ・栄螺 wreath shell, turban shell, turbo

sé *n* 背 1. height, stature (= **sei** せい・背, **se-take** 背丈, **shinchō** 身長): ~ **ga takái/hikúi** 背が高い/低い is tall/short 2. back (*of body*) (= **senaka** 背中)

se-biro *n* 背広 (*man's*) business suit, lounge suit

se-bone *n* 背骨 backbone, spine

séi *n* せい・背 height, stature (= **sé** 背, **se-take** 背丈, **shinchō** 身長): **sei-kurabe** 背比べ comparing heights with someone

se-naka *n* 背中 back of body: ~ **awase** 背中合わせ back to back

se-nobi *n* 背伸び 1. standing on tiptoe: ~ **shimásu** 背伸びします stands on tiptoe 2. trying to do more than one is able to do

se-suji *n* 背筋 the muscles along the spine: ~ **o nobashimásu** 背筋を伸ばします straightens up

segare *n* 倅・せがれ 1. [HUMBLE] my son 2. [rather IN NEGATIVE SENSE] child/young person

sehyō *n* 世評 one's reputation (= **seken no hyōka** 世間の評価)

séi (-) *n* 性 nature; sex; gender

sei-betsu *n* 性別 gender

sei-byō *n* 性病 venereal disease

séi-kō *n* 性交 [BOOKISH] (*sexual*) intercourse (= **sékkusu** セックス): ~

shimásu 性交します has sex

sei-teki (na) *adj* 性的(な) sexual

séi *n* 姓 family name, last name

séi-mei *n* 姓名 (*one's*) full name (= **shi-mei** 氏名)

sei-... *prefix* 聖... sacred, holy

sei-chi *n* 聖地 holy place

sei-bo *n* 聖母 the Holy Mother

sei-dō *n* 聖堂 sacred building (*temple, church, mosque, etc.*): **dai-seidō** 大聖堂 cathedral

sei-iki *n* 聖域 sanctuary

séi-ka *n* 聖歌 hymn (= **sanbi-ka** 賛美歌, **san-ka** 賛歌)

Séi-sho *n* 聖書 Bible (= **Baiburu** バイブル, **Shin-yaku seisho** 新約聖書, **Kyū-yaku seisho** 旧約聖書)

séi-... *prefix* 西... west, western

séi-bu *n* 西部 the west, the western part: **seibu-geki** 西部劇 cowboy movie

sei-hō *n* 西方 (the) west (*general direction/area*); **seihō no** 西方の western (= **nishi no** 西の)

sei-nan *n* 西南 southwest

sei-reki *n* 西暦 the Western (*Christian*) calendar: **seireki ...´-nen** 西暦 ...年 the year ... A.D.

Séi-yō *n* 西洋 the West, Europe and Americas (= **ōbei-shokoku** 欧米諸国): **séiyō-fū (no)** 西洋風(の) Western-style

sei-... *prefix* 声... voice, vocal

sei-gaku *n* 声楽 vocal music: **sei-gaku-ka** 声楽家 vocalist

sei-iki *n* 声域 range of voice

sei-ryo *n* 声量 volume of one's voice

sei-tai *n* 声帯 vocal cords

sei-yū *n* 声優 voice actor

sei(-) n, *prefix* 生(...) life (= **seimei** 生命, **ínochi** 命)

sei-katsu *n* 生活 life, (*daily*) living, livelihood (= **kurashi** 暮らし, **seikei** 生計); **nichijo-seikatsu** 日常生活 daily life; **seikatsú-hi** 生活費 living costs; **seikatsu-kyōdō-kumiai** 生活協同組合, **seikyō** 生協 cooperative society, consumer cooperative (*coop*)

sei-kei *n* 生計 livelihood, the way of (*earning*) one's living (= **kurashi** 暮らし): ~ **o tatemásu** 生計を立てます earns one's living

séi-mei *n* 生命 life (= **ínochi** 命, **sei** 生): **seimei-rinri** 生命倫理 bioethics

séi-shi *n* 生死 life and death

… **séi** *suffix* …せい [IN NEGATIVE SENSE] cause, effect, influence, fault: … **no séi de** …のせいで because of …, due to …: … **séi ka** …せいか perhaps because of …

…'-sei *suffix* …生 student: **shōgaku-sei** 小学生 elementary school student: **chūgaku-sei** 中学生 junior high school student: **kōkō'-sei** 高校生 highschool student: **daigaku-sei** 大学生 college/ university student

…'-sei *suffix* …製 made in …, made of …: **nihon-sei** 日本製 made in Japan: **gaikoku-sei** 外国製 foreign-made: **kinzoku-sei** 金属製 made of metal: **moku-sei** 木製 made of wood

…'-sei *suffix* …星 (*name of certain, kinds of*) star: **waku-sei** 惑星 planet: **kō-sei** 恒星 fixed star

séibun *n* 成分 ingredient, component: **arukōru-seibun** アルコール成分 alcohol component

séibutsu *n* 生物 a living thing, a creature (= **ikimono** 生き物): **seibutsú-gaku** *n* 生物学 biology: **seibutsugaku-teki na** 生物学的な biological

seibutsu-gáku-sha *n* 生物学者 biologist

séibutsu *n* 静物 [BOOKISH] still object: **seibutsu-ga** 静物画 still-life painting

seichō *n* 成長 growth: ~ **shimásu** 成長します grows; grows up; **kōdo-keizai-seichō** 高度経済成長 high economic growth

séido *n* 制度 system (= **shisutemu** システム)

seidō *n* 青銅 bronze (= **buronzu** ブロンズ)

sieki *n* 精液 semen

séifu *n* 政府 government

seifuku *n* 制服 uniform (*of school, office, etc.*)

seigén *n* 制限 limit, restriction: ~ **shimásu** 制限します limits, restricts

seigen-jikan *n* 制限時間 time limit

seihin *n* 製品 product, manufactured goods

seii *n* 誠意 sincerity (= **magokoro** 真心): ~ **o komete** 誠意を込めて sincerely

seiji *n* 政治 politics: **seiji-ka** 政治家 politician: **seiji-mondai** 政治問題 political issue: **kokusai-seiji** 国際政治 international politics

seijin *n* 成人 adult (= **otona** 大人・おとな): ~ **no hí** 成人の日 Coming-of-Age Day (*honoring 20-year-olds*) on 2nd Monday of January

seijitsu (na) *adj* 誠実 (な) sincere

seijuku *n* 成熟 ripening, maturing: ~ **shimásu** 成熟します ripens, matures

séika *n* 成果 [BOOKISH] good result, outcome (= **yoi kekka** 良い結果)

séika *n* 正価 net price

séika-ichiba *n* 青果市場 vegetable market

seikaku *n* 性格 character (*personal traits*)

seikaku (na) *adj* 正確 (な) exact, accurate, correct

seikaku (na) *adj* 精確 (な) minute, correct and precise

seiketsu (na) *adj* 清潔 (な) clean; pure

séiki *n* 世紀 century: **kon-seiki** 今世紀 this century: **rai-seiki** 来世紀 next century

seikō *n* 成功 success: ~ **shimásu** 成功します succeeds

seikyū *n* 請求 claim, demand, request: ~ **shimásu** 請求します claims, demands, requests

seikyū-sho *n* 請求書 bill

seimitsu (na) *adj* 精密 (な) precise, detailed, minute, thorough, accurate

seimon *n* 正門 the front (*main*) gate

seinen *n* 青年 young person, youth, adolescent

seinén-ki *n* 青年期 (*one's*) youth; adolescence (= **seishún-ki** 青春期)

seinen-gáppi *n* 生年月日 date of birth

séiri *n* 生理 physiology: **séiri-teki na** 生理的な physiological; **séiri-yō nápukín** 生理用ナプキン sanitary pad

seiri-gaku *n* 生理学 physiology

séiri *n* 整理 adjustment, arrangement: ~ **shimásu** 整理します adjusts, arranges, (re-)orders, (re-)organizes

seiri-seiton *n* 整理整頓 keeping everything in order

seiritsu *n* 成立 formation, finalization, conclusion: ~ **shimásu** 成立します gets formed (*organized*), comes into being, gets finalized/concluded; **kōshō-seiritsu** 交渉成立 completion of the deal

Seiron *n* セイロン Ceylon (= **Suri-ránka** スリランカ Sri Lanka)

seiryō *n* 清涼 [BOOKISH] refreshing: **seiryō (inryō)sui** 清涼（飲料）水 refreshing drink

séiryoku *n* 勢力 power, energy; influence (= **iryoku** 威力)

seisaku *n* 政策 (*political*) policy

seisaku *n* 制作・製作 manufacture, production (= **purodyūsu** プロデュース): ~ **shimásu** 制作［製作］します manufactures, produces

seisan *n* 生産 production, manufacture: ~ **shimásu** 生産します produces

seisan *n* 清算 clearance, liquidation: ~ **shimásu** 清算します clears, liquidates

seiseki *n* 成績 results, marks, grades, record: **seiseki-hyō** 成績表 report card

seishi *n* 静止 stillness: **seishi-ga(zō)** 静止画（像） still image (*photo, etc.*)

seishi *n* 精子 spermatozoon

seishiki (no/na) *adj* 正式（の/な） formal, official

séishin *n* 精神 soul, mind, spirit, psyche: **séishin (no)** 精神（の） mental

seishitsu *n* 性質 character (*of things*), quality, disposition, nature

seishoku *n* 生殖 reproduction, procreation: ~ **shimásu** 生殖します produces, procreates

seishoku-ki *n* 生殖期 reproductive period

seishún *n* 青春 adolescence: **seishun-ki** 青春期 adolescence

seisō *n* 清掃 cleaning (= **sōji** 掃除): ~ **shimásu** 清掃します cleans

seisō-in *n* 清掃員 cleaning person

séito *n* 生徒 pupil, student

seitō *n* 政党 political party

seitō *n* 正当 [BOOKISH] propriety, validity, reasonableness: ~ **na riyū** 正当な理由 good/fair reason

seitō *n* 正統 legitimacy, orthodoxy (= **ōsodokkusu** オーソドックス)

seiyu *n* 製油 oil manufacturing

seiyu-gaisha *n* 製油会社 oil manufacturing company

seiyu-jo *n* 製油所 (*oil*) refinery

seiza *n* 正座 sitting straight on one's knees: ~ **shimásu** 正座します sits on the floor Japanese style (*sit with one's legs folded under one*)

seiza *n* 星座 constellation: **seiza-haya-mihyō** 星座早見表 planisphere

seiza *n* 静座 sitting quietly, meditation: ~ **shimásu** 静座します sits quietly, meditates

séizei *adv* せいぜい at most, at best

seizō *n* 製造 production, manufacture: **seizō-moto** 製造元 maker (*manufacturer*): ~ **shimásu** 製造します manufactures, produces

seizon *n* 生存 existence, surviving: ~ **shimásu** 生存します exists, survival

seizon-ritsu *n* 生存率 survival rate

seizu *n* 星図 star chart

seizu *n* 製図 drafting a (*technical*) drawing: **kikai-seizu** 機械製図 mechanical drawing: **kenchiku-seizu** 建築製図 architectural drafting

seji *n* 世辞 (**o-seji** お世辞) compliment, flattery

sékái *n* 世界 world; **sekai-jū** 世界中 throughout the world, worldwide; **sekai-teki (na)** 世界的（な） worldwide, international

séken *n* 世間 the public, people, the world, society (= **shakai** 社会, **yo-no-naka** 世の中)

seken-bánashi *n* 世間話 chat(-ting) (= **yomoyama-banashi** よもやま話)

seken-tei *n* 世間体 appearances, reputation, decency: ~ **o kinishimásu** 世間体を気にします cares about appearances

seki *n* せき・咳 cough: **seki-dome-shiroppu** せき止めシロップ cough syrup: ~ **o shimásu** 咳をします coughs

séki *n* 籍 1. (*one's*) family register (= **koseki** 戸籍): ~ **o iremásu** 籍を入れます legally marries and has a name entered in the family register, registers one's marriage (= **nyū-seki** 入籍) → **kekkon** 結婚 2. membership: **... ni ~ o okimásu** …に籍を置きます is a member of

séki *n* 席 seat, (*assigned*) place (= **o-seki** お席)

séki-ryō *n* 席料 cover charge

seki-... *prefix* 赤... red
seki-han *n* 赤飯 (**o-sékihan** お赤飯) rice boiled with red beans (*commonly for celebration dinner*)
Seki-jū´ji *n* 赤十字 Red Cross
seki-men *n* 赤面 a blush: **~ shimásu** 赤面します blushes

...-seki *suffix* ...隻 (*counts ships/vessels; commonly replaced by* **...-sō** ...艘)

Seki-dō *n* 赤道 equator

sekigaisen *n* 赤外線 infrared rays

sekinin *n* 責任 responsibility, obligation; **sekinín-sha** 責任者 responsible person: **~ o torimásu** 責任を取ります takes responsibility

sékiri *n* 赤痢 dysentery

sekitán *n* 石炭 coal
sekitan-san *n* 石炭酸 carbolic acid

sekitatemásu, sekitateru *v* 急き立てます, 急き立てる urges

sekitóri *n* 関取 (*ranking*) sumo wrestler

sekiyu *n* 石油 petroleum, oil, kerosene: **sekiyu-sutó´bu** 石油ストーブ kerosene heater

sékkai *n* 石灰 lime (*mineral*)

sekkakú *adv* せっかく [+ NEGATIVE verb] with much effort/devotion (*but*); on purpose, taking the trouble **Sekkakú desu ga ...** せっかくですが ... It is kind of you (*to ask*), but ...

sekkei *n* 設計 designing, planning (*of machine, etc.*): **~ shimásu** 設計します designs, plans
shekkei-sha *n* 設計者 designer (*of machine, etc.*) (= **dezainā** デザイナー)
shekkei-zu *n* 設計図 draft (= **zumen** 図面) blueprint (= **aojashin** 青写真)

sekken *n* 石けん・石鹼 soap (= **sōpu** ソープ)

sekkin *n* 接近 approach(ing): **sekkin-sen** 接近戦 close game, close contest (= **sessen** 接戦): **... ni ~ shimásu** ...に接近します approaches, draws near

sekkō *n* 石こう・石膏 plaster

sekkú *n* 節句; **Tángo no sekkú** 端午の節句 Boys Festival (5 May)

sékkusu *n* セックス sex (= **seikō** 性交)

~ (o) shimásu セックス（を）します has sex

sekkyō´ *n* 説教 (**o-sekkyō´** お説教) sermon: **~ shimásu** 説教します preaches

sekkyoku-teki (na) *adj* 積極的(な) positive, energetic, vigorous

semái *adj* 狭い **1.** narrow, tight, small (*space*): **semai-michi** 狭い道 narrow street, path (= **hoso-michi** 細道) **2.** narrow, limited: **shiya ga ~** 視野が狭い has a narrow outlook; **katami ga ~** 肩身が狭い is ashamed **3.** narrow, little, small (*mind*) (= **kyōryō** 狭量): **ryōken/kokoro ga ~** 了見/心が狭い is narrow-minded

sememásu, seméru *v* 攻めます, 攻める attacks, assaults

sememásu, seméru *v* 責めます, 責める censures, reproaches, criticizes

semento *n* セメント cement

sémete *adv* せめて at least; at most

sémete *v* 攻めて・責めて → **sememásu** 攻めます・責めます

semi *n* セミ・蟬 cicada, locust

seminā *n* セミナー seminar, workshop

sén *n* 千 1,000 (= **is-sén** 一千・1,000) thousand (= **is-sén** 一千)
sén-ba *n* 千羽 1,000 (*birds, rabbits*)
sen-bai *n* 千倍 a thousand-fold, 1,000 times as much
sén-bai *n* 千杯 1,000 cupfuls
sén-biki *n* 千匹 1,000 (*fishes/bugs, small animals*)
sén-bon *n* 千本 1,000 (*pencils/bottles, long objects*)
sen-en *n* 千円 a thousand yen
sén-zoku *n* 千足 1,000 pairs of footwear

sén *n* 線 **1.** line (= **shasen** 斜線): **kyoku-sen** 曲線 curved line: **choku-sen** 直線 straight line **2.** outline **3.** electron beam (= **āsu-sen** アース線) **4.** (*name of electric train line*): (**jē āru**) **Yama no te-sen** (JR)山手線 JR Yamanote Line

sén *n* 栓 plug, cork, stopper
sen-nuki *n* 栓抜き corkscrew, bottle opener

sen-... *prefix* 船... ship
sénchō *n* 船長 captain (*of ship*)
sen'in *n* 船員 ship's crew (*member*), sailor

(...´-) sen *suffix* (...) 船 (*name of certain*) ship

sen-.../...-sen *prefix, suffix* 戦.../...戦 war

sen-go *adv* [BOOKISH] 戦後 postwar, after/since the war

sén-ji *adv* [BOOKISH] 戦時 wartime; **senji-chū** 戦時中 during the war

sen-sō *n* 戦争 war (= **ikusa** 戦)

sen-tō *n* [BOOKISH] 戦闘 battle: ~ **shimásu** 戦闘します has a battle

sen-zen (no) *adj* [BOOKISH] 戦前(の) prewar, before the war

shū-sen *n* [BOOKISH] 終戦 the end of a war: **shūsen-go** 終戦後 after the war

(...´-) sen (...) 戦 (*name of certain*) war

sen-... *prefix* 先... **1.** last, previous, before, former

sen-datté *adv* 先立って a few days ago, recently

sén-getsu *n, adv* 先月 last month

sen-jin *n* 先人 **1.** ancestor (= **sosen** 祖先, **senzo** 先祖) **2.** forerunner

sen-jitsu *n, adv* 先日 the other day

sen-ku-sha *n* 先駆者 pioneer, a fore-runner (= **paionia** パイオニア)

sen-nyū-kan *n* 先入観 preconceived idea, prejudice (= **omoikomi** 思い込み)

sen-rei *n* 先例 precedent, prior example

sen-sén-getsu *n* [BOOKISH] 先々月 month before last, two months ago

sen-sén-shū *n* [BOOKISH] 先々週 week before last

sen-shū *n* 先週 last week

sen'-yaku *n* 先約 previous appointment/engagement

sén-zo *n* 先祖 ancestor (= **sosen** 祖先)

sen-... *prefix* 先... head, front, top

sen-tan *n* 先端 **1.** tip, (*pointed*) end **2.** forefront: **sentan-gijutsu** 先端技術 high-technology (= **hai-teku** ハイテク)

sen-tō *n* 先頭 lead, head, front, top (= **riido** リード): ~ **ni tachimásu** 先頭に立ちます takes the lead, takes the initiative

sénbei *n* せんべい・煎餅 (**o-sénbei** お煎餅) (*also* **o-sénbe** おせんべ) rice crackers

(...-) sénchi (...) センチ, **senchimē´-toru** センチメートル centimeter

senchiméntaru (na) *adj* センチメンタル(な) sentimental (= **kanshōteki (na)** 感傷的(な))

senden *n* 宣伝 propaganda, publicity: **senden-kōkoku** 宣伝広告 promo

sén'i *n* 繊維 fiber

sénkō *n* 線香 (**o-sénkō** お線香) incense, joss stick: **katori-senkō** 蚊取り線香 mosquito coil: **senkō-hanabi** 線香花火 Japanese sparkler

senkō *n* 専攻 major (*study*): ~ **shimásu** 専攻します majors (*specializes*) in

sénkyo *n* 選挙 election: **senkyo-ken** 選挙権 right to vote: **senkyo-undō** 選挙運動 election campaign

senkyō´ *n* 宣教 mission work (= **dendō** 伝道, **fukyō** 布教)

senkyō´shi *n* 宣教師 missionary

senmen *n* 洗面 washing one's face

senmen-jó *n* 洗面所 lavatory (*to wash up at/in*), bathroom

senmen-ki *n* 洗面器 wash basin

senmon *n* 専門 specialty, major (*line/field/study*): **senmon-(yō)go** 専門(用)語 technical term, jargon; **senmon-ka** 専門家 specialist; **senmón-i** 専門医 (*medical*) specialist

senpai *n* 先輩 one's senior (*colleague, fellow student*)

senpō *n* 先方 the other side (*party*)

senpū´ *n* 旋風 [BOOKISH] whirlwind

senpū´-ki *n* 扇風機 electric fan

senritsu *n* 旋律 melody (= **merodii** メロディー, **fushi** 節)

senritsu *n* 戦慄 [BOOKISH] shudder of horror, shiver of horror: ~ **shimásu** 戦慄します trembles with fear

sénro *n* 線路 railroad track/line

senryō *n* 占領 military occupation: ~ **shimásu** 占領します occupies

senryū *n* 川柳 seventeen-syllable poem

sensai (na) *adj* 繊細(な) delicate, sensitive

sensaku *n* 詮索 prying, inquiry: ~ **shimásu** 詮索します pries, inquires sensaku-zuki (na) *adj* 詮索好き(な) nosy

senséi *n* 先生 teacher; doctor; maestro, master (*artisan/artist*) (= **kyōshi** 教師)

sensei *n* 宣誓 [BOOKISH] oath (= **chikai** 誓い): ~ **shimásu** 宣誓します swears an oath

sensé´shon *n* センセーション a sensation (*excitement*): ~ **o maki-okoshimásu** センセーションを巻き起こします makes a splash, creates a sensation, causes a sensation

sénshu *n* 選手 athlete; player: **orinpikku-sénshu** オリンピック選手 an Olympic athlete: **sénshu-ken** 選手権 championship, title

sensu *n* 扇子 (**o-sensu** お扇子) (*Japanese*) fan (*folding*)

sénsu *n* センス sense: ~ **ga ii/warui** センスがいい/悪い has good/poor taste

sensui *n* 潜水 submerging, diving: ~ **shimásu** 潜水します submerges, dives

sensui-fuku *n* 潜水服 diving suit

sensui-kan *n* 潜水艦 submarine

sentaku *n* 洗濯 (**o-séntaku** お洗濯) laundry, washing (= **sentaku-mono** 洗濯物・洗たくもの)

sentáku-ki *n* 洗濯機 washer (*washing machine*)

sentaku-mono-ire *n* 洗濯物入れ clothesbag (*for laundry*)

sentaku-ya *n* 洗濯屋 a laundry

sentaku *n* 選択 selection, choice

sentaku shimásu (suru) *v* 洗濯します (する) launders, washes

sentaku shimásu (suru) *v* 選択します (する) selects

séntensu *n* センテンス sentence (*linguistic*) (= **bun** 文)

(...-) sénto *suffix* (...) セント cent(s)

sentō *n* 銭湯 public bath

seoimásu, seou *v* 背負います, 背負う carries on the back

seppuku *n* 切腹 *harakiri*: ~ **shimásu** 切腹します commits *harakiri*

seppun *n* 接吻 [BOOKISH] kiss (= **kisu** キス): ~ **shimásu** 接吻します kisses

serí *n* 競り auction (= **ōkushon** オークション)

serí *n* せり・芹 Japanese parsley

serifu *n* せりふ・台詞 one's lines (*in a play*), dialogue

sérohan *n* セロハン cellophane: **sero(-han) tēpu** セロ(ハン)・テープ cellophane tape, scotch tape

séron *n* 世論 = **yoron** 世論 public opinion

sérori *n* セロリ celery

sē´ru *n* セール sale: **bāgen-sēru** バーゲン・セール bargain sale (= **ōyasu-uri** 大安売り)

sessen *n* 接線 tangent line

sessen *n* 接戦 close game, close contest

sésse-to *adv* せっせと diligently, hard (*laboriously*); frequently, often

ses-shimásu, ses-suru *v* 接します, 接する; (**... ni) ses-shimásu** (...に) 接します **1.** comes in contact (*with*), borders (*on*), is adjacent/contiguous (*to*) **2.** encounters, meets, receives, treats, handles

sesshoku *n* 接触 contact, touch: **...ni ~ shimásu** ...に接触します touches, comes into contact with

sesshoku *n* 節食 abstemious diet (= **daietto** ダイエット): ~ **shimásu** 節食します goes on diet

sesshō *n* 折衝 negotiation (= **kakehiki** 駆け引き, **kōshō** 交渉): ~ **shimásu** 折衝します negotiates

sē´tā *n* セーター sweater

setai *n* 世帯 a household (= **shotai** 所帯・世帯)

setchaku-zai *n* 接着剤 glue, adhesive

setogiwa *n* 瀬戸際 the last moment: **... no ~** ...の瀬戸際 on the verge of ...

setomono *n* 瀬戸物 porcelain, china(ware)

Seto-náikai *n* 瀬戸内海 the Inland Sea

sétsu *n* 節 occasion (*time or event*)

sétsu *n* 説 theory

sétsubi *n* 設備 equipment, facilities, accommodations

setsubi-go/-ji *n* 接尾語/辞 suffix

setsudan *n* 切断 [BOOKISH] cutting, cutoff: ~ **shimásu** 切断します cuts off

setsudo *n* 節度 moderation: ~ **no aru** 節度のある moderate: ~ **o mamorimásu** 節度を守ります is moderate

sétsuei *n* 設営 construction, setting up: ~ **shimásu** 設営します constructs, sets up

setsugen *n* 節減 reduction: ~ **shimásu** 節減します reduces; **keihi-setsugen** 経費節減 reducing the cost; **denryoku-**

setsugen 電力節減 energy conservation

setsugō n 接合 connection, conjugation, joining: ~ **shimásu** 接合します connects, conjugates, joins

setsujitsu (na/ni) adj, adv 切実 (な/に) urgent, serious, keenly, earnestly: ~ **na mondai** 切実な問題 serious problem

setsumei n 説明 explanation, description: ~ **shimásu** 説明します explains, describes

setsumei-shó n 説明書 written explanation, instructions, manual

sétsuna n 利那 [BOOKISH] moment, instant (= **shunkan** 瞬間)

setsuritsu n 設立 establishment, foundation: ~ **shimásu** 設立します establishes, founds; **hōjin-setsuritsu** 法人設立 incorporation; **setsuritsu-tōki** 設立登記 organizing registration

setsuyaku n 節約 economizing: ~ **shimásu** 節約します saves (economizes on), conserves

setsuzóku n 接続 connection: ~ **shimásu** 接続します connects: **densha no** ~ 電車の接続 train connections

setsuzóku-shi n 接続詞 a conjunction

séttai n 接待 business entertainment: ~ **shimásu** 接待します entertains business guests (clients, etc.)

séttei n 設定 setup, setting: ~ **shimásu** 設定します sets up; **shoki-settei** 初期設定 default (setting)

sétto n セット **1.** set (hair, etc.) **2.** a set meal

settō n 窃盗 theft: **settō-han** 窃盗犯 a thief

settō-go/-ji n 接頭語/辞 prefix

settoku n 説得 persuasion: ~ **shimásu** 説得します persuades, convinces

sewá n 世話 (**o-séwa** お世話) **1.** care, trouble, assistance, help; (...no) ~ **ni narimásu** (...の)世話になります becomes obliged (to one for help); → **o-sewa-sama** お世話さま **2.** meddling, minding other people's business

sewashíi adj 忙しい = **sewashi-nái** 忙しない busy, hectic

sezu v せず not doing (= **sezu ni** せずに, **shináide** しないで)

sha-.../...-sha prefix, suffix 社.../

... 社 company

sha-chō n 社長 president of a company

sha-dan n 社団 corporation

shá-in n 社員 employee (of a company)

shá-nai (no) adj 社内 (の) within the office/company, internal, in-house

sha-... prefix 車... vehicle

sha-dō n 車道 road(way), drive(way), street

shá-ko n 車庫 garage, car barn

sha-rin n 車輪 wheel

sha-shō n 車掌 conductor

...-sha suffix ...車 (name of certain) vehicle

...´-sha suffix ...者 person

shaberánai v 喋らない [INFORMAL] = **shaberimasén** 喋りません (not speak/talk)

shaberimásu, shabéru v 喋ります, 喋る [INFORMAL] speak/talk: **o-shaberi shimásu** お喋りします chatters

sháberu n シャベル shovel

shabétte v 喋って → **shaberimásu** 喋ります

shabon n シャボン soap (= **sekken** 石けん・石鹸)

shabon-dama n シャボン玉 soap bubble

shaburanai v しゃぶらない [INFORMAL] = **saburimasén** しゃぶりません (not suck)

shaburimásu, shaburu v しゃぶります, しゃぶる [INFORMAL] sucks (= **sū** 吸う)

shabu-shabu n しゃぶしゃぶ beef slices dipped in hot broth till ready to eat

shabutte v しゃぶって → **shaburimásu** しゃぶります

shadan n 遮断 interruption: ~ **shimásu** 遮断します interrupts

shagamimásu, shagamu v しゃがみます, しゃがむ squats, crouches on heels

shagande v しゃがんで → **shagamimásu** しゃがみます

shagare-goe n 嗄れ声 hoarse voice

shageki n 射撃 shooting (firing a rifle, shotgun, etc)

shajitsu n 写実 [BOOKISH] drawing/

writing realistically: **shajitsu-teki (na)** 写実的(な) realistic (= **riaru (na)** リアル(な)): **shajitsu-shugi** 写実主義 realism

Sháka n シャカ・釈迦 Buddha (*Sakyamuni*) (= **O-Shaka-sámá** お釈迦様)

shákai n 社会 society (= **seken** 世間, **yo-no-naka** 世の中): **shákai no** 社会の social

shakai-kágaku n 社会科学 social science(s)

shakai no shukuzu n 社会の縮図 society in miniature

shakai-shúgi n 社会主義 socialism; **shakai-shúgí-sha** 社会主義者 a socialist

sháke n シャケ・鮭 salmon (= **sáke** サケ・鮭)

shakkín n 借金 debt

shákkuri n しゃっくり hiccup: ~ **shimásu** しゃっくりします hiccups

sháko n シャコ squilla, mantis shrimp

shakō n 社交 social intercourse, socializing

shaku n 酌 (**o-shaku** お酌) serving/ pouring the rice wine: **o-shaku o shimásu** お酌をします serves the saké

shakuhachi n 尺八 vertical bamboo flute

shakunetsu adj 灼熱 **1.** burning: ~ **no taiyō** 灼熱の太陽 scorching sun **2.** passionate

shaku ni sawarimásu (sawaru) v 癪に障ります(障る) takes offense, gets irritated/provoked; **... ga ~** ...が癪に障ります is offensive, irritating

shákushi n 杓子 ladle (*large wooden*): [IDIOM] **neko mo ~ mo** 猫も杓子も all the world and his wife, everyone (= **dare mo ka(re) mo** 誰も彼も)

shákushi-jōgi n 杓子定規 formalism: ~ **ni yarimásu** 杓子定規にやります goes by the book

shamisen n 三味線 a three-stringed banjo

Shánhái n シャンハイ・上海 Shanghai

shanpán, shanpén n シャンパン, シャンペン champagne

shánpū n シャンプー shampoo

share n しゃれ・洒落 pun (= **dajare** 駄洒落): ~ **o iimásu** しゃれを言います puns

sharei (kin) n 謝礼(金) remuneration, reward, fee

shasei n 写生 sketching, sketch: ~ **shimásu** 写生します sketches

shasei n 射精 ejaculation, seminal emission

shashin n 写真 photo, picture: **shashin-chō** 写真帳 photo album: **shashin-ka** 写真家 photographer: ~ **o torimásu** 写真を撮ります takes a photograph (= **shashin satsuei (o) shimásu** 写真撮影(を)します)

shashín-ki n 写真機 camera (= **kamera** カメラ)

shátsu n シャツ undershirt

sháttā n シャッター shutter (*camera, etc.*): ~ **o kirimásu** シャッターを切ります releases the shutter

sháwā n シャワー shower: ~ **o abimásu** シャワーを浴びます takes a shower

shi n 詩 poetry, poem, verse

shijin n 詩人 poet

... shi *suffix* ...し and, and so, what with (*the fact that*) ...

shí n 死 death

shi-gai n 死骸 corpse

shi-in n 死因 cause of death

shi-nin n 死人 dead person: [IDIOM] ~ **ni kuchi nashi** 死人に口なし Dead men tell no tales.

shi-shṓ-sha n 死傷者 casualties (*dead and wounded*)

shi-tai n 死体 corpse

shí n 四 four (= **yón** 四)

shi-go-... *prefix, adj* 四,五... four or five ...

shi-jū n 四十・40 forty (= **yón-jū** 四十・40)

shi-jū n 四重 quadruplex: **shi-jū-sō** 四重奏 quartet (= **karutetto** カルテット) (*musical instruments, two violins, viola, cello, etc.*): **gengaku-shijūsō-kyoku/dan** 弦楽四重奏曲/団 string quartet

shí n 市 city (= **tóshi** 都市)

shi-chō n 市長 mayor

shí-gai n 市外 outside the city: **shi-gai-denwa** 市外電話 out-of-city call

shí-min n 市民 citizen, civilian (= **kōmin** 公民)

shí-nai *n* 市内 within the city: **shinai-denwa** 市内電話 local telephone call

shí-ritsu (no) *adj* 市立(の) municipal

shi-yákusho *n* 市役所 city office, city hall

shiage *n* 仕上げ the finish(ing touch)

shiagemásu, shiagéru *v* 仕上げます, 仕上げる finishes up

shiagénai *v* 仕上げない = **shiagemásén** 仕上げません (not finish up)

shiágete *v* 仕上げて → **shiagemásu** 仕上げて

shiai *n* 試合 match, contest, tournament

shiasátte *n, adv* しあさって・明々後日 three days from now

shiawase *n* 幸せ・しあわせ happiness (= **kōfuku** 幸福, **saiwai** 幸い)

shiawase (na) *adj* 幸せ(な) happy

shiba *n* 柴 brushwood

shiba *n* 芝 turf, lawn

shibá-ebi *n* 芝エビ[海老] tiny shrimp

shiba-fu *n* 芝生 lawn, grass

shiba-karí-ki *n* 芝刈り機 lawn mower

Shíba *n* 芝 Shiba; **Shiba-Kō´en** 芝公園 Shiba Park

shibai *n* 芝居 1. a play (*drama*) (= **engeki** 演劇, **engi** 演技) 2. acting, pretending, fake: ~ **o uchimásu** 芝居を打ちます puts on an act

shibáraku *adv* しばらく (*for*) a while: ~ **shite** しばらくして after a while: **Shibáraku desu ne** しばらくですね. It's nice to see you again.

shibaránai *v* 縛らない = **shibarimásén** 縛りません (not tie up)

shibarimásu, shibáru *v* 縛ります, 縛る tie up

shíba shíba *adv* しばしば often, repeatedly

Shíberia *n* シベリア Siberia

shibin *n* しびん bedpan (*urinal*)

shibiré *n* しびれ・痺れ numbness: ~ **o kirashimásu** しびれを切らします loses patience

shibiremásu, shibiréru *v* 痺れます, 痺れる gets numb, (*a leg, etc.*) goes to sleep

shibō *n* 脂肪 fat (*lard, blubber*) (= **abura** 脂)

shibō *n* 志望 a desire, a wish: **haiyū/**

joyū-shibō 俳優/女優志望 a would-be actor/actress: **daiichi-shibō no ...** 第一志望の... one's first choice ...

shiboránai *v* 絞らない = **shiborimásén** 絞りません not wring it

shiborimásu, shibóru *v* 絞ります, 絞る wrings (*out*), squeezes, strains (*through cloth*)

shibótte *v* 絞って → **shiborimásu** 絞ります

shibu *n* 支部 branch office

shibúi *adj* 渋い 1. taste, astringent (*tea*), bitter (*wine*) rough 2. (*face*) wry, sour: ~ **kao o shimásu** 渋い顔をします makes a wry face 3. appearance cool (*sedate, sober, elegant, tasteful*): ~ **engi** 渋い演技 low-keyed performance

shibui kaki *n* 渋い柿, **shibu-gaki** 渋柿 sour persimmon

shibui iroi *n* 渋い色 elegant color

Shibuya *n* 渋谷 Shibuya; **Shibuyá-Eki** 渋谷駅 Shibuya Station

shichí *n* 七・7 seven (= **nána** 七・7)

Shichi-go-san *n* 七五三 the "seven-five-three" day when children of those ages visit shrines (*15 November*)

shichi-jū *n* 七十・70 seventy (= **naná-jū** 七十・70)

shichí *n* 質 a pawn (*something pawned*) shichí-ya *n* 質屋 pawnbroker, pawn-shop

Shichi-gatsú *n* 七月・7月 July

shichimen-chō *n* シチメンチョウ・七面鳥 turkey

shichū´ *n* シチュー stew

shída *n* シダ・羊歯 fern

shidai *n* 次第・しだい 1. circumstances 2. *suffix* ([NOUN, VERB] -i い) ~ **desu** 次第です it depends on ...; ([VERB] **-i** い) **-shídai** 次第 as soon as ...

shidashi-ya *n* 仕出し屋 caterer, catering shop

shidō *n* 指導 guidance, direction, leadership, counsel(ing), coaching: ~ **shimásu** 指導します guides, directs, leads, counsels, coaches

shidō-sha *n* 指導者 guide, director, leader, coach

shifuku *n* 私服 plain clothes; civilian clothes

shígā *n* シガー cigar (= **hamaki** 葉巻)

shi-gachi (na) *suffix, adj* しがち(な) apt to do, tends to

shigarétto *n* シガレット cigarette(s) (= **tabako** たばこ・タバコ・煙草): **sigaretto-kēsu** シガレットケース cigarette case

Shi-gatsú *n* 四月・4月 April

shigeki *n* 刺激 stimulation: ~ **shimásu** 刺激します stimulates; ~ **o ukemásu** 刺激を受けます gets stimulated

shigerimásu, shigéru *v* 茂ります, 茂る it grows thick(ly)/luxuriant(ly)

shígoku *adv* 至極 extremely

shigoto *n* 仕事 (**o-shígoto** お仕事) job, work, task, undertaking, business; operation: ~ **(o) shimásu** 仕事(を)します works; ~ **ni ikimásu** 仕事に行きます goes to work

shigure *n* 時雨 an on-and-off drizzle (*in early winter*): **semi-shigure** 蝉時雨 cicada shower, cicada chorus

shihái, shíhai *n* 支配 management, control: ~ **shimásu** 支配します rules, controls

shihái-nin *n* 支配人 manager

shihái-sha *n* 支配者 ruler

shihanki *n* 四半期 quarter (*year*): **dai ni-shihanki** 第二四半期 the second (*business*) quarter (*of a company*)

shiharai *n* 支払い paying out, payment, disbursement

shihei *n* 紙幣 paper money, currency (*bill*) (= **(o-)satsu** (お)札)

shihó' (-happō) *n* 四方(八方) all sides/directions

shihon (kin) *n* 資本(金) capital, funds: **shihon-ka** 資本家 capitalist; **shihon-shúgi** 資本主義 capitalism

shiīému *n* シーエム・CM TV commercial, CM (= **komāsharu** コマーシャル)

shiin *n* 子音 consonant (= **shion** 子音)

shíin *n* シーン scene (= **bamen** 場面)

shiítake *n* シイタケ・椎茸 large brown mushrooms, shiitake mushrooms: **hoshi-shiitake** 干し椎茸 dried shiitake mushrooms

shiite *v* 敷いて → **shikimásu** 敷きます

shiíte *adv* 強いて forcibly: ~ **sase-másu** 強いてさせます forces one to do

shíito *n* シート **1.** sheets; **biniiru shiito** ビニール・シート vinyl sheet **2.** seat; **shiito-béruto** シート・ベルト seatbelt

shiítsu *n* シーツ for sheet (*bed*) (= **beddo (no) shítsu** ベッド(の)シーツ)

shíizun *n* シーズン **1.** the season (= **kisetsu** 季節) **2.** high season; **yakyū (no) shíizun** 野球(の)シーズン baseball season

shiji *n* 支持 [BOOKISH] support, maintenance (= **sapōto** サポート): ~ **shimásu** 支持します supports, endorses

shíji *n* 指示 [BOOKISH] indication, instruction, directions: ~ **shimásu** 指示します indicates, points out

shíji *n* 師事 [BOOKISH] studying under someone: **... ni ~ shimásu** ...に師事します studies under someone at ...

shíji *n* 私事 [BOOKISH] **1.** personal matter (= **watakushi-goto** 私事) **2.** privacy

shijō *n* 市場 market (= **māketto** マーケット)

shijū *adv* 始終 all the time

shika *n* シカ・鹿 deer

shiká *n* 歯科 dentistry

shiká-i *n* 歯科医 dentist (= **há-isha** 歯医者)

...shika *conj* ...しか [+ NEGATIVE] (nothing) but, except for; (= **...daké ...** だけ [+ POSITIVE]) only, just

shikake *n* 仕掛け device (*gadget*)

shikaku *n* 資格 qualification(s), competency; ~ **shikaku** 在留資格 status of residence

shikakúi *adj* 四角い square

shiká-mo *adv* しかも moreover; and yet

shikanai *v* 敷かない = **shikimásén** 敷きません (not spread it)

shikaranai *v* 叱らない = **shikarimasén** 叱りません (not scold)

shikarimásu, shikaru *v* 叱ります, 叱る scolds

shikarō' *v* 叱ろう = **shikarimashō'** 叱りましょう (let's scold!)

shikáshi *conj* しかし [BOOKISH] but, however (= **demo** でも, **keredo(mo)** けれど(も))

shi-kata *n* 仕方 way (of doing), manner, method, means: ~ **ga arimasén** 仕方がありません there's nothing I/we can do about it, can't be helped

shikátte *v* 叱って → **shikarimásu** 叱ります

shikéba *v* 敷けば・しけば (if one spreads it) → **shikimásu** 敷きます

shikén *n* 試験 [BOOKISH] examination, test, trial, experiment (= **tesuto** テスト)
shiken-jó *n* 試験所 (*testing*) laboratory
shiken-jō *n* 試験場 exam room/place
shikén-kan *n* 試験管 test tube

shikí *n* 式 ceremony

shikí *n* 指揮 **1.** command **2.** conducting (*orchestra*)
shikí-sha *n* 指揮者 conductor (*orchestra*)

shikibetsu *n* 識別 discrimination: ~ **shimásu** 識別します discriminates, discerns, distinguishes

shiki-chi *n* 敷地 building lot; (*house*) site

shikii *n* 敷居 sill; threshold

shikí-kin *n* 敷金 security deposit (*for rental*)

shikimásu, shiku *v* 敷きます, 敷く spreads (*a quilt, etc.*)
shiki-búton *n* 敷布団 bottom quilt
shiki-fu *n* 敷布 (bed)sheet (= **shíitsu** シーツ)
shiki-mono *n* 敷物 a spread; rug, mat, cushion

shikín *n* 資金 fund, capital

shi-kiremasén, shi-kirénai *v* し切れません, し切れない = **dekimasén** できません, **dekínai** できない (cannot do it)

shikíri *n* 仕切り partition (= **pātéshon** パーテーション)

shikiri ni *adv* しきりに incessantly; intently, hard

shikkári *adv* しっかり firmly, resolutely

shikke, shikki *n* 湿気 dampness, humidity

shikki *n* 漆器 lacquer(ware)

shíkko *n* しっこ, **o-shíkko** おしっこ (*slang/baby talk*) urine, urinating (= **nyō** 尿)

shikkui *n* 漆喰 plaster, stucco, mortar

shikō *n* 嗜好・し好 liking, fancy, taste; **...ni ~ ga arimásu** …に嗜好があります has a taste/liking for…

shikō-hin *n* 嗜好品・し好品 articles of taste, amenities of life

Shikóku *n* 四国 Shikoku: **Shikóku-chihō** 四国地方 the Sikoku area of Japan (*Tokushima, Kagawa, Ehime, Kōchi prefectures*)

shiku *v* 敷く = **shikimásu** 敷きます (spreads it)

shikyō-hin *n* 試供品 tester, free sample (*for customers*) (→ **sanpuru** サンプル)

shikyū *adv* 至急 urgently: **shikyū (no)** 至急(の) urgent

shima *n* 島 island

shima *n* 縞 stripes (= **sutoraipu** ストライプ): **shima-moyō** 縞模様 stripe pattern

shimai *n* 終い・仕舞(い) = **o-shimai** おしまい・御仕舞(い) the end: **shimai (no)** しまい(の) the final/last

shimaimásu, shimau *v* しまいます, しまう puts away, finishes; **shite shimau** してしまう finishes doing, ends up by doing (*after all*), does anyway, does it all

shimaō *v* しまおう = **shimaimashō´** まいましょう (let's put it away; let's finish)

shimaránai *v* 閉まらない = **shimari-masén** 閉まりません (not shut; not …)

shimarimásu, shimáru *v* 閉まります, 閉まる it shuts, closes, locks

shimarimásu, shimáru *v* 締まります, 締まる gets steady, braces oneself

shimarimásu, shimáru *v* 締まります, 締まる gets thrifty, frugal

shimasén, shinai *v* しません, しない doesn't

shimasén deshita, shinákatta *v* しませんでした, しなかった didn't

shimáshita *v* しました = **shita** した (did)

shimashō´ *v* しましょう = **shiyō´** しよう (let's do it): **shimashō´ ka** しましょうか Shall we do it?

shimásu, suru *v* します, する does (it); it happens; wears … ni ([ADJECTIVE] **-ku**) shimásu …に…(く)します makes it so that (*it is*), makes it into; decides on (= **... ni kimemásu** …に決めます)

… (shiyō) to shimásu …（しよう）とします goes (tries, is about) to do

… (suru) koto ni shimásu …（する）事にします decides to (do)

… to shíte(´ mo) …として(も) (*even*) as a …

shímatsu *n* 始末 managing, dealing with; outcome, upshot, climax; ~ **shimásu** 始末します deals with, manages, settles, disposes of

shimatta *v* しまった = **shimaimáshita** しまいました (finished)

shimátta *v* 閉まった・締まった = **shimarimáshita** 閉まりました・締まりました (it shut, closed, locked)

shimátta *interj* しまった! Damn!, Good heavens

shimau *v* しまう = **shimaimásu** しまいます (puts away, finishes)

shimauma *n* シマウマ zebra

shimawanai *v* しまわない = **shimaimásen** しまいません (not put away)

shime-gane *n* 締め金 buckle

shimei *n* 使命 mission (= **misshon** ミッション): **shimei-kan** 使命感 sense of mission

shi-mei *n* 氏名 (*one's*) full name (= **sei-mei** 姓名)

shimei *n* 指名 designation: ~ **shimásu** 指名します nominates

shimei-tsū´wa *n* 指名通話 person-to-person call

shimei-tehai *n* 指名手配 listing a person (*criminal*) on the wanted list: ~ **shimásu** 指名手配します puts a person (*criminal*) on the wanted list

shimekiri *n* 締め切り・〆切 **1.** closing **2.** "Closed", deadline: ~ **kígen/kíjitsu** 締め切り期限/期日 deadline, due date

shimemásu, shiméru *v* 閉めます, 閉める shuts (closes, locks) it

shimemásu, shiméru *v* 締めます, 締める **1.** ties, fastens, tightens it (*necktie, belt, kimono sash, seatbelt, etc.*) **2.** tightens up on: **neji o ~** ネジを締めます tightens up a screw **3.** economizes on: [IDIOM] **saifu no himo o shimeru** 財布の紐を締める tightens one's belt

shiménai *v* 閉めない = **shimemásén** 閉めません (not shut it)

shimeppói *adj* 湿っぽい damp; humid

shimerasemásu, shimerasu *v* 湿らせます, 湿らす moistens/dampens it, wets it

shimerimásu, shimeru *v* 湿ります, 湿る gets damp

shiméru *v* 閉める = **shimemásu** 閉めます (closes it)

shiméru *v* 締める = **shimemásu** 締めます (fastens, closes it)

shimeshimásu, shimésu *v* 示します, 示す shows, indicates

shímeta *v* 閉めた = **shimemáshita** 閉めました (closed it)

shímeta *v* 締めた = **shimemáshita** 締めました (fastenend it, closes it)

shímete *v* 閉めて → **shimemásu** 閉めます

shímete *v* 締めて → **shimemásu** 締めます

shimetta *v* 湿った = **shimerimáshita** 湿りました (got damp)

shimette *v* 湿って → **shimerimásu** 湿ります: ~ **imásu** 湿っています is damp

shimi *n* 染み・しみ **1.** stain, blot, blotch, spot

shimi *n* 衣魚・シミ clothes moth

shimijími (to) *adv* しみじみ(と) deeply (*feels*), fully (*appreciates*)

shimimásu, shimiru *v* 染みます, 染みる penetrates, soaks

shimimásu, shimiru *v* 沁みます, 沁みる smarts, is stimulated (*body*), is deeply moved (*heart*): **… ga kokoro ni ~** …が心に沁みます it is deeply moved by …: **honemi ni ~** 骨身に沁みます touches one to the quick

shimó *n* 霜・しも frost: ~ **ga orimásu** 霜が降ります frosts

shí mo *suffix* しも [+ NEGATIVE verb] ~ **shimasén** しもしません nor do, not do either/even

shimon *n* 指紋 fingerprint

shimon *n* 諮問 [BOOKISH] inquiry: ~ **shimásu** 諮問します inquires, consults

shimon *n* 試問 [BOOKISH] questioning, interviewing, examination; **kōtō-shí-mon** 口頭試問 oral examination

shín *n* 芯 core, pith, heart: **rōsoku no ~**

219

ロウソク[蝋燭]の芯 candlewick: **ringo no ~**リンゴ[林檎]の芯 apple core

shín-... *prefix* 心... heart, spirit

shín-chū *n* 心中 in one's heart

shin-pai *n* 心配 worry, uneasiness, concern, anxiety, fear: **~ shimásu** 心配 します worries about, fears; **shinpai (na)** 心配(な) uneasy; **(... ni) ~ o kakemásu** (...に)心配をかけます causes (*one*) worry/concern; [HONORIFIC] **Go-shinpai náku.** ご心配なく Please do not worry about it.

shín-ri *n* 心理 psychology, mentality

shin-rí-gaku *n* 心理学 (*science/study of*) psychology; **shinri gákú-sha** 心理学者 psychologist

shín-soko *n* 心底 (*at*) the bottom of one's heart

shin-zō *n* 心臓 heart (*organ*)

shín-... *prefix* 新... ... new

shin-geki *n* 新劇 modern drama

shín-nen *n* 新年 new year: **Shín-nen akemashite omedetō (gozaimásu)** 新年 明けましておめでとう(ございます)! Happy New Year!

shin-sen (na) *adj* 新鮮(な) fresh (= **furesshu** フレッシュ)

Shin-yaku Seisho *n* 新約聖書 the New Testament

shin-... *prefix* 神... god, deity

shin-den *n* 神殿 the sanctuary of a shrine

shín-dō *n* 神童 child prodigy

shín-pu *n* 神父 priest (*Christian*), Father, Reverend

Shín-tō, Shín-dō *n* 神道 Shinto(ism)

shin-wa *n* 神話 myth, mythology

shina *n* 品 **1.** articles, goods (= **shina-mono** 品物) **2.** quality (= **hinshitsu** 品質): **ii shina** 良い品 good/high quality products

shina-mono *n* 品物 goods, articles (= **shina** 品)

shi-nagara しながら while doing

shinai *v* しない = **shimasén** しません (doesn't do it)

shináide *v* しないで not doing it, instead of doing it: **~ imásu** しないでいます keeps on not doing it; **~ kudasai** しないで下さい Please don't do it!; **~**

okimásu しないでおきます neglects to do it, leaves it undone; **~ mimásu** しないでみます tries not doing it; **~ sumimásu** しないで済みます gets by without doing it, needs not do it, doesn't have to do it

shinai to *v* しないと = **shinákereba** しなければ (unless one does it)

shinákatta *v* しなかった = **shimasén deshita** しませんでした (didn't do it)

shinákereba *v* しなければ unless one does it: **~ narimasén** しなければなりません must do it

shinákute mo *v* しなくても even not doing it; **~ íi desu** しなくてもいいです gets by without doing it, needs not do it, doesn't have to do it

shinákya *v* しなきゃ [INFORMAL] = **shinákereba** しなければ

shinanai *v* 死なない = **shinimasén** 死にません (does/will not die)

shinánákatta *v* 死ななかった = **shini-masén deshita** 死にませんでした (didn't die)

shi-naoshimásu, shi-naósu *v* し直します, し直す redoes it, fixes/improves it

Shínbashi *n* 新橋 Shinbashi; **Shin-bashí-Eki** 新橋駅 Shinbashi Station

shínbō *n* 辛抱 [BOOKISH] endurance, patience, forbearance (= **gaman** 我慢, **nintai** 忍耐): **~ shimásu** 辛抱します endures, bears, stands, puts up with

shinbun *n* 新聞 newspaper: **shinbun-kíshá** 新聞記者 newsperson; **shinbun-úriba** 新聞売り場 newsstand; **shinbun-úri** 新聞売り news vendor

shinbun-dai *n* 新聞代 newspaper bill

shinbún-sha *n* 新聞社 newspaper company

shinchō *n* 身長 height, stature (= **sé** 背, **séi** せい・背, **setake** 背丈): **~ o hakari-másu** 身長を測ります measures one's height

shinchū *n* 真鍮 brass

shinda *v* 死んだ = **shinimáshita** 死にました (died) ((*human*)) = **nakunari-mashita** 亡くなりました, **o-nakunari ni narimashita** [HONORIFIC] お亡くなりになりました)

shindai *n* 寝台 bed, berth, bunk; **shindái-ken** 寝台券 berth ticket; **shindái-sha** 寝台車 sleeping car

shinde *v* 死んで → **shinimásu** 死にます: ~ **imásu** 死んでいます is dead

shindō *n* 振動 vibration (= **baiburēshon** バイブレーション): ~ **shimásu** 振動します vibrates: **hageshii** ~ 激しい振動 thumping vibration

Shinetsu-chihō *n* 信越地方 the Shinetsu area of Japan (*Niigata, Nagano prefectures*)

shingō *n* 信号 signal: **shingō-ki** 信号機 traffic light: **shingō-mushi** 信号無視 running a red light: **ao-shingō** 青信号 green light: **aka-shingō** 赤信号 red light

shíngu *n* 寝具 bedding

shínguru *n* シングル **1.** = **shinguru-rū'mu** シングル・ルーム a single (*room*) **2.** single, unmarried (= **dokushin** 独身), bachelor

shinimásu, shinu *v* 死にます, 死ぬ dies (= **nakunarimásu** 亡くなります, **o-nakunari ni narimásu** [HONORIFIC] お亡くなりになります (*for human*)

shínja *n* 信者 a believer; **Kirisuto-kyo (no) shínja** キリスト教(の)信者 a Christian

shin-jimásu, shin-jíru *v* 信じます, 信じる believes in, trusts

shin-jínai *v* 信じない = **shin-jimasén** 信じません (don't believe/trust)

shin-jínakatta *v* 信じなかった = **shin-jimasén deshita** 信じませんでした (didn't believe/trust)

shínjitsu *n* 真実 truth (= **hontō no koto** 本当のこと, **makoto** 誠・真)

shinju *n* 真珠 pearl; **Shinjú-wan** 真珠湾 Pearl Harbor

shinjū *n* 心中 double suicide, lovers' suicide

Shinjuku *n* 新宿 Shinjuku; **Shinjukú-Eki** 新宿駅 Shinjuku Station

shinkánsen *n* 新幹線 bullet train (*line*), **Shinkansen**

shínkei *n* 神経 nerve: ~ **ni sawarimásu** 神経に障ります gets on one's nerves: **chūsū-shínkei** 中枢神経 central nerve shinkéi-shitsu (na) *adj* 神経質(な) nervous

shinkoku (na) *adj* 深刻(な) serious, grave

shinobánai *v* 忍ばない = **shinobi-masén** 忍びません (not bear, not put up with)

shinobimásu, shinobu *v* 忍びます, 忍ぶ bears, puts up with

shinónde *v* 忍んで → **shinobimásu** 忍びます

shínpi *n* 神秘 mystery; **shinpí-teki (na)** 神秘的(な) mysterious, esoteric, miraculous

shínpo *n* 進歩 progress: ~ **shimásu** 進歩します makes progress

shínpuru (na) *adj* シンプル(な) simple

shinrai *n* 信頼 trust, confidence, reliance shinrai-sei *n* 信頼性 reliability: ~ **ga takái** 信頼性が高い highly reliable

shínri *n* 真理 truth, veritas: **fuhen no ~** 不変の真理 eternal truth, everlasting truth (= **eien no shínri** 永遠の真理)

shinrui *n* 親類 a relative (= **shinseki** 親戚, **shinzoku** 親族)

shinryaku *n* 侵略 invasion, aggression: ~ **shimásu** 侵略します invades

shinsatsu *n* 診察 medical examination: ~ **shimásu** 診察します examines

shinsei *n* 申請 application (*for a permit*): ~ **shimásu** 申請します applies (*for a permit*) shinsei-nin *n* 申請人 an applicant shinsei-shó *n* 申請書 application form (*for a permit*)

shinseki *n* 親戚 a relative (= **shinrui** 親類, **shinzoku** 親族)

shínsetsu *n* 親切 (**go-shínsetsu** ご親切) kindness, goodwill, favor shínsetsu na *adj* 親切(な) kind, cordial

shínshi *n* 紳士 gentleman

shinshitsu *n* 寝室 bedroom

shíntai (no) *adj* 身体(の) physical; **shintai-kénsa** 身体検査 physical exam; **shintai-shōgáisha** 身体障害者 handicapped person

shinu *v* 死ぬ = **shinimásu** 死にます (dies)

shín'ya n, adv 深夜 late at night

shin'yō *n* 信用 trust, confidence; credit: ~ **shimásu** 信用します trusts

shinzoku n 親族 relatives (= **shinseki** 親戚, **shinrui** 親類)

shió n 潮 tide (→ **kanchō** 干潮, **manchō** 満潮)

shió n 塩 (**o-shío** お塩) salt
shio-karái adj 塩辛い salty (= **shoppai** しょっぱい)
shio-yáki n 塩焼き broiled salt-coated fish

shion n 子音 consonant (= **shiin** 子音)

shióri n しおり bookmark (*a thin marker made of paper, card, etc.*)

shippai n 失敗 failure, blunder, defeat: ~ **shimásu** 失敗します fails, misses

shippó n しっぽ・尻尾 tail (= **o** 尾)

shira-... *prefix* 白... white
shira-gá n 白髪 gray hair
shira-su n シラス・白子 baby sardines
shirá-taki n シラタキ・白滝 fine white threads of Konnyaku (こんにゃく)
shira-uo n シラウオ・白魚 icefish, white fish

shirábe ro v 調べろ [IMPERATIVE] (investigate!) → **shirabemásu** 調べます

shirabemásu, shirabéru v 調べます, 調べる investigates, examines, checks

shirabénai v 調べない = **shirabemásén** 調べません (not investigate)

shirábeta v 調べた = **shirabemáshita** 調べました (investigated)

shirábete v 調べて → **shirabemásu** 調べます

shirafu (no) adj しらふ(の)(*undrunk*) sober

shirami n シラミ louse, lice

shiranai v 知らない = **shirimásén** 知りません (not know): **shiranai hitó** 知らない人 a stranger (= **tanin** 他人)

shiraremásu, shirareru v 知られます, 知られる gets (*widely*) known; becomes famous

shirarenai v 知れない = **shiraremásén** 知れません (not get known; not be clear)

shirase n 知らせ (= **o-shirase** お知らせ) report, notice, information

shirasemásu, shiraseru v 知らせます, 知らせる announces (*informs of*), lets one know, notifies

shirase ro 知らせろ [IMPERATIVE] (let me/someone know!) → **shirasemásu** 知らせます

shiréba v 知れば (if one learns/knows) → **shirimásu** 知ります

shiréi n 司令 command (*in army, etc.*)
shiréi-bu n 司令部 headquarters

shiréi n 指令 command (= **meirei** 命令, **sashizu** 指図)
shiréi-kan n 指令官 commander

shiremásu, shireru v 知れます, 知れる gets known; is identified; becomes clear/evident

shirí n 尻 (**o-shiri** お尻) butt(ock), hip, bottom, seat

shiriai n 知り合い acquaintance

shirimasén, shiranai v 知りません, 知らない does not know

shirimásu, shiru v 知ります, 知る acquaints oneself with, finds out, learns; **shitte imásu** 知っています knows

shiri-tai v 知りたい curious about, want(ing) to know

shíritsu (no) adj 私立(の)(= **watakushí-ritsu** 私立) privately established entity/organization

shirizóita v 退いた = **shirizokimáshita** 退きました (retreated)

shirizóite v 退いて → **shirizokimásu** 退きます

shirizokánai v 退かない = **shirizoki-masén** 退きません (not retreat)

shirizokimásu, shirizóku v 退きます, 退く retreats, withdraws, retires

shiro n 城 (**o-shiro** お城) castle

shíro n 白 white: **shiro-kuma** 白熊・シロクマ white bear, polar bear (= **Hokkyoku-guma** ホッキョクグマ・北極熊)
shiró-mi n 白身 white (*of an egg*), albumen; white meat
shiró-i adj 白い white

shi ro *suffix* (v) しろ; [IMPERATIVE] do it! (= **sé yo** せよ) → **shimásu** します

shirō´ v 知ろう = **shirimashó´** 知りましょう (let's learn/know it!)

shíróppu n シロップ syrup

shírō´to n 素人 an amateur, a novice

shiru v 知る = **shirimásu** 知ります (learns; knows)

shíru *n* 汁 juice, gravy; broth, soup

shirukó *n* しるこ・汁粉 (**o-shiruko** おしるこ・お汁粉) a sweet redbean-paste soup

shirushi *n* 印・徴 (**o-shirushi** お印・お徴) indication, token, sign, symptom; effect(iveness)

shíryo *n* 思慮 [BOOKISH] consideration, thought(-fulness)

shíryō *n* 資料 materials; data

shíryoku *n* 視力 vision, eyesight, visual acuity

shisei *n* 姿勢 posture; attitude

shisen *n* 支線 branch (*of rail line*)

shisen *n* 視線 eye direction

shísetsu (no) *adj* 私設(の) private

shísetsu *n* 施設 facility, institution, establishment, installation

shíshi *n* シシ・獅子 lion (= **raion** ライオン)

shishū *n* 刺繍 embroidery

shishún-ki *n* 思春期 adolescence

shiso *n* シソ・紫蘇 perilla, beefsteak plant

shisō *n* 思想 thought, concept

shíson *n* 子孫 descendants; posterity

...-shi-sō (na) *suffix, adj* しそう(な) likely/about to do it: **~ mo nái** しそうもない unlikely to do it

shíssō (na) *adj* 質素(な) simple, plain, frugal, rustic

shi-sugimásu, shi-sugíru *v* し過ぎます, し過ぎる over(does)

shita *v* した = **shimáshita** しました (did, has done): **~ áto de** した後で after doing; **~ bákari désu** したばかりです just (now) did it; **~ hō´ga íi** した方がいい ought to do it, better do it; **~ kotóga arimasén** したことがありません has never done it; **~ monódesu** したものです used to do it

shita(-...) *n, prefix* 下(...) below, under, bottom, lower; (= **toshi-shita** 年下) younger, youngest

shita-baki *n* 下穿き underpants

shita-baki *n* 下履き (*outdoor*) shoes

shita-gi *n* 下着 underwear

shita-machi *n* 下町 downtown

shitá *n* 舌 tongue

shita-bírame *n* シタビラメ・舌平目 sole (*fish*)

shitagaimásu, shitagau *v* 従います, 従う: **...ni ~** ...に従います conforms to ..., accords with ...

shi-tagarimásu, shi-tagáru *v* したがります, したがる wants (*is eager*) to do

shitagatte *adv, conj* 従って accordingly, therefore; **... ni ~** ...に従って according to ..., in conformity with/to ...

shi-tagátte *v* したがって → **shi-tagari-másu** したがります

shi-tai *v* したい wants to do it

shi-tákatta *v* したかった wanted to do it

shitaku *n* 支度 preparation, arrangement

shi-taku *v* したく: **~ arimasén** したくありません is unwilling to do it: **~ narimásu** したくなります gets so one wants to do it

shitára *v* したら if/when one does it

shitári (... shimásu) *v* したり (...します) does/is such things as; sometimes does/is

shitashíi *adj* 親しい intimate, familiar

shitate-ya *n* 仕立屋 tailor

shitátte *v* したって = **shitémo** しても even doing, even if it does

shite *v* して doing; does and; **shité kara** してから (next) after doing; **shité mo íi** してもいい may do it, it is OK to do it; **shité wa ikemasén/ikenai/damé** してはいけません/いけない/だめ mustn't do it, don't do it!

shitei *n* 指定 designation, appointment: **~ shimásu** 指定します designates, appoints

shitei-seki *n* 指定席 reserved seat(s)

shitéi-shi *n* 指定詞 the copula (**désu, dá, ná, nó, ní, dé, ...** です, だ, な, の, に, で,...)

shiteki shimásu (suru) *v* 指摘します(する) indicates, points out

shiten *n* 支店 branch shop

shitetsu *n* 私鉄 private railroad

shitsu *n* 質 quality, nature

...´-shitsu *suffix* ...室 (*name of certain*) room

shitsū *n* 歯痛 toothache (= **ha-ita** 歯痛)

shitsubō *n* 失望 disappointment: **~ shimásu** 失望します disappoints

shitsúdo *n* 湿度 humidity

shitsugyō *n* 失業 unemployment; **shitsugyō´-sha** 失業者 unemployed person

shitsuke *n* しつけ・躾 training (*of children, …*), discipline, upbringing

shi-tsuke *n* 仕付け basting, tacking (*with thread*); **shitsuke-íto** 仕付け糸 basting/tacking thread

shitsukemásu, shitsukéru *v* しつけ[躾け]ます, しつけ[躾け]る trains (*children, …*), disciplines, brings up

shi-tsukemásu, shi-tsukéru *v* 仕付け ます, 仕付ける bastes, tacks (*with thread*)

shitsumon *n* 質問 question: ~ **shimásu** 質問します asks a question

shitsurakuen *n* 失楽園 Paradise Lost

shitsúrei *n* 失礼 discourtesy: ~ **shimásu** 失礼します does a discourtesy, excuses oneself (*leaves*); **Shitsúrei desu ga ...** 失礼ですが... Excuse me for asking, but ...

shitsúrei (na) *adj* 失礼 (な) impolite

shitsuren *n* 失恋 disappointment in love: ~ **shimásu** 失恋します gets brokenhearted

shitsuteki (na) *adj* 質的 (な) qualitative

shitta *v* 知った = **shirimáshita** 知りま した (learned, found out)

shitte *v* 知って → **shirimásu** 知りま す: ~ **imásu** 知っています knows

shitto *n* 嫉妬 jealousy: ~ **bukai** 嫉妬深 い jealous

shiwa *n* しわ・シワ・皺 wrinkle, crease: ~ **ga dekimásu** しわができま す, ~ **ni narimásu** しわになります it wrinkles

shiwaza *n* 仕業 act, deed: **Aitsu no ~ ni chigainai.** アイツの仕業に違いない I bet he is the one who is behind it.

shi-yasúi *v* しやすい **1.** easy to do **2.** likely to do it, tends to do it

shi-yō *n* 仕様 method, means, way (= **shi-kata** 仕方); (*for products, etc.*) specifications: ~ **ga nái** しようがない hopeless, beyond remedy (= **shō ga nái** しょうがない)

shiyō *n* 使用 use, employment: ~ **shimásu** 使用します uses, employs

shiyō-chū 使用中 in use, occupied (*toilet, etc.*)

shiyō-nin *n* 使用人 servant

shiyō´-sha *n* 使用者 user

shiyō *n* 私用 private use/business (= **jibun-yō** 自分用): shiyō no 私用の private

shiyō *v* しよう = **shimashō** しましょう (let's do it): ~ **to shimásu** しようとし ます tries/starts to do it

shizen *n* 自然 nature: **shizen (no)** 自 然(の) natural; **shizen (na)** 自然(な) natural, spontaneous

shízuka (na) *adj* 静か(な) quiet, still

shizumanai *v* 沈まない = **shizumi-masén** 沈みません (not sink)

shizumaránai *v* 静まらない・鎮まら ない = **shizumarimasén** 静まりませ ん・鎮まりません (not get quiet)

shizumarimásu, shizumáru *v* 静ま ります・鎮まります,静まる・鎮まる gets quiet/calm, quiets/calms down

shizumatte *v* 静まって・鎮まって → **shizumarimásu** 静まります・鎮ま ります (gets quiet)

shizumemásu, shizuméru *v* 静め ます・鎮めます, 静める・鎮める soothes, quiets, calms, pacifies

shizumemásu, shizumeru *v* 沈めま す, 沈める sinks it

shizúménai *v* 静めない・鎮めない = **shizumemasén** 静めません・鎮めませ ん (not soothe it)

shizumenai *v* 沈めない = **shizume-masén** 沈めません (not sink it)

shizumete *v* 沈めて → **shizume-másu** 沈めます

shizumete *v* 静めて・鎮めて → **shizumemásu** 静めます・鎮めます

shizumimásu, shizumu *v* 沈みます, 沈む it sinks

shizunde *v* 沈んで → **shizumimásu** 沈みます (it sinks)

sho- *prep* 諸 [*makes definite plurals of certain nouns*] **sho-ji** 諸事 all matters; everything; **sho-tō** 諸島 (*a group of*) islands; an archipelago

shō´ *n* 性 nature, disposition, quality

shō´ *n* 賞 prize, reward

shō´-batsu *n* 賞罰 rewards and punishments

shō-hin *n* 賞品 prize (*object*)

shō-kin *n* 賞金 prize money; reward

shō´-yo *n* 賞与 bonus; **shōyó-kin** 賞与金 bonus money

shō´ *n* 笙 a traditional Japanese reed instrument

shō-... *prefix* 商... sales, business

shō´-bai *n* 商売 trade, business: **mizu-shōbai** 水商売 chancy trade (*restaurant, bar, cabaret, etc.*)

shō´-gyō *n* 商業 commerce, trade, business

shō´-hin *n* 商品 goods, merchandise, (*sales*) product

shō´-nin *n* 商人 merchant, trader

shō´-ten *n* 商店 shop, store: **shōten-gai** 商店街 shop street(s), shopping area

...´-shō *suffix* ...商 dealer (*seller of ...*): **gyō-shō** 行商 peddling

...´-shō *suffix* ...省 **1.** (*name of certain*) Ministry **2.** (*name of certain*) province (*China*)

shōátsú-ki *n* 昇圧機 booster (*of current*)

sho´-batsu *n* 処罰 [BOOKISH] punishments: **~ shimásu** 処罰します punishes

shōbén *n* 小便 urine, urinating (*very informal, mostly male*): **~ shimásu** 小便します urinates

shōbō *n* 消防 fire fighting; **shōbō´-sha** 消防車 fire engine; **shōbō´-shi** 消防士 fire fighter; **shōbō-shó** 消防署 fire house/station, fire department

shō´bu *n* 勝負 match, contest

shō´bu *n* ショウブ・菖蒲 iris

shóbun *n* 処分 [BOOKISH] disposition, abolition: **~ shimásu** 処分します disposes of

sho´chi *n* 処置 [BOOKISH] dealing with: **~ shimásu** 処置します deals with

shōchi *n* 承知 agreement, understanding; **Shōchi shimáshita** 承知しました [HUMBLE] I understand (*and consent*). (*on business e-mail, etc.*) Yes, sir/ma'am.

shōchō *n* 所長 institute director

shōchō *n* 象徴 symbol: **~ shimásu** 象徴します symbolizes

shōchū´ *n* 焼酎 distilled liquor made from yams or rice

shōdaku *n* 承諾 [BOOKISH] consent, acceptance: **~ shimásu** 承諾します consents, accepts

shodō *n* 書道 calligraphy (= **shūji** 習字)

shōdokú-yaku/-zai *n* 消毒薬/剤 disinfectant

shoéba *v* しょえば [INFORMAL] (if one shoulders it) → **shoimásu** しよいます

shō-fuda *n* 正札 price tag

shōga *n* ショウガ・生姜 ginger

shōgai *n* 障害 impediment, obstacle, hindrance; **shōgái-sha** 障害者 handicapped person

shō´gai *n* 生涯 life(long), for all one's life (time)

shōgakkō *n* 小学校 primary (*elementary*) school (= **gakkō** 学校)

shōgáku-sei *n* 小学生 primary school student

shō ga nai *adj* しょうがない [INFORMAL] = **shi-yō ga nái** しようがない hopeless, beyond remedy; **...-kute ~** ...くてしょうがない, **... de ~** ...でしょうがない is ever so ..., is terribly ...

Shōgatsú *n* 正月 (**O-shōgatsu** お正月) January; New Year

shōgi *n* 将棋 (*Japanese*) chess: **shōgi-ban** 将棋盤 chessboard

shō´go *n* 正午 noon (*exactly*)

shōhi *n* 消費 consumption; **shōhí-sha** 消費者 consumer

shōhi-zei *n* 消費税 consumption tax

shohō *n* 処方 prescription, prescribing: **~ shimásu** 処方します prescribes (*medicine*)

shohō-sen *n* 処方箋 prescription (slip)

shō´i *n* 少尉 2nd lieutenant; ensign

shoimásu, shou *v* しょいます[背負い]ます, しょう・背負う [INFORMAL] carries on the back, shoulders it

shōji *n* 障子 translucent sliding door

shōjíkí (na) *adj* 正直（な) honest: **shōjíkí ni** 正直に honestly

shō-jimásu, shō-jiru *v* 生じます, 生じる **1.** produces, comes about, occurs **2.** arises, happens

shōjin-ryō´ri *n* 精進料理 vegetarian cuisine

shójo *n* 処女 virgin (*female*)

shō´jo *n* 少女 young girl (= **onna no ko** 女の子)

shōjū *n* 小銃 rifle

shōka *n* 消化 digestion: **~ shimásu** 消化します digests
shōka-fúryō *n* 消化不良 indigestion
shōkai *n* 紹介 (**go-shōkai** ご紹介) introduction (*of a person*): **~ shimásu** 紹介します introduces
shōká-ki 消火器 fire extinguisher
shōka-sen *n* 消火栓 fireplug, hydrant
shōken *n* 証券 security (*stock, bond*)
shóki *n* 書記 secretary
shoki *n* 初期 [BOOKISH] beginning
  shoki-settei *n* 初期設定 default (*setting*)
shōki (no) *adj* 正気(の) sober, sane; in one's right mind
shōkin *n* 賞金 award, prize money
shōkin *n* 正金 hard cash
shōkin *n* 償金 → **baishōkin** 賠償金 (*indemnity, reparation*)
shokken *n* 食券 meal ticket
shokki *n* 食器 tableware (*dish, plate, chopsticks, etc.*); **shokkí-dana** 食器棚 dish rack; **shokki-tódana** 食器戸棚 cupboard, **shokkí-shitsu** 食器室 pantry
shokkō *n* 職工 factory worker; workman (= **kōin** 工員)
shókku *n* ショック shock
shōko *n* 証拠 proof, evidence, witness
shō´kō *n* 将校 military officer
shoku *n* 職 office, occupation
  shokú-gyo *n* 職業 occupation, vocation, job, profession
  shoku-reki *n* 職歴 professional experience
shoku *n* (…´-shoku …食) food; (*counts meals*)
  shoku-dō *n* 食堂 dining room; restaurant
  shoku-dō´-sha *n* 食堂車 dining car, diner
  shokú-en *n* 食塩 table salt
  shoku-go (ni) *adv* 食後(に) after a meal (= **shokuji no áto de** 食事の後で)
  shoku-hin *n* 食品 foodstuffs, groceries
  shoku-ji *n* 食事 (**o-shokuji** お食事) a meal; eating, having a meal: **~ shimásu** 食事します dines, eats (*a meal*)
  shoku (-ji) tsuki (no) *n* 食(事)付き(の) with meals (*included*); **chōshoku-**

tsuki (no) 朝食付き(の) with breakfast
  shokú-motsu *n* 食物 food(s)
  shoku-pán *n* 食パン bread
  shoku-ryō-hin *n* 食料品 foodstuffs, groceries: **shokuryōhín-ten** 食料品店 grocery store
  shoku-taku *n* 食卓 dinner table; **sho-kutakú-en** 食卓塩 table salt
  shoku-yoku *n* 食欲 appetite
  shoku-zen *n* 食膳 (*low*) individual meal table
  shoku-zen (ni) *adv* [BOOKISH] 食前(に) before a meal (= **shokuji no máe ni** 食事の前に)
shokúbutsu *n* 植物 (*botanical*) plant; **shokubutsú-en** 植物園 botanical garden
shokumín-chi *n* 植民地 colony
shōkyoku-teki (na) *adj* 消極的(な) negative; conservative
shōkyū *n* 昇給 rise in pay
shōkyū *n* 昇級 promotion
shomei *n* 署名 signature: **~ shimásu** 署名します signs one's name
shōmei *n* 証明 proof, verification, attestation, certification: **~ shimásu** 証明します proves, verifies, attests, certifies
  shōmei-shó *n* 証明書 certificate; note of authentication
shōmei *n* 照明 lighting, illumination: **shōmei-kígu** 照明器具 lighting fixtures
shōmén *n* 正面 the face (*front side*)
shomotsu *n* 書物 [BOOKISH] book (= **hón** 本)
shōmyō´ *n* 声明 chanting of Buddhist scriptures
shōnen *n* 少年 boy, lad, youngster (= **otoko no ko** 男の子)
shō´ni *n* 小児 infant, child; **shōnimáhi** 小児麻痺 infantile paralysis, polio
shōni-ka *n* 小児科 pediatrics; pediatrician (= **shōniká-i** 小児科医)
shōnin *n* 証人 a witness
shoppái *adj* しょっぱい [INFORMAL] salty (= **shio-karai** 塩辛い [FORMAL])
shóppingu *n* ショッピング shopping (= **kaimono** 買い物): **shoppingu-bággu** ショッピングバッグ, **shoppingu-bákku** ショッピングバック shopping

bag; **shoppingu-séntā** ショッピングセ
ンター shopping center

shō´rai *n, adv* 将来 future (= **yukusue**
行く末, **mirai** 未来)

shōrei *n* 奨励 encouragement,
promotion: ~ **shimásu** 奨励します
encourages, promotes

shóri *n* 処理 managing, disposing of,
transacting, dealing with: ~ **shimásu**
処理します manages, handles, takes
care of, deals with

shori-jō *n* 処理場 [sewage] treatment
plant

shō´ri *n* 勝利 victory: ~ **shimásu** 勝利
します [BOOKISH] wins (= **kachimásu**
勝ちます)

shōrí-sha *n* 勝利者 winner, victor

shorui *n* 書類 form, document,
paper(s), writing

shōryaku *n* 省略 abbreviation, omission
(= **ryaku** 略): ~ **shimásu** 省略します
abbreviates, omits

shōsa *n* 少佐 major; lieutenant
commander

shosai *n* 書斎 a study, library (*room*)

shōsai *n* 詳細 [BOOKISH] details

shóseki *n* 書籍 books, publications
(= **hón** 本)

shōsetsu *n* 小説 fiction, a novel

shō´shō *adv* 少々 a little
[DEFERENTIAL] (= **chótto** ちょっと)

shō´shō *n* 少将 major general; rear
admiral

shōshū *n* 召集・招集 conscription,
(*military*) draft: ~ **saremásu** 召集[招
集] されます gets drafted: ~ **shimásu**
召集[招集] します drafts, conscripts

shōsoku *n* 消息 news, word (*from/of*
…): ~ **nyúsu** ニュース

shotái *n* 所帯・世帯 a household;
housekeeping (→ **onna-jotai** 女所帯,
otoko-jotai 男所帯) (= **setai** 世帯)

shō´tai *n* 招待 invitation: ~ **shimásu**
招待します invites

shōtái-jō *n* 招待状 invitation (card)

shótchū *adv* しょっちゅう all the time

shoten *n* 書店 bookshop

shō´ten *n* 焦点 focus, focal point

shō´to *n* ショート a short (*circuit*);
short story; short stop

…-shótō *n* …諸島 (*name of certain*)
islands

shotoku *n* 所得 income; **shotokú-zei**
所得税 income tax

shōtotsu *n* 衝突 collision: ~ **shimásu**
衝突します collides

shotte *v* しょって → **shoimásu** しょ
います・背負います [INFORMAL]

shou *v* しょう・背負う = **shoimásu** し
ょいます・背負います [INFORMAL]
(carries on the back)

Shōwa-jidai *n* 昭和時代 Showa Period
(*1926–1989*)

showanai *v* しょわない・背わない =
shoimasén しょいません・背いません
[INFORMAL] (not carry on the back)

shoyū (no) *adj* 所有(の) possessed,
owned, belonging; one's own

shoyū-butsu/-hin *n* 所有物/品
belongings, possessions

shoyū´-sha *n* 所有者 (*legal*) owner

shōyu *n* しょうゆ・醤油 (**o-shōyu** お醤
油) soy sauce

shozai *n* 所在 whereabouts

shōzō *n* 肖像 portrait

shōzō-ga *n* 肖像画 portrait (*drawing
and/or painting*)

shu *n* 朱 vermilion

shu-niku *n* 朱肉 red ink pad

shu´, …-shū *n, suffix* 州, …州 (*name
of certain*) state (*U.S., Australia*);
province (*Canada*); county (*Britain*)

shū´, …-shū *n, suffix* 週, …週 (=
shūkan 週間) week

shū-matsu *n* 週末 weekend

shū-kan *n* 週間 week: **shūkan-tenki-
yohō** 週間天気予報 weather forecast
for a week: **dokusho-shūkan** 読書週間
book week

shūbun *n* 秋分 autumnal equinox:
Shūbun-no-hí 秋分の日 Autumnal
Equinox Day

shuchō *n* 主張 assertion: ~ **shimásu**
主張します asserts, claims, maintains

shūchū *n* 集中 concentration: ~
shimásu 集中します concentrates,
centers (*on*)

shúdan *n* 手段 ways, means, measures,
steps (= **hōhō** 方法): **saigo no ~** 最後の
手段 last resort

shūdan *n* 集団 group, collective body: **shūdan-seikatsu** 集団生活 group living, communal living (= **kyōdō-seikatsu** 共同生活): **busō-shūdan** 武装集団 armed group: **bo-shūdan** 母集団 a population

shūden *n* 終電 the last train (= **saishū densha** 最終電車)

shūdó´-in *n* 修道院 convent

shúfu *n* 主婦 housewife

shúfu *n* 首府 → **shutó** 首都

shūgeki *n* 襲撃 attack, charge, raid: ~ **shimásu** 襲撃します attacks, charges, raids

shúgi *n* 主義 principle, doctrine, -ism

shūgi-in *n* 衆議院 House of Representatives: **shūgi-in-senkyo** 衆議院選挙 House of Representatives election

shúgo *n* 主語 subject (*of a sentence*)

shūgō *n* 集合 assembly, gathering: ~ **shimásu** 集合します congregates, gathers, meets (*as a group*)

shugyō *n* 修行・修業 (*getting one's*) training, ascetic practices, meditation: ~ **shimásu** 修行します・修業します gets training

shūgyō *n* 就業 starting one's work(-day): ~ **shimásu** 就業します goes to (*starts*) work

shūgyō´-jikan *n* 就業時間 working hours

shū´ha *n* 宗派 sect

shūhen *adj* 周辺 circumference, en-virons, surroundings (= **shūi** 周囲): **tóshi no ~** 都市の周辺 outskirts (*of city*); **shūhen no …** 周辺の… the surrounding …

shū´i *n* 周囲 circumference; surroundings (= **shūhen** 周辺)

shuin *n* 手淫 [BOOKISH] masturbation (= **masutā-bēshon** マスターベーション, **onanii** オナニー)

shūji *n* 習字 (**o-shūji** お習字) calligraphy (*handwriting*) practice

shújin *n* 主人 **1.** husband; **go-shújin** ご主人 your husband **2.** master, owner, landlord, boss, host (**go-shújin(-sama)** ご主人(様), **danna(-san/sama)** 旦那(さん/様))

shúju (no) *adj* 種々(の) all kinds of (=

samazama (na) 様々(な), **iroiro (na)** 色々(な), **iron na** いろんな)

shújutsu *n* 手術 surgical operation, surgery; ~ **(o) shimásu** 手術(を)します performs an operation, operates

shūkaku *n* 収穫 harvest, crop: ~ **shimásu** 収穫します harvests, reaps

shukan *n* 主観 subjectivity: **shukan-teki (na)** 主観的(な) subjective

shūkan *n* 習慣 custom, practice, habit (= **kuse** 癖)

shū´ki *n* 秋期 autumn (*period/term*)

shū´ki *n* 周期 cycle (*length*)

shū´ki *n* 臭気 bad smell, stink (= **akushū** 悪臭)

shūki-dome *n* 臭気止め deodorant (*household, etc.*) (= **nioi-keshi** におい消し)

shukkin *n* 出勤 office attendance: ~ **shimásu** 出勤します goes to work

shuku-choku *n* 宿直 night duty

shukudai *n* 宿題 **1.** homework (*at school*) **2.** unsolved problem

shukuga *n* 祝賀 congratulation: **shuku-ga-kai** 祝賀会 a celebration

shukujitsu *n* 祝日, **shuku-saijitsu** 祝祭日 national holiday

shū-kuríimu *n* シュークリーム a cream puff, an éclair: ~ **no kawa** シュークリームの皮 puff shell

shukuten *n* 祝典 celebration ceremony

shū´kyo *n* 宗教 religion

shūmai *n* シューマイ pork meatballs steamed in thin pastry

shúmi *n* 趣味 taste, interest, liking, hobby (= **hobii** ホビー)

shumoku *n* 種目 **1.** item: **eigyō-shumoku** 営業種目 item of business **2.** (*competition*) event: **kyōgi-shumoku** 競技種目 athletic event

shunbun *n* 春分 vernal equinox: **Shunbun-no-hí** 春分の日 Vernal Equinox Day

shunga *n* 春画 pornography (*of Ukiyo-e*)

shúngiku *n* シュンギク・春菊 (*tasty leaves of*) garland chrysanthemum

shunkan *n* 瞬間 a moment, an instant (= **shunji** 瞬時, **matatakuma** 瞬く間): **tsugi no ~** 次の瞬間 next moment

shūnyū *n* 収入 earnings, income: **shūnyū-ínshi** 収入印紙 tax (*revenue*) stamp (= **inshi** 印紙)

shuppan *n* 出版 publishing: ~ **shimásu** 出版します publishes

shuppán-butsu *n* 出版物 publication(s)

shuppán-sha *n* 出版社 publishing company

shuppán-sha *n* 出版者 publisher

shuppatsu *n* 出発 departure; **shuppátsú-ten** 出発点 point of departure: ~ **shimásu** 出発します departs, leaves

shuppin *n* 出品 exhibit(ing): ~ **shimásu** 出品します exhibits; **shuppín-sha** 出品者 exhibitor

shū´ri *n* 修理 repair: ~ **shimásu** 修理します repairs

shūrí-kō *n* 修理工 repairman, mechanic

shūrō *n* 就労 [BOOKISH] work: ~ **shimásu** 就労します works (*for company, etc.*)

shúrui *n* 種類 type, sort, kind, variety

shū´shi *n* 修士 master's degree: **shūshi-rónbun** 修士論文 master's thesis: **shūshi-gō** 修士号 master's degree

shūshí *n* 終止 [BOOKISH] ending (= **oshimai** おしまい)

shūshí-fu *n* 終止符 [BOOKISH] period, full stop (*punctuation*)

shū´shin *n* 修身 ethics, morals

shū´shin *n* 終身 all one's life (= **isshō** (-**gai**) 一生(涯), **shōgai** 生涯, **shūsei** 終生)

shū´shin-kei *n* 終身刑 life imprisonment

shū´shin-koyō *n* 終身雇用 lifetime employment

shushō *n* 首相 prime minister

shūshoku *n* 就職 getting a job, finding employment: ~ **shimásu** 就職します gets a job, finds employment

shūshū *n* 収集 **1.** collecting (*trash, etc.*): **gomi-shū-shū-sha** ゴミ収集車 garbage truck **2.** collection (*as one's hobby, for research, etc.*) (= **korekushon** コレクション, **saishū** 採集): **shūshū-ka** 収集家 collector (= **korekutā** コレクター)

shusse *n* 出世 making a success in life: ~ **shimásu** 出世します makes a success in life

shussei *n* 出生 [BOOKISH] birth (= **umare** 生まれ): **shussei-chi** 出生地 (*one's*) birthplace

shusseki *n* 出席 attendance, presence (= **sanka** 参加): ~ **shimásu** 出席します attends, is present

shusséki-sha *n* 出席者 those present

shusshin *n* 出身 alumnus (of …); coming (*from* …): **shusshin-chi** 出身地 (*one's*) hometown

shúsu *n* 繻子 satin

shutchō *n* 出張 business trip: ~ **shimásu** 出張します makes a business trip

shūten *n* 終点 terminus, end of the line, last stop, destination

shutó *n* 首都 capital city

shutó-ken *n* 首都圏 Tokyo metropolitan area (= **kantō-chihō** plus Yamanashi *prefecture* 関東地方+山梨県) → **kantō-chihō** 関東地方

shūtome *n* 姑 common spoken term for one's mother-in-law

shuyō (na) *adj* 主要(な) leading, chief; **shuyō-tóshi** 主要都市 major city

shūzen *n* 修繕 [BOOKISH] repair: ~ **shimásu** 修繕します repairs; **shūzén-kō** 修繕工 repairman

si... → **shi...**

sō *n* 僧 Buddhist priest (= **sōryo** 僧侶, **obō-san** お坊さん)

sō´ *interj* そう [hearsay]: ... (**suru**, **shita**; **dá**, **dátta**), **sō´** (**desu**, **da/na**, **de**, **ni**) ... (**する**, した; だ, だった), そう (です, だ/な, で, に) it is reported (*said/written*) that, I hear that, they say that …; reportedly …

...-sō *suffix* ...そう, **...-sō´** ...そう: **shisō** (**désu**, **dá/na**, **dé**, **ní**) しそう(です,だ/な, で, に) looking (*as though*), about to (*happen*); will at any moment; **abuna-sō** (**désu**, **ni miemásu**) 危なそう(です, に見えます) looks dangerous, **jōbu-sō níwa miemasén** 丈夫そうには見えません doesn't look sturdy; **ochi-só´desu** 落ちそうです is about to fall

...-sō *suffix* ...艘 (*counts ships/boats*; commonly replaced by **...-seki** ...隻)

229

sóba *n* そば・側 (**o-soba** お側) near/close(-by), (be-)side

sóba *n* そば・ソバ・蕎麦 (**o-soba** おそば・お蕎麦) buckwheat noodles

soba-gara *n* そば殻・ソバ殻 buckwheat chaff (*used as pillow stuffing*)

soba-ya (**o-sobaya**) *n* そば[蕎麦]屋 (おそば[蕎麦]屋) Japanese noodle shop

sōbetsu *n* 送別 farewell; send-off; **sōbetsú-kai** 送別会 farewell party (*reception*)

sobiemásu, sobiéru *v* そびえます, そびえる rises, looms

sóbo *n* 祖母 grandmother [FORMAL] (= **obá´-san** おばあさん・お祖母さん, **obā-chan** おばあちゃん)

soboku na *adj* 素朴な simple, naive

soboro *n* そぼろ・ソボロ parched minced fish; fish meal

só´chi *n* 装置 equipment, apparatus

sochira *pron* そちら **1.** there, that way **2.** that one (*of two*) **3.** you
sochira-gawa *n* そちら側 your side

sō´dā *n* ソーダー soda water (= **sōdá-sui** ソーダ水)

sō da *v* そうだ = **só´ desu** そうです that's right, yes

sodachí *n* 育ち (**o-sodachi** お育ち) growing up, one's early years: ~ **ga yoi/warui** 育ちが良い/悪い well-bred/ill-bred

sodachimásu, sodátsu *v* 育ちます, 育つ grows up, is raised (reared)

sōdai na *adj* 壮大な magnificent, grand

sōdan *n* 相談 conference (*personal*), talk, consultation, *advice*: **sōdan-aite** 相談相手 someone to turn to for *advice*; (**… to**) ~ **shimásu** (…と)相談します consults (*with*), discusses, talks it over

sōdá-sui *n* ソーダ水 soda water (= **sidā** サイダー)

sodatánai *v* 育たない = **sodachimásen** 育ちません (not grow up)

sodaté *v* 育てて [IMPERATIVE] (grow up!) → **sodachimásu** 育ちます

sodatemásu, sodatéru *v* 育てます, 育てる raises, rears, educates

sodaténai *v* 育てない = **sodatemásén** 育てません (not raise)

sodate-no-oyá *n* 育ての親 a foster parent

sodaté ro *v* 育てろ [IMPERATIVE] (raise them!) → **sodatemásu** 育てます

sodatéru *v* 育てる = **sodatemásu** 育てます (raises, rears, educates)

sodátete *v* 育てて → **sodatemásu** 育てます

sodátsu *v* 育つ = **sodachimásu** 育ちます (grows up, is raised (reared)

sodátte *v* 育って → **sodachimásu** 育ちます

sode *n* 袖・そで (**o-sode** お袖) sleeve (→ **naga-sode** 長袖)

só´ (desu) *v* そう(です) That's right, yes
Só desu ka. そうですか. **1.** Oh? How interesting! **2.** Is that right/so?
Só desu ne. そうですね. Well, now;
Let me see.

sō´dō *n* 騒動 unrest, disturbance, tumult, strife; riot (= **bōdō** 暴動, **sawagi** 騒ぎ): ~ **ga okimásu** 騒動が起きます disturbance occurs: **oie-sōdō** お家騒動 family trouble

soéba *v* 沿えば (if it follows) → **soimásu** 沿います

soemásu, soeru *v* 添えます, 添える adds, throws in extra, attaches

soenai *v* 添えない = **soemásen** 添えません (not add)

soeru *v* 添える = **soemásu** 添えます (adds, throws in extra, attaches)

soete *v* 添えて → **soemásu** 添えます

soé ya shinai *v* 添えやしない = **soé wa shinai** 添えはしない = **soenai** 添えない (not add)

soeyō *v* 添えよう = **soemashō´** 添えましょう (let's add it!)

sófu *n* 祖父 grandfather [FORMAL] (= **ojii´-san** おじいさん・お祖父さん, **ojii-chan** おじいちゃん)

sófuto-kuriimu *n* ソフトクリーム soft ice cream

sofuto(wéa) *n* ソフト(ウェア) (*computer*) software

sōgan-kyō *n* 双眼鏡 binoculars

sōgi-ya *n* 葬儀屋 undertaker (*funeral director*)

sōgō *n* 総合 synthesis
sōgō-teki (na) *adj* 総合的(な) composite, comprehensive, overall, synthesized

sō´go no *adj* 相互 mutual, reciprocal
sō´go ni *adv* 相互に mutually, reciprocally (= **otagai ni** お互いに)

sōi *n* 相違[相異] discrepancy, difference: … **ni sōi nai** … に相違[相異]ない must be …

soimásu, sou *v* 沿います, 沿う runs along, follows

soitsu *pron* そいつ that damn one; **soitsú-ra** そいつら those damn ones

sō´ ja arimasén *v* そうじゃありません [INFORMAL] (= **sō de wa arimasén** そうではありません) not that way, not like that

sō´ ja nái to *adv* そうじゃないと [INFORMAL] (= **sō de naito** そうでないと), **sō´ ja nákereba** そうじゃなければ (= **sō de nakereba** そうでなければ) otherwise

sōji *n* 掃除 (**o-sō´ji** お掃除) cleaning, sweeping (= **seisō** 清掃): **~ shimásu** 掃除します cleans, sweeps: **nenmatsu no ōsōji** 年末の大掃除 year-end cleaning
sōji-ki *n* 掃除機 a sweeper

sōjū *n* 操縦 handling, operation: **~ shimásu** 操縦します manipulates, handles, controls, operates

sōkei *n* 総計 [BOOKISH] the grand total (= **gōkei** 合計)

sokétto *n* ソケット socket, plug

sōkin *n* 送金 remittance: **~ shimásu** 送金します remits

sokki *n* 速記 shorthand: **~ shimásu** 速記します takes shorthand notes

sokkō-jó *n* 測候所 weather observatory/station

sokkúri *adj* そっくり entirety, completely: **sokkúri (no)** そっくり (の) just like

sókkusu *n* ソックス anklets, socks (= **kutsushita** 靴下)

soko *pron* そこ there, that place

soko *n* 底 bottom: **umi no ~** 海の底 bottom of the ocean (= **kaitei** 海底); **kokoro no ~** 心の底 bottom of one's heart; **soko-nuke (no)** 底抜け(の)

bottomless (= **soko-nashi (no)** 底無し(の))

soko-mame *n* 底まめ bunion, corn, blister

sō´ko *n* 倉庫 warehouse

sókoku *n* 祖国 homeland, mother country (= **bokoku** 母国)

sokonaimásu, sokonáu *v* 損ないます, 損なう harms, injures, hurts; [VERBS INFINITIVE +] fails in doing; **yari-sokonaimásu** やり損ないます botches, misses

…-sokú *suffix* …足 (*counts pairs of footwear*)

sókudo *n* 速度 speed (= **supíido** スピード); **"Sókudo otóse"** 速度落とせ Reduce Speed.

sokutatsu *n* 速達 special delivery, express

sómatsu na *adj* 粗末な crude, coarse; **o-sómatsu-sama** お粗末さま Please excuse the poor fare (*reply to* **gochisō-sama** ご馳走さま・ごちそうさま)

somemásu, someru *v* 染めます, 染める dyes

sō´men *n* そうめん・素麺 thin white wheat-flour noodles (*cf.* **hiyamúgi** 冷や麦・ひやむぎ)

somete *v* 染めて → **somemásu** 染めます

somúite *v* 背いて → **somukimásu** 背きます

somukimásu, somúku *v* 背きます, 背く; **(… ni) ~** (…に) 背きます disobeys, goes against, violates; rebels, revolts

Sōmu-shō *n* 総務省 Ministry of Internal Affairs and Communications (MIC)

són *n* 損 damage, loss; disadvantage: **son-toku kanjō** 損得勘定 profit-and-loss arithmetic; **son'eki-keisan-sho** 損益計算書 profit and loss statement (P/L)

…´-son *suffix* …村 (*name of certain*) village

sonáé *n* 備え preparations, provisions; defenses: [IDIOM] **~ areba urei nashi** 備えあれば憂いなし If you are prepared, you don't have to worry.

sonáé ro *v* 備えろ [IMPERATIVE] (prepare it!) → **sonaemásu** 備えます

sonaemásu, sonáeru *v* 備えます, 備える prepares, fixes, installs, furnishes; possesses

sonáenai *v* 備えない = **sonaemasén** 備えません (not prepare it)

sonáete *v* 備えて → **sonaemásu** 備えます

sōnan *n* 遭難 disaster, accident, shipwreck, train wreck: ~ **shimásu** 遭難します has an accident (*a disaster*); (*a ship/train*) is wrecked

songai *n* 損害 damage, harm, loss

sonkei *n* 尊敬 respect, esteem: ~ **shimásu** 尊敬します respects, esteems

sonna ... *adj* そんな… [INFORMAL] such (*a*) …, that kind of …: **sonna ni** そんなに to that extent, that much, so (very/much)

sono ... *adj* その … that; **sono áto** その後, **sono-go** その後 since then; **sono mamá (de/ni/no)** そのまま (で/に/の) intact

sonó-hoka *n* その他[外] and others

sonó-ta *n* その他 [BOOKISH] and others (= **sonó-hoka** その他[外])

sono-tóki *n, adv* その時 at that time

sono-uchi *adv* そのうち soon, before long, sometime in the future

sono-ue´ ni *adv* そのうえに moreover, also, besides

sono-yō´ na *adj* そのよう[様](な) such (*-like*); **sono-yō´ni** そのよう[様] に like that, that way

sono-koro (wa) *adv* その頃(は) (*at*) that time, then, (*in*) those days (= **tó´ji (wa)** 当時(は), **aono-koro (wa)** あの頃 (は))

sore jíshin/jítai *n* それ自身/自体 itself

... sono-mónó *adv* …そのもの (*in*) itself, the very …

són-shimásu, són-suru *v* 損します, 損する = **són o suru** 損をする loses, suffers a loss

sonshitsu *n* 損失 a loss (= **son** 損, **rosu** ロス)

sonzai *n* 存在 existence; being/person (*in existence*), personage, figure: ~ **shimásu** 存在します exists

sō-on *n* 騒音 noise

sóppa *n* 反っ歯 bucktooth (= **deppa** 出っ歯)

sóra *n* 空 sky

sóra de *adv* そらで by heart, from memory

soránai *v* 剃らない = **sorimasén** 剃り ません (not shave)

soránai *v* 反らない = **sorimasén** 反り ません (not bend/curve)

sorasánai *v* 逸さない = **sorashi-masén** 逸しません (not dodge/warp)

sorashimásu, sórasu *v* 逸らします, 逸らす **1.** dodges, turns aside **2.** warps it

soráshite *v* 逸らして → **sorashi-másu** 逸らします

sore *pron* それ that one, it

sore de *conj* それで and (*then/so/also*)

sore démo *conj* それでも still, yet, even so

sore dé wa *conj* それでは = **sore ja/ jā** それじゃ/じゃあ [INFORMAL] well, well now/then: ~ **shitsúrei shimásu** それでは失礼します excuse me but I'll be on my way; good-bye

sore hodo *conj* それほど to that extent, so

sore kara *conj* それから and (*then*); after that, since then

sore máde *conj* それまで until then: **sore máde ni** それまでに by them

sore náno ni *conj* それなのに nevertheless, nonetheless, and yet

sore nára *conj* それなら then, in that case

sore ni *conj* それに on top of that, moreover, in addition, plus

soré-ra *pron* それら those, they/them

sore-tómo *conj* それとも or else

sóreba *v* 剃れば (if one shaves) → **sorimásu** 剃ります

sóreba *v* 反れば (if one bends) → **sorimásu** 反ります

soremásu, soréru *v* 逸れます, 逸れる deviates, strays, digresses

soremásu, soréru *v* 剃れます, 剃れ る can shave

soremásu, soréru *v* 反れます, 反れる can bend/warp

soréru *v* 逸れる = **soremásu** 逸れます (deviates)

soréru v 剃れる = **soremásu** 剃れます (can shave)

soréru v 反れる = **soremásu** 反れます (can bend/range)

sórete v 逸れて・剃れて・反れて → **soremásu** 逸れます・剃れます・反れます

sore wa sore wa *interj* それはそれは My my! My goodness!

sorézóre *adv* それぞれ respectively, severally (= **onoono** おのおの・各々)

sorí n そり・反り a warp, curve, bend

sorí n そり・剃り shaving

sorí n そり・ソリ sled

sōri-dáijin n 総理大臣 prime minister

sorimásu, sóru v 剃ります, 剃る shaves

sorimásu, sóru v 反ります, 反る bends (*back*), warps

sōritsu n 創立 establishment

soroban n そろばん・算盤 abacus, counting beads

soroé n 揃え an array

soroemásu, soroéru v 揃えます, 揃える puts in order; collects; completes a set

soróí n 揃い a set (of …)

sōron n 争論 quarrel, dispute

sōron n 総論 general remarks, outline, introduction

sórosoro *adv* そろそろ (*leave*) before long, it is about time to

sóru v 剃る = **sorimásu** 剃ります (shaves)

sóru v 反る = **sorimásu** 反ります (bends, warps)

sō'(ryo) n 僧(侶) Buddhist priest

sō-ryó'ji n 総領事 consul general

sū'sa n 操作 operation, handling; ~ **shimásu** 操作します operates, handles

sōsaku n 創作 creation; ~ **shimásu** 創作します creates

sōsaku n 捜索 search, investigation; ~ **shimásu** 捜索します searches, investigates; **sōsaku-negai** 捜索願(い) an application to the police to search for (*a missing person*); **kataku-sōsaku** 家宅捜索 house search; **sōsaku-tai** 捜索隊 search party

sō'sē'ji n ソーセージ sausage

sósen n 祖先 ancestor (= **senzo** 先祖)

sóshiki n 組織 system, structure, setup, organization

sōshiki n 葬式 (**o-sōshiki** お葬式) funeral

soshite *conj* そして, **sōshite** そうして and then

soshō n 訴訟 lawsuit

sōshoku n 装飾 ornament, decoration

sosogimásu, sosogu v 注ぎます, 注ぐ pours (into)

sosoide v 注いで → **sosogimásu** 注ぎます

sō'su n ソース sauce, gravy

sotchí *pron* そっち [INFORMAL] = **sochira** そちら (there, that way; that one (*of two*); you)

sotchoku (na) *adj* 率直(な) frank

sóto n 外 outside, outdoors

sōtō (na) *adv, adj* 相当(な) **1.** rather, quite, fairly **2.** suitable, proper

soto-bori n 外堀 outer moat

soto-gawa n 外側 the outside: **soto-gawa (no)** 外側(の) external

soto-umi n 外海 high sea (= **gaikai** 外海)

sotsugyō n 卒業 graduation: ~ **shimásu** 卒業します graduates

sotsugyō'-sei n 卒業生 a graduate

sotsugyō'-shiki n 卒業式 commencement, graduation ceremony

sotta v 沿った = **soimáshita** 沿いました (followed)

sótta v 剃った = **sorimáshita** 剃りました (shaved; bent, warped)

sótta v 反った = **sorimáshita** 反りました (shaved; bent, warped)

sotte v 沿って → **soimásu** 沿います

sótte v 剃って, 反って → **sorimásu** 剃ります

sou v 沿う = **soimásu** 沿います (it runs along, follows)

Sóuru n ソウル Seoul

sowanai v 沿わない = **soimasén** 沿いません (not follow)

sō yū (**sō iu**)… *adj* そうゆう(そういう) [INFORMAL] …that kind/sort of …; such … (= **sonna** そんな, **sono-yō' na** その様な)

sōzō n 想像 imagination: ~ **shimásu** 想像します imagines

sōzōshíi *adj* 騒々しい noisy

su *n* 巣 nest

sú *n* 酢(**o-su** お酢) vinegar
  sú-no-mono *n* 酢の物 vinegared
  dishes
  sú-buta *n* 酢豚 sweet and sour pork

sū´ *n* 数 number (= **kázu** 数); **sūji** 数字
  numeral
  sū-gaku *n* 数学 (*junior/senior high
  school, college, university, graduate
  school*) mathematics (= **sansū** 算数);
  sūgáku-sha 数学者 mathematician
  sū-ji *n* 数字 numeral, figure (= **kazu** 数)

sū´-... *prefix* 数... several
  sū´-jitsu *n*, *adv* 数日 several days
  sū´-nen *n*, *adv* 数年 several years
  sū´-nin *n* 数人 several people

sū *v* 吸う = **suimásu** 吸います(sips,
  sucks, smokes, breathes in)

subarashíi *adj* すばらしい・素晴しい
  wonderful, splendid: **subaráshiku** すば
  らしく・素晴らしく splendidly

suberí-dai *n* すべり台・滑り台 a slippery slide

suberimásu, suberu *v* 滑ります, 滑る
  slides, slips, skates

sube-sube (no) *adj* すべすべ(の)
  smooth, slippery (= **nameraka na** 滑ら
  かな)

súbete *n*, *adv* すべて all

subétte *v* 滑って → **suberimásu** 滑り
  ます

suchuwā´desu *n* スチュワーデス
  stewardess, flight attendant

suchuwā´do *n* スチュワード steward,
  flight attendant

sudare *n* すだれ・簾 curtain (*bamboo*)

sude *n* 素手 bare hands

súde ni *adv* すでに・既に already
  (= **mŏ´** もう)

sue *n* 1. 末 end, close 2. 末 future
  (= **shōrai** 将来): **... no yuku-sue** ...の
  行く末 one's future: **yuku-sue wa** 行く
  末は in the future

súe *v* 吸え [IMPERATIVE] (suck!) →
  suemásu 吸えます

suéba *v* 吸えば (if one sips/sucks/
  smokes) → **suimásu** 吸います

suemásu, sueru *v* 据えます, 据える
  sets it up

suemásu, sueru *v* 吸えます, 吸える
  can sip (*suck, smoke*)

suemásu, suéru *v* すえます, すえる
  it spoils, goes bad

suete *v* 据えて, 吸えて → **suemásu**
  据えます, 吸えます

súete *v* すえて → **suemásu** すえます

súgata *n* 姿(**o-súgata** お姿) form, figure, shape: **hare-sugata** 晴れ姿 one
  in his/her Sunday best: **kimono-sugata**
  着物姿 one in his/her kimono

sugi *n* 杉 cryptomeria, Japanese cedar
  ...-sugi *suffix* ...過ぎ past (*the hour*)

sugimásu, sugíru *v* 過ぎます, 過ぎる
  passes, exceeds; **(shi-)sugimásu** (し)
  過ぎます overdoes: *adj* ... **sugimásu**
  ... 過ぎます is overly/excessively/too

sugínai *v* 過ぎない = **sugimasén** 過ぎ
  ません (not pass; not exceed); **(... ni)**
  sugínai (...に)過ぎない is nothing
  more/other than, only

sugói *adj* すごい・凄い 1. swell,
  wonderful, marvelous, terrific 2. fierce,
  dreadful, ghastly, weird, uncanny

súgoku *adv* すごく・凄く awfully,
  terribly

sugoshimásu, sugósu *v* 過ごします,
  過ごす passes (*time*)

súgu (ni) *adv* すぐ(に) at once, right
  away, immediately; in a minute;
  directly, right (*there*)

sugureteimásu, suguréru *v* 優れてい
  ます, 優れている excels: **(... ni/yóri)**
  sugureteimásu (...に/より)優れてい
  ます surpasses, is superior (*to*): is
  excellent; **sugúreta ...** 優れた...
  excellent ...

súgu sóba (ni) *adv* すぐそば(に) right
  near (at hand)

suichoku (no) *adj* 垂直(の) vertical;
  perpendicular

suidō *n* 水道 water system, water
  service, running water; plumbing
  suidō-kan *n* 水道管 water pipe
  suidō´-kyoku *n* 水道局 the Waterworks
  Bureau; municipal water service
  (*headquarters*)
  suidō-ya (san) *n* 水道屋(さん) plumber

suiei *n* 水泳 swimming; **suiei-jō** 水泳場
  swimming pool

suiéi-gí *n* 水泳着 swim suit (= **mizuki** 水着)

súifu *n* 水夫 seaman, sailor

suigara *n* 吸い殻 cigarette/cigar butt

súihei *n* 水兵 navy enlisted person, sailor, seaman

suihei (no) *adj* 水平(の) horizontal, level: **suihei-sen** 水平線 (*sea*) horizon

suii *n* 水位 water level

suijun *n* 水準 **1.** water level **2.** standard

suika *n* スイカ・西瓜 watermelon

Sui, Kin, Chi, Ka, Moku, Do, Ten, Kai 水金地火木土天海 (= 水星、金星、地球、火星、木星、土星、天王星、海王星) "My Very Educated Mother Just Showed Us Nine (*planets*)" Mercury, Venus, Earth, Mars, Jupiter, Saturn, Uranus, Neptune (*eight planets in the solar system*)

sui-kuchi *n* 吸い口 cigarette holder

suimásu, sū *v* 吸います、吸う sips, sucks, smokes, breathes in

suimasén *interj* すいません [INFORMAL] **1.** Excuse me. Sorry. **2.** Thank you. (= **sumimasén** すみません)

suimin *n* 睡眠 sleep; **suimín-zai** 睡眠剤, **suimín-yaku** 睡眠薬 sleeping pill(s)

sui-mono *n* 吸い物 clear soup

sui-sei *adj* 水性 water-based: **suisei-inku** 水性インク water based ink: **suisei-toryō** 水性塗料 water based paint

sui-sei *adj* 水生 aquatic: **suisei-dōbutsu** 水生動物 aquatic animal

Sui-sei *n* 彗星 comet: **Harē-suisei** ハレー彗星 Halley's comet

Sui-sei *n* 水星 Mercury

suisen *n* 水洗 flushing: **suisen-tóire** 水洗トイレ flush toilet

suisen *n* 推薦 recommendation: ~ **shimásu** 推薦します recommends

suisen-jō *n* 推薦状 letter of recommendation

súiso *n* 水素 hydrogen

suisō *n* 水槽 water tank

suisoku *n* 推測 conjecture, guess, surmisal, supposition; ~ **shimásu** 推測します guesses, surmises

Súisu *n* スイス Switzerland: **Súisu no** スイスの Swiss

Suisú-jin *n* スイス人 a Swiss

suítchi *n* スイッチ switch; ignition switch: ~ **o iremásu** スイッチを入れます turns/switches it on, turns on the ignition; ~ **o kirimásu** スイッチを切ります turns/switches it off

suitei *n* 推定 inference, presumption, estimation: ~ **shimásu** 推定します infers, presumes, estimates

suitō-gákari *n* 出納係 cashier

suitorí-gami *n* 吸い取り紙 blotter

Suiyō´(bi) *n* 水曜(日) Wednesday

suizókúkan *n* 水族館 aquarium (= **akuariumu** アクアリウム)

súji *n* 筋 tendon, muscle, fiber, line

...súji *suffix* ...筋 plot (→ **ōsuji** 大筋): **arasuji** あらすじ summary, outline, synopsis

sukā´fu *n* スカーフ scarf; (*military*) sash

sukā´to *n* スカート skirt

sukébē (na) *adj* 助平(な)・すけべえ(な)・スケベ(な) lecherous; lewd (= **etchi (na)** エッチ(な))

sukē´to *n* スケート skate(s); skating: **sukēto-bōdo** スケートボード skate board: **sukēto-gutsu** スケート靴 (*a pair of*) skates: ~ **(o) shimásu** スケート(を)します skates

suki *n* すき・透き crack; opening; opportunity (= **suki-ma** すき間・透き間・隙間)

sukí (na) *adj* 好き(な) one's favorite: **o-súki (na)** お好き(な) (*your/someone else's*) favorite

sukídesu, sukida *v* 好きです、好きだ likes

sukii *n* スキー ski, skiing: ~ **o shimásu** スキーをします skis

suki-ma *n* すき間・透き間・隙間 crack; opening; opportunity

sukimásu, suku *v* 空きます、空く gets empty/clear

sukimásu, suku *v* 鋤きます、鋤く plows

sukimásu, suku *v* すき[梳き]ます、すく・梳く combs

sukimásu, suku *v* 好きます、好く → **sukídesu, sukida** 好きです、好きだ

sukimu-míruku *n* スキムミルク skim milk

sukiyaki *n* すき焼き・すきやき thin-sliced beef cooked in an iron pan (*with leeks, mushrooms, bean curd, etc.*)

su̱kkári *adv* すっかり completely, all

su̱kóshi *adv* 少し a little, a bit: **su̱kóshi (no)** 少し(の) some, a few; somewhat: **su̱koshí mo** 少しも [+ NEGATIVE] not in the least; **su̱koshí-zútsu** 少しずつ bit by bit, a bit of/for each, a little at a time, gradually

su̱kuimásu, su̱kū *v* 救います, 救う helps, rescues, saves

su̱kuimásu, su̱kū *v* すく[掬い]います, すくう・掬う scoops

su̱kunái *adj* 少ない few, meager, scarce, little; **yori ~** より少ない fewer, less

su̱kúnaku *adv* 少なく (*so as to be*) few, little: **~ shimásu** 少なくします lessens

su̱kúnaku-tomo *adv* 少なくとも at (*the*) least

su̱kuranburu-éggu *n* スクランブルエッグ scrambled eggs

su̱kuríin *n* スクリーン (*movie*) screen

su̱kutte *v* 救って → **su̱kuimásu** 救います

su̱kutte *v* すく[掬い]って → **su̱kuimásu** すく[掬い]います

su̱kū *v* 救う = **su̱kuimásu** 救います (helps, rescues, saves)

su̱kū *v* すくう・掬う = **su̱kuimásu** すく[掬い]います (scoops)

su̱kuwatto *n* スクワット squat (*bending and stretching exercises, power lifting, etc.*)

su̱kyándaru *n* スキャンダル scandal

súmai *n* 住まい (**o-súmai** お住まい) residence

sumánai, sumimasén *v, interj* すまない, すみません 1. it never ends 2. Thank you 3. Excuse me 4. I apologize (for what I did).

sumasemásu, sumaséru *v* 済ませます, 済ませる finishes, concludes it

sumashimásu, sumásu *v* 済ませます, 済ます 1. finishes, concludes it 2. puts up with (*things as they are*)

sumā́ to (na) *adj* スマート (な) smart, stylish, fashionable

sumā́ tofon *n* スマートフォン smartphone (*multifunctional mobile phone*)

súmi *n* 隅 an inside corner

sumí *n* 炭 charcoal

sumí *n* 墨 India ink, ink stick

sumi-e *n* 墨絵 Indian ink painting

sumimasén *v* すみません 1. Excuse me. 2. Sorry. 3. Thank you. (= **sumánai** すまない)

sumimásu, súmu *v* 済みます, 済む comes to an end

sumimásu, súmu *v* 住みます, 住む lives, takes up residence, resides

sumire *n* スミレ・菫 violet

sumō *n* 相撲・すもう Japanese wrestling, sumo

sumṓ *v* 住もう = **sumimashṓ** 住みましょう (let's reside!)

sumomo *n* スモモ・李 plum

sumṓ -tóri *n* 相撲取り a sumo wrestler

súmu *v* 済む = **sumimásu** 済みます (comes to an end)

súmu *v* 住む = **sumimásu** 住みます (lives)

...-sún *suffix* ...寸 inch (*Japanese*)

suna *n* 砂 sand

suna-búkuro *n* 砂袋 sandbag

sunákku *n* スナック 1. a snackshop 2. an after-hours bar 3. refreshiment

sunakkú-gashi *n* スナック菓子 munch, snack

súnao (na) *adj* 素直(な) docile, gentle, obedient, submissive, meek

sunáwachi *adv* すなわち・即ち namely, to wit; that is to say; in other words

súnda *v* 済んだ = **sumimáshi̱ta** 済みました (ended)

súnda *v* 住んだ = **sumimáshi̱ta** 住みました (lived)

súnde *v* 住んで → **sumimásu** 住みます: **~ imásu** 住んでいます lives, resides

suné *n* すね・臑・脛 shin, leg: [IDIOM] **oya no ~ o kajiru** 親の脛をかじる sponges off one's parents

sunpō *n* 寸法 measurements

sū́ pā *n* スーパー = **sū́ pā-mā́ketto** スーパーマーケット supermarket

supái *n* スパイ spy

supai-wea *n* スパイウェア spyware (*computer*)

supaisu *n* スパイス spice (= **kōshinryō** 香辛料)

supamu-mēru *n* スパムメール (= **mei-waku-mēru** 迷惑メール) spam e-mail, spam mail, e-mail spam (*Internet*)

supána *n* スパナ wrench

supein *n* スペイン Spain
Supein-go *n* スペイン語 Spanish (*language*)
Supein-jin *n* スペイン人 Spaniard, a Spanish person

supéringu *n* スペリング, **supéru** スペル spell (= **tsuzuri** つづり・綴り)

supēsu *n* スペース 1. space (= **kūkan** 空間) 2. blank (= **kūhaku** 空白)

supíido *n* スピード speed (= **sokudo** 速度, **hayasa** 速さ): kokusai-supiido-yūbin 国際スピード郵便 EMS (*Express Mail Service*)

supíikā *n* スピーカー (loud)speaker

suponji *n* スポンジ sponge; swab: **suponji-kēki** スポンジケーキ sponge cake

suponsā *n* スポンサー 1. sponsor (= **kōkoku-nushi** 広告主, **bangumi-teikyō-sha** 番組提供者) 2. patron (= **kōen-sha** 後援者, **patoron** パトロン)

supō´tsu *n* スポーツ sport(s), athletics (= **undō** 運動)

suppái *adj* すっぱい[酸っぱい] sour, acid: **suppai-aji** すっぱい[酸っぱい] 味 sour flavor, sour taste (= **san-mi** 酸味)

suppon *n* すっぽん・スッポン snapping turtle

supponpon *n* すっぽんぽん (IN-FORMAL, *slang*) full monty, complete nudity (= **suppadaka** 素っ裸)

sū´pu *n* スープ soup

supū´n *n* スプーン spoon (= **saji** さじ・サジ・匙)

surákkusu *n* スラックス slacks

suránai *v* 擦らない = **surimasén** 擦り ません (not rub)

suránai *v* 摺ら[摺ら]ない = **surimasén** 摺り[摺り]ません (not file/grind)

suránai *v* 刷らない = **surimasén** 刷り ません (not print)

suránai *v* すらない = **surimasén** すり ません (not pick one's pocket)

sure *v* 擦れ [IMPERATIVE] (rub!) → suremásu 擦れます

sure *v* 摺れ[摺れ] [IMPERATIVE] (file/ grind!) → suremásu 摺れ[摺れ]ます

sure *v* 刷れ [IMPERATIVE] (print!) → suremásu 刷れます

suréba *v* すれば (if one does) → shimásu します

súreba *v* 擦れば (if one rubs) → surimásu 擦ります

suréba *v* 摺れば (if one files/ grinds) → surimásu 摺ります

súreba *v* 刷れば (if one prints) → surimásu 刷ります

súreba *v* すれば (if one picks one's pocket) → surimásu すります

suremásu, suréru *v* 擦れます, 擦れる 1. it rubs/grazes 2. can rub/graze

suremásu, suréru *v* 刷れます, 刷れ る can print

surénai *v* 擦れない = **suremasén** 擦れ ません (cannot rub)

surénai *v* 刷れない = **suremasén** 刷れ ません (cannot print)

suréreba *v* 擦れれば (if it rubs; if one can rub) → suremásu 擦れます

suréreba *v* 刷れれば (if it prints; if one can print) → suremásu 刷れます

surí *n* 刷り print(ing)

súri *n* すり・スリ・掏り pick-pocket

suríbachi *n* すり鉢 earthenware kitch-en-mortar with wooden pestle

surii *n* スリー three

surimásu, súru *v* 擦ります, 擦る rubs

surimásu, súru *v* 摺り[摺り]ます, 摺 る[摺る] files; grinds

surimásu, súru *v* 刷ります, 刷る prints

surimásu, súru *v* すります, する picks one's pocket

suríppa *n* スリッパ slippers

suríppu *n* スリップ slip(ping); **surippu-jíko** スリップ事故 slipping accident

Suriránka *n* スリランカ Sri Lanka

súriru *n* スリル thrill

surō´ *v* 擦ろう = **surimashō´** 擦りまし ょう (let's rub!)

surō´ *v* 摺[摺]ろう = **surimashō´** 摺り [摺り]ましょう (let's file/grind it!)

surō´ ν 刷ろう = **surimashō´** 刷りましょう (let's print it!)

surō´ ν すろう = **surimashō´** すりましょう (let's steal it!)

surō´gan n スローガン slogan

surō´ (na) adj スロー（な） slow

surō´pu n スロープ ramp

suru ν する = **shimásu** します (does)
suru koto n すること: **... ~ ga arimásu (arimasén)** …することがあります（ありません) does do it sometimes; has something (nothing) to do; **... ~ arimasén** …することはありません never does it; **... shita koto ga arimásu** …したことがあります has done it before; **... shita koto wa arimasén** …したことはありません has never done it; **... (suru/shinai) koto wa arimasén** …(する/しない)ことはありません isn't that one (does/doesn't, will/won't do it); **... ~ ni shimásu** …することにします decides to (do it)

súru ν 擦る = **surimásu** 擦ります (rubs)

súru ν 摺る[擂る] = **surimásu** 摺り[擂り]ます (files, grinds)

súru ν 刷る = **surimásu** 刷ります (prints)

súru ν する = **surimásu** すります (picks one's pocket)

surudói adj 鋭い sharp, acute

surume n スルメ dried cuttlefish

sushi n すし・スシ・寿司・鮨 (**o-súshi** お寿司・お鮨) sushi (rice seasoned with sweetened vinegar with raw fish)
sushí-ya n 寿司[鮨]屋 (**osushi-ya** お寿司[お鮨]屋) a sushi bar

suso n すそ・裾 hem: **~ o agemásu** 裾を上げます takes a hem up

súsu n すす・煤 soot: **~ o haraimásu** すすを払います sweeps off soot

susume ν 進め [IMPERATIVE] (forward!) → **susumimásu** 進みます

susumemásu, susumeru ν 進めます, 進める furthers, advances

susumemásu, susumeru ν 勧めます, 勧める encourages, recommends, advises, counsels; persuades, urges

susumimásu, susumu ν 進みます, 進む goes forward, progresses; goes too fast, gets ahead

susumō´ ν 進もう = **susumimashō** 進み

ましょう (let's go forward!)

susunde ν 進んで **1.** → **susumimásu** 進みます: **~ imásu** 進んでいます is advanced, (clock) is fast **2.** **~ yarimásu** 進んでやります go ahead voluntarily, willingly

sutā n スター star (actor) (= **hanagata** 花形)

sutajio n スタジオ studio (= **satsuei-jo** 撮影所)

sutando n スタンド **1.** stand (for selling things): gasorin-sutándo ガソリンスタンド gas(oline)/service station **2.** = **denki sutándo** 電気スタンド) desk/floor lamp

sute ro ν 捨てろ [IMPERATIVE] (throw it away!, drop it!) → **sutemásu** 捨てます

sute-ba n 捨て場 dump site (= **gomi-suteba** ごみ捨て場)

sute-mi (de) adv 捨て身(で) in desperation

suteki (na) adj すてき[素敵](な) fine, splendid, swell

sutē´ki n ステーキ (beef) steak: biifu sutē´ki ビーフステーキ

sutékki n ステッキ walking stick, cane

sutemásu, suteru ν 捨てます, 捨てる throws away, abandons, dumps

sutereo n ステレオ stereo (sound/player)

sutēshon n ステーション railroad station (= **eki** 駅)

sutó n スト = **sutoráiki** ストライキ strike (job action)

sutō´bu n ストーブ stove, heater

sutōkā n ストーカー stalker

sutoráiku n ストライク strike (baseball)

sutóresu n ストレス stress, tension: sutoresu-kaishō ストレス解消 stress relieving, stress release (= **sutoresu hassan** ストレス発散)

sutoretchi n ストレッチ stretch (exercises)

sutoríppu n ストリップ striptease, strip show, burlesque

sutórō n ストロー straw (to drink with)

sū´tsu n スーツ suit

sūtsukē´su n スーツケース suitcase

sutte ν 吸って → **suimásu** 吸います

238

suwanai v 吸わない = **suimasén** 吸いません (not sip, …)

suwaremásu, suwareru v 座れます, 座れる can sit; seats are available

suwarikomi(-súto) n 座り込み(スト) sit-in (*strike*)

suwarimásu, suwaru v 座ります, 座る sits (*especially Japanese style*)

suwatte v 座って → **suwarimásu** 座ります

suzu n スズ・鈴 little bells

súzu n スズ・錫 tin

suzuki n スズキ・鱸 sea bass

suzume n スズメ・雀 sparrow

suzumé-bachi n スズメバチ・スズメ蜂 hornet

suzurí n すずり・硯 inkstone: **suzurí-bako** すずり[硯]箱 inkstone case

suzushíi adj 涼しい cool

sy... → **sh...**

T

tá n た・他 = **hoka** 他, **sono-ta, sono-hoka** その他 other(s)

ta-hō´ n 他方 a different direction, another place: **~ de wa** 他方では on the other hand

tá (ni) adv 他(に) to/for/as others, additionally (= **hoka (ni)** 他[外](に))

ta-nin n 他人 outsider, stranger; others (*people*) (= **ta-sha** 他者): **aka no tanin** 赤の他人 a complete stranger

tá (no) adj 他(の) = **hoka (no)** 他[外](の) other

tá-sha n 他社 other companies

tá-sha n 他者 [BOOKISH] others (*people*) (= **ta-nin** 他人)

tá n 田 rice field (= **tanbo** 田んぼ)

ta-nbo n 田んぼ [INFORMAL] rice field (= **ta** 田)

ta-ué n 田植え rice planting

...-ta v ...た = **...-máshita** ...ました did

tába n 束 bundle, bunch: **satsu-taba** 札束 bundle of bills

tabako n タバコ・煙草 tobacco; cigarettes (= **shigaretto** シガレット)

tabakó-ire n タバコ[煙草]入れ cigarette case (= **sigaretto kēsu** シガレットケース)

tabemásu, tabéru v 食べます, 食べる eats

tabé-mónó n 食べ物 food (= **shoku-motsu** 食物)

taberaremásu, taberaréru v 食べられます, 食べられる can eat

tabé ro v 食べろ [IMPERATIVE] (eat!) → **tabemásu** 食べます

tabesasemásu, tabesaséru v 食べさせます, 食べさせる feeds

tábete v 食べて → **tabemásu** 食べます

tabeyō´ v 食べよう = **tabemashō´** 食べましょう (let's eat!)

tábi n たび・タビ・足袋 split-toe socks

tabí n 旅 journey (= **ryokō** 旅行)

tabí n 度・たび time, occasion; **... tabí (ni)** ...度[たび](に) every time that ...

tabitabi adv たびたび・度々 often (= **shibashiba** しばしば, **nando-mo** 何度も)

tabō (na) adj 多忙(な) [BOOKISH] busy (= **isogashíi** 忙しい): [HONORIFIC] **go-tabō no tokoro ...** ご多忙のところ ... ... in your busyness

tábu n タブ a tab

tabū n タブー taboo (= **kinki** 禁忌, **go-hatto** ご法度)

tábun adv たぶん・多分 probably, likely; perhaps, maybe (**~ ... deshō´** たぶん ...でしょう, **~ ... ká mo shire-masén** たぶん ...かも知れません)

tabun (ni) adv 多分(に) [BOOKISH] a lot, much

taburetto n タブレット **1.** tablet **2.** Tablet PC

taburoido n タブロイド tabloid

táchi n たち・質 nature, disposition

...´-tachi suffix ...達・たち [*animate plural*]; and others: **watashi-tachi** わたし[私達] we: **anata-tachi** あなた達 you (*people*); **kimi-tachi** 君たち[達] you guys

tachi-agarimásu, tachi-agaru v 立ち上がります, 立ち上がる rises, stands up

tachi-bá *n* 立場 viewpoint, standpoint, situation

tachi-domarimásu, tachi-domaru *v* 立ち止まります, 立ち止まる comes to a stand

"Tachiiri kinshi" *n* 立ち入り禁止. No Trespassing. Off Limits.

tachimachi *adv* たちまち immediately, instantly (= **at-toiuma ni** あっという間 に, **matatakuma ni** 瞬く間に)

tachimásu, tátsu *v* 立ちます, 立つ stands (up)

tachi-bánashi *n* 立ち話 *(wayside)* a stand for talking, a stand for chatting: ~ **(o) shimásu** 立ち話(を)します stands chatting, stands talking

tachi-mi *n* 立ち見 a stand for watching: ~ **shimásu** 立ち見します sees as a standee; **tachimi-kyaku** 立ち見客 standee; **tachimi-seki** 立ち見席 the gallery, standing room

tachimásu, tátsu *v* 発ちます, 発つ leaves *(for a far place)* (= **shuppatsu shimásu** 出発します)

tachimásu, tátsu *v* 経ちます, 経つ elapses

tachimásu, tátsu *v* 断ちます, 断つ [BOOKISH] cuts off

táda *n* ただ free, gratis, no fee/charge (= **muryō** 無料)

tádachi ni *adv* ただちに [BOOKISH] immediately

tadáima *adv* ただいま just now; in a minute (= **tatta-íma** たった今)

Tadaima *interj* ただいま I'm back!, I'm home! *(said on returning to one's residence)* *(abbreviated phrase of "Tadaima kaerimáshita", meaning "I just came back home.")*

táda (no) *adj* ただ(の) **1.** only, just **2.** ordinary

tádashi *conj* 但し provided

tadashíi *adj* 正しい right; correct; **tadáshiku** 正しく rightly, correctly

tadō´-shi *n* 他動詞 transitive verb

tadotadoshii *adj* たどたどしい halting, not smooth (= **tsutanai** 拙い)

taema-náku *adv* 絶え間なく continuously, without interruption (= **táezu** 絶えず)

taemásu, taéru *v* 堪えます, 堪える bears, puts up with

taemásu, taéru *v* 絶えます, 絶える ceases

taénai *v* 堪えない = **taemasén** 堪えま せん (not bear)

taénai *v* 絶えない = **taemasén** 絶えま せん (not cease)

taeraremásu, taeraréru *v* 堪えられま す, 堪えられる (can bear)

taerarénai *v* 堪えられない = **taerare-masén** 堪えられません (cannot bear)

taéru *v* 堪える = **taemásu** 堪えます (bears, puts up with)

taéru *v* 絶える = **taemásu** 絶えます (ceases)

táete *v* 堪えて・絶えて → **taemásu** 堪えます・絶えます

táezu *adv* 絶えず continuously, without interruption (= **taemanáku** 絶え 間なく)

tagá *n* たが a barrel hoop: [IDIOM] ~ **o shimeru** たがを締める braces oneself; [IDIOM] ~ **ga yurumu/hazureru** たがが 緩む/外れる becomes less disciplined, loses one's spirits

tagai (no) *adj* 互い(の) (**o-tagai (no)** お互い(の)) mutual, reciprocal, for each other

tagai (ni) *adv* 互い(に) (**o-tagai (ni)** お 互い(に)) mutually, reciprocally, with each other

tagaku *n* 多額 large sum

...-tagarimásu, -tagaru *suffix, v* ... たがります, ...たがる wants to ..., is eager to ...

tagayashimásu, tagayásu *v* 耕しま す, 耕す plows

tágetto *n* ターゲット object, target (= **taishō** 対象)

tagu-bōto *n* タグボート tug boat

tái *n* タイ・鯛 sea bream, red snapper

Tái *n* タイ Thailand

Tai-go *n* タイ語 Thai *(language)*

Tai-jin *n* タイ人 a Thai

tái *n* 体 **1.** form **2.** style **3.** body (= **karada** 体, **shintai** 身体)

tai-... *prep* 対..., ...´-**tai** ...対 versus, towards, against; **rokú-tai yón** 六対四, 6対4 4 to 6 *(score)*

tai-... *prefix* 退... leaving, retire

tai-gaku *n* 退学 **1. ~ shimásu** 退学します leaves school: **chūto-taigaku** 中途退学, **chū-tai** 中退 dropout **2.** expulsion from school (= **taigaku-shobun** 退学 〔処分〕)

tai-i *n* 退位 abdication: **~ shimásu** 退位します abdicates

tai-in *n* 退院: **~ shimásu** 退院します leaves the hospital

tai-shoku *n* 退職 retirement: **~ shimásu** 退職します retires: **taishoku-kin** 退職金 retirement allowance: **taishoku-negai** 退職願 letter of resignation

tai-... *prefix* 大... great, large

tai-bō, tai-mō *n* 大望 ambition, great willingness (= **taishi** 大志)

tai-ryō *n* 大量 large quantity: **tairyō-seisan** 大量生産 mass production

tai-sa *n* 大佐 (*army*) colonel; (= **daisa** 大佐) (*navy*) captain

tái-sa *n* 大差 [BOOKISH] a great difference (= **ōkina sa** 大きな差): **tái-sa de** 大差で by a wide margin

tai-sen *n* 大戦 a great war, a world war (= **ōkina sensō** 大きな戦争): **dai-ichi-ji sekai-taisen** 第一次世界大戦 World War I: **dai-ni-ji sekai-taisen** 第二次世界大戦 World War II

tai-shi *n* 大志 ambition (= **taibō, taimō** 大望); [IDIOM] **shōnen yo ~ o idake** 少年よ大志を抱け Boys, be ambitious!

tái-shō *n* 大将 (*general*) admiral: **o-yama no ~** お山の大将 king of the mountain: **gaki-daishō** がき〔ガキ〕大将 boss of the kids

tai-shoku *n* 大食 gluttony (= **ōgui** 大食い); **taishoku-kan** 大食漢 a big eater, glutton (= **ōgurai** 大食らい)

tái-sō *adj, adv* たいそう・大層 [BOOKISH] very: **tái-sō (na)** たいそう〔な〕 a great many/much; = **go-táisō** ごたいそう exaggerated

...-tái *suffix* ... 帯 belt; zone: **anet-tai** 亜熱帯 subtropical zone: **anzen/kiken chi-tai** 安全/危険地帯 safety/danger zone

...-tai *suffix v* ...たい wants to, is eager to

tabe-tai *suffix v* 食べたい wants to eat

shi-tai *suffix v* したい, **yari-tai** やりたい wants to do: **~ hōdai** したい放題 whatever one feels like doing [IN NEGATIVE SENSE]

taibō (no) *adj* 待望(の) long-awaited

taichō *n* 体調 (*physical condition*) tone (= **guai** 具合): **~ ga ii/yoi/warui** 体調がいい/〔良い〕/悪い is in good/poor health condition

taidan *n* 対談 [BOOKISH] conversation between two people, dialogue: **~ shimásu** 対談します has a conversation; **taidan-bangumi** 対談番組 TV talk show

táido *n* 態度 attitude, disposition, behavior: **~ ga ōkii** 態度が大きい acts big; **aimai na ~** あいまいな態度 ambiguous attitude

taidō *n* 胎動 fetal movement

taifū *n* 台風 typhoon

taigai *adv* 大概・たいがい **1.** in general; for the most part; practically (= **taitei** たいてい・大抵) **2.** probably, like(ly), like as not

taigen *n* 体言 substantive words, indeclinable words (*grammar*)

taigū *n* 待遇 **1.** treatment, reception **2.** pay, working conditions **3.** official position, post

taihai-teki (na) *adj* 退廃的(な) decadent

Taihéiyō *n* 太平洋 Pacific Ocean (→ **taiyō** 大洋)

Taiheiyō-sensō *n* 太平洋戦争 Pacific War

taihen *adv* たいへん・大変 **1.** very, exceedingly, terribly, enormously (= **hijō ni** 非常に): **Taihen osewa ni narimáshita.** 大変お世話になりました Thank you so much for everything you have done for me. **2.** laboriously, seriously, disastrously: **sorewa (hontō ni) taihen desu ne** それは(本当に)大変ですね It must be (*really*) hard for you.

taihen (na) *adj* たいへん〔大変〕(な) **1.** exceeding, enormous: **~ na bijin** 大変な美人 very beautiful **2.** serious, disastrous, tough, terrible, difficult: **~ na shigoto** 大変な仕事 tough work

taihi *n* 対比 [BOOKISH] contrast, comparison (= **hikaku** 比較): ~ **shimásu** 対比します contrasts, compares

táiho *n* 逮捕 arrest(ing): ~ **shimásu** 逮捕します arrests

taihō *n* 大砲 cannon

táii *n* 大尉 captain (*army*); lieutenant (*navy*) (= **dáii** 大尉)

taii *n* 大意 [BOOKISH] outline, summary, drift: ~ **o tsukamimásu** 大意をつかみます catches the drift

taii *n* 体位 body position, posture (= **shisei** 姿勢)

tái(i)ku *n* 体育 physical education, athletics: **Tái(i)ku-no-hí** 体育の日日 Sports Day (*2nd Monday of October*) **tai(i)kú-kan** *n* 体育館 gymnasium

taiji *n* 胎児 fetus, unborn baby, embryo

taiji *n* 退治 extermination: ~ **shimásu** 退治します exterminates; **oni-taiji** 鬼退治 demon extermination

taijū *n* 体重 body weight: **taijū-kei** 体重計 scales: ~ **ga fuemásu/herimásu** 体重が増え/減ります gains/loses weight

táika *n* 大家 authority (= **kyoshō** 巨匠)

táika *n* 対価 compensation, consideration

táika *n* 退化 degeneration: ~ **shimásu** 退化します degenerates

taikai *n* 大会 mass meeting; convention, conference; tournament: **zenkoku-taikai** 全国大会 national convention: **sekai-senshuken-taikai** 世界選手権大会 world championships

taikái *n* 大海 ocean, high sea (= **taiyō** 大洋)

taikaku *n* 体格 body build, physique

taikei *n* 体系 a system

taiken *n* 体験 personal experience: ~ **shimásu** 体験します experiences

taiko *n* 太鼓 (*Japanese*) drum

taikō *n* 対抗 confrontation, opposition; ... **ni ~ shimásu** ...に対抗します opposes, stands against, confronts; ... **ni ~ shite** ...に対抗して in opposition to, against, in rivalry with

taikutsu (na) *adj* 退屈 (な) boring, dull

taiman (na) *adj* 怠慢 (な) negligent, careless, neglectful

táimatsu *n* たいまつ・松明 torch

taimen *n* 対面 interview

taimen *n* 体面 one's dignity, sense of honor, "face": ~ **o tamochimásu** 体面を保ちます keeps up appearances

taimingu *n* タイミング timing (= **ma-ai** 間合い)

taiō *n* 対応 correspondence, handling: (... **ni**) ~ **shimásu** (...に) 対応します corresponds (*to*); is equivalent (*to*) (= **sōō** 相応)

taion *n* 体温 body temperature; **taion-kei** 体温計 (*clinical*) thermometer

taipo *n* タイポ typo, typing error

táipu *n* タイプ **1.** type, style (= **kata** 型): **atarashii ~** 新しいタイプ new type (= **shin-gata** 新型) **2.** = **kónomi** 好みのタイプ one's type **3.** typewriting, typewriter

taipuráitā *n* タイプライター typewriter (= **taipu** タイプ)

tairagemásu, tairageru *v* 平らげます, 平らげる [INFORMAL] eats up

taira-gi *n* タイラギ pin/razor/fan shell (*a kind of scallop*)

taira (na) *adj* 平ら (な) even, smooth, flat; ~ **ni shimásu** 平らにします flattens

tairiku *n* 大陸 continent: ~ **(no)** 大陸 (の) continental

tairitsu *n* 対立 confronting, opposing: ~ **shimásu** 対立します confronts, opposes

táiru *n* タイル tile (*floor, wall*)(*made of plastic, etc.*)

tairyoku *n* 体力 stamina (= **sutamina** スタミナ): ~ **ga arimásu** 体力があります has stamina

taisei *n* 体制 system: **seiji-taisei** 政治体制 political system: **kyōiku-taisei** 教育体制 education system

taisei *n* 体勢 posture (= **shisei** 姿勢): ~ **o kuzushimásu/tatenaoshimásu** 体勢を崩します/立て直します loses/regains one's balance

taisei *n* 耐性 tolerance: **arukōru-taisei** アルコール耐性 tolerance to alcohol

taisei *n* 大勢 general situation (= **nariyuki** なりゆき)

taisei *n* 態勢 preparedness: ~ **ga totonoimásu** 態勢が整います is ready

Taiséiyō *n* 大西洋 Atlantic Ocean (→ **taiyō** 大洋)

taisen *n* 対戦 match, competition:

taisen-aite 対戦相手 one's opponent

taisetsu (na) *adj* 大切(な) **1.** important (= **daiji (na)** 大事(な), **jūyō (na)** 重要(な)): ~ **na shorui** 大切な書類 important documents **2.** valuable, precious (= **daiji (na)** 大事(な), **kichō (na)** 貴重(な)): ~ **na omoide** 大切な思い出 precious memories

taisetsu-ni-shimásu (suru) *v* 大切にします(する) cherishes, treats carefully, gives importance (= **daiji-ni-shimásu** 大事にします): (**dōzo) o-karada o ~ ni shitekudasai** (どうぞ)お体を大切にして下さい Please take care of yourself.

táishaku *n* 貸借 debit and credit, lending and borrowing

táishaku-taishō hyō *n* 貸借対照表 balance sheet (B/S)

táishi *n* 大使 ambassador

taishí-kan *n* 大使館 embassy

tai-shimásu, tai-súru *v* 対します, 対する: (**… ni) ~** (…に)対します confronts, opposes; **… ni tái-shite** …に対して **1.** against; toward; as against, as compared with, in contrast to **2.** with respect to, in regard to

tái-shita … *adj* たいした・大した… important; serious; immense

taishitsu *n* 体質 (*physical*) constitution

taisho *n* 対処 handling of matters: ~ **shimásu** 対処します handles, copes with

taishō *n* 対象 object, target (= **tāgetto** ターゲット)

taishō *n* 対照 contrast: ~ **shimásu** 対照します contrasts; **hikaku-taishō** 比較対照 comparison and contrast (→ **táishaku-taishō-hyō** 貸借対照表)

taishō *n* 対称 symmetry: **sayū-taishō** 左右対称 bilateral symmetry: **taishō na** 対称な symmetrical

Táishō-jidai *n* 大正時代 Taisho Period (*1912–1926*)

taishū *n* 体臭 body odor (BO)

taishū *n* 大衆 the general public, the masses: **taishū (no)** 大衆(の) popular, mass: **taishū-ka** 大衆化 popularization

taisō *n* 体操 calisthenics, physical exercises

taita *v* 炊いて = **takimáshita** 炊きました (cooked)

taite *v* 炊いて → **takimásu** 炊きます

taite *v* 焚いて → **takimásu** 焚きます

taitei *adv* たいてい・大抵: **taitei no …** たいていの …the usual …, most …

taitō (no) *adj* 対等(の) equal, equivalent (= **dōtō (no)** 同等(の))

táitoru *n* タイトル **1.** title (= **hyōdai** 表題) **2.** title, championship: **taitoru-matchi** タイトルマッチ title match **3.** caption, subtitle (= **jimaku** 字幕)

taiwa *n* 対話 conversation, dialogue

Taiwán *n* 台湾 Taiwan; **Taiwan-jín** 台湾人 a Taiwanese

taiya *n* タイヤ a tire

taiyō *n* 大洋 ocean (= **taikai** 大海): **go-taiyō** 五大洋 five oceans (*Pacific Ocean, Indian Ocean, Atlantic Ocean, Arctic Ocean, Antarctic Ocean*) (→ **Taiheiyō** 太平洋, **Taiseiyō** 大西洋)

taiyō *n* 大要 summary (= **gaiyō** 概要, **yōyaku** 要約, **samarii** サマリー)

táiyō *n* 太陽 **1.** sun (= **ohisama** お日様) **2.** joy to someone

taiyō-enerugii *n* 太陽エネルギー solar energy

taiyō-kei *n* 太陽系 solar system

táiyō-kō 太陽光 [FORMAL] sunshine (= **nikkō** 日光, **taiyō no hikari** 太陽の光)

taiyō-nensū *n* 耐用年数 lifespan of thing, expected lifetime

taiyō-sei *n* 耐用性 durability

taizai *n* 滞在 a stay (*away from home*), a sojourn: ~ **shimásu** 滞在します stays (*away from home*), sojourns; **taizai-saki** 滞在先 place of sojourn

taka *n* タカ・鷹 hawk

taka no tsume *n* タカノツメ・鷹の爪 red pepper (= **tōgarashi** トウガラシ・唐辛子)

táká *n* 高 quantity: ~ **ga shireteimásu** 高が知れています is limited, not amount to a hill of beans

takaga *adj* たかが no(thing) more than

takái *adj* 高い high, tall; costly, expensive; loud

takanai *v* 焚かない = **takimasén** 焚きません (not make a fire)

takanai ν 炊かない = **takimasén** 炊きません (not cook)

takará n 宝 (**o-takara** お宝) a treasure (= **takara-mono** 宝物)
  takará-kuji n 宝くじ lottery
  takara-mono n 宝物 a treasure

tákasa n 高さ height (= **kōdo** 高度)

take n 竹 bamboo
  take-no-ko n タケノコ・竹の子・筍 bamboo shoot
  take-záiku n 竹細工 bambooware

take n タケ・茸 (*compounds/dialect*) mushroom (= **kínoko** キノコ)

take ν 炊け [IMPERATIVE] (cook it!) → **takimásu** 炊きます

takéba ν 焚けば (if one makes a fire) → **takimásu** 焚きます

takéba ν 炊けば (if one cooks/burns it) → **takimásu** 炊きます

takemásu, takeru ν 焚けます, 焚ける can make a fire

takemásu, takeru ν 炊けます, 炊ける can cook; can burn it

taki n 滝 waterfall

takigi n たきぎ・薪 firewood, fuel

takimásu, taku ν 焚きます, 焚く makes a fire
  taki-bi n 焚き火 bonfire
  taki-tsuke n 焚き付け kindling

takimásu, taku ν 炊きます, 炊く cooks; burns it
  takikomi-góhan n 炊き込みご飯 a rice dish that includes adding seasonal ingredients to the rice

takishiido n タキシード tuxedo

takkuru n タックル tackle

táko n タコ octopus
  tako-yaki n たこ焼き griddled dumplings with octopus bits inside

táko n 凧・たこ kite
  takó-áge n 凧揚げ kite-flying

táko n たこ callus, corn

takō´ ν 焚こう = **takimashō´** 焚きましょう (let's make a fire!)

takō´ ν 炊こう = **takimashō´** 炊きましょう (let's cook!; let's burn it!)

takokuseki (no) adj 多国籍(の) multinational: **takokuseki-kigyō** 多国籍企業 multinational company

taku n 宅 1. my house 2. (*your/someone else's*) house (= **o-taku** お宅) 3. [HUMBLE] my husband

tak-kyū-bin n 宅急便 express delivery service

taku-hai-bin n 宅配便 delivery service

taku ν 焚く = **takimásu** 焚きます (cooks; burns)

taku ν 炊く = **takimásu** 炊きます (makes a fire)

taku n 卓 table, desk
  tak-kyū n 卓球 table tennis
  taku-jō n, adv 卓上 on one's table/desk

takúan, takúwan n たくあん, たくわん yellow pickles made from sliced daikon

takumashii adj たくましい・逞しい 1. strong, robust (*body*) 2. strong (*will*)

takumi n 巧み skill
  takumi na adj 巧み(な) skillful
  takumi ni adv 巧みに skillfully

takurami n 企み plan, scheme, plot

takuramimásu, takurámu ν 企みます, 企む plans, schemes, plots

takuránde ν 企んで → **takuramimásu** 企みます 1. intentionally, on purpose, with forethought 2. (*... to* **takuránde**) ...と企んで in collusion/cahoots with ...

takusán (no) adj たくさん[沢山](の) lots (*of*), much/many, a lot (*of*)

tákushii n タクシー taxi: ~ (**no**) **untenshu** タクシー(の)運転手 taxi driver: ~ **noriba** タクシー乗り場 taxi stand: **takushii-dai** タクシー代 taxi fare (= **takusii-unchin** タクシー運賃, **takusii-ryōkin** タクシー料金)

takuwae n 蓄え savings, a reserve, a stock (= **chochiku** 貯蓄)

takuwaemásu, takuwaéru ν 蓄えます, 蓄える saves up, hoards

takúwan, takuan n たくわん, たくあん yellow pickles made from sliced daikon

tamá n 1. 玉 1. ball: **keito-damá** 毛糸玉 ball of wool; **pachinko-damá** パチンコ玉 pachinko ball 2. round thing, bead: **bii-damá** ビー玉 marble 3. testicle(s) (= **kōgan** 睾丸, **kin-tama** 金玉) 4. ~ **no yō na** 玉のような sweetest, precious and/or lovely thing

tamá n 玉・珠 jewel; bead; drop;

[IDIOM] ~ **no koshi ni noru** 玉の輿に乗る marries a rich man

tamá *n* 球 **1.** globe (= **chikyū** 地球) **2.** (*light*) bulb (= **denkyū** 電球)

tamá *n* 弾 bullet (= **dangan** 弾丸)

tamágo *n* 卵・玉子・タマゴ egg: ~ **no kara** 卵の殻 eggshell: **tamago-yaki** 卵[玉子]焼き rolled egg

tama-négi *n* タマネギ・玉葱 onion (*round bulb*)

tama (no/ni) *adj, adv* たま(の/に) occasional(ly), infrequent(ly), now and then, at times, once in a while

tamaranai *v* 溜らない = **tamarimasén** 溜りません (does/will not accumulate)

tamaranai *v* 貯まらない = **tamarimasén** 貯まりません (does/will not save)

tamaranai *v* 堪らない = **tamarimasén** 堪りません (is intolerable, insufferable, unbearable)

tamari *n* 溜まり・たまり = **tamari-ba** たまり場 (a gathering place (*hangout, haunt*))

tamari-ba *n* たまり場 a gathering place (*hangout, haunt*)

tamarimasén, tamaranai *v* 溜まりません, 溜まらない does/will not accumulate

tamarimasén, tamaranai *v* 貯まりません, 貯まらない does/will not save (*money*)

tamarimasén, tamaranai *v* たまりません, たまらない is intolerable, insufferable, unbearable; (**...te tama-nai** ...てたまらない does/is) unbearably, insufferably

tamarimásu, tamaru *v* 溜まります, 溜まる it accumulates

tamarimásu, tamaru *v* 貯まります, 貯まる it saves (*money*)

támashii *n* 魂 soul

tamatama たまたま occasionally

tamá-tsuki *n* 玉突き billiards (= **biri-yádo** ビリヤード)

tamá-tsuki jiko *n* 玉突き事故 pileup

tamatte *v* 溜まって → **tamarimásu** 溜まります

tamatte *v* 貯まって → **tamarimásu** 貯まります

... tamé *suffix* ...為・ため **1.** for the

sake (good, benefit) of **2.** for the purpose of **3.** because (*of*), due to

tameiki *n* ため息 sigh

tamemásu, tameru *v* 溜めます, 溜める amasses/accumulates

tamemásu, tameru *v* 貯めます, 貯める saves (*money*)

tameraimásu, tameráu *v* ためらいます, ためらう hesitates

tame ro *v* 溜めろ [IMPERATIVE] (amass it!; accumulate it!) → **tamemásu** 溜めます

tame ro *v* 貯めろ [IMPERATIVE] (save it!) → **tamemásu** 貯めます

tameshí *n* 試し trial, test, experiment: **tameshí ni** 試しに as a trial/test

tameshimásu, tamésu *v* 試します, 試す tries, attempts, experiments with

tamete *v* 溜めて・貯めて → **tamemásu** 溜めます・貯めます

tāminaru *n* ターミナル terminal

ta-minzoku (no) *adj* 多民族(の) multiracial: **ta-minzoku-kokka** 多民族国家 multiracial country

tamochimásu, tamótsu *v* 保ちます, 保つ keeps, preserves, maintains

tamótánai *v* 保たない = **tamochimasén** 保ちません (not keep)

tamotó *n* たもと・袂 sleeve; edge, end

tamótte *v* 保って → **tamochimásu** 保ちます

tamushi *n* タムシ・田虫 ringworm; athlete's foot (= **mizumushi** 水虫)

...ʹ-tan *suffix* ...反 bolt (*of cloth*)

tana *n* 棚 shelf, rack (→ **shokkí-dana** 食器棚)

tana-age *n* 棚上げ shelving: **mondai o ~ shimásu** 問題を棚上げします shelves the issue

tana kara botamochi *n* 棚からぼた餅 windfall (= **tana-bota** 棚ぼた)

tana-oroshi *n* 棚卸し stocktaking

Tanabata *n* 七夕・たなばた the Festival of the Weaver Star (*7 July*)

... tanbí (ni) *suffix, adv* ...たんび(に) [INFORMAL], **tabí (ni)** 度・たび(に) every time that ...

tandoku *n* 単独 alone (= **tanshin** 単身): **tandoku-kōdō** 単独行動 independent action

táne n 種 1. seed 2. source, cause 3. material 4. secret, trick to it 5. **hanashi no ~** 話の種 subject, topic

tango n 単語 word(s), vocabulary

tango n タンゴ tango (*music*)

Tángo no sekku n 端午の節句 Boys' Festival (5 May)

tani, tani-ma n 谷, 谷間 valley

tán'i n 単位 unit

tanitsu-minzoku n 単一民族 single race

tanjō´bi n 誕生日 (**o-tanjō´bi** お誕生日) birthday: **(o-)tanjōbi-pātii** (お) 誕生日パーティ birthday party

tanjun (na) adj 単純 (な) simple; simplehearted, simpleminded (*not complicated*): **tanjun-ka** 単純化 simplification: **tanjun-meikai** 単純明快 simple and clear

tánka n 短歌 31-syllable poem (*traditional Japanese poem*)

tánka n 担架 stretcher, litter: **~ de hako-baremásu** 担架で運ばれます is carried on a stretcher

tánka n 単価 unit cost, unit price

tánka n 啖呵 [BOOKISH] caustic words (*during a quarrel*): **~ o kirimásu** 啖呵を切ります blusters out

tanki n 短期 short period

tanki-dáigaku n 短期大学 junior college, two-year college

tankō n 炭鉱 coal mine

tanmatsu n 端末 computer terminal

tanmono n 反物 draperies, dry goods

tán naru ... adj 単なる... only, mere [BOOKISH] = **táda no** ただの: **~ uwasa ni sugimasén** 単なる噂にすぎません That's just a rumor.

tán ni adv 単に only, merely (= **táda** ただ)

tannin n 担任 (*teacher*) in charge; **... o ~ shimásu** ...を担任します takes charge (*is in charge*) of

tanomí n 頼み a request (= **tanomi-goto** 頼みごと, **onegai** お願い): **~ no tsuna** 頼みの綱 one's one and only hope, mainstay: **o-tanomi-shitai koto ga arunodesuga...** お願みしたいことがあるのですが ... Would you mind doing me a favor?

tanomimásu, tanómu v 頼みます, 頼む 1. requests, begs 2. relies upon, entrusts with 3. hires, engages (*a professional*)

tanónde v 頼んで → **tanomimásu** 頼みます

tanoshii adj 楽しい pleasant, enjoyable

tanoshími n 楽しみ (**o-tanoshími** お楽しみ) a pleasure, an enjoyment; **... (surú) no ~ ni shimás̱u** ...(するの) を楽しみにします 1. takes pleasure in (doing) 2. looks forward to ...ing

tanoshimimásu, tanoshímu v 楽しみます, 楽しむ enjoys, takes pleasure in

tanoshínde v 楽しんで → **tanoshimimásu** 楽しみます

tanpakú-shitsu n 蛋白質・たんぱく質 protein

tanpen-shōsetsu n 短編小説 short story (*novel*)

tánpo n 担保 mortgage, pledge (= **teitō** 抵当): **jinteki-tanpo** 人的担保 guarantee: **tanpo-bukken** 担保物件 collateral: **mu-tanpo no** 無担保の unsecured

tánpon n タンポン tampon

tánpopo n タンポポ・たんぽぽ dandelion

tansan n 炭酸 carbonic acid

tansán-sui n 炭酸水 soda water

tanseki n 胆石 gall stone

tanshi n 端子 a terminal (*electronics*)

tanshin n 単身 [BOOKISH] alone (= **tandoku** 単独)

tanshin-funin n 単身赴任 job transfer away from one's home

tánsho n 短所 shortcoming, fault, weak point: **to chōsho** 長所 短所と長所 weak and strong points

tansu n たんす・タンス・箪笥 chest of drawers

tantei n 探偵 detective: **tantei-shōsetsu** 探偵小説 detective fiction: **shiritsu-tantei** 私立探偵 private eye

tantō n 担当 responsibility, charge: **~ shimásu** 担当します takes charge of

tantō´-sha n 担当者 person in charge, responsible person (→ **tannin** 担任)

tantō-chokunyū (na) adj 単刀直入 (な) point-blank: **~ na iken** 単刀直入な意見 straightforward opinion: **~ ni iu**

to *adv* 単刀直入に言うと put bluntly

tánuki *n* タヌキ・狸 **1.** raccoon dog (*not* badger **anaguma** 穴熊) **2.** sly person: [IDIOM] **~ neiri** 狸寝入り play possum

tánzen *n* 丹前 padded bathrobe (= **dot-era** どてら)

taoremásu, taoréru *v* 倒れます, 倒れる falls down, tumbles, collapses

táoru *n* タオル towel: **basu-taoru** バスタオル bath towel

taóse *v* 倒せ [IMPERATIVE] (knock it down!) → **taoshimásu** 倒します

taoshimásu, taósu *v* 倒します, 倒す knocks down, overthrows

tapesutorii *n* タペストリー tapestry

tappú-dansu *n* タップダンス tap dance

tappúri *adv* たっぷり fully, more than enough

tára *n* タラ・鱈 cod (*fish*)

…-tára *suffix, conj* …たら if, when

tarafuku *adv* たらふく [INFORMAL] (*eat, drink*) one's fill

tarai *n* たらい tub, basin: **tarai-mawashi** たらい回し shifted from one section to another

tarako *n* タラコ・鱈子 cod roe

taráppu *n* タラップ gangway

tarashimásu, tarásu *v* 垂らします, 垂らす dangles, drops, spills

tarashimásu, tarásu *v* たらします, たらす = **tarashi-komimásu (-komu)** たらし込みます(込む) seduces; wheedles

taré *n* たれ・タレ gravy, (*cooking*) sauce

taremásu, taréru *v* 垂れます, 垂れる hangs down, dangles; drips

tarento *n* タレント a TV personality, (*person of*) talent

…-tári (shimásu/desu) …たり(します/です) doing representatively/sometimes/alternately: **…-tári …-nákáttari** …たり…なかったり doing off and on, sometimes does and sometimes doesn't

tarimásu, tariru *v* 足ります, 足りる is enough/sufficient, suffices

tarinai *v* 足りない = **tarimasén** 足りません (is not enough, is insufficient)

tariru *v* 足りる = **tarimásu** 足ります (is enough/sufficient, suffices)

taru *n* たる・樽 barrel, keg, cask

taru *v* 足る [*dialect, literary*] = **tarimásu** 足ります (is enough/sufficient, suffices)

táru *n* タール tar: **kōru-táru** コール・タール coal tar: **sekiyu-táru** 石油タール petroleum tar

tarumimásu, tarumu *v* 弛みます, 弛む gets slack (*loose*), relaxed

tarunde *v* 弛んで → **tarumimásu** 弛みます

taruto *n* タルト tart (pastry)

taryō *n* 多量 large quantity

tasanai *v* 足さない = **tashimasén** 足しません (not add)

tase *v* 足せ [IMPERATIVE] (add!) → **tashimásu** 足します

taséba *v* 足せば (if one adds) → **tashimásu** 足します

tashi *n* 足し: **~ ni shimásu** 足しにします make up

táshika *adv* 確か if I remember rightly, probably

táshika ni *adj* 確かに for sure, surely, undoubtedly; indeed

táshika na *adv* 確かな safe, sure, certain

tashikamemásu, tashikaméru *v* 確かめます, 確かめる makes sure, ascertains

tashimásu, tasu *v* 足します, 足す **1.** adds **2. yō o ~** 用を足します does one's business, relieves oneself, goes to the bathroom

tashite *v* 足して → **tashimásu** 足します

tashō *adj* 多少 **1.** (*large and/or small*) number, quantity, amount **2. tashō (no)** 多少(の) more or less; somewhat; some

tasogare *n* たそがれ・黄昏 twilight (= **yūgure** 夕暮れ)

tassha (na) *adj* 達者(な) healthy; skillful, expert, good at

tas-shimásu, tas-suru *v* 達します, 達する accomplishes; reaches

tas-shinai *v* 達しない = **tas-shimasén** 達しません (not accomplish/reach)

tasū′ *n* 多数 large number; majority

tasukarimásu, tasukáru *v* 助かります, 助かる is saved; is relieved

tasukemásu, tasukéru v 助けます, 助ける **1.** helps **2.** saves

tasukénai v 助けない = **tasukemasén** 助けません (not help; not save)

tasuké ro v 助けろ [IMPERATIVE] (help!) → **tasukemásu** 助けます

tasukéte v 助けて → **tasukemásu** 助けます

tasuki n タスキ・襷 a sleeve cord

tatáite v 叩いて → **tatakimásu** 叩きます

tatakaemásu, tatakaéru v 戦えます, 戦える can fight

tatakaenai v 戦えない = **tatakaemasén** 戦えません (cannot fight)

tatakaete v 戦えて → **tatakaemásu** 戦えます

tatakaimásu, tatakau v 戦います, 戦う fights; makes war/game: **teki to ~** 敵と戦います battles an enemy

tatakaimásu, tatakau v 闘います, 闘う struggle, fights (with, against): **byōki to ~** 病気と闘います fights the disease

tatakánai v 叩かない = **tatakimasén** 叩きません (not strike)

tatakátte v 戦って → **tatakaimásu** 戦います

tatakátte v 闘って → **tatakaimásu** 闘います

tatakau v 戦う = **tatakaimásu** 戦います (fights; makes war/game)

tatakau v 闘う = **tatakaimásu** 闘います (fights, struggles)

tatakawanai v 戦わない = **tatakaimasén** 戦いません (not fight/make war/game)

tatakemásu, tatakéru v 叩けます, 叩ける can strike (hit, knock, clap)

tatakénai v 叩けない = **tatakemasén** 叩けません (cannot strike)

tatákete v 叩けて → **tatakemásu** 叩けます

tatakí n **1.** 叩き pounding; bashing; mincing; **Nihon-tátaki** 日本叩き Japan-bashing **2.** たたき concrete/cement floor

tatakimásu, tatáku v 叩きます, 叩く strikes, hits, knocks; pounds (fish/meat to tenderize or mince it), minces: **té o ~** 手を叩きます claps

tatami n 畳 floor mat(ting), matted floor

tatamimásu, tatamu v 畳みます, 畳む folds up

tatánai v 立たない = **tachimasén** 立ちません (not stand)

tatanda v 畳んだ = **tatamimáshita** 畳みました (folded up)

tatande v 畳んで → **tatamimásu** 畳みます

tátchi n タッチ touch; **~ no sa de** タッチの差で by the turn of a hair

tate n 盾・楯 shield: **~ ni toru** 盾[楯]に取る use something as an excuse

tate n 縦 length, height, longitudinal

tate-gaki n 縦書き vertical writing

tate-ito n 縦糸 warp (vertical threads)

táte no 縦の adj vertical

táte ni 縦に adv vertically, lengthwise

táte v 立て [IMPERATIVE] (stand up!) → **tachimásu** 立ちます

táteba v 立てば (if one stands) → **tachimásu** 立ちます

taté-fuda n 立(て)札 signboard

tatekae n 立(て)替え paying for someone: **tatekaemásu** 立(て)替えます pays for someone

tatekae-kin n 立(て)替え金 advance money

tatekae n 建(て)替え reconstruction, rebuilding: **tatekaemásu** 建(て)替えます rebuilds

tatémae n 建て前 principle, policy: **... o ~ to shimásu** ...を建て前とします makes ... one's policy

tate-mashi n 建て増し house addition/extension, annex

tatemásu, tatéru v 建てます, 建てる erects, builds, raises; sets up, establishes

tatemásu, tatéru v 立てます, 立てる can stand

taté-móno n 建物 building

taténai v 建てない = **tatemasén** 建てません (not build)

taténai v 立てない = **tatemasén** 立てません (cannot stand)

tateraremásu, tateraréru v 建てられます, 建てられる can build it

tateraréreba v 建てられれば (if one can build) → **tateraremásu** 建てられれます

248

tatéreba *v* 建てれば (if one builds) → **tatemásu** 建てます

tatéreba *v* 立てれば (if one can stand) → **tatemásu** 立てます

táte ro *v* 建てろ [IMPERATIVE] (build it!) → **tatemásu** 建てます

taté-tsubo *n* 建て坪 floor space

tateyō´ *v* 建てよう = **tatemashō´** 建てましょう (let's build it!)

tatō´ *v* 立とう = **tachimashō´** 立ちましょう (let's stand!)

tatoé *conj* たとえ even if

tatóe 例え・たとえ *n* an example, an instance; a simile, an analogy

tatóeba *adv* 例えば・たとえば for example, for instance

tatoemásu, tatoéru *v* 例えます・喩えます, 例える・喩える gives an example, compares (*draws a simile to*)

tátsu *v* 立つ = **tachimásu** 立ちます (stands (up))

tátsu *v* 発つ = **tachimásu** 発ちます (leaves)

tátsu *v* 経つ = **tachimásu** 経ちます (elapses)

tátsu *v* 断つ = **tachimásu** 断ちます (cuts off)

tatsu *n* 竜・龍 dragon (= **doragon** ドラゴン)

Tatsu-doshi *n* 辰年 year of the Dragon

tatsu no otoshigo *n* タツノオトシゴ・竜の落とし子 sea horse (= **umi-uma**, **kaiba** 海馬)

tatta *adj* たった just, merely, only

tátta *v* 立った = **tachimáshita** 立ちました; etc. (stood up; …)

tatta-íma *n*, *adv* たった今 just now; in (*just*) a minute

tátte *v* 立って → **tachimásu** 立ちます: **~ imásu** 立っています is standing

tawā *n* タワー tower, pagoda (= **tō** 塔); **Tōkyō-tawā** 東京タワー Tokyo Tower

tawará *n* たわら・俵 straw bag; bale

tawashi *n* たわし scrub(bing) brush; swab

tayasúku *adv* たやすく easily

tayoránai *v* 頼らない = **tayorimasén** 頼りません (not rely on)

táyori 頼り *n* reliance: **~ ni shite(i)másu** 頼りにして(い)ます I'm counting on

you.: **~ nai** 頼りない undependable, unreliable

táyori *n* 便り communication, correspondence, a letter, word (*from someone*), news (= **shōsoku** 消息); **kaze no ~** 風の便り a little bird, rumor

tayorimásu, tayóru *v* 頼ります, 頼る relies on, depends on

tayō-sei *n* 多様性 diversity

tayótte *v* 頼って → **tayorimásu** 頼ります

tazuna *n* 手綱 reins: **~ o shimemásu** 手綱を締めます tightens the reins

tazunemásu, tazunéru *v* 尋ねます, 尋ねる **1.** asks (*a question*) **2.** looks for

tazunemásu, tazunéru *v* 訪ねます, 訪ねる visits

tazuné ro *v* 尋ねろ [IMPERATIVE] (ask!) → **tazunemásu** 尋ねます

tazuné ro *v* 訪ねろ [IMPERATIVE] (visit!) → **tazunemásu** 訪ねます

té *n* 手 **1.** hand, arm **2.** trick, move **3.** kind **4.** person **5.** help: **~ ni hairimásu** 手に入ります = **~ ni iremásu** 手に入れます obtains, gets it

te-árai *n* 手洗い **1.** hand wash **2. o-teárai** お手洗い washroom, rest room, toilet (= **keshō-shitsu** 化粧室, **toire** トイレ)

té-ate *n* 手当て treatment; reparation, provision

té-ate *n* 手当 (**o-téate** お手当) allowance

te-búkuro *n* 手袋 gloves

te-dori *n* 手取り take-home pay

te-fuki *n* 手拭き (**o-tefúki** お手拭き) hand towel (= **te-nugui** 手拭い)

te-gákari *n* 手掛かり a hold, a place to hold on; a clue (= **itoguchi** 糸口)

te-gami *n* 手紙 (**o-tégami** お手紙) letter (= **shokan** 書簡 [BOOKISH])

te-gata *n* 手形 a note, a bill: **yakusoku-tegata** 約束手形 promissory note: **kawase-tegata** 為替手形 draft bill of exchange

te-gatái *adj* 手堅い safe; reliable; steady

te-gókoro *n* 手心 discretion

te-gótae *n* 手応え response, effect: **~ ga aru** 手応えがある response on my fishing rod té-guchi *n* 手口 way (*of doing bad things*), trick

te-gúruma *n* 手車 hand cart

té-hái *n* 手配 (*setting up*) a search for a criminal, a dragnet: ~ **shimásu** します sets up a dragnet; **tehai-sháshin** 手配写真 photograph of a wanted criminal

té-hazu *n* 手はず・手筈 arrangements

te-hón *n* 手本 (**o-tehon** お手本) model, pattern (= **mihon** 見本)

té-kubi *n* 手首 wrist

té-mane *n* 手まね・手真似 gesture with hand(s) (= **(te no) jesuchā** (手の)ジェスチャー)

té-máneki *n* 手招き beckoning

té-mari *n* 手まり・手毬 (*decorated small*) handball

té-nímotsu *n* 手荷物 hand luggage

té-nó-hira *n* 手のひら・掌 palm (*of hand*)

te-nugui *n* 手拭い hand towel (= **te-fuki** 手拭き (**o-tefuki** お手拭き))

te-ono *n* 手斧 hatchet, hand axe

te-ori (no) *adj* 手織り(の) handweaving

te-sage *n* 手提げ・手さげ handbag

te-záiku *n* 手細工 handiwork

te-zawari *n* 手ざわり texture, touch, hand feeling

te-zúkuri (no) *adj* 手作り(の) homemade, made by hand (= **hōmu meido (no)** ホームメイド(の), **hando meido (no)** ハンドメイド(の), (**o-**) **te-sei** (no) (お)手製(の))

...**-te** *suffix* ...て (*does/did*) and, and then, and so; doing; [+ AUXILIARY] (→ **shite** して)

tēburu *n* テーブル table; **tēburú-kake** テーブル掛け tablecloth (= **tēburu kurosu** テーブルクロス); **dainingu-tēburu** ダイニングテーブル dining table (= **shoku-taku** 食卓)

tei-... *prefix* 定... fixed, appointed, set

tei-ka *n* 定価 the set price, fixed price

téiki (no) *adj* 定期(の) fixed, regular, periodic, scheduled: **teiki-yokin** 定期預金 time deposit

tei-ki-ken *n* 定期券 pass (*commuter ticket*), season ticket

tei-shoku *n* 定食 a set meal, table

d'hôte; a complete meal

tei-... *prefix* 低... low

tei-ka *n* 低下: ~ **shimásu** 低下します falls, drops, declines, descents

tei-kétsúatsu *n* 低血圧 low blood pressure

tei-kíatsu *n* 低気圧 low (*barometric*) pressure

tei-soku *n* 低速 low speed: **teisoku-gia/giya** 低速ギア/ギヤ low gear

tei-... *prefix* 停... stop

tei-den *n* 停電 power failure/outage

tei-ryū *n* 停留 stop, stopping: **tei-ryū-jo** 停留所 stop (*of bus, streetcar, etc.*)

tei-sha *n* 停車 stopping (*of a vehicle*): ~ **shimásu** 停車します stops (*a vehicle*)

tei-shi *n* 停止 suspension, interruption: ~ **shimásu** 停止します suspends; **ichiji-teishi** 一時停止 pause, suspension

teian *n* 提案 proposal, suggestion: ~ **shimásu** 提案します proposes

teibō *n* 堤防 dike, embankment (= **tsutsumi** 堤)

téido *n* 程度 degree, extent, level

teikei *n* 提携 [BOOKISH] cooperation, affiliation: ~ **shimásu** 提携します cooperates, affiliates

teikō *n* 抵抗 resistance: ~ **shimásu** 抵抗します resists

téikoku *n* 帝国 empire

téikoku (no) *adj* 帝国(の) imperial

teikoku-shúgi *n* 帝国主義 imperialism

téinei (na) *adj* ていねい[丁寧](な) (**go-téinei (na)** ごていねい[丁寧](な)) polite; careful

te-iré *n* 手入れ repair; upkeep, care

teisai *n* 体裁 appearance, get-up, form, format, layout

teisetsu (na) *adj* 貞節(な) chaste, principled: ~ **na tsuma** 貞節な妻 faithful wife

téishu *n* 亭主 1. host (*at Japanese tea ceremony*) 2. landlord 3. (*my*) husband

teitō *n* 抵当 mortgage, pledge (= **tanpo** 担保)

téjina *n* 手品 jugglery, magic (*tricks*) tejiná-shi *n* 手品師 juggler, magician

tejun *n* 手順 order, procedure, program (= **dandori** 段取り)

...**-té kara** *suffix* ...てから after (doing),

after one does/did, does/did and then
(*next*)

teki *n* 敵 **1.** enemy, foe **2.** opponent;
kō-teki-shu 好敵手 rival (= **raibaru** ラ
イバル): [IDIOM] **~ ni shio o okuru** 敵に
塩を送る help one's enemy when they
are in trouble

...-teki *suffix* ...滴 a drop

...-teki (na) *suffix, adj* (の) ...ic, ...
ical, ...al, ...ly: **chi-teki (na)** 知的(な)
intellectual: **shi-teki (na)** 私的(の)
private, personal (= **kojin-teki (na)** 個人
的(な)): **shi-teki (na)** 詩的(な) poetic:
-teki ni ...的に ...ically, ...ally: **kanjō-
teki** 感情的 emotional: **kiseki-teki** 奇跡
的 miraculously

tékido *n* 適度 [BOOKISH] moderation

tékido na *adj* 適度な reasonable,
moderate: **~ undō** 適度な運動
moderate exercise

tékigi *adv* 適宜 [BOOKISH] suitably,
fitly, properly (= **tekitō (ni)** 適当(に)):
tékigi (no) 適宜の suitable, fit, proper

tekikaku (na) *adj* 適格(な) qualified,
eligible: **tekikaku-sha** 適格者 qualified
person (= **teki-nin** 適任)

tekikaku (na/ni) *adj, adv* 的確・適確
(な/に) precise(ly), accurate(ly),
exact(ly): **~ na handan** 的確[適確]な
判断 accurate judgement

teki-nin 適任 qualified person
(= **tekikaku-sha** 適格者)

teki-sánai *v* 適しません = **tekishimasén**
適しません (is not suitable)

tekisetsu (na) *adj* 適切(な) appropriate, to the point

teki-shimásu, teki-su 適します、適
す is suitable, qualified

tekí-shite *v* 適して → **teki-shimásu**
適します

tékísuto *n* テキスト **1.** textbook (=
kyōka-sho 教科書) **2.** original text

tekitō (na) *adj* 適当(な) **1.** suitable,
proper **2.** irresponsible, haphazard,
random, half-hearted (= **iikagen (na)**
いい加減(な)): **~ na henji** 適当な返事
vague answer

tekitō (ni) *adv* 適当(に) **1.** suitably,
properly (= **tekigi** 適宜) **2.** irrespon-
sibly, haphazardly, randomly, half-

heartedly (= **iikagen (ni)** いい加減
(に)): **~ ni erabimásu** 適当に選びます
chooses randomly

tekk(-...) *n, prefix* 鉄(...) iron, steel

tek-ka(-maki) *n* 鉄火(巻き) seaweed-
rolled sushi with tuna inside

tek-ki 鉄器, **tekkí-rui** 鉄器類 hardware (items)

tek-kyō *n* 鉄橋 iron bridge

teko *n* てこ・挺子・梃子 lever: **~ demo
ugokanai** てこでも動かない will not
move at all

...-te kudasái *interj* ...て下さい please
(*do*)

temá *n* 手間 (**o-téma** お手間) time and
effort (*taken up*); one's trouble (= **tesū**
手数 (**o-tesū** お手数))

tē'ma *n* テーマ theme, topic (= **shudai**
主題): **tēma-songu** テーマソング
theme song (= **shudai-ka** 主題歌)

temae *n* **1.** 手前・てまえ this side (of
...); I/me **2.** 手前 (**o-témae** お手前)
prowess, skill, ability

temae *n* 点前 (**o-témae** お点前) tea ceremony procedures

...-temásu *suffix, v* ...てます = **...-te
imásu** ...ています

temáwari *n* 手回り personal effects;
luggage (= **temawarí-hin** 手回り品)

...-témo *suffix* ...ても even doing/
being, even if (*one does/is*); **shítémo íi**
してもいい it is OK to do, one may do

ten *n* 点 point, dot, spot; score (*points*)

ten-sū' *n* 点数 score, points

tén *n* 天 **1.** sky **2.** heaven (= **ten-goku**
天国)

tén-goku *n* 天国 paradise, heaven
(= **ten** 天)

ten-jō *n* 天井 ceiling

tén-ki *n* 天気 (**o-ténki** お天気) **1.**
weather; **ten-ki-yóhō** 天気予報 weather
forecast **2.** fair weather

ten-kō *n* 天候 weather

ten-mon (no) *n* 天文(の) astronomical:
ten-mon-dai 天文台 (*astronomical*)
observatory: **ten-mon-gaku** 天文学
astronomy

tén-shi *n* 天使 angel

tén *n* テン ten; **besutó-tén** ベストテン
the best ten

ten-.../...-ten *prefix, suffix* 天.../
...天 → ten-pura 天ぷら・天麸羅
ten-don *n* 天丼 a bowl of rice with tenpura shrimp on top
ten-pura *n* テンプラ・天ぷら・天麸羅 tempura, food fried in batter, especially shrimp
ten-.../...-ten *prefix, suffix* 店.../...店 shop
ten'-in *n* 店員 shop clerk, salesclerk, salesperson
ten-po *n* 店舗 [BOOKISH] store, shop (= **mise** 店 (**o-mise** お店))
ten-shu *n* 店主 shopkeeper
ten-tō *n* 店頭 store front
tenbō 1. 展望 looking over, a view **2.** prospecting, prospects
  tenbō-dai *n* 展望台 (*sightseeing*) observatory
tengu *n* テング・天狗 **1.** a long-nosed goblin **2.** conceited person
ténisu *n* テニス tennis: **tenisu-kōto** テニスコート tennis court: **tenisu-shūzu** テニスシューズ tennis shoes
tenjí *n* 展示 exhibit: **~ shimásu** 展示します exhibits
  tenjí-kai *n* 展示会 exhibition
ten-jimásu, ten-jiru *v* 転じます, 転じる [BOOKISH] changes, shifts; gets transferred
ten-kin *n* 転勤 job transfer (= **tennin** 転任): **~ shimásu** 転勤します gets transferred (*to another location*)
ten-kō *n* 転校 school transfer: **~ shimásu** 転校します transfers to another school
ten-nin *n* 転任 job transfer (= **tenkin** 転勤): **~ shimásu** 転任します gets transferred
tennen *n* 天然 nature (= **shizen** 自然)
  tennen-boke *n* 天然ボケ goofy, dopey by nature [IN POSITIVE SENSE]
  tennen-gasu *n* 天然ガス natural gas
  tennen (no) *adj* 天然(の) natural
  tennen-tō *n* 天然痘 smallpox
Tennō´ *n* 天皇 the Emperor; **Tennō-héika** 天皇陛下 His Majesty the Emperor
  Tennō-tanjō´bi *n* 天皇誕生日 the Emperor's Birthday (*national holiday in Japan*)

tenōru *n* テノール tenor
  tenōru-kashu *n* テノール歌手 a tenor (*singer*)
ténpi *n* 天火 oven (= **ōbun** オーブン)
tenpo *n* テンポ tempo
tenrán-kai *n* 展覧会 exhibition (= **tenji-kai** 展示会)
tensai *n* 天才 genius
ténsei *n* 天性 disposition, temperament
ténto *n* テント tent
tepp-... *prefix* 鉄... iron, steel
  tep-pan *n* 鉄板 iron plate: **teppan-yaki** 鉄板焼き sliced meat, etc. grilled at table
  tep-pō *n* 鉄砲 gun, rifle: **mizu-deppō** 水鉄砲 squirt gun, water pistol
teppén *n* てっぺん [INFORMAL] top, highest part (= **chōjō** 頂上)
té´pu *n* テープ tape; **sero(han)-tēpu** セロ(ハン)テープ scotch tape; **tēpu-rekō´dā** テープレコーダー tape recorder
terá *n* 寺 (**o-tera** お寺) Buddhist temple (= **jiin** 寺院)
teránai *v* 照らない = **terimásen** 照りません (not shine)
terashi-awasémásu, terashi-awaséru *v* 照らし合わせます, 照らし合わせる collates
terashimásu, terásu *v* 照らします, 照らす illuminates, lights it up, shines on; compares, collates, checks; **... ni teráshite** ...に照らして in the light of..., in view of ...
térasu *n* テラス terrace, balcony
tére *v* 照れ = **terekusai** 照れくさい feels embarrassed
...-teréba ...てれば = **...-te iréba** ...ていれば: **sō shite(i)réba yokatta** そうして(い)ればよかった if one does so
téreba *v* 照れば (if it shines) → **terimásu** 照ります
térebi *n* テレビ television
  terebi-bangumi *n* テレビ番組 TV show
  terebi-denwa *n* テレビ電話 videophone
  terebi-gēmu *n* テレビゲーム video game
  terebi-kaigi *n* テレビ会議 teleconference

terehonkādo *n* テレホンカード telephone card

teremásu, teréru *v* 照れます, 照れる feels embarrassed, awkward, flustered

terénai *v* 照れない = **teremasén** 照れません (not feel embarrassed)

terepashii *n* テレパシー telepathy

teréreba *v* 照れれば (if one feels embarrassed) = **teremásu** 照れます

térete *v* 照れて → **teremásu** 照れます

terimásu, téru *v* 照ります, 照る it shines

teriyaki *n* 照り焼き (*fish, chicken, etc.*) broiled with soy sauce and sweeteners

tero (risuto) *n* テロ (リスト) terrorism, terrorist

...-teru *suffix, v* ...てる [INFORMAL] = **...-te iru** ...ている = **...-te imásu** ...ています

...-terya *suffix, v* ...てりゃ [INFORMAL] = **...-te irya** ... ていりゃ [INFORMAL] = **...-te iréba** ...ていれば

tesū́ *n* 手数 (**o-tesū** お手数) [BOOKISH] trouble (taken up), time and effort (= **tema** 手間 (**o-tema** お手間))

tesū́-ryō *n* 手数料 handling/service charge

tésuto *n* テスト test (= **shiken** 試験)

...-téta *suffix, v* ...てた = **...-te ita** ... ていた = **-te imáshita** ...ていました (was doing)

...-tête *suffix, v* ...てて = **...-te ite** ...ていて (was doing)

tetsu *n* 鉄 iron, steel

tetsu-bō *n* 鉄棒 **1.** horizontal bar (*gymnastics*) **2.** iron bar

tetsu-dō *n* 鉄道 railroad, railway

tetsudáe *v* 手伝え [IMPERATIVE] (you should help!) → **tetsudaimásu** 手伝います

tetsudái *n* 手伝い **o-tétsudai** お手伝い assistance, help

tetsudaimásu, tetsudáu *v* 手伝います, 手伝う helps

tetsudaṓ *v* 手伝おう = **tetsudaimashṓ** 手伝いましょう (let's help!)

tetsudátte *v* 手伝って → **tetsudaimásu** 手伝います

tetsúgaku *n* 哲学 philosophy; **tetsugáku-sha** 哲学者 philosopher

tetsuya *n* 徹夜 staying up all night

te-tsúzuki *n* 手続き formalities, procedure (= **tejun** 手順)

tétte *v* 照って → **terimásu** 照ります

tettei-teki (na/ni) *adj, adv* 徹底的 (な/に) thorough(ly)

...-té wa *suffix, v* ...ては doing/being, if one does/be [+ NEGATIVE verb] : **-té wa ikemasén** ...てはいけません mustn't

ti... → **chi...**

tii-kappu *n* ティーカップ Western-style tea cup

tii-supūn *n* ティースプーン Western-style teaspoon (= **ko-saji** 小匙・小さじ)

tisshu(-pḗpā) *n* ティッシュ (ペーパー) tissue(s) (= **chiri-kami, chiri-gami, chiri-shi** ちり紙)

to *n* 戸 door

to-dana *n* 戸棚 cupboard, enclosed shelves

to *n* 都 **1.** capital (= **shu-to** 首都) **2.** Tokyo (= **Tōkyō-to** 東京都)

to-chi-ji *n* 都知事 Governor of Tokyo

to-chō *n* 都庁 the Tokyo Metropolitan Government

to-den *n* 都電 Toei (*Tokyo metropolitan*) streetcar

to-ei *n* 都営 Toei, metropolitan (*run by Tokyo*), metro; **Toei-sen** 都営線 (subway) Toei Line; **Toei-basu** 都営バス Toei Bus

to-kai *n* 都会 city, town; **tokái-jin** 都会人 city dweller, urbanite

to-min *n* 都民 Tokyoite (= **Tōkyō-tomin** 東京都民)

tó-nai *n, adv* 都内 within the metropolis (of Tokyo)

tó-shi *n* 都市 city; **toshi (no)** 都市 (の) urban; **toshi-gasu** 都市ガス city gas; **toshi-ginkō** 都市銀行 city bank

... to *prep* ...と with [CONCATENATES A NOUN]: **... to issho ni** ...と一緒に ... with (someone)

... to ... *conj* ...と ... and [CONCATENATES A NOUN]: **anata to watashi** あなたと私 you and I

... to *suffix* ...と (*said/thought/seemed*) that ...; "..." (*quote-*) unquote: **kare wa ... to itta** 彼は...と言った he said that ...

... to iu *suffix* ...という which says; which is (*called*), called; which is (*in effect*)

to iú no wa ... *suffix* というのは... What that means (*What that amounts to*) is that ...

... to *suffix* ...と **1. (su)-ru to** (す)ると when(ever), if; ...and thereupon, ... whereupon; **moshika suru to** もしかすると perhaps, possibly **2. (shi)-nai to** (し)ないと unless: **nantoka shi-nai to** なんとかしないと have to do something

tō´ *n* 十 ten (= **jū** 十)

tō´ *n* 籐 rattan, cane

tō´ *n* 塔 tower, pagoda (= **tawā** タワー); **Efferu-tō** エッフェル塔 Eiffel Tower

tō´-... *prefix* 東... east, eastern
　tō´-bu *n* 東部 the east, the eastern part
　tō-hō *n* 東方 the east
　tō-nan *n* 東南 southeast: **tōnan-ajia** 東南アジア Southeast Asia
　Tō´-yō *n* 東洋 the East, the Orient
　tō-zai *n* 東西 east and west, the East and the West

...´-tō *suffix* ...頭 (*counts large animals*) head [go-tō 五頭 *unaccented* (five heads)]

...-tō *suffix* ...等 class

Tō´a *n* 東亜 → **Higashi-Ájia** 東アジア

tobaku *n* 賭博 [BOOKISH] gambling (= **ganburu** ギャンブル, **bakuchi** 博打)

tō´ban *n* 当番 (**o-tō´ban** お当番) person on duty

tobanai *v* 跳ばない = **tobimasén** 跳びません (not jump)

tobanai *v* 飛ばない = **tobimasén** 飛びません (not fly)

tobashimásu, tobasu *v* 飛ばします, 飛ばす lets fly; skips, omits; hurries

tobe *v* 跳べ [IMPERATIVE] (jump!) → **tobimásu** 跳びます

tobe *v* 飛べ [IMPERATIVE] (fly!) → **tobimásu** 飛びます

tobéba *v* 跳べば (if one jumps) → **tobimásu** 跳びます

tobéba *v* 飛べば (if one flies) → **tobimásu** 飛びます

tobemásu, toberu *v* 跳べます, 跳べる can jump

tobemásu, toberu *v* 飛べます, 飛べる can fly

tobete *v* 跳べて・飛べて → **tobemásu** 跳べます・飛べます

tobi-dashimásu, tobi-dásu *v* 跳び出します・跳び出す jumps out

tobi-dashimásu, tobi-dásu *v* 飛び出します, 飛び出す runs/bursts out; it sticks out, protrudes; **uchi o ~** 家を飛び出します runs away (*from home*) (= **iede shimásu** 家出します)

tobimásu, tobu *v* 跳びます, 跳ぶ jumps

tobimásu, tobu *v* 飛びます, 飛ぶ flies

tobira *n* 扉 **1.** a door wing, a door of a gate **2.** title page

toboshíi *adj* 乏しい scarce, meager, scanty

tobu *v* 跳ぶ = **tobimásu** 跳びます (jumps)

tobu *v* 飛ぶ = **tobimásu** 飛びます (flies)

tōbun *n* 糖分 [BOOKISH] sugar content

tōbun *n* 等分 dividing equally: **~ shimásu** 等分します divides equally

tōbun *n* 当分 for the time being

tōchaku *n* 到着 arrival: **~ shimásu** 到着します arrives

tochi *n* 土地 ground, earth, soil; a piece of land

tochū (de/no) *adv, adj* 途中 (で/の) on the way; **tochū-gesha** 途中下車 stopover (*train*)

tōdai *n* 燈台 lighthouse

Tō-dai *n* 東大 Tokyo University (= **Tōkyō-Dáigaku** 東京大学)

todóite *v* 届いて → **todokimásu** 届きます

todoké *n* 届け (**o-todoke** お届け) notification, notice, report

todokemásu, todokéru *v* 届けます, 届ける **1.** delivers **2.** reports it (*to*), notifies

todokeraremásu, todokeraréru *v* 届けられます, 届けられる can deliver

todoké ro *v* 届けろ [IMPERATIVE] (deliver! notify!) → **todokemásu** 届けます

todoke-saki *n* 届け先 address (for delivery)

tódokete *v* 届けて → **todokemásu** 届けます

todokimásu, todóku ν 届きます, 届く reaches; arrives; gets delivered

todomarimásu, todomáru ν とどまります, とどまる it stops; it remains

todomátte ν とどまって → **todomarimásu** とどまります

todomé ro ν とどめろ [IMPERATIVE] (stop it!) → **todomemásu** とどめます

todomemásu, todoméru ν とどめます, とどめる stops it

todómete ν とどめて → **todomemásu** とどめます

todoróite ν 轟いて → **todorokimásu** 轟きます

todorokimásu, todoróku ν 轟きます, 轟く [BOOKISH] roars, rumbles

tóeba ν 問えば (if one inquires) → **toimásu** 問います

tōfu n 豆腐 (**o-tōfu** お豆腐) bean curd

togamé n とがめ (**o-togame** おとがめ) [BOOKISH] rebuke, censure, blame

togamemásu, togaméru ν とがめます, とがめる [BOOKISH] blames, rebukes, reproves, finds fault with: **ki ga** ~ 気がとがめます suffers from a guilty conscience

togarasemásu, togaráseru ν とがらせ[尖らせ]ます, とがらせる・尖らせる sharpens, points

togarimásu, togáru ν とがります・尖ります, とがる・尖る gets sharp (pointed)

togé n とげ・刺・棘 thorn

tóge ν 研げ [IMPERATIVE] (sharpen it!) → **togimásu** 研ぎます

tōgé n 峠 mountain pass; **...-tō´ge** ...峠 ...Pass

tōgei n 陶芸 ceramic art, ceramics

togemásu, togéru ν 遂げます, 遂げる achieves, accomplishes

togemásu, togéru ν 研げます, 研げる can sharpen (grind, polish)

tógete ν 遂げて・研げて → **togemásu** 遂げます・研げます

togimásu, tógu ν 研ぎます, 研ぐ sharpens, grinds, polishes

tōhenboku n 唐変木 damned fool

tōhoku-chihō 東北地方 The Tōhoku area of Japan (*Aomori, Iwate, Miyagi, Akita, Yamagata, Fukushima prefectures*)

tōhon n 謄本 full copy: **koseki-tōhon** 戸籍謄本 full copy of one's family register

tōhyō n 投票 ballot, vote

toi n 問い question (= **shitsumon** 質問); query

tói n とい・樋 drain pipe, gutter

tōi adj 遠い 1. far-off, distant 2. **mimí ga** ~ 耳が遠い is hard of hearing

toiawase n 問い合わせ (**o-toiawase** お問い合わせ) inquiry

tóida ν 研いだ = **togimáshita** 研ぎました (sharpened it)

tóide ν 研いで → **togimásu** 研ぎます

toimásu, tóu ν 問います, 問う inquires

tóire n トイレ toilet, bathroom

tóiretto-pé´pā n トイレットペーパー toilet paper

tóita ν 解いた = **tokimáshita** 解きました (undid;...) → **tokimásu** 解きます

...-tóita ...といた = **...-te óita** ...ておいた = **...-te okimáshita** ...ておきました: **yametóita hō ga ii** 止めといた方がいい You'd be better off just giving up.

...-tóita ra ...といたら = **...-te óita ra** ...ておいたら: **yametóita ra yokatta** 止めといたら良かった It just had to give it up.

...-tóita ri ...といたり = **...-te óita ri** ...ておいたり: **koko ni oitóita ri shinaide kudasái** ここに置いといたりしないで下さい don't put it here please

...-tóite ...といて = **...-te óite** ...ておいて: **himitsu ni shitóite kudasái** 秘密にしといて下さい Keep it on the downlow.

tóite ν 解いて → **tokimásu** 解きます

tōitsu n 統一 unification, standardization: ~ **shimásu** 統一します unifies, standardizes

tōji n 冬至 winter solstice

tōji n 湯治 hot-spring cure: **tōji-ba** 湯治場 spa; ~ **shimásu** 湯治します takes (*goes for*) the baths (= ~ **ni ikimásu** 湯治に行きます)

tō´ji (wa) adv 当時 (は) (*at*) that time, then, (*in*) those days (= **anokoro (wa)** あの頃 (は), **sono-koro (wa)** その頃 (は))

tojimásu, tojíru v 閉じます, 閉じる closes (*a book, door wings, …*)

tojínai v 閉じない = **tojimasén** 閉じません (not close)

tójite v 閉じて → **tojimásu** 閉じます

tójitsu n 当日 the day in question, that very day, on the day

tōjō n 搭乗 boarding a plane: **tōjō-chū** 搭乗中 (*in the midst of*) boarding: ~ **shimásu** 搭乗します boards

tōjō´-ken n 搭乗券 boarding pass

tōjō n 登場 entry upon the stage: ~ **shimásu** 登場します appears on stage

… tóka …とか or something (*like it*)

tōka n 十日 **1.** 10th day (*of a month*) **2.** (*for*) ten days (= **tōka-kan** 十日間)

tokage n トカゲ・蜥蜴 lizard

tokai n 都会 city: **dai-tókai** 大都会 metropolis (= **tóshi** 都市)

tōkai-chíhō n 東海地方 The Tōkai area of Japan (*Mie, Aichi, Gifu, Shizuoka prefectures*)

tokaku (… shimásu) adv とかく (…します) apt/liable (*to do*): ~ **no uwasa** とかくの噂 unsavory rumors

tokánai v 解かない = **tokimasén** 解きません (not undo it; not…)

tokasánai v 溶かさない = **tokashimasén** 溶かしません (not melt/dissolve)

tokasánai v とかさ[梳かさ]ない = **tokashimasén** とかし[梳かし]ません (not comb)

tokáse v 溶かせ [IMPERATIVE] (melt it!) → **tokashimásu** 溶かします

tokáse v とかせ・梳かせ [IMPERATIVE] (comb it!) → **tokashimásu** とかし[梳かし]ます

tokasemásu, tokaséru v 溶かせます, 溶かせる can melt/dissolve it

tokasemásu, tokaséru v とかせ[梳かせ]ます, とかせる・梳かせる can comb it

tokaséru v 溶かせない = **tokasemasén** 溶かせません (cannot melt/dissolve)

tokaséru v とかせ[梳かせ]ない = **tokasemasén** とかせ[梳かせ]ません (cannot comb)

tokashimásu, tokásu v 溶かします, 溶かす melts/thaws/dissolves it

tokashimásu, tokásu v とかし[梳か

し]ます, とかす・梳かす combs

tóke v 解け [IMPERATIVE] (undo!; …!) → **tokimásu** 解きます

tókeba v 解けば, etc. (if one undoes it; if …) → **tokimásu** 解きます, etc.

tokei n 時計 time piece; clock; watch

tōkei n 統計 statistics

tokemásu, tokéru v 溶けます, 溶ける it melts/thaws/dissolves

tokemásu, tokéru v 解けます, 解ける comes undone; gets solved

tókete v 溶けて・解けて → **tokemásu** 溶けます・解けます

tokí n 時 time

tokí n トキ・朱鷺・鴇 crested ibis (*bird*)

tō´ki n 陶器 pottery, ceramics, china → **jíki** 磁器

tō´ki n 登記 registration: ~ **shimásu** 登記します registers

tō´ki n 冬期 winter (*period/term*): **tōki-orinpikku** 冬季オリンピック Winter Olympics

tō´ki n 投機 speculation: ~ **shimásu** 投機します speculates

tō´ki n 投棄 dumping: ~ **shimásu** 投棄します dumps, throws away

tokidoki 時々・ときどき sometimes

tokimásu, tóku v 解きます, 解く undoes, unties; solves

tokimásu, tóku v 説きます, 説く explains, persuades, preaches

tokimásu, tóku v とき[梳き]ます, とく・梳く comb

…-tókimásu v …ときます = **…-te okimásu** …ておきます: **yametóki-másu** 止めときます will pass

tóki ni adv …時に at the time that …, when …

tokí ni adv ときに・時に by the way, incidentally; sometimes

tokkakari n 取っ掛かり a hold, a place to hold on; a clue (= **tegakari** 手掛かり)

tokkan kōji n 突貫工事 eleventh-hour job

tokki n 突起 projection, protuberance

tokki n 特記 special mention: **tokki-jíkō** 特記事項 special comments, special instruction

tokku (ni) adv とっく(に) long before (= ~ **no mukashi (ni)** とっくの昔(に))

tokkumiaimásu, tokkumiau *v* 取っ組み合います, 取っ組み合う grapple

tokkuri *n* とっくり・徳利 saké bottle/pitcher, ceramic decanter for serving saké

tokkyo *n* 特許 patent

tokkyū *n* 特急 special express (*train*); **tokkyū´-ken** 特急券 special-express ticket

tokkyū *n* 特級 special class; (*best*) quality

toko *n* 床 (**o-toko** お床) bed: ~ **ni tsukimásu** 床に就きます takes to one's bed, goes to bed

... **tokó** *suffix* …とこ [INFORMAL] place (= … **tokoró** …所)

tokonoma *n* 床の間 alcove in Japanese room

tokoro, ... tokoró *suffix* 所, …所
1. place 2. address

tokoro, ... tokoró ところ, …ところ circumstance, time: **shíta ~ desu** した ところです has just done it; **shíte iru ~ desu** しているところです is (*in the midst of*) doing it; **suru ~ desu** する ところです is about to do it

tokoró-de *conj* ところで by the way; well now

tokoro-dókoro *n, adv* ところどころ various places, here and there

tokoró-ga *conj* ところが but, however

... **tokoró ga** *suffix, conj* …ところが however

tokoro-gaki *n* 所書き [BOOKISH] address (*written*) (= **atesaki** 宛先, **jū´sho** 住所)

tokoroten *n* ところてん seaweed gelatin strips served cold in a tangy soy sauce

toko-ya *n* 床屋 barber(shop)

toku-... *prefix* 特… special (= **tokube-tsu** 特別)

toku-betsu (no) *adj* 特別(の) special, particular, extra
tokubetsu ni *adv* 特別に especially
toku-chō *n* 特徴 special feature/quality, (*a distinguishing*) characteristic
toku-shoku *n* 特色 special feature, characteristic
toku-shu (na) *adj* 特殊(な) special, particular

toku-yū (no) *adj* 特有(の) special, particular

toku *n* 徳 virtue

toku *n* 得 (**o-toku** お得) profit, advantage, gain
toku (na) *adj* 得(な) profitable, advantageous

tóku *v* 説く = **tokimásu** 解きます (undoes)

tóku *v* 説く = **tokimásu** 説きます (explains)

tóku *v* とく・梳く = **tokimásu** とき [梳き]ます (combs)

...-**toku** *suffix* …とく [INFORMAL] = ...-**te oku** …ておく: **ato de yattoku** あとでやっとく I will do it later.

tōkú *adv* 遠く 1. the distance, far off 2. so as to be far/distant → **tōi** 遠い

tokuhon *n* 読本 reader, reading book

tokúi *n* 得意 1. pride; forte, strong point 2. **o-tokui** お得意 (regular) customer, patron 3. prosperity
tokúi (na) *adj* 得意(な) favorite, proud, exultant

tokúi (na/no) *adj, adv* 特異(な/の) unique, peculiar

tóku (ni) *adv* 特(に) in particular, especially

tokuten *n* 得点 points obtained, score (= **sukoa** スコア)

Tōkyō *n* 東京 Tokyo
Tōkyō´-Dáigaku *n* 東京大学 Tokyo University (= **Tō-dai** 東大)
Tōkyō´-Eki *n* 東京駅 Tokyo Station
Tōkyō´-jin *n* 東京人 a Tokyoite
Tōkyō´-to *n* 東京都 the metropolis of Tokyo

tō´kyoku *n* 当局 the authorities

tománai *v* 富まない = **tomimasén** 富みません (not abound)

tomare *v* 止まれ [IMPERATIVE] (stop!) → **tomarimásu** 止まります

tomare *v* 泊まれ [IMPERATIVE] (stay over for the night!) → **tomarimásu** 泊まります

tomaremásu, tomareru *v* 泊まれます, 泊まれる can stay overnight

tomaremásu, tomareru *v* 止まれます, 止まれる can stop

tomarete *v* 泊まれて・止まれて →

257

tomaremásu 泊まれます・止まれます

tomari *n* 泊まり staying overnight; night duty

tomarimásu, tomaru *v* 止まります・止まる it stops

tomarimásu, tomaru *v* 泊まります, 泊まる stays overnight

tomarṓ´ *v* 泊まろう = **tomarimashṓ´** 泊まりましょう (let's stay overnight!)

tomaru *v* 泊まる = **tomarimásu** 泊まります (stays overnight): ~ **tokoró** 泊まる所 accommodation(s), place to stay

tomatte *v* 止まって・泊まって → **tomarimásu** 止まります・泊まります

tōmawari *n* 遠回り detour

tōmáwashi *n* 遠回し oblique statement

tómeba *v* 富めば (if it abounds) → **tomimásu** 富みます

tōmei (na) *adj* 透明(な) transparent, clear

tomemásu, tomeru *v* 止めます, 止める stops it

tomemásu, tomeru *v* 泊めます, 泊める puts one up overnight

tomemásu, tomeru *v* 留めます, 留める fastens (*firmly attaches*)

tome-bári *n* 留め針 pin

tōmen *adv* 当面 for now (= **sashiatari** 差し当たり)

tōmen (no) *adj* 当面(の) immediate, present; ~ **no mondai** 当面の問題 immediate problem

tomenai *v* 止めない = **tomemasén** 止めません, etc. (not stop it; …)

tomeraremásu, tome(ra)reru *v* 止められます, 止められる can stop it

tomeraremásu, tome(ra)reru *v* 泊められます, 泊められる can put one up overnight

tomerarenai *v* 止められない = **tomeraremasén** 止められません, etc. (cannot stop it; …)

tomeyṓ *v* 止めよう = **tomemashṓ´** 止めましょう (let's stop it!; …)

tómi *n* 富 wealth, fortune, riches, abundance

tomimásu, tómu *v* 富みます, 富む is rich; abounds

tōmin *n* 冬眠 hibernation

tómo *n* 友 [BOOKISH] friend (= **yūjin** 友人)

tomodachi *n* 友達 (**o-tomodachi** お友達) friend

tómo *n* 伴 (**o-tómo** お伴) one's companion, company (= **dōhan-sha** 同伴者)

… tó-mo! *interj* …とも！: **ii tó mo** いいとも Of course!

tó-mo-kaku *adv* ともかく anyway, anyhow, at any rate

tomonaimásu, tomonáu *v* 伴います, 伴う; **… ni ~** …に伴います accompanies

tomo ni *adv* 共に together (= **issho ni** 一緒に)

tō-mórokoshi *n* トウモロコシ corn (*on the cob*) (= **kōn** コーン); **tōmorokoshí-ko** とうもろこし粉 cornstarch (= **kōnsutáchi** コーンスターチ)

tomoshimásu, tomósu *v* 灯します, 灯す burns (*a light*)

tómu *v* 富む = **tomimásu** 富みます (is rich; abounds)

tonaemásu, tonáeru *v* 唱えます, 唱える advocates; shouts; recites; calls; claims

tonaé ro *v* 唱えろ [IMPERATIVE] (advocate!; shout!; recite!; call!; claim!) → **tonaemásu** 唱えます

tonáete *v* 唱えて → **tonaemásu** 唱えて

tōnan *n* 盗難 (*suffering*) theft

tonari *n* 隣 next-door, neighbor(ing)

tonbo *n* トンボ・蜻蛉 dragonfly

tonda *adj* とんだ outrageous, terrible, shocking

tonda *v* 跳んだ = **tobimáshita** 跳びました (jumped)

tonda *v* 飛んだ = **tobimáshita** 飛びました (flew)

tónda *v* 富んだ = **tomimáshita** 富みました (was rich; abounded)

tonde *v* 跳んで・飛んで → **tobimásu** 跳びます・飛びます

tónde *v* 富んで: ~ **imásu** 富んでいます is rich, abundant → **tomimásu** 富みます

tonde-mo arimasén *adj* とんでもありません Oh, no. No way.

tonde-mo nái *adj* とんでもない = **tonde-mo arimasén** とんでもありません outrageous, terrible, shocking

tó-ni-kaku とにかく anyway, anyhow

ton-katsu *n* 豚カツ・トンカツ pork cutlet

tónma *n* とんま・トンマ・頓馬 idiot, fool

tonma *n* とんま dullness, fool, idiot, boob (= **manuke** まぬけ, **noroma** のろま)

tonneru *n* トンネル tunnel

ton-ya *n* 問屋 wholesale store (= **oroshi-uri** 卸売り)

tōnyō-byō *n* 糖尿病 diabetes

tōnyū *n* 豆乳 soybean milk

tōnyū *n* 投入 [BOOKISH] **1.** a throw (*into*) **2.** investment, investing: **~ shimásu** 投入します throws into, invests

toppatsu *n* 突発 [BOOKISH] outbreak: **toppatsu-jiko** 突発事故 sudden accident; **toppatsu-jiken** 突発事件 unforeseen accident; bombshell

toppu *n* トップ top

tora *n* トラ・虎 tiger

toraberāzu chekku *n* トラベラーズチェック traveler's check

toraburu *n* トラブル trouble: **toraburu-mēkā** トラブルメーカー troublemaker

Tora-doshi *n* 寅年 year of the Tiger

toraemásu, toráéru *v* 捕らえます、捕らえる catches, seizes, captures, arrests

toraiaru *n* トライアル trial: **toraiaru-koyō** トライアル雇用 trial employment

torákku *n* トラック **1.** truck **2.** track (*for running*)

torakutā *n* トラクター tractor

toránai *v* 取らない = **torimasén** 取りません、etc. (not take; not …)

toránku *n* トランク (*clothes/car*) trunk

toránkusu *n* トランクス trunks

toranpétto *n* トランペット trumpet

toranporin *n* トランポリン trampoline

toránpu *n* トランプ playing cards

toranshiibā *n* トランシーバー transceiver, walkie-talkie

tóre *v* 取れ [IMPERATIVE] (take it!; … !) → **torimásu** 取ります

tóreba *v* 取れば (if one takes) →

torei *n* トレイ tray

toremásu, toréru *v* 取れます、取れる **1.** (*button, etc.*) comes off **2.** can take

torénā *n* トレーナー sweatshirt

torénai *v* 取れない = **toremasén** 取れません (not come off; cannot take)

torendo *n* トレンド trend (*fashion, etc.*) (= **keikō** 傾向)

torēningu *n* トレーニング training (*exercise, etc.*) workout: **torēningu-uea** トレーニングウエア training wear: **torēningu-shūzu** トレーニングシューズ training shoes: **torēningu-jimu** トレーニングジム training gym

torēreba *v* 取れれば (if it comes off; if one can take) → **toremásu** 取れます

torēshingu-pē´pā *n* トレーシングペーパー = **torepe** トレペ tracing paper

tórete *v* 取れて → **toremásu** 取れます

tori *n* トリ・鳥 bird (→ **ko-tori** 小鳥)

tori-kago *n* トリカゴ・鳥籠 bird cage

torí-gai *n* トリガイ・鳥貝 Japanese cockle

tori-i *n* 鳥居 the gate to a Shinto shrine

tori *n* トリ・鶏 chicken (= **niwa-tori** 鶏・ニワトリ)

tori-niku *n* トリニク・鶏肉 chicken meat

tori-… *prefix* 取り … [VERB PREFIX]: takes and …

tōrí *n* 通り street, avenue; passage (= **michi** 道)

tō´ri *n* とおり・通り way (of doing), manner: **… no ~ ni** …のとおりに like … (= **(no) yō ni** (の)様に)

tori-agemásu, tori-ageru *v* 取り上げます、取り上げる takes up; takes away

tori-atsukai *n* 取り扱い handling, treatment, management, transaction

tori-atsukaimásu, tori-atsukau *v* 取り扱います、取り扱う handles, deals with, manages

tori-awase *n* 取り合わせ assortment

tori-bun *n* 取(り)分 share (= **torimae** 取り前)

Tori-doshi *n* 酉年 year of the Rooster

tórí-hiki *n* 取り引き・取引 transaction, deal, business, trade

tori-kae *n* 取り替え change, replacement

tori-kaemásu, tori-kaeru v 取り替えます, 取り替える replaces it

tori-kaenai v 取り替えない = **tori-kae-masén** 取り替えません (not replace it)

tori-kaeraremásu, tori-kaerareru v 取り替えられます, 取り替えられる can replace it

tori-kaerarenai v 取り替えられない = **tori-kaerararemasén** 取り替えられません (cannot replace it)

tori-kae ro v 取り替えろ [IMPERATIVE] (replace it!) → **tori-kaemásu** 取り替えます

tori-kesanai v 取り消さない = **tori-keshimasén** 取り消しません (not cancel)

tori-keshi n 取り消し cancellation, revocation; deletion, erasure

tori-keshimásu, tori-kesu v 取り消します, 取り消す cancels, revokes; deletes, erases

tori-keshite v 取り消して → **tori-keshimásu** 取り消します

tori-kesó' v 取り消そう = **tori-keshi-mashó'** 取り消しましょう (let's cancel it!, I will cancel it)

toriko n とりこ・虜 1. captive, prisoner (= **horyo** 捕虜) 2. person who is crazy about something/someone

tori-kumi n 取り組み・取組み wrestling match/bout/program

torimásu, tóru v 取ります, 取る 1. takes; takes away, removes 2. passes (*the salt, sugar, etc.*) 3. takes (*a course*)

torimásu, tóru v 撮ります, 撮る takes (*a picture*)

tōrimásu, tō'ru v 通ります, 通る passes by, passes through

tōrimásu, tō'ru v 透ります, 透る penetrates

tōri-michi n 通り道 passage(way) (= **tsūro** 通路)

torishimari n 1. 取り締まり・取締り control, management, supervision 2. 取締 (= **torishimari-yaku** 取締役) managing director

tori-shimarimásu, tori-shimaru v 取り締まります, 取り締まる controls, manages, supervises, directs

toritsugi 1. 取り次ぎ・取次ぎ answering the door 2. 取次 an usher; an agency

toriwake adv とりわけ especially, in particular

tóro n とろ・トロ fatty tuna (*cf.* **chū-toro** 中とろ・中トロ, **aka-mi** 赤身)

torō' v 取ろう = **torimashó'** 取りましょう (let's take it!)

torō n 徒労 vain effort

tōrō n 灯籠 a stone lantern: ~ **nagashi** 灯籠流し floating lanterns on a river

tōroku n 登録 registration: ~ **shimásu** 登録します registers, enrolls

tō'ron n 討論 [BOOKISH] debate, discussion, dispute

tororo n トロロ・とろろ grated yam; **tororo-kónbu** とろろ昆布 kelp flakes

tóru v 取る = **torimásu** 取ります (takes; takes away)

tō'ru v 通る = **tōrimásu** 通ります (passes by, passes through)

tō'ru v 透る = **tōrimásu** 透ります (penetrates)

Tóruko n トルコ Turkey

toryō n 塗料 coating compositions (*paint, Japanese lacquer, varnish, etc.*)

tōsaku n 倒錯 [BOOKISH] perversion: **seiteki-tōsaku** 性的倒錯 paraphilia

tōsaku n 盗作 plagiarism

tōsan n 倒産 bankruptcy (= **hasan** 破産): ~ **shimásu** 倒産します goes bankrupt

tōsan n 父さん (*mostly male*) dad (= **oyaji** 親父, **tō-chan** 父ちゃん)

tōsánai v 通さない = **tōshimasén** 通しません (not let through/in)

tō'se v 通せ [IMPERATIVE] (let them through/in!) → **tōshimásu** 通します

tōsei n 統制 control (*of prices, etc.*)

tōsemásu, tōséru v 通せます, 通せる can let through/in

tōsemásu, tōséru v 透せます, 透せる can let through/penetrate

tōsénai v 通せない = **tōsemasén** 通せません (cannot let through/in)

tōsenbo, tōsenbō n 通せんぼ・通せん坊 blocking a person's way

toshí n 年 1. year 2. 年・歳 (お年・お歳) age: ~ **o torimásu** 年を取ります gets old toshi-ake *n* 年明け new year

toshi-koshi soba *n* 年越しそば[蕎麦] buckwheat noodles eaten traditionally on New Year's Eve

toshi-otoko *n* 年男 a man born in a year with the same Chinese zodiac sign as the current year

toshi-onna *n* 年女 a woman born in a year with the same Chinese zodiac sign as the current year

toshi-go *n* 年子 child born within a year of another

toshi-kakkō *n* 年格好 one's age (= **toshi-goro** 年頃)

toshi-ma *n* 年増 middle-aged woman

toshi-shita (no) *adj* 年下(の) younger, junior

toshi-ue (no) *adj* 年上(の) older, senior

toshi-yóri *n* 年寄り (**o-toshiyori** お年寄り) an old person (= **kōrei-sha** 高齢者)

tóshi *n* 都市 city: **dai-tóshi** 大都市 big city, metropolis (= **tokai** 都会)

tōshi *n* 投資 investment, investing: ~ **shimásu** 投資します invests

tōshi *n* 凍死 freezing to death, frost-killing: ~ **shimásu** 凍死します is frozen dead

tō´shi *n* 闘志 [BOOKISH] fighting spirit

tō´shi (no) *adj* 通し(の) direct, through (*to destination*): **tōshi-gíppu** 通し切符 a through ticket: **tōshi-bangō** 通し番号 serial number

tōshimásu, tō´su *v* 通します, 通す lets through/in, admits; shows in; pierces

tōshimásu, tō´su *v* 透します, 透す penetrates

tōshin-dai *n* 等身大 life size

tōshin (jisatsu) *n* 投身(自殺) committing suicide by throwing oneself (*into water, off the platform, etc.*) (= **minage** 身投げ)

tō´shite *v* 通して → **tōshimásu** 通します

tósho *n* 図書 library (*book collection*): **tósho-gákari** 図書係 the librarian (*in charge*), (*book*) custodian

toshó-kan *n* 図書館 library (*building*); **toshokán-in** 図書館員 a librarian

toshó-shitsu *n* 図書室 library (*book room*)

tō´sho *n* 投書 letter to the editor

tō´sho (wa) *adv* 当初(は) [BOOKISH] at first, initially, originally (= **saisho (wa)** 最初(は), **hajime** (wa) 初め(は))

tōshu *n* 党首 party leader

tōshu *n* 投手 a pitcher (*baseball, etc.*) (= **pitchā** ピッチャー)

tōshū *n* 踏襲 following predecessor's way: ~ **shimásu** 踏襲します follows, adheres

tóso *n* とそ・屠蘇 (**o-tóso** お屠蘇) spiced saké drunk at New Year's

tōsō *n* 闘争 fight, labor struggle: ~ **shimásu** 闘争します fights, struggles

tōsō *n* 逃走 [BOOKISH] escape: ~ **shimásu** 逃走します escapes, runs away

tossa no *adj* とっさの prompt

tossa ni *adv* とっさに in an instant, promptly, immediately

tō´su *v* 通す = **tōshimásu** 通します (lets through/in, admits; shows in)

tō´su *v* 透す = **tōshimásu** 透します (lets pierce, penetrates)

tō´sutā *n* トースター toaster

tō´suto *n* トースト toast

… totan ni …途端に (*at*) the instant/ moment that …

tōtei *adv* 到底 [+ NEGATIVE VERB] absolutely not

totemo *adj* とても [INFORMAL] very (= **tottemo** とっても, **taihen** 大変)

tō´tō *adv* とうとう at last, finally (= **tsuini** ついに)

totonoemásu, totonóeru *v* 整えます, 整える regulates, adjusts; prepares

totonoénai *v* 整えない = **totonoemasén** 整えません (not regulate/adjust/ prepare)

totonoimásu, totonóu *v* 整います, 整う is in order; is ready

totonowánai *v* 整わない = **totonoi-masén** 整いません (is not ready)

totsuzen *adv* 突然 suddenly, abruptly (= **kyū ni** 急に): **totsuzen no** 突然の sudden, abrupt

tótta *v* 取った = **torimáshita** 取りました (took)

totte *v* 取って = **tótte** 取って (taking) [*before verbs of movement*]

totté *n* 取っ手・把手 a handle, knob

tótte *v* 取って → **torimásu** 取ります [*but* **totte** 取って *before verbs of movement*]

tótte *v* ...とって: (…に) とって (*with reference*) to, for

totte ikimásu (iku) *v* 取っていきます (いく) takes, brings it there

totte kimásu (kúru) *v* 取ってきます (くる) brings it (here)

tottemo *adj* とっても terribly, extremely, completely (= **totemo** とても)

tótte okimásu (oku) *v* 取っておきます (おく) puts aside, reserves, holds

tóu *v* 問う = **toimásu** 問います (inquires)

tōwaku *n* 当惑 embarrassment, puzzlement (= **konwaku** 困惑): ~ **shimásu** 当惑します gets embarrassed/puzzled

towanai *v* 問わない = **toimásén** 問いません (not inquire)

tōza *n* 当座, **tōza-yókin** 当座預金 current deposit, checking account

tōza no *adj* 当座 (の) [BOOKISH] temporary

tózan *n* 登山 mountain-climbing (= **yama-nobori** 山登り): ~ **shimásu** 登山します climbs a mountain

tozán-sha *n* 登山者 mountain-climber

tōzen *adv* 当然 naturally, surely; **tōzen no** 当然の proper, deserved

tōzoku *n* 盗賊 burglar

tsū *n* 通 **1.** an authority, an expert **2.** (*counts letter*): **ít-tsū** 一通 one letter

tsūā *n* ツアー tour **1.** group tour (= **dantai-ryokō** 団体旅行) **2.** short trip (= **shō-ryokō** 小旅行)

tsubá *n* つば・唾 spit, saliva

tsúba *n* つば・鍔 sword-guard

tsubakí *n* つばき・唾 = **tsubá** つば・唾 (spit)

tsúbaki *n* ツバキ・椿 camellia

tsubame *n* ツバメ・燕 swallow (bird)

tsubasa *n* つばさ・翼 wing

tsubo *n* つぼ・壷・壺 jar, crock

tsubo *n* 坪 *tsubo* (6 sq. ft.)

tsubomarimásu, tsubomaru *v* つぼまります, つぼまる it puckers up; gets puckered up, is shut; it narrows

tsubomemásu, tsubomeru *v* つぼめます, つぼめる puckers it; shuts it;

narrows it

tsubome ro *v* つぼめろ [IMPERATIVE] (pucker it!) → **tsubomemásu** つぼめます

tsubomi *n* つぼみ・蕾 flower bud

tsúbu *n* 粒 grain

tsuburemásu, tsubureru *v* 潰れます, 潰れる it collapses/smashes

tsuburemásu, tsubureru *v* つぶれます, つぶれる can shut/close one's eyes: **mé ga ~** 目がつぶれます lose one's eyesight

tsuburimásu, tsuburu *v* つぶります, つぶる: **mé o ~** 目をつぶります shuts/closes one's eyes

tsubushimásu, tsubusu *v* 潰します, 潰す smashes (*crushes, squeezes*) it

tsubuyakimásu, tsubuyaku *v* つぶやきます, つぶやく murmur; (**tsuittā de**) **tsubuyaku** (ツイッターで) つぶやく tweet (*internet*)

tsuchí *n* 土 earth, ground

tsuchí *n* 槌 hammer (= **hánmā** ハンマー, **hánma** ハンマ)

tsūchi *n* 通知 report, notice, notification

tsūchō *n* 通帳 passbook, bankbook: **yokin-tsūchō** 預金通帳 deposit book: **chokin-tsūchō** 貯金通帳 savings book

tsúe *n* 杖 cane, walking stick

tsūgaku *n* 通学: ~ **shimásu** 通学します commutes to school

tsūgaku-ro *n* 通学路 school route

tsuganai *v* 注가ない = **tsugimasén** 注ぎません; etc. (not pour it; not …)

tsuge *n* つげ・ツゲ・柘植 boxwood

tsuge *v* 注げ [IMPERATIVE] (pour it!) → **tsugimásu** 注ぎます

tsuge-guchi (ya) *n* 告げ口 (屋) (tattle)tale, (= **chikuri-ya** チクリ屋 [INFORMAL]): ~ **shimásu** 告げ口します tattles (= **chikurimásu** チクリます [INFORMAL])

tsugemásu, tsugeru *v* 告げます, 告げる tells, informs

tsugemásu, tsugeru *v* 注げます, 注げる can pour

tsugemásu, tsugeru *v* 継げます, 継げる can inherit

tsugemásu, tsugeru *v* 接げます, 接げる can join it

262

tsugenai *v* 告げない = **tsugemasén** 告げません (will not tell)

tsugenai *v* 注げない = **tsugemasén** 注げません (cannot pour)

tsugenai *v* 継げない = **tsugemasén** 継げません (cannot inherit)

tsugenai *v* 接げない = **tsugemasén** 接げません (cannot join in it)

tsuge ro 告げろ [IMPERATIVE] (tell it!) → **tsugemásu** 告げます

tsugi *n* 継ぎ patch; (... ni) ~ o atemásu (...に)継ぎを当てます patches in

tsugí *n* 次 (o-tsúgi お次) next, the following; **tsugí no** 次の the next one

tsugimásu, tsugu *v* 注ぎます, 注ぐ pours it

tsugimásu, tsugu *v* 継ぎます, 継ぐ inherits, succeeds to

tsugimásu, tsugu *v* 接ぎます, 接ぐ joins it, grafts, glues

tsugi-me *n* 継ぎ目・接ぎ目 joint, seam

tsugitashi-kō´do *n* 継ぎ足しコード extension cord (= **enchō-kō´do** 延長コード)

tsugí-tsugi (ni) *adv* 次々(に) one after another

tsugō *n* 都合 (**go-tsugō** ご都合) circumstances, convenience, opportunity: ~ **ga íi/warúi** 都合がいい/悪い (it is) convenient/inconvenient; ~ **no yoi** 都合のよい expedient: **go-tsugō shugi** ご都合主義 expediency, opportunism

tsui *n* 対 a pair (= **pea** ペア): ~ **ni narimásu** 対になります becomes/makes/forms a pair

tsúi *adv* つい **1.** unintentionally, inadvertently **2.** just (*now*): ~ **imashí-gata** つい今しがた just now; ~ **saki-hodo** つい先程 [BOOKISH] just a little while ago (= **tsúi sakki** ついさっき)

tsuide *v* 注いで・継いで・接いで → **tsugimásu** 注ぎます・継ぎます・接ぎます

tsúide *adv* 次いで next, in succession, subsequently; ... **ni** ~ ...に次いで following ..., next after/to ... (*in importance*)

tsuide *n* ついで opportunity, occasion, convenience: **tsuide no setsu/sai/toki ni** ついでの節/際/時に at your/one's

convenience; **tsuide ga arimásu** ついでがあります has occasion to...

... **tsuide (ni)** *suffix* ...ついで(に) on the occasion of/that ..., incidentally to ...; while ...; along the way

tsuihō *n* 追放: ~ **shimásu** 追放します purges

tsuín *n* ツイン, **tsuin-rū´mu** ツインルーム twin(-bed)room

tsuin-béddo *n* ツインベッド twin beds

tsúi ni *adv* ついに at last, finally (= **tōtō** とうとう)

tsuiraku *n* 墜落 (*plane*) crash: ~ **shimásu** 墜落します (*a plane*) crashes

tsui-shi(kén) *n* 追試(験) makeup exam (= **sai-shi(ken)** 再試(験))

tsuitachí *n* 一日 first day of a month

tsuitate *n* 衝立 partition

tsuite *v* 突いて → **tsukimásu** 突きます

tsúite *suffix* ついて ... **ni tsúite (no)** ...について(の) about, concerning; ... **ni tsúite (wa)** ...について(は) as far as ... is concerned

tsúite *v* 付いて → **tsukimásu** 付きます

tsúite imasén (inai) *v* ついていません(いない) is unlucky, fails to strike it lucky (= **tsúitemasén** ついてません)

tsúite imasén (inai) *v* 付いていません(いない) is not attached; un-.... (= **tsúitemasén** 付いてません)

tsúite imasén (inai) *v* 点いていません(いない) is not turn on (lights) (= **tsúitemasén** 点いてません)

tsúite nai *v* ついてない = **tsúitemasén** ついてません (is unlucky, fails to strike it lucky)

tsuittā *n* ツイッター Twitter (*Internet*)

tsuji *n* 辻 crossroads; road(side), street: **yotsu-tsuji** 四つ辻 crossroad (= **jūji-ro** 十字路)

tsū-ji *n* 通じ **1.** (**o-tsū´-ji** お通じ) bowel movement **2.** effect

tsū-jimásu, tsū-jiru *v* 通じます, 通じる gets through, communicates; transmits; connects, runs; is understood; is well versed in; one's bowels move; (... **o**) **tsū-ji te** (...を)通じて through (*the medium of*)

tsūjín *n* 通人 an expert, an authority; a man of the world

tsūjō *adv* 通常 usually, ordinarily (= **futsū** 普通, taitei たいてい・大抵)

tsūjō (no) *adj* 通常(の) usual, ordinary

tsuká *n* 塚 mound

tsukáe *n* つか・柄 hilt

tsūka *n* 通貨 currency (*money*) (= **kahei** 貨幣)

tsūkā no naka *n* つーかー[ツーカー]の仲 those who are very close and know what each other is thinking

tsukae *v* 使え [IMPERATIVE] (use it!) → **tsukaimásu** 使います

tsukáe *n* つかえ obstruction

tsukaeba *v* 使えば (if one uses it) → **tsukaimásu** 使います

tsukaemásu, tsukaeru *v* 使えます, 使える can use it; be useful

tsukaemásu, tsukáéru *v* つかえます, つかえる **1.** gets clogged up, obstructed, busy: **nodo ga tsukaemásu** 喉がつかえます has difficulty in swallowing: **mune ga tsukaemásu** 胸がつかえます **2.** feels stuffed up (*physically*) **3.** feels a pressure on one's chest (*mentally*)

tsukaenai *v* 使えない = **tsukaemásen** 使えません (cannot use it)

tsukáénai *v* つかえない = **tsukaemásen** つかえません (not get obstructed)

tsukaeréba *v* 使えれば (if one can use it) → **tsukaemásu** 使えます

tsukáeréba *v* つかえれば (if it is obstructed) → **tsukaemásu** つかえます

tsukaete *v* 使えて → **tsukaemásu** 使えます

tsukáete *v* つかえて → **tsukaemásu** つかえます

tsukai *n* 使い **1.** message, errand **2.** messenger

tsukai-hashiri, tsukai-bashiri *n* 使い走り, **tukai-ppashiri** 使いっ走り errand runner

tsukaimásu, tsukau *v* 使います, 使う uses; spends; employs; handles

tsukamaemásu, tsukamaeru *v* 捕まえます, 捕まえる catches, seizes, arrests

tsukamaenai *v* 捕まえない = **tsuka-**

maemásen 捕まえません (not catch)

tsukamae ro *v* 捕まえろ [IMPERATIVE] (catch!) → **tsukamaemásu** まえます

tsukamánai *v* つかまない = **tsukami-masén** つかみません (not seize)

tsukamemásu, tsukaméru *v* つかめます, つかめる can seize

tsukaménai *v* つかめない = **tsukame-másen** つかめません (cannot seize)

tsukámete *v* つかめて → **tsukame-másu** つかめます

tsukamimásu, tsukámu *v* つかみます, つかむ seizes, grasps, clutches

tsukamō´ *v* つかもう = **tsukamimashō** つかみましょう (let's seize it!)

tsukanai *v* 突かない = **tsukimasén** 突きません (not stab, ...)

tsukánai *v* 付かない = **tsukimasén** 付きません (not come in contact, ...)

tsukánde *v* つかんで → **tsukami-másu** つかみます

tsukaō *v* 使おう = **tsukaimashō´** 使いましょう (let's use it!)

tsukaremásu, tsukaréru *v* 疲れます, 疲れる gets tired

tsukatte *v* 使って → **tsukaimásu** 使います

tsukau *v* 使う = **tsukaimásu** 使います (uses)

tsukawanai *v* 使わない = **tsukaimásen** 使いません (not use)

tsuke *v* 突け [IMPERATIVE] (stab it!) → **tsukimásu** 突きます

tsuké *n* 付け bill, account: **~ de kaimásu** 付けで買います buys it on credit

tsuké *v* 着け [IMPERATIVE] (arrive!) → **tsukimásu** 着きます

tsukeawase *n* 付け合わせ garnish, relish

tsukéba *v* 突けば (if one stabs) → **tsukimásu** 突きます

tsukéba *v* 付けば (if it comes in contact) → **tsukimásu** 付きます

tsukemásu, tsukeru *v* 漬けます, 漬ける pickles; soaks

tsukemásu, tsukeru *v* 突けます, 突ける can stab/thrust/poke/push

tsukemásu, tsukéru *v* 付けます, 付ける attaches, sticks on, adds, applies

tsukemásu, tsukéru v 点けます, 点ける turns on (*lights*)

tsukemásu, tsukéru v 着けます, 着ける = **mi ni tsukemásu** 身に着けます puts on, wears

tsuke-mono n 漬物 Japanese pickles

tsuke ro v 漬けろ [IMPERATIVE] (soak it!) → **tsukemásu** 漬けます

tsuké ro v 付けろ [IMPERATIVE] (attach it!) → **tsukemásu** 付けます

tsukenai v 漬けない = **tsukemasén** 漬けません (not pickle/soak)

tsukenai v 突けない = **tsukemasén** 突けません (cannot stab/thrust/poke/push)

tsukénai v 付けない = **tsukemasén** 付けません (not attach/stick on/add/apply)

tsukénai v 点けない = **tsukemasén** 点けません (not turn on (lights))

tsukénai v 着けない = **tsukemasén** 着けません (not puts on/wears)

tsukete v 漬けて・突けて → **tsukemásu** 漬けます・突けます

tsukéte v 点けて・着けて → **tsukemásu** 点けます・着けます

tsukeyō v 漬けよう = **tsukemashō´** 漬けましょう (let's pickle/soak it!)

tsukeyō´ v 付けよう = **tsukemashō´** 付けましょう (let's attach/... it!)

tsukeyō v 点けよう = **tsukemashō´** 点けましょう (let's turn on (*lights*)!)

tsukeyō´ v 着けよう = **mi ni tsukemashō´** 身に着けましょう (let's put on/wear!)

tsukí n 月 moon; month
tsuki-hi n 月日 time (*days and years*)
tsuki-mí n 月見 (**o-tsuki-mi** お月見) moon viewing
tsuki-yo n 月夜 moonlight (*night*)

...-tsuki (no) ...付き(の) with (... attached)

tsuki-ai 付き合い n **o-tsukíai** お付き合い association, social company, friendship (= **kōsai** 交際)

tsuki-aimásu, tsuki-áu v 付き合い, 付き合う: **... to** ...と付き合います associates (*with*), enjoys the company of, goes out (*with one's lover*)

tsuki-atari n 突き当たり the end of a street/corridor

tsuki-atarimásu, tsuki-atáru v 突き当たります, 突き当たる runs into; comes to the end of (*a street*)

tsuki-dashimásu, tsuki-dásu v 突き出します, 突き出す makes it protrude, sticks it out

tsuki-demásu, tsuki-déru v 突き出ます, 突き出る protrudes, sticks out

tsukimásu, tsuku v 突きます, 突く stabs, thrusts, pokes, pushes

tsukimásu, tsúku v 付きます, 付く
1. comes in contact **2.** sticks to; joins; follows; touches

tsukimásu, tsúku v 着きます, 着く arrives (= **tōchaku shimásu** 到着します)

tsukimásu, tsúku v 点きます, 点く burns, is turned (*on*), is lit

tsukimásu, tsukíru v 尽きます, 尽きる comes to an end, runs out

tsūkin n 通勤 commuting to work: **~ shimásu** 通勤します commutes to work; **tsūkin-jíkan** 通勤時間 commuting time

tsukínai v 尽きない = **tsukimasén** 尽きません (not come to an end)

tsukíru v 尽きる = **tsukimásu** 尽きます (comes to an end)

tsuki-sashimásu, tsuki-sásu v 突き刺します, 突き刺す stabs

tsúkite v 尽きて → **tsukimásu** 尽きます

tsukiyō´ v 尽きよう: **~ to shiteimásu** 尽きようとしています is about to come to an end → **tsukimásu** 尽きます

tsukō´ v 付こう: **~ to shimásu** 付こうとします is about to come in contract, ... → **tsukimásu** 付きます

tsukō´ v 突こう = **tsukimáshō´** 突きましょう (let's stab/poke/thrust!)

tsūkō n 通行 passing, passage, transit: **~ shimásu** 通行します = **tōrimásu** 通ります passes (*by/through*); **tsūkō-dome** 通行止め closed to traffic, No Passage; **tsūkō-nin** 通行人 passer-by

Tsukúba n つくば・筑波 Tsukuba Tsukuba-Dáigaku n 筑波大学 Tsukuba University

tsukuda-ni n 佃煮 conserves boiled down from fish or seaweed

tsuke n 机 desk (= **desuku** デスク)

tsukuránai v 作らない = **tsukurimasén** 作りません (not make it)

tsukúre v 作れ [IMPERATIVE] (make it!) → **tsukurimásu** 作ります

tsukúreba v 作れば (if one makes it) → **tsukurimásu** 作ります

tsukuremásu, tsukuréru v 作れます, 作れる can make it

tsukurénai v 作れない = **tsukuremásén** 作れません (cannot make it)

tsukuréreba v 作れれば (if one can make it) → **tsukuremásu** 作れます

tsukúrete v 作れて → **tsukuremásu** 作れます

tsukurí n 作り 1. makeup, toilette 2. artistically arranged slices of raw fish

tsukurí n 造り a structure, build

tsukurí-banashi n 作り話 (*stories*) fiction

tsukurimásu, tsukúru v 作ります 作る makes, forms, creates, produces, grows, manufactures, prepares (*fixes*) (*small or intangible things*); **jikan o ~** 時間を作ります makes (*sets aside*) time, sets up a time

tsukurimásu, tsukúru v 造ります, 造る makes, forms, creates, grows, manufactures, builds (*big things*)

tsukuróe v 繕え [IMPERATIVE] (mend it!) → **tsukuroimásu** 繕います

tsukuróeba v 繕えば (if one mends it) → **tsukuroimásu** 繕います

tsukuroemásu, tsukuroeru v 繕えます, 繕える can mend it

tsukuroénai v 繕えない = **tsukuroe-masén** 繕えません (cannot mend it)

tsukuroéreba v 繕えれば (if one can mend it) → **tsukuroemásu** 繕えます

tsukurói n 繕い mending, repair

tsukuroimásu, tsukuróu v 繕います, 繕う mends, repairs

tsukuroō´ v 繕おう = **tsukuroimashō´** 繕いましょう (let's mend it!)

tsukurowánai v 繕わない = **tsukuroi-masén** 繕いません (not mend)

tsukusánai v 尽くさない = **tsukushi-masén** 尽くしません (not exhaust)

tsukúse v 尽くせ [IMPERATIVE] (exert yourself!) → **tsukushimásu** 尽くします

tsukúseba v 尽くせば (if one exhausts) → **tsukushimásu** 尽くします

tsukusemásu, tsukuséru v 尽くせます, 尽くせる can exhaust

tsukusénai v 尽くせない = **tsukuse-masén** 尽くせません (cannot exhaust)

tsukuséreba v 尽くせれば (if one can exhaust) → **tsukusemásu** 尽くせます

tsukúsete v 尽くせて → **tsukuse-másu** 尽くせます

tsukushimásu, tsukúsu v 尽くします, 尽くす exhausts, runs out of; exerts oneself, strives

tsukúshite v 尽くして → **tsukushi-másu** 尽くします

tsukusō´ v 尽くそう = **tsukushimashō´** 尽くしましょう (let's exert ourselves!)

tsukútta v 作った = **tsukurimáshita** 作りました (made it)

tsukútte v 作って → **tsukurimásu** 作ります

tsúma n 妻 1. my wife (= **kanai** 家内) 2. (*your/someone else's*) wife (= **oku-san** 奥さん)

tsumá n つま・褄 skirt (*of Kimono*)

tsumá n ツマ sashimi garnishings

tsumamanai v 摘まない = **tsumami-masén** 摘みません (not pinch)

tsumami n 摘み・つまみ 1. a knob; a pinch 2. n = **tsumamimono** つまみ物, **o-tsúmami** おつまみ things to nibble on while drinking (= **sakana** さかな・肴)

tsumamimásu, tsumamu v 摘みます, 摘む pinches, picks; summarizes

tsumanai v 積まない = **tsumimasén** 積みません (not pile it up)

tsumanai v 摘まない = **tsumimasén** 摘みません (not gather/pluck)

tsumánnai adj つまんない [INFORMAL] → **tsumaránai** つまらない

tsumaránai adj つまらない worthless, no good, boring, trivial

tsumaránai v 詰まらない = **tsumari-masén** 詰まりません (is not clogged)

tsúmari adv つまり after all; in short (= **kekkyoku (no tokoro)** 結局(のとこ

ろ), **yōsuruni** 要するに)

tsumarimásu, tsumáru ν 詰まります, 詰まる is clogged up, choked; is stuck; is shortened; is crammed

tsumáru tokoro つまるところ = **tsú-mari** つまり (after all)

tsumasaki n つま先・爪先 toe, toe tip(s)

tsumashíi adj つましい・倹しい is thrifty, frugal

tsumátte ν 詰まって → **tsumarimásu** 詰まります

tsuma-yōji n つまようじ・爪楊枝 toothpick

tsuma-zuite ν つまずいて → **tsuma-zukimásu** つまずきます

tsuma-zukánai ν つまずかない = **tsuma-zukimasén** つまずきません (not stumble)

tsuma-zukimásu, tsuma-zuku ν つまずきます, つまずく stumbles

tsume n 爪 **1.** claw (= **kagizume** 鉤爪) (→ **taka-no-tsume** 鷹の爪) **2.** hoof

tsume-kíri ν 爪切り nail clippers

tsume-yásuri n 爪やすり nail file, emery board

tsume ν 積め [IMPERATIVE] (pile it up!) → **tsumimásu** 積みます

tsume ν 摘め [IMPERATIVE] (pluck it!) → **tsumemásu** 摘みます

tsumemásu, tsumeru ν 積めます, 積める can pile it up; accumulates

tsumemásu, tsumeru ν 摘めます, 摘める can gather/pluck it

tsumemásu, tsuméru ν 詰めます, 詰める **1.** stuffs, crams **2.** cans

tsumenai ν 積めない = **tsumemasén** 積めません (cannot pile it up)

tsumenai ν 摘めない = **tsumemasén** 摘めません (cannot gather/pluck it)

tsuménai ν 詰めない = **tsumemasén** 詰めません (not stuff/cram, not can it)

tsumenai ν 積めない = **tsumemasén** 積めません (not accumulate)

tsumeraremásu, tsumeraréru ν 詰められます, 詰められる can stuff/can it

tsumeraremásu, tsumerareru ν 積められます, 積められる can accumulate

tsumerarénai ν 詰められない = **tsumeraremasén** 詰められません (cannot stuff)

tsumerárete ν 詰められて → **tsumeraremásu** 詰められます

tsumé ro ν 詰めろ [IMPERATIVE] (stuff it!) → **tsumemásu** 詰めます

tsumeru ν 積める = **tsumemásu** 積めます (can pile up; can gather/pluck it)

tsumeru ν 摘める = **tsumemásu** 摘めます (can pile up; can gather/pluck it)

tsuméru ν 詰める = **tsumemásu** 詰めます, etc. (stuffs, ...)

tsumeta ν 積めた = **tsumemáshita** 積めました; etc. (could pile it up; ...)

tsúmeta ν 詰めた = **tsumemáshita** 詰めました, etc. (stuffed, ...)

tsumetai adj 冷たい cold (to the touch)

tsumete ν 積めて・摘めて → **tsumemásu** 積めます・摘めます

tsúmete ν 詰めて → **tsumemásu** 詰めます

tsumeyō ν 詰めよう = **tsumemashō** 詰めましょう (let's stuff it!)

tsúmi n 罪 crime, sin, guilt, fault: **tsumi-bukai** 罪深い sinful

tsumi-(i)re n つみれ (つみいれ) fish-balls (for soup)

tsumimásu, tsumu ν 積みます, 積む piles it up, accumulates it; deposits; loads

tsumimásu, tsumu ν 摘みます, 摘む gathers, plucks, clips, picks

tsumitate-kin n 積立金 reserve fund: = **tsumitate-chókin** 積立貯金 installment savings

tsumō ν 積もう = **tsumimashō** 積みましょう (let's pile it up!)

tsumō ν 摘もう = **tsumimashō** 摘みましょう (let's pluck it!)

...-tsumori ... つもり intention, plan, (what one has in) mind, purpose, expectation: **(watashi wa) mada wakai-tsu-mori desu.** (私は)まだ若いつもりです I think I am still young.

...-tsumori (de)wa/ja... ... つもり (で) は/じゃ [+ NEGATIVE verb] didn't/don't mean to, had/have no intention of: **kau-tsumori wa arimasen** 買うつもりはありません I have no intention of buying: **kare o kizutukeru-tsumori wa arimasendeshita** 彼を傷つけるつもりはありませんでした I didn't mean to hurt him.

tsumu v 積む = **tsumimásu** 積みます (piles it up, accumulates it, etc)

tsumu v 摘む = **tsumimásu** 摘みます (gathers, plucks, picks, etc)

tsumují-kaze n つむじ風・旋風 whirlwind

tsuná n 綱 rope, cord, cable (= **rōpu** ロープ) (→ **tanomi no tsuna** 頼みの綱, **tazuna** 手綱)

tsuna watari n 綱渡り walking a tight-rope, balancing act

tsúna n ツナ tuna(fish) (canned)

tsuna-sándo n ツナサンド tuna-fish sandwich

tsunagari n つながり・繋がり connection, relation

tsunagarimásu, tsunagaru v つながります, つながる is connected, linked

tsunagatte v つながって → **tsunagaru** つながる; in a string (line, chain), in succession, in a row

tsunage v つなげ [IMPERATIVE] (link them!) → **tsunagimásu** つなぎます

tsunagemásu, tsunageru v つなげます, つなげる can connect, link, tie

tsunagete v つなげて → **tsunagemásu** つなげて

tsunagi n つなぎ a link, a connection

tsunagimásu, tsunagu v つなぎます, つなぐ connects, links, ties

tsunaide v つないで → **tsunagimásu** つなぎます

tsunami n 津波 tsunami

tsunda v 積んだ = **tsumimáshita** 積みました (piled it up; …)

tsunde v 積んで・摘んで → **tsumimásu** 積みます・摘みます

tsúne (no) adj 常(の) usual, ordinary

tsunerimásu, tsunéru v つねります, つねる pinches

tsunézune n つねづね・常々 all the time, usually (= **fudan** 普段, **itsumo** いつも)

tsunó n 角 horn (of an animal): **sai no ~** サイの角 rhinoceros horn

tsū-píisu n ツーピース a two-piece woman's suit

tsurá n 面・つら (slipshod Japanese) 1. face (= **kao** 顔): [IDIOM] **~ no kawa ga**

atsui 面の皮が厚い is thick-skinned, is brazenfaced 2. surface, appearance (= **uwa(t)-tsura** 上(っ)面, **uwa-be** うわべ・上辺)

tsurai adj つらい・辛い painful, cruel, hard

tsuranai v 吊らない → **tsurimásén** 吊りません (not hang it)

tsuranai v 釣らない → **tsurimásén** 釣りません (not fish)

tsuranukimásu, tsuranuku v 貫きます, 貫く 1. goes through, penetrates (= **kantsū shimásu** 貫通します) 2. accomplishes: **shinnen o ~** 信念を貫きます has the courage of one's convictions

tsurara n ツララ・氷柱 icicle

tsure n 連れ = **o-tsúre** お連れ company, companion

tsure v 吊れ [IMPERATIVE] (hang it!) → **tsurimásu** 吊ります

tsure v 釣れ [IMPERATIVE] (fish!) → **tsurimásu** 釣ります

tsuréba v 吊れば (if one hangs) → **tsurimásu** 吊ります

tsuréba v 釣れば (if one fishes) → **tsurimásu** 釣ります

tsurimásu, tsureru v 連れます, 連れる brings along, is accompanied by (= brings/takes one along)

tsurimásu, tsureru v 吊ります, 吊れる can hang it

tsurimásu, tsureru v 釣れます, 釣れる can fish

tsurenai v 連れない = **tsuremasén** 連れません (not bring along)

tsurenai v 吊れない = **tsuremasén** 吊れません (cannot hang)

tsurenai v 釣れない = **tsuremasén** 釣れません (cannot fish)

tsurenái adj つれない coldhearted, cruel

tsureraremásu, tsurerareru v 連れられます, 連れられる (… ni) **tsureraremásu** (…に)連れられます gets brought along (by …)

tsureréba v 連れれば (if one brings along) → **tsuremásu** 連れます

tsureréba v 吊れれば (if one can hang) → **tsuremásu** 吊れます

tsureréba v 釣れれば (if one can fish) → **tsuremásu** 釣れます

tsurete v 連れて → **tsuremásu** 連れます

tsurete v 吊れて・釣れて → **tsuremásu** 吊れます・釣れます

tsureyō v 連れよう 1. = **tsuremashō´** 連れましょう (let's bring him along!) 2. = **o-tsureshimashō´** お連れしましょう (I'll take you along.)

tsuri n つり・釣り (o-tsuri おつり, **tsuri-sen** つり銭) (small) change

tsuri n 釣り fishing: **sakana-tsuri** 魚釣り fishing for: **ippon-zuri** 一本釣り single hook fishing

　tsuri-bari n 釣り針 fishhook

　tsuri-dōgu n 釣り道具 fishing gear

　tsuri-ito n 釣り糸 fishing line

　tsuri-zao n 釣り竿 fishing rod

tsuri n つり・吊り hanging (things), hanging for: **kubi-tsuri jisatsu** 首吊り自殺 suicide by hanging: **zubon-tsuri** ズボンつり[吊り] suspender, galluses

　tsuri-bashi n つり[吊り]橋 suspension bridge

　tsuri-gane n つり[吊り]鐘 big bell (temple, etc.)

　tsuri-kawa n つり[吊り]革 strap to hang on to (electric train, bus, etc.)

tsuriai n 釣り(り)合い・つりあい balance, equilibrium, symmetry (= **baransu** バランス, **chōwa** 調和)

tsurimásu, tsuru v 吊ります, 吊る hangs it (by a line), suspends, strings up

tsurimásu, tsuru v 釣ります, 釣る fishes

tsū´ro n 通路 1. passage(way) (= **tōri-michi** 通り道) 2. aisle (= **rōka** 廊下) 3. thoroughfare

tsuru v 吊る = **tsurimásu** 吊ります (hangs it)

tsuru v 釣る = **tsurimásu** 釣ります (fishes)

tsurú n ツル・蔓 vine; earpieces of a glass frame

tsurú n つる・弦 string (of bow or violin)

tsurú n つる・鉉 handle

tsúru n ツル・鶴 crane (bird)

tsurugí n 剣・つるぎ sword

tsūshin n 通信 1. correspondence:

tsūshin-kōza 通信講座 correspondence course: **tsūshin-hanbai** 通信販売 mail order 2. report, news: **gakkyū-tsūshin** 学級通信 class report/news 3. communications: **tsūshin-shudan** 通信手段 means of communication

tsutá n ツタ・蔦 ivy

tsutaé n 伝え (o-tsutae お伝え) → **dengon** 伝言, **messēji** メッセージ

tsutaemásu, tsutaeru v 伝えます, 伝える passes it on to someone else; reports, communicates; transmits; hands down

tsutaenai v 伝えない = **tsutaemasén** 伝えません (not transmit)

tsutaeraremásu, tsutaerareru v 伝えられます, 伝えられる can transmit it

tsutaerarenai v 伝えられない = **tsutaeraremasén** 伝えられません (cannot transmit it)

tsutaerarete v 伝えられて → **tsutae-raremásu** 伝えられます

tsutaeréba v 伝えれば (if one transmits it) → **tsutaemásu** 伝えます

tsutae ro v 伝えろ [IMPERATIVE] (trasmit!) → **tsutaemásu** 伝えます

tsutaete v 伝えて → **tsutaemásu** 伝えて

tsutanai adj つたない・拙い halting, unskillful, poor (= **heta** 下手): **~ Nihongo** つたない日本語 poor Japanese

tsutawaranai v 伝わらない = **tsutawari-masén** 伝わりません (not get transmitted)

tsutawáréba v 伝われば (if it be transmitted) → **tsutawarimásu** 伝わります

tsutawarimásu, tsutawaru v 伝わります, 伝わる is passed on; is reported, communicated; is transmitted; is handed down

tsutawatte v 伝わって → **tsutawari-másu** 伝わります

tsuto n つと・苞 straw wrapping, straw-wrapped package

tsuto adv つと [BOOKISH] quickly

tsutomé n 勤め (o-tsutome お勤め) [BOOKISH] work(ing), job (post)

　tsutome-nin n 勤め人 office worker

　tsutome-saki n 勤め先 place of employment, one's office

tsutomé n 務め (**o-tsutome** お務め) duty, role

tsutomemásu, tsutoméru ν 勤めます, 勤める [BOOKISH] is employed, works; works as

tsutomemásu, tsutoméru ν 努めます, 努める [BOOKISH] exerts oneself, strives, endeavors

tsutomé ro ν 勤めろ [IMPERATIVE] (work!) → **tsutomemásu** 勤めます

tsutomé ro ν 努めろ [IMPERATIVE] (endeavor!) → **tsutomemásu** 努めます

tsutómete ν 勤めて・努めて → **tsutomemásu** 勤めます・努めます

tsutomeyō´ ν 努めよう = **tsutome-mashō´** 努めましょう (let's exert ourselves!)

tsutsu n 筒 cylinder, pipe (= **kuda** 管, **kan** 管)

...´tsutsu suffix ...つつ [LITERARY]
1. = ...-**nágara** ...ながら (while doing)
2. ... (shi)tsutsu arimásu ...(し)つつ あります is about to ... (= ...-**te imásu** ...ています)

tsutsúji n ツツジ azalea

tsutsukimásu ν つつきます → **tsu(t)-tsukimásu** つ(っ)つきます

tsutsumánai ν 包まない = **tsutsumi-masén** 包みません (not wrap it up)

tsutsúme ν 包め [IMPERATIVE] (wrap it up!) → **tsutsumimásu** 包みます

tsutsúmeba ν 包めば (if one wraps it up) → **tsutsumimásu** 包みます

tsutsumemásu, tsutsuméru ν 包めます, 包める can wrap it up

tsutsuménai ν 包めない = **tsutsume-masén** 包めません (cannot wrap it up)

tsutsuméreba ν 包めれば (if one can wrap it up) → **tsutsumemásu** 包めます

tsutsúmete ν 包めて → **tsutsume-másu** 包めます

tsutsumí n 包み package, bundle: **tsutsumi-gami** 包み紙 package paper (= **hōsō-shi** 包装紙)

tsutsumí n 堤 **1.** dike, bank, embank-ment (= **dote** 土手, **teibō** 堤防) **2.** reservoir (= **chosui-chi** 貯水池)

tsutsúmi n 包み pack; parcel

tsutsumimásu, tsutsúmu ν 包みます, 包む wraps it up

tsutsumō´ ν 包もう = **tsutsumimashō´** 包みましょう (let's wrap it up!)

tsutsúnde ν 包んで → **tsutsumi-másu** 包みます

tsutsushimi n 慎み prudence, discretion

tsutsushimimásu, tsutsushimu ν 慎みます, 慎む is discreet, is careful; refrains from: **kotoba o** ~ 言葉を慎み ます is careful about how one speaks and behaves

tsutsushimimásu, tsutsushimu ν 謹みます, 謹む is humble, is reverent

tsutsushínde ν 慎んで → **tsutsu-shimimásu** 慎みます

tsutsushínde ν 謹んで: ~ **go-meifuku o oinori itashimásu** 謹んでご冥福を お祈りいたします I offer my deepest condolences → **tsutsushimimásu** 謹みます

tsutte ν 吊って・釣って → **tsurimásu** 吊ります・釣ります

tsu(t)tsúite ν つ(っ)ついて = **tsu(t)-tsukimásu** つ(っ)つきます [INFORMAL]

tsu(t)tsukimásu, tsu(t)tsúku ν つ(っ) つきます, つ(っ)つく [INFORMAL] pecks at

tsuya n ツヤ・艶 gloss, shine, luster (= **gurosu** グロス, **kōtaku** 光沢) **tsuya-keshi** ツヤ[艶]消し matte

tsuya n 通夜 (**o-tsuya** お通夜) lyke-wake

tsū´yaku n 通訳 interpreter; interpret-ing: **tsūyaku-sha** 通訳者 an interpreter: ~ **shimásu** 通訳します interprets

tsuyo-bi n 強火 high flame

tsūyō shimásu (suru) ν 通用します (する) **1.** is used commonly **2.** is accepted among people, is valid

tsuyói adj 強い strong; **tsúyosa** 強さ strength

tsuyu n つゆ・梅雨 rainy season (in Japan)

tsúyu n 露 dew

tsúyu n つゆ・汁 (**o-tsúyu** おつゆ) light (clear) soup

tsuzuite ν 続いて → **tsuzukimásu** 続きます

tsuzukanai ν 続かない = **tsuzukimasén** 続きません (it does/will not continue)

tsuzukemásu, tsuzukeru v 続けます、続ける continues it, goes on (with it)

tsuzukenai v 続けない = **tsuzukemasén** 続けません (does not continue it)

tsuzukerarenai v 続けられない = **tsuzukeraremasén** 続けられません (cannot continue it)

tsuzukerarete v 続けられて → **tsuzukeraremásu** 続けられます

tsuzukete 続けて **1.** *adv* continuously, in succession, going on (*to the next*) **2.** → **tsuzukemásu** 続けて

tsuzukeyō v 続けよう = **tsuzukemashō´** 続けましょう (let's continue!)

tsuzuki n 続き continuation, sequel, series

tsuzukimásu, tsuzuku v 続きます、続く it continues (will continue); adjoins

tsuzuku 続く To Be Continued

tsuzumarimásu, tsuzumáru v つづまります、つづまる [BOOKISH] it shrinks, gets shortened (= **chijimarimásu**, 縮まります、chijimaru 縮まる)

tsuzumí n 鼓・つづみ drum (*hourglass-shaped*)

tsuzuranai v 綴らない = **tsuzurimasén** 綴りません (not spell/... it)

tsuzure n 綴れ **1.** rags **2.** hand-woven brocade

tsuzúre v 綴れ [IMPERATIVE] (spell/... it!) → **tsuzurimásu** 綴ります

tsuzuremásu, tsuzureru v 綴れます、綴れる can spell; can compose; can patch, bind, sew (together)

tsuzurenai v 綴れない = **tsuzuremasén** 綴れません (cannot spell/... it)

tsuzuri 1. n 綴り・つづり spelling (= **superu** スペル) **2.** binding, bound (*sewn*) pages **3.** v 綴り → **tsuzurimásu** 綴ります

tsuzurimásu, tsuzuru v 綴ります、綴る **1.** spells **2.** composes, writes **3.** patches; binds; sews (*together/up*)

tsuzurō´ v 綴ろう = **tsuzurimashō´** 綴りましょう (let's spell/compose/ bind it!)

tsuzutte v 綴って → **tsuzurimásu** 綴ります

tu... → **tsu...**

ty... → **ch...**

U

u n ウ・鵜 cormorant (*fishing bird*): [IDIOM] **u-nomi ni suru** 鵜呑みにする swallows (*someone's words, talk, etc.*), believes every word someone says **u-kai** n 鵜飼い cormorant fishing

uba n 乳母 nanny (*who cares for baby/babies in a household*) **uba-guruma** n 乳母車 baby carriage (= **bebii-kā** ベビーカー)

ubaimásu, ubáu v 奪います、奪う seizes, robs, plunders

ubátte v 奪って → **ubaimásu** 奪います

ubawánai v 奪わない = **ubaimasén** 奪いません (not seize)

uchi n うち・家 **1.** **o-uchi** おうち[お家] house, home; family: ~ **no náka de/ ni** うち[家]の中で/に indoors **2.** ~ **uchi** ...うち、... **uchi (no)** うち(の) [INFORMAL] we/us; I/me; our, my: ~ **no kazoku** うちの家族 my family

uchi n 内: **... no uchí (de)** ...の内(で) inside; among

uchi n うち: **...-(shi)nai uchí ni ...** ...(し)ないうちに before it happens (*while it has not yet happened*)

uchi-... *prefix* 内... inside, inner **uchi-benkei** n 内弁慶 a lion at home and a mouse abroad **uchi-bori** n 内堀 inner moat **uchi-gawa** n 内側 the inside **uchi-ki (na)** *adj* 内気(な) shy (= **shai (na)** シャイ(な)) [IN POSITIVE SENSE]: ~ **na seikaku** 内気な性格 shy disposition **Uchi-mō´ko, Uchi-mongoru (jichi-ku)** n 内蒙古, 内モンゴル(自治区) Inner Mongolia (= **Nai mō´ko** 内蒙古, **Nai-mongoru (jichi-ku)**, 内モンゴル(自治区)) **uchi-wa** n 内輪 **1.** the family circle; the inside: **uchiwa (no)** 内輪(の) private: ~ **no hanashi** 内輪の話 private matter,

family affair **2. uchiwa (na)** 内輪（な）
moderate, modest, conservative
uchi-wake *n* 内訳 breakdown, particulars, details (= **meisai** 明細): **shishutsu
no ~** 支出の内訳 breakdown of expen-
ditures
uchi-age *n* 打ち上げ **1.** launch (*rocket*)
2. close (*performance, project, etc.*)
uchi-akemásu, uchi-akeru *v* 打ち明
けます, 打ち明ける confesses, frankly
reveals, confides
uchi-awase *n* 打ち合わせ・打合せ
consultation, meeting (*in the office,
etc. by appointment*) (= **kaigi** 会議,
miitingu ミーティング)
uchi-awasemásu, uchi-awaséru *v*
打ち合わせます, 打ち合わせる hold a
meeting/consultation
uchi-keshi *n* 打ち消し denial;
negation, negative
uchi-keshimásu, uchi-kesu *v* 打ち消
します, 打ち消す denies (*a rumor, etc.*),
takes back a remark
uchi-koroshimásu, uchi-korósu *v*
撃ち殺します, 撃ち殺す shoots to death
uchimásu, útsu *v* 打ちます, 打つ hits,
strikes, hammers; sends a telegram
uchi-mí *n* 打ち身 bruise
uchimásu, útsu *v* 撃ちます, 撃つ
fires, shoots (*a gun*)
uchíwa *n* うちわ・団扇 (*Japanese*) a
flat fan
uchōten *n* 有頂天 rapturous delight,
going into raptures, being beside
oneself with joy, being in seventh
heaven, being carried away, being
overjoyed: **~ ni narimásu** 有頂天にな
ります goes into raptures
úchū *n* 宇宙 universe, (*outer*) space
uchū-fuku *n* 宇宙服 spacesuit
uchū-hikō-shi *n* 宇宙飛行士 astronaut
uchū-sen *n* 宇宙船 spaceship
udé *n* 腕 **1.** arm **2.** special skill
ude-dókei *n* 腕時計 wristwatch
ude-gumi *n* 腕組み folding one's arms;
~ shimásu 腕組みします folds one's arms
ude-jiman (no) *adj* 腕自慢（の）proud
of one's skill
ude-kiki (no) *adj* 腕利き（の）skilled,
competent, able

ude-maé *n* 腕前 prowess, skill, ability
ude-wa *n* 腕輪 bracelet (= **buresuretto**
ブレスレット)
ude-zuku (de) *adv* 腕ずく（で）forcibly
údo *n* ウド・独活 Japanese celery
udon *n* うどん (**o-údon** おうどん)
Japanese wheat-flour noodles: **udon-ya**
うどん屋 Japanese noodle shop
U-doshi *n* 卯年 year of the Rabbit
ue *n* 上 **1. …ué** …上 above, upper part,
surface, top: **… no ue (de/ni/no)** …の上
（で/に/の）on, on top of **2. ué** 上
(= **toshi-ue** 年上) older, oldest
ue *n* 飢え hanger, starvation
uédingu-… *prefix* ウエディング…
wedding
uédingu-doresu *n* ウエディングドレ
ス wedding dress (= **hanayome-ishō**
花嫁衣裳）
uédingu-kēki *n* ウエディングケーキ
wedding cake
uédingu-pātii *n* ウエディングパーテ
ィ wedding party (= **kekkon-shukuga-
kai** 結婚祝賀会, **kekkon-hirōen** 結婚
披露宴）
uédingu-ringu *n* ウエディングリング
wedding ring (= **kekkon-yubiwa** 結婚
指輪）
uehāsu *n* ウエハース wafer
ueki *n* 植木 garden/potted plant
uekí-bachi *n* 植木鉢 flowerpot
ueki-ya *n* 植木屋 gardener
uemásu, ueru *v* 植えます, 植える
plants, grows plant
uemásu, uéru *v* 飢えます, 飢える
starves (*hungers*)
uenai *v* 植えない = **uemásén** 植えま
せん (not plant)
uénai *v* 飢えない = **uemásén** 飢えま
せん (not starve)
Ueno *n* 上野 Ueno; **Uenó-Eki** 上野駅
Ueno Station; **Ueno-Kō´en** 上野公園
Ueno Park
ueraremásu, uerareru *v* 植えられます,
植えられる can plant
ueréba *v* 植えれば (if one plants) →
uemásu 植えます
uéreba *v* 飢えれば (if one starves) →
uemásu 飢えます
uérudan *n* ウエルダン well-done (beef)

uésuto *n* ウエスト waist (= **koshi** 腰); **uesuto-pōchi** ウエストポーチ belt bag

ueta *v* 植えた = **uemáshita** 植えました (planted)

úeta *v* 飢えた = **uemáshita** 飢えました (starved)

uē´tā *n* ウエーター waiter

uete *v* 植えて → **uemásu** 植えます

úete *v* 飢えて → **uemásu** 飢えます

uē´toresu *n* ウエートレス waitress

ueyō *v* 植えよう = **uemashō´** 植えましょう (let's plant it!)

ugai *n* うがい a gargle
ugai (o) shimásu (suru) うがい(を)します(する) gargles

ugóita *v* 動いた = **ugokimáshita** 動きました (one/it moved)

ugokanai *v* 動かない = **ugokimasén** 動きません (not move)

ugokasánai *v* 動かさない = **ugokashimasén** 動かしません (not move it)

ugokáse *v* 動かせ [IMPERATIVE] (move it!) → **ugokashimásu** 動かします

ugokasemásu, ugokaséru *v* 動かせます, 動かせる can move it

ugokasénai *v* 動かせない = **ugokasemasén** 動かせません (cannot move it)

ugokásete *v* 動かせて → **ugokasemásu** 動かせます

ugokashimásu, ugokásu *v* 動かします, 動かす moves it

ugokáshite *v* 動かして → **ugokashimásu** 動かします

ugóke *v* 動け [IMPERATIVE] (move!) → **ugokimásu** 動きます

ugokemásu, ugokéru *v* 動けます, 動ける one/it can move

ugokénai *v* 動けない = **ugokemasén** 動けません (cannot move)

ugókete *v* 動けて → **ugokemásu** 動けます

ugokí *n* 動き movement, motion; trend

ugokimásu, ugóku *v* 動きます, 動く one/it moves

ugúisu *n* ウグイス・鴬 bush warbler

uindo-burē´kā *n* ウインドブレーカー windbreaker

uindō shoppingu *n* ウィンドウショッピング window shopping

uinkā *n* ウインカー car turn signal

uínku *n* ウインク wink(ing) (= **wínku** ウィンク, **mekubase** 目配せ)

uirusu *n* ウイルス virus; **uirusu-taisaku-sofuto** ウイルス対策ソフト antivirus software (= **anchi uirusu sofuto (-uwea)** アンチウイルスソフト(ウェア))

uísúkii *n* ウイスキー, **wísukii** ウィスキー whisky

uita *v* 浮いた = **ukimáshita** 浮きました (floated)

uite *v* 浮いて → **ukimásu** 浮きます

új í *n* 氏 clan, family; family name (= **sei** 姓)

uji-gami *n* 氏神 tutelary deity (*guardian spirit*)

uji (mushi) *n* ウジ(ムシ)・蛆(虫) maggot

ukabanai *v* 浮かばない = **ukabimasén** 浮かびません (not float)

ukabasemásu, ukabaseru *v* 浮かばせます, 浮かばせる lets float it

ukabe *v* 浮かべ [IMPERATIVE] (float!) → **ukabimásu** 浮かびます

ukabéba *v* 浮かべば (if it floats) → **ukabimásu** 浮かびます

ukabemásu, ukaberu *v* 浮かべます, 浮かべる lets/makes it float, floats it; shows (*a look*); brings to mind

ukabenai *v* 浮かべない = **ukabemasén** 浮かべません (not float it)

ukaberéba *v* 浮かべれば (if one floats it) → **ukabemásu** 浮かべます

ukabe ro *v* 浮かべろ [IMPERATIVE] (float it!) → **ukabemásu** 浮かべます

ukabete *v* 浮かべて → **ukabemásu** 浮かべます

ukabimásu, ukabu *v* 浮かびます, 浮かぶ floats

ukagaemásu, ukagaeru *v* 伺えます, 伺える can visit; can inquire

ukagaemásu, ukagaeru *v* 窺えます, 窺える can watch for

ukagaenai *v* 伺えない = **ukagaemasén** 伺えません (cannot visit/inquire)

ukagaenai *v* 窺えない = **ukagaemasén** 窺えません (cannot watch for)

ukagaete *v* 伺えて・窺えて → **ukagaemásu** 伺えます・窺えます

ukagai *n* 伺い (**o-ukagai** お伺い) visit;

inquiry, consultation

ukagaimásu, ukagau v 伺います, 伺う [HUMBLE] I visit (*you*); I inquire; I hear

ukagaimásu, ukagau v 窺います, 窺う keeps a watchful eye on (*the situation*): **kikái/chansu o ~** 機会/チャンスを窺います watches for (*an opportunity*)

ukagatte v 伺って・窺って → **ukagaimásu** 伺います・窺います

ukagawanai v 伺わない = **ukagaimasén** 伺いません (not visit/inquire)

ukagawanai v 窺わない = **ukagaimasén** 窺いません (not watch for)

ukai n 迂回・う回: **~ shimásu** 迂回します detours

ukanai v 浮かない = **ukimasén** 浮きません (not float)

ukande v 浮かんで → **ukabimásu** 浮かびます

ukárimásu, ukáru v 受かります, 受かる passes, succeeds

ukatsu うかつ・迂闊 carelessness, inattentiveness, thoughtlessness: **~ ni mo** うかつ[迂闊]にも carelessly, inattentively, thoughtlessly

uke v 浮け [IMPERATIVE] (float!) → **ukimásu** 浮きます

ukéba v 浮けば (if one floats) → **ukimásu** 浮けます

uke-iremásu, uké-ireru v 受け入れます, 受け入れる accepts

ukemásu, ukeru v 浮けます, 浮ける can float

ukemásu, ukéru v 受けます, 受ける accepts; receives; takes; gets; suffers, incurs

ukemi n 受身 1. passive voice (= **judō-tai** 受動態) 2. passive (*attitude*)

uke-mochimásu, uke-mótsu v 受け持ちます, 受け持つ takes/accepts/has charge of

ukenai v 浮けない = **ukemasén** 浮けません (cannot float)

ukénai v 受けない = **ukemasén** 受けません (not accept)

uke-óe v 請け負え [IMPERATIVE] (contract to do it!) → **uke-oimásu** 請け負います

uke-óeba v 請け負えば (if one contracts to do it) → **uke-oimásu** 請け負います

uke-oemásu, uke-oéru v 請け負えます, 請け負える can contract to do it

uke-oénai v 請け負えない = **uke-oemasen** 請け負えません (cannot contract to do it)

uke-óereba v 請け負えれば (if one can contract to do it) → **uke-oemásu** 請け負えます

uke-óete v 請け負えて → **uke-oemásu** 請け負えます

uke-oi n 請負・請け負い a contract (*to undertake work*)

ukeoi-gyōsha n 請(け)負(い)業者 a contractor

ukeoi-shigoto n 請(け)負(い)仕事 contract work

uke-oimásu, uke-óu v 請け負います, 請け負う contracts (*to undertake work*)

ukeoi-nin n 請負人 contractor

uke-oō´ v 請け負おう = **uke-oimashō´** 請け負いましょう (let's contract to do it!)

uke-ótte v 請け負って → **uke-oimásu** 請け負います

uke-owánai v 請け負わない = **uke-oimasén** 請け負いません (not contract to do it)

ukeraremásu, ukerareru v 受けられます, 受けられる can accept; can receive; …

ukerarénai v 受けられない = **ukera-remasén** 受けられません (cannot accept)

ukeárete v 受けられて → **ukerare-másu** 受けられます

ukeréba v 浮ければ (if one can float) → **ukemásu** 浮けます

ukéreba v 受ければ (if one accepts) → **ukemásu** 受けます

ukeru v 浮ける = **ukemásu** 浮けます (can float)

ukéru v 受ける = **ukemásu** 受けます (accepts)

uké ro v 受けろ [IMPERATIVE] (*accept it!*) → **ukemásu** 受けます

uketamawarimásu, uketamawáru v 承ります, 承る I (*humbly*) hear/listen/consent

ukete v 浮けて → **ukemásu** 浮けます

úkete *v* 受けて → **ukemásu** 受けます

uke-toranai *v* 受け取らない = **uke-torimasén** 受け取りません (not accept)

uke-tóre *v* 受け取れ [IMPERATIVE] (receives it!) → **uke-torimásu** 受け取ります

uke-toréba *v* 受け取れば (if one accepts) → **uke-torimásu** 受け取ります

uke-toremásu, uke-toréru *v* 受け取れます, 受け取れる can accept/take

uke-torénai *v* 受け取れない = **uke-tore-masén** 受け取れません (cannot accept)

uke-toréréba *v* 受け取れれば (if one can accept) → **uke-toremásu** 受け取れます

uke-tori *n* 受け取り・受取 receipt

uke-torimásu, uke-toru *v* 受け取ります, 受け取る accepts, receives, takes; takes it (= understand it)

uke-torō´ *v* 受け取ろう = **uke-torimashō´** 受け取りましょう (let's accept it!)

uke-tótte *v* 受け取って → **uke-tori-másu** 受け取ります

uketsugimásu, uketsugu *v* 受け継ぎます, 受け継ぐ succeeds to

uke-tsuke *n* 受付 acceptance; information desk; receptionist

uke-tsukemásu, uke-tsukéru *v* 受け付けます, 受け付ける accepts, receives

uke-uri *n* 受け売り borrowing someone else's ideas

ukeyō´ *v* 受けよう = **ukemashō´** 受けましょう (let's accept it!)

uké-zara *n* 受け皿 saucer (*for cup*)

uki *n* 雨季・雨期 rainy season

ukiashi dachimásu (dátsu) *v* 浮き足立ちます (立つ) is wavering, is ready to run away (= **nige-goshi ni narimásu (náru)** 逃げ腰になります(なる))

uki-bori *n* 浮き彫り relief (*sculpture consisting of shapes carved on a surface*) (= **reriifu** レリーフ): **shinjitsu o ~ ni shimásu** 真実を浮き彫りにします call attention to the fact that ...

ukimásu, uku *v* 浮きます, 浮く floats

ukiwa *n* 浮き輪 inner tube (*swimming*)

ukiyo *n* 浮世 [BOOKISH] this fleeting world, transient world

ukiyo-banare *n* 浮世離れ unworldliness

ukiyo-e *n* 浮世絵 Japanese woodblock prints

ukkári *adv* うっかり absentmindedly (= **tsui** つい)

ukō *v* 浮こう = **ukimashō** 浮きましょう (let's float!)

umá *n* ウマ・馬 horse: [IDIOM] **~ no mimi ni nenbutsu** ウマ[馬]の耳に念仏 in one ear and out the other

Uma-doshi *n* 午年 year of the Horse

uma ga aimásu (au) *v* ウマ[馬]が合います(合う) gets on well, gets along well

umái *adj* うまい・旨い・美味い (*commonly male*) tasty, delicious (= **oishii** 美味しい)

umái *adj* うまい・上手い **1.** skillful, good (= **jōzu** 上手) **2.** successful, profitable

úmaku *adv* うまく・旨く・美味く so as to be tasty

úmaku *adv* うまく・上手く **1.** skillfully **2.** successfully

umanai *v* 産まない = **umimasén** 産みません (not bear)

umánai *v* 膿まない = **umimasén** 膿みません (not fester)

ūman ribu *n* ウーマンリブ women's liberation

umare *n* 生まれ・産まれ birth

umaremásu, umareru *v* 生まれ[産まれ]ます, 生まれ[産まれ]る is born

umarimásu, umaru *v* 埋まります, 埋まる gets buried (= **uzumarimásu** うずまり[埋まり]ます)

ume *n* ウメ・梅 Japanese apricot ("plum")

ume-boshi *n* 梅干し pickled plum/apricot

ume-shu *n* 梅酒 apricot wine

ume *n* 産め [IMPERATIVE] (bear!) → **umimásu** 産みます

uméba *v* 産めば (if one bears) → **umimásu** 産みます

úmeba *v* 膿めば (if it festers) → **umimásu** 膿みます

umeite *v* うめいて・呻いて → **ume-kimásu** うめきます・呻きます

umekí *n* うめき・呻き a groan

umekimásu, uméku *v* うめきます・呻きます, うめく・呻く groans

275

umemásu, umeru v 埋めます, 埋める buries (= **uzumemásu** うずめます・埋めます)

umemásu, umeru v 生め[産め]ます, 生め[産め]る can give birth to, can bear (*a baby*)

umenai v 埋めない = **umemasén** 埋めません (not bury)

umenai v 生め[産め]ない = **umemasén** 生め[産め]ません (cannot bear)

umereba v 埋めれば (if one buries) → **umemásu** 埋めます

umereba v 生め[産め]れば (if one can bear) → **umemásu** 生め[産め]ます

umete v 埋めて → **umemásu** 埋めます

umete v 生め[産め]て → **umemásu** 生め[産め]ます

umeyō v 埋めよう = **umemashō** 埋めましょう (let's bury it!)

umi n 生み・産み birth: **umi (no)** 生み・産み(の) (*by giving*) birth, natal

umí n うみ・膿 pus

úmi n 海 sea

umibe n 海辺 (sea-) shore, seaside

umi-sen yama-sen 海千山千 **1.** knowing every trick in the book **2.** a sly old fox

umi no hi n 海の日 Marine day, Ocean Day (*3rd Monday of July*)

umimásu, umu v 生みます・産みます, 生む・産む gives birth to, bears

umimásu, úmu v 膿みます・膿む, 膿む festers

umō n 羽毛 feather

umō v 生もう・産もう = **umimashō´** 生み[産み]ましょう (let's give birth!)

umu v 生む・産む = **umimásu** 生みます・産みます (gives birth)

úmu n 有無 existence (*or non-existence*): **~ o iwasazu** 有無を言わさず forcibly (= **muriyari** 無理やり)

úmu v 膿む = **umimásu** 膿みます (festers)

ún n 運 fate, luck (→ **fu-un (na)** 不運(な), **kōun** 幸運)

ún ga íi adj 運がいい lucky

ún ga warui adj 運が悪い unlucky (= **fu-un** 不運, **tsuiteinai** ついて(い)ない・ツイて(い)ない)

ún-mei n 運命 destiny, fate (= **shuku-mei** 宿命): **~ no itazura** 運命のいたずら[悪戯] quirk of fate: **~ no akai-ito**

運命の赤い糸 red string of fate, red thread of destiny

ún-waruku adv 運悪く unluckily

ún-yoku adv 運良く luckily (= **saiwai** 幸い)

ún interj うん = **n** ん [INFORMAL] yeah, yes

unagashimásu, unagásu v 促します, 促す stimulates, urges (*on*)

unagi n ウナギ・鰻 eel

una-don n うな丼 a bowl of rice topped with broiled eel

uná-jū n うな重 broiled eel on rice in a lacquered box

unagi nobori n うなぎ登り[上り]・鰻登り[上り] rising rapidly and steadily (*prices, etc.*)

unarí n 唸り・うなり a roar; a growl; (= **umekí** うめき・呻き) a groan

unarimásu, unáru v 唸ります, 唸る roars; growls; (= **umekimásu** うめきます・呻きます) groans

unazukimásu, unazuku v うなずきます・頷きます, うなずく・頷く nods

únchin n 運賃 fare (*transportation*)

unda v 生んだ・産んだ = **umimáshita** 生み[産み]ました (gave birth)

únda v 膿んだ = **umimáshita** 膿みました (festered)

unde v 生んで・産んで = **umimásu** 生みます・産みます

únde v 膿んで = **umimásu** 膿みます

undei no sa n 雲泥の差 [IDIOM] great difference (= **taisa** 大差)

undō n 運動 **1.** movement: **shakai-undō** 社会運動 social movement: **senkyo-undō** 選挙運動 election campaign **2.** exercise; sports; athletics: **undō-jō** 運動場 athletic field, playground; **undō-senshu** 運動選手 athlete

únga n 運河 canal

úni n ウニ・雲丹 sea urchin (*roe*)

unpan n 運搬 transport(-ation) (*of goods and/or people*): **~ shimásu** 運搬します transports

unsō n 運送 transport(-ation) (*of goods*) (= **unpan** 運搬): **~ shimásu** 運送します transports

unsō-gyō-sha 運送業者 n transportation company

unsō-ya *n* 運送屋 express/forwarding agent; (*house*) mover (= **hikkoshi-ya** 引っ越し屋)

unten *n* 運転 operation, operating, running, working, driving: **~ shimásu** 運転します operates (*a vehicle*), drives

untén-menkyo (-shō) *n* 運転免許(証) driver's license

untén-shu *n* 運転手 driver (= **doraibā** ドライバー)

unto *adv* うんと much, a good deal, greatly

unubore ga tsuyói *adj* うぬぼれが強い vain, conceited

"un-un" *interj* うんうん = **n'n** んん

unyu *n* 運輸 transport(ation) (*of goods*) (= **unsō** 運送)

unzári shimásu (suru) *v* うんざりします(する) gets bored, gets sick and tired

uo *n* ウオ・魚 fish (= **sakana** サカナ・魚)

uo no me *n* うおのめ・魚の目 foot corn

uppun *n* うっぷん・鬱憤 frustration, pent-up anger, pent-up discontent: **~ o harashimásu** うっぷんを晴らします vents one's anger

urá *n* 裏 reverse (*side*), back; lining; what's behind it; the alley

urá *n* 裏 sole (*of foot*): **~ no urá** 足の裏 sole of foot

ura-dō'ri *n* 裏通り back street, alley

ura-gáeshi (no) *adj* 裏返し(の) inside-out

ura-gáeshimásu, ura-gáesu *v* 裏返します、裏返す turns over; turns inside out

ura-guchi *n* 裏口 back door: **ura-guchi-nyūgaku** 裏口入学 buying one's way into a school

ura-ji *n* 裏地 lining (*material*)

ura-kata *n* 裏方 sceneshifter

ura-me ni demásu (deru) *v* 裏目に出ます(出る) backfires, turns out badly

ura-mon *n* 裏門 back gate

ura-omote no aru hito *n* 裏表のある人 two-faced person

urá *n* 浦 bay (= **irie** 入り江)

urabon *n* うら[盂蘭]盆 the Bon Festival (= **o-bón** お盆)

ura-girí *n* 裏切り a double-cross, betrayal, treachery

ura-girimásu, ura-gíru *v* 裏切ります、裏切る betrays, double-crosses

uramí *n* 恨み grudge, resentment, ill will, enmity

urami o kaimásu (kau) *v* 恨みを買います(買う) incurs someone's enmity

uramimásu, urámu *v* 恨みます、恨む begrudges, resents

uranai *v* 売らない = **urimasén** 売りません (not sell)

uranái *n* 占い fortune-telling; **uranái-shi** 占い師 fortune-teller

urayamashii *adj* 羨ましい・うらやましい enviable; envious

urayamimásu, urayámu *v* 羨みます・うらやみます、羨む・うらやむ envies

ure *v* 売れ [IMPERATIVE] (sell it!) → **urimásu** 売ります

uréba *v* 売れば (if one sells) → **urimásu** 売ります

ure-kuchi *n* 売れ口 sales outlet

uremásu, ureru *v* 売れます、売れる **1.** it sells, is in demand; thrives; is popular **2.** can sell

urenai *v* 売れない = **uremasén** 売れません (not sell); cannot sell

ureréba *v* 売れれば (if it sells; if one can sell) → **uremásu** 売れます

ureshii *adj* うれしい・嬉しい glad, delightful, pleasant, wonderful, happy

urete *v* 売れて → **uremásu** 売れます

úri *n* ウリ・瓜 fruit of the gourd family, *Cucurbitaceae*, melon (cucumbers = **kyūri** キュウリ[胡瓜]), watermelons (= **suika** スイカ[西瓜]), pumpkin (= **kabocha** カボチャ[南瓜]), loofah (= **hechima** ヘチマ[糸瓜]), wax gourd (= **tōgan** トウガン[冬瓜]), *etc.*)

úri futatsu *n* ウリ二つ・瓜二つ like two peas in a pod (*not to literally mean, "two melons"*) (= **sokkuri** そっくり)

uri-ba *n* 売り場 (*shop*) counter, stand; shop, store

uri-dashi *n* 売り出し (*special*) sale; **uri-dashimásu** 売り出します puts on sale/market; launches

uri-kake *n* 売り掛け credit sales

uri-kire *n, adj* 売り切れ sellout; sold out

uri-ko *n* 売り子 salesclerk (*salesgirl/saleswoman/salesman*); shopgirl uri-mono *n* 売り物 sales goods/item, (*something*) for sale

uri-nushi *n* 売り主 seller (= **uri-te** 売り手)

uri-te *n* 売り手 seller (= **uri-nushi** 売り主)

uri-kíre *n* 売り切れ sell out

uri-kiremásu, uri-kíreru *v* 売り切れます, 売り切れる sells out, runs out of

urimásu, uru *v* 売ります, 売る sells

urō´ *v* 売ろう = **urimashō** 売りましょう (let's sell!)

uroko *n* ウロコ・鱗 scales (*on a fish*)

urotsukimásu, urotsuku うろつきます, うろつく hangs around

ū´ru *n* ウール wool

urū´-doshi *n* うるう[閏]年 leap year

urume (-íwashi) *n* ウルメ（イワシ）・潤目（鰯）large (*and usually dried*) sardine

urusái *adj* うるさい annoying, noisy (= **sawagashii** 騒がしい)

urushi *n* ウルシ・漆 lacquer; **urushi-nuri no utsuwa** 漆塗りの器 lacquerware (= **shikki** 漆器)

uruwashii *adj* うるわしい・麗しい [BOOKISH] **1.** beautiful **2.** heartwarming

usa-barashi *n* 憂さ晴らし distraction (*from emotional pain, suffering, etc.*), diversion, break, something to cheer one up: ~ **o shimásu** 憂さ晴らしをします diverts oneself (= **usa o harashimásu** 憂さを晴らします)

usagi *n* ウサギ・兎 rabbit, hare

usan kusai *adj* うさんくさい・胡散臭い fishy, suspicious-looking

usetsu shimásu (suru) うせつ右折します (する) turns right

ushi *n* ウシ・牛 ox, oxen; cow, cattle

Ushi-doshi *n* 丑年 year of the Ox

ushinaimásu, ushinau *v* 失います, 失う loses

ushinatte *v* 失って → **ushinaimásu** 失います

ushiro *n* 後ろ behind; (*in*) back

úso *n* うそ・嘘 lie, fib, false(hood): [IDIOM] ~ **mo hōben** うそ[嘘]も方便 a lie is sometimes expedient

usó-tsuki *n* うそつき・嘘つき liar

úsu *n* うす・臼 (*utensil*) mortar

usu-cha *n* 薄茶 weak powdered tea (= **o-úsu** お薄)

usui *adj* 薄い thin

utá *n* 歌 **1.** song **2.** (*Japanese*) 31-syllable poem

utá *n* 詩 modern poem

utaemásu, utaeru *v* 歌えます 歌える can sing

utaenai *v* 歌えない = **utaemásén** 歌えません (cannot sing)

utagaemásu, utagaeru *v* 疑えます, 疑える can doubt

utagaenai *v* 疑えない = **utagaemásén** 疑えません (cannot doubt)

utagai *n* 疑い a doubt: ~ **náku** 疑いなく undoubtedly, doubtless

utagaimásu, utagau *v* 疑います, 疑う doubts

utagawanai *v* 疑わない = **utagaimásén** 疑いません (not doubt)

utagawashii *adj* 疑わしい doubtful

utai *n* 謡 [BOOKISH] chanting a Noh libretto

utaimásu, utau *v* 歌います, 歌う sings; recites, chants

utaimásu, utau *v* うたい[謡い]ます, うたう・謳う expressly states; extols

utánai *v* 打たない = **uchimásén** 打ちません (not hit)

utaō *v* 歌おう = **utaimashō´** 歌いましょう (let's sing!)

utawanai *v* 歌わない = **utaimasen** 歌いません (not sing)

úte *v* 打て [IMPERATIVE] (hit it!) → **uchimásu** 打ちます

úte *v* 撃て [IMPERATIVE] (shoot it!) → **uchimásu** 撃ちます

úteba *v* 打てば (if one hits) → **uchimásu** 打ちます

utemásu, utéru *v* 打て ます, 打てる can hit; can send (*a telegram*)

utemásu, utéru *v* 撃てます, 撃てる can shoot (*a gun*)

uten *n* 雨天 [BOOKISH] rainy weather: **uten-kekkō** 雨天決行 rain or shine: **uten-jun'en** 雨天順延 Postponed in case of rain.: **uten-chūshi** 雨天中止 Canceled in case of rain.

uténai *v* 打てない = **utemásén** 打てません (cannot hit)

uténai ν 撃てない = **utemasén** 撃てません (cannot shoot)

utéreba ν 打てれば (if one can hit) → **utemásu** 打てます

utéreba ν 撃てれば (if one can shoot) → **utemásu** 撃てます

utó´ ν 打とう = **uchimashō** 打ちましょう (let's hit!)

utó´ ν 撃とう = **uchimashō** 撃ちましょう (let's shoot!)

utói *adj* うとい・疎い; **... ni ~** ...に疎い [うとい] out of touch with ..., not abreast of ...; estranged from ...

útouto *adv* うとうと drowsing (off) (= **utsura utsura** うつらうつら); **~ shimásu** うとうとします drowses, dozes

útsu ν 打つ = **uchimásu** 打ちます (hits)

utsubuse *n* うつぶせ・俯せ lying on one's stomach

utsukushíí *adj* 美しい beautiful

utsumukemásu, utsumukeru ν うつむけます, うつむける turns (face) downward; **kao o ~** 顔を~ turns one's face down

utsumukimásu, utsumúku ν うつむきます, うつむく lowers one's eyes, looks down, hangs one's head

utsurí *n* 映り reflection, picture quality; (*a becoming*) match

utsurimásu, utsúru ν 移ります, 移る 1. one/it moves, shifts (= **idō shimásu** 移動します) 2. changes 3. moves house/residence (= **hikkoshimásu** 引越します)

utsurimásu, utsúru ν 映ります, 映る is reflected; can be seen (*through*); is becoming

utsurimásu, utsúru ν 写ります, 写る comes out (*photograph*)

utsuro (na) *adj* うつろ・虚ろ (な) hollow, empty, vacant: **~ na hyōjó´ o mísete** うつろ[虚ろ]な表情を見せて with a blank look

utsúse ν 移せ [IMPERATIVE] (move it!) → **utsushimásu** 移します

utsúshí *n* 写し copy (= **kopii** コピー, **fukusha** 複写)

utsushimásu, utsúsú ν 移します, 移す moves/transfers it

utsushimásu, utsúsú ν うつします, うつす infects, gives another person a disease (*illness*)

utsushimásu, utsúsú ν 写します, 写す copies; takes a picture of; projects a picture

utsushimásu, utsúsú ν 映します, 映す reflects, mirrors

utsúshite ν 移して・写して → **utsushimásu** 移します・写します

utsúshite ν 映して → **utsushimásu** 映します

utsutsu o nukashimásu (nukasu) ν うつつを抜かします (抜かす) is engrossed, is addicted

utsútte ν 移って・映って → **utsurimásu** 移ります・映ります

utsuwa *n* 器 1. receptacle, utensil, container (= **yōki** 容器) 2. tool (= **kigu** 器具, **dōgu** 道具) 3. ability, personality: **~ ga/no ōkii hito** 器が/の大きい人 person of high caliber

utta ν 売った = **urimáshita** 売りました (sold)

útta ν 打った = **uchimáshita** 打ちました (hit)

uttae *n* 訴え complaint, lawsuit

uttaemásu, uttaéru ν 訴えます, 訴える accuses, sues: **kujō o ~** 苦情を訴える complains

utte ν 売って → **urimásu** 売ります

útte ν 打って → **uchimásu** 打ちます

uttetsuke (no) *adj* うってつけ (の) the most suitable; just right, just the ..., just the one/ticket

uttóri (to) *adv* うっとり (と) absorbed, fascinated: **~ (to) shimásu** うっとりします is fascinated, spellbound, is enchanted

uttōshíí *adj* うっとうしい gloomy, dismal, dreary: **~ tenki** うっとうしい天気 gloomy weather

uwabaki *n* 上履き・上ばき indoor footwear (*slippers, etc.*)

uwabe *n* 上辺・うわべ 1. surface (= **hyōmen** 表面) 2. outer appearances (= **gaikan** 外観): **~ o tsukuroi másu** うわべをつくろい[繕い]ます puts up a front

uwagaki *n* 上書き 1. address (*written on envelope, etc.*) 2. overwriting:

uwagaki-hozon 上書き保存 overwrite save: **uwagaki-mōdo** 上書きモード overwrite mode
uwagi n 上着 coat, jacket, blouse
uwagoto n うわごと・うわ言 raving, delirium
uwaki n 浮気: ~ (o) shimásu 浮気(を)します is unfaithful, has an (*extramarital*) affair; **uwaki (na)** 浮気(な) fickle
uwa-mawarimásu, uwa-mawaru v 上回ります, 上回る exceeds
uwasa n うわさ・噂 rumor, gossip (= **goshippu** ゴシップ)
uyamai n 敬い reverence, respect
uyamaimásu, uyamáu v 敬います, 敬う reveres, respects
uyamátte v 敬って → **uyamaimásu** 敬います
uyamuya n うやむや obscurity, vague-

ness (= **aimai** あいまい・曖昧)
uyamuya ni shimásu (suru) v うやむやにします(する) is wishy-washy, obscures the issue
uyoku n 右翼 (*political party*) the right wing, rightists
úzu n 渦, **uzú-maki** 渦巻き whirlpool (uzu-maki) rōru-kēki n (渦巻き)ロールケーキ swiss roll
uzu-shio n 渦潮 whirling current: **Naruto no ~** 鳴門の渦潮 Naruto whirlpool
uzumarimásu, uzumaru v うずまります・埋まります, うずまる・埋まる gets buried
uzumemásu, uzumeru v うずめます・埋めます, うずめる・埋める buries
uzura n ウズラ・鶉 quail: ~ **no tamago** ウズラ[鶉]の卵 quail egg

W

wá n 輪 circle; wheel; link; ring; loop (= **wak-ka** 輪っか)
wa-gomu n 輪ゴム rubber band
wa n 和 **1.** peace (= **hei-wa** 平和, **wa-hei** 和平) **2.** harmony (= **chō-wa** 調和, **kyō-wa** 協和)
wa-hei kōshō n 和平交渉 [BOOKISH] peace negotiations
wa-hei jōyaku n 和平条約 [BOOKISH] peace treaty
wa-... *prefix* 和 ... Japanese ...
wa-ei n 和英 Japanese-English (= **nichi-ei** 日英); **waei-jíten** 和英辞典 Japanese-English dictionary
wa-fū n 和風 [BOOKISH] Japanese style
wa-fuku n 和服 Japanese traditional clothes; kimono
wa-gáshi n 和菓子 Japanese cakes/sweets
wá-ka n 和歌 (*Japanese*) 31-syllable poem
wa-sei-eigo n 和製英語 "Made in Japan" English, Japanese English (= **japaniizu ingurisshu** ジャパニーズイングリッシュ)
wá-shi n 和紙 Japanese paper

wa-shitsu n 和室 Japanese-style room
wa-shoku n 和食 Japanese food
wa-yaku n 和訳 translation into Japanese; **ei-bun wa-yaku** 英文和訳 translation from English into Japanese
...-wa *suffix* ... 羽 (*counts birds, rabbits*)
... wa *particle* ...は as for ..., speaking of ..., let's talk about (*change the subject to*) ...; ..., guess what —; if it be (= **...déwa** ... では = **... nára** ...なら)
... wa *interj* ...わ (*mostly female*) indeed, you see
wā *interj* わあ (*female or children*) Wow!; Gee!; Gosh!
wabí n わび・侘び a liking for simple things; simple tastes
wabi n 詫び = **o-wabi** お詫び apology
wabimásu, wabiru v 詫びます, 詫びる [BOOKISH] apologize (= **o-wabishimasu** お詫びします)
wabínai v 詫びない = **wabimasén** 詫びません (not apologize)
wabishíi v 詫びしい・侘しい miserable; lonely
wábite v 詫びて → **wabimásu** 詫びます

wa-chū *n* 話中 [BOOKISH] busy (*on the phone*) (= **hanashi-chū** 話し中): **wachū-on** 話中音 busy tone

wa-dachi *n* わだち・ワダチ・轍 (*wheel*) ruts

wadai *n* 話題 topic of conversation, subject (*of talk*)

wá-ga ... *adj* 我が・わが… [BOOKISH] my, our: **wá-ga kuni** 我が国・わが国 our (*this*) country (*commonly Japan*)

wá-ga-hai *pron* 我(が)輩・吾(が)輩 [BOOKISH] I/me: "**Wa-ga-hai wa neko de aru**" 「吾輩は猫である」 "I am a cat"

waga-mámá (na) *adj* わがまま(な) selfish (= **mi-gatte (na)** 身勝手(な), **jibun-katte (na)** 自分勝手(な))

wágon (sha) *n* ワゴン(車) station wagon

wai-fai *n* ワイ・ファイ, Wi-Fi (= **musen-ran** 無線 LAN) Wi-Fi, wireless LAN (*computer*)

wáin *n* ワイン wine: **aka-wain** 赤ワイン red wine: **shiro-wain** 白ワイン white wine: **wain-gurasu** ワイングラス wine glass

wáipā *n* ワイパー windshield wiper

wáiro *n* わいろ・賄賂 bribe(ry); graft

waisetsu *n* わいせつ obscenity (= **midara** 淫ら, **iyarashii** いやらしい): **waisetsu na** わいせつな obscene

wai-shatsu *n* Yシャツ shirt

waita *v* 沸いた = **wakimáshita** 沸きました (boiled)

waita *v* 湧いた = **wakimáshita** 湧きました (gushed)

waite *v* 沸いて・湧いて → **wakimásu** 沸きます・湧きます

wakai *n* 和解 reconciliation: ~ **shimásu** 和解します is reconciled

wakái *adj* 若い young
  waka-ba *n* 若葉 young leaves: **Wakaba-máku** 若葉マーク Wakaba mark (*a mark displayed on the windshield to indicate brand new driver*)
  waka-dori *n* 若鶏 broiler chicken
  waka-mono *n* 若者 young person, youth
  waka-te *n* 若手 young person; **wakate-sákka** 若手作家 young writer

wakame *n* ワカメ・若布 a kind of seaweed

wakanai *v* 沸かない = **wakimásen** 沸きません (not boil)

wakanai *v* 湧かない = **wakimásen** 湧きません (not gush)

wakaránai *v* 分からない・解らない = **wakarimásen** 分かりません・解りません (not understand)

wakaré *n* 別れ (**o-wakare** お別れ) parting, farewell

wakaré *n* 分かれ branch(ing), fork(ing), division

wakáre *n* 別れ breakup; farewell; leave

wakáre *v* 分かれ [IMPERATIVE] (understand!) → **wakarimásu** 分かります

wakaremásu, wakaréru *v* 別れます, 別れる they part, separate

wakaremásu, wakaréru *v* 分かれます, 分かれる it branches off, splits

wakareme *n* 分かれ目 turning point

wakaténai *v* 別れない = **wakaremásen** 別れません (not part)

wakaré ro *v* 別れろ [IMPERATIVE] (part!) → **wakaremásu** 別れます

wakarí *n* 分かり comprehension (= **nomikomi** 呑み込み): ~ **ga hayái** 分かりが早い quick-witted, ~ **ga íi** 分かりがいい intelligent; **(mono)wakarí ga warúi** (もの)分かりが悪い dull(-witted), stupid

Wakarimáshita *v* 分かりました.
  1. Yes, I see. **2.** Yes, I will (*comply with your request*).

wakarimásu, wakáru *v* 分かります, 分かる it is clear (*understood*); understands; finds out; has good sense

wakari-yasúi *v* 分かりやすい clear, easy to understand

wakashimásu, wakasu *v* 沸かします, 沸かす boils it

wakátta *v* 分かった = **wakarimáshita** 分かりました (understood)

wakátte *v* 分かって → **wakarimásu** 分かります: ~ **imásu** 分かっています it is understood, it is (*now*) clear

wáke *n* わけ・訳 **1.** reason (= **riyū** 理由) **2.** meaning (= **imi** 意味), content (= **naiyō** 内容) **3.** case, circumstance (= **jijō** 事情)

waké ro ν 分けろ [IMPERATIVE] (divide it!) → **wakemásu** 分けます

wáke n 訳: **(... suru/shinai) wáke ni wa ikanai** ...（する/しない）訳にはいかない cannot help (doing)

wakéba ν 沸けば (if it boils) → **wakimásu** 沸きます

wakéba ν 湧けば (if it gushes) → **wakimásu** 湧きます

wakemae n 分け前 share, portion

wakemásu, wakéru ν 分けます, 分ける divides (*splits, distributes*) it; separates them

wake-mé n 分け目 dividing line, part(ing) (*in hair*)

wáke arimasén (nái) ν 訳ありません（ない）is no problem, is a cinch; easy

wakénai ν 分けない = **wakemasén** 分けません (not divide it; not separate it)

wáke-nai ν 訳ない・わけない easy, simple, ready; **wake-naku** 訳なく・わけなく easily, simply, readily

wakeraremásu, wakeraréru ν 分けられます, 分けられる 1. it gets divided; they get separated 2. can divide it

wakerarénai ν 分けられない = **wake-raremasén** 分けられません (cannot divide it)

wakeraréreba ν 分けられれば (if it gets divided; if we can divide it) → **wakeraremásu** 分けられます

wakerárete ν 分けられて → **wake-raremásu** 分けられます

wakereba ν 分ければ (if we divide it) → **wakemásu** 分けます

wákete ν 分けて → **wakemásu** 分けます

wakeyō´ ν 分けよう = **wakemashō´** 分けましょう (let's divide it!)

wakí n わき・脇 side (= **yoko** 横）

waki-bara n わき腹・脇腹 flank (= **yoko-bara** 横腹）

waki-mi n わき見・脇見 looking off (= **yoso-mi** よそ見); **wakimi-unten** 脇見運転 inattentive driving

waki-michi n わき道・脇道 sideroad; **hanashi ga ~ ni soremásu** 話が脇道にそれます strays from the subject

wakí n わき・腋 side of the body

waki-ga n わきが・腋臭 armpit smell,

body odor

waki-nó-shita n わき[脇・腋]の下 1. armpit 2. under one's arms

waki-mizu n 湧き水 spring water

waki aiai n 和気あいあい in happy harmony

wakimásu, waku ν 沸きます, 沸く it boils: **o-yu ga ~** お湯が沸きます the water boils

wakimásu, waku ν 湧きます, 湧く it gushes, springs forth: **yūki ga waki-máshita** 勇気が湧きました I was given courage., I got courage.: **kibō ga wakimáshita** 希望が湧きました I was given hope., I got hope.

waku ν 沸く = **wakimásu** 沸きます (it boils)

waku ν 湧く = **wakimásu** 湧きます (it gushes, springs forth)

wakú n 枠 1. frame, framework (= **waku-gumi** 枠組) 2. reel, limit, a confine

waku-gumi n 枠組 1. frame, framework (= **waku** 枠) 2. outline (= **autorain** アウトライン, **ōsuji** 大筋)

wákuchin n ワクチン vaccine

wakusei n 惑星 planet

waku-waku shímásu (suru) ν わくわくします（する）is thrilled, is excited

waméite ν わめいて・喚いて → **wamekimásu** わめきます

wamekimásu, waméku ν わめきます・喚きます, わめく・喚く yells

wan n 碗 (**o-wan** お碗) bowl: **cha-wan** 茶碗 rice-bowl: **cha-wan-mushi** 茶碗蒸し pot-steamed hotchpotch

wán n 湾 bay, gulf: **Tōkyō-wan** 東京湾 Tokyo Bay

wan-gan n 湾岸 gulf coast: **wangan-sensō** 湾岸戦争 Gulf War

wán n ワン one

wán-man n ワンマン 1. one-man, operator-only (*bus*); **wanman-shō´** ワンマンショー one-man show, solo performance 2. dictator: **wanman-keiei** ワンマン経営 Caesar management

wan-píisu n ワンピース (*one-piece*) dress

wan-rū´mu n ワンルーム one-room (*studio*) apartment

wána n わな・ワナ・罠 trap; lasso: ~

ni kakarimásu わな[罠]にかかります gets trapped/snared

wáni *n* ワニ crocodile, alligator

waní-ashi (no) *adj* わに足（の）bow-legged (= **ganimata (no)** がに股（の））

wánisu *n* ワニス varnish

wanpaku *n* わんぱく・腕白 rudeness: **wanpaku-kozō** わんぱく[腕白]小僧 brat, mischievous boy

wanpaku (na) *adj* 腕白・わんぱく（な）naughty, mischievous (*commonly used for children*) (= **yancha (na)** やんちゃ（な））

wánryoku *n* 腕力 arm strength, physical force, physical strength

wán-wan *interj* ワンワン bow-wow! (*bark*)

wappu *n* 割賦 allotment, installment (= **kappu** 割賦)

wā-puro *n* ワープロ word processor

wára *n* ワラ・藁 rice straw: [IDIOM] ~ **ni mo sugaru omoi de** ワラ[藁]にもすがる思いで grasping at straws

warabanshi *n* わら半紙 coarse paper, rough paper

warabe *n* わらべ・童 [BOOKISH] child(ren) (= **jidō** 児童): **warabe-uta** わらべ歌・童歌 Japanese traditional children's song

warabi *n* ワラビ bracken

warae *v* 笑え [IMPERATIVE] (laugh!) → **waraimásu** 笑います

waraéba *v* 笑えば (if one laughs) → **waraimásu** 笑います

waraemásu, waraeru *v* 笑えます, 笑える can laugh

waraenai *v* 笑えない = **waraemásén** 笑えません (cannot laugh)

waraéreba *v* 笑えれば (if one can laugh) → **waraemásén** 笑えません

warai *n* 笑い a laugh, laughter; smile **warai-banashi** *n* 笑い話 funny story

warai *n* わらい・嗤い ridicule, sneer, mockery

waraimásu, warau *v* 笑います, 笑う laughs; laughs at; smiles

waraimásu, warau *v* わらい[嗤い] ます, わらう・嗤う ridicules, sneers, mocks (= **chōshō shimásu** 嘲笑します, **aza-waraimásu** 嘲笑います)

waranai *v* 割らない = **warimásén** 割り ません (not break/divide/dilute it)

waraō *v* 笑おう = **waraimashō´** 笑いま しょう (let's laugh!)

warawanai *v* 笑わない = **waraimásén** 笑いません (not laugh)

warawanai *v* わらわ[嗤わ]ない = **warai-másén** わらい[嗤い]ません (not ridicule)

warawaremásu, warawareru *v* 笑わ れます, 笑われる gets laughed at

warawaremásu, warawareru *v* わらわ [嗤わ]れます, わらわ[嗤わ]れる is ridiculed at

warawarenai *v* 笑われない = **wara-waremásén** 笑われません (not get laughed at)

warawarenai *v* わらわ[嗤わ]れない = **warawaremásén** わらわ[嗤わ]れま せん (is not ridiculed at)

warawaréréba *v* 笑われれば (if one gets laughed at) → **warawaremásu** 笑われます

warawaréréba *v* わらわ[嗤わ]れれば (if one is ridiculed at) → **waraware-másu** わらわ[嗤わ]れます

warawarete *v* 笑われて・わらわ[嗤わ] れて → **warawaremásu** 笑われます ・わらわ[嗤わ]れます

wáre *pron* 我 [BOOKISH] **1.** oneself **2.** I/ me (= **wata(ku)shi** わた（く）し・私) **ware ni kaerimásu (kaeru)** *v* 我に返り ます（返る）comes to oneself **ware o wasuremásu (wasureru)** *v* 我を忘れます（忘れる）**1.** is hooked on, is carried away (= **muchū ni narimásu (náru)** 夢中になります（なる））**2.** is stunned (= **bōzen-jishitsu to narimásu (náru)** 茫然自失となります（なる）) **ware-ware** *pron* 我々・われわれ [BOOKISH] we; us

ware *v* 割れ [IMPERATIVE] (divide it!) → **warimásu** 割ります

waremásu, wareru *v* 割れます, 割れる **1.** it cracks, it splits **2.** can divide/ break/dilute it **ware-me** *n* 割れ目 crack, crevice, gap **ware-mono** *n* 割れ物 fragile

warenai *v* 割れない = **waremásén** 割れ ません (not crack; cannot divide/ break/dilute)

warete ν 割れて→ **waremásu** 割れます

wari n 割 1. (…-wari …割) tens of percent; percentage; **sán-wari** 三割 = **sanjup-pāsénto** 30パーセント・30% thirty percent 2. profit(ability): ~ **ni aimasén** 割に合いません it doesn't pay (off); ~ **ga íi** 割がいい profitable: ~ **ga warúi** 割が悪い unprofitable

wari-ai n 割合 rate, percentage: **wari-ai (ni)** 割合(に) comparatively, relatively

wariate n 割り当て quota, allotment

waribashi n 割り箸 throwaway chopsticks

wari-biki n 割引 discount

wari-kan n 割り勘 splitting the bill; (going) Dutch treat: ~ **ni shimashō** 割り勘にしましょう Let's split the bill.

warikómimásu, warikómu ν 割り込みます, 割り込む cuts in (into), breaks in; breezes in

wari-mae n 割り前 share, portion

warimásu, waru ν 割ります, 割る divides/splits it, breaks it, dilutes it

wari (ni) adv わり(に)・割(に) relatively, comparatively (= **wariai (ni)** 割合(に))

warízan n 割り算 division

warō ν 割ろう → **warimashō** 割りましょう (let's divide/break/ dilute it!)

warú n 悪 bad, evil (= **aku** 悪)

warú-i adj 悪い 1. bad, poor; wrong; vicious 2. at fault

Warú-i! interj 悪い! Sorry.

warú-fuzake n 悪ふざけ practical joke

warú-gashikoi adj 悪賢い sly, cunning, crafty, wily (person) (= **zuru-gashikoi** ずる賢い, **kōkatsu (na)** 狡猾(な))

warú-gi n 悪気 evil intent, malice (= **akui** 悪意)

warú-jie n 悪知恵 cunning, craft

warú-kuchi/-guchi n 悪口 (verbal) abuse, slander: ~ **o iimásu** 悪口を言います speaks ill (of)

waru-mono n 悪者 bad guy/fellow, villain, scoundrel: ~ **atsukai** 悪者扱い demonize

warú-yoi n 悪酔い getting sick from drink: ~ **shimásu** 悪酔いします gets sick from drink

warutsu n ワルツ waltz

wásabi n ワサビ・山葵 horseradish

washi n ワシ・鷲 eagle

washi pron わし (archaic old male) I/me (= **wata(ku)shi** わたくし)

Washinton n ワシントン Washington

wasure ro ν 忘れろ [IMPERATIVE] (forget it!) → **wasuremásu** 忘れます

wasuremásu, wasureru ν 忘れます, 忘れる forgets

wasure-mono n 忘れ物 1. leaving something behind 2. a thing left behind (forgetfully)

wasurenái de ν 忘れないで: ~ (… shite) kudasái 忘れないで(…して)下さい don't forget (to do …)

wasurep-pói adj 忘れっぽい forgetful

wasureraremásu, wasurerareru ν 忘れられます, 忘れられる can forget

wasurerarenai ν 忘れられない = **wasureraremasén** 忘れられません (cannot forget)

wasurerareréba ν 忘れられれば (if one can forget) → **wasureraremásu** 忘れられます

wasureta ν 忘れた = **wasuremashita** 忘れました (I forgot.)

wasurete ν 忘れて → **wasuremásu** 忘れます

wasureyō ν 忘れよう = **wasuremashō** 忘れましょう (let's forget it!)

watá n 綿 cotton (= **kotton** コットン)

watá-ame n 綿アメ cotton candy (= **wata-gashi** 綿菓子)

wata-bokori n 綿ぼこり dustball

watá-gashi n 綿菓子 cotton candy (= **wata-ame** 綿アメ)

wata-ge n 綿毛 fluff, cotton fiber: **tanpopo no ~** タンポポの綿毛 pappus of a dandelion

wata-íre n 綿入れ (cotton-) padded garment

watá n 腸 guts, intestines (= **harawatá** はらわた・腸)

watakushi pron わたくし・私 [BOOKISH], **watashi** わたし・私 [HUMBLE] I/me; **watakushí-tachi** わたくし[私]達, **watáshí-táchi** わたし[私]達 we/us

watakushí-ritsu (no) adj 私立(の) private(-ly established); **watakushí-**

ritsu (no) gakkō 私立(の)学校 private school

watakushi-shōsetsu *n* 私小説 I-Novel (*a novel writing about oneself*) (= **shi-shōsetsu** 私小説)

wataranai *v* 渡らない = **watarimasén** 渡りません (not cross over)

watare *v* 渡れ [IMPERATIVE] (cross over!) → **watarimásu** 渡ります

wataremásu, watareru *v* 渡れます, 渡れる can cross over

watarenai *v* 渡れない = **wataremasén** 渡れません (cannot cross over)

waterete *v* 渡れて → **wateremásu** 渡れます

watari *n* 渡り crossing, ferry (*place*): **~ o tsukemásu** 渡りをつけます forms an understanding with, gets in touch with; **~ ni fúne** 渡りに船 a timely rescue, a convenient escape/excuse

watarimásu, wataru *v* 渡ります, 渡る crosses over

watarō´ *v* 渡ろう = **watarimashō´** 渡りましょう (let's cross over!)

watasanai *v* 渡さない = **watashi-masén** 渡しません (not hand it over; not ferry)

watase *v* 渡せ [IMPERATIVE] (hand it over!) → **watashimásu** 渡します

wataséba *v* 渡せば (if one hands it over; if one ferries) → **watashimásu** 渡します

watasemásu, wataseru *v* 渡せます, 渡せる can hand it over; can ferry

watasenai *v* 渡せない = **watasemasén** 渡せません (cannot hand it over; cannot ferry)

wataséba *v* 渡せれば (if one can hand it over; if one can ferry) → **wa-tasemásu** 渡せます

watásete *v* 渡せて → **watasemásu** 渡せます

watashi *pron* 私・わたし = [BOOKISH] **watakushi** 私・わたくし I/me

watashi-búne *n* 渡し舟 ferryboat

watashimásu, watasu *v* 渡します, 渡す hands it over; ferries

watáshí-táchi *pron* わたし[私]達 we, us (= **watakushí-tachi** わたくし[私]達)

watashite *v* 渡して → **watashimásu** 渡します

watasō *v* 渡そう = **watashimashō´** 渡しましょう (let's hand it over!; let's ferry them over!)

watasu *v* 渡す = **watashimásu** 渡します (hands it over; ferries)

watatte *v* 渡って → **watarimásu** 渡ります

watta *v* 割った = **warimáshita** 割りました (divided/ … it)

watte *v* 割って → **warimásu** 割ります

watto *n* ワット watt

waza *n* 業 trick, feat

waza *n* 技 skill, technique, art (= **gijutsu** 技術)

wáza-to *adv* わざと deliberately, on purpose, intentionally (= **ito-teki ni** 意図的に, **koi ni** 故意に, **aete** あえて)

wazawai *n* 災い misfortune, mishap, disaster, calamity (= **sainan** 災難)

wázawaza *adv* わざわざ expressly, especially; purposely (= **wáza-to** わざと, **ito-teki ni** 意図的に, **koi ni** 故意に, **aete** あえて)

wazuka *adj* わずか a few, a little (= **sukoshi** 少し)

wazurai *n* 煩い・わずらい [BOOKISH] trouble, worry

wazurai *n* 患い [BOOKISH] illness (= **byōki** 病気)

wazuraimásu, wazurau *v* 煩います, 煩う worries about, is troubled by

wazuraimásu, wazurau *v* 患います, 患う has trouble with (*one's eyes*), suffers from (*an ailment*): **mé o ~** 目を患います has trouble with one's eyes

wazuratte *v* 煩って・患って → **wazuraimásu** 煩います・患います

wazurawanai *adj* 煩わない = **wazu-raimasén** 煩いません (not worry …)

wazurawashíi *adj* 煩わしい troublesome; complicated

web *n* ウェブ World Wide Web, Internet

websaito *n* ウェブサイト website

weburogu *n* ウェブログ(= **burogu** ブログ) weblog, blog (*Internet*)

wísukii *n* ウィスキー whisky

witto *n* ウィット wit (= **kichi** 機知, **tonchi** とんち・頓知・頓智)

285

Y

yá *n* 矢 arrow
ya-jirushi *n* 矢印 arrow sign (*such as* "→", "←", "↑", "↓")

ya-..., **...-ya** *prefix, suffix* 夜... , ... 夜 night (= **ban** 晩): **shū-ya** 終夜 all night (= **ōru-naito** オールナイト)

yá-gu *n* 夜具 [BOOKISH] bedclothes; top quilt

yá-kan *n* 夜間 [BOOKISH] (*at*) night

ya-kei *n* 夜景 night view

ya-kin *n* 夜勤 nightwork

ya-kō-ressha *n* 夜行列車 night train

ya-... *prefix* 野... wild, field

ya-chō *n* 野鳥 wild bird

ya-ei *n* 野営 camp, bivouac

yá-gai *n* 野外 outdoors, in the field (= **auto-doa** アウトドア): **yagai-katsudō** 野外活動 outdoor activity

ya-jū *n* 野獣 [BOOKISH] wild beast

ya-ken *n* 野犬 wild dog

ya-sei (no) *adj* 野性(の) wild, not cultivated

ya-sen *n* 野戦 open battle: **yasen-byōin** 野戦病院 field hospital

... ya ... *conj* ...や... and ... and ... (*choosing typical items*)

... -ya *suffix* ...屋 (*name of certain*) shop, shopkeeper, dealer; house (→ (**o-)sobá-ya** (お)蕎麦屋: **rāmen-ya** ラーメン屋 Ramen shop: **karē-ya** カレー屋 curry shop

yā´ *interj* やあ hi! hello! (*mostly male. very INFORMAL. Cannot be used to address a superior*)

yabái *adj* やばい 1. (*very INFORMAL*) dangerous (*will get you into trouble*) 2. (SLANG) awesome

yaban (na) *adj* 野蛮(な) barbarous, barbarian, savage: **yaban-jín** 野蛮人 a barbarian, a savage

yabō *n* 野望 ambition [IN NEGATIVE SENSE] (= **yashin** 野心, **taishi** 大志, **taibō** 大望 [IN NEGATIVE SENSE])

yábo (na) *adj* 野暮(な) rustic, inelegant

yabo-yō *n* 野暮用 small errand to run

yabu *n* ヤブ・薮 bush, thicket

yabu-hebi *n* やぶ蛇 boomerang (*something injures the originator*), waking a sleeping giant

yabu-isha *n* ヤブ[薮]医者 quack doctor

yabu-ka *n* ヤブカ・薮蚊 striped mosquito

yabúite *v* 破いて → **yabukimásu** 破きます

yabukánai *v* 破かない = **yabukimasén** 破きません (not tear it)

yabúke *v* 破け [IMPERATIVE] (tear it!) → **yabukimásu** 破きます

yabukemásu, yabukéru *v* 破けます, 破ける 1. it tears, bursts; is frustrated 2. can tear/burst it (= **yaburemásu** 破れます)

yabukénai *v* 破けない = **yabukemasén** 破けません (it does not tear)

yabúkete *v* 破けて → **yabukemásu** 破けます

yabukimásu, yabúku *v* 破きます, 破く tears (*bursts*) it; frustrates; violates; defeats

yaburánai *v* 破らない = **yaburimasén** 破りません (not tear it)

yabure *v* 破れ [IMPERAITIVE] (tear it!) → **yaburimásu** 破ります

yabure-kabure *n* やぶれ[破れ]かぶれ desperation (= **jibōjiki** 自暴自棄)

yaburemásu, yaburéru *v* 破れます, 破れる 1. it tears, bursts; is frustrated 2. can tear/burst it

yaburemásu, yaburéru *v* 敗れます, 敗れる loses

yaburénai *v* 破れない = **yaburemasén** 破れません (it does not tear)

yaburénai *v* 敗れない = **yaburemasén** 敗れません (it does not lose)

yabúrete *v* 破れて・敗れて → **yaburemásu** 破れます・敗れます

yaburimásu, yabúru *v* 破ります, 破る tears (*bursts*) it; frustrates; violates; defeats

yabusaka de (wa) arimasen (nai) *v* やぶさかで(は)ありません (ない) is willing to do

yabútte *v* 破って → **yaburimásu** 破ります

yá-chin *n* 家賃 house rent

yádo, yado-ya *n* 宿, 宿屋 inn

yagate *adv* やがて before long; in time (= **mamonaku** まもなく)

yági *n* ヤギ・山羊 goat

yahári *adv* やはり also; either; after all; just we/I thought! (= **yappari** やっぱり)

yaiba *n* やいば・刃 blade; sword

yaite *v* 焼いて・妬いて → **yakimásu** 焼きます・妬きます

yáji *n* やじ・野次 heckling

yajiuma *n* やじうま・野次馬 rubbernecker: **yajiuma-konjō** やじうま根性 extreme curiosity

yakamashíi *adj* やかましい [INFORMAL] noisy, boisterous, clamorous; annoying; overly strict [IN NEGATIVE SENSE]

yakan *n* やかん teakettle

yakanai *v* 焼かない = **yakimásén** 焼きません (not burn it)

yakanai *v* 妬かない = **yakimásén** 妬きません (is not jealous, not envy)

yake *n* やけ・自棄 [IMPERATIVE] (burn/broil it!) → **yakimásu** 焼きます

yáke *n* やけ・自棄 desperation(= **jibō-jiki** 自暴自棄): **yáke ni** やけに excessively, unbearably, terribly; ~ **(-kuso) ni nátte** やけ(くそ)になって desperately, from (*out of*) despair

yakéba *v* 焼けば (if one burns/broils it) → **yakimásu** 焼きます

yakéba *v* 妬けば (if one is jealous, if one envies) → **yakimásu** 妬きます

yakedo *n* やけど・火傷 burn, scald (*on the skin*) (= **nesshō** 熱傷)

yakemásu, yakeru *v* 焼けます, 焼ける **1.** it burns; it is baked **2.** can burn it

yakemásu, yakeru *v* 妬けます, 妬ける is jealous, envies

yakenai *v* 焼けない = **yakemásén** 焼けません (it does not burn; cannot burn it)

yakenai *v* 妬けない = **yakemásén** 妬けません (is not jealous, not envy)

yakete *v* 焼けて・妬けて → **yakemásu** 焼けます・妬けます

yaki *n* 焼き baking, burning, broiling; tempering; exposure

yaki-... *prefix* 焼き… roast: **(ishi-)yaki**

imo (石) 焼き芋 (stone-)baked yam

yaki-dō'fu *n* 焼き豆腐 broiled bean curd

yakí-guri *n* 焼き栗 roasted chestnuts

yaki-gushi *n* 焼き串 skewer, spit

yaki-meshi *n* 焼き飯 fried rice

yaki-móchi *n* やきもち・焼き餅 jealousy (= **shitto** 嫉妬)

yaki-mochi *n* やきもち・焼き餅 toasted rice-cake

yaki-mono *n* 焼き物 **1.** pottery **2.** broiled food/dishes

yaki-niku *n* 焼き肉・焼肉 grilled slices of meat

yaki-soba *n* 焼きそば・やきそば chow mein; fried Chinese noodle

yaki-tori *n* 焼き鳥・やきとり chicken shishkebab (*skewers*): **yakitori-ya** 焼き鳥屋 a *yakitori* shop/stand

...-yaki *suffix* …焼 (*ceramic*) ware from …; **Imari-yaki** 伊万里焼 Imari (*ware*)

yakimásu, yaku *v* 焼きます, 焼く burns/broils it, bakes (*roasts, toasts*) it

yakimásu, yaku *v* 妬きます, 妬く is jealous, envies

yákkai *n* 厄介・やっかい (**go-yákkai** ご厄介) trouble, bother (= **meiwaku** 迷惑, **go-meiwaku** ご迷惑): **yákkai (na)** 厄介・やっかい(な) troublesome, annoying

yakko *n* やっこ・奴 **1.** servant, slave **2.** [IN NEGATIVE SENSE] (*undesirable*) person/one: **yakko-san** やっこ[奴]さん that guy, he/him (= **yatsu** やつ・奴, **aitsu** あいつ). **3.** = **yakko-dō'fu** やっこ[奴]豆腐 (*parboiled*) tofu (*bean-curd cubes*); **hiya-yakko** 冷や奴 cold tofu

yakkyoku *n* 薬局 pharmacy, drugstore

yaku *v* 焼く = **yakimásu** 焼きます (burns it, bakes it)

yaku *v* 妬く = **yakimásu** 妬きます (is jealous, envies)

yaku *n* ヤク yak (*animal*)

yakú *n* 訳 translation, translated word (→ **honyaku** 翻訳, **tsūyaku** 通訳)

yáku(...) *adj* 約(…) approximately, about … (= **oyoso** およそ, **daitai** 大体)

yaku *n* 役 **1.** (*cast of*) players **2.** part, role, duty

yaku-mé *n* 役目(**o-yakume** お役目) duty, function (= **yakuwari** 役割)

yaku-sha *n* 役者 actor (= **haiyū** 俳優), actress (= **joyū** 女優)

yaku-wari *n* 役割 role, part (= **yakume** 役目)

yaku-... 役...(**o-yaku...** お役...) service (*government, official*), use
o-yaku ni tatereba saiwai desu お役に立てれば幸いです [HUMBLE] I hope I/it can be of some help to you.
o-yaku ni tatezu (ni) sumimasen お役に立てず(に)すみません [HUMBLE] I am sorry for not being able to help you.

yaku-nin *n* 役人 (**o-yaku-nin** お役人) public servant, government official (= **kōmuin** 公務員)

yaku-sho *n* 役所 (**o-yaku-sho** お役所) government office (→ **shi-yakusho** 市役所, **ku-yakusho** 区役所)

yaku *n* 薬 drug (= **mayaku** 麻薬) (→ **kusuri** 薬)

...-yaku, yaku-... *suffix, prefix* ...-薬, 薬... medicines, drugs

yaku-hin *n* 薬品 drugs; chemicals

yaku-mi *n* 薬味 1. spice (→ **supaisu** スパイス, **kōshin-ryō** 香辛料), condiment 2. drug ingredient

yaku-sō *n* 薬草 medicinal herb

yaku-zai *n* 薬剤 [BOOKISH] pharmaceuticals, medicines (= **kusuri** 薬): **yaku-zai-shi** 薬剤師 pharmacist

yaku-dachimásu, yaku-dátsu *v* 役立ちます, 役立つ serves a purpose, is useful

yaku-datánai *v* 役立たない = **yaku-dachimasén** 役立ちません (not useful)

yakú-datemásu, yakú-datéru *v* 役立てます, 役立てる puts it to use

yakú ni tachimásu (tátsu) *v* 役に立ちます(立つ) → **yaku-dachimásu** 役立てる

yakú ni tatemásu (tatéru) *v* 役に立てます(立てる) puts it to use (= **yakú-datemásu** 役立てます)

yakusánai *v* 訳さない = **yakushimasén** 訳しません (not translate)

yakúse *v* 訳せ [IMPERATIVE] (translate!) → **yakushimásu** 訳します

yakusemásu, yakuséru *v* 訳せます, 訳せる can translate

yakusénai *v* 訳せない = **yakusemasén**

訳せません (cannot translate)

yakúsete *v* 訳せて → **yakusemásu** 訳せます

yakushimásu, yakúsú *v* 訳します, 訳す translates

yakúshite *v* 訳して → **yakushimásu** 訳します

yakusó´ *v* 訳そう = **yakushimashō´** 訳しましょう (let's translate!)

yakusoku *n* 約束 (**o-yakusoku** お約束) promise, agreement, appointment, engagement, date, commitment: ~ **shimásu** 約束します promises, agrees

yakusoku-goto *n* 約束事 a promise

yakuza *n* やくざ gangster, hoodlum

yákuza (na) *adj* やくざ(な) no-good, worthless; ~ **na kagyō** やくざな稼業 improper work; coarse

yakyū *n* 野球 baseball (= **bēsubōru** ベースボール)

yakyū-jō *n* 野球場 ball park, (*baseball*) stadium

yamá *n* 山 1. mountain 2. heap, pile, bunch: **shorui no** ~ 書類の山 pile of documents 3. speculation, venture 4. → **yamá(-ba)** 山(場)

yama-arashi *n* ヤマアラシ・山荒 porcupine

yama-arashi *n* 山嵐, mountain storm

yama-aruki *n* 山歩き trekking (= **haikingu** ハイキング)

yamá(-ba) *n* 山(場) climax

yama-biko *n* やまびこ・山彦 echo (= **kodama** こだま・木霊)

yama-buki *n* ヤマブキ・山吹 Japanese rose: **yamabuki-iro** 山吹色 bright yellow

yama-goya *n* 山小屋 cabin, mountain lodge

yama-imo *n* ヤマイモ・山芋 yam

yama-neko *n* ヤマネコ・山猫 wild cat

yama-nóbori *n* 山登り mountain-climbing (= **tozan** 登山)

yama no fumoto *n* 山のふもと[麓] the base of a mountain (= **yamasuso** 山裾)

yama-otoko *n* 山男 1. mountaineer 2. woodsman 3. monster living in the heart of a mountain

yama-suso *n* 山裾 the base of a moun-

tain (= **yama no fumoto** 山のふもと
[麓])

yamanai ν やまない = **yamimásén** やみ
ません (not stop)

yama-shi n 山師 speculator

yamashíi adj やましい ashamed of
oneself; has guilty feeling

yama-te n 山手, yama-no-te 山手・山
の手 uptown; the bluff: **Yama-no-te-
sen** 山の手線 Yamanote Line

Yámato n 大和 Japan (an ancient name)

yamato-kotoba n 大和言葉 words of
Japanese origin, native Japanese words
(= **wago** 和語)

yamato-nadeshiko n ヤマトナデシ
コ・大和撫子 1. dianthus (flower)
2. beautiful and modest Japanese
woman

yame ro ν 止めろ [IMPERATIVE] (stop
it!) → **yamemásu** 止めます

yaméba ν 止めば (if it stops) → yamimásu 止めます

yamemásu, yameru ν 止めます, 止め
る stops it; abolishes, abstains from,
gives up

yamemásu, yameru ν 辞めます, 辞め
る resigns, quits

yamenai ν 止めない = **yamemasén** 止
めません (not stop it)

yameraremásu, yamerareru ν 止めら
れます, 止められる can stop it

yamerarenai ν 止められない =
yameraremasén 止められません
(cannot stop it)

yameréba ν 止めれば (if one stops it)
→ **yamemásu** 止めます

yamete ν 止めて → **yamemásu** 止め
ます

yameyō ν 止めよう = **yamemashō´**
止めましょう (let's stop it!)

yamí n 闇 1. darkness (= **kurayamí**
暗闇) 2. disorder 3. black market (=
yamí-ichí 闇市) 4. anything illicit,
the dark (= **fuhō na** 不法な)

yamí-ichi(ba) n 闇市(場) black market

yamí-kumo (ni) adv 闇雲(に) at
random, in a blind way

yamí-sōba n 闇相場 black-market price

yamimásu, yamu ν 止みます, 止む
it stops

yamō´ ν 止もう → yamimásu 止みま
す (about to stop)

yamome n やもめ widow

yámori n ヤモリ・守宮 gecko

yamu ν 止む = **yamimásu** 止みます
(it stops)

yamu-o-énai ν やむを得ない = **yamu-
o-émasén** やむを得ません unavoidable
(= **sakerarénai** 避けられない)

yanagi n ヤナギ・柳 willow

yancha (na) adj やんちゃ(な)
naughty, mischievous (commonly used
for boys) (= **wanpaku (na)** 腕白・わん
ぱく(な))

yanda ν 止んだ = **yamimáshita** 止みま
した (it stopped)

yande ν 止んで → **yamimásu** 止みます

yáne n 屋根 roof

yaní n やに・脂 resin, gum → meyaní
目やに・目脂

yánushi n 家主 landlord, landlady
(= **ōya(-san)** 大家(さん))

yaochō n 八百長 fixed game

yaoya n 八百屋 greengrocer, vegetable
market

yappári adv やっぱり [INFORMAL] also;
either; as I thought (= **yahári** やはり)

yarakashimásu, yarakasu ν やらかし
ます, やらかす [INFORMAL] does it [IN
NEGATIVE SENSE] (= **shimásu** します);
héma o ~ へまをやらかします makes
a damn mess of it

yaranai ν やらない = **yarimasén** やり
ません (not give/send/do/…)

yararemásu, yarareru ν やられます,
やられる gets had/hit (= beaten),
outwitted, robbed, ripped off, beset (by
illness), wounded, killed, …

yare ν やれ [IMPERATIVE] (give/send/
do/… !) → **yarimásu** やります

yaréba ν やれば (if one does) →
yarimásu やります

yaremásu, yareru ν やれます, やれる
1. can give 2. can do

yaremásu, yareru ν 遣れます, 遣れる
can send

yarenai ν やれない = **yaremásén** やれ
ません (cannot give/do)

yarete ν やれて → yaremásu やれ
ます

yari *n* やり・槍 spear
yari-kata *n* やり方 way, method, process, manner
yarimásu, yaru *v* やります, やる does
yarimásu, yaru *v* やります, やる・遣る・遣る **1.** gives **2.** sends: **tegami o yarimásu** 手紙をやります send a letter **3.** **íp-pai yarimásu** 一杯やります has a drink **4.** has sex
yari-naoshimásu, yari-naósu *v* やり直します, やり直す redoes it, does it over (*again*)
yari-sokonaimásu, yari-sokonáu *v* やり損ないます, やり損なう botches, misses
yarō´ *v* やろう = **yarimashō´** やりましょう (let's do …!)
yaru *v* やる = **yarimásu** やります (does; gives; sends; etc.)
yasai *n* 野菜 (**o-yásai** お野菜) vegetables
yasashii *adj* 優しい・やさしい gentle; kind, generous (= **shinsetsu** 親切)
yasashii *adj* 易しい・やさしい easy, simple
yasashiku *adj* 優しく・やさしく gently; politely
yase-gaman *n* やせ[痩せ]我慢: ~ **shimásu** やせ我慢します plays the martyr
yasemásu, yaseru *v* 痩せます, 痩せる gets thin; **yasete imásu** 痩せています is thin
yáshi *n* ヤシ・椰子 (*coconut*) palm
yáshin *n* 野心 ambition [IN NEGATIVE SENSE] (= **yabō** 野望; **taishi** 大志, **taibō** 大望)
yashinai *n* 養い foster(ing)
yashinaimásu, yashinau *v* 養います, 養う brings up, rears; fosters; nourishes
yashinatte *v* 養って → **yashinaimásu** 養います
yashinawanai *v* 養わない = **yashinaimásén** 養いません (not rear)
… -yasu, yasu-… *suffix, prefix* …安, 安… cheap(er/lower) by … ; **hyakuén-yasu** 百円安 down/off by ¥100
yasúi *adj* 安い cheap, low(-priced)
yasu-mono *n* 安物 cheap stuff
yasu-ne *n* 安値 low price

yasu-ukeai *n* 安請け合い easy promise
yasu-uri *n* 安売り bargain (= **bāgen** バーゲン)
yasude *n* ヤスデ millipede (*animal*)
yasúi *adj* やすい・易い (= **shi-yasúi** しやすい) easy (*to do*)
yasúi *adj* やすい (= **shi-yasúi** しやすい) likely/apt to (*do*), tends to
yasúme *v* 休め [IMPERATIVE] (rest!) → **yasumimásu** 休みます
yasúmeba *v* 休めば (if one rests) → **yasumimásu** 休みます
yasumemásu, yasuméru *v* 休めます, 休める **1.** rest/relax it, let it rest; ease it **2.** can rest
yasuméreba *v* 休めれば (if we let it rest) → **yasumemásu** 休めます
yasumeyō´ *v* 休めよう = **yasumemashō´** 休めましょう (let's let it rest!)
yasumí *n* 休み (**o-yasumi** お休み) **1.** rest = [BOOKISH] **kyūkei** 休憩) **2.** break, pause (= **teishi** 停止, **chūdan** 中断) **3.** recess (= **kyūkei jikan** 休憩時間) **4.** time off, vacation, holiday (= **kyūka** 休暇) **5.** → **O-yasuminasái** おやすみなさい
yasumimásu, yasúmu *v* 休みます, 休む rests, relaxes, takes time off; stays away (from school); goes to bed, sleeps
yasumō´ *v* 休もう = **yasumimashō´** 休みましょう(let's rest!)
yasúnde *v* 休んで → **yasumimásu** 休みます
yasuraka (na/ni) *adj, adv* 安らか(な/に) peaceful(ly)
yasuri *n* やすり file, rasp
yasurí-gami *n* やすり紙 sandpaper (= **kami-yásuri** 紙やすり)
yatai *n* 屋台 street stall; stand
yatara *adv* やたら: **yatara na** やたらな indiscriminate, reckless, random: **yatara ni** やたらに indiscriminately, randomly, recklessly, blindly, unduly
yatō *n* 野党 opposition party
yatóe *v* 雇え [IMPERATIVE] (hire them!) → **yatoimásu** 雇います
yatóeba *v* 雇えば (if one hires) → **yatoimásu** 雇います
yatoéreba *v* 雇えれば (if one can hire) → **yatoemásu** 雇えます

yatoéru v 雇える = **yatoemásu** 雇えます (can employ/hire)

yatói n 雇い employment

yatoimásu, yatóu v 雇います, 雇う employs, hires

yatótte v 雇って → **yatoimásu** 雇います

yatóu v 雇う = **yatoimásu** 雇います (employs)

yatowánai v 雇わない = **yatoimasén** 雇いません (not hire)

yatsú n 八つ eight (= **yattsú** 八つ)

yatsuatari n 八つ当たり・やつあたり: ~ **shimásu** 八つ当たりします takes out on

yátsu n やつ・奴 [INFORMAL] **1.** guy, fellow [IN NEGATIVE SENSE] (*undesirable*) person/one (= **aitsu** あいつ) **2.** (*undesirable*) thing/one **3.** he/him

yatsude n ヤツデ fatsia

yattekimásu, yattekúru v やってきます, やってくる comes, comes along

yatto adv やっと at last; barely, with difficulty

yattoko n やっとこ pincers, pliers

yattsú n 八つ eight; eight years old

yawarakái adj 軟らかい・柔らかい soft, mild

yáya adj やや a little, slightly: ~ **átte** ややあって after a little while

yaya(k)koshíi adj やや(っ)こしい complicated; puzzling; tangled; troublesome

ye... → **e...**

yó n 世 the world at large, the public

yo-nó-naka n 世の中 the world at large, society

yó-ron n 世論 public opinion

yó n 代 the age, the times; one's lifetime

yó n 夜 night (= **yóru** 夜)

yo-aké n 夜明け dawn

yo-fúkashi n 夜更かし staying up late: ~ **o shimásu** 夜更かしをします stays up late

yo-máwari n 夜回り night watchman

yo-naká n 夜中 middle of the night

yóru n 夜 night

yo-... prefix 四 four

yó-ji n 四時 four o'clock

yo-jō´-han n 四畳半 four-and-a-half

mat area, a small Japanese room

yo-ban, yón-ban n 四番 number four

yo-nen n 四年 **1.** fourth year **2.** four years (= **yonén-kan** 四年間)

yon-én-sei n 四年生 **1.** fourth-year student (*at elementary school*) **2.** senior (*at university/college*)

yo-nín n 四人 four people

... yo interj ...よ **1.** indeed, mind you, I tell/warn/alert you **2.** (*reinforces* IMPERATIVE)

yō´ n 要 gist (= **yō´shi** 要旨, **yōryō´** 要領)

yō´ n 用 (go-yō ご用) **1.** business; errand (= **yōji** 用事) **2.** use, service **3.** going to the bathroom

yō-ji n 用事 business, errand

yō-ken n 用件 business (*something to tell, something to do*)

yō-mú-in n 用務員 custodian, janitor, servant (*in the school, office, etc.*)

yō-táshi n 用足し business, errand

yō-... prefix 洋... Western

yō-fuku n 洋服 (o-yōfuku お洋服) (Western-style) clothes, a suit, a dress (= **fuku** 服): (yō)fuku-ya (洋)服屋 tailor, clothing shop; **yōfuku-burashi** 洋服ブラシ cloth-brush; **yōfuku-dansu** 洋服ダンス wardrobe

yō-ga n 洋画 **1.** foreign movie **2.** Western-style painting

yō-gaku n 洋楽 Western-style music

yō-gása n 洋傘 (*Western-style*) umbrella (= **kasa** 傘)

yō-gáshi n 洋菓子 western cakes/sweets

yō-hin n 洋品 haberdashery

yō-kan n 洋館 Western-style building

yō-ma n 洋間 Western-style room

yō-sai n 洋裁 dressmaking; **yōsáishi** 洋裁師 dressmaker

yō-shi n 洋紙 Western paper

yō-shoku n 洋食 foreign (*Western*) food

yō-shu n 洋酒 liquor (*Western*)

yō-... prefix 養... foster, protection

yō-fubo n 養父母 adoptive parents

yō´-jo n 養女 adopted daughter; (... **o**) ~ **ni shimásu** (...を)養女にします adopts (*a girl*)

yō-shi n 養子 adopted child; (... **o**)

~ **ni shimásu** (…を)養子にします
adopts a child

yō-iku n 養育 [BOOKISH] **1.** bringing up
children, education: ~ **shimásu** 養育し
ます brings up; **yōiku-hi** 養育費 expense
of bringing up children **2.** protection
(of old people, orphan children, sick
people, etc.); **yōiku-in** 養育院 asylum

yō-rōin n 養老院 old people's home (=
rōjin hōmu 老人ホーム)

yobanai v 呼ばない = **yobimasén** 呼び
ません (not call/invite)

yobe v 呼べ [IMPERATIVE] (call!) →
yobimásu 呼びます

yobéba v 呼べば (if one calls/invites)
→ **yobimásu** 呼びます

yobemásu, yoberu v 呼べます、呼べ
る **1.** can call **2.** can invite

yobenai v 呼べない = **yobemasén** 呼べ
ません (cannot call/invite)

yobete v 呼べて → **yobemásu** 呼べ
ます

yóbi n 予備 preparation: **yóbi (no)** 予備
(の) reserve, spare

yobi-kō n 予備校 prep school, cram
school

yobi-sénkyo n 予備選挙 a primary
election

yobimásu, yobu v 呼びます、呼ぶ
1. calls; names; summons **2.** invites

yobō v 呼ぼう = **yobimashō´** 呼びまし
ょう (let's call/invite!)

yobō n 予防 precaution, prevention: ~
shimásu 予防します prevents, wards off
yobō-sesshu 予防接種 = **yobō-
chū´sha** 予防注射 inoculation, vaccination (injection)

yōbō n 要望 strong desire

yōbō n 容貌 facial appearance

yobun (no/ni) adj, adv 余分(の/に)
extra, excess

yōbun n 養分 nutrient substance
(= **eiyōbun** 栄養分)

yóchi n 余地 [BOOKISH] room, space,
margin, leeway (= **yutori** ゆとり, **yoyū**
余裕): **giron no ~ ga arimasen** 議論の
余地がありません There is no room for
debate.: **utagai no ~ ga arimasen** 疑い
の余地がありません There is no doubt
about it (at all).

yóchi n 予知 prediction: ~ **shimásu**
予知します predicts, forecasts, foresees,
foretells

yochi-nōryoku 予知能力 ability to
foresee the future

yochi (na) adj 幼稚(な) childish: ~ **na
kangae** 幼稚な考え childish idea
yōchi-en 幼稚園 kindergarten

yodare n よだれ drool: ~ **ga déru** よだ
れが出る drool comes out

yōdai n 容態・容体・様態 health
condition (commonly of patient)
(= **yōtai** 容態, **byōjō** 病状)

yō´do n ヨード iodine

yóeba v 酔えば = **yóya** 酔や (if one
gets drunk) → **yoimásu** 酔います

yōeki n 溶液 liquid solution

yōen adj 妖艶 seductive beauty,
fascinatingly elegant, bewitching
(= **adeyaka** あでやか・艶やか)

yoga n ヨガ yoga

yō´gan n 溶岩 lava

yogen n 予言 prediction: ~ **shimásu**
予言します predicts

yōgí-sha n 容疑者 a suspect

yogo n 予後 prognosis: **yogo-furyō**
予後不良 poor prognosis: **yogo-ryōkō**
予後良好 good prognosis: **yogo-inshi**
予後因子 prognostic factor

yōgo n 擁護 [BOOKISH] protection,
support: ~ **shimásu** 擁護します
protects, supports; **jinken-yōgo** 人権
擁護 protection of human rights;
dōbutsu-yōgo-dantai 動物擁護団体
animal protection association

… **yōgo** suffix …用語 (special) term
(technical word, etc.): **kōyōgo** 公用語
national language: **senmon-yōgo** 専門
用語 technical term: **sabetsu-yōgo** 差別
用語 discriminatory words

yogore n 汚れ dirt, smudge, blot, blotch

yogoremásu, yogoreru v 汚れます、
汚れる gets soiled, smudged; **yogorete
imásu** 汚れています is dirty

yogorenai v 汚れない = **yogoremasén**
汚れません (not get soiled)

yogosanai v 汚さない = **yogoshimasén**
汚しません (not soil)

yogoshimásu, yogosu v 汚します、汚
す soils, dirties, stains

yōˊgu *n* 用具 tools, implements, instruments, kit; **yōgu-búkuro** 用具袋 kit bag; **yōgú-bako** 用具箱 tool box

yōguruto *n* ヨーグルト yogurt

yoha *n* 余波 after-effect (*of typhoon, etc.*), aftermath

yohaku *n* 余白 margin, blank (*space*) (= **supēsu** スペース)

yōhin *n* 用品 = **...-yōˊhin** ...用品 utensils, appliances, supplies, necessities; **nichi-yōhin** 日用品 daily necessities; **jimu-yōhin** 事務用品 office supplies

yohō *n* 予報 forecast, prediction; **tenki-yóhō** 天気予報 weather forecast

yohodo *adv* よほど・余程 considerably, a good deal (= **yoppodo** よっぽど); **~ no koto ga nai kagiri** よほどのことがない限り unless something really important comes up

yoi *n* 宵 [BOOKISH] early part of the night, just after nightfall; **yoi no myōjō** 宵の明星 Venus in the evening sky

yói *adj* 良い・よい (= **íi** いい) good [NEGATIVE] **yóku arimasén** 良くありません; (*past*) **yókatta desu** 良かったです was good

yoi *n* 酔い **1.** intoxication, drunkenness **2.** motion sickness (*seasick, carsick, airsick, etc.*); **kuruma-yoi** 車酔い car sickness; **norimono-yói** 乗り物酔い travel sickness

yōˊi *n* 用意 preparation; caution (= **junbi** 準備); **... no ~ o shimásu** ...の用意をします prepares for ...

yoimásu, yóu *v* 酔います, 酔う gets drunk; gets seasick, carsick, airsick

yoisho *interj* よいしょ upsy-daisy!, alley-oop!, heave-ho!

yōji *n* 楊枝・ようじ toothpick = **tsuma-yōˊji** つまようじ・爪楊枝

yōˊji *n* 幼児 [BOOKISH] infant

yōˊji *n* 幼時 [BOOKISH] childhood: **yōji-taiken** 幼時体験 childhood experiences

yōˊjin *n* 用心 precaution, caution, care; **"hi no yōˊjin"**「火の用心」 "Be careful of fire!"

yōjin-bō *n* 用心棒 bodyguard (= **bodii gādo** ボディーガード)

yōjin-bukái *adj* 用心深い cautious,

careful (= **shinchō** 慎重)

yoka *n* 余暇 spare time (= **hima (na jikan)** 暇(な時間))

yōka *n* 八日 **1.** 8th day (*of a month*) **2.** (*for*) eight days (= **yōka-kan** 八日間)

yokan *n* 予感 premonition, foreboding

yōˊkan *n* ヨウカン・羊羹 sweet bars of bean paste and agar-agar flavored with chestnut, plum, etc.

yokei (na) *adj* 余計(な) superfluous, unnecessary, uncalled-for: **yokei ni** 余計に unnecessarily

yokemásu, yokéru *v* 避けます, 避ける avoids, keeps away from

yoken *n* 予見 prediction (= **yochi** 予知): **~ shimásu** 予見します predicts, forecasts

yokénai *v* 避けない = **yokemásen** 避けません (not avoid)

yokeyōˊ *v* 避けよう = **yokemashōˊ** 避けましょう (let's avoid!)

yoki *n* 予期 expectation, anticipation: **~ shimásu** 予期します expects, anticipates

yōki *n* 容器 container, receptacle (= **iremono** 入れ物, **utsuwa** うつわ・器)

yōki *n* 陽気 **1.** weather **2.** cheerfulness, brightness, liveliness

yōki (na) *adj* 陽気な cheerful, bright, lively

yokin *n* 預金 deposit (*of money*)

yokin-kōˊza *n* 預金口座 bank account

yokin-tsūˊchō *n* 預金通帳 bankbook

yokka *n* 四日 **1.** 4th day (*of a month*) **2.** (*for*) four days (= **yokka-kan** 四日間)

yokkyū *n* 欲求 greed; desire, want (= **yoku** 欲, **yokubō** 欲望, **negai** 願い): **sandai-yokkyū** 三大欲求 three basic desires (*food appetite, sexual desire, and desire to sleep*) (*also known as part of the four Primitive Fountains: Food, Sleep, and Sex*)

yokkyū-fuman *n* 欲求不満 frustration (= **furasutorēshon** フラストレーション)

yoko *n* 横 **1.** side (= **soba** 側, **waki** 脇) **2.** the width (= **haba** 幅) **3.** sideways **4.** sidewise

yoko-chō *n* 横町 sidestreets, alley

yoko-ito *n* 横糸 woof (*horizontal threads*)

yoko-girimásu, yoko-gíru *v* 横切り
ます, 横切る crosses, cuts across,
intersects, passes

Yokohama *n* 横浜 Yokohama

Yokohamá-Eki *n* 横浜駅 Yokohama
Station

Yokohamá-kō *n* 横浜港 the port of
Yokohama

yokoku *n* 予告 advance notice; **eiga
no yokoku-hen** 映画の予告編 movie
trailer (= **torērā** トレーラー)

yoko ni narimásu (náru) *v* 横にな
ります(なる) lies down (= **yoko-tawárimásu** 横たわります)

yoko ni shimásu (suru) *v* 横にします
(する) lays down (= **yokotaemásu**
横たえます)

yokoshimásu, yokósu *v* 寄越します,
寄越す sends (*here*), hands over to me

Yō´koso. *interj* ようこそ Welcome!;
Nihon e Yōkoso 日本へようこそ
Welcome to Japan! (= **Yōkoso Nihon e**
ようこそ日本へ)

yokozuna *n* 横綱 grand champion
sumo wrestler

yokú *n* 欲 greed; desire, want (= **yokubō**
欲望)

　yokubō *n* 欲望 greed; desire, want
　(= **yoku** 欲)

　yoku o ieba 欲を言えば [IDIOM] if I
　am allowed to wish more

　yoku o kaku 欲をかく [IDIOM] gets
　greedy (= **yoku baru** 欲張る)

… yoku *suffix* …欲 desire: **shoku-yoku**
食欲 food appetite, desire for food or
drink; **sei-yoku** 性欲 sexual desire;
suimin-yoku 睡眠欲 desire to sleep (→
sandai-yokkyū 三大欲求)

yóku *adv* 良く・よく well, better; **kare
no koto wa ~ shitte imasu** 彼のことは
よく知っています I know him very
well.; **hayaku ~ narimasu-yōni** 早く良
くなりますように Hope you feel better
soon. (*to a sick person*)

　Yóku irasshaimáshita. *interj* よくいら
　っしゃいました. Welcome! (= **Yōkoso
　(irasshaimashita)** ようこそ(いらっし
　ゃいました))

yóku *adv* よく lots, much, thoroughly,
carefully; **~ yonde kudasai** よく読んで

下さい Please read it carefully.

yóku *adv* よく lots, often, frequently

yóku (-) … *prefix* 翌… the next (*day,
night, month, year;* date)

yoku-ban *n* 翌晩 [BOOKISH] the following night, the next night

yoku-getsu *n* 翌月 [BOOKISH] the following month, the next month

yoku-jitsu *n* 翌日 [BOOKISH] the following day, the next day

yoku-shū *n* 翌週 [BOOKISH] the following week, the next week

yoku-toshi *n* 翌年 [BOOKISH] the following year, the next year

yokubári *n* 欲張り a greedy person

yokubári (na) *adj* 欲張り(な) greedy

yokubarimásu, yokubáru *v* 欲張りま
す, 欲張る is greedy

yoku (-) … *prefix* 浴… bath (→
yukata 浴衣)

　yoku-jo *n* 浴場 [BOOKISH] bathhouse;
　kōshū-yokujō 公衆浴場 public bath (=
　(o-)furo-ya (お)風呂屋)

　yoku-shitsu *n* 浴室 bathroom (= **(o-)
　furo-ba** (お)風呂場)

　yoku-sō *n* 浴槽 bathtub

yōkyū *n* 要求 requirement, demand,
claim, request (= **yōsei** 要請)

yománai *v* 読まない = **yomimasén** 読み
ません (not read)

yome *n* 嫁 **1.** daughter-in-law **2.** bride
(= **o-yome-san** お嫁さん) **3.** = **yome-
san** 嫁さん [INFORMAL] (*my*) wife (=
óku-san 奥さん)

yómeba *v* 読めば (if one reads) →
yomimásu 読みます

yomi *n* 読み **1.** reading **2.** expectation,
forecast **3.** pronunciation; **on-yomi**
音読み Chinese pronunciation of
Kanji/Chinese characters; **kun-yomi**
訓読み Japanese pronunciation of
Kanji/Chinese characters

yomi-kata *n* 読み方 **1.** how to read
2. how to pronounce the Kanji/Chinese
characters

yomimásu, yómu *v* 読みます, 読む **1.**
reads **2.** reads out, pronounces
3. foresees, guesses

yōmō *n* 羊毛 wool

yón *n* 四・4 four

yon-bai n 四倍 four-fold, four times as much

yon-banmé (no), yo-banmé (no) adj 四番目(の) fourth

yón-ban n 四番 number four

yón-dai n 四台 four (machines, vehicles)

yón-do n 四度 four degrees; four times (= yón-kái 回回, yón-hén 四遍)

yon-do-mé n 四度目 the fourth time

yón-fun, yón-pun n 四分 four minutes

yón-hai n 四杯 four cupfuls

yón-hén n 四遍 four times

yón-hiki n 四匹 four (fishes/bugs, small animals)

yón-hon n 四本 four (pencils/bottles, long objects)

yón-hyaku n 四百・400 four hundred

yón-jū n 四十・40 forty

yon-kágetsu n 四か月 four months

yón-kai n 四階 four floors/stories; fourth floor

yón-kái n 四回 four times; yon kai-mé 四回目 the fourth time

yón-mai n 四枚 four sheets (flat things, papers, dishes, etc.)

yón-méi n 四名 four people (also yo-mei 四名, yo-nín 四人)

yon-mán n 四万 40,000 forty thousand

yón-pun n 四分 four minutes (also yón-fun 四分)

yón-satsu n 四冊 four copies (books, magazines)

yón-sén n 四千・4,000 four thousand

yón-tō n 四頭 four (horses/oxen, large animals)

yón-wa n 四羽 four (birds, rabbits) (also yón-ba 四羽)

... yō´ (na) suffix, adj ...よう[様](な) seem(ing) to be: yō ni ...よう[様]に (so as to be) like ...; suru yō ni iimásu するよう[様]に言います tells one to do it

yondokoro-nai adj よんどころない inevitable

yōniku n 羊肉 [BOOKISH] lamb (meat, includes mutton)

...-yō (no) adj ...用(の) for the use of ...

yopparai n 酔っ払い drunk (person)

yopparaimásu, yopparau v 酔っ払います, 酔っ払う gets drunk

yoppodo adv よっぽど considerably, a good deal (= yohodo よほど・余程)

yoranai v 拠らない = yorimasén 寄りません (not drop in)

yoranai v 拠らない = yorimasén 拠りません (not rely)

yoranai v 撚らない = yorimasén 撚りません (not twist)

yore v 寄れ [IMPERATIVE] (drop in!) → yorimásu 寄ります

yóre v 撚れ [IMPERATIVE] (twist it!) → yorimásu v 撚ります

yoréba v 拠れば (if one relies) → yorimásu 拠ります

yoréba v 寄れば (if one drops in) → yorimásu 寄ります

yoréba v 撚れば (if one twists) → yorimásu 撚ります

yoremásu, yoreru v 寄れます, 寄れる can drop in; can approach

yoremásu, yoréru v 撚れます, 撚れる can twist/twine

yorenai v 寄れない = yoremásén 寄れません (cannot drop in)

yorénai v 撚れない = yoremasén 撚れません(cannot twist)

yoreréba v 寄れれば (if one can drop in) → yoremásu 寄れます

yoréreba v 撚れれば (if one can twist) → yoremásu 撚れます

yorete v 寄れて → yoremásu 寄れます

yórete v 撚れて → yoremásu 撚れます

yori-... adj より... [+ADJECTIVE] more ..., ...-er [BOOKISH]

... yóri conj ...より 1. (more/rather/ other) than 2. from, out of; since

yoridori-midori n よりどりみどり choosing whichever one likes

yorigónomi n より好み・選り好み: ~ shimásu より好みします is choosy

yorimásu, yoru v 寄ります, 寄る drops in; approaches, comes near; meets

yorimásu, yoru v 拠ります, 拠る relies on; ... ni yotte ...によって, ... ni yoru to ...によると, ... ni yoréba ...によれば according to ...: tenki-yohō ni

yoreba 天気予報によれば according to the weather forecast

yorimásu, yóru v 撚ります, 撚る twists, twines (= **nejirimasu** 捻ります, **nejiru** 捻る)

yoro v 寄ろう = **yorimashố** 寄りましょう (let's drop in!; let's approach!)

yorố v 撚ろう = **yorimashố** 撚りましょう (let's twist it!)

yoroi n 鎧 armor

yoroi-do n よろい戸・鎧戸 shutter (*house*) (= **shattā** シャッター)

yorokobi n 喜び joy

yorokobimásu, yorokóbu v 喜びます, 喜ぶ is glad, happy, delighted; rejoices

yorokónde 喜んで **1.** adv gladly **2.** v → **yorokobimásu** 喜びます

yoro-mekí n よろめき an (*extramarital*) affair

yoro-mekimásu, yoro-méku v よろめきます, よろめく totters, falters, staggers; has an (*extra-marital*) affair

Yōróppa n ヨーロッパ Europe (= **Ōshū** 欧州)

yoroshii adj よろしい・宜しい very well; satisfactory

yoroshikáttara adv よろしかったら if you don't mind; if you like

yoroshiku n よろしく・宜しく **1.** (…ni) ~ (itte kudasái/o-tsutae kudasái) (…に)よろしく(言って下さい/お伝え下さい) Give my regards to … **2.** → **yoroshii** よろしい・宜しい **3.** Dố zo ~. どうぞよろしく. How do you do?; Please favor (*my request, me, mine*).

yóroyoro (to) adj, adv よろよろ(と) tottering, faltering, staggering; having an affair: ~ **(to) shimásu** よろよろ(と)します (= **yoromekimásu** よろめきます)

yoru v 寄る = **yorimásu** 寄ります (drops in)

yoru v 拠る・因る = **yorimásu** 拠る[因る]ます (relies); … **ni yoru to** …によると according to …

yóru v 撚る = **yorimásu** 撚ります (twists)

yōryō n 要領 **1.** gist: ~ **o enai kaitō** 要領を得ない回答 pointless answer, unclear answer **2.** knack: ~ **ga ii** 要領がいい is efficient (*person*)

yōsai n 要塞 fortress (*military facility*)

yosan n 予算 budget

yōsan n 養蚕 raising silkworms, silk farming, sericulture

yosánai v よさない = **yoshimásén** よしません (not stop doing it) (= **yamemasén** やめません)

yose n 寄席 vaudeville (*theater*)

yóse v 止せ [IMPERATIVE] (stop doing it!) → **yoshimásu** 止します

yóseba v 止せば (if they stop doing it) → **yoshimásu** 止します

yōseki n 容積 volume of a container

yosemásu, yoseru v 寄せます, 寄せる **1.** lets approach, brings near **2.** collects, gathers **3.** adds **4.** sends

yosen n 予選 preliminary; primary

yose-nabe n 寄せ鍋 chowder

yosenai v 寄せない = **yosemásen** 寄せません (not let approach; …)

yose-nami 寄せ波 surf

yoseréba v 寄せれば (if we let them approach; …) → **yosemásu** 寄せます

yose ro v 寄せろ [IMPERATIVE] (let them approach!) → **yosemásu** 寄せます

yosete v 寄せて → **yosemásu** 寄せます (lets approach; …)

yóshi n 由 reason; meaning; circumstance; means

Yóshi! interj よし! OK; very well

yō´shi n 用紙 forms, blanks, papers: **genkō-yóshi** 原稿用紙 manuscript paper used for writing Japanese vertically: **ankēto-yóshi** アンケート用紙 questionnaire (*originally came from French word "enquete"*)

yō´-shi n 要旨 summary, abstract (*gist*) (= **shu-shi** 主旨)

yoshimásu, yósu v 止します, 止す stops doing it (= **yamemásu** 止めます)

yō-shimásu, yō-súru v 要します, 要する needs, requires, takes, costs; summarizes, sums it up

yóshite v よして → **yoshimásu** よします (can stop doing it)

yōshoku n 養殖 raising, farming, culture: **yōshoku-shínju** 養殖真珠 cultured pearls

yoshū n 予習 preparatory study: ~ **shimásu** 予習します prepares, studies (*ahead*)

yosó *n* よそ・余所 somewhere else; alien, strange

yoso-mono *n* よそ者 outsider, stranger (= **yoso no hitó** よその人)

yosō *n* 予想 expectation, presumption: **~ shimásu** 予想します expects, anticipates, presumes; **~ íjō** 予想以上 above/beyond expectations

yosō´ *v* よそう = **yoshimashō´** よしましょう (let's stop doing it!)

yō´so *n* 要素 element

yosoku *n* 予測 forecast, prediction, estimate: **~ shimásu** 予測します forecasts, predicts, estimates

yósu *v* 止す = **yoshimásu** 止します (stops doing it)

yōsu *n* 様子・ようす circumstances; aspect; appearance, look

yōsui *n* 用水 diversion of water, service water, irrigation water

yōsui-ro *n* 用水路 irrigation canal

yō-súru *v* 要する = **yō-shimásu** 要します (needs, requires, takes, costs; summarizes, sums it up)

yō-súru ni *v* 要するに in summary, to sum it up, in short; in effect, what it amounts to (*boils down to*) is …; after all

yotamono *n* よた者・与太者 hoodlum

yotei *n* 予定 expectation, plan: **~ shimásu** 予定します schedules, plans

yōtén *n* 要点 gist, point

yotō *n* 与党 ruling party

yotsu-kado *n* 四つ角 intersection (*of two streets*), crossroads

yotta *v* 寄った = **yorimáshita** 寄りました (dropped in)

yotta *v* 拠った = **yorimáshita** 拠りました (relied)

yótta *v* 撚った = **yorimáshita** 撚りました (twisted)

yótta *v* 酔った = **yoimáshita** 酔いました (got drunk)

yotte *v* 寄って・拠って → **yorimásu** 寄ります・拠ります

yótte *v* 撚って → **yorimásu** 撚ります

yótte *v* 酔って → **yoimásu** 酔います

yotto *n* ヨット yacht

yottsú *n* 四つ four

yóu *v* 酔う = **yoimásu** 酔います (gets drunk; gets seasick; etc.)

yowái *adj* 弱い weak; frail; poor at (*math, etc.*); **sake ni ~** 酒に弱い easily intoxicated

yowa-mi *n* 弱み weakness, weak point

yowa-mushi *n* 弱虫 a cream puff, wimp

yowánai *v* 酔わない = **yoimasén** 酔いません (not get drunk)

yowasemásu, yowaséru *v* 酔わせます, 酔わせる gets one drunk, lets one get drunk

yoyaku *n* 予約 reservation, subscription, booking, appointment: **~ shimásu** 予約します makes a reservation

yōyaku *adv* ようやく finally, at last; barely

yōyaku *n* 要約 a summary: **~ shimásu** 要約します summarizes

yoyū *n* 余裕 room, leeway, margin, excess, surplus

yú *n* 湯 (**o-yu** お湯) hot water, warm water: **o-yu o wakashimásu** お湯を沸かします boils water

yu-dō´fu *n* 湯豆腐 tofu (*bean-curd*) cubes boiled in an earthen-ware pot

yu-ge *n* 湯気 steam

yu-nomi *n* 湯飲み, **yunomi-jáwan** 湯飲み茶碗 Japanese teacup

yu-tánpo *n* 湯たんぽ hot-water bottle

yu-wákashi *n* 湯沸かし teakettle, boiler (*for heating water*)

yu-zámashi *n* 湯冷まし cooled boiled water

yú *n* 湯 (**o-yu** お湯) = (**o-)furu** (お)風呂 bath: **o-yu ga wakimáshita** お湯が沸きました The bath is ready.: **otoko-yu** 男湯 men's section of a bathhouse: **on'na-yu** 女湯 women's section of a bathhouse

yú-bune *n* 湯船 bathtub

yu-zame *n* 湯冷め feeling chilly after taking a bath

yū *n* ゆう・言う = **iu** 言う, **iimásu** 言います (says)

yū *n* 結う = **yuu** 結う, **yuimásu** 結います does up one's hair

yū *n* 優 excellent (*grade*)

yū´-retsu *n* 優劣 relative merits (*superiority or inferiority*)

yū-ryō (na) *adj* 優良な superior

yū-shō n 優勝 (*winning*) the victory/championship: ~ **shimásu** 優勝します wins (*the victory*); **yūshō-sha** 優勝者 the winner, victor

yū-shū (na) adj 優秀な excellent, superior

yū-tō-sei n 優等生 model student

yū n 夕 evening (= **yū-gata** 夕方)

yū-bé n タベ evening

yū-dachi n 夕立 a sudden shower during afternoon or evening

yū-gao n 夕顔 moonflower

yū-gata n 夕方 evening

yū-giri n 夕霧 evening mist

yū-gure n 夕暮れ twilight (= **tasogare** たそがれ・黄昏); **yū-gure-doki** 夕暮れ 時 evening during the twilight hours

yū-han n 夕飯 = **yū-meshi** 夕飯 supper, dinner (= **yū-shoku** 夕食)

yū-hi n 夕日・夕陽 setting sun

yū-kan n 夕刊 evening paper

yū-kaze n 夕風 evening breeze

yū-moya n 夕もや・夕靄 evening fog

yū-shoku n 夕食 evening meal (*supper, dinner*) (= **yū-han, yū-meshi** 夕飯)

yū-yake n 夕焼け (*red sky at*) sunset

yū-... prefix 友... friend

yū-jin n 友人 [BOOKISH] friend (= **tomo** 友, **tomo-dachi** 友だち・友達)

yū-jō n 友情 friendship

yū-kō n 友好 [BOOKISH] (*official*) friendship, friendly relationship (*among countries, etc.*)

yū-be n ゆうべ・昨夜 last night (= **kinō no ban/yoru** 昨日の晩/夜, **saku-ban/ya** 昨夜/晩)

yūben n 雄弁 eloquence: **yūben (na)** 雄弁 (な) eloquent

yūben-ka n 雄弁家 eloquent speaker

yubi n 指 1. finger (= **te no yubi** 手の指) 2. toe (= **ashi no yubí** 足の指)

yubi-ningyō n 指人形 finger puppet

yubi-núki n 指貫き thimble

yubi-saki n 指先 fingertip

yubi-sashimásu, yubi-sasu n 指差し ます, 指差す points (*commonly indicates something with an extended index finger*)

yubi-wa n 指輪 ring: **konyaku-yubiwa** 婚約指輪 engagement ring

yūbin n 郵便 mail: **yūbin-chókin** 郵便

貯金 postal savings; **yūbin-fúrikae** 郵便振替 postal transfer; **yūbin-káwase** 郵便為替 (*postal*) money order; **yūbin-uke** 郵便受け mailbox

yūbin-bako n 郵便箱 mailbox

yubin-bángo n 郵便番号 zip code; ZIP Code

yūbin-butsu n 郵便物 mail

yūbin-kyoku n 郵便局 post office

yūbin-posuto n 郵便ポスト Red post box (= **posuto** ポスト)

yūbin-ya (san) n 郵便屋 (さん) mail carrier, mailman, postman

yū´bi (na) adj 優美な elegant, graceful

yūboku n 遊牧 nomadism: **yūboku-min** 遊牧民 nomad

yūbō (na) adj 有望 (な) promising (= **zento yūbō (na)** 前途有望 (な)): **yūbō-kabu** 有望株 growth stock

yudan n 油断 negligence, carelessness, sloppines

yudanemásu, yudanéru v 委ねます, 委ねる entrusts, commits

yudané ro v 委ねろ [IMPERATIVE] (entrust it!) → **yudanemásu** 委ねます

Yudayá-jin n ユダヤ人 Jew; **Yudaya-kyō** ユダヤ教 Judaism

yudemásu, yudéru v 茹でます, 茹で る boils (*food*)

yude-támago n ゆで卵 boiled egg

yúdete v 茹でて → **yudemásu** 茹で ます

yue v 結え [IMPERATIVE] (do up your hair!) → **yuimásu** 結います

yué n 故・ゆえ [BOOKISH] reason, grounds; ... yué ni ...故に・ゆえに for the reason that ..., because ...

yuéba v 結えば (if one does up one's hair) → **yuimásu** 結います

yuemásu, yueru v 結えます, 結える can do up one's hair

yuenai v 結えない = **yuemásen** 結えま せん (cannot do up one's hair)

yūenchi n 遊園地 amusement park

yueréba v 結えれば (if one can do up one's hair) → **yuemásu** 結えます

yūfō n ユーフォー・UFO unidentified flying object (= **mi-kakunin hikō-buttai** 未確認飛行物体)

yū´fuku (na) adj 裕福 (な) rich, wealthy

yū´ga (na) adj 優雅(な) elegant, refined

yugamanai v 歪まない = **yugamimásén** 歪みません (not get distorted/warped)

yugamemásu, yugameru v 歪めます, 歪める distorts, warps

yugamenai v 歪めない = **yugamemásén** 歪めません (not distort/warp)

yugámete v 歪めて → **yugamemásu** 歪めて

yugami n 歪み distortion, warp

yugamimásu, yugamu v 歪みます, 歪む gets distorted/warped

yugande v 歪んで → **yugamimásu** 歪みます

yūga-tō n 誘蛾灯 light trap

yūgi n 遊戯(o-yūgi お遊戯) playgame: **yūgi-shitsu** 遊戯室 playroom

yūhei n 幽閉 confinement

yūhodō n 遊歩道 promenade (= **puro-munādo** プロムナード)

yuigon n 遺言 1. leaving a will 2. a will, testament (= **yuigon-jō** 遺言状, **yuigon-sho** 遺言書)

yúiitsu (no) adj 唯一(の) [BOOKISH] the only (= **tada hitotsu no** ただひとつの・唯一つの)

yuimásu, yū (yuu) v 結います, 結う does up one's hair

yūjū-fudan n 優柔不断 indecisiveness

yuka n 床 floor (= **furoa** フロア): **yuka-ita** 床板 floor board

yúkai (na) adj 愉快(な) merry, happy, gay; funny, droll

yūkai n 誘拐 kidnap(ping): ~ **shimásu** 誘拐します kidnaps

yūkai-han n 誘拐犯 kidnapper

yūkaku n 遊郭 red-light district

yūkan (na) adj 勇敢(な) brave

yūkari n ユーカリ eucalyptus

yukata n 浴衣・ゆかた (light) bathrobe

yuketsu n 輸血 blood transfusion

yuki v 行き・ゆき [LITERARY] = **iki** 行き (goes) [INFINITIVE]

yuki n 雪 snow: ~ **ga furimásu** 雪が降ります it snows

yuki-dama n 雪玉 snowball

yuki-daruma n 雪だるま snowman

yuki-doke n 雪解け 1. melting snow 2. thaw (reduction or easing in tension or hostility)

yuki-gassen n 雪合戦 snowball fight

yuki-nádare n 雪なだれ snowslide, avalanche (= **nadare** 雪崩・なだれ)

yuki-onna n 雪女 snow woman (spirit of snow)

yuki-otoko n 雪男 yeti

yū´ki n 勇気 courage

yukimásu v 行きます・ゆきます [LITERARY] = **ikimásu** 行きます (goes)

yū´ki (no) adj 有機(の) organic: **yūki-yasai** 有機野菜 organic vegetables: **yūki-kagaku** 有機化学 organic chemistry

yukkúri adv ゆっくり 1. slowly 2. at ease; **Go-yukkúri.** ごゆっくり. Take it easy. Don't feel you have to rush.

yūkō (na) adj 有効(な) effective, valid **yūkō-kigen** n 有効期限 expiration date (except food. → **shōmi-kigen** 賞味期限)

yuku v 行く・ゆく = **iku** 行く (goes)

yukue-fumei n 行方不明 missing (person, pet, etc.): **yukue-fumei-sha** 行方不明者 a missing person

yumé n 夢 dream 1. succession of images during sleep 2. aspiration, wish; ~ **ga kanaimashita** 夢が叶いました (My) dream came true!

yūmei (na) adj 有名(な) famous, well-known

yumi n 弓 bow (for archery or violin) **yumi-gata** n 弓形 curve, arch, bow

yū´moa n ユーモア humor, wit

yunifōmu n ユニフォーム uniform (of athlete, etc.)

yuniiku n ユニーク unique (= **kosei-teki** 個性的, **dokutoku** 独特)

yunikōdo n ユニコード unicode

yunikōn n ユニコーン unicorn (= **ikkaku-jū** 一角獣)

yunitto basu n ユニットバス prefabricated bath

yūnō (na) adj 有能(な) capable, efficient: ~ **na hisho** 有能な秘書 efficient secretary

yunyū n 輸入 import(ing)

yunyū-hin n 輸入品 imported goods **yunyū´-zei** n 輸入税 (import) duty

yūran n 遊覧 excursion

yūrashia n ユーラシア Eurasia

yure n 揺れ tremor, shock

yū´rei n 幽霊 Japanese ghost (commonly lacks legs and feet) (= **bō-rei** 亡霊)

yuremásu, yureru ν 揺れます, 揺れる it shakes, sways, swings, rocks, rolls

yurenai ν 揺れない = **yuremásén** 揺れません (not shake it)

yureréba ν 揺れれば (if it shakes) → **yuremásu** 揺れます

yurete ν 揺れて → **yuremásu** 揺れます

yuri n ユリ・百合 lily

yuri-kago n 揺りかご cradle
yuri-kago kara hakaba made 揺りかごから墓場まで (*slogan*) From the cradle to the grave

yū´ri (na) *adj* 有利(な) profitable, advantageous

yurúi *adj* 緩い・ゆるい loose, slack; lenient; slow

yurushí n 許し (**o-yurushí** お許し) permission

yurushimásu, yurúsu ν 許します, 許す allows, permits; pardons, forgives

yūryō n 有料 pay (*not free*), charge, fee: **yūryō-chū´shajō** 有料駐車場 paid parking

yūryoku (na) *adj* 有力(な) strong, powerful, influential

yusaburimásu, yusaburu ν 揺さぶります, 揺さぶる shakes (*sways, swings, rocks, shocks*) it

yūsen n 優先 priority: **yūsen-jun'i** 優先順位 order of priority

yūsha n 勇者 brave man (→ **yūkan** 勇敢)

yūshi n 融資 financing (*of bank, etc.*): ~ **shimásu** 融資します finances

yūshi n 有志 volunteer, supporter, interested person

yūshi-téssen n 有刺鉄線 barbed wire

yūshutsu n 輸出 export(ing)
yushutsu-hin n 輸出品 export goods
yushutsu-zei n 輸出税 (*export*) duty

yūshoku-jinshu n 有色人種 colored races

yusō n 輸送 transport(ation): ~ **shimásu** 輸送します transports

yūsō n 郵送 mailing: ~ **shimásu** 郵送します mails
yūsō´-ryō n 郵送料 postage

yusuburimásu, yusuburu ν 揺すぶります, 揺すぶる shakes (*sways, swings, rocks*) it

yusugimásu, yusugu ν ゆすぎます, ゆすぐ rinses (= **susugu** すすぐ)

yūsu-hósuteru n ユースホステル youth hostel

yusuranai ν 揺すらない = **yusuri-masén** 揺すりません (not shake it)

yusuréba ν 揺すれば (if one shakes it) → **yusurimásu** 揺すります

yusuri n ゆすり・強請り blackmail, extortion

yusuri ν 揺すり: **binbō-yusuri** 貧乏揺すり nervous shaking of one's leg(s)

yusurimásu, yusuru ν 揺すります, 揺する shakes (*sways, swings, rocks*) it

yusurimásu, yusuru ν 強請ります, 強請る blackmails, extorts

yusurō´ ν 揺すろう = **yusurimashō´** 揺すりましょう (let's shake it!)

yútaka (na) *adj* 豊か(な) abundant, plentiful; wealthy (= **hōfu (na)** 豊富(な)

yū-tā´n n ユー[U]ターン U-turn

Yuta-shū n ユタ州 Utah

yutori *adj* ゆとりleeway, breadth of mind, space; **yutori-kyōiku** ゆとり教育less strenuous education (*primary education with reduced hours and/or content of the curriculum*)

yútte ν 結って → **yuimásu** 結います (does up one's hair)

yutte ν ゆって・言って = **itte** 言って (saying, says that)

yūutsu (na) *adj* 憂うつ・憂鬱(な) melancholy, gloom

yūwaku n 誘惑 temptation; seduction: ~ **shimásu** 誘惑します seduces

yuwanai ν 結わない = **yuimásén** 結いません (not do up one's hair)

yuwanai ν ゆわない・言わない = **iwanai** 言わない (not say)

yūzai (no) *adj* 有罪(の) guilty

yúzu n ユズ・柚子 citron

yūzū n 融通 **1.** financing: ~ **shimásu** 融通します finances, lends/advances money **2.** adaptability, versatility
yūzū no/ga kiku *adv* 融通の/がきく adaptable, versatile

yuzuranai ν 譲らない = **yuzurimásén** 譲りません (not cede)

yuzure ν 譲れ [IMPERATIVE] (cede!) → **yuzurimásu** 譲ります

yuzuréba ν 譲れば (if one cedes) → **yuzurimásu** 譲ります

yuzuremásu, yuzureru *v* 譲れます, 譲れる can give up/in; can cede

yuzurenai *v* 譲れない = **yuzuremásen** 譲れません (cannot cede)

yuzuréreba *v* 譲れれば (if we can cede) → **yuzuremásu** 譲れます

yuzurete *v* 譲れて → **yuzuremásu**

譲れます (can cede)

yuzuri *v* 譲り: inheritance; **... yuzuri no** ...譲りの inherited from ...

yuzurimásu, yuzuru *v* 譲ります, 譲る gives up; gives in; yields; cedes; is inferior

yuzutte *v* 譲って → **yuzurimásu** 譲ります

Z

zá *n* 座 **1.** theater (→ **kabuki-za** 歌舞伎座) **2.** seat

za-búton *n* 座布団 Japanese flat square cushion to sit on

za-dan *n* 座談 [BOOKISH] chat; **zadán-kai** 座談会 round-table discussion

za-isu *n* 座椅子 backrest (= *legless chair*)

za-kō *n* 座高 sitting height

za-kyo *n* 座興 entertainment (*at drinking party, etc.*)

za-seki *n* 座席 seat: **zaseki-bángō** 座席番号 seat number; **kōbu-zaseki-béruto** 後部座席ベルト rear seat belts (= **kōbu-zaseki (no) siitoberuto** 後部座席（の）シートベルト)

za-shiki *n* 座敷 (**o-zashiki** お座敷) **1.** tatami room, drawing room **2.** tatami-floored seating area in Japanese-style restaurant

za-zen *n* 座禅 meditation (*Zen*)

za-... *prefix* 雑... miscellaneous

zak-ka *n* 雑貨 miscellaneous goods, sundries; **zakka-ten** 雑貨店 variety shop

za-tsuon *n* 雑音 noise(s), static, miscellaneous sounds

zap-pi *n* 雑費 miscellaneous expenses

zas-shi *n* 雑誌 magazine, periodical, miscellaneous articles

zas-sō *n* 雑草 (*miscellaneous*) weeds

zatsudan *n* 雑談 (*miscellaneous*) chat: **~ shimásu** 雑談します has a chat

zat-ta (na) *adj* 雑多（な） sundry, miscellaneous

zái *n* 材 (= **zaimoku** 材木) lumber; (= **zairyō** 材料) material

zai-moku *n* 材木 lumber, wood

zai-ryōˊ *n* 材料 raw material(s),

ingredient(s): **kenchiku-zairyō** 建築材料 building materials: **sūpu no** ~ スープの材料 ingredients for the soup

zái *n* 財 (= **záisan** 財産) wealth

zai-batsu *n* 財閥 a big financial group

zai-dan *n* 財団 a foundation

zai-gen *n* 財源 financial resources

zai-hō *n* 財宝 treasures, riches (*money, jewels, etc.*)

zai-kai *n* 財界 financial circles

zai-ryoku *n* 財力 financial power, economic power

zái-san *n* 財産 one's property, wealth, fortune

zai-sei *n* 財政 finance

zai-... *prefix* 在... (*resident*) in

zai-gaku(-chū) *adv* 在学(中) in school; in college; at university: **zaigaku-shōmeisho** 在学証明書 certificate of enrollment

zai-ryū *n* 在留 [BOOKISH] residing, residence: **zairyū-shíkaku** 在留資格 status of residence

zai-seki(-chū) *adv* 在籍(中) **1.** in school; in college; at university (= **zaigaku(-chū)** 在学(中)) **2.** in association: **zaiseki-sha** 在籍者 registered person/student

zai-taku *adj* 在宅 [BOOKISH] being at home: **zaitaku-kinmu** 在宅勤務 working at home

zai-... *prefix* 罪... sin, crime

zái-aku *n* 罪悪 sin: **záiaku-kan** 罪悪感 feeling/sense of guilt

zai-nin *n* 罪人 criminal

zaiko *n* 在庫 inventory

zaiko-hyō *n* 在庫表 inventory list

zaiko-shobun seˉru *n* 在庫処分セール

clearance sale (= **zaiko-issō sēru** 在庫一掃セール)

Zaimu-shō n 財務省 Ministry of Finance

záiru n ザイル a mountain-climbing rope

zamā´-miro interj ざまあ見ろ (mostly male. Very INFORMAL) It serves you/them right!

zandaka n 残高 (remaining money) balance: (**ginkō**) **yokin-zandaka** (銀行)預金残高 bank balance

zangai n 残骸 **1.** wreck(age) which does not preserve its original shape **2.** thrown corpse which does not preserve its original shape

zángé n 懺悔 confession (of sins): ~ **shimásu** 懺悔します confesses

zangyaku (na) adj 残虐(な) merciless and cruel/brutal (to animals, people), atrocious; **zangyaku-kó´i** 残虐行為 an atrocity

zangyō n 残業 overtime (work): ~ **shimásu** 残業します works late

zankoku (na) adj 残酷(な) cruel to, brutal to, harsh towards (animals, people): ~ **na shiuchi** 残酷な仕打ち cruel treatment

zannén (na) adj 残念(な) regrettable, disappointed; too bad, a pity; **zannen-nagara** 残念ながら regrettably (= **ikan-nagara** 遺憾ながら [BOOKISH])

zannin (na) adj 残忍(な) brutal, cruel (= **zankoku (na)** 残酷(な)): ~ **na hito** 残忍な人 cruel person

zara ni adv さらに found everywhere, very common

zárazara (shita) adj ざらざら(した) rough(-textured)

zarigani n ザリガニ crawfish

zarú n ざる・ザル a bamboo sieve/colander

zāsai n ザーサイ Chinese pickles

zasetsu n 挫折 falling by the wayside, frustration, setback, fail; **zasetsú-kan** 挫折感 feeling of frustration, sense of failure; ~ **shimásu** 挫折します gets frustrated, falls by the wayside, fails; ~ **sasemásu** 挫折させます frustrates, defeats

zatsu (na) adj 雑(な) coarse, crude

zatto adv ざっと roughly; briefly

zé-hi adv ぜひ・是非 **1.** without fail, for sure **2.** [BOOKISH] right and wrong, pros and cons; **shikei (seido) no ~** 死刑(制度)の是非 pros and cons of the death penalty

zéi n 税 tax (= **zei-kin** 税金); **shōhi-zei** 消費税 consumption tax; **shotoku-zei** 所得税 income tax; **gensen-chōshū-zei** 源泉徴収税 withholding income tax; **jūmin-zei** 住民税 resident tax

zei-kan n 税関 customs, custom house

zei-kin n 税金 tax (= **zei** 税)

zei-mu sho n 税務署 tax office

zeitakú n ぜいたく・贅沢 luxury, extravagance: **zeitakú (na)** ぜいたく・贅沢(な) luxurious

zeitaku-hin n ぜいたく[贅沢]品 luxury (goods), luxuries

zékken n ゼッケン an athlete's number: ~ **o tsukemásu** ゼッケンを付けます attaches/assigns a number (to an athlete)

zekkō (no) adj 絶好(の) best: **zekkō-chō** 絶好調 best condition

zémi n ゼミ, **zeminá´ru** ゼミナール seminar

zén n 善 goodness: **zén-aku** 善悪 good and evil, right and wrong

zén'-i n 善意 goodwill

zén-sho n 善処 [BOOKISH]: ~ **shimásu** 善処します will do my best (about the matter) = Don't expect me to do anything.

Zén n 禅 Zen (Buddhism)

zen n 膳 (**o-zen** お膳, **gó-zen** 御膳) (traditional individual low) meal table, dining tray

zén-... prefix 全... all, total, whole, complete, the whole

zén-bu adv 全部 everything, completely: **zén-bu de** 全部で altogether

zen'-in n 全員 everyone

zén-koku (no) adj 全国(の) nationwide

zen-men n 全面 the entire surface

zen-metsu n 全滅 annihilation

zen-shin n 全身 the whole body, body as a whole

zen-tai *n* 全体 the whole, entirety: **zentai no** 全体の entire, whole; **zentai ni** 全体に wholly, generally

zén-yaku *adv* 全体 originally, primarily (= **gánrai** 元来)

zen-yaku *n* 全訳 complete translation

zen-zen *adv* 全然・ぜんぜん [+ NEGATIVE verb] (not) at all, (not) ever **2.** [INFORMAL] completely, altogether

zén-... *prefix* 前...[BOOKISH] former, earlier (= **máe no ... 前の...**)

zen-chō *n* 前兆 omen, sign

zén-go *n* 前後 **1.** before and after; ahead and behind; back and forth **2.** sequence, order

...-zén-go *suffix* ...前後 approximately, around, about (= **teido** 程度)

zen-han *n* 前半 the first half

zen-men *n* 前面 the front side

zen-pō *n* 前方 the front direction

zen-rei *n* 前例 precedent, prior example

zén-sha *n* 前者 the former

zen-shin *n* 前進 advance: ~ **shimásu** 前進します advances

zen-tei *n* 前提 premise

zén-to *n* 前途 the future, prospects: ~ **yūbō (na)** 前途有望(な) promising (= **yūbō (na)** 有望(な))

zén'-ya *n* 前夜 the night before

zenmai *n* ぜんまい・ゼンマイ **1.** a spring, hairspring, clock-spring **2.** royal fern, osmund

zensoku *n* ぜんそく・喘息 asthma

zeppeki *n* 絶壁 precipice

zérii *n* ゼリー jelly

zéro *n* ゼロ zero

zetsubō *n* 絶望 despair: ~ **shimásu** 絶望します despairs

zetsuen shimásu *v* 絶縁します insulates

zi... → j...

zō *n* 像 **1.** statue (= **chō-zō** 彫像) **2.** image: **terebi ei-zō** テレビ映像 images on TV screen: **ga-zō** 画像 picture, image **3.** portrait (= **shō-zō** 肖像)

zō *n* ゾウ・象 elephant

zō-... *prefix* 増... increase

zō-dai *n* 増大 enlargement, increase: ~

shimásu 増大します enlarges, increases

zō'-ho *n* 増補 supplement: ~ **shimásu** 増補します supplements

zō-ka *n* 増加 increase, growth: (...ga) ~ **shimásu** (...が)増加します increases

zō-ryō *n* 増量 increase (*quantity*): (...o) ~ **shimásu** (...を)増量します increases it

zō-satsu *n* 増刷 reprint (*publishing*): (...o) ~ **shimásu** (...を)増刷します reprints

zō-shin *n* 増進 promotion, betterment, increase: ~ **shimásu** 増量します promotes

zōgan *n* 象眼 inlaid work; damascene

zōgo *n* 造語 coined word

zōka *n* 造花 artificial flower

zōkei *n* 造詣 profound knowledge (*of academics, arts, technologies, etc.*): ~ **ga fukai** 造詣が深い is well versed

zōkin *n* ぞうきん・雑巾 rag, dustcloth

zoku *n* 賊 robber, bandit, thief (→ **kai-zoku** 海賊, **tō-zoku** 盗賊, **san-zoku** 山賊)

...'-zoku *suffix* ...族 (*name of certain*) tribe/gang/group of ...; the ...s

zokugo *n* 俗語 slang (= **surangu** スラング)

zoku (na) *adj* 俗(な) common, vulgar; popular

zokusánai *v* 属さない = **zokushimasén** 属しません (not belong)

zoku-shimásu, zoku-súru *v* 属します, 属する belongs (= **zokúsú** 属す)

zokú(-)shite *v* 属して → **zoku(-)shimásu** 属します

zokú zoku *adv* ぞくぞく・続々 one right after another, in rapid succession

zóku zoku (suru) *v* ぞくぞくします(する) **1.** is thrilled with excitement **2.** shivers with chill

zonbún (ni) *adv* 存分(に) as much as one likes

zóngai *adv* 存外 beyond expectations

zōni *n* 雑煮・ぞうに (**o-zōni** お雑煮) rice cakes boiled with vegetables (*eaten as New Year's soup*)

zon-jiagemásu, zon-jiageru *v* 存じあげます, 存じあげる [HUMBLE] thinks, feels; knows

zon-jimásu, zon-jíru v 存じます, 存じる [HUMBLE/DEFERENTIAL] thinks, feels; knows → **go-zon-ji** ご存じ

zon-jínai v 存じない = **zon-jimasén** 存じません (not think/feel/know)

zón jite v 存じて → **zon-jimásu** 存じます

zonzái (na) adj ぞんざい(な) slovenly, rough, carelessly, sloppy

zōri n 草履 straw sandals

zórozoro adv ぞろぞろ in streams/ crowds, in large numbers

zōsen n 造船 shipbuilding: **~ shimásu** 造船します builds a ship

zōsen-jó n 造船所 shipyard

zōsho n 蔵書 book collection, library

zōsui n 雑炊 rice boiled in a soup

zō-tei n 贈呈 [HUMBLE] presentation: **~ shimásu** 贈呈します presents

zotto adv ぞっと: **~ shimásu** ぞっとします shudders, shivers, thrills (is thrilled)

zu n 図 picture, drawing, chart, map, diagram, figure: **~ ni norimásu** 図に乗ります pushes a good thing too far, takes advantage of a person

zu-an n 図案 sketch, design

zu-hyō n 図表 chart, diagram (= **chāto** チャート)

zu-kai n 図解 illustration, diagram

...-zu suffix ...ず, **...-zu ni** ...ずに = **...-nái de** ...ないで (not doing, instead of doing)

zubari adv ずばり: **~ iimásu** ずばり言います comes directly to the point

zubón n ズボン trousers, pants, slacks

zubon-shita n ズボン下 underpants, shorts

zubon-tsuri n ズボン吊り suspenders

zubutoi adv 図太い **thick-skinned**, impudent: **~ shinkei** 図太い神経 nerves of steel

zúibun adv ずいぶん・随分 1. fairly, rather 2. very, quite, extremely (= **kanari** かなり)

zuihitsu n 随筆 essays (= **essei** エッセイ)

zúii (no) adj 随意(の) voluntary,

optional (= **nin'i (no)** 任意(の))

zúiji adv 随時 as needed, at anytime as one likes

-zuke suffix 付け dated: **honjitsu-zuke de** 本日付けで effective today

...-zuki suffix ...好き a lover of ..., a great ... fan

zúkku n ズック canvas; duck (fabric)

...-zúkuri suffix ...造り made of ...

zūmu n ズーム zoom (camera)

zúnō n 頭脳 [BOOKISH] brains, head, intellect (= **atama** 頭)

zurashimásu, zurasu v ずらします, ずらす shifts

zuré n ずれ discrepancy, lag, gap

zuremásu, zuréru v ずれます, ずれる slips out of place, gets loose

zurénai v ずれない = **zuremasén** ずれません (not get loose)

zúrereba v ずれれば (if it gets loose) → **zuremásu** ずれます

zúrete v ずれて → **zuremásu** ずれます

zurō´su n ズロース panties; drawers

zúru n ずる cheating

zuru-gashikoi adj ずる賢い cunning, wily

zurúi adj ずるい sly, cunning, tricky

zuru-yásumi n ずる休み skipping (school): **~ shimásu** ずる休みします skips (school)

zusan (na) adj ずさん(な) sloppy, slipshod, careless, slovenly

...´zútsu suffix ...ずつ (offor) each, apiece, at a time

zutsū n 頭痛 headache: **~ no táne** 頭痛の種 one's biggest headache; **~ ga shimásu** 頭痛がします has a headache

zutto adv ずっと 1. directly 2. by far, much (more): **~ máe** ずっと前 way back (before), a long time ago 3. all the way through, all the time

zūzūshíi adj ずうずうしい・図々しい brazen, shameless, bold, impudent (= **atsukamashii** 厚かましい)

zy... → **j...**

A

a, an → one (*but usually omitted in Japanese*)

aardvark *n* tsuchíbutá ツチブタ

abacus *n* soroban そろばん

abacus rod *n* keta けた・桁

abalone *n* áwabi アワビ・鮑

abandon *v* sutemásu (suteru, sutete) 捨てます(捨てる, 捨てて)

abandoned cat *n* suteneko 捨て猫

abase *v* otoshimásu (otósu, otoshite) 落とします(落とす, 落として), (*be humble*) hige shimásu (suru, shite) 卑下します(する, して)

abate *v* **1.** (*loses steam*) osamarimásu 治まります, yawaragimásu 和らぎます **2.** herashimásu 減らします **3.** (*excludes*) haijo shimásu (suru, shite) 排除します(する, して); (*resolve*) mukō ni shimásu (suru, shite) 無効にします(する, して) **4.** ~ *a tax* genzei shimásu (suru, shite) 減税します(する, して)

abbreviate *v* ryakushimásu (ryakúsu, ryakushite) 略します(略す, 略して)

abbreviation *n* ryakugo 略語, shōryaku 省略

abdicate *v* **1.** shirizokimásu (shirizoku, shirizoite) 退きます(退く, 退いて), jinin shimásu (suru, shite) 辞任します(する, して) **2.** ~ *the throne* taii shimásu (suru, shite) 退位します(する, して)

abdomen *n* onaka おなか, fu-kubu 腹部, hara 腹

abduct *v* yūkai shimásu (suru, shite) 誘拐します(する, して)

aberration *n* dassen 脱線, itsudatsu 逸脱, seishin ijō 精神異常

abet *v* keshikakemásu (keshikakeru, keshikakete) けしかけます(けしかける, けしかけて)

abeyance *n* ichiji teishi 一時停止, horyū 保留

abhor *v* **1.** (*dislike intensely*) nikumimásu (nikumu, nikunde) 憎みます(憎む, 憎んで), (*not favored*) kiraimásu (kirau, kiratte) 嫌います(嫌う, 嫌って) **2.** ... o sakemásu (sakeru, sakete) ...を

abide *v* **1.** (*stays*) nokórimásu (nokoru, nokotte) 残ります(残る, 残って), todomarimásu (todomaru, todomatte) 留まります(留まる, 留まって) **2.** (*dwells*) sumimásu (sumu, sunde) 住みます(住む, 住んで) **3.** (*suffers*) gaman shimásu (suru, shite) 我慢します(する, して), ...ni taemásu (taeru, taete) ...に耐えます(耐える, 耐えて) **4.** (*accepts*) ukeiremasu (ukeireru, ukeirete) 受け入れます(受け入れる, 受け入れて)

ability *n* **1.** (*skill*) nōryoku 能力, udemae 腕前, temae 手前 (o-témae お手前); (*stuff*) kiryō 器量, utsuwa 器 **2.** (*function*) hataraki 働き; (*proficiency*) jitsuryoku 実力 **3.** (*talent*) sái(nō) 才(能)

abject *adj* **1.** mijime (na) 惨め(な), hisán (na) 悲惨(な), zetsubō-teki (na) 絶望的(な) **2.** iyashii 卑しい **3.** hikutsu na 卑屈な

ablaze *adj* **1.** (*shiny*) kagayaiteiru 輝いている **2.** (*burning*) moeteiru 燃えている **3.** (*excited*) kōfun 興奮している

able → can

abnormal *adj* (*abnormality*) ijō (na) 異常(な)

aboard *v* **gets ~** norimásu (noru, notte) 乗ります(乗る, 乗って); *puts ~* nosemásu (noseru, nosete) 乗せます(乗せる, 乗せて)

abode *n* ie 家, jūkyo 住居, jūtaku 住宅

abolish *v* **1.** (*demolish*) haishi shimásu (suru, shite) 廃止します(する, して), yamemásu (yameru, yamete) 止めます(止める, 止めて) **2.** (*destroy*) ... o horoboshimásu (horobosu, horoboshite) ...を滅ぼします(滅ぼす, 滅ぼして)

aborigine *n* aborijini アボリジニ, aborijinii アボリジニー, genjūmin 原住民, senjūmin 先住民

abort *v* chūshi shimásu (suru, shite) 中止します(する, して)

abortion *n* datai 堕胎, ninshin chū´zetsu 妊娠中絶; *has an* ~ oroshimásu (orósu, oróshite) 下ろします(下ろす, 下ろして)

abound *v* tomimásu (tómu, tónde) 富みます(富む, 富んで)

about *prep* **1.** (*an amount*) yáku ... 約..., ... gúrai ...位, ... hodo ...程, ...-zéngo... 前後, ...-kéntō ...見当 → **almost**, **around 2.** (*a time*) ... gòro (ni) ... 頃(に) **3.** (*concerning*) ... ni tsúite (no)... について(の); *talk ~ ...* ni tsúite hanashimásu (hanasu, hanashite) ...について話します(話す, 話して)
is about to happen (su-)ru tokoró desu (す)るところです, (shi-)yō to shimásu (し)ようとします, (shi-)sō désu (し)そうです
about when itsu goro いつ頃

above *prep* ... (no) ué (ni) ...(の)上(に)

aboveground *n* chijō 地上

abrade *v* **1.** (*to wear down*) surihera shimásu (suriherasu, suriherashite) すり減らします(すり減らす, すり減らして), (*to be worn away*) mamō sasemásu (saseru, sasete) 磨耗させます (させる, させて) **2.** (*chafe*) iraira sasemasu (saseru, sasete) イライラさ せます(させる, させて)

abreast *adv* yokó ni narande 横に並ん で; *not ~ of* ...ni utói ...に疎い

abridge *v* (*shorten*) tanshuku shimásu (suru, shite) 短縮します(する, して), yōyaku shimásu (suru, shite) 要約しま す(する, して); (*abate*) hera shimásu (herasu, herashite) 減らします(減ら す, 減らして)

abroad *adv* gaikoku (de) 外国(で), káigai (de) 海外(で)
study abroad *n* ryūgaku 留学

abrupt *adj* totsuzen (no) 突然(の)

abruptly *adv* totsuzen 突然

abscess *n* nōyō 膿瘍

abscond *v* nigemásu (nigeru, nigete) 逃げます(逃げる, 逃げて)

absence *n* kesseki (no) 欠席(の), (*from home*) rúsu (no) 留守(の)

absent *v* kesseki shimásu (suru, shite) 欠席します(する, して)

absentee *n* kesséki-sha 欠席者

absent-minded *adj* bon'yári shimásu (suru, shite) ぼんやりします(する, して)

absent-mindedly *adv* ukkári shite うっかりして

absolute *adj* zettai (no) 絶対(の)

absolutely *adv* zettai ni 絶対に, honto (hontō) ni 本当(ほんとう)に; *~ can-not* tōtei 到底 + [NEGATIVE]

absorbed *adj* (*fascinated*) uttóri (to) うっとり(と); *gets ~ in* ... ni korimásu (kóru, kótte)...に凝ります(凝る, 凝 って)

absorbent cotton *n* dasshí-men 脱脂綿

absorption *n* kyūshū 吸収

abstain *v* **1.** (*stop*) yamemásu (yameru, yamete) 止めます(止める, 止めて), (*refrain from*) tsutsushimimasu (tsutsushimu, tsutsushinde) 慎みます (慎む, 慎んで); *~ from* ... o yame másu (yameru, yamete) ...をやめま す(やめる, やめて), tachimásu (tátsu, tátte) 断ちます(断つ, 断って) **2.** (*do not vote*) kíken shimásu (suru, shite) 棄権します(する, して)

abstainer *n* kinshu-ka 禁酒家

abstention *n* kiken 棄権

abstinence *n* jisei 自制, sessei 節制, kinshu 禁酒

abstract *adj* **1.** *adj* chūshō-teki (na) 抽象 的(な) **2.** *n* (*summary*) yō´shi 要旨

absurd *adj* baka-rashíi ばからしい

abundance *n* tómi 富

abundant *adj* yútaka (na) 豊か(な) → **abound**

abuse 1. *n* warú-kuchi/-guchi 悪口 **2.** → **scold**, **mistreat**

abusive *adj* ranbō (na) 乱暴(な), kuchigitanai 口汚い, warui 悪い

abut *v* sesshimásu (sessu(ru), sesshite) 接します(接する, 接して)

abysmal *adj* hidói ひどい, sokonuke (no) 底抜けの, hakarishirenai 計り知 れない; *~ darkness* (mak-)kurayami (no) (真っ)暗闇(の)

abyss *n* chi no soko 地の底, shin'en 深 遠, naraku 奈落, donzoko どん底

AC, alternating current *n* kōryū 交流

academic *adj* akádemikku アカデミッ ク, gakumon 学問

academy *n* gakkō 学校

accede *v* tsugimásu (tsugu, tsuide) 継ぎます(継ぐ, 継いで), dōi shimásu (suru, shite) 同意します(する, して)

accede to *v* ... ni ō-jimásu (ō-jiru, ō-jite) ...に応じます(応じる, 応じて)

accelerate *v* kasóku shimásu (suru, shite) 加速します(する, して)

accelerator *n* ákuseru アクセル

accent *n* ákusento アクセント → pronunciation, dialect

accept *v* 1. ukemásu (ukéru, úkete) 受けます(受ける, 受けて), uke-torimásu (uke-toru, uke-totte) 受け取ります(受け取る, 受け取って), uke-tsukemásu (uke-tsukeru, uke-tsukete) 受け付けます(受け付ける, 受け付けて) 2. (*consents*) shōdaku shimásu (suru, shíte) 承諾します(する, して)

acceptance *n* 1. shōdaku 承諾 2. (*resignation*) akirame 諦め

access; *seeks ~ to* ... ni sekkin o haka-rimásu (hakáru, hakátte) ...に接近を図ります(図る, 図って)

accessible *adj* (*easy to get to*) iki-yasúi 行きやすい

accessory *n* (*clothing accessory; belt, handbag, etc.*) akusesarii アクセサリー, (*car accessory, etc.*) kā akusesarii カーアクセサリー

accident *n* 1. jíko 事故, dekígoto 出来事 2. (*disaster*) sōnan 遭難; *has an ~* sōnan shimásu (suru, shíte) 遭難します(する, して)

accidental *adj* gūzen (no) 偶然(の)

accidentally *adv* gūzen ni 偶然に, hyótto ひょっと

acclaim 1. *n* shōsan 称賛 2. *v* shōsan shimásu (suru, shite) 称賛します(する, して)

accommodate *v* shukuhaku sasemásu (saseru, sasete) 宿泊させます(させる, させて), tekiō shimásu (suru, shite) 適応します(する, して)

accommodation *n* (*place to stay*) shukuhaku shisetsu 宿泊施設; (*facilities*) sétsubi 設備

accompany *v* 1. *~ ... to* issho ni ikimásu (iku, itte) (...と)一緒に行きます(行く, 行って); o-tómo shimásu (suru, shíte) お供します(する, して); ...ni tomonaimásu (tomonáu, tomonátte) ...に伴います(伴う, 伴って) 2. *is accompanied by* (= *brings along*) ... o

tsuremásu (tsureru, tsurete) ... を連れます(連れる, 連れて)

accomplice *n* kyōhansha 共犯者, ichimi 一味

accomplish *v* 1. (*shite*) shimaimásu (shimau, shimatte) (して)しまいます(しまう, しまって); hatashimásu (hatásu, hatáshite) 果たします(果たす, 果たして); togemásu (togéru, tógete) 遂げます(遂げる, 遂げて) 2. (*attains*) ...ni tas-shimásu (tas-suru, tas-shite) ...に達します(達する, 達して); ... ga kanaimásu (kanáu, kanátte) ... がかないます(かなう, かなって)

accord; *v ~ with* (...ni) kanaimásu (kanáu, kanátte) (...に)かないます(かなう, かなって); (... to) itchi shimásu (suru, shíte) (...と)一致します(する, して)

accordance *n* itchi 一致; *in ~ with* ... ni ō-jite ...に応じて; ... ni shitagátte ...にしたがって

according (to) *adj* 1. (*relying on*) ... ni yoru to ...によると, ... no hanashíde (wa) ...の話で(は) 2. (*in conformity with*) ... ni shitagátte ...に従って

accordingly *adv* shitagátte 従って

accordion *n* acōdion アコーディオン

accost *v* kóe o kakemásu (koe o kakeru, koe o kakete) 声をかけます(声をかける, 声をかけて), hanashikakemásu (hanashikakeru, hanashikakete) 話しかけます(話しかける, 話しかけて)

account *n* 1. (*bill*) kanjō 勘定 (o-kanjō お勘定) 2. (*credit*) tsuké つけ 3. (*bank account*) kōza 口座, yokin 預金 on account of ... no séi de ... のせいで → because → sake (for the) takes into account kō'ryo ni iremásu (ireru, irete) 考慮に入れます(入れる, 入れて)

accountable *adj* sekinín ga aru 責任がある, setsumei dekíru 説明できる

accountant *n* kaikei (-gákari) 会計 (係), kaikéi-shi 会計士

accounts *n* (o-)kaikei (お)会計

accumulate *v* 1. (*it accumulates*) tsu-morimásu (tsumóru, tsumótte) 積もります(積もる, 積もって), tamarimásu (tamaru, tamette) たまります(たまる,

307

たまって); tsumemásu (tsumeru, tsumete) つめます(つめる、つめて); atsumarimásu (atsumáru, atsumátte) 集ま
ります(集まる、集まって) **2.** (*accumulates it*) tsumimásu (tsumu, tsunde)
積みます(積む、積んで), tamemásu
(tameru, tamete) ためます(ためる、
ためて); atsumemásu (atsúmeru,
atsúmete) 集めます(集める、集めて)

accurate *adj* seikaku (na) 正確(な)

accuse *v* uttaemásu (uttaeru, uttaete)
訴えます(訴える、訴えて); (*criticizes*)
hínan shimásu (suru, shite) 非難しま
す(する、して)

accustom *v* ~ *oneself to* ... ni naremásu (naréru, nárete) ... に慣れます
(慣れる、慣れて)

accustomed *adj* jū´rai no 従来の

ache 1. *v* (*it aches*) itamimásu (itámu,
itánde) 痛みます(痛む、痛んで) **2.** *n*
(*an ache*) itamí 痛み

achieve → **accomplish**

achievement *n* (*work*) hataraki 働き

acid 1. *n* sán 酸 **2.** *adj* suppái 酸っぱい

acknowledge *v* mitomemásu (mitomeru, mitomete) 認めます(認める、
認めて)

acorn *n* dónguri どんぐり

acoustic *n* **1.** akō´sutíkku (gakki) アコ
ースティック(楽器); ~ *guitar*
akōsutikku gitā アコースティック・
ギター **2.** onkyō 音響

acquaint; *v* ~ *oneself with* (... o)
shirimásu (shiru, shitte) (...を) 知りま
す(知る、知って); *is acquainted with*
... o shitte imásu (iru, ite) ... を知って
います(いる、いて)

acquaintance *n* shiriai 知り合い,
[BOOKISH] chijin 知人

acquiesce *v* fukujū shimásu (suru,
shite) 服従します(する、して)

acquire → **get**

acquit *v* **1.** shakuhō´ shimásu (suru,
shite) 釈放します(する、して), kaihō
shimásu (suru, shite) 解放します(す
る、して), muzai ni shimásu (suru,
shite) 無罪にします(する、して)

acre *n* ēkā エーカー

acrobat *n* akurobátto アクロバット,
kyokugei 曲芸

acronym *n* kashira moji 頭文字

across *prep, adv* ... (no) mukō(ni) ...
(の)向こう(に), múkō 向こう **goes
across** → **cross**
across the way mukō 向こう, mukō-
gawa 向こう側; *cuts* ~ yoko-girimásu
(yoko-gíru, yoko-gítte) 横切ります(横
切る、横切って); *goes* ~ ōdan shimásu
(suru, shite) 横断します(する、して)

act *n* **1.** → **do** **2.** (*deed*) shiwaza しわ
ざ, okonai 行い, kō´i 行為; ~ *of God*
fuka kō´ryoku 不可抗力 **3.** (*of play*)
makú 幕; dán 段 **4.** hōritsu 法律; ~ *of
Congress* kokkai seiteihō 国会制定法

acting 1. *n* (*play acting*) éngi 演技
2. → **temporary** → **agent**; ~ *as
agent* daikō 代行

action *n* **1.** katsudō 活動 **2.** (*conduct*)
okonai 行い; (*behavior*) kōdō 行動 →
activity

activate *v* ugokashimásu (ugokasu,
ugokashite) 動かします(動かす、動か
して), sádō sasemásu (saseru, sasete)
作動させます(させる、させて)

active *adj* kappatsu (na) 活発(な); *is* ~
katsuyaku shimásu (suru, shite) 活躍
します(する、して)

activity *n* **1.** katsudō 活動, katsuyaku
活躍 **2.** (*work*) hataraki 働き **3.**
(*agency*) kikán 機関 → **exercise** →
movement

actor *n* yakusha 役者, haiyū 俳優

actress *n* joyū 女優

actual *adj* jissai (no) 実際(の); ~ *conditions* genjitsu 現実

actuality *n* jitchi 実地

actually *adv* jitsú wa 実は, jitsu ní 実に

acupuncture *n* hári 鍼

acute *adj* **1.** (*sharp*) surudói 鋭い
2. (*severe*) hageshíi 激しい **3.** (*sudden*)
kyūsei (no) 急性(の)

ad → **advertisement**

adage *n* kotowaza ことわざ, kakugen
格言

adamant *adj* katái 硬い・固い, gánko
(na) 頑固(な), dánko (to shita) 断固
(とした)

adapt *v* tekigō´ sasemásu (saseru,
sasete) 適合させます(させる、させて)

adaptability *n* yūzū 融通; *is adaptable*

yūzū ga kikimásu (kiku, kiite) 融通が
ききます(きく、きいて)

adapter n adáputā´ アダプター

add v kuwaemásu (kuwaeru, kuwaete)
加えます(加える、加えて); (*supple-
ments it with*) soemásu (soeru, soete)
添えます(添える、添えて); yosemásu
(yoseru, yosete) 寄せます(寄せる、寄
せて); (*attaches*) tsukemásu (tsukéru,
tsukéte) 付けます(付ける、付けて)

addict n jōyō´-sha 常用者, chūdoku
(-sha) 中毒(者), izón-sha 依存者;
drug addict mayaku jō´yō´/chūdoku
(-sha) 麻薬常用者/中毒(者)

addition n tsuiká 追加, tenká 添加;
house ~ tate-mashi 建て増し; *in ~
to*...no hoka (ni) ...の他(に); *food
additive* shokuhin tenkábutsu 食品
添加物

additionally adv hoka ni 他に, [BOOKISH]
tá ni 他に

address n 1. jūsho 住所, (...) saki
(...)先, (*house number*) banchi 番地,
(*written*) tokoro-gaki 所書き, adoresu
アドレス; (*on envelope*) uwagaki
上書き

contact address n renraku-saki 連絡先
e-mail address n mēru ádoresu
(meru-ado) メールアドレス(メルアド)
address book n adoresu chō´ アドレ
ス帳
addressed to v ...-ate (no) ...あて(の)
2. enzetsu 演説 3. v torikumimásu
(torikumu, torikunde) 取り組みます
(取り組む、取り組んで)

addressee n uketori-nin 受取人,
jushin-sha 受信者

adequate adj ...-no tame (ni) ...のため
(に)

adhere v kuttsukimásu (kuttsuku,
kuttsuite) くっつきます(くっつく、く
っついて); fucháku shimásu (suru,
shite) 付着します(する、して)

adhesive tape n nenchaku tē´pu 粘着
テープ; bansōkō ばんそうこう

ad hoc adj tokubetsu (no) 特別(の),
sonoba shinogi (no) その場しのぎの)

adios adj sayōnará さようなら

adjacent adj 1. → next 2. *is ~ to* ...ni
ses-shimásu (ses-suru, ses-shíte) ...に

adjective n keiyō´shi 形容詞

adjoining → next

adjust v totonoemásu (totonoéru,
totonóete) 整えます(整える、整えて),
chōsei/séiri/kagen shimásu (suru, shite)
調整/整理/加減します(する、して)

adjustment n chōsei 調整, séiri 整理,
kagen 加減, chōsetsu 調節

administer v (*of government*)
osámemásu (osámeru, osámete) 治め
ます(治める、治めて); kánri shimásu
(suru, shite) 管理します(する、して)

administration n 1. (*of government*)
gyōsei 行政 2. (*of business*) keiei 経営,
kánri 管理

admirable adj mígoto (na) 見事(な),
rippa (na) 立派(な)

admirably adv mígoto ni 見事に, rippa
ni 立派に

admiral n táishō 大将; *vice ~* chū´jō 中
将; *rear ~* shō´shō 少将

admire v kanshin shimásu (suru, shite)
感心します(する、して), homemásu
(homéru, hómete) 褒めます(褒める、
褒めて), akogaremásu (akogareru,
akogarete) あこがれ[憧れ]ます(あこ
がれる、あこがれて)

admission n (*to hospital*) nyūin 入院;
(*to school*) nyūgaku 入学; (*to a place*)
nyūjō 入場
admission fee n nyūjō´-ryō 入場料
admission ticket n nyūjō´-ken 入場券

admit v 1. (*lets in*) iremásu (ireru, irete)
入れます(入れる、入れて), tōshimásu
(tō´su, tō´shite) 通します(通す、通し
て) 2. (*acknowledges*) mitomemásu
(mitomeru, mitomete) 認めます(認め
る、認めて); (*confesses*) uchi-akemásu
(uchi-akeru, uchi-akete) 打ち明けます
(打ち明ける、打ち明けて)

admittance n nyūjō (kyoka) 入場(許
可), nyūkai 入会

admonish v chūkoku shimásu (suru,
shite) 忠告します(する、して), chūi
shimásu (suru, shite) 注意します(する、
して), kankoku shimásu (suru, shite)
勧告します(する、して)

adolescence n seinén-ki 青年期,
seishún-ki 青春期, shishún-ki 思春期

adolescent n seinen 青年

adopt v (a boy) yōshi ni shimásu (suru, shíte) 養子にします(する, して); (a girl) yō'jo ni shimásu (suru, shíte) 養女にします(する, して)

adopted adj (son) yōshi (ni natta) 養子(になった); (daughter) yō'jo (ni natta) 養女(になった)

adorable adj kawaíi かわいい, kawairashíi かわいらしい, airashíi 愛らしい

adore v akogaremásu (akogareru, akogarete) あこがれ[憧れ]ます(あこがれる, あこがれて)

adrenalin n adorenarín アドレナリン

adult n otona おとな・大人, seijin 成人

adultery n kantsū 姦通, furin 不倫

advance 1. n zenshin 前進 2. n in ~ sono máe ni その前に; (beforehand) mae motte 前もって, jizen ni 事前に 3. v (goes ahead) susumimásu (susumu, susunde) 進みます(進む, 進んで), (advances it) susumemásu (susumeru, susumete) 進めます(進める, 進めて), (lends money) yūzū shimásu (suru, shíte) 融通します(する, して)

advance notice n yokoku 予告

advanced sale n maeuri 前売り

advanced-sale ticket maeuri-ken 前売り券

advantage n 1. toku 得 (o-toku お得), (benefit) ríeki 利益; takes ~ of ... o riyō shimásu (suru, shíte) ...を利用します(する, して) 2. (merit) chō'sho 長所

advantageous adj yū'ri (na) 有利(な), toku (na) 得(な)

advent n shutsugen 出現, tōrai 到来, kirisuto no kōrin キリストの降臨

adventure n bōken 冒険

adverb n fukushi 副詞

advergame n ado(ba) gēmu アド(バ)ゲーム

adversary n aité 相手 (o-aite お相手)

adverse adj fúri (na) 不利(な), gyakkyō (no) 逆境(の)

advertisement n kōkoku 広告

advice n 1. adobáisu アドバイス, chūkoku 忠告 2. (consultation) sōdan 相談

adviser n (consultant) komon 顧問, sōdan aite 相談相手

advocate v tonaemásu (tonaéru, tonáete) 唱えます(唱える, 唱えて)

aerial → antenna

aerobics n earobíkusu エアロビクス

aerology n kishōgaku 気象学

Aesop n Isóppu イソップ

aesthetic adj bi-teki (na) 美的な

afar adv tōku (ni) 遠く(に), enpō 遠方; from ~ tōku kara 遠くから

affable adj áiso/áisō ga ii あいそ/あいそう[愛想]がいい, hitoatari no ii 人当たりのいい, hitozuki no yoi 人好きのする, shitashimiyasui 親しみやすい

affair n 1. kotó 事, kotogara 事柄, jíken 事件, shigoto 仕事 2. (love affair) (extramarital) uwaki 浮気; has an ~ with … … to uwaki o shimásu (suru, shíte) …と浮気をします(する, して)

affect → influence

affectation n kidori 気取り, furí ふり, kíza きざ・気障

affected adj kidotta … 気取った…; is ~ kidotte imásu (iru, ite) 気取っています(いる, いて)

affection n nasake 情け (o-násake お情け), aijō 愛情; treats with ~ (... o) kawai-garimásu (kawai-gáru, kawai-gátte) (...を)かわいがります(かわいがる, かわいがって)

affiliate 1. v kamei shimásu (suru, shíte) 加盟します(する, して) 2. n ko-gaisha 子会社, shíten 支店

affirmation n kōtei 肯定

affix v setsuji 接辞, tenkábutsu 添加物

afflict v kurushimemásu (kurushiméru, kurushímete) 苦しめます(苦しめる, 苦しめて)

affliction n kurushimi 苦しみ

afford v (jūbun na) (o-)kane ga arimásu (áru, átte) (十分な)(お)金があります(ある, あって); yoyū ga arimásu (áru, átte) 余裕があります(ある, あって)

affront 1. v bujoku shimásu (suru, shíte) 侮辱します(する, して) 2. n bujoku 侮辱

Afghan 1. (person) Afuganísután-jin アフガニスタン人 2. (language) Afuganisután-go アフガニスタン語

Afghanistan n Afuganísután アフガニスタン

afire *adv* moete 燃えて, kōfunshite 興奮して

afloat *adj, adv* ukan da/de 浮かんだ/で
afloat cargo *n* okini 沖荷

afraid; *is ~ of* ... (...ga) kowái desu (...が) 怖いです, (...o) kowagarimásu (kowagáru, kowagátte) (...を) 怖がります (怖がる, 怖がって)

Africa *n* Afurika アフリカ

Afro-American *n* kokujin 黒人

after **1.** *prep* ... kará ...から, ... (no) áto de ...(の)後で; *~ doing* shitékara shite から, shita áto de した後で; **-go** 後; *~ that* sono-go その後 **2.** *adv* ... shita ato ni/de ...した後に/で

after a long time *adv* (*of absence*) hisashi-buri ni 久しぶりに

after a meal *n, adv* shokuji no áto 食事の後, [BOOKISH] shokugo 食後

after a while *adv* shibáraku shite しばらくして

after all *adv* kekkyokú 結局; yappári やっぱり; tsúmari つまり, [BOOKISH] tsumáru tokoro つまるところ, [BOOKISH] yō-súru ni 要するに; [BOOKISH] shosen しょせん

aftercare *n* afutā kea アフターケア

after the war *n, adv* sensō no áto 戦争の後, [BOOKISH] sengo 戦後

After you! *interj* Dōzo o-saki ni どうぞお先に

after-hours bar *n* sunákku スナック

afterlife *n* **1.** anoyo あの世, ráise 来世, shígo no sekai 死後の世界 **2.** bannen 晩年

afternoon *n, adv* hirú kara 昼から, gógo 午後

afters *n* dezāto デザート

after-school *adj* hōkago (no) 放課後 (の)

aftershave (lotion) *n* afutā-shē´bu (rōshon) アフターシェーブ (ローション)

aftertaste *n* ató-aji 後味; *leaves a bad ~* atóaji ga warúi 後味が悪い

after(ward) *adv* ato de 後で

afterwards *adv* áto de 後で

afterworld *n* anoyo あの世, ráise 来世, shígo no sekai 死後の世界

again *adv* mō ichi-dó もう一度, mō ik-kái もう一回; matá また; aratámete 改めて, kurikaeshimásu (ga) 繰り返します (が)

against *prep* **1.** (*in contrast to*) ...ni táishite ...に対して; (*contrary to*) ...ni hán-shite ...に反して; (*opposing*) ... ni hantai/taikō shite ...に反対/対抗して **2.** (*running into*) ... ni butsukatte ...にぶつかって **3.** (*leaning on*) ...ni motárete (no) ...にもたれて (の)

age **1.** *n* toshi 年・歳, nenrei 年齢; *your ~* (o-)toshi (お) 年, [BOOKISH] nenrei 年齢 **2.** *n* (*era*) jidai 時代 **3.** *v* (*gets old*) toshí o torimásu (tóru, tótte) 年を取ります (取る, 取って), fukemásu (fukéru, fukéte) 老けます (老ける, 老けて)

agency *n* **1.** dairi 代理, dairí-ten 代理店 **2.** (*organization*) kikán 機関

agent *n* dairi 代理, dairi-nin 代理人, (*proxy*) daikō´-sha 代行者; (*broker*) burō´kā ブローカー

aggravating *adj* haradatashíi 腹立たしい

aggression *n* shinryaku 侵略

aggressor *n* (*person*) shinryáku-sha 侵略者

agile *adj* kibin (na) 機敏 (な), binshō (na) 敏捷 (な), subayái すばやい

agitated; *v gets ~* dōyō shimásu (suru, shite) 動揺します (する, して) → **flustered**

agitation *n* **1.** dōyō 動揺 **2.** kōfun 興奮

agitator *n* (*person*) sendō-sha 扇動者

agnate *n, adj* chichigata (no shinzoku) 父方 (の親族)

ago *adv* ...máe ni ...前に; *a little while ~* (tsui) sákki (つい) さっき, [BOOKISH] (tsui) saki-hodo (つい) 先程

agony *n* kurushimi 苦しみ, kutsū 苦痛

agrarian *adj* nōgyō (no) 農業(の), nōchi (no) 農地(の), nōson (no) 農村 (の), nōmin (no) 農民(の)

agree *v* **1.** (*approves*) sansei shimásu (suru, shite) 賛成します (する, して); (*concurs*) dōi shimásu (suru, shite) 同意します (する, して) **2.** (*promises*) yakusoku shimásu (suru, shite) 約束します (する, して) **3.** (*accords with*) ... ni kanaimásu (kanáu, kanátte) ...にかないます (かなう, かなって), ... to

itchi shimásu (suru, shite) ...と一致し
ます(する、して); ~ *with* (*in harmony*)
... to chōwa shimásu (suru, shite) ...と
調和します(する、して)
agreeable *adj* aisó/aisō´ ga íi あいそ/
あいそう[愛想]がいい
agreement *n* **1.** (*promise*) yakusoku
約束; (*contract*) keiyaku 契約; (*treaty*)
jōyaku 条約 **2.** (*understanding*) shōchi
承知; (*consensus*) itchi 一致, dōi 同意,
gō´i 合意 **3.** (*harmony*) chōwa 調和
agriculture *n* nō´gyō 農業
ague *n* okóri おこり, mararia netsu
マラリア熱, okán 悪寒
ahead *adv* saki (ni) 先(に) (o-saki (ni)
お先(に)); *gets* ~ susumimásu
(susumu, susunde) 進みます(進む、進
んで)
ahead and behind zén go (ni) 前後
(に)
aid → help
AIDS *n* éizu エイズ, AIDS
aikido *n* aikídō 合気道
ail → sick
ailing *adj* byōki de 病気で, byōki
ryōyōchū (no) 病気療養中(の)
aim *n* **1.** nerai 狙い, méate 目当て; médo
目処・目途, meyasu 目安, kentō´ 見当;
(*target*) mato 的; *takes* ~ kentō´ o
tsukemásu (tsukéru, tsukéte) 見当をつ
けます(つける、つけて) **2.** (*goal*)
mokuteki 目的; (*direction*) hōshin 方針
aim at ... *v* **1.** o neraimásu (nerau,
neratte) ...を狙います(狙う、狙って)
2. ...o megakemásu (megakéru,
megákete) ...を目掛けます(目掛ける、
目掛けて)
aimless *adj* mokuteki ga/no nái 目的
が/のない
air 1. *n* kū´ki 空気 **2.** *n* (*manner*) furí
ふり; (*appearance*) fū´ 風 **3.** *n* (*tune*)
fushí 節 **4.** *v airs it* (*dry*) hoshimásu
(hósu, hóshite) 干します(干す、干して)
air base *n* kūgun kíchi 空軍基地
air conditioner, air conditioning *n*
kū´ra クーラー, eakon エアコン, reibō
(sō´chi) 冷房(装置)
aircraft *n* hikōki 飛行機
aircraft carrier *n* kōkū bokan 航空
母艦

air force *n* kūgun 空軍
airline *n* (*company*) kōkū-gáisha 航空
会社
airmail *n* kōkū-bin 航空便, kōkū
yū´bin 航空郵便, eamēru エアメール
airplane *n* hikō´-ki 飛行機
airport *n* kūkō 空港, hikōjō 飛行場
airsick *adv gets* ~ hikōki ni yoimásu
(yóu, yótte) 飛行機に酔います(酔う、
酔って)
airsick(ness) *n* hikō-yoi 飛行機酔い
airspace *n* ryōkū 領空
air terminal *n* tāminaru ターミナル
airy *adj* **1.** kaze tōshi no yoi 風通しの
よい **2.** keikai (na) 軽快(な) **3.** kei-
haku (na) 軽薄(な)
aisle *n* tsū´ro 通路
ajar *adj* **1.** sukoshi hiráite 少し開いて,
hanbiraki (de) 半開き(で) **2.** chōwa
shinái (de) 調和しない(で)
akin *adj* **1.** ketsuen (no) 血縁(の),
ketsuzoku (no) 血族(の) **2.** dōshu
(no) 同種(の), ruiji (no) 類似(の)
à la carte *adj, adv* ippin ryō´ri 一品料
理, arakaruto (no) アラカルト(の)
alarm *n* keihō 警報(装置)
alarm clock *n* arāmu アラーム,
mezámashi 目覚し, mezamashi-dókei
目覚し時計
alas *prep* áa ああ, āā あーあ
album *n* (*photograph*) arubamu アル
バム; (*stamp*) kitte-chō 切手帳
alchemy *n* renkinjutsu(shi) 錬金術
(師), arukemísuto アルケミスト
alcohol *n* arukōru アルコール
alcoholic *n* arukōru chūdoku-sha
アルコール中毒者
alcove *n* (*in Japanese room*) toko no
ma 床の間
alert *n* (*alarm*) keihō 警報, arāto アラ
ート
algebra *n* dáisū (gaku) 代数(学)
alias *n* gimei 偽名, betsumei 別名,
tsūshō 通称
alibi *n* aribái アリバイ
alien *n* **1.** yosó (no) よそ(の) **2.** (*an
alien*) → **foreigner 3.** uchūjin 宇宙
人, éirian エイリアン
alienate *v* sogai shimásu (suru, shite)
疎外します(する、して), tōzakemásu

(tōzakeru, tōzakete) 遠ざけます(遠ざ
ける, 遠ざけて), sodéni shimasu
(suru, shite) そでにします(する, して)

align v seiretsu shimasu (suru, shite)
整列します(する, して), narabimásu
(narabu, narande) 並びます(並ぶ, 並
んで)

alike adj onaji (yō´na) 同じ(ような),
nitéiru 似ている

alimentary adj eiyō (no) 栄養(の),
tabemono (no) 食べ物(の)

alimony n bekkyo téate 別居手当,
rikon téate 離婚手当, fujoryō 扶助料

alive adj **1.** is ~ íkite imásu (iru, ite)
生きています(いる, いて), **2.** keeps it
~ ikashimásu (ikásu, ikáshite) 生かしま
す(生かす, 生かして)

all pron **1.** minna みんな, zen'in 全員;
all (concerned/present) ichidō 一同 **2.**
zénbu 全部, súbete 全て; (everything)
íssai 一切, arayúru あらゆる; not at
~ どういたしまして **3.** (completely)
sukkári すっかり

all along adv (from the beginning)
móto kara 元から

all day (long) adv ichinichi-jū 一日中

all directions, all sides adv shíhō 四方

all kinds of adj samazama (na) さまざ
ま(な), iroiro (na/no) いろいろ(な/
の), shúshu (no) 種々(の)

all-out adj zenmen-teki (na) 全面的な,
zenryoku o ageta 全力をあげた

all over adv **1.** (everywhere) hōbō ほ
うぼう; ...-jū ...中 **2.** (finished) → end

all of a sudden adv totsuzen (ni) 突然
(に), fuini 不意に, ikinari いきなり

all the more adv issō いっそう, nao-
sara なおさら

all the time adv zutto ずっと, shótchū
しょっちゅう, shíjū/始終; (usually)
tsunezune 常々

all the way to adv ... máde ...まで

all the way through adv zutto ずっと

all together adv awásete 合わせて

allay v shizumemásu (shizumeru,
shizumete) 静めます(静める, 静めて),
yawáragemásu (yawárageru,
yawáragete) 和らげます(和らげる, 和
らげて)

allegation n **1.** shuchō 主張 **2.** mōshi-

tate 申し立て

allege v **1.** shuchō shimasu (suru, shite)
主張します(する, して) **2.** mōshitate-
másu (mōshitateru, mōshitatete) 申し
立てます(申し立てる, 申し立てて)

allegory n gūwa 寓話

allergy n arérúgii アレルギー

alleviate v **1.** yawáragemásu
(yawárageru, yawáragete) 和らげます
(和らげる, 和らげて) **2.** shizumemásu (shizumeru, shizmete) 静めます
(静める, 静めて) **3.** kanwa shimásu
(suru, shite) 緩和します(する, して)

alley n róji 路地; (back street) urá 裏,
ura-dō´ri 裏通り; (side street) yokochō
横町[横丁]

alliance n rengō 連合

allied adj rengōku no 連合国の,
dōmeikoku no 同盟国の

Allies n Rengōkoku 連合国

alligator n wáni ワニ

allocate v wariatemásu (suru, shite)
割り当てます(する, して), haibun
shimásu (suru, shite) 配分します(する,
して)

allot v kubarimásu (kubáru, kubátte) 配
ります(配る, 配って)

allotment n wariate 割り当て; (share)
buntan 分担

allow v. **1.** (permits) yurushimásu
(yurúsu, yurúshite) 許します(許す, 許
して) **2.** → give

allowance n (bonus) téate 手当 (o-téate
お手当); (grant) kyō´yo 供与; makes
~ for ...o kagen shimásu (suru, shite)
...を加減します(する, して)

alloy n gōkin 合金

all right adj (OK) dáijōbu (na) 大丈夫
(な); (permissible) íi いい, yoroshii
よろしい

allude v honomeka shimásu (su, shite)
ほのめかします(す, して), anji shi-
másu (suru, shite) 暗示します(する,
して)

allure 1. n miryoku 魅力, miwaku
魅惑 **2.** adj alluring miryoku-teki (na)
魅力的な, miwaku-teki (na) 魅惑的な

ally n dāmeikoku 同盟国

almanac n koyomi 暦, nenkan 年鑑

almond n āmondo アーモンド

313

almost *adv* hotóndo ほとんど; daitai 大体
　almost all, almost all the time *n* hotóndo ほとんど
　almost every day *n* máinichi no yō ni 毎日のように

alms *n* hodokoshi (mono) 施し(もの)

aloft *adj* kūchū ni/de 空中に/で, takaitokoro ni/de 高いところに/で

alone *adv* hítori (de) 一人[独り](で); (*somewhere*) *let ~* hotte/hōtte okimásu (oku, oite) 放っておきます(おく, おいて)

along 1. *prep, adv* ...ni sotte ...に沿って; (*somewhere*) ...no doko ka (de) ...のどこか(で) 2. *adv brings/takes ~* jisan shimásu (suru, shite) 持参します(する, して); (... o tsurete ikimásu (iku, itte) ...を連れて行きます(行く, 行って)

alongside *prep* ... no sóba ni ...のそばに

aloof *adj* takabisha (na) 高飛車(な), otákaku tomatta お高くとまった

aloud *adv* kóe o/ni dáshite 声を/に出して

alphabet (ABC) *n* arufabetto アルファベット, ē bii shíi エービーシー

alphabetical *adj* ē-bii-shii jun (no) ABC 順(の), arufabetto jun (no) アルファベット順(の)

Alps *n* arupusu アルプス

already *adv* mō'もう, súde-ni すでに

also *conj* 1. ...mo ...も,, mátá また 2. [INFORMAL] yappári やっぱり, [BOOKISH] yahári やはり

altar *n* saidan 祭壇
　household altar *n* (*Buddhist*) butsu-dan 仏壇; (*Shinto*) kami-dana 神棚

alter *v* 1. (*clothing*) naoshimásu (naósu, naóshite) 直します(直す, 直して) 2. aratamemásu (arataméru, aratámete) 改めます(改める, 改めて), kaemásu (kaeru, kaete) 変えます(変える, 変えて)

alternate; *v alternate (with)* kōtai shimásu (suru, shite) 交代[交替]します(する, して)

alternately *adv* kawaru-gáwaru 代わる代わる

alternating current *n* kōryū 交流

alternation *n* kōtai 交代・交替

alternative *adj, n* ... (no) hō´(ga) ... (の)方(が)

although *conj* ... no ni ...のに, ... daga ... だが, ... towaie ... とはいえ

altitude *n* kō´do 高度

altogether *adv* 1. zénbu de 全部で; minná de みんなで 2. (*completely*) mattakú まったく

altruism *n* ritá shugi 利他主義, ritá-teki (na) kōi 利他的(な)行為

aluminum *n* arumi(niumu) アルミ(ニウム)

alumna *n* joshi sotsugyōsei 女子卒業生, josei no sotsugyōsei 女性の卒業生

alumni *n* sotsugyōsei 卒業生
　alumni association *n* dōsō-kai 同窓会

alumnus (*of...*) *n* (...no) sotsugyō(-sei) ...(の)卒業(生), shusshin 出身

always *adv* 1. ítsu-mo いつも, (*usually*) fúdan ふだん・普段 2. (*from the beginning*) móto kara 元から
　as always *n* aikawarazu 相変わらず

am → **is**

a.m. *adv* (*morning*) gozen 午前, ē emu AM

amalgamate *v* 1. gappei shimásu (suru, shite) 合併します(する, して), heigō shimásu (suru, shite) 併合します(する, して) 2. yūgō shimásu (suru, shite) 融合します(する, して), maze-másu (mazeru, mazete) 混ぜます(混ぜる, 混ぜて)

amass *v* tamemásu (taméru, támete) ため[貯め・溜め]ます(ためる, ためて)

amateur *n* amachua アマチュア; (*novice*) shírō'to しろうと・素人

amaze *v gets amased* akiremásu (akireru, akirete) 呆れます(呆れる, 呆れて), bikkuri shimásu (suru, shite) びっくりします(する, して)

amazement *n* odoroki おどろき・驚き, kyōtan 驚嘆

ambassador *n* táishi 大使

amber *n* kohaku (iro) 琥珀(色)

ambition *n* (*hope*) netsubō 熱望, yashin 野心; (*energetic spirit*) háki 覇気

ambitious *adj* yashin-teki (na) 野心的(な)

ambivalent *adj* kokoro ga fúantei (na)

心が不安定(な), ánbibarensu (no)
アンビバレンス(の), kattō-teki (na)
葛藤的な

ambulance *n* kyūkyū-sha 救急車

ambush **1.** *n* machibuse 待ち伏せ,
harikomi 張り込み, fuiuchi 不意打ち,
kishū kōgeki 奇襲攻撃 **2.** *v* machibuse
shimásu (suru, shite) 待ち伏せします
(する, して), kishū kōgeki o kakemásu
(kakeru, kakete) 奇襲攻撃をかけます
(かける, かけて)

amenable *adj* jūjun (na) 従順(な),
sunao (na) 素直(な)

amend *v* shūsei shimásu (suru, shite)
修正します(する, して), kaisei shimásu
(suru, shite) 改正します(する, して)

amendment *n* shūsei 修正, kaisei 改正

amenity *n* **1.** kokochiyosa 心地よさ,
kaiteki-sa/sei 快適さ/性, reigi 礼儀
3. benri na shisetsu 便利な施設

America *n* Amerika アメリカ, Beikoku
米国

American *n* Ameriká-jin アメリカ人

amiable *adj* shakō-teki (na) 社交的
(な), hitozukiai no yoi 人付き合いの
よい, hitoatari no yoi 人当たりのよい,
kanji no yoi 感じのよい, aiso/aisō ga íi
あいそ/あいそう[愛想]がいい

amiss *adv* machigatte 間違って, fute-
kitō ni 不適当に, futsugō ni 不都合に,
hazurete はずれて・外れて

amity *n* yūkō 友好, shinboku 親睦,
shinzen 親善

ammonia *n* ánmonia アンモニア

ammunition *n* **1.** dan'yaku 弾薬, buki
武器 **2.** kōgeki shudan 攻撃手段, bōei
shudan 防衛手段

amnesia *n* kioku sōshitsu 記憶喪失,
kenbō-shō 健忘症

amnesiac *adj* kiokusōshitsu (no) 記憶
喪失(の)

amnesty **1.** *n* onsha 恩赦 **2.** *v* onsha o
ataemásu (ataeru, ataete) 恩赦を与え
ます(与える, 与えて)

among *prep* ... no náka/uchí (ni) ...
の中/内(に)

amoral *adj* dōtoku kannen no nai 道徳
観念のない

amorous *adj* **1.** iroppoi 色っぽい,
namámekashii なまめかしい **2.** kōsho-

ku (na) 好色(な) **3.** koi (no) 恋(の),
ren'ai (no) 恋愛(の)

amortize *v* shōkyaku shimásu (suru,
shite) 償却します(する, して), kenbō-
shō 健忘症

amount **1.** *n* (*sum*) gáku 額, kingaku
金額 **2.** *n* (*large and/or small*) ~ tashō
多少 **3.** *v* ~ *to* (*how much*) (íkura o-
ikura) ni narimásu (náru, nátte) いくら
(おいくら)になります(なる, なって)
4. *v* *what it amounts to is* ...yōsúru ni
要するに

amour **1.** *n* ren'ai 恋愛, jōji 情事
2. aijin 愛人

ample *adj* **1.** *n* hiroi 広い, kōdai na
広大な **2.** futotta 太った **3.** jūbun (na)
じゅうぶん・十分(な) → **enough**

amplifier *n* anpu アンプ

amplify *v* kakudai shimásu (suru, shite)
拡大します(する, して)

amulet *n* o-mamori お守り

amuse *v* warawasemásu (warawaseru,
warawasete) 笑わせます(笑わせる, 笑
わせて), tanoshimasemásu (tanoshi-
maseru, tanoshimasete) 楽しませます
(楽しませる, 楽しませて)

amusement *n* **1.** asobi 遊び **2.** nagusami 慰み, goraku 娯楽
amusement park *n* yūenchi 遊園地

amusing *adj* omoshirói おもしろい・
面白い; (*funny*) okashíi おかしい,
kokkei (na) こっけい・滑稽(な)

an → **a**

anal *adj* kōmon no 肛門の

analog *n*, *adj* anarogu (shiki) (no)
アナログ(式)(の)

analogy *n* **1.** tatoe 例え **2.** ruiji 類似

analysis *n* bunseki 分析

ancestor *n* sósen 祖先, sénzo 先祖

ancestry; *of ... ~* ...-kei (no) ... 系(の)
an American of Japanese ancestry *n*
Nikkei (no) Ameriká-jin 日系(の)ア
メリカ人, (Amerika no) Nikkéi-jin
(アメリカの)日系人

anchor *n* ikari いかり・錨・碇
anchor man *n* nyūsu kyásutā ニュー
スキャスター

ancient *adj* mukashi no 昔の, kodai no
古代の
ancient days ōmukashi 大昔

ancient times kodai 古代
and conj ... (including each item) ... to
...と; (choosing typical items) ...ya ...や;
(does/did) and [VERB]-te て; [VERB]-
rú/-tá shi る/たし; (is/was) and [NOUN]
dc で, [ADJECTIVE]-kute くて; [NOUN]
dá/dátta shi だ/だったし, [ADJECTIVE]-
í/-kátta shi い/かったし
and also ... oyobi ...および・及び
and now/then sá-te さて/それから
and/or mátá-wa または, ...ya ...や
and others ... -ra ...ら;... nádo ...など,
sonó-hoka そのほか, [BOOKISH] sonó-
ta その他
and so forth/on, and the like, and
what-not ... nádo ...など..., ... nánka ...な
んか
and yet sore démo それでも, shiká-
mo しかも, sore náno ni それなのに
anemia n hinketsu(-shō) 貧血(症)
anesthetic n másui(-yaku/zai) 麻酔
(薬/剤)
anew adv ataráshjku 新しく, aratámete
改めて, sára-ni さらに
angel n ténshi 天使, enjeru エンジェル
angel fish n énzeru fisshu エンゼルフ
イッシュ
anger n ikari 怒り
angina n angina アンギナ, kyōshin-
shō 狭心症
angle n 1. kákudo 角度, kaku 角
2. (viewpoint) kénchi 見地
angry; gets ~ okorimásu (okóru,
okótte) 怒ります(怒る, 怒って), hará
o tatemásu (tatéru, tátete) 腹を立てま
す(立てる, 立てて), atáma ni kimásu
(kuru, kite) 頭にきます(くる, きて),
kiremásu (kiréru, kirete) キレます(キ
レる, キレて)
animal n dōbutsu 動物, ikímono 生き
物; [IN NEGATIVE SENSE] ke(da)mono
け(だ)もの・獣 (1: ip-pjki 一匹,
2: ní-hjki 二匹, 3: sán-biki 三匹, how
many nán-biki 何匹)
animation n 1. animé アニメ, animēshon アニメーション, dōga 動画
2. kakki 活気
ankle n ashí-kúbi 足首
anklets n sókkusu ソックス (how many
nán-soku/-zoku 何足)

annex n 1. (building) bekkan 別館
2. (new) shinkan 新館 3. (addition)
tate-mashi 建て増し
annihilation n zenmetsu 全滅
anniversary n (day) kinén-bi 記念日
annotation n chū 注
announce v 1. (informs) shirasemásu
(shiraseru, shirasete) 知らせます(知
らせる, 知らせて) 2. (publishes)
happyō shimásu (suru, shite) 発表しま
す(する, して) 3. (wedding, etc.) hírō
shimásu (suru, shite) 披露します(す
る, して)
announcement n happyō 発表,
anáunsu アナウンス
announcer n anáunsā アナウンサー
annoyance n (trouble) méiwaku 迷惑
annoying adj urusái うるさい,
yakamashíi やかましい, méiwaku (na)
迷惑(な), wazurawashíi わずらわしい
annual 1. adj ichinen (no) 一年(の)
2. n nenkan 年刊, nenpō 年報
annuity n nenkin 年金
annul v haishi shimásu (suru, shite)
廃止します(する, して), mukō ni
shimásu (suru, shite) 無効にします
(する, して)
anomalous adj hensóku (no) 変則
(の), tókui (na) 特異(な)
anonymous adj mumei (no) 無名(の)
anorak n 1. anorákku アノラック
2. otáku オタク
another pron mō hitótsu もう一つ, mō
ichi-... もう一...
another person mō hitóri もう一人
another place yoso よそ
another time (some other time) ítsu-ka
いつか, izure いずれ
answer 1. n (an answer) kotáé 答え,
kaitō 解答, (a reply) henji 返事 (o-henji
お返事), [BOOKISH] hentō 返答 2. v
(answers it) kotaemásu (kotáéru,
kotáete) 答えます(答える, 答えて),
kaitō shimásu (suru, shite) 解答します
(する, して); ~ the phone denwa ni
demásu (déru, déte) 電話に出ます(出
る, 出て)
ant n ari アリ・蟻 (1: ip-pjki 一匹,
2: ní-hjki 二匹, 3: sán-biki 三匹; how
many nán-biki 何匹)

antagonism n tekii 敵意, tairitsu 対立, hánkan 反感, kikkō 拮抗

Antarctica n nánkyoku (tairiku) 南極 (大陸)

antenna n antena アンテナ

anthropology n jinrúi-gaku 人類学

anti- n han- 反

anti-American n, adj hanbei (no) 反米(の)

antibiotic(s) n kōsei bússhitsu 抗性 物質

antic(s) n kokkei na shigusa こっけい なしぐさ, odoketa shigusa おどけたし ぐさ, fuzaketa taido ふざけた態度

anticipate v machimásu (mátsu, mátte) 待ちます(待つ, 待って), kitai shimásu (suru, shite) 期待します(する, して); (presume) yosō shimásu (suru, shite); 予想します(する, して)

anticipation n → expectation → hope

anti-diarrhetic n geri-dome 下痢止め

antidote n 1. gedókuzai 解毒剤, dok(u)-késhí 毒消し 2. bōei shudan 防衛手段

antifreeze n futōeki 不凍液

antihistamine n kōhisutamín-zai 抗ヒ スタミン剤

anti-Japanese adj hannichi (no) 反日(の)

antipathy n hankan 反感, ken'o 嫌悪, fuítchi 不一致, tairitsu 対立

antiquated adj kyūshiki (no) 旧式 (の), táiko (no) 太古(の), kódai (no) 古代(の); [IN NEGATIVE SENSE] jidai okure (no) 時代遅れの(の); [IN POSITIVE SENSE] kófū (na) 古風(な)

antique n jidai-mono 時代物; (curio) kottō-hin 骨董品

antiquity n ōmukashi 大昔

antiseptic n bōfu-zai 防腐剤

antithesis n seihántai 正反対, taishō 対照, anchi-tēze アンチテーゼ

antiwar n, adj hansen (no) 反戦(の)

antler n edazunó 枝角, tsunó 角

antonym n hantai-go 反対語

anus n kōmon 肛門

anxiety n ki-zúkai 気遣い, shinpai 心配 → worry

anxious adj gets ~ harahara shimásu

(suru, shite) はらはらします(する, して) → worried, worry → eager

any adj ... ka ...か, ... mo ...も (but often omitted) → anything

anybody pron hito 人, dáre ka 誰か; (not anybody) dare mo 誰も anybody (at all) dare de mo 誰でも

anyhow adv 1. (nevertheless) tónikaku とにかく; (anyway) tómokaku ともか く, nanibun なにぶん, nánishiro なに しろ 2. (at all) dō de mo どうでも

anyone → anybody

anyplace → anywhere

anything pron 1. (something) náni ka 何か (but often omitted); (not anything) nani mo 何も 2. (at all) nan de mo 何でも

any time adv itsu de mo いつでも

anyway adv → anyhow

anywhere adv (somewhere) dóko ka (...) どこか(...); anywhere (at all) doko de mo どこでも; not anywhere → nowhere

apart; adv lives ~ bekkyo shimásu (suru, shite) 別居します(する, して); ~ from ... ...wa betso ni shite ...は別と して; quite ~ from ... ... tó wa betsu ni (shite) ... とは別に(して); takes it ~ barashimásu (barásu, baráshite) ばら します(ばらす, ばらして)

apartment (house) n apāto アパート, (luxury) mánshon マンション apartment complex n danchi 団地

apathetic adj mukándō (no) 無感動 (の), mukánjō (no) 無感情(の), mukán-shin (no) 無関心(の)

apathy n mukándō 無感動, mukánjō 無感情, mukanshin 無関心

ape 1. n sáru サル・猿 2. n noróma na hito のろまな人 3. v ... o mane(su)ru ... をまね(す)る, ... no mane o suru ... のまねをする

aperitif n aperitifu/aperichifu アペリティ フ/アペリチフ, shokuzen-shu 食前酒

aphorism n kakugen 格言, kingen 金言, keiku 警句

aphrodisiac n biyaku 媚薬, hore-gusuri ほれ薬, [FORMAL] seishin kyōsōzai 精神強壮剤

apiece *adv* (onóono/sorezore) ...zútsu (おのおの/それぞれ) ...ずつ

apologize *v* owabishimásu (suru, shite) おわび[お詫び]します(する, して), ayamarimásu (ayamáru, ayamátte) 謝ります(謝る, 謝って); *I apologize (for what I did).* Mōshiwaké arimasén/gozaimasén 申し訳ありません/ございません, sumimasén すみません, gomen nasái ごめんなさい

apology *n* wabi わび・詫び (o-wabi お詫び), ayamári 謝り

apoplexy *n* (nō) sotchū (脳)卒中, (nō) ikketsu (脳)溢血

appall *v* zotto shimásu (suru, shite) ぞっとします(する, して), gakuzen to shimásu (suru, shite) がく然とします(する, して)

apparatus *n* sṓchi 装置; kígu 器具

apparel *n* (i)fuku (衣)服

apparel industry *n* apareru gyōkai アパレル業界

apparent(ly) *adv* ... rashíi ...らしい

apparition *n* **1.** yūrei 幽霊, bōrei 亡霊 **2.** shutsu-gen 出現

appeal *v* (*appeal to one*) pin to kimásu (kúru, kíte) ぴんときます(くる, きて), ki ni irimásu (ki ni iru, ki ni itte) 気に入ります(気に入る, 気に入って)

appear *v* **1.** (*looks, seems*) miemásu (miéru, míete) 見えます(見える, 見えて) **2.** (*shows up*) demásu (déru, déte) 出ます(出る, 出て), arawaremásu (arawaréru, arawárete) 現れます(現れる, 現われて); (*occurs*) hassei shimásu (suru, shite) 発生します(する, して); *~ on stage* bútai ni demásu (déru, déte) 舞台に出ます(出る, 出て), tōjō shimásu (suru, shite) 登場します(する, して)

appearance *n* **1.** yōsu 様子・ようす, ...sama ...様 **2.** gaiken 外見; (*outer appearances*) uwabe うわべ・上辺, omoté 表 **3.** (*get-up, form*) teisai 体裁; (*shape*) kakkō かっこう・格好・恰好 • *personal appearance* **4.** (*air, manner*) ...fū́ ...風

appease *v* nadámemásu (nadameru, nadamete) なだめます(なだめる, なだめて), yawaragemásu (yawarageru,

yawaragete) 和らげます(和らげる, らげて), iyashimásu (iyasu, iyashite) いやします・癒します(癒す, 癒して)

append *v* fuka shimásu (suru, shite) 付加します(する, して), tsuketashimásu (tsuketasu, tsuketashite) 付け足します(付け足す, 付け足して), soemásu (soeru, soete) 添えます(添える, 添えて)

appendage *n* fuzoku-butsu 付属物

appendectomy *n* mōchō setsujojutsu 盲腸切除術, mōchō-en (no) shujutsu 盲腸炎(の)手術, chūsui setsujojutsu 虫垂切除術, chūsui-en (no) shujutsu 虫垂炎(の)手術

appendicitis *n* mōchō-en 盲腸炎, chūsui-en 虫垂炎

appetite *n* shokuyoku 食欲

appetizers *n* zensai 前菜; (*to go with drinks*) sakana さかな・肴, tsumami (mono) つまみ(もの), o-tsúmami おつまみ

appetizing *adj* oishisō (na) おいしそう(な)

applaud *v* hákushu shimásu (suru, shite) 拍手します(する, して), hákushu o okurimásu (okuru, okutte) 拍手を送ります(送る, 送って)

applause *n* hákushu 拍手

apple *n* ringo リンゴ・林檎 (*how many* nán-ko 何個)

apple pie *n* appuru pai アップルパイ

appliances *n* (katei) yṓgu (家庭)用具, katei yṓhin 家庭用品; (*electric*) denki-yṓhin 電気用品, katei-yō denki kigu 家庭用電気器具

applicant *n* mōshikomí-sha 申し込み者, kibō-sha 希望者

application *n* **1.** (*for a job, etc.*) mōshi-komi 申し込み, gánsho 願書; (*claim*) mōshi-de 申し出; (*for a permit*) shinsei-sho 申請書 **2.** (*putting to use*) ōyō 応用, jitsuyō 実用; (*for computer*) sofutowea ソフトウェア

apply *v* **1.** (*it applies*) atarimásu (ataru, attate) 当たります(当たる, 当たって); (*accordingly*) jun-jimásu (jun-jiru, jun-jite) 準じます(準じる, 準じて) **2.** (*applies it*) atemásu (ateru, atete) 当てます(当てる, 当てて), tsukemásu (tsukéru, tsukéte) 付けます(付ける, 付けて); ōyō shimásu (suru, shite) 応用します(する, して) **3.** (*applies for*) mōshi-komimásu (mōshi-komu, mōshi-konde) 申し込みます(申し込む, 申し込んで), ōbo shimásu (suru, shite) 応募します(する, して); (*claims*) mōshi-demásu (mōshi-deru, mōshi-dete) 申し出ます(申し出る, 申し出て)

appoint *v* (*nominates*) mei-jimásu (mei-jiru, mei-jite) 命じます(命じる, 命じて); (*designates*) shitei shimásu (suru, shite) 指定します(する, して)

appointed day *n* kíjitsu 期日

appointment *n* (*engagement, date, visit to a customer*) yakusoku 約束; (*to see doctor, ...*) yoyaku 予約

apportion *v* ... o wariatemásu (wariateru, wariatete) ... を割り当てます(割り当てる, 割り当てて), ... o bunpai shimásu (suru, shite) ... を分配します(する, して)

appraisal *n* hyōka 評価

appraise *v* hyōka shimásu (suru, shite) 評価します(する, して), kantei shimásu (suru, shite) 鑑定します(する, して)

appreciable *adj* kánari (no) かなり(の), sōtō (no) 相当(の)

appreciate *v* arigátaku omoimásu (omóu, omótte) ありがたく[有り難く] 思います(思う, 思って), kansha shimásu (suru, shite) 感謝します(する, して)

appreciation *n* kánsha 感謝, hyōka 評価

apprehend *v* **1.** ríkai shimásu (suru, shite) 理解します(する, して), sasshimásu (su(ru), shite) 察します(す(る), して) **2.** tsukamaemásu (tsukamaeru, tsukamaete) 捕まえます(捕まえる, 捕まえて), taiho shimásu (suru, shite) 逮捕します(する, して) **3.** shinpai shimásu (suru, shite) 心配します(する, して)

apprehensive *adj* kimí ga warúi 気味が悪い

apprentice *n* deshí 弟子

approach *v* (...ni) chika-zukimásu (chika-zúku, chika-zúite) (...に)近付

きます(近付く, 近付いて), yorimásu (yóru, yótte) 寄ります(寄る, 寄って); sekkin shimásu (suru, shite) 接近します(する, して); *lets one* ~ (... o) chika-zukemásu (chika-zukéru, chika-zúkete) (...を)近付けます(近付ける, 近付けて)

appropriate 1. *adj* (*suitable*) tekisetsu (na) 適切(な), tekitō (na) 適当(な) **2.** *v* (*sets aside (for)*) atemásu (ateru, atete) 当てます(当てる, 当てて) **3.** *v* → **seize**

approval *n* dōi 同意

approve *v* sansei shimásu (suru, shite) 賛成します(する, して)

approximate 1. *adj* daitai (no) 大体 (の), gaisan (no) 概算(の), chikái 近い **2.** *v* chikazukimásu (chikazuku, chikazuite) 近づきます(近づく, 近づいて), chikazukemásu (chikazukeru, chikazukete) 近づけます(近づける, 近づけて)

approximately *adv* daitai 大体; yáku ... 約...; ... gúrai ...位; ...-zéngo ...前後; ... -kéntō ...見当; ...-náigai (de) ...内外(で)

apricot *n* anzu アンズ・杏

April *n* Shi-gatsú 四月・4月

apron *n* épuron エプロン

apropos *adv* tekisetsu na/ni 適切な/に

apt; *adj* ~ *to (do)* (shi-)yasúi (し)やすい; [BOOKISH] tokaku (...shimásu) とかく(...します); [BOOKISH] ete-shite (...shimásu) 得てして(します)

aptitude *n* keikō 傾向, sáinō 才能, rikairyoku 理解力

aquarium *n* suizóku-kan 水族館

Aquarius *n* (*star sign*) Mizugame-za 水瓶座

Arab, Arabian *n, adj* Árabu (no) アラブ(の), (*person*) Arabú-jin (no) アラブ人(の)

Arabic *n* (*language*) Arabia-go アラビア語

arbiter *n* cyūsái-sha 仲裁者

arbitrary *adj* nin-i (no) 任意の, dokudan-teki (na) 独断的(な), kimáma (na) 気まま(な)

arbor *n* kokáge 木陰

arc *n* (en)ko (円)弧

arcade n ākēdo アーケード

archaeologist n kōko gákusha 考古学者

archaic adj sutáreta 廃れた

arch n yumi-gata 弓形, āchi(-gata) アーチ(形)

archer n ite, shashu 射手, yumí o iruhito 弓を射る人; yumí no meijin 弓の名人

archery n (the traditional art) kyūdō 弓道, kyūjutsu 弓術

archetype n genkei 原型, tenkei 典型

archipelago n rettō 列島, ...-rettō ...列島

architect n kenchíku-ka 建築家

architecture n kenchiku 建築

archive n kiroku (sho) 記録(書)

Arctic n Hokkyoku 北極

ardent adj nesshin (na) 熱心(な), netsuretsu(teki) (na) 熱烈(的)(な)

ardor n netsui 熱意, jōnetsu 情熱, nesshin 熱心, ikigomi 意気込み

arduous adj kónnan (na) 困難(な)

arid adj kánsō shita/shiteiru 乾燥した/している, fumō no/na 不毛の/に

are → is

area n 1. ménseki 面積 2. (district) chíhō 地方, chiiki 地域, eria エリア, chitai 地帯 → place → vicinity

argue v kenka shimásu (suru, shite) けんか[喧嘩]します(する, して); (discusses, debates) ron-jimásu (ron-jiru, ron-jite) 論じます(論ずる, 論じて)

argument n 1. kenka けんか, kuchi-génka 口げんか 2. (discussion) rón論, ronsō 論争 3. (logic) rikutsu 理屈

Aries n (star sign) O-hitsuji-za 牡羊座

arise v okimásu (okíru, ókite) 起きます(起きる, 起きて); (happens) shō-jimásu (shō-jiru, shō-jite) 生じます(生じる, 生じて)

ark shell n (blood clam) aká-gai 赤貝

arm n udé 腕

armor n yoroi よろい・鎧

armory n buki ko 武器庫, heiki ko 兵器庫

armpit n waki nó shita わきの下
armpit smell n (body odor) waki-ga わきが

arms n heiki 兵器, buki 武器

army n gúntai 軍隊; (vs. navy) rikú-gun 陸軍

aroma n ároma アロマ, (yoi) kaori (よい)香り, hōkō 芳香

around 1. adv (... no) mawari ni (...の)周りに; goes ~ (... o) mawarimásu (mawaru, mawatte) (...を)回ります (回る, 回って) 2. → about, approximately

arouse v shigeki shimásu (suru, shite) 刺激します(する, して), kōfun shimásu (suru, shite) 興奮します(する, して), kōfun sasemásu (saseru, sasete) 興奮させます(させる, させて)

arrange v 1. (lines them up) narabemásu (naraberu, narabete) 並べます (並べる, 並べて); ~ themselves narabimásu (narabu, narande) 並びます(並ぶ, 並んで) 2. (decides, sets) kimemásu (kimeru, kimete) 決めます(決める, 決めて); (a meeting/consultation) uchi-awasemásu (uchi-awaséru, uchi-awásete) 打ち合わせます(打ち合わせる, 打ち合わせて) 3. (puts together) matomemásu (matomeru, matomete) まとめます(まとめる, まとめて) 4. (flowers) (haná o) ikemásu (ikéru, íkete) (花を)生けます(生ける, 生けて)

arranged v 1. gets ~ (is put together) matomarimásu (matomaru, matomatte) まとまります(まとまる, まとまって), (as a set/array) soroimásu (soróu, sorótte) 揃います(揃う, 揃って); (gets decided/set) kimarimásu (kimaru, kimatte) 決まります(決まる, 決まって) 2. it has been ~ that ... kotó ni natte (i)másu ...ことになって(い)ます

arranged marriage n (o-)miai kékkon (お)見合い結婚

arrangement n 1. (settlement) kimari 決まり; (adjustment) séiri 整理 2. arrangements (preparations) júnbi 準備, shitaku 支度・仕度; (plans) téhazu 手はず・手筈

flower arrangement n ikébana 生け花・いけばな

prior arrangement n uchi-awase 打ち合わせ

array *n* soróe 揃え

arrears *n* tainō(kin) 滞納（金）

arrest *v* toraemásu (toráeru, toráete) 捕えます (捕える, 捕えて), tsukamae-másu (tsukamaeru, tsukamaete) 捕えます (捕える, 捕えて), táiho shimásu (suru, shite) 逮捕します (する, して)

arrival *n* tōchaku 到着; ... cháku ...着

arrive (at) *v* **1.** (... ni) tsukimásu (tsukú, tsuite) (...に) 着きます (着く, 着いて), tōchaku shimásu (suru, shite) 到着します (する, して), itarimásu (itaru, itatte) 至ります (至る, 至って) **2.** (*is delivered*) todokimásu (todóku, todóite) 届きます (届く, 届いて)

arriving at (TIME/PLACE) ... cháku (no) ...着 (の)

arrogant *adj* gōman (na) 傲慢 (な); *is/acts ~* ibarimásu (ibáru, ibátte) 威張ります (威張る, 威張って)

arrow *n* yá 矢; (*sign*) ya-jírushi 矢印

arrowroot *n* kuzu くず・葛

powdered arrowroot *n* kuzuko くず粉・葛粉

art *n* bíjutsu 美術, geijutsu 芸術

artery *n* **1.** dōmyaku 動脈 **2.** kansen dōro 幹線道路

artful *adj* kōmyō (na) 巧妙 (な), takumi (na) 巧み (な), kōkatsu (na) 狡猾 (な), jinkō (no) 人工 (の)

arthritis *n* kansetsu-en 関節炎

article *n* (*thing*) monó 物, (*goods*) shina(-mono) 品 (物); (*writeup*) kíji 記事, (*scholarly*) ronbun 論文

articulate **1.** *adj* hakkírishita はっきりした, meikai (na) 明快 (な) **2.** *v* hakkíri iimásu (iu, itte) はっきり言います (言う, 言って)

artifice *n* sakuryaku 策略, kōmyō sa 巧妙さ

artificial *adj* jinkō (no) 人工 (の), jinkō-teki (na) 人工的 (な)

artillery *n* taihō 大砲, buki 武器

artisan *n* shokunin 職人

artist *n* geijutsu-ka 芸術家; (*painter*) gaka 画家

arts *n* géi 芸, waza 技, āto アート

as **1.** *conj* (*like*) ... (no) yō´ (ni) ... (の) よう (に) **2.** (*so as to be*) ...ni..に

3. (*in the role of*) ... to shite ... として

as far as ... is concerned ... ni kákete wa ... にかけては; ...ni kan-shite wa ...に関しては

as for ... wa ...は

as much as ... gúrai ...位; ...hodo ...ほど; *~ one likes* zonbun ずん分

as much as possible dekiru-dake 出来るだけ

as regards ... ni kákete wa ...にかけては; ...ni kán-shite ...に関して; ni tsúite ...については

as to/for the matter at hand sá-te さて

as soon as ... (suru) to (súgu) ... (する) と (すぐ); ([shité] kara súgu (して) からすぐ; ([VERB]-i´-i) -shídai (ni) 次第 (に)

as usual/ever/always aikawarazu 相変わらず

Asakusa *n* Asakusa 浅草

ascent *n* jōshō 上昇, agáru koto 上がること

ascertain *v* tashikamemásu (tashikaméru, tashikámete) 確かめます (確かめる, 確かめて)

ascetic practices *n* shugyō 修行, gyō´行

ashamed *adj* hazukashíi 恥ずかしい; (*guilty feeling*) yamashíi やましい; *is ~ of* hajimásu (hajíru, hajíte) 恥ます (恥じる, 恥じて)

ash(es) *n* hai 灰; *volcanic ~* kazán-bai 火山灰

ashen *adj* hai iro (no) 灰色 (の), aojiroi 青白い, masáao (na) 真っ青 (な)

ashore *adv* kishi (ni) (mukatte) 岸 (に) (向かって), riku (ni) (mukatte) 陸 (に) (向かって)

ashtray *n* hai-zara 灰皿

Asian **1.** *adj* Ajia (no) アジア (の) **2.** *n* (*person*) Ajiá-jin アジア人

aside (from) *adv* ... wa betsu ni shite ...は別として

ask *v* **1.** (*a favor of a person*) (... ni ...o) tanomimásu (tanómu, tanónde) (...に...を) 頼みます (頼む, 頼んで), negai-másu (negau, negatte) 願います (願う, 願って); (*requires*) motomemásu (motoméru, motómete) 求めます

321

(求める, 求めて) **2.** (*asks a person a question*) (... ni) kikimásu (kiku, kiite) (...に)聞きます(聞く, 聞いて), tazunemásu (tazunéru, tazúnete) 尋ねます(尋ねる, 尋ねて), ukagaimásu (ukagau, ukagatte) 伺います(伺う, 伺って)

askance 1. *adv* utagatte 疑って **2.** *adj* nanáme (no) 斜め(の)

aslant *adv*, *adj* nanáme (no/ni) 斜め(の/に)

asleep *adv*, *adj* nemutte (iru) 眠って(いる)

asparagus *n* asupara (gásu) アスパラ(ガス)

aspect *n* **1.** yōsu 様子・ようす **2.** (*grammatical*) ásupékuto アスペクト, (soku/kyoku) men (側/局)面

aspersions *n* chūshō 中傷, hinan 非難

asphalt *n* asufáruto アスファルト

asphyxiate *v* chissoku shimásu (suru, shite) 窒息します(する, して), chissoku sasemásu (saseru, sasete) 窒息させます(させる, させて)

aspiration *n* ganbō 願望, yashin 野心, akogare 憧れ

aspire → **hope**

aspirin *n* asupirin アスピリン

ass 1. *n* róba ロバ・ろば **2.** *n* ganko-mono 頑固者; báka ばか **3.** *n* (o-)shíri (お)しり[尻] **4.** *v* (*act dumb*) báka na mane o shimásu (suru, shite) ばかな真似をします(する, して)

assail *v* kōgeki shimásu (suru, shite) 攻撃します(する, して), hínan shimásu (suru, shite) 非難します(する, して)

assault *v* osoimásu (osou, osotte) 襲います(襲う, 襲って) → **attack**

assemble *v* **1.** (*they collect*) atsumarimásu (atsumáru, atsumátte) 集まります(集まる, 集まって), shūgō shimásu (suru, shite) 集合します(する, して) atsumemásu (atsuméru, atsúmete) 集めます(集める, 集めて) **2.** (*fits parts together to make a whole*) kumi-awasemásu (kumi-awaseru, kumi-awasete) 組(み)合せます(組(み)合わせる, 組(み)合わせて), kumi-tatemásu (kumi-tateru, kumi-tatete) 組(み)立てます(組(み)立てる, 組(み)立てて)

assembly *n* **1.** (*gathering*) shūgō 集合 **2.** (*parliament*) kokkai 国会

assent *v* nattoku shimásu (suru, shite) 納得します(する, して) → **consent**

assert *v* shuchō shimásu (suru, shite) 主張します(する, して)

assertion *n* shuchō 主張

assimilate *v* dōka shimásu (suru, shite) 同化します(する, して); kyūshū shimásu (suru, shite) 吸収します(する, して)

assist *v* ōen shimásu (suru, shite) 応援します(する, して); tasukemásu (tasukéru, tasukete) 助けます(助ける, 助けて) → **help**

assistance *n* sewá 世話 (o-séwa お世話); tetsudái 手伝い(o-tétsudai お手伝い); hójo 補助, ōen 応援

assistant *n* joshu 助手, ashísutanto アシスタント

associate professor *n* jun-kyō′ju 准教授

associate with ...to tsuki-aimásu (tsuki-áu, tsuki-átte) ...と付き合います(付き合う, 付き合って); ...to maji-warimásu (majiwáru, majiwátte) ...と交わります(交わる, 交わって); ... o chika-zukemásu (chika-zukéru, chika-zúkete) ...を近付けます(近付ける, 近付けて)

association *n* **1.** kyōkai 協会; (*academic*) gakkai 学会; (*guild, union*) kumiai 組合 **2.** (*social company*) tsuki-ai 付き合い(o-tsukíai お付き合い) **3.** (*of thought*) rensō 連想

assortment *n* kumi-awase 組み合わせ, tori-awase 取り合わせ

assumed name *n* gimei 偽名

asterisk *n* hoshi-jírushi 星印; asutari-suku アスタリスク

asthma *n* zensoku 喘息

astonished; *adj* gets ~ odorokimásu (odoróku, odoróite) 驚きます(驚く, 驚いて)

astringent *adj* shibúi 渋い

astringent *n* (*facial*) asutorínzen アストリンゼン

astronomy *n* tenmón-gaku 天文学

asylum *n* hinán-jo 避難所, seishin byōin 精神病院

at *prep* ... de...で; (*being located at*) ... ni ...に
at any rate **tómokaku** ともかく
at best **séizei** せいぜい
at ease **yukkúri** ゆっくり
at last **iyoiyo** いよいよ, **yōyaku** ようやく, **tsúi-ni** ついに; (*after difficulty*) **yatto** やっと
at least **sukúnáku-tomo** 少なくとも, **sémete** せめて
at most **1.** ōku-temo 多くても, **séizei** せいぜい **2.** sémete せめて
at once **sassokú** 早速・さっそく
at one time **kátsute** かつて
atelier *n* **atorie** アトリエ, **gashitsu** 画室
athlete *n* (undō) sénshu (運動)選手
athlete's foot *n* **mizumushi** 水虫, **tamushi** 田虫
athletic field *n* undō-jō 運動場, kyōgi-jō 競技場
athletics *n* undō 運動, supō´tsu スポーツ; (*physical education*) tai(i)ku 体育, asurechíkku アスレチック
athletic supporter *n* sapōtā サポーター
Atlantic Ocean *n* Taiséiyō 大西洋
atmosphere *n* fun´iki 雰囲気
atom *n* génshi 原子
atomic *adj* genshí (-ryoku) 原子力(の)
atomic bomb *n* genshi bákudan 原子爆弾
atomic energy *n* genshí-ryoku 原子力
atomizer *n* supurē スプレー
atrocious *adj* (*brutal*) zangyaku (na) 残虐(な)
atrocity *n* zangyaku kō´i 残虐行為
attach 1. *v* (*sticks on*) tsukemásu (tsukéru, tsukéte) 付けます(付ける, 付けて) **2.** (*adds*) soemásu (soeru, soete) 添えます(添える, 添えて)
attached file *n* tenpu fáiru 添付ファイル
attachment *n* fuzoku 付属・附属, fuzoku-hin 付属品・附属品
attack 1. *n* (*an attack*) kōgeki 攻撃, shūgeki 襲撃 **2.** *v* (*makes an attack*) osóimásu (osou, osotte) 襲います(襲う, 襲って); sememásu (seméru, sémete) 攻めます(攻める, 攻めて); kōgeki/shūgeki shimásu (suru, shite) 攻撃/襲撃します(する, して)

attain → reach → accomplish
attempt 1. *n* tameshí 試し, kokoromi 試み; (*plot, scheme*) kuwadate 企て **2.** *v* (*attempts it*) tameshimásu (tamésu, taméshite) 試します(試す, 試して), kokoromimásu (kokoromíru, kokoró-mite) 試みます(試みる, 試みて); kuwadatemásu (kuwadatéru, kuwa-dátete) 企てます(企てる, 企てて)
attend *v* demásu (deru, dete) 出ます(出る, 出て); shusseki shimásu (suru, shite) 出席します(する, して)
attendance *n* shusseki 出席
office attendance *n* shukkin 出勤
attendant *n* (*in charge*) kakari 係, kakari-in 係員, ...-gákari ...係 → **clerk**
flight attendant *n* furaito aténdanto フライトアテンダント, suchuwādesu スチュワーデス, kyabin aténdanto キャビンアテンダント, kyakushitsu jōmu-in 客室乗務員
attention *n* **1.** chū´i 注意, chūmoku 注目 **2.** omoiyari 思いやり
attest *v* shōmei shimásu (suru, shite) 証明します(する, して)
attestation *n* shōmei 証明
attitude *n* táido 態度, shisei 姿勢
attorney *n* bengóshi 弁護士
attract *v* hikimásu (hiku, hiite) 引きます(引く, 引いて); (*charming*) miryoku ga arimásu (áru, átte) 魅力があります(ある, あって)
attraction *n* atorakushon アトラクション
attractive *adj* (*nice-looking*) kírei (na) きれい・綺麗(な); (*charming*) miryoku-teki (na) 魅力的(な)
attractiveness *n* (*charm*) aikyō あいきょう・愛矯
auction *n* serí 競り・セリ, kyōbai 競売, ōkushon オークション
audience *n* chōshu 聴衆, kankyaku 観客
audio *n, adj* onsei (no) 音声(の), ōdio オーディオ
audition *n* ōdishon オーディション, shínsa 審査
auditorium *n* kaidō 会堂, kōdō 講堂
aunt *n* (*father's or mother's elder sister*) obá(-san) 伯母(さん); (*father's or*

mother's younger sister) obá(-san) 叔母(さん); (*in general*) obá(-san) おば(さん)

auspicious *adj* medetái めでたい・目出度い(o-medetái おめでたい)

Australia *n* ōsutorária オーストラリア

Australian 1. *n* (*person*) ōsutorariá-jin オーストラリア人 **2.** *adj* ōsutorariá no オーストラリアの

authentic *adj* kakujitsu (na) 確実(な), honmono (nó) 本物(の), shōshinshōmei (no) 正真正銘(の)

authentication *n* (*certificate*) shōmei-sho 証明書

author *n* chó-sha 著者, sáku-sha 作者 → **writer**

authority *n* **1.** (*expert*) táika 大家, tsū 通 **2.** (*power*) ken'i 権威 **3.** (*basis*) kónkyo 根拠
  the authorities tōkyoku 当局, okámi お上; **~ concerned with ...** ... no kankéi-sha ... の関係者

authorized *adj* kōnin (no) 公認(の)

automatic *adj* jidō-teki (na) 自動的(な)

automatically *adv* jidō-teki ni 自動的に; (*spontaneously*) hitori-de ni ひとりでに, onozukara おのずから

automation *n* ōtomēshon オートメーション, jidō (-ka) 自動(化)

automobile *n* jidō-sha 自動車, kuruma 車 (*how many* nán-dai 何台)

autosuggestion *n* áki 秋
  autumn leaves mómiji もみじ・紅葉
  autumn period/term shū'ki 秋期

autumnal equinox *n* shūbun 秋分
  Autumnal Equinox Day Shūbun-no-hí 秋分の日

available *adj* (*things*) riyō dekiru 利用できる, (*person*) áiteiru 空いている;
  seats are ~ suwaremásu (suwareru, suwarete) 座れます(座れる, 座れて)
  available room(s) aki-beya/-ma/-shitsu 空き部屋/間/室
  available space aki-ma 空き間
  available taxi kūsha 空車

avalanche *n* nadare なだれ・雪崩; (*snowslide*) yuki-nádare 雪なだれ

avenue *n* tōri 通り, ōdō'ri 大通り, kaidō 街道; michi 道

average 1. *n* (*on the average*) heikin 平均
  average age heikin nenrei 平均年令; (*life span, lifetime*) heikin jumyō 平均寿命
  average score heikin ten 平均点 **2.** *adj* (*ordinary*) nami (no) 並(の), heibon (na) 平凡(な) **3.** *v* **averages it** narashimásu (narásu, naráshite) なら[均]します(ならす, ならして)

avert *v* **1.** sakemásu (sakéru, sákete) 避けます(避ける, 避けて) **2.** me o sorashimásu (sorasu, sorashite) 目をそらします(そらす, そらして)

aviary *n* torígoya 鳥小屋

aviation *n* kōkū (ki) 航空(機)

avoid *v* sakemásu (sakéru, sákete) さけ[避け]ます(さける, さけて), yoke-másu (yokéru, yókete) よけ[避け]ます(よける, よけて)

await → **wait for**

awake *v*, (*comes awake*) mezamemásu, (mezaméru mezámete) 目覚めます(目覚める, 目覚めて); *is* ~ (*not asleep*) nemurimasén (nemuranai, nemuranaide) 眠りません(眠らない, 眠らないで)

award 1. *n* shō 賞
  Academy Award academí shō アカデミー賞
  2. *v* (*gives*) (shō o) júyo shimásu (suru, shite) (賞を)授与します(する,して); okurimásu (okuru, okutte) 贈ります(贈る, 贈って)

awardee *n* jushō´-sha 受賞者

away *adj* tōku (ni) 遠く(に)
  away from home rúsu (no) 留守(の)
  right away súgu すぐ
  go away ikimásu (iku, itte) 行きます(行く, 行って)
  run away (*flees*) nigemásu (nigéru, nígete) 逃げます(逃げる, 逃げて)
  take away torimásu (tóru, tótte) 取ります(取る, 取って); tōku (ni) 遠く(に)

awesome *adj* (mono)sugói (もの)すごい・凄い, subárashíi すばらしい・素晴らしい, saikō 最高

awful *adj* osoroshíi 恐ろしい, hidói ひどい

awfully *adv* → **very**

awkward *adj* mazúi まずい, gikochinai
ぎこちない, buzama (na) ぶざま(な)

awl *n* kiri きり・錐

awning *n* hi-ói 日覆い, hiyoke 日よけ,
tenmaku 天幕

ax *n* ono おの・斧

axis, axle *n* jikú 軸; *x/y/z axis/axle*
ekkusu/wai/zetto jiku X/Y/Z 軸

azalea *n* tsutsúji ツツジ

B

babble *n* o-shaberi おしゃべり

baby **1.** *n* áka-chan 赤ちゃん, akanbo/
akanbō 赤ん坊 **2.** *n* (*lover*) koibito 恋
人 **3.** *v* (*pampers one*) ama-yakashi-
másu (ama-yakasu, ama-yakashite)
甘やかします(甘やかす, 甘やかして)

babysitter *n* bebii shittá ベビーシッタ
ー, (*professional*) komóri 子守

baby stroller *n* bebii kā ベビーカー

bachelor *n* **1.** dokushin dansei 独身男性,
hitori mónó ひとり者 **2.** gákushi 学士
bachelor's degree *n* gákushi (gō)
学士(号)

back **1.** *adv* (*behind*) ... no ushiro (de/
ni) ...の後ろ(で/に) **2.** *n* (*of body*)
senaka 背中, (*lower part*) koshi 腰; (*of
room etc.*) óku 奥; (*reverse side*) urá
裏 → support

back; *go ~* modorimásu (modóru,
modótte) 戻ります(戻る, 戻って); (*to
one's usual place*) kaerimásu (káeru,
káette) 帰ります(帰る, 帰って); *~
up* bákku shimásu (suru, shite) バッ
クします(する, して); bákku-appu
shimásu (suru, shite) バックアップし
ます(する, して)

I'll be right back. *interj* Chótto itte
kimásu. ちょっと行って来ます.

I'm back. *interj* Tadáima (kaerimáshita). ただいま(帰りました).

back and forth *adv* zéngo (ni) 前後(に);
goes ~ kayoimásu (kayou, kayotte)
通います(通う, 通って)

backbencher *n* hira-giin 平議員

backbone *n* sebone 背骨

backdate *v* hizuke o sakanoborasemásu
(sakanoboraseru, sakanoborasete) 日付
をさかのぼらせます(せる, せて)

back door *n* ura-guchi 裏口

back down *v* **1.** (*retreat*) kōtai shimásu
(suru, shite) 後退します(する, して)

2. (*withdraw*) hiki sagarimásu (sagaru,
sagatte) 引き下がります(下がる, 下
がって)

backdrop *n* haikei (maku) 背景(幕)

backed up *v* (*traffic*) jūtai shite imásu
(iru, ite) 渋滞しています(いる, いて)

backfire *n* ura-me ni demásu (deru,
dete) 裏目に出ます(出る, 出て)

back gate *n* ura-mon 裏門

background *n* **1.** haikei 背景, bákku
バック **2.** (*one's origin, education,
experience, etc.*) keireki 経歴 **3.** (*circumstances of the event, information*)
yobi chishiki 予備知識, bákku gura(u)
ndo バックグラ(ウ)ンド

backhand *n* (*sports*) bakku hando
バックハンド

backhanded **1.** *adj* (*sports*) bakku
hando (no) バックハンド(の) **2.** *adj*
(*ambiguous meaning*) aimai (na) あい
まい・曖昧(な) **3.** *adj* (*roundabout,
indirect*) mawarikudoi 回りくどい
4. *n* (*backhanded slap*) bakku hando
バックハンド

backhander *n* (*bribe*) wáiro わいろ

backing **1.** *n* (*support*) kōen 後援; enjo
援助 **2.** → lining

back issue *n* (*out-of-date or previous
issue of a periodical*) bakku nanbā
バックナンバー

backlash *n* handō 反動, hanpatsu 反発

backlog *n* **1.** (*reserve*) bichiku 備蓄
2. (*stock*) zaiko 在庫 **3.** (*work*) yarino-
koshi no shigoto やり残しの仕事

back number *n* → back issue

back-order *n* toriyose chūmon 取り寄
せ注文

backpack *n* ryukku-sakku リュックサ
ック

back pay *n* mibarai kyūyo 未払給与,
mibarai chingin 未払賃金

backrest n (*legless chair*) za-isu 座椅子

back room n nándo 納戸

back seat n kōbu zaseki 後部座席

backside n **1.** ushiro 後ろ, [BOOKISH] kōhō 後方 **2.** (*buttock*) shiri 尻 (o-shiri お尻)

backstage adj, adv butai ura (no/de) 舞台裏(の/で), gakuya (no/de) 楽屋 (の/で)

backstop n (*baseball*) bakku netto バックネット

back street n ura-dō´ri 裏通り

backstroke n seoyogi 背泳ぎ

backup n **1.** (*computer*) bákku appu バックアップ **2.** yobi 予備, hikae 控え

backwards adv (*contrariwise*) gyaku (ni) 逆(に); *move* ~ bakku shimásu (suru, shite) バックします(する, して), ushiro e/ni sagarimásu (sagáru, sagátte) 後ろに下がります(下がる, 下がって)

backwater n **1.** (*stagnant place*) teitai chi 停滞地 **2.** (*stagnant state*) teitai 停滞 **3.** (*held water*) yodonda mizu よどんだ水

backyard n ura-niwa 裏庭

bacon n bē´kon ベーコン
bacon and egg bēkon eggu ベーコン エッグ

bacteria n bakuteria バクテリア, saikin 細菌

bad adj **1.** warúi 悪い, damé (na) だめ (な); furyō (na) 不良(な), (*inept*) hetá (na) へた(な) **2.** fu- 不 ー
bad custom, bad practice n akushū 悪習
bad guy n furyō 不良, warumono 悪者
bad-tasting adj mazúi まずい
bad temper n tanki 短気

bad; *goes* ~ (*rots, sours*) kusarimásu (kusáru, kusátte) 腐ります(腐る, 腐っ て); *too* ~ (*regrettable*) zannen (na) 残 念(な); ikemasén (ikenai) いけません (いけない)

badge n bajji バッジ

badger n anaguma アナグマ (*not raccoon-dog* tánuki タヌキ)

badly adv **1.** waruku 悪く **2.** (*very*) totemo とても

badminton n badominton バドミン

トン; (*traditional Japanese version*) hané-tsuki 羽根突き

bag n **1.** fukuró 袋; (*paper*) kamibú-kuro 紙袋, (*plastic*) poribúkuro ポリ袋 **2.** → **suitcase 3.** → **handbag; purse**

baggage n nímotsu 荷物 (o-nimotsu お荷物)

baggy adj dabudabu (no) だぶだぶ(の)

Bahama Islands n bahama shotō バハマ諸島

bait n esa えさ・餌

bake v **1.** yakimásu (yaku, yaite) 焼き ます(焼く, 焼いて) **2.** *gets baked* yakemásu (yakeru, yakete) 焼けます (焼ける, 焼けて)

baker, bakery, bakeshop n pán-ya パ ン屋, bēkarii ベーカリー

baking n yaki 焼き
baking powder n bēkingu paudā ベーキングパウダー

balance n **1.** (*equilibrium*) tsurai 釣り 合い, baransu バランス **2.** (*remaining money*) zandaka 残高
balance sheet n (B/S) taishaku-taishō hyō 貸借対照表, bii-esu B/S

balcony n barukonii バルコニー

bald 1. adj hágeta ... はげた... **2.** v (*gets bald*) hagemásu (hagéru, hágete) はげます(はげる, はげて); (*is bald*) hágete imásu (iru, ite) はげています (いる, いて)

baldness n háge はげ (*bald spot*)

bale n tawará 俵

baleful adj yūgai (na) 有害(な)

ball n **1.** tamá 玉; *dragon* ~ ryū no tama 竜[龍]の玉; (*traditional Japanese handball*) mari まり, temari 手まり **2.** (*sports*) bō´ru ボール; *tennis* ~ tenisu bōru テニスボール; *basket* ~ basuketto bōru バスケットボール; *rugby* ~ ragubii (no) bōru ラグビー (の)ボール **3.** kyū 球; ~ *sport* kyūgi 球技
ball park n yakyū-jō 野球場, kyūjō 球場

ballad n (*Japanese traditional music*) min'yō 民謡; (*Western-style*) barādo バラード

ballerina n (*female ballet dancer*) bareriina バレリーナ

ballet n bárē バレエ

ballet company n barē dan バレエ団
ballet dancer n barē dansā バレエダ
ンサー, (*female dancer*) bareriina バレ
リーナ

balloon n **1.** fūsen 風船 **2.** (*hot-air balloon*) (netsu)kikyū (熱)気球 **3.** (*toy balloon*) fūsen-dama 風船玉 **4.** (*water balloon*) mizu-fūsen 水風船

ballot n tōhyō 投票

ballot paper n tōhyō yōshi 投票用紙
ballot results n tōhyō kekka 投票結果

ballpoint pen n bōru-pen ボールペン

balm n kōyu 香油

bamboo n take 竹 (**1:** íp-pon 一本, **2:** ní-hon 二本, **2:** sánbon 三本, *how many* nán-bon 何本)

bamboo blind n (*Japanese traditional*) misu 御簾, sudare すだれ → **blind**
bamboo hat n kása 笠
bamboo shoot n take-no-ko タケノコ・竹の子・筍
bamboo tea whisk n chasen 茶せん

bambooware n take-záiku 竹細工

ban 1. n kinshi 禁止 **2.** *bans it* v kinshi shimásu (suru, shite) 禁止します(する, して)

banal *adj* heibon (na) 平凡(な), arifureta ありふれた

banana n banana バナナ; *banana shake* banana sheiku バナナシェイク

band n **1.** (*group*) kumí 組 **2.** (*of musicians*) (*Western style*) gakudan 楽団, bando バンド; (*Japanese style*) hayashí はやし・囃(o-hayashi お囃し) **3.** (*watchband, etc.*) (tokei (時計)) bando バンド **4.** beruto ベルト
band leader n bando masutā バンドマスター

Band-Aid n bando-eido バンドエイド

bandage n hōtai 包帯

bandit n zoku 賊

bandwagon n gakutai-sha 楽隊車

bandy-legged *adj* OH-kyaku (no) O (oh) 脚の, ganimata (no) がに股(の)

bang n (*sound*) ban バン, batan バタン

bangle n **1.** (*wristlet*) ude wa 腕輪 **2.** kazari 飾り

banish v tsuihō shimásu (suru, shite) 追放します(する, して)

banister n tesuri 手すり

banjo n banjo バンジョー; *three stringed ~* shamisen 三味線

bank n **1.** ginkō 銀行 **2.** (*special storage place*) banku バンク **3.** (*bank of a river or lake*) kishí 岸
bank account n ginkō-kóza 銀行口座, yokin-kóza 預金口座
bankbook n tsū´chō 通帳, yokin-tsū´chō 預金通帳
bank clerk n ginkō´-in 銀行員
bank rate n ginkō waribiki-buai 銀行割引歩合
blood bank n ketsueki banku 血液バンク
sperm bank n seishi banku 精子バンク

bankruptcy n hasan 破産; *goes bankrupt* hasan shimásu (suru, shite) 破産します(する, して)

banner n **1.** (*flag*) hata 旗 **2.** (*motto, slogan, etc.*) hyōshiki 標識 **3.** (*hanging cloth or curtain over a street, entrance, etc.*) taremaku 垂れ幕 **4.** (*advertising*) banā (kōkoku) バナー(広告)

banquet n enkai 宴会

baptism n senrei 洗礼

bar n **1.** (*for drinking*) saka-ba 酒場, (*Western style*) bā バー, (*neighborhood pub*) nomí-ya 飲み屋, (*after-hours*) sunákku スナック **2.** bō 棒
bartender n bāten(-dā) バーテン(ダー)
iron bar n tetsu-bō 鉄棒
wooden bar n ki no bō 木の棒
a bar of soap n sekken ík-ko せっけん[石鹸]一個

barbarian n yaban-jín 野蛮人

barbarous *adj* yaban (na) 野蛮(な)

barbecue n bābekyū バーベキュー

barbed wire n yūshi-téssen 有刺鉄線

barber(shop) n tokoya 床屋, rihátsú-ten 理髪店, sanpatsu-ya 散髪屋

bar-code n bā-kōdo バーコード

bare *adj* **1.** (*scarce*) toboshii 乏しい **2.** (*mere*) honno wazuka (no) ほんのわずか(の) **3.** → **naked 4.** → **reveal**
barefoot *adj, adv* hadashi (no/de) はだし・裸足(の/で)

barely *adv* karōjite かろうじて, nantoka なんとか, girigiri ぎりぎり

bargain n (a real find) horidashi mono 堀出し物, bāgen バーゲン; (cut the price) bāgen sēru バーゲンセール

barge n hashike はしけ

bar hopping n hashigó-zake はしご酒, hashígo はしご

baritone n (male singing voice or a singer with the voice) bariton バリトン

barium n bariumu バリウム
　barium study bariumu kensa バリウム検査

bark n (of tree) kí no kawá 木の皮, [BOOKISH] juhi 樹皮

bark v (a dog barks) hoemásu (hóéru, hóete) 吠えます(吠える, 吠えて)

barley n ō-mugi 大麦
　barley tea n mugi-cha 麦茶

barn n naya 納屋

barometer n 1. (indicator) baromētā バロメーター 2. (atmospheric pressure measurement instrument) kiatsu-kei 気圧計

baron n (man with a barony) danshaku 男爵

baroness n (wife of a baron) danshaku fujin 男爵夫人; (woman with a barony) onna danshaku 女男爵

baroque 1. n (music, architecture) barokku バロック 2. adj barokku (yōshiki) no バロック(様式)の
　baroque architecture n barokku kenchiku バロック建築
　baroque music n barokku ongaku バロック音楽

barracks n 1. héisha 兵舎 2. barakku バラック

barracuda n kamásu カマス

barrage n shūchū hōka 集中砲火

barrel n taru 樽; ~ hoop tagá たが

barren adj 1. (land) yaseta やせた, fumō (na/no) 不毛(な/の) 2. (sterile) funin (no) 不妊(の) 3. (dull) ajike nai 味気ない, mumikansō (na) 無味乾燥(な)

barricade n barikēdo バリケード

barrier n 1. (fence) saku 柵 2. (obstacle) shōgai-butsu 障害(物) 3. (limit) genkai 限界 4. (limit or boundary) kyōkai 境界

barrow n (wheelbarrow) teoshi-guruma 手押し車

barter n butsubutsu kōkan 物々交換

base n 1. (military, etc.) kíchi 基地
　military base n gunji-kichi 軍事基地 2. (of a tree) ne-motó 根元 3. (foundation) kiso 基礎; is based on ... ni motozukimásu (motozúku, motozúite) ...に基づきます(基づく, 基づいて) 4. (baseball) rui 塁, bē′su ベース

baseball n yakyū 野球, bēsubō′ru ベースボール
　baseball stadium n yakyū-jō 野球場, kyūjō 球場
　baseball team n náin ナイン, chiimu チーム

basement n (floor) chikai 地階; (room) chiká (-shitsu) 地下(室)

bash v tatakimásu (tatáku, tatáite) 叩きます(叩く, 叩いて)

bashful → **shy**

bashing n tatakí 叩き, basshingu バッシング

basic adj kihon-teki (na) 基本的(な), konpon-teki (na) 根本的(な)

basically adv kihon-teki (ni) 基本的(に)

basin n 1. (for washing face) senmén-ki 洗面器 2. tarai たらい 3. hachí 鉢 4. (flat land surrounded by higher land) bonchi 盆地
　Kyoto basin n Kyōto bonchi 京都盆地

basis n 1. kihon 基本, konpon 根本, kijun 基準, kiso 基礎 2. (grounds) kónkyo 根拠

basket n kago かご・籠, basuketto バスケット

basketball n basuketto bōru バスケット・ボール, basuke バスケ

basking (in the sun) n hinatabokko ひなたぼっこ

bass n 1. (sea bass) suzuki スズキ 2. (music) basu バス, bēsu ベース

bastard n 1. (illegitimate child) [BOOKISH] hi-chakushutsu-shi 非嫡出子, (discriminatory word) shisei-shi/shisei-ji 私生子/私生児 2. (baseball) bátto バット

baste v 1. (sewing) ~ with thread shi-tsukemásu (shi-tsukéru, shi-tsúkete)

仕付けます(付ける, 付けて); *basting thread* shitsuke-íto 仕付け糸 **2.** (*cooking*) tare o kakemásu (kakéru, kakete) タレをかけます(かける, かけて)

bat n **1.** kô'mori コウモリ **2.** (*baseball*) bátto バット

bath n furó 風呂 (o-fúro お風呂), yokujō 浴場

bathing n nyūyoku 入浴; ~ *suit* mizu-gi 水着

bathrobe n basurōbu バスローブ

bathroom n **1.** (*for bathing*) furoba 風呂場 (o-furoba お風呂場), yoku-jō/shitsu 浴場/室 **2.** (*toilet*) tóire トイレ, keshō'-shitsu 化粧室, (o-)teárai (お)手洗い, (o-)benjó (お)便所; *goes to the* ~ yō' o tashimásu (tasu, tashite) 用を足します(足す, 足して)

bathtub n yúbune 湯舟, yokusō 浴槽

public bath n séntō 銭湯, kōshū yokujō 公衆浴場

steam bath n sauna(-buro) サウナ(風呂)

taking a bath n nyūyoku 入浴; *takes a bath* furó ni hairimásu (háiru, háitte) 風呂に入ります(入る, 入って), nyū-yoku shimásu (suru, shite) 入浴します(する, して)

baton n **1.** (*sports, such as race and rhythmic gymnastics*) baton バトン **2.** (*music*) shiki-bō 指揮棒

battalion n (*military*) daitai 大隊

batter n (*baseball*) battā バッター, dásha 打者

battery n denchi 電池, bátterii バッテリー

batting n (*baseball*) battingu バッティング

batting practice n furii batting フリーバッティング

battle **1.** n tatakai 戦い, arasoi 争い, [BOOKISH] sentō 戦闘 **2.** v tatakaimásu (tatakau, tatakatte) 戦います(戦う, 戦って)

battledore n hagó-íta 羽子板 (*wooden paddle used to play traditional Japanese badminton* hané-tsukí 羽根突き)

bay n wán 湾, urá 浦

bay area n wángan chiiki 湾岸地域; beieria ベイエリア

be → is → go → come

beach n hama 浜, bíichi ビーチ; (*seashore*) kaigan 海岸

bead n **1.** tamá 玉, biizu ビーズ; (*prayer*) *beads* juzú じゅず・数珠 **2.** *counting beads* → abacus

beagle n (*dog*) biiguru-ken ビーグル犬

beak n kuchibashi くちばし

beam n **1.** (*crossbeam*) keta けた・桁; *under the* ~ keta-shita 桁下 **2.** (*beam of light*) kōsen 光線

bean n mamé マメ・豆; (*soy beans*) daizu ダイズ・大豆

bean curd n tōfu 豆腐 (o-tōfu お豆腐); (*pot-boiled squares*) yu-dō'fu 湯豆腐; (*cooled cubes*) hiya-yakko 冷ややっこ (冷や奴); (*broiled*) yaki-dō'fu 焼き豆腐; (*deep-fried*) abúra-áge 油揚げ

bean-curd lees n o-kara おから

bean-flour threads n harusame 春雨

bean jam/paste n (*sweet*) án(ko) あん(こ); (*fermented*) míso みそ・味噌 (o-míso お味噌)

bear **1.** n (*animal*) kúma 熊 **2.** v (*puts up with*) shinobimásu (shinobu, shinonde) 忍びます(忍ぶ, 忍んで), taemásu (táeru, táete) 耐えます(耐える, 耐えて), shínbō shimásu (suru, shite) 辛抱します(する, して) **3.** → carry **4.** v → give birth **5.** v *bears fruit* minorimásu (minoru, minotte) 実ります(実る, 実って)

bear up (*stands firm*) ganbarimásu (ganbáru, ganbátte) がんばり[頑張り]ます(がんばる, がんばって)

beard n hige ひげ; (*chin-whiskers*) ago-hige あごひげ

bearings; n *one's* ~ hōgaku 方角

beat v **1.** (*hits*) nagurimásu (nagúru, nagútte) なぐり[殴り]ます(なぐる, なぐって); (*slaps*) hatakimásu (hatáku, hatáite) はたき[叩き]ます(はたく, はたいて) **2.** (*defeats*) makashimásu (makasu, makashite) 負かします(負かす, 負かして) **3.** (*heart throbs*) dókidoki shimásu (suru, shite) どきどきします(する, して); ~ *around the bush* (*is non-committal*) hanashí o bokashimásu (bokásu, bokáshite) 話をぼかします(ぼかす, ぼかして)

beaten; v *gets* ~ yararemásu (yarareru, yararete) やられます(やられる, やられて)

beautiful adj utsukushíi 美しい, kírei (na) きれい(な), mígoto (na) 見事(な)

beauty n **1.** [BOOKISH] bi 美, utsukushísa 美しさ **2.** (*beautiful woman*) bi-jin 美人, bi-jo 美女

beauty parlor n biyō'in 美容院

beaver n biibā ビーバー

eager beaver n ganbari-ya 頑張り屋

because conj ... kara ...から, ... tame ... ため, ... mono ... もの, ... no de ... ので, [BOOKISH] ... yué ni ... ゆえに; *perhaps* ~ *of* ... (no) séi ka ... (の) せいか

beckoning n temáneki 手招き

become v (... ni, ... -ku) narimásu (náru, nátte) (... に, ... く)なります(なる, なって); [HONORIFIC] o-nari ni narimásu (náru, nátte) おなりになります(なる, なって); *is becoming to ...* (*suits*) ... ni ai-aimásu (ni-áu, ni-átte) ... に似合います(似合う, 似合って)

bed n toko 床, (*Western*) béddo (bétto) ベッド(ベット), shindai 寝台; *goes to* ~ nemásu (neru, nete) 寝ます(寝る, 寝て), yasumimásu (yasúmu, yasúnde) 休みます(休む, 休んで); *takes to one's* ~ toko ni tsukimásu (tsukú, tsúite) 床に就きます(就く, 就いて)

bed-and-breakfast n minshuku 民宿

bedclothes, bedding n shíngu 寝具, yágu 夜具; (*Japanese quilt*) futon 布団 (o-fúton お布団)

bed making n beddo me¯kingu ベッドメーキング

bedroom n shinshitsu 寝室

bedroom community n beddotáun ベッドタウン

bedsheet n shíitsu シーツ, shikifu 敷布

bedside n makura-moto 枕元

bedspread n beddo kabā ベッドカバー

bedtime n shūshin jikoku 就寝時刻

bedlam n **1.** sawagi 騒ぎ; sōran 騒乱 **2.** (*confusion*) konran 混乱

bedpan n benki 便器; (*urinal*) shibin しびん; (*fecal*) omaru おまる

bedraggled adj **1.** (*limp and wet*) hikizutte nurashita 引きずって濡らした **2.** (*limp and soiled*) hikizutte yogoshita 引きずって汚した

bee n hachi ハチ・蜂

beehive n mitsubachi no subako ミツバチ[蜜蜂]の巣箱

beeswax n mitsurō ミツロウ・蜜蝋

honey bee mitsú-bachi ミツバチ

beef n gyūniku 牛肉, biifu ビーフ

beef hash (*over rice*) hayashi-ráisu ハヤシライス

beef slices dipped in hot broth shabu-shabu しゃぶしゃぶ

roast beef rōsuto biifu ロ-ストビーフ

beefsteak n sutēki ステーキ

beefsteak plant n (*perilla*) shiso シソ

been → is → go → come

beep n **1.** (*sound*) bii-tto iu oto ビーッという音 **2.** (*answering machine*) pii-tto iu oto ピーッという音 **3.** yobi-dashi-on 呼び出し音

beer n bíiru ビール

beer bottle/can n biirú-bin/kan ビール瓶/缶

beer hall n bia/ya hō'ru ビア/ビヤホ-ル

draft beer n nama-bíiru 生ビール, náma 生

beet n bíito ビート

beetle n (*insect*) kabutomushi カブトムシ

black beetle n gokiburi ゴキブリ

before adv (... no) máe (ni) (...の) 前 (に); ~ *it happens* (shi-) nai uchí (ni) (し)ないうちに

before a meal n, adv taberu mae (ni) 食べる前(に), [BOOKISH] shokuzen (ni) 食前(に)

before and after adv zéngo (ni) 前後 (に); máe mo áto mo 前も後も

before anything else adv mázu まず

before long adv ma-mó-naku まもなく, sórosoro そろそろ; (*eventually*) yagate やがて

before the war adv sensō no mae (no) 戦争の前(の), [BOOKISH] senzen (no) 戦前(の)

beforehand adv mae-motte 前もって, jizen (ni) 事前(に)

beg v tanomimás<u>u</u> (tanómu, tanónde) 頼みます(頼む, 頼んで), negaimás<u>u</u> (negáu, negátte) 願います(願う, 願って) I beg your pardon, but ... interj shits<u>u</u>réi des<u>u</u> ga ... 失礼ですが...

beggar n kojiki こじき・乞食

begin v (it begins) hajimarimás<u>u</u> (hajimaru, hajimatte) 始まります(始まる, 始まって); (begins it) hajimemás<u>u</u> (hajimeru, hajímete) 始めます(始める, 始めて)

beginner n shoshin-sha 初心者, biginā ビギナー

beginning n hajime 初め, (outset) saisho 最初, hajimari 始まり; from the ~ hajime (k)kara 初め(っ)から, móto kara もとから, [BOOKISH] mótó-yori もとより

begrudge v uramimás<u>u</u> (urámu, uránde) 恨みます(恨む, 恨んで); (be jealous of another's good fortune, etc.) h<u>i</u>to no kōun o netamimás<u>u</u> (netamu, netande) 人の幸運をねたみます(ねたむ, ねたんで)

behalf n 1. (support) shiji 支持 2. (benefit) rieki 利益; in/on ~ of ... (... no) tamé ... のため 3. (representative) in/on ~ of ... [INFORMAL] (... no) kawari ni ...の代わりに, (... o) dairi (de) ...の代理(で), (... o) daihyō shite ...を代表して

behavior n 1. (actions) kōdō 行動 2. (act) kōi 行為 3. (deportment) furumai 振る舞い 4. (manners) (o-)gyōgi (お)行儀 5. (attitude) táido 態度

behind 1. prep (... no) ushiro (de/ni) (... の)後ろ(で/に); (the other side) urá 裏 2. v falls/gets ~ okuremás<u>u</u> (okureru, okurete) 遅れます(遅れる, 遅れて); gets left ~, stay ~ nokorimás<u>u</u> (nokóru, nokótte) 残ります(残る, 残って); leaves ~ nokoshimás<u>u</u> (nokósu, nokóshite) 残します(残す, 残して), (forgets) wasuremono o shimás<u>u</u> (suru, shite) 忘れ物をします(する, して)

beige n bēju ベージュ

Beijing n pekin 北京

being 1. n (in existence; person) sonzai 存在; human ~ ningen 人間 2. (creature) ikimono 生き物 3. → is 4.

v comes into ~ seiritsu shimás<u>u</u> (suru, shite) 成立します(する, して) 5. ... ~ what it is (who one is) sasuga no ... さすがの...

belch 1. n geppu げっぷ 2. v geppu o shimás<u>u</u> (suru, shite) げっぷ(をします;する, して)

belfry n shōrō 鐘楼

Belgium n berugii ベルギー

believe v 1. believe (in) (... o) shinji-más<u>u</u> (shinjiru, shinjite) (... を)信じます(信じる, 信じて) 2. → think

bell n 1. (large) kane 鐘 2. (small) rín/suzu 鈴 3. (doorbell) béru ベル, yobi-rin 呼び鈴 4. (temple bell) tsurigane 釣り鐘
the bells on New Year's Eve joya no kane 除夜の鐘

bellboy n bōi ボーイ

bell pepper n píiman ピーマン

belly n hará 腹; fuku-bu 腹部; onaka お腹

bellybutton n heso へそ(o-heso おへそ)

belong (to) v (... ni) zokushimás<u>u</u> (zokusú(ru), zokúshite) (... に)属します(属する, 属して)

belonging adj (possessed) shoyū (no) 所有(の); belongings n mochímono 持ち物

beloved n 1. (person or pet) itoshii い としい・愛しい, saiai (no) 最愛(の) 2. (thing) aiyō (no) 愛用(の) 3. (thing or place) okiniiri (no) お気に入りの, daisuki (na) 大好き(な)
beloved daughter mana-musume 愛娘
beloved dog ai-ken 愛犬
beloved vehicle ai-sha 愛車
beloved wife ai-sai 愛妻

below prep, adv (... no) sh<u>i</u>tá (ni) (... の)下(に); (less than) ... íka (... no) ... 以下(... の), ... míman (... no) ... 未満(... の)

belt n 1. beruto ベルト, óbi 帯 2. (sumo wrestler's) mawashi まわし 3. (zone) (chi)tai 地帯
belt conveyor n = conveyor belt
beruto konbeyā/konbeā ベルト・コン ベヤー/コンベアー
belt line n kanjō-sen 環状線

beltway n kanjō dōro 環状道路

bemused adj **1.** (confused) konwakushita 困惑した, tōwakushita 当惑した **2.** (lost in thought) mono-omoi ni fuketta 物思いにふけった

bench n benchi ベンチ

bend v **1.** (it bends) oremásu (oréru, órete) 折れます(折れる, 折れて), (curves) magarimásu (magaru, magatte) 曲がります(曲がる, 曲がって), (warps) sorimásu (sóru, sótte) 反ります(反る, 反って) **2.** (bends it) orimásu (óru, ótte) 折ります(折る, 折って), magemásu (mageru, magete) 曲げます(曲げる, 曲げて), sorashimásu (sorásu, soráshite) 反らします(反らす, 反らして), (branch, etc.) tawamemásu (tawameru, tawamete) たわめます(たわめる, たわめて)

bend backward v karada o sorashimásu (sorasu, sorashite) 体を反らします(反らす, 反らして)

bend down v kagamimásu (kagamu, kagande) 屈みます(屈む, 屈んで)

bend forward v mae-kagami ni narimásu (naru, natte) 前屈みになります(なる, なって)

bend over v kagamimásu (kagamu, kagande) 屈みます(屈む, 屈んで)

beneath → below

benefactor n onjin 恩人

benefit n ríeki 利益; (... no) tamé (... の)為

benign 1. n (pathology) ryōsei 良性 **2.** adj (gracious) shinsetsu (na) 親切(な)

bent adj (curved) magatta 曲がった

beret n berē-bō ベレー帽

Berlin n Berurín ベルリン

berm n (road shoulder) rokata 路肩

berry n kí-no-mi 木の実, berii ベリー (includes nuts, fruits) → **strawberry** → **mulberry**

berth n shindai 寝台

berth ticket n shindái-ken 寝台券

beset (stricken); **gets ~** (by illness) yararemásu (yarareru, yararete) やられます(やられる, やられて)

beside prep, adv (next to) ... no sóba (de/ni) ... のそば(で/に), ... no tonari (de/ni) ...の隣り(で/に), ... no wakí (de/ni) ... のわき(で/に)

besides prep, adv (in addition to) sono ué (ni) その上(に), (sono) hoka (ni) (その)他(に)

best adj **1.** ichiban íi 一番いい[良い, 善い]; sairyō (no) 最良(の) **2.** (highest) saiko (no) 最高(の) **3.** (top-class) jōtō (no) 上等(の) **4.** (special-quality) tokkyū (no) 特級(の), zekkō (no) 絶好 (の) **5.** bésuto ベスト

at best adv séizei せいぜい

the best, one's best n saizen 最善

best-seller n besuto-serā ベストセラー

Please give my best wishes to ... ... ni yoroshiku (itte kudasái, o-tsutae kudasái) ... によろしく(言って下さい, お伝え下さい)

ten best n besutó-tén ベストテン

bet 1. n (act of betting) kake 賭け **2.** n (money) kake-kin 賭け金 **3.** v kakemásu (kakéru, kákete) 賭けます (賭ける, 賭けて), kaké o shimásu (suru, shite) 賭けをします(する, して)

betray v ura-girimásu (ura-gíru, ura-gítte) 裏切ります(切る, 切って)

betrayal n ura-giri 裏切り

betrayer n ura-giri-mono 裏切り者

betrothal n konyaku 婚約

betrothed n konyaku-sha 婚約者

better adj **1.** móttó íi/yoi もっといい/ 良い, (...) yóri íi/yoi (...) よりいい/良 い **2.** (preferable) ... (no hó) ga íi/yoi ...(の方)がいい/良い **3.** *had ~ do it* shita hō ga íi/yoi した方がいい/良い, *had ~ not do it* shinai hō ga íi/yoi し ない方がいい/良い **4.** (sick person, etc.) *feel ~* kibun ga (mae yori) ii/yoi 気分が(前より)いい/良い

betterment n zōshin 増進

between prep, adv (... no) aida (ni) (... の)間(に); ...-kan (...)...間

between acts maku no aida 幕の間, makuai ni 幕あい[合]に

beverage n nomí-mono 飲み物

beware v chūi shimásu (suru, shite) 注意します(する, して) (Please) beware ki o tsukete (kudasai) 気をつけて(ください)

beyond prep, adv (... no) mukō (ni) (... の)向こう(に); ~ *expectations* zongai 存外

beyond remedy shō (shi-yō) ga nái しょう(しよう・仕様)がない

BGM n (background music) bii jii emu ビージーエム

bias n **1.** (prejudice) henken 偏見, sennyū-kan 先入観 **2.** (statistics) baiasu バイアス

Bible n Séisho 聖書, Báiburu バイブル

bibliography n tosho mokuroku 図書目録, bunken mokuroku 文献目録

bicycle n jitén-sha, jidén-sha 自転車
bicycle races n keirin 競輪
bicycle shop n jitensha-ya, jidensha-ya 自転車屋

bid n **1.** v (to offer) nyūsatsu shimásu (suru, shite) 入札します(する、して) **2.** v (to command) meirei shimásu (suru, shite) 命令します(する、して) **3.** v (to express) ii másu (iu, itte) 言います(言う、言って) **4.** n nyūsatsu 入札

bidder n nyūsatsu-sha 入札者

bidding n nyūsatsu 入札, seri 競り

big adj **1.** ōkíi 大きい, [INFORMAL] dekai (dekkai) でかい(でっかい) **2.** (spacious) hirói 広い
big brother áni 兄, (o-)níi-san (お)兄さん
big dipper n jettokōsutā ジェットコースター
big-head n unubore うぬぼれ
big news n sukūpu スクープ
big shot n ō-mono 大物
big sister ane 姉, (o-)nē´-san (お)姉さん

bigot n henkutsu-mono 偏屈者, ganko-mono 頑固者

bike n **1.** (bicycle) jitén-sha, jidén-sha 自転車 **2.** (motorbike) baiku バイク, ōtobai オートバイ (abbreviation for the word "autobike")

bilingual n, adj bairingaru (no) バイリンガル(の)

bill n **1.** (to pay) kanjō 勘定(o-kanjō お勘定); denpyō 伝票, o-aiso おあいそ; daikin 代金, ...-dai ... 代; (account) tsuké つけ **2.** (bank bill, promissory note) tegata 手形 **3.** (currency note) (o-)satsu (お)札 **4.** (handbill) bira びら・ビラ
separate bill/charge (restaurant)

betsu-ryōkin 別料金; (Dutch treat) warikan 割り勘

billfold → wallet

billiards n biriyādo ビリヤード

billion n jū´-oku 十億 (U.S.); chō´ 兆, ít-chō 一兆 (Britain)

billy-club n konbō こん棒

bin n trash ~ gomi-bako ゴミ箱

bind v **1.** (pages, sheets) tsuzurimásu (tsuzuru, tsuzutte) 綴ります(綴る、綴って) **2.** → tie

binding (a book) n **1.** seihon 製本 **2.** (bound pages) tsuzuri 綴り

bine n tsuru ツル・蔓

binge n donchan-sawagi どんちゃん騒ぎ

bingo n (game) bingo ビンゴ

binoculars n sōgan-kyō 双眼鏡

biography n denki 伝記

biological adj seibutsugaku-teki (na) 生物学的(な)

biologist n seibutsu gáku-sha 生物学者

biology n seibutsú-gaku 生物学

biotechnology n baio(-tekunorojii) バイオ(テクノロジー), seibutsu kōgaku 生物工学

bird n tori 鳥, (... -wa ... 羽, **1:** ichí-wa 一羽, **2:** ní-wa 二羽, **3:** sánba 三羽, **6:** róp-pa 六羽, **10:** júp-pa 十羽; how many nán-ba 何羽)
bird-watching n bādo uotchingu バードウオッチング; yachō-kansatsu 野鳥観察
small bird n ko-tori 小鳥

birth n **1.** (being born) umare 生まれ, [BOOKISH] shussei 出生 **2.** (origin) tanjō 誕生; give ~ to ... o umimásu (umu, unde) ... を生みます(生む、生んで), o-san shimásu (suru, shite) お産します(する、して) **3.** (roots) hassei/hasshō 発生

birthstone n tanjō´seki 誕生石

birthday n tanjō´bi 誕生日 (o-tanjō´bi お誕生日); bāsudē バースデー
birthday cake n (o-)tanjō´bi kēki (お)誕生日ケーキ; bāsudē kēki バースデーケーキ
birthday card n (o-)tanjō´bi kādo (お)誕生日カード; bāsudē kādo バースデーカード

birthday present n (o-)tanjō´bi pure-
zento（お）誕生日プレゼント，bāsudē
purezento バースデープレゼント

birthplace n kókyō 故郷, furusato ふる
さと

biscuit n (*cookie*) bisuketto ビスケット

bisexual n (*ambisexual*) bai-seku-
shuaru バイセクシュアル, bai-seku-
sharu バイセクシャル, ryōseiai-sha
両性愛者

bit n 1. (*a little*) sukóshi 少し; [INFORMAL]
chótto ちょっと

bitch n 1. (*female dog*) mesu-inu 雌犬
2. (*malicious and lewd woman*)
abazure あばずれ

bite 1. v kamimásu (kámu, kánde)
かみます(かむ, かんで), kamitsuki-
másu (kami-tsúku, kami-tsuite) かみ
つきます(かみつく, かみついて)
2. n one ~ hitó-kuchi ひとくち・一口
3. n (*hurt*) sashikizu 刺傷

bitter adj 1. (*taste, hard to bear, painful*) nigái 苦い 2. (*awful*) hidói ひどい
bitter experience nigai keiken 苦い
経験
bitter orange n daidái ダイダイ・橙;
~ juice pónsu/ponzú ポン酢
bitter taste nigai aji 苦い味

bivouac n yaei 野営, bibāku ビバーク

black adj kurói 黒い; kúro (no) 黒(の);
jet ~ makkúro (na) 真っ黒(な)
black box n burakku bokkusu ブラック
ボックス
black coffee n burakku kōhii ブラック
コーヒー
blacklist n burakku risuto ブラックリ
スト
black mark n battén ばってん
black market n yami-ichi 闇市, yamí-
íchiba 闇市場
black person (*people*) n kokujin 黒人
black tea n kōcha 紅茶

blackboard n kokuban (*usually in
school*) 黒板

black-hearted adj hara gurói 腹黒い

blackmail n yusuri ゆすり, kyōkatsu
恐喝

bladder n bōkō 膀胱

blade n 1. (*razor*) (kamisóri no) há
（かみそりの）刃 2. (*sword*) yaiba

やいば・刃 3. (*leaf*) ha 葉 4. (*metal
part of an ice skate*) burēdo ブレード
5. (*swordsman*) ken-shi 剣士

blah adj tsumaranai つまらない,
taikutsu (na) 退屈(な)

blah blah blah adj nantoka (kantoka)
何とか(かんとか), kakukakushikajika
かくかくしかじか

blame 1. n (*censure*) togamé とがめ
(o-togameおとがめ), hínan 非難 2. v
(*rebukes one*) togamemásu (togaméru,
togámete) とがめます(とがめる, とが
めて), hínan shimásu (suru, shite)
非難します(する, して) 3. →
responsibility

blanch v (*bleach*) hyōhaku shimásu
(suru, shite) 漂白します(する, して)

bland adj 1. (*tasteless*) aji ga usui 味が
薄い 2. (*gentle*) odayaka (na) 穏やか
(な) 3. (*insipid*) tsumaranai つまらな
い, omoshirokunai 面白くない

blank 1. n (*space*) kūsho 空所, yohaku
余白 2. n (*form*) yōshi 用紙 3. adj
hakushi (no) 白紙(の) 4. adj (*expression*) utsuro (na) うつろ・虚ろ・虚ろ
(な); with a ~ look utsuro na hyōjō o
mísete うつろな表情を見せて

blanket n mō´fu 毛布, buranketto
ブランケット

blast-off n hassha 発射

bleach n hyōhaku-zai 漂白剤

bleak adj 1. (*hopeless*) kibō no nai
希望のない; ~ future kurai shōrai 暗
い将来 2. (*desolate*) wabishii わび
しい, sappūkei (na) 殺風景(な)
3. (*cold*) samui 寒い

bleed v chi ga demásu (déru, déte)
血が出ます(出る, 出て), shukketsu
shimásu (suru, shite) 出血します(す
る, して)

blemish n 1. (*scarring*) kizu 傷 2. (*defect*)
ketten 欠点 3. (*stain*) oten 汚点

blend n burendo ブレンド, kongō 混合

blender n míkisā ミキサー

bless v 1. bless with ... o megumimásu
(megumu, megunde) ... を恵みます
(恵む, 恵んで) 2. gets blessed with
...ni megumaremásu (megumareru,
megumarete) ...に恵まれます(恵まれ
る, 恵まれて)

Bless you. *interj* (*to sneezer*) Odaiji ni お大事に

blessed *adj* **1.** megumareta 恵まれた, shukufuku sareta 祝福された **2.** (*holy*) shinsei (na) 神聖(な), seinaru 聖なる; ***Blessed Virgin Mary*** seibo maria 聖母マリア

blessed event (*pregnancy, childbirth, marriage, etc.*) omedeta おめでた, [BOOKISH] keiji 慶事

blessing *n* megumi 恵み, shukufuku 祝福

blessedly *adv* saiwai 幸い

blind *n* **1.** (*person*) mōjin 盲人 **2.** (*sunshade*) hi-ō'i 日覆い, hi-yoke 日よけ, buraindo ブラインド → **bamboo blind**

blindfold *n* me-kákushi 目隠し

blindly *adv* yatara (ni) やたら(に)

blink *v* ma-tátaki/ma-bátaki shimásu (suru, shíte) またたき/まばたき/瞬きします(する, して)

blister *n* mizu-búkure 水膨れ; (*corn*) mamé まめ, soko mame 底まめ

blizzard *n* (mō-/ō-) fúbuki (猛/大)吹雪

bloc *n* ken 圏, burokku ブロック

block **1.** *n* (*city block*) The closest equivalent is chōme 丁目, *a square of several blocks. For distances, use* ...-chō ... 町; *It is three [stretches of] blocks from here.* ... Michi o mittsu watari-másu ... 道を三つ渡ります. ... *You cross three streets.* **2.** *n ~ of wood* kakuzai 角材 **3.** *n* (*toy*) tsumiki 積み木, burokku ブロック **4.** *v* (*clogs, impedes*) fusagimásu (fusagu, fusaide) ふさぎます(ふさぐ, ふさいで), burokku shi-másu (suru, shíte) ブロックします(する, して)

blocked (off) *v* **gets ~** fusagarimásu (fusagaru, fusagatte) ふさがります(ふさがる, ふさがって); **the road is ~** dō'ro ga fusagátte imásu 道路がふさがっています

blockade **1.** *n* fūsa 封鎖 **2.** *v* fūsa shimásu (suru, shite) 封鎖します(する, して)

blond *adj* kinpatsu (no) 金髪(の), burondo (no) ブロンド(の)

blood *n* chi 血, [BOOKISH] ketsueki 血液

blood type *n* ketsueki-gata 血液型

bloodless *adj* mu-ketsu (no) 無(血)の

blood pressure *n* ketsuatsu 血圧; ***~ gauge*** ketsuatsu-kei 血圧計, ***takes one's ~*** ketsuatsu o hakarimásu (hakáru, hakátte) 血圧を計ります(計る, 計って)

bloodshot; *adj* **with ~ eyes** chimánako ni nátte 血眼になって

bloody *adj* chinamagusái 血生臭い

bloom *v* sakimásu (saku, saite) 咲きます(咲く, 咲いて)

blossom → **bloom** → **flower**

blot, blotch *n* shimi しみ・染み, yogore 汚れ

blotter *n* suitorí-gami 吸い取り紙

blouse *n* (*woman's, child's*) buráusu ブラウス

blow *v* fukimásu (fukú, fúite) 吹きます(吹く, 吹いて); ***blows one's nose*** hana o kamimásu (kamu, kande) 鼻をかみます(かむ, かんで)

blowfish *n* fúgu フグ・河豚

blowout *n* panku パンク

blowup *n* bakuhatsu 爆発, bakuha 爆破

bludgeon *n* konbō こん棒

blue *adj* **1.** áoi 青い; áo (no) 青(の) **2.** (*feel blue*) burū ブルー, yūutsu 憂うつ

dark (navy) blue kon-iro (no) 紺色(の)

light (sky) blue sora-iro (no) 空色(の)

blue-collar worker *n* burū karā ブルーカラー; nikutai rōdō-sha 肉体労働者

bluejeans *n* jii-pan ジーパン

blueprint *n* ao-jáshin 青写真

blunder *n* shippai 失敗; chónbo ちょんぼ; (*faux pas*) bu-sáhō 不[無]作法

blunt *adj* (*dull-edged*) kirénai 切れない; (*dull-pointed*) nibúi 鈍い; (*rude*) bu-sáhō 不[無]作法(な); (*curt*) bu-áisō (na) 無愛想(な), bukkírábō (na) ぶっきらぼう(な)

blush *v* kao ga akaku narimásu (náru, nátte) 顔が赤くなります(なる, なって), [BOOKISH] sekimen shimásu (suru, shite) 赤面します(する, して)

board **1.** *n* (*plank*) íta 板 **2.** *n* (*meals*) (o-)shokuji (お)食事 **3.** *v* (*gets on a train/bus*) jōsha shimásu (suru, shíte) 乗車します(する, して), (*a plane*)

tōjō shimásu (suru, shite) 搭乗します
（する，して）

boarder n geshuku-nin 下宿人

boarding area/place n nori-ba 乗り場

boarding house n **1.** geshuku (-ya) 下
宿（屋）**2.** (dormitory) kishúkusha 寄
宿舎, ryō´ 寮

boarding pass n tōjō´-ken 搭乗券,
bōdingu-kādo ボーディングカード,
bōdingu-pasu ボーディングパス

boarding school n zenryōsei (no)
gakkō 全寮制（の）学校

boast v jiman shimásu (suru, shite)
自慢します（する，して）

boat n fúne 舟・船; (small) kobune
小舟・小船, bō´to ボート; (how many)
nán-sō/seki 何艘/隻

boat people n bōto-piipuru ボートピ
ープル

boat race n bōto-rēsu ボートレース

bock beer n kuro-bíiru 黒ビール

body n **1.** karada 体・身体; (whole) ~
zenshin 全身; ~ **build** taikaku 体格;
~ **odor** waki-ga わきが・腋臭; taishū
体臭; ~ **temperature** taion 体温; ~
weight taijū 体重 **2.** (collective body,
group) shūdan 集団

bodybuilding n bodii-biru ボディビル

bodyguard n bodii-gādo ボディガー
ド, goei 護衛

body lotion n bodii-rōshon ボディー
・ローション

bogged down; v **gets** ~ iki-zumarimásu (iki-zumáru, iki-zumátte) 行き詰
まります（行き詰まる，行き詰まって）

bog rhubarb n fuki フキ・蕗

bohemian n bohemian ボヘミアン

boil v **1.** **boils water** o-yu o wakashimásu (wakasu, wakashite) お湯を沸
かします（沸かす，沸かして）; **water
boils** o-yu ga wakimásu (waku, waite)
お湯が沸きます（沸く，沸いて）**2.**
boils (food) nimásu (niru, nite) 煮ま
す（煮る，煮て）, yudemásu (yudéru,
yúdete) ゆでます（ゆでる，ゆでて）;
(soup, rice) takimásu (taku, taite) 炊き
ます（炊く，炊いて）**3.** **it boils** niemásu
(nieru, niete) 煮えます（煮える，煮
えて）; **what it boils down to** (is ...)
yō-súru ni 要するに

boil n (on skin) hare-mono はれもの,
dekí-mónó できもの（o-déki おでき）

boiled eggs n yude-támago ゆで卵

boiled fish n nizakana 煮魚

boiled foods n ni-mono 煮物; (assorted) o-dén おでん, dengaku 田楽

boiled greens n (usually spinach,
served cold with seasoning) o-hítashi
おひたし

boiled vegetables n nishime 煮しめ,
o-níshime お煮しめ

boiled water n o-yu お湯, (cooled for
drinking) yu-zámashi 湯冷まし

boiler n bóirā ボイラー; (gas-fired
instant hot-water maker) shunkan
yu-wa'kashiki 瞬間湯沸かし器; (hot-
water maker) yu-wakashiki 湯沸かし
器; (pot) kama かま・釜, nábe 鍋

boisterous adj yakamashíi やかまし
い, sawagashii 騒がしい

bok choi n (Chinese cabbage) hakusai
白菜

bold adj daitán (na) 大胆（な）, yūkan
(na) 勇敢（な）

bolt n (of door) kannuki かんぬき・
閂; (of nut and bolt) boruto ボルト; (of
cloth) ... -maki ... 巻き, -tan 反

bomb **1.** n (a bomb) bakudan 爆弾 **2.** n
(bombing) bakugeki 爆撃 **3.** v (bombs
it) bakugeki shimásu (suru, shite) 爆撃
します（する，して）

bomber n bakugékí-ki 爆撃機

bombing n bakugeki 爆撃

bombshell n bakudan 爆弾; ~
statement bakudan hatsugen 爆弾発言

Bon; the Bon Festival (o-)bón （お）盆,
urabon うら盆

bond n (debenture) saiken 債券

bone n honé 骨

bonehead n (idiot) baka ばか・馬鹿

bonfire n taki-bi たき火

bong n gōn ゴーン

bonito n katsuo カツオ・鰹; (dried)
katsuo-bushi かつお節・鰹節

bonnet → **hat** → (car) **hood**

bonus n **1.** (wage) bō´nasu ボーナス,
shō´yo 賞与 **2.** (extra) omake おまけ

booboo n chónbo ちょんぼ

boo-hoo interj (sound of crying)
1. ēn ēn エーンエーン(mostly children's

crying), wān wān ワーンワーン (*louder*) **2.** ōi ōi オーイオーイ

book 1. n hón 本 (*how many* nán-satsu 何冊), [BOOKISH] shómotsu 書物; (*publications*) shoseki 書籍 **2.** n ~ *of* (*commuting*) *tickets* kaisū-ken 回数券 **3.** n (*book of account*) chōbo 帳簿 **4.** *books* v (*reserves*) yoyaku shimás<u>u</u> (suru, sh<u>i</u>te) 予約します(する、して)

bookcase n hónbako 本箱

book collection n zōsho 蔵書, tósho 図書

book cover n hon no hyōshi 本の表紙

book up v gets ~ f<u>u</u>sagarimás<u>u</u> (f<u>u</u>sagaru, f<u>u</u>sagatte) ふさがります(ふさがる、ふさがって)

bookends n hón-tate 本立て

bookfair n bukku-fea ブックフェア

bookie n kaké-ya 賭け屋, nomiya ノミ屋

booking n **1.** yoyaku 予約 **2.** bóki 簿記

bookshelf n hón-dana 本棚

bookshop, bookstore n hón-ya 本屋, shoten 書店

book title n sho-mei 書名

bookkeeper n chōbo-gákari 帳簿係

bookkeeping n bóki 簿記

bookmark n shiori しおり

bookworm n no mono no mushi 本の虫

boom n **1.** (*prosperity*) (niwaka) keiki (にわか)景気; keiki (ga ii) 景気(がいい) **2.** (*fad*) bú'mu ブーム (= ryūkō 流行) **3.** (*sound*) dón ドン

boomerang n būmeran ブーメラン

booster n (*of current*) shōátsú-ki 昇圧器

booth n **1.** (*selling things*) baiten 売店 **2.** (*in a tavern, etc.*) bókkusu-seki ボックス席 **3.** (*telephone*) denwa bókkusu 電話ボックス **4.** (*office*) būsu ブース

boot(s) n naga-gutsu 長靴, būtsu ブーツ, (*rubber*) gomu-naga ゴム長; *to boots* (*extra*) omake (ni) おまけ(に)

border n **1.** (*boundary*) sakái 境, (*of a district, etc.*) kyōkai 境界, (*of a country*) kokkyō 国境; (*edging*) herí へり・縁 **2.** ~ *on* v ... ni ses-shimás<u>u</u> (ses-suru, ses-sh<u>i</u>te) ... に接します(接する、接して), rinsetsu shimás<u>u</u> (suru, sh<u>i</u>te) 隣接します(する、して)

borderline **1.** n kyōkai-sen 境界線, bōdārain ボーダーライン **2.** adj kyōkai-senjō no 境界線上の, girigiri no ぎりぎりの

bored; v gets ~ unzári sasemás<u>u</u> (saseru, sasete) うんざりさせます(させる、させて)

boring adj (*dull*) taikutsu (na) 退屈 (な), tsumará-nai つまらない

born **1.** gets ~ v umaremás<u>u</u> (umareru, umarete) 生まれます(生まれる、生まれて) **2.** ~ *in/of* adj ... no de/umare ... の出/生まれ, ...-úmare (no) ... 生まれ(の)

borrow (*from ...*) v (... ni) karimás<u>u</u> (kariru, karite) (... に)借ります(借りる、借りて); [HUMBLE] haishaku shimás<u>u</u> (suru, sh<u>i</u>te) 拝借します(する、して)

bosom n f<u>u</u>tokoro 懐・ふところ

boss n **1.** shújin 主人 **2.** (*head of company*) shachō 社長 **3.** (*a leader*) jōshi 上司 **4.** (*ring-leader*) óyá-bun 親分, bosu ボス

Boston n bosuton ボストン

Boston bag n bosuton-baggu ボストンバッグ

botanical garden n shokubutsú-en 植物園

botch v yari-sokonaimás<u>u</u> (yari-sokonáu, yari-sokonátte) やり損ないます(損なう、損なって)

both **1.** pron ryōhō 両方 **2.** adj ryōhō no 両方の **3.** adv dochira mo どちらも; ~ ... *and* ... ... mo ... mo ...も...も

both directions/sides n ryōmen 両面, ryō-gawa 両側

bother n mendó' 面倒, méiwaku 迷惑; (*intrusion*) jama じゃま・邪魔; (*care*) sewá 世話 (o-séwa お世話), o-sewa-sama お世話様, yákkai やっかい・厄介 (go-yákkai ご厄介) → worry; ~ *a person* h<u>i</u>to no jama o shimás<u>u</u> (suru, sh<u>i</u>te) 人のじゃまをします(する、して)

bothersome adj mendō-kúsai 面倒くさい, yákkai (na) やっかい・厄介(な), jama (na) じゃま・邪魔(な)

bottle n **1.** bín 瓶 **2.** (*a bottle of liquor*) *a ~ of whiskey* wisukii-botoru (ippon) ウィスキーボトル(一本); *a ~ of beer* bíiru íp-pon ビール一本, *1.8-liter bottle (of saké)* isshó´-bin 一升瓶; *keeping one's own bottle at a bar* botoru-kiipu ボトルキープ

bottle cap *n* (bín no) kyáppu (瓶の)キャップ, (bín no) ōkan (瓶の)工冠

bottle opener *n* sen-nuki 栓抜き

bottom *n* soko 底; (*underneath*) shita 下, ... shitá ...下; (*buttock*) shirí 尻 (o-shiri お尻); (*bottommost, minimum, minimal*) *adj* saitei (no) 最低(の)

bottoms up (*toast*) kanpai 乾杯

bottom-up management *n* botomu-appu ボトムアップ

bounce *v* hazumimásu (hazumu, hazunde) 弾みます(弾む, 弾んで)

bound 1. *v* → bind; *~ pages* tsuzuri 綴り **2.** → jump

bound for ... ...-iki (no) ... 行き(の); *is ~ ...* ...e ikimásu (iku, itte) ... へ行きます(行く, 行って)

bound to (*do*) *v* kítto ...(suru) deshō きっと...(する)でしょう

boundary *n* sakái 境

bouquet *n* haná-tába 花束

bourbon *n* bā´bon バーボン

boutique *n* butikku ブティック

bow *n* (*archery or violin*) yumí 弓; (*shape*) yumi-gata 弓形; (*of ribbon*) chō-músubi ちょう結び

bow 1. *n* (*of head, etc.*) o-jigi おじぎ・お辞儀 **2.** *v* o-jigi o shimásu (suru, shite) お辞儀をします(する, して)

bowel *n* chō 腸; *bowels* naizō 内臓

bowel movement *n* (o-)tsū-ji (お)通じ; *has a ~* tsū-ji ga arimásu (arú, atte) 通じがあります(ある, あって)

bowl *n* wan 碗(o-wan お碗); (*ricebowl*) chawan 茶碗 (o-cháwan お茶碗); (*basin, pot*) hachí 鉢; *~ of rice with topping* ...-don ... どん・丼, donburi (mono) どんぶり・丼(もの)

bowlegged *adj* gani-mata (no) がにまた(の), waní-ashi (no) わに足(の)

bowl(ful) *n* ...-hai ... 杯 (**1:** íp-pai 一杯, **2:** ní-hai 二杯, **3:** sánbai 三杯)

bowling *n* bōringu ボウリング; *~ competition* bōringu-taikai ボウリング大会, *~ alley* bōringu-jō ボウリング場, *~ ball* bōringu (no) bōru ボウリング(の)ボール

bow-wow! *n* wán-wan ワンワン

box *n* hako 箱; *~ lunch* bentō 弁当 (o-bentō お弁当), (*sold at station*) eki-ben 駅弁; *small measuring ~* masú 升

boxer *n* bokusā ボクサー

boxing *n* kentō 拳闘, bókushingu ボクシング; *~ glove* gurōbu グローブ

box office *n* **1.** (*ticket office*) chiketto-uriba チケット売り場 **2.** (*receipts from a play, film, etc.*) kōgyō-shūnyū 興行収入, bokkusu-ofisu ボックスオフィス

boxtree, boxwood *n* tsuge つげ

boy *n* **1.** otokó-no-ko 男の子, shōnen 少年, bō´ya 坊や, bótchan 坊ちゃん; *big~* (*male*) otokó 男 **2.** (*waiter*) bōi ボーイ

boyfriend *n* bōi-furéndo ボーイフレンド; káre-shi 彼氏

boyish *adj* bōisshu ボーイッシュ, otoko-no-ko rashii 男の子らしい

Boy Scouts *n* bōi sukauto ボーイスカウト

Boys' Festival (*5 May*) *n* Tángo no sekku 端午の節句

boycott *n* boikotto ボイコット

bra *n* bura ブラ = burajā ブラジャー

brace oneself *v* shimarimásu (shimaru, shimatte) 締まります(締まる, 締まって)

bracelet *n* ude-wa 腕輪, buresuretto ブレスレット

bracing *adj* (*refreshing*) sawáyaka (na) さわやか・爽やか(な)

bracket *n* kakko 括弧; *square bracket* (*such as "[]")* kaku-kakko 角括弧

brag *v* hóra o fukimásu (fukú, fúite) ほらを吹きます(吹く, 吹いて)

brag about *v* jiman (o) shimásu (suru, shite) 自慢(を)します(する, して), hokorimásu (hokóru, hokótte) 誇ります(誇る, 誇って)

braid *v* amimásu (ámu, ánde) 編みます(編む, 編んで)

brain(s) *n* nō(-míso) 脳(みそ), zunō 頭脳, atamá 頭 (= *head*)

brainstorming *n* burein sutōmingu ブレインストーミング

brake n burḗki ブレーキ

branch n **1.** (of tree) eda 枝 **2.** (of store) shiten 支店 **3.** (of rail line) shisen 支線 **4.** (of school) bún-kō 分校 **5.** (of office) bu 部

branch off v it branches off wakaremásu (waka-réru, wakárete) 分かれます(分かれる、分かれて)

brand n burando ブランド, meigara 銘柄, shōhyō 商標; famous ~ goods yūmei burando-hin 有名ブランド品

brandy n burandē ブランデー

brand-new adj shinpin no 新品の

brass n shinchū 真ちゅう・真鍮

brassiére n burájā ブラジャー

brat n wanpaku-kozō わんぱく小僧, gakí がき・餓鬼

brave adj yūkan (na) 勇敢(な), tsuyói 強い

bravo interj burabō ブラボー

brazen adj zūzūshíi ずうずうしい

brazier n híbachi 火鉢

Brazil n Burajiru ブラジル

bread n pán パン, shoku-pan 食パン
    bread crumbs n pan-kó パン粉, pankúzu パンくず[屑]
    bread flour n kyōriki-kó 強力粉, pan senyō-ko パン専用粉

breadth n haba 幅

break n **1.** (rift or pause) kire-mé 切れ目 **2.** (rest) yasumí 休み(o-yasumi お休み), kyūkei 休憩

break v **1.** it breaks v kowaremásu (kowaréru, kowárete) 壊れます(壊れる、壊れて), (in two) oremásu (oréru, órete) 折れます(折れる、折れて), (it splits) waremásu (wareru, warete) 割れます(割れる、割れて), (it smashes) kudakemásu (kudakéru, kudákete) 砕けます(砕ける、砕けて); (it opens up, it dawns) akemásu (akeru, akete) 開け[明け]ます(開け[明け]る、開け[明け]て) **2.** breaks v kowashimásu (kowású, kowáshite) 壊します(壊す、壊して), (in two) orimásu (óru, ótte) 折ります(折る、折って), (splits) warimásu (waru, watte) 割ります(割る、割って), (smashes it) kudakimásu (kudáku, kudáite) 砕きます(砕く、砕いて); break in wari-kómimásu (wari-

kómu, wari-kónde) 割り込みます(割り込む、割り込んで)

break down **1.** it breaks down (crumbles) kuzuremásu (kuzuréru, kuzúrete) 崩れます(崩れる、崩れて), (stops working) koshō shimásu (suru, shite) 故障します(する、して) **2.** breaks (demolishes) it kuzushimásu (kuzúsu, kuzúshite) 崩します(崩す、崩して)

break off (ends it) kirimásu (kíru, kítte) 切ります(切る、切って); (it ends) kiremásu (kiréru, kírete) 切れます(切れる、切れて)

break out (appears) hassei shimásu (suru, shite) 発生します(する、して) → occur

breakable adj koware-yasúi 壊れやすい

breakdown n **1.** (crash) koshō 故障 **2.** (item by item) meisai 明細, uchiwake 内訳

breakfast n chōshoku 朝食, asa-góhan 朝ご飯; (mostly male, [INFORMAL] asameshi 朝飯)

bream n sea ~ tái タイ・鯛

breast n (chest) muné 胸; (woman's) chichí 乳, chibusa 乳房, (baby talk, slang) óppai おっぱい; ~ cancer nyūgan 乳がん・乳癌

breath n íki 息; a breath hitó-iki 一息; draws/takes one's last ~ íki o hikitorimásu (hiki-tóru, hiki-tótte) 息を引き取ります(引き取る、引き取って)

breathe v íki o shimásu (suru, shite) 息をします(する、して); kokyū shimásu (suru, shite) 呼吸します(する、して); ~ a sigh of relief hótto shimásu (suru, shite) ほっとします(する、して)

breathe (it) in v (... o) suimásu (sū, sutte) (...を)吸います(吸う、吸って)

breechcloth n fundoshi ふんどし・褌

breed n **1.** (species of plant, etc.) hinshu 品種 **2.** (kind) shurui 種類 **3.** (lineage) kettō 血統

breeze n (soyó-)kaze (そよ)風; ~ in wari-komimásu (wari-kómu, warikónde) 割り込みます(割り込む、割り込んで)

brevity n kanketsu (sa) 簡潔(さ), mijikasa 短さ

brew *n* jōzō 醸造
brewery *n* jōzō-sho 醸造所
bribe(ry) *n* wáiro わいろ・賄賂
bric-a-brac *n* oki-mono 置物
brick *n* rénga レンガ・煉瓦
bride *n* haná-yome(-san) 花嫁(さん), (o-)yome(-san) (お)嫁(さん)
bridegroom *n* hana-múko(-san) 花婿 (さん), (o-)múko(-san) (お)婿(さん)
bridge *n* **1.** hashí 橋; *(steel)* tekkyō 鉄橋; *(card)* burijji ブリッジ koto-ji 琴柱; *Rainbow Bridge (Tokyo)* Reinbō-burijji レインボーブリッジ **2.** *(card)* burijji ブリッジ
brief *adj (short)* mijikái 短い; *(simple)* kantan (na) 簡単(な)
briefcase *n* kaban かばん・鞄, buriifu kēsu ブリーフケース
briefing *n* jōkyō setsumei 状況説明
briefly *adj (in brief)* zatto ざっと
brier *n* ibara イバラ
brigadier general *n* junshō 准将
bright *adj* **1.** akarui 明るい **2.** *(sunny)* hogáraka (na) 朗らか(な) **3.** *(colorful)* hanáyaka (na) 華やか(な) **4.** *(gaudy)* hadé (na) 派手(な) **5.** *(of spirit)* yōki (na) 陽気(な)
brilliant *adj* subarashii すばらしい・素晴らしい, sugoi すごい・凄い
brim *n* fuchi ふち・縁, heri へり・縁
brine *n* shiomizu 塩水
bring *v (a thing)* motte/tótte kimásu (kúru, kité) 持って/取って来ます (来る, 来て); *~ along (a person)* tsurete kimásu (kúru, kité) 連れて来ます(来る, 来て). *– But "~ to you/them"* motte/tótte/tsurete ikimásu (iku, itte) 持って/取って/連れて行きます (行く, 行って)
bring about *v* okoshimásu (okósu, okóshite) 起こします(起こす, 起こして)
bring close/near *v* chika-zukemásu (chika-zukéru, chika-zúkete) 近付けます(近付ける, 近付けて), yosemásu (yoseru, yosete) 寄せます(寄せる, 寄せて)
bring up *v (rears)* sodatemásu (sodatéru, sodátete) 育てます(育てる, 育てて); yashinaimásu (yashinau, yashinatte) 養います(養う, 養って);

yōiku shimásu (suru, shite) 養育します(する, して); *(trains)* shitsukemásu (shitsukéru, shitsúkete) しつけます(しつける, しつけて)
brink *n* kiwá 際
Britain → England
British → English
brittle *adj* morói もろい・脆い
broad *adj* hirói 広い
broadband *n, adj* burōdo-bando ブロードバンド, [BOOKISH] kōtai-iki 広帯域
broadcast **1.** *n* hōsō 放送 **2.** *v* hōsō shimásu (suru, shite) 放送します(する, して)
broadcasting station *n* hōsō'-kyoku 放送局
broadly *adj* hiróku 広く
broad-minded *adj* kanyō (na) 寛容(な)
brocade *n* níshiki 錦
broccoli *n* burokkorii ブロッコリー
brochure *n* panfuretto パンフレット, katarogu カタログ
broil *v* yakimásu (yaku, yaite) 焼きます(焼く, 焼いて)
broiled foods *n* yaki-mono 焼物; *broiled salt-coated fish* shioyaki 塩焼き
broke *adj (without money)* kinketsu 金欠
broken *adj (not working)* damé desu (da/na, de, ni) だめ[駄目]です(だ/な, で, に); koshō shita 故障した
brokenhearted; *gets ~* shitsuren shimásu (suru, shite) 失恋します(する, して)
broker *n* burōkā ブローカー, nakagai 仲買い, nakadachí 仲立ち
brokerage *n (commission)* tesúryō 手数料, komisshon コミッション
bronze *n* seidō 青銅, buronzu ブロンズ
brooch *n* burōchi ブローチ
brook *n* ogawa 小川
broom *n* hōki ほうき・箒
broth *n* sūpu スープ
brother *n (otoko)* kyō'dai (男) 兄弟; *(older)* (o-)nii-san (お)兄さん, áni 兄; *(younger)* otōtó 弟, *(your younger brother)* otōto-san 弟さん
brother-in-law *n* gíri no áni/otōtó (kyō'dai) 義理の兄/弟(兄弟)
brothers and sisters *n* kyō'dai 兄弟, *(female sisters)* shimai 姉妹

brought up; gets ~ (*is reared*)
sodachimásu (sodátsu, sodátte) 育ちま
す(育つ、育って)

brow n **1.** (*eyebrow*) máyu 眉 **2.** (*forehead*) hitai 額

brown adj cha-iro (no/i) 茶色(の/い)

brown bread n kuro-pan 黒パン

bruise n uchimí 打ち身、daboku-shō
打撲傷

brush 1. n búrashi ブラシ、haké 刷毛;
(*for writing or painting*) fude 筆 **2.** v
~ aside haraimásu (haráu, harátte) 払
います(払う、払って)

brushing n burasshingu ブラッシング

brush up n burasshu appu ブラッシュ
アップ

brushwood n shiba 柴

brusque adj bu-áisō (na) 無愛想(な)、
bukkírábō ぶっきらぼう(な)

Brussels sprouts n me-kyábetsu
芽キャベツ

brutal adj mugói むごい、zankoku (na)
残酷(な)、zangyaku (na) 残虐(な)、
zannin (na) 残忍(な)

brutality n mugósa むごさ、zankoku
残酷、zangyaku 残虐、zannin 残忍、
mujihi 無慈悲

bubble n awá 泡、abukú あぶく; (*soap*)
shabon-dama シャボン玉; **~ economy**
baburu (keizai) バブル(経済)

bubble bath n baburu-basu バブルバ
ス; awa-buro 泡風呂

bubble gum n fūsen-gámu 風船ガム

bucket n **1.** baketsu バケツ **2.** (*rice*)
(o)-hachi お鉢、(o)-hitsu おひつ、
meshi-bitsu 飯びつ

buckle n shime-gane 締め金、bákkuru
バックル

buck private n heisotsu 兵卒

buck tooth n déppa 出っ歯、sóppa
反っ歯

buckwheat n soba そば・蕎麦

buckwheat chaff n soba-gara そばがら

buckwheat noodles n (o-)sóba (お)そ
ば[蕎麦]

bud n **1.** (*of leaf*) mé 芽 **2.** (*of flower*)
tsubomi つぼみ・蕾

Buddha n Hotoke(-sámá) 仏(様)、
(*Sakyamuni*) Shaka 釈迦 = O-shaka-
sama お釈迦様; (*statue of Buddha*)

Butsu-zō 仏像

Buddhism n Bukkyō 仏教

Buddhist n Bukkyō-to 仏教徒

Buddhist priest n (o-)bō-san (お)坊さ
ん、sō´ryo 僧侶、[INFORMAL] bō´zu 坊
主

Buddhist temple n (o-)terá (お)寺

budding willow n ao yagi 青やぎ・青
柳、ao-yánagi 青柳

buddy → friend

budge → move

budget n yosan 予算

buffet n byuffe ビュッフェ

bug n mushi ムシ・虫 (**1:** ip-piki 一匹、
2: ní-hiki 二匹、**3:** sánbiki 三匹; **how
many** nán-biki 何匹)

bugle n rappa ラッパ

build v (*erects*) tatemásu (tatéru, tátete)
建てます(建てる、建てて)、ki-zuki-
másu (ki-zúku, ki-zúite) 築きます(築
く、築いて); (*creates*) tsukurimásu
(tsukúru, tsukútte) 造ります(造る、造
って); kōsaku shimásu (suru, shite) 工
作します(する、して); **body ~** taikaku
体格

builder n (*person*) kenchiku-sha 建築
者; kenchiku-gyōsha 建築業者

building n taté-mono 建物、bíru ビル

building lot n shiki-chi 敷地

bulb n tamá 玉; **light ~** denkyū 電球

bulge n fukurami ふくらみ・膨らみ

bulk n ōkisa 大きさ、kasá かさ; **in ~**
bára de ばらで・バラで

bull n **1.** (*bullshit*) baka/muda-bánashi
ばか/無駄話、(*bragging*) hóra ほら・
ホラ; **shoots the ~** muda-bánashi o
shimásu (suru, shite) 無駄話をします
(する、して) **2.** o-ushi 雄牛

bulldozer n burudózā ブルドーザー

bullet n tamá 弾、[BOOKISH] dangan 弾丸

bulletin n keiji 掲示

bulletin board n keiji-ban 掲示板

bulletproof adj bōdan (no) 防弾(の)

bullet train n shinkánsen 新幹線

bullfight(ing) n tōgyū 闘牛

bully n (*children*) ijimekko いじめっ子

bump n **1.** (*swelling*) kobú こぶ・瘤;
(*with*) **bumps** bótsubotsu (ga dekite)
ぽつぽつ(ができて) **2.** (*in road*)
dekoboko でこぼこ・凸凹

bump into *v* ... ni butsukarimásu (butsukaru, butsukatte) ... にぶつかります(ぶつかる、ぶつかって); (*happens to meet*) de-aimásu (de-au, de-atte) 出会います(出会う、出会って)

bun *n* (*steamed*) manjū まんじゅう, (*pork-stuffed*) niku-man 肉まん; (*beanjam-stuffed*) an-man あんまん

bunch *n* 1. (*cluster*) fusá 房 2. (*pile*) yamá 山 3. (*bundle*) tába 束 4. (*group*) muré 群れ
bunch of *n* (*lots of*) takusan (no) たくさんの

bundle *n* tsutsumí 包み; (*bunch*) tába 束

bungalow *n* (*cottage*) bangarō バンガロー

bungle 1. *n* héma へま 2. *v* héma o shimásu (suru, shite) へまをします(する、して)

bunion *n* mamé まめ, soko-mame 底まめ

bunk *n* (*bed*) shindai 寝台

bunny *n* 1. (*rabbit*) usagi (chan) ウサギ(ちゃん) 2. (*alluring young woman*) sekushii na onna (no ko) セクシーな女(の子); **~ girl** banii gāru バニーガール

burden *n* ní 荷, (*on one's mind*) omo-ni 重荷

burdock (*root*) *n* gobō ゴボウ; **fried ~ and carrot strips** kinpira キンピラ

bureau *n* 1. (*department*) kyóku 局, ...-kyoku ... 局 2. (*chest*) tansu たんす・箪笥

bureaucracy *n* kanryō-seido 官僚制度
bureaucrat *n* kanryō 官僚
burglar *n* dorobō 泥棒・どろぼう
burglar alarm *n* bōhan béru 防犯ベル, (tōnan) keihō-ki (盗難)警報器

burial *n* maisō 埋葬
buried → bury
burlesque *n* 1. sutorípputi ストリップ 2. (*parody*) parodii パロディ
Burma *n* Bíruma ビルマ

burn 1. *v* (*it burns*) yakemásu (yakeru, yakete) 焼けます(焼ける、焼けて); (*fire burns*) moemásu (moeru, moete) 燃えます(燃える、燃えて) 2. *v* (*burns it*) yakimásu (yaku, yaite) 焼きます(焼く、焼いて); (*burns a fire; wood, coal*) takimásu (taku, taite) 焚きます

(焚く、焚いて), (*burns a light*) tomoshimásu (tomósu, tomóshite) ともし[点し]ます(ともす、ともして) 3. *n* (*on the skin*) yakedo やけど・火傷

burp *n* geppu (o shimásu; suru, shite) げっぷをします;する、して)

burst *v* (*it bursts*) yaburemásu (yaburéru, yabúrete) 破れます(破れる、破れて), (*explodes*) bakuhatsu shimásu (suru, shite) 爆発します(する、して); (*bursts it*) yaburimásu (yabúru, yabútte) 破ります(破る、破って); **~ out** tobi-dashimásu (tobi-dásu, tobi-dáshite) 飛び出します(飛び出す、飛び出して)

bury *v* uzumemásu (uzumeru, uzumete) うずめます(うずめる、うずめて), umemásu (umeru, umete) 埋めます(埋める、埋めて); **gets buried** uzumarimásu (uzumaru, uzumatte) うずまり[埋まり]ます(うずまる、うずまって), umarimásu (umaru, umatte) 埋まります(埋まる、埋まって)

bus *n* básu バス
bus driver *n* básu no untenshu バスの運転手
bus information booth *n* básu no annai-jo バスの案内所
bus stop *n* teiryū-jo 停留所; básu nori-ba バス乗り場
bus terminal *n* basu tāminaru バスターミナル
bus tour guide *n* basu gaido(-san) バスガイド(さん)

bush *n* shigemi 茂み, [BOOKISH] kanboku 灌木・潅木
Bushido *n* bushi-dō 武士道
bush warbler *n* ugúisu ウグイス

business *n* 1. (*job*) shigoto 仕事 (o-shígoto お仕事), bijinesu ビジネス 2. (*line of business*) shō'bai 商売 3. (*office work*) jímu 事務 4. (*transaction*) tóri-hiki 取り引き・取引 5. (*errand*) yōji 用事, (go-)yō´ (ご)用, yō-táshi 用足し 6. (*enterprise*) jígyō 事業, jitsugyo 実業 7. (*commerce*) shō'gyō 商業 8. **having no ~** muyō (no) 無用(の) 9. **It's not your ~.**, **Mind your own ~.** Yokei na o-sewa désu 余計なお世話です。

business concern *n* shōsha 商社
business conditions *n* keiki 景気
business hours *n* eigyō-jíkan 営業時間
businesslike *adj* bijinesu raiku ビジネスライク, jimu-teki(na) 事務的(な)
businessman *n* jitsugyō-ka 実業家, bijinesu-man ビジネスマン
business suit *n* sebiro 背広
business trip *n* shutchō 出張
bust → burst
bustle *n* (*energetic activity*) kakki 活気
bustling *adj* nigíyaka (na) にぎやか・賑やか(な)
busy *adj* isogashíi いそがしい・忙しい, sewashíi せわしい, sewashínai せわしない; [BOOKISH] tabō (na) 多忙(な); (*in the midst of work*) shigoto-chū 仕事中, (*in conference*) kaigi-chū 会議中; *The line is ~* (O-)hanashi-chū désu (お)話中です
busybody *n* osekkai-yaki (na hito) おせっかい焼き(な人), sewa-zuki 世話好き
but *conj* 1. [BOOKISH] shíkashi しかし, tokoró-ga ところが 2. démo でも 3. ([INFORMAL] *or child talk*) dátte だって; ... ga ... が, (...) kéredo (-mo) (...)けれど(も), ... tokoróga ... ところが; ippō´ (de) 一方(で)
butcher (*shop*) *n* nikú-ya 肉屋
butcher knife *n* nikukiri-bō´chō 肉切り包丁
butt *n* 1. (*cigarette, cigar*) suigara 吸いがら 2. → buttock
butter *n* báta バター, báta バタ; *~ roll* batā-rō´ru バターロール
butterfly *n* chō´ ちょう・蝶, chōchō ちょうちょう, chōcho ちょうちょ
buttock *n* shirí 尻 (o-shiri お尻), (*mostly male* [VERY INFORMAL]) ketsu けつ・尻・穴
button 1. *n* botan ボタン 2. *v* (*buttons it*) ... no botan o kakemásu (kakéru, kákete) ... のボタンをかけます(かける、かけて)

buxom *n* (*full-bosomed*) hōman na mune (no) 豊満な胸の, fukuyoka (na) ふくよか(な)
buy *v* kaimásu (kau, katte) 買います(買う、買って); motomemásu (motoméru, motómete) 求めます(求める、求めて); *~ up* kai-torimásu (kai-tóru, kai-tótte) 買い取ります(買い取る、買い取って)
buyer *n* 1. kai-te 買い手 2. (*professional*) báiyā バイヤー
buzz *n* 1. (*phone call*) denwa no yobi-dashi-on 電話の呼び出し音 2. (*rumor*) uwasa 噂・うわさ 3. (*humming sound of insect*) (mushi no) haoto (虫の)羽音
buzzer *n* búzā ブザー
by 1. *prep* (*no later than*) ... máde ni ... までに; (*means of*) ... de ... で; *by and by* → soon
by ... at the latest *adv* ... máde ni wa ... までには
by chance *adv* hyótto suruto ひょっと(すると), gūzen (ni) 偶然(に), futo ふと
by far *adv* zutto ずっと; háruka (ni) はるか(に)
gets by *v* (*lives*) kurashimásu (kurasu, kurashite) 暮らします(暮らす、暮らして)
by heart/memory *adv* sóra de そらで
by itself/nature *adv* hitori-de ni ひとりで・独りでに, motomoto もともと・元々, móto-yori もと[元]より
by oneself *adv* jibun de 自分で
by the way → way
bye (-bye) → good-bye
bygone *n* kako no koto 過去のこと, sugita koto 過ぎたこと
bylaw *n* kisoku 規則
bypass *n* (*highway, surgery*) baipasu バイパス
by-product *n* fukusanbutsu 副産物
bystander *n* kenbutsu-nin 見物人
byte *n* (*computer*) baito バイト

C

cab → taxi

cabaret n kyábarē キャバレー

cabbage n kyábetsu キャベツ; (*Chinese*) hakusai 白菜・ハクサイ

cabin n koya 小屋; (*mountain lodge*) yama-goya 山小屋

cabin cruiser n ōgata mōtā bōto 大型モーターボート, kurūzā クルーザー

cabinet n (*government*) náikaku 内閣

cable n 1. tsuná 綱, kē´buru ケーブル 2. (*telegram*) kaigai-dénpō 海外電報

cable car n kēburú-kā´ ケーブルカー

cable television n kēburú-terebi ケーブルテレビ, yūsen-terebi 有線テレビ

cache n (*computer*) kyasshu キャッシュ

cactus n saboten サボテン

cadaver n shitai 死体

caddie n kyadii キャディー

cadence n rizumu リズム, hyōshi 拍子

cadet n shikan kōho sei 士官候補生

cadge v nedarimásu (nedaru, nedatte) ねだります(ねだる, ねだって); takarimásu (takaru, takatte) たかります(たかる, たかって)

cafe n (*coffee shop*) kissa-ten 喫茶店, kafe カフェ

cafeteria n kafeteria カフェテリア, shokudō 食堂; *school* ~ gaku-shoku 学食, gakusei shokudō 学生食堂; *company* ~ shain-shokudō 社員食堂

caffeine n kafein カフェイン

cage n 1. (*for bird*) kago かご・籠, tori-kago 鳥かご 2. (*for animal*) orí 檻

cagey adj nukeme-no-nai 抜け目のない, yōjin-bukai 用心深い

cahoots; *in ~ with* ... to takuránde ... と企[たくら]んで

Cairo n kairo カイロ

cajole v odatemásu (odateru, odatete) おだてます(おだてる, おだてて); kangen de damashimásu (damasu, damashite) 甘言でだまします・騙します(騙す, 騙して)

cajolery n obekka おべっか, kuchi-guruma 口車, [BOOKISH] kangen 甘言

cake n 1. kē´ki ケーキ; (*spongecake*)

kasutera カステラ 2. (o-)káshi (お)菓子; (*Japanese*) wa-gáshi 和菓子 3. (*rice cake*) mochi もち・餅 4. → bar (*of soap*)

cake v *it cakes* (mud) (doró ga) katamarimásu (katamaru, katamatte) (泥が)固まります(固まる, 固まって)

calamity n sainán 災難, wazawai 災い

calcium n karushium カルシウム

calculate v keisan shimásu (suru, shite) 計算します(する, して)

calculation n 1. keisan 計算 2. (*estimate*) mitsumori 見積もり

calculator n keisán-ki 計算機; *desk* ~ dentaku 電卓

calculus n 1. (*mathematics*) biseki-bun-gaku 微積分学 2. (*pathology*) kesseki 結石

calendar n koyomí 暦; karéndā カレンダー

calf n 1. (*young cow*) ko-ushi 子牛 2. (*leg below the knee*) fukurahagi ふくらはぎ

calfskin n ko-ushi no kawa 子牛の皮

caliber n 1. (*bore caliber*) kōkei 口径 2. (*ability*) sainō 才能

calisthenics n biyō taisō 美容体操, jūnan taisō 柔軟体操

call 1. n (*phone call*) denwa 電話 2. n (*visit*) hōmon 訪問; (*of solicitude*) (o-)mimai (お)見舞 3. v yobimásu (yobu, yonde) 呼びます(呼ぶ, 呼んで); (*phone*) denwa o shimásu (suru, shite) 電話をします(する, して) 4. v (*call on*) → visit; call to mind → recall

call box n hijōyō denwa 非常用電話

call center n kōru sentā コールセンター

call girl n kōru gāru コールガール

called; *is ~* ... to iimásu (iu, itte/yutte) ... と言います(言う, 言って/ゆって)

caller n (*visitor*) raikyaku 来客

calligraphy n shodō 書道; (*handwriting practice*) (o-)shūji (お)習字

calling n 1. (*vocation*) shokugyō 職業 2. (*summons*) shōshū 召集

calling card n meishi 名刺 (= *busi-*

ness card, *name card*); ~ *case* meishí-ire 名刺入れ

callous *adj* **1.** (*having calluses*) táko no dekita たこのできた **2.** (*insensitive, unfeeling*) mu-shinkei (na) 無神経(な), mu-kankaku (na) 無感覚(な) **3.** (*unsympathetic*) omoiyari ga nai 思いやりがない, mu-jō (na) 無情(な)

callus *n* táko たこ

calm *adj* (*quiet*) shízuka (na) 静か(な), odáyaka (na) 穏やか(な), reisei (na) 冷静(な); nódoka (na) のどか(な); *gets* ~ shizu-marimásu (shizumáru, shizumátte) 静まります(静まる, 静まって); *calms, makes* ~ shizumemásu (shizuméru, shizumete) 静めます(静める, 静めて); *calms down* (*regains composure*) ochitsukimásu (ochi-tsuku, ochitsuite) 落ち着きます(落ち着く, 落ち着いて)

calmly *adv* ochi-tsuite 落ち着いて; (*unperturbed*) heiki de 平気で

calorie *n* karorii カロリー

calorie calculation *n* karorii keisan カロリー計算

Cambodia *n* kanbojia カンボジア

camcorder *n* bideo kámera ビデオカメラ

came → **come**

camel *n* rakuda ラクダ

camellia *n* tsúbaki ツバキ・椿

cameo *n* kameo カメオ

camera *n* kámera カメラ, shashín-ki 写真機

cameraman *n* kamera-man カメラマン

camouflage *n* kamufurāju カムフラージ

camp **1.** *n* kyánpu キャンプ; (*bivouac*) yaei 野営 **2.** *v* kyánpu (o) shimásu (suru, shite) キャンプ(を)します(する, して)

campaign *n* kyanpēn キャンペーン, undō 運動

camper *n* **1.** (*a person who camps*) kyanpu (o) suru hito キャンプ(を)する人 **2.** (*vehicle*) kyanpingukā キャンピングカー, kyanpā キャンパー

campfire *n* kyánpu-faiyā キャンプファイヤー

camping *n* kyanpu キャンプ, kyanpu-

seikatsu キャンプ生活

campsite *n* kyanpu-jō キャンプ場; yaei-chi 野営地

campus *n* kyánpasu キャンパス, (*within the university*) daigakú-kōnai 大学構内; kōtei 校庭

can **1.** *n* (*tin can*) kán 缶 (**1:** íp-pon 一本, **2:** ní-hon 二本, **3:** sánbon 三本, *how many* nán-bon 何本) **2.** *cans it* *v* (kán ni) tsumemásu (tsuméru, tsúmete) (缶に)詰めます(詰める, 詰めて)

canned beer *n* kan bíiru 缶ビール

can opener *n* kan-kírí 缶切り

can *modal v* (*can do it*) (... ga) dekimásu (dekíru, dékite) (... が)出来ます(出来る, 出来て), (*suru*) kotó ga dekimásu (する)事が出来ます; (... ga) kanaimásu (kanáu, kanátte) (... が)叶います(叶う, 叶って) [NOTE] *A potential* ("can") *version of almost every verb can be made by replacing ... -ru ... る with ... -(ra)reru ... (ら)れる, or ...-u ...う with ...-eru ...える. Most of the potentials will be found in the Japanese-English section. Some Japanese frown upon the ...-reru ...れる forms, and use only the longer ...-rareru ...られる; some use ...-eru ...える as well as ...-rareru (=...-reru) ...られる(=...れる)*

can see (... ga) miemásu (miéru, míete) (... が)見えます(見える, 見えて)

can hear (... ga) kikoemásu (kikoeru, kikoete) (... が)聞こえます(聞こえる, 聞こえて)

Canada *n* Kánada カナダ

Canadian *n* Kanadá-jin カナダ人

canal *n* únga 運河

canary *n* kanari(y)a カナリア[ヤ]

cancel *v* tori-keshimásu (tori-kesu, tori-keshite) 取り消します(取り消す, 取り消して); keshimásu (kesu, keshite) 消します(消す, 消して)

cancellation *n* tori-keshi 取り消し; kyánseru キャンセル

cancellation mark/stamp *n* keshi-in 消印

cancelled flight *n* kekkō 欠航 = *flight cancellation*

cancer *n* gán がん・癌; (*lung*) haigan

345

肺がん・肺癌; (*stomach*) i-gan 胃がん・胃癌; (*breast*) nyū´gan 乳がん・乳癌
Cancer n (*star sign*) Kani-za カニ座
candid adj sotchoku (na) 率直(な)
candidate n kōhó-sha 候補者
candid(ly) adv sotchoku (ni) 率直に, ó´pun (ni) オープン(に) → frank
candle n rōsókú ろうそく, kyándoru キャンドル
candleholder n rōsókú date ろうそく立て, shoku-dai 燭台
candlelight n rōsókú no hikari ろうそくの光
candlestick n rōsókú-date ろうそく立て, shokudai 燭台
candor n socchoku (sa) 率直(さ)
candy n kyándii キャンディー, (*wheat-gluten*) ame アメ・飴
candy floss n (*sweet*) watagashi 綿菓子
candy store n (o-)kashí-ya (お)菓子屋
cane n 1. (*walking stick*) sutékki ステッキ; (*staff*) tsúe 杖 2. (*rattan*) tó´ 藤
canine n 1. (*dog*) inu 犬; *canidae* inu-ka 犬科 2. (*canine teeth*) kenshi 犬歯
canister n yōki 容器, kan 缶
canna n kanna カンナ
cannabis n taima 大麻, marifana マリファナ
canned (*food*) adj kanzúmé (no) 缶詰(の)
cannibal n kanibaru カニバル, hitokui 人食い
cannon n taihō 大砲
cannot modal v [NEGATIVE] dekimasén (dekínai) でき[出来]ません(でき[出来]ない); (shi-) kiremasén (shi-kírénai) (し)切れません(し切れない); ~ *stand it* gáman dekimasén (dekínai) がまん[我慢]でき[出来]ません(でき[出来]ない), tamarimasén (tamaranai) たまりません(たまらない)
canoe n kanū カヌー
canon n (*music*) kanon カノン
canopy n tengai 天蓋・てんがい
cantankerous adj kimuzukashii 気難しい, tsumujimagari (no) つむじ曲がり(の)
canteen n shokudō 食堂

canvas n kyanbasu キャンバス
canvas shoes n (*sneakers*) suniikā スニーカー
canyon n kyōkoku 峡谷; *Grand Canyon* Gurando kyanion グランドキャニオン
cap n 1. → hat 2. (*of a pen*) kyáppu キャップ 3. (*of a bottle*) kyáppu キャップ, ōkan 王冠 4. (*of a mushroom*) kása かさ・笠
capability n 1. (*ability*) nōryoku 能力 2. (*possibility*) kanō-sei 可能性 3. (*potential*) shōrai-sei 将来性
capable adj nōryoku ga aru 能力がある; yūnō (na) 有能(な)
capacity n kyapa(sitii) キャパ(シティー) 1. (*ability*) nōryoku 能力 2. (*measure of contents*) yōseki 容積
cape n 1. (*promontory*) misaki 岬 2. (*sleeveless garment*) kēpu ケープ
caper n kēpā ケーパー
capital n 1. (*city*) shútó 首都 2. (*money*) shihon 資本
capitalism n shihon-shúgi 資本主義
capitalist n shihon-ka 資本家
capitalize v 1. (*write or print in capital letters*) ōmoji de kakimásu (kaku, kaite) 大文字で書きます(書く, 書いて) 2. (*supply with capital*) shusshi shimásu (suru, shite) 出資します(する, して)
capital letter n ōmoji 大文字
capital punishment n shi-kei 死刑
capitulate v kōfuku shimásu (suru, shite) 降伏します(する, して), kōsan shimásu (suru, shite) 降参します(する, して)
caprice n kimagure 気まぐれ
capricious adj kimagure (na) 気まぐれ(な)
Capricorn n (*star sign*) Yagi-za 山羊座
capsize v tenpuku shimásu (suru, shite) 転覆します(する, して), tenpuku sasemásu (saseru, sasete) 転覆させます(させる, させて)
capsule n kápuseru カプセル
captain n (*army*) tái i 大尉; (*navy*) taisa 大佐; (*airplane*) kíchō´ 機長; (*ship*) sénchō 船長, (*warship*) kanchō 艦長; (*team*) kyáputen キャプテン

346

caption *n* kyapushon キャプション **1.** (*situation*) midashi 見出し **2.** (*text of a speech of movie, etc*) jimaku 字幕 **3.** (*explanation*) setsumei bun 説明文

captivate *v* miwaku shimásu (suru, shite) 魅惑します(する、して)

captive *n* horyo 捕虜

captivity *n* kankin 監禁

capture *v* toraemásu (toráéru, toráete) 捕らえます(捕らえる、捕らえて)

car *n* kuruma 車, jidō-sha 自動車 (*how many* nán-dai 何台); *Car Number (Six)* (roku)-gō´sha (六)号車; *what (number)* ~ nan-gō´sha 何号車

car barn *n* shako 車庫

car ferry *n* kā ferii カーフェリー

car park *n* chūsha-jō 駐車場

carafe *n* mizu-sashi 水差し

caramel *n* kyarameru キャラメル

carat *n* karatto カラット

caravan *n* **1.** taishō 隊商, kyaraban キャラバン **2.** (*large vehicle*) kyaraban-kā キャラバンカー, kanpingu-kā キャンピングカー

carbohydrate *n* tansuikabutsu 炭水化物

carbolic acid *n* sekitan-san 石炭酸

carbon *n* tanso 炭素

carbon copy *n* kābon-kopii カーボンコピー; (*e-mail*) shiishii CC

carbon dioxide *n* ni-sanka-tanso 二酸化炭素

carbon monoxide *n* issanka-tanso 一酸化炭素

carbon paper *n* kābon-shi カーボン紙

carbonated drink *n* tansan inryō 炭酸飲料

carbonated water *n* tansan sui 炭素水

carbonic acid *n* tansan 炭酸

carburetor *n* kyaburétá キャブレター

carcass *n* shitai 死体, shigai 死骸

card *n* **1.** fuda 札, kā´do カード; (*playing card*) toránpu (ichí-mai) トランプ(一枚) **2.** (*calling card, name card*) meishi 名刺 **3.** (*postcard*) hagaki はがき・葉書(o-hágaki お葉書) *New Year's card* nengajō 年賀状

card game *n* toranpu トランプ

card index *n* kādo-shiki sakuin カード式索引

cardboard *n* bōru-gami ボール紙; (*corrugated*) danbō´ru 段ボール

cardiac 1. *n* (*medicine*) kyōshin-zai 強心剤 **2.** *adj* shizō (no) 心臓(の)

cardigan *n* kādigan カーディガン

cardinal *n* shuyō (na) 主要(な), kihonteki (na) 基本的(な)

care *n* (*caution*) yōjin 用心, nén 念; (*upkeep*) te-iré 手入れ; *take ~ of (a person)* ... no sewá o shimásu (suru, shite), ... の世話(o-séwa お世話)します(する、して), ... no mendó o mimásu (míru, míte) ... の面倒を見ます(見る、見て); (*a matter*) ... o shóri shimásu (suru, shite) ... を処理します(する、して)

care for *v* → like, love, want → look after

career *n* (*occupation*) shokúgyō 職業; kyaria キャリア; (*history*) rireki 履歴, (*summary, resume*) kei-reki 経歴; shoku-reki 職歴

carefree *adj* kiraku (na) 気楽(な), nónki (na) のんき・呑気(な)

careful *adj* chūibukai 注意深い; *is ~* ki o tsukemásu (tsukéru, tsukéte) 気を付けます(付ける、付けて); nén o iremásu (ireru, irete) 念を入れます(入れる、入れて); chūi-bukái 注意深い

carefully *adv* chūibukaku 注意深く

careless *adj* mutón-chaku/-jaku (na) 無頓着(な), zusan (na) ずさん(な), zonzái (na) ぞんざい(な), taiman (na) 怠慢(な), fuchū´i (na) 不注意(な)

carelessly *adv* (*casually*) muzō´sa ni 無造作に

carelessness *n* fuchū´i 不注意, yudan 油断

carer *n* kaigo-nin 介護人

caress 1. *n* aibu 愛撫, hōyō 抱擁 **2.** *v* aibu/hōyō shimásu (suru, shite) 愛撫/抱擁します(するして)

caretaker 1. *n* (*custodian*) kanri-nin 管理人 **2.** (*person who takes care of another*) kaigo-nin 介護人, sewa-nin 世話人

carnival *n* kānibaru カーニバル, shaniku-sai 謝肉祭

carouse n (*drink deeply*) dáiku 大工

carp n (*fish*) kói コイ・鯉
  carp streamers n (*for the Boys' Festival*) koi-nóbori こいのぼり・鯉のぼり

carpenter n dáiku 大工

carpentry n daiku shigoto 大工仕事

carpet n jū´tan じゅうたん・絨毯, kā´petto カーペット

carpet bombing n jū´tan bakugeki じゅうたん爆撃

carpet sweeper n jū´tan sōji-ki じゅうたん掃除機

carriage n 1. (*four-wheeled horse-drawn passenger*) basha 馬車 2. (*transporting*) unpan 運搬 3. (*carrying expense*) unsōryō 運送料 4. (*movable part of a machine*) (kikai no) kadōbu (機械の) 可動部 5. (*bearing*) mi no konashi 身のこなし

carrier n 1. (*transportation*) yusō 輸送, unsō 運送 2. (*of disease*) hokin-sha 保菌者, hoin-sha 保因者 3. (*mail carrier*) yūbin haitatsu(-nin) 郵便配達(人); (*newspaper carrier*) shinbun haitatsu(-nin) 新聞配達(人) 4. (*aircraft carrier*) kōkū bokan 航空母艦, kūbo 空母

carrot n ninjin ニンジン・人参

carry v 1. (*transportation*) motte/tótte ikimásu (iku, itte) 持って/取っていきます(いく、いって); (*loads aboard*) nosemásu (noseru, nosete) 載せます(載せる、載せて); (*conveys*) hakobimásu (hakobu, hakonde) 運びます(運ぶ、運んで) 2. (*dangling from the hand*) sagemásu (sagéru, ságete) 提げます(提げる、提げて); **~ on one's back/shoulders** shoimásu (shou, shotte) しょいます(しょう、しょって), ninaimásu (nináu, ninátte) 担います(担う、担って), katsugimásu (katsúgu, katsúide) 担ぎ[かつぎ]ます(担ぐ、担いで); (*piggyback*) oimásu (ou, otte) 負います(負う、負って), obuimásu (obú´, obútte) おぶ[負ぶ]います(おぶう、おぶって), ónbu shimásu (suru, shite) おんぶします(する、して)
  carry out (*performs*) okonaimásu (okonau, okonatte) 行います(行う、

行って); (*brings about*) genjitsu-ka shimásu (suru, shite) 現実化します(する、して)

carry-cot n keitai bebii beddo 携帯ベビーベッド

carry-on 1. n (*luggage*) te-nimotsu 手荷物 2. adj kinai-mochikomi (yō no) 機内持ち込み(用の)

carsick; gets ~ (kuruma ni) yoimásu (yóu, yótte) (車に)酔います(酔う、酔って)

cart n teoshi-gúruma 手押し車, daisha 台車

cartel n karuteru カルテル

cartilage n nankotsu 軟骨

carton → **box**

cartoon n manga マンガ・漫画

cartridge n 1. (*ink cartridge*) kātorijji カートリッジ 2. (*cartridge in gun*) danyaku-tō 弾薬筒

carve v (*inscribe*) kizamimásu (kizamu, kizande) 刻みます(刻む、刻んで), horimásu (hóru, hótte) 彫ります(彫る、彫って)

carving n horí-monó 彫り物, (*sculpture*) chōkoku 彫刻
  carving knife n nikukiri-bō´chō 肉切り包丁; chōkokutō 彫刻刀

cascade n (*small waterfall*) chiisana taki 小さな滝

case n 1. (*situation*) ba(w)ai 場合, ... wáke... 訳, (*event*) ... dán ... 段; (*matter*) kotó 事, jiken 事件, (*particular instance*) kē´su ケース 2. (*box*) hako 箱
  case by case kēsu-bai-kē´su ケース・バイ・ケース
  in this case kono ba(w)ai この場合
  in that case sorenára それなら; (*sore*) déwa (それ)では, ja じゃ, jā じゃあ
  in case of ... ni sái-shite... に際して; ... no bāi/tokí ni... の場合/時に
  just in case nen no tame 念のため, ichiō 一応

cash n 1. (*money*) genkín 現金; **petty ~** koguchi genkin 小口現金 2. shōkin 賞金
  cashbook n genkin-suitō-chō 現金出納帳
  cashbox n (chiisai) kinko (小さい)金庫

cash card n kyasshu-kādo キャッシュ
カード

cash dispenser n genkin jidō
shiharai-ki 現金自動支払機

cash envelope n (registered mail)
genkin-kákitome 現金書留

cash flow n kyasshu furō キャッシュ
フロー

cash register n reji レジ
3. v (a check) genkín ni kaemásu
(kaéru, káete) 現金にかえます・換えま
す(換える、換えて)、genkín ni shimásu
(suru, shite) 現金にします(する、して)
4. v (into smaller bills/coins) koma-
káku shimásu (suru, shite) 細かくしま
す(する、して)、kuzushimásu (kuzúsu,
kuzúshite) くずします(くずす、くず
して)

cashew nut n kashū nattsu カシュー
ナッツ

cashier n suitō-gákari 出納係、réji-
gákari レジ係

cashmere n kashimia(/ya) カシミア
(/ヤ)

casino n kajino カジノ

cask n taru たる・樽

casket n **1.** (coffin) hitsugi 棺・ひつぎ
2. (jewel box) hōseki-bako 宝石箱

casserole n kyaserōru キャセロール

cassette n kasetto (tēpu) カセット
(テープ)

cast 1. n (throwing) hito nage 一投げ
2. n (selecting actors, selected actors)
kyasuto キャスト、haiyaku 配役 **3.** v
(throw) nagemásu (nagéru, nágete) 投
げます(投げる、投げて) **4.** v (select
actors) kyasutingu shimásu (suru,
shite) キャスティングします(する、
して)、haiyaku o kimemásu (kimeru,
kimete) 配役を決めます(決める、決
めて)

castaway n **1.** (shipwrecked person)
hyōryū-sha 漂流者 **2.** (outcast)
misuterareta hito 見捨てられた人

caste n kāsuto カースト

cast iron n chū-tetsu 鋳鉄・ちゅうてつ

castle n (o-)shiro (お)城; (name of
certain) ...-jō ... 城

castor oil n himashi-abura ヒマシ油

castrate n kyosei-sha 去勢者

casual adj nanige-nái 何気ない; kigaru
(na) 気軽(な); kajuaru (na) カジュア
ル(な)

casual clothes n kajuaru na hukusō/
kakkō カジュアルな服装/格好

casual sex n yukizuri no sekkusu
行きずりのセックス

casuals n fudan-gi 普段着

casually adv (effortlessly; carelessly)
muzō´sa ni 無造作に

casualty n (injury, damage) higai
被害; (victim) higái-sha 被害者; (dead
and injured) shishō´-sha 死傷者

cat n néko 猫・ネコ (**1:** ip-píki 一匹,
2: ní-hiki 二匹, **3:** sánbiki 三匹, how
many nán-biki 何匹)

cat's cradle n ayatori あやとり

cat's-eye n nekome-ishi 猫目石

catalog n katarogu カタログ; mokuroku
目録; (directory) meibo 名簿

catalyst n shokubai 触媒

catapult n (airplane) funsha-ki 噴射
機、kataparuto カタパルト

cataract n **1.** (large waterfall) ookina
taki 大きな滝 **2.** (downpour) gōu 豪雨
3. (ophthalmology) hakunai-shō 白内障

catarrh n kataru カタル

catastrophe n dai-sanji 大惨事, dai-
saigai 大災害, katasutorofi カタストロ
フィ

catastrophic adj hakyoku-teki (na)
破局的(な)

catch 1. v (seizes) tsukamaemásu
(tsukamaeru, tsukamaete) 捕まえます
(捕まえる、捕まえて); torimásu (tóru,
tótte) 取ります(取る、取って); (attracts)
hikimásu (hiku, hiite) 引きます(引く、
引いて) **2.** v (a disease) (byōki ni)
kakarimásu (kakáru, kakátte) (病気に)
かかります(かかる、かかって) **3.** n
a good ~ 獲物・えもの **4.** n (trap)
wana わな・ワナ **5.** n (clasp)
tomegane 留め金

catch a cold kaze o hikimásu (hiku,
hiite) かぜ[風邪]をひきます(ひく、
ひいて)、[HONORIFIC] kaze o o-meshi
ni narimásu (náru, nátte) かぜ[風邪]
をお召しになります(なる、なって)

catch-phrase kyacchi furēzu キャッチ
フレーズ

catch up (*with*) (... ni) oi-tsukimásu (oi-tsúku, oi-tsúite) (... に) 追いつきます (追いつく, 追いついて)

category *n* kategorii カテゴリー

caterer, catering shop *n* shidashi-ya 仕出し屋

catering *n* (*food delivered to order*) demae 出前, kētaringu ケータリング

caterpillar *n* kemushi 毛虫・ケムシ

catfish *n* namazu ナマズ

cathedral *n* dai-seidō 大聖堂

Catholic *n* Katoríkku (kyō) カトリック (教), (*person*) Katoríkku kyōto カトリック教徒

cattle *n* (*bulls and cows*) ushi 牛・ウシ (*how many*) nán-tō 何頭

catty *adj* ijiwaru (na) 意地悪(な), zurui ずるい

caucho *n* gomu ゴム

caucus *n* tōin shūkai 党員集会

cauldron *n* kama かま・釜

cauliflower *n* karifurawā カリフラワー

cause *n* (*of an effect*) gen'in 原因, moto 元; (*negative effect*) ... séi ... せい; (*source*) táne 種; (*reason*) wáke 訳, riyū 理由; (*purpose, benefit*) tame ため・為

cause (*one*) concern/worry (... ni) shinpai o kakemásu (kakéru, kákete) (... に) 心配をかけます(かける, かけて)

cause (*one*) trouble (... ni) méiwaku o kakemásu (kakéru, kákete) (... に) 迷惑をかけます(かける, かけて)

cause (*someone to do*) ... ni sasemásu (saseru, sasete) ... にさせます(させる, させて)

caustic **1.** *n* fushoku-zai 腐食剤 **2.** *adj* fushoku-sei (no) 腐食性(の)

caution **1.** *n* yōjin 用心; (*precaution*) yō´i 用意, nén-ge 念; *as* (*a word of caution*) nen no tamé (ni) 念のため[為] (に) **2.** *v* (*warns*) keikai shimásu (suru, shite) 警戒します(する, して)

cautious *adj* yōjin-bukái 用心深い

cautiously *adv* shinchō (ni) 慎重に, yōjin-bukaku 用心深く, chūi-bukaku 注意深く

cavalier *adj* gōman (na) 傲慢(な), ōhei (na) 横柄(な)

cavalry *n* **1.** (*horsemen*) kihei-tai 騎兵隊 **2.** (*military*) kikō-butai 機甲部隊

cave *n* hora-ana 洞穴・ほら穴, hórá dō 洞・ほら; ... -dō ... 洞

caveman *n* **1.** (*human living in caves*) kekkyo-jin 穴居人, genshi-jin 原始人 **2.** (*crude man*) soya na otoko 粗野な男, (*brutal man*) yaban na otoko 野蛮な男

cavern *n* dai-dōkutsu 大洞窟

caviar *n* (*roe*) kábia キャビア; (*salmon/ trout roe*) ikura イクラ, sujiko 筋子, suzuko すずこ; (*cod roe*) tarako たらこ

cavity *n* **1.** (*hole*) ana 穴 **2.** (*hollow area*) kūdō 空洞 **3.** (*tooth cavity*) mushiba 虫歯

CD player *n* shii-dii pureiyā CDプレイヤー

cease *v* yamimásu (yamu, yande) やみます・止みます(止む, 止んで), taemásu (taéru, táete) 絶えます(絶える, 絶えて)

cease-fire *n* teisen 停戦

ceaseless *adj* taemanai 絶え間ない

cedar; *cryptomeria, Japanese ~* sugi 杉・スギ

cede *v* yuzurimásu (yuzuru, yuzutte) 譲ります(譲る, 譲って)

ceiling *n* tenjō 天井

celeb, celebrity *n* serebu セレブ, yūmei-jin 有名人

celebrate *v* iwaimásu (iwáu, iwátte) 祝います(祝う, 祝って)

celebration *n* (*party*) iwái 祝い (o-iwai お祝い)

celery *n* sérori セロリ; *Japanese ~* údo ウド・独活

celestial *adj* ten (no) 天(の), tentai (no) 天体(の)

celibacy **1.** *n* (*single person/people*) dokushin-sha 独身者 **2.** *adj* dokushin (no) 独身(の)

cell *n* **1.** (*biology*) saibō 細胞 **2.** (*prison*) dokubō 独房, rōya 牢屋

cellar *n* (*storehouse*) kurá 倉・蔵; (*basement*) chiká-shitsu 地下室

cello *n* chéro チェロ

cellophane *n* sérohan セロハン cellophane tape *n* serohan-tēpu セロハンテープ

Celt *n* **1.** (*a Celt*) keruto-jin ケルト人 **2.** (*ethnic*) keruto-zoku ケルト族

cement *n* semento セメント
　cement floor *n* tatakí たたき
cemetery *n* haka-bá 墓場, bóchi 墓地
cenotaph *n* (senbotsu-sha) kinen-hi
　(戦没者) 記念碑
censor **1.** *n* ken'etsu-kan 検閲官 **2.** *v*
　ken'etsu shimásu (suru, shite) 検閲し
　ます(する, して)
censorship *n* ken'etsu 検閲
censure **1.** *n* (*blame*) hínan 非難
　2. *v* (*blames one*) hínan shimásu (suru,
　shite) 非難します(する, して), seme-
　másu (seméru, sémete) 責めます(責め
　る, 責めて)
census *n* kokusei-chōsa 国勢調査
centennial *n* hyakushūnen 百周年
center *n* mannaka 真ん中, chūō 中央,
　chūshin 中心; (*institution*) séntā セ
　ンター
centigrade *n* sésshi 摂氏, seshi セ氏;
　... -do ... 度
centimeter *n* sénchi センチ, senchi-
　mḗtoru センチメートル
centipede *n* mukade ムカデ・百足
central *adj* mannaka no 真ん中の,
　chūshin no 中心の, chūō no 中央の
　Central America *n* chūbei 中米, chūō-
　amerika 中央アメリカ
　central area *n* chūshín-chi 中心地
　central heating *n* sentoraru hiitingu
　セントラルヒーティング
　central office *n* hónbu 本部
　central park *n* chūō kōen 中央公園;
　(*Manhattan*) *Central Park* sentoraru
　pāku セントラルパーク
　central reservation *n* chūō-bunri-tai
　中央分離帯
century *n* séiki 世紀
ceramics *n* seramikku セラミック;
　(*ceramic art*) tōgei 陶芸; (*ceramic ware*)
　tōʹki 陶器; (*pottery*) yaki-mono 焼き物
cereal *n* **1.** kokúmotsu 穀物, kokúrui
　穀類 **2.** (*breakfast food prepared from
　grain*) siriaru シリアル
cerebral *adj* nō (no) 脳(の)
ceremony *n* shikí 式, gíshiki 儀式;
　wedding ~ kekkon-shiki 結婚式
certain *adj* táshika (na) 確か・たしか
　(な); kakujitsu (na) 確実(な); (*specific,
　particular*) áru ... ある...

certainly *adv* mochíron もちろん;
　táshika ni 確かに; mása-ni まさに
certainty *n* kakujitsu 確実, kakujitsu-
　sei 確実性
certificate *n* shōmei-sho 証明書
certification *n* shōmei 証明
certified *adj* kōnin (no) 公認(の)
　certified public accountant (CPA) *n*
　kōnin-kaikéishi 公認会計士
　certified mail *n* kakitome yūbin 書留
　郵便
certify *v* shōmei shimásu (suru, shite)
　証明します(する, して)
cervical *adj* shikyū-keibu (no) 子宮
　頚部(の)
cesarean *n* teiō-sekkai 帝王切開
cesspool *n* osui-dame 汚水溜め,
　gesui-dame 下水溜め
Ceylon *n* Seiron セイロン = *Sri Lanka*
　Suriránka スリランカ
chafe *v* surimukimásu (surimuku,
　surimuite) 擦りむきます(擦りむく, 擦
　りむいて)
chaff *n* momigara もみ殻・もみがら
chagrin *n* kuyashisa 悔しさ
chain *n* kusari 鎖, chēn チェーン;
　(*linked*) ***in a*** ~ tsunagatte つながって
　chain smoker ~ chēn sumōkā チェー
　ンスモーカー
　chain store *n* chēn-ten チェーン店,
　chēn sutoa チェーンストア
　chain mail *n* chēn mēru チェーンメー
　ル
　chain of islands rettō 列島
chair *n* isu イス・椅子, koshi-káké 腰
　掛け
chair-lift *n* (*ski lift*) sukii rifuto スキー
　リフト
chairperson *n* kaichō 会長, gichō 議長
chalet *n* sharē シャレー, sansō 山荘
chalk *n* chōʹku チョーク (*piece of chalk*;
　1: íp-pon 一本, **2:** ní-hon 二本, **3:** sán-
　bon 三本, ***how many*** nán-bon 何本)
challenge **1.** *n* chárenji チャレンジ,
　chōsen 挑戦 **2.** *v* (*tries*) idomimásu
　(idómu, idonde) 挑みます(挑む, 挑ん
　で), chárenji shimásu (suru, shite) チ
　ャレンジします(する, して); (*tests*)
　tameshimásu (tamésu, taméshite) 試し
　ます(試す, 試して)

challenger *n* charenjā チャレンジャー, chōsen-sha 挑戦者

chamber **1.** *n* (*room*) heya 部屋 **2.** *n* (*meeting hall*) kaigi-shitsu 会議室 **3.** *n* (*compartment in a firearm*) yakushitsu 薬室 **4.** *n* (*palace room*) ō-shitsu 王室 **5.** *n* (*legislative hall*) giin 議院 **6.** *n* (*legislative officer*) giin 議員

chamber *v* (*enclose bullets*) tama o komemásu (komeru, komete) 弾をこめます(こめる、こめて)

chamber of commerce *n* shōkō kaigisho 商工会議所

chamber-pot *n* omaru おまる

chameleon *n* kamereon カメレオン

champagne *n* shanpán シャンパン, shanpén シャンペン

champion *n* yūshō-sha 優勝者, chanpíon チャンピオン; (*sumo wrestler*) ō´-zeki 大関; *grand ~ sumo wrestler* yokozuna 横綱

championship *n* senshu-ken 選手権, chanpion shippu チャンピオンシップ

chance *n* **1.** (*opportunity*) kikái 機会, chánsu チャンス **2.** (*impulse*) hazumi 弾み → **by chance**

chancellor *n* (*minister*) daijin 大臣

chandelier *n* shanderia シャンデリア

change **1.** *n* (*small money*) kozeni 小銭, komakái (o)kane 細かい(お)金 **2.** *n* (*money returned*) o-tsuri お釣り・おつり, tsuri-sen 釣り銭 **3.** *n* hénka 変化; (*in health*) o-kawari お変わり; (*abnormality*) ijō 異常; (*of trains*) norikae 乗り換え; (*of clothing*) kigae 着替え **4.** *v it changes* kawarimásu (kawaru, kawatte) 変わります(変わる、変わって); hénka shimásu (suru, shite) 変化します(する、して); utsurimásu (utsúru, utsútte) 移ります(移る、移って) **5.** *v changes it* kaemásu (kaeru, kaete) 変えます(変える、変えて); aratamemásu (arataméru, aratámete) 改めます(改める、改めて) **6.** *v* (*clothes*) kigaemásu (kigáeru, kigáete) 着替えます(着替える、着替えて) **7.** *v* (*train, bus, plane*) nori-kaemásu (nori-káeru, nori-káete) 乗り換えます(乗り換える、乗り換えて)

for a change *adj* kibun-tenkan (ni) 気分転換(に), ikinuki (ni) 息抜き(に)

changeable *n* kōi-shitsu 更衣室

channel *n* **1.** (*for radio or television*) channeru チャンネル **2.** kaikyō 海峡; suiro 水路

chant *v* utaimásu (utau, utatte) 歌い[謡い]ます(歌[謡]う、歌[謡]って); *chanting Buddhist scriptures* shōmyō 声明; *chanting a Noh libretto* utai 謡

chaos *n* kaosu カオス, muchitsujo 無秩序, konton 混沌

chaotic *adj* muchitsujo (no) 無秩序(の), konton to shita 混沌とした

chap *n* **1.** (*crack*) hibi ひび **2.** (*capped skin*) akagire あかぎれ **3.** (*fellow*) yatsu やつ

chapel *n* chaperu チャペル, reihai-dō 礼拝堂

chapter *n* (*book*) shō 章, chaputā チャプター

char *v* **1.** *become charred* kogemásu (kogeru, kogete) 焦げます(焦げる、焦げて) **2.** *chars it* kogashimásu (kogasu, kogashite) 焦がします(焦がす、焦がして)

character *n* **1.** (*quality*) seishitsu 性質 **2.** (*personal traits*) seikaku 性格, kosei 個性 **3.** (*written*) jí 字, móji 文字; *Chinese character* kanji 漢字 **4.** (*part or role in a play or film*) kyarakuta キャラクタ, kyarakutā キャラクター

characteristic **1.** *n* (*an earmark*) tokushoku 特色, (*a distinguishing characteristic*) tokuchō 特徴 **2.** *adj* (*typical*) daihyō-teki (na) 代表的(な); (*specific*) koyū (no) 固有(の), tokuchō-teki (na) 特徴的(な)

characterize *v* tokuchō zukemásu (zukeru, zukete) 特徴づけます(づける、づけて)

charade *n* misekake 見せかけ

charcoal *n* sumí 炭・スミ, mokután 木炭

charcoal brazier *n* híbachi 火鉢

charge *n* **1.** (*fee*) ryōkin 料金, daikin 代金, ... -ryō ... 料, ... -dai ... 代; (*with fee*) yūryō (no) 有料(の); *no ~* muryō (no) 無料(の), [INFORMAL] tada (no) ただ(の); *Is there a ~?* Yūryō désu ka. 有料ですか。 **2.** *in ~* (*teacher*)

tannin 担任; tantō 担当; *takes/accepts*
(*is in*) ~ *of* ... o tannin/tantō shimás<u>u</u>
(suru, sh<u>i</u>te) ... を担任/担当します
(する, して), uke-mochimás<u>u</u> (uke-
mótsu, uke-mótte) 受け持ちます(受
け持つ, 受け持って); *takes* (*is in*)
partial ~ of ... o buntan shimás<u>u</u> (suru,
sh<u>i</u>te) ... を分担します(する, して) **3.**
(*an attack*) shūgeki 襲撃
charge *v* **1.** seikyū shimás<u>u</u> (suru,
sh<u>i</u>te) 請求します(する, して) **2.**
v (*attacks*) shūgeki shimás<u>u</u> (suru,
sh<u>i</u>te) 襲撃します(する, して) **3.** *v*
(*fill or furnish*) (*rechargeable public
transport card*) chāji shimás<u>u</u> (suru,
sh<u>i</u>te) チャージします(する, して),
(*cellphone*) jūden shimás<u>u</u> (suru, sh<u>i</u>te)
充電します(する, して)
charisma *n* karisuma カリスマ
charitable *adj* jizen (no) 慈善(の)
charity *n* hodokoshi 施し, jizen 慈善,
charitii チャリティー; (*mercy*)
megumi 恵み
　charity concert *n* charitii konsáto
　チャリティーコンサート
charm *v* (.. o) uttori-sasemás<u>u</u> (uttori-
saseru, uttori-sasete) うっとり
させます(うっとりさせる, うっとり
させて)
charm *n* (*good-luck piece*) o-mamori
お守り; (*attraction*) miryoku 魅力,
(*attractiveness*) aikyō´ あいきょう・
愛敬・愛嬌
charming *adj* chāmingu チャーミング,
miryoku-teki na 魅力的な; *is* ~ miryoku/
aikyō´ ga arimás<u>u</u> (áru, átte) 魅力/あ
いきょうがあります(ある, あって)
chart *n* zuhyō 図表, zu 図, chāto チャ
ート
charter *n* tokkyo jō 特許状, chātā チャ
ーター
chartered;
　chartered accountant *n* kōninkaikéi-
　shi 公認会計士
　chartered plane *n* chātā´-ki チャータ
　ー機
　chartered bus *n* kash<u>i</u>kiri-básu 貸し
　切りバス
chase *v* oi-kakemás<u>u</u> (oi-kakéru, oi-
kákete) 追いかけます(追いかける,

追いかけて), oimás<u>u</u> (ou, otte) 追い
ます(追う, 追って), tsuiseki shimás<u>u</u>
(suru, sh<u>i</u>te) 追跡します(する, して)
chasm *n* wareme 割れ目
chaste *adj* teisetsu (na) 貞節(な),
junsui (na) 純粋(な)
chastise *v* korashimemás<u>u</u> (korashi-
meru, korashimete) 懲らしめます(懲
らしめる, 懲らしめて)
chastity *n* teisetsu 貞節, junketsu 純潔
chat *n* **1.** *n* oshaberi おしゃべり, seken-
bánashi 世間話, muda-banashi 無駄
話, zatsu-dan 雑談 **2.** *v* oshaberi o
shimás<u>u</u> (suru, sh<u>i</u>te) おしゃべりをし
ます(する, して)
chatter *v* shaberimás<u>u</u> (shabéru,
shabétte) しゃべり[喋り]ます(しゃべ
る, しゃべって)
chatterbox *n* o-sháberi おしゃべり
chauffeur *n* okakae unténshu お抱え
運転手
chauvinism *n* **1.** (*aggressive
patriotism*) kyōshin-teki aikokushin
狂信的愛国心 **2.** (*sexism*) sei-sabetsu
shugi 性差別主義
cheap *adj* yasúi 安い; *cheaper by
¥100* hyakuén-yasu 百円安
cheat *v* (*deceives*) damashimás<u>u</u>
(damás<u>u</u>, damásh<u>i</u>te) だまします(だま
す, だまして), gomakashimás<u>u</u> (gomakásu, gomakash<u>i</u>te) ごまかします(ご
まかす, ごまかして); (*dissembles,
shirks, tricks*) zúru o shimás<u>u</u> ずるを
します; (*on one's spouse*) fútei o hataraki-
más<u>u</u> (hataraku, hataraite) 不貞をはた
らきます(はたらく, はたらいて)
cheating *n* kan'nin'gu カンニング
check *n* **1.** (*bank*) kogítte 小切手,
chékku チェック **2.** (*chit*) tuda 札 **3.**
(*pays money at the restaurant*) kanjō´
勘定(o-kanjō お勘定), denpyō 伝票,
o-aisó おあいそ
　Check please! O-ikura dés<u>u</u> ka. おいく
　らですか.
check *v* **1.** *checks it* (*baggage*)
azukemás<u>u</u> (azukéru, azúkete) 預けま
す(預ける, 預けて) **2.** (*investigates*)
shirabemás<u>u</u> (shirabéru, shirábete)
調べます(調べる, 調べて), chékku
shimás<u>u</u> (suru, sh<u>i</u>te) チェックします

(する,して); (*inspects*) kénsa shimásu (suru, shi̱te) 検査します(する,して); (*compares*) terashimásu (terásu, terashi̱te) 照らします(照らする, 照らして)

check in (*registers*) chekkúin shimásu (suru, shi̱te) チェックインします(する,して)

check out (*of hotel*) chekkuáuto shimásu (suru, shi̱te) チェックアウトします(する,して)

checkbook n (*bank*) kogítte chō 小切手帳

checking account n tōza-yókin 当座預金

checkpoint kenmon-jo 検問所

check room n (*cloakroom*) kurō´ku クローク; azukari-jo 預かり所

check-up n 1. kénsa 検査 2. (*medical checkup*) kenkō shindan 健康診断

cheek n hō´ 頬・ほお, hoho 頬・ほほ, [INFORMAL] hoppéta ほっぺた

cheekbone n hoho-bone, hō-bone 頬骨 [ほほ骨, ほお骨]

cheeky adj namaiki (na) 生意気(な)

cheer n ōen 応援; ~ *for* ōenshimásu (suru, shi̱te) 応援します(する,して)

cheerful adj (*in a good mood*) kigen ga ii 機嫌がいい, (*full of energy*) genki ga ii 元気がいい, (*merry, blitheful*) hogáraka (na) ほがらか(な), yōki (na) 陽気(な)

cheerleader n (*female*) chia gāru チアガール

cheerless adj genki ga nai 元気がない

Cheers interj 1. (*See you later*) mata (ne) また(ね) 2. (*toast*) kanpai! 乾杯!

cheese n chíizu チーズ

cheesecloth n kanreisha 寒冷紗

chef n shefu シェフ, ryōri chō 料理長, (*chef of Japanese food*) itamae(-san) 板前(さん)

chemicals n kagaku-séihin 化学製品; (*pharmaceuticals*) yakuhin 薬品, kagaku-yakuhin 化学薬品

chemist n 1. kágaku-sha 化学者 2. (*pharmacist*) yakuzai-shi 薬剤師

chemistry n kágaku 化学, bakegaku 化学

chemotherapy n kagaku ryōhō 化学療法

cherish v daijí ni shimásu (suru, shi̱te) 大事にします(する,して)

cherry n (*tree*) sakura no ki 桜の木; (*fruit*) sakuranbo サクランボ・桜んぼ

cherry blossoms n sakura (no haná) 桜(の花)

cherry tree n sakura no ki 桜の木

chess n 1. chesu チェス 2. (*Japanese chess*) shōgi 将棋

chessboard n (*Japanese chess*) shōgi-ban 将棋盤

chest n 1. (*of body*) muné 胸 2. (*box*) hako 箱; (*drawers*) tansu たんす・タンス

chestnut 1. n kurí 栗・クリ; *roasted chestnut* yaki-guri 焼き栗 2. adj (*color*) kuri iro (no) 栗色(の)

chew v kamimásu (kámu, kánde) 噛みます(噛む, 噛んで); ~ *the fat* (*idly talk*) daberimásu (dabéru, dabétte) だべります(だべる, だべって)

chewing gum n gamu ガム, chūin-gamu チューインガム

chiao-tze n (*jiaozi*) gyōza 餃子・ギョーザ

chic adj shikku (na) シック(な), iki (na) 粋(な), jōhin (na) 上品(な)

chicken n tori 鶏・トリ, niwatori 鶏・ニワトリ; ~ (*etc.*) *boiled into hot broth* mizutaki 水炊き; *skewered grilled* ~ yaki-tori 焼き鳥・やきとり, (*shop*) yaki̱tori-ya 焼き鳥屋

chide v tashinamemásu (tashinameru, tashinamete) たしなめます(たしなめる, たしなめて), shikarimásu (shikaru, shikatte) 叱ります(叱る, 叱って)

chief 1. n (*head*) chō 長, chōkan 長官, chiifu チーフ, (*ringleader*) óyá-bun 親分 2. adj (*main*) shuyō (na) 主要(な), ómo na 主な, hon-... 本...

chiefly adv moppara 専ら・もっぱら, ómo ni 主に

chieftain n 1. (*of a group*) shuchō 首長 2. (*of a clan or a tribe*) zokuchō 族長

child n kodomo 子供・子ども, ko 子, (*elementary school student*) jídō 児童; *your* ~ o-ko-san/sama お子さん/さま・様

childhood n kodomo no toki̱ 子供の時, kodomo no koro 子供の頃, kodomo jidai 子供時代

childish *adj* osanái 幼い; yōchi (na) 幼稚(な); kodomoppoi 子供っぽい

childlike *adj* kodomo rashii 子供らしい; junshin (na) 純真(な)

children *n* kodomó-tachi 子供たち; ***Children's Day*** (*5 May*) Kodomo no hí こどもの日

chili *n* chiri チリ

chili pepper *n* chiri peppā チリペッパー, tōgarashi トウガラシ・唐辛子

chili powder *n* chiri paudā チリパウダー

chill *v* **chill it** hiyashimásu (hiyásu, hiyáshite) 冷やします(冷やす, 冷やして)

chilled *n* reizō 冷蔵; ~ **wheat-flour noodles** hiyamúgi ひやむぎ・冷や麦

chilly *adj* samúi 寒い, hieru 冷える

chime *n* chaimu チャイム

chimney *n* entotsu 煙突・えんとつ

chimpanzee *n* chinpanjii チンパンジー

chin *n* agó あご・顎

China *n* Chū́goku 中国

China dress *n* Chaina doresu チャイナドレス

Chinatown *n* Chaina taun チャイナタウン

china (ware) *n* (*porcelain*) setomono 瀬戸物

Chinese *n* (*language*) Chugoku-go 中国語; (*person*) Chugokú-jin 中国人

Chinese:

Chinese cabbage *n* (*bok choi*) hakusai 白菜・ハクサイ

Chinese character *n* kanji 漢字, jí 字

Chinese cooking *n* chūka-ryṓri 中華料理

Chinese egg rolls *n* haru-maki 春巻・ハルマキ

Chinese fried noodles *n* yakisoba 焼きそば

Chinese fried rice *n* chā́han チャーハン

Chinese meatballs *n* niku-dángo 肉団子

Chinese noodles *n* (*with soup*) rā́men ラーメン, chūkamen 中華麺; (*with tidbits*) gomoku-sóba 五目そば

Chinese pickles *n* zāsai ザーサイ

Chinese restaurant *n* chūka-ryōrí-ten

中華料理店, Chūka resutoran 中華レストラン

Chinese word/vocabulary (*in Japanese*) *n* kango 漢語

chip *n* (*of wood*) kóppá 木っ端; (*crack*) kizu 傷; (*electronic engineering*) chippu チップ

chips *n* (*potato chip*) poteto chippusu ポテトチップス

chirp *n* saezuri さえずり

chisel *n* nómi ノミ

chives *n* asátsuki アサツキ・浅葱

chlorine *n* énso 塩素

chocolate *n* choko(rḗto) チョコ(レート)

chocolate bar *n* ita-choko 板チョコ

chocolate milk *n* míruku-kokoa ミルクココア

choice **1.** *n* (*selection*) sentaku 選択 **2.** *adj* (*best-quality*) jōtō (na) 上等(な)

choir *n* **1.** (*chorus group*) gasshō-dan 合唱団 **2.** (*chorus group in church*) seika-tai 聖歌隊

choke *v* **1.** (*he chokes*) íki ga tsumari-másu (tsumaru, tsumátte) 息がつまります・詰まります(詰まる, 詰まって) **2.** (*chokes him*) ... no íki o tomemásu (tomeru, tomete) ... の息を止めます(止める, 止めて)

cholera *n* kórera コレラ

cholesterol *n* koresuterōru コレステロール

choose *v* **1.** erabimásu (erábu, eránde) えらびます・選びます(選ぶ, 選んで); [BOOKISH] sentaku shimásu (suru, shíte) 選択します(する, して) **2.** (*decides on*) ... ni shimásu (suru, shíte) ... にします(する, して)

choosy *adj* yorigónomi ga hageshíi より好みがはげしい・激しい, yorigóno-mi o shimásu (suru, shíte) より好みをします(する, して)

chop **1.** *v* (*chops it*) kizamimásu (kizamu, kizande) 刻みます(刻む, 刻んで); (*fire wood*) (takigi o) warimásu (waru, watte) 薪を割ります(割る, 割って) **2.** *n* (*signature seal*) hankó はんこ, hán はん・判

chopped meat *n* híki-niku 挽き肉・ひき肉

355

chopping board *n* manaita まないた
choppy *adj* (*having many waves*) nami no arai 波の荒い
chopstick rest *n* hashí-óki 箸置き
chopsticks *n* (o-)háshi (お)はし・箸; (*throw-away*) wari-bashi 割り箸・わりばし (*1 pair* ichí-zen 一膳)
chorale *n* **1.** (*choir*) gasshō tai 合唱隊 **2.** (*chorus*) gasshō-kyoku 合唱曲
chord *n* **1.** (*music*) waon 和音; (*guitar chord*) kōdo コード **2.** (*emotion*) kokoro no kinsen 心の琴線
chore *n* zatsuyō 雑用
choreography *n* furitsuke 振り付け
chorus *n* kō'rasu コーラス, (*music sang by a group*) gasshō-kyoku 合唱曲, (*group of singers*) gasshō-dan 合唱団
chow → **food**
chowder *n* chaudā チャウダー, (*Japanese style*) yose-nabe 寄せ鍋
chow mein *n* yaki-soba 焼きそば
Christ *n* Kirisuto キリスト
Christian 1. *adj* Kirisuto-kyo no ... キリスト教の... **2.** *n* (Kirisuto-kyō no) shínjá (キリスト教の)信者
Christianity *n* Kirisuto-kyō キリスト教
Christian name *n* senrei mei 洗礼名, kurisuchan nēmu クリスチャンネーム
Christmas *n* Kurísúmasu クリスマス
Christmas card *n* kurisumasu kādo クリスマスカード
Christmas Eve *n* kurisumasu ibu クリスマスイブ
Christmas present *n* kurisumasu purezento クリスマスプレゼント
Christmas tree *n* kurisumasu tsurii クリスマスツリー
chromosome *n* senshokutai 染色体
chronic *adj* mansei (no) 慢性(の)
chronicle *n* nendai-ki 年代記
chronological *adj* nendai-jun (no) 年代順(の)
chrysalis *n* sanagi サナギ・蛹
chrysanthemum *n* kikú 菊・キク; (*tasty leaves*) **garland ~** shungiku 春菊・シュンギク
chubby *adj* fukkurashita ふっくらした, futome (no) 太めの
chuck *v* **1.** (*throws*) nagemásu (nageru,

nagete) 投げます(投げる, 投げて) **2.** (*tosses*) hōrimásu (hōru, hōtte) 放ります(放る, 放って)
church *n* kyōkai 教会
cider *n* (*fizzy lemon soda*) sáidā サイダー, ringo shu リンゴ酒
cigar *n* shígā シガー, ha-maki 葉巻
cigar shop/store *n* tabako-ya たばこ屋
cigarette *n* tabako タバコ・煙草, maki-tábako 巻きたばこ, shígarétto シガレット (**1:** íppon 一本, **2:** ní-hon 二本, **3:** sánbon 三本, *how many* nán-bon 何本; (*packs*) **1:** hitó-hako 一箱, **2:** futá-hako 二箱, **3:** mí-hako, san-pako 三箱, *how many packs* nán-pako 何箱)
cigarette/cigar butt *n* suigara 吸い殻
cigarette case *n* tabakó-ire たばこ入れ
cigarette holder *n* páipu パイプ, sui-kuchi 吸い口
cigarette lighter *n* raitā ライター
cinch *n* (*an easy thing to do*) wáke mo nái (kotó) わけもない(こと)
cinder(s) *n* moegara 燃えがら
cinema → **movies**
cinnamon *n* shinamon シナモン
cipher *n* **1.** (*zero*) zero ゼロ・零 **2.** (*secret code*) angō 暗号
circle 1. *n* maru 丸, én 円, (*ring*) wá 輪, (*orbit*) kidō 軌道; *traffic circle* rō'tarii ロータリー **2.** *v* maru/en de kakomimásu (kakomu, kakonde) 丸/円で囲みます(囲む, 囲んで)
circular *adj* kanjō (no) 環状(の)
circulate *v* (*it circulates*) mawarimásu (mawaru, mawatte) 回ります(回る, 回って); (*circulates it*) mawashimásu (mawasu, mawashite) 回します(回す, 回して)
circulation *n* (*cycle*) junkan 循環; (*of money*) ryūtsū 流通
circumference *n* shū'i 周囲, shūhen 周辺, enshū 円周
circumstance *n* **1.** ba(w)ai 場合; kotó koto, ... wáke ... わけ ... tokoró ... ところ **2.** jijō 事情, jōtai 状態, jōkyō 状況; yóshi 由, ... shidai ... 次第 **3.** yōsu 様子・ようす **4.** (*convenience*) tsugō 都合(go-tsugō ご都合)

circumstances n (*details*) ikisatsu いきさつ・経緯

circus n sākasu サーカス

cistern n suisō 水槽, chosui tanku 貯水タンク

citation n inyō bun 引用文

cite v 1. (*quotes*) inyō shimásu (suru, shite) 引用します(する, して) 2. (*refers*) genkyū shimásu (suru, shite) 言及します(する, して)

citizen n shímin 市民; (*national*) kokumin 国民

citizenship n shimin-ken 市民権

citron n yúzu ユズ・柚; ~ *bath* ユズ湯

citrus n kankitsu-rui かんきつ類・柑橘類

city 1. n shí 市, (*town*) machí 町, (*metropolis*) tóshi 都市, tokai 都会 (*dweller*) tokái-jin 都会人
   city office n shi-yákusho 市役所
   city council n shi-gikai 市議会
   2. *adj.* (*within the city*) shí-nai (no) 市内(の)

civilian n minkan no hito 民間の人, minkan-jin 民間人

civilian clothes n shifuku 私服, heijō-fuku 平常服

civility n reigi tadashisa 礼儀正しさ

civilization n bummei 文明, (*culture*) búnka 文化

civilize v 1. bunmei-ka shimásu (suru, shite) 文明化します(する, して) 2. senren shimásu (suru, shite) 洗練します(する, して)

claim 1. n (*demands*) yōkyū/seikyū (shimásu, suru, shite) 要求/請求(します; する, して) 2.v (*maintains*) shuchō shimásu (suru, shite) 主張します(する, して), tonaemásu (tonáeru, tonáete) 唱えます(唱える, 唱えて)

clairvoyant 1. n senrigan 千里眼 2. *adj* senrigan (no) 千里眼(の)

clam n hamáguri ハマグリ・蛤; *short-necked* ~ asari アサリ・浅蜊; *blood(y)* ~ aká-gai 赤貝・アカガイ

clamber v yojinoborimásu (yojinoboru, yojinobotte) よじ登ります(よじ登る, よじ登って)

clamor 1. n (*a clamor*) sáwagi 騒ぎ, kensō 喧騒; 2.v (*makes a clamor*) sawagimásu (sawágu, sawáide) 騒ぎます(騒ぐ, 騒いで)

clamorous *adj* sōzōshii 騒々しい

clamp 1. n (*a piece of metal for fastening*) tomegane 留め金 2. v (*fastens or fixes*) koteishimásu (suru, shite) 固定します(する, して)

clan n ichizoku 一族, ikka 一家 (*historically, a social grouping affiliated through blood and allegiance relationships*)

clandestine *adj* himitsu (no) 秘密(の)

clang 1. n gachan ガチャン 2.v (*rings loudly*) (gachan to) narashimásu (narasu, narashite) (ガチャンと)鳴らします(鳴らす, 鳴らして) 3.v (*sounds*) narimásu (naru, natte) 鳴ります(鳴る, 鳴って)

clannish *adj* haitateki (na) 排他的(な)

clap (*one's hands*) v té o tatakimásu (tatáku, tatáite) 手を叩きます(叩く, 叩いて), hákushu shimásu (suru, shite) 拍手します(する, して)

clarification n setsumei 説明

clarify v 1. (*makes clear*) akiraka ni shimásu (suru, shite) あきらか[明らか]にします(する, して) 2. (*becomes clear*) akiraka ni narimásu (naru, natte) あきらか[明らか]になります(なる, なって), hakkiri shimásu (suru, shite) はっきりします(する, して)

clarinet n kurarinetto クラリネット

clarity n 1. (*transparency*) tōmei do 透明度 2. seichō sa 清澄さ 3. meiryō sa 明瞭さ

clasp (*one's hands*) v (té o) kumimásu (kúmu, kúnde) (手を)組みます(組む, 組んで)

class n 1. kúrasu クラス, kyū´ 級, (*in school*) gakkyū 学級
   class instruction n 1. júgyō 授業, kōshū 講習 2. kaikyū 階級; **the middle class** chūryū kaikyū 中流階級
   classmate n dōkyū´-sei 同級生, (*former classmate*) dōkí-sei 同期生
   class reunion n dōsō´-kai 同窓会
   classroom n kyōshitsu 教室; *classroom teaching* júgyō 授業

classic n kurashikku クラシック, koten 古典

classical *adj* koten (no) 古典(の)
  classical music *n* kurashikku ongaku クラシック音楽, koten ongaku 古典音楽
  classical literature *n* koten bungaku 古典文学, (*Japanese*) kobun 古文

clatter *v* gátagata shimásu (suru, shite) がたがたします(する, して)

claw *n* tsume 爪・ツメ; (*of crab*) hasamí ハサミ; (*animal*) kagitsume 鉤爪(かぎづめ)

claw hammer *n* kugi-nuki 釘抜き

clay *n* néndo 粘土

clean 1. *adj* kírei (na) きれい(な), seiketsu (na) 清潔(な); (*fresh*) sappári shita さっぱりした **2. cleans it** (*up*) *v* kírei ni shimásu (suru, shite) きれいにします(する, して), (*tidies*) katazukemásu (katazukéru, katazúkete) 片づけます(片づける, 片づけて), (*sweeps*) sōji shimásu (suru, shite) 掃除します(する, して)

cleaner *n* seiso-in 清掃員; **cleaners** *n* kuriíningu-ya クリーニング屋

cleaning *n* (*dry*) (dorai-) kuríiníngu (ドライ)クリーニング; (*sweeping up*) sōji 掃除・そうじ (o-sṓji お掃除)

clear 1. *adj* (*bright*) akarui 明るい, (*sunny*) hárete imásu 晴れています, harete ... 晴れた ...; (*transparent*) tōmei (na) 透明(な) **2.** *adj* (*evident*) akíraka (na) 明らか, (*obvious, explicit*) meihaku (na) 明白(な); (*understood*) wakátte imásu 分かっています, wakátta 分かった... **3.** *adj* (*easy to see*) miyasúi 見やすい; (*easy to understand*) wakari-yasúi 分かりやすい **4.** *adj* (*unimpeded*) jama ga nái じゃま[邪魔]がない **5.** *v* (*takes away from the table*) sagemásu (sagéru, ságete) 下げます(下げる, 下げて) **6. gets ~** (*empty*) sukimásu (suku, suite) すきます(すく, すいて) **7. becomes ~** (*evident*) shiremásu (shireru, shirete) 知れます(知れる, 知れて)

clearly *adv* (*distinctly*) hakkíri はっきり; (*obviously, explicitly*) meihaku ni 明白に

clear soup *n* sui-mono 吸い物; (o-) tsúyu (お)つゆ・汁

clear weather *n* haré 晴れ

cleaver *n* hōchō 包丁; *meat* ~ nikukiri-bṓchō 肉切り包丁

clerk *n* (*in shop*) ten'in 店員; (*in office*) jimú-in 事務員; (*in bank*) ginkṓ-in 銀行員

clever *adj* rikō (na) 利口(な); (*nimble with fingers*) kíyō (na) 器用(な); (*skilled*) jōzú (na) じょうず[上手](な)

cliff *n* gake がけ・崖

climate *n* kikō 気候

climax *n* yamá 山, chṓten 頂点; (*upshot*) ketsumatsu 結末; shímatsu 始末

climb *v* noborimásu (noboru, nobotte) 登ります(登る, 登って)

clinch *n* (*boxing*) kurinchi クリンチ

cling *v* kuttsukimásu (kuttsuku, kuttsuite) くっつきます(くっつく, くっついて), shigamitsukimásu (shigamitsuku, shigamitsuite) しがみつきます(しがみつく, しがみついて)

clinic *n* byōin 病院

clip 1. clips it *v* tsumimásu (tsumu, tsunde) 摘みます(摘む, 摘んで); kirimásu (kíru, kitté) 切ります(切る, 切って) **2.** *n* kuríppu クリップ → **paperclip**

clippers *n* hasamí はさみ・鋏; (*nail*) tsumekíri 爪切り; (*barber's*) barikan バリカン

clipping *n* (*from newspaper, etc.*) kirinuki 切り抜き

clique *n* renchū/renjū 連中, habatsu 派閥

cloak *n* mánto マント

  cloakroom *n* kurṓku クローク, (te-nimotsu) azukarijo (手荷物)預かり所

clock *n* tokei 時計; *alarm clock* mezamashi dokei 目覚まし時計; *around the* ~ nijūyojikan 24時間, ichinichi-jū 一日中

clockspring *n* zemmai ぜんまい

clockwise *adv* migi-máwari (ni) 右回り(に)

clogged; gets ~ (*up*) fusagarimásu (fusagáru, fusagátte) ふさがります(ふさがる, ふさがって)

clogs 1. *n* (*wooden shoes*) getá げた・下駄 **2.** *v* (*it clogs up, gets clogged*) tsumarimásu (tsumáru, tsumátte) 詰まります(詰まる, 詰まって),

tsukaemásu (tsukáeru, tsukáete) つか
えます (つかえる, つかえて)
cloisonné n shippō-yaki 七宝焼
close 1. v *closes it (shuts)* shimemásu
(shiméru, shímete) 閉めます (閉める,
閉めて); *(a book, etc.)* tojimásu
(tojíru, tójite) 閉じます (閉じる, 閉じ
て); ~ *one's eyes* mé o tsuburimásu
(tsuburu, tsubutte) 目をつぶります (つ
ぶる, つぶって); *(obstructs)* fusagimásu
(fusagu, fusaide) ふさぎます (ふさぐ,
ふさいで); *(ends)* owarimásu (owaru,
owatte) 終わります (終わる, 終わっ
て) **2.** *it closes* shimarimásu (shimáru,
shimátte) 閉まります (閉まる, 閉まっ
て) → **end 3.** adj *(near)* chikái 近い;
~ *by* sóba (no) そば (の) (o-soba (no)
おそば (の)); *(intimate)* missetsu (na)
密接 (な); *(humid)* mushi-atsúi
蒸し暑い **5.** n *(the end)* owari 終わり,
sue 末, matsu 末
closely adv pittári (to) ぴったり (と)
closet n *(Japanese)* oshi-ire 押し入れ,
nándo 納戸; *(Western)* kurōzetto クロ
ーゼット
clot n *(a clot)* katamari 固まり・塊;
(it clots) **2.** v katamarimásu (katamaru,
katamatte) 固まります (固まる, 固ま
って)
cloth n ori-mono 織物, kíji 生地, nuno
布; *(a piece of)* kiré 切れ, nuno-gire 布
切れ; *(dustcloth)* zōkin ぞうきん・雑巾;
(dishcloth) fukín ふきん; *(traditional
wrapper)* furoshiki ふろしき・風呂敷
clothes n fukú 服, fukusō 服装;
(Western) yōfuku 洋服; *(Japanese
traditional style)* kimono 着物, wafuku
和服
    clothes moth n íga いが, shimi しみ
clothesbag n *(for laundry)*
sentakumono-ire 洗濯物入れ
clothesbrush n yōfuku-búrashi 洋服
ブラシ
clothesline n monohoshi-zuna 物干
し綱
clothing shop n yōfuku-ya 洋服屋
cloud n kúmo 雲
cloudburst n gōu 豪雨
cloudiness n kumori 曇り・くもり
cloudy; *gets* ~ kumorimásu (kumóru,

kumótte) 曇ります (曇る, 曇って); ~
weather kumorí 曇り・くもり
clover n kuróba⁻ クローバー; *four-
leaf* ~ yotsuba no kurōba 四つ葉のク
ローバー
cloves n chō'ji 丁字, kuróbu クローブ
clown n dōke-shi 道化師
club n **1.** *(group; card suit)* kúrabu ク
ラブ **2.** *(stick)* konbō こん棒; *(golf)*
(gorufu) kurabu (ゴルフ) クラブ
clue n tegákari 手掛かり, itóguchi 糸口
clump n katamari 塊・かたまり
clumsy adj hetá (na) へた [下手] な,
bu-kíyō (na) 不器用 (な); gikochi-nái
ぎこちない
cluster → bunch
clutch 1. v *(grasps)* nigirimásu (nigiru,
nigitte) 握ります (握る, 握って),
tsukamimásu (tsukámu, tsukánde) つ
かみます (つかむ, つかんで) **2.** n
(of car) kurátchi クラッチ *(pedal)*
kuratchí-pédaru クラッチペダル
CM → commercial *(message)*
coach 1. v *(coaches them)* shidō
shimásu (suru, shíte) 指導します (す
る, して) **2.** n *(director)* shidō'-sha
指導者; *(sports)* kō'chi コーチ **3.** n
(railroad) kyakusha 客車
    coach station n *(depot)* basu no
hatchaku-jō バスの発着場
coal n sekitán 石炭
    coal mine n tankō 炭鉱
coarse adj arai 粗い・荒い; sómatsu
(na) 粗末 (な); zatsu-... 雑...
coast n engan 沿岸, kaigan 海岸
coat n uwagi 上着, kō'to コート;
(overcoat) gaitō 外套, ō'bā オーバー;
(traditional Japanese) haori 羽織
coax v odatemásu (odateru, odatete) お
だてます (おだてる, おだてて)
cobweb n kúmo no su クモの巣; kúmo
no íto クモの糸
cocaine n kokáin コカイン
cock n ondori オンドリ・雄鶏
cockle n torí-gai トリガイ [貝]
cockpit n kokkupitto コックピット,
sōjū-seki 操縦席, sōjū-shitsu 操縦室
cockroach n gokiburi ゴキブリ
cocktail (party) n kákuteru (pātii)
カクテル (パーティー)

359

cocky *adj* unuboreta うぬぼれた, namaiki (na) 生意気(な)

cocoa *n* kókóa ココア

coconut *n* kókónáttsu ココナッツ
coconut palm *n* yáshi ヤシ・椰子

cocoon *n* máyu マユ・繭

C.O.D. (collect on delivery) *n* daikin hiki-kae (de) 代金引き換え(で)

cod *n* (fish) tára タラ・鱈
cod roe *n* tarako タラコ

code *n* kō′do コード; (secret) angō 暗号

co-ed *n* jo (-shi) gákusei 女(子)学生

coeducation *n* dánjo kyōgaku 男女共学

co-existence *n* kyōson/kyōzon 共存

coffee *n* kōhíi コーヒー
coffee cup *n* kōhii-káppu/jáwan コーヒーカップ/茶碗
coffee pot *n* kōhii-pótto コーヒーポット

coffee machine *n* **1.** kōhii-mēkā コーヒーメーカー **2.** *n* (vending machine) kōhii-jidōhanbaiki/jihanki コーヒー自動販売機/自販機

coffee shop/house *n* kōhii-ten コーヒー一店, kíssa-ten 喫茶店

coffin *n* hitsugi 棺・ひつぎ

cog *n* (wheel) ha-gúruma 歯車

coherence *n* (shubi) ikkan-sei 首尾一貫性

coherent *adj* (shubi) ikkan shita 首尾一貫した

cohesion *n* danketsu 団結, ketsugō 結合

coil *n* koiru コイル

coin *n* kō′ka 硬貨, kóin コイン; (brass or copper) dō′ka 銅貨; (¥10) jū-en-dama 十円玉; (¥100) hyaku-en-dama 百円玉; tosses a coin kōka/koin o nagete ura-omote de kimemásu (kimeru, kimete) 硬貨/コインを投げて裏表で決めます(決める, 決めて)
coin locker *n* koin-rókkā コインロッカー

coincidence *n* gūzen 偶然

coincidental *adj* gūzen itchi shita 偶然一致した

coincidentally *adv* gūzen 偶然, gūzen itchi shite 偶然一致して

coitus *n* seikō 性交

cola *n* kō′ra コーラ

colander *n* mizu-kírí 水切り; (bamboo) zarú ざる

cold 1. *adj* samúi 寒い; (to touch) tsumetái 冷たい; gets ~ sámuku/tsumétaku narimásu (náru, nátte) 寒く/冷たくなります(なる, なって); same-másu (saméru, sámete) 冷めます(冷める, 冷めて); hiemásu (híeru, híete) 冷えます(冷える, 冷えて) **2.** *n* kaze かぜ[風邪]; catches a cold kaze o hikimásu (híku, hiite) かぜ[風邪]をひきます(ひく, ひいて) [HONORIFIC] kaze o omeshi ni narimásu (náru, nátte) かぜ[風邪]をお召しになります(なる, なって)
cold medicine *n* kaze-gúsuri かぜ[風邪]薬

cold-blooded *adj* reiketsu (no) 冷血(の), reikoku (na) 冷酷(な), chi mo namida mo nai 血も涙もない

coldhearted *adj* turenái つれない

coldness *n* tsumetasa 冷たさ, samusa 寒さ

cold water *n* mizu 水, (o-)híya (お)冷や

coleslaw *n* kōru-surō コールスロー, kyabetsu-sárada キャベツサラダ

collaborate *v* **1.** (cooperates) kyōryoku shimásu (suru, shite) 協力します(する, して) **2.** (works collaboratively) kyōdōsagyō shimásu (suru, shite) 共同作業します(する, して)

collaboration *n* kyōryoku 協力

collapse *v* taoremásu (taoréru, taórete) 倒れます(倒れる, 倒れて); (gets smashed) tsuburemásu (tsubureru, tsuburete) つぶれます(つぶれる, つぶれて)

collar *n* **1.** (of coat) kárā カラー, erí えり・襟 **2.** (of dog) kubi-wa 首輪

collarbone *n* sakotsu 鎖骨

collate *v* (compares) terashimásu (terásu, terá-shite) 照らします(照らす, 照らして), terashi-awasémásu (terashi-awaséru, terashi-awaséte) 照らし合わせます(照らし合わせる, 照らし合わせて)

collateral *n* tanpo 担保

colleague *n* **1.** (professional colleague) (shokuba no) dōryō (職場の)同僚 **2.** (academic colleague) gakuyū 学友

collect *v* **1.** *collects them* atsumemásu (atsuméru, atsúmete) 集めます(集める, 集めて), yosemásu (yoseru, yosete) 寄せます(寄せる, 寄せて), (*completes a set*) soroemásu (soroéru, soroéte) 揃えます(揃える, 揃えて); (*gathers up*) shūshū shimásu (suru, shite) 収集します(する, して); (*recruits*) boshū shimásu (suru, shite) 募集します(する, して), (*reaps, brings in*) osamemásu (osaméru, osámete) 納めます(納める, 納めて), (*levies taxes etc.*) chōshū shimásu (suru, shite) 徴収します(する, して); **~ tickets** shūsatsu shimásu (suru, shite) 集札します(する, して) **2.** *they ~* (*come together*) atsumarimásu (atsumáru, atsumátte) 集まります(集まる, 集まって)

collect call *n* korekuto kōru コレクトコール

collect (*on delivery*), **C.O.D.** *adv* daikin híki-kae (de) 代金引き換え(で), dai-biki (de) 代引き(で), chakubarai (de) 着払い(で)

collection *n* **1.** (*of books*) zōsho 蔵書, korekushon コレクション **2.** (*of taxes etc.*) chōshū 徴収

collector *n* shūshū-ka 収集家, korekutā コレクター

college *n* daigaku 大学; karejji カレッジ; *in ~* zaigaku(-chū) 在学(中)

college student *n* daigaku-sei 大学生

collide *v* shōtotsu shimásu (suru, shite) 衝突します(する, して)

collision *n* shōtotsu 衝突

colloquial 1. *n* (*language, word*) kōgo 口語 **2.** *adj* kōgo-teki (na) 口語的(な)

collusion; *in ~ with* ... to takuránde ... と企んで

colonel *n* taisa 大佐

colony *n* shokumín-chi 植民地

color *n* iró 色, kárā カラー; *what color* nani-iro (no) 何色(の), dónna iró (no) どんな色(の)

color-blind *adj* **1.** (*ophthalmology*) shikikaku ijō (no) 色覚異常(の) **2.** (*nonracialism*) jinshusabetsu o shinai 人種差別をしない

colored paper *n* irógami 色紙

colorful *adj* (*bright*) hanáyaka (na) 華

やか(な), karafuru (na) カラフル(な)

colorless *adj* **1.** (*without color*) mushoku (no) 無色(の) **2.** (*lacking animation*) seiki no nai 生気のない **3.** (*insipid*) tsumaranai つまらない

colossal *adj* kyodai (na) 巨大(な)

colt *n* (*young male horse*) osu no ko-uma 雄の子馬

column *n* **1.** rán 欄, koramu コラム; (*page column*) dán 段; (*numerical column*) keta けた・桁 **2.** → **pillar**

columnist *n* koramunisuto コラムニスト

coma *n* konsui 昏睡

comb 1. *n* kushí くし・櫛 **2.** *v* (*the hair*) kamí o sukimásu (suku, suite) 髪をすきます(すく, すいて), tokimásu (tóku, tóite) ときます(とく, といて), tokashimásu (tokásu, tokáshite) とかします(とかす, とかして)

combat *n* sentō 戦闘

combatant *n* sentō-in 戦闘員

combination *n* **1.** kumi-awase 組み合わせ, konbinēshon コンビネーション **2.** (*union*) gappei 合併, gōdō 合同

combine *v* **1.** (*combines them*) kumi-awasemásu (kumi-awaseru, kumi-awasete) 組み合わせます(組み合わせる, 組み合わせて), awasemásu (awaséru, awásete) 合わせます(合わせる, 合わせて); (*dually serves as*) kanemásu (kanéru, kánete) 兼ねます(兼ねる, 兼ねて) **2.** *v* (*they unite*) gappei/gōdō shimásu (suru, shite) 合併/合同します(する, して)

combined *adj* gōdō no ... 合同の...

combustion *n* **1.** (*burning*) nenshō 燃焼 **2.** (*oxidation*) sanka 酸化 **3.** (*tumult*) sawagi 騒ぎ **4.** (*agitation*) dōyō 動揺

come *v* kimásu (kúru, kíte) 来ます(来る, 来て); (*I/we come to you*) ikimásu (iku, itte) 行きます(行く, 行って)

come about shō-jimásu (shō-jiru, shō-jite) 生じます(生じる, 生じて); genjitsu-ka shimásu (suru, shite) 現実化します(する, して)

come along yatte-kimásu (yatte-kúru, yatte-kíte) やってきます(くる, きて)

come back itte kimásu (kúru, kíte)

行ってきます(くる、きて); kaerimásu (káeru, káette) 帰ります(帰る、帰って)

come down kudarimásu (kudaru, kudatte) 下ります(下る、下って); (on the price) makemásu (makeru, makete) 負けます(負ける、負けて)

come in hairimásu (háiru, háitte) 入ります(入る、入って), háitte kimásu (kúru, kíte) 入ってきます(くる、きて)

come near yorimásu (yoru, yotte) 寄ります(寄る、寄って), chika-zukimásu (chika-zúku, chika-zúite) 近づきます(近づく、近づいて)

come off (button, etc.) toremásu (toréru, tórete) 取れます(取れる、取れて); nukemásu (nukeru, nukete) 抜けます(抜ける、抜けて); hazuremásu (hazureru, hazurete) 外れます(外れる、外れて)

come on, ...! (urging an invitation) sá゛ さあ, hora ほら

come out demásu (déru, déte) 出ます(出る、出て), déte kimásu (kúru, kíte) 出てきます(くる、きて); (appears) arawaremásu (arawaréru, arawárete) 現れます(現れる、現れて); (photographs) utsurimásu (utsúru, utsútte) 写ります(写る、写って)

come to (reaches) ... ni itarimásu (itaru, itatte) ... に至ります(至る、至って)

come to an end sumimásu (súmu, súnde) 済みます(済む、済んで), owari-másu (owaru, owatte) 終わります(終わる、終わって), tsukimásu (tsukiru, tsukíte) 尽きます(尽きる、尽きて)

come to the end of (a street) tsuki-atarimásu (tsuki-ataru, tsuki-atatte) 突き当たります(突き当たる、突き当たって)

come what may nán to itté mo なんと言っても

comedy n kígeki 喜劇, komedii コメディ

comely no 1. (pleasing in appearance) yōshi no íi 容姿のいい, kiryō no yoi 器量の良い 2. (attractive) miryoku-teki (na) 魅力的(な)

comet n hōki-boshi ほうき星, suisei 彗星・すい星

comfort 1. n anraku 安楽, kiraku 気楽 2. n (consolation) nagusame 慰め, ian 慰安 3. v (consoles) nagusamemásu (nagusameru, nagusamete) 慰めます(慰める、慰めて)

comfortable 1. adj rakú (na) 楽(な), anraku (na) 安楽(な), kiraku (na) 気楽(な); kaiteki (na) 快適(な), kimochi ga íi 気持ちがいい 2. → relax 3. adj (easy to wear) ki-yasúi 着やすい, (easy to sit on) suwariyasúi 座りやすい

comforter n 1. (down quilt) hane-buton 羽布団 2. (person that comforts) nagusameru hito 慰める人 3. (thing that comforts) nagusameru mono 慰めるもの 4. **Comforter** seirei 聖霊

comic;
  comic book n manga (-bon) 漫画(本); komikku コミック
  comics n manga マンガ・漫画
  comic storytelling n rakugo 落語
  comic storyteller n rakugo-ka 落語家
  comic strip n koma wari manga こま割りマンガ[漫画]

comical adj hyōkín (na) ひょうきん(な) → funny

Coming-of-Age Day (2nd Monday of January) n Seijin no hí 成人の日

comma n konma コンマ

command 1. n (order, instructions) meirei 命令; (historic term) sátá 沙汰 2. v (orders a person) ... ni ii-tsukemásu (ii-tsukéru, ii-tsukéte) ... に言い付けます(言い付ける、言い付けて), mei-jimásu (mei-jiru, mei-jite) 命じます(命じる、命じて) 3. v (leads) híkiimásu (híkiíru, híkiíte) 率います(率いる、率いて)

commander n shiréi-kan 司令官; (navy) chūsa 中佐

commemorate v kinen shimásu (suru, shíte) 記念します(する、して)

commemoration n kinen 記念

commemorative stamp n kinen-kítte 記念切手

commencement n (ceremony) sotsugyō゛-shíki 卒業式

commend v (praises) homemásu (homeru, homete) ほめます(ほめる、ほめて)

comment 1. n (*explanation*) kaisetsu 解説 **2.** n (*critique, opinion*) hyōron 評論 **3.** n komento コメント → remark **4. comments on** v (*explains*) kaisetsu shimásu (suru, shite) 解説します(する, して); (*criticizes*) hyōron shimásu (suru, shite) 評論します(する, して)

commentary n **1.** (*interpretation*) kaisétsu 解説 **2.** (*explanatory note*) chūshaku 注釈 **3.** (*records*) kiroku 記録 **4.** (*on-the-spot broadcasting*) jikkyō hōsō 実況放送

commentator n komentētā コメンテーター **1.** (*explicator*) kaisétsu-sha 解説者 **2.** (*critic*) hyōron-ka 評論家, hyōron-sha 評論者

commerce n shó´gyō 商業; (*trade*) bōeki 貿易

commercial (*message*) n komásharu コマーシャル, shiiému (*CM*) シーエム

commercialize v **1.** (*makes commercial*) shōgyō-ka shimásu (suru, shite) 商業化します(する, して) **2.** (*makes profitable*) eiri-ka shimásu (suru, shite) 営利化します(する, して) **3.** (*makes profitable at the expense of quality*) hinshitsu o gisei ni shite eiri-ka shimásu (suru, shite) 品質を犠牲にして営利化します(する, して)

commission 1. n (*handling charge*) tesū-ryō 手数料; (*brokerage fee*) sáya さや **2.** v (*commissions ... to do it*) (sore o ... ni) irai shimásu (suru, shite) (それを... に) 依頼します(する, して)

commissioner n riji 理事, chōkan 長官

commit v **1.** (*entrusts*) yudanemásu (yudanéru, yudáhete) ゆだねます(ゆだねる, ゆだねて) **2.** (*perpetrates*) okashimásu (okasu, okashite) 犯します(犯す, 犯して); hatarakimásu (hataraku, hataraite) 働きます(働く, 働いて) → do **3. commit oneself** → promise → say

commitment n **1.** (*promise*) yakusoku 約束 **2.** (*duty*) gimu 義務 **3.** (*responsibility*) sekinin 責任

committee n iín-kai 委員会

committee member(s) n fin 委員

commodity n shōhin 商品

commodity prices n bukka 物価

common adj futsū (no) 普通(の); kyōtsū (no) 共通(の); (*average*) nami (no) 並(の); (*vulgar, popular*) zoku (na) 俗(な); **very ~** (*is prevalent*) hayari (no) はやり・流行(の); [IN NEGATIVE SENSE](*is found everywhere*) arifureta ありふれた; arikitari (no) ありきたり(の)

commoner n shomin 庶民, ippan-jin 一般人

commonplace adj heibon (na) 平凡(な), arifureta ありふれた

common sense n (ippan) jōshiki 一般常識

commonwealth n renpō 連邦

commotion n **1.** (*tumult*) sawagi 騒ぎ **2.** (*agitation*) dōyō 動揺 **3.** (*confused movement*) konran 混乱

commune 1. v danwa shimásu (suru, shite) 談話します(する, して) **2.** n chihō jichitai 地方自治体

communicate v tsutaemásu (tsutaeru, tsutaete) 伝えます(伝える, 伝えて); tsūjimásu (tsū-jiru, tsū-jite) 通じます(通じる, 通じて)

communicated; gets ~ tsutawarimásu (tsutawaru, tsutawatte) 伝わります(伝わる, 伝わって)

communication n (*traffic*) kōtsū 交通, ōrai 往来; (*message, news*) táyori 便り, tsūshin 通信

communique n kōshiki seimei 公式声明

Communism n kyōsan -shúgi 共産主義

Communist n kyōsan shugí-sha 共産主義者

community n komyuniti コミュニティ, komyunitii コミュニティー, (*society*) shákai 社会 → town, village

community college n (*junior college*) tanki-dáigaku 短期大学

commute v kayoimásu (kayou, kayotte) 通います(通う, 通って); **~ to work** tsūkin shimásu 通勤します(する, して)

commuter n (*to work*) tsūkin-sha 通勤者; (*goes to school*) tsūgaku-sha 通学者

commuting;
commuting to work *n* tsūkin 通勤
commuting hours *n* tsūkin-jíkan 通勤
時間; *peak* ~ tsūkin-jíkan-tai 通勤時間
帯

companion *n* nakamá 仲間; tsure 連れ
(o-tsure お連れ), tómo 供 (o-tómo お
供), tomodachi 友達; aité 相手 (o-aite
お相手)

company *n* (*firm*) kaisha 会社, ... -sha
... 社; (*within the office/company*) shánai
(no) 社内(の); (*group*) kumí 組; (*social*)
tsuki-ai 付き合い, kōsai 交際; (*guests*)
raikyaku 来客, (o-)kyaku (お)客,
o-kyaku-san/sámá お客さん/さま・様
company secretary *n* sōmu buchō
総務部長
keep one company ... to tsuki-aimásu
(tsuki-áu, tsuki-átte) ... と付き合いま
す(付き合う, 付き合って)
keep company with ... o chika-zukemásu (chika-zukéru, chika-zúkete) ...
を近付けます（近付ける, 近付けて）

comparatively *adv* hikaku-teki (ni)
比較的(に), wari ni 割に, wariai (ni)
割合(に)

compare *v* kurabemásu (kuraberu,
kurabete) 比べます(比べる, 比べて),
hikaku shimásu (suru, shite) 比較しま
す(する, して); taishó/taihi shimásu
(suru, shite) 対照/対比します(する,
して); (*collates*) terashimásu (terásu,
teráshite) 照らします(照らす, 照らし
て); *as compared with* ... ni tái-shite
... に対して

comparison *n* hikaku 比較; taishō
対照, taihi 対比

compass *n* (*for directions*) rashinban
羅針盤; (*for drafting*) konpasu コンパス

compassion *n* nasake 情け (o-násake
お情け)

compatibility *n* aishō´ 相性

compatible *adj* aishō´ ga(/no) íi 相性
が(/の)いい

compensate *v* mukuimásu (mukuíru,
mukuite) 報います(報いる, 報いて);
(*indemnifies*) hoshō shimásu (suru,
shite) 補償します(する, して); (*certify*)
hoshō shimásu (suru, shite) 保証しま
す(する, して)

compensation *n* (*indemnity money*)
hoshō-kin 補償金, benshō 弁償, baishō
賠償; (*allowance*) kyō´yo 供与

compete *v* kisoimásu (kisóu, kisótte)
競います(競う, 競って), kyōsō shimásu
(suru, suite) 競争します(する, して)

competency *n* (*qualification*) shikaku
資格

competition *n* kyōsō 競争

competitive *adj* **1.** (*fiercely-competi-
tive*) kyōsō no hageshii 競争の激しい
2. (*strong desire to compete*) kyōsō-
shin no tsuyoi 競争心の強い

competitor *n* kyōsō-áite 競争相手

complain *v* (*gives utterance*) fuhei/
mónku o iimásu (iu, itte/yutte) 不平/
文句を言います(言う, 言って/ゆっ
て); (*guchi o*) koboshimásu (kobósu,
kobóshite) (愚痴を)こぼします(こ
ぼす, こぼして); (*mutters to oneself*)
butsu-butsu iimásu (iu, itte) ぶつぶ
つ言います(言う, 言って); kujō o
iimásu (iu, itte) 苦情を言います(言う,
言って); (*makes a formal accusation*)
uttaemásu (uttaeru, uttaete) 訴えます(
訴える, 訴えて)

complaint *n* fuhei 不平, mónku 文句,
kujō 苦情, kogoto 小言 (o-kógoto お
小言), guchi ぐち・愚痴; (*lawsuit*)
uttae 訴え

complement *n* hosoku 補足, hojū 補充

complete 1. *becomes* ~ *v* (*full*) michimásu (michíru, michíte) 満ちます
(満ちる, 満ちて) **2.** *completes it* *v*
kansei shimásu (suru, shite) 完成し
ます(する, して); (*a set*) soroemásu
(soroéru, soróete) 揃えます(揃える,
揃えて) **3.** oginaimásu (ogináu,
oginatte) 補います(補う, 補って)

complete *adj* (*exhaustive*) mō´ra shita
... 網羅した

completely *adv* mattakú まったく,
to(t)temo と(っ)ても, sukkári すっか
り, sokkúri そっくり; (+ [NEGATIVE])
zenzen 全然; (*all*) zénbu 全部, minná
みんな・皆; (*the whole*...) zén(-) ... 全...

completion *n* kansei 完成

complex *n* konpurekkusu コンプレッ
クス, rettō-kan 劣等感

complexation *n* sakuka 錯化

complexion *n* kao-iro 顔色

complexities *n* (*details*) ikisatsu いきさつ

compliance; *in ~ with* ... ni ō-jite, ... に応じて, ... ni junkyo shite ... に準拠して

complicated *adj* fukuzatsu (na) 複雑（な）, komi-itta 込み入った, yaya(k)koshíi やや(っ)こしい, wazurawashii 煩わしい; hanzatsu (na) 煩雑（な）; *gets ~* kojiremásu (kojiréru, kojírete) こじれます(こじれる, こじれて), motsuremásu (motsureru, motsurete) もつれます(もつれる, もつれて)

complications *n* (*details*) ikisatsu いきさつ; (*entanglements*) motsure もつれ

compliment *n* seji 世辞, o-seji お世辞, home-kotoba ほめ言葉

comply; *~ with* *v* ... ni ō-jimásu (ō-jiru, ō-jite) ... に応じます(応じる, 応じて); ... o nattoku shimásu (suru, shite) ... を納得します(する, して)

component *n* séibun 成分

compose *v* (*writes*) tsuzurimásu (tsuzuru, tsuzutte) 綴ります(綴る, 綴って), tsukurimásu (tsukúru, tsukutte) 作ります(作る, 作って)

composed *adj* (*unperturbed*) heiki (na) 平気（な）; reisei (na) 冷静（な）

composite *adj* sōgō-teki (na) 総合的（な）

composition *n* (*writing*) sakubun 作文; (*constituency*) kōsei 構成

compound *n* (*word*) fukugō-go 複合語, jukugo 熟語

comprehend → understand → include → comprise → consist of

comprehension *n* rikai 理解

comprehension ability *n* rikái-ryoku 理解力

comprehensive *adj* (*composite*) sōgō-teki (na) 総合的（な）

compress *v* 1. (*constricts*) asshuku shimásu (suru, shite) 圧縮します(する, して) 2. (*presses*) appaku shimásu (suru, shite) 圧迫します(する, して) 3. (*shorten*) tanshuku shimásu (suru, shite) 短縮します(する, して)

comprise *v* (*includes all items*) mō´ra

shimásu (suru, shite) 網羅します(する, して)

compromise 1. *n* dakyō 妥協; (*makes a compromise*) *v* dakyō shimásu (suru, shite) 妥協します(する, して)

compulsion *n* 1. (*psychology*) shōdō kyōhaku 衝動強迫 2. (*forcing*) kyōsei 強制

compulsive *adj* 1. (*psychology*) kyōhaku kan'nen no aru 強迫観念のある, osaerarenai 抑えられない 2. (*very interesting or compelling*) hito (no kokoro) o hikitsukeru 人(の心)を引きつける

compulsory *adj* 1. (*stipulated*) kitei (no) 規定（の） 2. (*obligatory*) gimu-teki (na) 義務的（な） 3. (*required*) hissu (no) 必須（の） 4. (*compelling*) kyōsei-teki (na) 強制的（な）

compulsory education *n* gimu-kyō´iku 義務教育

computation *n* keisan 計算

compute *v* keisan shimásu (suru, shite) 計算します(する, して)

computer *n* konpyū´ta コンピュータ, konpyū´tā コンピューター

computer game *n* konpyū´ta/ konpyū´tā gēmu コンピュータ/コンピューター・ゲーム

computerize *v* konpyū´ta-ka/ konpyū´tā-ka shimásu (suru, shite) コンピュータ化/コンピューター化します(する, して)

computer programmer *n* konpyū´ta/ konpyū´tā puroguramā コンピュータ/コンピューター・プログラマー

computer science *n* konpyū´ta-ka/ konpyū´tā saiensu コンピュータ/コンピューター・サイエンス, jōhō kagaku 情報科学, jōhō kōgaku 情報工学

comrade *n* (...) dō´shi (...) 同志, (...) nakama (...) 仲間

con *n* sagi 詐欺

con man *n* sagi-shi 詐欺師・サギ師, peten-shi ペテン師

concave *adj* ōmen 凹面

conceal → hide → cover up

conceit *n* [INFORMAL] unubore うぬぼれ, [BOOKISH] kadai hyōka 過大評価

conceited person n tengu 天狗・てんぐ, unuboreta hito うぬぼれた人

concentrate v shūchū shimás<u>u</u> (suru, shi<u>t</u>e) 集中します(する, して)

concentration n shūchū 集中

concept n gáinen 概念, shisō 思想

conception n **1.** (concept) gáinen 概念, shisō 思想 **2.** (fertilization) jusei 受精 **3.** (inception of pregnancy) jutai 受胎, kainin 懐妊

concern 1. n (relevance) kankei 関係, (interest) kanshin 関心; (worry) shinpai 心配; (business) kaisha 会社 **2.** v (relates to) ... ni kanshimás<u>u</u> (kansúru, kánshi<u>t</u>e) ... に関します (関する, 関して), (centers on) ... o megurimás<u>u</u> (meguru, megu<u>t</u>te) ... を巡ります(巡る, 巡って)

concerning prep ... ni kán-shi<u>t</u>e ... に関して, ... o megu<u>t</u>te ... を巡って

concert n ongák(u) -kai 音楽会, ensō´-kai 演奏会, consāto コンサート

concert hall n consāto hōru コンサート・ホール

concerto n koncheruto コンチェルト, kyōsō-kyoku 協奏曲

concession n **1.** (compromise) jōho 譲歩 **2.** (right) tokken 特権

conciliate v nadamemás<u>u</u> (nadameru, nadamete) なだめます(なだめる, なだめて); wakai sasemás<u>u</u> (saseru, sasete) 和解させます(させる, させて); chōtei shimás<u>u</u> (suru, shi<u>t</u>e) 調停します(する, して)

concise adj kanketsu (na) 簡潔(な)

conclude v (brings to an end) sumashimás<u>u</u> (sumás<u>u</u>, sumáshi<u>t</u>e) 済まします (済ます, 済まして); (ends a discussion) ketsuron shimás<u>u</u> (suru, shi<u>t</u>e) 結論します(する, して); (finalizes) seiritsu shimás<u>u</u> (suru, shi<u>t</u>e) 成立します(する, して)

conclusion n **1.** (of discussion) ketsuron 結論; in ~ ketsuron to shi<u>t</u>e 結論として **2.** (finalization) seiritsu 成立

concoct v koshiraemás<u>u</u> (koshiraeru, koshiraete) こしらえます(こしらえる, こしらえて), tsukuriagemás<u>u</u> (tsukuriageru, tsukuriagete) 作り上げます(作り上げる, 作り上げて)

concrete 1. n (cement) konkuríito コンクリート **2.** adj (not abstract) gutai-teki(na) 具体的(な)

concrete floor n tatáki たたき

concubine n mekaké 妾・めかけ, o-mekaké(-san) お妾(さん)

concur v (agrees) dōi shimás<u>u</u> (suru, shi<u>t</u>e) 同意します(する, して), (coincides) itchi shimás<u>u</u> (suru, shi<u>t</u>e) 一致します(する, して)

concurrent adj (occurring at the same time) dōji ni okoru 同時に起こる

concurrently adv (serves as) ... o kanemás<u>u</u> (kanéru, kánete) を兼ねます (兼ねる, 兼ねて)

concussion n (brain) nō-shintō 脳しんとう

condemn v hinan shimás<u>u</u> (suru, shite) 非難します(する, して)

condense v **1.** (concentrates) gyōshuku shimás<u>u</u> (suru, shite) 凝縮します(する, して), nōshuku shimás<u>u</u> (suru, shite) 濃縮します(する, して) **2.** (liquefies) ekika shimás<u>u</u> (suru, shite) 液化します(する, して) **3.** (summarizes) yōyaku shimás<u>u</u> (suru, shite) 要約します(する, して)

condensed milk n rennyū 練乳, kondensu miruku コンデンスミルク

condition n (state) ari-sama 有様・ありさま, jōtai 状態, jijō 事情, jissai 実際, guai 具合, chōshi 調子; (weather) hiyori 日和・ひより; (stipulation) jōken 条件; best ~ zekkō-chō 絶好調; be in good (bad) ~ chōshi ga ii (warui) 調子がいい(悪い)

condolence n okuyami お悔やみ

condom n kondōmu コンドーム

condominium n kondominiamu コンドミニアム, bunjō manshon 分譲マンション, bunjō apāto 分譲アパート

condone v mokunin shimás<u>u</u> (suru, shite) 黙認します(する, して)

conduct 1. n (behavior) okonai 行い **2.** v michibimás<u>u</u> (michibiku, michibiite) 導きます(導く, 導いて), shiki shimás<u>u</u> (suru, shite) 指揮します(する, して)

conductor n (train) shashō(-san) 車掌 (さん); (orchestra) shikísha 指揮者

cone *n* ensui(-kei) 円錐(形), kōn コー
ン; *ice cream ~* (aisukuriimu) kōn
(アイスクリーム)コーン

confection *n* (o-)káshi (お)菓子

confectionery *n* (*confectioner*) (o-)
kashí-ya (お)菓子屋; (*candy*) (o-)
kashí (お)菓子

confederacy *n* rengō 連合, dōmei
(koku) 同盟(国)

confederate *n* (*person*) kyōhan-sha 共
犯者, kyōbō-sha 共謀者

confer *v* **1.** hanashi-aimásu (hanashi-
au, hanashi-atte) 話し合います(話し
合う, 話し合って) **2.** → grant

conference *n* (*personal*) sōdan 相談;
kaígi 会議, taikai 大会; (*discussion*)
kyō´gí 協議, (*negotiation*) hanashi-ai
話し合い

confess *v* **1.** hákujō shimásu (suru,
shíte) 白状します(する, して), jihaku
shimásu (suru, shite) 自白します(す
る, して), kokuhaku shimásu (suru,
shite) 告白します(する, して);
(*confess the sin*) zángéshimásu (suru,
shíte) [懴悔]します(する, し
て) **2.** (*frankly reveals*) uchi-akemásu
(uchi-akeru, uchi-akete) 打ち明けます
(打ち明ける, 打ち明けて)

confession *n* hákujō 白状; (*of sins*)
zángé ざんげ・懴悔

confidence *n* shin'yō 信用, shinrai
信頼, tánomi 頼み; (*self-confidence*)
jishin 自信; (*secure feeling*) anshin
安心

confidential *adj* naisho (no) 内緒(の)

confirm *v* (*a reservation*) (yoyaku o)
kakunin shimásu (suru, shíte) (予約を)
確認します(する, して)

confirmation *n* kakunin 確認

conflict *n* tatakai 戦い

confluence *n* gōryū 合流

conform (*with/to*) *v* ... ni shitagaimásu
(shitagau, shitagatte) ... に従います
(従う, 従って), ... ni motozukimásu
(motozúku, motozúite) ... に基づきま
す(基づく, 基づいて)

confront *v* ... ni tai-shimásu (tai-súru,
tái-shite) ... に対します(対する, 対
して); ... to tairitsu shimásu (suru,
shíte) ... と対立します(する, して);

... ni taikō shimásu (suru,
shíte) ... に対抗します(する, して)

confrontation *n* taikō 対抗

confound *v* **1.** kondō shimásu (suru, shíte)
混同します(する, して) **2.** (*perplexes*)
konwaku sasemásu (saseru, sasete)
困惑させます(させる, させて)

Confucianism *n* Júkyō 儒教

Confucius *n* Kōshi 孔子

confused; *gets ~* komarimásu (komáru,
komátte) 困ります(困る, 困って),
(*flustered*) awatemásu (awateru, awatete)
慌てます(慌てる, 慌てて); (*in a panic,
mistakenly*) mechamecha めちゃめちゃ

confusion *n* (*disorder*) konran 混乱,
kónzatsu 混雑

congeal *v* **1.** *it congeals* katamarimásu
(katamaru, katamatte) 固まります(固
まる, 固まって) **2.** *congeals it* katamemásu (katameru, katamete) 固めます
(固める, 固めて)

congenial *adj* aishō´ ga(/no) íi 相性が
(/の)いい

congeniality *n* aishō´ 相性

conger eel *n* anago アナゴ・穴子

congested (*traffic*) jūtai-jō´kyō 渋
滞状況; *is ~* jūtai shite imásu (shiteiru,
shiteite) 渋滞しています(している,
していて)

congestion *n* jūtai 渋滞

conglomerate *n* konguromaritto コン
グロマリット, fukugō-kigyō 複合企業

congratulate *v* (o-)iwai shimásu (suru,
shíte) お祝いします(する, して)

congratulation *n* shukuga 祝賀,
o-iwai お祝い; *Congratulations!*
O-medetō gozaimásu. おめでとうご
ざいます

congregate *v* shūgō shimásu (suru, shíte)
集合します(する, して)

congregation *n* atsumari 集まり,
shūkai 集会

congress → Diet; conference

congruence *n* gōdō 合同

conjecture **1.** *n* suisoku 推測, sas-shi
察し(o-sasshi お察し), **2.** *v* (*guesses,
supposes*) sas-shimásu (sas-suru, sas-
shite) 察します(察する, 察して)

conjugal *adj* fūfu (no) 夫婦(の),
kon'in (no) 婚姻(の)

conjugate v (*grammar*) (dōshi o) katsuyō sasemásu (saseru, sasete) (動詞を)活用させます(させる, させて)

conjunction n setsuzókú-shi 接続詞

connect (*with*) v (... to) tsunagimásu (tsunagu, tsunaide) (... と)つなぎます(つなぐ, つないで); ... to renraku shimásu (suru, shite) ... と連絡します(する, して); tsū-jimásu (tsū-jiru, tsū-jite) 通じます(通じる, 通じて)

connected; *is ~* (*with* ...) (...to) tsunagarimásu (tsunagaru, tsunagatte) (... と)つながります(つながる, つながって), (... ni) kan-shimásu (kan-súru, kán-shite) (... に)関します(関する, 関して)

connection n renraku 連絡; (*relevance*) kankei 関係; (*relation*) tsunagari つながり; (*link*) tsunagi つなぎ; (*"pull", avenue of influence*) kone コネ

conscience n ryō´shin 良心

conscientious adj majime (na) まじめ・真面目(な); ryōshin-teki (na) 良心的(な)

consciousness n íshiki 意識, obóé 覚え; *loses ~* íshiki o ushinaimásu (ushinau, ushinatte) 意識を失います(失う, 失って)

conscription n (*for military service*) shōshū 召集・招集

consent v shōchi/shōdaku/dōi shimásu (suru, shite) 承知/承諾/同意します(する, して), nattoku shimásu (suru, shite) 納得します(する, して); [HUMBLE] uketamawarimásu (uketamawaru, uketamawatte) 承ります(承る, 承って)

consequence → result

conservative adj hoshu-teki (na) 保守的(な); shōkyoku-teki (na) 消極的(な); (*moderate*) uchiwa (na) 内輪(な)

conserve 1. v (*saves*) setsuyaku shimásu (suru, shite) 節約します(する, して) 2. n (*fruit jam*) jamu ジャム; *~ boiled down from fish or seaweed* tsukuda-ni つくだ煮・佃煮

consider v kangaemásu (kangáeru, kangáete) 考えます(考える, 考えて); (*takes into account*) kō´ryo ni iremásu (ireru, irete) 考慮に入れます(入れる, 入れて)

considerable adj sōtō (na) 相当(な), yohodo (no) 余程(の), yoppodo (no) よっぽど(の)

considerably adv kanari かなり, zuibun ずいぶん

consideration n (*being kind*) omoiyari 思いやり; (*thought*) kō´ryo 考慮, shíryo 思慮; *takes into ~* kō´ryo ni iremásu (ireru, irete) 考慮に入れます(入れる, 入れて)

consist; *~ of* ...kara nátte imásu (iru, ite) ... から成っています(いる, いて)

consolation n nagusame 慰め・なぐさめ, ian 慰安

console v nagusamemásu (nagusameru, nagusamete) 慰めます・なぐさめます(慰める, 慰めて)

consommé n konsome コンソメ

consonant n shion/shiin 子音

conspicuous adj ichijirushíi 著しい・いちじるしい; medátta ... 目立った..., medátte imásu 目立っています

conspicuously adv ichijirúshiku 著しく; medátte 目立って

constant adj chakujitsu (na) 着実(な); fuhen (no) 不変の

constantly → always

constipation n benpi 便秘

constitute v kōsei shimásu (suru, shite) 構成します(する, して)

constitution n 1. (*basic laws*) kénpō 憲法; *Constitution (Memorial) Day* (*3 May*) Kenpō-kínénbi 憲法記念日 2. (*physical*) taishitsu 体質 3. (*composition*) kōsei 構成

constrained adj kyū´kutsu (na) 窮屈・きゅうくつ(な)

constricted place, waist n kubire くびれ

construct → build

construction n (*work*) kō´ji 工事; *under ~* kōji-chū 工事中; (*building*) kensetsu 建設; (*constitution*) kōsei 構成

construe v káishaku shimásu (suru, shite) 解釈します(する, して)

consul n ryō´ji 領事 consul general n sō-ryō´ji 総領事

consulate n ryōjí-kan 領事館

consult v (*a person*) ... to sōdan

shimásu (suru, shíte) ... と相談します
（する、して）

consultant *n* kómon 顧問, konsárutanto コンサルタント

consultation *n* ukagai 伺い (o-ukagai
お伺い), sōdan 相談 (go-sōdan ご相
談); (*by appointment*) uchi-awase 打
ち合わせ

consumer *n* shōhí-sha 消費者

consuming *adj* hageshii 激しい

consumption *n* shōhi 消費
consumption tax *n* (*duty*) shōhi-zei 消
費税

contact 1. *n* sesshoku 接触; *comes in
~ (with ...)* (... ni) furemásu (fureru,
furete) (... に) 触れます (触れる, 触
れて), ses-shimásu (ses-suru, ses-
shíte) 接します (接する, 接して),
sesshoku shimásu (suru, shíte) 接触
します (する, して) **2. contacts** *n* →
contact lenses コンタクトレンズ
3. *v* (*contacts a person*) ... to renraku
shimásu (suru, shíte) と連絡します (す
る, して), ... ni aimásu (áu, átte) ... に
会います (会う, 会って)
contact lenses *n* kontakuto-rénzu コ
ンタクトレンズ, kontákuto コンタク
ト; *wears ~* kontákuto o shíte imásu
コンタクトをしています

contagion *n* densen 伝染

contagious disease *n* densenbyō
伝染病

contain *v* ... ga háitte imásu (iru, ite)
... が入っています (いる, いて); ... o
fukumimásu (fukúmu, fukúnde) ... を
含みます (含む, 含んで)

container *n* ire-mono 入れ物, yō′ki
容器; (*box*) hako 箱; (*for transporting
goods*) kóntena コンテナ

contamination *n* osen 汚染

contempt *n* keibetsu 軽蔑

contented *adj* ... de mánzoku shimásu
(suru, shíte) ... で満足します (する, し
て); osamarimásu (osamáru, osamátte)
治まります (治まる, 治まって)

contention *n* arasoi 争い

contents *n* nakámi 中身, naiyō 内容;
(*table of contents*) mokuji 目次, midashi
見出し

contest *n* konkū′ru コンクール, kón-

tesuto コンテスト; (*competition*)
kyōsō 競争; (*sports*) kyō′gi 競技,
(*match*) shō′bu 勝負, (*meet*) shiai 試合

contiguous *adj is ~ to* ... ni ses-
shimásu (ses-suru, ses-shíte) ... に接し
ます (接する, 接して)

continent *n* tairiku 大陸

continuation *n* tsuzuki 続き

continue *v* (*it continues*) tsuzukimásu
(tsuzuku, tsuzuite) 続きます (続く,
続いて); (*continues it*) tsuzukemásu
(tsuzukeru, tsuzukete) 続けます
（続ける, 続けて)

continuity *n* renzoku-sei 連続性

continuously *adv* taema-náku 絶え間
なく, táezu 絶えず; (*without resting*)
yasumánaide 休まないで; tsuzukete
続けて

contraceptive *n* **1.** hinín-yaku 避妊薬,
(*pills*) keikō-hinín-yaku 経口避妊薬
2. (*device*) hinín-gu 避妊具; (*condom*)
kondó′mu コンドーム

contract 1. *n* (*an agreement*) keiyaku
契約 **2.** *v* (*agrees to undertake work*)
ukeoimásu (ukeóu, ukeótte) 請け負い
ます (請け負う, 請け負って)

contractor *n* ukeói-nin 請け負い人

contradict *v* ... ni sakaraimásu
(sakaráu, sakarátte) ... に逆らいます
（逆らう, 逆らって) → **deny**

contradiction *n* (*inconsistency*) mujun
矛盾

contradictory *adj* (*inconsistent*)
mujun shíte imásu (iru, ite) 矛盾して
います (いる, いて)

contrary *adj* hantai (no) 反対 (の);
gyaku (no) 逆 (の); *~ to* ... ni hán-shite...
に反して; *acts ~ to* (*goes against*) ...
ni han-shimásu (han-suru, han-shite)
... に反します (反する, 反して), ... ni
sakaraimásu (sakaráu, sakarátte) ...
に逆らいます (逆らう, 逆らって); *~
expectations* káette かえって

contrast 1. *n* taishō/taihi (shimásu;
suru, shíte) 対照/対比 (します; する,
して) **2.** *v* (*compares*) kurabemásu
(kuraberu, kurabete) 比べます (比べ
る, 比べて); *in ~ to/with* ... ni tái-
shite ... に対して, ... ni hán-shite ... に
反して

control 1. n shíhai 支配, kánri 管理; (of prices, etc.) tōsei 統制 **2.** v (supervises it) tori-shimarimásu (tori-shimaru, tori-shimatte) 取り締まります(取り締まる, 取り締まって); (restrains) osaemásu (osáeru, osáete) 抑えます(抑える, 抑えて); (operates equipment) sōjū shimásu (suru, shite) 操縦します(する, して)

controversy n ronsō 論争

convenience n tsugō 都合 (go-tsugō ご都合), tsuide ついでに; at your ~ tsuide no sai ついでの際, tsuide no toki ni ついでの時に

convenience store n konbini コンビニ

convenient adj bénri (na) 便利(な), bén ga íi 便がいい; chō´hō (na) 重宝 (な); (easy to arrange) tsugō ga íi 都合がいい

convent n shūdō´-in 修道院

convention → conference, meeting

conventional adj heibon (na) 平凡(な)

conversation n (ordinary) hanashí 話, danwa 談話; (in language class, etc.) kaiwa 会話

conversion n henkan 変換; conversion key henkan-kíi 変換キー

convert v henkan-kaemásu (hiki-káeru, hiki-káete) 引き変えます(引き換える, 引き換えて)

converter n henkán-ki 変換器; (AC-DC) henryū´-ki 変流器; (transformer) hen'atsú-ki 変圧器

convey v hakobimásu (hakobu, hakonde) 運びます(運ぶ, 運んで)

cook 1. n ryōri-nin 料理人, kókku(-san) コック(さん), (Japanese chef) itamae 板前 **2.** v (cooks it) ryō´ri shimásu (suru, shite) 料理します(する, して), (boils it) nimásu (niru, nite) 煮ます(煮る, 煮て); (rice, soup) taki-másu (taku, taite) 炊きます(炊く, 炊いて) **3.** v (it boils) niemásu (nieru, niete) 煮えます(煮える, 煮えて)

cooked rice n meshí 飯, góhan ご飯

cooking n ryōri 料理
cooking stove n rénji レンジ

cool 1. adj suzushíi 涼しい; (calm) reisei (na) 冷静(な); (unperturbed) heiki (na) 平気(な) **2.** v it cools off/

down samemásu (saméru, sámete) 冷めます(冷める, 冷めて), hiemásu (híeru, híete) 冷えます(冷える, 冷えて); (cools it) hiyashimásu (hiyásu, hiyáshite) 冷やします(冷やす, 冷やして)

cooperation n kyōryoku 協力; (joint activity) kyōdō 共同

cop → policeman

copper n aka-gane アカガネ・銅, dō´ 銅

copula n shitei-shi 指定詞, keiji 繋詞 (= désu, dá, ná, nó, ní, dé, ... です, だ, な, の, に, で, ...)

copy 1. n (of a book) ... -bu ... 部, ichí-bu 一部 **2.** n (photocopy) kópii コピー (how many nán-mai 何枚) **3.** n (reproduction) fukusha 複写, fukusei 複製; two-sided copy ryōmen-kopii 両面コピー **4.** v (copies it) utsushi-másu (utsúsú, utsúshite) 写します(写す, 写して), fukusha/fukusei shimásu (suru, shite) 複写/複製します(する, して); (imitates) nisemásu (niseru, nisete) 似せます(似せる, 似せて); (makes a copy) kópii o torimásu (tóru, tótte) コピーをとります(とる, とって)

coral n sángo サンゴ・珊瑚

cord n himo ひも・紐, nawá なわ・縄, kō´do コード

cordial adj shínsetsu (na) 親切(な), kokoro no komotta 心のこもった

core n shín しん・心・芯

cork n kóruku コルク, sén 栓, korukú-sen コルク栓

corkscrew n korukú-nuki コルク抜き, sen-nuki 栓抜き

cormorant n u ウ・鵜
cormorant fishing n ukai 鵜飼い

corn 1. (maize) tō-mórokoshi トウモロコシ, kōn コーン **2.** (on skin) uonome 魚の目; (callus) táko たこ, (bunion) mamé まめ; soko-mame 底まめ

corner n (outside) kádo 角; (inside) súmi 隅

cornstarch n kōn-sutá´chi コーンスターチ, tōmorokoshí-ko トウモロコシ粉

corporation n **1.** (joint-stock

corporation) kabushiki-gáisha 株式
会社 **2.** (*incorporated association*)
shadan 社団 **3.** (*public corporation*)
kōdan 公団

corps *n* gundan 軍団; *Marine Corps*
kaiheitai 海兵隊; *Peace Corps* heiwa-
bútai 平和部隊; *medical corps* eisei-tai
衛生隊

corpsman *n* (*medical*) eiséi-hei 衛生兵

corpse *n* shitai 死体, nakigara なきが
ら・亡骸, shigai 死骸

correct 1. *adj* tadashíi 正しい **2.** *v*
atarimásu (ataru, atatte) 当たります
(当たる, 当たって); (*corrects it*) naoshimásu (naósu, naóshite) 直します(直
す, 直して), aratamemásu (arataméru,
aratámete) 改めます(改める, 改めて)

correction *n* naoshi 直し, teisei 訂正
(= *correcting*)

correctly *adv* tadáshiku 正しく

correspond (*to ...*) *v* (... ni) taiō
shimásu (suru, shite) (... に)対応しま
す(する, して)

correspondence *n* (*messages*) tsūshin
通信; (*equivalence*) taiō 対応

corridor *n* rōka 廊下

corrugated cardboard *n* danbō'ru
段ボール

cosmetics *n* keshō' 化粧(o-keshō
お化粧), keshō-hin 化粧品

cost 1. *n* (*expense*) híyō 費用 **2.** *v*
it costs (*how much*) (ikura) shimásu
(suru, shite) (いくら)します(する, し
て); (*requires*) yō-shimásu (yō-súru,
yō'-shite) 要します(要する, 要して)
at any cost nán to shité mo 何として
も, náni ga nánde mo 何が何でも

costly → **expensive**

costume *n* fukusō 服装

cotton *n* wata 綿, momen 木綿, kotton
コットン; *absorbent ~* dasshí-men
脱脂綿; *cotton-padded* (*garment*)
watairé 綿入れ

cotton belt *n* kotton beruto コットン
・ベルト

couch *n* ne-isu 寝椅子, naga-isu
長椅子

cough *v* sekí o shimásu (suru, shite) 咳
をします(する, して)

could → **can; maybe**

counsel 1. *n* (*guide, coach*) shidōsha
指導者 **2.** *v* (*counsels them*) shidō
shimásu (suru, shite) 指導します(す
る, して)

count *v* kazoemásu (kazoéru, kazóete)
数えます(数える, 数えて); *~ on*
one's fingers yubí o ótte kazoemásu
指を折って数えます; *is counting on*
... o ate ni shite imásu (iru, ite) ... を当
てにしています(いる, いて)

counter *n* (*shop counter*) uri-ba 売り場

counterclockwise *adj* hidari-máwari
(ni) 左回り(に)

counterfeit 1. *adj* nise (no) 偽(の)
2. *v* nisemásu (niseru, nisete) 似せます
(似せる, 似せて)

counterfeit bill *n* (*currency*) nisesatsu
にせ[偽・贋]札

countless *adj* kazoe-kirenai 数え切れ
ない, musū (no) 無数(の)

country *n* **1.** kuni 国;... -koku ... 国
(*how many countries* nan-kákoku 何
カ国) **2.** (*countryside*) inaka いなか・
田舎; (*outdoors*) yagai 野外

county *n* gún 郡 (*U.S.*); shū' 州 (*Britain*)

couple → **two**; **a couple** *n* (*husband
and wife*) fū'fu 夫婦, (*on a date*)
abékku アベック

coupon ticket *n* kaisū'-ken 回数券

courage *n* yū'ki 勇気

course *n* kō'su コース; (*in school*)
kamoku 科目; (*of action*) hōshin 方針;
(*of time*) keika 経過; (*development*)
nariyuki 成り行き; *in the ~ of*
(*during*) ...-chu (ni) 中(に)

course → **of course**

court *n* **1.** (*of law*) saiban-sho 裁判所,
hōtei 法廷 **2.** (*sports*) kōto コート
3. (*imperial/royal*) kyūtei 宮廷

court dances and music *n* búgaku 舞
楽

courtesy *n* reigí 礼儀

cousin *n* itóko いとこ・従兄弟・従
姉妹

cover *n* (*lid*) futa ふた・蓋; kabā
カバー; (*book, magazine, etc.*) hyōshí'
表紙

cover *v* **1.** (*covers it*) ōimásu (ōu, ōtte)
覆[おお]います(覆う, 覆って);
(*includes all items*) mō'ra shimásu

371

(suru, shíte) 網羅します(する, して)
2. ~ with a roof ... no yáne o fukimásu
(fuku, fuite) ... の屋根をふきます
(ふく, ふいて) **3. ~ up** (conceals)
fusemásu (fuséru, fuséte) 伏せます(伏
せる, 伏せて)

cover charge n (restaurant) seki-
ryō 席料, sābisú-ryō サービス料;
(admission) nyūjō´-ryō 入場料

cow n ushi 牛・ウシ (how many nán-
tō 何頭)

coward n okubyō-mono 臆病[憶病・
おくびょう]者; **cowardice** n okubyō´
臆病・憶病・おくびょう; **cowardly**
adj okubyō´ (na) 臆病[憶病・おくび
ょう](な)

crab n kani カニ・蟹 (**1:** ip-píki 一匹,
2: ní-hiki 二匹, **3:** sánbiki 三匹, how
many nán-biki 何匹)

crack 1. n suki (-ma) 透き(間); (wide)
ware-me 割れ目; (fine) hibí ひび;
(flaw) kizu 傷 **2. it cracks** v waremásu
(wareru, warete) 割れます(割れる, 割
れて)

crackers n kurákka クラッカー, bisukétto ビスケット

cradle n yuri-kago ゆりかご[籠]

crag n iwá 岩

cram; crams it in v tsumemásu
(tsuméru, tsúmete) 詰めます(詰める,
詰めて); **it is crammed in** tsumarimásu
(tsumáru, tsumátte) 詰まります(詰ま
る, 詰まって)

cram school n júku 塾

cramp n **1.** (leg) tsuru つる **2.** (stomach) ikeiren 胃痙攣・胃けいれん

crane n **1.** (bird) tsúru ツル・鶴
2. (machine) kurē´n クレーン

crash n (plane) tsuiraku 墜落;
(collision) shōtotsu 衝突

crass adj egetsunái えげつない

crate n wakú 枠, hako 箱

crater n funka -kō 噴火口

crawl v haimásu (háu, hátte) はい[這
い]ます(はう, はって)

crawly adj múzumuzu (shimásu; suru,
shíte) むずむず・ムズムズ(します; す
る, して)

crazy adj **1.** ki-chigái (no) 気違い・き
ちがい(の); **2. is ~ about ...** ni muchū

désu ... に夢中です

cream n kuríimu クリーム
cream puff n shū-kurímu シュークリ
ーム

crease n **1.** shiwa しわ・皺 **2.** (pleat)
orímé 折り目

create v tsukurimásu (tsúkuru, tsukutte)
造[創]ります(造[創]る, 造[創]って)

creator n (god) sōzō-shu 創造主,
(artists) kurieitā クリエイター

creature n séibutsu 生物, kuriichā
クリーチャー

credit n **1.** shin'yō 信用 **2.** (one's
credit) noren のれん・暖簾 **3.** (on
credit) kaké kaké 掛け掛け; **buys it on ~ on
one's account** tsuké de kaimásu (kau,
katte) つけで買います(買う, 買って)
credit sales n kakeuri 掛け売り, uri-
kake 売り掛け

credit card n kurejitto-kā´do クレジ
ットカード

credit limit n kurejitto (kā´do) no
gendo-gaku クレジット(カード)の限
度額

creed n shinjō 信条

creek n ogawa 小川

creep 1. v haimásu (hau, hatte) はい
[這い]ます(這う, 這って); (baby) hai
hai shimásu (suru, shíte) はいはいしま
す(する, して) **2. that creep** n aitsu
あいつ

creeper n tsuru shokubutsu つる植物

creepy adj múzumuzu (shimásu; suru,
shíte) むずむず・ムズムズ(します; す
る, して)

cremation n kasō 火葬, shōkyaku 焼却

crematorium n kasō-ba 火葬場

crescent n mikazuki 三日月, shingetsu
新月

crest; family crest n monshō 紋章,
món 紋, kamon 家紋

crested ibis n tóki トキ・朱鷺

crevice n ware-me 割れ目

crew n (member) norikumí-in 乗組員,
(of ship) sen'in 船員

crew cut n kurū-katto クルーカット,
kakugari 角刈り

crew neck n kurū-nekku クルーネック

crime n tsúmi 罪, hanzai 犯罪

criminal n (culprit) hánnin 犯人

crimson *adj* makká (na) 真っ赤(な)

cripple *n* shintai shōgaisha 身体障害者; *is crippled* ashí ga fú-jiyū desu 脚が不自由です

crisis *n* (*critical moment*) kíkí 危機

crisp *adj* paripari (no) パリパリ(の)

criterion *n* (*standard of judgment*) monosáshí ものさし・物差し・物指し, kijun 基準

critic *n* hihyō-ka 批評家, (*judge*) hihán-sha 批判者; (*commentator*) hyōron-ka 評論家

critical *adj* (*judgmental*) hihan-teki (na) 批判的(な); (*urgent*) kinkyū (na) 緊急(な)

critical moment *n* kíkí 危機

criticism *n* **1.** hihyō 批評; (*favorable*) kōhyō 好評; (*unfavorable*) akuhyō 悪評 **2.** (*commentary*) hyōron 評論

criticize *v* hihyō shimásu (suru, shite) 批評します(する, して); (*judges*) hihan shimásu (suru, shite) 批判します (する, して); (*comments on*) hyōron shimásu (suru, shite) 評論します(す る, して); (*censures*) sememásu (seméru, sémete) 責めます(責める, 責めて)

crock *n* tsubo つぼ・壷

crocodile *n* wáni ワニ・鰐

crony *n* nakama 仲間

crop *n* (*harvest*) minori 実り, shūkaku 収穫

cross 1. *n* (*symbol*) júji 十字; (*wooden*) jūji-ka 十字架 **2.** *n* ("×") bátsu ばつ (*vs.* maru 丸 "○")

cross *v* **1.** (*goes across*) watarimásu (wataru, watatte) 渡ります(渡る, 渡っ て), yoko-girimásu (yoko-gíru, yoko-gítte) 横切ります(横切る, 横切って); (*goes over a height*) koemásu (koeru, koete) 越えます(越える, 越えて) **2.** (*crosses one's legs*) ashí o kumimásu (kúmu, kúnde) 脚を組みます(組む, 組んで)

crossbeam *n* keta けた・桁

crossing *n* (*street intersection*) kōsaten 交差点; (*crossing over*) ōdan 横断

crossroads *n* jūji-ro 十字路, tsuji 辻 → intersection

cross-talk comedy *n* manzái 漫才

crossword puzzle *n* kurosuwādo (pazuru) クロスワード(パズル)

crotch *n* matá また・股

crouch *v* shagamimásu (shagamu, shagande) しゃがみます(しゃがむ, し ゃがんで); (*so as not to be seen*) mi o fusemásu (fuséru, fuséte) 身を伏せま す(伏せる, 伏せて)

crow *n* kárasu カラス・烏・鴉

crowd *n* gunshū 群衆, renjū/renchū 連中; *in crowds* zórozoro ぞろぞろ

crowded; gets ~ komimásu (kómu, kónde) こみます・混みます(こむ, こ んで); *is ~* kónde imásu (iru, ite) こん で[混んで]います(いる, いて)

crown *n* ōkan 王冠

Crown Prince *n* Kōtáishi 皇太子, Kōtáishi-sama 皇太子様; *Crown Princess* Kōtáishi-hi 皇太子妃

crucian carp *n* fúna フナ・鮒

crude *adj* sómatsu (na) 粗末(な), zatsu (na) 雑(な)

cruel *adj* mugói むごい, tsurai つらい ・辛い, hakujō (na) 薄情(な), zankoku (na) 残酷(な), zangyaku (na) 残虐(な)

cruelly *adv* hídoku ひどく

cruise *n* kurūzu クルーズ, funa-tabi 船旅

cruiser *n* kurūzā クルーザー

crumble *v* (*it crumbles*) kudakemásu (kudakéru, kudákete) 砕けます(砕け る, 砕けて); (*crumbles it*) kudakimásu (kudáku, kudáite) 砕きま す(砕く, 砕いて)

crumb(s) *n* pan-kúzu パンくず, pan-kó パン粉

crush *v* (*crushes it*) tsubushimásu (tsubusu, tsubu-shite) つぶします (つぶす, つぶして); (*it gets crushed*) tsuburemásu (tsubureru, tsuburete) つ ぶれます(つぶれる, つぶれて)

crust *n* kawá 皮

crutch *n* matsuba-zúe 松葉杖

cry *v* nakimásu (naku, naite) 泣きます (泣く, 泣いて); (*cries out*) sakebimásu (sakébu, sakénde) 叫びます(叫ぶ, 叫 んで)

cryptomeria *n* (*Japanese cedar*) sugi 杉・スギ

crystal *n* suishō 水晶, kesshō 結晶, kurisutaru クリスタル

cub *n* ko 子

cubbyhole *n* 1. (*snug room/place*) igokochi no yoi heya/basho 居心地の良い部屋/場所 2. (*small room/place*) chiisai heya/basho 小さい部屋/場所

cube *n* rippō (-tai) 立方(体)

cubic *adj* rippō-tai (*no*) 立方体(の), rippō (*no*) 立方(の)

cuckoo *n* kákkō カッコウ; (*little*) hototógisu ホトトギス

cucumber *n* kyū́ri キュウリ; (*sushi-bar term*) kappa カッパ

cuff *n* káfusu カフス

cuff link *n* kafusu botan カフスボタン

culprit *n* hánnin 犯人

cult *n* karuto カルト

cultivate *v* tagayashimásu (tagayasu, tagayashite) 耕します(耕す, 耕して)

cultural festival *n* bunká-sai 文化祭

cultural shock *n* karuchā-shokku カルチャーショック

culture *n* (*refinement*) kyōyō 教養; (*farming*) yōshoku 養殖; (*civilization*) búnka 文化; *Culture Day* (*3 November*) Búnka no hí 文化の日

culture center *n* karuchā sentā カルチャーセンター

cultured pearls *n* yōshoku-shínju 養殖真珠

cunning *adj* zurúi ずるい

cup *n* chawan 茶碗 (o-cháwan お茶碗), koppu コップ; (*with handle*) káppu カップ; (*cupful*) ... -hai ... 杯 (1: íp-pai 一杯, 2: ní-hai 二杯, 3: sánbai 三杯, *how many* nán-bai 何杯)

cupboard *n* (*enclosed shelves*) todana 戸棚; (*for dishes*) shokki-tódana 食器戸棚; (*closet*) oshi-ire 押し入れ

curb 1. *n* (*of road*) hodó no fuchí 歩道の縁・ふち → sidewalk 2. *v* yokusei shimásu 抑制します 3. *v* (*restrains*) yokusei shimásu (suru, shite) 抑制します(する, して)

cure *v* naoshimásu (naósu, naóshite) 治します(治す, 治して)

curios *n* kottō-hin 骨董品 → antiques

curiosity *n* kōkíshin 好奇心

curious *adj* (*inquisitive*) monózukí

(na) 物好き(な); (*novel*) mezurashíi めずらしい・珍しい; *I'm ~ about something.* Shiri-tái kotó ga arimásu. 知りたいことがあります.

curly *v become ~* chijiremásu (chijireru, cnijirete) 縮れます(縮れる, 縮れて)

currant *n* rēzun レーズン; hoshibudō 干しブドウ

currency *n* (*bill/note*) satsu 札 (o-satsu お札); shihei 紙幣

current 1. *adj* (*present*) génzai no ... 現在の..., gén (-) ... 現...

current address *n* gen-jū́sho 現住所

current deposit *n* tōza-yókin 当座預金

2. *n* (*tide*) chōryū 潮流

current affairs *n* jiji(mondai) 時事 (問題)

currently *adv* génzai 現在

curriculum *n* karikyuramu カリキュラム

curriculum vitae *n* rirekisho 履歴書

curry *n* karē カレー; (*with rice*) karē-ráisu カレーライス

curry powder *n* karē ko カレー粉

curse 1. *n* noroi のろい・呪い 2. *v* (*utters a curse*) noroimásu (noróu, norótte) のろい[呪い]ます(のろう, のろって), (*reviles*) nonoshirimásu (nonoshíru, nonoshitte) ののしり[罵り]ます(ののしる, ののしって)

cursor *n* (*computer*) kāsoru カーソル

cursory *adj* 1. (*hasty*) isogi (no) 急ぎ(の) 2. (*superficial*) hyōmen-teki (na) 表面的(な) 3. (*perfunctory*) ozanari (na) おざなり(な)

curt *adj* bu-áisō (na) 無愛想(な), bukkírábō (na) ぶっきらぼう(な)

curtail *v* herashimásu (herasu, herashite) 減らします(減らす, 減らして)

curtain *n* kā́ten カーテン; (*bamboo*) sudare すだれ; (*stage*) makú 幕

curtain rod *n* kāten-róddo カーテンロッド

curtain time *n* kaien-jíkan 開演時間

curve 1. *n* magari 曲がり; (*road*) kábu カーブ; (*bend*) sorí そり・反り, (*arch*) yumi-gata 弓形 2. *it curves v* magarimásu (magaru, magatte) 曲がります(曲がる, 曲がって) 3. *curves it v*

magemásu (mageru, magete) 曲げます（曲げる、曲げて）

cushion n (*seat*) zabúton 座布団; (*spread*) shíki-mono 敷物; kusshon クッション

custard n kasutādo (kuriimu) カスタード（クリーム）

custard pudding n kasutādo purin カスタードプリン

custodian n **1.** (*janitor*) kózukai 小使い、yōmu-in 用務員 **2.** (*administrator*) kanri-nin 管理人

custody n (*child custody*) yōiku-ken 養育権

custom n **1.** shūkan 習慣 **2.** (*tradition*) dentō 伝統

customary adj jū´rai (no) 従来(の)

customer n (o-)kyaku (お)客、o-kyaku-sámá お客様; (*patron*) otokui お得意、tokui-saki 得意先

customer center n kasutamā sentā カスタマーセンター

customer service n kasutamā sābisu カスタマーサービス

custom-made adj ōda meido (no) オーダーメイド(の)

customs n (*place*) zeikan 税関; (*tariff*) kanzei 関税、zéi 税

customs duty n kanzei 関税

customs officer n zeikan shokuin 税関職員

customs official n zeimukan 税務官

cut 1. v kirimásu (kíru, kítté) 切ります（切る、切って）; (*mows*) karimásu (karu, katte) 刈ります（刈る、刈って）; (*it cuts well*) kiremásu (kiréru, kiréte) 切れます（切れる、切れて）**2.** n (*of cloth*) kata 型; (*share*) wake-mae 分け前; (*percentage*) rítsu 率

cuts the price v makemásu (makeru, makete) 負けます（負ける、負けて）

cut across v yoko-girimásu (yoko-gíru, yoko-gítte) 横切ります（横切る、横切って）

cut back v sakugen shimásu (suru, shite) 削減します（する、して）

cut class v saborimásu (sabóru, sabótte) さぼります（さぼる、さぼって）

cut down v (*lessens*) herashimásu (herasu, herashíte) 減らします（減ら

す、減らして）; (*reduces*) chijimemásu (chijiméru, chijímete) ちぢめます（ちぢめる、ちぢめて）; (*dilutes*) warimásu (waru, watte) 割ります（割る、割って）

cut in (into) v wari-kómimásu (wari-kómu, wari-kónde) 割り込みます（割り込む、割り込んで）

cut off v kirimásu (kíru, kítté) 切ります（切る、切って）; tachimásu (tátsu, tátte) たち[裁ち・断ち・絶ち]ます（たつ[裁つ・断つ・絶つ]、たって[裁って・断って・絶って]）

cut out v (*eliminates*) habukimásu (habúku, habúite) 省きます（省く、省いて）

cutback n sakugen 削減

cute adj **1.** kawaíi かわいい、kawai-rashíi かわいらしい **2.** (*handsome*) kakkoii かっこいい

cuticle n **1.** (*nail*) amakawa 甘皮 **2.** (*hair*) kyutikuru キューティクル

cutlery n (*cutting instruments*) há-mono 刃物 **2.** (*tableware*) shokki-rui 食器類

cutlet n kátsu(retsu) カツ（レツ）

pork cutlet n tonkatsu 豚カツ・トンカツ

cutout n anzen sōchi 安全装置

cut-rate adj waribiki (no) 割引(の)、yasu-uri (no) 安売り(の)

cutthroat n hitogoroshi 人殺し

cuttlefish n (*squid*) ika イカ

dried cuttlefish n surume スルメ

cyanide n shian kabutsu シアン化物、seisan kabutsu (na) 青酸化物

cyberspace n saibā-supēsu サイバースペース

cycle n (*circulation*) junkan 循環、saikuru サイクル

cycling n saikuringu サイクリング

cyclist n saikurisuto サイクリスト

cyclone n saikuron サイクロン、teikiatsu 低気圧

cygnet n wakai hakuchō 若いハクチョウ[白鳥]

cylinder n tsutsu 筒、shirindā シリンダー

cymbal n shinbaru シンバル

cynic n hiniku-ya 皮肉屋

cynical adj hiniku (na) 皮肉(な)、shinikaru (na) シニカル(な)

cynicism *n* shinikaru na taido シニカルな態度
cypress *n* **1.** hinoki ヒノキ・檜 **2.** itosugi イトスギ
Cypriot *adj* kipurosu (no) キプロス(の)
Cyprus *n* kipurosu キプロス
cyst *n* nōhō 嚢胞; nōshu 脳腫

cystitis *n* bōkō-en 膀胱炎
Czechoslovakia *n* chekosurobakia チェコスロバキア
Czechoslovakian *n* **1.** (*language*) chekosurobakia-go チェコスロバキア語 **2.** (*people*) chekosurobakia-jin チェコスロバキア人

D

dab *n* hitonuri ひと塗り
daddy, dad *n* papa パパ
daffodil *n* rappa-zuisen ラッパズイセン
dagger *n* tanken 短剣
daily *n* **1.** *n* (*newspaper*) nikkan(-shi) 日刊(紙) **2.** *adj* (*everyday*) mainichi(no) 毎日(の)
dainty *adj* **1.** (*delicate beauty*) yūbi (na) 優美(な), **2.** *n* (*something delicious*) oishii-mono おいしい[美味しい]もの
dairy *n* (*milk shop*) gyūnyū-ya 牛乳屋
dais *n* endai 演台
daisy *n* hinagiku ヒナギク・ひな菊, deijii デイジー
dam *n* dámu ダム
damage 1. *n* songai 損害; són 損, gái 害, higai 被害, daméji ダメージ **2.** *damages it* v itamemásu (itaméru, itamete) 傷めます(傷める, 傷めて), arashimásu (arásu, aréte) 荒らします(荒らす, 荒れて); sokonaimásu (sokonau, sokonátte) 損ないます(損なう, 損なって)
damascene *n* zō'gan 象眼・象嵌
damask *n* dónsu どんす・緞子
dame *n* (*woman, sometimes offensive*) onna 女・おんな
Damn! *interj* Shimátta! しまった！
damn (*fool*) *n* …-me …め; **~ idiot** baka-me ばかめ
damp 1. *adj* shimeppoi 湿っぽい; **2.** *gets* ~ v shimerimásu (shimeru, shimette) 湿ります(湿る, 湿って), nuremásu (nureru, nurete) ぬれます(ぬれる, ぬれて)
dampen v nurashimásu (nurasu, nurashite) ぬらします(ぬらす, ぬらして), shimeshimásu (shimesu, shimeshite) 湿します(湿す, 湿して)

damp (hand-)towel *n* o-shíbori おしぼり
dampness *n* shikki 湿気, shikke 湿気・しっけ
dance 1. *n* odori 踊り・おどり, dansu ダンス **2.** *dances* v odorimásu (odoru, odotte) 踊ります(踊る, 踊って)
dancer *n* (*Japanese-style*) odori-te 踊り手; (*Western-style*) dansā ダンサー
dandelion *n* tánpopo タンポポ
dandruff *n* fuke ふけ
dandy 1. *n* (*fancy dresser*) osháre おしゃれ **2.** *v* osháre (na) おしゃれ(な)
Dane *n* (*people*) dēn-zoku デーン族, denmáku no minzoku デンマークの民族
danger *n* kiken 危険・キケン; (*crisis*) kyū 急; (*fear/worry lest …*) …osoré/shinpai …恐れ/心配
dangerous *adj* abunai 危ない, kiken (na) 危険(な); yabái やばい; (*delicate, ticklish*) kiwadói きわどい
dangle v (*dangles it*) sagemásu (sagéru, ságete) 下げます(下げる, 下げて), tarashimásu (tarásu, taráshite) 垂らします(垂らす, 垂らして); (*it dangles*) taremásu (taréru, tárete) 垂れます(垂れる, 垂れて)
dangling *adj* (*idly*) búrabura ぶらぶら
Danish 1. *n* (*language*) denmáku-go デンマーク語; (*person*) denmáku-jin デンマーク人 **2.** *n* (*pastry*) denishu デニッシュ **3.** *adj* (*concerning Denmark*) denmáku-go(-jin) no デンマーク語(人)の
dare (*to do*) v áete (shimásu) あえて(します)
dark 1. *adj* kurai 暗い; (*color*) kói [COLOR NAME] (no) 濃い [COLOR NAME] (の)

2. the dark n higure 日暮れ, yamí 闇;
it gets ~ hi ga kuremásu (kureru,
kurete) 日が暮れます (暮れる, 暮れて)

dark blue n kón 紺, kon-iro (no) 紺色(の)

dark glasses n sangurasu サングラス

darkness n (kura-)yami (暗)闇・やみ

darling adj kawaíi かわいい,
kawairashíi かわいらしい

darts n dātsu ダーツ

dash n dasshu ダッシュ

dashboard n dasshu-bōdo ダッシュボード

data n dḗta データ, shiryō 資料

database n dētabēsu データベース

date n **1.** (of month) hizuke 日付 (け);
(complete) nengáppi 年月日; *~ of
birth* seinen-gáppi 生年月日 **2.**
(engagement) yakusoku 約束 (o-yakusoku お約束) **3.** (a couple) dēto (shimásu; suru, shíte) デート (します; す
る, して)

date n (fruit) natsume なつめ

dated adj [DATE]-zuke [...日] 付け

daughter n musume(-san) 娘・むす
め (さん); (your) ojō′ san お嬢さん;
eldest ~ chōjo 長女

daughter-in-law n **1.** (wife of your
son) musuko no tsuma 息子の妻 **2.**
(wife of someone's son) o-yome-san
お嫁さん

dawn n yoaké 夜明け, akegata 明け方

day n hi 日, ...hí ...日; (daytime) hirú
昼 (o-híru お昼), hirumá 昼間; *the ~
in question, that very ~* tō′jitsu 当日;
(fixed) hinichi 日にち

day after tomorrow n asátte あさっ
て・明後日, myō′go-nichi 明後日

day before last/yesterday n ototói お
ととい・一昨日, issakú-jitsu 一昨日

day in and day out n aketémo kuretémo
明けても暮れても

day off n yasumí (no hí) 休み (の日),
kyūka 休暇

daybreak n akegata 明け方, yoake 夜
明け

daydream 1. n kūsō′ 空想, hakuchūmu
白昼夢 **2.** v bon'yári shimásu (suru,
shíte) ぼんやりします (する, して)

daylight n nitchū 日中, hiru no hikari
昼の光

days n **1** day ichi-nichí 一日, **2 days**
futsuka 二日, **3 days** mikka 三日, **4
days** yokka 四日, **5 days** itsuka 五日,
6 days muika 六日, **7 days** nanoka 七
日, **8 days** yōka 八日, **9 days** kokonoka
九日, **10 days** tō′ka 十日, **14 days** jú-
yokka 十四日, **24 days** ní-jū yokka 二
十四日; (others) ...-nichi ...日; *how
many days* nán-nichi 何日

daytime n hirú 昼 (o-híru お昼), hiru-
má 昼間

dazed; gets ~ bō′tto shimásu (suru,
shíte) ぼうっとします (する, して),
madoimásu (madóu, madótte) 惑いま
す (惑う, 惑って)

dazzling adj mabushíí まぶしい,
mabayui まばゆい

DC, direct current n chokuryū 直流

dead adj shinda ...死んだ...; *is
~* shinde imásu (iru, ite) 死んでい
ます (いる, いて) **2. dead person** n
nakunatta hitó 亡くなった人, shinda
hitó 死んだ人, shinin 死人

deaden v **1.** (becomes dead) shinimásu
(sinu, shinde) 死にます (死ぬ, 死んで)
2. (makes less sensitive) mu-kankaku
ni shimásu (suru, shíte) 無感覚にします
(する, して) **3.** (weakens) yowamari-
másu (yowamaru, yowamatte) 弱まり
ます (弱まる, 弱まって) **4.** (makes
impervious to sound) bōon ni shimásu
(suru, shite) 防音にします (する, して)

dead end n ikidomari 行き止まり

dead heat n dōchaku 同着

deadline n shimekiri 締め切り・しめ
きり, (saishū-)kígen (最終) 期限,
kíjitsu 期日

deaf 1. n (person) mimí no kikoenai
hitó 耳の聞こえない人; *is ~* mimí ga
fú-jiyū desu 耳が不自由です **2.** adj
mimí no kikoenai 耳の聞こえない,
mimí ga fujiyū na 耳が不自由な

deafness n nanchō 難聴

deal 1. n (transaction) torí-hiki 取引
2. v (cards) kubarimásu (kubáru,
kubátte) 配ります (配る, 配って); *a
good/great ~* → lots, much

deal in (sells) urimásu (uru, utte) 売り
ます (売る, 売って), hanbai shimásu
(suru, shíte) 販売します (する, して)

deal with tori-atsukaimásu (tori-atsukau, tori-atsukatte) 取り扱います (取り扱う, 取り扱って); (*treats a person*) ashiraimásu (ashiráu, ashirátte) あしらいます(あしらう, あしらって); (*copes*) shóri/shóbun/shóchi shimásu (suru, shíte) 処理/処分/処置します (する, して); (*disposes of a matter*) shímatsu shimásu (suru, shíte) 始末します(する, して)

dealer *n* kouriten 小売店, (*retail outlet*) hanbái-ten 販売店, diirā ディーラー; (*seller of …*) …shō′ …商, …-ya …屋

dealing *n* torihiki 取(り)引(き)

dean *n* gakubu-chō 学部長

dear *adj* 1. (*beloved*) itoshíi いとしい・愛しい, natsukashíi 懐かしい 2. (*precious*) taisetsu (na) 大切(な); **Dear Sir/Madam** Haikei 拝啓; **Dear dear!** *interj* Oyaoya! おやおや!; **Dear me!** *interj* (*feminine*) Mā! まあ! 3. → **expensive**

dearly *adv* hijō (ni) 非常(に), kokoro-kara 心から

death *n* shí 死

death penalty *n* shí-kei 死刑

death toll *n* shibō-sha sū 死亡者数

debacle *n* hōkai 崩壊, dōraku 道楽

debatable *adj* giron no yochi ga aru 議論の余地がある

debate *n* tō′ron 討論, ronsō′ 論争 2. *debates it* *v* ron-jimásu (ron-jiru, ron-jite) 論じます(論じる, 論じて)

debauchery *n* hōtō 放蕩

debit *n* fusai 負債, (*bookkeeping*) karikata 借方

debris *n* zangai 残骸

debt *n* shakkín 借金

debug *n* debaggu デバッグ

debut *n* debyū デビュー

decade *n* jū nen-kan 十[10]年間

decadence *n* taihai 退廃

decaffeinated *adj* kafein nuki (no) カフェイン抜き(の)

decanter *n* mizusashi 水差し

decay 1. *v* kuchimásu (kuchiru, kuchite) 朽ちます(朽ちる, 朽ちて); kusarimásu (kusaru, kusátte) くさります(くさる, くさって) 2. *n* [BOOKISH] fuhai 腐敗

decayed tooth *n* mushi-ba 虫歯

deceased *n the deceased* kojin 故人

deceive → **cheat**

deceit *n* 1. (*lie*) itsuwari 偽り 2. (*fraud*) sagi 詐欺・サギ

deceitful *adj* fu-shōjiki (na) 不正直 (な)

deception *n* (*cheat*) gomakashi ごまかし, (*fraud*) sagi 詐欺・サギ

December *n* Jūni-gatsú 十二月・12月

decency *n* reigi 礼儀

decent *adj* (*respectable*) jō′hin (na) 上品(な), rippa (na) 立派・りっぱ(な)

decibel *n* deshiberu デシベル

decide *v* kimemásu (kimeru, kimete) 決めます(決める, 決めて); kettei shimásu (suru, shíte) 決定します(する, して)

decider *n* 1. (*person*) kettei-sha 決定者 2. (*game*) kettei-sen 決定戦

decimal *n* shōsū 小数; ~ *point* shōsū-ten 小数点

decision *n* kettei 決定

deck *n* 1. (*of ship*) kanpan 甲板, dékki デッキ 2. → **pack** (*of cards*)

deckchair *n* dekki chea デッキチェア

decline *v* 1. (*refuses*) kotowarimásu (kotowáru, kotowátte) 断わります(断わる, 断わって), jitai shimásu (suru, shíte) 辞退します(する, して) 2. (*it fades*) otoroemásu (otoróéru, otoróete) 衰えます(衰える, 衰えて)

declutch *v* kuratchi o kirimásu (kiru, kitte) クラッチを切ります(切る, 切って)

decode *v* kaidoku shimásu (suru, shite) 解読します(する, して)

decompose *v* (*rots*) fuhai shimásu (suru, shite) 腐敗します(する, して)

decor *n* sōshoku (hin) 装飾品

decorate *v* kazarimásu (kazaru, kazatte) 飾ります(飾る, 飾って)

decoration *n* kazari(-mono) 飾り(物), sō′shoku 装飾, dekorēshon デコレーション

decorative *adj* sōshoku teki (na) 装飾的(な)

decorator *n* sōshoku-sha 装飾者

decorum *n* reigi (sahō) 礼儀(作法)

decoy *n* otori おとり

decrease 1. *v* (*it decreases*) herimásu (heru, hette) 減ります(減る、減って)、genshō shimásu (suru, shite) 減少します(する、して); herashimásu (herasu, herashite) 減らします(減らす、減らして) 2. *n* genshō 減少

decrepit *adj* 1. (*infirm*) rōsui shita 老衰した 2. (*dilapidated*) rōkyūka shita 老朽化した

decry *v* kenashimásu (kenasu, kenashite) けなします(けなす、けなして)

dedicate *v* sasagemásu (sasageru, sasagete) 捧げます(捧げる、捧げて)

dedication *n* kenshin 献身

deduct *v* hikimásu (hiku, hiite) 引きます(引く、引いて)

deed *n* (*act*) shiwaza 仕業・しわざ、kō'í 行為、okonai 行い

deep *adj* 1. fukái 深い 2. (*saturated color*) kói 濃い; ~ red makká (na) 真っ赤(な)

deeply *adv* fukáku 深く、(*feeling deeply*) shimijími (to) しみじみ(と)

deer *n* shika 鹿・シカ

deface *v* gaikan o sokonaimásu (sokonau, soko-natte) 外観を損ないます(損なう、損なって)

defamation *n* chūshō 中傷; (*defamation of character*) meiyo-kison 名誉棄損

default *n* deforuto デフォルト、shoki-settei 初期設定

defeat 1. *n* make 負け、shippai 失敗 2. *v* (*defeats*) makashimásu (makasu, makashite) 負かします(負かす、負かして)、yaburimásu (yabúru, yabutte) 破ります(破る、破って); (*is defeated*) makemásu (makeru, makete) 負けます(負ける、負けて)、mairimásu (máiru, máitte) 参ります(参る、参って); (*falls behind*) okure o torimásu (tóru, tótte) 遅れを取ります(取る、取って)

defecate *v* daibén o shimásu (suru, shite) 大便をします(する、して); *defecation n* daibén 大便

defect *n* ketten 欠点、kizu 傷・キズ

defective *n* furyō-hin 不良品、kekkan-hin 欠陥品

defend *v* mamorimásu (mamóru, mamótte) 守ります(守る、守って);

kabaimásu (kabau, kabatte) 庇います(庇う、庇って)

defendant *n* hikoku(-nin) 被告(人)

defense *n* (*military*) bōei 防御、(*sport*) bōgyo 防御、difensu ディフェンス; *The Ministry of Defense* bōei-shō 防衛省

defensive *adj* bōei (no) 防衛(の)、shubi (no) 守備(の)

defer *v* nobashimásu (nobásu, nobáshite) 延ばします(延ばす、延ばして)

deference *n* 1. (*obedience*) fukujū 服従 2. (*respect*) keii 敬意

defiance *n* hankō 反抗

defiant *adj* hankō-teki (na) 反抗的(な)

deficiency *n* fusoku 不足、ketsubō 欠乏、kekkan 欠陥

deficit (*figures*) *n* aka-ji 赤字

defile *v* yogoshimásu (yogosu, yogoshite) 汚します(汚す、汚して)

define *v* teigi shimásu (suru, shite) 定義します(する、して)

definite *adj* (*certain amount of*) ittei (no) 一定(の)

definitely *adv* (*firmly*) kippári (to) きっぱり(と)

definitive *adj* kakujitsu (na) 確実(な)

deformity *n* kikei 奇形

defy *v* ...ni sakaraimásu (sakaráu, sakarátte) ...に逆らいます(逆らう、逆らって)

degenerate *adj* daraku shiteiru 堕落している、daraku shita 堕落した

degrade *v* (*to lower in dignity*) otoshimemásu (otoshimeru, otoshimete) おとしめます(おとしめる、おとしめて)

degree *n* 1. (*extent*) téido 程度、dó 度、kagen 加減; ... 2. *degrees* (*temperature*) ...-do ...度; (*higher learning*) gákúi 学位

dehydrate *v* dassui-jōtai ni narimásu (naru, natte) 脱水状態になります(なる、なって)

deify *v* shinkaku-ka shimásu (suru, shite) 神格化します(する、して)、shinsei-shi shimásu (suru, shite) 神聖視します(する、して)

deity *n* shinsei 神性、kami 神

dejection *n* rakutan 落胆、iki shōchin 意気消沈

delay v (*delays it*) okurasemásu (oku-raseru, okurasete) 遅らせます(遅らせる, 遅らせて); (*gets delayed*) oku-remásu (okureru, okurete) 遅れます(遅れる, 遅れて)

delegate 1. n (*representative*) daihyō 代表 2. n (*alternate*) dairi (-nin) 代理(人) 3. v (*commits to another*) inin shimásu (suru, shite) 委任します(する, して)

delete v tori-keshimásu (tori-kesu, tori-keshíte) 取り消します(取り消す, 取り消して)

deletion n tori-keshi 取り消し, sakujo 削除

deliberate adj (*intentional*) kói (no) 故意(の); (*careful*) shinchō´ (na) 慎重(な)

deliberately adv wáza to わざと, wázawaza わざわざ, kói (ni) 故意(に)

delicate adj (*fine*) bimyō´ (na) 微妙(な); (*risky*) kiwadói きわどい

delicatessen n derikatessen デリカテッセン, chōri-zumi shokuhin(-ten) 調理済み食品(店)

delicious adj oishii おいしい・美味しい, [INFORMAL] umái うまい

delight 1. adj *is delighted* yorokobi-másu (yorokóbu, yorokónde) 喜びます(喜ぶ, 喜んで); *with great ~* ō´-yóro-kobi (de) 大喜び(で) 2. n yorokobi 喜び, tanoshimi 楽しみ

delightful adj ureshii うれしい

delimit v kagirimásu (kagíru, kagítte) 限ります(限る, 限って)

delinquency n hikō 非行

delinquent n (*juvenile delinquent*) hikō shōnen shōjo 非行少年少女, furyō 不良

deliria n (*pathology*) senmō せん妄

delirium n (*pathology*) seishin sakuran 精神錯乱, (*excitement*) kōfun 興奮

deliver v todokemásu (todokéru, todókete) 届けます(届ける, 届けて)

delivered food n demae 出前

delivery n 1. haitatsu 配達, deribarii デリバリー; *restaurant ~* (*service/person*) demae 出前; *~ person* demáé-mochi 出前持ち 2. (*giving birth*) shussan 出産

delta n 1. (*Greek alphabet*) deruta デルタ 2. (*mathematics*; *incremental change*) sabun 差分 3. (*plain*) sankaku-su 三角州

deluge n (*great flood*) dai-kōzui 大洪水, (*downpour*) gōu 豪雨

delusion n sakkaku 錯覚

deluxe adj jō´上, jō´tó´(no) 上等(の), gō´ka (na) 豪華(な)
    deluxe article n tokutō-hin 特等品
    deluxe edition n gōka-ban 豪華版

demand 1. n yō´kyū/seikyū (shimásu; suru, shite) 要求/請求(します; する, して) 2. v motomemásu (motoméru, motómete) 求めます(求める, 求めて); *is in ~* (*sells*) uremásu (ureru, urete) 売れます(売れる, 売れて)

demanding adj (*overly strict*) yakamashii やかましい

democracy n minshu-shúgi 民主主義, demokurashii デモクラシー

democrat n minshu-shúgi-sha 民主主義者, minshu-tō-in 民主党員

democratic adj minshu-shúgi (no) 民主主義の, minshu-teki (na) 民主的(な)

demolish v kuzushimásu (kuzúsu, kuzúshite) 崩します(崩す, 崩して); hakai shimásu (suru, shite) 破壊します(する, して)

demon n akuma 悪魔, dēmon デーモン

demonize v warumono atsukai 悪者扱い

denial n uchi-keshi 打ち消し, hitei 否定

denim n denimu デニム, denims jiinzu ジーンズ

denomination → **sect**

denominator n bunbo 分母

dense adj kói 濃い, mítsu (na) 密(な), missetsu (na) 密接(な)

density n mitsudo 密度

dent n kubomi 窪み・くぼみ

dentifrice n ha-mígaki 歯みがき

dentist n há-isha 歯医者

dentistry n shika 歯科

denture n ireba 入れ歯

deny v uchi-keshimásu (uchi-kesu, uchi-keshíte) 打ち消します(打ち消す, 打ち消して), hitei shimásu (suru, shite) 否定します(する, して)

deodorant n (*personal*) shō´shū-zai 消臭剤; (*household, etc.*) hōkō-zai 芳香剤

departing at/from v [TIME/PLACE] … hátsu (no) …発(の)

department n (*university, hospital*) ká-ka 科; (*company, office*) bumon 部門, bu 部, ka 課; *Department of Health Education and Welfare* hoken kyōiku fukushi-shō 保健教育福祉省; *Department of Humanitarian Affairs* jindō mondai-kyoku 人道問題局

department store n depā´to デパート, hyakká-ten 百貨店

departure n shuppatsu 出発; [TIME/PLACE] … hátsu (no …) …発(の…)
point of departure n shuppátsú-ten 出発点
departure platform n hassha-hōmu 発車ホーム
departure lobby n shuppátsú-robii 出発ロビー
departure time n shuppátsú-jikoku 出発時刻

depend v; **v ~ on** (… ni) tayorimásu (tayóru, tayótte) (…に)頼ります(頼る, 頼って), izon shimásu (suru, shíte) 依存します(する, して); *it depends* (*on …*) (… ni) yorimásu (yóru, yotte) (…に)よります(よる, よって), ([NOUN], [VERB] -i i) -shídai desu しだいです

dependence n izon 依存

dependent n fuyō-kazoku 扶養家族

depiction n byōsha 描写

depilatory n datsumō´-zai 脱毛剤

deposit 1. v azukemásu (azukéru, azukéte) 預けます(預ける, 預けて); (*money*) yokin/chokin shimásu (suru, shíte) 預金/貯金します(する, して), tsumimásu (tsumu, tsunde) 積みます(積む, 積んで) **2.** → *downpayment*

depositor n yokin-sha 預金者

depot n **1.** (*railroad station*) eki 駅 **2.** (*bus station*) basu hatchaku-jō バス発着場 **3.** (*warehouse*) sōko 倉庫

depressed adj (*feeling*) ki ga omoi 気が重[おも]い **2.** *gets ~* (*concave*) hekomimásu (hekomu, hekonde) へこみます(へこむ, へこんで)

depressing adj yūtsu (na) 憂うつ(な)

depression n (*hard times*) fukéiki 不景気; (*hollow*) kubomi 窪み・くぼみ

depth n fukása 深さ; (*of color*) kósa 濃さ

derail v dassen shimásu (suru, shíte) 脱線します(する, して); *derailment* n dassen 脱線

derision n azakeri あざけり, reishō 冷笑

derivative n (*word*) hasei-go 派生語

descend v kudarimásu (kudaru, kudatte) 下ります(下る, 下って)

descendant n shíson 子孫

descent n **1.** (*going down*) kudari 下り・くだり **2.** (*family line*) kakei 家系

describe v (*pictures it*) byōsha shimásu (suru, shíte) 描写します(する, して), (*elaborates it*) (no kobto) o kuwáshiku iimásu (iu, itte/yutte) …(のこと[事])を詳しく言います(言う, 言って/ゆって); (*explains it*) setsumei shimásu (suru, shíte) 説明します(する, して) → *relate*

description n setsumei 説明

desert n sabaku 砂漠

deserving adj (*proper*) tō´zen (no) 当然(の)

design 1. n (*sketch*) zuan 図案; dezain デザイン **2.** v (*plans it*) hakarimásu (hakáru, hakátte) 図ります(図る, 図って); dezain shimásu (suru, shíte) デザインします(する, して)

designate v atemásu (ateru, atete) 当てます(当てる, 当てて); shitei shimásu (suru, shíte) 指定します(する, して) → *name*

designation n shitei 指定, shimei 指名 → *name*

desirable adj nozomashii 望ましい, hoshíi 欲しい; *most ~* (*ideal*) motte-kói (no) もってこい(の)

desire 1. n nozomi 望み, omói 思い, nén 念; (*hope*) kibō 希望 **2.** *desires it* v (… ga) hoshíi (…が)欲しい; (*wants to do*) (shi-) tái desu (し)たいです; (*hopes for*) nozomimásu (nozomu, nozonde) 望みます(望む, 望んで)

desk n tsukue 机, taku 卓; (*desk-top*) takujō´ 卓上; *~ lamp* sutando スタンド, denki sutándo 電気スタンド

despair *n* zetsubō´ 絶望, yáke やけ

desperate *adj* hisshi (no) 必死(の)

desperately *adv* (*hard*) isshō´-kénmei (ni) 一生懸命(に); (*out of despair*) yáke ni nátte やけになって

desperation *n* zetsubō´ 絶望, yáke やけ

despise *v* keibetsu shimásu (suru, shite) 軽蔑します(する, して)

despite (*that*) *prep* …ni mo kakawarazu …にもかかわらず[関わらず]

despot *n* dokusai-sha 独裁者, bōkun 暴君

dessert *n* dezā´to デザート

destination *n* iki sakí 行き先, mokutekí chi 目的地; (*last stop*) shūten 終点

destiny *n* únmei 運命

destroy *v* kowashimásu (kowásu, kowáshite) 壊します(壊す, 壊して); hakai shimásu (suru, shite) 破壊します(する, して); horoboshimásu (horobosu, horoboshite) 滅ぼします(滅ぼす, 滅ぼして)

detach *v* hanashimásu (hanásu, hanáshite) 離します(離す, 離して)

detailed *adj* kuwashíi 詳しい; bisai (na) 微細(な); (*machine, etc.*) seimitsu (na) 精密(な)

details *n* kuwashíi koto 詳しいこと, shō´sai 詳細; (*complexities*) ikisatsu いきさつ

detect → see → smell → hear → discover → discern

detective *n* 1. (*consulting detective*) tantei 探偵 2. (*police*) kéiji 刑事 3. (*investigator*) sōsa-kan 捜査官

detective agency *n* kōshin-jo 興信所

detective story (*writer*) *n* suiri-shōsetsu (sakka) 推理小説(作家)

deteriorate *v* (*weather*) kuzuremásu (kuzuréru, kuzúrete) 崩れます(崩れる, 崩れて)

determination *n* (*decision*) kettei 決定; (*resolve*) késshín 決心

determine (*to do*) *v* kettei shimásu (suru, shite) 決定します(する, して)

determined *adj* ketsuzen to shita 決然とした

detest *v* nikumimásu (nikúmu, nikúnde) 憎みます(憎む, 憎んで)

detour *n* mawari-michi 回り道・まわり道, ukai 迂回, tō´máwari 遠回り

devastate *v* arashimásu (arásu, aráshite) 荒らします(荒らす, 荒らして)

develop *v* 1. (*it unfolds*) hattatsu/hatten shimásu (suru, shite) 発達/発展します(する, して) 2. (*processes film*) genzō´ shimásu (suru, shite) 現像します(する, して)

developing nation *n* hatten tojō´-koku 発展途上国, kōshinkoku 後進国

development *n* hattatsu 発達, hatten 発展, kaihatsu 開発, (*process*) nariyuki 成り行き・なりゆき, (*course*) keika 経過; *housing ~* danchi 団地

deviate *v* soremásu (soréru, sórete) それ[逸れ]ます(それる, それて)

device *n* (*gadget*) shikake 仕掛け・しかけ; (*scheme*) kufū 工夫

devil *n* (*ogre*) oní 鬼・オニ, (*Satan*) ákuma 悪魔

devil's-tongue *n* (*root made into gelatin*) konnyáku コンニャク・蒟蒻

dew *n* tsúyu 露・つゆ

diabetes *n* tō´nyō´-byō´ 糖尿病

diagonal *adj* nanáme (no) 斜め(の)

diagram *n* zu 図, zuhyō´ 図表, zukai 図解

dial *n* (*telephone*) daiyaru ダイヤル

dialect *n* hō´gén 方言; (*regional accent*) namarí なまり

dialogue *n* 1. (*lines*) serifu せりふ 2. (*conversation*) taiwa 対話, kaiwa 会話

dial tone *n* hasshin-on 発信音

diameter *n* chokkei 直径

diamond *n* daiya ダイヤ, daiyamóndo ダイヤモンド, kongō´-seki 金剛石

diapers *n* oshíme おしめ, omútsu おむつ

diarrhea *n* geri 下痢・げり

diary *n* nikki 日記, daiarii ダイアリー

dice *n* saikóro さいころ・サイコロ

dichotomy *n* nibun 二分

dictation *n* kakítori 書き取り, dikutēshon ディクテーション

dictator *n* dokusái-sha 独裁者, wánman ワンマン

dictatorship *n* dokusai-seiji 独裁政治, dokusai-seiken 独裁政権

dictionary *n* jibikí 字引(き), jishó 辞書, jiten 辞典
dictionary entry *n* midashi 見出し, midashi-go 見出し語
did *v* shimáshita (shita, shite) しました (した, して)
didn't *v* shimasén deshita (shinákatta, shináide) しませんでした (しなかった, しないで)
die 1. *v* shinimásu (shinu, shinde) 死に ます(死ぬ, 死んで), naku-narimásu (naku-naru, naku-natte) 亡くなります (亡くなる, 亡くなって); íki o híki- torimásu (hiki-tóru, hiki-tótte) 息を引 き取ります (引き取る, 引き取って)
2. → *dice*
diesel *n* diizeru ディーゼル
diet *n* kitéi-shoku 規定食, daietto-shoku ダイエット食; daietto (shimásu; suru, shite) ダイエット(します; する, して)
Diet *n* (*parliament*) kokkai 国会, gikai 議会; (*building*) (kokkai) giji-dō 国会)議事堂
differ *v* kotonarimásu (kotonáru, koto- nátta) 異なります (異なる, 異なって); **~ in opinion** íken ga chigaimásu (chi- gau, chigatte) 意見が違います(違う, 違って)
difference *n* chigai 違い, sō´i 相違, sa 差, sái 差異; (*a big difference*) táisa 大差; **~ in time** jísa 時差; **it makes no ~** kamaimasén (kamawánai, kamawá- naide) 構いません(構わない, 構わな いで)
different *adj is* ~ chigaimásu (chigau, chigatte) 違います(違う, 違って); kotonarimásu (kotonáru, kotonátte) 異なります(異なる, 異なって); **a ~ direction** tahō´ 他方; **~ opinion/view** iron 異論 (= *objection*)
differentiation *n* kúbetsu 区別
difficult *adj* muzukashii 難しい・むず かしい; kónnan (na) 困難(な); (*hard to do*) shi-nikúi しにくい, shi-gatai し がたい; (*requires much effort*) honé ga oremásu (oréru, órete) 骨が折れます (折れる, 折れて)
difficulty *n* kónnan 困難; (*hardship*) kurō´ 苦労; (*problem*) mondai 問題; (*nuisance*) mendó´ 面倒・めんどう;

with ~ yatto やっと
diffusion *n* fukyū´ 普及; **gets diffused** fukyū shimásu (suru, shite) 普及しま す(する, して)
dig *v* horimásu (hóru, hótte) 掘ります (掘る, 掘って)
digest *v* konashimásu (konasu, konas- híte) こなします(こなす, こなして), shō´ka shimásu (suru, shite) 消化しま す(する, して)
digestion *n* shō´ka 消化
digit *n* **1.** (*Arabic figures*) (arabia) sūji (アラビア)数字 **2.** (*digit number*) ketasū 桁数 **3.** (*finger or toe*) yubi 指
digital *n* dejitaru デジタル
dignified *adj* igen no aru 威厳のある
dignitary *n* kōkan 高官
dignity *n* **1.** (*nobility*) hin(-sei) 品(性), kihin 気品 **2.** (*respect and honor*) songen 尊厳; **death with ~** songen-shi 尊厳死
digress *v* soremásu (soréru, sórete) それ[逸れ]ます(それる, それて)
digression *n* dassen 脱線, yodan 余談
dike *n* (*levee*) tsutsumí 堤・つつみ, dote 土手, teibō´ 堤防
dilapidated; gets ~ aremásu (areru, arete) 荒れます(荒れる, 荒れて)
dilemma *n* tō´waku 当惑, jirenma ジレンマ
diligent *adj* kinben (na) 勤勉(な), mame (na) まめ(な)
diligently *adv* kinben ni 勤勉に; sésse- to せっせと
dilute 1. *v* (*dilutes it*) (mizu de) wari- másu (waru, watte) (水で)割ります (割る, 割って), usumemásu (usumeru, usumete) 薄めます(薄める, 薄めて) **2.** *adj* (*dilute acid*) nōdo ga usui 濃度 が薄い
dim 1. *adj* (*faint*) kásuka (na) かすか・ 微か(な), (*dark*) kurai 暗い **2.** *v* (*gets dim, hazy*) kasumimásu (kasumu, kasunde) かすみ[霞み]ます(かすむ, かすんで)
dime *n* jussento kōka 10セント硬貨
dimple *n* ékubo えくぼ
din *n* sōon 騒音
dine *v* shokuji (o) shimásu (suru, shite) 食事(を)します(する, して)

diner *n* (*dining car*) shokudō´-sha 食堂車

dingey, dinghy *n* (*boat*) (kogata) bōto (小型)ボート

dining room *n* shokudō´食堂, daini'ngu rūmu ダイニングルーム

dinner *n* (*meal*) shokuji 食事, góhan ご飯・ごはん, (*supper*) ban góhan 晩ご飯, yūshoku 夕食, yū gohan 夕ご飯, yū-han/yū-meshi 夕飯

dinner jacket *n* takishiido タキシード

dinosaur *n* kyōryū 恐竜

diploma *n* **1.** menjō´ 免状 **2.** (*graduation diploma*) sotsugyō-shōsho 卒業証書

diplomacy *n* gaikō´ 外交

diplomat *n* (*diplomatic official*) gaikō´-kan 外交官; (*diplomatic person*) gaikō´-ka 外交家

diplomatic *adj* gaikō´-teki (na) 外交的(な); gaikō´ (no) 外交(の); ~ *in manner* sotsu no nai… そつのない
diplomatic relations *n* gaikō´ 外交

direct 1. *adj* chokusetsu (no) 直接(の); *goes* ~ (*through to destination*) chokusetsu ikimásu 直接行きます **2.** *v* (*tells the way*) (michi o) oshiemásu (oshieru, oshiete) (道を)教えます(教える, 教えて) **3.** *v* (*guides, coaches*) shidō´ shimásu (suru, shite) 指導します(する, して); (*a film*) kantoku (suru, shite) 監督します(する, して)

direct current *n* chokuryu 直流

direction *n* **1.** hō´kō´ 方向; kentō´ 見当; hō´mén 方面; … (no) hō´ …(の)方; hō´gaku 方角 **2.** *directions* (*instructions*) shíji 指示, oshie 教え; *gives directions (to a destination)* michi o oshiemásu (oshieru, oshiete) 道を教えます(教える, 教えて)

directive *n* shirei 指令

directly *adv* chokusetsu (ni) 直接(に), zutto ずっと, jika-ni じかに・直に, (*immediately*) sugu ni すぐに, (*shortly*) ma-mó-naku 間もなく・まもなく

director *n* **1.** (*coach*) shidō´-sha 指導者 **2.** (*of a film*) kantoku 監督, direkutā ディレクター

directory *n* (*telephone*) denwa-chō´ 電話帳; (*list of names*) meibo 名簿

dirt *n* yogore 汚れ; (*filth*) doró 泥・ドロ; (*grime*) aká あか・垢; (*soil*) tsuchí 土

dirt-cheap *adj* kakuyasu (no) 格安(の), tada dōzen (no) ただ同然(の)

dirty 1. *adj* kitanái 汚い, fuketsu (na) 不潔(な) **2.** *adj* (*dirty-minded*) gehin (na) 下品(な); étchi (na) エッチ(な); ~ *story* hiwai na hanashi 卑猥[ひわい]な話 **3.** *v gets* ~ yogoremásu (yogoreru, yogorete) 汚れます(汚れる, 汚れて) **4.** *v dirties it* yogoshimásu (yogosu, yogoshite) 汚します(汚す, 汚して)

disability *n* shintai-shōgai 身体障害

disadvantage *n* són 損, fúri 不利; (*shortcoming*) ketten 欠点, mainasu マイナス, tánsho 短所

disagreeable *adj* iyá (na) 嫌・いや(な), fuyukai (na) 不愉快(な)

disagreement *n* fu-itchi 不一致

disappointed *adj* zan'nen (na) 残念(な); *gets* ~ gakkári shimásu (suru, shite) がっかりします(する, して)

disappointing *adj* shitsubō saseru 失望させる

disappointment *n* shitsubō´ 失望, kitai hazure 期待はずれ, rakutan 落胆; (*in love*) shitsuren 失恋

disapprobation *n* fu-sansei 不賛成

disapproval *n* **1.** (*disapprobation*) fu-sansei 不賛成, (*nonrecognition*) fu-shōnin 不承認 **2.** (*accusation*) hinan 非難

disarmament *n* busō-kaijo 武装解除, gunbi-shukushō 軍備縮小

disarray *n* konran 混乱, mu-chitsujo 無秩序

disassemble *v* barashimásu (barásu, baráshite) ばらします(ばらす, ばらして)

disaster *n* sō´nan 遭難, sainán 災難, wazawai 災い; *has a* ~ sō´nan shimásu (suru, shite) 遭難します(する, して)

disaster area *n* hisai-chi 被災地

disastrous *adj* taihen (na) 大変(な)

discard *v* sutemásu (suteru, sutete) 捨てます(捨てる, 捨てて)

discern *v* **1.** (*discriminates*) shikibetsu shimásu (suru, shite) 識別します(する, して) **2.** → see

discharge v (*from employment*) káiko shimásu (suru, shite) 解雇します(する, して)

disciple n deshí 弟子

discipline 1. n kiritsu 規律, chitsujo 秩序; shitsuke しつけ **2.** v (*drills, trains*) kitaemásu (kitaéru, kitáete) 鍛えます(鍛える, 鍛えて), (*brings up children, ...*) shitsukemásu (shitsukéru, shitsúkete) しつけます(しつける, しつけて)

disclose v (*public*) kōkai shimásu (suru, shite) 公開します(する, して); abakimásu (abaku, abaite) 暴きます (暴く, 暴いて); *is disclosed* barémásu (baréru, baréte) ばれます(ばれる, ばれて)

disco n disuko ディスコ

discomfort n fukai(-kan) 不快(感)

disconnect v hazushimásu (hazusu, hazushite) 外します(外す, 外して), hanashimásu (hanásu, hanáshite) 離します(離す, 離して), kirimásu (kiru, kitte) 切ります(切る, 切って)

disconnected; gets ~ (*comes off*) hazuremásu (hazureru, hazurete) 外れます(外れる, 外れて)

discontent n (*grumbling*) fuhei 不平, fuman 不満

discontented adj fuman (na) 不満(な)

discount n wari-biki 割引, ne-biki 値引き

discourage v ki o kujikimásu (kujíku, kujíite) 気をくじきます(くじく, くじいて); *gets discouraged* ki ga kujikemásu (kujikéru, kujíkete) 気がくじけます(くじける, くじけて)

discourtesy n búrei 無礼, shitsúrei 失礼

discover v **1.** (*finds*) mitsukemásu (mitsukeru, mitsukete) 見つけます(見つける, 見つけて), hakken shimásu (suru, shite) 発見します(する, して) → *find out* **2.** *is discovered* baré-másu (baréru, baréte) ばれます(ばれる, ばれて); abakaremásu (abakareru, abakarete) 暴かれます(暴かれる, 暴かれて)

discovery n hakken 発見; *Discovery Channel* disukabarii channeru ディスカバリー・チャンネル

discrepancy n chigai 違い, sa 差, sṓi 相違, kuichigai 食い違い; (*gap*) zuré ずれ

discretion n tsutsushimi 慎み・つつしみ, funbetsu 分別

discriminate v (*distinguishes them*) mi-wakemásu (mi-wakeru, mi-wakete) 見分けます(見分ける, 見分けて), shikibetsu shimásu (suru, shite) 識別します(する, して)

discrimination n sábetsu 差別; kúbetsu 区別; (*distinguishing*) shiki-betsu 識別

discuss v (*talks it over*) hanashi-aimásu (hanashi-au, hanashi-atte) 話し合います(話し合う, 話し合って), sō'dan shimásu (suru, shite) 相談します(する, して); (*debates, argues*) ron-jimásu (ron-jiru, ron-jite) 論じます(論じる, 論じて)

discussion n hanashi-ai 話し合い; hanashí 話・はなし; kyō'gi 協議, (*argument*) rón 論, (*debate*) tō'ron 討論, ronsō' 論争; (*roundtable discussion*) zadán-kai 座談会

disease n byō'ki 病気

disembark v jō'riku shimásu (suru, shite) 上陸します(する, して)

disgrace n hají 恥・はじ; chijoku 恥辱, ojoku 汚辱; *~ oneself* hají o kakimásu (káku, káite) 恥をかきます (かく, かいて)

disgraceful adj hazukashíi 恥ずかしい

disgusted; gets ~ akiremásu (akireru, akirete) 呆れます(呆れる, 呆れて); iyá ni narimásu (náru, nátte) 嫌に[いやに]なります(なる, なって)

disgusting adj iyá (na) 嫌・いや(な)

dish n sara 皿 (o-sara お皿); shokki 食器; (*how many*) nán-mai 何枚

dishcloth, dishtowel n fukín ふきん・布巾

dishearten → discourage

dishonest adj fu-seijitsu (na/no) 不誠実(な/の), fu-shōjiki (na/no) 不正直(な/の), fusei (na/no) 不正(な/の)

dishpan n arai-óke 洗い桶

dish rack n shokkí-dana 食器棚

dishwasher n shokkí arai-ki 食器洗い機

disinfectant *n* shō´dokú-yaku/zai 消毒薬/剤

dislikable *adj* nikúi 憎い, iyá (na) 嫌・いや(な)

dislike *v* ... ga kirai désu (iyá desu) ...が嫌いです(嫌です・いやです)...o iya-gari-másu (iya-gáru, iya-gátte) ...を嫌がります(嫌がる, 嫌がって)

dismal *adj* (*gloomy*) uttō´shíí うっとうしい

dismiss *v* (*from employment*) káiko shimásu (suru, shite) 解雇します(する, して)

dismissal *n* (*from employment*) káiko 解雇; (*of servant*) hima 暇・ひま

disobedient *adj* hankō-teki (na) 反抗的(な)

disobey *v* ... ni somukimásu (somúku, somúite) ...に背きます(背く, 背いて)

disorder *n* konran 混乱, kónzatsu 混雑, midaré 乱れ・みだれ, yamí 闇; *in* ~ mechamecha めちゃめちゃ

disorderly *adj* ranbō´ (na) 乱暴(な)

dispatched from/at [TIME/PLACE] ... hátsu (no) ...発(の)

dispensary *n* yakkyoku 薬局

disperse *v* (*they scatter*) chirimásu (chiru, chitte) 散ります(散る, 散って)

display → **show**

displease *v* fu-yúkai ni shimásu (suru, shite) 不愉快にします(する, して)

displeased *adj* fu-kigen (na) 不機嫌(な)

displeasing *adj* fu-yúkai (na) 不愉快(な)

dispose *v* shímatsu shimásu (suru, shite) 始末します(する, して); shóri shimásu (suru, shite) 処理します(する, して)

disposition *n* **1.** seishitsu 性質; (*nature*) táchi たち・質, shō´性; (*temperament*) ténsei 天性; (*attitude*) táido 態度 **2.** (*dealing with*) shóri 処理, shóbun 処分, shóchi 処置

dispute *n* arasoi 争い, tō´ron 討論, sō´ron 争論

dissatisfied *adj* fuman (na) 不満(な)

dissertation *n* ronbun 論文, (*for a degree*) gakui-rónbun 学位論文, (*doctoral*) hakase-rónbun 博士論文

dissipation *n* dō´raku 道楽

dissolve *v* (*dissolves it*) tokashimásu (tokasu, tokáshite) 溶かします(溶かす, 溶かして); (*it dissolves*) tokemásu (tokéru, tókete) 溶けます(溶ける, 溶けて)

distance *n* kyóri 距離

distant *adj* (*far*) tō´i 遠い, háruka (na) はるか・遥か(な); *gets* ~ hedatarimásu (hedatáru, hedátte) 隔たります(隔たる, 隔たって)

distilled liquor *n* (*from yam or rice*) shō´chū´ 焼酎

distilled water *n* jō´ryū´-sui 蒸留水

distinct *adj* hakkíri to shimásu (suru, shite) はっきりとします(する, して)

distinctly *adv* hakkíri はっきり

distinguish *v* (*discriminates*) mi-wakemásu (mi-wakeru, mi-wakete) 見分けます(見分ける, 見分けて), shikibetsu shimásu (suru, shite) 識別します(する, して)

distort *v* yugamemásu (yugameru, yugamete) ゆがめます(ゆがめる, ゆがめて); *gets distorted* yugamimásu (yugamu, yugande) ゆがみます(ゆがむ, ゆがんで)

distortion *n* yugami ゆがみ・歪み

distract *v* ki o chirashimásu (chirasu, chirashite) 気を散らします(散らす, 散らして)

distress 1. *n* nayamí 悩み, kurushimi 苦しみ **2.** *v* (*afflicts*) kurushimemásu (kurushiméru, kurushímete) 苦しめます(苦しめる, 苦しめて); *gets distressed* kurushimimásu (kurushímu, kurushínde) 苦しみます(苦しむ, 苦しんで)

distribute *v* kubarimásu (kubáru, kubátte) 配ります(配る, 配って); wakemásu (wakéru, wákete) 分けます(分ける, 分けて)

distribution *n* ryūtsū 流通

district *n* chihō 地方; hō´mén 方面, ...-hō´men ...方面

disturb *v* (... no) jama o shimásu (suru, shite) (...の)じゃま[邪魔]をします(する, して)

disturbance *n* (*intrusion*) (o-)jama (お)じゃま・邪魔; (*unrest*) sō´dō´ 騒動; (*strife*) arasoi 争い, rán 乱

disused adj fuyō´ (no) 不要(の)

ditch 1. n mizo 溝; horí 堀 **2.** v mizo o horimásu (horu, hotte) 溝を掘ります(掘る、掘って)

dive (under) v mogurimásu (mogúru, mogútte) 潜ります(潜る、潜って), tobikomimásu (tobikomu, tobikonde) 飛び込みます(飛び込む、飛び込んで), daibingu shimásu (suru, shite) ダイビングします(する、して)

diver n daibā´ ダイバー; (woman pearl diver) áma 海女・あま

diverse adj sama zama (na) さまざま・様々(な)

divide v (divides it) warimásu (waru, watte) 割ります(割る、割って), wakemásu (wakéru, wákete) 分けます(分ける、分けて); (it divides) waremásu (wareru, warete) 割れます(割れる、割れて); wakaremásu (wakaréru, wakárete) 分かれます(分かれる、分かれて); ~ roughly (into main categories) taibetsu shimásu (suru, shite) 大別します(する、して)

diving (sports) n sensui 潜水, daibingu ダイビング

diving board n tobikomi-dai 飛び込み台, tobikomi-ban 飛び込み板

dividing line n wake-mé 分け目

divine message n otsuge お告げ

division n bú 部; (army) shídan 師団; (branching) wakaré 分かれ; (math calculation) warízan 割り算

divorce 1. n rikon 離婚; gets divorced from …to rikon shimásu (suru, shite) …と離婚します(する、して) **2.** v rikon shimásu (suru, shite) 離婚します(する、して)

DIY adj (do-it-yourself; building or repairing things for oneself) nichiyō-daiku (no) 日曜大工(の)

dizzy adj **1.** me ga mararu 目が回る; feel ~ memai ga shimásu (suru, shite) めまいがします(する、して) **2.** baka-geta ばかげた

do v shimásu (suru, shite) します(する、して), yarimásu (yaru, yatte) やります(やる、やって); nashimásu (násu, náshite) なします(なす、なして); (performs) okonaimásu (okonau,

okonatte) 行います(行う、行って); [HONORIFIC] nasaimásu (nasáru, nasátte, nasaimáshite) なさいます(なさる、なさって、なさいまして); [HUMBLE, DEFERENTIAL] itashimásu (itasu, itashite, itashimáshite) 致します・いたします(致す、致して、致しまして); ~ it (deprecating object) yarakashimásu (yarakasu, yarakashite) やらかします(やらかす、やらかして); ~ it over (again) yari-naoshimásu (yari-naósu, yari-naóshite) やり直します(やり直す、やり直して)

docile adj súnao (na) 素直(な)

dock n dókku ドック, ganpeki 岸壁

doctor n **1.** (physician) (o-)isha(-san) (お)医者(さん), sensái 先生 **2.** (Ph.D.) hákase 博士・はかせ

   doctor's office n (clinic) byō´in 病院, íin 医院

doctoral degree n hakase gō 博士号

doctoral dissertation n hakase rónbun 博士論文

doctrine n shúgi 主義

document n shorui 書類, bunsho 文書, bunken 文献

documentary n dokyumentarii ドキュメンタリー

dodge v (turns it aside) sorashimásu (sorásu, soráshite) そらします(そらす、そらして)

does → do; doesn't → don't

dog n inú 犬・イヌ (**1:** ip-pikí 一匹, **2:** ní-hiki 二匹, **3:** sánbiki 三匹; how many nán-biki 何匹)

   dog tag (dog license) inú no kansa-tsu 犬の鑑札; (name tag) na fuda 名札

doll n ningyō´ 人形・にんぎょう (o-ningyō´ お人形); festival ~ hina-níngyō´ ひな人形・雛人形

   Doll's Festival n (3 March) Hina-mátsuri ひな祭(り)・雛祭(り)

dollar n dóru ドル

dolphin n iruka イルカ

domestic adj (not foreign) kokúnai (no) 国内(の); (domestically made) kokusan (no) 国産(の)

   domestic help n otetsudai(-san) お手伝い(さん), kaji-tetsudai 家事手伝い

domesticate v narashimásu (narásu,

narásh<u>i</u>te) 慣らします(慣らす, 慣らして)

domino *n* domino ドミノ

done *v* (*ready*) dekimásh<u>i</u>ta 出来ました, dék<u>i</u>te imás<u>u</u> (iru, ite) 出来ています(いる, いて); (*finished*) (sh<u>i</u>-)te sh<u>i</u>maimásh<u>i</u>ta (shimatta, shimatte) (し)てしまいました(しまった, しまって)

half-done *adj* (*cooked medium*) hanyake (no) 半焼け(の)

underdone *adj* (*cooked rare*) namayake (no) 生焼け(の), (*beef*) réa レア

well-done *adj* yóku yaketa 良[よ]く焼けた, (*beef*) wérudan ウェルダン

donkey *n* róba ロバ

don't *v* shimasén (shinai, shináide) しません(しない, しないで)

don't (do it)! *interj* (sh<u>i</u>té wa) damé desu/da (しては)だめです/だ, ikemasén (ikenai) いけません(いけない); (sh<u>i</u>-)náide kudasai (し)ないで下[く]さい; *Don't be shy/ reticent.* Go-enryo náku. ご遠慮なく., *Don't feel you have to rush.* Go-yukkúri. ごゆっくり., *Don't go to any trouble.* Okamai náku. おかまいなく., *Don't worry about it.* Go-shinpai náku. ご心配なく.

doodling *n* rakugaki 落書き・らくがき

door *n* to 戸, dóa ドア; (*hinged*) hirakido 開き戸; (*opaque sliding*) fusuma ふすま・襖; **~ wing, ~ of a gate** tobira 扉・とびら

doorbell *n* suzu 鈴・スズ, béru ベル, yobirin 呼び鈴

doorknob *n* doa nobu ドアノブ

dope *n* (*narcotic*) mayaku 麻薬

dormitory *n* sh<u>i</u>shúkusha 寄宿舎, ryō´ 寮

dose *n* ikkai-ryō 一回量, ikkai-bun 一回分

dot *n* ten 点・てん, póchi ぽち, pótsu ぽつ; (*with*) *dots* bótsu bótsu ぽつぽつ

double 1. *adj* bai (no) 倍(の), (*two-layer*) ni-jū (no) 二重(の)

double bed *n* daburu-béddo ダブルベッド

double boiler *n* nijū-nábe 二重なべ

double (room) *n* dáburu ダブル, daburu-rū´mu ダブルルーム, daburu-

beddo-tsuki no heya ダブルベッド付きの部屋

doubles *n* (*tennis*) dáburusu ダブルス

double(-size) drink *n* dáburu ダブル **2.** *doubles it* *v* (…o) bai ni shimás<u>u</u> (suru, sh<u>i</u>te) (…を)倍にします(する, して)

double bass *n* kontorabasu コントラバス

double-breasted suit *n* dáburu ダブル

double-check *v* nén o oshimás<u>u</u> (osu, oshite) 念を押します(押す, 押して); saíkakunin shimás<u>u</u> (suru, sh<u>i</u>te) 再確認します(する, して)

double-cross 1. *n* (*treachery*) uragiri 裏切り **2.** *v* ura-girimás<u>u</u> (ura-giru, ura-gítte) 裏切ります(裏切る, 裏切って)

double-decker *n* nikaidate basu 二階建てバス

double plug *n* (*two-way socket*) futamata-sokétto 二又ソケット

double suicide *n* shinjū 心中

doubt 1. *n* gimon 疑問, utagai 疑い, fushin 不審 **2.** *v* (*doubts it*) utagaimás<u>u</u> (utagau, utagatte) 疑います(疑う, 疑って), fushin ni omoimás<u>u</u> (omóu, omótte) 不審に思います(思う, 思って)

douche *n* chūsúi-ki 注水器

dough *n* pan-kíji パン生地

doughnut *n* dōnatsu ドーナツ

dove *n* háto 鳩・ハト

down *prep, adv* sh<u>i</u>ta e 下へ; *down* (*lower in price by*) *¥100* hyaku én-yasu 百円安

get down orimás<u>u</u> (oríru, órite) 下ります[降ります]・おります(下りる, 下りて)

go down kudarimás<u>u</u> (kudaru, kudatte) 下ります・くだります(下りる, 下りて), sagarimás<u>u</u> (sagáru, sagátte) 下ります・さがります(下る, 下がって)

hang down taremás<u>u</u> (taréru, tárete) 垂れます(垂れる, 垂れて), sagemás<u>u</u> (sagéru, ságete) 下げます(下げる, 下げて)

lie down nemás<u>u</u> (neru, nete) 寝ます(寝る, 寝て)

take down oroshimás<u>u</u> (orósu, oróshite) 下ろします(下ろす, 下ろして)

download v (*computer*) daunrōdo shimásu (suru, shite) ダウンロードします(する, して)

downpayment n atama-kin 頭金

downpour n gō´u 豪雨, doshaburi 土砂降り; *local downpour* shūchū-gō´u 集中豪雨

downstairs n kaika 階下

downtown n hanka-gai 繁華街

doze v úto uto shimásu (suru, shite) うとうとします(する, して); *~ off* inemúri shimásu (suru, shite) 居眠りします(する, して)

dozen n (ichi-) dā´su (一) ダース, jū-ní 十二・12

Dr. … n (*physician*) … senséi …先生

draft 1. n (*rough*) shitagaki 下書き, dorafuto ドラフト; (*military conscription*) shō´shū (shimásu; suru, shite) 召集((します; する, して) 2. n (*beer*) náma 生, náma bíiru 生ビール 3. n (*call-up*) shō´shū/chōhē (shimásu; suru, shite) 召集/徴兵(します; する, して)

drag v hipparimásu (hippáru, hippátte) 引っ張ります(引っ張る, 引っ張って), hikimásu (hiku, hiite) 引きます(引く, 引いて), hiki-zurimásu (hiki-zuru, hiki-zutte) 引きずります(引きずる, 引きずって)

dragnet n téhái 手配; *sets up a ~* téhái shimásu (suru, shite) 手配します(する, して)

dragon n ryū 竜・龍, tatsu 竜・たつ, doragon ドラゴン

dragonfly n tonbo トンボ

drain 1. n (*kitchen*) gesui 下水; (*ditch*) mizo 溝 2. *it drains off* v hakemásu (hakéru, hákete) はけます(はける, はけて); *it drains well* (mizu) haké ga íi désu (水)はけがいいです

drain pipe n tói とい・樋

drama n engeki 演劇, géki 劇, dorama ドラマ

dramatic adj géki-teki (na) 劇的(な)

draperies k tanmono 反物

drapes n kā´ten カーテン

draw 1. v (*a picture*) egakimásu (egáku, egáite) 描きます(描く, 描いて) 2. v (*pulls*) hikimásu (hiku, hiite) 引きます(引く, 引いて); *~ out* hiki-dashimásu (hiki-dasu, hiki-dashite) 引き出します(引き出す, 引き出して); *~ an underline* kasen o hikimásu (hiku, hiite) 下線を引きます(引く, 引いて) 3. v (*water etc.*) kumimásu (kumu, kunde) 汲みます(汲む, 汲んで) 4. v *~ apart* hiki-wakemásu (hiki-wakeru, hiki-wakete) 引き分けます(引き分ける, 引き分けて) 5. n (*game*) hikiwake 引き分け

drawer n (*of desk, etc.*) hiki-dashi 引き出し・ひきだし

drawers n (*underwear*) zubon-shíta ズボン下, momohíki 股引き, (*for woman*) zurō´su ズロース

drawing n (*diagram*) zu 図; (*picture*) é 絵

drawing room n (*parlor*) kyakuma 客間

draw near → approach

dread v 1. osoremásu (osoreru, osorete) 恐れます(恐れる, 恐れて)

dreadful adj osoroshíi 恐ろしい, sugói すごい, hidoi ひどい

dream n yumé (o mimásu; míru, míte) 夢(をみます; みる, みて); *American ~* american doriimu アメリカンドリーム

dreary adj uttō´shíi うっとうしい

dregs n kásu かす; ori おり

dress 1. n ki-mono 着物; yō´-fuku 洋服, fukú 服, fukusō 服装, (*woman's*) wanpíisu ワンピース, dóresu ドレス 2. v (*wears*) fukú o kimásu (kiru, kíte) 服を着ます(着る, 着て) 3. (*dresses vegetables, fish*) aemásu (aéru, áete) 和えます(和える, 和えて)

dressing gown n gaun ガウン

dressmaker n yō´sai-shi 洋裁師, doresu-mē´ka ドレスメーカー

dressmaking n yō´sai 洋裁

dried 1. adj hoshí-…, hí-…; *~ persimmons* hoshí-gaki 干し柿 2. → dry

dried bonito fish n katsuo-bushi カツオブシ・鰹節

dried gourd strips n kanpyō´カンピョウ

drill 1. n (*tool*) kíri きり・錐 2. n (*practice*) doriru ドリル, (o-)kéi ko (お)けいこ・稽古; (*study*) renshū

練習; (*training*) kúnren 訓練 **3.** *v*
(*trains*) nerimásu (néru, nétte) 練り
ます(練る, 練って), kúnren shimásu
(suru, shite) 訓練します(する, して),
(*disciplines*) kitaemásu (kitaeru,
kitáete) 鍛えます(鍛える, 鍛えて)
drink 1. *n* (*beverage*) nomí-mono 飲み
物・のみもの; **one ~** hitó-kuchi 一口;
has a ~ íp-pai nomimásu/yarimásu 一
杯飲みます/やります **2.** *v* nomimásu
(nómu, nónde) 飲みます(飲む, 飲
んで); [HONORIFIC] meshiagarimásu
(meshiagaru, meshiagatte) 召し上がり
ます・めしあがります(召し上がる,
召し上がって); [HUMBLE] itadakimásu
(itadaku, itadaite) いただきます(いた
だく, いただいて)
drinkable; is ~ nomemásu (noméru,
nómete) 飲める(飲める, 飲めて)
drinking water *n* nomí-mizu 飲み水
drip *v* taremásu (taréru, tárete) 垂れま
す(垂れる, 垂れて)
drive *v* (*a car*) unten shimásu (suru,
shite) 運転します(する, して), doraibu
shimásu (suru, shite) ドライブします
(する, して)
drive *n* (*what one is driving at*) iitai-koto
言いたい事, nerai ねらい・狙い
drive-in *n* nori-komi 乗り込み
driver *n* untén-shu 運転手, doraibā
ドライバー
driver license *n* untén-menkyo-shō
運転免許証
driveway *n* shadō' 車道
drizzle *n* kosame 小雨; (*on-and-off*)
shigure 時雨・しぐれ
droll *adj* yúkai (na) ゆかい・愉快(な)
→ *funny*
drool *v* **is drooling** yodare ga deteimásu
(déteiru, déteite) よだれが出ています
(出ている, 出ていて)
droop *v* naemásu (naéru, náete) 萎え
[なえ]ます(萎える, 萎えて)
drop 1. *v* (*drops it*) otoshimásu (otósu,
otóshite) 落とします(落とす, 落と
して), (*lets it fall, spills*) tarashimásu
(tarásu, taráshite) 垂らします(垂らす,
垂らして) **2.** *v* (*it drops*) ochimásu
(ochíru, óchite) 落ちます(落ちる, 落
ちて) **3.** *n* (*a drop*) tsúbu 粒, tamá 玉;

(*counting*) …-teki …滴
drop in *v* yorimásu (yoru, yotte) 寄り
ます(寄る, 寄って)
drop off *v* (*a person from a vehicle*)
oroshimásu (orósu, oróshite) 降ろしま
す(降ろする, 降ろして)
drown *v* obore-jini shimásu (suru,
shite) おぼれ死にします(する, して)
drowse *v* útouto shimásu (suru, shite)
うとうとします(する, して)
drowsy *adj* nemui 眠い; darui ダルい
drudge *v* ákuseku hatarakimásu
(hataraku, hataraite) あくせく働きま
す(働く, 働いて)
drug *n* (*for patient*) kusuri 薬(o-kusúri
お薬), (*chemical substances*) yakuhin
薬品
drug addict *n* mayaku-chūdoku-sha 麻
薬中毒者
druggist *n* kusuri-ya (san) 薬屋(さん)
drugstore *n* kusuri-ya 薬屋, yakkyoku
薬局
drum *n* (*Japanese-style*) taiko 太鼓・
たいこ, (*large*) ō'-daiko 大太鼓;
(*hourglass-shaped*) tsuzumí 鼓・つづ
み, (*small*) ko-tsúzumi 小鼓, (*Western-
style*) doramu ドラム
drunk; gets ~ yopparaimásu (yopparau,
yopparatte) 酔っぱらいます(酔っぱ
らう, 酔っぱらって); yoimásu (yóu,
yótte) 酔います(酔う, 酔って)
dry *v* (*it dries*) kawakimásu (kawáku,
kawáite) 乾きます(乾く, 乾いて),
kansō shimásu (suru, shite) 乾燥します
(する, して); (*dries it*) kawakimásu
(kawakasu, kawakáshite) 乾か
します(乾かす, 乾かして), (*foodstuff*)
hoshimásu (hósu, hóshite) 干します
(干す, 干して)
dry cleaning *n* dorai-kuríiníngu ドラ
イクリーニング
dry goods *n* tanmono 反物, gofuku 呉服
dry land *n* oka おか・陸
dub *v* (*names*) nazukemásu (nazukéru,
nazúkete) 名付けます(名付ける, 名
付けて)
duck *n* (*wild*) kámo カモ・鴨, (*tame*)
ahiru アヒル; (*canvas*) zúkku ズック
dude *n* mekashiya めかし屋; yatsu や
つ・奴

due 1. *dues* *n* kaihi 会費, ryōkin 料金
2. *adj* (*payment*) kijitsu no 期日 (の)
due date → **deadline**
due to → **because**
dull *adj* nibui 鈍い・にぶい, norói の
ろい; (*uninteresting*) taikutsu (na) 退
屈 (な), (*long-winded*) kudói くどい;
(*dull-witted*) wakarí ga waruí 分かり
が悪い
dumb *adj* **1.** (*stupid*) baka (na) ばか・
馬鹿 (な) **2.** (*unable to speak*) kuchi no
kikenai 口の利けない
dump 1. *v* (*discards*) sutemásu (suteru,
sutete) 捨てます (捨てる, 捨てて) **2.**
n (*dump site*) sute-ba 捨て場
dumpling *n* dango だんご・団子
(o-dango お団子); (*large stuffed bun*)
manjū まんじゅう・饅頭; (*small
meat-stuffed crescent*) gyō´za ギョウ
ザ・餃子
dune *n* sakyū 砂丘
dung *n* kusó クソ・糞, fún フン・糞
→ **excrement**
dupe *n* kámo カモ
duplicate *n, adj* **1.** (*double*) ni-jū (no)
二重 (の) **2.** → **copy**
during *prep* (...) no aida (ni) (...)の間
(に); ...-chū (ni) ...中 (に); **~ *the war***
senji-chū 戦時中
dust 1. *n* (*in air*) hokori ほこり・埃;
(*on ground, floor, etc.*) chiri ちり・塵;

(*in house*) gomí ごみ **2.** *v* (*dusts it*)
hatakimásu (hatáku, hatáite) はたきま
す (はたく, はた いて)
dustbin *n* gomi-bako ゴミ箱・ごみ箱
dustcloth *n* zō´kin ぞうきん・雑巾
duster *n* zō´kin ぞうきん・雑巾;
hatakí はたき
dustpan *n* chiri-tóri ちり取り
Dutch 1. *adj* Oranda no オランダの **2.**
n (*language*) Oranda-go オランダ語
3. *n* (*person*) Orandá-jin オランダ人
Dutch treat *n* wari-kan 割り勘・ワ
リカン
duty *n* **1.** (*obligation*) gímu 義務 **2.**
(*function*) yakumé 役目 (o-yakume
お役目), yakú 役 (o-yaku お役),
honbun 本分; (*job, post*) tsutomé 務め
(o-tsutome お務め), yakú 役 (o-yaku
お役); (*work, service*) kínmu 勤務;
those on ~ kinmú-sha 勤務者; *the
person on ~* tō´ban 当番 (o-tō´ban お
当番) **3.** (*import tax*) kanzei 関税,
yunyū-zei 輸入税 **4.** → **off duty**
dwarf trees *n* bonsai 盆栽
dwindle *v* herimásu (heru, hette) 減りま
す (減る, 減って), sukúnaku narimásu
(náru, nátte) 少なくなります (なる, な
って)
dye (*it*) *v* somemásu (someru, somete)
染めます (染める, 染めて)
dysentery *n* sékiri 赤痢

E

each *pron* [NUMBER, QUANTITY +] ...
zútsu ...ずつ; (*every*) mai-...毎...,
káku(-) ... 各..., ... goto (ni) ...毎・
ごと (に)
each other *pron* o-tagai (ni) お互い
(に); [VERB-i] -aimásu (-au/-áu, -atte/-
átte) [VERB-い] 合います (合う, 合って)
eager *adj* nésshín (na) 熱心 (な),
setsubō shiteiru 切望している; **~ *to*** (*do*)
zé-hi ... (shi-) tai ぜひ...(し) たい,
(*concerning another person's
behavior*) (shi-) tagarimásu (tagáru,
tagátte) (し) たがります (たがる, た
がって)
eager beaver *n* ganbari-ya 頑張り屋

・がんばり屋, (*workaholic*) shigoto
no mushi 仕事の虫
eagerly *adv* nésshín (ni) 熱心 (に)
eagerness *n* netsui 熱意, netsuretsu
熱烈, nesshin 熱心
eagle *n* washi ワシ・鷲
ear *n* mimí 耳・みみ
  earache *n* mimi no itamí 耳の痛み
  ear buzzing *n* mimi-nari 耳鳴り
  ear doctor *n* jika-i 耳科医
  ear pad *n* mimiate 耳あて
eardrum *n* komaku 鼓膜・こまく
earl *n* hakushaku 伯爵
earlier *adj* (*former*) máe no ... 前の...;
[BOOKISH] zén(-) ... 前...

early 1. *adj* hayái 早い **2.** *adv* háyaku 早く; (*ahead of time*) hayame (ni) 早め (に); *one's ~ years* kodomo no koro 子供の頃

early bird *n* hayaoki (no hito) 早起き (の人)

earn *v* kasegimásu (kaségu, kaséide) 稼ぎます (稼ぐ, 稼いで)

earnest *adj* majime (na) まじめ(な), (*serious*) honki (no) 本気(の)

earnings *n* (*income*) shūnyū 収入, shotoku 所得

earphone *n* iyahon イヤホン, iyahōn イヤホーン

earpick *n* mimi-káki 耳かき

earpiece *n* (*of glass frame*) (megane no) tsurú (めがねの)つる; (*telephone*) juwá-ki 受話器

earplug *n* iya-puragu イヤプラグ, mimi-sen 耳栓

earring *n* íyaringu イヤリング, mimi-kázari 耳飾り

earshot *n* mimi no todoku kyori 耳の届[とど]く距離, kikoeru kyori 聞こえる距離

earth 1. *n* tsuchí 土, tochi 土地 **2.** *the Earth* chikyū 地球

earth and sand *n* dosha 土砂

earth axis *n* chi-jiku 地軸

what on earth *adv* ittai-zentai 一体全体

earthenware *n* doki 土器; tōki 陶器

earthquake *n* jishin 地震

earthworm *n* mimizu ミミズ

ease 1. *n* (*comfort*) rakú 楽

at ease jiyū (ni) 自由(に), yukkúri ゆっくり **2.** *eases it* *v* yasumemásu (yasuméru, yasúmete) 休めます (休める, 休めて)

easel *n* iizeru イーゼル, gaka 画架

easily *adv* **1.** tayásuku たやすく, wáke-naku わけなく, kantan (ni) 簡単(に), muzó'sa (ni) 無造作(に); assári (to) あっさり(と) **2.** → **undoubtedly**

easily broken koware-yasúí 壊れ[こわれ]やすい

easily intoxicated sake ni yowái 酒に弱い[よわい]

east *n* higashi 東, tō-... 東...; (*the east*) tōhō 東方, (*the eastern part*)

tō'bu 東部

East Asia *n* Higashi-Ájia 東アジア, Tō'a 東亜

east coast *n* higashi-káigan 東海岸

Easter *n* iisutā イースター, fukkatsu-sai 復活祭

Easter egg *n* iisutā eggu イースターエッグ

Easter holidays *n* fukkatsu-sai no kyūka 復活祭の休暇

easterly (*wind*) *n* higashi-yori (no kaze) 東寄り(の風)

East Europe *n* Higashi-yōroppa 東ヨーロッパ, Tō'ō 東欧

easy *adj* **1.** yasashii やさしい, tayasui たやすい, wákenai わけない, kantan 簡単, muzó'sa (na) 無造作(な); *easy (to do)* (shi-) yasúí (し)やすい; *~ to get to* ikiyasúí 行きやすい, *~ to understand* wakari-yasúí 分かりやすい **2.** → **comfortable**

easy chair *n* anraku isu 安楽いす

easy death *n* anraku-shi 安楽死

easy delivery *n* anzan 安産

easygoing *adj* nónki (na) のん気(な), kiraku (na) 気楽(な)

easy money *n* abukú-zéni あぶく銭

eat *v* tabemásu (tabéru, tábete) 食べます (食べる, 食べて), (*vulgar form*) kuimásu (kuu, kútte) 食います (食う, 食って); (*has a meal*) shokuji shimásu (suru, shíte) 食事します (する, して); [HONORIFIC] meshiagarimásu (meshiagaru, meshiagatte) 召し上がります (召し上がる, 召し上がって); [HUMBLE] itadakimásu (itadaku, itadaite) いただきます (いただく, いただいて)

eat out *v* gaishoku shimásu (suru, shíte) 外食します (する, して)

eat-in kitchen *n* dii-ke' (DK) ディーケー, dainingu-kítchin ダイニングキッチン

eaves *n* noki 軒, hisashi ひさし

ebauche *n* shitae 下絵

ebb 1. *n* hiki-shio 引き潮, kanchō 干潮 **2.** *v* otoroemásu (otoroeru, otoroéte) 衰えます (衰える, 衰えて)

ebb and flow *n* **1.** (*tide*) shio no michi-hiki 潮の満ち引き **2.** (*life*) (eiko) seisui (栄枯)盛衰

eccentric *n* **1.** fūgawari na hito 風変わりな人, ekisentorikku エキセントリック **2.** (*freak*) hen-jin 変人, ki-jin 奇人

echo *n* hibikí 響き, kodama こだま, hankyō 反響, ekō エコー **2.** *v* (*it echoes*) hibikimásu (hibíku, hibíite) 響きます (響く, 響いて)

éclair *n* ekurea エクレア

eclipse *n* **1.** (*sun*) nisshoku 日食 **2.** (*moon*) gesshoku 月食

ecologist *n* seitai-gakusha 生態学者

ecology *n* seitai-gaku 生態学, ekorojii エコロジー, seitai-kankyō 生態環境

e-commerce *n* denshi shō-torihiki 電子商取引, ii komāsu e-コマース

economic *adj* keizai-gaku (no) 経済学 (の), keizai (no) 経済(の)

economical *adj* keizai-teki (na) 経済 的(な); toku (na) (お)徳(な)

economics *n* kéizai 経済; (*science/ study*) keizái-gaku 経済学

economize *v* ... o ken'yaku/setuyaku shimásu (suru, shite) ...を倹約/節約 します(する, して), shimemásu (shiméru, shiméte) 締めます・しめます

economizing *n* (*saving*) setsuyaku 節約

economy *n* **1.** (*saving*) setsuyaku 節約 **2.** (*economics*) keizai 経済

economy class *n* ekonomii-kurasu エコノミークラス

economy-class syndrome *n* ekonomii-kurasu shōkō-gun エコノミークラス症候群

economy hotel *n* bijinesu hoteru ビジネスホテル

economy size *n* o-kaidoku saizu お買い得サイズ, o-toku saizu お得サイズ

ecstasy *n* **1.** (*sexual ecstasy, name of drug*) ekusutashii エクスタシー **2.** kōkotsu 恍惚; *in an ~ of* muga-muchū (de) 無我夢中で

ecumenical *n* (*general*) fuhen-teki (na) 普遍的(な) **2.** (*ecumenical movement*) kyōkai itchi undō (no) 教会一致運動(の) **3.** (*of Christian unity throughout the world*) sekai no kirisuto-kyōkai (no) 世界のキリスト教会(の)

eczema *n* shisshin 湿疹・しっしん

edge *n* fuchí ふち・縁, hashi 端・はし, hashikko/hajikko はしっこ/はじっこ, háta 端・はた, ejji エッジ, (*rim*) herí へり, (*brink*) kiwá 際, (*end*) tamotó たもと, (*nearby*) sóba そば; (*of knife*) ha (-saki) (刃)先

edacious *adj* kuishinbō (no) 食いしん坊・くいしん坊

edacity *n* taishoku 大食

edgy *adj* irairashita イライラした

edible **1.** *n* shokuryō-hin 食品料品 **2.** *adj* shokuyō (no) 食用(の)

edict *n* **1.** (*government decree*) seirei 政令 **2.** (*act*) hōrei 法令 **3.** (*command*) meirei 命令

edifice *n* (*large building*) dai-kenzō-butsu 大建造物, kyodai-kenchiku 巨大建築

edition *n* ban 版

editor *n* henshū-chō 編集長, editā エディター

editorial *n* shasetsu 社説

educate *v* (*rears*) sodatemásu (sodatéru, sodátete) 育てます(育てる, 育てて) → **teach**

education *n* kyōiku 教育; (*learning*) gakúmon 学問, (*culture*) kyōyō 教養; (*bringing up*) yōiku 養育
Ministry of Education, Culture, Sports, Science and Technology *n* Monbú Kagaku-shō 文部科学省

educational *adj* kyōiku-teki (na) 教育 的(な), kyōiku-jō (no) 教育上(の)

educational background *n* gakureki 学歴

education-related *adj* kyōiku-kanren (no) 教育関連(の)

eel *n* unagi ウナギ・鰻; (*conger eel*) anago アナゴ・穴子
broiled eel *n* kabayaki 蒲焼き, (*on rice in a lacquered box*) uná-jū うな重; (*on a bowl of rice*) una-don うな丼

effect *n* (*result*) kekka 結果, (*cause*) ... (no) séi ...(の)せい; (*effectiveness*) kiki-me 効き目, shirushi しるし, kōka 効果; (*gist*) muné 旨・むね
in effect yō-súru ni 要するに
has/takes effect kikimásu (kiku, kiite) 効きます(効く, 効いて)
side/after-effect *n* fukú-sayō 副作用

effective *adj* yūkō (na) 有効(な), kōka-teki (na) 効果的(な)

effeminate *adj* (*feminine*) memeshii 女々しい, onna no yō(na) 女のよう(な)

efficiency *n* nōritsu 能率, kōritsu 効率

efficient *adj* nōritsu-teki (na) 能率的(な), kōritsu teki (na) 効率的(な)

effort *n* hone-órí 骨折り (o-hone ori お骨折り), dóryoku 努力, kúrō 苦労(go-kúrō ご苦労)

with much effort (but) sekkakú せっかく

requires much effort honé ga ore-másu (oréru, órete) 骨が折れます(折れる, 折れて)

makes an effort doryoku shimásu (suru, shite) 努力します(する, して)

effortless *adj* muzó´sa (na) 無造作(な); *effortlessly* *adv* muzó´sa (ni) 無造作(に)

e.g. *adv* tatoeba 例えば・たとえば

egg *n* tamago 卵・玉子・タマゴ (*how many* nán-ko 何個)

egg on *v* sosonokashimásu (sosonokasu, soso-nokashite) そそのかします(そそのかす, そそのかして)

hard-boiled *adj* (*egg*) katayude (no) 固ゆで(の)

soft-boiled *adj* (*egg*) hanjuku (no) 半熟(の)

egg cup *n* yude-tamago ire ゆで卵入れ, eggu-kappu エッグカップ

eggplant *n* násu ナス・茄子, násubi ナスビ

egg rolls *n* haru-maki 春巻・ハルマキ

eggshell *n* tamago no kara 卵の殻

ego *n* jíga 自我, ego エゴ

egoism *n* (*selfishness*) riko-shugi 利己主義, wagamama わがまま (*= egotism*)

egoist *n* riko-shugi-sha 利己主義者, egoisuto エゴイスト (*= egotist*)

Egypt *n* Ejiputo エジプト

Egyptian *n* **1.** (*language*) Ejiputo-go エジプト語 **2.** (*person*) Ejiputo-jin エジプト人

eight *n* hachí 八・8, yattsú 八つ・やっつ; (*8-oared racing boat*) éito/ḗ´to エイト/エート; *~ days* yōka 八日

eight; 8 pieces (*small things*) hachi-ko, hák-ko 八個, **8 trees** (*or long things*)

háp-pon 八本; *8 sheets* (*flat things*) hachí-mai 八枚; *8 cars* (*or machines/vehicles*) hachí-dai 八台; *8 copies* (*books/magazines*) has-satsú 八冊; *8 cats* (*or small animals*) hap-piki 八匹; *8 cows* (*or large animals*) hát-tō´ 八頭; *8 birds/rabbits* háp-pa 八羽; *8 cupfuls* háp pai 八杯; *8 days* yōka 八日, yōka-kan 八日間; *8 o'clock* hachi-ji 八時・8時; *8 hours* hachi-jíkan 八時間; *8 minutes* hachi-fun, háp-pun 八分・8分; *8 months* hachi-/hak-kágetsu 八ヶ月; hakkagetsú-kan 八ヶ月間; *8 years* hachi-nen 八年, hachí nén-kan 八年間; *8 years old* yattsú 八つ, hás-sai 八歳; *8 people* hachi-nín 八人; *8 yen* (*money*) hachi-en 八円; *8 degrees* hachi-dó 八度; *8 times* hachi-do 八度, hachi/hak-kai 八回; hap-pén 八遍; *8 floors/stories* hachi/hak-kai 八階

eighteen *n* jū-hachí 十八・18

eighth *adj* hachi-banmé (no) 八番目(の), yattsu-mé (no) 八つ目(の)

the eighth day *n* yōka-mé 八日目, (*the day of the month*) yōka 八日

eight hundred *n* hap-pyakú 八百・800

eight thousand *n* has-sén 八千・8,000

eighty *n* hachi-jū 八十・80; *~ thousand* *n* hachi-mán 八万・80,000

Eire *n* airurando アイルランド

either one *adv* dochira demo どちらでも

eke *v* yarikuri shimásu (suru, shite) やりくりします(する, して), maniawasemásu (maniawaseru, maniawasete) 間に合わせます(まにあわせる, まにあわせて)

elaborate 1. *adj* (*complex*) fukuzatsu (na) 複雑(な) **2.** (*diligent*) kinben (na) 勤勉(な) **3.** kuwashiku setsumei shimásu (suru, shite) 詳しく説明します(する, して), kuwashiku nobemásu (noberu, nobete) 詳しく述べます(述べる, 述べて)

elapse *v* tachimásu (tátsu, tátte) 経ちます(経つ, 経って), hemásu (héru, héte) 経ます(経る, 経て), keika shi-másu (suru, shite) 経過します(する, して)

elastic n (*material*) → rubber
elastic band n wagomu 輪ゴム
elation n jōkigen 上機嫌, ōyorokobi 大喜び
elbow n hijí 肘・肱・ひじ
eldest son n chō´nán 長男
elect v erabimásu (erábu, eránde) 選びます(選ぶ、選んで)
election n sénkyo 選挙
electric adj dénki (no) 電気・でんき(の)
electric;
electric appliances n kaden 家電, denki-kígu 電気器具, denki-yō´hin 電気用品, denka-seihin 電化製品
electric car n densha 電車; (also *electrified train*, *electric train*)
electric fan n senpú´-ki 扇風機
electric heater n denki-sutō´bu 電気ストーブ
electric hot plate n denki-kónro 電気コンロ
electric shaver n denki-kámisori 電気かみそり
electric vacuum cleaner n (denki) sōjíki (電気)掃除機
electric wire n densen 電線
electrician n denki-ya (san) 電気屋(さん)
electricity n dénki 電気・でんき
electron n dénshi 電子
electronic adj dénshi (no) 電子(の)
electronic account settlement n denshi-kessai 電子決済
electronic accounting n denshi-kaikei 電子会計
elegance n hin 品, (o-)jōhín (お)上品, fū´ryu 風流
elegant adj fū´ryu (na) 風流(な), yū´bi (na) 優美(な), yū´ga (na) 優雅(な), (o-)jōhín (na) (お)上品(な)
element n yō´so 要素, eremento エレメント
elementary school n (*primary school*) shōgakkō 小学校
elementary school student n shōgáku-sei 小学生
elephant n zō 象・ゾウ
elevator n erebē´tā エレベーター
eleven n jū ichí 十一・11
eliminate v habukimásu (habuku,

habúite) 省きます(省く、省いて), nozokimásu (nozoku, nozoite) 除きます(除く、除いて); háijo shimásu (suru, shite) 排除します(する、して)
elimination n háijo 排除
elite **1.** n eriito エリート **2.** adj ichiryū (no) 一流(の)
else adv hoka (no/ni) 他・ほか(の/に) or else mátá-wa または, sore-tómo それとも, aruiwa 或いは・あるいは
somewhere else (dokoka) yosó (no/ni) (どこか)よそ(の/に), (dokoka) betsu no basho (no/ni) (どこか)別の場所(の/に)
email n mēru メール
embankment n teibō 堤防, tsutsumí 堤・つつみ
embarrass v komarasemásu (komaraséru, komarásete) 困らせます(困らせる、困らせて), kurushimemásu (kurushiméru, kurushímete) 苦しめます(苦しめる、苦しめて); ~ *oneself* hají o kakimásu (káku, káite) 恥をかきます(かく、かいて)
embarrassed; **1.** *gets* ~ komarimásu (komáru, komátte) 困ります(困る、困って); kurushimimásu (kurushímu, kurushínde) 苦しみます(苦しむ、苦しんで) **2.** *feels* ~ teremásu (teréru, térete) 照れます(照れる、照れて), kimari ga warúi (desu) きまりが悪い(です) **3.** *is* ~ (*ashamed, shy*) hazukashíi 恥ずかしい
embarrassment n tōwaku 当惑; kómaru kotó 困る事; hají 恥
embassy n taishí-kan 大使館
emblem n kishō 記章; (*symbol*) shōchō 象徴, hyōshō 表象; (*heraldic emblem*) monshō 紋章
embroidery n shishū 刺しゅう・刺繍
emerge v demásu (déru, déte) 出ます(出る、出て), arawaremásu (arawaréru, arawárete) 現れます(現れる、現れて)
emergence (*appearance*) n shutsugen 出現
emergency n hijō (jitai) 非常(事態), kinkyū (jitai) 緊急(事態), (*temporary*) rinji 臨時; (*crisis*) kíki 危機
emergency brake n hijō-burē´ki 非常ブレーキ

emergency exit *n* hijō-guchi 非常口
emergency phone *n* hijō-dénwa 非常
電話
in an emergency tossa no toki (ni)
とっさのとき (に)
for emergencies kyūkyū (no) 救急(の)
emery board *n* tsume-yásuri 爪やすり
emigrant *n* imin 移民, ijū-sha 移住者
Emoticon *n* (*computer*) kaomoji 顔文
字, emōtikon エモーティコン
emotion *n* kanjō 感情; (*feeling*) kandō
感動, kangeki 感激
emotional *adj* kanjo-teki (na) 感情的
(な)
Emperor *n* 1. (*Japanese*) Tennō 天皇,
His Majesty the Emperor Tennō-héika
天皇陛下 2. kōtei 皇帝
emphasis *n* kyōchō 強調
emphasize *v* kyōchō shimásu (suru,
shite) 強調します(する, して)
empire *n* téikoku 帝国
employ *v* 1. tsukaimásu (tsukau, tsukatte) 使います(使う, 使って), yatoimásu (yatóu, yattótte) 雇います(雇
う, 雇って) 2. *is employed* tsutómete
imásu (iru, ite) 勤めています(いる, い
て); yatówarete imásu (iru, ite) 雇われ
ています(いる, いて)
employee *n* jūgyō-in 従業員; (*of a
company*) sha-in 社員, kaishá-in
会社員
employer *n* koyō-sha 雇用者, koyō-
nushi 雇用主
employment *n* (*use*) shiyō 使用;
(*hiring*) koyō 雇用, yatói 雇; (*job*)
tsutomé (o-tsutome) 勤め (お勤め)
finding employment *n* shūshoku
就職
place of employment *n* tsutome-saki
勤め先
seeking employment *n* kyūshoku
求職
Empress *n* Kōgō (-in) sama 皇后(様・さ
ま); *Her Majesty the Empress* Kōgō-
héika 皇后陛下
empty 1. *adj* kara (no) 空・から(の),
karappo (no) からっぽ(の); (*with
nothing in it*) nani mo háitte inai ...
何も入っていない...; (*hollow*) utsuro
(na) うつろ(な); (*futile*) munashii

空しい・虚しい・むなしい; (*is vacant*)
aite imásu (iru, ite) 空いています(い
る, いて) 2. *adj* aki-...空[あ]き...
empty bottle *n* aki-bin 空[あ]き瓶
empty box *n* aki-bako 空[あ]き箱
empty can *n* aki-kan 空[あ]き缶
empty house *n* aki-ya 空[あ]き家
empty room/office *n* aki-ma 空[あ]
き間, aki-shitsu 空[あ]き室
3. *gets* ~ *v* akimásu (aku, aite) 空きま
す(空く, 空いて), sukimásu (suku,
suite) すきます(すく, すいて) 4.
empties it *v* akemásu (akeru, akete)
空けます(空ける, 空けて); (*drinks
to the bottom*) kanpai shimásu (suru,
shite) 乾杯します(する, して)
enclose *v* (*in envelope*) dōfu shimásu
(suru, shite) 同封します(する, して)
encompass *v* fukumimásu (fukumu,
fukunde) 含みます(含む, 含んで),
kakomimásu (kakomu, kakonde) 囲み
ます(囲む, 囲んで)
encounter *v* ... ni de-aimásu (de-áu,
de-átte) ...に出会います(出会う, 出会
って), sōgū shimásu (suru, shite) 遭遇
します(する, して)
encourage *v* susumemásu (susumeru,
susumete) 勧めます(勧める, 勧めて)
hagemashimásu (hagemásu, hagemás-
hite) 励まします(励ます, 励まして)
encouragement *n* shōrei 奨励
encouraging *adj* kokoro-zuyoi 心強い
encroach upon *v* okashimásu (okasu,
okashite) 侵します(侵す, 侵して)
encyclopedia *n* hyakka-jíten 百科事典
end *n* (*the ending*) owari 終わり ・
おわり, o-shimai おしまい, kirí 切り
・きり; (*close*) sue 末; (*of street*) tsuki-
atari 突き当たり; (*edge*) hashi/haji 端
= hashíkko/hajikko はしっこ, tamotó
たもと; (*purpose*) mokuteki 目的
end of the year *n* (toshi no) kure (年
の) 暮れ, nenmatsu 年末
to the (very) end ákú-made (mo) あく
まで(も)
2. *v* (*it ends, ends it*) owarimásu
(owaru, owatte) 終わります(終わる,
終わって), (*comes to an end*) sumimásu (súmu, súnde) 済みます(済む,
済んで), (*runs out*) tsukimásu (tsukiru,

tsukite) 尽きます（尽きる、尽きて）
3. *v goes to the ~ (of a road, etc.)*
tsuki-atarimásu (tsuki-ataru, tsuki-atatte) 突き当たります（突き当たる、突き当たって）
end up (doing) *v* shite shimaimásu (shimau, shimatte) してしまいます（しまう、しまって）
endeavor *v* tsutomemásu (tsutoméru, tsutómete) 努めます（努める、努めて）、dóryoku shimásu (suru, shite) 努力します（する、して）
ending *n* owari 終わり, ketsumatsu 結末
　ending address *n* shūryō adoresu 終了アドレス
　ending balance *n* kimatsu-zandaka 期末残高
　ending of a word *n* gobi 語尾
　ending point *n* shūten 終点
　happy ending *n* happii endo ハッピーエンド
endless *adj (no limit)* owari no nai 終わりのない, kirí ga nai きりがない; *(forever)* eien (no) 永遠（の）
endorse → sign → support
endurance *n (patience)* shínbō 辛抱
endure *v (puts up with)* shínbō shimásu (suru, shite) 辛抱（する、して）
enema *n* kanchō 浣腸
enemy *n* teki 敵
energetic *adj* génki (na) 元気（な）, eneruǵísshu (na) エネルギッシュ（な）; *(vigorous)* sekkyoku-teki (na) 積極的（な）
energetically *adv* génki (ni) 元気（に）, ikíói yóku 勢いよく
energy *n* **1.** ikíói 勢い **2.** enérúgii エネルギー **3.** *(pep)* génki 元気 (o-génki お元気)
engage *v* **1.** *(hires a professional)* tanomimásu (tanómu, tanónde) 頼みます（頼む、頼んで）**2.** *~ in (an activity)* ...ni jū'ji shimásu (suru, shite) ...に従事します（する、して）
3. *gets engaged (booked up, occupied)* fusagarimásu (fusagáru, fusagátte) ふさがります（ふさがる、ふさがって）
engaged *adj (to be married)* kon'yaku shite imásu (iru, ite) 婚約しています（いる、いて）

engagement *n (date)* yakusoku 約束
engine **1.** *n* kikan 機関, *(automobile)* énjin エンジン; *the engine starts* énjin ga kakarimásu (kakáru, kakátte) エンジンがかかります（かかる、かかって）
2. *n* → fire engine **3.** *starts the engine* *v* énjin o kakemásu (kakéru, kákete) エンジンをかけます（かける、かけて）
engineer *n* gíshi 技師
engineering *n* kōgaku 工学
England *n* Igirisu イギリス, Eikoku 英国
English *n (language)* Eigo 英語; *(person)* Igirisú-jin イギリス人
　English conversation *n* eikaiwa 英会話
　English-Japanese *n* ei-wa 英和; *English-Japanese dictionary* eiwa-jíten 英和辞典
　English-Japanese translation *n* eibun wayaku 英文和訳, nichiei-honyaku 日英翻訳
　English text *n* eibun 英文
　English translation *n* eiyaku 英訳
engrave *v* chōkoku shimásu (suru, shite) 彫刻します（する、して）, kizamimásu (kizámu, kizánde) 刻みます（刻む、刻んで）
engraving → woodblock print
engrossed; *gets ~ in* ...ni muchū ni narimásu (náru, nátte) ...に夢中になります（なる、なって）; ...ni korimásu (kóru, kótte) ...に凝ります（凝る、凝って）
enjoy *v* tanoshimimásu (tanoshímu, tanoshínde) 楽しみます（楽しむ、楽しんで）; enjói shimásu (suru, shite) エンジョイします（する、して）; *the company of* ... to tsuki-aimásu (tsuki-áu, tsuki-átte) ...と付き合います（付き合う、付き合って）
enjoyable *adj* tanoshíi 楽しい
enjoyment *n* tanoshimi 楽しみ, enjói エンジョイ
enlargement *n* zōdai 増大
enlightenment *n* satori 悟り
enliven; *~ with* kakki-zukemásu (kakki-zukeru, kakki-zukete) 活気づけます（活気づける、活気づけて）; nigiyaka ni

shimásu (suru, shite) にぎやかにします(する、して)

enormous *adj* bakudai (na) 莫大(な); bōdai (na) 膨大(な); taihen (na) 大変・たいへん(な)

enough *adj* **1.** jūbún (na) 十分(な); tappúri たっぷり; kékkō 結構・けっこう **2.** *is ~* tarimásu (tariru, tarite) 足ります(足りる、足りて) **3.** *gets (more than) ~ of* akimásu (akíru, ákite) 飽きます(飽きる、飽きて)

enquiry *n* shitumon 質問, toiawase 問い合わせ

enroll (*in school*) *v* nyūgaku shimásu (suru, shite) 入学します(する、して)

ensign *n* (*naval officer*) shōi 少尉

entangled; *gets ~* kojiremásu (kojiréru, kojírete) こじれます(こじれる、こじれて), motsuremásu (motsureru, motsurete) もつれます(もつれる、もつれて)

entanglement *n* motsure もつれ

enter *v* … (no naka) ni hairimásu (háiru, háitte) … (の中[なか])に入ります(入る、入って); (*appears on stage*) tōjō shimásu (suru, shite) 登場します(する、して)

entering;
entering a company nyūsha 入社
entering a country nyūkoku 入国
entering a hospital nyūin 入院
entering a school nyūgaku 入学

enterprise *n* jígyō 事業

entertain *v* (*with food*) gochisō shimásu (suru, shite) ごちそう[ご馳走]します(する、して)

entertainer *n* geinō´-jin 芸能人

entertainment *n* entātei(n)mento エンターテイ(ン)メント, goraku 娯楽

enthusiastic *adj* nésshín (na) 熱心(な)

enthusiastically *adv* nésshín (ni) 熱心(に)

entire *adj* zentai (no) 全体(の)
entire surface zenmen 全面
throughout the entire … …-jū …中

entirety *n* zenzen 全然・ぜんぜん, sokkúri そっくり → **all** → **completely**

entrance *n* iriguchi 入(り)口, toguchi 戸口; (*front entry*) génkan 玄関
entrance exam *n* (*school*) nyūgaku

shikén 入学試験; (*company*) nyūsha-shikén 入社試験
entrance gate **1.** (*wicket*) madoguchi 窓口 **2.** (*station*) kaisatsuguchi 改札口

entranced; *gets ~ with* … ni muchū ni narimásu (náru, nátte) …に夢中になります(なる、なって)

entrust (*one with it*) *v* (sore o …ni) azukemásu (azukéru, azukéte) (それを…に)預けます(預ける、預けて); yudanemásu (yudanéru, yudanéte) 委ねます(委ねる、委ねて); makasemásu (makaséru, makásete) 任せます(任せる、任せて); tanomimásu (tanómu, tanónde) 頼みます(頼む、頼んで); irai shimásu (suru, shite) 依頼します(する、して)

entry *n* **1.** (*head word of dictionary*) midashi 見出し, midashi-go 見出し語・見だし語 **2.** (*entry upon the stage*) tōjō 登場 **3.** sanka 参加 **4.** (*registration*) tōroku 登録 **5.** (*computer*) nyūryoku 入力 **6.** → **enter 7.** → **entrance**

envelope *n* fūtō 封筒・ふうとう (*how many* nán-mai 何枚)

enviable/envious *adj* netamashíi ねたましい・妬ましい, urayamashíi うらやましい・羨ましい

environment *n* kankyō 環境
environmental pollution *n* kankyō-osen 環境汚染
environmental protection *n* kankyō-hogo 環境保護

environs *n* shūhen 周辺

envy *v* urayamimásu (urayámu, urayánde) うらやみ[羨み]ます(うらやむ、うらやんで), netamimásu (netámu, netánde) ねたみ[妬み]ます(ねたむ、ねたんで)

epidemic *n* ryūkō-byō 流行病; densen-byō 伝染病

episode *n* **1.** (*story*) episōdo エピソード, sōwa 挿話 **2.** (*TV series*) *an episode* ichi-wa 一話; *two episodes* ni-wa 二話; *final ~* saishū-kai 最終回

equal *adj* **1.** byōdō (na) 平等(な); (*on an equal level*) taitō (no) 対等(の); (*equivalent to*) … to hitoshíi …と等しい **2.** (*extends to*) … ni oyobimásu (oyobu, oyonde) …に及び[およ]ます

(及ぶ、及んで) **3.** (*constitutes*) …
désu (dá/ná/nó, dé, ní) … です(だ／な／の、で、に)

equality *n* byōdō 平等

equation *n* (*equation form*) hōtei-shiki 方程式

equator *n* sekidō 赤道

equilibrium *n* tsuriai 釣り合い

equipment *n* (*apparatus*) sō´chi 装置、kiki 機器、(*facilities*) sétsubi 設備

equivalence *n* taiō 対応

equivalent *adj* taitō (no) 対等(の)；
~ to … to hitoshíi …と等しい；… ni sōtō shimásu (suru, shite) …に相当します(する、して)

era *n* jidai 時代；…jídai …時代
Edo-era *n* Edo-jídai 江戸時代

erase *v* keshimásu (kesu, keshíte) 消します(消す、消して)、tori-keshimásu (tori-kesu, tori-keshíte) 取り消します(取り消す、取り消して)

eraser *n* (*pencil*) keshi-gomu 消しゴム；(*blackboard*) kokubán-fuki 黒板拭き、kokubán-keshi 黒板消し

erasure *n* tori-keshi 取り消し

erect *v* tatemásu (tatéru, tátete) 立てます(立てる、立てて)、(*builds*) tatemásu (tatéru, tátete) 建てます(建てる、建てて)

erotic *adj* iroppói 色っぽい、kōshoku (na) 好色(な)

err *v* ayamarimásu (ayamáru, ayamátte) 誤ります(誤る、誤って)

errand *n* yōji 用事、tsukai 使い、yō-táshi 用足し
errand runner *n* tsukai bashiri (tsukai-ppashiri) 使い走り

error *n* machigai 間違い・まちがい、ayamári 誤り、erā エラー；*is in ~* machigaemásu (machigáéru, machigá-éte) 間違えます(間違える、間違えて)

erupt *v* funka shimásu (suru, shite) 噴火します(する、して)

eruption *n* funka 噴火；(*skin eruption*) hasshin 発疹・はっしん、hosshin 発疹・ほっしん；fukidemono 吹き出物

escalator *n* esukarē´tā エスカレーター

escape *v* nigemásu (nigéru, nígete) 逃げます(逃げる、逃げて)；nukemásu (nukeru, nukete) 抜けます(抜ける、抜けて)

esoteric *adj* (*mysterious*) shinpi-teki (na) 神秘的(な)

especially *adv* tokubetsu (ni) 特別(に)、kóto(-ni) こと(に)；toriwake とりわけ；sekkakú せっかく；*~ when* … sekkaku … na no ni せっかく…なのに

essay *n* zuihitsu 随筆、essē エッセー、zuisō-roku 随想録、sakubun 作文；shōron 小論

essential *adj* (*necessary*) hitsuyō (na) 必要(な)

essentials *n* (*supplies*) hitsuju-hin 必需品；*daily essentials* seikatsu hitsuju-hin 生活必需品

establish *v* tatemásu (tattéru, tátete) 建てます(建てる、建てて)；okoshimásu (okósu, okóshite) 起こします(起こす、起こして)

establishment *n* **1.** (*founding*) sōritsu 創立 **2.** (*facility*) shisetsu 施設 **3.** → company

esteem *n* sonkei 尊敬

estimate **1.** *n* (*an estimate*) mitsumori 見積もり、kentō´ 見当、suitei 推定、(*forecast*) yosoku 予測 **2.** *v* (*estimates it*) mi-tsumorimásu (mi-tsumoru, mi-tsumotte) 見積もります(見積もる、見積もって)、(*makes a guess*) kentō´ o tsukemásu (tsukéru, tsukéte) 見当をつけます(つける、つけて)、(*infers*) suitei shimásu (suru, shite) 推定します(する、して)、(*forecasts*) yosoku shimásu (suru, shite) 予測します(する、して)

estimation *n* (*inference, presumption*) suitei 推定 → judgment

estrange *v* **1.** *gets entangled* hedatari-másu (hedatáru, hedatátte) 隔たります(隔たる、隔たって) **2.** *becomes entangled from reality* hedatemásu (hedatéru, hedatéte) 隔てます(隔てる、隔てて)

estranged *adj* utói うとい・疎い

eternal *adj* eien (no) 永遠(の)

eternally *adv* eien (ni) 永遠(に)、eikyū (ni) 永久(に)

eternity *n* eien 永遠、eikyū 永久

ethics *n* rínri 倫理、dōtoku 道徳

ethnic *n* minzoku 民族

etiquette *n* reigí 礼儀、echikétto エチケット

etymology *n* gogen 語源
euro *n* yūro ユーロ
Europe *n* Yōróppa ヨーロッパ, Ō´shū 欧州
Europe and America *n* Ō-Bei 欧米, Séiyō 西洋
European *n* (*person*) Yōróppa-jin ヨーロッパ人, Ō´shū-jin 欧州人
European Union *n* Ō´shū-rengō 欧州連合
evacuate *v* (*to escape*) hinan shimásu (suru, shite) 避難します(する, して), (*gets repatriated*) hiki-agemásu (hiki-agéru, hiki-ágete) 引き揚げます(引き揚げる, 引き揚げて)
evacuation *n* (*escape*) hinan 避難, (*repatriation*) hikiage 引き揚げ
evacuee *n* (*refugee*) hinan-min 避難民, (*repatriated*) hikiagésha 引き揚げ者
evaluation score *n* hyōten 評点
evaporated milk *n* eba-míruku エバミルク
even 1. *adj* (*smooth, flat*) taira (na) 平ら(な) **2.** *adj* dōtō (no) 同等(の); ... to hitoshíi ...と等しい; kinitsu na 均一な **3.** *adj* gokaku no 互角の **4.** *adv* ... mo ...も; ... (de) sae (で)さえ; ~ *doing* (*if it does*) (shi-) té mo/(shi-)tátte (し)ても/(し)たって; ~ *being* (*if it is*) [ADJECTIVE] -kute mo/kutatte くても/くたって, [NOUN] démo/dátte でも/だって
even so (sore) démo (それ)でも
evening *n* ban 晩, yūgata 夕方, yoi 宵
evening at school *n* hōkago 放課後
evening paper *n* yūkan 夕刊
evening performance *n* yóru no bú 夜の部
evening dress *n* ibuningu doresu イブニングドレス, yakai-fuku 夜会服
evening meal *n* yūshoku 夕食
event *n* kotó 事・こと; (*incident*) jíken 事件; (*case*) dán 段; (*ceremony*) gyō´jí 行事, ibento イベント; (*game*) kyō´gí (shumoku) 競技(種目)
eventually *adv* (*come what may*) nán to itté mo 何と言っても; (*in due time*) sono uchi ni そのうちに; saishū-teki ni(wa) 最終的に(は) → **finally, at last**
ever 1. *adv* (*always*) ítsu-mo いつも;

as ~ aikawarazu 相変わらず **2.** *adv* (*once*) ítsu-ka いつか, ... kotó ga ari-másu (áru, átte) 事があります(ある, あって)
ever since *adv* ... írai ...以来
ever so many *adv* íkutsu mo いくつも, nán- [COUNTER] mo 何 [COUNTER]も
ever so much *adv* íkura mo いくらも; dōmo どうも
every ... *adj* dóno ... démo どの...でも; ... goto (ni) ... ごと・毎(に), mai- ... 毎...; arayuru あらゆる
every chance one gets *adv* koto áru góto (ni) 事あるごと(に)
every day *adv, n* máinichi 毎日, higo-to (ni) 日毎(に), híbi 日々; *almost* ~ máinichi no yō´ni 毎日のように
every month *adv, n* mai-tsúki 毎月, mai-getsu 毎月
every morning *adv, n* mái-asa 毎朝
every night *adv, n* mai-ban 毎晩, mai-yo 毎夜
every other ... *adv* ... oki ni ...おきに
every station *n* kaku-eki 各駅
every time *adv, n* maido 毎度; ~ *that* ...tabí(ni) ...度(に)
every week *adv, n* maishū 毎週
every which way *adv* hō´bō 方々
every year *adv, n* mai-toshi 毎年, mainen 毎年
everybody *pron* mi(n)náな み(ん)な・皆, miná-san 皆さん; dare demo 誰でも (= *everyone*)
everyday ... *adj* (*daily*) máinichi no ... 毎日の...; (*usual*) fúdan no ... 普段の...
everyday clothes *n* fudán-gí 普段着
everyone *pron* zen'in 全員
everyplace → **everywhere**
everything *pron* minná みんな・皆, zénbu 全部, nan demo 何でも, íssai 一切; monógoto 物事
everywhere *adv* doko demo どこでも, dóko ni mo どこにも, hō´bō 方々
evidence *n* shōko 証拠; (*basis*) kónkyo 根拠
evil *n* **1.** → **bad 2.** (*a devil*) ákú 悪
evil spirit *n* ákuma 悪魔
exact *adj* (*detailed*) kuwashíi 詳しい, komakái 細かい; (*correct*) seikaku (na) 正確(な)

exactly *adv* chōdo ちょうど, mattakú 全く・まったく, pittári ぴったり, hakkíri はっきり; másani まさに・正に; ... daké ...だけ

exaggerate *v* kochō shimásu (suru, shite) 誇張します（する, して）

exaggerated *adj* ōgesa (na) 大げさ（な）, (go-)táisō (na) （ご）大層（な）

exaggeration *n* kochō 誇張; (*bragging*) hóra ほら

examination *n* **1.** (*test*) shikén 試験 **2.** (*inquiry*) chō´sa 調査 **3.** (*inspection*) kénsa 検査, (*medical*) shinsatsu 診察
examination place *n* shiken-jō 試験場
examination room *n* shinsatsu-shitsu 診察室

examine *v* **1.** (*investigates*) shirabemásu (shiraběru, shirábete) 調べます（調べる, 調べて） **2.** kentō shimásu (suru, shite) 検討します（する, して） **3.** (*medically*) mimásu (míru, míte) 診ます（診る, 診て）, shinsatsu shimásu (suru, shite) 診察します（する, して） **4. ~ tickets** (*at wicket*) kaisatsu shimásu (suru, shite) 改札します（する, して）; (*aboard*) kensatsu shimásu (suru, shite) 検札します（する, して）

example *n* réi 例, ichi-rei 一例, tatoe 例え・たとえ, tatoi 例い・たとい; *follows* (*learns from*) *the ~ of* ... o mi-naraimásu (mi-narau, mi-naratte) ...を見習います（見習う, 見習って）
for example tatóeba 例えば・たとえば

excavate *v* horimásu (hóru, hótte) 掘ります（掘る, 掘って）

exceed *v* sugimásu (sugíru, súgite) 過ぎます（過ぎる, 過ぎて）, chōka shimásu (suru, shite) 超過します（する, して）; koshimásu (kosu, koshite) 超します（超す, 超して）, uwa-mawarimásu (uwa-mawaru, uwa-mawátte) 上回ります（上回る, 上回って）

exceedingly *adv* móttómo 最も, góku ごく・極, taihen 大変, hijō ni 非常に

excel *v* sugúrete imásu (iru, ite) 優れています（いる, いて）

excellent *adj* sugúreta 優れた, yūshū (na) 優秀（な）; kékkō (na) 結構（な）;

is ~ sugúrete imásu (iru, ite) 優れています（いる, いて）

except (*for*) *prep* ...no hoka ...の他, ...ígai ...以外

exception *n* reigai 例外; *without ~* (*all*) íssai 一切

excess *n* chōka 超過, kajō 過剰; (*leeway, margin*) yoyū 余裕; *is in ~* amarimásu (amáru, amátte) 余ります（余る, 余って）

excessive *adj* yokei (na) 余計（な）, hōgai (na) 法外（な）; (*extreme*) kageki (na) 過激（な）, kyokután na 極端（な）

excessively *adv* yáke ni やけに, (*extremely*) kyokután ni 極端（に）

exchange *v* (tori-)kaemásu (kaeru, kaete) （取り）替えます（替える, 替えて）, hiki-kaemásu (hiki-káeru, hiki-káete) 引き換えます（引き換える, 引き換えて）, kōkan shimásu (suru, shite) 交換します（する, して）

exchange rate *n* kawase rēto 為替レート

excited 1. *gets ~* ki ga tachimásu (tátsu, tátte) 気が立ちます（立つ, 立って）, nes-shimásu (nes-suru, nes-shite) 熱します（熱する, 熱して） **2.** *is excited* kōfun shite imásu (iru, ite) 興奮しています（いる, いて）

excitement *n* kōfun 興奮

exciting *adj* wakuwaku saseru ワクワクさせる, kōfun saseru 興奮させる, kōfun suru 興奮する

exclude *v* hájio shimásu (suru, shite) 排除します（する, して）

excluded *adj* (*not included*) fukumarete inai 含まれていない

exclusion *n* hájio 排除

excrement *n* daibén 大便, kusó 糞・クソ

excursion *n* ensoku 遠足, yūran 遊覧

excuse *n* ii-wake 言い訳, mōshiwake 申し訳, (*pretext*) kōjitsu 口実; *makes ~* (*apologizes*) ii-wake o shimásu (suru, shite) 言い訳をします（する, して）; (*declines*) kotowarimásu (kotowáru, kotowátte) 断ります（断る, 断って）

Excuse me. Sumimasén すみません; Osóre-irimásu. 恐れ入ります; Dō´mo. どうも; Gomen nasái. ごめんなさい;

Shitsúrei shimásu. 失礼します.

Excuse me but I'll be on my way.
Sore déwa shitsúrei (ita)shimásu. それ
では失礼(いた)します.

Excuse me for having interrupted/
bothered you. O-jama shimáshita.
おじゃま[お邪魔]しました.

Excuse me for interrupting/bothering
you. (but) O-jama deshô ga … おじゃ
ま[お邪魔]でしょうが….

Excuse me for being the first to leave.
O-saki ni shitsúrei shimásu. お先に失
礼します.

Excuse me for going first. O-saki ni.
お先に

exempt v *is ~ from* … o manukaremásu
(manukaréru, manukárete) … を免れ
ます(免れる, 免れて)

tax-exempt *adj* menzei (no) 免税(の)

exercise 1. n (*physical*) undō 運動,
(*calisthenics*) taisō 体操; (*study*)
renshū 練習, (*practice*) dóríru ドリル,
kéiko 稽古・けいこ (o-keiko お稽古)
2. v undō shimásu (suru, shite) 運動し
ます(する, して)

exercise book n nōto ノート, renshū-
chō 練習帳

exert v (*exerts oneself*) tsutomemásu
(tsutoméru, tsutómete) 努めます(努め
る, 努めて); tsukushimásu (tsukúsu,
tsukúshite) 尽くします(尽くす, 尽く
して)

exhaust 1. n haiki 排気; (*fumes*)
haiki-gásu 排気ガス **2.** ~ *it* v tsukaihatashimásu (tsukai-hatásu, tsukai-
hatáshite) 使い果たします(使い果
たす, 使い果たして); (*runs out of*)
kirashimásu (kirásu, kiráshite) 切らし
ます(切らす, 切らして)

exhaust fan n haikí-sen 排気扇,
kankí-sen 換気扇

exhaustive *adj* téttē'tékí (na) 徹底的
(な), mō'ra shita 網羅した

exhibit 1. n tenji(-kai) 展示(会),
tenrán-kai 展覧会 **2.** v *exhibits it*
misemásu (miséru, mísete) 見せます
(見せる, 見せて); shuppin shimásu
(suru, shite) 出品します(する, して)

exhibition n tenjí-kai 展示会, tenrán-
kai 展覧会, hakuránkai 博覧会;

(*display*) misemóno 見世物

exhibitor n shuppín-sha 出品者

exist v sonzai shimásu (suru, shite)
存在します(する, して)

existence n (*survives or does not
survive*) sonzai 存在, seizon 生存; (*or
exists or does not exist*) úmu 有無

exit 1. n dé-guchi 出口; *north/south/
east/west ~* kita/minami/higashi/
nishi-guchi 北/南/東/西口 **2.** v taijō
shimásu (suru, shite) 退場します(す
る, して)

exorbitant *adj* hogai (na) 法外(な)

expand v hirogarimásu (hirogaru, hirogatte) 広がります(広がる, 広がって);
bōchō shimásu (suru, shite) 膨脹しま
す(する, して) → **develop** → **grow**
→ **spread**

expansion → **development** → **growth**

expect v (*awaits*) mátte imásu (iru, ite)
待っています(いる, いて), kitai shi-
másu (suru, shite) 期待します(する,
して); (*anticipates*) yosō shimásu
(suru, shite) 予想します(する, して);
as we might ~ sasuga (ni) さすが(に)
expect to (*do*) … (suru) tsumori dé su
…(する)つもりです

expectation n mikomi 見込み, ate 当
て, tsumori つもり, yosō 予想, yotei
予定; kitai 期待; …hazu …はず

expediency n (*convenience*) kōtsugō
好都合

expedient *adj* tsugō no yoi 都合のよい

expense n híyō 費用, kei-hi 経費;
…-hi …費

expensive *adj* (ne ga) takái (値が)高い

experience 1. n keiken 経験, (*personal*)
taiken 体験; (*a sometime happening*)
…koto …事; (*professional*) shokureki
職歴 **2.** v (*experiences, undergoes*)
keiken shimásu (suru, shite) 経験しま
す(する, して), …mé ni aimásu (áu,
átte) …目にあいます(あう, あって)

experiment 1. n jikken (o shimásu;
suru, shite) 実験(をします; する, し
て); (*test*) shíken 試験, tameshi 試し
2. v ~ *with* … o tameshimásu (tamésu,
taméshite) …を試します(試す, 試して)

expert 1. *adj* jōzú (na) じょうず[上手]
(な), tassha (na) 達者(な) **2.** n meijín
名人

名人, tsū 通, tsūjin 通人, (*veteran*) kúró'to くろうと・玄人, ekisupāto エキスパート, beteran ベテラン, (*specialist*) senmon-ka 専門家

expire v (*contract, rights, etc.*) shikkō shimásu (suru, shite) 失効します(する, して)

explain v setsumei shimásu (suru, shite) 説明します(する, して); tokimásu (tóku, tóite) 説きます(説く, 説いて); káishaku shimásu (suru, shite) 解釈します(する, して)

explanation n setsumei 説明; (*interpretation*) kái-shaku 解釈; (*excuse*) ii-wake 言い訳

explanatory notes n hanrei 凡例

explicit adj meihaku (na) 明白(な)

explicitly adv meihaku (ni) 明白(に)

explode v bakuhatsu shimásu (suru, shite) 爆発します(する, して)

exploit 1. n tegara 手柄 **2.** v riyō shimásu (suru, shite) 利用します(する, して)

explosion n bakuhatsu 爆発

export 1. n (*exporting*) yushutsu 輸出
  export goods n yushutsu-hin 輸出品
  2. v *exports it* yushutsu shimásu (suru, shite) 輸出します(する, して)

expose (*a secret*) v barashimásu (barásu, baráshite) ばらします(ばらす, ばらして)

exposition n **1.** (*a fair*) hakurán-kai 博覧会 **2.** (*explanation*) káishaku 解釈

expound v káishaku shimásu (suru, shite) 解釈します(する, して)

express 1. n (*train, bus*) kyūkō 急行 **2.** v (*puts into words*) ii-arawashimásu (ii-arawásu, ii-arawáshite) 言い表します(言い表す, 言い表して), (*tells*) iimásu (iu, itte/yutte) 言います(言う, 言って/ゆって)
  express mail n sokutatsu (yū-)bin 速達(郵)便
  express train n kyūkō-ressha 急行列車

expression n (*way of saying*) iikata 言い方, (*phrase*) hyōgen 表現, (*on face*) hyōjō 表情, kao 顔・かお; *has/ wears an ~ of ...* (no) kao o shite imásu (iru, ite) ...(の)顔をしています(いる, いて)

extend v **1.** (*extends it*) nobashimásu (nobásu, nobáshite) 延ばします(延ばす, 延ばして), enchō shimásu (suru, shite) 延長します(する, して) **2.** (*it extends*) nobimásu (nobíru, nóbite) 伸びます(伸びる, 伸びて), (*reaches*) oyobimásu (oyobu, oyonde) 及びます(及び, 及んで)

extension n (*cord*) enchō-kō'do 延長コード; (*phone line, inside*) naisen 内線, (*outside*) gaisen 外線

extent n kágirí 限り; hodo 程; teido 程度; kagen 加減 → scope → degree; *to what ~* dónna ni どんなに; *to this ~* konna ni こんなに; *to that ~* sonna ni そんなに, anna ni あんなに

exterior n gáibu 外部, gaimen 外面

external adj soto-gawa (no) 外側(の); gáibu/gaimen (no) 外部/外面(の); gai-... 外...

extinguish v keshimásu (kesu, keshite) 消します(消す, 消して); *gets extinguished* kiemásu (kieru, kiete) 消えます(消える, 消えて)

extinguisher → fire extinguisher

extol v homemásu (homéru, hométe) ほめ[褒め]ます(ほめる, ほめて)

extortion n yusuri ゆすり

extra 1. n (*actor/actress*) ekisutora エキストラ **2.** n (*bonus*) omake おまけ **3.** adj yobun (no/ni) 余分(に/の), betsu (no/ni) 別・べつ(の/に); (*special*) tokubetsu no 特別(の)
  extra charge n betsu-ryō'kin 別料金

extract n ekisu エキス

extraordinary adj rinji (no) 臨時(の); namihazureta 並外れた

extravagance n muda-zúkai 無駄使い, rōhi 浪費

extravagant adj zeitakú (na) ぜいたく・贅沢(な); ogorimásu (ogoru, ogótte) おごり[驕り]ます(おごる, おごって)

extreme adj kyokután (na) 極端(な); (*radical*) kageki (na) 過激(な)

extremely adv hijō (ni) 非常(に), kiwámete 極めて, hanahada はなは

だ・甚だ, góku ごく・極, shigoku しごく, itatte 至って, kyokután (ni) 極端(に), to(t)temo と(っ)ても, monosúgóku ものすごく・物凄く, zúibun ずいぶん・随分; (*more than one might expect*) nakanaka なかなか

extremist *n* kageki-ha 過激派

exultant *adj* tokui (na) 得意(な)

eye *n* **1.** mé 目 [眼] **2.** (*detective*) tantei 探偵; (*of a needle*) médo めど; (*with*) *wide eyes* me o maruku shimásu (suru, shite) 目を丸くします(する, して)

public eye *n* seken no me 世間の目

typhoon's eye *n* taifū no me 台風の目

eye area *n* mejiri 目尻・めじり

eye ball *n* gankyū 眼球, medama 目玉

eyebrow *n* máyu(ge) 眉・まゆ(毛)

eye camera *n* ai kamera アイ・カメラ

eye doctor *n* mé-isha 目医者・眼医者

eye drops *n* me-gúsuri 目薬

eye fatigue *n* gansei-hirō 眼精疲労

eyeglasses *n* mégane 眼鏡・めがね・メガネ; *puts on* (*wears*) *eyeglasses* mégane o kakemásu (kákete imásu) 眼鏡[メガネ]をかけます(かけています)

eyelashes *n* mátsuge まつげ

eyelid *n* mábuta まぶた

eye lotion *n* me-gúsuri 目薬

eye shadow *n* ai-shadō アイシャドウ

eyesight *n* shíryoku 視力

F

fable *n* gūwa 寓話

fabric *n* ori-mono 織物, kíji 生地

fabrication *n* **1.** (*fiction*) tsukuri-banashi 作り話, detchiage でっちあげ **2.** (*making*) seizō 製造

fabulous *adj* subarashii すばらしい・素晴らしい, wakuwaku suru ワクワクする

face **1.** *n* kao 顔, tsurá つら・面; (*one's honor*) taimen 体面 **2.** *n* (*front*) shō´men 正面 **3.** *v* (*faces it*) mukimásu (muku, muite) 向きます(向く, 向いて) **4.** *v* atarimásu (ataru, atatte) 当たります(当たる, 当たって)

face cream *n* bigan kuriimu 美顔クリーム

face powder *n* oshiroi おしろい・白粉

face towel *n* fēsu taoru フェースタオル

Facebook *n* (*Internet*) feisu bukku フェイスブック

facelift *n* biyō-seikei 美容整形, seikei-shujutsu 整形手術

facial *adj* kao (no) 顔(の)

facile *adj* tegaru (na) 手軽(な), tayasui たやすい

facility, facilities *n* shísetsu 施設, sétsubi 設備; bén 便・べん

facing *adv* mukai no 向かいの (o-múkai お向かいの)

facsimile *n* fakushimiri ファクシミリ, fákkusu ファックス → fax

fact *n* kotó 事・こと, jíjitsu 事実; *in fact* jitsú wa 実は, jissai (wa) 実際(は), iyó-iyo いよいよ, jítai 事態

faction *n* habatsu 派閥

factory *n* kō´ba/kō´jō´ 工場

factory worker *n* kō´in 工員, shokkō´ 職工

fad *n* ichiji-teki ryūkō 一時的流行

fade *v* **1.** samemásu (saméru, sámete) さめます(さめる, さめて), asemásu (aseru, asete) あせます・褪せます (あせる, あせて) **2.** (*grows weak*) otoroemásu (otoróéru, otoróete) 衰えます(衰える, 衰えて) **3.** (*vanishes*) kiemásu (kieru, kiete) 消えます(消える, 消えて)

fade-in *n* fēdo in フェードイン

fade-out *n* fēdo auto フェードアウト

fail *v* **1.** shippai shimásu (suru, shite) 失敗します(する, して) **2.** (*exam*) ochimásu (ochíru, óchite) 落ちます (落ちる, 落ちて), rakudai shimásu (suru, shite) 落第します(する, して) **3.** (*is wide off the mark*) hazuremásu (hazureru, hazurete) 外れます(外れる, 外れて) **4.** (*engine etc. breaks down*) koshō´ shimásu (suru, shite) 故障します(する, して)

without fail zé-hi ぜひ・是非, kana-razu 必ず

failed *adj* fugó´kaku (no) 不合格(の)

failure *n* **1.** shippai 失敗 **2.** (*exam*) rakudai 落第, fugó´kaku 不合格
power failure *n* teiden 停電

faint **1.** *adj* (*dim*) kásuka (na) かすか [微か](な) **2.** *v* (*loses consciousness*) ki o ushinaimásu (ushinau, ushinatte) 気を失います(失う, 失って)

fair *n* (*market*) íchi 市, íchi-ba 市場, (*temple festival*) én-nichi 縁日

fair *adj* (*just, impartial*) kō´hei (na) 公平(な); (*sunny*) hárete imásu (háreta ...) 晴れています(晴れた…); ~ **weather** haré 晴れ, (o-)ténki (お)天気

fairly *adv* (*rather*) kánari かなり, sō´tō´ 相当, zúibun ずいぶん・随分
fairly well (*sufficiently*) kékkō´ 結構

fairy *n* yōsei 妖精

fairy tale *n* dōwa 童話, otogibánashi おとぎ話

faithful *adj* seijitsu (na) 誠実(な), chūjitsu (na) 忠実(な), makoto (no) 誠(の)

fake **1.** *adj* nise (no) にせ・偽(の), inchiki (na) いんちき・インチキ(な) **2.** *n* (*thing*) nise-mono にせもの・偽物, inchiki いんちき・インチキ, feiku フェイク **3.** *v* detchiagemásu (detchi-ageru, detchiagete) でっちあげます(でっちあげる, でっちあげて)

falcon *n* taka タカ・鷹, hayabusa ハヤブサ・隼

falconry *n* taka-gari タカ・鷹狩り

fall **1.** *n* (*autumn*) áki 秋 **2.** *v* (*it falls*) ochimás<u>u</u> (ochíru, óchite) 落ちます(落ちる, 落ちて), okkochimás<u>u</u> (okkochíru, okkóchite) 落っこちます(落っこちる, 落っこちて) **3.** *v* (*falls and scatters*) chirimás<u>u</u> (chiru, ch<u>i</u>tte) 散ります(散る, 散って)

fall behind okuremás<u>u</u> (okureru, okurete) 遅れます(遅れる, 遅れて); okure o torimás<u>u</u> (tóru, tótte) 後れを取ります(取る, 取って)

fall down taoremás<u>u</u> (taoréru, taorete) 倒れます(倒れる, 倒れて), korobi-más<u>u</u> (korobu, koronde) 転びます(転ぶ, 転んで)

fall in love with ... ni horemás<u>u</u> (hore-ru, horete) …にほれ[惚れ]ます(ほれる, ほれて), kói ni ochimás<u>u</u> (ochiru, ochite) 恋に落ちます(落ちる, 落ちて)

fallacy *n* goshin 誤信

fallout *n* **1.** (*radioactive particles*) hōsha-sei kōka-butsu 放射性降下物, shi no hai 死の灰

falls *n* taki 滝 (= *waterfalls*)

false *adj* (*falsehood*) úso (no) うそ・嘘・ウソ(の), itsuwari (no) いつわり・偽り(の); (*fake*) nise (no) にせ・偽(の), (*artificial*) jinzó´ (no) 人造(の)
false alarm *n* go-hō 誤報

falsehood *n* úso うそ・ウソ・嘘, itsu-wari いつわり・偽り

false teeth *n* ire-ba 入れ歯

falter *v* yoro-mekimás<u>u</u> (yoro-méku, yoro-méite) よろめきます(よろめく, よろめいて), yóro-yoro shimás<u>u</u> (suru, sh<u>i</u>te) よろよろします(する, して)

fame *n* **1.** (*reputation*) hyō´ban 評判 **2.** → **honor**

familiar *adj* sh<u>i</u>tashíi 親しい → **accustomed** → **know**

family *n* uchi 家・うち, ... uchí …家 (o-uchi お家); kázoku 家族, (*household*) (*clan*) úji 氏, …-ke …家; ~ **crest** (ka)món (家)紋, monshō´ 紋章; (*bio-logical taxonomy*) ká 科

family circle *n* uchiwa 内輪

family inn *n* minshuku 民宿

family name *n* (*surname*) sei 姓, (*as written*) myō´ji, miyoji 名字・苗字, úji 氏, kámei 家名

family room *n* (*Japanese family room*) (o-)cha-no-ma (お)茶の間

famine *n* ue 飢え, kikin 飢饉

famous *adj* yūmei (na) 有名(な), na-dakái 名高い, hyoban (no) 評判(の); *gets* ~ shiraremás<u>u</u> (shirareru, shirarete) 知られます(知られる, 知られて), yūmei ni narimás<u>u</u> (náru, nátte) 有名になります(なる, なって)

fan *n* **1.** ō´gí 扇, (*folding*) sensu 扇子, (*flat*) uchiwa うちわ, (*electric*) senpū´-ki 扇風機 **2.** (*enthusiast*) fán ファン; …-zuki …好き・…ずき
fan club *n* fan-kurabu ファンクラブ

fan letter *n* fan-retā ファンレター

baseball fan *n* yakyū-fan 野球ファン

fancy *adj* (*high-grade*) kō'kyū (no) 高級(の)

fancy dresser *n* osháre na hito おしゃれな人

fancy dress party *n* kasō pātii 仮装パーティー

fancy goods *n* kō'kyū-hin 高級品

fanfare *n* fanfāre ファンファーレ

fang *n* kiba 牙・キバ

fan shell *n* (*a kind of scallop*) taira-gí たいらぎ

fantastic *n* subarashii 素晴らしい

fantasy *n* (*imaginary*) kūsō 空想, fantajii ファンタジー

far *adj* tō'i 遠い, háruka (na) はるか・遥か(な); háruka (ni) はるか・遥か(に)

how far donogurai/donokurai どの位, dóko made どこまで

as far as it goes ichiō' 一応

by far zutto ずっと, háruka (ni) はるか・遥か(に)

farce; *traditional Noh farce* kyō'gen 狂言, chaban 茶番

fare *n* (*fee*) ryō'kin 料金, (*transportation*) únchin 運賃

Far East *n* kyokutō' 極東

farewell *n* wakaré 別れ, (o-wakare お別れ)

farewell party *n* sō'bétsukai 送別会, o-wakare-kai お別れ会

farm *n* nō'jō' 農場

farm house/family *n* nō'ka 農家

farm land *n* nō'chi 農地

farmer *n* nō'ka 農家, nō'min 農民

farmhand *n* nō'jō-rōdō-sha 農場労働者

farmhouse *n* nō'ka 農家

farming *n* **1.** nō'gyō' 農業 **2.** yōshoku 養殖

far-off *adj* tō'i 遠い, háruka (na) はるか・遥か(な)

farsighted *adj* enshi (no) 遠視(の); (*forward-looking*) mae-muki (no) 前向き(の); senken no mei (no/ga aru) 先見の明(の/がある)

fart *n* onara (o shimásu; suru, shite) おなら(をします; する, して), [INFOR-MAL] hé (o hirimásu; híru, hítté) へ・屁(をひります; ひる, ひって)

fascinated *adj* uttóri (to) うっとり(と); *is ~* uttóri shimásu (suru, shite) うっとりします(する, して)

fascination *n* miryoku 魅力

fascism *n* fashizumu ファシズム

fascist *n* fashisuto ファシスト

fashion 1. *n* (*way*) ryūkō' 流行, hayari はやり [流行り], fásshon ファッション; (...) fū (...)風 **2.** *is in ~* hayari-másu (hayáru, hayátte) はやり [流行り]ます(はやる, はやって)

fashion show *n* fasshon shō ファッションショー

fashionable *adj* hayari (no) はやり [流行り](の), ryūkō' (no) 流行(の); haikara (na) ハイカラ(な), sumā'to (na) スマート(な)

fast *adj* háyaku 速く; hayái 速い; (*clock runs fast*) susunde imásu (iru, ite) 進んでいます(いる, いて)

fasten *v* **1.** (*firmly attaches*) tomemásu (tomeru, tomete) 留めます(留める, 留めて) **2.** (*tightens, secures*) shimemásu (shiméru, shímete) 締めます(締める, 締めて); *Fasten your seat belts.* Shiito béruto o shímete kudasai. シートベルトを締めて下さい。

fastener *n* fasunā' ファスナー, chakku チャック

fast food *n* fāsuto fūdo ファーストフード, insutanto (shokuhin) インスタント(食品)

fastidious → choosy

fat 1. *n* (*grease*) abura あぶら・脂, (*lard, blubber*) shibō' 脂肪 **2.** *gets ~* futorimásu (futóru, futótte) 太ります(太る, 太って), koemásu (koéru, kóete) 肥えます(肥える, 肥えて); (*is fat*) futótte imásu (iru, ite) 太っています(いる, いて) **3.** *adj* (*plump*) futói 太い, debu (no) デブ(の), futotta 太った

fate *n* ún 運, únmei 運命, shukumei 宿命

father *n* otō'san お父さん, chichí 父, chichi oya 父親

Father *n* (*Reverend*) ...shínpu san ...神父さん

father-in-law *n* gifu 義父

fatigue *n* hirō 疲労

fatso *n* debu でぶ・デブ

fatty *adj* abrakkói 脂っこい; ***fatty tuna***
tóro とろ・トロ

faucet *n* jaguchi 蛇口

fault 1. *n* (*defect*) kizu きず; (*short-coming*) tánsho 短所; (*guilt*) tsúmi 罪;
(*cause*) …séi …せい 2. *at* ~ warúi 悪
い; *it is my* ~ watashi ga warúi/wáru-
katta わたし [私] が悪い/悪かった
3. *finds* ~ *with* toga-memásu (togáméru,
togámete) とがめ [咎め] ます (とがめ
る, とがめて)

faust *adj* minikui 醜い・みにくい

faux pas *n* bu-sáhō´ 無 [不] 作法

favor 1. (*kindness*) shínsetsu 親切
(go-shínsetsu ご親切), (*goodwill*)
kō´i 好意; (*request*) o-nagai お願い
2. *does a* ~ kō´i o misemásu (miséru,
mísete) 好意を見せます (見せる, 見
せて); *does me/us the* ~ *of* …*ing* …
te kudasaimásu (kudasáru kudasátte)/
kuremásu (kureru, kurete) …て下さい
ます (下さる, 下さって)/くれます (く
れる, くれて) 3. *favors v* (*a choice*)
… (no) hō´ga íi to omoimásu (omóu,
omótte) … (の) 方が [ほうが] いいと思
います (思う, 思って)

favorite *adj* dái-suki (na) 大好き (な),
(ichiban) sukí (na) (一番) 好き (な);
o-kiniiri (no) お気に入り (の); konomí
(o-konomi) no …好み (お好み) の…;
tokui (na/no) 得意 (な/の)

favoritism *n* ekohiiki えこひいき

fax *n* fákkusu ファックス

fear 1. *n* (*a fear*) osoré 恐れ, kyō´fu
恐怖; shinpai 心配 2. *fears it v* osoremásu (osoréru, osórete) 恐れます
(恐れる, 恐れて); kowagarimásu
(kowagáru, kowagátte) 怖がります
(怖がる, 怖がって); (*worries about*)
shinpai shimásu (suru, shite) 心配しま
す (する, して)

fearful *adj* osoroshíi 恐ろしい

feat *n* waza 業・わざ; (*deed*) shiwaza
仕業・しわざ

feather *n* hane 羽, umō´ 羽毛; ke 毛

feature *n* tokuchō 特徴

feature article *n* tokushū-kiji 特集記事

feature film *n* chōhen-eiga 長編映画

February *n* Ni-gatsú 二月・2月

feces *n* kusó くそ・糞, fún ふん・糞;
bén 便, daibén 大便

federation *n* renmei 連盟

fee *n* ryō´kin 料金; …-ryō´ …料;
(*remuneration*) sharei 謝礼, rei 礼;
***membership* ~** kaihi 会費; ***student* ~**
gakusei-ryō´kin 学生料金;
***transportation* ~** unsō´ryō 運送料

feeble → weak

feed *v* tabesasemásu (tabesaséru,
tabesásete) 食べさせます (食べさせる,
食べさせて); [INELEGANT] kuwasemásu (kuwaséru, kuwásete) 食わせま
す (食わせる, 食わせて)

feel 1. *v* (*by touch*) sawarimásu
(sawaru, sawatte) さわり [触り] ます
(さわる, さわって) 2. (*by emotion*)
kan-jimásu (kan-jiru, kan-jite) 感じ
ます (感じる, 感じて) 3. (*thinks*)
omoimásu (omóu, omótte) 思います
(思う, 思って) 4. zon-jimásu (zon-
jiru, zon-jite) 存じます (存じる, 存
じて); zon-jiagemásu (zon-jíageru,
zon-jiagéte) 存じあげます (存じあげ
る, 存じあげて) 5. (*body reaction*)
moyō´shimásu (moyō´su, moyō´shite)
催します (催す, 催して) 6. *it feels*
good/bad kimochi ga íi/warúi 気持ち
がいい/悪い

feeling *n* kimochi 気持ち, kanji 感じ,
ki 気, nén 念; (*sense*) kimí 気味;
kokóro 心, omói 思い; (*mood*) kokoro-
mochi 心持ち, kíbun 気分; (*true inner*)
honne 本音, honshin 本心; (*one's view*)
íkō´ 意向; (*health*) (karada no) guai
(体の) 具合; (*compassion*) nasake 情け
(o-násake お情け), nínjō´ 人情

fellow *n* (*person*) hito 人・ひと, …
hitó …人; monó 者, yátsu やつ・奴;
(*comrade*) fellow …… dō´shi …同志;
(*man*) otoko 男

female *n* onná (no hito) 女 (の人),
josei 女性; ***female* …** (*animal*) mesu
no …・メスの…

female flower *n* mebana 雌花

female impersonator *n* (*in Kabuki*)
onna-gata 女形, óyama おやま・女形

female student *n* jo (-shi) gákusei
女 (子) 学生

fence *n* kakíne 垣根, (*wall*) hei 塀

fencing n fenshingu フェンシング; *the art of Japanese fencing* (*with bamboo swords*) kéndō´ 剣道

fermented adj 発酵した

fermented bean paste míso みそ・味噌 (o-míso お味噌)

fermented soy beans nattō´ 納豆・ナットウ

fern n shída しだ・シダ

royal fern n (*osmund*) zenmai ぜんまい・ゼンマイ

ferry (*them over*) v watashimásu (watasu, watashite) 渡します(渡す、渡して)

ferryboat n watashi-búne 渡し舟[船]

fester v umimásu (umu, unde) うみ[膿み]ます(うむ、うんで)

festival n matsuri 祭り (o-matsuri お祭り)

feudal (*period, system*) adj hō´ken (-jídai/-séido) no 封建(時代/制度)の

feudal lord n daimyō´大名 (o-daimyō´お大名)

fever n netsú 熱 (o-netsú お熱); fiibā フィーバー; *became feverish* fiibā shimásu (suru, shite) フィーバーします(する、して)

few adj sukóshi (no) 少し(の); sukunái 少ない

a few wazuka わずか; sukoshi 少し→ **several**

a few days ago sendatté せんだって・先だって, senjitsu 先日

fewer adj (yori) sukunái (より)少ない

fib n (*lie*) úso うそ・嘘

fiber n sén'i 繊維; (*line*) súji 筋・すじ

synthetic fiber n kasen 化繊

fickle adj uwaki (na) 浮気(な)

fiction n shō´setsu 小説, tsukuri-banashi 作り話, fikushon フィクション

science fiction n saiensu fikushon サイエンスフィクション, esu-efu (shōsetsu) SF(小説)

fief n ryóchi 領地

field n (*dry*) hatake 畑; nóhara 野原, nó 野, hárappa 原っぱ; (*rice paddy*) tá 田, tanbo 田んぼ; (*specialty*) senmon 専門; (*out in the field*) yagai 野外

field day n 1. (*military*) yagai-enshū-bi 野外演習日 2. (*athletic festival*)

undō-kai 運動会 3. (*picnic*) pikunikku ピクニック

field study/trip/work n kengaku 見学

fielder n yashu 野手

fierce adj hageshíi 激しい, sugói すごい・凄い

fifteen n jū´-go 十五・15

fifth adj go-banmé (no) 五番目(の), itsutsu-mé (no) 五つ目(の)

the fifth day itsuka-me 五日目, (*of the month*) itsuka 五日

fifth floor n go-kai 五階

fifty n go-jū´ 五十・50

fifty thousand go-mán 五万・50,000

fig n ichíjiku いちじく・イチジク

fight v tatakaimásu (tatakau, tatakatte) 戦います(戦う、戦って) → **argue**

figure → **count; number; think; shape; body; being; person; diagram**

file n 1. (*nail file, etc.*) yasuri やすり 2. (*computer*) fairu ファイル 3. → **folder** 4. v (*grinds*) surimásu (súru, sutté) すります(する、すって) 5. v (*submit*) teishutsu shimásu (suru, shite) 提出します(提出する、提出して); ~ *income tax* kakutei o shinkoku shimásu 確定申告をします 6. v (*store document*) shorui o tojimásu (tojíru, tojite) 書類を綴じます(綴じる、綴じて)

filet n (*of pork etc.*) hire ヒレ

Filipino n (*language*) Firipin-go フィリピン語; (*person*) Firipin-jin フィリピン人

fill v 1. ippai ni shimásu (suru, shite) いっぱいにします(する、して); mitashimásu (mitásu, mitáshite) 満たします(満たす、満たして); *fills the tank, fills it up* man-tan ni shimásu (suru, shite) 満タンにします(する、して) 2. (*fulfills*) konashimásu (konasu, konashite) こなします(こなす、こなして), ~ *an order* chūmon o ko-nashimásu 注文をこなします 3. ~ *in* (*information*) kaki-iremásu (kaki-ireru, kaki-irete) 書き入れます(書き入れる、書き入れて), ki-nyū shimásu (suru, shite) 記入します(する、して)

filling station → **gas station**

film n f(u)irumu フィルム(フィルム);

(*movie*) eiga 映画

filter 1. *n* f(u)írutā フィルター（フィルター） **2.** *v* (*filters it*) koshimásu (kosu, koshíte) こします（こす、こして）

filth *n* obutsu 汚物

filthy → dirty

fin *n* hire ひれ・ヒレ

final *adj* saigo (no) 最後（の）, saishū (no) 最終

finalization *n* seiritsu 成立; *gets finalized* seiritsu shimásu (suru, shíte) 成立します（する、して）

finance 1. *n* kin'yū 金融; kéizai 経済; zaisei 財政

Ministry of finance *n* Zaimú-shō 財務省; (*financing*) yūzū 融通

2. finances it *v* yūzū shimásu (suru, shíte) 融通します（する、して）

financial circles *n* zaikai 財界

financial institution *n* kinyū-kíkan 金融機関

find 1. *v* mitsukemásu (mitsukeru, mitsukete) 見つけます（見つける、見つけて） **2.** *n* (*bargain*) horidashi-mono 掘り出し物

find fault with togamemásu (togaméru, togámete) とがめ[咎め]ます（とがめる、とがめて）

find out (*hears*) (… ga) mimí ni hairi-másu (háiru, háitte) (…が)耳に入ります（入る、入って）; (… ga) wakarimásu (wakáru, wakátte) (…が)分かります（分かる、分かって）

fine 1. *adj* (*small/detailed*) komakái 細かい, (*minute*) bisai (na) 微細（な）, (*delicate*) bimyō´ (na) 微妙（な） **2. → OK, good, splendid, fair 3.** (*penalty*) bakkin 罰金

finger *n* yubí 指・ゆび

finger food *n* o-tsúmami おつまみ, tsumami つまみ・ツマミ

fingernail *n* (yubi no) tsume（指の）つめ・爪・ツメ

fingerprint *n* shimon 指紋

finish 1. *n* → **end 2.** *v* (*finishes …ing*) …te shimaimásu (shimau, shimatte) …てしまいます（しまう、しまって）

Finland *n* Finrando フィンランド

Finn *n* (*person*) Finrando-jin フィンランド人

Finnish *adj* (*language*) Finrando-go no フィンランド語の; (*person*) Finrando-jin no フィンランド人の

fir *n* mómi もみ・モミ

fire 1. *n* hí 火, (*accidental*) kájí 火事, kasai 火災; (*bonfire*) takibi たき火 **2.** *v* (*lays off disemploys*) kubi ni shimásu (suru, shíte) 首にします（する、して）, kotowarimásu (kotowáru, kotowátte) 断ります（断る、断って）, káiko shimásu (suru, shíte) 解雇します（する、して）; *got fired* kubi ni narimáshita 首になりました

fire alarm *n* kasai-kéihō´ 火災警報; (*device*) kasai-hō´chíki 火災報知器

fire department *n* shō´bō-sho 消防署

fire engine *n* shō´bō´-sha 消防車

fire extinguisher *n* shō´ká-ki 消火器

fire fighter *n* shō´bō´-shi 消防士

fire fighting *n* shō´bō´ 消防

fire house/station *n* shō´bō-sho 消防署

fireman → fire fighter

fireplug *n* shō´ka-sen 消火栓

firewood *n* taki-gi たきぎ・薪, maki まき・薪

fireworks *n* hána-bi 花火・はなび

fireworks exhibition *n* hanabi-taikai 花火大会

firm 1. *adj* jō´bu (na) 丈夫（な）; (*hard*) katai 固い・硬い・堅い **2.** *n* (*business*) → **company**

firmly *adv* kataku 固く・硬く・堅く; (*securely*) chanto ちゃんと; (*resolutely*) shikkári しっかり; (*definitely*) kippári (to) きっぱり（と）

first *adj* hajime (no) 初め（の）, saisho (no) 最初（の）, hatsu (no) 初（の）; (*number one*) ichí-ban 一番（の）; *the first* daiichi (no) 第一（の） *adv* (*first of all*) dái-ichi (ni) 第一（に）, mázu まず・先ず; (*ahead of others*) saki (ni) 先（に）

first aid *n* ō´kyū´-téate 応急手当; ~ *kit* kyūkyū´-bako 救急箱

first class *adj* ik-kyū 一級; (*ticket, seat*) it-tō´ 一等; (*hotel, school*) ichiryū (no) 一流（の）

first day of the month *n* tsuitachí 一日・ついたち

409

first day of the year n ganjitsu 元日, gantan 元旦

first floor n ik-kai 一階

first generation n is-sei 一世

first time adj hajímete (no) 初めて(の)

first volume (of a set of 2 or 3) n jō´-kan 上巻, jō´ 上

first-rate adj ichiryū (no) 一流(の); jō´tō (no) 上等(の)

first-run movie n rō´do-shō´ ロードショー

first-year student n ichinén-sei 一年生

fish 1. n sakana 魚・さかな (o-sakana お魚), uo 魚: 1: ip-piki 一匹, 2: ní-hiki 二匹, 3: sánbiki 三匹, how many nán-biki 何匹; sliced raw ~ sashimi 刺身・さしみ 2. v (angles) tsurimásu (tsuru, tsutte) 釣ります(釣る, 釣って)

fishballs n (for soup) tsumire つみれ

fish cake n (steamed) kamaboko かまぼこ; (boiled) hanpén はんぺん; (broiled) chikuwa ちくわ・竹輪; (deep-fried) Satsumá-age さつま[薩摩]揚げ

fish dealer/market n sakana-ya 魚屋

fish meal n soboro そぼろ

fisherman n ryō´shi 漁師, gyo´fu 魚夫

fishhook n tsuribari 釣り針・つり針

fishing n (as sport) (sakaná-) tsuri (魚)釣り, ryō´ 漁; (business) gyogyō´ 漁業

fishy adj (questionable) kusái 臭い・くさい; fishy-smelling namagusái 生臭い

fist n kobushi こぶし・拳, genkotsu げんこつ・拳骨, genko げんこ

fit 1. adj (suitable) tekigi (no) 適宜・てきぎ(の); fits ... nicely ...ni yóku aimásu (aū, átte) ...に良く合います(合う, 合って) 2. v fits it to ... ni ate-hamemásu (ate-haméru, ate-hámete) ...に当てはめます(当てはめる, 当てはめて) 3. n (a good fit) saizu ga atteiru サイズが合っている

five n gó 五・5; itsútsu 五つ; fáibu ファイブ

five; five days itsu-ká 五日・いつか; 5 pieces (small things) gó-ko 五個,

5 trees (or long things) go-hon 五本; 5 sheets (flat things) go-mai 五枚; 5 cars (or machines/vehicles) go-dai 五台; 5 copies (books/magazines) gó-satsu 五冊; 5 cats (or small animals) gó-hiki 五匹; 5 cows (or large aminals) go-tō´ 五頭; 5 birds/rabbits gó-wa 五羽; 5 cupfuls go-hai 五杯; 5 days itsuka 五日, itsuka-kan 五日間; 5 o'clock gó-ji 五時・5時; 5 hours go-jikan 五時間; 5 minutes go-fun 五分; 5 months go-kágetsu 五ヶ月, gokágetsu-kan 五ヶ月間; 5 years go-nen 五年, go nén-kan 五年間; 5 years old itsútsu 五つ・いつつ, go-sai 五歳; 5 people go-nín 五人; 5 yen (money) go-en 五円; 5 degrees gó-do 五度; 5 times go-dó 五度, go-kái 五回, go-hén 五遍; 5 floors/stories go-kai 五階

five hundred n go-hyakú 五百・500

five o'clock shadow n bushō´-hige 無精[不精]ひげ

five thousand n go-sén 五千・5,000

fix 1. v (repairs) naoshimásu (naósu, naóshite) 直します(直す, 直して); (makes) tsukurimásu (tsukúru, tsukutte) 作ります(作る, 作って); (prepares) sonaemásu (sonáeru, sonáete) 備えます(備える, 備えて); (settles) sadame-másu (sadaméru, sadámete) 定めます(定める, 定めて) 2. n (plight) hamé はめ・羽目, kukyō 苦境

fixed 1. adj (settled) ittei (no) 一定(の); (periodic) téiki (no) 定期(の); tei-...shi- 定... 2. gets ~ (repaired) naori-másu (naóru, naótte) 直ります(直る, 直って); (settled) sadamarimásu (sadamáru, sadamátte) 定まります(定まる, 定まって)

fixedly (staring) adv jitto じっと

fixture n kígu 器具

flag n hatá 旗; (national) kokki 国旗

flame n honō´ 炎・ほのお

flannel n néru ネル, furanneru フランネル

flap 1. n (of envelope, etc.) futa ふた・蓋, furappu フラップ 2. v ~ the wings habatakimásu (habatáku, habatáite) 羽ばたきます(羽ばたく, 羽ばたいて)

flare *n* hatsuen-tō 発煙筒, furea フレア

flashing *n* pikápika ぴかぴか・ピカピカ

flashlight *n* kaichū-déntō´ 懐中電灯, dentō´ 電灯

flashy *adj* hadé (na) 派手(な)

flask *n* furasuko フラスコ

flat **1.** *n* heimen 平面 **2.** *n* (*apartment*) furátto フラット, apāto アパート **3.** *v* taira ni shimásu (suru, shite) 平らにします(する, して) **4.** *adj* taira (na) 平ら(な), hiratai 平たい; (*flavorless*) ajikenái 味気ない

flat land *n* heichi 平地

flat rate *n* kin'itsu-ryōkin 均一料金

flat tire *n* panku パンク; *gets a ~* panku shimásu (suru, shite) パンクします(する, して)

flatfish *n* karei カレイ・鰈

flathead *n* (*fish*) kochi コチ・鯒

flatter *v* o-seji o iimásu (iu/yū, itte/yutte) お世辞を言います(言う, 言って/ゆって); goma o surimásu (súru, sutté) ごま[胡麻・ゴマ]をすります(する, すって)

flattery *n* o-seji お世辞; gomasuri ごま[胡麻・ゴマ]すり

flatulate *v* onara o shimásu (suru, shite) おならをします(する, して), [INFORMAL] hé o hirimásu (híru, hítté) 屁をひります(ひる, ひって)

flatulence *n* onara おなら・オナラ, hé へ・屁

flavor **1.** *n* aji 味・あじ, fū´mí 風味; (*seasoning*) chō´mi 調味, kagen 加減 **2.** *v* (*seasons it*) … ni aji o tsukemásu (tsukéru, tsukéte) …に味を付け[つけ]ます(付ける, 付けて)

flavor sprinkles (*to top rice*) *n* furikake ふりかけ・フリカケ

flavorless *adj* ajike-nái 味気ない

flaw *n* kizu 傷, (*defect*) ketten 欠点

flax *n* asá 麻・あさ

flea *n* nomí ノミ・蚤

flee *v* nigemásu (nigéru, nígete) 逃げます(逃げる, 逃げて)

fleet *n* (*fleet of ships*) kantai 艦隊

fleeting *adj* (*transitory*) hakánai はかない・儚い

fleeting moments *n* hakánai isshun

はかない一瞬, tsukanoma つかの間

flesh *n* nikutai 肉体

flicker *n* chiratsuki ちらつき; chika-chikashita hikari チカチカした光

flies → fly

flight (*number* …) *n* …-bin …便

flight attendant *n* kyakushitsu jō´muin 客室乗務員, furaito-atendanto フライト・アテンダント

flint (*for lighter*) *n* (ráitā no) ishí (ライターの)石

float **1.** *v* (*it floats*) ukabimásu (ukabu, ukande) 浮かびます(浮かぶ, 浮かんで), ukimásu (uku, uite) 浮きます(浮く, 浮いて); (*floats it*) ukabemásu (ukaberu, ukabete) 浮かべます(浮かべる, 浮かべて) **2.** *n* (*swimming float*) ukiwa 浮き輪

floating assets *n* ryūdō shisan 流動資産

floating exchange rate *n* hendō (kawase) rēto 変動(為替)レート, hendō kawase sōba 変動為替相場

flock **1.** *n* muré 群れ **2.** *v* *they ~ together* muragarimásu (muragáru, muragátte) 群がります(群がる, 群がって)

flood **1.** *n* kō´zui 洪水, ō´mízú 大水 **2.** *v* hanran shimásu (suru, shite) 氾濫[はんらん]します(する, して)

floor *n* yuka 床, furoa フロア; (*story*) (-)kai 階, *What ~?* nan-gai/kai 何階 (*1st ~* ik-kai 一階, *2nd ~* ni kai 二階, *3rd ~* san-gai 三階, san kai 三階); *mezzanine* (*floor*) chū-ní-kai 中二階

floor lamp *n* (*denki*) sutándo (電気)スタンド

floor mat(ting) *n* tatami タタミ・畳

floor space *n* taté-tsubo 建て坪 (*in units of tsubo; 3.954 sq. yards*)

floppy (*disku*) *n* furoppii (disuku) フロッピー・ディスク, FD

florist *n* haná-ya 花屋

flounder *n* hirame ヒラメ・平目

flour *n* koná 粉・こな, kó 粉; (*wheat*) komugi-ko 小麦粉

flourish *v* sakaemásu (sakáeru, sakáete) 栄えます(栄える, 栄えて)

flourishing *adj* nigíyaka (na) にぎやか[賑やか](な)

flow **1.** *it flows v* nagaremásu (nagaréru, nagárete) 流れます(流れる, 流れて) **2.** *it flows* v nagashimásu (nagásu, nagáshite) 流します(流す, 流して) **3.** n (*outflow*) de 出, nagaré 流れ

flower 1. n haná 花 (o-hana お花) **2.** v (*blooms*) (hana ga) sakimásu (saku, saite) (花が)咲きます(咲く, 咲いて)

flower arrangement n (*arranging*) o-hana お花, ikébana 生け花・いけばな, [BOOKISH] kadō 華道, furawā arenjimento フラワーアレンジメント; (*in a tall vase*) nage-ire 投げ入れ, (*in a low basin*) moribana 盛り花

flower bed n kadan 花壇・花だん

flower bud n tsubomi つぼみ・蕾

flower cards n (*game*) haná-fuda 花札, hana-káruta 花かるた・花カルタ

flowerpot n uekí-bachi 植木鉢

flower scissors n hana-basami 花ばさみ

flower shop → **florist**

flower vase n kabin 花瓶, káki 花器

flower viewing n hana-mí 花見 (o-han-amiお花見)

flu n infuruénza インフルエンザ

fluent adj ryū´chō´ (na) 流ちょう[流暢](な); (*can speak it fluently*) jiyū (/ryū´chō´) ni hanasemásu (hanaséru, hanásete) 自由(/流暢)に話せます (話せる, 話せて)

fluent(ly) adj (adv) (*speaking*) pera-pera (to) ぺらぺら・ペラペラ(と); (*writing*) surasura (to) すらすら(と)

fluorescent light n keikō´-tō´ 蛍光灯

flush n (*the flush on one's face*) sekimen (shimásu; suru, shite) 赤面 (します; する, して)

flush v (*flush the toilet*) (toire o) naga-shimásu (nagasu, nagashite) (トイレを)流します(流す, 流して)

flush toilet n suisen-tóire 水洗トイレ

flustered; gets ~ awatemásu (awateru, awatete) あわてます・慌てます(あわてる, あわてて); *feels ~* teremásu (teréru, térete) 照れます(照れる, 照れて); *a person easily ~* awate-mono あわて者・慌て者

flute n fue 笛・ふえ; furúto フルート; *vertical bamboo ~* shakuhachi 尺八

flutter; one's heart flutters dókidoki

shimásu (suru, shíte) どきどき[ドキドキ]します(する, して)

fly 1. n (*insect*) hae 蝿・ハエ (**1:** ip-píki 一匹, **2:** ní-hiki 二匹, **3:** sánbiki 三匹, *how many* nánbiki 何匹) **2.** *your ~ is open* (*unzipped/unbuttoned*) máe (chákku) ga aite imásu 前(チャック)が開いています **3.** v (*moves in air*) tobimásu (tobu, tonde) 飛びます(飛ぶ, 飛んで); (*flies it*) tobashimásu (tobasu, tobashite) 飛ばします(飛ばす, 飛ばして), *flies a kite* táko o agemásu (ageru, agete) 凧をあげます(あげる, あげて); (*pilots*) sō´jū shimásu (suru, shíte) 操縦します(する, して); (*goes by plane*) hikō´-ki de ikimásu (iku, itte) 飛行機で行きます(行く, 行って)

foam → **bubble**

focus 1. n (*camera*) pinto ピント; (*focal point*) shō´ten 焦点; *out-of-focus* pinboke ピンぼけ **2.** v shōten o awasemásu (awaseru, awasete) 焦点を合わせます (合わせる, 合わせて); shūchū-sasemasu (shūchū-saseru, shūchū-sasete) 集中させます(集中させる, 集中させて)

fodder n shiryō 飼料

fog n kiri 霧・きり

foggy adj kiri ga fukái 霧が深い

fold 1. n ori-mé 折り目 **2.** v (*folds it*) orimásu (óru, ótte) 折ります(折る, 折って), (*folds it up*) tatamimásu (tatamu, tatande) 畳みます(畳む, 畳んで); (*it folds*) oremásu (oréru, órete) 折れます(折れる, 折れて); *folds one's arms* udé o kumimásu (kúmu, kúnde) 腕を組みます(組む, 組んで)

folder n **1.** *file ~* kami-básami 紙挟み, fairu ファイル **2.** (*computer*) foruda フォルダ, forudā フォルダー

folding money n (o-)satsu (お)札

fold up v (ori-) tatamimásu (tatamu, tatande) (折り)畳みます(畳む, 畳んで)

foliage n ha 葉

folk adj minkan no 民間の

folkcraft n mingei 民芸, mingei-hin 民芸品

folk dance n fōku dansu フォークダンス, minzoku-buyō 民族舞踊

412

folk dancer *n* minzoku-buyō-ka 民族舞踊家

folk medicine *n* (*medicine*) minkan-yaku 民間薬, (*treatment*) minkan-ryōhō 民間療法

folks → people; parents; family

folk song *n* min'yō´民謡, fōku songu フォークソング

follow *v* (*follows it*) … no áto o tsuke-másu (tsukéru, tsukéte) …のあとをつけます(つける, つけて); (*adheres to*) … ni tsukimásu (tsukú, tsúite) … に付きます(付く, 付いて); (*conforms to*) … ni shitagaimásu (shitagau, shitagatte) … に従います(従う, 従って); (*runs along*) … ni soimásu (sou, sotte) …に沿います(沿う, 沿って); ~ *the example of* … o mi-naraimásu (mi-narau, mi-naratte) …を見習います(見習う, 見習って)

follower *n* (*adherent*) shijisha 支持者; (*follower of a stronger person or boss*) kobun 子分

following **1.** *adj* tsugí (no) 次(の), ika (no) 以下(の), kaki (no) 下記(の) **2.** *n* (*a following*) fan ファン **3.** *prep* … no ato ni 一の後に

folly *n* gukō 愚行, orokasa 愚かさ

fond of → like

fondness *n* konomi 好み

fondue *n* fondu フォンデュ

font *n* **1.** fonto フォント **2.** (*church*) senrei-ban 洗礼盤 (= *baptismal bowl*)

food *n* **1.** tabe-mónó 食べ物, góhan ご飯, shokúmotsu 食物; (*meal*) shoku 食, (*Western*) yō´-shoku 洋食, (*Japanese*) wa-shoku 和食 **2.** *n* (*stuff*) → groceries

food cooked and served in a pan nabé-mono 鍋物

food delivered to order demae 出前

food poisoning shoku-chūdoku 食中毒, shoku-atari 食あたり

food with rice (*food poured over rice*) donburí-mono どんぶり物, don-mono 丼物

fool **1.** *n* báka ばか・馬鹿, tónma とんま・頓馬

fool around *v* fuzakemásu (fuzakeru, fuzakete) ふざけます(ふざける, ふざ

けて) **2.** *fool (someone)* *v* karakai-másu (karakau, karakatte) からかいます(からかう, からかって)

foolish *adj* baka-rashíí ばか[馬鹿]らしい, báka (na) ばか[馬鹿](な)

foolproof *adj* machigae yō no nai 間違えようのない, dare ni de mo dekiru 誰にでもできる

foot *n* ashí 足; (*of a mountain*) fumotó ふもと・麓; *at the ~ of* … no fumotó(de) … のふもと[麓](で)

football *n* (*American*) (amerikan) futto-bōru (アメリカン) フットボール, amefuto アメフト

footing *n* ashi-ba 足場, kiso 基礎

footlight *n* futto-raito フットライト, kyakkō 脚光

footnote *n* kyakuchū 脚注

footprint *n* ashi-áto 足跡

foot sore (*from shoe rubbing*) *n* kutsu-zure 靴ずれ・靴擦れ

footstool *n* ashi-nosé-dai 足乗せ台

footwear *n* hakimono 履物・はきもの

for *prep* … (no) tamé (ni)…(の)ため(に); … ni (wa) … に(は); … ni tótte … にとって; …no… の…; (*for the use of*) …-yō´(no) …用(の); (*suitable for*) …-muki (no) …向き(の); (*bound/ intended for*) …-muke (no) …向け(の) do it for me/us, they do it for you … -te kuremásu (kureru, kurete) …てくれます(くれる, くれて) [HONORIFIC] kudasaimásu (kudasáru, kudasátte) くださいます(くださる, くださって) do it for you/them, you do it for them … -te agemásu (ageru, agete) …てあげます(あげる, あげて)/[HONORIFIC] sashi-agemásu (sashi-ageru, sashi-agete) さし[差し]あげます(さし[差し]あげる, さし[差し]あげて)

for a long time *adv* (*now*) zutto máe kara ずっと前から

for a while *adv* shibáraku しばらく, hitómazu ひとまず

for example, for instance *adv* tatóeba 例えば・たとえば

for sure *adv* kanarazu 必ず, zéhi 是非・ぜひ, táshikani 確かに; (*not forgetting*) wasurenáide 忘れないで

for the first time *adv* hajímete 初めて

for the most part *adv* taigai たいがい・大概, ō´kata おおかた・大方

for the reason that … *adv* to iu riyū de … という理由で, …yué ni …故に・ゆえに

for the time being *adv* tō´bun 当分, hitómazu ひとまず

forbearance *n* shínbō´ 辛抱

forbid *v* kin-jimásu (kin-jiru, kin-jite) 禁じます(禁じる, 禁じて)

force 1. *n* (*power*) jitsuryoku 実力 2. *v* forces one (*to do*) múri o (or shíite) sasemásu (saseru, sasete) 無理に[強いて]させます(させる, させて)

forced landing *n* fujichaku 不時着

forceps *n* pinsetto ピンセット

forcible *adj* gō´in (na) 強引(な); forcibly gō´in ni 強引に, shíite 強いて

ford *n* asase 浅瀬

foreboding *n* yokan 予感

forecast 1. *n* yohō´ 予報, yosoku 予測; weather ~ tenki-yóhō´ 天気予報 2. forecasts it *v* (*predicts, estimates*) it yosoku shimásu (suru, shite) 予測します(する, して)

forehead *n* hitai 額, odéko おでこ

foreign *adj* gaikoku (no) 外国(の), gai-… 外…, (*Western*) yō´… 洋…

foreign currency operations *n* gaikoku-kawase (gaitame) 外国為替 (外為)

foreign language *n* gaikoku-go 外国語

foreign minister *n* gaimu-daijin 外務大臣

Foreign Ministry *n* gaimu-shō 外務省

Foreign Office *n* gaikō-kikan 外交機関

foreign policy *n* gaikō-seisaku 外交政策

foreign student(s) *n* ryūgaku-sei 留学生

foreigner *n* gaijin 外人, gaikokú-jin 外国人

foreigner card *n* gáikokujin tōrokushō (/kādo) 外国人登録証(/カード)

forest *n* mori 森, (*grove*) hayashi 林

forever *adv* ítsu mo いつも, eien ni 永遠に, eikyū ni 永久に

forwarding *adj* tensō (no) 転送(の), unsō (no) 運送(の)

forwarding address *n* tensō-saki (no) jūsho 転送先(の)住所

forwarding agency *n* unsō-gyōsha 運送業者

forwarding business *n* unsō-gyō 運送業

forwarding of e-mail *n* mēru (no) tensō メール(の)転送

foreword *n* jobun 序文, mae-gaki 前書き

forward planning *n* keikaku 計画

forge *v* 1. (*a signature, document, etc.*) nisemásu (niseru, nisete) 似せます (似せる, 似せて) 2. (*tempers metal*) kitaemásu (kitáéru, kitáete) 鍛えます (鍛える, 鍛えて)

forger *n* gizō-sha 偽造者

forgery *n* (*making a fake copy*) gizō´ 偽造; (*a fake*) nise-mono にせもの

forget *v* wasuremásu (wasureru, wasurete) 忘れます(忘れる, 忘れて); don't ~ to do it wasurenáide shite kudasai 忘れないで下さい

forgetful *adj* wasureppói 忘れっぽい

forget-me-not *n* wasurena-gusa 忘れな草・ワスレナグサ

forgive *v* yurushimásu (yurúsu, yurúshite) 許します(許す, 許して)

forgiveness *n* yurushi 許し

fork 1. *n* fō´ku フォーク 2. (*forking, branching*) wakare 分かれ, matá 又・叉, futa-matá 二叉[股]

fork out money (*for …*) (… ni) okane o dashimasu (dasu, dashite) (…に)お金を出します(出す, 出して)

forked *adj* (*bifurcate*) futamata (no) 二叉[股](の)

forklift *n* fōku rifuto フォークリフト

form 1. *n* katachi 形, katá 型, (*figure*) súgata 姿 (o-súgata お姿), kakkō´ かっこう・格好・恰好; narí なり (o-nári おなり), (*style*) tái 体; (*appearance*) teisai 体裁, (*blank paper*) yō´shi 用紙; (*document*) shorui 書類 2. *v* (*creates it*) nashimásu (násu, náshite) 成します(成す, 成して), tsukurimásu (tsukúru, tsukutte) 作ります(作る, 作って)

formal *adj* seishiki (na/no) 正式(な/の); fōmaru (na) フォーマル(な);

keishikiteki (na) 形式的(な); (*procedure, red tape*) te-tsúzuki 手続き

formality *n* fōmaru フォーマル; keishikiteki 形式的

format **1.** *n* (*book, magazine*) teisai 体裁, hankei 版型; (*data*) fó´matto フォーマット **2.** *v* (*format a disk*) (disuku o) fōmatto(-ka) shimásu (suru, shite) (ディスクを)フォーマット(化)します(する, して)

formation *n* (*getting formed*) seiritsu 成立

formed; **gets ~** (*organized*) seiritsu shimásu (suru, shite) 成立します(する, して)

former *adj* máe (no) 前(の); móto (no) もと[元](の); [BOOKISH] zén... 前...; *the former* zénsha 前者

formerly *adv* móto wa もと[元]は; kátsute かつて

fortnight *n* ni-shūkan 2週間・二週間

fortuitous (*accidental*) *adj* gūzen (no) 偶然(の)

fortunate *adj* saiwai (na) 幸い(な)

fortunately *adv* saiwai ni (mo) 幸いに(も)

fortune *n* (*property*) zaisan 財産; (*luck*) ún 運, únmei 運命; (*good luck*) saiwai 幸い, shiawase 幸せ; (*written*) (o)mikuji (お)みくじ

fortune-teller *n* uranái-shi 占い師

fortune-telling *n* uranai 占い

forty *n* yón jū 四十・40, shi-jū 四十

forty thousand *n* yon mán 四万・40,000

forward **1.** *adv* (*ahead*) máe e/ni 前[まえ]へ/に; *goes ~* susumimásu (susumu, susunde) 進みます(進む, 進んで) **2.** *adj* (*pushy*) bu-énryo (na) 無遠慮(な)

forwarding agent *n* unsō´-ya 運送屋

foster *v* yashinaimásu (yashinau, yashinatte) 養います(養う, 養って)

foster child *n* sodate-go 育て子, sato-go 里子

foster parent *n* sodate no oyá 育ての親, sato-oya 里親

foul **1.** *n* hansoku 反則 **2.** *v* hansoku shimásu (suru, shite) 反則します(する, して) → **dirty**

found **1.** → **find**; **gets ~** mitsukarimásu (mitsukaru, mitsukatte) 見つかります(見つかる, 見つかって) **2.** → **establish**

foundation *n* (*base*) kisó 基礎, (*basis*) konpon 根本, kihon 基本; (*non-profit organization*) zaidan 財団

fountain *n* funsui 噴水

fountain pen *n* mannén-hitsu 万年筆

four *n* yón 四・4, shí 四・4, yottsú 四つ・よっつ; (*4-oared racing boat*) foa (fō´) フォア(フォー); *number ~* yo-ban (*also* yónban) 四番

four; **4 pieces** (*small things*) yón ko 四個, (*long things*) yón hon 四本; **4 sheets** (*flat things*) yónmai (yo-mai) 四枚; **4 machines/vehicles** yón-dai 四台; **4 copies** (*books/magazines*) yón-satsu 四冊; (*small animals*) yón-hiki 四匹; (*large animals*) yón-hiki 四匹; **4 birds/rabbits** shí-wa/yón-wa 四羽; **4 cupfuls** yón-hai 四杯; **4 days** yokka 四日, yokká-kan 四日間; **4 o'clock** yó-ji 四時・4時; **4 hours** yo-jíkan 四時間; **4 minutes** yóm -pun 四分・4分 (*also* yón-fun 四分・4分); **4 months** yon-kágetsu 四ケ月; yonkagetsú-kan 四ケ月間; **4 years** yo-nen 四年, yo-nén-kan 四年間; **4 years old** yottsú 四つ, yón-sai 四歳; **4 yen** (*money*) yó(n)-en 四円; **4 people** yo-nín 四人, yo-nín 四人; **4 degrees** yón-do 四度; **4 times** yón-do 四度, yón kái 四回 yónhén 四遍; **4 floors/ stories** yon-kai 四階; **four-and-a half mat area** yo-jō´-han 四畳半

fourfold, two times doubled *n* yonbai 四倍

four hundred *n* yón-hyaku 四百・400

four or five *n* shi-go-... 四、五...

fourteen *n* jū-yón, jū-shí 十四・14; **~ days** jū-yokka 十四日; **14th** (*day of month*) jū-yokka 十四日; **~ people** jū´yo-nin 十四人; **~ years, the year 14** jū´yo-nen 十四年

fourteenth *adj* jūyo(m) -banmé (no) 十四番目(の); *the ~ day* jūyokka-mé 十四日目, (*of the month*) jū´-yokka 十四日

fourth *adj* yo-banmé (no) (*also* yonbanmé) 四番目(の), yottsu-mé (no) 四つ目(の); *the ~ day* yokka-mé 四日目, (*of the month*) yokka 四日; *~ floor*

415

four thousand

yon-kai 四階; **~ time** yon do-mé 四度目, yon kai-mé 四回目; **fourth-year student** yo-nén-sei 四年生

four thousand *n* yon-sén 四千・4,000

fowl *n* kakin 家禽・かきん

fox *n* kitsune キツネ・狐

fraction *n* **1.** ichibu 一部 **2.** (*mathematics*) bunsū 分数

fragile *adj* koware-yasúi 壊れやすい; (*thing*) koware-mono こわれもの, waremono われもの・割れ物

fragrance *n* kaori 香り・かおり

fragrant *adj* kaorimásu (kaoru, kaotte) 香ります(香る, 香って)

frail *adj* morói もろい・脆い; yowái 弱い

frame *n* wakú 枠, fuchí ふち・縁, kamachí かまち・框; (*of picture*) gaku-buchi 額縁; (*of glasses*) mégane no fuchí 眼鏡のふち

framework *n* kumi-tate 組み立て, honegumi 骨組み, furēmu wāku フレームワーク

France *n* Furansu フランス

frank *adj* sotchoku (na) 率直(な), assárishita ... あっさりした...; (*unreserved*) enryo ga/no nái 遠慮が/のない, enryo shinai 遠慮しない, bu-énryo (na) 無遠慮(な); (*uninhibited*) sappári shita ... さっぱりした...

frankly *adv* sotchoku ni 率直に, assári (to) あっさり(と); (*unreservedly*) enryo shináide 遠慮しないで; zubari ずばり

frantically *adv* chi-mánako ni nátte 血眼になって

fraud *n* sági 詐欺・サギ, inchiki いんちき

freak *n* hen-jin 変人

freckle *n* sobakasu そばかす

free *adj* (*gratis*) táda (no) ただ(の), (*as part of the service*) sābisu サービス; (*no fee/charge*) muryō´ (no) 無料(の); (*unrestrained*) jiyū (na) 自由(な); (*unoccupied*) hima (na) 暇(な); **sets ~** (*releases*) hanashimásu (hanásu, hanáshite) 放します(放す, 放して) → **liberate**

free-of-charge, FOC *adj* muryō no 無料の

free parking muryō-chūshajō 無料駐車場

free seat (*unreserved*) jiyū´-seki 自由席

freedom *n* jiyū´ 自由

freelance, freelancing *n* (*work*) jiyū´-gyō 自由業

freely *adv* jiyū´ ni 自由に

freeway *n* kō´soku-dō´ro 高速道路

freeze *v* (*it freezes*) kō´rimásu (kō´ru, kō´tte) 凍ります(凍る, 凍って); (*freezes it*) kō´rasemásu (kō´raseru, kō´rasete) 凍らせます(凍らせる, 凍らせて), reitō shimásu (suru, shite) 冷凍します(する, して)

Freeze! Ugokuna! 動くな!

freezer *n* reitōko 冷凍庫

freezer bags *n* reitō-yō baggu 冷凍用バッグ

French *n* (*language*) Furansu-go フランス語; (*person*) Furansú-jin フランス人

French beans (*kidney beans*) ingen インゲン, ingénmame インゲンマメ

French fries → fried potatoes

French kiss *n* furenchi-kisu フレンチキス

frequently → often

fresh *adj* atarashíi 新しい, shinsen (na) 新鮮(な), furesshu (na) フレッシュ(な); **~ from ...** ...-tate (no) ...たて(の), ...-ágari (no) ...上がり(の)

freshman *n* **1.** (*first year grade*) ichinén-sei 一年生 **2.** (*new student*) shinnyu-sei 新入生 **3.** (*new employee*) shinnyu-shain 新入社員

friction *n* masatsu 摩擦

Friday *n* Kin'yōbi 金曜日

Friday prayers *n* kinyō-reihai 金曜礼拝

Friday the 13th *n* jūsan-nichi no Kin'yōbi 13日の金曜日

fried chicken *n* (tori no) kara-age (鶏の)唐揚げ, furaido chikin フライドチキン

fried eggs *n* medama-yaki 目玉焼(き)

fried potatoes *n* furaido poteto フライドポテト

fried rice *n* chā´han チャーハン, yaki-meshi 焼き飯・ヤキメシ

fried shrimp *n* (*in batter*) ebi-ten えび

fuel

[海老・エビ]天, (*in bread crumbs*)
ebi-fúrai えび[海老・エビ]フライ
friend *n* tomodachi 友達 (o-tomodachi
お友達); furendo フレンド; tómó 友;
yūjin 友人, (*pal*) nakama 仲間 (o-nakama お仲間); aibō 相棒; (*accomplice*)
mikata 味方
  best friend *n* ichiban no shinyū 一番の
  親友; muni no tomodachi 無二の友達
  close friend *n* sinyū 親友
friendly *adj* yūkō-teki (na) 友好的(な);
furendorii (na) フレンドリー(な)
friendship *n* (*keeping company*) tsuki-
ai 付き合い (o-tsukiai お付き合い)
frightened → afraid
frightful *adj* kowái 怖い・こわい
frizzy *adj* chijireta 縮れた; ~ *hair*
chijireta kami(no ke) 縮れた髪(の毛)
frock *n* doresu ドレス
frog *n* **1.** kaeru カエル・蛙 **2.**
(*pinholder for flowers*) kénzan 剣山
frogman *n* daibā ダイバー
from *prep* ... kara ...から; ~ *now on*
kore kara これから, kongo 今後; ~ ...
to ...kara ...máde ...から...まで,
[BOOKISH] ... náishi ...ないし...
front **1.** *n* máe 前, (*ahead*) saki 先;
zenpō 前方; (*side*) omoté 表 **2.** *adj*
(*surface*) shō'mén (no) 正面(の),
zenmen (no) 前面(の)
  front gate/entrance *n* seimon 正門,
  omote-mon 表門; → **front door**
  front cover *n* hyōshi 表紙
  front desk *n* furonto フロント
  front door *n* omote-genkan 表玄関,
  shōmen-genkan 正面玄関, furonto-doa
  フロントドア
frontier *n* (*international border*)
kokkyō 国境
frost *n* shimó 霜・しも
frostbite *n* tōshō 凍傷, shimo-yake
しもやけ・霜焼け
frosted glass *n* suri-garasu すりガラス
frosting *n* furosutingu フロスティン
グ, aishingu アイシング
frown *v* **1.** nigái/shibui kao o shimásu
(suru, shite) 苦い/渋い顔をします
(する, して), kao o shikamemásu
(shikameru, shikamete) 顔をしかめま
す(しかめる, しかめて) **2.** *n* jūmen

shibui kao 渋い面
frozen; *is* ~ kō'tte imásu 凍っています
frozen food *n* reitō-shokuhin 冷凍食
品 (= *frozen meal*)
frozen heart *n* reitan na kokoro 冷淡
な心
frugal *adj* tsumashíi つましい, ken'-
yaku (na) 倹約(な), shísso (na) 質素
(な)
fruit *n* **1.** kudámono くだもの・果物,
kí-no mi 木の実, mi 実・み
  fruit juice *n* kajū 果汁, furūtsu jūsu
  フルーツジュース
  fruit market/shop *n* kudamónó-ya
  くだもの屋・果物屋
  fruit salad *n* furūtsu sarada フルーツ
  サラダ
2. (*product, outcome*) sanbutsu 産物
→ **result** → **crop**
fruitful *adj* minori no ōi 実りの多い,
yūeki (na) 有益(な)
frustrate *v* yaburimásu (yabúru,
yabútte) 破ります(破る, 破って),
zasetsu sasemásu (saseru, sasete) 挫
折させます(させる, させて); (*a plan*)
kujikimásu (kujíku, kujíite) くじき[挫
き]ます(くじく, くじいて)
frustrated; *gets* ~ yaburemásu
(yabúreru, yabúrete) 破れます(破れる,
破れて), zasetsu shimásu (suru, shite)
挫折します(する, して); (*a plan*)
kujikemásu (kujikéru, kujíkete) くじ
け[挫け]ます(くじける, くじけて)
frustration *n* zasetsu 挫折; (*feeling
of frustration*) zasetsú-kan 挫折感,
(*cause to lose hope*) shitsubo sasemásu
(saseru, sasete) 失望させます(させる,
させて), (*cause to despair*) rakutan
sasemásu (saseru, sasete) 落胆させま
す(させる, させて)
fry *v* agemásu (ageru, agete) 揚げ[あ
げ]ます(揚げる, 揚げて); (*pan fries,
sautés*) itamemásu (itaméru, itámete)
炒めます(炒める, 炒めて)
  frying pan *n* furai-pan フライパン
ftp *n* (= *file transfer protocol*) efu-tii-
pii, ftp エフ・ティー・ピー
fuel *n* nenryō' 燃料; (*firewood*) taki-gi
たきぎ; (*gasoline*) gasorin ガソリン
  fuel tank *n* nenryō'-tanku 燃料タンク

fugitive *n* tōbō-sha 逃亡者
Fujiyama *n* Fúji (-san) 富士(山)
fulfill *v* konashimásu (konasu, kona-shíte) こなします(こなす, こなして)
→ **accomplish**; *a desire is fulfilled* nozomiga kanaimásu (kanáu, kanátte) 望みが叶います(叶う, 叶って)
full *adj* ippai (no) いっぱい(の); (*of people*) man'in (no) 満員(の); *gets ~* michimásu (michíru, míchite) 満ちます(満ちる, 満ちて)
full coverage insurance *n* zengaku-hoken 全額保険
full dinners *n* furu-kōsu フルコース
full moon *n* mangetsu 満月
full name *n* furu nēmu フルネーム, shimei 氏名
full stop *n* (*period*) shūshí-fu 終止符, piriodo ピリオド
full tank *n* man-tan 満タン
full-time Japanese housewife *n* sengyō-shufu 専業主婦
full-time worker *n* jōkin rōdō-sha 常勤労働者
fully *adv* tappúri たっぷり; mán(-) …満… maru(-) … まる…; (*appreciating*) shimijími (to) しみじみ (と); *~ maturing* enjuku 円熟
fun *n* omoshirói (kotó) おもしろい[面白い](こと); asobi 遊び・あそび
function *n* **1.** yakumé 役目 (o-yakume お役目); hataraki 働き; kinō 機能 **2.** (*mathematics*) kansū 関数; (*function as…*) …to shite kinō shimásu (suru, shíte) …として機能します(する, して)
fund *n* shikín 資金, (*capital*) shihon 資本
fundamental *adj* konpon-teki (na) 根本的(な), kihon-teki (na) 基本的(な)
fundamentally *adv* konpon-teki (ni) 根本的(に), kihon-teki (ni) 基本的(に)
funeral *n* (o-)sō´shiki (お)葬式
funeral home *n* (o-)sō´shiki-jō (お)葬式場, sō´gi-jō 葬儀場
funfair *n* yūen-chi 遊園地
funicular *n* kēburu-kā ケーブルカー
fun-loving *adj* omoshiroi-koto zuki

(no) 面白いこと好き(の), omoshiroi-koto ga suki (na) 面白いことが好き (な), tanoshii-koto ga suki (na) 楽しいことが好き(な)
funnel *n* jō´go じょうご, [BOOKISH] rō´to ろうと・漏斗
funny *adj* okashíi おかしい, okáshi na おかしな; (*comical*) kokkei (na) こっけい・滑稽(な), hyōkín (na) ひょうきん(な), (*droll*) yúkai (na) ゆかい・愉快(な), (*strange*) hén (na) 変(な), fushigi (na) 不思議・ふしぎ(な)
fur *n* ke-gawa 毛皮
fur coat *n* ke-gawa no kōto 毛皮のコート
furious *adj* gekido-shita 激怒した
furlough *n* hima 暇・ひま
furnace *n* ro 炉; kamado かまど, danbō (sō´chi) 暖房(装置)
furnish *v* (*provides*) sonaemásu (sonáeru, sonáete) 備えます(備える, 備えて)
furnished *adj* (*with household goods*) kagu-tsuki (no) 家具付き(の)
furniture *n* kágu 家具
furniture store *n* kagú-ya 家具屋
furry *adj* kegawa no yō (na) 毛皮のよう(な)
further 1. *adv* (*more*) mótto saki (ni) もっと先(に), (*elsewhere*) hoka no basho (de) 他の場所(で) **2.** (*advances it*) *v* mótto susumemásu (susumeru, susumete) 進めます(進める, 進めて)
fuse *n* hyū´zu ヒューズ
fusion *n* gō´dō´ 合同
fuss *n* sáwagi 騒ぎ, ō´-sáwagi 大騒ぎ
fussy *adj* ki-muzukashíi 気難しい → **choosy**
futile *adj* muda (na) 無駄(な), muna-shii 空しい・虚しい・むなしい
futon *n* futon ふとん・布団
future *n* shō´rai 将来, mírai 未来, saki 先(o-saki お先); zénto 前途, sue 末
in the future kongo 今後
in the near future chikái uchí (ni) 近いうち(に)
futures *n* sakimono-torihiki 先物取引

G

gabble v hayakuchi ni hanashimásu (hanasu, hanashite) 早口に話します (話す, 話して), pechakucha shaberimásu (shaberu, shabette) ぺちゃくちゃしゃべり[喋り]ます(しゃべる, しゃべって)

gable n kirizuma 切妻・きりづま

gaffe n bu-sahō 無作法・不作法

gaiety n o-matsuri sawagi お祭り騒ぎ

gain 1. n toku 得 (o-toku お得), (income) shotoku 所得 **2.** v → get

gait n aruki-kata 歩き方

gale n bōfū 暴風

gall bladder n (medical) tannō 胆嚢・胆のう

gallery n gyararii ギャラリー, garō 画廊

gallon n garon ガロン

gallop 1. n gyaroppu ギャロップ **2.** v kakemásu (kakéru, kákete) 駆けます(駆ける, 駆けて)

galoshes n amá-gutsu 雨靴

gambling n kaké(-goto) 賭け事, tobaku とばく・賭博, bakuchi ばくち・博奕

game 1. n asobi 遊び, gḗmu ゲーム; **card ~** toranpu トランプ **2.** (athletic) kyōgi 競技

gang n renchū/renjū 連中, nakama 仲間

gangway n taráppu タラップ

gap n suki-ma すき間・隙間, suki すき・隙; ware-me 割れ目, kire-mé 切れ目; zuré ずれ, gyáppu ギャップ

garage n gárḕji ガレージ, sháko 車庫

garbage n gomí ごみ・ゴミ, (kitchen waste) nama-gomi 生ごみ

garbage bag n gomi-búkuro ごみ袋
garbage bin/can n gomi-bako ごみ箱
garbage collector n gomí-ya (san) ごみ屋(さん)
garbage dump n gomi-sute ba ごみ捨て場

garden n niwa 庭 (o-niwa お庭)

gardener n ueki-ya 植木屋, niwa-shi 庭師

gardening n engei 園芸, gēdeningu ガーデニング

gargle v ugai shimásu (suru, shite) うがいします(する, して)

garlic n ninniku ニンニク・大蒜, gḗrikku ガーリック

garnishings n (to go with sashimi) tsumá つま・ツマ, tsukeawase つけ合わせ

garter n gā´ta ガーター

gas n **1.** (natural) gásu ガス **2.** (a gas, vapor) kitai 気体 **3.** (gasoline) gasorin ガソリン

gas bill n gasú-dai ガス代
gas company n gasu-gaisha ガス会社
gas mask n gasu-masuku ガスマスク
gas meter n gasu-mḗtē ガスメーター
gas range n gasu-rénji ガスレンジ
gas pedal ákuseru アクセル; **steps on the ~** ákuseru o fumimásu (fumu, funde) アクセルを踏みます[ふみます](踏む, 踏んで)

gas(oline) station n gasorin sutándo ガソリンスタンド

gasp v aegimásu (aégu, aéide) あえぎ[喘ぎ]ます(あえぐ, あえいで)

gate n món 門, (gateway) deiriguchi 出入り口, (of shrine) torii 鳥居; (front) omote-mon 表門, (back) uramon 裏門, (main [front]) seimon 正門; (at airport terminal) gē´to ゲート

gatekeeper n mónban 門番

gather 1. v (they gather) atsumarimásu (atsumáru, atsumátte) 集まります(集まる, 集まって), (to make a set) soroimásu (soróu, sorótte) 揃います(揃う, 揃って), (congregate) shūgō shimásu (suru, shite) 集合します(する, して); (gathers them) atsumemásu (atsuméru, atsúmete) 集めます(集める, 集めて), yosemásu (yoseru, yosete) 寄せます(寄せる, 寄せて) **2.** v (plucks, clips) tsumimásu (tsumu, tsunde) 摘みます(摘む, 摘んで) **3.** n (pleat) hida ひだ, gyazā ギャザー

gathering n shūgō 集合
gathering place n tamari-ba たまり場

gaudy adj hadé (na) 派手(な)

gauze n gā´ze ガーゼ

gave → give

gaze v mi-tsumemásu (mi-tsumeru, mi-tsúmete) 見つめます(見つめる, 見つめて), nagamemásu (nagaméru, nagámete) 眺めます(眺める, 眺めて)

gay adj 1. akarui 明るい, yúkai (na) ゆかい・愉快(な) 2. (homosexual) hómo (no) ホモ(の), gei (no) ゲイ(の)

gear n gí(y)a ギア[ギヤ], hagúruma 歯車

gear box n gí(y)a bokkusu ギア[ギヤ]ボックス, hensoku-sōchi 変速装置

high gear n kōsoku-gí(y)a 高速ギア[ギヤ]

low gear n teisoku-gí(y)a 低速ギア[ギヤ]

gearshift n hensoku-réba 変速レバー, shifuto-réba シフトレバー

gecko n yámori ヤモリ・守宮

Gee! interj wā! わあ！, ā! ああ！, sugoi! すごい！

geisha n geisha 芸者

gel n geru ゲル, jeru ジェル

gelatine n zerachin ゼラチン; (from tengusa 天草・テングサ seaweed) kanten 寒天・カンテン

gem n hōseki 宝石

gem dealer n hōsekí-shō 宝石商

Gemini n (star sign) Futago-za ふたご座・双子座

gender n séi 性

gene n idenshi 遺伝子

general 1. adj (over all) ippan (no) 一般(の); (common) kyōtsū (no) 共通(の) 2. n (army) táishō 大将

in general daitai 大体・だいたい, taigai たいがい・大概, ippan ni 一般に, futsū 普通 (= generally)

the general public taishū 大衆

general remarks (outline) sōron 総論

major general shō´shō 少将

generally adv ippanteki ni 一般的に, zentai ni 全体に; daitai 大体・だいたい, taigai たいがい・大概

generation n sedai 世代, dōjidai 同時代

generations after generations, for generations dáidai 代々

generator n hatsudén-ki 発電機

generous adj kimae ga íi 気前がいい, kandai (na) 寛大(な)

genius n tensai 天才

gentle adj yasashii 優しい・やさしい, (well-behaved) otonashíi おとなしい, (docile) súnao (na) すなお[素直](な), (calm) odáyaka (na) 穏やか(な)

gentleman n dánsei 男性, shínshi 紳士; (middle-aged man) ojisan おじさん, (old man) ojíisan おじいさん

gently adv yasashiku 優しく・やさしく, otonáshiku おとなしく

gentry n shinshi-kaikyū 紳士階級, kizoku 貴族

gents' n shinshi-yō toire 紳士用トイレ, dansei-yō toire 男性用トイレ

gents' underwear n shinshi-yō shitagi 紳士用下着

genuine adj hontō (no) 本当(の), honmono (no) 本物(の), makoto (no) 真(の)

geoduck n (surf clam) mirú-gai ミル貝

geographical adj chiri-teki (na) 地理的(な), chiri-jō (no) 地理上(の)

geography n chíri 地理; (study/science) chirí-gaku 地理学

geology n (of a place) chishitsu 地質; (study/science) chishitsú-gaku 地質学

geranium n zeraniumu ゼラニウム

germ n saikin 細菌, baikin ばい菌・バイキン

German n (language) Doitsu-go ドイツ語; (person) Doitsú-jin ドイツ人

Germany n Dóitsu ドイツ

gesture n miburi 身振り; jesuchā ジェスチャー, (hand gesture) temane 手まね, (motion) dōsa 動作

get v (receives) moraimásu (morau, moratte) もらい[貰い]ます(もらう, もらって), [HUMBLE] itadakimásu (itadaku, itadaite) いただき[頂き]ます(いただく, いただいて)

get (someone) to do it v 1. (hito ni) shite moraimásu (morau, moratte) (人に)してもらいます(もらう, もらって) 2. [BOOKISH] emásu (éru, éte) ます(得る, 得て)

get caught (in) between v hasamari-másu (hasamaru, hasamátte) 挟まります(挟まる, 挟まって)

get down v (descends) orimásu (oríru, órite) 降ります(降りる, 降り

て); (*crouches*) mi o fusemásu (fuséru, fuséte) 身を伏せます(伏せる、伏せて)

get in *v* (*enters*) hairimásu (háiru, háitte) 入ります(入る、入って); (*puts it in*) iremásu (ireru, irete) 入れます (入れる、入れて)

get into *v* (*a vehicle*) (… ni) norimásu (noru, notte) (…に)乗ります(乗る、乗って)

get off *v* (*gets down*) orimásu (oríru, órite) 降ります(降りる、降りて)

get old *v* toshí o torimásu (tóru, tótte) 年を取ります(取る、取って), fukemásu (fukéru, fukéte) 老けます(老ける、老けて)

get out *v* (*leaves*) demásu (déru, déte) 出ます(出る、出て); (*gets it out*) dashimásu (dásu, dáshite) 出します (出す、出して)

get out of the way *v* dokimásu (doku, doite) どきます(どく、どいて), nokimásu (noku, noite) の[退]きます (の[退]いて)

get to be → **become**

get up *v* (*arises*) okimásu (okíru, ókite) 起きます(起きる、起きて)

getting aboard *n* (*into a car, etc.*) jōsha 乗車

getting a job *n* shūshoku 就職

Getting off! *interj* Orimásu! 降ります!

get-together party *n* konshín-kai 懇親会

get-up *n* (*appearance*) teisai 体裁

geyser *n* kankessen 間欠泉, kanketsu-onsen 間欠温泉

Ghana *n* Gēna ガーナ

ghastly *adj* sugói すごい・凄い; *adv* sugóku waruí すごく[凄く]悪い

ghetto *n* gettō ゲットー

ghetto blaster *n* ōgata rajikase 大型ラジカセ

ghost *n* yū´rei 幽霊, gōsuto ゴースト; (*goblin*) obáke お化け・オバケ, bakemónó 化け物

giant *n* kyojin 巨人, ōótoko 大男; (*baseball team*) **the Giants** Kyójin-gun 巨人軍

gibberish *n* chinpunkanpun no/na hanashi ちんぷんかんぷんの/な話; detarame でたらめ

gift *n* purezento プレゼント gifuto

ギフト → **present**

gift shop *n* miyagemono-ya みやげ[土産]物屋

gifted *adj* sugureta sainō no aru 優れた才能のある, sainō ni megumareta 才能に恵まれた

giga byte, GB *n* (*computer*) giga-baito ギガ・バイト

gigantic *adj* **1.** (*vast amounts of*) bōdai (na) 膨大(な) **2.** kyodai (na) 巨大(な)

gill *n* era エラ・えら

gilt *n* kinpaku 金箔, kinmekki 金メッキ

gimmick *n* gimikku ギミック, shikake 仕掛け

gin *n* jin ジン

ginger *n* shōga ショウガ・生姜

ginger ale *n* jinja-ēru ジンジャエール, jinjā-ēru ジンジャーエール

ginger beer *n* jinja-biiru ジンジャビール, jinjā-biiru ジンジャービール

Japanese ginger *n* (*buds*) myōga ミョウガ・茗荷

pickled ginger *n* sushó´ga 酢しょうが, gári がり・ガリ

gingerbread *n* (*bread*) shōga-iri kashi-pan ショウガ入り菓子パン, shōga-iri kēki ショウガ入りケーキ

gingerbread man *n* (*nigyō no katachi no*) shōga-kukkii (人形のかたちの)ショウガクッキー

gingko *n* (*tree*) ichō イチョウ・銀杏

gingko nuts *n* ginnán ギンナン・銀杏

giraffe *n* kirin キリン

girder *n* keta けた・桁; *under the ~* keta-shíta けた下・桁下

girdle *n* **1.** (*belt*) óbi 帯 **2.** gādoru ガードル

girl *n* musume(-san) 娘(さん); onná-no-ko 女の子; jóshi 女子

girl friend *n* gāru-furéndo ガールフレンド; káno-jo 彼女

girlish *adj* shōjo rashii 少女らしい; onná-no-ko rashii 女の子らしい

giro system *n* furikae-seido 振替制度

girth *n* shūi 周囲

gist *n* muné 旨; yō´shi 要旨, shushi 主旨, yōten 要点, yōryō´ 要領, kosshi 骨子

give *v* **1.** (*they to you/me, you to me*) kuremásu (kureru, kurete) くれます

(くれる, くれて), kudasaimásu (kuda-sáru, kudasátte) 下さいます(下さる, 下さって) **2.** (*I to you/them, you to them, they to them*) agemásu (ageru, agete) あげます(あげる, あげて), yarimásu (yaru, yatte) やります(や る, やって); [HUMBLE, DEFERENTIAL] sashi-agemásu (sashi-ageru, sashi-agete) 差し上げます(差し上げる, 差 し上げて) **3.** (*provides*) ataemásu (ataeru, ataete) 与えます(与える, 与え て), motasemásu (motaséru, motásete) 持たせます(持たせる, 持たせて); *gives mercifully* (*in charity*) megu-mimásu (megumu, megunde) 恵みま す(恵む, 恵んで) **4.** (*entrusts temporarily*) azukemásu (azukéru, azúkete) 預けます (預ける, 預けて) **5.** (*a party, etc.*) (pátii o) hirakimásu (hiraku, hiraite) (パーティーを)開きます(開く, 開 いて); moyōshimásu (moyóu, moyōshíte) 催します(催す, 催して)
give birth to ... *v* umimásu (umu, unde) ...を生み[産み]ます(生む, 生 んで)
give in/up *v* (*cedes, concedes*) yuzurimásu (yuzuru, yuzutte) 譲りま す(譲る, 譲って)
give up (on) ... *v* akiramemásu (akiraméru, akirámete) ...を諦めます (諦める, 諦めて)
glacial *adj* hyōga-ki (no) 氷河期(の)
glacial age *n* hyōga-ki 氷河期
glacier *n* hyōga 氷河
glad *adj* ureshíi うれしい; *is* ~ yoroko-bimásu (yorokóbu, yorokónde) 喜びま す(喜ぶ, 喜んで)
glad to ... *v* yorokonde ... o shimásu (suru, shite) 喜んで...をします(する, して)
gladly *adv* yorokónde 喜んで
glamor *n* guramē グラマー
glamorous *adj* miryoku-teki (na) 魅力 的(な), miwaku-teki (na) 魅惑的(な)
gland *n* sen 腺・せん
glare *v* ... o niramimásu (nirámu, niránde) ...をにらみ[睨み]ます(にら む, にらんで)
glaring *adj* (*dazzling*) mabushíi まぶし い・眩しい

glass *n* (*the substance*) garasu ガラス; (*the container*) koppu コップ, gúrasu グラス
glass, glassful ...-hai ...杯 (**1:** íp-pai 一杯, **2:** ní-hai 二杯, **3:** sánbai 三杯; *how many* nán-bai 何杯)
glasses *n* mégane メガネ・眼鏡
glassy *adj* utsuro (na) うつろ・虚ろ (な), seiki no nai 生気のない, donyori (to) shita どんより(と)した, mu-hyōjō (na) 無表情(な)
glazier *n* garasu-ya ガラス屋
gleam, glitter *v* kagayakimásu (kagayáku, kagayáite) 輝きます(輝く, 輝いて)
glittering *adj* pikapika/kirakira kaga-yaku ぴかぴか・ピカピカ/きらきら ・キラキラ輝く
glen *n* tani-ma 谷間
glider *n* guraidē グライダー
gliding *n* kakkū 滑空
glimmer *n* (*light*) kasuka na hikari かすかな[微かな]光
globe *n* (*shape*) tamá 球; (*map*) chikyū´-gi 地球儀
gloom *n* (*depression*) yūutsu 憂うつ [鬱]
gloomy *adj* uttōshíi うっとうしい, kurai 暗い, yūutsu (na) 憂うつ(な), inki (na) 陰気(な)
glorious *adj* hanáyaka (na) 華やか(な)
glory *n* méiyo 名誉
gloss *n* **1.** (*shine*) tsuya つや・艶 **2.** (*lipstick*) gurosu グロス
glove *n* tebúkuro 手袋; (*baseball, boxing*) gúrabu グラブ, gúrōbu グロ ーブ
glow 1. *v* hikarimásu (hikáru, hikátte) 光ります(光る, 光って) **2.** *n* (*shine*) kagayaki 輝き, (*glow of sunset*) yūyake 夕焼け
glucose *n* budō-tō ブドウ糖, gurukōsu グルコース
glue 1. *n* setchakuzai 接着剤, nori のり ・糊, nikawa ニカワ・膠 **2.** *v* (*glues it*) setchakuzai de tsukemásu (tsukéru, tsukéte) 接着剤で付けます(付ける, 付 けて), tsugimásu (tsugu, tsuide) 接ぎ ます(接ぐ, 接いで)
glum *adj* shibúi 渋い, inki (na) 陰気(な)

glut *n* kajō 過剰

glutinous rice *n* mochi-gome もち米

glutton *n* kúi-shínbō 食いしん坊・く
いしんぼう, taishoku-ka 大食家

gluttonous *adj* kúi-shínbō (na) 食いし
ん坊・くいしんぼう(な)

gluttony *n* ōgui 大食い

glycerin *n* guriserin グリセリン

gnarl *n* fushí 節

gnat *n* buyo ブヨ

gnaw *v* kajirimásu (kajíru, kajítte) かじ
り[齧り]ます(かじる, かじって)

go *v* ikimásu (iku, itte) 行きます(行く,
行って)

go against ... *v* ni somukimásu (somúku, somúite) ...に背きます(背く, 背い
て); ...ni han-shimásu (han-súru, hán-
shite) ...に反します(反する, 反して)

go ahead *interj* (*to driver*) ōrai オー
ライ; sā dōzo さあどうぞ

go around *v* (*a curve*) magarimásu
(magaru, magatte) 曲がります(曲が
る, 曲がって); (*revolves*) mawarimásu
(mawaru, mawatte) 回ります(回る, 回
って)

go away *v* ikimásu (iku, itte) 行きま
す(行く, 行って); sarimásu (saru, satte)
去ります(去る, 去って)

go back *v* modorimásu (modóru,
modótte) 戻ります(戻る, 戻って),
kaerimásu (káeru, káette) 帰ります
(帰る, 帰って)

go back *v* (*in time*) to ... ni sakanoborimásu (sakanobóru, sakanobótte)
... にさかのぼり[遡り]ます(さかの
ぼる, さかのぼって)

go back and forth *v* ittari kitari shimásu (suru, shite) 行ったり来たりし
ます(する, して); kayoimásu (kayou,
kayotte) 通います(通う, 通って)

go down *v* orimásu (oríru, órite) 下り
ます(下りる, 下りて); kudarimásu
(kudaru, kudatte) 下ります(下る, 下っ
て); sagarimásu (sagáru, sagátte) 下が
ります(下がる, 下がって); (*on the
price*) makemásu (makeru, makete)
負けます(負ける, 負けて); (*dwindles*)
herimásu (heru, hette) 減ります(減
る, 減って)

go forward *v* susumimásu (susumu,

susunde) 進みます(進む, 進んで)

go home *v* kaerimásu (káeru, káette)
帰ります(帰る, 帰って)

go in *v* hairimásu (hairu, háitte) 入り
ます(入る, 入って), háitte ikimásu (iku,
itte) 入って行きます(行く, 行って)

go out *v* demásu (déru, déte) 出ます
(出る, 出て), déte ikimásu (iku, itte)
出て行きます(行く, 行って); (*of
the house*) dekakemásu (dekakeru,
dekakete) 出かけ[掛け]ます(出かける,
出かけて), gaishutsu shimásu (suru,
shite) 外出します(する, して); (*appears*)
arawaremásu (arawaréru, arawárete)
現れます(現れる, 現れて); (*lights,
fire, etc.*) kiemásu (kieru, kiete) 消えま
す(消える, 消えて)

go over *v* (*exceeds*) sugimásu
(sugíru, súgite) 過ぎます(過ぎる, 過
ぎて), chōka shimásu (suru, shite) 超
過します(する, して); koshimásu
(kosu, koshite) 超[越]します(超[越]
す, 超[越]して); (*revises*) fukushū
shimásu (suru, shite) 復習します(す
る, して)

go to *v* (*reaches*) itarimásu (itaru,
itatte) 至ります(至る, 至って)

go to bed *v* yasumimásu (yasúmu,
yasúnde) 休みます(休む, 休んで),
nemásu (neru, nete) 寝ます(寝る, 寝て)

go too far *v* (*to excess*) do o koshimásu
(kósu, kóshite) 度を越します(越す,
越して)

go too fast *v* (*clock*) susumimásu
(susumu, susunde) 進みます(進む, 進
んで)

go to the end of *v* (*a street*) tsuki-
atarimásu (tsuki-atáru, tsuki-atátte)
突き当たります(突き当たる, 突き当
たって)

go to work *v* (*start work*) shigoto ni
ikimásu (iku, itte) 仕事に行きます
(行く, 行って), shūrō shimásu (suru,
shite) 就労します(する, して)

go up *v* agarimásu (agaru, agatte)
上がります(上がる, 上がって),
noborimásu (noboru, nobotte) 上りま
す(上る, 上って)

go upstream *v* (*goes against the
stream*) sakanoborimásu (sakanobóru,

sakanobótte) さかのぼり[遡り]ます
（さかのぼる、さかのぼって）

Go n (board game) gó 碁、ígo 囲碁
Go board n go-ban 碁盤

goal n mokuteki 目的、ate 当て；
(destination) mokutekí-chi 目的地；
(sports) gó´ru ゴール

goalkeeper n gōru kiipā ゴールキー
パー

goat n yági ヤギ・山羊

gobang n (simplified version of Go)
gomoku-nárabe 五目並べ

go-between n (intermediary)
chūkaisha 仲介者、nakadachí 仲立ち；
(match-maker) nakō´do 仲人

goblin n (long-nosed) tengu 天狗

goby n (fish) háze はぜ・ハゼ

God, gods n kámi(-sama) 神(様)

godchild n nazuke-go 名付け子

goddaughter n nazuke-musume 名付
け娘

goddess n megami 女神

godfather, godmother n nazuke-oya
名付け親

godown n (storeroom) kurá 蔵・倉

godsend n ten no megumi 天の恵み

godson n nazuke-go 名付け子、
nazuke-musuko 名付け息子

goggle n gōguru ゴーグル

Goh → Go

gold n kín 金、gōrudo ゴールド

golden adj (color) kin-iro (no) 金色
(の)

Golden Week (29 April–5 May) n
gōruden-wíiku ゴールデンウィーク

goldfish n kíngyo 金魚・キンギョ

gold lacquer n (kin-)mákie (金)蒔絵

goldsmith n kin-zaiku shokunin 金細
工職人

golf n górufu ゴルフ
golf ball n gorufu-bōru ゴルフボール
golf club n gorufu-kurabu ゴルフクラ
ブ
golf course n gorufu-jō ゴルフ場、
gorufu-kōsu ゴルフコース

golfer n gorufā ゴルファー

gondola n gondora ゴンドラ

gong n gongu ゴング、dora どら

gone → go; v is ~ itte imásu (iru, ite)
行っています（いる、いて）

gonorrhea n rinbyō りん病・淋病

good adj fi いい・良い・好い・善い、
yói 良い・好い・善い・よい
good at (… ga) umái (…が)うまい、
jōzú (na) じょうず[上手](な)、o-jōzu
お上手、tassha (na) 達者(な)
a good deal adv yohodo よほど・余
程、yoppodo よっぽど；unto うんと；
takusán (no) たくさん・沢山(の)
for the good of … adv no tamé ni …
のため[為]に
Good afternoon. interj konnichi wa.
こんにちは・今日は.
good-bye interj sayonara さよなら、
sayōnára さようなら；sore déwa では
では；go- kigen yō´. ごきげんよう.
Good evening. interj konban wa. こ
んばんは・今晩は.
good-looking adj hansamu (na) ハン
サム(な)、kakkoii かっこ[格好]いい、
kakkōii かっこう[格好]いい；rukkusu
no ii ルックスのいい
Good morning. interj O-hayō (gozaimásu). おはよう[お早う]ございます.
Good night. interj O-yasumi nasái. お
やすみ[お休み]なさい.
no good furyō (no) 不良(の)

good and evil n zén-aku 善悪

good fortune n kōun 幸運、saiwai
幸い・さいわい

good-hearted adj shinsetsu (na) 親切
(な)、omoiyari no aru 思いやりのある、
yasashii 優しい・やさしい

good heavens/grief interj shimatta し
まった、oya-mā おやまあ、(feminine)
mā まあ

good-looking adj kírei (na) きれい
[綺麗](な)

good-luck piece n o-mamori お守り

good-natured adj kidate no yoi 気立
ての良い

goodness n zén 善

good offices; through the ~ of …
n assen de …のあっせん[斡旋]で

goods n shina(mono) 品(物)；(merchandise) shōhin 商品

goodwill n kō´i 好意、kokorozashi 志、
shínsetsu 親切(go-shínsetsu ご親切)、
zén´i 善意

goof 1. n (blunder) hema へま・ヘマ、

doji どじ・ドジ, chónbo チョンボ
2. *v goof (up)* hema o shi-másu (suru, shite) へま(を)します(する, して)
3. *v goof off* → loaf

Google 1. *n (Internet search engine)* gūguru グーグル **2.** *v* ... o gūguru de shirabemásu (shiraberu, shirabete) を Google で調べます(調べる, 調べて)

goose *n* gachō ガチョウ・鵞鳥

gorgeous *adj* gōka (na) 豪華(な); rippa (na) 立派(な); hanáyaka (na) 華やか(な)

Gosh! *interj* wā わあ

gossip *n* **1.** uwasa うわさ・噂; muda-/baka-bánashi 無駄/ばか話 **2.** *(a gossip)* oshábéri おしゃべり

gourd *n* hyōtán ヒョウタン・瓢箪
gourd strips *n (dried)* kanpyō カンピョウ・干瓢
sponge gourd *n* hechima ヘチマ・糸瓜

gourmand *n* taishokukan 大食漢

gourmet *n, adj* gurume (no) グルメ (の), shokutsū (no) 食通(の), bishokuka (no) 美食家(の)

govern *v* osamemásu (osaméru, osámete) 治めます(治める, 治めて)

government *n* séifu 政府; *(cabinet)* náikaku 内閣; *(nation)* kuni (no) 国 (の), *(national)* kokuritsu (no) 国立 (の); *(the authorities)* tō´kyoku 当局, okámi お上
government office *n* (o-)yaku-sho (お)役所
government official *n* yakunin 役人
government worker/employee *n* kōmú in 公務員

governor *n* chíji 知事
gown *n* gaun ガウン
grab → seize
graceful *adj* yū´bi (na) 優美(な)
gradation *n* guradēshon グラデーション

grade 1. *n (value, quality)* tōkyū 等級, *(class)* kyū 級, gakkyu 学級; *(step)* dán 段; *(evaluation score)* hyōten 評点, hyō´ka 評価; *(academic record)* seiseki 成績 **2.** *v (to grade a test paper)* saitenshimásu (suru, shite) 採点します (する, して), seiseki o tsukemásu

(tsukéru, tsukete) 成績をつけます(つける, つけて)

grade school *n* shōgakkō 小学校
grade school children *n* shōgaku-sei 小学生

gradually *adv* dandan だんだん, jojo ni 徐々に, sukoshízútsu 少しずつ, sórosoro (to) そろそろ(と); *(finally)* yōyaku ようやく

graduate 1. *v* sotsugyō shimásu (suru, shite) 卒業します(する, して); ~ *from* (daigaku o) demásu (deru, dete) (大学を)出ます(出る, 出て) **2.** *n* sotsugyō´-sei 卒業生; *(graduate of ...)* ...no de ...の出
graduate school *n* daigakú-in 大学院
graduate student *n* daigakuín-sei 大学院生

graft 1. *n (bribery)* wáiro わいろ・賄賂, oshoku 汚職 **2.** *n* tsugiki 接ぎ木 **3.** *v (attaches)* tsugimásu (tsugu, tsuide) 接ぎます(接ぐ, 接いで)

grain *n* **1.** tsúbu 粒 **2.** *(cereal)* kokúmotsu 穀物, kokúrui 穀類 **3.** *(texture)* kimé きめ・木目・肌理

gram *n* gúramu グラム

grammar *n* bunpō 文法, guramā グラマー

grand *adj* subarashíi すばらしい・素晴らしい, erái 偉い, sōdai (na) 壮大(な)

grandchild *n* magó 孫 (o-mago-san お孫さん)

grandfather *n* ojíi-san おじいさん・お祖父さん, sófu 祖父

grandmother *n* obā´-san おばあさん・お祖母さん, sóbo 祖母

grandson *n* mago (musuko) 孫(息子)

grandstand *n (seats)* kamán-seki 観覧席
grandstand play sutando-purē スタンドプレー

grand total *n* sōkei 総計

granite *n* kakó´-gan 花崗岩・かこう岩, mikagé-ishi 御影石・みかげ石

grant 1. *n* hojokin 補助金, joseikin 助成金 **2.** *v (grants it)* ataemásu (ataeru, ataete) 与えます(与える, 与えて)

grapefruit *n* gurēpufurūtsu グレープフルーツ

grapes *n* budō ブドウ・葡萄

graph n grafu グラフ

graphic n zukei 図形, gurafikku グラフィック

grasp v tsukamimásu (tsukámu, tsukánde) つかみ[掴み]ます(つかむ, つかんで); nigirimásu (nigiru, nigitte) 握ります(握る, 握って)

grass n kusá 草; (lawn) shibafu 芝生

grasshopper n (locust) batta バッタ, inago イナゴ, (long-horned grasshopper) kirigirisu キリギリス

grassland n sōgen 草原

grated v suri-oroshita すりおろした

grated radish n daikon-óroshi 大根おろし[下ろし]

grated yam n tororo とろろ・トロロ

grateful adj arigatái ありがたい・有り難い

I am grateful arigatáku zon-jimásu (zon-jiru, zon-jite) ありがたく存じます(存じる, 存じて)

feels grateful/obliged kyōshuku shimásu (suru, shite) 恐縮します(する, して)

grater n oroshí-gane 下ろし金

gratification n manzoku 満足

grating n kōshi 格子

gratis → **free**

gratitude n kansha 感謝

gratuity n kokoro-zuke 心付け

grave n (tomb) haká 墓(o-haka お墓)

graveyard n haka-bá 墓場, bóchi 墓地

grave adj (serious) omoi 重い, shinkoku (na) 深刻(な)

gravel n jari 砂利・じゃり

gravy n taré たれ; (o-)sō´su (お)ソース; niku-jū/jíru 肉汁

gray adj hai-iro (no) 灰色(の), nezumi-iro (no) ねずみ色(の); gurē´ no グレーの

gray hair n shiragá 白髪・しらが

gray mullet n bora ぼら・ボラ

graze v kasurimásu (kasúru, kassute) かすり[掠り]ます(かする, かすって); kasumemásu (kasumeru, kasumete) かすめ[掠め]ます(かすめる, かすめて)

grease n abura 脂・油・アブラ

greasy adj aburakkói 脂っこい; kudói くどい

great adj (superior) idai (na) 偉大(な), erái 偉い; ōki (na) 大き(な), dai- 大… → **big** → **good** → **grand**

a great difference taisa 大差

a great many táisō (na) たいそう・大層(na) たいそう・大層

a great war taisen 大戦

Great Britain n Eikoku 英国, igirisu イギリス

great-grandfather n sō-sofu 曽祖父, hii ojiisan ひいおじいさん

great-grandmother n sō-sobo 曽祖母, hii obēsan ひいおばあさん

great-great-grandfather n hii hii ojiisan ひいひいおじいさん

great-great-grandmother n hii hii obēsan ひいひいおばあさん

greatly adv ōi ni 大いに, unto うんと, totemo とても; hijō ni 非常に → **extremely**

Greece n Gírisha ギリシャ

greed n yokubári 欲張り, yokú 欲

greedy adj yokubári (na) 欲張り(な), kúi-shínbō (na) 食いしん坊(な); yokubarimásu (yokubáru, yokubátte) 欲張ります(欲張る, 欲張って); a ~ person yokubári 欲張り

Greek 1. n (langage) Girisha-go ギリシャ語, (people) Girisha-jin ギリシャ人 2. adj Girisha-/-jin/-go (no) ギリシャ/人/語(の)

green adj 1. mídori (no) 緑(の), aói 青い; guríin (no) グリーン(の) 2. (inexperienced) osanái 幼い

Green Car n (deluxe coach) guríin-sha グリーン車

greengrocer n yao-ya 八百屋

greenhouse n onshitsu 温室

green light n (signal) ao-shíngō 青信号

green onion n nira ニラ・韮; naganagi 長ねぎ[葱] nira ニラ・韮; naganegi 長ねぎ[葱]; (chives, scallion) asátsuki アサツキ・浅葱

green pepper n píiman ピーマン

greens n náppa 菜っ葉, ná 菜; (boiled greens served cold with seasoning) o-hitáshi おひたし

green tea n (o-)cha (お)茶

Green Window n (for special train tickets) mídori no madóguchi みどりの窓口

greet v (welcomes, receives) áisatsu (o) shimásu (suru, shite) あいさつ[挨拶](を)します(する, して); de-mukaemásu (de-mukaeru, de-mukaete) 出迎えます(出迎える, 出迎えて)

greeting n áisatsu あいさつ・挨拶; réi 礼

grenade n shuryūdan 手榴弾

grief n nakeí 嘆き, kanashimí 悲しみ

grievance n fuhei 不平, fuman 不満

grieve v nagekimásu (nagéku, nagéite) 嘆きます(嘆く, 嘆いて); kokóro o itamemásu (itaméru, itámete) 心を痛めます(痛める, 痛めて)

grill v yakimásu (yaku, yaite) 焼きます(焼く, 焼いて), aburimásu (abúru, abútte) あぶり[炙り]ます(あぶる, あぶって)

grime n yogore 汚れ

grin n (hanikanda) egao はにかんだ笑顔 2. v (nit-to, niyat-to) waraimásu (warau, waratte) (にっと/にやっと)笑います(笑う, 笑って)

grind v surimásu (súru, sútte) すります(する, すって); (into powder) hikimásu (hiku, hiite) ひきます(ひく, ひいて) → **sharpen** → **polish**

grip v nigirimásu (nigiru, nigitte) 握ります(握る, 握って)

gripe 1. n (complaint) guchi ぐち・愚痴 **2.** v (complains) guchi o koboshimásu (kobósu, kobóshite) ぐち[愚痴]をこぼします(こぼす, こぼして), gúzu-guzu iimásu (yū, itte/yutte) ぐずぐず言います(言う, 言って/ゆって), boyakimásu (boyáku, boyáite) ぼやきます(ぼやく, ぼやいて)

groan 1. n (a groan) umekí うめき・呻き **2.** v (groans) umekimásu (uméku, uméite) うめき[呻き]ます(うめく, うめいて); fuman o iimásu (iu, itte) 不満を言います(言う, 言って)

grocer n shokuryō-hin-ten 食料品店

groceries n shokuryō-hin 食料品, shokuhin 食品

grocery (store) n shokuryō-hin-ten 食料品店

groin n matá 股・また

groom n hanamuko 花婿, shinrō 新郎

groove n mizo 溝

grope v sagurimásu (saguru, sagutte) 探ります(探る, 探って)

groper n (molester) chikan 痴漢

gross adj (crass) egetsunai えげつない; (rude) gehin (na) 下品(な)

grotesque n gurotesuku グロテスク

grotto n dōkutsu 洞窟・洞くつ

ground 1. n (land) tochi 土地, jí 地, (earth) tsuchí 土・つち; (surface) jímen 地面, (playground) guraundo グラウンド **2.** n (basecoat) shitanuri 下塗り **3.** adj hiita 挽いた **4.** v (to be grounded) ... o gaishutsu kinshi ni shimásu (suru, shite) ...を外出禁止にします(する, して)

ground meat n hiki-niku 挽き肉・ひき肉

ground floor n ik-kai 一階

groundless adj konkyo no nai 根拠のない

grounds n (reason) riyū 理由, yué 故・ゆえ

group n gurū´pu グループ, dantai 団体; shūdan 集団; (class) kúrasu クラス; (throng, flock) muré 群れ

groupie n gurū´pii グルーピー, okkake 追っかけ

grove n hayashi 林

grow v 1. (it grows) seichō shimásu (suru, shite) 成長します(する, して); (gets big) ō´kiku/ō´ku narimásu (náru, nátte) 大きく/多くなります(なる, なって); (increases) fuemásu (fuéru, fúete) 増えます(増える, 増えて); (teeth, hair, mold, ...) haemásu (haéru, háete) 生えます(生える, 生えて); (appears) hassei shimásu (suru, shite) 発生します(する, して); (develops) hatten shimásu (suru, shite) 発展します(する, して) **2.** (grows it) (a plant) uemásu (ueru, uete) 植えます(植える, 植えて); (a crop) tsukurimásu (tsukúru, tsukútte) 作ります(作る, 作って); (hair, teeth, ...) hayashimásu (hayásu, hayáshite) 生やします(生やす, 生やして) **3.** (becomes) (... ni, ...-ku) narimásu (náru, nátte) (...に, ...く)なります(なる, なって)

grow late v (yó ga) fukemásu (fukéru, fukéte) (夜が)更けます(更ける, 更けて)

grow up *v* sodachimásu (sodatsu, sodátte) 育ちます(育つ, 育って); seichō shimásu (suru, shite) 成長します(する, して)

grower *n* saibai-sha 栽培者, shiiku-sha 飼育者

growing up *n* seichō 成長; sodachí 育ち

growl 1. *n* (*a growl*) unarí (goe) うなり・唸り (声) **2.** *v* (*growls*) unarimásu (unáru, unátte) うなり[唸り]ます(うなる, うなって)

growth *n* seichō 成長; (*increase*) zōka 増加; (*development*) hatten 発展

grow thick(ly) *v* shigerimásu (shigéru, shigétte) 茂り[繁り]ます(茂[繁]る, 茂[繁]って)

grow weak *v* otoroemásu (otoróeru, otoróete) 衰えます(衰える, 衰えて)

grudge *n* uramí 恨み

gruel *n* (*rice*) (o-)kayu (お)かゆ[粥]

grumble *v* boyakimásu (boyáku, boyáite) ぼやきます(ぼやく, ぼやいて), gúzuguzu shimásu (suru, shite) ぐずぐずします(する, して), (guchi o) koboshimásu (kobósu, kobóshite) (愚痴を)こぼします(こぼす, こぼして)

grumbling *n* fuhei 不平

guarantee *n, v* hoshō (shimásu; suru, shite) 保証(します; する, して)

letter of guarantee *n* hoshō-sho 保証書

guard 1. *n* bán 番, gādo-man ガードマン, (*gate keeper*) mónban 門番, shuei 守衛; (*vigilance*) keikai 警戒 **2.** *v guards it* mamorimásu (mamóru, mamótte) 守ります(守る, 守って), keibi shimásu (suru, shite) 警備します(する, して); *guards against* ... o keikai shimásu (suru, shite) ...を警戒します(する, して)

guard dog *n* banken 番犬

guardian *n* hogo-sha 保護者, kōken-nin 後見人

guardian angel *n* shugo-tenshi 守護天使

guardian spirit *n* (*tutelary deity*) uji-gami 氏神

guarding *n* keibi 警備

guess 1. *n* (*conjecture*) sas-shi 察し (o-sasshi お察し), (*estimate*) suisoku 推測, kentō 見当 **2.** *v* (*guesses*) sas-shimásu (sas-suru, sas-shite) 察します(察する, 察して), suisoku shimásu (suru, shite) 推測します(する, して), kentō o tsukemásu (tsukéru, tsukéte) 見当をつけます(つける, つけて); (*correctly*) sas-shi ga tsukimásu (tsukú, tsúite) 察しがつきます(つく, ついて), atemásu (ateru, atete) 当てます(当てる, 当てて)

guest *n* (o-)kyaku (お)客, okyaku-san/-sámá お客さん/様・さま; (*caller*) raikyaku 来客

guest of honor *n* shuhin 主賓[ひん], kihin 貴賓[ひん]

guest room *n* kyakuma 客間

guesthouse *n* gesuto hausu ゲストハウス

guesstimate 1. *n* ate-suiryō 当て推量 **2.** *v* suisoku de mitsumorimásu (mitsumoru, mitsumotte) 推測で見積もります(見積もる, 見積もって)

guidance *n* annai 案内 (go-annai ご案内); (*direction, counseling*) shidō 指導

guide 1. *n* (*person*) annai-gákari 案内係, annai-nin 案内人, annái-sha 案内者, gáido ガイド; (*coach, counsel*) shidō'-sha 指導者; (*book*) annai-sho 案内書, gaido bukku ガイドブック, (*travel*) ryokō-ánnai(-sho) 旅行案内(書); (*visual*) méate 目当て, meyasu 目安 **2.** *v* (*guides them*) annái shimásu (suru, shite) 案内します(する, して), michibikimásu (michibíku, michibíite) 導きます(導く, 導いて); (*directs, counsels*) shidō shimásu (suru, shite) 指導します(する, して)

guided tour *n* gaido-tsuki no tsuē ガイド付きのツアー

guild *n* (*union*) kumiai 組合, giruɗo ギルド

guillotine *n* girochin ギロチン

guilt *n* tsúmi 罪; *feeling/sense of ~* záiaku-kan 罪悪感

guilty *adj* yūzai (no) 有罪(の)

guilty-feeling *n* yamashíi やましい

guinea pig *n* morumotto モルモット, jikken-dōbutsu 実験動物

guitar *n* gitā ギター

guitarist *n* gitarisuto ギタリスト

gulf *n* wán 湾

gull *n* kamome カモメ・鴎
gullet *n* shokudō 食道
gullible *adj* baka-shō´jiki (na) ばか正直(な)
gully *n* kyōkoku 峡谷
gulp **1.** *n* ikki ni nomu 一気に飲む, hitoiki de nomu 一息で飲む **2. gulps down** *v* gutto/gabugabu nomimásu (nomu, nonde) ぐっと/がぶがぶ飲みます(飲む, 飲んで)
gum *n* (*chewing*) (chūin) gámu (チューイン)ガム; (*mucus from eye*) me-yaní 目やに; (*teethridge*) háguki 歯茎
gum-boot *n* gomu(-naga) gutsu ゴム(長)靴
gun *n* jū´ 銃, teppō 鉄砲
gunfire *n* happō 発砲
gunpowder *n* kayaku 火薬
gunshot → gunfire
gush *v* hotobashirimásu (hotobashiru, hotobashitte) ほとばしります(ほとばしる, ほとばしって), wakimásu (waku, waite) わき[湧き・涌き]ます(わく, わいて)
guts *n* harawata はらわた・腸・腑, watá わた・腸; → courage
gutter *n* mizo 溝; (*ditch*) dobu どぶ; (*drain pipe*) tói 樋
guy *n* yátsu やつ・奴; *that ~* aitsu あいつ, (*polite*) sono/ano hitó その/あの人
gym *n* tai(f)kú-kan 体育館
gymnast *n* taisō-senshu 体操選手
gym shoe *n* undō-gutsu 運動靴, suniikē スニーカー
gymnasium *n* tai(f)kú-kan 体育館, jímu ジム
gymnastics *n* taisō 体操
gynecologist *n* fujin-ka 婦人科
gypsy *n* jipushii ジプシー

H

haberdashery *n* (*notions*) koma-mono 小間物, yōhin 洋品; (*shop*) yōhín-ten 洋品店, zakka-ya/-ten 雑貨屋/店
habit *n* shūkan 習慣; (*bad habit*) kusé くせ・癖
habitable *adj* sumukoto ga dekiru 住むことができる; sumeru 住める
habitat *n* seisoku-chi 生息地; sumika 住処・すみか
habitation *n* kyojū-chi 居住地; sumai 住まい
habitual *adj* shūkan (no) 習慣(の); itsumono いつもの
hack *n* hakkingu ハッキング, (*computer*) hakkā ハッカー
hacker *n* (*computer*) hakkā ハッカー
had → have; *gets ~ (by …)* *v* (…ni) yararemásu (yarareru, yararete) (…に)やられます(やられる, やられて)
hag *n* (oni) baba (鬼)ばば
haggard *adj* yatsureta やつれた, yatsureteiru やつれている
haggle *n* ii-arasoi 言い争い, ronsō 論争
hail **1.** *n* arare/hyō´ **2.** *v* arare/hyō´ ga furimásu (fúru, fútte) あられ/ひょうが降ります(降る, 降って)

hailstone → hail
hair *n* (*on head*) kamí 髪, kamí no ke 髪の毛; (*general*) ke 毛
hair oil *n* kami ábura 髪油, pomā´do ポマード
hair spray *n* hea supurē ヘアスプレー
hair style *n* hea sutairu ヘアスタイル, kamigata 髪型
hairbrush *n* (hea) burashi (ヘア)ブラシ
haircut *n* rihatsu 理髪, sanpatsu 散髪, hea katto ヘアカット; *gets/gives a ~* rihatsu/sanpatsu shimásu (suru, shite) 理髪/散髪します(する, して)
hairdresser → beauty parlor → barber (*shop*)
hair-dryer *n* (hea) doraiyā (ヘア)ドライヤー
hairpin *n* heapin ヘアピン
hairspring *n* zenmai ぜんまい
hairy *adj* kebukai 毛深い
hale *adj* genki ga yoi 元気が良い, genki (na) 元気(な)
half *n* hanbún 半分; *half a …* han-… 半…, *…no hanbún* …の半分; *and a ~* …- hán …半; *the first ~* zenhan 前半

half a day *n* han-nichí 半日

half a month *n* han-tsukí 半月

half a week *n* sán-yokka 三、四日 = *3 or 4 days*

half a year *n* han-toshí 半年

halfbeak *n* (*fish*) sayori サヨリ・細魚

half brother *n* **1.** (*different mother*) ibo kyōdai 異母兄弟 **2.** (*different father*) ifu kyōdai 異父兄弟

half-cooked *adj* (*meat*) nama-nie (no) 生煮え(の)

half-done *adj* (*meat*) han'yake (no) 半焼け(の), namayake (no) 生焼け(の)

halfhearted *adj* ii-kagen (na) いい加減(な)

half-hour *n* san juppun 30分・三十分

half price *n* hangaku 半額; *half-price* hangaku (no) 半額(の)

half sister *n* **1.** (*different mother*) ibo shimai 異母姉妹 **2.** (*different father*) ifu shimai 異父姉妹

half term *n* chūkan kyūka 中間休暇

halfway *adj* tochū (no) 途中(の)

hall *n* (*building*) kaikan 会館; (*lecture hall*) kōdō 講堂, hōru ホール; (*entrance*) génkan 玄関

hallmark *n* ken'in 検印

hallucination *n* genkaku 幻覚

hallway *n* tsūro 通路, rōka 廊下

halt → **stop**

ham *n* hámu ハム

ham and eggs *n* hamu éggu ハムエッグ

ham sandwich *n* hamu sándo ハムサンド

hamburger *n* (*sandwich*) hanbā´gā ハンバーガー; (*ground beef*) hanbā´gu ハンバーグ

hamlet *n* chiisai mura 小さい村

hammer **1.** *n* kanazuchi かなづち・金槌, hánmā/hánma ハンマー/ハンマ, tsuchí tsuchí・つち, (*small*) kózuchi 小槌 claw hammer *n* kuginuki 釘抜き **2.** *v* (*hits*) uchimásu (útsu, útte) 打ちます (打つ、打って)

hamper *n* (*basket*) kago かご・カゴ

hamster *n* hamusutā ハムスター

hand *n* té 手; (*of clock*) hári 針; *has on ~* (*in stock*) mochi-awasemásu (mochi-awaseru, mochi-awasete) 持ち

合わせます(持ち合わせる、持ち合わせて)

hand down *v* tsutaemásu (tsutaeru, tsutaete) 伝えます(伝える、伝えて); *gets handed down* tsutawarimásu (tsutawaru, tsutawatte) 伝わります(伝わる、伝わって)

hand over *v* watashimásu (watasu, watashite) 渡します(渡す、渡して); (*to me*) yokoshimásu (yokosu, yokoshite) よこします(よこす、よこして)

hand up *v* kōsan shimásu (suru, shite) 降参します(する、して); *Hands up!* te o agero! 手を挙げろ!

handbag *n* hando bággu (hando bákku) ハンドバッグ(ハンドバック), tesage 手提げ・手さげ

handball *n* hando bōru ハンドボール

handbill *n* bira びら・ビラ

handbook *n* hando bukku ハンドブック, tebiki-sho 手引(き)書

handbrake *n* saido burē´ki サイドブレーキ

handcraft *v* kōsaku shimásu (suru, shite) 工作します(する、して)

handcrafted *adj* tesei (no) 手製(の)

handcuff *n* te jō 手錠

handful *n* shōryō 少量, hito-nigiri 一握り

handicap *n* handikyappu ハンディキャップ, handekyappu ハンデキャップ, handi ハンディ, hande ハンデ

handicapped *adj* (*physically*) karada ga fú-jiyū (na) 体が不自由(な) handicapped person *n* (*shintai*) shōgái-sha (身体)障害者

handicraft *n* shukōgei-hin 手工芸品

handiwork *n* te-záiku 手細工, saiku 細工, te-shigoto 手仕事

handkerchief *n* hankachi ハンカチ

handle **1.** *n* totté 取っ手, handoru ハンドル, tsuru´ つる・ツル, é 柄 **2.** *v* tori-atsukaimásu (tori-atsukau, tori-atsukatte) 取り扱います(取り扱う、取り扱って); (*copes with it*) shóri shimásu (suru, shite) 処理します(する、して); (*uses a tool*) tsukaimásu (tsukau, tsukatte) 使います(使う、使って); (*controls, operates*) sōjū shimásu (suru, shite) 操縦します(する、して); (*receives*) …

ni ses-shimásu (ses-suru, ses-shite) …
に接します(接する, 接して) → sell
→ touch
handlebar n handoru ハンドル, sōsa
rebā 操作レバー
Handle With Care Kowaremono chū´i
こわれ物[コワレモノ]注意
handling n tori-atsukai 取り扱い;
(operation) sōjū 操縦; ~ charge tesū´-
ryō 手数料
hand luggage n te-nímotsu 手荷物
handshake n ákushu 握手
handsome n hansamu ハンサム,
nimai-me 二枚目
hand towel n te-nugui 手ぬぐい,
tefuki 手ぬき, o-téfuki お手ふき;
(damp) o-shíbori おしぼり
handwriting n te-gaki 手書き, niku-
hitsu 肉筆
handy adj bénri (na) 便利(な)
handyman n (or his shop) benri-ya
便利屋
hang v 1. it hangs kakarimásu (kakáru,
kakátte) 掛かります(掛かる, 掛かっ
て) 2. hangs it kakemásu (kakéru,
kákete) 掛けます(掛ける, 掛けて),
(suspends it) tsurimásu (tsuru, tsutte)
吊ります(吊る, 吊って) 3. hangs
one's head utsumukimásu (utsumuku,
utsumuite) うつむき[俯き]ます(うつ
むく, うつむいて) 4. hangs around
urotsukimásu (urotsuku, urotsuite) う
ろつきます(つく, ついて)
hang down v 1. it hangs down
taremásu (taréru, tárete) 垂れます(垂
れる, 垂れて); sagarimásu (sagáru,
ságatte) 下がります(下がる, 下がっ
て); bura-sagarimásu (bura-sagaru,
bura-sagatte) ぶら下がります(ぶら下
がる, ぶら下がって) 2. hangs it down
sagemásu (sagéru, ságete) 下げます
(下げる, 下げて); bura-sagemásu
(bura-sageru, bura-sagete) ぶら下げま
す(ぶら下げる, ぶら下げて)
hang in there v ganbarimásu (ganbáru,
ganbátte) がんばり[頑張り]ます(が
んばる, がんばって)
hang up v (phone) (denwa o)
kirimásu (kíru, kítte) (電話を)切りま
す(切る, 切って)

hanger n (clothes hanger) hángā ハン
ガー
hang gliding n hangu-guraidā-nori
ハンググライダー乗り
hanging scroll n scroll
hangout n tamari-ba 溜まり場
hangover n futsuka-yoi 二日酔い
hankering n netsubō 熱望, setsubō
切望
haphazard adj ii-kagen (na) いい加減
(な)
happen v okorimásu (okóru, okótte)
起こります(起こる, 起こって); ~ to
see/observe mi-ukemásu (mi-ukeru,
mi-ukete) 見受けます(見受ける, 見受
けて); ~ to see/meet de-aimásu (de-áu,
de-átte) 出会います(出会う, 出会って)
happening n (incident) dekígoto 出来
事, jíken 事件, hapuningu ハプニング;
(event) koto 事
happi coat n happi はっぴ・法被,
hanten 半天・はんてん
happiness n kōfuku 幸福, shiawase
幸せ
happy adj ureshíi うれしい・嬉しい,
yúkai (na) ゆかい・愉快(な), kōfuku
(na) 幸福(な), shiawase (na) 幸せ(な);
(cheerful) yōki (na) 陽気(な); (auspicious)
medetái めでたい; (is delighted)
yorokobimásu (yorokóbu,
yorokónde) 喜びます(喜ぶ, 喜んで)
→ lucky
happy-go-lucky adj nónki (na) のん
気(な), rakuten-teki (na) 楽天的(な),
nōtenki (na) 能天気(な)
Happy New Year interj Shínnen/
Akemáshite o-medetō gozaimásu.
新年/あけ[明け]ましておめでとうご
ざいます.
harakiri n seppuku 切腹, harakiri 腹切
(り)
harangue n netsuben 熱弁, sekkyō
説教
harbinger n mae-bure 前触れ・前ぶ
れ, zenchō 前兆
harbor → port
hard adj 1. katai 固い・硬い・堅い;
(difficult) muzukashii 難しい, (hard
to do) shi-nikúi しにくい; (onerous)
kurushíi 苦しい, (trying) tsurai つら

い・辛い; (*requires much effort*) honé ga oremásu (oréru, órete) 骨が折れます (折れる、折れて); (*cruelly, terribly*) hídoku ひどく **2.** (*working hard*) yóku よく; (*laboriously*) ákuseku あくせく, sésse-to せっせと; (*intently*) shikiri ni しきりに **3.** *adv* (*zealously*) nésshín ni 熱心に; (*seriously*) majime ni まじめ[真面目]に; *works ~* hagemimásu (hagému, hagénde) 励みます(励む、励んで)

hard cash *n* genkín 現金, shōkin 正金

harden *v* **1.** *it hardens* katamarimásu (katamaru, katamatte) 固まります(固まる、固まって) **2.** *hardens it* katamemásu (katameru, katamete) 固めます(固める、固めて)

hard disk *n* hādo disuku ハードディスク

hardly *adv* hotóndo ほとんど・殆ど + [NEGATIVE]

hardness *n* katasa 硬さ

hard of hearing *adj* mimí ga tōi 耳が遠い

hardship *n* kónnan 困難, kúrō 苦労

hard times *n* fukéiki 不景気

hard to hear *adj* kiki-nikui 聞きにくい, kiki-zurai 聞きづらい

hardware *n* **1.** kanamono 金物; (*items*) tekki 鉄器; (*store*) kanamono-ya 金物屋 → **houseware**; (*machine*) kikai setsubi 機械設備 **2.** (*computer*) hādowéa ハードウェア

hard work *n* kúrō 苦労 (go-kúrō ご苦労)

hard worker, hardworking staff *n* hataraki-mono 働き者

hardworking *adj* kinben (na) 勤勉(な)

hare *n* usagi ウサギ・兎

harm 1. *n* gái zoku 害, songai 損害 **2.** *harms it* *v* sokonaimásu (sokonáu, sokonátte) 損ないます(損なう、損なって); *without ~* (*incident*) buji (ni) 無事 (に); *no ~* ...shite mo mondai nai ...しても問題ない

harmful *adj* yūgai (na) 有害(な)

harmless *adj* mugai (na) 無害(な)

harmonica *n* hāmonika ハーモニカ

harmony *n* chōwa 調和; *is in ~ with* ... to chōwa shimásu (suru, shite) ...と調

和します(する、して)

harp *n* (*Japanese*) (o-)kóto (お)琴; (*Western*) hāʹpu ハープ

harpoon *n* mori 銛・モリ

harpsichord *n* hāpushikōdo ハープシコード

harsh *adj* (*cruel*) zankoku (na) 残酷 (な)

harvest 1. *n* minori 実り, shūkaku 収穫 **2.** *v* (*harvests it*) osamemásu (osaméru, osámete) 収めます(収める、収めて)shūkaku shimásu (suru, shite) 収穫します(する、して)

has → **have**

hash → **beef hash**

haste *n* isogí 急ぎ・いそぎ

hasten → **hurry**

hasty *adj* (*hurried*) isogí no 急ぎの; (*rash*) keisotsu (na) 軽率(な)

hat *n* bōshi 帽子; *bamboo ~* kása 笠・カサ

hatch *n* fuka 孵化

hatchet *n* nata なた, óno 斧・オノ, te-ono 手斧

hate *v* (*... ga*) iyádesu (áru, átte) (...が) 嫌です; (*... o*) nikumimásu (nikúmu, nikúnde) (...を) 憎みます(憎む、憎んで)

haughty *adj* gōman (na) 傲慢(な); *is/acts ~* ibarimásu (ibáru, ibátte) 威張ります(威張る、威張って)

haul *n* (*goods in transit*) yusō-hin 輸送品

haunch *n* den-bu 臀部, koshi 腰

haute couture *n* (*high fashion*) ōtokuchūʹru オートクチュール

have *v* (*...ga*) arimásu (áru, átte) (...が) あります(ある、あって), (...o) mótte imásu (iru, ite) (...を) 持っています(いる、いて); (*keeps, retains*) kakaemásu (kakaeru, kakaete) 抱えます(抱える、抱えて)

have someone do it *v* (hito ni sore o) sasemásu (saseru, sasete) (人にそれを) させます(させる、させて), (*as a favor*) shite moraimásu (morau, moratte) して もらいます(もらう、もらって)

have it done *v* (*by someone to another*) (hito ni sore o) saremásu (sareru, sarete) (人にそれを) されます(され る、されて)

have no ... v (...ga) arimasén (nái, nákute) (...)が ありません(ない, なくて)

have to → must

Hawaii n Háwai ハワイ

hawk n taka タカ・鷹

hay n magusa まぐさ・秣, hoshi-gusa 干し草; **~ fever** kafun-shō 花粉症, arérúgii アレルギー

hazard n hazādo ハザード, (danger) kiken 危険

haze n móya もや・靄, (mist) kasumi かすみ・霞

hazelnut n hēzeru nattsu ヘーゼルナッツ

hazy; gets ~ kasumimásu (kasumu, kasunde) かすみ[霞み]ます(かすむ, かすんで)

he n káre 彼, anó-hito あの人 (but use name, title, or role; often omitted); (that guy) yátsu やつ・奴, yakko san やっこさん

he-... (animal) ... no osú ...の雄[オス]

head n atamá 頭・あたま, kashirá 頭・かしら (o-kashira お頭); (brains) zunō 頭脳, (leader) kashirá 頭, chō′ 長, (of a school) kōchō 校長

head for ... v ni mukaimásu (mukau, mukatte) ...に向かいます(向かう, 向って); ... o mezashimásu (mezásu, mezáshite) ...を目指します(目指す, 目指して)

head over heels adv massáka-sama ni まっさかさま[真っ逆さま]に

headache n zutsū 頭痛; **have a ~** zutsū ga shimásu (suru, shite) 頭痛がします(する, して), atamá ga itái 頭が痛い

heading n (caption) midashi 見出し, (title) taitoru タイトル

headland n misaki 岬・みさき

headlight(s) n heddo ráito ヘッドライト, zenshōtō 前照灯

headline n midashi 見出し, heddo rain ヘッドライン

head office n honten 本店, (corporate headquarter) honsha 本社

headquarters n hónbu 本部; (building; military) shiréi-bu 指令(司令)部; (corporate headquarter) honsha 本社

headstone n boseki 墓石, bohyō 墓標

headteacher n kōchō 校長

headway n zenshin 前進, shinpo 進歩

heady adj sēkyū (na) 性急(な)

heal v iyashimásu (iyasu, iyashite) 癒します(癒す, 癒して)

health n kenkō 健康, (one's health) karada 体・身体, (state of one's health) (go-)kigen (ご)機嫌, o-kagen お加減; (hygiene, sanitation) eisei 衛生

health service n (hospital) byōin 病院

health insurance n kenkō hoken 健康保険

healthy adj kenkō (na) 健康(な), génki (na) 元気(な), tassha (na) 達者(な), mame (na) まめ(な); (sturdy) jōbu (na) 丈夫(な); (good for one's health) karada ni ii 体にいい

heap 1. n yamá 山, (one) hitó-yama 一山 **2. ~ it up** v morimásu (moru, motte) 盛ります(盛る, 盛って)

hear v kikimásu (kiku, kiite) 聞きます(聞く, 聞いて); [HUMBLE] ukagaimásu (ukagau, ukagatte) 伺います(伺う, 伺って); uke-tamawarimasu (uke-tama-waru, uke-tamawatte) 承ります(承る, 承って)

hearer n kiki-te 聞き手

hearing test n **1.** (checkup) chōryoku kensa 聴力検査 **2.** (exam) hiyaringu tesuto ヒヤリング・テスト, hiyaringu shiken ヒヤリング試験, kikitori shiken 聞き取り試験

hearsay n (rumor) uwasa うわさ・噂

hearse n reikyū-sha 霊柩車

heart n shinzō 心臓; (as seat of emotions) kokóro 心 (o-kokoro お心); (the very center) chūshin 中心; (core, spirit) shín 芯・シン; (mind) muné 胸, omói 思い; (spirit) ki 気

by heart adv (from memory) sóra de 空で

heartache n shintsū 心痛

heart attack n shinzō mahi 心臓麻痺, shinzō hossa 心臓発作

heartbreak n hitsū 悲痛; (lost love) shitsuren 失恋

heartburn n mune-yake 胸焼け

heartening adj kokoro-zuyoi 心強い

heartfelt adj kokóro kara (no) 心から(の)

heartless adj mujō (na) 無情(な), hakujō (na) 薄情(な)

heat 1. n átsu-sa 熱さ・暑さ, netsú 熱 **2.** *heats it* v átsuku shimásu (suru, shite) 熱くします(する, して), nes-shimásu (nes-suru, nes-shite) 熱します (熱する, 熱して) → **warm it up 3.** *it heats up* v átsuku narimásu (naru, natte) 熱く[暑く]なります(なる, なっ て), nes-shimásu (nes-suru, nes-shite) 熱します(熱する, 熱して)

heat island (effect) n hiito airando ヒートアイランド(現象)

heater n sutóʾbu ストーブ, híitā ヒー ター, kanetsú-ki 加熱器

heath n are-chi 荒(れ)地

heating n (of room, etc.) danbō 暖房; *Japanese traditional quilt-covered heating device* kotatsu こたつ(o-kóta おこた)

heating saké n (o-)kan (お)燗, kán-zake 燗酒

heatstroke n nissha-byō 日射病, nessha-byō 熱射病

heat wave n neppa 熱波

heaven n tén 天; (*sky*) sóra 空; (*paradise*) téngoku 天国

heavy n omoi 重い; (*onerous*) kurushíi 苦しい

heavy rain n ō-áme 大雨; (*torrential downpour*) gōʾu 豪雨

heavy snow n ō-yuki 大雪

heavy task n tsurai shigoto つらい仕 事, kitsui shigoto きつい仕事, jūrōdo 重労働

heavy tax n jū-zei 重税

heavy work (load) → **heavy task**

heckling n yáji やじ・野次

hedge n ikegaki 生け垣

hedonism n kairaku shugi 快楽主義, kyōraku shugi 享楽主義

heed n chūi 注意

heel n kakato かかと・踵

height n takasa 高さ; (*stature*) séi 背・ せい = sé 背

heir n sōzoku-nin 相続人

helicopter n herikoputā ヘリコプター

helium n heriumu ヘリウム

hell n jigokú 地獄

hellish adj jigoku no yō (na) 地獄[じ

ごく]のよう(な), hisan (na) 悲惨(な)

hello 1. (*on phone*) móshi moshi もし もし **2.** (*saying at door*) [FORMAL] Gomen kudasái ごめん下さい. [CASUAL] konnichi wa. こんにちは **3.** (*on encounter*) ā ああ + [NAME] and/or [TITLE]; yā やあ; gokigen yō ご きげんよう

help 1. n (*assistance*) tetsudái (otétsudai) 手伝い(お手伝い); (*good offices*) assen あっせん・斡旋, sewá 世話; (*aid*) énjo 援助, hójo 補助; (*support*) ōen 応援; *with the ~ of …* no assen/ sewá de …のあっせん/世話で **2.** v (*assists*) tetsudaimásu (tetsudáu, tetsudátte) 手伝います(手伝う, 手伝っ て); (*rescues*) tasukemásu (tasukéru, tasukete) 助けます(助ける, 助けて); (*saves*) sukuimásu (sukū, sukutte) 救 います(救う, 救って); (*supports*) ōen shimásu (suru, shite) 応援します(す る, して)

helper n joshu 助手; *household helper* o-tétsudai(-san) お手伝い(さん)

helping; *a second ~* (of rice, etc.) o-káwari お代わり

hem n suso 裾

hemorrhoids n ji 痔・ぢ

hen n mendori 雌鳥・メンドリ

henchman n kó-bun 子分

hepatitis n kan'en 肝炎

her → she; **herself →** oneself

herb n kusá 草; yakusō 薬草, hāʾbu ハーブ

herd n mure 群れ

here n koko ここ; kochira こちら, kotchí こっち; *is here* kitéimásu (iru, ite) 来ています(いる, いて); *Here!* (*answering roll call*) exclam Hái! は い! *Here (you are)!* Hái (kore désu)! はい(これです)! [HONORIFIC] Dōzo (kochira désu)! どうぞ(こちらです)!

here and there achí-kóchi あちこち; (*various places*) tokoro dókoro ところ どころ・所々

hero n eiyū 英雄, hiirō ヒーロー

heroine n eiyū 英雄, hiroin ヒロイン

herpes n hōshin 疱疹, hérupesu ヘ ルペス

herring n níshin ニシン・鰊

hers (= *of her*) → she

hesitate *v* tameraimás̱u (tamerá̱u, tamerátte) ためらい[躊躇]います(ため らう、ためらって); chūcho shimás̱u (suru, shi̱te) ちゅうちょ[躊躇]します (する、して); enryo shimás̱u (suru, shi̱te) 遠慮します(する、して)

hey! *interj (masculine)* ói! おい!, tchotto! ちょっと!, *(feminine)* nē! ねえ!, ano né! あのね!

hi! *interj (masculine)* yá やあ! → hello → hey

Hibiya *n* Hibiya 日比谷

Hibiya Park *n* Hibiya kō'en 日比谷 公園

hiccup *n* shákkuri しゃっくり

hide **1.** *v (hides it)* kaḵushimás̱u (kaḵusú, kaḵushi̱te) 隠します(隠す、 隠して); *(it hides)* kaḵuremás̱u (kaḵuréru, kaḵúrete) 隠れます(隠れ る、隠れて) **2.** *n (skin of an animal)* kawa 皮, híḵaku 皮革, *(skin of a human)* hifu 皮膚

hi-fi *n* haifai ハイファイ, sutereo ステ レオ

high *adj* táḵai 高い; kō-… 高…; *highest (maximum, top)* saikō (no) 最高(の), saijō (no) 最上(の); *higher by ¥100* hyaḵuén-daka 百円高; *the highest (degree)* saikō-géndo 最高限度

high (barometric) pressure *n* kō-kíatsu 高気圧

high blood pressure *n* kō-kétsúatsu 高血圧

highball *n* haibō'ru ハイボール; *(of shōchū* 焼酎) chū-hai 酎ハイ・チュ ーハイ; *(whisky-and-water)* mizuwari 水割り

highbrow **1.** *n* interi インテリ **2.** *adj (intellectual)* chiteki (na) 知的(な)

high-class *adj (high-grade/-ranking)* kōkyū (na) 高級(な), haiḵurasu (no) ハイクラス(の)

high degree *n* kō'do 高度

highest *adj/adv* ichiban táḵai 一番高 い, saikō (no) 最高(の); ichiban ue 一番上, saijō (no) 最上(の)

high fashion *n* ōtoḵuchū'ru オートク チュール

high-fiber *adj* sen'i no ōi 繊維の多い

high-fidelity *adj* kōseinō (no) 高性能 (の)

high gear *n* kōsoku gí(y)a 高速ギア [ヤ]

highhanded *adj* gōin (na) 強引(な)

highhandedly *adv* gōin ni 強引に

highland *n* kōchi 高地

highlight *n* midokoro 見所, medama 目玉, hairaito ハイライト

highly *adv* ōi ni おおいに, hijō ni 非常 に, kiwamete 極めて

highpoint *n* chō'ten 頂点

highrise *adj* kōsō (no) 高層(の)

high-rise (office) building *n* kōsō ofisubiru 高層(オフィス)ビル

high school *n* kōtō-gákkō 高等学校, kō-kō 高校

high school student *n* kōkō'-sei 高校生

high sea *n* taikai/daikai 大海; soto-umi/gaiyō 外洋

high speed *adj* kōsoku 高速

highway *n* kaidō 街道, kokudō 国道, kōdō 公道; *(expressway)* kōsoku-dōro 高速道路

hijack **1.** *v (airplane)* nottorimás̱u (nottóru, nottótte) 乗っ取ります(乗っ取る、 乗っ取って) **2.** *n* haijakku ハイジャック

hijacker *n* nottorí-han 乗っ取り犯

hijacking *n* nottori-jíken 乗っ取り事件

hike, hiking *n* háikíngu (o shimás̱u; suru, shi̱te) ハイキング(をします; する、して)

hilarious *adj* yukai (na) 愉快(な)

hilarity *n* tanoshii/yukai na kibun 楽し い/愉快な気分

hill *n (slope)* saká 坂; *(small mountain)* ōka 丘, koyama 小山

hilt *n* tsuká 塚

him → he; himself → oneself

hind *adj* ushiro (no) 後ろ(の)

hind leg *n* ato-ashi 後肢, ushiro ashi 後ろ肢[あし]

hinder *v* samatagemás̱u (samatageru, samatagete) 妨げます(妨げる、妨げて)

hindrance *n* sashi̱tsukae 差し支え, (o-)jama (お)じゃま[邪魔]; koshō 故 障; shōgai 障害

hinge **1.** *n* chō-tsúgai ちょうつがい・ 蝶番 **2.** *v ~ on* … ni sayū-saremás̱u (sayū-sareru, sayū-sarete) ...に左右されれます(左右される、左右されて)

hinged door n hiraki-do 開き戸

hint 1. n hínto ヒント, honomekashí ほのめかし, anji 暗示, tegakari 手掛かり 2. v (hints it) hono-mekashimásu (hono-mekásu, hono-mekáshite) ほのめかします(ほのめかす、ほのめかして), anji shimásu (suru, shite) 暗示します(する、して)

hinterland n oku-chi 奥地, nairiku-chi 内陸地

hip 1. n (buttock) shirí 尻 (o-shiri お尻), (thigh) mómo もも・股; (loins) koshi 腰, hippu ヒップ 2. adj [SLANG] ikashita いかした, iketeru イケてる

hippopotamus n kaba カバ・河馬

hiragana n hirágáná ひらがな・平仮名

hire v yatoimásu (yatóu, yatótte) 雇います(雇う、雇って); (a professional) tanomimásu (tanómu, tanónde) 頼みます(頼む、頼んで)

his (of him) → he

historian n rekishi-ka 歴史家

history n rekishi 歴史; one's personal history rireki 履歴, keireki 経歴, (resume) rirekisho 履歴書

hit 1. n híttó ヒット; atari 当たり 2. v butsukemásu (butsukeru, butsukete) ぶつけます(ぶつける、ぶつけて), uchimásu (útsu, útte) 打ちます(打つ、打って); (strike) tatakimásu (tatáku, tatáite) 叩きます(叩く、叩いて) atemásu (ateru, atete) 当てます(当てる、当てて) 3. v atarimásu (ataru, atatte) 当たります(当たる、当たって); gets ~ (robbed, beset, wounded, killed) yararemásu (yarareru, yararete) やられます(やられる、やられて)

hit and run adj 1. hikinige ひき逃げ 2. (baseball) hitto endo ran ヒット・エンド・ラン

hitch 1. n (knot) musubi-me 結び目 2. n (barrier) shōgai 障害 3. n,v (hitchhike) hit-tchi-haiku (shimásu; suru, shite) ヒッチハイク(します; する、して)

hitherto n jū´rai 従来

hit home (with/to one) pin to kimásu (kúru, kíte) ぴんときます(くる、きて)

hives n jinmashin じん麻疹

hoard v takuwaemásu (takuwaeru, takuwaete) 蓄えます(蓄える、蓄えて), (buys up) kaidame shimásu (suru, shite) 買いだめします(する、して)

hoarse adj hasukii (na) ハスキー(な); shiwa-gareta しわがれた

hobby n shúmi 趣味; hobii ホビー; ohako おはこ・十八番 (= hobbyhorse)

hoe n kuwa くわ・鍬

Hokkaido n Hokkaidō 北海道

hold 1. v (té ni) mochimásu (mótsu, mótte) (手に)持ちます(持つ、持って), mótte imásu (iru, ite) 持っています(いる、いて); (in arms) dakimásu (daku, daite) 抱きます(抱く、抱いて), (or under the arm) kakaemásu (kakaeru, kakaete) 抱えます(抱える、抱えて); (an open umbrella) sashimásu (sásu, sáshite) 差します(差す、差して); (keeps in reserve) tótte okimásu (oku, oite) 取って置きます(置く、置いて); (gives an event) moyōshimásu (moyōsu, moyōshite) 催します(催す、催して); ~ in the mouth (kuchi ni) fukumimásu (fukúmu, fukúnde) (口に)含みます(含む、含んで)

hold back v (hesitates) (go-)enryo shimásu (suru, shite) (ご)遠慮します(する、して)

hold it v (sonomama de) machimásu (matsu, matte) (そのままで)待ちます(待つ、まって), taiki shimásu (suru, shite) 待機します(する、して)

hold it up v (lift) sashi-agemásu (sashi-ageru, sashi-agete) 差し上げます(差し上げる、差し上げて) 2. n (place to hold on) tegakari 手掛かり

hole n aná 穴・あな; (opening) kuchi 口・クチ

hole-punch n kíri きり・錐

holiday n yasumí 休み・やすみ, kyūjitsu 休日; (official) saijitsu 祭日, shukujitsu 祝日

Holland n Oranda オランダ

hollow 1. adj (empty) utsuro (na) うつろ(な) 2. n (a dent) kubomi くぼみ・窪み; gets ~ hekomimásu (hekomu, hekonde) へこみ[凹み]ます(へこむ、へこんで)

holly *n* hiiragi ヒイラギ

holocaust *n* dai-gyakusatsu 大虐殺;
the Holocaust yudaya-jin (no) dai-gyakusatsu ユダヤ人(の)の大虐殺

home *n* uchi 家 (o-uchi お家), ... uchí
...家; (*one's residence*) jitaku 自宅;
(*household*) katei 家庭; (*of a product/
crop*) sánchi 産地; *goes ~* kaerimásu
(káeru, káette) 帰ります(帰る, 帰って)
home and abroad náigai 内外
(*one's*) home area kuni 国(o-kuni
お国), inaka いなか・田舎 (= *hometown*)
one's parent's home jikka 実家

home appliance *n* katei yō´gu/yō´hin
家庭用具/用品

homebody *n* de-bushō 出不精

home help *n* hōmu herupā ホームヘ
ルパー

homeland *n* sókoku 祖国,
(*motherland*) bókoku 母国

homeless *n* hōmuresu ホームレス,
furō´-sha 浮浪者

homely *adj* (*ugly*) bu-kíryō (na) 不器
用[ぶきよう](な)

homemade *adj* tesei (no) 手製(の),
tezúkuri (no) 手作り(の)
homemade cake *n* jikasei kēki 自家
製ケーキ, hōmu-meido kēki ホームメ
イドケーキ

homemaker *n* shufu 主婦

homesick *adj* hōmu shikku (no) ホー
ムシック(の)

home stay *n* hōmu sutei ホームステイ

hometown *n* kókyō 故郷; hōmu taun
ホームタウン; (*countryside*) inaka い
なか・田舎; sato 里 (o-sato お里)

homework *n* (*student*) shukudai 宿題

homicide *n* (*murder*) satsujin 殺人
2. (*killer*) satsujin-han 殺人犯

homosexual 1. *n* hómo ホモ **2.** *adj*
dōsei ai (no) 同性愛(の)

homosexuality *n* dōsei ai 同性愛

honest *adj* shōjíkí (na) 正直(な),
katagi (na) 堅気(な); (*proper*) tadashíi
正しい; (*earnest*) majime (na) まじめ
[真面目](な)

honestly *adv* shōjíkí ni 正直に

honewort *n* mitsuba 三ツ葉・ミツバ

honey 1. *n* mítsu 蜜・ミツ, hachi-
mitsu 蜂蜜・ハチミツ **2.** *interj* hanii
ハニー

Hong Kong *n* Hónkón ホンコン・
香港

Honolulu *n* Honoruru ホノルル

honor *n* méiyo 名誉; (= "*face*") taimen
体面; (*sense of obligation*) girí 義理

honorable *adj* (*respectable*)
sonkeidekiru 尊敬できる, rippa na
立派な; (*famous*) chomei na 著名な

honorific (*word*) *n* keigo 敬語;
honorific prefix o- お・御; go- ご・
御; (*for a few words*) on- 御, mi- み・
御, o-mi- おみ, gyo- 御

Honshu *n* Hónshū 本州

hood *n* **1.** (*of car*) bonnétto ボンネット
2. (*for head*) fūdo フード

hoodlum *n* yotamono よたもの・与太
者; chinpira ちんぴら・チンピラ

hoof *n* hizume ヒヅメ・蹄

hook 1. *n* kagí カギ・鈎; (*snap*) hókku
ホック; *fishing ~* tsuribari 釣り針
2. *v* (*to hook a fish*) (sakana o) tsurimásu (tsuru, tsutte) 釣ります(釣る,
釣って); *~ up* setsuzoku shimásu
(suru, shite) 接続します(する, して)
3. *v* (*to hang*) tsurushimásu (tsurusu,
tsurushite) 吊るします(吊るす, 吊る
して), hikkakémásu (hikkakéru,
hikkakéte) 引っ掛けます(引っ掛ける,
引っ掛けて)

hookey; *plays ~* saborimásu (sabóru,
sabótte) さぼります(さぼる, さぼっ
て), zuru-yásumi shimásu (suru, shite)
ずる休みします(する, して)

hoop *n* wa(-k-ka) 輪(っか); *a barrel ~*
tagá たが

hope 1. *n* nozomi 望み, kibō 希望,
(*anticipation*) mikomi 見込み, (*ambition*)
kokorozashi 志 **2.** *v hopes for v*
nozomimásu (nozomu, nozonde) 望み
ます(望む, 望んで), kibō shimásu
(suru, shite) 希望します(する, して);
I ~ that ... (da) to íi desu ...(だ)とい
いです

horizon *n* (*sea*) suihei sen 水平線,
(*land*) chihei sen 地平線

horizontal *adj* suihei (no) 水平(の)

hormone *n* horumon ホルモン

horn *n* (*of animal*) tsunó 角; (*of car*

keiteki 警笛, kurakushon クラクショ
ン; (music) hórun ホルン
hornet n suzumé-bachi スズメバチ
horrible adj osoroshíi 恐ろしい
horse n umá 馬 (1: i-tō, 2: ni-tō,
3: sán-tō; how many nán-tō 何頭)
horse mackerel n áji アジ・鯵
horseman n kishu 騎手
horsepower n bariki 馬力
horse racing n keiba 競馬
horseradish n (seiyō) wásabi (セイヨ
ウ) ワサビ・山葵
hose n hōsu ホース → **stockings**
hospital n byōin 病院; ~ admission
nyūin 入院; is in the ~ nyūin shite
imásu (iru, ite) 入院しています(い
る、いて)
hospital head/director n ínchō 院長
hospitality n o-motenashi おもてなし、
kantai 歓待
host n shújin 主人, téishu 亭主
hostage n (captive) hitójichi 人質
hostelry n minshuku 民宿
hostess n onna shújin 女主人;
hósutesu ホステス
hostile adj tekii/tekitaishin/hankan o
motta 敵意/敵対心/反感を持った
hostility n tekii 敵意
hot adj 1. atsúi 熱い・暑い; (pungent,
spicy) karai からい・辛い 2. gets ~
nes-shimásu (nes-suru, nes-shite) 熱し
ます(熱する、熱して)
hot air n (idle talk) baka-/muda-
bánashi ばか/無駄話
hot blast n neppū 熱風
hot blood n tanki 短気
hot cake n hotto-kēki ホットケーキ,
pan-kēki パンケーキ; sells like hot
cakes (popular) ninki no aru 人気の
ある
hot dog n hotto-doggu ホットドッグ
hotel n hóteru ホテル
hotel bill n hoterú-dai ホテル代
hothouse n onshitsu 温室
hotline n hottorain ホットライン
hot plate n (electric) denki kónro 電気
コンロ, hotto purēto ホットプレート、
(gas) gasu kónro ガスコンロ
hot spring n onsen 温泉
hot-spring cure tōji 湯治

hot water n oyu お湯, yú 湯, (burning
hot water) nettō 熱湯
hot-water bottle n yu-tánpo 湯たんぽ
hour n jikan 時間 (o-jíkan お時間)
hourglass n suna-dokei 砂時計
house n uchi 家 (o-uchi お家), …
uchí …家, ié 家 (1: íkken 一軒, 2: ní-
ken 二軒, 3: sán-gen 三軒; how many
nán-gen 何軒); taku 宅, …-ya …家
house addition/extension n tatemashi
建て増し
house dust n (ie no) hokori (家の)ほ
こり
house refuse n gomí ごみ・ゴミ
house rent n yá-chin 家賃
rental house n (house for rent or
rented house) kashi-ya 貸家
your house o-taku お宅
housefly n hae ハエ・蝿
household n katei 家庭; shótai 所帯
household altar n (Buddhist) butsu-
dan 仏壇, (Shinto) kami-dana 神棚
household helper n otétsudai(-san)
お手伝い(さん)
household budget n 家計
housekeeper n kaséi-fu 家政婦
housekeeping n kasei 家政, shótai
所帯
housekeeping book n kakei-bo 家計
簿
house sit; is house sitting (for) (…no)
kawari ni súnde imásu (…の)代わり
に住んでいます
houseware n (store) nichiyōhin-ten
日用品店
housewife n shúfu 主婦
housework n kaji 家事
housing development n danchi 団地
housing project n (kōei) danchi (公
営)団地
how adv dō どう, [DEFERENTIAL] ikága
いかが
How are you (feeling)? interj
Go-kigen (wa) ikága desu ka. ご機嫌
(は)いかがですか。O-génki desu ka.
お元気ですか。
how come adv dō´-shite どうして
How do you do? interj (on first being
introduced) Hajimemáshite. はじめま
して。

how far/long *adv* (*distance*) dono-gurai/kurai どの位・どのくらい

how long *adv* (*time length*) ítsu made いつまで; ítsu kara いつから

how many *adj* íkutsu いくつ (o-ikutsu おいくつ); nán-… 何…, íku-… いく・幾…; (*small things*) ~ *pieces* nán-ko 何個; (*long things*) nán-bon 何本; (*flat things*) ~ *sheets* nán-mai 何枚; (*small animals, fish/ bugs*) nán-biki 何匹; (*large animals*) nán-tō 何頭; (*birds, rabbits*) nán-ba 何羽; (*machines, vehicles*) nán-dai 何台; (*books, magazines*) ~ *copies* nán-satsu 何冊; ~ *days* nán-nichi 何日; ~ *people* nán-nin 何人, nánmei 何名; ~ *times* nán-do 何度, nán-kai 何回, nánbén 何遍 (*how many fold*); ~ *cupfuls* nán-bai 何杯; ~ *years* nán-nen 何年; ~ *years old* íkutsu いくつ(o-ikutsu おいくつ), nán-sai 何歳

how much *adj* íkura いくら (o-ikura おいくら), dono-gurai どの位, ika-hodo いか程; dónna ni どんなに

how old *adj* íkutsu いくつ(o-ikutsu おいくつ); nán-sai 何歳

how true *interj* naru-hodo (sō desu né) なるほど[成る程](そうですね)

however *adv* kéredo (mo) けれど(も), shíkashi しかし, démo でも, dátte だって, tokoróga ところが, tádashi ただし・但し; (*to be sure*) móttomo もっとも

hug *v* daki-shimemásu (daki-shiméru, daki-shímete) 抱き締めます(抱き締める, 抱き締めて)

huge *adj* kyodai (na) 巨大(な), bakudai (na) 莫大(な)

huh?! *exclam* hóra! ほら!, hē へー; *Interesting, huh?!* Omoshiroi-desho!? 面白いでしょ!?, (*male*) Omoshiroi-daro!? 面白いだろ!?

hull *n* 1. (*of grain, etc.*) kawa 皮, kara 殻, (*of strawberry*) heta へた 2. (*of boat*) sentai 船体

human being *n* ningen 人間; jínrui 人類

humankind → **human being**

human feelings/nature *n* nínjō 人情

humanities *n* jinbun kagaku 人文科学

humanity *n* ningen-sei 人間性, hyūmanitii ヒューマニティ

human rights *n* jinken 人権

humble *adj* (*modest*) kenkyo (na) 謙虚 (な)

humid *adj* (*in summer*) mushi-atsúi 蒸し暑い, (*gets sultry*) mushimásu (músu, múshite) 蒸します(蒸す, 蒸して); (*in winter*) shimeppoi 湿っぽい

humidity *n* shikki/shikke 湿気, shitsúdo 湿度

humiliating *adj* kuyashíi 悔しい

humor *n* yū´moa ユーモア

humorous *adj* yū´morasu na ユーモラ スな, yū´moa no aru ユーモアのある, kek-kei na 滑稽[こっけい]な

hunch up se o maruku shimásu (suru, shite) 背を丸くします(する, して)

hundred *n* hyakú 百・100; *how many* ~ nán-byaku 何百

hundred million *n* óku 億

hundred thousand *n* jū-mán 十万・100,000

hungry 1. *n gets* ~ o-naka ga sukimásu (suku, suite) おなかがすきます(すく, すいて), hara ga herimásu (heru, hette) 腹が減ります(減る, 減って) 2. *adj* kūfuku (no) 空腹(の)

hunt *v* kári/ryō´ o shimásu (suru, shite) 狩り/猟をします(する, して) → **look for**

hunter *n* káriudo 狩人, ryō´-shi 猟師, hantá ハンター

hunting *n* kári 狩り, ryō´ 猟

hurdle *n* (*obstacle*) shōgai (-butsu) 障害物, (*sport*) hādoru ハードル

hurray! *exclam* banzái! 万歳・バン ザイ!

hurricane *n* bōfū 暴風, harikēn ハリ ケーン

hurry *v* isogimásu (isógu, isóide) 急ぎ ます(急ぐ, 急いで); tobashimásu (tobasu, tobashite) 飛ばします(飛ば す, 飛ばして)

in a big hurry ō-ísogi (de/no) 大急ぎ (で/の)

hurt 1. *v it hurts* (*is painful*) *v* itái 痛い 2. *v gets hurt* kegá o shimásu (suru, shite) けが[怪我]をします(す る, して) 3. *adj* (*injures*) itamemásu

439

(itaméru, itámete) 傷めます(傷める、傷めて); (*damages*) sokonaimás̲u̲ (sokonáu, sokonátte) 損ないます(損なう、損なって) **4.** *n* kizu 傷, kega けが, kutsū 苦痛

husband *n* otto 夫, shújin 主人, danna-san/-sama 旦那さん/様, téishu 亭主
husband and wife *n* fūfu 夫婦; *both*
~ **fūfu-tomo** 夫婦共
my husband otto 夫, shújin 主人, taku 宅
your husband go-shújin ご主人

hut *n* koya 小屋
hydrant *n* → fireplug
hydrogen *n* súiso 水素
hygiene *n* eisei 衛生
hypothesis *n* katei 仮定, zentei 前提

I

I *n* [FORMAL *for male*] watashi わたし・私, [FORMAL] watakushi わたくし・私; [HUMBLE] temae 手前; (*male*) boku ぼく・僕; (*male, unrefined*) ore おれ・俺; (*female*) atashi あたし
I see! *interj* naru-hodo なるほど・成る程, wakatta わかった・分かった
…-ic, …-ical …-teki (na) …的(な)
ibis *n* toki トキ・鴇
ice *n* kōri 氷・こおり
iceberg *n* hyó̲zan 氷山
icebox *n* reizó̲ko 冷蔵庫, reitó̲ko 冷凍庫 → refrigerator
ice cream *n* aisu-kuríimu アイスクリーム
ice cube *n* kaku-hyō 角氷, kōri 氷
ice hockey *n* aisu-hokkē アイス・ホッケー
ice rink *n* sukēto-rinku スケート・リンク
ice skate *n* aisu-sukēto アイス・スケート
icicle *n* tsurara つらら・氷柱
icing *n* aishingu アイシング
icon *n* **1.** (*computer*) aikon アイコン; *icon box* aikon-bokkusu アイコン・ボックス **2.** (*image*) zō 像
icon memory *n* zanzō 残像
iconify *v* aikon-ka shimás̲u̲ (suru, sh̲i̲te) アイコン化します(する、して)
iconoclast *n* seizō-hakai-sha 聖像破壊者
idea *n* (*thought*) kangáe 考え, omói-tsu̲ki 思いつき; kokoro atari 心当たり; (*opinion*) íken 意見, (*your opinion*) go-íken ご意見; aidéa アイデア; (*intention, aim*) nerai 狙い → rough idea

ideal *adj* risō-teki (na) 理想的(な); (*most desirable*) motte-kói (no) もってこい(の)
idealism *n* risō-shugi 理想主義
idealist *n* risō-shugi-sha 理想主義者
identical *adj* h̲i̲toshíi 等しい → same
identical twins *n* ichiransei-sōsēji 一卵性双生児
identified; *gets* ~ shiremás̲u̲ (shireru, shirete) 知れます(知れる、知れて)
identity card *n* mibun-shōmei-sho 身分証明書, ai dii-kādo IDカード
ideologist *n* kannen ron-sha 観念論者
ideology *n* ideorogii イデオロギー, kannen 観念, shisō 思想, kangae 考え
idiot *n* (*fool*) báka ばか・バカ, manuke 間抜け・まぬけ
idle 1. *v* (*is lazy*) namakemás̲u̲ (namakéru, namákete) 怠けます(怠ける、怠けて); (*useless, unavailing*) **2.** *adj* muda (na) 無駄(な)
idle talk baka/muda-bánashi ばか/無駄話
idleness *n* taida 怠惰, bushō 無精
idly *adv* búrabura ぶらぶら・ブラブラ
i.e. *adv* sunawachi すなわち, iikaereba 言い換えれば
if *conj* móshi … (shi-) tára もし…(し)たら; … (no) ba(w)ai … (の)場合; **if by any chance** *conj* mán'ichi 万一
if you prefer/like *conj* nan-nára なんなら
if I remember rightly *conj* táshi̲ka 確か
if you don't mind *conj* yorosh̲i̲kattara よろしかったら・宜しかったら; nan-nára なんなら
if you don't want to/if you like *conj* nan-nára なんなら

if there be *conj* áreba あれば, árya
ありや

ignition *n* tenka 点火; (*car*) **~ switch**
(kuruma no) tenka suítchi (車の)点火
スイッチ; **turns on the ~** tenka suítchi
o iremásu (ireru, irete) 点火スイッチを
入れます(入れる, 入れて)

ignorance *n* múshi shimásu (suru, shite)
無視します(する, して)

ignore *n* múshi shimásu (suru, shite)
無視します(する, して)

ikebana *n* ikebana 生け花・いけばな

ileac *adj* kaichō (no) 回腸(の)

ileus *n* (*medical*) ireusu イレウス, chō-
heisoku 腸閉塞

ill → sick; bad

illegal *adj* fuhō (no) 不法(の), ihō (no)
違法(の)

illegal work(er) *n* fuhō shūrō(-sha)
不法就労(者)

illicit *adj* yami no 闇の, fuhō (na) 不法
(な), mumenkyo (no) 無免許(の),

illness *n* byōki 病気

ill-tempered *adj* íji ga waruí 意地が悪い

illuminate *v* terashimásu (terásu, teráshite) 照らします(照らす, 照らして)

illumination *n* iruminēshon イルミネ
ーション, shōmei 照明

illustration *n* zukai 図解, irasuto
(rēshon) イラスト(レーション)

illustrator *n* irasutorētā イラストレー
ター

ill-will *n* (*resentment*) urami 恨み,
(*hostile feeling*) teki-i 敵意

image *n* (ga)zō (画)像, imēji イメージ,
(*video picture*) eizō 映像; (*psychologi-
cal, social*) imē'ji イメージ

imagery *n* **1.** (*image*) imēji イメージ,
shinshō 心象 **2.** (*figure of speech*) hiyu
比喩

imaginary *adj* kakū (no) 架空(の),
sōzōjō (no) 想像上(の)

imagination *n* sōzō 想像, (*imaginative
power*) sōzō-ryoku 想像力

imagine *v* sōzō shimásu (suru, shite)
想像します(する, して) → suppose,
think

imbalance *n* fu-antei 不安定, anbaransu
アンバランス

imbecile **1.** *adj* teinō (na) 低脳(な)
2. *n* teinō na hito 低脳な人

imitate *v* ... no mane o shimásu (suru,
shite) ...のまね[真似]をします(する,
して), ...o manemásu (maneru, man-
ete) ...をまね[真似]します(する, し
て); nisemásu (niseru, nisete) 似せま
す(似せる, 似せて)

imitation *n* **1.** (*man-made*) jinzō 人造;
(*fake*) nise 偽, mozō-hin 模造品, nise-
mono 偽物 **2.** (*mimicry*) mane まね・
真似

imitator *n* mohō-sha 模倣者

immediate *adj* tōmen (no) 当面(の),
mokuzen (no) 目前(の)

immediately *adv* súgu (ni) すぐ(に),
sassokú 早速, jiki (ni) じき(に),
tádachi-ni 直ちに, tachimachi (ni) た
ちまち(に); (*without waiting*) matá-
naide 待たないで

immense *adj* tái-shita 大した; bakudai
(na) 莫大(な)

immigrant *n* imin 移民

immigrant laborer *n* imin-rōdō-sha
移民労働者

immigrate *v* ijū shimásu (suru, shite)
移住します(する, して)

immigration *n* (*entry*) nyūkoku 入国

immigration office *n* nyūkoku kanri-
kyoku 入国管理局

immigration control office *n* nyūkoku-
kanri-jimú-sho 入国管理事務所

imminent *adj* sashisematta 差し迫っ
た, majika (no) 間近(の)

immoderately *adv* múyami ni むやみに

immoral *adj* fu-dō'toku (na) 不道徳(な)

immorality *n* fu-dō'toku 不道徳

immortal *adj* fu-shi (no) 不死(の);
fu-metsu (no) 不滅(の); fu-kyū (no)
不朽(の)

immortal soul *n* fu-shi no tamashii
不死の魂

immortal work *n* fu-kyū no meisaku
不朽の名作

immunization *n* yobō-chūsha 予防注射

impartial *adj* kōhei (na) 公平(な);
kōsei (na) 公正(な)

impartiality *n* kōsei 公正

impatient *adj* ki ga mijikái 気が短い

impediment *n* shōgai 障害; (*hindrance*)
sashitsukae 差し支え

imperial *adj* téikoku (no) 帝国(の)

imperialism *n* teikoku-shúgi 帝国主義, teisei 帝政

impertinent *adj* namaiki (na) 生意気 (な)

impetus *n* hazumi 弾み・はずみ

impish *adj* itazura na いたずらな, wanpaku na わんぱくな

implant 1. *n* (*tooth*) sáshi-ba 差し歯, (*medical*) ishoku 移植 **2.** *v* umekomi-másu (umekomu, umekónde) 埋め込みます(埋め込む, 埋め込んで), ishoku shimásu (suru, shite) 移植します(する, して)

implement 1. *n* (*tool*) yóʹgu 用具; (*apparatus*) kígu 器具 **2.** *v* (*to carry out*) jik-kō shimásu (suru, shite) 実行します(する, して)

imply *v* **1.** fukumimásu (fukúmu, fukúnde) 含みます(含む, 含んで) **2.** → hint

impolite *adj* búrei (na) 無礼(な), shitsúrei (na) 失礼(な)

import *v* yunyū shimásu (suru, shite) 輸入します(する, して); (*goods*) yunyū-hin 輸入品

importance; a matter of ~ dáiji 大事, jū-dái-ji 重大事

important *adj* jūyō (na) 重要(な), taisetsu (na) 大切(な), jūdai (na) 重大(な), (*precious*) daijí (na) 大事(な), tái-shita (kotó) 大した(事); omoi 重い

importune *v* kongan shimásu (suru, shite) 懇願します(する, して), segamimásu (segamu, segande) せがみます(せがむ, せがんで)

impose; ~ it *v* kuwaemásu (kuwaeru, kuwaete) 加えます(加える, 加えて)

imposition *n* **1.** (*forcible*) kyōsei 強制 **2.** (*obligation*) gimu 義務

impossible *adj* dekínai 出来ない, fukánō (na) 不可能(な)
impossible! *interj* másaka まさか

imposter *n* sagi-shi 詐欺師

impotence *n* inpotensu インポテンス

impotent *adj* muryoku (na) 無力(な)

impression *n* inshō 印象

impressionism *n* inshō-shugi 印象主義

impressive *adj* inshō-teki (na) 印象的 (な)

imprisonment *n* tōgoku 投獄

improve *v* **1.** (*it improves*) naorimásu (naóru, naótte) 直ります(直る, 直って), yóku narimásu (náru, nátte) 良くなります(なる, なって) **2.** (*improves it*) naoshimásu (naósu, naóshite) 直します(直す, 直して), yóku shimásu (suru, shite) 良くします(する, して)

improvement *n* kaizen 改善

impudent *adj* atsukamashíi 厚かましい, zūzūshii ずうずうしい・図々しい

impulse *n* hazumi 弾み, shigeki 刺激, shōdō 衝動

impulsive *adj* shōdō-teki (na) 衝動的 (な)

impunity *n* buji 無事

in *prep* … de … で, (*located in*) …ni …に; (*inside*) …no náka (de/ni) …の中(で/に); (*resident in*) zai- … 在…
come in *v* (… ni) háitte kimásu (kúru, kité) (…に)入って来ます(来る, 来て)
go in *v* (… ni) hairimásu (háiru, háitte) …に入ります(入る, 入って), háitte ikimásu (iku, itte) 入って行きます(行く, 行って)
let/put in *v* (… ni) iremásu (ireru, irete) (…に)入れます(入れる, 入れて)

inadvertently *adv* tsúi つい, ukkari うっかり

inadvisable *adj* mazúi まずい

inbound (*to Tokyo*) *adj* nobori (no) 上り(の)

incense *n* kō 香; (o-)sénkó お線香, sénkō 線香

inception *n* kaishi 開始, hajimari はじまり・始まり

incessantly *adv* shíkiri-ni しきりに

incest *n* kinshin sōkan 近親相姦

incentive *n* dōki 動機

inch 1. *n* (…)ínchi (…)インチ; (*Japanese*) (…)- sún (…)寸 **2.** *v* (*to make very slowly*) yukkuri/sukoshi zutsu/ noronoro ugokimásu (ugoku, ugoite) ゆっくり/少しずつ/ノロノロ動きます(動く, 動いて)

incident *n* jíken 事件, jíhen 事変

incidentally *adv* (*by the way*) sore wa sóʹto それはそうと, tokoró de ところで, chinami ni ちなみ[因み]に, tsuide ni ついでに, tokí ni 時に

incision *n* sekkai 切開

incite *v* aorimásu (aóru, aótte) あおり
ます(あおる、あおって), shigeki
shimásu (suru, shite) 刺激します(す
る、して)

inclination *n* katamuki 傾き; (*intention*)
ikō 意向

include *v* iremásu (ireru, irete) 入れま
す(入れる、入れて), komemásu
(koméru, kómete) 込めます(込める、
込めて), fukumemásu (fukuméru,
fukúmete) 含めます(含める、含めて);
(*covers all items*) mō´ra shimásu
(suru, shite) 網羅します(する、して)

including ... *prep* o irete/fukúmete ...
を入れて/含めて; ...-tsuki ...付き

income *n* shotoku 所得, shūnyū 収入
income tax *n* shotokú-zei 所得税

inconsistency *n* mujun 矛盾

inconsistent *adj* **is inconsistent** mujun
shite imásu (iru, ite) 矛盾しています
(いる、いて)

inconvenience 1. *n* (*trouble taken*)
tesū´ 手数(o-tesū お手数), tékazu
手数, futsugō 不都合 **2.** ... ni meiwaku/
tesū o kakemásu (kakeru, kákéte)
...に迷惑/手数を掛けます(掛ける、
掛けて)

inconvenient *adj* fúben (na) 不便(な),
fú-jiyū (na) 不自由(な)

increase 1. *v* (*it increases/increases it*)
mashimásu (masu, mashite) 増します
(増す、増して); (*it/they increase(s)*)
fuemásu (fuéru, fúete) 増えます(増え
る、増えて), (*increases it/them*) fuyashimásu (fuyásu, fuyáshite) 増やします
(増やす、増やして) **2.** *n* (*an increase*)
mashi 増し; zōka 増加, zōdai 増大,
zōshin 増進

increasingly *adv* masú-masu ますま
す・益々

incur *v* (*unfair treatment, tribulation*)
kōmurimásu (kōmúru, kōmútte) 被り
ます(被る、被って)

indecent *adj* gehín (na) 下品(な);
(*obscene*) waisetsu (na) わいせつ・
猥褻(な)

indeed *adv* honto ni ほんと[本当]に,
hontō ni ほんとう[本当]に, jitsú ni
実に, tashika ni 確かに; (*of course*)
móttomo 最も; (*as we might expect*)

sasuga (ni) さすが(に)

indefinite *adj* futei (no) 不定(の),
fumeiryō (na) 不明瞭(な)

indemnify *v* hoshō shimásu (suru,
shite) 保証します(する、して)

indemnity *n* baishō(-kin) 賠償(金),
(*indemnity allowance*) hoshō-kin
補償金

indemnity insurance *n* songai hoken
損害保険

indemnity issue *n* baishō-kin mondai
賠償金問題

indemnity period *n* hoshō kikan 補償
期間

independence *n* dokuritsu 独立

independent *adj* dokuritsu shita
独立した...; *is* ~ dokuritsu shite imásu
(iru, ite) 独立しています(いる、いて)

index *n* sakuin 索引, midashi 見出し,
indekkusu インデックス

index card *n* sakuin kādo 索引カード

index finger *n* hitosashi yubi 人差し指

index function *n* shisū kansū 指数関数

India *n* Índo インド

Indian 1. Indó-jin インド人 **2.**
American indian Indian インディアン

India ink *n* sumí 墨;
India ink painting sumi-e 墨絵

indicate *v* shimeshimásu (shimesu,
shimeshite) 示します(示す、示して);
sashimásu (sásu, sáshite) 指します(指
す、指して); shiteki shimásu (suru, shite)
指摘します(する、して), shíji shimásu
(suru, shite) 指示します(する、して)

indication *n* shíji 指示, (*token, sign*)
shirushi しるし・印

indicator *n* (*car*) uinkā ウインカー

indict *v* kiso shimásu (suru, shite) 起訴
します(する、して)

indictment *n* kiso 起訴

indifferent to ... *adj* ni mu-kánshin
(no) ... に無関心(の)

indigent *n* (*people*) hinkon-sha 貧困者

indigestion *n* shōka-fúryō 消化不良

indignant; *adj gets* ~ fungai shimásu
(suru, shite) 憤慨します(する、して),
ikidōrimásu (ikidō´ru, ikidō´tte) 憤り
ます(憤る、憤って)

indignation *n* fungai 憤慨, ikidōri 憤り

indignity *n* bujoku 侮辱, kutsujoku 屈辱

indigo

indigo n (*Japanese indigo plant*) ái 藍;
(*Japanese indigo dye*) ái zome 藍染め

indirect adj kansetsu (no) 間接(の)
indirect kiss n kansetsu kisu 間接キス
indirect lighting n kansetsu shōmei 間
接照明

indirectly adv kansetsu ni 間接に

indiscreet adj keisotsu (na) 軽率(な)

indiscriminate adj musabetsu (no)
無差別(の), yatara na やたらな,
mechakucha (na) めちゃくちゃ・メチ
ャクチャ(な)

indiscriminately adv yatara ni やたら
に, múyami ni むやみに

indispensable adj hissu (no) 必須
(の), fukaketsu (no) 不可欠(の)

indispensability n fukaketsu 不可欠

individual 1. adj kojin-teki (na) 個人的
(な) 2. n (*a person*) kójin 個人

individuality n kosei 個性

individually adv betsu betsu ni 別々に

indolence n taida 怠惰, namake 怠け

Indonesia n Indonéshia インドネシア

Indonesian n (*language*) Indonesia-
go インドネシア語, (*person*)
Indonesiá-jin インドネシア人

indoors adv uchi (no náka) de/ni
家(の中)で/に

indoor shoes n 1. (*in school*) uwabaki
上履き 2. (*in room*) shitsunaibaki
室内履き

indulgent adj kandai (na) 寛大(な),
amai 甘い

industrialization n kō´gyō-ka 工業化,
sangyō-ka 産業化

industrious adj kinben (na) 勤勉(な)

industry n kō´gyō 工業, sangyō 産業,
gyōkai 業界
industry analyst n gyōkai anarisuto
業界アナリスト
industry bookkeeping n kōgyō boki
工業簿記

in effect yō-súru ni 要するに

inept adj hetá (na) へた[下手](な)

inequality n hu-kōhei 不公平,
fu-byōdō 不平等

inequilateral triangle n hu-tōhen
sankakkei 不等辺三角形

inequity n hu-kōhei 不公平, fu-kōsei
不公正

inertia n (*physics*) kansei 慣性, dasei
惰性

inevitable adj yondokoro-nái よんどこ
ろ無い, shikata-nái 仕方ない

inevitably adv kanarazu 必ず; nán to
shitémo 何としても; iyaō-naku いや
おう[否応]なく

inexpensive adj yasui 安い

inexperience n mu-keiken 無経験

inexperienced adj keiken busoku (no)
経験不足(の)

inexpert adj hetá (na) へた[下手](な)

infancy n (*childhood*) yōnen-ki 幼年期

infant n yō´ji 幼児, shō´ni 小児, akanbō
赤ん坊, aka-chan 赤ちゃん

infantile paralysis n shōni-máhi
小児麻痺

infantry n hohei 歩兵

infect v utsushimásu (utsúsú, utsúshite)
移します(移す, 移して)

infection n 1. kansen 感染 2.
(*infectious disease*) densenbyō 伝染病
virus infection uirusu kansen ウイル
ス感染

infer v suitei shimásu (suru, shite) 推定
します(する, して)

inference n suitei 推定

inferior adj furyō (no) 不良(の); *is ~*
ochimásu (ochíru, óchite) 落ちます
(落ちる, 落ちて), otorimásu (otoru,
ototte) 劣ります(劣る, 劣って);
yuzurimásu (yuzuru, yuzutte) 譲りま
す(譲る, 譲って), makemásu (makeru,
makete) 負けます(負ける, 負けて)

inferiority complex n konpurekkusu
コンプレックス, rettō-kan 劣等感

inflation n infure インフレ

influence n (*effect*) eikyō 影響, ...séi
...せい; (*power*) séiryoku 勢力

influential adj yūryoku (na) 有力(な)

influenza → flu

inform v kikasemásu (kikaseru, kikasete) 聞かせます(聞かせる, 聞かせて),
shirasemásu (shiraseru, shirasete) 知ら
せます(知らせる, 知らせて), tsuge-
másu (tsugeru, tsugete) 告げます(告げ
る, 告げて); (*instructs*) oshiemásu
(oshieru, oshiete) 教えます(教える, 教
えて); (*tells*) mimí ni iremásu (ireru,
irete) 耳に入れます(入れる, 入れて)

informal *adj* hi-kō´shiki (no) 非公式 (の)

information *n* jōhō 情報, shirase 知らせ; *(guidance)* annái 案内; *(reception desk)* uke-tsuke 受付

information desk *n* annai-jo 案内所, furonto フロント

information technology *n* jōhō gijutsu 情報技術, jōhō kōgaku 情報工学, infomēshon tekunorojii インフォメーション・テクノロジー

informed *adj* chishiki no aru 知識のある, jōhō ni motozuita 情報に基づいた

informer *n* mikkoku-sha 密告者, jōhō-ya 情報屋, jōhō-teikyō-sha 情報提供者

infotainment *n (documentary film)* dokyumentarii dorama ドキュメンタリードラマ

infraction *n (violation)* ihan 違反

infrared rays *n* sekigai-sen 赤外線

infrequent *adj* tama no たまの, mare na まれ[稀]な

infrequently *adv* tama ni たまに, mare ni まれ[稀]に

infringement *n* ihan 違反

infusion *n chūnyū* 注入, yueki 輸液

ingredient *n (component)* séibun 成分; *(raw material)* zairyó´ 材料; *(cooking ingredient)* shokuzai 食材

inherit *v (succeeds to)* tsugimásu (tsugu, tsuide) 継ぎます(継ぐ、継いで)

injection *n* chūsha 注射
preventive injection yobō-chūsha 予防注射

injure *v* **1.** kega (o) saseru 怪我(を)させる, itamemásu (itaméru, itámete) 傷めます(傷める、傷めて); *(damages it)* sokonaimásu (sokonáu, sokonátte) 損ないます(損なう、損なって)
2. injures it kizu tsukemásu (tsukeru, tsukete) 傷つけます(傷つける、傷つけて); kega o sasemásu (saseru, sasete) 怪我をさせます(させる、させて)

injured *adj* kizutsuita 傷ついた, fōshōshita 負傷した
injured person *n* kega-nin けが人

injury *n* kegá けが・怪我; *(damage)* gái 害, higai 被害

ink *n* inki インキ, inku インク
ink stick, India ink *n* sumí 墨

inkjet printer *n* inkujetto purintā インクジェット・プリンター

inkstone *n* suzurí 硯・スズリ
inkstone case *n* suzurí-bako 硯箱

inlaid work *n* zōgan 象眼・象嵌

inland *adj (domestic)* kokúnai (no) 国内(の)

Inland Sea *n* Seto-náikai 瀬戸内海

...-in-law *adj* giri no …義理の…

inlet *n (opening)* kuchi 口

inn *n (Japanese-style)* ryokan 旅館; yado-ya 宿屋, yádo 宿 (o-yado お宿)

inner *adj* **1.** *(inside)* naibu no 内部の, uchigawa no 内側の **2.** *(secret)* kakureta 隠れた **3.** *(one's mind)* naimen-teki na 内面的な
inner cloth *n* shitagi 下着
inner moat *n* uchi-bori 内堀(り)

innocent *adj (naive)* mújaki (na) 無邪気(な); *(not guilty)* múzai (no) 無罪(の)
innocent baby *n* muku na akanbō 無垢な赤ん坊
innocent lie *n* warugi no nai uso 悪気のない嘘[うそ]
innocent mischief *n* warugi no nai itazura 悪気のない悪戯[いたずら]

innumerable *adj* musū (no) 無数(の), kazoe-kire nai 数え切れない

inoculation *n* yobō-chūsha 予防注射

inordinate *adj* hogai (na) 法外(な)

in other words → word

in particular → particular

inpatient *n* nyūin-kanja 入院患者

in pieces → piece

inquire *v* toimásu (tou, tōte) 聞います(問う、問って) → **ask**

inquiry *n* (o-)toiawase (お)問い合わせ; (o-)ukagai (お)伺い; *(survey)* chō´sa 調査

inquisitive *adj* monózukí (na) 物好き(な)

inquisitiveness *n* kōkíshin 好奇心

in rapid succession → succession

insane *adj* ki-chígái (no) 気違い(の); *goes ~* ki ga kuruimásu (kurū´, kurútte) 気が狂います(狂う、狂って)

insect *n* konchū 昆虫, *(bug)* mushi

虫・ムシ (**1**: ip-piki 一匹, **2**: ní-hiki 二匹, **3**: sánbiki 三匹, *how many* nán-biki 何匹)

insecticide n bōchū-zai 防虫剤

insect repellent n mushi-yoke 虫よけ

insert v sashi-komimásu (sashi-komu, sashi-konde) 差し込みます(込む、込んで); (*puts it between*) hasamimásu (hasámu, hasánde) 挟みます(挟む、挟んで)

in short → short

inside adj, adv, prep (... no) náka (de/ni) (...の)中(で/に), ...-nai ...内; (*among*) (... no) uchí(de/ni) (...の)中(で/に); *the inside* uchi-gawa 内側, uchiwa 内輪, okunai 屋内, (*back/deep inside*) óku 奥; *is ~* háitte imásu (iru, ite) 入っています(いる、いて)

inside and out adv náigai no 内外の; nani mo ka mo 何もかも

inside corner n súmi 隅・すみ

inside information n naibu-jōhō 内部情報

inside-out adj uragáeshi (no) 裏返し(の)

insipid adj ajike-nái 味気ない

inspect v kénsa/kansatsu shimásu (suru, shite) 検査/監察します(する、して)

inspection n kénsa 検査, kansatsu 監察

install v sonaemásu (sonáeru, sonáete) 備えます(備える、備えて)

installation n shisetsu 施設

installment(s) n kappu/wappu 割賦; (*monthly payments*) geppu 月賦, bun-katsu barai 分割払い

installment savings n tsumitatekin 積立金

instance n (*example*) tatoe 例え・たとえ, tatoi 例い・たとい, réi 例, ichi-rei 一例

for instance tatóeba 例えば・たとえば

instant n (*moment*) shunkan 瞬間, sétsuna せつな・刹那

(at) the instant that ... totan ni 途端に

in an instant tachimachi (ni) たちまち(に), súgu すぐ, tossa ni とっさに

instantly adv tachimachi (ni) たちまち(に)

instead adv (sono) kawari ni (その)

代わりに

institute n (*research*) kenkyū-jo 研究所

institute director n shochō 所長

institution n shisetsu 施設

instruct → teach

instruction n (*teaching*) oshie 教え; (*leading*) shidō 指導

instructions n (*directions*) sáshizu 指図, shíji 指示; (*written explanation*) setsumei-sho 説明書

instructor n **1.** kyō´shi 教師, sénséi 先生 **2.** (*sports*) insutorakutā インストラクター

instrument n (*implement*) yō´gu 用具; (*instrumentality*) kikái 機械, kikan 機関; (*musical*) gakki 楽器

insufficiency n fusoku 不足, ...-búsoku ...不足

insufficient adj tarimasén (tarinai) 足りません(足りない)

insulate v zetsuen shimásu (suru, shite) 絶縁します(する、して)

insult 1. n bujoku 侮辱 **2.** v (*insults one*) bujoku shimásu (suru, shite) 侮辱します(する、して)

insurance n hoken 保険

insure (*it*) v (... ni) hoken o kakemásu (kakéru, kákete) (...に)保険をかけます(かける、かけて)

intact adj sono mamá (de/no) そのまま(で/の), mu-kizu (no) 無傷(の)

integrate v ... o matomemásu (matomeru, matomete) ...をまとめます(まとめる、まとめて), tōitsushimásu (tōitsuru, tōitsushite) 統一します(統一する、統一して)

integrity n seijitsu 誠実, shōjiki 正直

intellectual adj chiteki (na) 知的(な)

intelligence n **1.** (*information*) jōhō 情報 **2.** chisei 知性, chinō 知能; → **knowledge**

intelligent adj chiteki (na) 知的(な), rikō (na) 利口(な)

intelligentsia n (*intellectual(s)*) chishiki-jin 知識人, interi インテリ

intelligibility n rikaido 理解度

intend v *intend (to do)* (suru) tsumori désu (tsumori da, tsumori de) (する)つもりです(つもりだ、つもりで)

intent n muné 旨 → **intention**

intention n tsumori つもり, íto 意図, íshi 意思, kokoro-zashi 志・こころざし; (aim) nerai 狙い
That was not my intention. interj sonna tsumori dewa arimasendeshita. そんなつもりではありませんでした

intentionally adv wazato わざと, takuránde 企んで → **[on] purpose**

intently adv shikiri-ni しきりに; jitto じっと

intercourse n (social) shakō 社交; (sexual) seikō 性交

interest 1. n (on money) risoku 利息, ríshi 利子, rí 利; (pleasure) kyō´mí 興味, shúmi 趣味; (relevance) kankei 関係, (concern) kanshin 関心 2. v ...no kyōmi o hikimásu (hiku, hiite) ...の興味を引きます(引く、引いて)

interesting adj omoshirói おもしろい・面白い, kyōmi-bukái 興味深い
(Oh?) How interesting! Sō´ desu ka. そうですか。

interfere v jama ni narimásu (náru, nátte) じゃま[邪魔]になります(なる、なって), jama o shimásu (suru, shite) じゃま[邪魔]をします(する、して), kanshō shimásu (suru, shite) 干渉します(する、して)

interference n jama じゃま・邪魔; (meddling) kanshō 干渉

interior n okunai 屋内, shitsunai 室内; uchigawa 内側
interior decoration interia dezain インテリアデザイン

interjection n (word) kantō´shi 間投詞

intermediary n chūkai-sha 仲介者, shōkai-sha 紹介者

intermission n (between acts) makuai 幕あい・幕間

internal adj 1. uchi (no) 内(の), náibu (no) 内部(の), nai-teki (na) 内的(な) 2. (to the nation) kokúnai (no) 国内(の), náichi (no) 内地(の) 3. (within the office/company) shánai (no) 社内(の)
internal evidence nai-teki shō´ko 内的証拠

international adj kokusai-teki (na) 国際的(な); intānashonaru (na/no) インターナショナル(な/の); (worldwide) sekai-teki (na) 世界的(な)

Internet n (world wide web) (intā)netto （インター）ネット

interpret v tsu´yaku shimásu (suru, shite) 通訳します(する、して); (explains, construes) káishaku shimásu (suru, shite) 解釈します(する、して)

interpretation n tsu´yaku 通訳; (explanation, understanding) káishaku 解釈

interpreter n (translator) tsu´yaku(-sha) 通訳(者)

interrupt v (with a remark) (...no hanashí ni) kuchi o hasamimásu (hasamu, hasande) (...の話に)口をはさみます(はさむ、はさんで)
Am I interrupting you? interj jama-shita? 邪魔した? [FORMAL] O-jama-deshitaka? お邪魔でしたか?

interruption n shadan 遮断; (suspension) teishi 停止; (remark) sashideguchi 差し出口

intersect v yoko-girimásu (yoko-gíru, yoko-gítte) 横切ります(横切る、横切って)

intersecting n ōdan 横断

intersection (of streets) n kōsaten 交差点, yotsu-kado 四つ角

interval n aida 間・あいだ, ma 間; kankaku 間隔

interview n 1. kaiken 会見 2. taimen 体面 3. (meeting with) menkai 面会 4. (job interview) mensetsu 面接, intabyū インタビュー
interviewing n (questioning) shimon 諮問
press interview n kisha kaiken 記者会見

intestines n harawata はらわた・腸, watá わた・腸, chō 腸

intimate adj shitashíi 親しい; missetsu (na) 密接(な)

in time → **time**

intimidate v kowagarasemásu (kowagaraseru, kowagarasete) 怖がらせます(怖がらせる、怖がらせて)

intolerable adj tamarimasén (tamaranai) たまりません(たまらない), taeraremasén (taerarenai) 耐えられません(耐えられない)

intolerably *adv* yáke ni やけに; hidoku ひどく

intoxicated → drunk; *is easily* ~ sake ni yowái 酒に弱い

intoxication *n* yoi 酔い

intramural *adj* kō´nai (no) 校内(の), chō´nai/shinai (no) 町/市内(の)

intransitive verb *n* jidō´shi 自動詞

intravenous *n* jōmyaku (chūsha) 静脈(注射), tenteki 点滴

intravenous anesthesia *n* jōmyaku masui 静脈麻酔

intricate *adj* (*situation, subject*) komi-itta 込み入った

introduce *v* shōkai shimásu (suru, shite) 紹介します(する, して) Let me introduce you. Go-shōkai shimásu. ご紹介します。

introduction *n* shōkai 紹介 (go-shōkai ご紹介)

intrude *v* (*to force*) oshi-tsukémásu (oshi-tsukéru, oshi-tsukéte) 押し付けます(付ける, 付けて)

intrusive *adj* (o-)jama (na) (お)じゃま[邪魔](な)

intuition *n* chokkan 直観・直感

in vain → vain

invalid 1. *adj* (*not valid*) mukō (na) 無効(な) **2.** *n* (*ill person*) byōnin 病人

invasion *n* shinryaku 侵略

invention *n* hatsumei 発明

inventory *n* mokuroku 目録, zaiko 在庫; (*inventory list*) zaiko-hyō 在庫表

invest *v* oroshimásu (orósu, oróshite) 下ろします(下ろす, 下ろして); tōshi shimásu (suru, shite) 投資します(する, して)

investigate *v* shirabemásu (shirabéru, shirábete) 調べます(調べる, 調べて); kiwamemásu (kiwaméru, kiwámete) 究めます(究める, 究めて); kentō shimásu (suru, shite) 検討します(する, して)

investigation *n* **1.** (*research*) chōsa 調査 **2.** (*study*) kenkyū 研究

investment *n* tōshi 投資

invisible *n* (mé ni) miemasén (miénai) (目に)見えません(見えない)

invitation *n* sasoi 誘い, shō´tai 招待; (*card*) shōtai-jō 招待状

invite *v* yobimásu (yobu, yonde) 呼びます(呼ぶ, 呼んで), sasoimásu (sas-ou, sasotte) 誘います(誘う, 誘って), manekimásu (manéku, manéite) 招きます(招く, 招いて), shōtai shimásu (suru, shite) 招待します(する, して), mukaemásu (mukaeru, mukaete) 迎えます(迎える, 迎えて)

involuntary *adj* muíshiki (no/na) 無意識(の/な)

iodine *n* yō´do ヨード

i.q. 1. *adj* dōyō (no) 同様(の) **2.** *adv* dōyō ni 同様に

Iran *n* Iran イラン

Iraq *n* Iraku イラク

Ireland *n* Airurándo アイルランド

Irelander *n* Airurando-jin アイルランド人

iris *n* **1.** (*plant*) shō´bu ショウブ・菖蒲, ayame アヤメ・菖蒲 **2.** (*eye*) kōsai 虹彩

Irish *n* (*language*) Airurando-go アイルランド語; (*person*) Airurando-jin アイルランド人

Irish potato *n* jagaimo ジャガイモ・じゃが芋

iron *n* (*metal*) tetsu 鉄; (*clothes iron*) airon アイロン; *irons a shirt* wai-shatsu ni airon o kakemásu (kakéru, kákete) ワイシャツにアイロンをかけます(かける, かけて)

iron bar *n* tetsu-bo 鉄棒

iron bridge *n* tekkyō 鉄橋

ironic *adj* hiniku (na) 皮肉(な)

irregular *adj* fukísoku (na) 不規則(な)

irrelevant to … *adj* to mu-kánkei (no) …と無関係(の)

irresponsible *adj* mu-sékinin (na) 無責任(な)

irrigation *n* kangai 灌漑・かんがい

irritate *v* jira-shimasu (jira-su, jira-shite), irairasasemasu (-saseru, -sasete) じらしさせます(じらす, じらして), イライラさせます(させる, させて); *gets irri-tated/is irritating* shaku ni sawarimásu (sawaru, sawatte) しゃくに[癪]にさわります(さわる, さわって)

is (*am, are, be*); *v* **1.** (*it is*) …désu (dá/nó/ná, dé, ní) です(だ/の/な, で, に); [DEFERENTIAL] …de gozaimásu (de gozaimáshi̱te) …でございます(でございまして), [HONORIFIC] … de irasshaimás̱u (de irassháṟu, de irasshátte/irásẖite) …でいらっしゃいます(でいらっしゃる, でいらっしゃって/いらして) **2.** (*there is; it is there*) arimás̱u (áru, átte) あります(ある, あって); [DEFERENTIAL] gozaimás̱u (gozaimáshi̱te) ございます(ございまして) **3.** (*person is there*) imás̱u (iru, ite) います(いる, いて), [DEFERENTIAL, HUMBLE] orimás̱u (óru, ótte/orimásẖite) おります(おる, おって/おりまして), [HONORIFIC] irasshaimás̱u (irassháṟu, irasshátte/irásẖite/irasshaimásẖite) いらっしゃいます(いらっしゃる, いらっしゃって/いらして/いらっしゃいまして) **4.** (*is doing*) …te imás̱u (iru, ite) …ています(いる, いて), …te orimás̱u (óru, ótte/orimásẖite) …ております(おる, おって/おりまして), …te irasshaimás̱u (irassháṟu, irasshátte/irásẖite/irasshaimásẖite) …ていらっしゃいます(いらっしゃる, いらっしゃって/いらして/いらっしゃいまして) = …te oide ni narimás̱u (náru, nátte/narimásẖite) …ておいでになります(なる, なって/なりまして)

Islam *n* Isuramu-kyō イスラム教, kaikyō 回教

island *n* shimá 島; (*group of*) **islands** …-shōtō …諸島, (*archipelago*) rettō 列島, …-réttō …列島

(-)ism *n, suffix* shúgi 主義

isn't (*aren't*) **1.** *v* (*it isn't*) …ja

arimasén (ja nái, ja nákute)…じゃありません(じゃない, じゃなくて) **2.** (*there isn't*) arimasén (nái, nákute) ありません(ない, なくて)

isolation *n* koritsu 孤立

Israel *n* Isuraeru イスラエル

Israeli *n* Isuraeru-jin イスラエル人

issuance *n* hakkō 発行

issue 1. *n* hakkō(butsu) 発行(物); (*magazine issues*) -gatsu-gō 月号 **2.** *v* (*publishes*) hakkō shimás̱u (suru, shite) 発行します(する, して) → **put out**

it *pron* sore それ (*but usually omitted*)

Italian 1. *n* (*language*) Itaria-go イタリア語; (*person*) Itariá-jin イタリア人 **2.** *adj* Itaria (no) イタリア(の)

italic *n* itarikku(-tai) イタリック(体); shatai 斜体

Italy *n* Itaria イタリア

itch *n* kayúmi かゆみ・痒み

itchy *adj* kayúi かゆい・痒い; múzumuzu suru むずむずする

item 1. *n* kōmoku 項目 **2.** (*sports*) shumoku 種目 **3.** (*game*) aitemu アイテム

itinerary *n* nittei 日程

its *pron* sore no それの, are no あれの

itself *pron* sore jíshin/jítai それ自身/自体; … ~ (*as we might expect*) sasuga no …さすがの…; …(*in*) ~ … sono-mónó …そのもの, (sore) jítai (それ)自体; **of/by** ~ hi̱tori-de ni ひとりでに・独りでに

ivory *n* zōge 象牙・ゾウゲ

ivy *n* tsuta ツタ・蔦

J

jab *n* **1.** tsuki 突き **2.** (*boxing*) jabu ジャブ

jacket *n* uwagi 上着, jákétto ジャケット; *traditional workman's ~* hantén 半天・ハンテン, happi はっぴ・法被

jackknife *n* jakku naifu ジャックナイフ

jade *n* hi̱sui ヒスイ・翡翠

jail *n* keimú-sho 刑務所, rōgoku 牢獄, rōya 牢屋, [*uncommon*] orí おり・檻

jailer *n* kanshu 看守

jam *n* (*to eat*) jámu ジャム

Jamaica *n* jamaika ジャマイカ

janitor *n* kózukai 小使い, yōmúin 用務員; kanri-nin 管理人

January *n* Ichi-gatsú 一月・1月

Japan *n* Nihón 日本・にほん, Nippón 日本・にっぽん; *made in Japan* Nihon-sei (no) 日本製(の), meido in japan (no) メイド・イン・ジャパン(の), kokusan (no) 国産(の)

Japan Airlines, JAL *n* Nihon Kōkū 日本航空, Járu ジャル

Japan-bashing n Nihon-tátaki 日本叩き［たたき］

Japanese 1. n (*language*) Nihon-go 日本語; (*person*) Nihon-jín 日本人 **2.** adj (*of Japan*) Nihón no 日本の; wa-… 和;, nichi-; 日 …

Japanese cakes/sweets n wa-gáshi 和菓子

Japanese celery n údo ウド・独活

Japanese clothes n wa-fuku 和服

Japanese cuisine n Nihon-ryō´ri 日本料理, kappō´ 割烹; kaiseki-ryō´ri 懐石料理

Japanese-English dictionary n waei-jíten 和英辞典

Japanese food n wa-shoku 和食

Japanese ginger (*buds*) n myōga ミョウガ・茗荷

Japanese grapefruit n (*pomelo*) natsu-míkan 夏みかん・夏蜜柑

Japanese harp n (o-)kóto（お）琴

Japanese music n hōgaku 邦楽; (*traditional to the imperial court*) gágaku 雅楽, (*and dances*) búgaku 舞楽

Japanese noodles n (*wheat-flour*) udon うどん・ウドン; (*buckwheat-flour*) soba そば(o-soba おそば)

Japanese paper n wáshi 和紙

Japanese parsley n serí せり・芹

Japanese pepper n (*mild*) sanshō さんしょう・山椒

Japanese restaurant n kappō´ 割烹, (nihon)ryōrí-ya（日本）料理屋

Japanese style adj wafū 和風, nihon-fū 日本風

Japanese-style room n wa-shitsu 和室, Nihonma 日本間

Japanese-style wrestling n sumō 相撲・スモウ (= *Sumo wrestling*)

Japan Travel Bureau, JTB n Jei tii bii, JTB (JTB CORP.)

jar n (*with a large mouth*) kamé かめ・瓶; (*with a small mouth*) tsubo つぼ・壺; (*glass*) garasu-bin ガラス瓶, bín びん・瓶

jargon n senmon-go 専門語; tawagoto たわごと・戯言

jaundice n ōdan 黄疸・おうだん

jaunt n ensoku 遠足

javelin n nage-yari 投げ槍・投げやり

jaw n agó あご・顎

jazz n jazu ジャズ

jealous adj urayamashii うらやましい・羨ましい; *gets ~* (yaki-móchí o) yakimásu (yaku, yaite)（焼きもちを）焼きます(焼く, 焼いて), urayami-másu (urayamu, urayande) うらやみ［羨み］ます(うらやむ, うらやんで)

jealousy n yaki-móchí 焼きもち・やきもち, shitto 嫉妬

jeans n jiinzu ジーンズ, jiipan ジーパン

jeep n jiipu ジープ

jeer 1. n hiyakashi 冷やかし **2.** v hiyakashimásu (hiyakasu, hiyakashite) 冷やかします(冷やかす, 冷やかして)

jelly n zérii ゼリー, jérii ジェリー

jellyfish n kurage クラゲ・水母

jeopardy n kiki 危機, kiken 危険

jerk; *with a jerk* gui(t)to グイ(ッ)と

jerky 1. adj gikushakushita ぎくしゃくした **2.** n (*smoked/dried meat*) jākii ジャーキー

jersey n jáji ジャージ

Jesus Christ n iesu kirisuto イエス・キリスト

jet (*plane*) n jettó-ki ジェット機

jet lag n jisa-boke 時差ぼけ

jet black adj makkúro (na) 真っ黒(な)

jetty n bōha-tei 防波堤

Jew n Yudayá-jin ユダヤ人

jewel n hōseki 宝石, tamá 玉

jeweler n hōseki-shō 宝石商

jigsaw puzzle n jigusō-pazuru ジグソーパズル

job n shigoto 仕事(o-shígoto お仕事), tsutomé 勤め(o-tsutomé お勤め), (*place*) tsutome-saki 勤め先

getting a job shūshoku 就職

job hopping n tenshoku 転職

job hunting n kyūshoku 求職

job transfer n tenkin 転勤, tennin 転任

jockey n kishu 騎手

jockstrap n (*athletic supporting underwear*) sapō´tā サポーター

jog(ging) n jogingu (o shimásu; suru, shite) ジョギング(をします; する, して), marason マラソン

join v (*joins them together*) awasemásu (awaséru, awásete) 合わせます(合

わせる, 合わせて), (*grafts, glues*)
tsugimásu (tsugu, tsuide) 接ぎます(接
ぐ, 接いで); (*enters*) ...ni hairimásu
(háiru, háitte) ... に入ります(入る,
入って); (*in cooperation*) tsukimásu
(tsukú, tsúite) 付きます(付く, 付い
て); ~ (*forces*) gōdō shimásu (suru,
shite) 合同します(する, して)
joint 1. *n* fushi 節; (*of two bones*)
kansetsu 関節; (*of pipe*; *seam*) tsugi-
me 接ぎ目 2. *adj* (*combined*) gōdō no
... 合同の...
joint venture, JV *n* kyōdō/gōben jigyō
共同/合弁事業
joke *n* jōdán 冗談, share しゃれ・洒落
joss stick *n* (o-)sénkō (お)線香, sénkō
線香・せんこう
journal *n* 1. jānaru ジャーナル 2. (*diary*)
nikki 日記 3. (*newspaper*) shinbun
新聞 4. (*magazine*) zasshi 雑誌
journalist *n* 1. jānarisuto ジャーナリ
スト 2. (*newspaper journalist*)
shinbun-kíshá 新聞記者 3. (*reporter*)
kishá 記者
journey *n* tabi 旅, ryokō 旅行 → **trip**
jovial *adj* yōki 陽気, yōkí (na) 陽気(な)
joy *n* yorokobi 喜び・よろこび
joyful *adj* ureshii 嬉しい・うれしい,
tanoshii 楽しい・たのしい, yorokon-
deiru 喜んでいる
Judaism *n* Yudaya-kyō ユダヤ教
judge 1. *n* hánji 判事, saibánkan 裁判
官 2. *v* (*gives judgment*) hándan
shimásu (suru, shite) 判断します(す
る, して), (*criticizes*) hihan shimásu
(suru, shite) 批判します(する, して)
judgment *n* hándán 判断; (*criticism*)
hihan 批判
judicious *adj* kenmei (na) 賢明(な)
judo *n* jū'dō 柔道; ~ *outfit/suit* jūdō'-
gí 柔道着
jug *n* mizusashi 水差し
juggler *n* 1. (*magician*) tejiná-shi 手品
師 2. (*magic*) **jugglery** *n* tejina 手品
3. jagurā ジャグラー
juice *n* jū'su ジュース; ~ *of
bitter orange* pónsu ポンス, ponzu
ポン酢
juicy *adj* jū'shii (na) ジューシー(な),
shiruke no/ga ōi 汁気の/が多い

jujitsu *n* jūjutsu 柔術(= **judo**)
July *n* Shichi-gatsú 七月・7月
jumble *n* gotchamaze ごちゃ混ぜ,
yoseatsume 寄せ集め
jumbo shrimp *n* kurumá-ebi 車えび
[海老・エビ]
jump *v* tobimásu (tobu, tonde) 跳びま
す・とびます(跳ぶ, 跳んで), janpu
shimásu (suru, shite) ジャンプします
(する, して); *jumps out* tobi-dashimásu (tobi-dásu, tobi-dáshite) 飛び出
します(飛び出す, 飛び出して)
jumper *n* janpā ジャンパー
June *n* Roku-gatsú 六月・6月
jungle *n* mitsurin 密林, jánguru ジャン
グル
jungle gym *n* janguru-jímu ジャング
ルジム
junior *adj* (*younger*) toshi-shita (no)
年下(の); (*colleague, fellow student*)
kōhai 後輩; (*3rd-year student*) sannén-
sei 三年生
junior college *n* tanki-dáigaku 短期
大学
junior high school *n* chūgákkō 中学
校; ~ *student* chūgáku-sei 中学生
junk *n* kúzu くず・クズ, kuzu-mono
くず物, garakuta がらくた・ガラクタ
junk food *n* janku-fūdo ジャンクフ
ード
junkyard *n* sute-ba 捨て場
jurisconsult *n* hō gaku-sha 法学者
jurisdiction *n* shihō-ken 司法権
jurisprudence *n* hō(ritsu-)gaku
法(律)学
jurist *n* hōritsu-ka 法律家
juror *n* baishin-in 陪審員
jury *n* baishin (in dan) 陪審員団
just 1. *adv* (*exactly*) chōdo ちょうど・
丁度, mása ni まさに・正に; (*only*) ...
daké ...だけ, (*merely*) táda ただ 2.
adj (*equal, fair*) tadashii 正しい, kōsei
na 公正な
just a moment chótto ちょっと
just did it (shi-)ta bákari desu (し)た
ばかりです
just now tatta-íma たった今, tadáima
ただ今, tsúi imashígata つい今しがた
just right pittári ぴったり; uttetsuke
(no) うってつけ(の); *is ~ for me*

watashi ni pittári desu わたし[私]にぴったりです
just the (*one/thing/ticket*, ...) uttetsuke (no) うってつけ(の)
justice *n* **1.** (*rightness*) seigi 正義,
seitō-sei 正当性 **2.** (*judiciary*) shihō 司法
juvenile delinquent *n* hikō-shōnen 非行少年, chinpira ちんぴら・チンピラ

K

kana *n* kana かな・仮名
kangaroo *n* kangarū カンガルー
karate *n* (*weaponless self defense*) karate 空手・カラテ; ~ *outfit/suit* karaté-gí 空手着
katakana *n* katákána カタカナ・片仮名
kayak *n* kayakku カヤック
keen *adj* nesshin (na) 熱心(な)
keenly *adv* (*feels*) shimijími (to) しみじみ(と)
keep *v* tamochimásu (tamótsu, tamótte) 保ちます(保つ, 保って); (*retains*) kakaemásu (kakaeru, kakaete) 抱えます(抱える, 抱えて); (*takes in trust*) azukarimásu (azukáru, azukátte) 預かります(預かる, 預かって); (*raises animals*) kaimásu (káu, kátte) 飼います(飼う, 飼って)
keep away from *v* yokemásu (yokéru, yókete) よけ[避け]ます(よける, よけて)
keep company with *v* (...o) chika-zukemásu (chika-zukéru, chika-zúkete) (...を)近付けます(近付ける, 近付けて)
keep cool *v* (*calms down*) ochi-tsukimásu (ochi-tsuku, ochi-tsuite) 落ち着きます(落ち着く, 落ち着いて)
keep doing *v* (shi)-te imásu (iru, ite) (し)ています(いる, いて); (shi)-tsuzukemásu (-tsuzukéru, -tsuzúkete) (し)続けます(続ける, 続けて)
Keep it up! ganbare! 頑張れ！
keepsake *n* **1.** (*legacy*) katami 形見 **2.** (*remembrance*) kinen no shina 記念の品, kinen-hin 記念品
keg *n* taru たる・樽
kelp *n* kónbu 昆布・コンブ; ~ *flakes* tororo-kónbu とろろ昆布
kennel *n* inu-goya 犬小屋
kerchief *n* nekkachiifu ネッカチーフ
kernel *n* koku-tsubu 穀粒

kerosene *n* tōyu 灯油, sekiyu 石油
kerosene heater *n* sekiyu sutō'bu 石油ストーブ
ketchup *n* kecháppu ケチャップ
kettle *n* (*teakettle*) yakan やかん・薬缶, yu-wákashi 湯沸かし; (*cauldron*) kama かま・釜
key *n* kagí 鍵, kíi キー
keyhole *n* kagí-ana 鍵穴
"key money" (*to obtain rental lease*) kenri-kin 権利金
kick *v* kerimásu (kéru, kétte) 蹴ります(蹴る, 蹴って)
kick out *v* (*company*) kubi ni shimásu (suru, shite) クビにしますし(する, して), (*school*) yame/taigaku-sasemásu (-saseru, -sasete) 辞め/退学させます(させる, させて)
kick the habit *v* (tabako, sake o) yam-emásu (yameru, yamete) (たばこ, 酒) やめます(やめる, やめて)
kid *n* kodomo 子供・子ども, kozō 小僧 → **child**
kid around *v* fuzakemásu (fuzakeru, fuzakete) ふざけます(ふざける, ふざけて)
kids oneself about ... (*underestimates*) ... o amaku mimásu (míru, míte) ...を甘く見ます(見る, 見て)
no kidding! másaka まさか, uso (da/darō)! うそ(だ/だろう)！
kidnap 1. *n* yūkai 誘拐 **2.** *v* yūkai shimásu (suru, shite) 誘拐します(する, して)
kidnapper *n* yūkai-han 誘拐犯
kidnapping *n* yūkai 誘拐, rachi 拉致
kidney *n* jinzō 腎臓
kidney beans *n* íngen インゲン, ingén mame インゲンマメ[豆]
kill *v* koroshimásu (korosu, koroshite) 殺します(殺す, 殺して); [SLANG] ba-

rashimásu (barásu, baráshite) ばらし
ます(ばらす, ばらして)

killjoy n tanoshimi ni mizu o sasu hito
楽しみに水を差す人, ba o shira-kesa-
seru hito まをしらけさせる人

killed; gets ~ korosaremásu (korosareru,
korosarete) 殺されます(殺される,
殺されて), yararemásu (yarareru,
yararete) やられます(やられる, やら
れて)

killer n satsujin-han 殺人犯

kiln n kama かま・釜

kilogram n kíro キロ, kiroguramu キロ
グラム

kilometer n kíro キロ, kirométoru キロ
メートル

kiloliter n kíro キロ, kirorittoru キロリ
ットル

kilowatt n kíro キロ, kirowatto キロワ
ット

kimono n **1.** (Japanese attire) wa-fúku
和服, ki-mono 着物・キモノ; (long-
sleeved) furisode 振り袖 **2.** (light, for
summer) yukata ゆかた・浴衣, (gown)
tánzén 丹前

kin n (relatives) shinseki 親戚, ketsuen
血縁

kind 1. n (variety) shúrui 種類, té 手
a kind of … no ís-shu …の一種 (ís-
shu no …一種の …)
all kinds of samazama (na) 様々(な),
iroiro (na/no) 色々(な/の)
kinds of …-rui …類
2. adj (nice) (go-)shínsetsu (na) (ご)
親切(な)

kindergarten n yōchíen 幼稚園

kindling n taki tsuke たきつけ

kindly adv atatakáku あたたかく・温
かく; (kindly does) (shi-)te kuremásu
(kureru, kurete) (し)てくれます(く
れる, くれて), kudasaimásu (kudasáru,
kudasátte) /下さいます・くださいま
す(下さる, 下さって)

kindness n ón 恩・おん(go-ón ご恩),
(o-)kokoro-zashi (お)志・こころざし,
shínsetsu 親切(go-shínsetsu ご親切),
omoiyari 思いやり

king n ō 王, ō-sama 王様

kingdom n ō-koku 王国

king-size adj kingu-saizu (no) キング
サイズ(の), tokudai (no) 特大(の)

kink n nejire ねじれ・捩れ

kinky adj **1.** (twisted) nejireta ねじれた
・捩れた **2.** (sexually perverse) hentai
(no) 変態(の), seiteki ni tōsakushita
性的に倒錯した

kinsfolk → kin

kinship n shinzoku 親族

kiosk n (selling things) baiten 売店,
kiosuku キオスク

kiss n ki(s)su (shimásu; suru, shite)
キ(ッ)ス(します;する, して), seppun
(shimásu; suru, shite) 接吻(します;す
る, して)

kit (of tools) n yō'gu 用具, kitto キット;
~ bag yōgu-búkuro 用具袋

kitchen n daidokoro 台所, katte 勝手
(o-katte お勝手), (Western-style)
kitchin キッチン

kitchen door n katte-guchi 勝手口

kitchen range/stove n (old Japanese
style) kamado かまど; (gas, electricity)
konro コンロ, renji レンジ

kitchen sink n nagashí 流し

kitchen utensils n daidokoro-dō'gu 台
所道具

kitchenware n daidokoro yō'hin
台所用品

kite n táko 凧・たこ; **flies a ~** táko o
agemásu (ageru, agete) 凧をあげます
(あげる, あげて); **kite-flying** takó-áge
凧あげ

kitten n konéko 子猫・子ネコ

Kleenex n (tissue) tisshu-pē'pā ティ
ッシュペーパー; hanagami 鼻紙,
chiri-gami ちり紙

knack n kotsú こつ; yōryō' 要領

knapsack n **1.** ryúkku リュック,
ryukkusákku リュックサック
2. (elementary school bag) randóseru
ランドセル

knead v nerimásu (néru, nétte) 練りま
す(練る, 練って)

knee n hiza ひざ・膝

kneecap n hizagashira ひざがしら・
膝頭

kneel v hizamazukimásu (hizamazuku,
hizamazuite) ひざまずき[跪き]ます
(ひざまずく, ひざまずいて)

knew → know

knife *n* **1.** náifu ナイフ **2.** (*kitchen knife*) hōchō 包丁・ホウチョウ, (*butcher knife*) nikukiri-bō´chō 肉切り包丁

knight *n* naito ナイト, kishi 騎士

knit *n* amimásu (ámu, ánde) 編みます (編む, 編んで)

knitted goods *n* meriyasu メリヤス, amí-mono 編み物・あみもの

knob *n* (*bump*) kobú こぶ, (*gnarl*) fushí 節; *door* ~ hiki-te 引き手, totte 取っ手, doa nobu ドアノブ

knock 1. *v* (*hits*) nagurimásu (nagúru, nagútte) 殴ります (殴る, 殴って) **2.** *v* (*on door*) (to o) tatakimásu (tatáku, tatáite) (戸を) 叩きます (叩く, 叩いて), nókku shimásu (suru, shite) ノックします (する, して) **3.** *n* nokku ノック

knock down *v* taoshinásu (taósu, taóshite) 倒します (倒す, 倒して)

knockout *n* (*boxing*) nokkuauto ノックアウト

knot *n* musubi (-me) 結び・むすび (目); (*gnarl*) fushí 節

know *v* ... o shitte imásu (iru, ite) ...を知っています (いる, いて), [DEFERENTIAL] zon-ji(age)másu (zon-jí(age)ru, zon-ji (agé)te) 存じ (あげ) ます (存じ (あげ) る, 存じ (あげ) て), [HONORIFIC] gozónji (désu) ご存じ (です), (*understands*) ... ga wakarimásu (wakáru, wakátte) ... が分かります (分かる, 分かって); *doesn't* ~ shirimasén (shiranai, shiranáide) 知りません (知らない, 知らないで), wakarimasén (wakaránai, wakaránaide) 分かりません (分からない, 分からないで)

know-it-all *n* shittakaburi 知ったかぶり

know-how *n* nōhau ノウハウ; yarikata やり方

knowledge *n* chíshiki 知識; (*learning, academics*) gakúmon 学問

knowledgeable (*about ...*) ni kuwashíi ...に詳しい

known; *gets* ~ shiremásu (shireru, shirete) 知れます (知れる, 知れて), (*widely*) shiraremásu (shirareru, shirarete) 知られます (知られる, 知られて)

known as ... (*so-called*) iwáyuru ... いわゆる

knuckle *n* yubi-kansetsu 指関節

knuckle down *v* isshōkenmei yarimásu (yaru, yatte) 一生懸命やります (やる, やって)

knuckle under *v* kōsan shimásu (suru, shite) 降参します (する, して)

Kobe *n* Kōbe 神戸; *the port of kobe* Kōbe-kō 神戸港; *Kobe Station* *n* Kōbé-Eki 神戸駅

Korea *n* **1.** (*South Korea*) Kánkoku 韓国 **2.** (*North Korea*) Kita-chōsen 北朝鮮

Korean *n* (*person*) Kankokú-jin 韓国人; (*language*) Kankoku-go 韓国語

kumquat *n* kinkan キンカン・金柑

Kurile (*Islands*) *n* Chishíma 千島, Chishíma-réttō 千島列島

Kyoto *n* Kyōto 京都; *Kyoto Station* Kyōtó-Eki 京都駅; *Kyotoite* *n* Kyōtó-jin 京都人; *Kyoto-style cooking/dishes* *n* Kyō ryō´ri 京料理

Kyūshu *n* Kyū´shū 九州

L

lab *n* rábo ラボ; (*research*) kenkyūjo 研究所; (*testing*) shiken jo 試験所

label 1. *n* retteru レッテル, (*tag*) fuda 札・ふだ, rabel ラベル **2.** *n* (*record*) rēberu レーベル **3.** *v* raberu o tsukemásu/harimásu (tsukeru, tsukete/haru, hatte) ラベルを付けます/貼ります (付ける, 付けて/貼る, 貼って)

label requirement *n* hinshitsu hyōji 品質表示

grade labeling *n* tōkyū hyōji 等級標示

labor *n* rōdō 労働; *Labor Thanksgiving Day* Kinrō kánsha no hí 勤労感謝の日

labor union *n* rōdō kumiai 労働組合

laboratory *n* **1.** (*research room*) kenkyū-shitsu 研究室 **2.** (*experimental laboratory*) jikken-shitsu 実験室, rabo ラボ

laborer *n* rōdō-sha 労働者

laboring adj **1.** (*hard*) hone ga oreru 骨が折れる **2.** (*painful*) kurushii 苦しい

laboriously adv ákuseku あくせく

lace n **1.** rḗsu レース, mṓru モール **2.** → **shoelace**

lack 1. n (*shortage*) fusoku 不足 **2.** v (*is not available*) …ga arimasén (nái) …がありません(ない)

lackey n tsuishō-sha 追従者, gomasuri ごますり

lackluster adj **1.** saenai さえない, patto shinai ぱっとしない **2.** (*object*) tsuya no nai つやのない

lacquer 1. n urushi 漆・ウルシ, nuri 塗り・ぬり; *raised lacquer* maki-e 蒔絵

lacquer ware nuri mono 塗り物, shikki 漆器

2. v (*lacquers it*) nurimásu (nuru, nette) 塗ります(塗る, 塗って)

lad n **1.** (*boy*) shōnen 少年 **2.** (*young man*) wakamono 若者, seinen 青年

ladder n hashigo はしご・梯子

laden adj tsunda 積んだ

laden weight n sekisai jūryō 積載重量

ladle 1. n hishaku ひしゃく・柄杓; (*large wooden*) shákushi しゃくし・杓子 **2.** *ladle it* v kumimásu (kumu, kunde) 汲みます(汲む, 汲んで)

lady n fujin 婦人, óku-san/-sama 奥[おく]さん/様; (*young*) ojō-san お嬢さん, redii レディ, (*middle-aged*) oba-san おばさん, (*old*) obāsan おばあさん → **woman**

lady-killer, ladies' man n onna(t) tárashi 女(っ)たらし

lag 1. n (*a lag*) okure 遅れ, [BOOKISH] chien 遅延 **2.** v (*lags behind*) okuremásu (okureru, okurete) 遅れます(遅れる, 遅れて)

time lag n jisa 時差

lake n mizū'mi 湖, …-ko …湖

lake-side n kohan 湖畔

lakeshore n kogan 湖岸

lake trout n masú マス・鱒

lamb n ko-hítsuji 子羊・子ヒツジ; (*meat, includes mutton*) yōniku 羊肉; ramu ラム

lamb chop n yōniku 羊肉; ramu niku ラム肉

lame 1. adj ashí ga fú-jiyū (na) 足が不自由(な) → **cripple(d) 2.** n (*fabric*) rame ラメ

lament v nagekimásu (nagéku, nagéite) 嘆きます(嘆く, 嘆いて)

lamentation n nagekí 嘆き・なげき

lamp n ránpu ランプ; akari 明かり; dentō 電灯・電燈; *desk/floor ~* (den-ki-) sutándo (電気)スタンド

lampoon n fūshi 風刺, hiniku 皮肉

lampshade n ránpu no kasa ランプのかさ

lance n yari 槍・やり

land 1. n riku 陸, oka 丘, jí 地; (*a piece of land*) tochi 土地 → **country** → **earth** → **place 2.** v (*comes ashore*) jōriku shimásu (suru, shite) 上陸します(する, して); (*from the air*) chakuriku shimásu (suru, shite) 着陸します(する, して)

landing n chakuriku 着陸, jōriku 上陸

landing gear n chakuriku sōchi 着陸装置

landlady n **1.** (*traditional Japanese inn, etc.*) okámi おかみ・女将, okami-san おかみ[女将]さん; (*apartment, etc.*) ō'ya(-san) 大家(さん), yanushi 家主 **3.** (*rental manager*) kanri-nin 管理人

landlord n ō'ya(-san) 大家(さん), yanushi 家主; (*owner*) ōnā オーナー; (*rental manager*) kanri-nin 管理人

landmark n mejirushi 目印

landowner n ji-nushi 地主

landscape n fū'kei 風景, keshiki 景色

landslide 1. n (*earth slide*) ji-súberi 地すべり **2.** adj (*overwhelming*) taisa (no) 大差(の), attō-teki (na) 圧倒的(な)

lane n (*traffic, swim*) kō'su コース; (*path*) komichi 小道; *Lanes Merge* "Gōryū Chū'i" "合流注意"

language n kotobá 言葉・ことば, [BOOKISH] géngo 言語; …-go …語; *what ~* nan-kákokugo 何ヵ国語; *~ learning* gogaku gakushū 語学学習; *foreign ~* gaikoku-go 外国語; *How many languages do you know?* Gaikoku-go wa íkutsu dekimásu ka. 外国語はいくつできますか.

languid *adj* (ke-)darui （気)だるい

lanky *adj* yaseta やせた・痩せた, hosoi 細い

lantern *n* (of paper) chōchin ちょうちん・堤灯; (traditional night-light) andon あんどん・行灯

lap *n* hiza ひざ・膝

lapel *n* eri えり・襟

lapse *n* **1.** (time lapse) toki no keika 時の経過 **2.** (small error) kashitsu 過失, chiisana machigai 小さな間違い

laptop *n* rapputoppu (-gata) pasokon ラップトップ（型)パソコン, nōto (-gata) pasokon ノート（型)パソコン

larceny *n* settō (-zai) 窃盗(罪)

large *adj* ōkii 大きい, ō'ki-na 大きな; (wide, spacious) hirói 広い

large crowd *n* ōzéi 大勢

large number *n* tasū 多数

large quantity *n* taryō 多量, tairyō 大量

large-size (model) *adj* ōgata 大型

lasso *n* nage-nawa 投げなわ[縄], wána わな・罠

last *adj* **1.** (final) owari no 終わりの, sáigo no 最後の; (the tail end) bíri (no) びり(の) **2.** (the preceding ...) kono máe no 前の, the sen-... 先, saru 去る (+ DATE); *it lasts* mochimásu (mótsu, mótte) 持ちます(持つ, 持って)

at last tō'tō とうとう, yatto (no kotóde) やっと(のことで), iyó-iyo いよいよ, tsúini ついに, yōyaku ようやく

last breath *n* (deathbed) rinjū 臨終

last call *n* rasuto ōdā ラスト・オーダー

last century *n* zenseiki 前世紀

last chance *n* saigo no chansu 最後のチャンス, rasuto chansu ラストチャンス

last day (of month) *n*, *adv* getsumatsu 月末, misoka みそか・晦日; (of year) ō-mísoka 大みそか・大晦日; *the Last Day* saigo no shinpan (no hi) 最後の審判(の日)

last month *n*, *adv* séngetsu 先月

last night *n*, *adv* kinō no ban きのう[昨日]の晩, kinō no yoru きのう[昨日]の夜, sakúban 昨晩, yūbé ゆうべ・昨夜

last stop *n* shūten 終点

last time *adv* kono máe この前

last volume *n* (of a set of 2 or 3) gekan 下巻, gé 下

last week *n*, *adv* senshū 先週

last year *n*, *adv* kyónen 去年, sakunen 昨年

late 1. *adj* osoi 遅い; (lags, fails to be on time) okuremásu (okureru, okurete) 遅れます(遅れる, 遅れて); *is too ~ (for it)* ma ni aimasén (awánai, awánaide) 間に合いません(合わない, 合わないで); *till ~* osokú made 遅くまで; *till ~ at night* yóru osokú made 夜遅くまで, shín'ya made 深夜まで; *the night grows ~* yó ga fukemásu (fukéru, fukéte) 夜が更けます(更ける, 更けて) **2.** *adv* osoku 遅く; *~ for* chikoku shimásu (suru, shite) 遅刻します(して)

lately *adv* **1.** (other day) kono aidá この間, konaidá こないだ **2.** (recently) chikágoro 近頃, saikin 最近

later *adv* áto no 後の, áto (de) 後（で), áto no ... 後の..., nochihodo のちほど・後程, [BOOKISH] kō'(-) ...後...; *does for ~* (shi-)teokimásu (-teoku, -teoite) (し)ておきます(ておく, ておいて)

See you later. *interj* Jā mata. じゃあまた, Jāne. じゃあね

Talk to you later. *interj* Jā mata. じゃあまた; Jāne. じゃあね

latest 1. *n* saishin (no mono) 最新(の物) **2.** *adj* (newest) saishin (no) 最新(の)

at the latest ... máde ni wa ...まで[迄]には, osóku tomo 遅くとも

Latin *n* Raten-go ラテン語; *Latin letters* rōmá-ji ローマ字

latter *adj* áto no ... 後の, [BOOKISH] kō'(-) ... 後...; *the latter* kō'sha 後者

laugh *v* **laugh at** (... o) waraimásu (warau, waratte) (...を)笑います(笑う, 笑って)

loud laugh (laugh out loud) ōwarai 大笑, bakushō 爆笑

laugh maker *n* o-warai sakka お笑い作家

laughingstock *n* (o-)warai-gusa （お)笑い草, warai mono 笑いもの

laughter *n* warai 笑い

launch *n* hassha 発射, uchiage 打ち上げ

launder *v* sentaku shimás<u>u</u> (suru, sh<u>i</u>te) 洗濯します(する, して)

laundry *n* sentaku(-mono) 洗濯(物), o-séntaku お洗濯; (*a laundry*) sentaku-ya 洗濯屋; (*cleaner*) kuriiningu-ya クリーニング屋

laurel *n* gekkei 月桂・ゲッケイ, gekkéi-ju 月桂樹・ゲッケイジュ

lava *n* yōgan 溶岩

lavatory *n* (*to wash up in*) senmen-jo 洗面所, keshō-shitsu 化粧室 → **bathroom, toilet**

law *n* hōritsu 法律, hō 法; (*rule*) hōsoku 法則; (*science/study*) hōgaku 法学 → **...-in-law**

lawn *n* shiba 芝, shibafu 芝生

lawn mower *n* shibakarí-ki 芝刈り機

lawsuit *n* soshō 訴訟, uttae 訴え

lawyer *n* bengó-shi 弁護士

lax *adj* yurúi 緩い・ゆるい

laxative *n* gezai 下剤

lay *v* (*puts*) okimás<u>u</u> (oku, oite) 置きます(置く, 置いて); (*did lie down*) nemáshita (neta) 寝ました(寝た)

lay aside *v* sutemás<u>u</u> (suteru, sutete) 捨てます(捨てる, 捨てて), mizu ni nagashimás<u>u</u> (nagasu, nagash<u>i</u>te) 水に流します(流す, 流して)

lay down *v* yoko ni shimás<u>u</u> (suru, sh<u>i</u>te) 横にします(する, して); yoko-taemás<u>u</u> (yokotaeru, yokotaete) 横たえます(横たえる, 横たえて)

lay it face down *v* f<u>u</u>semás<u>u</u> (f<u>u</u>séru, f<u>u</u>séte) 伏せます(伏せる, 伏せて)

lay off *v* kaiko shimás<u>u</u> (suru, sh<u>i</u>te) 解雇します(する, して)

lay on its side *v* nekashimás<u>u</u> (nekasu, nekash<u>i</u>te) 寝かします(寝かす, 寝かして)

layman *n* mongái-kan 門外漢

layout *n* (*format*) teisai 体裁, reiauto レイアウト

lazy *adj* namaketa 怠けた; *gets lazy* namakemás<u>u</u> (namakéru, namákete) 怠けます(怠ける, 怠けて); (*shirks*) okotarimás<u>u</u> (okotaru, okotatte) 怠ります(怠る, 怠って); *lazy person* namake-mono 怠け者・なまけもの

lead **1.** *n* (*metal*) namari 鉛・なまり **2.** *v* (*guides them*) annái shimás<u>u</u> (suru, sh<u>i</u>te) 案内します(する, して), michibikimás<u>u</u> (michibíku, michibíite) 導きます(導く, 導いて), riído shimás<u>u</u> (suru, sh<u>i</u>te) リードします(する, して); (*coaches them*) shidō shimás<u>u</u> (suru, sh<u>i</u>te) 指導します(する, して); (*commands them*) h<u>i</u>ki-imás<u>u</u> (h<u>i</u>ki-íru, h<u>i</u>ki-ite) 率います(率いる, 率いて)

leader *n* chō 長; (*director, coach*) shidō'-sha 指導者; riídā リーダー

group leader *n* han chō 班長

leader of a sect *n* kyōso 教祖

team leader *n* han chō 班長, chiimu riídā チームリーダー

leadership *n* (*guidance*) shidō 指導; riídāshippu リーダーシップ

leading *adj* (*chief*) shuyō 主要 (na) (な), omo (na) 主(な)

leaf *n* happa 葉っぱ, ha 葉 (*how many leaves* nán-mai 何枚)

leaflet *n* chirashi ちらし・チラシ, bira びら・ビラ

leak *v* **1.** *it leaks* morimás<u>u</u> (móru, mótte) 漏ります(漏る, 漏って), more-más<u>u</u> (moréru, mórete) 漏れます(漏れる, 漏れて) **2.** *leaks it* morashimás<u>u</u> (morásu, morásh<u>i</u>te) 漏らします(漏らす, 漏らして)

lean **1.** *v* katamuku 傾く; ... o katamukeru ～を傾ける; *~ against* ... ni motaremás<u>u</u> (motaréru, motárete) にもたれます(もたれる, もたれて); *~ toward* ... no hō'ni katamukimás<u>u</u> (katamúku, katamúite) ...の方に傾きます(傾く, 傾いて); (*to one side*) kata-yorimás<u>u</u> (kata-yóru, kata-yótte) 片寄ります(片寄る, 片寄って); *~ out of* ... kara nori-dashimás<u>u</u> (nori-dásu, nori-dásh<u>i</u>te) ...から乗り出します(乗り出す, 乗り出て) **2.** (*meat/fish*) akami (no) 赤味(の)

leap → **jump**

leap year *n* urū'doshi うるう[閏]年

learn *v* naraimás<u>u</u> (naráu, narátte) 習います(習う, 習って), manabimás<u>u</u> (manabu, manande) 学びます(学ぶ, 学んで); (*finds out*) shirimás<u>u</u> (shiru, sh<u>i</u>te) 知ります(知る, 知って),

(*hears*) … ga mimí ni hairimás̲u (háiru, háitte) …が耳に入ります(入る, 入って)

learning n gakúmon 学問, gaku 学; (*study of a basic subject*) gakushū 学習

least adj (*smallest*) saishō (no) 最小 (の)

at least sukúnaku-tomo 少なくとも, sémete せめて; (*anyway*) tó-ni-kaku とにかく

leather n kawá 皮・革

leave v demás̲u (déru, déte) 出ます(出る, 出て); sarimás̲u (saru, satte) 去ります(去る, 去って); (*for a far place*) tachimás̲u (tátsu, tátte) 発ちます(発つ, 発って); (*to go home*) kaerimás̲u (káeru, kátte) 帰ります(帰る, 帰って); (*withdraws*) hiki-agemás̲u (hiki-agéru, hiki-ágete) 引き揚げます(引き揚げる, 引き揚げて), hiki-torimás̲u (hiki-tóru, hiki-tótte) 引き取ります(引き取る, 引き取って); (*leave one's seat*) seki o hazushimás̲u (hazusu, hazushite) 席を外します(外す, 外して)

leave it behind v nokoshimás̲u (nokósu, nokóshite) 残します(残す, 残して); (*forgetfully*) wasure-mono o shimás̲u (suru, shite) 忘れ物をします(する, して), oki-wasurémás̲u (oki-wasuréru, oki-wasuréte) 置き忘れます(忘れる, 忘れて)

leave it empty v akemás̲u (akeru, akete) 空けます(空ける, 空けて)

leave it intact v (*untouched*) sono mamá ni shimás̲u (suru, shite) そのままにします(する, して)

leave it undone v shináide okimás̲u (oku, oite) しないでおきます(おく, おいて)

Leave me alone! interj hōtteoite/hottoite (kudasai) 放っておいて/ほっといて(ください), (watashi ni) kamawanaide (kudasai) (私に)構わないで(ください), hitori ni shite (oite) (kudasai) 一人[独り・ひとり]にして(おいて)(ください)

leave out (*skips*) nukashimás̲u (nukasu, nukashite) 抜かします(抜かす, 抜かして)

leave-taking n itoma 暇・ひま

lecherous adj sukébe (na) 助平・スケベ(な), kōshoku (na) 好色(な)

lecture n kōgi 講義, (*talk*) kōen 講演; ~ **platform** endan 演壇, kōdan 講壇

lecturer n 1. (*instructor*) kō'shi 講師 2. (*public speaker*) kōen-sha 講演者

ledger n daichō 台帳

leech n híru ヒル・蛭

leek n nira ニラ・韮; négi ネギ・葱 (= naga-negi 長ネギ[葱])

leeway n yoyū 余裕, yochi 余地

left 1. adj (*not right*) hidari (no) 左の 2. → **leave** 3. → **rest**

left; **gets ~ behind** nokorimás̲u (nokóru, nokótte) 残ります(残る, 残って); **gets ~ over** (*in excess*) amarimás̲u (amáru, amátte) 余ります(余る, 余って) → **left behind**

left-handed (*person*) hidari-kiki/-giki (no) 左利き(の); gícho (no) ぎっちょ(の)

leftover n nokorí 残り; (*surplus*) amarí 余り; **leftovers** n nokori-mono 残り物

leg n ashí 脚・足・あし, (*shin*) suné すね・脛・臑

legacy n isan 遺産

legal adj 1. hōritsu-jō (no) 法律上(の), hōteki (na) 法的(な) 2. (*lawful*) gōhō (na) 合法(な)

legend n mukashi-bánashi 昔話, densetsu 伝説, monogátari 物語

leisure n 1. (*spare time*) hima 暇, ma 間, yoka 余暇 2. réjā レジャー

leisure center n rejā sentā レジャーセンター

leisure land n rejā rando レジャーランド

leisure time n hima na jikan 暇な時間, yoka 余暇

lemon n remon レモン; **lemonade** remón-sui レモン水, remonḗ'do レモネード; ~ **soda** ramune ラムネ

lend v kashimás̲u (kasu, kashite) 貸します(貸す, 貸して); **lends money** (*finances it*) yūzū shimás̲u (suru, shite) 融通します(する, して)

length n nágasa 長さ

lengthen v (mótto) nágaku shimás̲u (suru, shite) (もっと)長くします(す

る、して); (*prolongs it*) nobashimásu (nobásu, nobáshite) 伸ばします(伸ばす、伸ばして); enchō shimásu (suru, shite) 延長します(する、して)

lengthwise *adj* táte (no/ni) 縦(の/に)

lenient *adj* yurúi ゆるい・緩い; amai 甘い・あまい

lens *n* **1.** rénzu レンズ (*how many* nán-ko 何個) **2.** (*eye*) suishōtai 水晶体
contact lens *n* kontakuto renzu コンタクトレンズ
eye lens *n* gan renzu 眼レンズ
lens eye *n* suishōtai 水晶体

Leo *n* (*star sign*) shishi-za 獅子座

leopard *n* hyō ヒョウ・豹

lesbian *n* rezu(-bian) レズ(ビアン)

less *adj* (yori) sukunái (より)少ない; (*minus*) mainasu マイナス
less than (…) íka (…)以下、… míman …未満
no less than (…) íjō (…)以上、... mo no ...もの (= *as many as*)

lessee *n* chinshaku-nin 賃借人

lessen *v* sukúnaku/chíisaku shimásu (suru, shite) 少なく/小さくします(する、して) herashimásu (herasu, herashite) 減らします(減らす、減らして)

lesson *n* …-ka …課、réssun レッスン; *takes lessons (in)* (…)o naraimásu (naráu, narátte) (…を)習います(習う、習って)

lessor *n* chintai-nin 賃貸人

let *v* lets (one) do it (… ni sore o) sasemásu (saseru, sasete) (…にそれを)させます(させる、させて); yurushimásu (yurúsu, yurúshite) 許します(許す、許して); (*as a favor*) (…ni sore o) sasete (…にそれを)させて + [GIVE]
let approach *v* yosemásu (yoseru, yosete) 寄せます(寄せる、寄せて)
let fly *v* tobashimásu (tobasu, tobashite) 飛ばします(飛ばす、飛ばして)
let get away *v* nigashimásu (nigásu, nigáshite) 逃がします(逃がす、逃がして)
let go *v* (*releases*) hanashimásu (hanásu, hanáshite) 放します(放す、放して)
let in *v* (*air, the sun, light*) iremásu (ireru, irete) 入れます(入れる、入れて); *let through/in* tōshimásu (tōsu, tōshite) 通します(通す、通して)

let off/out *v* (*of a vehicle*) oroshimásu (orósu, oróshite) 降ろします(降ろす、降ろして)
let me know *interj* O-shirase kudasai お知らせください; Go-renraku kudasai ご連絡ください
let me see *interj* (*well now*) sā´sa さ´あ; Sō´desu ne. そうですね。
let's (*do it*) (shi-)mashō´ (し)ましょう

lethal *adj* chimei-teki (na) 致命的(な)

lethargy *n* mukiryoku 無気力

letter *n* tegami 手紙 (o-tégami お手紙), (*news*) táyori 便り; (*of alphabet*) móji 文字, (*character*) jí 字; ~ *of guarantee* hoshō-sho 保証書; ~ *of recommendation, reference* ~ suisen-jō 推薦状

letter box *n* yūbin posuto 郵便ポスト

love letter *n* rabu retā ラブレター, koibumi 恋文

letter paper and envelope *n* retā setto レターセット

lettuce *n* rétasu レタス

level *adj* (*flat*) taira (na) 平ら(な); (*extent*) téido 程度; (*standard; water level*) suijun 水準, reberu レベル; *advanced* ~ jōkyū 上級, *academic* ~ kyōiku suijun 教育水準

lever *n* teko てこ・挺子, rébā レバー

levity *n* keisotsu 軽率

levy *v* chōshū shimásu (suru, shite) 徴収します(する、して)

levying *n* chōshū 徴収

lewd *adj* sukébē (na) 助平・スケベ(な), midara (na) みだら・淫ら(な), hiwai (na) ひわい・卑猥(な)

liable to (*do*) → apt to

liaison *n* renraku 連絡

liar *n* usó-tsuki うそ[嘘]つき

liberate *v* kaihō shimásu (suru, shite) 解放します(する、して)
liberation *n* kaihō 解放

libertine *n* hōtō-mono/sha 放蕩者

libido *n* ribidō リビドー, seiteki shōdō 性的衝動

Libra *n* (*star sign*) tenbin-za 天秤座・てんびん座

librarian *n* tosho-gákari 図書係, toshokán-in 図書館員, shisho 司書

library *n* (*building*) toshó-kan 図書館; (*room*) toshó-shitsu 図書室, (*home* *study*) shosai 書斎; (*collection*) zōsho 蔵書

main library *n* chūō-toshokan 中央図書館

National Diet Library *n* kokuritsu kokkai toshokan 国立国会図書館

lice *n* shirami シラミ・虱

license *n* ménkyo 免許, ráisensu ライセンス, menkyo-shō/-jō 免許証/状; menjō 免状; *license (tag)* kansatsu 鑑札; (*car*) ~ *plate* nánbā ナンバー, nanbā-purē'to ナンバープレート
driver's license *n* unten menkyo(-shō) 運転免許(証), menkyo(-shō) 免許(証)
license agreement *n* raisensu keiyaku ライセンス契約

lick *v* namemásu (naméru, námete) なめ[舐め]ます (なめる, なめて)

lid *n* futa ふた・蓋 (*how many* nánmai 何枚)

lie 1. *n* (*falsehood*) úso うそ・嘘, itsuwari 偽り・いつわり; *a* ~ *comes to light* uso ga baremásu (baréru, baréte) うそがばれます (ばれる, ばれて) 2. *v lies down* nemásu (neru, nete) 寝ます (寝る, 寝て); yoko ni narimásu (náru, nátte) 横になります (なる, なって); yoko-tawárimásu (yoko-tawáru, yoko-tawátte) 横たわります (横たわる, 横たわって)

lieutenant *n* (*1st Lt, Lt JG*) chū'i 中尉; (*2nd Lt*) shō'i 少尉; (*navy full*) dáii/táii 大尉
lieutenant colonel *n* chūsa 中佐
lieutenant commander *n* shōsa 少佐
lieutenant general *n* chūjō 中将

life *n* ínochi 命, seimei 生命; (*daily living*) seikatsu 生活; (*lifetime*) shō'gai 生涯, isshō 一生, yo 世; (*a one's life*) jínsei 人生; *brings* ~ *to* … o ikashimásu (ikásu, ikáshite) …を生かします (生かす, 生かして)
life boat *n* kyūmei bōto 救命ボート
life care *n* raifu kea ライフケア
lifeguard *n* raifu gādo ライフガード, kyūjo-in 救助員
life insurance *n* seimei hoken 生命保険
life partner *n* (*spouse*) shōgai no hanryo 生涯の伴侶

life preserver *n* kyūmei (yō-)gu 救命(用)具
lifestyle *n* raifu sutairu ライフスタイル, ikikata 生き方

lift 1. *v* mochi-agemásu (mochi-ageru, mochi-agete) 持ち上げます (持ち上げる, 持ち上げて), agemásu (ageru, agete) 上げます (上げる, 上げて) 2. → elevator

light 1. *n* hikári 光・ひかり, akari 明かり, (*ray*) kōsen 光線; (*electric*) dénki 電気, dentō 電灯; *in the light of* … ni teráshite …に照らして 2. *lights it up* *v* terashimásu (terásu, teráshite) 照らします (照らす, 照らして) 3. *adj* (*not heavy*) karui 軽い; (*bright*) akarui 明るい; (*pale*) usui 薄い; (*simple*) assári shita… あっさりした…; *light rain* kosame 小雨
lightbulb *n* denkyū 電球
lighter *n* (*cigarette*) ráitā ライター
lighthearted *adj* kigaru (na) 気軽(な)
lighthouse *n* tōdai 灯台
lighting *n* (*illumination*) shōmei 照明, raitingu ライティング; *lighting fixtures* shōmei kígu 照明器具
lighting-up time *n* tentō jikoku 点灯時刻
lightning *n* inabíkari 稲光り, inazuma 稲妻・イナズマ

like 1. *v* (*is fond of*) …ga sukídesu …が好きです, … o konomimásu (konómu, konónde) …を好みます (好む, 好んで); *would like* → want, wish 2. *prep* (*similar*) … no yō'(na) …の様(な); (*is similar to*) … ni nite imásu (iru, ite) …に似ています (いる, いて)
like that *adj* sō (sō' + [PARTICLE]/désu) そう (そう + [PARTICLE]/です); sonna … そんな…; ā (ā' + [PARTICLE]/désu) ああ (ああ + [PARTICLE]/です), anna …あんな…
like this *adj* kō (kō' + [PARTICLE]/désu) こう (こう + [PARTICLE]/です); konna … こんな…
likely 1. *adj* ari-sō'(na) ありそう(な) (shi-)sō'(na) (し)そう(な) 2. *adv* (*probably*) tábun たぶん・多分
like(ly) as not *adv* taigai たいがい・大概

likely to *adv* (*do*) (shi-)yasúi（し）やす
い

liking *n* (*a fancy*) shikō 志向, konomí
好み (o-konomi お好み)

lily *n* yuri ユリ・百合

lime 1. *n* (*fruit*) ráimu ライム **2.** (*mineral*)
sékkai 石灰

limit 1. *n* kágiri 限り, seigén 制限; gendo
限度; hodo 程・ほど; hán'i 範囲;
rimitto リミット; *time ~* taimu rimitto
タイムリミット, seigen (jikan) 制
限(時間) **2.** *limits* (*delimits*) *it* v
kagirimásu (kagíru, kagítte) 限ります
(限る, 限って); (*restricts*) gentei
shimásu (suru, shite) 限定します(す
る, して), seigén shimásu (suru, shite)
制限します(する, して)

limitation *n* gentei 限定, seigén 制限

limited edition *n* gentei-ban 限定版

limited time offer *n* kikan gentei 期間
限定

limited-time product *n* kisetsu gentei
shōhin 季節限定商品

limousine for hire *n* háiyā ハイヤー

line *n* sén 線, rétsu 列, (*of letters*) gyō´
行; (*plot*) súji 筋; (*in a play*) serifu せり
ふ・台詞; *the ~ is busy* (o-)hanashi
chu (お)話し中です; (*of work*)
shokúgyō 職業, gyō´業

lined garment *n* (*kimono*) awasé あわ
せ・袷

linen 1. *n* áma 亜麻・アマ, asa 麻・ア
サ, rinneru リンネル **2.** (*sheet*) shiitsu
シーツ

line up *v* (*they line up*) narabimásu
(narabu, narande) 並びます(並ぶ, 並
んで); (*lines them up*) narabemásu
(naraberu, narabete) 並べます(並べ
る, 並べて)

linguist *n* **1.** gogaku ni tannōna hito 語学
に堪能な[たんのうな]人 **2.** (*language
scholar*) gengo gakusha 言語学者

linguistics *n* (*language learning*)
gogaku 語学; (*science of language*)
gengó-gaku 言語学

lining *n* urá-ji 裏地; **lining of a sleeve** *n* sode ura 袖裏

link 1. *n* wá 輪 **2.** *links them* *v* tsunagimásu (tsunagu, tsunaide) つなぎ[繋
ぎ]ます(つなぐ, つないで)

link address *n* (*computer*) rinku
adoresu リンクアドレス, rinku saki
リンク先

linked; is ~ (*with ...*) (... *to*) tsunagarimásu (tsunagaru, tsunagatte) (...と)
つながり[繋がり]ます(つながる, つ
ながって)

lion *n* raion ライオン, shíshi 獅子・シシ

lip *n* kuchibiru くちびる・唇

lipstick *n* kuchi-beni 口紅

liquid *n* eki(-tai) 液(体); mizu 水

liquor *n* (o-)sake (お)酒, (*Western*)
yōshu 洋酒; (*distilled from yam or rice*)
shōchū´焼酎

lisp *v* shi tága motsuremásu (motsuréru,
motsúrete) 舌がもつれます(もつれる,
もつれて)

list 1. *n* (*of items*) hyō 表, mokuroku
目録, rísuto リスト; (*of names*) meibo
名簿 **2.** *v* (*lists them*) hyō ni shimásu
(suru, shite) 表にします(する, して),
(*puts it in a list*) rísuto ni) iremásu
(ireru, irete) (リストに)入れます(入
れる, 入れて)

listen *v* kikimásu (kiku, kiite) 聞きま
す(聞く, 聞いて); [HUMBLE] uketamawarimásu (uketamawaru, uketamawatte)
承ります(承る, 承って)

listener *n* kiki-te 聞き手, risunā リス
ナー

lit; is lit tsúite imásu (iru, ite) ついて
[点いて]います(いる, いて)

liter *n* rittoru リットル

literary 1. *adj* (*literature*) búngaku
(no) 文学(の); (*bookish*) bungo-teki
(na) 文語的(な) **2.** *n* **literary style**
bungo-tai 文語体

literature *n* búngaku 文学

litter 1. *n* (*rubbish*) kúzu くず・屑, kuzu-
mono くず物・屑物, garakuta がらく
た **2.** *n* (*stretcher*) tánka 担架 **3.** *v* (*to
throw litter*) (gomi o) chirakashimásu
(chirakasu, chirakashite) (ゴミを) 散
らかします(散らかす, 散らかして)

little *adj* (*in size*) chiisái 小さい,
chíisa-na 小さな, (*child*) chítchai ちっちゃい,
chítcha-na ちっちゃな; (*in quantity*)
sukunái 少ない, sukóshi (no) 少し(の)
a little sukóshi 少し, wazuka わずか;
(*somewhat*) yáya やや

461

a little at a time sukoshí-zútsu 少しずつ

a little while ago saki-hodo 先程, sákki さっき

little by little sukoshí zútsu 少しずつ; sórosoro そろそろ

live 1. v (*resides*) súnde imásu (iru, ite) 住んでいます(いる, いて); (*is alive*) íkite imásu (iru, ite) 生きています(いる, いて); (*gets along*) kurashimásu (kurasu, kurashite) 暮らします(暮らす, 暮らして); *lets/makes it ~* ikashimásu (ikásu, ikáshite) 生かします(生かす, 生かして) **2.** adj (*animal*) ikita 生きた, (*broadcast*) raibu (no) ライブ(の), nama/jikkō hōsō (no) 生/実況放送(の) **3.** adv (*broadcast*) raibu de ライブで, nama/jikkō hōsō de 生/実況放送で, (*live performance*) nama de 生で

livelihood n seikei 生計

lively adj (*cheerful*) yōki (na) 陽気(な), (*peppy*) kappatsu (na) 活発(な), ikiiki (to) shita 生き生き(と)した, génki (na) 元気(な), (*flourishing*) nigíyaka (na) にぎやか(な)・賑やか(な)

live-out adj kayoi (no) 通い(の)

liver n kimó 肝, kanzō 肝臓; (*as food*) rébā レバー

liver transplant n kan(-zō) ishoku 肝(臓)移植

livestock n kachiku 家畜

living allowance n seikatsu-hi teate 生活費手当(て)

living costs n seikatsú-hi 生活費

living room n imá 居間, (*Japanese-style*) zashikí 座敷 (o-zashiki お座敷), (*Western-style*) ribingu (rūmu) リビング(ルーム)

living thing n ikímono 生き物

lizard n tokage トカゲ・蜥蜴

loach n dojō どじょう・ドジョウ

load 1. n nímotsu 荷物 (o-nímotsu お荷物), ní 荷 **2.** *loads it* v (*piles it on*) tsumimásu (tsumu, tsunde) 積みます(積む, 積んで), (*puts it aboard*) nosemásu (noseru, nosete) 載せます(載せる, 載せて)

loaf v (*around*) búrabura shimásu (suru, shíte) ぶらぶらします(する, して); (*on the job*) saborimásu (sabóru, sabótte) さぼり[サボリ]ます(さぼる, さぼって)

loaf n (*of bread*) katamari 固まり・塊・かたまり, hitó-kátamari 一固まり[塊]・ひとかたまり

loaf cake n rōfu kēki ロープケーキ

sandwich loaf n shoku-pan 食パン

loan → lend

lobby n róbii ロビー

lobster n ise ebi 伊勢エビ[海老]・イセエビ, robusutā ロブスター

local 1. adj chihō (no) 地方(の), rōˊkaru (no) ローカル(の); (*of the city*) machí (no) 町(の), (*within the city*) shínai (no) 市内(の) **2.** n jimoto 地元

local downpour n shūchū-gōˊu 集中豪雨

local paper n chihōˊ-shi 地方紙, chihōˊ-shinbun 地方新聞

local specialty n méibutsu 名物

local telephone call n shinai dénwa 市内電話

local train n kakueki téisha (no ressha) 各駅停車(の列車); (*non-express*) futsū dénsha 普通電車

location 1. n íchi 位置, basho 場所 **2.** (*computer*) rokēshon ロケーション **3.** (*shooting place*) roke-chi ロケ地

location of offices n kaisha (no) shozai-chi 会社(の)所在地, jimusho (no) shozai-chi 事務所(の)所在地

lock 1. n jōˊ(-mae) 錠(前), kagí 鍵, rokku ロック **2.** *locks* v (*a door*) (to ni) kagí o kakemásu (kakéru, kákete) (戸に)鍵を掛けます(掛ける, 掛けて); (*shuts it*) shimemásu (shiméru, shímete) 閉めます(閉める, 閉めて) **3.** *it locks* v kagí ga kakarimásu (kakáru, kakátte) 鍵が掛かります(掛かる, 掛かって), (*it shuts*) shimarimásu (shimáru, shimátte) 閉まります(閉まる, 閉まって)

locker n rókkā ロッカー; (*coin-operated*) *baggage lockers* koin rókkā コインロッカー

lodging n (*lodging house*) geshuku (-ya) 下宿(屋)

log n maruta 丸太 (**1:** íp-pon 一本, **2:** ní-hon 二本, **3:** sánbon 三本, *how many* nán-bon 何本)

logic n rónri 論理, rikutsu 理屈

logical adj ronri-teki (na) 論理的(な), rojikaru (na) ロジカル(な)

login n (*computer*) roguin ログイン, setsuzoku 接続

loincloth n fundoshi ふんどし・褌, sarumata 猿股, koshi-maki 腰巻き

loin(s) n koshi 腰

London n Róndon ロンドン

loneliness n kodoku 孤独

lonely adj hitori (no) ひとり・独り(の), sabishíi 寂[淋]しい・さびしい, wabishíi わびしい・侘びしい, kokoro-bosói 心細い

　feel lonely sabishíi 寂しい・淋しい・さびしい

long 1. adj nagái 長い 2. adv nágaku 長く 3. longs for v machi-kogaremásu (machi-kogareru, machi-kogarete) 待ちこがれます(待ちこがれる, 待ちこがれて)

　for a long time adv nágaku 長く, nagái aida 長い間, (*in the past*) máe kara 前から

　after a long time adv (*of absence*) hisashi-buri ni 久しぶりに

　how long (a time) adv dono-gurai どの位・どのぐらい

　long ago adv mukashi 昔・むかし; súde-ni 既に・すでに

　long and slender/narrow adj hosói 細い

　long awaited adj machidōshíi 待ち遠しい

　long before adv daibu máe ni だいぶ[大分]前に; súde-ni 既に・すでに; ma-mó-naku 間もなく・まもなく, sórosoro そろそろ, yagate やがて

long-distance adj chō-kyóri (no) 長距離(の)

　long distance telephone n chō-kyori denwa 長距離電話

　long distance runner n chō-kyori rannā 長距離ランナー

longer adj mótto (nágaku) もっと(長く); no ~, not any ~ mō´ もう + [NEGATIVE]

long-nosed goblin n tengu 天狗・てんぐ

long-period adj (*time*) chō´ki 長期

long-range adj chō´ki 長期

longsighted → farsighted

longsleeved kimono n furisode 振り

袖・ふりそで

long-term contract n chō´ki keiyaku 長期契約

long-time bills n chō´ki-tegata 長期手形

long-winded adj kudó´i くどい

loofah → luffa

look 1. n (*appearance*) yōsu 様子・ようす; (*personal appearance*) kíryō 器量, kao 顔; (*a look in one's eyes*) mé-tsuki 目付き・目つき 2. it looks like v (*as though*) ... yō´/mítai desu (da/na, de, ni) ...よう/みたいです(だ/な, で, に); [NOUN] dátta yō´/mítai desu (da/na, de, ni) ...だったよう/みたいです(だ/な, で, に); [VERB]-(r)u/-ta yō´/mítai desu (da/na, de, ni) う[る]/た よう/みたいです(だ/な, で, に); [ADJECTIVE]-i/-kátta yō´/mítai desu (da/na, de, ni) い/かった よう/みたいです(だ/な, で, に) 3. look (at) v (... o) mimásu (míru, míte) (...を)見ます(見る, 見て), [HUMBLE] haiken shimásu (suru, shite) 拝見します(する, して), [HONORIFIC] goran ni narimásu (náru, nátte) ご覧になります(なる, なって)

　look after v ... no sewá o shimásu (suru, shite) ...の世話をします(する, して), ... no mendō´ o mimásu (míru, míte) ...の面倒を見ます(見る, 見て), (*a matter*) shóri o shimásu (suru, shite) 処理をします(する, して); (*takes over*) hiki-torimásu (hiki-tóru, hiki-tótte) 引き取ります(引き取る, 引き取って)

　look around for v (*shop around for*) busshoku shimásu (suru, shite) 物色します(する, して)

　look back v furi-kaerimásu (furi-kaeru, furi-kaétte) 振り返ります(振り返る, 振り返って)

　look down v utsumukimásu (utsumuku, utsumuite) うつむき[俯き]ます(うつむく, うつむいて)

　look for 1. (*searches*) sagashimásu (sagasu, sagashite) 捜し[探し]ます(捜す, 探す, 捜し[探し]て); 2. motome-másu (motoméru, motómete) 求めます(求める, 求めて), tazunemásu (tazunéru, tazúnete) 尋ねます(尋ねる, 尋ねて), ukagaimásu (ukagau, ukagatte)

伺います(伺う, 伺って) **2.** (*expects*) machimásu (mátsu, mátte) 待ちます (待つ, 待って)

look out on, look out to *v* ... o nozo-mimásu (nozomu, nozonde) ...を望み ます(望む, 望んで)

look up *v* (*a word*) hikimásu (hiku, hiite) 引きます(引く, 引いて)

loom *n* hatá機

loop *n* **1.** (*ring*) wá 輪 **2.** (*shape*) kanjō 環状; *loop line* kanjō-sen 環状線 **3.** (*computer*) rūpu ループ

loophole *n* (*hole*) aná 穴・あな

loose 1. *adj* yurúi ゆるい・緩い, bára (de) ばら(で) **2.** *lets it* ~ *v* (*releases*) hanashimásu (hanásu, hanáshite) 放 します(放す, 放して) **3.** *gets/comes loose v* zuremásu (zuréru, zúrete) ず れます(ずれる, ずれて), (*slack*) tarumimásu (tarumu, tarunde) たるみ [弛み]ます(たるむ, たるんで)

loot *n* ryakudatsu-hin 略奪品

looting *n* ryakudatsu 略奪

loquacious *adj* taben (na) 多弁(な), oshaberi (na) おしゃべり・お喋り(な)

loquat *n* bíwa ビワ・枇杷

lord *n* (*feudal*) daimyō 大名; ryōshu 領主; go-shujin-sama ご主人様; **Lord** kyō 卿

lorry *n* torakku トラック

Los Angeles *n* Rosanzérusu ロサンゼ ルス, Rosu ロス

lose *v* nakushimásu (nakusu, nakushite) なくします(なくす, なく して), ushinaimásu (ushinau, ushinatte) 失います(失う, 失って); (*gets defeated*) makemásu (makeru, makete) 負けます(負ける, 負けて), mairimásu (máiru, máitte) 参ります(参る, 参って)

lose color *v* (iró ga) samemásu (saméru, sámete) 色がさめます(さめ る, さめて)

lose consciousness *v* ki/íshiki o ushi-naimásu (ushinau, ushinatte) 気/意識 を失います(失う, 失って)

lose patience *v* shibiré o kirashimásu (kirásu, kiráshite) しびれを切らしま す(切らす, 切らして)

loss *n* **1.** songai 損害, sonshitsu 損失 **2.** (*defeat*) make 負け shippai 失敗

lost 1. *it gets* ~ *v* naku-narimásu (naku-naru, naku-natte) なくなります(なく なる, なくなって) **2.** (*a person*) *gets* ~ *v* (michi ni) mayoimásu (mayóu, mayótte) (道に)迷います(迷う, 迷っ て) **3.** *n* (*item*) otoshimono 落とし物

lost child *n* máigo 迷子

lot 1. *n* (*in a lottery*) kúji くじ・クジ; (*vacant land*) aki-chi 空き地; *parking* ~ chūsha-jō 駐車場 **2.** *a lot, lots adj* (*much/many*) takusán (no) たくさん [沢山] (の), ō'i 多い, ō'ku no 多くの; ō'ku 多く, tábun ni 多分に; yóku よく

lottery *n* takará-kuji 宝くじ, fukubiki 福引(き)

lotus *n* hasu ハス・蓮, ~ *root* renkon レ ンコン・蓮根

loud *adj* (*noise*) ōkíi 大きい, ō'ki-na 大きな; *in a* ~ *voice* ō'góe de 大声 で, kowadaka (ni) 声高(に); (*color*) hadé(na) 派手(な)

loudspeaker *n* kakuséi-ki 拡声器, supíkā スピーカー

lounge *n* **1.** (*break room*) kyūkéi-shitsu 休憩室 **2.** (*in a hotel, etc.*) raunji ラウ ンジ **3.** (*chair*) ne-isu 寝椅子

louse → **lice**

lovable *adj* kawaíi かわいい・可愛い, kawairashíi かわいらしい・可愛らしい

love 1. *n* kói 恋, ren'ai 恋愛, ái 愛, rabu ラブ; ~ *marriage* ren'ai-kékkon 恋 愛結婚 **2.** *n* (*tennis*) rabu ラブ **3.** *v* aishimásu (aisúru, áishite) 愛します (愛する, 愛して); kawai-garimásu (kawai-gáru, kawai-gátte) かわい[可 愛]がります(かわいがる, かわいが って) → **like**; *falls in* ~ (*with*) ... ni horemásu (horeru, horete) ...に惚れ [ほれ]ます(惚れる, 惚れて), kói ni ochimásu (ochiru, ochite) 恋に落ちま す(落ちる, 落ちて)

love affair *n* ren'ai-kánkei 恋愛関係, rómansu ロマンス

lovely *adj* **1.** airashii 愛らしい **2.** (*beautiful*) utsukushii 美しい・うつ くしい **3.** (*pretty*) kawaii 可愛い・ かわいい

lover *n* koibito 恋人, íi-hito いい人; (*devotee of ...*) (...no) aikō-ka (...の) 愛好家, ...-zuki ...好き; *lovers'* *suicide* shinju 心中

low *adj* (*short*) hikúi 低い; (*cheap*) yasúi 安い; *low gear* teisoku gí(y)a 低速ギア[ヤ]

low (*barometric*) **pressure** *n* tei-kíatsu 低気圧

low blood pressure *n* tei-kétsúatsu 低血圧

low voice *n* kogoe 小声

low-wage *adj* tei-chingin (no) 低賃金 (の)

lower 1. *adj* shita (no) 下(の); *lower* (*cheaper*) *by ¥100* hyakuén-yasu 百円 安 **2.** *~ it* v sagemásu (sagéru, ságete) 下げます・さげます(下げる, 下げ て), oroshimásu (orósu, oróshite) 下ろ します・おろします(下ろす, 下ろ して); *~ one's eyes* mé o fusemásu (fuséru, fuséte) 目を伏せます(伏せる, 伏せて), utsumukimásu (utsumuku, utsumuite) うつむき[俯き]ます(うつ むく, うつむいて)

lowest *adj* (*minimum, minimal*) sáika (no) 最下(の), (*bottom*) saitei (no) 最低(の); *the lowest* (*degree*) saitei géndo 最低限度

lowly *adj* (*shabby*) iyashii いやしい・ 卑しい

loyal *adj* chūjitsu (na) 忠実(な), seijitsu (na) 誠実(な)

luck *n* **1.** ún 運 **2.** (*fate*) únmei 運命 **3.** (*happiness*) shiawase 幸せ

good luck 1. *interj* ganbatte (kudasai). 頑張って・がんばって(下さい・くだ さい) **2.** *n* kōun 幸運

bad luck 1. *adj* un ga warui 運が悪い **2.** *n* aku-un 悪運, fu-un 不運

luckily *adv* ún-yoku 運良く

lucky *adj* ún ga íi 運がいい; shiawase (na) 幸せ(な); (*strikes it lucky*) tsúite imásu (iru, ite) ついています(いる, いて)

lucky bag *n* fuku-bukuro 福袋

lucky charm *n* o-mamori お守り

lucky seventh *n* rakkii sebun ラッキー ・セブン

lucky star *n* kōun no hoshi 幸運の星

lucky shot *n* magure atari まぐれ当たり

luffa *n* (*sponge gourd*) hechima ヘチマ ・糸瓜

luggage *n* (te-)nímotsu (手)荷物, temá- wari 手回り, temawari-hin 手回り品

lukewarm *adj* nurúi ぬるい

lumber *n* zaimoku 材木, zái 材

lump *n* katamari 固まり・塊・かたまり

lunch *n* hiru góhan 昼ご飯(hirú 昼, o-híru お昼), chūshoku 昼食, ránchi ランチ; (*box*) bentō´ 弁当(o-bentō お 弁当)

lunch break *n* hiru yasumi 昼休み, hiru kyūkei 昼休憩

luncheon special *n* ranchi sā´bisu ランチサービス

lung cancer *n* hai-gan 肺がん・肺癌

lungs *n* hai 肺

lure 1. *n* (*decoy*) otori おとり **2.** *n* (*fishing*) ruā ルアー **3.** *v* obikidashi- másu (obikidásu, obikidáshite) おびき 出します(おびき出す, おびき出して)

lurid *adj* **1.** (*horrible*) zottosuru ぞっ とする **2.** (*shocking*) shokkingu (na) ショッキング(な) **3.** (*bright red*) makka (na) 真っ赤(な)

lush *adj* (midori no) shigetta (緑の) 茂った, aoao to shita 青々とした, mizumizushii みずみずしい

lute *n* (*Japanese lute*) bíwa 琵琶

luxury, luxurious *adj* zeitákú (na) ぜいたく[贅沢](な); (*deluxe*) gō´ka (na) 豪華(な)

luxury goods, luxuries *n* zeitaku-hin ぜいたく[贅沢]品

lyrics *n* kashi 歌詞

M

macabre *adj* zotto suru ぞっとする

macaroni *n* makaroni マカロニ

machination *n* inbō 陰謀, keiryaku 計略, takurami たくらみ

machine *n* kikái 機械, mashin マシン (*how many* nán-dai 何台)

machine gun *n* kikan-jū 機関銃, mashin gan マシンガン

machiner *n* kikái kō 機械工

machinery *n* kikái 機械

mackerel *n* saba サバ・鯖

mackerel pike *n* sanma サンマ・秋刀魚

mad *adj* (*insane*) ki-chigái (no) 気違い(の); (*goes mad*) ki ga kuruimásu (kurū´, kurútte) 気が狂います(狂う, 狂って); muchū ni narimásu (náru, nátte) 夢中になります(なる, なって); *gets mad* (*angry*) okorimásu (okóru, okótte) 怒ります(怒る, 怒って)

Madam *n* óku-san/-sama 奥さん/様, madamu マダム

made → **make**

made in …-sei; …製; *made in Japan* Nihon-sei (no) 日本製(の), meido in japan メイド・イン・ジャパン

madman *n* kichigai 気違い

madness *n* kyōki 狂気

maestro *n* (*great musician/artist*) … senséi …先生, maesutoro マエストロ

magazine *n* zasshi 雑誌 (*how many* nán-satsu 何冊), magajin マガジン

magic (*tricks*) *n* tejína 手品; majikku マジック

magical *adj* mahō (no) 魔法(の); *magical world* mahō no sekai 魔法の世界

magician *n* tejiná-shi 手品師

magistrate *n* hanji 判事

magnate *n* yūryokusha 有力者

magnesium *n* maguneshium マグネシウム

magnet *n* jíshaku 磁石, magunetto マグネット

magnetic *adj* jíki (no) 磁気(の), jíshaku (no) 磁石(の)

magnificent *adj* subarashíi すばらしい・素晴らしい; sōdai (na) 壮大(な)

magnifying *adj* kakudai (shita) 拡大(した)

magnifying glass *n* rūpe ルーペ, mushi megane 虫メガネ; *magnifying glass icon* mushi megane no aikon 虫メガネのアイコン

magnitude *n* magunichūdo マグニチュード

magnolia *n* mokuren モクレン・木蓮

magpie *n* kasasagi カササギ・鵲

mahjong *n* majan マージャン・麻雀

mahjong parlor *n* mājan-ya マージャン[麻雀]屋

mahjong tile *n* pái パイ

mahogany *n* mahoganii マホガニー

maid *n* (*servant*) otétsudai(-san) お手伝い(さん), mé´do/meido メード/メイド

maiden *n* otome 乙女・おとめ, (*girl*) shōjo 少女

maiden name *n* kyūsei 旧姓

mail 1. *n* yūbin 郵便 **2.** *v* (*mails it*) (tegami o) dashimásu (dásu, dáshite) (手紙を)出します(出す, 出して), yūsō shimásu (suru, shite) 郵送します(する, して)

mail box *n* yūbínbako 郵便箱, pósuto ポスト

mail drop *n* pósuto ポスト

mail officer *n* yūbin kyoku-in 郵便局員

mail order *n* tsūshin hanbai 通信販売

mailing *n* yūsō 郵送

mailman, mail deliverer *n* yūbin-ya (san) 郵便屋(さん)

main *adj* ómo (na) 主(な), shuyō (na) 主要 (な); hon-… 本…

main course *n* mein kōsu メインコース

main road/route *n* honsen 本線; *main road to a shrine* omote sándō 表参道

main store *n* honten 本店

main street *n* ōdō´ri 大通り; mein sutoriito メインストリート

mainland *n* hondo 本土

mainly adv ómo ni 主に

mainstay n (person) daikokubashira 大黒柱

mainstream n honryū 本流

maintain v (preserves) hóshu shimásu (suru, shite) 保守します(する, して); (supports) shíji/iji shimásu (suru, shite) 支持/維持します(する, して); (insists) shuchō shimásu (suru, shite) 主張します(する, して)

maintenance n (preservation) hóshu 保守; (support) shíji 支持, (upkeep) iji 維持

majesty n ō zoku 王族
Your Majesty interj Heika 陛下

major n (army) shōsa 少佐; (line/field/study) senmon 専門; (mainstream) mejā メジャー; (study) senkō (shimásu; suru, shite) 専攻(します; する, して) → main → big

major city n shuyō tóshi 主要都市

major general n shō´shō 少将

Major League Baseball n mejā riigu メジャーリーグ

majority n dai-búbun 大部分, dai-tasū´ 大多数, (more than half) kahansū 過半数

make 1. v (does) shimásu (suru, shite) します(する, して); (creates) tsukurimásu (tsukúru, tsukútte) 作ります(作る, 作って), (concocts) koshiraemásu (koshiraeru, koshiraete) こしらえます(こしらえる, こしらえて). **2.** n seizō 製造, (type) kata(-shiki) 型(式)

make a fire v (hí o) takimásu (taku, taite) (火を)焚きます(焚く, 焚いて)

make a living v kurashimásu (kurasu, kurashite) 暮らします(暮らす, 暮らして)

make do v (with ...) (...de) ma-ni-awasemásu (ma-ni-awaséru, ma-ni-awásete) (...で)間に合わせます(間に合わせる, 間に合わせて)

make good, make up for v ...o oginaimásu (ogináu, oginátte) ...を補います(補う, 補って)

make money v (profit) (kane o) mōkemásu (mōkéru, mō´kete) (金を)もうけ[儲け]ます(もうける, もうけて)

make one do v (... ni ... o) sasemásu (saseru, sasete) (...に...を)させます(させる, させて)

make sure v tashikamemásu (tashikaméru, tashikámete) 確かめます(確かめる, 確かめて)

make the most of ... v o ikashimásu (ikásu, ikáshite) ...を生かします(生かす, 生かして)

make-believe adj mise-kake (no) 見せかけ(の)

maker n (manufacturer) mē´kā メーカー, seizō-moto 製造元

makeshift adj ma-ni-awase 間に合わせ

makeup n keshō´ 化粧 (o-keshō お化粧), mēkyáppu メーキャップ; (cosmetics) keshō hin 化粧品; (structure) kumi-tate 組み立て, kōzō 構造

makeup exam n tsui-shikén 追試験, sai-shikén 再試験

malady n byōki 病気

malaria n mararia マラリア

male 1. n otokó 男, dansei 男性; (animal) (...no) osú (...の)雄; **male and female** dánjo 男女 **2.** adj (gender) otokó (no) 男(の), dansei (no) 男性(の); (animal) osú (no) 雄(の)

malefactor n 1. (bad man) akunin 悪人 **2.** (criminal) hannin 犯人

malevolence n akui 悪意

malevolent adj akui no aru 悪意のある

malfunction n koshō 故障

malice n ákúi 悪意

malicious adj akui no aru 悪意のある, iji no warui 意地の悪い

malignant adj akushitsu (na) 悪質(な)

mall n (shoppingu) mōru (ショッピング)モール

mallet n kizuchi 木槌
mallet of luck n uchide no kozuchi 打ち出の小槌

malt n bakuga 麦芽

malt beer n moruto biiru モルトビール

malt beverage n bakugashu 麦芽酒

malum n byōki 病気, shikkan 疾患

mama n mama ママ, o-kāsan おかあさん・お母さん, o-kāchan おかあちゃん・お母ちゃん

mammal n honyū-rui 哺乳類, honyū dōbutsu 哺乳動物

mammoth n manmosu マンモス

man n 1. (*male*) otokó 男, otoko no hito/katá 男の人/方, dánshi 男子, (*middle-aged*) oji-san おじさん, (*old*) ojíisan おじいさん, (*young*) o-níi-san お兄さん 2. (*person*) hito 人, ... hitó ...人

manage v (*treats*) tori-atsukaimásu (tori-atsukau, tori-atsukatte) 取り扱います(取り扱う, 取り扱って); (*copes with*) shóri shimásu (suru, shite) 処理します(する, して); (*runs a business*) keiei shimásu (suru, shite) 経営します (する, して); (*a team*) kantoku shimásu (suru, shite) 監督します(する, して)

manage to (*do*) dō´ni ka shimásu (suru, shite) どうにかします(する, して); konashimásu (konasu, konashite) こなします(こなす, こなして)

management n keiei 経営; manēji-mento マネージメント; (*control*) shíhai 支配; (*handling*) tori-atsukai 取り扱い

manager n shihái-nin/-sha 支配人/者, kanri-nin 管理人, máné´jā マネージャー; (*sports*) kantoku 監督

Manchuria n Mánshū 満州

Mandarin Chinese n Mandarin マンダリン, Chūgoku hyōjun-go 中国標準語, pekin-go 北京語

mandarin orange → tangerine

mandate n shirei 指令

mandatory adj kyōsei-teki (na) 強制的 (な)

mane n tategami たてがみ

man-eater n (*seductress*) otoko tárashi 男たらし

maneuver n sakusen 作戦, enshū 演習

manga n (*comic*) manga マンガ・漫画

manganese n mangan マンガン

mangle v zutazuta ni shimásu (suru, shite) ずたずたにします(する, して), mechamecha ni shimásu (suru, shite) めちゃめちゃにします(する, して)

mango n mangō マンゴー

mangy adj kitanarashii 汚らしい, misuborashii みすぼらしい, fuketsu (na) 不潔(な)

manhandle v teara ni atsukaimásu (atsukau, atsukatte) 手荒に扱います (扱う, 扱って)

manhood n 1. (*manly*) otoko rashisa 男らしさ 2. (*adult male*) seijin danshi 成人男子, seinen dansei 成年男性

mania n mania マニア

maniac n maniakku マニアック

manicure n manikyua マニキュア

manifest 1. adj akiraka (na) 明らか (な) 2. v arawaremásu (arawaréru, arawárete) 現れます(現れる, 現れて), (*make it clear*) akiraka ni shimásu (suru, shite) 明らかにします(する, して)

manifestation n meiji 明示, hyōmei 表明

manifesto n sengen 宣言, seimei 声明

Manila n Mánira マニラ

manipulate v sōjū shimásu (suru, shite) 操縦します(する, して), (*a person*) (hito o) ayatsuru (人を)操る

mankind n jinrui 人類

manliness n otokorashisa 男らしさ

manly adj otokorashii 男らしい

mannequin n manekin (ningyō) マネキン(人形)

manner (*of doing*) n yari-kata やり方, shi-kata 仕方; furí ふり; (*fashion*) (...) fū (...)風・ふう

manners n gyōgi 行儀, sáhō 作法, manā マナー; → etiquette

manor n shōen 荘園

mantelpiece n rodana 炉棚, danro no mae no tana 暖炉の前の棚

mantis shrimp n shákó シャコ・蝦蛄

manual n manyuaru マニュアル, tebikisho 手引き書

manufacture v seisan/seizō shimásu (suru, shite) 生産/製造します(する, して), tsukurimásu (tsukúru, tsukutte) 作り[造り]ます(作る[造る], 作って[造って])

manuscript n genkō 原稿

many adj takusán (no) たくさん[沢山] (の), ō´ku (no) 多く(の); *are/have many* ... ga ō´i ...が多い; *how many* íkutsu いくつ, nán-... 何...

map n chízu 地図, mappu マップ, (*diagram*) zu 図; (*how many* nán-mai 何枚)

maple n kaede カエデ・楓, mómiji モミジ・紅葉

maple syrup n mēpuru shiroppu メープルシロップ

marathon n marason マラソン; *marathon runner* marason senshu マラソン選手, marason rannā マラソンランナー; *marathon relay race* ekiden 駅伝

marble n (*marble stone*) dairi-seki 大理石

marbles n o-hájiki おはじき, biidama ビー玉

march 1. n kōshin 行進, māchi マーチ **2.** (*music*) kōshin kyoku 行進曲 **3.** v kōshin shimásu (suru, shite) 行進します(する, して)

March n Sán-gatsu 三月・3月

mare n (*horse*) meuma 雌馬

margarine n māgarin マーガリン

margin n (*white space*) yohaku 余白; (*leeway*) yoyū 余裕, yochi 余地; (*price difference*) rizáya 利鞘・利ざや, mājin マージン

marijuana n marifana マリファナ

marina n mariina マリーナ

marine(s), Marine Corps n kaihei tai 海兵隊

mariner n suifu 水夫

marionette n ayatsuri ningyō 操り人形, marionetto マリオネット

marital adj kon'in (no) 婚姻(の)

mark 1. n (*sign*) shirushi 印, kigō 記号, māku マーク, ato 跡 **2.** n (*vestige*) konseki 痕跡; *leaves a mark* konseki o nokoshimásu (nokósu, nokóshite) 痕跡を残します(残す, 残して) **3.** n (*score point*) ten 点, (*score*) tensū´ 点数; (*school grades*) seiseki 成績 **4.** v (*makes a mark on*) (... ni) shirushi/kigō/ten o tsukemásu (tsukéru, tsukéte) (...に)印/記号/点を付けます(付ける, 付けて)

market 1. n íchi(-bá) 市(場), shijō 市場, mā´kétto マーケット; *vegetable market* seika íchiba 青果市場

marketing n māketingu マーケティング

marketplace n íchi-bá 市場

marksman n shashu 射手

marmalade n māmarēdo マーマレード

maroon n, adj kuri iro (no) 栗色・くり色(の)

marriage n kekkon 結婚; *marriage proposal* endan 縁談

marron glacé n marongurasse マロングラッセ

marrow n kotsuzui 骨髄; *spinal marrow* sekizui 脊髄

marry v (... to) kekkon shimásu (suru, shite) (...と)結婚します(する, して)

Mars n kasei 火星
　Martian n kaséijin 火星人

marsh n numa (chi) 沼(地)

marshy adj nukarunda ぬかるんだ

martial n bújutsu 武術, búdō 武道; *martial arts hall* dō jō 道場

marvelous adj suteki (na) すてき[素敵](な), sugói すごい・凄い

mask n men 面(o-men お面), kamen 仮面, másuku マスク; (*Noh drama*) nō-men 能面

mash v suritsubushi másu (suritsubusu, suritsubushite) すり潰します(すりつぶす, すりつぶして)

mashed potatoes n masshu poteto マッシュポテト

marshmallow n mashumaro マシュマロ

masochism n mazo(-hizumu) マゾ(ヒズム), jigyaku 自虐

mason n sekkō 石工

masque n kamen geki 仮面劇

masquerade n kasō pātii 仮装パーティ, kamen budō kai 仮面舞踏会

mass n **1.** (*Buddhist*) hōji 法事, (*Catholic*) mísa ミサ **2.** (*lump*) katamari 固まり・塊; (*people*) taishū 大衆, kōshu 公衆, minshū 民衆
　mass communications n masu-komi マスコミ
　mass media n マスメディア
　mass meeting n taikai 大会

massacre 1. n daigyakusatsu 大虐殺, minagoroshi 皆殺し **2.** v gyakusatsu shimásu (suru, shite) 虐殺します(する, して)

massage 1. n massā´ji マッサージ, anma あんま・按摩 **2.** v (*rubs with both hands*) momimásu (momu, monde) 揉みます(揉む, 揉んで)

masseur

masseur *n* massājí-shi マッサージ師, anma あんま・按摩

massive *adj* bōdai (na) 膨大(な)

mast *n* hashira 柱, masuto マスト

master *n* **1.** (*of house*) shújin 主人, danna-san/-sama 旦那さん/様 **2.** (*of shop*) masutā マスター, danna 旦那 **3.** (*owner*) (mochí)-nushi (持ち)主 **4.** (*college degree*) shū´shi 修士 **5.** (*maestro*) senséi 先生, (*artisan*) oyakata 親方, shishō 師匠; **grand master** (*martial arts*) shihan 師範

masterpiece *n* kessaku 傑作, meisaku 名作

master's thesis *n* shūshi-rónbun 修士論文

mastery *n* **1.** (*conversance*) seitsū 精通 **2.** (*control*) shihai 支配

masturbate *v* jíí/shuin o shimásu (suru, shite) 自慰/手淫をします(する, して), onanii o shimásu (suru, shite) オナニーをします(する, して)

mat *n* shikí-mono 敷物, mátto マット; (*Japanese floor*) tatami タタミ・畳, (*thin*) gozá ござ・ゴザ; (*how many*) nán-mai 何枚

match 1. *n* (*sports*) shiai 試合, kyō´gi 競技; (*contest*) shō´bu 勝負 **2.** *v* (*matches, equals, is a match for*) ... ni kanaimásu (kanáu, kanátte) ...にかないます(かなう, かなって), ...to yóku aimásu (áu, átte) ...とよく合います (合う, 合って)

matchbook *n* kami-mátchi 紙マッチ (*how many*) íkutsu いくつ

matchbox *n* matchí-bako マッチ箱

match(es) *n* (*for fire*) mátchi マッチ; (1: íppon 一本, 2: níhon 二本, 3: sánbon 三本; *how many* nán-bon 何本)

matchmaker *n* **1.** matchí seizō gyō-sha マッチ製造業者 **2.** nakōdo 仲人

mate *n* **1.** (*friend*) nakama 仲間, tomodachi 友達・ともだち **2.** (*spouse*) haigū-sha 配偶者

classmate *n* dōkyū-sei 同級生, kurasu meito クラスメイト

workmate *n* shigoto nakama 仕事仲間, (*colleague*) dōryo 同僚

material *n* **1.** (*cloth*) kíji 生地 **2.** **raw material** zairyō 材料, zái 材 **3.** (*topic*)

táne 種; → **substance**

material *adj* (*physical*) busshítsuteki (na) 物質的(な)

materialism *n* busshítsu-shúgi 物質主義

materialize *v* genjítsu-ka shimásu (suru, shite) 現実化します(する, して)

materials *n* zairyō´ 材料, genryō´ 原料, shíryō 資料

mathematical *adj* sūgaku (no) 数学(の)

mathematics *n* **1.** sūgaku 数学; **mathematician** sūgáku-sha 数学者 **2.** (*subject of elementary school, calculation*) sansū 算数・さんすう

matinee *n* máchínē マチネー; hiru no bú 昼の部

matter *n* **1.** kotó 事・こと, (*problem*) mondai 問題 **2.** (*something that is*) **the matter** (*amiss, wrong*) ijō 異常, (*hitch*) komátta kotó 困った事[こと], (*bad aspect/point/thing*) waruí tokoró/ten/ kotó 悪いところ/点/事

What's the matter? *interj* Dō´shita n desu ka. どうしたんですか.

It doesn't matter. *interj* Kamaimasén 構いません.

mattress *n* mattoresu マットレス

mature *v* (*growth, developed*) seijuku shimásu (suru, shite) 成熟します(する, して); **fully matures** enjuku shimásu (suru, shite) 円熟します(する, して)

maturity *n* seijuku 成熟

maudlin *adj* kanshō-teki (na) 感傷的 (な), namida moroi 涙もろい

mausoleum *n* (*an Imperial tomb*) ryō´ 陵, (dai)reibyō 霊廟

maxim *n* kakugen 格言

maximal *adj* (*greatest*) saidaigen (no) 最大限(の); (*highest*) saikō (no) 最高 (の)

maximum 1. *n* saidai-gén 最大限 **2.** *adj* → **maximal**

May *n* Gó-gatsu 五月・5月

may *v* (*perhaps*) ...kámo shiremasén ...かもしれません; (*it is OK to do*) (shi)-témo íi desu (し)てもいいです

maybe *adv* tábun (... deshō´) 多分(... でしょう), ... kámo shiremasén ...か もしれません; hyótto shita ra/shite/ suru to ひょっとしたら/して/すると;

470

arúi-wa あるいは・或いは

mayonnaise n mayonēzu マヨネーズ

mayor n shichō´ 市長

maze n meiro 迷路, meikyū 迷宮

me *pron* watashi わたし・私, watakushi わたくし・私; *(male)* boku ぼく・僕, *[unrefined]* ore おれ・俺; watashi/watakushi (o/ni) 私(を/に); *(male)* boku/ore (o/ni) 僕/俺(を/に)

meadow n sōgen 草原, kusahara 草原, kusachi 草地

meager *adj* sukunái 少ない, toboshii 乏しい

meal n (o-)shokuji (お)食事; (o-)shokuji o shimásu; suru, shite (お)食事をします; する, して), góhan ご飯 (góhan o tabemásu; tabéru, tábete ご飯を食べます; 食べる, 食べて); *(1:* isshoků 一食, *2:* ní-shoku 二食, *3:* sánshoku 三食, *how many*; nán-shoku (何食)
a set/complete meal n teishoku 定食; *a set meal (of house choices)* sétto セット, kō´su コース
with meals *(included)* *adj* shoku(-ji) tsuki (no) 食事付き[つき](の)

meal ticket n shokken 食券 *(how many*; nán-mai (何枚)

mean *v it means ...* ... to iu ími desu …という意味です; ... o ími shimásu (suru, shite) …を意味します(する, して); *what I mean is ...* ii-tai kotó wa … 言いたい事は…

meaning n ími 意味, wáke 訳・わけ; *(significance)* ígi 意義; *(what one wants to say)* ii-tai kotó 言いたい事

meaningful *adj* ími ga aru 意味がある, yūigi (na) 有意義(な)

meaningless *adj* mu-ími (na) 無意味(な)

means n **1.** shúdan 手段, hōhō 方法, shi-kata 仕方, shi-yō 仕様 **2.** → mean
by all means zé-hi 是非・ぜひ
by some means *(or other)* nán to ka shíte 何とかして
means of transportation n kōtsū shudan 交通手段, kōtsū kikan 交通機関
use any means hudan o erabimasen (erabanai, erabanaide) 手段を選びません(選ばない, 選ばないで)

mean-spirited *adj (mean spirited)* ijí no warúi 意地の悪い → **stingy**

meantime n aida 間・あいだ
in the meantime *adv* sono aida (ni) そのあいだ[間](に), sono-uchi (ni) そのうち(に)

meanwhile *adv* sono-uchi (ni) そのうち(に); *(on the other hand)* ippō´ 一方

measles n hashika はしか

measure 1. n → **a means 2.** n *(ruler)* mono-sáshí 物差し, mejā メジャー **3.** *measures it* v hakarimásu (hakáru, hakátte) 計ります(計る, 計って)
measuring tape n maki-jaku 巻き尺

measurement(s) n sunpō 寸法

meat n nikú 肉・ニク (o-níku お肉); *grilled ~* yaki-niku 焼肉・ヤキニク

meatballs n *(Chinese)* niku-dángo 肉団子, miito bōru ミートボール

meat cleaver n nikukiri-bō´chō 肉切り包丁

mechanic n *(car repairman)* shūri kō 修理工, seibi-shi 整備士; *automobile mechanic* jidōsha seibishi 自動車整備士

mechanical *adj* kikai-teki (na) 機械的(な), kikai (no) 機械(の)

mechanics n rikigaku 力学

medal n medaru メダル, kunshō 勲章; *gold medal* kin medaru 金メダル; *silver medal* gin medaru 銀メダル; *bronze medal* dō medaru 銅メダル

medallion n ōgata medaru 大型メダル

meddle v o-sékkai o yakimásu (yáku, yaíte) おせっかい[お節介]を焼きます(焼く, 焼いて)

meddling n o-sékkai おせっかい・お節介; kanshō 干渉; sewá 世話(o-séwa お世話)

media n (masu-)media (マス)メディア → **mass**

mediation n *(good offices)* assen あっせん・斡旋; chōtei 調停

mediator n assen-sha あっせん・斡旋者; chōtei-sha 調停者; chūsai-nin 仲裁人

medical *adj* igaku no 医学の, naika no 内科の
medical department n ígaku bu 医学部, íkyoku 医局

medical examination *n* shinsatsu 診察, kenkō´ shindan 健康診断

medicine *n* **1.** kusuri 薬・くすり (o-kusúri お薬), [BOOKISH] yakuzai 薬剤 **2.** (*doctoring*) ígaku 医学

meditation *n* mokusō 黙想; meisō 瞑想; meditḗshon メディテイション; (*ascetic training*) shugyō 修行, gyō´行; (*Zen*) zazen 座禅

Mediterranean *n* chichū-kai 地中海

medium 1. *adj* chūkan (no) 中間(の) **2.** *n* chūkan 中間; baitai 媒体

medium-fat tuna *n* chū-toro 中トロ

medium-rare *adj* (*meat*) han-yake (no) 半焼け(の), midiamu rea ミディアム・レア

medium-size *n* (*model*) chūgata 中型

medley *n* (*music*) medorē メドレー

meek *adj* súnao (na) すなお[素直] (な)

meet *v* **1.** (*sees a person*) …ni aimásu (áu, átte) …に会います(会う, 会って); (*welcomes*) …o mukaemásu (mukaeru, mukaete)…を迎えます(迎える, 迎えて), … o de-mukaemásu (de-mukaeru, de-mukaete)…を出迎えます(出迎える, 出迎えて) (*happens to meet*) de-aimásu (de-au, de-atte) 出会います(出会う, 出会って), (*encounters*) sesshimásu (ses-suru, ses-shite) 接します(接する, 接して) **2.** (*they assemble*) atsumarimásu (atsumáru, atsumátte) 集まります(集まる, 集まって), shūgō shimásu (suru, shite) 集合します(する, して)

meeting *n* **1.** kái 会; (*mass meeting*) taikai 大会; (*conference*) káigí 会議, miitingu ミーティング **2.** (*interview*) menkai 面会; (*of prospective bride and groom*) miai 見合い **3.** (*by prior arrangement*) uchi-awase 打ち合わせ

megahertz (MHz) *n* megaherutsu メガヘルツ

megaphone *n* megahon メガホン

melancholy *n, adj* yūutsu (na) 憂うつ (な), merankorii (na) メランコリー (な)

mellow *v* (*gets mellow*) enjuku shimásu (suru, shite) 円熟します(する, して)

melodrama *n* merodorama メロドラマ

melody *n* merodii メロディー, senritsu 旋律

melon *n* méron メロン; úri 瓜・ウリ

melt *v* (*it melts*) tokému (tokéru, tókete) 溶けます(溶ける, 溶けて); (*melts it*) tokashimásu (tokásu, tokáshite) 溶かします(溶かす, 溶かして)

member *n* ménbā メンバー, kai-in 会員; (*ichi*-)in (一)員

membership *n* ménbā shippu メンバーシップ, kai-in 会員

memo(random) *n* mémo メモ

memorial *n* kinen hi 記念碑

memorial service *n* (*remembrance ceremony*) tuitō-shiki 追悼式; (*funeral*) kokubetsu-shiki 告別式; (*100 days after the death*) hyákkanichi 百か日

memorize *v* anki shimásu (suru, shite) 暗記します(する, して)

memory *n* obóe 覚え, monoóboe 物覚え, kioku 記憶, (*computer*) memori メモリ, memorii メモリー, (*capacity*) kiokú-ryoku 記憶力; (*a recollection*) omoide 思い出; *by/from ~* sóra de そらで, anki shite 暗記して

memory stick *n* memori stikku メモリスティック

men → man

mend *v* **mend it** naoshimásu (naósu, naóshite) 直します(直す, 直して), tsukuroimásu (tsukuróu, tsukurótte) 繕います(繕う, 繕って)

mending *n* shū´ri 修理, naoshí 直し → **repair**

menstruation *n* gekkei 月経, seiri 生理

menswear *n* otoko mono 男物

mental *adj* séishin (no) 精神(の)

mental care *n* seishin-teki na kea 精神的なケア, mentaru kea メンタルケア

mental disease *n* seishin-byō 精神病, seishin shōgai 精神障害, seishin shikkan 精神疾患

mentality *n* shínri 心理, kangaekata 考え方

mention 1. *v* …ni furemásu (fureru, furete) …に触れます(触れる, 触れて), [BOOKISH] …ni genkyū shimásu (suru, shite) …に言及します(する, して) **2. → say**

Don't mention it. *interj* Dō´ itashima-shite. どういたしまして.

mentor *n* (yoki) jogen-sha (良き)助言者, shidō-sha 指導者, senpai 先輩

menu *n* kondate 献立, ményū メニュー

merchandise *n* shōhin 商品

merchant *n* shō´nin 商人

mercy *n* megumi 恵み; nasake 情け

mere *adj* hon no ... ほんの...; táda ただ; [BOOKISH] tán naru ... 単なる...

merely *adv* táda ただ, tatta たった; [BOOKISH] tán no 単に

merge *v* (*they unite*) gappei shimásu (suru, shite) 合併します(する, して); (*they flow together*) gōryū shimásu (suru, shite) 合流します(する, して)
Lanes Merge (*Ahead*), Merge (*Lanes*) "Gōryū chū´i" "合流注意"

merger *n* gappei 合併; (*confluence*) gōryū 合流

merit *n* (*strong point*) chō´sho 長所

merry *adj* yúkai (na) ゆかい・愉快 (な), nigíyaka (na) にぎやか・賑やか(な)
Merry Christmas. *interj* Kurísúmásu omedetō クリスマスおめでとう

mess *n* (*disorder*) konran 混乱; (*predicament*) komátta koto 困った事, (*plight*) (kurushíi) hamé (苦しい)羽目; (*bungle*) héma へま・ヘマ; *makes a damn ~ of it* héma o yarakashimásu へまをやらかします; *It's a ~.* Taihen désu né. 大変ですね. *I'm in a ~.* Komátte imásu. 困っています.

message *n* kotozuke ことづけ・言付け, kotozute ことづて・言伝て, mésséji メッセージ, o-tsuge お告げ
message board *n* dengonban 伝言板, (*bulletin board*) keijiban 掲示板

messenger *n* tsukai 使い, (*Internet*) messenjā メッセンジャー
messenger boy *n* tsukaihashiri (no shōnen) 使い走り(の少年)
messenger of God *n* kami no tsukai 神の使い
messenger RNA *n* messenjā āru enu ē メッセンジャーRNA

messiah *n* kyūsei-shu 救世主, meshia メシア

messy *adj* kitanái 汚い, chirakatte(i)ru

chirakatte(i)ru 散らかって(い)る
messy situation *n* konran 混乱

metal *n* kínzoku 金属, metaru メタル
heavy metal *n* (*music*) hebimeta ヘビメタ

meter *n* **1.** (*of length*) mētoru メートル **2.** (*device*) kéiki 計器, mētā メーター

method *n* shi-kata 仕方; shi-yō 仕様, hōhō 方法, ... hō´...法

metro(politan) *adj* tokai (no) 都会(の); (*run by Tokyo*) toei 都営

Mexico *n* mekishiko メキシコ

mezzanine (*floor*) *n* chū-ní-kai 中二階

microcomputer *n* maikuro konpyūta/konpyūtā マイクロコンピュータ/コンピューター

microphone *n* maiku マイク, maikurohon マイクロホン

microscope *n* kenbi-kyō 顕微鏡

microwave *n* **1.** (*wave*) maikuro-ha マイクロ波 **2.** (*kitchen microwave*) denshi renji 電子レンジ

midday *n* mahiru 真昼, shōgo 正午

middle **1.** *n* náka 中, mannaka 真ん中, chūshin 中心; naka ba 半ば; chūkan 中間; (*medium size*) chū´ 中 **2.** *adj* mannaka (no) 真ん中(の), chūkan (no) 中間(の)
the middle of (*month*) *n* chūjun 中旬, nakaba 半ば
middle of the night *n* (ma)yonaka 真夜中
middle volume *n* (*of a set of three*) chū-kan 中巻, chū´ 中

middle age *n* chū-nen 中年
middle-aged *adj* chū-nen (no) 中年 (の)

middle school *n* (*junior high*) chūgákkō 中学校

midget *n* chíbi ちび・チビ

midnight *n* ma-yónaka 真夜中

midst *n* (... no) sáichū (...の)最中

midsummer/midyear gift *n* (o-)chū-gen (お)中元

might **1.** *n* → perhaps **2.** *v* → power

mild *adj* yawarakái 柔らかい; (*taste*) maroyaka まろやか; (*moderate*) odayaka (na) 穏やか(な)

mildew *n* kabi かび・カビ

mile *n* mairu マイル

military *n, adj* gunrai (no) 軍隊(の), gunjin (no) 軍人(の
military base *n* (gunji) kíchí (軍事)基地
military occupation *n* senryō 占領
military officer *n* shō´kō 将校
military person *n* gunjin 軍人
military uniform *n* gunpuku 軍服

milk *n* míruku ミルク, gyūnyū 牛乳; *mother's milk* chíchi 乳, bonyū 母乳, [BABY TALK, SLANG] óppai おっぱい

milkman *n* gyūnyū-ya 牛乳屋, gyūnyū haitatsu(-nin) 牛乳配達(人)

milkshake *n* miruku sē´ki ミルクセーキ

millet *n* áwa アワ・粟

milligram *n* miriguramu ミリグラム

million *n* hyaku mán 百万・1,000,000

millionaire *n* mirionerā ミリオネラー, hyaku man chōja 百万長者

million city *n* hyaku man toshi 百万都市

million dollar *n* mirion darā ミリオン・ダラー, ichi oku-en purēyā 1億円プレーヤー

million-seller *n* mirion serā ミリオンセラー

mimic *n* ... no mane (o shimásu; suru, shíte) ...のまね[真似](をします; する, して)

mimicry *n* mane まね・真似

minced meat *n* hiki-niku ひき肉

mincing (*fish/meat*) *n* tatakí 叩き, ...-tátaki ...叩き

mind *n* kokóro 心, omói 思い・想い, séishin 精神; muné 旨・むね; ki 気; kokorozashi 志, (*what one has in mind*) tsumori つもり, ikō 意向
bear/keep in mind fukumimásu (fukúmu, fukúnde) 含みます(含む, 含んで); oboemásu (oboéru, obóete) 覚えます(覚える, 覚えて)
Do you mind? *interj* Íi desu ka? いいですか?
if you don't mind *adv* nan-nára なんなら, yoroshikáttara よろし[宜し]かったら
Never mind. *interj* Kamaimasén 構いません.
one's right mind *n* shōki 正気
set one's mind *v* kokoro-zashimásu (kokoro-zasu, kokoro-zashite) 志します(志す, 志して)

mine *pron* (*my*) wata(ku)shi no わた(く)しの・私の

mine *n* (*coal, etc.*) kō´zan 鉱山

miner *n* tankō sagyōin 炭坑作業員

mineral water *n* mineraru wōtā ミネラルウォーター

minimal *adj* (*smallest, least*) saishō no 最小の; (*lowest*) saitei (no) 最低(の), sáika (no) 最下(の)

minimum 1. *n* (*degree*) saishō-gén 最小限 **2.** *adj* → **minimal**
minimum rate *n* saitei chingin 最低賃金
minimum standard of living *n* saitei seikatsu suijun 最低生活水準

minister *n* (*pastor*) bokushi 牧師; (*cabinet*) dáijin 大臣

Ministry *n* ...-sho ...省
Ministry of Agriculture, Forestry and Fisheries of Japan (MAFF) *n* Nōrin-Suisan-shō 農林水産省
Ministry of Defense *n* Bōei-shō 防衛省
Ministry of Economy, Trade and Industry *n* Keizai Sangyō-shō 経済産業省
Ministry of Education, Culture, Sports, Science and Technology (MEXT) *n* Monbú Kagaku-shō 文部科学省
Ministry of Finance *n* Zaimú-shō 財務省
Ministry of Health, Labour and Welfare *n* Kōsei-Rōdō-shō 厚生労働省
Ministry of Internal Affairs and Communications (MIC) *n* Sōmu-shō 総務省
Ministry of Justice *n* Hōmu-shō 法務省
Ministry of Land, Infrastructure, Transport and Tourism (MLIT) *n* Kokudo-Kōtsū-shō 国土交通省
Ministry of the Environment (MOE) *n* Kankyō-shō 環境省

minus *n* mainasu マイナス

minute *n* ...-fun ...分 (1: íp-pun 一分, 2: ni-fun 二分, 3: sánpun 三分, 4: yón-pun 四分, 5: gó-fun 五分, 6: róp-pun 六分, 7: naná-fun 七分, 8: háp-pun 八分, 9: kyū´-fun 九分, 10: júp-pun 十分; *how many* nán-pun 何分)

in a minute *adv* súgu (ni) すぐ(に); tadáima ただ今・ただいま

minutes after *adv* chokugo (ni) 直後(に)

minute *adj* (*fine, detailed*) bisai (na) 微細(な), seimitsu (na) 精密(な)

minutes *n* gijiroku 議事録

mirror **1.** *n* kagamí 鏡・カガミ **2.** *v* (*reflects it*) utsushimásu (utsúsú, utsúshite) 映します(映す, 映して)

side mirror *n* (*car*) saido mirā サイドミラー

rearview mirror *n* (*car*) bakku mirā バックミラー

miscarriage *n* ryū´zan 流産

miscast *v* haiyaku o ayamarimásu (ayamaru, ayamatte) 配役を誤ります(誤る, 誤って)

miscellaneous *adj* samazama (na) 様々(な), zatta (na) 雑多(な); *miscellaneous goods* zakka 雑貨

mischief *n* itazura いたずら・悪戯

mischievous *adj* wanpaku (na) 腕白・ワンパク(な); *mischievous child* itazurakko いたずらっ子

miserable *adj* wabishíi わびしい・侘しい, nasake-nái 情けない, mijime (na) みじめ・惨め(な)

"Les Miserables" *n* (*title*) "ā mujō" 『ああ無情』

misfortune *n* fukō´ 不幸, wazawai 災い

mishap *n* kegá けが・怪我 (o-kéga おけが[怪我]), wazawai 災い → **accident**

misrepresent *v* gomakashimásu (gomakasu, gomakashite) ごまかし[誤魔化し]ます(ごまかす, ごまかして)

miss **1.** *n* (*mistake*) mísu ミス **2.** *v* (*goes wide off the mark*) hazuremásu (hazureru, hazurete) 外れます(外れる, 外れて), (*fails*) shippai shimásu (suru, shite) 失敗します(する, して) **3.** *v* (*is not in time for*) (...ni) ma ni aimasén (awánai, awánaide) (...に)間に合いません(合わない, 合わないで) **4.** *v* (*yearns for*) ...ga natsukashíi ...が懐かしい; (*feels lonely without*) ...ga inakute/nákute sabishíi ...がいなくて/なくて寂しい

Miss *n* ... san ...さん, ... san no ojō´-san ...さんのお嬢さん

missing **1.** *n* (*person*) yukue fumei no hito 行方不明の人, yukue fumei-sha 行方不明者; (*it*) *is* ~ arimasén (nái, nákute) ありません(ない, なくて); (*he*) *is* ~ imasén (inai, ináide) いません(いない, いないで) **2.** *adj* yukue fumei (no) 行方不明(の), miataranai 見当たらない, mitsukaranai 見つからない, fusoku shita 不足した

mission *n* (*task*) ninmu 任務, (*operation*) sakusen 作戦, (*Christianity*) fukyō (katsudō) 布教(活動)

missionary *n* senkyō´shi 宣教師

mist *n* kasumi かすみ・霞, kiri きり・霧, móya もや・靄

mistake **1.** *n* machigái 間違い, ayamári 誤り, ayamáchi 過ち, mísu ミス, misuteíku ミステイク **2.** *v* (*makes a mistake*) machigaimásu (machigáu, machigátte) 間違います(間違う, 間違って), ayamarimásu (ayamáru, ayamátte) 誤ります(誤る, 誤って) **3.** *mistakes it* *v* machigaemásu (machigáeru, machigáete) 間違えます(間違える, 間違えて)

mistletoe *n* yadorigi ヤドリギ

mistreat *v* gyakutai shimásu (suru, shite) 虐待します(する, して)

mistress **1.** *n* (*Madam*) óku-san/-sama 奥さん/様 **2.** (*lover*) káno-jo 彼女; (*concubine*) mekáke 妾・めかけ, o-mekake-san お妾さん

misty; *gets* ~ kasumimásu (kasumu, kasunde) かすみ[霞み]ます(かすむ, かすんで)

misunderstand *v* gokai shimásu (suru, shite) 誤解します(する, して)

mix *v* (*mixes it in with*) (... ni sore o) mazemásu (mazéru, mázete) ...(にそれを)混ぜます(混ぜる, 混ぜて); (*it mixes*) mazarimásu (mazáru, mazátte) 混ざります(混ざる, 混ざって), majirimásu (majíru, majítte) 混じります(混じる, 混じって); *mixing one's foods/drinks* chánpon ちゃんぽん

mixed bathing kon'yoku 混浴

mixture *n* (*assortment*) kumiawase 組み合わせ, kongō 混合

moan *v* nagekimásu (nagéku, nagéite) 嘆きます(嘆く, 嘆いて)

moat *n* horí 堀; *inner ~* uchi-bori 内堀, *outer ~* soto-bori 外堀

mobile 1. *n* keitai (denwa) 携帯(電話) **2.** *adj* mochi-hakoberu 持ち運べる

mobile phone *n* keitai (denwa) 携帯 (電話)

model *n* mohan 模範, tehón 手本(o-tehon お手本); (*mold*) mokei 模型; (*type*) katá 型, ...-gata ...型, ...-kei ...型; móderu モデル

fashion model *n* fasshon moderu ファッション・モデル

supermodel *n* sūpā moderu スーパーモデル

moderate 1. *adj* (*reasonable*) tekido (no) 適度(の); (*properly limited/ restrained*) odayaka (na) 穏やか(な); (*conservative*) hikaeme (na) 控えめ (な) **2. moderates it** *v* kagen shimásu (suru, shíte) 加減します(する, して)

moderation *n* tékido 適度, setsudo 節度; kagen 加減

modern *adj* géndai (no) 現代(の), kindai (no) 近代(の), modan モダン

modern dance *n* modan dansu モダンダンス

modern music *n* kindai ongaku 近代音楽

modern people *n* gendai-jin 現代人

modern state *n* kindai kokka 近代国家

modernization *n* gendai-ka 現代化, kindai-ka 近代化

modest *adj* kenkyo (na) 謙虚(な), hikaeme (na) 控え目(な), uchiki (na) 内気(な); (*small*) ō'kiku nái 大きくない

Mohammed *n* mohameddo モハメッド, muhanmado ムハンマド

moisten *v* shimeshimásu (shimesu, shimeshíte) 湿します(湿す, 湿して)

mold 1. *n* (*pattern*) katá 型; (*model*) mokei 模型 **2.** (*growth*) kabi かび・黴; *is moldy* kabi ga háete imásu かびが生えています **3.** *v* katachi-zuku-rimásu (katachi-zukuru, katachi-zukútte) 形作ります(形作る, 形作って)

mole *n* (*on skin*) hokuro ほくろ・ホクロ; (*rodent*) mogura モグラ・土竜

molester *n* (*sexual*) chikan 痴漢・ちかん

moment *n* (*instant*) shunkan 瞬間, sétsuna せつな・刹那

at the moment isshun 一瞬

just a moment chótto matte kudasai ちょっと待って下さい

on the spur of the moment tokí no hazumi de 時の弾みで

(at) the moment that ... totan ni ... とたん[途端]に

momentum *n* hazumi 弾み・はずみ

Monday *n* Getsuyō'(-bi) 月曜(日); *Monday-Wednesday-Friday* ges-sui-kin 月水金

money *n* (o-)kane (お)金; (*money given as a New Year's gift*) otoshi-dama お年玉 → **cash** → **finance**

money-changer *n* (*money-changing machine*) ryōgáe-ki 両替機

money changing/exchange *n* ryōgae 両替

money market *n* kin'yū shíjō 金融市場

money offering (*to a shrine*) *n* (o-)saisen (お)さい銭[賽銭]

money order *n* kawase 為替; (*postal*) yūbin káwase 郵便為替

Mongolia *n* Mongoru モンゴル

monk *n* (*Buddhist*) bō'zu 坊主, obō-san お坊さん; *young monk* kozó' 小僧, kozō-san 小僧さん

monkey *n* sáru 猿・サル(o-saru お猿)

monorail *n* monorē'ru モノレール

monster *n* kaibutsu 怪物, kaijū 怪獣, monsutā モンスター

month *n* tsukí 月, ...-getsu ...月 (*how many months* nan-kágetsu 何ヵ月)

month after next *n* sarai-getsu 再来月

month before last *n* sensén-getsu 先々月

monthly *adj* maitsuki (no) 毎月(の); ~ *installments/payments* geppu 月賦; ~ *salary* gekkyū 月給

monument *n* monyumento モニュメント, kinen hi 記念碑

mood *n* kíbun 気分, kokoro-mochi 心持ち, mūdo ムード

good mood *n* jō-kigen 上機嫌, (go-)kigen (ご)機嫌

moody *adj* kigen ga warúi 機嫌が悪い

moon *n* tsukí 月, ó-tsuki-sama お月様

moon-faced *adj* marugata (no) 丸型

(の); marugao (no) 丸顔(の); (*moon-faced woman*) okáme おかめ

moonlight night *n* tsukí-yo 月夜

moonrise *n* tsuki no de 月の出

moon viewing *n* tsuki-mí-mi 月見 (o-tsu-kimi お月見)

mop *n* móppu モップ

moral **1.** *n* moraru モラル **2.** *adj* dōtoku-teki (na) 道徳的(な)

morality, morals *n* dōtoku 道徳; (*ethics*) shū´shin 修身

more *adj* mótto もっと, mō sukóshi もう少し, mō もう + [NUMBER]; (*some more*) sára-ni さらに・更に

a little more *adj* mō sukóshi もう少し

a lot more *adj* mótto takusán もっとたくさん[沢山]

all the more ..., still/much ~ ... *adv* issō ...いっそう...・一層..., nao-sara なおさら・尚更

the more ... the more *adv* ...-suréba suruhodo/dake ...すれば する程/だけ... (issō ... いっそう...)

more and more *adv* masú-masu ますます・益々, iyó-iyo いよいよ

more or less *adv* tsúmari つまり; tashō 多少

more than anything *adv* náni yori mo 何よりも

more than enough *adv* tappúri たっぷり

moreover *adv* sono ue (ni) その上 (に), matá 又・また, náo 尚, shiká-mo しかも, kótoni ことに・殊に

morning *n* ása 朝・あさ, go zen 午前; *this* ~ kesa 今朝

Good morning. O-hayō (gozaimásu). おはよう[お早う]ございます。

morning glory *n* (*flower*) ásagao 朝顔・アサガオ

morning meal *n* chōshoku 朝食, asa-góhan 朝ご飯

morning paper *n* chōkan 朝刊

morning sun *n* ásahi 朝日

morphine *n* moruhine モルヒネ

mortar *n* (*utensil*) úsu うす・臼; surí-bachi すり鉢; (*material*) morutaru モルタル, shikkui しっくい・漆喰

mortifying *adj* kuyashíi 悔しい

Moscow *n* Mosukuwa モスクワ

mosquito *n* ka 蚊・カ

mosquito net *n* kaya かや・蚊帳

moss *n* koke こけ・苔

most *adj* ichiban 一番, móttomo 最も

most of the ... *adj* ... no daibúbun ...の大部分

at most *adv* ō´kute 多くて, sémete せめて, séizei せいぜい

for the most part *adv* ōkata おおかた・大方, taigai たいがい・大概, ō´ku 多く

the most *adj* (*largest*) saidai (no) 最大(の)

most recent *adj* (+ [DATE]) saru ... 去る...; kono mae/aida (no) この前/間 (の); tsui saikin (no) つい最近(の)

moth *n* ga ガ・蛾; (*clothes moth*) íga イガ・衣蛾, shimi しみ・衣魚, mushi 虫・ムシ

mothballs *n* bōchū´-zai 防虫剤; mushi-yoke 虫よけ

mother *n* okā´-san お母さん, háha 母, haha-oya 母親; ofukuro おふくろ

mother country *n* bókoku 母国, sókoku 祖国

mother-in-law *n* gíbo 義母; (*husband or wife's mother*) shūtome 姑, o-shū-tome-san お姑さん

mother's milk *n* chichí 乳, bonyū 母乳; [*baby talk*] óppai おっぱい

motion *n* ugokí 動き; mō´shon モーション; *~ sickness* norimono-yoi 乗物酔い

motivation, motive *n* dōki 動機; yaruki やる気

motor *n* hatsudō´-ki 発動機, mō´tā モーター → **automobile**

motorcycle *n* ōtóbai オートバイ (*how many* nán-dai 何台)

motor race, motor racing *n* jidōsha rēsu 自動車レース, kā rēsu カーレース

motto *n* hyōgo 標語, mottō モットー

mould → **mold**

mound *n* tsuká 塚; (*burial*) ryō´ 陵

mount *v* (*ride*) ... ni norimásu (noru, notte) ...に乗ります(乗る, 乗って); (*sits astride*) ... ni matagarimásu (matagáru, matagátte) ...にまたがり[跨り]ます(またがる, またがって); (*climb*) ... ni noborimásu (noboru, nobotte) ...に登ります(登る、登って)

mountain n yamá 山; ...-san ...山

mountain bicycle/ bike n maunten baiku マウンテンバイク

mountain-climber n tozán-sha 登山者

mountain-climbing n yama nóbori 山登り、tozan 登山; ~ *rope* záiru ザイル

mountain lodge n yama-goya 山小屋

mountain pass n tōgé 峠

mountain range n sanmyaku 山脈

Mount Fuji n Fúji-san 富士山

mouse n 1. nezumi ネズミ・鼠, hatsuka nézumi 二十日ネズミ[鼠] 2. (*computer*) mausu マウス

mousetrap n nezumí-tori ネズミ[鼠]取り[捕り]

mouth n 1. (*human*) kuchi 口 2. (*river mouth*) kakō 河口

mouthful n (*one mouthful*) hitó-kuchi 一口

mouth organ n hāmonika ハーモニカ

movable type n katsuji 活字

move 1. v (*it moves*) ugokimásu (ugóku, ugóite) 動きます(動く、動いて); (*moves it*) ugokashimásu (ugokásu, ugokáshite) 動かします(動かす、動かして) 2. (*moves residence*) utsurimásu (utsúru, utsútte) 移ります(移る、移って)、(*changes residence*) hikkoshimásu (hikkósu, hikkóshite) 引っ越します(引っ越す、引っ越して); (*moves into an apartment*) nyūkyo shimásu (suru, shite) 入居します(する、して)

movement n ugokí 動き; katsudō 活動; undō 運動; (*gesture*) miburi みぶり・身振り、dōsa 動作

mover n (*household mover*) hikkoshi-ya 引っ越し屋、(hikkoshi no) unsō-ya (引っ越しの)運送屋

movie(s) n eiga 映画

   movie theater n eigá-kan 映画館

   movie projector n eishá-ki 映写機

   movie actor/actress n eigá haiyū/joyū 映画俳優/女優

moving n (*one's household*) hikkoshi 引っ越し; *moving man* → **mover**

   mover's van n hikkoshi torákku 引っ越しトラック

mow v karimásu (karu, katte) 刈ります(刈る、刈って)

moxibustion n (o-)kyū (お)きゅう[灸]

Mr. n ... san ...さん; *Mrs.* ... san (no óku-san) ...さん(の奥さん)、...-fujin ...夫人; *Mr. and Mrs.* ... fusái ...夫妻; *Ms.* ... san ...さん、...jóshi ...女史

much adj, adv takusán (no) たくさん[沢山](の)、ō'ku (no) 多く(の)、un to うんと

   is/has much adj ... ga ō'i ...が多い

   not (very) much adv anmari あんまり + [NEGATIVE]

   how much adv íkura いくら・幾ら (o-ikura おいくら)、dono-gurai どの位・どのぐらい

   as much as adv ... gúrai ...位、...no yō'ni ...のように[様]に; ~ *one likes* (omóu) zonbun ni (思う)存分に

   much more adv mótto takusán もっとたくさん[沢山]、zutto ō'ku ずっと多く; (*still more*) issō いっそう・一層、nao-sara なおさら・尚更

much → **how much**

muck → **mud**

mucus n (*nasal*) hana (mizu) 鼻(水)

mud n doró 泥・土

muddy adj doro-dárake (no) 泥だらけ(の); *gets* ~ nigorimásu (nigóru, nigótte) 濁ります(濁る、濁って)

mudfish n dojō どじょう・ドジョウ

muffin n mafin マフィン

muffler n mafurā マフラー

mug n 1. (*cup*) magu kappu マグカップ 2. (*beer mug*) jokki ジョッキ

mugged; *gets* ~ (*robbed*) gōtō ni osowaremásu (osowareru, osowarete) 強盗に襲われます(襲われる、襲われて)

muggy adj mushi-atsúi 蒸し暑い

mulberry n kúwa クワ・桑

mule n (*animal*) raba ラバ・騾馬

multiply v 1. (*grows*) fuemásu (fúeru, fúete) 増えます(増える、増えて) 2. (3 by 5 sán ni góo) kakemásu (kakéru, kákete) (3に5を)かけ[掛け]ます(掛ける、掛けて) 3. (*increases*) fuyashimásu (fuyásu, fuyáshite) 増やします(増やす、増やして)

mummy n miira ミイラ

mumps n otafuku kaze おたふく風邪

municipal adj shí (no) 市(の)、shiritsu (no) 市立(の)、kōritsu (no) 公立(の)、

(*urban*) shínai (no) 市内（の）
municipality *n* chihō jichitai 地方自治体
mural painter *n* hekiga-ka 壁画家
mural painting *n* hekiga 壁画
murder *n* satsujin 殺人, hitogóroshi 人殺し → **kill**
murmur → **whisper**
muscle *n* kínniku 筋肉, súji 筋; (*power*) kínryoku 筋力, chikará 力
muscle pains *n* kinniku-tsū 筋肉痛
museum *n* hakubútsú-kan 博物館; (*art gallery*) bijútsú-kan 美術館
mushroom *n* kínoko キノコ・茸; (*thumb-like*) matsutake 松茸・マツタケ; (*large brown*) shíitake 椎茸; (*straw*) enokí-dake/-take エノキ[榎]茸
music *n* óngaku 音楽, myūjikku ミュージック, (*traditional to the imperial court*) gágaku 雅楽
musical *n* myūjikaru ミュージカル
musical instrument *n* gakki 楽器; *musical instrument score* gakufu 楽譜
musician *n* ongaku-ka 音楽家, myūjishan ミュージシャン
musk *n* jakō ジャコウ
muskmelon *n* masuku meron マスクメロン
Muslim *n* **1.** isuramu kyōto イスラム教徒, kai kyōto 回教徒 **2.** isuramu kyō (no) イスラム教（の）, kai kyō(no) 回教（の）
mussel *n* igai イガイ; *blue mussel*

mūru-gai ムール貝
must *verbal auxiliary* **~ do** (shi-)nákereba narimasén (し)なければなりません; **~ not** (*do*) (shi-)té wa ikemasén (し)てはいけません
mustache *n* kuchi hige 口ひげ[髭]
mustard *n* karashi からし・芥子, masutādo マスタード
mutt *n* (*dog*) zasshu (ken) 雑種（犬）
mutton *n* maton マトン, hitsuji no niku 羊の肉 → **lamb**
mutual *adj* o-tagai (no) お互い（の）; [BOOKISH] sō´go (no) 相互（の）
mutually *adv* o-tagai ni お互いに; [BOOKISH] sō´go ni 相互に
my *pron* wata(ku)shi no わた（く）し[私]（の）; *my wife* kánai 家内
My my! My goodness! [EXCLAM] Sore wa sore wa それはそれは
myopic *adj* kingan (no) 近眼（の）, kin-shi (no) 近視（の）
myringa *n* (*medical*) komaku 鼓膜
myself *pron* jibun 自分, (watakushi) jíshin (私)自身
by myself jibun jíshin de 自分自身で
mysterious *adj* (*strange*) fushigi (na) 不思議（な）, (*esoteric*) shinpi-teki (na) 神秘的（な）
mystery *n* nazo 謎・ナゾ, misuterii ミステリー, (*secret*) himitsu 秘密
myth *adj* shinwa 神話
mythologist *n* shinwa gakusha 神話学者

N

Nagasaki *n* Nagásaki 長崎; *Nagasaki City* Nagasakí-shi 長崎市; *Nagasaki Prefecture* Nagasakí-ken 長崎県
nail *n* kugi 釘・くぎ; (*finger, toe*) tsume 爪・ツメ
nail clippers *n* tsumekírí 爪切り
nail polish *n* manikyua (eki) マニキュア（液）
nail polish remover *n* jokō eki 除光液
naive *adj* mújaki (na) 無邪気（な）, soboku (na) 素朴（な）, naiibu (na) ナイーブ（な）
naked *adj* hadaka (no) 裸（の）→ **nude**

naked eye *n* ragan 裸眼
name 1. *n* namae 名前, (o-namae お名前), na 名 **2.** *v* (*calls*) (…to) yobimásu (yobu, yonde) (…と)呼びます（呼ぶ、呼んで）, (*dubs*) nazukemásu (nazukéru, nazúkete) 名付けます（名付ける、名付けて）; (*says the name of*) …no namae o iimásu (iú, itte/yutte) …の名前を言います（言う、言って/ゆって）
list of names *n* meibo 名簿
name card *n* meishi 名刺
name plate/tag *n* na fuda 名札
name seal/stamp *n* (*"chop"*) hankó ハンコ

nam<u>e</u>less *adj* mumei (no) 無名（の）

namely *adv* sunáwachi すなわち・即ち; tsumari つまり

namesake *n* dōmei no hito 同名の人

nap *n* hiru-ne (o shimásu; suru, sh<u>i</u>te) 昼寝（をします; する, して）; **takes a ~** h<u>i</u>tó-nemuri 一眠り

napkin *n* nápukín ナプキン, f<u>u</u>kín ふきん・布巾

narcotic(s) *n* mayaku 麻薬

narration *n* nar<u>ē</u>shon ナレーション

narrative *n* monogatari 物語; naratibu ナラティブ

narrator *n* nar<u>ē</u>tā ナレーター; katari-te 語り手

narrow *adj* semái 狭い; hosói 細い
narrow mind *n* henkyō na kokoro 偏狭な心; kyōryō na kokoro 狭量な心
narrow road *n* hosomichi 細道

NASA *n* nasa NASA; beikoku kōkū uchū kyoku 米国航空宇宙局

nasal mucus *n* hana-jiru 鼻汁 → **snivel**

nasty *adj* iyá (na) 嫌（な）, akuratsu (na) 悪らつ・悪辣（な）

nation *n* (*country*) kuni 国, kókka 国家; (*people*) kokumin 国民; **how many nations** nan-kákoku 何か国

national *adj* kuni (no) 国（の）; koku-…国…; kokuritsu (no) 国立（の）; kokumin (no) 国民の; nashonaru ナショナル

national defense *n* kokubō 国防

National Foundation Day *n* (*11 February*) Kenkoku-kínen no hi 建国記念の日

national park *n* kokuritsu kōen 国立公園

nationalist *n* kokka shugi-sha 国家主義者; (*patriot*) aikoku shugi-sha 愛国主義者

nationality *n* kokuseki 国籍

national(s) *n* kokumin 国民

nation-wide *adj* zénkokuteki (na/ni) 全国的（な/に）

native *adj* bokoku (no) 母国（の）; umaretsuki (no) 生まれつき（の）; neitibu ネイティブ
native American *n* Amerika senjūmin アメリカ先住民, Indian インディアン

native land *n* bokoku 母国

native language *n* bokoku-go 母国語

native place *n* sh<u>u</u>sshin-chi 出身地; kuni 国 (o-kuni お国)

natural *adj* **1.** shizen (no, na) 自然（の, な）; tennen (no) 天然（の）; nachururu ナチュラル **2.** *adj* (*proper, deserved*) tōzen (no) 当然（の） **3.** (*to be expected*) … (suru) monó desu …（する）ものです

natural food *n* shizen shoku (-hin) 自然食（品）

natural gas *n* tennen-gásu 天然ガス

naturally *adv* shizen ni 自然に; (*by nature*) motomoto もともと・元々 → **spontaneously** → **of course**

nature *n* **1.** shizen 自然 **2.** seishitsu 性質, shō 性, séi 性; (*quality*) sh<u>i</u>tsú 質; (*disposition*) táchi 質; **human ~** nínjō 人情 **3.** **by ~** mótó-yori もとより, motomoto もともと・元々

naughty *adj* wanpaku (na) 腕白・わんぱく（な）, itazura (na) いたずら・悪戯（な）
naughty child *n* itazurákko いたずらっ子・悪戯っ子; (*boy*) wanpaku-bōzu 腕白坊主, (*girl*) otenba お転婆

nausea *n* hakike 吐き気, (*medical term*) oshin 悪心, ōki 嘔気

nauseate *v feels nauseated* hakiké ni moyōshimásu; moyōsu, moyōsh<u>i</u>te 吐き気（を催します; 催す, 催して） → **queasy**

navel *n* (o-)heso （お）へそ

navigate *v* kōkai shimásu (suru, sh<u>i</u>te) 航海します（する, して）; annái shimásu (suru, sh<u>i</u>te) 案内します（する, して）

navigation *n* kōkai 航海; (*car navigation system*) kānabi カーナビ

navy *n* káigun 海軍

navy blue *n* neibii burū ネイビーブルー, (nō)kon （濃）紺

near *adj* ch<u>i</u>kái 近い; *adv* ch<u>i</u>kaku (ni) 近く（に）

near-miss *n* niamisu ニアミス

near (by) *adj* sóba (no) そば・側（の）; ch<u>i</u>káku (no) 近く（の）

nearly *adv* hotóndo ほとんど・殆ど; mázu まず; hóbo ほぼ

nearsighted *adj* (*myopic*) kingan (no)

近眼(の), kinshi (no) 近視(の)

neat *adj* (*tidy*) kichín-to shite imásu (iru, ite) きちんとしています(いる、いて); (*attractive*) kírei (na) きれい[綺麗](な)

necessarily *adv* kanarazu 必ず; *not ~* kagirimasen (kagiranai) 限りません(限らない)

necessary *adj* hitsuyō (na) 必要(な), (*needed*) nyūyō (na) 入用(な); ...ga irimásu (iru, itte) ...が要ります(要る、要って)

necessity *n* hitsuyō 必要

neck *n* kubi 首; (*of a bottle*) kubire くびれ

necklace *n* kubi-kázari 首飾り, nékkuresu ネックレス

necktie *n* nékutai ネクタイ; *puts on* (*wears*) *a necktie* nékutai o musubimásu (musubu, musunde) ネクタイを結びます(結ぶ、結んで), nékutai o shimásu (suru, shite) ネクタイをします(する、して)

need 1. *v needs to do* (... ga) irimásu (iru, itte) (...が)要ります(要る、要って), (... o) yō-shimásu (yō-súru, yō-shite) (...を)要します(要する、要して); (*suru*) hitsuyō ga arimásu (áru, átte) (する)必要があります(ある、あって), (shi)-nákereba narimasén (し)なければなりません; *needs not do* (shi) nákute mo íidesu (し)なくてもいいです **2.** *n* (*necessity*) hitsuyō 必要; (*poverty*) hinkon 貧困, fújiyū 不自由; *is in ~* (*of help*) komarimásu (komáru, komátte) 困ります(困る、困って)

needle *n* hári 針

sewing needle *n* núibari 縫い針

needlework *n* hari-shígoto 針仕事

needy *adj* mazushíi 貧しい, fú-jiyū (na) 不自由(な), hinkon (na) 貧困(な)

negation *n* uchi-keshi 打ち消し, hitei 否定

negative 1. *adj* shōkyoku-teki (na) 消極的(な), hitei-teki (na) 否定的(な), negatibu (na) ネガティブ(な) **2.** *n* (*film*) nega ネガ

neglect 1. *v* (*disregards*) múshi shimásu (suru, shite) 無視します(する、

して); (*leaves undone*) hōtte okimásu (oku, oite) 放っておきます(おく、おいて); (*shirks*) okotarimásu (okotaru, okotatte) 怠ります(怠る、怠って); *~ to write/visit* (go-)busata shimásu (suru, shite) (ご)無沙汰します(する、して) **2.** *n* ikuji-hōki 育児放棄

neglectful *adj* hanashi-aimásu 怠慢(な); *I have been ~* (*in not keeping in touch with you*). Go-busata itashimáshita. ご無沙汰しました.

negligee *n* negurije ネグリジェ

negligence *n* taiman 怠慢; (*carelessness*) yudan 油断, fuchūi 不注意

negligent *adj* taiman (na) 怠慢(な), zubora (na) ずぼら(な)

negligible *adj* wazuka (na) わずか(な)

negotiable *adj* kōshō no yochi ga aru 交渉の余地がある

negotiate *v* hanashi-aimásu (hanashi-au, hanashi-atte) 話し合います(話し合う、話し合って); kōshō 交渉

negotiation *n* hanashi-ai 話し合い, kōshō (shimásu; suru, shite) 交渉(します; する、して)

negotiator *n* kōshō-nin 交渉人

neighborhood *n* (go-)kínjo (ご)近所

neighbor(ing) *adj* tonari (no) 隣り(の)

neither ... nor ... *adv* ... mo... mo... も...も + [NEGATIVE]

neither one dóchira (no ...) mo どちら(の...)も + [NEGATIVE]

nephew *n* oi おい・甥; *your nephew* oigo-san 甥子さん

nerve *n* shínkei 神経; *gets on one's nerves* shínkei ni sawarimásu (sawaru, sawatte) 神経に障ります(障る、障って)

nervous *adj* **1.** shinkéi-shitsu (na) 神経質(な) **2.** (*feels self-conscious*) agarimásu (agaru, agatte) 上がります(上がる、上がって) **3.** (*gets agitated*) dōyō shimásu (suru, shite) 動揺します(する、して) → **flustered 4.** (*feeling apprehensive*) kimí ga warúi 気味が悪い → **worried**

nervous breakdown *n* shinkei suijaku 神経衰弱

nest *n* su 巣

nest egg *n* hesokuri へそくり

nested boxes *n* jūbako 重箱(o-jū お重)
net *n* **1.** ami 網, nétto ネット **2.** = *internet* nettó ネット
Netbook *n* (*computer*) netto-bukku ネットブック
Netherlander *n* Oranda-jin オランダ人
Netherlandic *n, adj* (*language*) Orando-go (no) オランダ語(の); (*person*) Oranda-jin (no) オランダ人(の)
Netherlands *n* Oranda オランダ
Netizen *n* (*Internet*) netto-shimin ネット市民 (*from* **Internet** *+* **citizen**)
net price *n* séika 正価
network *n* **1.** nettowāku ネットワーク, jōhō-mō 情報網 **2.** (*human network*) jinmyaku 人脈
  network administrator *n* nettowāku kanri-sha ネットワーク管理者
  computer network *n* konpyūta/ konpyūtā nettowāku コンピュータ/ コンピューターネットワーク
neurotic *adj* noirōze (no) ノイローゼ(の)
neutral(ity) *adj* chūritsu (no) 中立(の), nyūtoraru ニュートラル
never *adv* kesshíte 決して + [NEGATIVE]; **has ~ (done)** (shi)-ta kotó ga arimasén (nái) (し)た事がありません(ない); **~ (does)** (su)-ru kotó wa arimasén (nái) (す)る事はありません; **~ mind** kamaimasén (kamawánai) 構いません(構わない)
never-ending *adj* owari no nai 終わりのない
nevertheless *adv* sore náno ni それなのに, tó-ni-kaku とにかく
new *adj* atarashíi 新しい; shín(-) … 新…; shínki (no) 新規(の), nyū ニュー …
  new address *n* **1.** (*home*) shin-jūsho 新住所 **2.** (*email*) atarashii adoresu 新しいアドレス
  new age *n* nyū eiji ニューエイジ
  newborn baby *n* shinseiji 新生児
  new moon *n* shin-getsu 新月, mikazuki 三日月
  new movie *n* shin-saku (eiga) 新作(映画)
  new version *n* atarashii bājon 新しいバージョン, shin bājon 新バージョン
  new world *n* shin-sekai 新世界
  new year *n* shínnen 新年; *Happy new*

year. (Shínnen/Akemáshite) o-medetō (新年/明けまして)おめでとう.
  New Year's (day) *n* ganjitsu 元日, gantan 元旦; O-shōgatsu お正月
  New Year's eve ō-mísoka 大みそか・大晦日
newcomer *n* shinjin 新人
newest *adj* saishin (no) 最新(の)
newly *adv* ataráshiku 新しく, arátamete 改めて
newlyweds *n* shinkon fūfu 新婚夫婦
news *n* nyū´su ニュース, tsūshin 通信; (*newspaper item*) kíji 記事; (*word from*) táyori 便り, shōsoku 消息
news agency *n* tsūshin-sha 通信社
newscaster *n* nyūsu kyasutā ニュースキャスター
newsflash *n* nyūsu sokuhō ニュース速報
newsletter *n* nyūsu retā ニュースレター, kaihō 会報
newspaper *n* shinbun 新聞; (*morning*) chōkan 朝刊, (*evening*) yūkan 夕刊; (*company*) shinbún-sha 新聞社; *newspaper bill* shinbun-dai 新聞代
newsperson *n* shinbun-kísha 新聞記者
newsstand *n* (*at the station*) baiten 売店, (*kiosk*) kiosuku キオスク
news vendor *n* shinbun-úri 新聞売り
newt *n* imori イモリ
New York *n* Nyūyōku ニューヨーク
New Zealand *n* Nyūjiirándo ニュージーランド; *New Zealander* n Nyūjiirándo-jin ニュージーランド人
next *adj* (*time/order*) tsugí (no) 次(の), (*date etc.*) yóku(-) … 翌…; (*the next one*) tsugí 次, tsugí no 次の; (*going on to the next*) tsuzukete 続けて; **~ to** (*in space*), **~ door to …** no tonari (no) …の隣り(の); **~ on the left/right** hidari-/migi-dónari (no) 左/右隣り(の); **~ after/to …** (*in importance*) … ni tsúide (no) …に次いで(の)
  next day *n, adv* yokujitsu 翌日, tsugi no hi 次の日
  next evening *n, adv* yokuban 翌晩, tsugi no hi no yo(ru) 次の日の夜
  next month *n, adv* ráigetsu 来月

next morning *n, adv* yokuasa 翌朝, tsugi no hi no asa 次の日の朝

next time *n, adv* kóndo 今度, jikai 次回, kono-tsugí この次

next week *n, adv* raishū 来週

next year *n, adv* rainen 来年

nibble *v* kajirimásu (kajíru, kajítte) か じり [齧り]ます(かじる, かじって)

nice *adj* **1.** ii/yoi いい/良い → **good 2.** oishii おいしい → **delicious 3.** kirei na きれい(な), utsukushii 美し い, hare (no) 晴れ(の) → **fair 4.** shin-setsu (na) 親切(な), yasashii やさしい → **kind 5.** → **delicate**

nice weather *n* íi ténki (いい) 天気 (o-tenki お天気)

nicely *adv* shinsetsu (ni) 親切に, kirei (ni) きれいに(に)

nick *v* kizamimásu (kizamu, kizande) 刻みます(刻む, 刻んで)

nickname *n* adana あだ名, aishō 愛称, nikkunēmu ニックネーム

niece *n* méi めい・姪; *your niece* meigo-san めいご [姪子]さん

night *n* yóru 夜, yó 夜; ban 晩; *(at) night* yakan 夜間, *late at ~* yóru osoku 夜遅く, shín'ya 深夜; *~ before last* issakú-ban/-ya 一昨晩/夜; *the ~ before (… no)* zen'ya (…の)前夜; *one night* hitóban 一晩, *two nights* futá-ban 二晩

night(s) of lodging …-haku …泊 (**1:** ip-paku 一泊, **2:** ni-haku 二泊, **3:** san-paku 三泊; *how many nights (will you stay?)* Nánpaku shimásu ka. 何泊(し ますか.)

night bus *n* yakō basu 夜行バス

nightcap *n* naito kyappu ナイトキャ ップ; nezake 寝酒

nightclothes *n* pajama パジャマ

nightclub *n (cabaret)* kyábariē キャバ レー; naito kurabu ナイトクラブ

nightdress → nightclothes

night duty *n* shukuchoku 宿直

night game *n (of baseball)* náitā ナイ ター

night-light *(Japanese traditional paper-covered)* *n* andon あんどん・ 行灯

nightmare *n* akumu 悪夢

night school *n* yakan gakkō 夜間学校

night shift *n* yakin 夜勤

night-watch(man) *n* yakei 夜警; yakei-in 夜警員

Nikko *n* Níkkō 日光

nil *n* zero ゼロ

nimble *adj* kíyō (na) 器用(な)

nine *n* kyū 九・9, kú 九・9, kokónotsu 九つ; náin ナイン

nine; *9 pieces (small things)* kyū´-ko 九個, *9 trees (or long things)* kyū-hon 九本, *9 sheets (flat things)* kyū´-mai 九 枚; *9 cats (or small animals)* kyū-hiki 九匹; *9 cows (or large aminals)* kyū´-tō 九頭; *9 birds/rabbits* kyū´-wa 九羽; *9 cars (or machines/vehicles)* kyū´-dai 九台; *9 copies (books/magazines)* kyū´-satsu 九冊; *9 floors/stories* kyū-kai 九 階; *9 people* kyū´-nin, ku-nin 九人, kyū´-mei 九名; *9 fold* kyū-bai 九倍; *9 degrees* kyū´-do 九度; *9 times* kyū-dó 九度 kyū´-kái 九回, kyū´-hén 九遍; *9 o'clock* kú-ji 九時; *9 hours* kú-jíkan 九時間; *9 days* kokonoka 九日; *9 weeks* kyū´-shūkan 九週間; *9 months* kyū´-ka-getsu 九ヶ月; *9 years* kyū´-nen 九年, kyū-nénkan 九年間; *9 years old* kokónotsu 九つ, kyū´-sai 九歳

nine hundred *n* kyū´-hyaku 九百・ 900

nineteen *n* jū´-ku 十九・19, jū-kyū 十九・19

nine thousand *n* kyū-sén 九千・9,000

ninety *n* kyū´-jū 九十・90, ku-jū´ 九十; *~ thousand* kyū-mán 九万 ・90,000

ninja *n* nínja 忍者

ninjitsu, ninjutsu *n* nínjutsu 忍術

ninth *adj* kyū-banme (no) 九番目(の) ・9番目(の) ku-banmé (no) 九番目 (の), kokonotsumé (no) 九つ目(の); *the ~ day* kokonoka-mé 九日目・9日目, *(of the month)* kokonoka 九日・9日

no *adv* iie いいえ *(or just say the negative verb)*

no charge/fee *n, adj* múryō (no) 無料 (の), tada (no) ただ(の)

no doubt *adv (surely)* kitto きっと; *There's no doubt about it.* sore wa machigai arimasen. それは間違いあり ません.

No kidding! *interj exclam* Másaka!
まさか!, *(male)* Jōdan daro! 冗談だろ!,
(female) Jōdan desho! 冗談でしょ!

no good *adj* tsumaránai つまらない;
damé (na) だめ〔駄目〕(な); furyō (na)
不良(な); *(futile)* muda (na) 無駄(な);
(worthless) yákuza (na) やくざ(な)

no later than *adj* … máde ni wa …ま
でには

no need to worry *interj, adj* daijō´bu
(na) 大丈夫(な); shinpai nai/(go)-
muyō 心配ない/(ご)無用

No parking chūsha kinshi 駐車禁止

No passing oi-koshi kinshi 追越し禁止

No smoking kin'en 禁煙

No, thank you. *interj* Kékkō desu.
結構です.

No trespassing tachiiri kinshi 立ち入
り禁止

no use *adj* damé (na) だめ〔駄目〕(な)

No war! *interj* Sensō hantai! 戦争反対!

No way! *interj* Tonde-mo arimasén
(nái) とんでもありません(ない);
(Absolutely not.) Zettai ni dame desu.
絶対にだめです.

noble *adj* kidakai 気高い, kōketsu (na)
高潔(な), sūkō (na) 崇高(な)

nobody *pron* dare mo 誰も + [NEGATIVE]

nod *v* unazukimásu (unazuku, unazuite)
うなずき〔頷き〕ます(うなずく, うな
ずいて)

Noh *n (Japanese classical theater)* nō
能, o-nō お能; *traditional Noh farce*
kyōgen 狂言

noise *n* otó 音; *(unwanted)* sōon 騒音,
(static) zatsuon 雑音; *(boisterous)*
sáwagi 騒ぎ

noisy *adj* yakamashíi やかましい,
sōzōshíi 騒々しい, urusai うるさい

nomad *n* yūboku-min 遊牧民

nomadic *adj* yūboku-min (no) 遊牧民
(の)

nominal *adj* meimoku-jō (no) 名目上
(の)

nominate *v* shimei shimásu (suru, shite)
指名します(する, して); mei-jimásu
(mei-jiru, mei-jite) 命じます(命じる,
命じて); suisen shimásu (suru, shite)
推薦します(する, して); nominēto
shimásu (suru, shite) ノミネートしま

す(する, して)

non- *prefix* fu- 不

non-alcohol *n, adj* sofuto dorinku (no)
ソフトドリンク(の); non arukōru (no)
ノンアルコール(の)

noncommittal *adj (beats around the
bush)* hanashi o bokashimásu (bokásu,
bokáshite) 話をぼかします(ぼかす,
ぼかして)

nondrinker *n* geko 下戸; (o-)sake o
nomanai hito (お)酒を飲まない人

none *pron (nothing)* nani mo 何も +
[NEGATIVE]; *(not even one)* hitotsu mo
一つも + [NEGATIVE], *(person)* hitori
mo 一人も + [NEGATIVE]

non-fatty tuna (maguro no) aka-mi
(マグロ〔鮪〕の)赤身

nonetheless *adv* sore náno ni それなの
のに

nonsense *n* baka na kotó ばかなこと;
baka-bánashi ばか話; detarame でた
らめ; tawagoto たわごと・戯言;
nansensu ナンセンス

nonsmoker *n* non-sumōkā ノンスモ
ーカー; tabako o suwanai hito タバコ
〔煙草〕を吸わない人; hi-kitsuen-sha
非喫煙者

no(n)-smoking *n* kin'én seki 禁煙席

no(n)-smoking car *n* kin'én-sha
禁煙車

nonspecialist *n* mongái-kan 門外漢

nonstop *adj (flight)* mu-chákuriku (no)
無着陸(の)

noodles *n* mén(-rui) めん〔麺〕(類);
(o-)sóba (お)そば・蕎麦; *(Japanese
wheat-flour)* udon うどん・udón
おうどん, *(thin)* sōmen そうめん・
冷や麦; *(chilled)* hiya-múgi ひやむぎ・冷や
麦; *(Chinese)* rā´men ラーメン

cup noodle *n* kappu nūdoru カップヌ
ードル

noodle shop *n* (o-)sobá-ya (お)そば
〔蕎麦〕屋; udon-ya うどん屋

noon *n* hirú 昼(o-híru お昼); *(exactly
noon)* shō´go 正午

nope *adv (no)* iya いや

no place → nowhere

norm *n (standard)* kikaku 規格, hyōjun
標準

normal *adj* hyōjun (no) 標準(の),

futsū (no) 普通(の)、**nōmaru (no)** ノーマル(の) → usual

normally adv hyōjun-teki (ni) 標準的(に)、futsū (ni) 普通(に)

north n kita 北、hoku-… 北…；(the north) hoppō 北方、(the northern part) hókubu 北部；**north and south** nánboku 南北

North America n Kita-Ámerika 北アメリカ、Hoku-Bei 北米

northeast n hokutō 北東

northerly adj (wind) kita-yori (no kaze) 北寄り(の風)

North Pole n Hokkyoku 北極

North Sea n Hokkai 北海

northwest n hokusei 北西

Norway n Noruwei ノルウェイ

Norwegian n (language) Noruwei-go ノルウェイ語；(person) Noruwei-jin ノルウェイ人

nose n hana 鼻(o-hana お鼻)

nosebleed n hanaji 鼻血

nose hair n hanage 鼻毛

not adv **does not** [VERB]-masén (-nai, -náide) ません(ない、ないで)；**is not** [ADJECTIVE]-ku arimasén (-ku nái, -ku nákute) くありません(くない、くなくて)；[NOUN] ja arimasén (ja nái, ja nákute じゃありません(じゃない、じゃなくて)

not as/so much as … adj…hodo…ほど・程 + [NEGATIVE]

not at all adv **1.** sappári さっぱり；kesshíte 決して + [NEGATIVE] **2.** (you're welcome) dō´ itashimashíte どういたしまして

not working properly adj guai ga warúi 具合が悪い

not yet adv máda まだ + [NEGATIVE]

non-past (… -masén …ません、…-nai …ない)

notch 1. v (makes a notch) kizamimásu (kizamu, kizande) 刻みます(刻む、刻んで)、kizami-me/kirikomi o iremásu (ireru, irete) 刻み目/切り込みを入れ(入れむ、入れて) **2.** n kizami-me 刻み目

note n (memorandum) mémo メモ；chū´chū 注；(reminder) chū´i 注意；(promissory note) tegata 手形 → letter → notice,

explanatory notes → sound

notebook n nō´to ノート、nōtobúkku ノートブック

noted adj chomei (na) 著明(な)

note pad n memo-chō メモ帳

nothing pron nani mo 何も + [NEGATIVE]；**nothing (at all)** nan to mo 何とも + [NEGATIVE]

there is nothing like (better than) … ni kagirimásu (kagíru, kagítte) …に限ります(限る、限って)

notice 1. v …ni ki ga tsukimásu (tsukú, tsúite) …に気が付きます(付く、付いて)、kizukimásu (kizúku, kizúite) 気が付きます(気が付く、気付いて) **2.** n (notification) shirase 知らせ(o-shirase お知らせ)、todoké 届け(o-todoke お届け)、tsūchi 通知；(reminder) chū´i 注意

with short notice adv kyū na (o-)shirase (de) 急な(お)知らせ(で)；totsuzen no shirase (de) 突然の知らせ(で)

without notice adv mudan de 無断で；kotowári mo náku 断りもなく

notification → notice

notify v shirasemásu (shiraseru, shirasete) 知らせます(知らせる、知らせて)、(notifies formally or officially) tsūchi shimásu (suru, shite) 通知します(する、して)；todokemásu (todokéru, todókete) 届けます(届ける、届けて)

notion n kangae 考え、iken 意見 → idea → concept

notions n (haberdashery) koma-mono 小間物

noun n meishi 名詞

nourish v yashinaimásu (yashinau, yashinatte) 養います(養う、養って)

nourishment n eiyō 栄養

novel 1. n (fiction) shōsetsu 小説 **2.** (curious) adj mezurashíi 珍しい

novelist n shōsetsu-ka 小説家、sak-ka 作家

November n Jūichi-gatsú 十一月・11月

now adv íma 今、(already) mō´ もう

from now on kore kara これから、kongo 今後

just now tadáima ただ今、tsúi imashígata つい今しがた

until now ima-máde 今まで
well now (sore) ja (それ)じゃ, jā´ じゃあ, déwa では, sá-te さて
now then, and now sá-te さて
now and then tama ni たまに
nowhere *adv* doko (de/ni/e) mo どこ(で/に/へ)も + [NEGATIVE]
nuclear *adj* káku (no) 核(の)
nuclear weapon *n* kaku hēki 核兵器
nude 1. *adj* hadaka (no) 裸(の), nūdo (no) ヌード(の); ratai (no) 裸体(の) **2.** *n* nū´do ヌード; (*picture*) ratai-ga 裸体画 → **naked**
nuisance *n* mendō 面倒
numb *adj* mu-kánkaku (na) 無感覚(な); **goes/gets ~** shibiremásu (shibiréru, shibírete)しびれます(しびれる, しびれて)
number *n* kázu 数, sū´ 数, nanbā ナンバー; bán 番, ...-ban ...番; (*written numeral*) sūji bangō´ 数字番号, (*assigned*) bangō´ 番号, (*on an athlete*) zékken ゼッケン; (*large and/or small*) tashō 多少
a number of ... íkutsu ka no ... いくつかの..., nan-[COUNTER] ka no ... 何 [COUNTER] かの..., sū-[COUNTER] no ... 数 [COUNTER] の...
in large numbers ōzéi 大勢, dóndon どんどん, zorozoro ぞろぞろ

the number of days nissū´ 日数, hin-ichi 日にち
the number of people nínzū 人数
the number of times kaisū 回数
numbering *n* nanbaringu ナンバリング
number one *adj* ichí-ban (no) 一番(の)
numbness *n* shibiré しびれ
numeral *n* sūji 数字, sū´ 数
numerous → many
nun *n* áma 尼
nurse 1. *n* kangó-fu 看護婦, nāsu ナース **2.** *v* (*nurses a patient*) kángo shimásu (suru, shite) 看護します(する, して)
nursery *n* takuji-jo 託児所
nursery school *n* (*pre-kindergarten*) hoikú-en 保育園
nursing (*a patient*) *n* kángo 看護, kanbyō 看病
nutrition *n* eiyō 栄養
nuts 1. *n* náttsu ナッツ, kurumi クルミ・胡桃, kí-no-mi 木の実 (*includes fruits and berries*), mi 実・み **2.** *adj* (*mad*) (atama no) ikareta (頭の)イカれた; *Are you nuts?* atama okashiinjanai? 頭おかしいんじゃない?
nylon *n* náiron ナイロン
nymph *n* ninfu ニンフ

O

Oahu *n* Oafu-tō オアフ島
oak *n* ōku オーク
oar *n* kai 櫂・かい, ōru オール
oasis *n* oashisu オアシス
oat *n* ōto mugi オートムギ, karasu mugi カラスムギ
oath *n* chikai (no kotoba) 誓い(の言葉)
obedient *adj* súnao (na) すなお[素直](な)
obeisance *n* (*salute*) keirei 敬礼
obelisk *n* oberisuku オベリスク
obesity *n* himan 肥満
obey (*a person*) *v* (... ga) yū/iu kotó o kikimásu (kiku, kiite) (...が)言う事を聞きます(聞く, 聞いて)
obituary *n* shibō kiji 死亡記事
object 1. *n* taishō 対象; (*thing*) monó

物; buttai 物体; obujekuto オブジェクト; (*objective, goal*) mokuteki 目的, ate 当て; (*aim*) nerai 狙い **2.** *v object to* (*opposes*) ... ni hantai shimásu (suru, shite) ...に反対します(する, して)
objective *n* mokuhyō 目標
obligation *n* (*duty*) gímu 義務, (*responsibility*) sekinin 責任; (*sense of obligation*) girí 義理 (o-giri お義理); (*for a kindness*) ón 恩 (go-ón ご恩)
obliged *adj* **1.** *becomes ~* (*to ... for help*) (...no) sewá ni narimásu (naru, natte) (...の)世話になります(なる, って); *I'm much ~ for all your help.* Iroiro o-séwa ni narimáshita. いろいろ[色々]お世話になりました. **2.** *feels ~* (*grateful*) kyōshuku shimásu (suru,

shite) 恐縮します(する, して)

oblique *adj* (*diagonal*) naname (no) 斜め(の), (*slanting*) hasu (no) はす(の); (*oblique statement*) tōmawashi (no) 遠回し(の)

obliquely *adv* naname ni 斜めに, hasu ni はすに

oblong *n* **1.** (*box*) chōhō-kei 長方形 **2.** (*oval*) chōdaen-kei 長だ円形

obscene *adj* waisetsu (na) わいせつ・猥褻(な)

obscure *adj* (*unknown*) fumei (no) 不明(の); (*unrenowned*) mumei (no) 無名(の) → **dark**

observation *n* kansatsu 観察, kansoku 観測

observatory *n* (*astronomical*) tenmon-dai 天文台; (*weather station*) sokkō-jo 測候所, kishō-dai 気象台; (*sightseeing*) tenbō-dai 展望台

observe *v* **1.** (*happens to see*) kizukimásu (kizuku, kizuite) 気付きます(気付く, 気付いて) **2.** (*watches*) kansatsu/kansoku shimásu (suru, shite) 観察/観測します(する, して) **3.** → **say**

observe a rule *v* okite o mamorimásu (mamoru, mamotte) 掟を守ります(守る, 守って)

observer *n* kansatsú-sha 観察者; tachiai-nin 立会人

obstacle *n* sashitsukae 差し支え; (o-)jama (お)じゃま[邪魔]; shōgai 障害 → **hindrance**

obstruct *v* (*hinders*) samatagemásu (samatageru, samatagete) 妨げます(妨げる, 妨げて); *gets obstructed* (*clogged*) tsukaemásu (tsukáeru, tsukáete) つかえます(つかえる, つかえて)

obstruction *n* shōgai 障害, samatage 妨げ

obtain *v* té ni iremásu (ireru, irete) 手に入れます(入れる, 入れて) → **get**

obvious *adj* meihaku (na) 明白(な), akiraka (na) 明らか(な)

obviously *adv* (*clearly*) meihaku (ni) 明白(に), akiraka (ni) 明らか(に) → **certainly, of course**

occasion *n* (*time*) tokí 時・とき, (*at*

that time) koro 頃・ころ; (*event*) sétsu 節, sái 際, orí おり, jísetsu 時節; (*opportunity*) kikái 機会, tsuide ついで; (*circumstance*) ba(w)ai 場合; *on the occasion of* … ni sái-shite … に際して

occasional *adj* (*infrequent*) tama no たまの; tokidoki no 時々[ときどき]の

occasionally *adv* tamatama たまたま; tama ni たまに; tokidoki 時々

Occident *n* (*the West/Western*) Séiyō 西洋; *Occidental adj* yō-… 洋…

occult *n* okaruto オカルト

occultism *n* shinpi-gaku 神秘学

occultist *n* okaruto shinkō-sha オカルト信仰者

occupant *n* kyojū-sha 居住者

occupation *n* (*job*) shokugyō 職業, shoku 職; (*military*) senryō 占領

occupied *adj* **1.** *is* ~ (*toilet, etc.*) shiyōchū 使用中; (*I'm in here*) Háitte imásu はいっています **2.** (*a seat*) (*They're coming!*) Kimásu 来ます **3.** → **busy** **4.** *gets* ~ (*booked up*) fusagarimásu (fusagaru, fusagatte) ふさがります(ふさがる, ふさがって)

occur *v* okorimásu (okóru, okótte) 起ります(起こる, 起こって), hassei shimásu (suru, shite) 発生します(する, して), shōjimásu (shō-jiru, shō-jite) 生じます(生じる, 生じて); genjitsu-ka shimásu (suru, shite) 現実化します(する, して)

occurrence *n* hassei 発生

ocean *n* taiyō 大洋, taikai/daikai 大海

o'clock *adv* …-ji …時 (4 o'clock yó-ji 四時)

October *n* Ju-gatsú 十月・10月

octopus *n* táko タコ・蛸; *baby* ~ íidako イイダコ・飯蛸

oculist *n* mé-isha 目[眼]医者

odd *adj* (*peculiar, strange*) hén (na) 変(な); kawatta 変わった; kawatteiru 変わっている; okashina おかしな

odor → **smell**

of … *prep* … no …の

of course mochíron もちろん・勿論, muron むろん・無論, móttómo もっとも

off; *time* ~ yasumí 休み; *time* ~ *in lieu of* daikyū 代休; *day* ~ ofu (no hi) オフ

(の日), hiban (no hi) 非番（の日）; *off* (*down in price by*) *¥100* hyakeún-yasu 百円安

off *adv* (*turns*) *off* (*light, radio, etc.*) …o keshimásu (kesu, keshite) …を消します(消す, 消して); (*button, etc.*) *comes ~* toremásu (toréru, tórete) 取れます(取れる, 取れて); (*slips off*) nuke-másu (nukeru, nukete) 抜けます(抜ける, 抜けて); *gets ~* (*a vehicle*) orimásu (oríru, órite) 降ります(降りる, 降りて); *takes ~* (*clothes, shoes*) nugimásu (núgu, núide) 脱ぎます(脱ぐ, 脱いで); *does/ is ~ and on* …-tári/-káttari/dáttari shimásu (suru, shite) …たり/かったり/だったりします(する, して); *gets ~ the track* dassen shimásu (suru, shite) 脱線します(する, して)

off duty (*taxi*) kaisō(-chū) 回送(中); *off duty taxi* kaisō´-sha 回送車

Off Limits "tachiiri kinshi" "立入り禁止"

off-line *n* ofu rain オフライン

off screen **1.** *adj* gamen-gai (no) 画面外(の) **2.** *adv* gamen-gai de 画面外で

off season *n* ofu shiizun オフシーズン, kansanki 閑散期

off the record *n* ofureko オフレコ

offend *v* **1.** (*violates*) … ni ihan shimásu (suru, shite) …に違反します(する, して) **2.** → displease **3.** → anger

offense *n* burei 無礼; ihan 違反

offensive *adj* shaku ni sawaru しゃく [癪]に障る

offer **1.** *n* mōshi-komi 申し込み, ofā オファー; (*makes an offer*) mōshidemásu (mōshideru, mōshidete) 申し出ます(申し出る, 申し出て) **2.** *v* (*propose*) teian shimásu (suru, shite) 提案します(する, して), (*recommend*) susumemásu (susumeru, susumete) 勧めます(勧める, 勧めて)

job offer *n* saiyō 採用

offering *n* mōshi-de 申し出, mōshi-komi 申し込み; (*public*) mōshi-ire 申し入れ; o-sonae お供え

office *n* (*business*) jimú-sho 事務所; (*government*) yakusho 役所 (o-yakusho お役所); (*within the company*) shánai 社内, ofisu オフィス; (*job*) shoku 職,

tsutomé 勤め (o-tsutome お勤め), (*post*) yakú 役; (*place of employment*) tsutome-saki 勤め先

office attendance *n* shukkin 出勤

office clerk/worker *n* jimú-in 事務員

office lady *n* ōeru OL・オーエル

officer *n* (*military*) shō´kō 将校; *police officer* omáwari-san おまわりさん, [FORMAL] keikan 警官

office work *n* jímu 事務

official **1.** *adj* (*public*) ōyake (no) 公(の) **2.** *n* (*a government official*) kōmu-in 公務員; yakunin 役人

offing, offshore *n* oki 沖; *~ from* oki …の沖

often *adv* yóku よく, tabitabi たびたび, hinpan (ni) 頻繁(に), shíbashiba しばしば, sésse-to せっせと

ogre *n* oní 鬼・オニ

oh *interj* wā わあ; ā´ ああ; *oh?* sō´ desu ka そうですか, árá あら; *oh well* mā´ まあ (*tends to be a female expression*)

oil *n* abura 油, (*petroleum, machine oil*) sekiyu 石油, (*for lubricating cars*) óiru オイル; *hair oil* pomā´do ポマード

ointment *n* nuri-gúsuri 塗り薬, nankō 軟膏

O.K. **1.** *adv* íi desu いいです; (*I approve*) sansei (désu) 賛成(です); (*safe; functioning*) daijōbu (désu) 大丈夫(です); ōkē (désu) オーケー(です) **2.** *adj O.K.!* Yóshi! よし!

Okhotsk *n* Ohōtsuku オホーツク; *Sea of Okhotsk* Ohōtsuku-kai オホーツク海

Okinawa *n* Okinawa 沖縄; Ryūkyū´ 琉球

old **1.** *adj* (*not new*) furúi 古い, (*from way back*) mukashi karáno 昔からの, kyū´(-) … 旧… **2.** *adj* (*not young*) toshi-tótta toshi取った, rō-… 老…; *gets old* toshi o torimásu (tóru, tótte) 年を取ります(取る, 取って), fukemásu (fukéru, fukéte) 老けます(老ける, 老けて) **3.** *n* (*old person*) rōjin 老人

how old íkutsu いくつ (o-ikutsu おいくつ), nán-sai 何歳; (*age*) toshí 年

old friend *n* mukashi kará no tomodachi/yūjin 昔からの友達/友人, furuku kará no yūjin 古くからの友人; [BOOKISH] kyū´yū 旧友

488

old maid *n* (*card game*) baba-núki
ばば抜き

older *adj* toshi-ue (no) 年上(の)

older brother *n* áni 兄; (o-)níi-san (お)
兄さん

older sister *n* ane 姉; (o-)né-san (お)
姉さん

oldest *adj* ichiban (toshi-)ue (no) 一番
(年)上(の)

old person *n* toshiyóri 年寄り (o-toshiyori お年寄り), rōjin 老人, kōrei-sha
高齢者, kōrei no hito/kata 高齢の人/方;
(*man*) ojíi-san おじいさん, (*woman*)
obā´-san おばあさん

olive *n* oríibu (no ki) オリーブ (の木)

olive oil *n* oríibu-yu オリーブ油,
oríibu-oiru オリーブオイル

olive branch *n offer an olive branch*
wakai o mōshideru 和解を申し出る

...ology *n* ...-gaku ...学; *biology*
seibutsu-gaku 生物学

omelet *n* omuretsu オムレツ; *omelet
wrapped around rice* omu-ráisu オム
ライス

omen *n* engi 縁起, zenchō 前兆

omission *n* shōryaku 省略, ryaku 略

omit *v* 1. otoshimásu (otósu, otóshite)
落とします(落とす, 落として), habu-
kimásu (habúku, habúite) 省きます
(省く, 省いて), nokemásu (nokeru,
nokete) のけ[除け]ます(のける, のけ
て), nukimásu (nuku, nuite) 抜きます
(抜く, 抜いて), nozokimásu (nozoku,
nozoite) 除きます(除く, 除いて), (*skips*)
tobashimásu (tobasu, tobashite) と
ばし[飛ばし]ます(とばす, とばし
て), (*curtails*) ryakushimásu (ryakúsú,
ryakúshite) 略します(略す, 略して)
2. *gets omitted* ochimásu (ochíru, óchite)
落ちます(落ちる, 落ちて); nukemásu
(nukeru, nukete) 抜けます(抜ける, 抜
けて); moremásu (moréru, mórete) 漏
れます(漏れる, 漏れて)

on *prep* 1. ... de ...で, (*located*) ... ni
...に; (*atop*) ... no ue (de/ni) ...の上
(で/に) 2. *has/puts ~* (*clothes, etc.*)
→ *wear* 3. *turns ~* (*light, radio, etc.*)
... o tsukemásu (tsukéru, tsukéte) ...を
付けます(付ける, 付けて)

on the way tochū 途中

on the whole daitai だいたい・大体

once *adv* ichi-dó 一度, ik-kái 一回;
ichiō 一応・いちおう; (*sometime*) ítsu
ka いつか; *~ did* shitakotó ga arimásu
(áru, átte) 〜した事があります(ある, あ
って); *~ in a while* tama ni たまに

one *n* ichí 一; hítotsu 一つ・ひとつ;
hito-... ひと..., ichi-... いち..., wán ワン;
(*person*) hítori 一人・ひとり (o-hítori
お一人), ichí-mei 一名; *~ of a pair,
the other ~* katáhō 片方, katáppō 片っ
方, katáppo 片っぽ

one after another tsugí-tsugi ni 次々
に, zokuzoku 続々, áitsuide 相次いで

one and the same hítotsu 一つ・ひと
つ

one by one ichi-ichi 一々; (*objects*)
hítotsu-zutsu 一つ[ひとつ]ずつ,
(*people*) hítori-zutsu 一人[ひとり]ずつ

one; *1 piece* (*small thing*) ík-ko 一個,
1 tree (*or long things*) íp-pon 一本;
1 sheet (*flat thing*) ichi-mái 一枚; *1 cat*
(*or small animals*) ip-piki 一匹; *1 cow*
(*or large aminals*) ít-tō 一頭; *1 bird/
rabbit* ichí-wa 一羽; *1 car* (*or machines/
vehicles*) ichí-dai 一台; *1 copy* (*book/
magazine*) is-satsú 一冊; *1 person*
hitó-ri ひとり・一人, ichí-mei 一名;
1 time ichi-dó 一度, ik-kái 一回, ip-pén
一遍; *1 degree* ichí-do 一度; *1 o'clock*
ichí-ji 一時; *1 hour* ichí-jikan 一時間;
1 day ichi-nichí 一日; *1 week* is-shūkan
一週間; *1 month* íkkágetsu 一ヶ月;
íkkagetsu-kan 一ヶ月間; *1 year* ichí-
nen 一年, ichí-nénkan 一年間; *1 year
old* hítotsu 一つ, ís-sai 一歳; *1 yen*
ichi-en 一円

one day *n* ichi-nichí 一日; (*a certain day*)
áru hi ある日; (*someday*) ichijitsú 一日

one leg/foot *n* kata-ashi 片足

one-room (studio) apartment *n* wan-
rū´mu ワンルーム

oneself *pron* jibun 自分; wáre 我;
oneself (as we might expect) sasuga
no ... さすがの...; *talking to ~* hítori-
goto 独り言

one side *n* ippō´ 一方

one-time *adj* ichí-ji (no) 一時(の),
kátsute (no) かつて(の), ízen (no)
以前(の)

one word *n* ichí-go 一語
one-way *adj* (*ticket*) katamichi-(-kíppu) 片道(切符); (*traffic*) ippō-tsū´kō 一方通行
onion *n* (*green*) négi ネギ・葱, naga-negi 長ねぎ・ナガネギ; (*green chive*) nira ニラ・韮; (*round bulb*) tama- négi 玉ねぎ・タマネギ
only *adj* táda … ただ…, tatta … たった…, … daké…だけ, …bákari …ばかり; … ni sugínai (sugimasén) …に過ぎない(過ぎません)
Ontario *n* Ontario オンタリオ
oops *interj* otto おっと, o' おっ, a' あっ
opaque *adj* futōmei (na) 不透明(な)
opal *n* opáru オパール
OPEC *n* (*Organization of Petroleum Exporting Countries*) Sekiyu yushutsu-koku kikō 石油輸出国機構
open *v* **1.** *opens it* akemásu (akeru, akete) 開けます(開ける, 開けて), (*opens it up*) hirakimásu (hiráku, hiráite) 開きます(開く, 開いて); (*begins it*) hajimemásu (hajimeru, hajimete) 始めます(始める, 始めて) **2.** *it opens* akimásu (aku, aite) 開きます(開く, 開いて); (*it begins*) hajimarimásu (hajimaru, hajimatte) 始まります(始まる, 始まって), (*a place, an event*) ō´pun shimásu (suru, shíte) オープンします(する, して), kaijō shimásu (suru, shíte) 開場します(する, して), (*a shop/business*) kaiten shimásu (suru, shíte) 開店します(する, して) **3.** *~ to the public* kōkai (no) 公開(の); *opens it to the public* kōkai shimásu (suru, shíte) 公開します(する, して)
open door *n* (*admission free*) nyūjō muryō 入場無料
open-minded *adj* **1.** (*broad-minded*) kokoro no hiroi 心の広い **2.** (*unprejudiced*) henken no nai 偏見のない
open-mouthed *adj* (*dumbfounded*) azen to shita 唖然とした
opener *n* (*can*) kan-kírí 缶切り; (*bottle*) sen-nuki 栓抜き
opening *n* **1.** (*inlet*) kuchi 口 **2.** (*gap*) suki(-ma) 透き/隙(間) **3.** (*of a place*) kaijō 開場, ō´pun オープン; *~ ceremony* kaijō/kaikai-shiki 開場/開

公式; *~ time* kaijō-jíkan 開場時間
4. (*book*) bōtō 冒頭
job opening *n* shūshoku-guchi 就職口
open(ly) *adv* (*publicly*) kōzen (no/to) 公然(の/と), ōyake (no/ni) 公(の/に); (*candid*) ō´pun (na/ni) オープン(な/に), sotchoku (na/ni) 率直(な/に)
open (public) space *n* (*plaza*) híro-bá 広場
open space parking *n* okugai chūsha-jō 屋外駐車場
opera *n* kágeki 歌劇, ópera オペラ
operate *v* (*machinery*) sōjū shimásu (suru, shíte) 操縦します(する, して); (*vehicle*) unten shimásu (suru, shíte) 運転します(する, して); (*machinery*) ugokashimásu (ugokásu, ugokáshite) 動かします(動かす, 動かして); (*business*) keiei shimásu (suru, shíte) 経営します(する, して)
operation *n* (*surgical*) shújutsu 手術; (*driving*) unten 運転; (*handling*) sōjū 操縦; (*management*) keiei 経営; (*working*) sagyō 作業, shigoto 仕事
operator *n* (*telephone*) (denwa) kōkánshu (電話)交換手; operēta オペレーター **2.** (*vehicle*) unténshu 運転手 **3.** (*business*) keiéisha 経営者
opinion *n* íken 意見, go-íken ご意見, kangáe 考え, hyō´ka 評価; (*outlook*) mikomi 見込み, (*observation*) kansoku 観測; *public opinion* yóron 世論
opium *n* ahen アヘン・阿片
opponent *n* (*sports*) aité 相手 (o-aite お相手); taikō-sha 対抗者; (*rival*) teki 敵
opportunity *n* kikái 機会; chansu チャンス; (*opening*) suki(-ma) 透き/隙(間); (*opportune time*) jíki 時機, jísetsu 時節; (*convenience*) tsugō 都合, tsuide ついで
oppose *v* … ni hantai shimásu (suru, shíte) …に反対します(する, して), … o kobamimásu (kobámu, kobánde) …を拒みます(拒む, 拒んで); (*resists*) … ni hankō shimásu (suru, shíte) …に反抗します(する, して); … to tairitsu shimásu (suru, shíte) …と対立します(する, して), …ni taikō shimásu (suru, shíte) …に対抗します(する, し

て); (*faces*) … ni mukaimásu (mukau, mukatte) …に向かいます(向かう、向かって)

opposite *adj* (*facing*) mukō (no) 向こう(の), (o-)múkai (no) (お)向かい(の), (*contrary*) gyaku (no) 逆(の), (*opposing*) hantai (no) 反対(の)

opposite side *n* hantai-gawa 反対側, mukō-gawa 向こう側

opposition *n* (*resistance*) hankō 反抗; (*confrontation*) taikō 対抗; *in opposition to* … ni taikō shíte …に対抗して; *opposition party* yatō 野党

oppress *v* appaku shimásu (suru, shite) 圧迫します(する、して)

oppression *n* appaku 圧迫

optimism *n* rakkan/rakuten (shugi) 楽観/楽天(主義)

optimistic *adj* rakkan-teki (na) 楽観的(な)

optional *adj* zuii (no) 随意(の), nin'i (no) 任意(の)

or *conj* … ka …か; mátá-wa または・又は
or else sore-tómo それとも, mátá-wa または・又は, arúiwa あるいは・或いは
or something (*like it*) … tó ka … とか

oral *adj* **1.** kuchi no 口の, kuchi kará no (口からの); keikō(-) 経口(-); *oral contraceptive* keikōhinín'yaku 経口避妊薬 **2.** (*verbal*) kōtō (no) 口頭(の); *oral examination* kōtō-shímon 口頭試問

orange *n* orénji オレンジ, (*Mandarin orange, tangerine*) míkan みかん・蜜柑, (*bitter*) daidái ダイダイ・橙

orange drink/soda pop (*orange juice*) orenji-jū´su オレンジジュース

orbit *n* kidō 軌道

orchestra *n* ōkesutora オーケストラ

orchid *n* rán 蘭・ラン

order 1. *n* júnjo 順序, jun 順; *alphabetical ~* ē-bii-shii (ABC)-jun エービーシー[ABC]順; (*turn*) junban 順番 **2.** *n* (*grade, step*) dán 段, dankai 段階 **3.** *n* (*procedure*) tejun 手順 **4.** *n* (*rule*) kimari 決まり; chitsujo 秩序 **5.** *n* (*command*) meirei 命令 **6.** *v* (*clothes, meal, etc.*) chūmon shimásu (suru, shite) 注文します(する、して)

7. *v* (*a person to do something*) … ni ii-tsukemásu (ii-tsukéru, ii-tsukéte) …に言い付けます(言い付ける、言い付けて), meijimásu (meijiru, meijite) 命じます(命じる、命じて)
puts in order (*tidies up*) katazukemásu (katazukéru, katazukéte) 片付けます(片付ける、片付けて); (*arranges as a set*) soroemásu (soroéru, soroete) 揃えます(そろえる、そろえて)

ordinarily *adv* heijō (ni) 平常(に), futsū (ni) 普通・ふつう(に), fúdan (wa) 普段・ふだん(は)

ordinary *adj* futsū (no) 普通・ふつう(の), tsūjō (no) 通常(の), túsne (no) 常(の), fúdan (no) 普段・ふだん(の), táda (no) ただ(の); (*average*) nami (no) 並(の)

organic *adj* ōganikku (no) オーガニック(の), yūki (no) 有機(の)

organization *n* (*setup*) soshiki 組織; (*structure*) kumi-tate 組み立て, kōzō 構造; (*group*) dantai 団体

organize *v* (*sets up*) kumi-tatemásu (kumi-tateru, kumi-tatete) 組み立てます(組み立てる、組み立てて); hensei shimásu (suru, shite) 編成します(する、して)

Orient *n* Tō´yō 東洋; Oriento オリエント

Orient Express *n* Oriento kyūkō オリエント急行

Oriental *adj* Tō´yō (no) 東洋(の)

origin *n* kígen 起源, (*cause*) gen'in 原因, moto 元, okorí 起こり, hassei 発生; (*historical origin*) engi 縁起; (*a person's origins*) de 出

originally *adv* móto wa 元は, moto moto もともと・元々, hónrai wa 本来は, gánrai wa 元来は; (*in itself*) jitai 自体

Orion *n* **1.** orion オリオン **2.** (*star sign*) Orion-za オリオン座

ornament *n* kazari(-mono) 飾り(物), sōshoku-hin 装飾品, (*decoration*) sōshoku 装飾, (*bric-a-brac*) oki-mono 置き物

ornamentation *n* sōshoku-hin 装飾品

ornate *adj* karei (na) 華麗(な)

orphan *n* kóji 孤児; *orphanage* *n* kojí-in 孤児院

Osaka *n* Ōsaka 大阪; *Osaka Station* Osaká-Eki 大阪駅

Oscar *n* Osukā オスカー

Oslo *n* Osuro オスロ

other *adj* hoka (no) 他(の), betsu (no) 別(の); [BOOKISH] tá (no) 他(の);
other companies tásha 他社 → every other

in other words *conj* sunáwachi すなわち, 即ち

the other day *adv* kon[o]aidá こないだ[この間]

the other fellow *n* aité 相手 (o-aite お相手)

the other side *n* senpō 先方

on the other hand tahō de wa 他方では

other than … yóri …より

otherwise *adv* sá-mo nákereba さもなければ, sō´shinai to そうしないと

otherwise known as *adj* betsumei 別名

Ottawa *n* Otawa オタワ

otter *n* kawauso カワウソ

ouch! *interj* itái! 痛い!, itái! イタ(ッ)!

ought to *auxiliary verb* **ought to (do)** (shi)-ta hố´ga íi deshō (し)た方がいいでしょう, [BOOKISH] (su)-ru béki desu (す)るべきです

ounce *n* onsu オンス

our(s) *pron* watakushí-tachi no (watáshí-táchi no) わたくし[私]達の (わたし[私]達の)

out 1. *adv* sóto e/ni 外へ/に; (*away from home*) (…)rúsu (desu) (お)留守(です), gaishutsu-chū (désu) 外出中(です); *come/go out* (… kara) demásu (déru, déte) (…から)出ます(出る, 出て); *let out* (*of a vehicle*) oroshimásu (orosu, oroshíte) 降ろします(降ろす, 降ろして) **2.** *adj* (*baseball*) áuto (no) アウト(の)

out loud *adv* kóe o dáshite 声を出して

out of order; *gets* ~ kuruimásu (kurū´, kurútte) 狂います(狂う, 狂って); (*broken machine*) koshō shiteimásu (shiteiru, shiteite) 故障しています(している, していて)

out of place *n* ba-chígai (no) 場違い(の); *slips* ~ zuremásu (zuréru, zúrete) ずれます(ずれる, ずれて)

out of service *n, adj* kaisō(-chū) 回送(中); *a car* ~ kaisō-sha 回送車

out of the way; *gets* ~ dokimásu (doku, doite) どき[退き]ます(どく, どいて), nokimásu (noku, noite) のき[退き]ます(のく, のいて)

out of touch with … *adj* ni utói …にうとい・疎い

outage *n* (*power outage*) teiden 停電

out-and-out *adv* kanzen (na) 完全(な); tettei-teki (na) 徹底的(な); tettei-shita 徹底した

outback *n* okuchi 奥地

out-box *n* (*e-mail*) sōshin bokkusu 送信ボックス

outbound *adj* (*from Tokyo*) kudari 下り

outbreak *n* toppatsu 突発; hassei 発生

outbuilding *n* hanare 離れ

outburst *n* bakuhatsu 爆発

outcome *n* (*of situation*) ketsumatsu 結末; (*result*) séika 成果; (*product*) sanbutsu 産物; (*medical diagnosis*) tenki 転帰

outdoor(s) *adj* (*adv*) sóto no (/de/ni/e) 外の(/で/に/へ); yagai no (/de) 野外の(/で); autodoa (no) アウトドア(の); okugai no (/de/ni/e) 屋外の(/で/に/へ); *outdoor bath* noten-búro 野天風呂

outer *adj* ~ *appearance* uwabe うわべ・上辺; ~ *lane/track* auto-kố´su アウトコース; ~ *moat* soto-bori 外堀; ~ *side/surface* omoté 表; ~ *space* úchū 宇宙

outfit *n judo* ~ jūdō´-gi 柔道着; *karate* ~ karaté-gí 空手着

outflow *n* de 出; ryūshutsu 流出

outing *n* (*picnic etc.*) ensoku 遠足

outlet *n* **1.** déguchi 出口; (*for water/ emotion/goods*) haké-kuchi/-guchi はけ口; (*sales outlet*) uri-kuchi 売れ口; (*store*) chokubái-ten 直売店 **2.** (*electric outlet*) kónsénto コンセント; (*plug*) sashi-komi 差し込み, puragu プラグ

outline *n* **1.** (*synopsis*) gaiyō 概要, auto rain アウトライン **2.** (*line*) rinkaku 輪郭

outlook *n* mikomi 見込み, mitōshi 見通し

output *n* auto putto アウトプット, seisan 生産, sanshutsu 産出

outrage *n* ranbō 乱暴 → **indignation**

outrageous *adj* tonde-mo nái とんでもない, tonda とんだ

outset *n* (*beginning*) hána はな・端, saisho 最初, shoppana しょっぱな

outside **1.** *adv* sóto (de/ni) 外(で/に); ~ *of* (*other than*) … no hoka …の他、… ígai …以外 **2.** *adj* soto-gawa 外側(の), sóto (no) 外(の) **3.** *n the outside* soto-gawa 外側, hata はた・端, gáibu 外部, gaimen 外面

outside corner *n* kádo 角

outsider *n* (*stranger*) yosó no hitó よその人, yoso-mono よそ者, tanin 他人, mongái-kan 門外漢, bugaisha 部外者

outsize *adj* tokudai 特大(の)

outskirts *n* (*suburb*) shígai 市外, kōgai 郊外, (tóshi no) shūhen (都市の)周辺

outsourcing *n* autosōshingu アウトソーシング, gyōmu itaku 業務委託, gai-chū 外注, gaibu hatchū 外部発注

outspread *adj* hirogatta 広がった

outstanding *adj* medátta 目立った, kencho (na) 顕著(な), medátte imásu 目立っています

outstandingly *adv* medátte 目立って, ichijirushiku 著しく・いちじるしく

outward **1.** *adj* soto (no) 外の, (*ostensible*) mikake jō no 見かけ上(の), hyōmen jō (no) 表面上(の) **2.** *adv* soto e 外へ

outward appearance *n* mikake 見かけ

outwardly *adv* mikake wa 見かけは

outwitted; *gets ~* (*tricked*) goma-kasaremásu (gomakaséreru, goma-kasárete) ごまかされ[誤魔化され]ます(ごまかされる, ごまかされて)

oval **1.** *n* daen(-kei) 楕円・だ円(形) **2.** *adj* daen-kei (no) 楕円[だ円]形(の)

ovation *n* daikassai 大喝采; *standing ~* sutandingu obēshon スタンディング・オベーション

ovary *n* ransō 卵巣, (*plant*) shibō 子房

oven *n* ōbun オーブン, témpi 天火, kama かま・窯, kamado かまど・竈

oven-proof *adj* ōbun tainetsu-sei (no) オーブン耐熱性(の)

over **1.** *prep* (*above*) … no ue (de/ni) …の上(で/に), … o ōimásu (ōu, ōtte) …を覆います(覆う, 覆って); (*more than*) … ijō 以上; … yori ōku …より多く; … o sugimásu (sugiru, sugite) …を過ぎます(過ぎる, 過ぎて); … o koemásu (koeru, koete) …を超えます(超える, 超えて) **2.** *adj* (*above*)… no ue (no) …の上(の) **3.** *adv* (*above*) ue (ni) 上(に); (*covered*) ichimen (ni) 一面(に); (*finished*) owarimashita (owatta, owatte) 終わりました(終わった, 終わって); (*run over*) kurikae-shimásu (kurikaesu, kurikaeshite) 繰り返します(繰り返す, 繰り返して) **4.** *v* (*recover*) (byōki ga) naorimásu (naoru, naotte) (病気が)治ります(治る, 治って)

over there mukō 向こう, mukai 向かい, sochira/sotchi そちら/そっち, achira/atchi あちら/あっち, (*other side*) mukō gawa ni 向こう側に

over again → **again**

overage *adj* tekirei(-ki) o sugita 適齢(期)を過ぎた, nenrei seigen o koeta 年齢制限を越えた

overall **1.** *adj* (*composite*) sōgō-teki (na) 総合的(な), zentai-teki (na) 全体的(な) **2.** *adv* sōgō-teki (ni) 総合的(に), zentai-teki (ni) 全体的(に)

overalls *n* (*coveralls*) tsunagi つなぎ

overcharge *v* ~ (*for*) fukkakemásu (fukkakéru, fukkákete) ふっかけます(ふっかける, ふっかけて); *gets overcharged for* fukkakeraremásu (fukkakeraréru, fukkakerárete) ふっかけられます(ふっかける, ふっかけられて)

overcoat *n* ō'bā オーバー, kōto コート, gaitō 外套

overcome *v* uchikachimásu (uchi-katsu, uchikatte) 打ち勝ちます(打ち勝つ, 打ち勝って), kokufuku shimásu (suru, shite) 克服します(する, して)

overdo *v overdo (it)* múri o shimásu (suru, shite) 無理をします(する, して), (sore o) múri ni yarimásu (yaru, yatte) (それを)無理にやります(やる, やって)

overeducate *v* kajō (ni) kyōiku shimásu (suru, shite) 過剰(に)教育します(する, して)

overestimate 1. n kadai hyōka 過大評価 **2.** v kadai hyōka shimásu (suru, shite) 過大評価します(する, して)

overemphasize v kyōchō shisugimásu (shisugiru, shisugite) 強調し過ぎます(しすぎる, しすぎて)

overexcited adj kajō ni kōfun shita 過剰に興奮した

overexpose v roshutsu shisugimásu (shisugiru, shisugite) 露出し過ぎます(しすぎる, しすぎて)

overexposure n roshutsu kado 露出過度

over-familiar adj narenareshii なれなれしい・馴れ馴れしい

overflow v afuremásu (afuréru, afúrete) あふれ[溢れ]ます(あふれる, あふれて); hanran shimásu (suru, shite) 氾濫します(する, して)

overflowing n hanran 氾濫

overheat 1. n kanetsu 過熱, (engine, etc.) ōbā hiito オーバーヒート **2.** v kanetsu shimásu (suru, shite) 過熱します(する, して), (engine, etc.) ōbā hiito shimásu (suru, shite) オーバーヒートします(する, して)

overhype v hade ni senden shimásu (suru, shite) 派手に宣伝します(する, して)

overlap v kasanarimásu (kasanaru, kasanatte) 重なります(重なる, 重なって), [INFORMAL] daburimásu (dabúru, dabútte) だぶります(だぶる, だぶって)

overly adv amari ni mo あまりにも; ... -sugimásu (-sugíru, -súgite) ...過ぎます(過ぎる, 過ぎて); ~ **strict** yakamashíi やかましい

over-optimism n chō rakkan shugi 超楽観主義, chō rakuten-teki/ka 超楽天的/家

overprice v takane o tsukesugimásu (tsukesugiru, tsukesugite) 高値を付け過ぎます(付け過ぎる, 付け過ぎて)

overprint v **1.** surikasanemásu (surikasaneru, surikasanete) 刷り重ねます(刷り重ねる, 刷り重ねて) **2.** surisugimásu (surisugiru, surisugite) 刷り過ぎます(刷り過ぎる, 刷り過ぎて)

overseas adj káigai 海外; ~ **travel** kaigai-ryokō 海外旅行

oversee v kantoku shimásu (suru, shite) 監督します(する, して)

overseer n kantoku 監督

overshoes n ōbāshū'zu オーバーシューズ

overshoot v ikisugimásu (ikisugiru, ikisugite) 行き過ぎます(行き過ぎる, 行き過ぎて)

overtake v ... ni oi-tsukimásu (oi-tsukú, oi-tsúite) ...に追い付きます(追い付く, 追い付いて)

overthrow v taoshimásu (taósu, taóshite) 倒します(倒す, 倒して), hikkuri kaeshimásu (kaésu, kaéshite) ひっくり返します(返す, 返して)

overtime; runs ~ jikan ga ō'bā shimásu (suru, shite) 時間がオーバーします(する, して); ~ **work** zangyō 残業

overwork v múri o shimásu (suru, shite) 無理をします(する, して)

owe v (borrow money) (hito ni kane o) karite imásu (iru, ite) (人に金を)借りています(いる, いて)

owing adj ~ **to** ... (no) séi de... (の)せいで → **because**

owl n fukúrō' フクロウ・梟

own 1. v (possesses) mótte imásu (iru, ite) 持っています(いる, いて) **2.** adj (one's own) jibun no 自分の, shoyū no 所有の

owner n (mochí-)nushi (持ち)主, shoyūsha 所有者; (master) shújin 主人, ōnā オーナー; (landowner) ji-nushi 地主

ox n (cattle) ushi 牛・ウシ, (male) o-ushi 雄牛 (plural; oxen) (how many nán-tō 何頭)

oxidant n sanka-zai 酸化剤, okishidanto オキシダント

oxter n waki no shita 脇の下・わきの下

oxydol n okishidōru オキシドール

oxygen n sánso 酸素

oxygenate v sanka shimásu (suru, shite) 酸化します(する, して)

oxygen mask n sanso masuku 酸素マスク

oyster n káki カキ・牡蠣, oisutā オイスター

ozone n ozon オゾン
ozone layer n ozon sō オゾン層

P

pace n pḗsu ペース, hochō 歩調
  walking pace n aruku hayasa 歩く速
  さ, aruku sokudo 歩く速度
pacemaker n pḗsu mḗkā ペースメー
  カー
Pacific Ocean n Taiheiyō 太平洋
pacifier n (for baby) o-sháburi おしゃ
  ぶり
pacifism n heiwa shugi 平和主義
pacifist n heiwa shugi-sha 平和主義者,
  hansen shugi-sha 反戦主義者
pacify v shizumemásu (shizuméru,
  shizúmete) 静め[鎮め]ます(静め[鎮
  め]る, 静め[鎮め]て); (soothes) nadamemásu (nadaméru, nadámete) なだ
  めます(なだめる, なだめて); (suppresses
  an uprising) osamemásu (osaméru,
  osámete) 収めます(収める, 収めて)
pack 1. n (of cards) (toránpu) hitó-kumi
  (トランプ)一組; (package of
  cigarettes) (tabako) hitó-hako (たばこ)
  一箱 2. v (one's bags) ni-zúkuri o
  shimásu (suru, shite) 荷造りをします
  (する, して) 3. v (wraps it up)
  tsutsumimásu (tsutsúmu, tsutsúnde)
  包みます(包む, 包んで); hōsō shimásu
  (suru, shite) 包装します(する, して)
package n kozútsumi 小包, nimotsu
  荷物, pakkḗji パッケージ → **package**
package deal n setto hanbai セット
  販売
package tour n pakkḗji tsuā パッケー
  ジツアー, pakku ryokō パック旅行
packed adj 1. (full) tsumatte(i)ru 詰ま
  って(いる), tsumatta 詰まった
  2. (crowded) konde(i)ru 混んで(いる),
  konda 混んだ
  packed train n man'in densha 満員
  電車
packer n (person) konpō gyōsha 梱包
  業者
packet n (kogata) hōsō´-butsu (小型)
  包装物, kozútsumi 小包
pact n kyōtei 協定, jōyaku 条約
pad n (note pad) memo-chō メモ帳
  sketch pad n suketchi bukku スケッ
  チブック

  shin pad n sune-ate 脛当て・すね当て
shoulder pad n kata-ate 肩当て, kata
  paddo 肩パッド
padded; **~ garment** wata-iré 綿入れ; **~
  bathrobe** tánzén 丹前, dotera どてら;
  ~ quilt futon 布団 (o-futón お布団)
paddle n kai 櫂
paddy n suiden 水田
padlock n nankinjō 南京錠
page n pḗji ページ・頁
pagoda n tō´ 塔
pagurian n yadokari ヤドカリ
pail n te-oke 手桶
pain 1. n itamí 痛み; (suffering) kurushimi 苦しみ, (trouble, bother) mendō
  面倒; takes (great) pains honé o orimásu
  (óru, ótte) 骨を折ります(折る, 折って)
  2. v (distresses) kurushimemásu (kurushiméru, kurushímete) 苦しめます(苦
  しめる, 苦しめて)
painful adj itái 痛い; kurushíi 苦しい,
  tsurai 辛い
paint 1. n penki ペンキ, enogu 絵の具,
  tosō 塗装 2. v (penki o) nurimásu (nuru,
  nutte) (ペンキを)塗ります(塗る, 塗
  って); (picture) e o kakimásu (káku,
  káite) 絵を描きます(描く, 描いて)
paintbox n enogubako 絵の具箱
paintbrush n efude 絵筆
painter n (artist) gaka 画家; (house-
  painter) penki-ya ペンキ屋
painting n (picture) é 絵, (oil color)
  abura e 油絵, ...-ga ...画; (watercolor)
  suisai-ga 水彩画
pair n (it-) tsui (一)対; pea ペア; (of
  foot-wear) is-sokú 一足 → **two**
  a pair of n (it-)tsui (no) (一)対(の);
  hitokumi (no) 一組(の); (animal)
  tsugai (no) つがい(の)
paisley n (of pattern) (moyō) (no)
  pēzurii (模様) (no)
  ペーズリー(模様)(の)
pajamas n pajama パジャマ; nemaki
  寝巻き
Pakistan n Pakisutan パキスタン
Pakistani adj Pakisutan (no) パキスタ
  ン(の), (person) Pakisutan-jin (no)
  パキスタン人(の)

pal n nakamá 仲間 (o-nakama お仲間)
　pen pal n pen paru ペンパル, pen
　furendo ペンフレンド, buntsū nakama
　文通仲間, buntsū tomodachi 文通友達
palace n (in Tokyo) kō´kyo 皇居;
　(in Kyoto) gósho 御所; (in general)
　kyūden 宮殿, paresu パレス
Palau n (republic nation of south
　Pacific ocean) Parao パラオ
pale adj **1.** (color) (iro ga) usui (色が)
　薄い; usui […iro] (no) 薄い[…色] (の)
　2. (face) (kao ga) aói (顔が) 青い, (kao
　ga) aojiroi (顔が) 青白い; **turns ~** kao
　ga áoku narimásu (náru, nátte) 顔が青
　くなります (なる, なって)
Palestine n Paresuchina パレスチナ
palette n paretto パレット
palindrome n kaibun 回文
palladium n parajiumu パラジウム
palm n (tree) yáshi ヤシ・椰子; (palm
　of hand) té-nó-hira 手のひら・掌
palmistry n tesō 手相
pamper v amayakashimásu (amaya-
　kasu, amayakashite) 甘やかします (甘
　やかす, 甘やかして)
pamphlet n pánfurétto パンフレット;
　(leaflet, handbill) bira びら・ビラ,
　chirashi ちらし・チラシ
pan n nábe 鍋 (o-nabe お鍋); **food
　cooked and served in a pan** nabé-mono
　鍋物; nabe-ryōri 鍋料理
panacea n bannō-yaku 万能薬
Panama n Panama パナマ
Panama Canal n Panama unga パナ
　マ運河
pancake n pankēki パンケーキ,
　hottokēki ホットケーキ; **seasoned ~**
　okonomiyaki お好み焼き; **pancake
　mix** hottokēki no moto ホットケー
　キの素
pancreas n suizō 膵臓・すい臓
panda n panda パンダ
Pandora's box n pandora no hako
　パンドラの箱
pandowdy n (baked fruit pie) appuru
　pai アップルパイ
panel n paneru パネル
　panel discussion n paneru
　disukasshon パネルディスカッション
　panel house n baishun yado 売春宿

panelist n kaitō-sha 解答者・回答者,
　shutsujō-sha 出場者
pan-fry v itememásu (itaméru, itámete)
　炒めます (炒める, 炒めて)
panic n pánikku パニック, [BOOKISH]
　kyōkō 恐慌
pant v (for breath) aegimásu (aégu,
　aéide) あえぎ[喘ぎ]ます (あえぐ, あ
　えいで)
panther n hyō ヒョウ・豹, pyūma
　ピューマ
panties n pántii パンティー, pántsu
　パンツ
pantomime n pantomaimu パントマイム
pantry n (dish cupboard) shokki(tó)
　dana 食器 (戸) 棚; (room) shokuryō´-
　ko 食料庫
pants n zubón ズボン, (slacks)
　surákkusu スラックス; (underpants)
　zubon-shita ズボン下; (women's)
　pántaron パンタロン
panty hose n pantii stokukkingu
　(pansuto) パンティーストッキング
　(パンスト)
papa n papa パパ, o-tōsan おとうさん
　・お父さん, o-tōchan おとうちゃん・
　お父ちゃん
papaya n papaiya パパイヤ
paper n **1.** kamí 紙; yōshi 用紙,
　(squared) genkōyō´shi 原稿用紙,
　(tissues) chiri-gami ちり紙, tisshu
　ティッシュ; (Japanese) wáshi 和紙;
　colored ~ irógami 色紙 **2.** (news-
　paper) shinbun 新聞, (morning) chōkan
　朝刊, (evening) yūkan 夕刊 **3.** (research
　report) happyō 発表 **4. →** document
　paper bag n kami-búkuro 紙袋
　paperclip n kami-básami 紙挟み,
　kuríppu クリップ
　paperfolding (art) n orígami 折り紙
　・おりがみ
　paper-hanger/-repairer n hyōgu-ya
　表具屋 (picture-framer)
　paper money n shihei/shíhei 紙幣,
　(o-)satsu (お) 札; (currency bills)
　…-satsu …札 (two $100 bills hyaku-
　dorú-satsu ní-mai 百ドル札二枚)
　paperweight n bunchin 文鎮
Papist n katorikku kyōto カトリック
　教徒

paprika *n* papurika パプリカ
Papua New Guinea *n* Papua nyūginia パプアニューギニア
papyrus *n* papirusu パピルス
parable *n* [BOOKISH] gūwa 寓話
parabola *n* hōbutsu sen 放物線
　parabola antenna *n* parabora antena パラボラアンテナ
parachute *n* parashūto パラシュート
parade *n* parēdo パレード, gyōretsu 行列, (*march*) kōshin 行進; demo kōshin デモ行進
　fancy-dress parade *n* kasō gyōretsu 仮装行列
　parade ground *n* [BOOKISH] eppei-jō 閲兵場
paradise *n* tengoku 天国, gokuraku 極楽, paradaisu パラダイス
paradox *n* paradokkusu パラドックス, gyakusetsu 逆説, mujun 矛盾
paraffin *n* parafin パラフィン
paraglider *n* paraguraidā パラグライダー
paragraph *n* danraku 段落, setsu 節, paragurafu パラグラフ
Paraguay *n* Paraguai パラグアイ
parakeet *n* inko インコ
parallel *n* heikō 並行
　parallel bars *n* heikō bō 平行棒
　parallel lines *n* heikō sen 平行線
paralysis *n* (*medical*) mahi 麻痺;
　infantile paralysis (*polio*) shōni-mahi 小児麻痺
paralytic *n* mahi kanja 麻痺患者
Paramatman *n* (*Hindy belief*) taiga 大我
paramecium *n* zōri mushi ゾウリムシ
parameter *n* paramēta パラメータ, paramētā パラメーター; hensū 変数
paramount *adj* saikō (no) 最高(の); shijō (no) 至上(の)
paraphrase *n* parafurēzu パラフレーズ
parasite *n* parasaito パラサイト, isōrō 居候, (*worm*) kiseichū 寄生虫
parasol *n* hi-gása 日傘; (*beach umbrella*) parasoru パラソル
parcel *n* kozútsumi 小包, nimotsu 荷物
parcel post *n* kozutsumi-yū´bin 小包郵便
parchment *n* yōhishi 羊皮紙

pardon *v* yurushimásu (yurúsu, yurú-shite) 許します(許す, 許して)
　Pardon? (*say once more*) [POLITE] Mō ichido osshatte kudasai. もう一度おっしゃって下さい.; (*male*) Nandatte! 何だって!; (*female*) Nandesutte! 何ですって!; Shitsúrei desu ga. 失礼ですが. → **Sorry?, Excuse me.**
　Pardon me! Shitsúrei shimásu. 失礼します; Sumimasén すみません; Gomennasai. ごめんなさい.
pare *v* (*peels it*) mukimásu (muku, muite) むき[剥き]ます(むく, むいて)
paregoric *n* (*medicine*) geri-dome 下痢止め
parent *n* oyá 親, kata oya 片親, *your parent* oyagosan 親御さん; *one's parents* oyátachi 親達, (*father and mother*) ryō´shin 両親, *your parents* go-ryō´shin ご両親
　parent and child *n* óyako 親子
　parent directory *n* (*computer*) oya direkutori 親ディレクトリ
　parent-teacher association *n* pii tii ei PTA
parentage *n* kakei 家系; umare 生まれ
parenthesis *n* (maru) kakko (丸)括弧・カッコ
parenting *n* ikuji 育児; kosodate 子育て
paresthesia *n* (*medical*) kankaku ijō 感覚異常; chikaku ijō 知覚異常
parfait *n* pafe パフェ
Paris *n* Pári パリ
parish *n* kyō(-kai) ku 教(会)区
park *n* kōen 公園; (*parking lot*) chūsha-jō 駐車場
park *v* (*a car*) chūsha shimásu (suru, shite) 駐車します(する, して)
parking *n* chūsha 駐車
　free parking *n* muryō chū´shajō 無料駐車場
　No parking *n* chūsha kinshi 駐車禁止
　paid parking *n* yūryō chūshajō 有料駐車場
　parking fee *n* chūsha ryōkin 駐車料金
　parking lot *n* chūsha-jō 駐車場
　parking meter *n* pākingu mēta パーキングメーター, chūsha ryōkin-kei 駐車料金計

parking ticket *n* chūsha ihan no kippu 駐車違反の切符

parliament → Diet

parliamentary *adj* gikai (no) 議会(の)

parlor *n* (*drawing room*) kyakuma 客間
  beauty parlor *n* biyōin 美容院, byūtii saron ビューティサロン
  ice-cream parlor *n* aisu kuriimu-ten アイスクリーム店, aisu kuriimu pārā アイスクリームパーラー
  mahjong parlor *n* mājan-ya マージャン[麻雀]屋; jansō 雀荘

parody *n* parodii パロディ; mojiri もじり

parrot *n* ōmu オウム・鸚鵡

parsley *n* paseri パセリ; *Japanese parsley* serī セリ・芹

part *n* **1.** búbun 部分, ichí-bu 一部; (*portion*) bún 分, (*section*) bú 部; *I for my* ~ watashi wa watashi de わたし[私]はわたし[私]で **2.** (*passage of a text*) ...tokoró ...所; *this* ~ koko ここ **3.** (*parting of hair*) wake-me 分け目 **4.** (*role*) yakuwari 役割, yakú 役 **5.** *v* (*to divide*) wakemásu (wakéru, wákete) 分けます(分ける, 分けて); (*they separate*) wakaremásu (wakaréru, wakárete) 別れます(別れる, 別れて); ~ *with* ... o hanashimásu (hanásu, hanáshite) ...を離します(離す, 離して)

Parthenon *n* (*ancient Greek temple*) Parutenon shinden パルテノン神殿

partial *adj* ichibu (no) 一部(の), ichibubun 一部分

participant *n* sanká-sha 参加者

participate *v* sanka shimásu (suru, shite) 参加します(する, して)

particle *n* **1.** (*auxiliary word*) joshi 助詞 **2.** (*physics*) ryūshi 粒子

particular *adj* **1.** (*especial*) tokubetsu no 特別の; (*separate*) betsu no 別の; (*peculiar, unique*) tókushu na 特殊な, tokuyū to tokoró (no) áru ..., kore to iú/yū ... これと言う/ゆう... → **choosy**
  in particular *adv* tóku-ni 特に, tori-wake とりわけ

particularly *adv* toku ni 特に, tokubetsu ni 特別に, toriwake とりわけ, koto ni 殊に; *not* ~ betsu ni 別に + [NEGATIVE]

particulars → details

parting *n* (*separation*) wakaré 別れ (o-wakare お別れ)

partition *n* shikiri 仕切り, (*computer*) pātishon パーティション

partner *n* aité 相手 (o-aite お相手), pātonā パートナー

parts *n* buhin 部品; bubun 部分, pātsu パーツ

part-time *adj* arubáito (no) アルバイト(の), baito (no) バイト(の); pāto taimu (no) パートタイム(の), pāto (no) パート(の); hi-jōkin (no) 非常勤(の)
  part-time high school *n* teiji-sei kōkō 定時制高校
  part-time job *n* arubáito (no shigoto) アルバイト(の仕事), baito バイト; pāto taimu (no shigoto) パートタイム(の仕事), pāto (no shigoto) パート(の仕事)
  part-time teacher *n* hi-jōkin kōshi 非常勤講師, rinji kyōin 臨時教員
  part-time worker *n* arubáito (no hito) アルバイト(の人), baito (no hito) バイト(の人), pāto (no hito) パート(の人), [BOOKISH] hi-jōkin (kinmu-sha) 非常勤(勤務者)

party *n* **1.** enkai 宴会, pá'ti パーティ, pá'tii パーティー, ...kai ...会 → **reception 2.** *political* ~ seitō 政党
  birthday party *n* tanjōbi kai 誕生日会, bāsudē pati/pāti(i) バースデー・パーティ/パーティー
  drinking party *n* nomi kai 飲み会, enkai 宴会
  farewell party *n* sōbetsu kai 送別会
  opposition party *n* yatō 野党
  ruling party *n* yotō 与党
  year-end party *n* bōnen kai 忘年会
  welcome party *n* kangei kai 歓迎会

parvenu *n* (*newly-rich*) narikin 成金

pass *n* **1.** (*commuter ticket*) teikíken 定期券 **2.** (*mountain pass*) tōge 峠, ...-tō´ge ...峠 **3.** (*sexual overture*) kudoku 口説く, iiyoru 言い寄る; *makes a* ~ *at* ... o kudokimásu (kudóku, kudóite) ...口説きます(口説く, 口説いて); nanpa shimásu (suru, shite) ナンパします(する, して)

pass *v* **1.** (*goes past*) ...o tōrimásu

(tō´ru, tō´tte) …を通ります(通る, 通
って); (*exceeds*) sugímásu (sugíru,
súgite) 過ぎます(過ぎる, 過ぎて);
(*hands over*) watashimásu (watasu,
watashite) 渡します(渡す, 渡して)
(*hands around*) mawashimásu
(mawasu, mawashite) 回します(回す,
回して); (*salt, sugar, etc.*) torimásu
(tóru, tótte) 取ります(取る, 取って)
2. (*exam*) (shikén ni) gōkaku shimásu
(suru, shite) (試験に)合格します(する,
して), ukárimásu (ukáru, ukátte) 受か
ります(受かる, 受かって), (shikén o)
pásu-shimásu (pásu-suru, pásu-shite)
(試験を)パスします(パスする, パス
して) **3.** (*time passes*) tachimásu
(tátsu, tátte) 経ちます(経つ, 経って),
hemásu (héru, héte) 経ます(経る, 経っ
て), keika shimásu (suru, shite) 経過し
ます(する, して); (*passes time*) sugoshimásu (sugósu, sugóshite) 過ごします
(過ごす, 過ごして) **4.** (*overtakes and
passes a vehicle*) … o oi-koshimásu
(oi-kósu, oi-kóshite) …を追い越します
(追い越す, 追い越して) *No passing*
oi-koshi kinshi 追い越し禁止 **5.** v
passes it on tsutaemásu (tsutaeru,
tsutaete) 伝えます(伝える, 伝えて);
is passed on tsutawarimásu (tsutawaru,
tsutawatte) 伝わります(伝わる, 伝わ
って)
pass out 1. (*loses consciousness*)
íshiki o ushinaimásu (ushinau,
ushinatte) 意識を失います(失う, 失っ
て) **2.** → **distribute**
passage n tsūkō 通行; (*thorough-fare*)
tōri 通り, tsū´ro 通路, (*corridor*) rōka
廊下; (*of text*) … tokoró…ところ,
issetsu 一節
passbook n tsūchō 通帳
passenger n jōkyaku 乗客, ryokyaku
旅客; **~ car** (*automobile*) jōyō-sha 乗
用車, (*train*) kyakusha 客車; **~ ticket**
jōshá-ken 乗車券
passer-by n tsūkō-nin 通行人
passion n jōnetsu 情熱, gekijō 激情,
netchū 熱中
passionate adj jōnetsu-teki (na)
情熱的(な)
passive adj judō-teki (na) 受動的

(na), shōkyoku-teki (na) 消極的(な)
passive voice n judō-tai 受動態,
ukemi 受身
passport n ryoken 旅券, pasupō´to
パスポート
password n pasuwādo パスワード
past adv (*the past*) káko 過去; (*… past
the hour*) …- (fún-) sugi …(分)過ぎ
pasta n pasuta パスタ
paste 1. n nori のり・糊 **2.** (*pate*)
pēsuto ペースト, neri-mono 練り
物 **3.** v (*pastes it*) norízukeshimásu
(norizukéru, norizukéte) のり付けしま
す(のり付ける, のり付けて)
pastel n pasuteru パステル
pastel color n pasuteru karā パステル
カラー
pasties n (*covering for nipples*)
supankōru スパンコール
pastime n dōráku 道楽; goraku 娯楽,
shúmi 趣味
pasting n [BOOKISH] kanpai 完敗
pastor n bokushi 牧師
pastry n (o-)káshi (お)菓子, kashi-pan
菓子パン, pesutorii ペストリー, pai
kiji パイ生地
pat v (*karuku*) tatakimásu (tataku,
tataite) (軽く)たたき[叩き]ます(た
たく, たたいて)
patch 1. v (*patches it*) (… ni) tsugi o
atemásu (ateru, atete) (…に)継ぎを当
てます(当てる, 当てて), tsuzurimásu
(tsuzuru, tsuzutte) つづり[綴り]ます
(つづる, つづって) **2.** n (*a patch*)
tsugi 継ぎ, patchi パッチ **3.** → **field**
patent n tokkyo 特許, tokkyo-ken
特許権
path n **1.** komichi 小道, michi 道
2. (*computer*) pasu パス
patience n gáman 我慢, konki 根気,
[BOOKISH] nintai 忍耐, shinbō 辛抱;
loses ~ shibiré o kirashimásu (kirásu,
kiráshite) しびれを切らします(切ら
す, 切らして)
patient 1. adj (*puts up with it*) gáman
shimásu (suru, shite) 我慢します(す
る, して); (*has patience*) gaman-zuyói
我慢強い, nintai-zuyói 忍耐強い
2. n (*medical*) kanja 患者, (*ill person*)
byōnin 病人, byōki no hito 病気の人

patiently *adv* jitto じっと; gáman shite 我慢して

patina *n* [BOOKISH] rokushō 緑青

patio *n* nakaniwa 中庭; terasu テラス

patriot *n* aikoku-sha 愛国者

patriotism *n* aikoku-shin 愛国心

patrol *n* patorōru パトロール; junkai 巡回

patrol car *n* patokā パトカー

patrolman *n* junsa 巡査

patron *n* (*customer, client*) tokui-saki 得意, suponsā スポンサー; patoron パトロン

pattern *n* patā´n/patán パターン/パタン, moyō 模様, tehon 手本 (o-tehon お手本), katá 型, gara 柄

paulownia *n* (*tree/wood*) kiri 桐

pauper *n* seikatsu-hogo-sha 生活保護者, hinmin 貧民; "The Prince and The Pauper" "Ōji to Kojiki" 『王子と乞食』 (→ beggar)

pause 1. *n* (*rest*) yasumí 休み (o-yasumi お休み); pōzu ポーズ; (*break in talk etc.*) kire-mé 切れ目 **2.** *v* hitoiki-tsuki-másu (hitoiki-tsúku, hitoiki-tsuite) 一息つきます (一息つく, 一息ついて); tameraimásu (tameráu, tameratte) ためらいます (ためらう, ためらって)

pavement *n* (*roadway*) shadō 車道; (*walkway*) hodō 歩道

paw *n* ashi 足; te 手

pawn *n* **1.** (*something pawned*) shichí 質 **2.** (*chess*) pōn ポーン

pawnbroker/pawnshop *n* shichí-yá 質屋

pay 1. *n* (*one's wage*) kyū´ryo 給料 (o-kyūryō お給料), chingin 賃金 **2.** *adj* (*not free*) yūryō (no) 有料(の) **3.** *v pays (out)* haraimásu (haráu, haratte) 払います (払う, 払って), dashi-másu (dásu, dáshite) 出します (出す, 出して); (*taxes*) osamemásu (osaméru, osámete) 納めます (納める, 納めて); ~ *attention to* … ni chū´i o haraimásu (haráu, haratte) …に注意を払います (払う, 払って), … ni nén o iremásu (ireru, irete) …に念を入れます (入れる, 入れて); ~ *compliments* o-seiji o iimásu (iu, itte/yutte) お世辞を言います (言う, 言って/ゆって); ~ *one's*

share buntan shimásu (suru, shite) 分担します (する, して); (*profitable*) wari ni aimásu (au, atte) 割に合います (合う, 合って)

pay parking *n* yūryō-chū´shajo 有料駐車場

pay phone *n* kōshū-dénwa 公衆電話 (*public telephone*)

pay raise *n* bēsu-appu (béa) ベースアップ (ベア)

payday *n* kyūryō´-bi 給料日

payment *n* shiharai 支払い, (*of taxes*) [BOOKISH] nōzei 納税

peace *n* heiwa 平和, heion 平穏, heian 平安; ~ *of mind* anshin 安心

Peace Corps *n* heiwa-bútai 平和部隊; (*member*) heiwa-butái-in 平和部隊員

peaceful *adj* odáyaka (na) 穏やか(な), nódoka (na) のどか(な)

peach *n* momo もも・桃

peacock *n* kujaku クジャク・孔雀

peak *n* itadaki 頂, chōjō´ 頂上; miné 峰; (*highpoint*) chō´ten 頂点

peanuts *n* pīnátsu ピーナツ, pīnáttsu ピーナッツ, rakkasei 落花生,

pear *n* nashí なし・梨

pearl *n* shinju 真珠, pāru パール

pearl diver *n* (*woman*) áma 海女

Pearl Harbor *n* Shinju-wan 真珠湾

peas *n* éndō エンドウ・豌豆, endō´-mame えんどう豆・エンドウ豆

pebble *n* koishi 小石; jari 砂利

peck (*at*) *v* (… o) tsu(t)tsukimásu (tsu(t)tsúku, tsu(t)tsúite) (…を) つ(っ)つきます (つ(っ)つく, つ(っ)ついて)

peculiar *adj* okashíi おかしい・可笑しい, okashina おかしな・可笑しな, kímyō (na) 奇妙(な), hén (na) 変(な) → particular

pedal *n* **1.** pédaru ペダル **2.** → gas pedal

pedestrian *n* hokō-sha 歩行者

pedestrian crossing *n* ōdan hodō 横断歩道

pediatrician *n* shōniká-i 小児科医

pediatrics *n* shōni-ka 小児科

pedometer *n* manpo-kei 万歩計

peek *v* (… o) nozokimásu (nozoku, nozoite) (…を) のぞき [覗き] ます (のぞく, のぞいて)

peel 1. n (rind) kawá 皮 **2.** v peels it …no kawá o mukimásu (muku, muite) …の皮をむきます(むく、むいて); **peels it off** hagimásu (hágu, háide) はぎ[剥ぎ]ます(はぐ、はいて); **it peels off** hagemásu (hagéru, hágete) はげ[剥げ]ます(はげる、はげて)

peep (at/into) → **peek**

peephole n nozoki-ana のぞき[覗き]穴

peeping Tom n nozoki-ya のぞき[覗き]屋

peewee n (small kids) (o)chíbi(-san) (お)ちび(さん)

peg n kugi くぎ・釘

Peking n Pékin ペキン・北京

pen n pén ペン; (ballpoint) bōrupen ボールペン; (fountain) mannén-hitsu 万年筆

penalty n **1.** (fine) bakkin 罰金 **2.** batsu 罰; penarutii ペナルティ

pence n pensu ペンス

pencil n enpitsu 鉛筆 (**1:** íp-pon 一本, **2:** ní-hon 二本, **3:** sánbon 三本, **10:** jíp-pon 十本; **how many** nánbon 何本)

penetrate v **1.** tōrimásu (tōˊru, tōtte) 通り[透り]ます(通[透]る、通[透]って), tōshimásu (tōˊsu, tōˊshite) 通し[透し]ます(通[透]す、通[透]して) **2.** (soaks in, permeates) shimimásu (shimiru, shimite) 染みます(染みる、染みて) **3.** minukimásu (minuku, minuite) 見抜きます(見抜く、見抜いて)

penguin n pengin ペンギン

peninsula n hantō 半島

penis n pénisu ペニス, dankon 男根; [BABY TALK] (o)-chínchin (お)ちんちん, chínko ちんこ; (medical) inkei 陰茎

pension n **1.** nenkin 年金, taishoku-nénkin 退職年金 **2.** (bed & breakfast) penshon ペンション

people n hito 人, … hitó…人; hitó-tachi 人達・人たち; hitóbito 人々, (at large) séken 世間; (of a nation) kokumin 国民; (populace, civilians) minshū 民衆; [COUNTED] …-nin …人, [BOOKISH] …-mei …名 (**1:** person hitóri 一人, ichi-mei 一名, **2:** futari 二人, ni-mei 二名, **3:** san-nín 三人, sanmei 三名; **how many** nán-nin 何人,

nanmei 何名)

pep n génki 元気

pepper n (black) koshōˊ コショウ・胡椒, (Japanese mild) sanshō さんしょう・山椒; (green/bell) píiman ピーマン; (red) tōgarashi とうがらし・唐辛子

peppermint n hakka ハッカ・薄荷. pepāminto ペパーミント

pepper sprout n kí-no-me/kónome 木の芽

peppery adj karái 辛い

perceive v **1.** kizukimasu (kizuku, kizuite) 気付きます(気づく、気づいて) **2.** …o rikai shimásu (suru, shite) ～を理解します(する、して)

perceivable adj chikaku dekiru 知覚できる

percent n (…-) pāsénto (…)パーセント; **ten ~** ichí-wari 一割, **one ~** ichí-bu 一分

percentage n wari 割, wariai 割合; rítsu 率

perfect 1. adj kanzen (na) 完全(な), kanpeki (na) 完璧(な), pāfekuto (no/na) パーフェクト(の/な) **2.** v perfects it kansei sasemásu (saseru, sasete) 完成させます(させる、させて) perfect circle, perfectly round manmaru (no) 真ん丸(の)

perfectly adv kanzen ni 完全に, kanpeki (ni) 完璧(に), pittári ぴったり, pittáshi ぴったし → **absolutely**, **totally**

perform v okonaimásu (okonau, okonatte) 行います(行う、行って), (act) enjimásu (enjiru, enjite) 演じます(演じる、演じて); (music, etc.) ensō shimásu (suru, shite) 演奏します(する、して); **~ an operation** shújutsu shimásu (suru, shite) 手術します(する、して)

performance n **1.** (of a task, duty) jikkō 実行 **2.** (daytime/evening performance) (hirú/yóru no) bú (昼/夜の)部 **3.** (artistic) éngi 演技, pafōmansu パフォーマンス; (musical instrument) ensō 演奏; **beginning a ~** kaien 開演; **during the ~** kaien-chū 開演中 → **show**

performer n engí-sha 演技者, (*musical performer*) ensō-sha 演奏者

perfume n kōsui 香水

perfunctory adj ii-kagen (na) いい加減(な)

perhaps adv ... ká mo shiremasén/shirenai ...かも知れません/知れない, ... ká mo wakarimasén/wakaránai...かも分かりません/分からない, moshi-ka-shitara もしかしたら, moshi-kasuru to もしかすると, tábun ... (deshō) 多分...(でしょう), [BOOKISH] osoraku ... (deshō) 恐らく...(でしょう)

peril n kiken 危険, [BOOKISH] kiki, 危機

perilla n (*plant*) shiso しそ・紫蘇

period n (*of time*) kikan 期間, (*limit*) kígen 期限; (*era*) jidai 時代, ...jídai ...時代, (*punctuation*) shūshí-fū 終止符; (*end*) owari 終わり, oshimai おしまい; ijō 以上

periodic adj téiki (no) 定期(の)

perish v horobimásu (horobiru, horobite) 滅びます(滅びる, 滅びて)

permanent adj eien (no) 永遠(の); funen (no) 不変(の); kawaranai 変わらない

 permanent residence n eijū 永住, honseki 本籍; **~ place** n honséki-chi 本籍地

 permanent visa n eijū biza 永住ビザ

 permanent wave n pā´ma パーマ

permanently adv eien (ni) 永遠(に), eikyū (ni) 永久(に)

permission n kyóka 許可, ninka 認可; menkyo 免許, ráisensu ライセンス; *without ~* mudan de 無断で, kotowárí mo náku 断りもなく

permissive adj amai 甘い

permit n kyóka (-shō) 許可(証), ráisensu ライセンス → *allow* → *permission* → *license*

pernicious adj akushitsu (na) 悪質(な)

perpendicular adj suichoku (no) 垂直(の)

perpetrate v (tsumi o) okashimásu (okasu, oka-shite) (罪を)犯します(犯す, 犯して)

perplexed; gets ~ komarimásu (komáru, komátte) 困ります(困る, 困って); mayoimásu (mayóu, mayótte) 迷います(迷う, 迷って)

persecute n hakugai shimásu (suru, shite) 迫害します(する, して)

persecution n hakugai 迫害

perseverance n gáman 我慢

persevere v gáman shimásu (suru, shite) 我慢します(する, して)

persist v koshitsu shimásu (suru, shite) 固執します(する, して), jizoku shimásu (suru, shite) 持続します(する, して)

persimmon n (*fruit*) kaki 柿・カキ

person n hito 人, ... hitó ...人; (*honored*) ...katá ...方; ... monó ...者, ...yátsu ...やつ・奴; ko 個, te 手; ...-jin ...人, ...-nin ...人; ...-sha ...者; hitóri 一人; (*being*) sonzai 存在 → *people*

personage n jínbutsu 人物; (*being*) sonzai 存在

personal adj kojin-teki (na) 個人的(な); kojin-yō (no) 個人用(の), (*for one's own use*) jibun-yō (no) 自分用(の); shiteki (na) 私的(な)

Act for Protection of Computer Processed Personal Data held by Administrative Organs n kojin jōhō hogo hō 個人情報保護法

 personal appearance n mi (mi-) narí (身)なり; kíryō 器量

 personal business n shiyō 私用, shiji 私事

 personal computer n paso-kon パソコン, pii shii PC

 personal effects n temáwari 手回り, temawari-hin 手回り品

 personal experience n taiken 体験, kojin-teki na keiken 個人的な経験

 personal history n rireki 履歴; (*resume*) rireki-sho 履歴書

 personal opinion n kojin-teki na iken 個人的な意見; [BOOKISH] kojin-teki (na) kenkai 個人的な見解

personality n kosei 個性, pāsonaritii パーソナリティ

personally adv jíka-ni じか[直]に, kojin-teki ni 個人的に

personnel n **~ department** jinji-ka 人事課; **~ cost** jinken-hi 人件費

person-to-person adj man tsū man

マンツーマン, ittaiichi 一対一
person-to-person call *n* shimei-tsū´wa 指名通話
perspire → **sweat**
persuade *v* settoku shimás̲u (suru, sh̲ite) 説得します（する、して）; (... ni sore o) nattoku sasemás̲u (…にそれを) 納得させます
persuasion *n* settoku 説得 → **belief**
pertain *v* **-to** ... ni kan-shimás̲u (kan-súru, kán-sh̲ite) …に関します（関する、関して）
pessimism *n* h̲ikan 悲観; **pessimistic** *adj* h̲ikan-teki (na) 悲観的（な）
pessimist *n* h̲ikan ron-sha 悲観論者
pessimistic *adj* h̲ikan-teki (na) 悲観的（な）
pet **1.** *n* pétto ペット **2.** *v* (*strokes, pats*) nademás̲u (nadéru, nádete) なで[撫で]ます（なでる、なでて）
petrol → **gasoline**
petroleum *n* sekiyu 石油
petticoat *n* pech̲ikōto ペチコート
petty *adj* sásai (na) ささい[些細]な, sasáyaka (na) ささやか（な）; **~ cash** koguchi-genkin 小口現金
pharmaceuticals *n* yakuzai 薬剤
pharmacist *n* yakúzai-shi 薬剤師
pharmacy *n* yakkyoku 薬局
pheasant *n* kiji きじ・雉
phenomenon *n* genshō 現象
phial *n* kusuri bin 薬瓶
Philippines *n* Fírípin フィリピン
philosopher *n* tetsugáku-sha 哲学者
philosophy *n* tetsugaku 哲学
phone *n* denwa 電話; (*cell-phone, mobile-phone*) keitai dénwa 携帯電話 → **telephone**
　　phone book *n* denwa-chō 電話帳
　　phone booth *n* kōshū denwa 公衆電話
　　phone number *n* denwa bangō 電話番号
phonograph *n* ch̲ikuón-ki 蓄音機
phony *adj* nise (no) にせ・偽（の）
photo, photograph **1.** *n* shashin 写真 (*how many* nánmai 何枚); **~ of a wanted criminal** tehaisháshin 手配写真 **2.** *v* (*takes a photograph of*) ... no shashin o torimás̲u (tóru, tótte) …の写真を撮ります（撮る、撮って）

photographer *n* shashin-ka 写真家, kamera-man カメラマン
phrase *n* mónku 文句, kú 句, furēzu フレーズ
physical *adj* karada (no) 体（の）, shín-tai (no) 身体（の）
physical assault *n* bōkō-jiken 暴行事件
physical exam *n* shintai-kénsa 身体検査
physical exercises *n* taisō 体操
physician *n* isha 医者, o-isha(-san) お医者（さん）
physicist *n* butsuri gákú-sha 物理学者
physics *n* butsuri-gaku 物理学
physiology *n* seiri-gaku 生理学; seiri (kinō) 生理（機能）
physiological *adj* seiri-teki (na) 生理学的（な）
physique *n* taikaku 体格
pianist *n* (*professional*) pianisuto ピアニスト
piano *n* piano ピアノ; **plays the ~** piano o h̲ikimás̲u (h̲iku, hiite) ピアノを弾きます（弾く、弾いて）
pick *v* **1.** → **choose 2.** (*plucks*) tsumimás̲u (tsumu, tsunde) 摘みます（摘む、摘んで）; **picks it up** ... o hiroi-más̲u (hirou, hirotte) …を拾います（拾う、拾って）; **picks one up** (*by car, etc.*) mukae ni ikimás̲u (iku, itte) 迎えに行きます（行く、行って）; tsumamimás̲u (tsumamu, tsumande) つまみます（つまむ、つまんで）; **picks one's pocket** surimás̲u (súru, sútté) すります（する、すって）
pickle **1.** *n* tsukemono 漬物; o-shinko おしんこ・お新香, (*Chinese*) zāsai ザーサイ **2. pickles it** *v* tsukemás̲u (tsukeru, tsukete) 漬けます（漬ける、漬けて）
pickled daikon (*radish*) *n* takú(w)an たくあ（わ）ん・沢庵
pickled ginger *n* gári ガリ, amazu shō´ga 甘酢ショウガ[生姜]
pickled plum/apricot *n* umeboshi 梅干し・うめぼし
pickpocket *n* súri すり
picnic *n* ensoku 遠足, píkuníkku ピクニック; **~ boxes** jūbako 重箱 (o-jú お重)

picture n é 絵; (*photo*) shashin 写真; (*diagram, drawing*) zu 図; (*films*) eizō 映像; **~ book** e-hón 絵本; **~ postcard** e-hágaki 絵葉書; *the ~ quality* utsurí 映り; *takes a ~* shashin o torimásu (tóru, tótte) 写真を撮ります(撮る, 撮って); utsushimásu (utsúsú, utsúshite) 映します(映す, 映して)

picture-framer n hyōgu-ya 表具屋

pie n pái パイ

piece n (*one*) *piece* (ík-)ko (一)個, (hitó-)tsu (一)つ; (*a cut*) kiré 切れ, hitó-kire 一切

in pieces *adv* barabara (ni) ばらばら(に), mechamecha めちゃめちゃ・メチャメチャ

into pieces *adv* barabara ni narimásu (naru, natte) ばらばらになります(なる, なって)

pier n sanbashi 桟橋, hato-ba 波止場

pierce v tōshimásu (tṓsu, tṓshite) 通します(通す, 通して)

pig n buta 豚・ブタ

pigeon n háto 鳩・ハト

pile n **1.** (*stake*) kúi くい・杭 **2.** (*heap*) (hitó-)yama (一)山

pile v **1.** *piles them up* kasanemásu (kasaneru, kasanete) 重ねます(重ねる, 重ねて); *they ~ up* kasanarimásu (kasanaru, kasanatte) 重なります(重なる, 重なって) **2.** *piles it up* tsumimásu (tsumu, tsunde) 積みます(積む, 積んで), morimásu (moru, motte) 盛ります(盛る, 盛って)

piles → **hemorrhoids**

pill n (*medicine*) kusuri 薬, o-kusúri お薬, (*specifically*) gan'yaku 丸薬, jōzai 錠剤; (*contraceptive*) keikō-hinin-yaku 経口避妊薬, piru ピル

pillar n hashira 柱 (**1:** íp-pon 一本, **2:** ní-hon 二本, **3:** sánbon 三本; *how many* nánbon 何本)

pillow n mákura まくら・枕 (*how many* nán-ko 何個)

pilot n pairótto パイロット; (*plane captain*) kichṓ 機長

pimp n ponbiki/ponpiki ぽん引き

pimple n níkibi にきび, dekímónó できもの・出来物, o-déki (おでき)

pin n (*for hair*) (hea-)pín (ヘア)ピン,

pin-dome ピン留め; (*for sewing*) hári 針, mushi-pin 虫ピン

pin money n kózukai 小遣い

pin number n pasuwādo パスワード, anshō bangō 暗証番号

pin shell n (*a kind of scallop*) taira-gi たいらぎ

pinball (machine) n (*Japanese style*) pachinko パチンコ

pincers n yattoko やっとこ

pinch n pínchi ピンチ, [BOOKISH] kíki 危機

pinch v tsunerimásu (tsunéru, tsunétte) つねります(つねる, つねって), tsuma-mi-másu (tsumamu, tsumandé) つまみます(つまむ, つまんで)

pine n (*tree*) mátsu (no kí) 松(の木)

pineapple n paináppuru パイナップル

pinholder n (*frog for flowers*) kénzan 剣山

pink n (*adj*) momo-iro (no) 桃色(の), pínku (no) ピンク(の)

pinpoint v seikaku ni shimeshimásu (shimesu, shimeshite) 正確に示します(示す, 示して)

pinup n pinnappu shashin ピンナップ写真

pioneer n paionia パイオニア, kaitaku-sha 開拓者, senku-sha 先駆者

pipe n páipu パイプ; (*tube*) tsutsu 筒, kúda 管

pipeline n páipu rain パイプライン; rūto ルート, yusōkanro 輸送管路

pipsqueak n chíbi ちび

pirate n kaizoku 海賊

pirate ship n kaizoku-sen 海賊船

pirated *adj* kaizoku-ban (no) 海賊版(の)

Pisces n (*star sign*) Uo-za 魚座・うお座

piss n shōbén 小便; [BABY TALK] shikko しっこ (o-shikko おしっこ) → **urine; urinate**

pissoir → **urinal**

pistol n pisutoru ピストル, kenjū 拳銃

pitch n (*baseball*) tōkyū 投球, (*cricket*) pitchi ピッチ

pitcher n tōshu 投手; pitchā ピッチャー; *water ~* mizu-sáshi 水差し; *saké ~* (*decanter*) tokkuri とっくり・徳利

pith n shín 芯

pitiful, pitiable adj kawai-sō´ (na) か
わいそう・可哀想(な), (o-)ki no dókú
(na) (お)気の毒(な)

pittance n shōryō 少量
small pittance n wazuka na teate/
shūnyū わずかな手当/収入

pituitary n kasuitai 下垂体

pity 1. v (pities) dōjō shimásu (suru,
shite) 同情します(する, して) **2.** n (it
is a pity) zannen (na) ... 残念(な)...,
kinodoku (na) 気の毒(な), dōjō 同情

pizza n píza ピザ

pizza crust, pizza dough n píza no
kiji ピザの生地

pizza delivery n píza no haitatsu ピザ
の配達, píza no takuhai ピザの宅配

place 1. n tokoró 所, basho 場所;
(assigned seat) seki 席 (o-séki お席);
(for something) ba 場, ...-ba ...場; (to
put something) oki-ba 置き場 (**how
many places** nan-kásho 何か所) **2.**
v → put
out of place, not from the right/best
place adj ba-chígai (na/no) 場違い
(な/の)
takes place → happen
takes the place of v ... ni kawarimásu (kawaru, kawatte) ...に代わりま
す(代わる, 代わって)
place of employment n tsutomesaki
勤め先; [BOOKISH] kinmu saki 勤務先,
shoku-ba 職場
place of residence n kyoju-chi 居住地

plain 1. adj (not gaudy) jimí (na) 地味
(な), (simple, frugal) shísso (na) 質素
(な) **2.** n (flat land) heiya 平野, heichi
平地
plain taste n tanpaku na aji 淡白な味
plain yogurt n purēn yōguruto プレー
ンヨーグルト

plainly adv (clearly) hakkíri (to) はっ
きり(と); (simply) assári (to) あっさり
(と)

plan 1. n keikaku 計画; kikaku 企画;
puran プラン; (schedule) yotei 予定;
(scheme) takurami たくらみ・企み;
kuwadate 企て; (intention) tsumori
つもり, íto 意図 **2.** v keikaku shimásu
(suru, shite) 計画します(する, して);

kikaku shimásu (suru, shite) 企画しま
す(する, して); kuwadatemásu
(kuwadáteru, kuwadátete) 企てます
(企てる, 企てて); (schedule) yotei
shimásu (suru, shite) 予定します(す
る, して); (devises) takuramimásu
(takurámu, takuránde) たくらみ[企み]
ます(たくらむ, たくらんで)

plane n (airplane) hikō-ki 飛行機
plane crash n tsuiraku (jiko) 墜落(事故)

planet n wakusei 惑星

planetarium n puranetariúmu プラネ
タリウム

plank n íta 板

plant 1. n (a plant) shokúbutsu 植物;
(herb) kusá 草, (shrub) kí 木; (garden/
potted) ueki 植木 **2.** n (factory) kōjō
工場 **3.** v (plants sth) uemásu (ueru,
uete) 植えます(植える, 植えて)

plaster 1. n sekkō 石こう[膏];
adhesive ~ bansōkō ばんそうこう・
絆創膏 **2.** (stucco) shikkui しっく
い・漆喰

plastic n purásuchíkku プラスチック;
(vinyl) bíniru/biníru ビニル/ビニール;
(polyethylene) pori(-) ポリ; ~ **bag**
poribúkuro ポリ袋, biniirubúkuro ビニ
ール袋; ~ **model** puramóderu プラ
モデル

plate n sara 皿 (o-sara お皿); shokki 食
器, purēto プレート

platform n **1.** (at station) hō´mu ホー
ム, nori-ba 乗り場; ~ (non-passenger
entry) **ticket** nyūjō´-ken 入場券 **2.**
(lecture platform) endan 演壇, kōdan
講壇

platonic adj puratonikku (na) プラト
ニック(な); kannen-teki (na) 観念的
(な)
platonic love n puratonikku rabu
プラトニックラブ

plausible adj mottomorashii もっとも
らしい

play v asobimásu (asobu, asonde) 遊
びます(遊ぶ, 遊んで); (a game)
shimásu (suru, shite) します(する, し
て); (a stringed instrument or piano)
hikimásu (hiku, hiite) 弾きます(弾く,
弾いて); (musical instrument) ensō
shimásu (suru, shite) 演奏します(す

る、して）; (*baseball, football, hockey, etc.*) (yakyū, sakkā, hokkē,...) o shimásu (suru, shíte) （野球、サッカー、ホッケー）をします（する、して）; ~ *it safe* daijío torimásu (tóru, tótte) 大事をとります（とる、とって）

play *n* (*drama*) shibai 芝居, engeki 演劇
Shakespeare's plays *n* sheikusupia no gikyoku シェイクスピアの戯曲

playboy *n* purei bōi プレイボーイ

player *n* (*sports*) sénshu 選手, (*instrument*) purēyā プレーヤー
CD player *n* shiidii purēyā CDプレーヤー
music player *n* myūjikku purēyā ミュージックプレーヤー
video player *n* bideo purēyā ビデオプレーヤー

playground *n* undō-jō 運動場

playing cards *n* toránpu トランプ

playmate *n* asobi nakama 遊び仲間

plaza *n* híró-bá 広場; puraza プラザ

pleasant *adj* tanoshíi 楽しい; omoshirói おもしろい・面白い; ureshíi うれしい・嬉しい; kaiteki (na) 快適（な）

Please ... *interj* Dō´zo ...どうぞ...; (*Do me a favor.*) O-negai shimásu. お願いします。; ...(shi)te kudasái ...（し）て下さい, [INFORMAL] ... (shi)te chōdai. ...（し）てちょうだい。

pleasure *n* tanoshimi 楽しみ (o-tano-shimi お楽しみ)

pleat *n* ori-mé 折り目; puriitsu プリーツ

pledge 1. *n* chikai 誓い **2.** *v* (*swears it*) chikaimásu (chikau, chikatte) 誓います（誓う、誓って）→ **promise**

Pleiades *n* (*cluster of stars*) Pureadesu プレアデス, Pureiadesu プレイアデス

plentiful *adj* yútaka (na) 豊か（な）

plenty *n* takusán たくさん・沢山

pliers *n* (*pincers*) pénchi ペンチ, yattoko やっとこ・鋏

plight *n* (*one gets into*) hamé はめ・羽目

plot *n* (*story line*) súji 筋; (*scheme, trick*) keiryaku 計略, hakarigoto はかりごと・謀, inbō 陰謀

plop *v* **1.** (*it drops*) dosun (dosa´, dobun, pochan, poton, *etc.*) to ochimásu (ochiru, ochite) ドスン（ドサッ、ドブン、ポチャン、ポトン）と落ちます

（落ちる、落ちて） **2.** (*drops it*) dosun (dosa´, dobun, pochan, poton, *etc.*) to otoshimásu (otosu, otoshite) ドスン（ドサッ、ドブン、ポチャン、ポトン）と落とします（落とす、落として）

plow 1. *n* (*a plow*) suki すき・鋤 **2.** *v* (*plows it*) tagayashimásu (tagayásu, tagayátte) 耕します（耕す、耕して）, sukimásu (suku, suite) すき[鋤き]ます（すく、すいて）

pluck *v* tsumimásu (tsumu, tsunde) 摘みます（摘む、摘んで）

plug *n* sén 栓; (*electricity*) puragu プラグ, sashikomi 差し込み, kónsénto コンセント

plum *n* **1.** sumomo スモモ・李 **2.** (*Japanese apricot*) ume 梅・ウメ; *pickled* ~ ume-boshi 梅干し・ウメボシ; *plum* ~ *wine* ume 梅・ウメ; ~ *wine* ume-shu 梅酒・ウメ酒

plumber *n* suidō-ya (san) 水道屋（さん）; (*city water department*) suidō-kyoku 水道局

plumbing *n* (*water line*) suidō (sét-subi) 水道（設備）

plump *adj* futói 太い

plunder *v* ubaimásu (ubáu, ubátte) 奪います（奪う、奪って）, ryakudatsu shimásu (suru, shite) 略奪します（する、して）

plural *n* fukusū 複数

plus *n* purasu プラス

p.m. *adv* (*afternoon*) gógo 午後, pii emu PM

pneumonia *n* haien 肺炎

poached eggs *n* pōchido-eggu ポーチドエッグ

poacher *n* (*person*) [BOOKISH] mitsuryō-sha 密猟者

pocket *n* pokétto ポケット; kaichū (no) 懐中（の）

pocketbook *n* **1.** handobággu ハンドバッグ → **purse 2.** (*paperback*) bunko-bon 文庫本

pocket money *n* kózukai こづかい・小遣い, (o-)kózukai（お）小遣い

pockmark *n* abata あばた

pockmarked face *n* abata-zura あばた面

pod *n* sáya さや・サヤ

podium n endan 演壇, shiki dai 指揮台

poem n shi 詩, utá 歌 → **verse**

poet n shijin 詩人, kajin 歌人

point n ten 点, (*points obtained*) tokuten 得点, (*in a statement*) fushí 節; (*gist*) yōten 要点; (*tip, end*) saki 先; *to the ~* tekisetsu (na/ni) 適切(な/に)

point v (*puts a point on*) togarasemásu (togaráseru, togarásete) とがらせ[尖らせ]ます(とがらせる, とがらせて); *points at/to …* o sashimásu (sásu, sáshite) …を指します(指す, 指して); *points out* shiteki shimásu (suru, shite) 指摘します(する, して); shíji shimásu (suru, shite) 指示します(する, して)

pointed; *gets ~* togarimásu (togáru, togátte) とがり[尖り]ます(とがる, とがって)

point of departure n shuppátsúten 出発点

poison n dokú 毒, [BOOKISH] doku-so 毒素

poke v tsukimásu (tsuku, tsuite) 突きます(突く, 突いて); *~ fun at* karakaimásu (karakáu, karakátte) からかいます(からかう, からかって)

pole n (*rod*) bō 棒, saó さお・竿, pōru ポール; *telephone/light ~* denchū 電柱

police n keisatsu 警察; *~ box* kōban 交番; *~ station* keisatsu-sho 警察署
police car n patokā パトカー
policeman, police officer n omáwarisan お巡り[おまわり]さん, keikan 警官, [BOOKISH] junsa 巡査

policy n hōshin 方針, tatémae 建て前, porishii ポリシー, (*political*) seisaku 政策; *makes … one's ~* o tatémae to shimásu (suru, shite) …を建て前とします(する, して)

polio n shōni-máhi 小児麻痺

polish v (*shines*) migakimásu (migaku, migaite) 磨きます(磨く, 磨いて); (*grinds*) togimásu (tógu, tóide) 研ぎます(研ぐ, 研いで)

polished rice n hakúmai 白米

polite adj (go-)téinei téinei (na) (ご)丁寧(な), (*well-behaved*) otonashíi おとなしい・大人しい, reigi-tadashíi 礼儀正しい

politely adv téinei ni 丁寧に, otoná-

shiku おとなしく・大人しく, yasashiku 優しく・やさしく

politician n seiji-ka 政治家

politics n seiji 政治

pollution n osen 汚染, kō´gai 公害; *air pollution* n taiki-osen 大気汚染; *environmental pollution* n kankyō-osen 環境汚染; *water pollution* n suishitsu-osen 水質汚染

polyethylene n pori(-) ポリ, poriechiren ポリエチレン

polyvinyl n bíniru ビニル, biníiru ビニール

pomade n pomā´do ポマード

pomelo n (*Japanese*) natsu-míkan 夏みかん・夏蜜柑

pond n iké 池

pony n ponii ポニー

ponytail n (*hairstyle*) ponii tēru ポニーテール

pool; *motor ~* (*parking (lot)*) mōtā pū´ru モータープール, chūsha-jō 駐車場; *swimming ~* pū´ru プール

poor adj (*needy*) bínbō 貧乏, bínbō (na) 貧乏(な), mazushíi 貧しい; (*clumsy*) hetá (na) へた[下手](な); (*bad*) warúi 悪い; (*pitiful*) kawaisō (na) かわいそう[可哀相](な)

pop 1. n (*soda water*) sōda ソーダ, jūsu ジュース 2. v (*it pops*) hajikemásu (hajikéru, hajíkete) はじけます(はじける, はじけて) 3. v (*pops it*) hajikesasemásu (hajikesaséru, hajikesásete) はじけさせます(はじけさせる, はじけさせて)

popcorn n poppukō´n ポップコーン

popular adj 1. ninki (no aru) 人気(のある); taishū (no) 大衆(の); zoku (na) 俗(な); hayari (no) はやり・流行り(の); hyoban (no) 評判(の) 2. *is ~* ninki ga arimásu (áru, átte) 人気があります(ある, あって); hayatte imásu (iru, ítte) はや[流行]っています(いる, いて); urete imásu (iru, ite) 売れています(いる, いて); (*a person is well liked*) motemásu (motéru, mótete) もてます(もてる, もてて)

popularity n ninki 人気; ryūkō 流行

popularization n fukyū 普及; *gets*

popularized fukyū shimásu (suru, shíte) 普及します(する、して)

popular music *n* poppusu ポップス

population *n* **1.** jinkō 人口; nínzu 人数、nínzū 人数 **2.** (*populace*) → people

porcelain *n* setomono 瀬戸物、jíki 磁器 → china(ware)

porch *n* **1.** (*entrance hall*) génkan 玄関、pōchi ポーチ、beranda ベランダ **2.** (*veranda*) engawa 縁側

pork *n* buta-niku 豚肉、pōku ポーク

pork cutlet *n* ton-katsu 豚カツ・とんかつ

pork dumpling *n* (*meatballs steamed in thin pastry*) shūmai シューマイ・焼売

porno film *n* poruno-éiga ポルノ映画

pornography *n* póruno ポルノ、ero-hon エロ本; (*traditional*) shunga 春画

porpoise *n* iruka イルカ

porridge *n* (o-)kayu (お)かゆ[粥]

port *n* minato 港; *Port of (Yokohama)* (Yokohama)-kō (横浜)港

portable shrine *n* (*for festival parades*) (o-) mikoshi (お)みこし[御輿]

porter *n* pō´tā ポーター; (*redcap*) akabō 赤帽

portion *n* búbun 部分、bún 分、ichí-bu 一部、wari-mae 割り前; (*serving*) …-ninmae …人前

portrait *n* shōzō(-ga) 肖像(画)、zō 像

position *n* **1.** íchi 位置、pojishon ポジション **2.** (*status, rank*) chíi 地位 **3.** → place → job

positive *adj* **1.** sekkyoku-teki (na) 積極的(な)、pojitibu ポジティブ **2.** → sure

positive thinking *n* maemuki (na) shikō 前向き(な)思考、pojitibu shinkingu ポジティブ・シンキング

possess *v* **1.** *is possessed of* shoyū-shiteimásu (shoyūsuru, shoyūshite) 所有しています(所有する、所有して) → have → own **2.** sonaemásu (sonáeru, sonáete) 備えます(備える、備えて)

possessed *adj* toritsukareta 取り憑かれた

possession *n* (*thing owned*) shoyū-butsu 所有物、shoyū-hin 所有品

possibility *n* kanō-sei 可能性、jitsugen-sei 実現性

possible *adj* kanō (na) 可能(な); *is ~* dekimásu (dekíru, dékite) でき[出来]ます(できる、できて)、kanaimásu (kanáu, kanátte) かない[叶い]ます(かなう、かなって)

possibly *adv* hyótto shitára/shite/suru to ひょっとしたら/して/すると、arúi-wa あるいは・或いは

possum *n* fukuro nezumi フクロネズミ

post *n* **1.** yūbin 郵便; *a post* yūbin-bustu 郵便物; (*mailbox*) yūbin-posuto 郵便ポスト → mail **2.** hashira 柱 → pole, stake **3.** (*duty*) yakú 役、(*job*) shoku 職

postage *n* yūbin-ryō´ kin 郵便料金、yūsō´-ryō 郵送料; *~ stamp* kitte 切手、yūbin-kítte/-gítte 郵便切手/切手

postal *n*; *~ savings* yūbin-chókin 郵便貯金; *~ transfer* yūbin-fúrikae 郵便振替

postcard *n* hagaki 葉書(o-hágaki お葉書); (*picture*) e-hágaki 絵葉書

poster *n* posutā ポスター

posterity *n* shíson 子孫

postman *n* yūbin-ya (san) 郵便屋(さん)

post office *n* yūbín-kyoku 郵便局

postpone *v* enki shimásu (suru, shíte) 延期します(する、して)、nobashimásu (nobasu, nobashite) 延ばします(延ばす、延ばして)

postponement *n* enki 延期

posture *n* shísei 姿勢

postwar *adj* sengo (no) 戦後(の)

pot *n* **1.** (*piece of pottery*) yakimono 焼き物 **2.** (*for cooking*) kama かま・釜; (*pan*) nábe 鍋(o-nabe お鍋); (*kettle*) pótto ポット **3.** (*for plants*) hachí 鉢; *potted plant* hachiue 鉢植え、hachí-mono 鉢物、ueki 植木

potage *n* (*thick soup*) potā´ju ポタージュ

potassium *n* kariumu カリウム

potato *n* póteto ポテト; (*Irish*) jagaimo じゃがいも (o-jága おじゃが)・ジャガイモ; (*sweet*) imó 芋・イモ(o-imo お芋)、Satsuma-imo さつま[薩摩]芋・サツマイモ; (*baked sweet potato*) yaki-imo 焼き芋・ヤキイモ

potato starch *n* katakúríko 片栗粉

pot-au-feu *n* (*food*) potofu ポトフ

potency *n* senzai-ryoku 潜在力

potential n (*possibility*) kanōsei 可能性, (*potentiality*) senzaisei 潜在性
  potential ability n senzai nōryoku 潜在能力

potter's wheel n rokuro ろくろ

pottery n yaki-mono 焼き物, tō'ki 陶器

pouch n pōchi ポーチ, fukuro 袋
  pouch of a kangaroo n kangarū no fukuro カンガルーの袋

pouched animal n [BOOKISH] yūtai-rui (dōbutsu) 有袋類(動物)

poultice n shippu 湿布

poultry n [BOOKISH] kakin 家禽

pound 1. n (*weight or money*) póndo ポンド

pound v **pounds it** tatakimásu (tatáku, tatáite) 叩きます(叩く, 叩いて)

pour v **1.** tsugimásu (tsugu, tsuide) つぎ [注ぎ]ます(つぐ, ついで), sosogimásu (sosogu, sosoide) そそぎ [注ぎ]ます(そそぐ, そそいで); *pour-ing the saké/beer* (o-)shaku (お)酌 **2.** *pours on* abisemásu (abiseru, abisete) 浴びせます(浴びせる, 浴びせて)

pout v fukuremásu (fukureru, fukurete) ふくれます(ふくれる, ふくれて)

poverty n hinkon 貧困, binbō 貧乏

powder n koná 粉(o-kóna お粉); funmatsu 粉末; paudā パウダー; (*face*) oshiroi おしろい・白粉
  powder magazine n kayaku-ko 火薬庫, danyaku-ko 弾薬庫
  powder snow n kona yuki 粉雪
  powder soap n kona sekken 粉石鹸・粉せっけん

powdered arrowroot n kuzuko くず粉

powdered medicine n kona-gúsuri 粉薬

powdered milk n kona-míruku 粉ミルク

powdered sugar n kona zatō 粉砂糖

power n chikará 力, jituryoku 実力, kenryoku 権力; (*person of power*) kenryoku-sha 権力者; (*energy, influence*) séiryoku 勢力; (*electricity*) dénki 電気
  power company n denryoku-gaisha 電力会社
  power failure/outage n teiden 停電
  power line n densen 電線

powerful adj yūryoku (na) 有力(な); kyōryoku (na) 強力(な); pawafuru

(na) パワフル(な)

practical adj jitchi (no) 実地(の), jis-senteki (na) 実践的(な); jitsuyōteki (na) 実用的(な)
  practical use n jitsuyō 実用

practically adv taigai たいがい・大概; jitsuyōteki (ni) 実用的(に)

practice n **1.** (*drill*) renshū 練習; (*artistic*) (o-)kéiko (お)けいこ [稽古] **2.** (*realization*) jikkō 実行, (*reality*) jissai 実際; (*habit*) shūkan 習慣; (*putting to*) ~ jitchi 実地; *puts to* ~ jisshi shimásu (suru, shite) 実施します(する, して)

praise 1. n (*homage*) home-kótoba ほめ[褒め]言葉, homé 褒め, [BOOKISH] shōsan 称賛 **2.** v (*lauds*) homemásu (homéru, hómete) ほめ[褒め]ます(ほめる, ほめて)

prank n itazura いたずら・悪戯

prawn n kurumá-ebi 車えび[海老]・クルマエビ

pray v inorimásu (inóru, inótte) 祈ります(祈る, 祈って)

prayer n inorí 祈り(o-inori お祈り)

preach v sekkyō shimásu (suru, shite) 説教します(する, して), (oshie o) tokimásu (tóku, tóite) (教えを)説きます(説く, 説いて)

preacher n (*priest*) bokushi(-san) 牧師(さん)

preamble n maeoki 前置き

prearrange v uchi-awasemásu (uchi-awaséru, uchi-awásete) 打ち合わせます(打ち合わせる, 打ち合わせて)

precaution n (*care*) yō'jin 用心, keikai 警戒, nén 念; (*prevention*) yobō 予防; *as a* ~ nen no tamé (ni) 念の為(に)

precedent n senrei 先例, zenrei 前例, réi 例

precious adj taisetsu (na) 大切(な), daijí (na) 大事(な), kichō (na) 貴重(な); oshíi 惜しい

precipice n (*cliff*) zeppeki 絶壁; kiki 危機

precipitate v (*rains, snows*) furimásu (fúru, fútté) 降ります(降る, 降って)

precipitous adj kyu (na) 急(な), kewashíi 険しい

precise adj seimitsu (na) 精密(な)

precisely adv kichín-to きちんと; seikaku ni 正確に; kikkari (ni) きっかり(に)

precision n seikaku 正確; [BOOKISH] seimitsu 精密

predicament n kyūchi 窮地, kukyō 苦境

predicate n jutsugo 述語; jutsubu 述部

predict v yogen shimásu (suru, shite) 予言します(する, して)

prediction n (weather, etc.) yohō 予報, yogen 予言

preface n jobun 序文, maegaki 前書き

prefabricated house n purehabu-jūtaku プレハブ住宅

prefectural adj kenritsu (no) 県立(の), kōritsu (no) 公立(の)

prefecture n kén 県, ...-ken ...県; **prefecture office** kenchō 県庁

prefer v ... no hō´ ga sukídesu ...の方が好きです; ... no hō´ o konomimásu (konómu, konónde) ...の方を好みます(好む, 好んで)

preferably adv isso いっそ, múshiro むしろ

prefix n settō-go 接頭語, settō-ji 接頭辞

pregnancy n ninshin 妊娠; (gets pregnant) ninshin shiteimásu (shiteiru, shiteite) 妊娠しています(している, していて)

prehistoric adj senshi jidai (no) 先史時代(の), yūshi izen (no) 有史以前(の)

prehistory n senshi jidai 先史時代, [BOOKISH] yūshi izen 有史以前

prejudice n henken 偏見, sennyūkan 先入観, sabetsu 差別

pre-kindergarten n hoikú-en 保育園

preliminary n yosen 予選

prelude n (music) pureryūdo プレリュード, zensō kyoku 前奏曲, jokyoku 序曲

premature adj hayasugiru 早過ぎる, [BOOKISH] jiki shōsō (no) 時期尚早(の) **premature baby** n sōzan-ji 早産児, mijuku-ji 未熟児

premeditated adj (not accidental, pre-planned) keikakuteki (ni) 計画的(に); (intentionally) koi (ni) 故意(に)

premiere n puremia プレミア, (film) hatsu kōkai 初公開

premise n zentei 前提, katei 仮定

premium n puremiamu プレミアム, (bonus) [BOOKISH] hōshōkin 報奨金; shōhin 賞品; omake おまけ, keihin 景品

premonition n yokan 予感

preparation(s) n yō´i 用意, júnbi 準備; shitaku したく・支度; (anticipatory steps) yóbi 予備; (advance study) yoshū 予習; (provisions) sonáé 備え

prep(aratory) school n yobi-kō 予備校

prepare v **1.** ... no yō´i/júnbi o shimásu (suru, shite) ...の用意/準備をします(する, して) **2.** (arranges) no shitaku o shimásu (suru, shite) ...のしたく[支度]をします(する, して) **3.** (studies ahead) yoshū shimásu (suru, shite) 予習します(する, して) **4.** (readies it) totonoemásu (totonóeru, totonóete) 整えます(整える, 整えて) **5.** (makes it) tsukurimásu (tsukúru, tsukútte) 作ります(作る, 作って) **6.** (sets up, provides) mōkemásu (mōkeru, mōkete) 設けます(設ける, 設けて)

prepared; **is ~ for** (resigned to) kákúgo shimásu (suru, shite) 覚悟します(する, して)

prescribe v **1.** (prescribes medicine) shohō shimásu (suru, shite) 処方します(する, して) **2.** (stipulates) kitei shimásu (suru, shite) 規定します(する, して)

prescription n shohō 処方; **~ slip** shohō-sen 処方せん[箋]

present 1. adj (the present time) génzai (no) 現在(の); íma (no) 今(の); kóndo (no) 今度(の) **2.** adj (in attendance) shusseki (no) 出席(の) n génzai 現在; íma 今; hon- ...本..., kon- ...今...; **at ~** íma wa 今は, génzai wa 現在は; **up to the ~** imamáde これまで, koremáde これまで; **the ~ conditions/state** genjō 現状

present n (gift) okuri-mono 贈り物, purézento プレゼント; o-rei お礼; kokorozashi 志 (o-kokorozashi お志); (as a souvenir) (o-)miyage (お)みやげ[土産], [BABY TALK] o-míya おみや、

(*midyear*) (o)-chūgen (お)中元, (*year-end*) (o)-seibo (お)歳暮

present *v* (*gives*) agemásu (ageru, agete) あげます(あげる, あげて), sashi-agemásu (sashi-ageru, sashi-agete) 差し上げます(差し上げる, 差し上げて); okurimásu (okuru, okutte) 贈ります(贈る, 贈って)

presently *adv* **1.** (*by and by*) íma ni 今に, yagate やがて → **soon** **2.** (*at present*) íma wa 今は

preservation *n* [BOOKISH] hozon 保存; hogo 保護
  Peace Preservation Law *n* Chian iji hō 治安維持法
  preservation of environment *n* kankyō hogo 環境保護, kankyō hozen 環境保全
  preservation of order *n* chitsujo no iji 秩序の維持
  preservation of the species *n* shu no hozen 種の保全
  wildlife preservation *n* yasei seibutsu no hogo 野生生物の保護

preservative *n* bōfu-zai 防腐剤; hozon-ryō 保存料

preserve *v* tamochimásu (tamótsu, tamótte) 保ちます(保つ, 保って), hozon shimásu (suru, shíte) 保存します(する, して); mamorimásu (mamóru, mamótte) 守ります(守る, 守って)

president *n* (*of a nation*) daitṓryō 大統領, (*of a company*) shachō 社長; (*of a university, college, etc.*) gakuchō 学長; (*of a school*) kōchō 校長

press **1.** *v presses (on)* oshimásu (osu, oshíte) 押します(押す, 押して); (*press ... (up)on ...*) oshitsukémásu (oshitsukéru, oshitsukéte) 押し付けます(押し付ける, 押し付けて) **2.** *v* (*iron*) airon o atemásu (ateru, atete) アイロンをあてます(あてる, あてて); (*hug*) daki-shimemásu (daki-shiméru, daki-shimete) 抱きしめます(抱きしめる, 抱きしめて) **3.** *n* (*printing press*) insatsu-ki 印刷機; (*publishing*) shuppan-ka 出版界; (*press corps*) kishadan 記者団

pressed; *feels ~* aserimásu (aséru, asétte) 焦ります(焦る, あせって)

pressure *n* atsuryoku 圧力; appaku 圧迫; puresshā プレッシャー; *puts ~ on* appaku shimásu (suru, shíte) 圧迫します(する, して)

prestige *n* meiyo 名誉; meiyo 名誉

presumably *adv* dōmo... rashii どうも...らしい; tabun ... da to omou たぶん ... だと思う

presume *v* **1.** suitei/yosō shimásu (suru, shíte) 推定/予想します(する, して) → **think** **1.** *~ on someone's goodwill* amaemásu (amaéru, amaéte) 甘えます(甘える, 甘えて)

presumption *n* suitei 推定, yosō 予想; katei 仮定

prêt à porter *n* (*ready to wear*) puretapórute プレタポルテ

pretend *v* ... (no) furí o shimásu (suru, shíte) ...(の)ふりをします(する, して)

pretend(ed) *adj* (*sham*) misekake (no) 見せかけ(の); (*fake*) nise (no) ニセ(の), omocha (no) おもちゃ(の)

pretense *n* furí ふり; misekake 見せかけ

pretension *n* misekake 見せかけ

pretext *n* kōjitsu 口実; iiwake 言い訳

pretty **1.** *adj* kírei (na) きれい[綺麗](な), kawaii かわいい → **fairly**, **rather** **2.** *adv* (*very*) kanari かなり, [BOOKISH] hijō ni 非常に

prevalence *n* fukyū 普及
  prevalence of diseases *n* byōki no ryūkō 病気の流行
  prevalence of the Internet *n* intānetto no fukyū インターネットの普及
  prevalence rate *n* fukyū ritsu 普及率, (*disease*) [BOOKISH] rikan ritsu 罹患率, yūbyō ritsu 有病率

prevent *v* **1.** (*hinders*) (... no) jama o shimásu (suru, shíte) (...の)じゃま[邪魔]をします(する, して); (*thwarts*) habamimásu (habámu, habánde) 阻みます(阻む, 阻んで) **2.** (*blocks*) fusegimásu (fuségu, fuséide) 防ぎます(防ぐ, 防いで), (*wards off*) yobō shimásu (suru, shíte) 予防します(する, して)

prevention *n* yobō 予防, bōshi 防止

preview *n* **1.** shitami 下見 **2.** shisha 試写

preview party *n* shisha-kai 試写会
preview room *n* shisha-shitsu 試写室
previous *adj* máe no 前の
previous appointment/engagement
sen'yaku 先約
previous story *n* (*TV, etc.*) zenkai no
(o-)hanashi 前回の(お)話・はなし
previously *adv* izen ni 以前に,
maemotte 前もって
prewar *adj* senzen (no) 戦前(の)
prey *n* (*sacrifice*) gisei 犠牲
price *n* nedan 値段(o-nédan お値段),
kakaku 価格, ne 値; (*the set/regular/
net price*) teika 定価; *commodity
prices* bukka 物価
price control *n* kakaku/bukka-tōsei
価格/物価統制
price difference/differential *n* rizáya
利ざや
price index *n* bukka-shisū 物価指数
price rise *n* ne-age 値上げ
price tag *n* shō-fuda 正札, ne fuda
値札
price war *n* kakaku-kyōsō 価格競争
pride *n* hokori 誇り; puraido プライド,
(*boast*) jiman 自慢; (*strong point*)
tokui 得意
priest *n* (*Christian*) shínpu(-san) 神父
(さん), bokúshi 牧師; (*Buddhist*)
sō´(ryo) 僧侶; (*Shinto*) kánnushi 神主
priggish *adj* katakurushii 堅苦しい,
kuchi urusai 口うるさい
prim *adj* kichintoshita きちんとした,
totonotta 整った
primrose *adj* sakurasō サクラソウ
primarily *adv* gánrai 元来, zéntai 全体
primary *adj* daiichi (no) 第一(の);
shokyū (no) 初級(の)
primary cancer *n* (*medical*) genpatsu-
gan 原発がん・原発癌
primary election *n* yobi-sénkyo
予備選挙
primary school → elementary
school
prime minister *n* sōri-dáijin 総理大臣,
shushō 首相
prince *n* miya(-sama) 宮(様), ōji(-
sama) 王子(様), purinsu プリンス;
Crown Prince kōtaishi(-sama) 皇太子
(様)

"The Little Prince" *n* "Hoshi no ōji-
sama" 『星の王子さま』
princess *n* híme 姫, ohíme-sama お姫
様; ōjo (-sama) 王女(様), purinsesu プ
リンセス; *Crown Princess* kōtaishi-hi
皇太子妃
principal **1.** *n* (*head of a school*) kōchō
校長, shuyaku 主役 **2.** *adj* (*main*) ómo
(na) 主(な)
principally *adv* ómo ni 主に, moppara
もっぱら・専ら
principle *n* (*policy*) hōshin 方針;
(*doctrine*) gensoku 原則, shúgi 主義
print *n* (*woodblock*) mokuhan (-ga) 木
版(画), hanga 版画; insatsu 印刷
print *v* (*prints it*) insatsu shimásu
(suru, shte) 印刷します(する, して),
purinto shimásu (suru, shte) プリント
します(する, して), surimásu (súru,
sútté) 刷ります(刷る, 刷って); (*in
print*) katsuji ni shimásu (suru, shte)
活字にします(する, して)
printed matter *n* insatsú-butsu 印刷物
printer *n* (*for personal computer*)
puríntā プリンター
prior *adj* jizen (no) 事前(の), saki (no)
先(の)
prior arrangement *n* uchi-awase
打ち合わせ
priority *n* yūsen(-ken) 優先(権); *first
~* sai-yūsen 最優先; *order of ~* yūsen-
jun('i) 優先順(位)
prism *n* purizumu プリズム
prison *n* keimusho 刑務所, (*slang*)
musho ムショ, buta-bako ブタ箱,
[BOOKISH] kangoku 監獄 → jail
privacy *n* puraibashii プライバシー;
shiseikatsu 私生活
private *adj* (*use*) jibun-yō (no) 自分用
(の), shiyō (no) 私用(の); (*undisturbed*)
jama sarenai じゃま[邪魔]されない;
(*confidential*) naishó (no) 内緒(の),
(*secret*) himitsu (no) 秘密(の),
puraibēto プライベート; (*within
the family*) uchiwa (no) 内輪(の);
(*privately established*) watakushí-
ritsu/shiritsu (no) 私立(の), shísetsu
(no) 私設(の)
private company *n* minkan kigyō
民間企業

private railroad *n* shitetsu 私鉄
private room *n* koshitsu 個室
private school *n* shiritsu (gakkō) 私立学校, watakushiritsu 私立・わたくしりつ
private talk *n* uchiwa no hanashí 内輪の話, naisho-bánashi 内緒話
private time *n* jibun no jikan 自分の時間
privatization *n* min'eika 民営化
privilege *n* tokken 特権, tokuten 特典, kenri 権利
prize 1. *n* shō´賞, ...-shō ...賞, *(object)* shōhin 賞品, *(money)* shōkin 賞金; ~ **contest** konkū´ru コンクール; **grand** ~ taishō 大賞, guranpuri グランプリ **2.** *n (reward)* go-hō´bi ごほうび・ご褒美 **3.** *v (highly esteems it)* daijí ni shimásu (suru, shite) 大事にします(する、して)
pro *n* **1.** = **professional** puro プロ **2.** *(supporter)* shiji-sha 支持者
probably *adv* tábun たぶん・多分, osóraku おそらく・恐らく, ōkata おおかた・大方, taigai たいがい・大概; ... (surú/shitá) deshō´...(する/した)でしょう
problem *n* mondai 問題, kadai 課題
difficult problem *n* nanmon 難問
If you have any problems, please let me know. *interj* Nani ka mondai ga arimashitara (dōzo) oshirasekudasai. 何か問題がありましたら(どうぞ)お知らせください。
No problem at all. *interj* Mattaku mondai arimasen. 全く問題ありません。
problematic *adj* mondai no aru 問題のある
procedure *n (formalities)* tetsúzuki 手続き; *(program)* tejun 手順
proceed *v* **1.** susumimasu (susumu, susunde) 進みます(進む、進んで) **2.** tsuzukemásu (tsuzukeru, tsuzukete) 続けます(続ける、続いて)
proceeding *n* gijiroku 議事録; sinkō 進行
process 1. *n (method)* yari-kata やり方, hōhō 方法, *(course, stage)* katei 過程, purosesu プロセス; *(development)* nariyuki 成り行き **2.** *v (handles)* shóri

shimásu (suru, shite) 処理します(する、して); *(industrially treats)* kakō shimásu (suru, shite) 加工します(する、して)
produce 1. *v (produces it)* ... ga dekimásu (dekíru, dékite) ...ができ[出来]ます(できる、できて), ... o tsukurimásu (tsukúru, tsukútte) ...を作ります(作る、作って), ... o seizō/seisaku shimásu (suru, shite) ...を製造/制作します(する、して) **2.** *v (brings it about)* ... o shō-jimásu (shō-jiru, shō-jite) ...を生じます(生じる、生じて) **3.** → **product**
producer *n* seisan-sha 生産者; *(movie, drama, etc.)* seisaku-sha 制作者, purodyūsā プロデューサー, enshutsuka 演出家
product *n* (sei)sanbutsu (生)産物; seihin 製品
production *n (manufacture)* seisan 生産, seizō 製造; *(movie, drama, etc.)* seisaku 制作, purodakushon プロダクション
production company *n* seisaku-gaisha 制作会社
profession *n (vocation)* shokúgyō 職業
professional *n (an expert)* kúrō´to くろうと・玄人, púro プロ
professional baseball *n* puro yakyū プロ野球
professional experience *n (career)* shokureki 職歴
professional wrestling *n* puro-resu プロレス
professor *n* kyōju 教授
proficiency *n* jitsuryoku 実力
profile *n* purofiiru プロフィール; *(face in profile)* yokogao 横顔; *(side view)* sokumen (zu) 側面(図)
profit 1. *n* ríeki 利益; toku 得(o-toku お得); *(interest)* rí 利 **2.** *v (makes a profit)* mōkemásu (mōkéru, mō´kete) もうけ[儲け]ます(もうける、もうけて)
profit and loss *n* son eki 損益, son toku 損得
profit-and-loss arithmetic *n* son toku kanjō 損得勘定
profit-and-loss statement *n* son eki keisansho 損益計算書; pii eru P/L

profit-earning *adj* shūeki-sei no aru
収益性のある

profitable *adj* yū´ri (na) 有利(な),
toku (na) 得(な); umái うまい; (*pay*)
rieki ni naru 利益になる; mōkaru 儲か
る; wari ga íi 割がいい

profound *adj* fukai 深い, [BOOKISH]
shin'en (na) 深遠(な)

program *n* (*TV, etc.*) bangumi 番組,
purogúramu プログラム; (*plan*)
keikaku 計画, (*itinerary, routine*)
nittei 日程; (*procedure*) tejun 手順;
(*computer program*) puroguramu プロ
グラム, sofuto(wea) ソフト(ウェア)

programmer *n* (*computer program*)
purogúrāmā プログラマー

progress 1. *n* shinkō 進行, shínpo
進歩, shínchoku 進捗; keika 経過 2. *v*
(*it progresses*) susumimásu (susumu,
susunde) 進みます(進む, 進んで),
shínpo shimásu (suru, shite) 進歩しま
す(する, して)

progression *n* zenshin 前進, shinkō
進行

prohibit *v* kinshi shimásu (suru, shite)
禁止します(する, して)

prohibition *n* kinshi 禁止

project 1. *v* (*a picture/movie*)
utsushimásu (utsúsu, utsúshite) 映しま
す(映す, 映して); keikaku shimásu
(suru, shite) 計画します(する, して)
2. *n* keikaku 計画, kikaku 企画,
purojekuto プロジェクト

projection *n* (*movie*) eishá 映写, tōei
投影

projector *n* (*movie*) eishá-ki 映写機,
purojekutā プロジェクター

prologue *n* purorōgu プロローグ,
jomaku 序幕, joron 序論

prolong → lengthen

promethium *n* puromechiumu プロメ
チウム

prominent *adj* ichijirushíi 著しい,
medatta 目立った, (*famous*) chomei (na)
著名(な)

prominently *adv* ichijirúshiku 著しく

promise 1. *n* (o-)yakusoku (お)約束,
yakusoku-goto 約束事; (*outlook*) mikomi
見込み 2. *v promises it* yakusoku
shimásu (suru, shite) 約束します(する,

shite); *fulfills a ~* yakusoku o hatashimásu (hatasu, hatashite) 約束を果たし
ます(果たす, 果たして)

promising *adj* mikomi no aru 見込み
のある, shōraisei no aru 将来性のある,
kitai dekiru 期待できる, [BOOKISH]
yūbō (na) 有望(な), zento yūbō (na)
前途有望(な)

promising candidate *n* yūbō na kōho-
sha 有望な候補者

promising enterprise *n* yūbō na
kigyō 有望(な)企業

promising future *n* akarui mirai 明る
い未来

promising job *n* shōraisei no aru
shigoto 将来性のある仕事

promising youth *n* zento yūbō na
wakamono 前途有望な若者, mikomi
no aru wakamono 見込みのある若者

promontory *n* misaki 岬

promotion *n* (*salary rise*) shōkyū
昇給; (*incentive*) shōrei 奨励;
(*betterment, increase*) zōshin 増進,
hanbai sokushin 販売促進

prompt *adj* sassokú (no) 早速(の),
[BOOKISH] jinsoku (na) 迅速(な),
(*instant*) tossa (no) とっさ(の)

prompt reply *n* jinsoku na hentō 迅速
な返答

promptly *adv* binsokú ni 敏速に,
jinsoku ni 迅速に, (*instantly*) tossa ni
とっさに

pronoun *n* daiméishi 代名詞

pronounce *v* hatsuon shimásu (suru,
shite) 発音します(する, して)

pronunciation *n* hatsuon 発音

pronunciation practice *n* hatsuon (no)
renshū 発音(の)練習

pronunciation symbol *n* hatsuon kigō
発音記号

proof *n* shōko 証拠, shōmei 証明

proofread *v* kōsei shimásu (suru,
shite) 校正します(する, して)

proofreader *n* kōsei-sha 校正者

prop 1. *n* (*a support*) sasae 支え 2. *n*
kodōgu 小道具 3. *v props it (up)* *v*
sasaemásu (sasaeru, sasaete) 支えます
(支える, 支えて)

propaganda *n* senden 宣伝, senden
katsudō 宣伝活動

propane *n* purópan プロパン; ~ *gas* puropan-gásu プロパンガス

propel *v* susumasemásu (susumaseru, susumasete) 進ませます(進ませる, 進ませて); suishin shimásu (suru, shite) 推進します(する, して)

propeller *n* puropera プロペラ

proper *adj* (*appropriate*) tekitō (na) 適当 (な), tekisetsu (na) 適切(な), kichinto-shita きちんとした, chanto shita ちゃんとした; (*expected, deserved*) tōzen (no) 当然(の); (*correct*) tadashíi 正しい proper noun *n* koyū meishi 固有名詞

properly *adv* tadáshiku 正しく; tekitō ni 適当に, tekisetsu ni 適切に, kichinto きちんと; chanto ちゃんと

property *n* (*fortune*) zaisan 財産; shoyū(ken) 所有(権) → belongings → land

prophet *n* yogen-sha 予言者 the prophet Muhammad *n* yogen-sha Mahometto 予言者マホメット

proportion *n* rítsu 率; wariai 割合; puropōshon プロポーション

proposal *n* 1. mōshi-komi 申し込み, mōshi-de 申し出 2. (*public*) mōshi-ire 申し入れ 3. (*suggestion*) kikaku (an) 企画(案), kikaku-sho 企画書, teian-sho 提案書; (*of marriage*) endan 縁談; kyūkon 求婚; puropōzu プロポーズ

propose *v* 1. teian shimásu (suru, shite) 提案します(する, して); mōshi-komimásu (mōshi-komu, mōshi-konde) 申し込みます(申し込む, 申し込んで); mōshi-demásu (mōshi-deru, mōshi-dete) 申し出ます(申し出る, 申し出て); (*publicly*) mōshi-iremásu (mōshi-ireru, mōshi-irete) 申し入れます(申し入れる, 申し入れて) 2. *proposes to* (*marriage*) kyūkon shimásu (suru, shite) 求婚します(する, して)

proprietor *n* keiéi-sha 経営者

prosecutor *n* kénji 検事

prospect(s) *n* (*outlook*) mikomi 見込み, mitōshi 見通し, [BOOKISH] zénto 前途

prospective *adj* mikomi no aru 見込みのある, kitai sareru 期待される prospective customer *n* mikomi kyaku 見込み客

prosper *v* sakaemásu (sakáeru, sakáete) 栄えます(栄える, 栄えて)

prosperity *n* (*relative business conditions*) keiki 景気; (*good business conditions*) kō-kéiki 好景気

prosperous *adj* sakan (na) 盛ん(な)

prostitute *n* baishún-fu 売春婦

prostitution *n* baishun 売春

protect *v* mamorimásu (mamóru, mamótte) 守ります(守る, 守って); (*safeguards*) hógo shimásu (suru, shite) 保護します(する, して); kabaimásu (kabau, kabatte) かばい[庇い]ます・(かばう, かばって)

protection *n* bōei 防衛, bōgyo 防御, purotekushon プロテクション

protein *n* tanpakú-shitsu たんぱく[蛋白]質・タンパク質

protest *v* kō´gi (shimásu; suru, shite) 抗議(します; する, して)

protester *n* kō´gi-sha 抗議者

Proteus *n* (*Greek god in mythology*) Puroteusu プロテウス

protocol *n* purotokoru プロトコル, gaikō girei 外交儀礼

proton *n* yōshi 陽子

protrude *v* tsuki-demásu (tsuki-déru, tsuki-déte) 突き出ます(突き出る, 突き出て), tobi-dashimásu (tobi-dásu, tobi-dáshite) 跳び[飛び]出します(跳び[飛び]出す, 跳び[飛び]出して)

protruding tooth *n* (*bucktooth*) déppa 出っ歯, sóppa 反っ歯

proud *adj* 1. tokui (na) 得意(な) 2. *is ~ of* ... o jiman shimásu (suru, shite) ...を自慢します(する, して)

prove *v* shōmei shimásu (suru, shite) 証明します(する, して)

proverb *n* kotowaza ことわざ・諺

provide *v* (*provides one with*) motasemásu (motaséru, motásete) 持たせます(持たせる, 持たせて); ataemásu (ataeru, ataete) 与えます(与える, 与えて) → give → prepare; ~ *a treat* gochisō shimásu (suru, shite) ごちそう[ご馳走]します(する, して)

provided *conj* moshi もし, tádashi ただし・但し → if

province *n* (*of old Japan*) (... no) kuni (...の)国; (*modern prefecture*) kén

県, …-ken …県; (*of Canada*) shū 州, …-shū …州; (*region*) chihō 地方

provision *n* (*supply*) kyōkyū 供給; (*allowance*) téate 手当 (o-téate お手当); (*stipulation*) jōken 条件; (*preparations*) sonáé 備え

provoke; *gets provoked, is provoking* shaku ni sawarimásu (sawaru, sawatte) しゃく［癪］に障ります(障る, 障って)

prowess *n* (*ability*) udemae 腕前; yūki 勇気

prudence *n* tsutsushimi 慎しみ

pseudo-... ese-...えせ..., gi-... 偽...

psyche *n* séishin 精神

psychiatric *adj* séishin-ka (no) 精神科(の)

psychiatrist *n* seishin-ka-i 精神科医

psychic powers *n* nenriki 念力, shin-rei nōryoku 心霊能力, saikikku pawā サイキックパワー

psychologist *n* shinrigákú-sha 心理学者

psychology *n* shínri 心理; (*science/study*) shinrí-gaku 心理学

pub *n* (*Western-style*) pabu パブ; (*Asian-style*) izakaya 居酒屋

public 1. *adj* kōshū (no) 公衆(の); kōkai (no) 公開(の); ōyake (no) 公(の); kōkyō (no) 公共(の); (*open*) kōzen (no) 公然(の); (*officially established*) kōritsu (no) 公立(の) **2.** *n* (*society*) yo-nó-naka 世の中, yo 世, séken 世間

public bath *n* séntō 銭湯, (o-)furo-ya (-san) (お)風呂屋(さん); (kōshū-) yokujō (公衆)浴場

public hall *n* kaikan 会館

public holiday *n* shukujitsu 祝日, saijitsu 祭日

public opinion *n* yóron 世論, séron 世論

public park *n* kōen 公園

public transportation *n* kōkyō no kōtsū kikan 公共の交通機関

publication *n* shuppan 出版; (*things*) shuppán-butsu 出版物; (*publishing*) hakkō 発行; (*books*) shoseki 書籍

publicity *n* senden 宣伝

publish *v* **1.** arawashimásu (arawasu, arawáshite) 著します(著す, 著して), shuppan shimásu (suru, shite) 出版します(する, して); hakkō shimásu

(suru, shite) 発行します(する, して) **2.** (*puts it in a newspaper*) nosemásu (noseru, nosete) 載せます(載せる, 載せて) → announce

publisher *n* (*person*) shuppan-sha 出版者, hakkō´-sha 発行者; (*company, etc.*) shuppan-moto 出版元

publishing 1. *n* shuppán-gyō 出版業 **2.** *adj* shuppan (no) 出版(の)

publishing company *n* shuppán-sha 出版社

publishing industry *n* shuppán gyōkai 出版業界

pucker *v puckers it up* subomemásu (subomeru, subomete) すぼめます(すぼめる, すぼめて); *it puckers up* subomarimásu (subomaru, subomatte) すぼまります(すぼまる, すぼまって)

pudding *n* pudingu プディング, purin プリン

puddle *n* mizutamari 水たまり

puff *n* (*cream puff*) shū-kuríimu シュークリーム

puffer fish *n* (*globefish*) fúgu フグ・河豚

puke → vomit

pull *v* hipparimásu (hippáru, hippátte) 引っ張ります(引っ張る, 引っ張って), hikimásu (hiku, hiite) 引きます(引く, 引いて); ~ *out* hikidashimásu (hikidasu, hikidashite) 引き出します(引き出す, 引き出して); ~ *up* (*refloats it*) hiki-agemásu (hiki-agéru, hiki-ágete) 引き上げます(引き上げる, 引き上げて); (*stop*) tomemásu (tomeru, tomete) 止めます(止める, 止めて)

pull *n* (*connnections*) kone コネ; *has ~ (with …)* kao ga kikimásu (kíku, kiíte) 顔がききます(きく, きいて), kóne ga arimásu (áru, átte) コネがあります(ある, あって)

pullover *n* sētā セーター, puruōbā プルオーバー

pulp *n* (*a material of paper*) parupu パルプ

pulse *n* myakú 脈, myakuhaku 脈拍

pulverize *v* funmatsu ni shimásu (suru, shite) 粉末にします(する, して), kona-gona in shimásu (suru, shite)

516

こなごなにします(する, して)

pumice n karuishi 軽石

pump n pónpu ポンプ

pumpkin n kabocha カボチャ・南瓜

pun n share しゃれ・洒落, dajare だ
じゃれ・駄洒落, goro-áwase ごろ[語
呂]合わせ

punch n panchi パンチ

punctual adj jikan o mamoru 時間を
守る, jikandóri (no) 時間通り(の)

punctually adv kichín-to きちんと,
jikandōri ni 時間通りに

punctuation n kugiri 区切り, kutō ten
句読点

puncture n (of tire) panku パンク

pungent adj karái からい・辛い

punish v bas-shimásu (bas-suru, bas-
shíte) 罰します(罰する, 罰して),
(punishes one's child) oshioki (o)
shimásu (suru, shíte) お仕置き(を)し
ます(する, して)

punishment n batsu 罰; (abuse)
gyakutai 虐待, (physical punishment)
táibatsu 体罰, oshioki お仕置き

punk n chinpira ちんぴら・チンピラ

pupil n 1. (student) séito 生徒;
(apprentice, disciple) deshi 弟子
2. (pupil of the eye) hitomi ひとみ・瞳

puppet n ayatsuri ningyō 操り人形
puppet show n ningyō-geki 人形劇;
(Japanese traditional) búnraku 文楽

puppy n koinu 小犬・コイヌ

purchase → buy

pure adj junsui (na) 純粋(な), jún (na)
純(な); (clean) seiketsu (na) 清潔(な)

purgative n gezai 下剤

purge n tsuihō 追放

purple adj murásaki (no) 紫(の)

purport n muné 旨

purpose n (intention) tsumori つもり
(o-tsumori おつもり), íto 意図,
kokorozashi 志; (goal) mokuteki 目的;
for the ~ of … (no) tamé (ni) …(の)
ため[為](に); on ~ wáza-to わざと,
wázawaza わざわざ, ito-teki ni 意図
的に, takuránde たくらんで・企んで;
serves a ~ → useful

purse n saifu 財布, gamaguchi がまぐち

pursue v oimásu (ou, otte) 追います
(追う, 追って)

pus n (medical) umí うみ・膿

push 1. v oshimásu (osu, oshite) 押し
ます(押す, 押して); (thrusts) tsukimásu (tsuku, tsuite) 突きます(突く,
突いて); oshitsukémasu (oshitsukéru,
oshitsukéte) 押し付けます(押し付け
る, 押し付けて); ~ a good thing too
far zu ni norimásu (noru, notte)
図に乗ります(乗る, 乗って) 2. n oshi
押し; (recommend) osusume おすす
め・お勧め; (pressure) atsuryoku 圧力

pusher n oshiuri 押し売り

pushy adj zūzūshíi ずうずうしい・図
々しい, bu-énryo (na) 無遠慮(な)

put v okimásu (oku, oite) 置きます(置
く, 置いて)

put aboard nosemásu (noseru, nosete)
載せます(載せる, 載せて)

put aside tótte okimásu (oku, oite) 取
っておきます(おく, おいて)

put away shimaimásu (shimau, shimatte) しまいます(しまう, しまって)

put in iremásu (ireru, irete) 入れます
(入れる, 入れて); ~ a call denwa o
iremásu (ireru, irete) 電話を入れます
(入れる, 入れて)

put in order soroemásu (soroéru,
soroéte) 揃えます(揃える, 揃えて);
(tidies it up) katazukemásu
(katazukéru, katazúkete) 片付けます
(片付ける, 片付けて)

put into words ii-arawashimásu (ii-
arawásu, ii-arawáshite) 言い表します
(言い表す, 言い表して)

put it another way ii-kaemásu (ii-
kaéru, ii-káete) 言い換えます(言い換
える, 言い換えて)

put it on its side nekashimásu (nekasu,
nekashíte) 寝かします(寝かす, 寝かし
て)

put it together (assembles it) kumi-
tatemásu (kumi-tateru, kumi-tatete) 組
み立てます(組み立てる, 組み立てて)

put it to use yakú ni tatemásu (tatéru,
tátete) 役に立てます(立てる, 立てて)

put on (clothes) kimasu (kiru, kite)
着ます(着る, 着て); (footwear)
hakimasu (haku, haite) はき[履き]
ます(はく, はいて); (headwear)
kaburimasu (kaburu, kabutte) かぶ

り[被り]ます(かぶる、かぶって);
(*glasses*) kakemasu (kakeru, kakete)
かけ[掛け]ます(かける、かけて) →
wear

put on airs kidorimásu (kidoru,
kidotte) 気取ります(気取る、気取って)

put one on top of another kasanemásu
(kasaneru, kasanete) 重ねます(重ね
る、重ねて)

put out dashimásu (dásu, dáshite) 出
します(出す、出して); (*extinguishes*)
keshimásu (kesu, keshite) 消します
(消す、消して)

put pressure on appaku shimásu
(suru, shite) 圧迫します(する、して)

put to bed/sleep nekashimásu
(nekasu, neka-shite) 寝かします(寝か
す、寝かして)

put together awasemásu (awaséru,

awásete) 合わせます(合わせる、合わ
せて); (*sets up*) kumimásu (kúmu,
kúnde) 組みます(組む、組んで)

put someone up overnight tomemásu
(tomeru, tomete) 泊めます(泊める、泊
めて)

put up with gáman shimásu (suru,
shite) 我慢します(する、して), shinobimásu (shinobu, shinonde) 忍びます
(忍ぶ、忍んで), taemásu (taéru, táete)
耐えます(耐える、耐えて), shínbō
shimásu (suru, shite) 辛抱します(す
る、して) sumashimásu (sumásu, su-
máshite) 済まします(済ます、済ま
して)

puzzle *n* nazo なぞ・謎, pázuru パ
ズル

puzzling *adj* yayakoshíi ややこしい

pyramid *n* piramíddo ピラミッド

Q

quack doctor *n* yabu isha やぶ医者

quadrangle *n* **1.** shikakukei, shika-
kkei 四角形 **2.** (*yard*) naka-niwa 中庭

quagmire *n* shitchi 湿地

quail *n* uzura ウズラ・鶉

qualification(s) *n* (*competency*)
shikaku 資格

qualified *adj* tekishita 適した, shikaku
ga aru 資格がある

qualify *v* (*suitable*) teki-shimásu (teki-
súru, tekí-shite) 適します(適する、適
して)

qualitative *adj* shitsu-teki (na) 質的な

quality *n* shitsu 質, hin 品, hinshitsu
品質; *best ~* tokkyū (no) 特級(の)

quality control *n* hinshitsu kanri 品質
管理

qualm *n* fuan 不安

quantitative *adj* ryō-teki (na) 量的(な)

quantity *n* ryō 量; táká 多寡; (*large*)
taryō 多量; tairyō 大量; (*large and/or
small*) tashō 多少

quantum *n* (*physics*) ryōshi 量子

quarrel *n, v* kenka (shimásu; suru; shite)
けんか[喧嘩](します; する、して),
kuchi-genka (shimásu; suru; shite) 口
げんか[口喧嘩](します; する、して),

kōron (shimásu; suru; shite) 口論(し
ます; する、して) → **argument** →
dispute

quarrelsome *adj* **1.** (*inclined to
quarrel*) kenka-zuki (no/na) 喧嘩好き
(の/な) **2.** (*argumentative*) giron-zuki
(no/na) 議論好き(の/な)

quart *n* kuwōto クォート

quarter *n* **1.** yonbun-no-ichi 四分の一
・4分の1; (*of a year*) shihanki 四半期
・4半期; (*time*) jūgo-fun 15分 **2.**
(*district*) hōmen 方面, …hō'men …
方面 → **area**

quartet *n* karutetto カルテット; (*music*)
shijū-sō kyoku 四重奏曲; (*group*)
shijū-sō-dan 四重奏団

quartz *n* (*crystal*) suishō 水晶

quay *n* hato-ba 波止場; futō 埠頭

queasy *adj* **1.** (*feels nauseated*)
múkamuka shimásu (suru, shite) むか
むかします(する、して), haki-kéga
shimásu 吐き気がします, haki-ké ga
moyōshimásu (moyōsu, moyoshite)
吐き気を催します(催す、催して)
2. (*feels anxious*) shinpai (na) 心配
(な), ochitsukanai 落ち着かない

queen *n* joō 女王, (*card*) kuiin クイーン

queen-size *adj* kuiin saizu (no) クイーンサイズ（の）

queer *adj* hén (na) 変（な）, okashíi おかしい; (*wondrous*) myō´ (na) 妙（な）

quest *n* tankyū 探求, tansaku 探索, tsuikyū 追求

question *n* shitsumon 質問; (*problem*) mondai 問題; (*doubt*, *query*) gimon 疑問

questionable *adj* ayashii 怪しい・あやしい, ikagawashíi いかがわしい, utagawashíi 疑わしい; (*fishy*) kusái くさい・臭い

questioning *n* (*interviewing*) shimon 試問

question mark *n* gimón-fu 疑問符

questionnaire *n* ankēto アンケート

queue *n* rétsu 列; *forms a ~* rétsu o tsukurimásu (tsukuru, tsukutte) 列を作ります（作る, 作って）

quick *adj* hayái 速い・早い・はやい

quickly *adv* háyaku 速く・早く・はやく

quick-witted *adj* kiten no kíku 機転のきく, atama no kaiten no yoi/hayai 頭の回転のよい/早い

quiet 1. *adj* shízuka (na) 静か（な）, odáyaka (na) おだやか・穏やか（な）, nódoka (na) のどか（な）; *gets ~* shizumarimásu (shizumaru, shizumatte) 静まります（静まる, 静まって）

2. *v* *quiets it*, *makes it ~* shizumemásu (shizumeru, shizumete) 静めます（静める, 静めて）

quietly *adv* shízuka ni 静かに; jitto じっと

quilt *n* (*padded*) futon ふとん・布団 (o-fúton お布団); *bottom ~* shiki-búton 敷布団; *top ~* kake-búton 掛け布団, yágu 夜具

quinine *n* kiníine キニーネ

quirk *n* kusé 癖・くせ

quit *v* yamemásu (yameru, yamete) やめ[止め, 辞め]ます（やめる, やめて）

quite *adv* sōtō 相当, daibu だいぶ・大分, zúibun ずいぶん・随分; (*completely*) mattakú 全く → **very** → **almost**, *quite a …* chótto shita …. ちょっとした…; *quite so* naru-hodo なるほど・成る程

quitter *n* okubyō-mono 臆病者, ikuji nashi 意気地なし

quiver *v* furuemásu (furueru, furuete) 震えます（震える, 震えて）

quiz *n* kuizu クイズ

quota *n* wariate 割り当て, noruma ノルマ

quotation *n* ínyō 引用

quote *v* in'yō shimásu (suru, shite) 引用します（する, して）

R

rabbi *n* rabi ラビ

rabbit *n* usagi ウサギ・兎
　rabbit hole *n* usagi no suana ウサギ［兎］の巣穴
　rabbit hutch *n* usagi-goya ウサギ［兎］小屋

raccoon *n* araiguma アライグマ

raccoon dog *n* tanuki たぬき・狸

race 1. *n* kyōsō 競争, rēsu レース; (*bike*) keirin 競輪; (*horse*) keiba 競馬 **1.** *n* (*of people*) jinshu 人種, minzoku 民族; *the human ~* jinrui 人類 **3.** *v* kyōsō shimásu (suru, shite) 競争します（する, して）; *~ the engine* énjin o fukashimásu (fukásu, fukáshite) エンジンを吹かします（吹かす, 吹かして）

boat race *n* kyōtei 競艇; bōto rēsu ボートレース

race of stars *n* hoshi no unkō 星の運行

race discrimination *n* jinshu-teki henken 人種的偏見

race issue *n* jinshu mondai 人種問題

racehorse *n* kyōsō-ba 競走馬

racetrack *n* keiba-jō 競馬場

racial *adj* jinshu (no) 人種（の）

racing car *n* rēshingu kā レーシングカー

racing driver *n* rē´sā レーサー

racism *n* jinshu sabetsu 人種差別

rack *n* tana 棚
　coat rack *n* kōto-kake コート掛け
　hat rack *n* bōshi-kake 帽子掛け

magazine rack *n* magajin rakku マガジンラック

racket *n* (*tennis, etc.*) rakétto ラケット

radar *n* rēdā レーダー

radiation *n* hōsha 放射; hōsha-sen 放射線

radiator *n* (*in house, etc.,*) danbō(-sōchi) 暖房(装置); (*car*) rajiētā ラジエーター

radical *adj* (*extremist*) kageki (na) 過激(な)

the radicals *n* kagekí-ha 過激派

radio *n* rajio ラジオ

radio program *n* rajio-bangumi ラジオ番組

radio cab *n* musen takushii 無線タクシー

radio calisthenics *n* rajio taisō ラジオ体操

radio cassette player *n* rajikase ラジカセ

radio station *n* rajio hōsō-kyoku ラジオ放送局

radio wave *n* denpa 電波

radioactive *adj* hōsha-sei (no) 放射性(の)

radioactive waste *n* hōsha-sei haikibutsu 放射性廃棄物

radioactivity *n* hōsha-sen 放射線, hōsha-nō 放射能

radiograph *n* hōsha-sen shashin 放射線写真, rentogen shashin レントゲン写真

radiotelegram *n* musen denpō 無線電報

radish *n* (*the giant white*) daikon 大根; ~ *pickles* taku(w)an たくあ(わ)ん・沢庵, (*radish, etc.*) (o-)shinko (お)しんこ[新香]

radium *n* rajiumu ラジウム

radius *n* hankei 半径

raffle *n* (*lottery*) fukubiki 福引き

raft *n* ikada いかだ・筏

rag *n* bóro ぼろ; kuzu くず・屑; (*dust cloth*) zōkin ぞうきん・雑巾

rage 1. *v* abaremásu (abareru, abarete) 暴れます(暴れる, 暴れて), aremásu (areru, arete) 荒れます(荒れる, 荒れて), (*be angry*) ikarimásu (ikaru, ikatte) 怒ります(怒る, 怒って), (*be furious*) ikarikuruimásu (ikarikurū,

ikarikurutte) 怒り狂います(怒り狂う, 怒り狂って) 2. *n* (*outrage*) gekido 激怒; (*passion*) jōnetsu 情熱

ragged *adj* boroboro (no) ボロボロ(の)

ragpicker *n* kuzu-hiroi くず拾い

raid 1. *n* (*attacking*) shūgeki 襲撃, kōgeki 攻撃; (*bombing*) bakugeki 爆撃 2. *v raids it* shūgeki/kōgeki/bakugekí shimásu (suru, shite) 襲撃/攻撃/爆撃します(する, して); (*invades, makes a raid on*) fumi-komimásu (fumi-kómu, fumi-kónde) 踏み込みます(踏み込む, 踏み込んで)

rail *n* rēru レール

railroad, railway *n* tetsudō 鉄道; ~ *line/track* sénro 線路; ~ *station* éki 駅, sutēshon ステーション

rain 1. *n* áme 雨; *light* ~ kosame 小雨; *heavy* ~ ō-ame 大雨, gō'u 豪雨 1. *v* (*it rains*) áme gafurimásu (fúru, fútté) 雨が降ります(降る, 降って)

rain boots *n* amá-gutsu 雨靴

rainbow *n* niji 虹

rainbow colors *n* niji iro 虹色

rain check; *takes a* ~ enryo shite okimásu (oku, óite) 遠慮しておきます(おく, おいて)

I'll take a rain check. *interj* Mata (kondo) sasotte kudasai. また(今度)誘ってください。

rain cloud *n* amagumo 雨雲

raincoat *n* reinkō'to レインコート

raindrop *n* amatsubu 雨粒

rainfall *n* kōu 降雨

rain shutters *n* amádo 雨戸

rain storm *n* bōfūu 暴風雨

rainy season *n* (*in Japan*) tsuyu つゆ・梅雨, nyūbai 入梅, (*outside Japan*) uki 雨季

raise 1. *v* agemásu (ageru, agete) あげ[上げ, 挙げ, 揚げ]ます(あげる, あげて); (*arouses*) okoshimásu (okósu, okóshite) 起こします(起こす, 起こして); (*increases*) mashimásu (másu, mashite) 増します(増す, 増して), (*price, wage, fee*) hiki-agemásu (hiki-agéru, hiki-ágete) 引き上げます(引き上げる, 引き上げて); (*erects*) tatemásu (tatéru, tátete) 立てます(立てる, 立てて) 2. *v* (*fosters, nourishes*) yashinaimásu (yashinau, yashinatte) 養います (養う, 養って); (*rears a child*) sodate-másu (sodatéru, sodátete) 育てます(育てる, 育てて); (*keeps animals, etc.*) kaimásu (káu, kátte) 飼います(飼う, 飼って); *is raised* (*reared*) sodachi-másu (sodátsu, sodátte) 育ちます(育つ, 育って) **3.** (*collects money*) tsunorimásu (tsunoru, tsunotte) 募ります(募る, 募って) **4.** *n* (*salary increase*) shōkyū 昇給; (*price increase*) neagari 値上り

raised lacquer *n* maki-e 蒔絵

raising *n* yōshoku 養殖; ~ **silkworms** yōsan 養蚕

raisin(s) *n* hoshi-búdō 干しぶどう[葡萄], rēzun レーズン

rake 1. *n* kumade 熊手 **2.** *v* (*rakes them up*) kaki-atsumemásu (kaki-atsuméru, kaki-atsumete) かき集めます(かき集める, かき集めて)

rally *n* shūkai 集会, kaigō 会合

ram *n* rámu ラム, hitsuji 羊・ヒツジ, o-hitsuji 雄羊

ramp *n* surō´pu スロープ, ránpu ランプ

rampage 1. *n* bōryoku 暴力, bōsō 暴走 **2.** *v* abaremásu (abareru, abarete) 暴れます(暴れる, 暴れて)

ranch *n* dai-bokujō 大牧場, dai-nōen 大農園

rancher *n* bokujō (no) keieisha 牧場 (の)経営者, nōen (no) keieisha 農園 (の)経営者

random *adj* iikagen (na) いいかげん・いい加減(な); detarame (na) でたらめ (な); yatara (na) やたら(な); (*math, computer*) musakui (no) 無作為(の); *at* ~ musakui (ni) 無作為(に), tekitō (ni) 適当(に), teatarishidai (ni) 手当たり次第(に), randamu (ni) ランダム(に)

randomly *adv* yatara ni やたらに

range *n* (*kitchen*) kamado かまど [竈], rénji レンジ; (*gas*) gasurénji ガスレンジ; (*mountains*) sanmyaku 山脈; (*scope*) han'i 範囲

age range *n* nenrei haba 年齢幅

a range of *adj* ichiren (no) 一連(の)

firing range *n* shatei 射程

long-range *adj* chōkyori (no) 長距離 (の)

mountain range *n* sanmyaku 山脈

price range *n* kakaku haba 価格幅

short-range *adj* tankyori (no) 短距離 (の)

rank 1. *n* kuraiā 位, …-i …位; chíi 地位, kaikyū 階級, kaisō 階層, ranku ランク **2.** *v* (*to grade*) chii o shime-másu (shiméru, shimete) 地位を占め ます(占める, 占めて)

first rank *n* ikkyū 一級; ichiryū 一流

high rank *n* kōkyū 高級; kōi 高位

high-ranked officer *n* kōkyū kanryō 高級官僚; kōkan 高官

ransom *n* minoshirokin 身代金

rape 1. *n* (*plant*) náppa 菜っ葉, ná 菜 **2.** *n* (*forcible intercourse*) gōkan 強 姦, reipu レイプ **3.** *v* **rapes** gōkan shimásu (suru, shite) 強姦します(す る, して)

rapid *adj* subayai 素早い; jinsoku (na) 迅速(な); kyūsoku (na) 急速(な) → **fast**

in rapid succession *adv* zokuzoku ぞくぞく・続々

rapid response *n* jinsoku na hentō 迅速 な返答

rapids *n* (*river*) kyūryū 急流

rare *adj* (*infrequent*) mare (na) まれ [稀](な), (*precious, curious*) mezurashíi 珍しい; (*uncooked*) náma no 生の, (*little cooked*) nama-yake (no) 生焼け(の), réa (no) レア(の)

rare case *n* mare na kēsu まれな[稀 な]ケース

rare chance *n* zekkō no chansu 絶好 のチャンス

rarely *adv* mare ni まれ[稀]に; (*occasionally*) tama ni たまに

rash 1. *n* (*medical*) hosshin 発疹・ほ っしん, hasshin 発疹・はっしん **2.** *adj* (*hasty*) keisotsu (na) 軽率(な), métta (na) めった(な), mukō´-mizu (na) 向こう見ず(な)

skin rash *n* (*medical*) hishin 皮疹

rasp *n* yasuri やすり

raspberry *n* razuberii ラズベリー

rat *n* nezumi ネズミ・鼠; dobu nezumi ドブネズミ・溝鼠

rate 1. *n* (*ratio*) rítsu 率, (*percentage*) wariai 割合; (*charge*) ryōkin 料金

2. v (*estimates it*) mitsumorimásu (mitsumoru, mitsumotte) 見積ります (見積もる、見積もって) **3.** → **at any rate**

admission rate n nyūin ritsu 入院率
discount rate n waribiki ritsu 割引率
employment rate n koyō ritsu 雇用率
infection rate n kansen ritsu 感染率
mortality rate n shibō ritsu 死亡率
tax rate n zei ritsu 税率
unemployment rate n shitsugyō ritsu 失業率

rather adv múshiro むしろ; (*preferably*) isso いっそ; (*fairly*) kánari かなり, ii-kagen いい加減 → **pretty, moderate**

ratio n ritsu 率, hiritsu 比率, (*percentage*) wariai 割合
birth ratio n shussei ritsu 出生率
ratio method n hiritsu hō 比率法

ration 1. n haikyū 配給 **2.** v (*rations it*) haikyū shimásu (suru, shite) 配給します(する、して)

rational adj gōri-teki (na) 合理的(な); risei-teki (na) 理性的(な)

rationalization n gōri-ka 合理化

rationalize v gōri-ka shimásu (suru, shite) 合理化します(する、して)

rattan n tō´藤・フジ

rattle v gáragara narimásu (naru, natte) がらがら鳴ります(鳴る、鳴って); (*clatters*) gátagata shimásu (suru, shite) がたがたします(する、して)

rattlesnake n garagara hebi ガラガラヘビ

ravine n kyōkoku 峡谷

raving n uwagoto うわごと・うわ言

raw adj náma (no, de) 生(の/で);
sliced ~ fish (o-)sashimí (お)刺身 刺身

raw material n zairyō 材料

raw silk n kí-ito 生糸

ray n kōsen 光線
a ray of sunlight n hizashi 日差し
X-ray n ekkusu sen X線, rentogen レントゲン

rayon n rēyon レーヨン

razor n kamisóri かみそり・剃刀; ~ *blade* kamisóri no ha かみそりの刃

razor shell n (*a kind of scallop*) tairagi たいらぎ

re-... prefix sai-... shimásu (suru, shite) 再...します(する、して); mō ichi-do... shimásu (suru, shite) もう一度...します(する、して); (*improves*) (shi)-naoshimásu ((shi)-naósu, (shi)-naóshite) (し)直します((し)直す、(し)直して)

reach 1. v (*it is delivered*) todokimásu (todóku, todóite) 届きます(届く、届いて); (*it extends to*) ... ni oyobimásu (oyobu, oyonde) ...に及びます(及ぶ、及んで), nobimásu (nobíru, nobíte) 伸びます(伸びる、伸びて); (*arrives at*) ...ni tsukimásu (tsukú, tsúite) ...に着きます(着く、着いて); (*achieves*) ...ni tas-shimásu (tas-suru, tas-shite) ...に達します(達する、達して) **2.** n (*within reach*) (te no) todoku hani/kyori (手の)届く範囲/距離

react v hannō shimásu (suru, shite) 反応します(する、して)

reaction n (*response*) hannō 反応; (*repercussion*) handō 反動
adverse reaction n (*medical*) yūgai hannō 有害反応
allergic reaction n arerugii hannō アレルギー反応
anaphylactic reaction n (*medical*) anafirakishii hannō アナフィラキシー反応

reactionary adj handō-teki (na) 反動的(な); *the reactionaries* n handō-ha 反動派

read v yomimásu (yómu, yónde) 読みます(読む、読んで)
read aloud v ondoku shimásu (suru, shite) 音読します(する、して)
read rapidly v sokudoku shimásu (suru, shite) 速読します(する、して)
read with pleasure, like to read v aidoku shimásu (suru, shite) 愛読します(する、して)
read silently v mokudoku shimásu (suru, shite) 黙読します(する、して)
read thoroughly v jukudoku shimásu (suru, shite) 熟読します(する、して)
read through v ichidoku shimásu (suru, shite) 一読します(する、して)

readable adj yomiyasui 読みやすい; yonde omoshiroi 読んで面白い

reader n (*person*) dokusha 読者;
(*book*) tokuhon 読本
readily adv (*easily*) wáke-naku わけな
く, muzō´sa ni 無造作に
reading n dokusho 読書
ready 1. adj (yō´i ga) dékíte imásu
(iru, ite) (用意が)出来ています(い
る, いて), dekimáshita 出来ました;
(*is arranged*) totonoimásu (totonoú,
totonótte) 整います(整う, 整って)
1. adj (*easy*) wáke-nai わけない **3.** adv
(*ready made*) kisei (no) 既成(の),
kizon/kison (no) 既存(の) **4.** v ~ *it*
(*provides*) sonaemásu (sonáeru,
sonáete) 備えます(備える, 備えて),
(*arranges it*) totonoemásu (totonóeru,
totonóete) 整えます(整える, 整えて)
ready cash/money n genkín 現金
ready-made 1. n kiseihin 既製品
2. adj kisei (hin) (no) 既製(品)(の),
dekiai (no) 出来合い(の)
ready to wear (*off the rack*) kiseifuku
(hin) 既製服(品), turushi つるし・吊し
real adj **1.** hontō (no) 本当(の); riaru
リアル → **genuine**; *the ~ thing* hon-
mono 本物 **2.** (*actual*) genjitsu (no) 現
実(の)
real estate n fudōsan 不動産
real income n jisshitsu shotoku 実質
所得
real intention n honne 本音; honshin
本心; shin'i 真意
real service n shin no sābisu 真のサ
ービス
real world n jisshakai 実社会; genjitsu
shakai 現実社会; genjitsu (no) sekai
現実(の)世界
realistic adj genjitsu-teki (na) 現実的
(な)
realistic person n genjitsu-teki na hito
現実的な人
realistic plan n genjitsu-teki na
keikaku/puran 現実的な計画/プラン
reality n jissai 実際; genjitsu 現実;
riaritii リアリティ
realization n **1.** jikkō 実行; genjitsu-
ka 現実化 **2.** → **understanding**,
enlightenment
realize v **1.** (*comprehends*) … ga
wakarimásu (wakáru, wakátte) …が分

かります(分かる, 分かって), satori-
másu (satoru, satotte) 悟ります(悟る,
悟って) **2.** (*carries out*) genjitsu-ka
shimásu (suru, shite) 現実化します
(する, して) **3.** (*notices*) kizukimásu
(kizuku, kizuite) 気づきます(気づく,
気づいて) → **accomplish**; *a desire is
realized* nozomi ga kanaimásu (kanáu,
kanátte) 望みが叶い[かない]ます(叶
う, 叶って)
really adv hontō/honto (ni) 本当/ほん
と(に), jitsú (ni) 実(に); *Really??*
(*No kidding!*) [EXCLAM] másaka まさか
realm n ryōdo 領土, kokudo 国土
reap v osamemásu (osaméru, osámete)
収めます(収める, 収めて), shūkaku
shimásu (suru, shite) 収穫します(す
る, して)
reaped; *gets* ~ osamarimásu (osamáru,
osamátte) 収まります(収まる, 収まっ
て), shūkaku saremásu (sareru, sarete)
収穫されます(される, されて)
rear 1. → **back, behind** → **tail end**
2. → **raise**
rear admiral n shō´shō 少将
rearview mirror n bakku-mírā バック
ミラー
reason n wáke わけ・訳, riyū 理由;
(*what is sensible*) dōri 道理; (*logic*)
rikutsu 理屈, ronri 論理; (*meaning*)
yóshi 由; (*grounds*) yué 故, kónkyo 根
拠; *for the ~ that* …to iu riyū de …と
いう理由で, …yuéni …故[ゆえ]に
good reason n seitō na riyū 正当な理
由
without reason adv riyū naku 理由なく
reasonable adj (*natural, proper*)
atarimae (no) 当り前(の); tekisetsu
(na) 適切(な); datō (na) 妥当(な);
(*rational*) gōri-teki (na) 合理的(な);
tegoro (na) 手頃(な) → **moderate** →
suitable → **sensible**
reasonable price n tegoro na kakaku
手頃な価格, datō na nedan 妥当な値段
rebate n haraimodoshi 払い戻し, ribēto
リベート
tax rebate n zeikin (no) kanpu 税金
(の)還付
rebel 1. n hangyaku-sha 反逆者 **2.** v
(*against*) … ni somukimásu (somúku,

somúite) …に背き[そむき]ます(背く、背いて)、hangyaku shimásu (suru, shite) 反逆します(する、して)、hanran o okoshimásu (okosu, okoshite) 反乱を起こします(起こす、起こして)

rebellion *n* hangyaku 反逆

rebuke 1. *n* (o-)togamé (お)とがめ [咎め]、[BOOKISH] shisseki 叱責 **2.** *v* (*blames*) togamemásu (togaméru, togámete) とがめ[咎め]ます(とがめる、とがめて)

recall 1. *n* (*of defective products*) rikōru リコール **2.** *v* (*remembers*) omoi-dashimásu (omoi-dasu, omoi-dashite) 思い出します(思い出す、思い出して)

receipt *n* uke-tori 受け取り、ryōshū-sho 領収書、juryō´-shō 受領書、reshiíto レシート

receive *v* moraimásu (morau, moratte) もらいます(もらう、もらって)、uke-másu (ukéru, úkete) 受けます(受ける、受けて)、uke-torimásu (uke-toru, uke-totte) 受け取ります(受け取る、受け取って)、uke-tsukemásu (uke-tsukeru, uke-tsukete) 受け付けます(受け付ける、受け付けて)；híki-torimásu (híki-tóru, híki-tótte) 引き取ります(引き取る、引き取って)、ses-shimásu (ses-suru, ses-shite) 接します(接する、接して)

receiver *n* (*telephone*) juwá-ki 受話器

recent *adj* saikin no 最近の、kono-goro no この頃の、chígoro no 近頃の
  the most recent *adj* saishin no 最新の

recently *adv* saikin 最近、kono-goro この頃、chígoro 近頃；(*a few days ago*) sendatté 先立って、senjitsu 先日

receptacle *n* yō´ki 容器、utsuwa 器

reception *n* resépushon レセプション；uketsuke 受付、(*get-together party*) konshín-kai 懇親会；(*welcome party*) kangéi-kai 歓迎会；(*farewell party*) sōbétsú-kai 送別会；(*engagement, wedding, etc.*) hirō´-kai 披露会、hirō´-en 披露宴
  reception room *n* ōsetsuma 応接間、ōsetsushitsu 応接室

receptionist *n* uketsuke no hito 受付の人；uketsuke-gakari 受付係

recess *n* yasumí 休み；[BOOKISH]

kyūkei 休憩

recession *n* fukéiki 不景気；keiki (no) kōtai 景気(の)後退

recipe *n* reshípi レシピ

reciprocal *adj* o-tagai (no) お互い (の)；[BOOKISH] sō´go (no) 相互(の)

reciprocally *adv* o-tagai ni お互いに；[BOOKISH] sō´go ni 相互に

recital *n* risaitaru リサイタル

recite *v* utaimásu (utau, utatte) 歌います(歌う、歌って)；tonaemásu (tonáeru, tonáete) 唱えます(唱える、唱えて)；anshō shimásu (suru, shite) 暗唱します(する、して)

reckless *adj* mubō (na) 無謀(な)、múcha (na) むちゃ[無茶](な)、métta (na) めった[滅多](な)、yatara (na) やたら(な)、mukō´-mizu (na) 向こう見ず(な)

recklessly *adv* yatara ni やたらに、múyami ni むやみ[無闇]に、mukō´-mizu ni 向こう見ず に

reckon *v* kazoemásu (kazoeru, kazoete) 数えます(数える、数えて)

reclamation *n* kaikon 開墾

recognition *n* ninshiki 認識

recognize *v* mitomemásu (mitomeru, mitomete) 認めます(認める、認めて)

recoil *v* atozusarimásu (atozusaru, atozusatte) 後ずさります(後ずさる、後ずさって)、[BOOKISH] kōtai shimásu (suru, shite) 後退します(する、して)

recollect *v* omoidashimásu (omoidasu, omoidashite) 思い出します(思い出す、思い出して)

recommend *v* susumemásu (susumeru, susumete) 勧め[薦め]ます(勧め[薦め]る、勧め[薦め]て)

recommendation *n* suisen 推薦、(*letter*) suisen-jō 推薦状

recompense *v* benshō shimásu (suru, shite) 弁償します(する、して)

reconcile *v* nakanaori shimásu (suru, shite) 仲直りします(する、して)、[BOOKISH] wakai shimásu (suru, shite) 和解します(する、して)

reconfirm 1. *n* sai-kákunin 再確認、(*flight*) rikonfāmu リコンファーム **2.** *v* (*reservations*) (yoyaku o) sai-kákunin shimásu (suru, shite) (予約を)

再確認します(する、して)

reconfirmation *n* sai-kákunin 再確認

record 1. *n* (*phonograph*) rekó'do レコード; (*results, marks*) seiseki 成績; (*historic*) kiroku 記録; *a new ~* (*an event*) shin-kiroku 新記録 **2.** *v records it* (*sound*) rokuon shimásu (suru, shite) 録音します(する、して); (*event*) kiroku shimásu (suru, shite) 記録します(する、して)

birth record *n* shussei kiroku 出生記録

death record *n* shibō kiroku 死亡記録

recorder *n* rokuón-ki 録音機; *tape ~* tēpu rekōdā テープレコーダー

recording *n* (*video*) rokuga 録画; (*music*) rokuon 録音

record player *n* (rekōdo) purēyā(レコード)プレーヤー

recover *v* kaifuku shimásu (suru, shite) 回復します(する、して)

recovery *n* kaifuku 回復

recreation *n* goraku 娯楽; ian 慰安; réjā レジャー, rekuriē'shon レクリエーション

recruit 1. *n* shinnyū-shain 新入社員, *v* boshū shimásu (suru, shite) 募集します(する、して); saiyō shimásu (suru, shite) 採用します(する、して)

recruitment *n* boshū 募集; saiyō 採用; rikurūto リクルート

recruitment agency *n* jinzai-gaisha 人材会社

recuperate → **recover**

recuperation → **recovery**

recycle *n, v* risaikuru (shimásu, suru, shite) リサイクル(します; する、して); sairiyō (shimásu, suru, shite) 再利用(します; する、して)

red *adj* akai 赤い; aka (no) 赤(の); *deep ~* makká (na) 真っ赤(な); *the red* (*deficit figures*) aka-ji 赤字

red bean *n* azukiあずき・小豆; *soup with ~ paste* shiruko 汁粉 (o-shiruko お汁粉)

redcap *n* (*porter*) akabō 赤帽

Red Cross *n* Sekijū'ji 赤十字

Junior Red Cross *n* Seishōnen Sekijū'ji 青少年赤十字

red light *n* (*signal*) aka-shíngō 赤信号

red snapper *n* tái タイ・鯛

redo *v* (*does it over* (*again*)) yari-naoshimásu (yari-naósu, yari-naóshite) やり直します(やり直す、やり直して)

reduce *v* **1.** herashimásu (herasu, herashite) 減らします(減らす、減らして), (*curtails*) habukimásu (habúku, habúite) 省きます(省く、省いて); (*summarizes*) tsuzumemásu (tsuzuméru, tsuzúmete) つづめます(つづめる、つづめて) → **lessen** → **lower** → **shorten 2.** (*loses weight*) yasemásu (yaseru, yasete) やせ[痩せ]ます(やせる、やせて)

Reduce Speed. "Sókudo otóse" "速度落とせ"

reduction → **discount**

reed *n* áshi/yóshi アシ/ヨシ・葦

reed organ *n* riido orugan リードオルガン

reef *n* anshō 暗礁

coral reef *n* sango-shō サンゴ礁・珊瑚礁

reel 1. *n* (*spool*) ito maki 糸巻き, riiru リール; (*frame*) waku 枠 **2.** *v* (*reels it*) kurimásu (kúru, kútté) 繰ります(繰る、繰って) **3.** → **stagger**

reentry *n* (*into the country*) sainyūkoku 再入国

reentry permit *n* sainyūkoku kyoka 再入国許可

reentry visa *n* sainyūkoku biza 再入国ビザ

refer *v* *~ to* ... ni furemásu (fureru, furete) ...に触れます(触れる、触れて); [BOOKISH] ... ni genkyū shimásu (suru, shite) ...に言及します(する、して); (*reference*) sanshō shimásu (suru, shite) 参照します(する、して)

referee *n* refurii レフリー, shinpan (-in) 審判(員)

reference *n* sanshō 参照

reference book *n* sankō-sho 参考書

reference literature *n* sankō bunken 参考文献

refined *adj* (*genteel*) (o-)jōhín (na) (お)上品(な), yū´ga (na) 優雅(な)

refinement *n* hin 品, jōhín 上品; (*culture*) kyōyō 教養

refinery *n* (*oil*) seiyu-sho 製油所

reflect *v* (*mirrors it*) utsushimásu

(utsúsú, utsúshite) 映します(映す、映して); *gets reflected* utsurimásu (utsúru, utsútté) 映ります(映る、映って); hansha shimásu (suru, shite) 反射します(する、して); *reflects on* hansei shimásu (suru, shite) 反省します(する、して)

reflection *n* utsurí 写り; hansha 反射; kage 影; (*consideration*) kō´ryo 考慮; hansei 反省

refloat *v* híki-agemásu (híki-agéru, híki-ágete) 引き上げます(引き上げる、引き上げて)

reform *v* (*starts a new life*) kōsei shimásu (suru, shite) 更生します(する、して)

reformation *n* **1.** (*improvement*) kairyō 改良、kaizen 改善 **2.** (*innovation*) kaikaku 改革 **3.** (*remedy*) kōsei 更生

reformatory *n* shōnen-in 少年院

refrain *v*; *~ from* ... o enryo shimásu (suru, shite) ...を遠慮します(する、して)

refresh *v* sawáyaka na kibun ni shimásu (suru, shite) さわやか[爽やか]な気分にします(する、して)

refreshing *adj* sawáyaka (na) さわやか・爽やか(な)

refreshments *n* (*food*) tabe-mónó 食べ物; (*drink*) nomí-mono 飲み物; (*tea*) o-cha お茶

refrigerate *v* hiyashimásu (hiyásu, hiyá-shite) 冷やします(冷やす、冷やして)

refrigerator *n* reizō´ko 冷蔵庫 (*how many* nán-dai 何台)

refugee *n* hinán-sha 避難者、nanmin 難民

asylum for refugees *n* nanmin higo 難民庇護

place of refuge *n* hinan-jo 避難所

refugee camp *n* nanmin kyanpu 難民キャンプ

refugee support *n* nanmin shien 難民支援

refund 1. *n* harai-modoshi 払い戻し、henkin 返金 **2.** *v* (*refunds it*) harai-modoshimásu (harai-modosu, harai-modoshite) 払い戻します(払い戻す、払い戻して)、henkin shimásu (suru, shite) 返金します(する、して)

tax refund *n* zeikin (no) kanpu 税金(の)還付

refusal *n* kotowarí 断り; kyóhi 拒否; kyozetsu 拒絶

refuse *n* (*rubbish*) kuzu くず・屑、gomi ごみ・ゴミ

refuse *v* kotowarimásu (kotowáru, kotowátte) 断ります(断る、断って); kyóhí shimásu (suru, shite) 拒否します(する、して); jitai shimásu (suru, shite) 辞退します(する、して); (*rejects it*) kobamimásu (kobámu, kobánde) 拒みます(拒む、拒んで)

regain *v* (*waste*) kúzu くず・屑

regard *v* mimásu (miru, mite) 見ます(見る、見て); kangaemasu (kangaeru, kangaete) 考えます(考える、考えて) → **look at**; **think**

regard *n* sonkei 尊敬、keii 敬意; *regards to* ... ni yoroshíku (itteku-dasái, o-tsutae kudasái) ...によろしく[宜しく](言って下さい、お伝え下さい)

regarding *prep* *in/with regard to* ... ni tái-shite (tai-súru ...) ...に対して(対する...)、... ni tsúite (no) ...について(の)

regardless → **nevertheless**; (**doesn't**) **matter**

regatta *n* regatta レガッタ

regeneration *n* kōsei 更生

reggae *n* regē レゲエ

region *n* chíhō 地方、chíiki 地域

regional *adj* chíhō (no) 地方(の)、chíiki (no) 地域(の)

register 1. *n* (*of names*) meibo 名簿、(*enrollment*) kiroku 記録 **2.** *v* (*checks into hotel*) chekkúín shimásu (suru, shite) チェックインします(する、して); (*enrolls, signs up*) tōroku shimásu (suru, shite) 登録します(する、して); *~ a letter* tegami o kakí-tome ni shimásu (suru, shite) 手紙を書留にします(する、して)

registered *adj* tōroku/tōki sareta 登録/登記された

registered mail *n* kakí-tome 書留

registered mail for cash *n* genkin kakí-tome 現金書留

registration *n* tōroku 登録、tō´ki 登記

regret 1. n kōˊkai 後悔 **2.** v (regrets it)
kōkai shimásu (suru, shite) 後悔し
ます(する, して), kuyamimásu
(kuyámu, kuyánde) 悔やみます(悔や
む, 悔やんで); **I regret that** … zannen/
ikan nagara …残念/遺憾ながら…

regrettable adj oshíi 惜しい, zannén
(na) 残念(な), ainiku (na) あいにく
(な), [BOOKISH] ikan (na) 遺憾(な)

regrettably adv zannen nagara 残念な
がら, [BOOKISH] ikan nagara 遺憾なが
ら

regular 1. adj (usual) futsū no 普通の,
(ordinary) nami no 並の, régyurā レギ
ュラー; (periodic/scheduled) téiki no 定
期の **2.** n (customer) jōren(-kyaku)
常連(客), otokui-sama お得意(様),
sei-kaiin 正会員; **regulars** (army) jōbi-
gun 常備軍
    regular customer n jōren kyaku 常連客,
    kotei kyaku 固定客, tokuisaki 得意先
    regular employee n seishain 正社員
    regular exam, regular examination n
    teiki shiken 定期試験
    regular life n kisoku tadashii seikatsu
    規則正しい生活
    regular size n futsū saizu 普通サイズ

regulate v (adjusts) totonoemásu
(totonóeru, totonóete) 整えます(整え
る, 整えて)

regulation n kísoku 規則, kítei 規定;
kimari 決まり

rehabilitation n rihabiri リハビリ

rehearsal n rihāsaru リハーサル

reincarnation n umarekawari 生まれ
変わり

reindeer n tonakai トナカイ

reign n chisei 治世

rein(s) n tázuna 手綱・たづな

reject v kobamimásu (kobámu,
kobánde) 拒みます(拒む, 拒んで);
kyóhí shimásu (suru, shite) 拒否しま
す(する, して)

rejection n kyozetsu 拒絶
    acute rejection n (medical) kyūsei
    kyozetsu hannō 急性拒絶反応

rejoice v yorokobimásu (yorokóbu,
yorokónde) 喜びます(喜ぶ, 喜んで)

relate v **1.** (tells) katarimásu (kataru,
katatte) 語ります(語る, 語って),

nobemásu (nobéru, nobete) 述べます
(述べる, 述べて) **2.** (is connected/
relevant to) … ni kanshimásu
(kansúru, kánshite) …に関します(関
する, 関して)

relation(ship) n kankei 関係; tsunagari
つながり, (between people) náka 仲,
aidagara 間柄

relative 1. n (person) shinrui 親類,
shinseki 親戚 **2.** adj kankei/kanren no
aru 関係/関連のある

relatively adv wari (ai) ni 割(合)に,
híkaku-teki ni 比較的に

relative merits n yūretsu 優劣

relax v (looses tension) tarumimásu
(tarumu, tarunde) たるみ[弛み]ます
(たるむ, たるんで); (gets comfortable)
kutsurogimásu (kutsurógu, kutsuróide)
くつろぎ[寛ぎ]ます(くつろぐ, くつ
ろいで); (rests oneself) yasumimásu
(yasúmu, yasúnde) 休みます(休む,
休んで), rirakkusu shimásu (suru,
shite) リラックスします(する, して),
(enjoys oneself) asobimásu (asobu,
asonde) 遊びます(遊ぶ, 遊んで)

relay n rirē リレー
    relay broadcast n chūkei hōsō 中継
    放送
    relay race n rirē kyōsō リレー競争

release 1. n (publication) hatsubai
発売, (movie) kōkai 公開; **press ~**
puresu ririisu プレスリリース **2.** v
(announce) happyō shimásu (suru, shite)
発表します(する, して); (let go) kahō
shimásu (suru, shite) 解放します(す
る, して)
    release date n hatsubai bi 発売日,
    kōkai-bi 公開日

relevance n renraku 連絡, kanren 関連

relevant adj (related) kanren/kankei
no aru 関連/関係のある; **is ~ to** … ni
kanren shimásu (suru, shite) …に関連
します(する, して)

reliability n shinrai-sei 信頼性

reliable adj (steady) te-gatai 手堅い;
(trustworthy) shinrai dekíru 信頼でき
る, **is highly ~** shinrai-sei ga takái 信
頼性が高い

reliance n ate 当て, tánomi 頼み,
shinrai 信頼

527

relief n (*rescue*) kyū´jo 救助; (*from worry*) anshin 安心; *breathes a sigh of ~* hótto shimásu (suru, shite) ほっとします(する, して)

relieve v 1. *is relieved* anshin shimásu (suru, shite) 安心します(する, して); (*gets saved*) tasukarimásu (tasukáru, tasukátte) 助かります(助かる, 助かって) 2. *relieves oneself* (*goes to the bathroom*) yō´o tashimásu (tasu, tashite) 用を足します(足す, 足して)

religion n shū´kyō 宗教, ...-kyō ...教

relish n *small dish of ~* tsukeawase 付け合せ

rely; *~ on* ... ni tayorimásu (tayóru, tayótte) ...に頼ります(頼る, 頼って), (*requests*) tanomimásu (tanómu, tanónde) 頼みます(頼む, 頼んで), irai shimásu (suru, shite) 依頼します(する, して)

remain v (*gets left behind*) nokorimásu (nokóru, nokótte) 残ります(残る, 残って), (*is in excess*) amarimásu (amáru, amátte) 余ります(余る, 余って); (*stops*) todomarimásu (todomáru, todomátte) とどまります(とどまる, とどまって); (*stays*) imásu (iru, ite) います(いる, いて), (*rather than go*) ikimasén (ikanai, ikanáide) 行きません(行かない, 行かないで)

remainder n (*leftover*) nokori 残り, (*surplus*) amari (o-ámari) 余り(お余り); áto no (mono, hító, ...) 後の(物, 人, ...)

remains n (*what remains*) nokori-mono 残り物; *the remaining* ... áto/nokori no ...後/残りの...

remark 1. *a remark* n kotobá 言葉, ... (yū/iu/itta) kotó ... (言う/言った)事; *uncalled-for ~* sashide-guchi 差し口 2. v → **say**

remarkable adj ijō 異常(な), ichijirushíi 著しい

remember v (*recalls*) omoi-dashimásu (omoi-dasu, omoi-dashite) 思い出します(思い出す, 思い出して); (*retains in memory*) obóete imásu (iru, ite) 覚えています(いる, いて)
Remember me to ... ... ni yoroshíku (itte kudasái, o-tsutae kudasái) ...によ

ろしく[宜しく](言って下さい, お伝え下さい)

remind; *~ one of* ... ... o omowase-másu (omowaséru, omowásete) ...を思わせます(思わせる, 思わせて); kizukasemásu (kizukaséru, kizukásete) 気付かせます(気付かせる, 気付かせて)

reminder n hínto ヒント, chū´i 注意, saisoku-jō 催促状, rimaindā リマインダー

remissness n yudan 油断

remit v sōkin shimásu (suru, shite) 送金します(する, して)

remittance n sōkin 送金

remodel v kaichiku shimásu (suru, shite) 改築します(する, して), rifōmu shimásu (suru, shite) リフォームします(する, して)

remote adj enkaku-chi 遠隔地
remote access n rimōto akusesu リモートアクセス, enkaku akusesu 遠隔アクセス
remote area n hekichi へき地・僻地
remote control n 1. enkaku seigyo 遠隔制御 2. (*TV, etc.*) rimo-kon リモコン

remove v torimásu (tóru, tótte) 取ります(取る, 取って), nozokimásu (nozoku, nozoite) 除きます(除く, 除いて); sarimásu (saru, satte) 去ります(去る, 去って); háijo shimásu (suru, shite) 排除します(する, して) → **take off** → **omit** → **move** (**house**)
snow removal n josetsu 除雪

remover n hakuri-zai 剥離剤
hair remover n datsumō-zai 脱毛剤

remuneration n sharei 謝礼; (*salary*) kyūryō 給料

renew v kōshin shimásu (suru, shite) 更新します(する, して)

renewal n kōshin 更新, rinyuaru リニューアル
contract renewal n keiyaku (no) kōshin 契約(の)更新
license renewal n menkyo (no) kōshin 免許(の)更新
renewal fee n kōshin-ryō 更新料

rent 1. n (*cost*) karí-chin 借り賃, (*house*) yá-chin 家賃; *rented/rental*

house kashi-ya 貸家; ***rented/rental room*** kashi-ma 貸間 **2.** *v* (*rents it out to*) kashimásu (kasu, kashíte) 貸します (貸す, 貸して); (*rents it from*) karimásu (kariru, karite) 借ります(借りる, 借りて)

rental *n, adj* chintai (no) 賃貸(の), rentaru (no) レンタル(の)

　rental car *n* rentákā´ レンタカー

　rental fee *n* shiyōryō 使用料, rentaru ryōkin レンタル料金

　rental house *n* kashiya 貸家

　rental safe *n* kashi-kinko 貸金庫

　rental shop *n* rentaru shoppu レンタルショップ

　rental video *n* rentaru bideo レンタルビデオ

renovate *v* **1.** (*repair*) shūri shimásu (suru, shite) 修理します(する, して) **2.** (*rebuild*) rifōmu shimásu (suru, shite) リフォームします(する, して)

reorder **1.** *v* (*adjusts*) séiri shimásu (suru, shite) 整理します(する, して) **2.** *n* sai-chūmon 再注文; tsuika-chūmon 追加注文

reorganization *n* sai-hensei 再編成

reorganize → **reorder**

repaint *v* nuri-kaemásu (nuri-káeru, nuri-káete) 塗り替えます(塗り替える, 塗り替えて)

repair **1.** *n* (*repairing*) naoshí 直し, shū´ri 修理, shūzen 修繕, tsukurói 繕い; (*upkeep, care*) te-iré 手入れ **2.** *v* *repairs it* naoshimásu (naósu, naó-shite) 直します(直す, 直して); (*mends, patches, sews*) tsukuroimásu (tsukuróu, tsukurótte) 繕います(繕う, 繕って), shū´ri/shūzen shimásu (suru, shite) 修理/修繕します(する, して); (*it gets repaired*) …ga naorimásu (naóru, naótte) …が直ります(直る, 直って), (*gets it repaired*) … o naóshite moraimásu (morau, moratte) …を直してもらいます(もらう, もらって)

repairman *n* shūrí-kō 修理工, shūzén-kō 修繕工

reparation *n* (*provision*) téate 手当て (o-téate お手当て); (*money*) baishō-kin 賠償金

repay *v* (*compensates*) mukuimásu (mukuíru, mukúite) 報います(報いる, 報いて)

repeat **1.** *v* mō ichi-do iimásu (iu/yū, itte/yutte) もう一度言います(言う, 言って/ゆって); kuri-kaeshimásu (kuri-kaesu, kuri-káeshite) 繰り返します(繰り返す, 繰り返して) **2.** *n* ripiito リピート; kurikaeshi 繰り返し; [BOOKISH] hanpuku 反復

　repeat function *n* ripiito kinō リピート機能

repeatedly *adv* (*often*) shíbashiba しばしば; (*ever so many times*) nán-do/-kai mo 何度/何回も

repeater *n* ripiitā リピーター

repel *v* (*water, etc.*) hajikimásu (hajíku, hajíite) 弾きます(弾く, 弾いて)

repercussion *n* handō 反動

repertory *n* repátorii レパートリー

repetition *n* kurikaeshi 繰り返し, hanpuku 反復

rephrase *v* ii-kaemásu (ii-káeru, ii-káete) 言い換えます(言い換える, 言い換えて)

replace *v* tori-kaemásu (tori-kaeru, tori-kaete) 取り換えます(取り換える, 取り換えて)

replacement *n* torikae 取り換え, sashikae 差し替え, [BOOKISH] chikan 置換

replica *n* fukúsei (-hin) 複製品, mozō(-hin) 模造品, repurika レプリカ

reply **1.** *n* kaitō 回答 **2.** *v* ~ *to* kaitō shimásu (suru, shite) 回答します(する, して) → **answer**

report **1.** *n* (*notice*) shirase (o-shirase) 知らせ(お知らせ), tsūchi 通知, todoké (o-todoke) 届け(お届け); (*announcement*) hōkoku 報告, repō´to レポート; (*message*) dengon 伝言; (*research paper*) happyō 発表; (*claim*) mōshi-de 申し出 **2.** *v* (*announces*) hōkoku shimásu (suru, shite) 報告します(する, して), (*relays, tells*) tsutaemásu (tsutaeru, tsutaete) 伝えます(伝える, 伝えて), (*is reported*) tsutawarimásu (tsutawaru, tsutawatte) 伝わります(伝わる, 伝わって), (*notifies*) todokemásu (todokéru, todókete) 届けます(届ける,

届けて）; (*presents research*) happyō
shimásu (suru, shite) 発表します（する、
して）; (*claims*) mōshi-demásu (mōshi-
deru, mōshi-dete) 申し出ます（申し出
る、申し出て）→ **inform → tell**; ~ *for
work* shukkin shimásu (suru, shite) 出勤
します（する、して）
report card *n* seiseki-hyō 成績表
reportedly *adv* … (da) sō desu …
（だ）そうです
reporter *n* ripōtā リポーター, (*news
reporter*) shinbun-kíshá 新聞記者,
(shuzai) kíshá（取材）記者
representative 1. *n* daihyō 代表,
daihyō´-sha 代表者 → **agent 2.** *adj*
(*typical, model*) daihyō-teki (na) 代
表的（な）
repress *v* osaemásu (osáeru, osáete)
抑えます（抑える、抑えて）
reprint *n, v* zōsatsu (shimásu; suru,
shite) 増刷（します; する、して）
reproach *n, v* hínan (shimásu; suru,
shite) 非難（します; する、して）,
sememásu (seméru, sémete) 責めます
（責める、責めて）
reproduce *v* (*replay*) saisei shimásu
(suru, shite) 再生します（する、して）;
(*replicates/copies it*) fukusei/fukusha
shimásu (suru, shite) 複製／複写します
（する、して）
reproduction *n* (*replication*) fukusei
複製, (*copy*) fukusha 複写; (*replay*)
saisei 再生
reprove *v* togamemásu (togaméru,
togámete) とがめ[咎め]ます（とがめ
る、とがめて）
reputation *n* hyōban 評判
request 1. *n* negái 願い, tanomí 頼み,
irai 依頼, rikuesuto リクエスト, (*a
demand*) yōkyū 要求, seikyū 請求;
(*requesting*) kói 請い **2.** *v* (*asks a
favor*) negaimásu (negáu, negátte) 願
います（願う、願って）, tanomimásu
(tanómu, tanónde) 頼みます（頼む、頼
んで）, irai shimásu (suru, shite) 依頼
します（する、して）; (*demands*) seikyū
shimásu (suru, shite) 請求します（す
る、して）
require *v* **1.** (*demands*) yōkyū shimásu
(suru, shite) 要求します（する、して）

2. → **need → take** (*time/money*) →
stipulate
requirement *n* yōkyū 要求;
(*qualification*) shikaku 資格
admission requirements *n* nyūgaku
shikaku 入学資格
entry requirements *n* tōroku hitsuyō
jōken 登録必要条件
job requirements *n* shokumu yōken
職務要件
rescue 1. *n* kyū´jo 救助 **2.** *v* tasukemásu (tasukéru, tasukéte) 助けます（助
ける、助けて）, sukuimásu (sukū, sukutte) 救います（救う、救って）; kyū´jo
shimásu (suru, shite) 救助します（す
る、して）
research 1. *v* kenkyū shimásu (suru,
shite) 研究します（する、して）, chōsa
shimásu (suru, shite) 調査します（す
る、して）, risāchi shimásu (suru, shite)
リサーチします（する、して）
2. (*investigation*) *n* chō´sa 調査
researcher *n* kenkyū-in 研究員,
kenkyū-sha 研究者, chōsa-in 調査員
resemblance *n* ruiji 類似
resemble *v* … ni nite imásu (iru, ite)
…に似ています（いる、いて）, nimásu
(niru, nite) 似ます（似る、似て）; … ni/
to ruiji shimásu (suru, shite) …に／と
類似します（する、して）; *closely* ~
… ni/to ni-kayoimásu (ni-kayóu, ni-
kayótte) …に／と似通います（似通う、
似通って）
resent *v* fungai shimásu (suru, shite)
憤慨します（する、して）; ikidōrimásu
(ikidō´ru, ikidō´tte) 憤ります（憤る、憤
って）; uramimásu (urámu, uránde)
恨みます（恨む、恨んで）
resentment *n* fungai 憤慨, ikidōri
憤り, uramí 恨み
reservation *n* (*booking*) yoyaku 予約,
mōshi-komi 申し込み
reserve *n* **1.** (*reticence*) enryo 遠慮;
shows ~ enryo shimásu (suru, shite)
遠慮します（する、して） **2.** (*spare*)
yobi 予備
reserve *adj* (*spare*) yóbi (no) 予備（の）
reserve fund *n* tsumitate-kin 積立金
reserve *v* (*makes a reservation*)
yoyaku shimásu (suru, shite) 予約し

す(する, して), mōshí-komimás<u>u</u>
(mōshí-komu, mōshí-konde) 申し込み
ます(申し込む, 申し込んで); (*puts
aside, holds*) tótte okimás<u>u</u> (oku, oite)
取って置きます(置く, 置いて)
reserved seat(s) *n* sh<u>i</u>tei-seki 指定席
reservoir *n* chosúi-chi 貯水池, jōsúi-
chi 浄水池
reside → **live**
residence *n* **1.** (*place*) súmái 住まい
(o-súmai お住まい), jū´sho 住所,
jūtaku 住宅; *one's ~ (home)* jitaku
自宅 **2.** (*residing*) zairyū 在留;
status of ~ zairyū-sh<u>í</u>kaku 在留資格;
permanent ~ honseki 本籍, (*place*)
honsék<u>i</u>-chi 本籍地
resident *n* (*person*) kyojū´-sha 居住者,
jūmin 住民; (*apartment tenant*)
nyūkyó-sha 入居者; *~ in* ... zai-...
在...
resign *v* (*job*) (sh<u>i</u>goto o) yamemás<u>u</u>
(yameru, yamete) (仕事を)辞めます
(辞める, 辞めて), jishoku shimás<u>u</u>
(suru, sh<u>i</u>te) 辞職します(する, して)
resignation *n* **1.** (*quitting a job*)
jishoku 辞職 **2.** (*acceptance*) akirame
諦め, kákugo 覚悟
resigned; *is ~ to* ... o kákúgo shimás<u>u</u>
(suru, sh<u>i</u>te) ...を覚悟します(する, し
て), akiramemás<u>u</u> (akiraméru, akirámete) 諦めます(諦める, 諦めて)
resin *n* yaní やに・ヤニ, (*pine*) matsu-
yani 松やに・マツヤニ; (*synthetic resin*)
gōsei jushi 合成樹脂
resist *v* ... ni hankō/teikō shimás<u>u</u>
(suru, sh<u>i</u>te) ...に反抗/抵抗します(す
る, して), kobamimás<u>u</u> (kobámu,
kobánde) 拒みます(拒む, 拒んで)
resistance *n* hankō 反抗, teikō 抵抗
resolutely *adv* sh<u>í</u>kkári しっかり
resolution *n* (*preparation*) kákúgo
覚悟
resolve 1. *n* (*determination*) késshín
決心 **2.** *v* *resolves to do* (shiyō to)
késshin shimás<u>u</u> (suru, sh<u>i</u>te) (しよう
と)決心します(する, して) **3.** *v*
(*medical*) shōsan shimás<u>u</u> (suru, sh<u>i</u>te)
消散します(する, して)
resolved; *is ~ (to do)* kákúgo shimás<u>u</u>
(suru, sh<u>i</u>te) 覚悟します(する, して)

resonance *n* hankyō 反響, kyōmei
共鳴, zankyō 残響
resonate *v* kyōmei shimás<u>u</u> (suru,
sh<u>i</u>te) 共鳴します(する, して)
resound *v* (*echo*) hibikimás<u>u</u> (hib<u>í</u>ku,
hib<u>í</u>ite) 響きます(響く, 響いて)
respect 1. *n* sonkei 尊敬, uyamai 敬
い **2.** *v* sonkei shimás<u>u</u> (suru, sh<u>i</u>te) 尊
敬します(する, して); uyamaimás<u>u</u>
(uyamáu, uyamátte) 敬います(敬う,
敬って); ogamimás<u>u</u> (ogámu, ogánde)
拝みます(拝む, 拝んで); *Respect-
for-the-Aged Day* (*the 3rd Monday of
September*) Keirō no hí 敬老の日 **3.**
→ **with respect to**
respectable *adj* katagi (na) 堅気(な),
(*proper*) chanto sh<u>i</u>ta ...ちゃんとし
た...; (*considerable*) chótto sh<u>i</u>ta ... ち
ょっとした...
respective *adj* sorézore no ... それぞ
れの..., onóono no ... 各々[おのお
の]の..., kaku ... 各...
respectively *adv* sorézóre それぞれ,
onóono 各々・おのおの
respiration *n* kokyū 呼吸
respond *v* kotaemás<u>u</u> (kotáéru,
kotáete) 答えます(答える, 答えて);
ō-jimás<u>u</u> (ō-jiru, ō-jite) 応じます(応じ
る, 応じて)
response *n* kotáé 答え, resuponsu
レスポンス, resu レス
audience response *n* **1.** (*at stadium,
theater, etc.*) kankyaku no hannō 観客
の反応 **2.** (*TV, etc.*) shichō-sha no
hannō 視聴者の反応
responsibility *n* sekinin 責任; (*charge*)
tantō 担当; (*cause*) gen'in 原因
sense of responsibility *n* sekinin-kan
責任感
responsible; *~ for* (*is in charge of*) ...
o tantō sh<u>i</u>te imás<u>u</u> (iru, ite) ...を担当
しています(いる, いて); (*is the cause
of*) ... no gen'in des<u>u</u> ...の原因です
responsible person *n* sekinín-sha
責任者; (*the one in charge*) tantō´-sha
担当者
rest 1. *n* (*a break/pause*) yasumí 休み
(o-yasumi お休み), [BOOKISH] kyukei
休憩 **2.** *n* *the rest* (*remainder*) nokorí
残り; (*thereafter*) sore kara áto (wa)

それから後(は) **3.** v *(takes a rest)*
yasumimás̱u (yasúmu, yasúnde) 休み
ます(休む, 休んで)

rest room n toire トイレ, keshó´-shítsu
化粧室, (o-)teárai (お)手洗い → **toilet**

restaurant n rés̱utoran レストラン,
shokudō 食堂; ryōrí-ten/-ya 料理店/屋

restless adj ochi-ts̱ukimasén 落ち着き
ません (ochi-ts̱ukanai 落ち着かない)

restoration n kaifuku 回復, fukugen
復元

restrain v osaemás̱u (osáéru, osáete)
抑えます(抑える, 抑えて); ***properly
restrained*** iikagen (na) いい加減(な)

restrict v seigen/gentei shimás̱u (suru,
sh̠ite) 制限/限定します(する, して)

restricted adj fú-jiyū (na) 不自由(な)

restriction n seigen 制限, gentei 限定

result n kekka 結果; *(outcome)* séika
成果; *(marks, grades)* seiseki 成績
experimental result n jikken kekka
実験成果
laboratory results n kensa kekka
検査結果
study results n kenkyū seika 研究成果

resume 1. n rireki-sho 履歴書 **2.** v
(continue) saikai shimás̱u (suru, sh̠ite)
再開します(する, して)

retail 1. n ko-uri 小売 **2.** v *(retails it)*
ko-uri shimás̱u (suru, sh̠ite) 小売りし
ます(する, して)
retail price n ko-uri kakaku 小売価格
retail shop n ko-uri-ten 小売店

retailer n ko-uri gyōsha 小売業者

retain v *(keeps it)* kakaemás̱u (kakaeru,
kakaete) 抱えます(抱える, 抱えて)

retentiveness n *(of memory)* kiokú-
ryoku 記憶力

reticence n enryo 遠慮 (go-enryo
ご遠慮)

retire v **1.** *(from job)* intai/taishoku
shimás̱u (suru, sh̠ite) 引退/退職します
(する, して) **2.** *(withdraws)* shirizoki-
más̱u (shirizoku, shirizóite) 退きます
(退く, 退いて) h̠íki-torimás̱u (h̠íki-
tóru, h̠íki-tótte) 引き取ります(引き取
る, 引き取って)

retirement n intai 引退, taishoku 退職
retirement allowance n taishokúkin
退職金

retirement pension n taishoku-nénkin
退職年金

retort 1. v *(refutes)* hanron shimás̱u
(suru, sh̠ite) 反論する, iikaeshimás̱u
(iikaesu, iikaeshite) 言い返します(言
い返す, 言い返して) **2.** v *(revenges)*
shikaeshi o shimás̱u (suru, sh̠ite) **3.** n
(answer back) iikaeshi 言い返し **4.** ~
food n retoruto shokuhin レトルト食品

retreat 1. n *(escape)* hinan 避難, *(retirement)* intai 引退, *(stay-at-home)* hikiko-
mori 引きこもり **2.** v shirizokimás̱u
(shirizoku, shirizóite) 退きます(退く,
退いて)

retribution n bachi 罰・ばち

return v **1.** *(reverses direction)* modo-
rimás̱u (modósu, modótte) 戻ります
(戻る, 戻って); *(goes back/home)*
kaerimás̱u (káeru, káette) 帰ります
(帰る, 帰って); *(comes back to where
one is now)* itte kimás̱u (kúru, kité)
行って来ます(来る, 来て); ~ *from
abroad* kíkoku shimás̱u (suru, sh̠ite)
帰国します(する, して) **2.** *returns
it* kaeshimás̱u (káesu, káeshite) 返し
ます(返す, 返して); modoshimás̱u
(modósu, modóshite) 戻します(戻す,
戻して); *(turns back)* h̠iki-kaeshimás̱u
(h̠iki-káesu, h̠iki-káeshite) 引き返し
ます(引き返す, 引き返して) **3.** n
(response) hentō 返答; *(replacement)*
henkyaku 返却; *(restoration)* kaifuku
回復

return ticket n ōfuku kippu 往復切符

return trip n ōfuku ryokō 往復旅行

returnee n kikokushijo 帰国子女

reveal v morashimás̱u (morásu,
moráshite) 漏らします(漏らす, 漏ら
して); arawashimás̱u (arawásu,
arawáshite) 現(わ)します(現(わ)す,
現(わ)して); *(makes it
public)* akíraka ni shimás̱u (suru, sh̠ite)
明らかにします(する, して)

revelation n otsuge お告げ

revenge v *(... no)* fukushū o shimás̱u
(suru, sh̠ite) (...の)復讐をします(する,
して)

revenue n **1.** *(governmental revenue)*
sainyū 歳入 **2.** *(income)* shūnyū 収入,
shūeki 収益

532

revenue stamp n shūnyū-ínshi 収入
印紙

revere v uyamaimásu (uyamáu,
uyamátte) 敬います(敬う, 敬って)

reverence n sonkei 尊敬; uyamai 敬い

Reverend n … bokushi …牧師, …
shínpu …神父

reverse 1. n, adj hantai (no) 反対(の),
gyaku (no) 逆(の); (back; lining) urá
(no) 裏(の), uragawa (no) 裏側(の)
2. v (to turn around) gyaku [sakasama/
hanten/hantai] shimásu (suru, shite)
逆[逆さま/反転/反対]にします(す
る, して), uragaeshimásu (uragaesu,
uragáeshite) 裏返します(裏返す, 裏
返して)

reversible adj ribāshiburu (no) リバー
シブル(の)

revert v modorimásu (modóru,
modótte) 戻ります(戻る, 戻って)

review 1. n rebyū レビュー, (study)
fukushū 復習; (criticism) híhyō 批評,
(commentary) hyōron 評論 **2.** v
(studies it) fukushū shimásu (suru,
shite) 復習します(する, して);
(criticizes it/comments on it) híhyō/
hyōron shimásu (suru, shite) 批評/評
論します(する, して); (considers it)
kentō shimásu (suru, shite) 検討しま
す(する, して)
book review n shohyō 書評
movie review n eiga hyōron 映画評論

reviewer n hyōron-ka 評論家

revise v kaitei shimásu (suru, shite)
改訂します(する, して)

revision n kaitei(-ban) 改訂(版), kōsei
校正

revival n (regeneration) fukkatsu 復活,
saisei 再生, ribaibaru リバイバル →
recover

revive v (brings back to life)
ikashimásu (ikásu, ikáshite) 生かしま
す(生かす, 生かして)

revoke v tori-keshimásu (tori-kesu,
tori-keshite) 取り消します(取り消す,
取り消して)

revolt 1. n hanran 反乱, hankō 反抗
2. v somukimásu (somúku, somúite)
背きます(背く, 背いて); hanran o
okoshimásu (okosu, okoshite) 反乱を起

こします(起こす, 起こして)

revolution n (political) kakumei 革命,
reboryūshon レボリューション;
(revolving) kaiten 回転
French Revolution n Furansu kakumei
フランス革命

revolve v mawarimásu (mawaru,
mawatte) 回ります(回る, 回って),
kaiten shimásu (suru, shite) 回転しま
す(する, して)

revolver n písutoru ピストル, riborubā
リボルバー

reward 1. n shōkin 賞金, shō'yo 賞与;
sharei 謝礼; (go-)hō'bi (ご)ほうび・
褒美 **2.** v rewards for (...shita) kai ga
arimásu (aru, atte) (...した)かいがあ
ります(ある・あって)
rewards and punishments shōbatsu
賞罰

rewrite; rewrite it kakí-naoshimásu
(kaki-naosu, kaki-naoshite) 書き直し
ます(書き直す, 書き直して), kakí-
kaemásu (kakí-kaéru, kakí-kaete) 書き
換えます(書き換える, 書き換えて)

rhino n sai サイ・犀

rhubarb n bog ~ fuki フキ・蕗

rhythm n rízumu リズム

rhythmical adj rizumikaru (na) リズ
ミカル(な)

rib n rokkotsu ろっ骨・肋骨,
abarabone あばら骨・肋骨

ribbon n himo ひも・紐, ríbon リボン
ink ribbon n inku ríbon インクリボン

rice n komé (o-kome) 米(お米);
(cooked) góhan ご飯, meshí 飯, (on
plate) ráisu ライス; (at store) o-kome
お米; (hulled) komé 米, (unhulled)
momí もみ・籾; (unpolished) génmai
玄米, (polished) hakúmai 白米; (plant)
íne 稲; Chinese fried ~ chā'han チャ
ーハン・炒飯; ~ boiled in a soup 雑
炊; ~ boiled with red beans sekíhan
(o-sekíhan) 赤飯(お赤飯); ~ topped
with something donburi どんぶり・
丼; dom(buri)-mono どん(ぶり)もの
・丼もの; (with chicken and onion
cooked in egg) oyako-dónburi/don
親子どんぶり[丼]; (with pork cutlet
cooked in egg) katsu-don カツ丼; (with
tenpura shrimp on top) ten-don 天丼;

533

~ with hot tea (o-)chazuke（お）茶漬け

rice bowl *n* chawan 茶碗(o-cháwan お茶碗)

rice bucket/tub *n* meshi-bitsu 飯びつ [櫃], o-hítsu おひつ[櫃], o-hachi お鉢

rice cake *n* (o-)mochi（お）もち・モチ・餅; **toasted ~** yaki-móchi 焼き餅; **~ in vegetable soup** zōni 雑煮・ぞう煮 (o-zōni お雑煮)

rice cooker *n* suihanki 炊飯器

rice crackers *n* sénbe(i) せんべい[煎餅], o-sénbe(i) おせんべ(い); (*cubes, tidbits*) arare あられ

rice curry *n* (*rice with curry*) karē-ráisu カレーライス

rice dealer *n* komé-ya (o-komeya) 米屋(お米屋)

rice field *n* tá 田, tanbo 田んぼ, suiden 水田

rice gruel/porridge *n* (o-)kayu （お）かゆ[粥]

rice paper *n* (*stationery*) hánshi 半紙

rice planting *n* taué 田植え

rice scoop *n* shamoji しゃもじ

rice straw *n* wára わら・藁

rice wine → saké

riceball *n* musubi むすび・結び (o-músubi おむすび); nigiri-meshi にぎり[握り]飯, o-nígiri おにぎり; **~ lunch(box)** makunóuchi(bentō) 幕の内(弁当)

rich *adj* (*wealthy*) kanemóchi (no) 金持ち(の), yūfuku (na) 裕福(な), ritchi (na) リッチ(な); (*abundant*) yútaka (na) 豊か(な), hōfu (na) 豊富(な); **is rich/ abundant in …** ni tomimásu (tómu, tónde) … に富みます(富む, 富んで)

rich person *n* okanemochi お金持ち

rickshaw *n* jinríkisha 人力車

riddle *n* nazo 謎, nazonazo なぞなぞ

ride **1.** *n* (*ride a vehicle*) jōsha 乗車, (*driving*) doraibu ドライブ, (*horse riding*) jōba 乗馬 **2.** *v …* ni norimásu (noru, notte) …に乗ります(乗る, 乗って), … ni notte ikimásu (iku, itte) …に乗って行きます(行く, 行って); (*sits astride*) matagarimásu (matagáru, matagátte) またがり[跨り]ます(またがる, またがって) **3.** *gives a ~ to …* v o nosemásu (noseru, nosete) … を乗

せます(乗せる, 乗せて)

ridge *n* (*of roof*) mune 棟

ridiculous *adj* bakageta ばかげた, bakabakashii ばかばかしい

rifle *n* shōjū 小銃, raifurú (-jū) ライフル(銃), teppō 鉄砲

right **1.** *adj* (*adv*) (*not left*) migi (no) 右(の) **2.** *adj* (*correct*) tadashíi (tadáshíku) 正しい(正しく), íi いい, yóku 良く **3.** *n* (*privilege*) kénri 権利 **just right** *adj* píttári ぴったり That's right. *interj* Sō' desu. そうです。, Sonotō'ri desu. その通りです。

right after *adv* chokugo (ni) 直後(に)

right there *adv* chōdo (a)soko (ni) ちょうど(あ)そこ(に)

voting right *n* tōhyō-ken 投票権, senkyo-ken 選挙権

You are so right. *interj* Naruhodo. なるほど。

right and wrong *n* zén-aku 善悪

right away *adv* (*at once*) sassokú 早速

right click *n* migi kurikku 右クリック

right-handed *adj* migi-kíki (no) 右利き(の)

right mind; **in one's ~** shōki (no) 正気(の)

right or wrong *n* zé-hi 是非

rightful *adj* seitō (na) 正当(な)

rightly *adv* tadashiku 正しく

rightness *n* (*justice*) seigi 正義

rigid *adj* katai 堅い・硬い

rim *n* herí へり・縁, fuchí ふち・縁

rind *n* kawa 皮

ring *n* (*on finger*) yubi-wa 指輪, ringu リング; (*circle*) wá 輪, maru 丸・円, en 円

engagement ring *n* konyaku yubi-wa 婚約指輪, engēji ringu エンゲージリング

ring finger *n* kusuri yubi 薬指

wedding ring *n* kekkon yubi-wa 結婚指輪

ring *v* (*a bell sounds*) narimásu (naru, natte) 鳴ります(鳴る, 鳴って); (*sounds a bell*) narashimásu (narasu, narashite) 鳴らします(鳴らす, 鳴らして)

ringleader *n* óya-bun 親分

ring-shaped *adj* kanjō (no) 環状(の)

ringtone *n* chaku mero 着メロ, chakushin-on 着信音

ringworm *n* tamushi タムシ・田虫, mizumushi 水虫・ミズムシ

rink *n* aisu sukēto-jō アイススケート場, (rōrā) sukēto-jō (ローラー)スケート場

rinse *v* yusugimásu (yusugu, yusuide) ゆすぎます(ゆすぐ, ゆすいで); susugimásu (susugu, susuide) すすぎます(すすぐ, すすいで)

riot *n* bōdō 暴動, sōdō 騒動

ripen *v* (*it gets ripe*) jukushimásu (jukúsú, jukúshite) 熟します(熟す, 熟して), seijuku shimásu (suru, shite) 成熟します(する, して); minorimásu (minoru, minotte) 実ります(実る, 実って)

ripped; gets ~ off (*overcharged*) boraremásu (boraréru, borárete) ぼられます(ぼられる, ぼられて), (*robbed*) yararemásu (yarareru, yararete) やられます(やられる, やられて)

rise 1. *n* (*in price, wage, fee*) híki-age 引き上げ; **gives ~ to** ... o okoshimásu (okósu, okóshite) ...を起こします(起こす, 起こして), shō-jimásu (shō-jiru, shō-jite) 生じます(生じる, 生じて) **2.** *v* (*gets up*) okimásu (okíru, ókite) 起きます(起きる, 起きて), (*goes up*) agarimásu (agaru, agatte) 上がります(上がる, 上がって), (*climbs, sun rises*) noborimásu (noboru, nobotte) 登り[昇り]ます(登[昇]る, 登[昇]って), (*stands up*) tachi-agarimásu (tachi-agaru, tachi-agátte) 立ち上がります(立ち上がる, 立ち上がって), (*looms*) sobiemásu (sobiéru, sobíete) そびえ[聳え]ます(そびえる, そびえて)

rising 1. *n* (*riot*) hanran 反乱, bōdō 暴動 **2.** *n, adj* (*uprise*) jōshō (shita) 上昇(した)

rising smoke *n* tachinoboru kemuri 立ち昇る煙

rising yen *n* endaka 円高

rising sun *n* ásahi 朝日; noboru taiyō 昇る太陽

flag of the Rising Sun *n* hi no maru 日の丸; [BOOKISH] nisshōki 日章旗

risk *n* risuku リスク; kiken 危険

risky *adj* risukii (na) リスキー(な); kiken (na) 危険(な)

rival *n* teki 敵; kyōgōsha 競合者, raibaru ライバル

rivalry *n* kyōsō 競争; **in ~ with** ... ni taikō shite ...に対抗して

river *n* kawá 川・河

riverbank *n* kawagishi 川岸

river trout *n* áyu あゆ・アユ・鮎, ái あい・アイ

rivet *n* ribetto リベット; byō 鋲・びょう

road *n* michi 道, dōʹro 道路, (*main road*) kaidō 街道; (*roadway*) shadō 車道; (*roadside*) tsuji 辻, michibata 道端

road rage *n* kōtsūjūtai de no iraira 交通渋滞でのイライラ

road-show attraction *n* rōdo-shō ロードショー

roadside *n* michibata 道端, robō 路傍, tsuji 辻

road sign *n* dōro-hyōʹshíki 道路標識, rojō hyōshiki 路上標識

roam *v* idō 移動

roar 1. *n* (*a roar*) unari うなり・唸り **1.** *v* (*roars*) unarimásu (unáru, unátte) うなり[唸り]ます(うなる, うなって) **3.** *v* (*rumbles*) todorokimásu (todoróku, todoróite) とどろき[轟き]ます(とどろく, とどろいて)

roast 1. *n* yaki-... 焼き..., ...-yaki ...焼き; rōʹsuto ロースト; **~ beef/chicken** rōsuto-bíifu/-chíkin ローストビーフ/チキン **2.** *v* (*roasts it*) yakimásu (yaku, yaite) 焼きます(焼く, 焼いて); irimásu (íru, ítte) いり[炒り]ます(いる, いって)

roasted chestnuts *n* yaki-guri 焼き栗

rob *v* (*steals*) nusumimásu (nusúmu, nusúnde) 盗みます(盗む, 盗んで); (*plunders*) ubaimásu (ubáu, ubátte) 奪います(奪う, 奪って); (*robs it of* ...) kasume-torimásu (kasume-tóru, kasume-tótte) かすめ取ります(かすめ取る, かすめ取って); **gets robbed** (*hit with a robbery*) (gōtō ni) yararemásu (yarareru, yararete) (強盗に)やられます(やられる, やられて)

robber *n* gōtō 強盗, dorobō どろぼう・泥棒; zoku 賊

robbery *n* gōtō 強盗

robin n komadori コマドリ

robot n robotto ロボット

rock n (*stone*) ishí 石, (*crag*) iwá 岩; (*music*) rókku ロック (also *rock'n'roll* rokkun-rōru ロックンロール)

rock v (*it rocks*) yuremásu (yureru, yurete) 揺れます(揺れる、揺れて)

rock-climbing n rokku kuraimingu ロッククライミング, iwanobori 岩登り

rocket n rokétto ロケット

rocking chair n yuriisu 揺り椅子

rocking horse n yurimokuba 揺り木馬

rocky adj iwa no ōi 岩の多い

Rocky Mountains n Rokkii maunten ロッキーマウンテン, Rokkii sanmyaku ロツキー山脈

rod n saó さお・竿; (*curtain, etc.*) róddo ロッド

roe n (*caviar*)*; salmon* ~ ikura イクラ, (*salmon/trout*) sujiko スジコ・筋子, suzuko スズコ, *cod* ~ tarákó タラコ・鱈子

role n yakuwari 役割, yakú 役, o-yaku-me お役目; tsutomé 務め (o-tsutome お務め)

roll 1. v (*it rolls*) korogarimásu (korogaru, korogatte) 転がります(転がる、転がって); (*sways*) yuremásu (yureru, yurete) 揺れます(揺れる、揺れて); (*rolls it*) korogashimásu (korogasu, korogashite) 転がします(転がす、転がして); (*rolls it up*) makimásu (maku, maite) 巻きます(巻く、巻いて) 2. n (*bread*) rōru-pan ロールパン, (batā-)rō´ru (バター)ロール 3. n (*a roll of toilet paper*) (toiretto-pē´pā) híto-maki (トイレットペーパー)一巻; ~ *of* (*currency*) *bills* satsu-taba 札束 4. n (*list of names*) meibo 名簿

roller n rō´rā ローラー

roller coaster n jetto kōsutā ジェットコースター

roller blade n rōrā burēdo ローラーブレード

roller skates n rōrā sukēto gutsu ローラースケート靴

roller-skating n rōrā sukēto ローラースケート

ROM (read only memory) n (*computer*) romu ロム

romance n rómansu ロマンス, ren'ai 恋愛, roman ロマン, rōman 浪漫

romance gray n romansu gurei ロマンスグレイ

romance novel n romansu shōsetsu ロマンス小説, ren'ai shōsetsu 恋愛小説

Romania n Rūmania ルーマニア

romanization n rōmá-ji ローマ字

romantic adj romanchikku (na) ロマンチック(な)

Rome n Rō´ma ローマ

roof 1. n yáne 屋根; (*rooftop floor*) okujō 屋上 2. v *roofs a house* uchi no yáne o fukimásu (fuku, fuite) 家の屋根をふき[葺き]ます(ふく、ふいて)

roofed adj yanetsuki (no) 屋根付き(の) roofed passageway n ā´kēdo アーケード

rookie n 1. shinjin 新人 2. (*player*) shinjin senshu 新人選手, rūkii ルーキー

room n 1. heyá 部屋 (o-heya お部屋), (…-) ma (…)間; …-shítsu …室; (*tatami room*) zashíki 座敷 (o-zashíki お座敷) 2. (*extra space*) yochi 余地, (*leeway*) yoyū 余裕

Japanese-style room n washitsu 和室

room and board n geshuku 下宿

rooming/boarding house n geshuku-ya 下宿屋

roommate n dōshítsú-sha 同室者, rūmu-meito ルームメイト

room number n heya (no) bangō´ 部屋(の)番号, …-gō shítsu …号室

Room No. 3 san-gō´shítsu 三号室

room service n rūmu-sā´bisu ルームサービス

rooms for rent n kashi-ma 貸間

tatami room n zashíkí (o-zashíki) 座敷(お座敷)

Western-style room n yōshitsu 洋室, yōma 洋間

root n né 根, *near the root* ne-motó 根元; (*cause*) gen'in 原因

root of all evil n shoaku no kongen 諸悪の根源

roots of a tree n ki no ne 木の根

root of a word n gogen 語源

rope *n* nawá 縄・繩・なわ, tsuná 綱・つな; rōpu ロープ; ***mountain-climbing ~*** záiru ザイル

rose *n* bara (no haná) バラ[薔薇](の花)

rosy *adj* bairairo (no) ばら色(の)

rot *v* kuchimásu (kuchiru, kuchite) 朽ちます(朽ちる, 朽ちて), kusarimásu (kusáru, kusátte) 腐ります(腐る, 腐って)

rotary → **traffic circle**

rotate *v* kaiten shimásu (suru, shite) 回転します(する, して)

rotation *n* kaiten 回転

rouge *n* béni べに・紅

rough 1. *adj* (*coarse*; *wild*) arai 荒い[粗い], zatsu-… 雑…; (*in texture*) zárazara (shíta …) ざらざら(した…); (*bumpy*) dekoboko (no) でこぼこ・凸凹(の); (*rambunctious*) ranbō (na) 乱暴(な); (*approximate*) ōyoso (no) およそ(の); ōmaka na おおまかな; daitai (no) 大体(の); (*sloppy*) zonzai (na) ぞんざい(な), zóppa (na) ざっぱ(な) **2.** *gets ~* aremásu (areru, arete) 荒れます(荒れる, 荒れて); ***gets a ~ idea of it*** kentō ga tsukimásu (tsukú, tsúite) 見当がつきます(つく, ついて)

　rough manners *n* busahō 不作法

　rough road *n* dekoboko (shita) michi でこぼこ(した)道

　rough schedule *n* ōmaka na yotei おおまかな予定, daitai no yotei 大体の予定

　rough work *n* arashigoto 荒仕事

roughly *adv* ōyoso おおよそ; daitai 大体, zatto ざっと; hóbo ほぼ; …-kéntō …見当

roughneck *n* abare-mono 暴れ者, abarenbō 暴れん坊

round 1. *n, adj* enkei (no) 円形(の), wa 輪, marui 丸い; ***~ thing*** tamá 玉・珠; ***make ~*** maruku shimásu (suru, shite) 丸くします(する, して) **2.** *n* (*game, match*) raundo ラウンド, shiai 試合 **3.** *rounds off* *v* shishagonyū shimásu (suru, shite) 四捨五入します(する, して) **4.** *adv* (*during*) … no aida-jū …の間中; marumeru 丸める

　final round *n* kesshō-sen 決勝戦

　first-round match *n* (dai) ikkai-sen 第1回戦, yosen 予選

round-up amount *n* gaisan 概算

round-eyed *adj* me o marukushita 目を丸くした

round face *n* marugao 丸顔

round figure *n* gaisū 概数

round screw *n* maru neji 丸ネジ

round shape *n* enkei 円形; marui katachi 丸い形

round-table *n* maru tēburu 丸テーブル, [BOOKISH] en taku 円卓

round-the-world *adj* sekai isshū (no) 世界一周の

round trip (ticket) *n* ōfuku(-kíppu) 往復(切符)

roundabout → **traffic circle**

roundly *adv* maruku 丸く

roundtable discussion *n* zadán-kai 座談会

rouse *v* okoshimásu (okósu, okóshite) 起こします(起こす, 起こして)

route *n* sén 線; rūto ルート; keiro 経路; (*bus, train*) rosen 路線

　administration route *n* (*medicine, etc.*) tōyo keiro 投与経路

routine *n* **1.** nikka 日課 **2.** (*computer*) rūchin ルーチン

　routine work *n* o-kimari no shigoto お決まりの仕事, kima(riki)tta shigoto 決ま(りき)った仕事; [BOOKISH] nichijō gyōmu 日常業務

roux *n* rū ルー

row 1. *n* (*line*) rétsu 列, narabi 並び, (*of trees*) namiki 並木; ***… are in a row*** … narande imásu (iru, ite) 並んでいます(いる, いて); (*linked*) *in a ~* tsunagatte つながって **1.** *v* (*a boat*) kogimásu (kógu, kóide) こぎ[漕ぎ]ます(こぐ, こいで) **3.** *v* (*to quarrel*) kenka shimásu (suru, shite) けんかします(する, して), kōron shimásu (suru, shite) 口論します(する, して)

　first row of seats *n* saizenretsu (no seki) 最前列(の席)

royal *adj* ō (no) 王(の)

　royal family *n* **1.** ōzoku 王族, ōshitsu 王室 **2.** (*Japanese*) kōshitsu 皇室

royalty *n* chosakuken ryō 著作権料, (*on a book*) inzei 印税

royalty basis *n* inzei hōshiki 印税方式

royal blend *n* roiyaru burendo ロイヤルブレンド

royal flush *n* roiyaru furasshu ロイヤルフラッシュ

royal jelly *n* roiyaru zerii ロイヤルゼリー

royal road *n* ōdō 王道, *(shortcut)* chikamichi 近道, *(easy way)* raku na hōhō 楽な方法

royal rule *n* ōsei 王政・王制

rub 1. *n* masatsu 摩擦; *(difficulty)* konnan 困難 2. *v (rubs it)* kosurimásu (kosúru, kosútte) こすります(こする, こすって), surimásu (súru, sútte) 擦ります(擦る, 擦って), masatsu shimásu (suru, shite) 摩擦します(する, して); *(with both hands)* momimásu (momu, monde) もみ[揉み]ます(もむ, もんで) 3. *(it rubs)* suremásu (suréru, súrete) 擦れます(擦れる, 擦れて)

rubber *n* gómu ゴム; *(condom)* sákku サック; ~ band wa-gomu 輪ゴム

rubbish *n* 1. gomí ごみ・ゴミ; kúzu くず・屑, kuzu-mono くず物, garakuta がらくた 2. *(failure)* dasaku 駄作 3. *v (to rubbish a rumor)* ... o kenashimásu (kenaru, kenashite) ...をけなします(けなす, けなして)

rubbish bin *n* gomí-bako ごみ箱・ゴミ箱

rubbish vehicle *n* gomí kaishū-sha ごみ・ゴミ回収車

rubella *n* hashika はしか; fūshin 風疹

ruble *n* rūburu ルーブル

ruby *n* rubii ルビー, kōgyoku 紅玉

rucksack *n* ryukkusakku リュックサック

rudder *n* káji かじ・舵

rude *adj* búrei (na) 無礼(な); buénryo (na) 無遠慮(な)

rudiment *n (basic)* kiso 基礎

ruffian *n* abare-mono 暴れ者

rug *n* shíki-mono 敷物, jū´tan じゅうたん・絨毯

rugby *n* ragubii ラグビー

ruin 1. *ruins it v* damé ni shimásu (suru, shite) だめ[駄目]にします(する, して); arashimásu (arásu, árete) 荒らします(荒らす, 荒れて); *ruins*

one's health karada o kowashimásu (kowásu, kowáshite) 体を[からだを]こわします(こわす, こわして) 2. *goes to ~ v* aremásu (areru, arete) 荒れます(荒れる, 荒れて) 3. *ruins n* iseki 遺跡

ruined; *gets ~* damé ni narimásu (náru, nátte) だめ[駄目]になります(なる, なって)

rule 1. *n (regulation)* kísoku 規則, kítei 規定; rū´ru ルール; *(law)* hōsoku 法則, hō´ 法 2. *v shihai shimásu (suru, shite) 支配します(する, して)

ruler *n (to measure with)* jō´gi 定規, *(foot rule)* monosáshi ものさし・物差し

ruling party *n* yōtō 与党

rum *n* ramu-shu ラム酒

rum-soaked raisins *n* ramu-zuke (no) rēzun ラム浸け(の)レーズン

rumble *v* todorokimásu (todoróku, todoróite) とどろき[轟き]ます(とどろく, とどろいて)

rumor *n* uwasa うわさ・噂

run 1. *n (dash)* kyōsō 競走; *(exercise)* ranning ランニング; *a ~ for one's money* doryoku ni miatta mikaeri 努力に見合った見返り 2. *v* hashirimásu (hashíru, hashítte) 走ります(走る, 走って), *(gallops)* kakemásu (kakéru, kákete) 駆けます(駆ける, 駆けて); *runs a marathon* marason o shimásu (suru, shite) マラソンをします(する, して) 3. *v (connects)* tsū-jimásu (tsū-jiru, tsū-jite) 通じます(通じる, 通じて) 5. *v (operates a machine)* unten shimásu (suru, shite) 運転します(する, して) 6. *v (manages, operates a business)* keihei shimásu (suru, shite) 経営します(する, して)

run along *v (side)* soimásu (sou, sotte) 沿います(沿う, 沿って)

run away *v (flees)* nigemásu (nigéru, nígete) 逃げます(逃げる, 逃げて), ochimásu (ochíru, óchite) 落ちます(落ちる, 落ちて); *(from home)* (uchi o) tobi-dashimásu (tobi-dásu, tobi-dashite) (家を)飛び出します(飛び出す, 飛び出して), iede shimásu (suru, shite) 家出します(する, して)

run fast *v (timepiece)* susumimásu

(susumu, susunde) 進みます(進む, 進んで)

run into v **1.** → **collide 2.** → **meet 3.** (*comes to the end of a street*) tsuki-atarimásu (tsuki-ataru, tsuki-atatte) 突き当たります(突き当たる, 突き当たって)

run out v **1.** (*dashes out*) tobi-dashi-másu (tobi-dásu, tobi-dáshite) 跳び[飛び]出します(跳び[飛び]出す, 跳び[飛び]出して) **2.** *it runs out* (*stock is exhausted*) kiremásu (kiréru, kírete) 切れます(切れる, 切れて), (*gets used up*) tsukimásu (tsukiru, tsukite) 尽きます(尽きる, 尽きて) **3.** *runs out of ...* o kirashimásu (kirásu, kiráshite) ...o 切らします(切らす, 切らして), ...o tsukaitsukushimásu (tsukaitsukúsu, tsukaitsukúshite) ...を使い尽くします(使い尽くす, 使い尽くして), tsukaihatashimásu (tsukaihatasu, tsukaihatashite) 使い果たします(使い果たす, 使い果たして), (*it sells out*) uri-kiremásu (uri-kiréru, uri-kírete) 売り切れます(売り切れる, 売り切れて)

run over v **1.** (*a person*) híkimásu (híku, hiite) ひきます・轢きます (ひく, ひいて); *gets ~ by* ... ni híkaremásu (híkareru, híkarete) ...に ひかれます[轢かれ]ます(ひかれる, ひかれて) **2.** → **exceed**

run overtime v jikan ga ō´bā shimásu (suru, shite) 時間がオーバーします (する, して), jikan o sugimásu (sugiru, sugite) 時間を過ぎます(過ぎる, 過ぎて)

run slow v (*it lags*) okuremásu (okureru, okurete) 遅れます(遅れる, 遅れて)

runaway n **1.** (*from home*) iede-nin 家出人 **2.** (*escapee*) tōbō-sha 逃亡者

rune n rūn moji ルーン文字

runlet n ogawa 小川

runner n rannā ランナー; sōsha 走者

long-distance runner n chōkyori rannā 長距離ランナー; chōkyori sōsha 長距離走者

running n ranningu ランニング

running togs n ranningu wea ランニングウェア

running water n suidō 水道

runt n (*deprecating a short person*) chíbi ちび

rupee n rupii ルピー

rural adj inaka (no) いなか・田舎(の)

rush v isogimásu (isógu, isóide) 急ぎます(急ぐ, 急いで); ō-ísogi de shimásu (suru, shite) 大急ぎでします (する, して); *with a ~* (*suddenly*) dotto どっと; *feels rushed* aserimásu (aséru, asétte) 焦ります(焦る, 焦って)

rush hour n rasshu-áwā ラッシュアワー

Russia n Róshia ロシア; (*Soviet Union*) Sóren ソ連

Russian n (*person*) Roshiá-jin ロシア人; (*language*) Roshia-go ロシア語

rust **1.** n sabí さび・錆 **2.** v (*it rusts*) sabimásu (sabíru, sábite) さび[錆び]ます(さびる, さびて)

rustic adj inaka (no) 田舎・いなか (の), shísso (na) 質素(な); yábo (na) やぼ[野暮](な), yábottai やぼった い・野暮ったい

rusticity n inaka rashisa 田舎らしさ

rustle n sarasara/kasakasa to iu oto サラサラ/カサカサという音

rustless **1.** (*rustproof*) sabínai さび [錆び]ない **2.** sabiteinai さびて[錆び て]いない

rustproof adj sabínai さび[錆び]ない

rusty n sabita さびた・錆びた

rut n wa-dachi わだち・轍

rutabaga n rutabaga ルタバガ

ruthless adj mujihi (na) 無慈悲(な); reikoku (na) 冷酷(な)

ruthlessly adv mujihi ni 無慈悲に; reikoku ni 冷酷に

Rwanda n Ruwanda ルワンダ

rye n raimugi ライ麦・ライムギ

rye bread n raimugi pan ライ麦・ラ イムギパン; kuro pan 黒パン

rye whisky, rye whiskey n rai wisukii ライウィスキー

Ryukyu (islands) n Ryūkyū´ 琉球 (= Okinawa)

S

Sabbath *n* ansoku-bi 安息日

sabbatical **1.** *n* ichinen kyūka 一年休暇 **2.** *adj* Sabbatical ansokubi (no) 安息日の

sabotage *n* bōgai kōsaku 妨害工作, hakai kōsaku 破壊工作, sabotāju サボタージュ

saccharin *n* sakkarin サッカリン

sack **1.** *n* (*bag*) fukuró 袋, (*large bag*) ōkina fukuro 大きな袋 **2.** (*pillage*) ryakudatsu 略奪 **3.** (*dismissal from employment*) kaiko 解雇 **4.** (*bed*) beddo ベッド, shindai 寝台

sack *v* **1.** kaiko shimásu (suru, shite) 解雇します(する, して) **2.** [INFORMAL] kubi ni shimásu (suru, shite) 首にします(する, して)

sacking *n* **1.** (*laying off*) kaiko 解雇 **2.** (*cloth*) asa nuno 麻布

sacrament *n* seireiten 聖礼典

sacred *adj* **1.** (*holy*) shinsei (na) 神聖(な) **2.** (*religious*) shūkyō-teki (na) 宗教的な, shūkyō (no) 宗教の
sacred building *n* sei-dō 聖堂

sacrifice **1.** *n* gisei 犠牲, ikenie 生(け)贄; *makes a ~* (*scapegoat*) *of ... o* gisei ni shimásu (suru, shite) ...を犠牲にします(する, して); *offers a ~* ikenie ni shimásu (suru, shite) 生(け)贄にします(する, して) **2.** *is sacrificed* *v* gisei ni narimásu (náru, nátte) を犠牲になります(なる, なって)

sacrificial *adj* gisei (no) 犠牲(の), ikenie (no) 生(け)贄(の)

sacrilege *n* [BOOKISH] bōtoku 冒涜

sacrosanct *adj* shinsei fukashin (no) 神聖不可侵(の)

sad *adj* **1.** kanashii 悲しい; *to be ~* kanashimimásu (kanashimu, kanashin-de) 悲しみます(悲しむ, 悲しんで) **2.** (*regrettable*) zannen (na) 残念(な) **3.** (*miserable*) mijime (na) 惨め(な) **4.** (*deplorable*) nagekawashii 嘆かわしい
look sad *v* kanashisō ni miemásu (mieru, miete) 悲しそうに見えます(見える, 見えて)

sadden *v* kanashimasemásu (kanashimaseru, kanashimasete) 悲しませます(悲しませる, 悲しませて); kanashikunarimásu (kanashikunaru, kanashikunatte) 悲しくなります(悲しくなる, 悲しくなって)

saddle **1.** *n* (*for horse*) kurá くら・鞍 **2.** *n* (*of bicycle*) sadoru サドル **3.** *v* owasemásu (owaseru, owasete) 負わせます(負わせる, 負わせて)

saddlebag *n* sadorubaggu サドルバッグ

sadism *n* sadizumu サディズム, sado サド

sadist *n* sadisuto サディスト, sado サド

sadistic *adj* sadisuto-teki (na) サディスト的(な), kagyaku-teki (na) 加虐的(な)

sadness *n* kanashimi 悲しみ

sae *n* = *self-addressed envelope* henshiyō fūtō 返信用封筒

safari *n* safari サファリ, shuryō (ryokō) 狩猟(旅行), tanken (ryokō) 探検(旅行)
safari park *n* safari pāku サファリパーク

safe **1.** *adj* (*harmproof*) anzen (na) 安全(な); (*reliable*) dai-jō´bu (na) 大丈夫(な), jōbu (na) 丈夫(な); (*steady*) te-gatai 手堅い; (*certain*) táshika (na) 確か(な); kakujitsu (na) 確実(な) **2.** *n* (*strongbox*) kínko 金庫 **3.** *to be on the ~ side* nen no tamé (ni) 念のため[為](に); *plays it ~* daijí o torimásu (tóru, tótte) 大事をとります(とる, とって)

safe-conduct *n* (anzen) tsūkō kyoka-shō (安全)通行許可証

safe and sound *adj* buji (ni) 無事(に)

safeguard **1.** *n* (*protection*) hogo 保護 **2.** *n* (*safety device*) anzen sōchi 安全装置 **3.** *v* hógo shimásu (suru, shite) 保護します(する, して)

safely *adv* (*harmfree, without incident*) búji (ni) 無事(に); (*for sure*) chanto ちゃんと, táshika (ni) 確かに

safety *n* anzen 安全

safety assessment *n* anzen-sei hyōka 安全性評価

safety belt *n* anzén beruto 安全ベルト

safety driving *n* anzén na unten 安全な運転

safety first *n* anzen daiichi 安全第一

safety pin *n* anzénpín 安全ピン

safety zone *n* anzen-chítai 安全地帯

safflower *n* benibana 紅花

saffron *n* safuran サフラン

sag *v* tarumimásu (tarumu, tarunde) たるみます(たるむ、たるんで)、tawamimásu (tawamu, tawande) たわみます(たわむ、たわんで)

saga *n* **1.** sāga サーガ **2.** (*tales of adventure*) bōken monogatari 冒険物語 **3.** *n* (*tale of heroism*) eiyūden 英雄伝、eiyū monogatari 英雄物語

sagacity *n* kibin (sa) 機敏(さ)、meibin (sa) 明敏(さ)、sōmei (sa) 聡明さ、kashikosa 賢さ、chisei 知性

sage *n* **1.** (*wise person*) kenja 賢者、kenjin 賢人 **2.** (*saint*) seija 聖者、seijin 聖人 → saint

Sagittarius *n* (*star sign*) Ite-za 射手座・いて座

Sahara *n* Sahara サハラ; *Sahara desert* Sahara sabaku サハラ砂漠

said *v* iimáshíta (itta/yutta) 言いました(言った/ゆった) → say

sail **1.** *n* ho 帆 **2.** *v* (*makes a voyage*) kōkai shimásu (suru, shite) 航海します(する、して)

sailboard *n* sēru bōdo セールボード

sailboat *n* (kogata) hansen (小型)帆船、yotto ヨット

sailing *n* kōkai 航海

sailing boat *n* yotto ヨット

sailor *n* funánori 船乗り、súifu 水夫、sērā セーラー; (*member of the crew*) sen'in 船員; (*navy enlisted person*) súihei 水兵

saint *n* seija 聖者、seijin 聖人

saintly *adj* seija/seijin no yō (na) 聖者・聖人のよう(な)

saké *n* (*rice wine*) (o-)sake (お)酒、Nihon-shu 日本酒; *sweet ~* (*for cooking*) mirin みりん・味醂; *~ bottle/pitcher* (*decanter*) tokkuri とっくり・徳利; *~ cup* (o-)chóko (お)ちょこ、sakazuki 杯(o-sakazuki お杯); *~ offered to the gods* miki 神酒 = o-miki お神酒

sake; *for the ~ of …* no tamé ni …のために[為]に、*for the ~ of doing …* suru tamé ni …するため[為]に

Sakhalin *n* (*an island in the Sea of Okhotsk*) saharin サハリン、karafuto 樺太

salad *n* sárada サラダ

fruit salad *n* furūtsu sarada フルーツサラダ

salad bowl *n* sarada bōru サラダボウル

salad cream → salad dressing

salad dressing *n* sarada (yō) doresshingu サラダ(用)ドレッシング

salad oil *n* sarada oiru サラダオイル、sarada abura サラダ油

vegetable salad *n* yasai sarada 野菜サラダ

salamander *n* sanshō-uo 山椒魚・サンショウウオ

salami sausage *n* sarami サラミ、sarami sōsēji サラミソーセージ

salaried man *n* sararii man サラリーマン、kaisha-in 会社員、kyūryō-tori 給料取り

salary *n* hōkyū 俸給、(o-)kyū'ryō (お)給料、sárarii サラリー; (*monthly*) gekkyū 月給

sale *n* hanbai 販売; hatsubai 発売; (*special*) uridashi 売り出し、(bāgen) seru (バーゲン)セール; *~ goods/item*, (*something*) *for* ~ uri-mono 売り物

sales agency *n* hanbai-moto 販売元、hanbai dairi-ten 販売代理店

sales assistant, salesclerk, salesperson *n* ten'in 店員、uriko 売り子、hanbai-in 販売員

sales outlet *n* hanbái-ten 販売店

sales tax *n* uriage-zei 売上税

sales volume *n* hanbai-daka 販売高

saliva *n* tsúba つば・唾、tsubakí つばき・唾、[BOOKISH] daeki 唾液・だえき

salmon *n* sáke サケ・鮭、sámon サーモン、sháke シャケ・鮭; *~ roe* ikura イクラ; sujiko スジコ・筋子、suzuko スズコ

salon *n* saron サロン

saloon *n* **1.** (*great hall*) (ō-) hiroma (大)広間 **2.** (*bar*) sakaba 酒場

salt *n* shió 塩, o-shío お塩; *table ~* shokúen 食塩

salt shaker *n* shió-ire 塩入れ

salty *adj* shio-karái 塩辛い, shoppái しょっぱい

salute 1. *(n)* keirei 敬礼 **2.** *v* keirei shimásu (suru, shíte) 敬礼します(する,して)

salvage *n* hiki-age 引き揚げ

salvation *n* kyūsai 救済
  Salvation Army *n* kyūsei gun 救世軍

salve *n* **1.** *(ointment)* nankō 軟膏 **2.** *(comfort)* nagusame 慰め・なぐさめ

salvo *n* issei shageki 一斉射撃

samba *n* sanba サンバ

same 1. *pron* onaji … 同じ…, [BOOK-ISH] dō´(-) … 同…, **2.** *adj/adv* onaji yō´ (na/ni) 同じ様(な/に); *one and the ~* onaji 同じ; *~ period* dō´ki 同期; *~ time* dōji 同時

sample 1. *n* mihon 見本, sanpuru サンプル **2.** *n (free sample)* shikyō-hin 試供品 **3.** *v (samples; tries doing)* (shi)-te mimásu (míru, míte) (し)てみます (みる, みて)

samurai *n (Japanese warrior)* samurai 侍・サムライ, búshi 武士; *the way of the ~* bushi-dō 武士道

sanatorium *n* sanatoriumu サナトリウム; hoyóchi 保養地; ryōyō-jo 療養所

sanctify *v* shinseika shimásu (suru, shíte) 神聖化します(する,して)

sanction *n* [BOOKISH] seisai (sochi) 制裁(措置)

sanctity *n* shinseisa 神聖さ

sanctuary *n* **1.** sei-iki 聖域 **2.** *(asylum)* hinanjo 避難所 **3.** *(church)* kyōkai 教会

sand *n* suna 砂; *~ dune* sakyū 砂丘
  sandbag *n* suna-búkuro 砂袋
  sandbox *n* suna-ba 砂場
  sandcastle *n* suna no shiro 砂の城
  sandstone *n* sagan 砂岩

sandal *n* sandaru サンダル; *(Japanese traditional style) straw sandals* zōri 草履

sandalwood *n* byakudan ビャクダン・白檀

sandpaper *n* sandopē´pā サンドペーパー, kami-yásuri 紙やすり, yasurí-gami やすり紙

sandwich 1. *n* sandoítchi サンドイッチ; …-sándo …サンド; *tuna-fish ~* tsuna-sándo ツナサンド, *egg ~* tamago-sando タマゴ・卵サンド, *vegetable ~* yasai-sando 野菜サンド, cutlet sandwich katsu-sando カツサンド **2.** *becomes ~ (in)* *v (between)* hasamarimásu (hasamáru, hasamátte) はさまり[挟まり]ます(はさまる, は さまって)

sandy *adj* suna no 砂の, suna no yō (na) 砂のよう(な)

sane *adj* shōki (no) 正気(の)

San Francisco *n* Sanfuranshísuko サンフランシスコ

sanguine 1. *adj* kaikatsu (na) 快活 (な), *(happy-go-lucky)* rakuten-teki (na) 楽天的(な) **2.** *(optimistic)* rakkan-teki (na) 楽観的(な)

sanitary *adj* eisei-teki (na) 衛生的(な), eisei (no) 衛生(の); *~ napkin* (seiri)-yō) nápukín (生理用)ナプキン

sanitation *n* eisei 衛生, kōshū eisei 公衆衛生

sanity *n* shōki 正気, funbetsu 分別

Santa Claus *n* Santa (kurōsu) サンタ (クロース), Santa-san サンタさん
  "Santa Claus Is Comin' To Town" *n* "Santa ga machi ni yattekuru" 『サンタが街にやって来る』

sap *v* yowarasemásu (yowaraseru, yowarasete) 弱らせます(弱らせる, 弱らせて)

sapling *n* **1.** *(tree)* naegi 苗木 **2.** *(person)* wakamono 若者

sapphire *n* safaia サファイア

sapphism *n (lesbianism)* rezubian レズビアン, rezu レズ

sarcasm *n* hiniku 皮肉, iyami 嫌味

sarcastic *adj* hiniku (na) 皮肉(な), iyami (na) 嫌味(な), iyamippoi 嫌味っぽい

sardine *n* iwashi イワシ・鰯; *(baby)* shirasu シラス・白子; *(large, usually dried)* urume(-íwashi) ウルメ(イワシ)・潤目(鰯)

sase *n = self-addressed stamped envelope* kitte o hatta henshiyō futō 切手を貼った返信用封筒

sash *n (girdle)* óbi 帯; *(military)*

542

sukā´fu スカーフ; (window-sash)
mado-waku 窓枠, sásshi サッシ,
sásshu サッシュ

Satan n satan サタン, ákuma 悪魔

satanic adj satan (no) サタン(の),
ákuma (no) 悪魔(の)

satchel n kaban かばん・鞄

sate 1. v (satiate) tannō sasemásu
(saseru, sasete) 堪能させます(させる,
させて) 2. n (skewered food) satē サ
テー

satellite n eisei 衛星; sateraito サテラ
イト artificial satellite n jinkō eisei
人工衛星

satellite transmission n eisei chūkei
衛星中継 satellite TV n eisei terebi
衛星テレビ

satellize v eisei-ka shimásu (suru,
shite) 衛星化します(する, して)

satiate v (sate) tannō sasemásu (saseru,
sasete) 堪能させます(させる, させて)

satin n shúsu しゅす・繻子, sáten
サテン

satire n fūshi 風刺

satirical adj fūshi (no) 風刺(の),
fūshi-teki (na) 風刺的(な)

satisfaction n manzoku 満足

satisfactory adj yoroshii よろしい・
宜しい, mánzoku (na) 満足(な), mánzoku dekiru 満足できる, nattoku (no)
iku 納得(の)いく

satisfied; v gets ~ mánzoku shimásu
(suru, shite) 満足します(する, して)

satisfy v mánzoku sasemásu (saseru,
sasete) 満足させます(させる, させて);
(fulfills) mitashimásu (mitásu, mitáshite)
満たします(満たす, 満たして)

saturate v (soaks) zubunure ni sasemásu (saseru, sasete) ずぶ濡れにさせ
ます(させる, させて)

saturated adj kói 濃い

saturation n [BOOKISH] hōwa 飽和
saturation point n hōwa ten 飽和点
saturation state n hōwa jōtai 飽和状態

Saturday n Doyō´bi 土曜日; Saturday-
Sunday dō-nichi 土日

Saturn n Dosei 土星

sauce n sō´su ソース, (cooking) taré
たれ・タレ; soy ~ (o-)shōyu (お)しょ
うゆ[醤油]

saucepan n nabe 鍋・ナベ

saucer n ko-zara 小皿 (o-kózara お小
皿), sara 皿 (o-sara お皿); (for cup)
uké-zara 受け皿

flying saucer n sora tobu enban 空飛
ぶ円盤

Saudi Arabia n Saujiarabia サウジア
ラビア

Saudi Arabian 1. adj Saujiarabia (no)
サウジアラビア(の) 2. n (person)
Saujiarabia-jin サウジアラビア人

sauna n sauna サウナ → steam bath

saurel n áji アジ・鯵

saury n sanma 秋刀魚・サンマ

saury-pike n kamásu かます・カマス

sausage n sō´sē´ji ソーセージ

sauté 1. n sotē ソテー 2. v itamemásu
(itaméru, itámete) 炒めます(炒める,
炒めて)

savage 1. adj yaban (na) 野蛮(な)
2. a savage n yaban-jín 野蛮人

savanna n sabanna サバンナ

save v 1. (saves up, hoards)
takuwaemásu (takuwaeru, takuwaete)
蓄えます(蓄える, 蓄えて), (deposits
money) chokin shimásu (suru, shite) 貯
金します(する, して); (accumulates)
tamemásu (tameru, tamete) ため[溜
め]ます(ためる, ためて) 2. (curtails,
omits) habukimásu (habúku, habúite)
省きます(省く, 省いて); (economizes
on) setsuyaku shimásu (suru, shite)
節約します(する, して), ken'yaku
shimásu (suru, shite) 倹約します(す
る, して) 3. → rescue

savings n takuwae 蓄え; installment ~
tsumitate-kin 積立金

savings account n yokin-kō´za 預金
口座, tsumitate-chókin 積立貯金
savings book n yokin-tsū´chō 預金
通帳

savings box n chokin-bako 貯金箱

savior n 1. (saver) kyūsai-sha 救済者
2. (messiah) kyūsei-shu 救世主

savor v (tastes) ajiwaimásu (ajiwau,
ajiwatte) 味わいます(味わう, 味わっ
て); ajiwai-tanoshimimásu (ajiwai-
tanoshimu, ajiwai-tanoshinde) 味わい
楽しみます(味わい楽しむ, 味わい楽
しんで)

saw **1.** n (*tool*) nokogírí のこぎり・鋸 **2.** v (*saws it*) nokogírí de hikimásu (hiku, hiite) のこぎり[鋸]で引きます (引く, 引いて)

sawdust n ogakuzu おがくず[屑]

sawmill n seizai kōjō 製材工場, seizaisho 製材所

sawmill machine, sawmill machinery n seizai kikai 製材機械

saw v (*did see*) mimáshita (míta) 見ました(見た); (*met a person*) … ni aimáshita (átta) …に会いました(会った)

saxophone n sakkusu サックス; sakusuhōn サクスホーン

saxophone player n sakkusu sōsha サックス奏者; sakusuhōn sōsha サクスホーン奏者

saxophonist → saxophone player

say v (*that …*) (… to) iimásu (iu/yu, itte/yutte) (…と)言います(言う/ゆう, 言って/ゆって); [HUMBLE] mōshimásu (mō´su, mōshíte/mōshimáshite) 申します(申す, 申して/申しまして), mōshi-agemásu (mōshi-ageru, mōshi-agete) 申し上げます(申し上げる, 申し上げて); [HONORIFIC] osshaimásu (ossháru, osshátte/osshaimáshite) おっしゃいます(おっしゃる, おっしゃって/おっしゃいまして)

say it another way v ii-kaemásu (ii-kaéru, ii-káete) 言い換えます(言い換える, 言い換えて)

Say there! interj Móshi-moshi! もしもし!

saying n kotowaza ことわざ・諺; kakugen 格言

scab n kasabuta かさぶた

scaffold n **1.** (*for the execution*) shokei dai 処刑台; shikei dai 死刑台; kōshu dai 絞首台 **2.** (*framework*) ashi ba 足場

scaffold n kasabuta かさぶた

scald **1.** n (*mark on the skin*) yakedo やけど・火傷 **2.** v (*scalds*) yakimásu (yaku, yaite) 焼きます(焼く, 焼いて), (*gets scalded*) yakemásu (yakeru, yakete) 焼けます(焼ける, 焼けて)

scale n **1.** sukēru スケール **2.** (*fish*) uroko うろこ・鱗

scale down v shukushō shimásu (suru, shite) 縮小します(する, して)

scale insect n kaigaramushi カイガラムシ

scale up v kakudai shimásu (suru, shite) 拡大します(する, して)

scales n (*weighing*) hakarí 秤

scallion n asátsuki アサツキ・浅葱

scallop(s) n hotaté-gai ホタテ[帆立]貝; (*pin/razor/fan shell*) taira-gi たいらぎ

scalp n [BOOKISH] tōhi 頭皮

scalpel n (geka-yō) mesu (外科用)メス

scamper v awatete hashirimásu (hashiru, hashitte) 慌てて走ります (走る, 走って), isoide hashirimásu (hashiru, hashitte) 急いで走ります (走る, 走って)

scan v sukyan shimásu (suru, shite) スキャンします(する, して)

scandal n sukyándaru スキャンダル, [BOOKISH] fushōji 不祥事; (*disgrace*) ojoku 汚辱

Scandinavia n Sukanjinabia スカンジナビア; *Scandinavia peninsula* Sukanjinabia hantō スカンジナビア半島

scanner n sukyanā スキャナー

scant, scanty adj toboshii 乏しい

scapegoat n sukēpugōto スケープゴート; migawari 身代わり → **sacrifice**

scar n kizu-ato 傷跡

scarce adj sukunái 少ない, toboshii 乏しい

scarcely adv hotóndo ほとんど・殆ど + [NEGATIVE]

scarcity n (*shortage*) fusoku 不足; (… ga) sukunái kotó (…が)少ない事

scare v odorokashimásu (odorokásu, odorokáshite) 驚かします(驚かす, 驚かして); bikkuri sasemásu (saseru, sasete) びっくりさせます(させる, させて); harahara sasemásu (saseru, sasete) はらはらさせます(させる, させて)

scarecrow n kakashi カカシ・案山子

scared adj obieta おびえた・怯えた

scarf n sukā´fu スカーフ

scarlet n, adj sukāretto (no) スカーレット(の), hiiro (no) 緋色(の)

scarlet fever n shōkō netsu しょうこう熱・猩紅熱

scarlet letter *n* hi moji 緋文字

scatter *v* chira(ka)shimásu (chira(ka)su, chira(ka)shite) 散ら(か)します(散ら(か)す、散ら(か)して); barabara ni narimásu (naru, natte) ばらばらになります(なる、なって)

scatterbrain *n* awate-mono 慌て者

scenario *n* shinario シナリオ; kyaku-hon 脚本

　scenario writer *n* shinario raitā シナリオライター; kyakuhon-ka 脚本家

scene *n* (*story, play*) shíin シーン; dán 段; bamen 場面; (*sight*) arisama 有り様

scenery *n* késhiki 景色, fū´kei 風景, (*view*) nagamé 眺め

scent *n* kaori 香り, hōkō 芳香

schedule **1.** *n* (*plan*) yotei 予定, sukejūru スケジュール **2.** *n* (*timetable*) yotei-hyō 予定表, sukejūru-hyō スケジュール表, jikan-hyō 時間表 **3.** *n* (*daily routine*) nittei 日程 **4.** *n* (*train*) daiya ダイヤ; (*train timetable*) jikoku-hyō 時刻表; (*list*) hyō 表 **5.** *v* yotei shimásu (suru, shite) 予定します(する、して), sukejūru o tatemásu (tateru, tatete) スケジュールを立てます(立てる、立てて), keikaku shimásu (suru, shite) 計画します(する、して)

scheduled *adj* (*periodic*) téiki (no) 定期(の)

scheme **1.** *n* (*plan*) keikaku 計画; (*device*) kufū 工夫; (*plot, trick*) keiryaku 計略, hakarigoto はかりごと・謀 **2.** *v* (*plot, plan*) ... no keikaku o tatemásu (tateru, tatete) ...の計画を立てます(立てる、立てて)

schizophrenia *n* (*medical*) tōgōshitchōshō 統合失調症

scholar *n* gakusha 学者; *scholarly society* gakkai 学会

scholarship *n* shōgaku-kin 奨学金; sukarashippu スカラシップ

school *n* (*educational establishment*) gakkō 学校; sūkūru スクール; *primary ~* shōgákkō 小学校, *middle* (*junior high*) *~* chūgákkō 中学校; *high ~* kōtō-gákkō 高等学校, kōkō 高校; *tutoring/cram ~* júku 塾; *in ~* zaigaku(-chū) 在学(中)

boys' school *n* danshikō 男子校

coed school *n* kyōgaku 共学

cooking school *n* ryōri gakkō 料理学校; kukkingu sukūru クッキングスクール

driving school *n* (jidōsha) kyōshūjo (自動車)教習所; (jidōsha) kyōshū gakkō (自動車)教習学校

girls' school *n* joshikō 女子校

school activity *n* kōnai katsudō 校内活動

school age *n* gakurei (ki) 学齢(期); shūgaku nenrei 就学年齢

school bag *n* randoseru ランドセル; tsūgaku kaban 通学かばん

schoolboy *n* danshi seito 男子生徒

school committee *n* kyōiku iinkai 教育委員会

school committee for discipline *n* fūki iinkai 風紀委員会

school festival *n* gakuen-sai 学園祭

school flag *n* kōki 校旗

schoolgirl *n* jo(shi) seito 女(子)生徒

school grounds, school field *n* kōtei 校庭

school hours *n* jugyō-jíkan 授業時間

school-house *n* kōsha 校舎

school teacher *n* gakkō no senséi 学校の先生

school textbook *n* (gakkō no) kyōkasho (学校の)教科書

school uniform *n* gakuséi-fuku 学生服, seifuku 制服

school year *n* gakunen 学年

schoolchild *n* gakudō 学童

schooling *n* (gakkō) kyōiku (学校)教育

schoolroom *n* kyōshitsu 教室

schoolmaster *n* sensei 先生, kyōshi 教師

schoolmate *n* gakuyū 学友

science *n* kágaku 科学, sáiensu サイエンス, (*study*) gaku 学, ríka 理科

science fiction *n* esu-efu SF (エス・エフ), saiensu fikushon サイエンス・フィクション

scientific *adj* kagaku-teki (na) 科学的(な)

scientist *n* kagákusha 科学者, saien-tisuto サイエンティスト

scissors n hasamí はさみ・鋏 (*how many pairs*) nán-chō 何丁)
scold v shikarimásu (shikaru, shikatte) しかり [叱り] ます(しかる、しかって)
scolding n kogoto 小言 (o-kógoto お小言), o-shikari おしかり・お叱り; (*abuse*) warú-kuchi/-guchi 悪口
scone n sukón スコーン
scoop 1. n sukoppu スコップ; [BOOKISH] hishaku ひしゃく・柄杓, (*one scoopful*) hitó-mori 一盛り **2.** v (*scoops it up*) kumimásu (kumu, kunde) くみ [汲み] ます(くむ、くんで), sukuimásu (sukū, sukutte) すくい [掬い] ます(すくう、すくって)
scooter n sukūtā スクーター
scope n hán'i 範囲
scorch v **1.** (*scorches it*) kogashimásu (kogasu, kogashite) 焦がします(焦がす、焦がして) **2.** (*it gets scorched*) kogemásu (kogéru, kógete) 焦げます(焦げる、焦げて)
score 1. n sukoa スコア, (*game*) tokuten 得点; (*score points*) tensū 点数; (*musical score*) gakufu 楽譜 **2.** (*makes a score*) ten o torimásu (tóru, tótte) 点を取ります(取る、取って)
scoreboard n sukoa bōdo スコア・ボード, tokuten keiji-ban 得点掲示板
Scorpio n (*star sign*) Sasori-za さそり座
scorpion n sasori サソリ
scotch n (*whisky*) sukotchi スコッチ
scotch tape n serohan tēpu セロハンテープ, serotēpu セロテープ
Scotland n sukottorando スコットランド
scoundrel n akutō 悪党
scramble v **1.** (*mixes*) kakimazemásu (kakimazeru, kakimazete) かき混ぜ [掻き混ぜ] ます(かき混ぜる、かき混ぜて) **2.** (*climbs*) hainoborimásu (hainoboru, hainobotte) はい登り [這い登り] ます(はい登る、はい登って) **3.** (*fights*) ubaiaimásu (ubaiau, ubaiatte) 奪いあいます(奪いあう、奪いあって)
scrambled eggs n iri-támago いり卵・炒り卵, sukuranburu-éggu スクランブルエッグ
scrap 1. n kúzu くず・屑, danpen 断片,

kuzu-mono くず物・屑物; (*refuse*) sukurappu スクラップ **2.** v sukurappu ni shimásu (suru, shite) スクラップにします(する、して)
scrapbook n sukurappu bukku スクラップブック
scrape v kosurimásu (kosúru, kosútté) こすり [擦り] ます(こする、こすって)
scratch 1. v (*scratches it*) (hikkakimásu (káku, káite) (ひっ)かきます(かく、かいて) **2.** n (*a scratch*) hikkaki-kizu 引っかき傷・ひっかき傷
scrawl 1. n hashiri-gaki 走り書き, nagurigaki 殴り [なぐり] 書き **2.** v hashirigaki shimásu (suru, shite) 走り書きします(する、して), nagurigaki shimásu (suru, shite) 殴り [なぐり] 書きします(する、して)
scrawny adj yase(koke)teiru やせ [痩せ] (こけ) ている, yaseta やせた・痩せた
scream 1. v himei o agemásu (ageru, agete) 悲鳴を上げます(上げる、上げて), sakebimásu (sakébu, sakénde) 叫びます(叫ぶ、叫んで), (*feminine*) kyā(t) to sakebimásu (sakébu, sakénde) きゃー(っ) [キャー(ッ)] と叫びます(叫ぶ、叫んで) **2.** n himei 悲鳴
screen 1. n (*folding*) byōbu びょうぶ・屏風 **2.** n (*TV, computer*) gamen 画面 **3.** n (*movie*) sukurīn スクリーン **4.** v (*examine*) kensa shimásu (suru, shite) 検査します(する、して) **5.** v (*movie*) ... o jōe shimásu (suru, shite) ...を上映します(する、して)
screen door n amí-do 網戸・あみど → window screen
screenplay n (*scenario*) kyakuhon 脚本, shinario シナリオ
screw 1. n néji ねじ・ネジ **2.** v (*tighten*) (kataku) shimemásu (shimeru, shimete) (堅く) 締めます(締める、締めて)
screw up v dainashi ni shimásu (suru, shite) 台無しにします(する、して), [INFORMAL] mechamecha ni shimásu (suru, shite) めちゃめちゃにします(する、して)
screwdriver n neji-máwashi ねじ回し
scribble n hashirigaki 走り書き, nagurigaki 殴り書き

scribbling *n* rakugaki 落書き

script *n* kyakuhon 脚本, daihon 台本

scroll *n* maki-mono 巻(き)物; (*hanging*) kaké-mono 掛け物, kakéjiku 掛軸, kakéji 掛け字

scrubbing brush *n* tawashi たわし・タワシ

scrum *n* sukuramu スクラム

scuba *n* sukyūba スキューバ

scuba diving *n* sukyūba daibingu スキューバダイビング

sculptor *n* chōkoku-ka 彫刻家

sculpture *n* chōkoku 彫刻

scuffle *n* tsukamiai つかみ[掴み]合い, tokkumiai 取っ組み合い

scurry *v* (*goes in haste*) awatete ikimásu (iku, itte) 慌てて行きます (いく、いって), (*goes quickly*) isoide ikimásu (iku, itte) 急いで行きます(行く、行って)

sea *n* úmi 海・うみ, ...-kai …海; *high sea* taikai (daikai) 大海; *Inland Sea* Seto-náikai 瀬戸内海, *Sea of Japan* Nihón-kai 日本海

sea bass *n* suzuki スズキ・鱸

sea bathing *n* kaisuiyoku 海水浴

sea bream *n* tái タイ・鯛

sea calf *n* azarashi アザラシ

sea captain *n* senchō 船長

sea chart *n* kaizu 海図

seadiver *n* (*woman seadiver*) áma 海女・アマ

seafood *n* shiifūdo シーフード, gyokairui 魚介類・魚貝類

seagull *n* kamome カモメ・鴎

sea horse *n* tatsu no otoshigo タツノオトシゴ・竜の落(と)し子

sea lion *n* ashika アシカ

sea level *n* kaibatsu 海抜

seamail *n* funabin 船便

seaman *n* súifu 水夫, (*navy*) súihei 水兵

seashell *n* kaigara 貝殻・貝ガラ

seashore *n* kaigan 海岸

seasick; *gets ~* (fúne ni) yoimásu (yóu, yótte) (船に)酔います(酔う、酔って)

seasickness *n* funayoi 船酔い

seaside *n* umibe 海辺

sea urchin *n* úni ウニ・海胆

seawater *n* kaisui 海水

seaweed *n* kaisō 海藻・カイソウ; (*green*) norí のり・海苔; wakáme わかめ・若布; (*kelp*) kónbu 昆布・こんぶ

seaweed-gelatin strips *n* tokoroten ところてん・トコロテン

seaweed-rolled sushi *n* norí-maki のり巻き; (*with cucumber*) kappa-maki かっぱ巻き; (*with tuna*) tekka-maki 鉄火巻き

seal 1. *n* (*for stamping one's name*) hán(kó) はん(こ)・判(子), ín 印 2. *n* (*animal*) azárashi あざらし・アザラシ・海豹, ottosei オットセイ 3. *v* (*seals a letter*) (tegami no) fū~ shimásu (suru, shite) (手紙の)封をします(する、して), mippū shimásu (suru, shite) 密封します(する、して), fusagimásu (fusagu, fusaide) ふさぎます(ふさぐ、ふさいで)

seam *n* nui-mé eaux い目, tsugi-me 接ぎ目

seamless *adj* nui-me no nai 縫い目のない, tsugi-me no nai 接ぎ目のない, tsunagi-me no nai つなぎ目のない, shiimuresu (no) シームレス(の)

seamy *adj* 1. uramen (no) 裏面(の) 2. (*unpleasant*) fukai (na) 不快(な)

sear *n* yakekoge 焼け焦げ

search 1. *n* sōsaku 捜索 2. *n* (*Internet*) kensaku 検索 3. *v searches for* (*seeks*) ... o sagashinásu (sagasu, sagashite) …を探し[捜し]ます (探す[捜す], 探して[捜して]); *a ~ for a criminal* téhái 手配

searching for a criminal *n* hannin-sagashi 犯人捜し

searching for a missing person/thing *n* sōsaku 捜索

searching for one's lost child *n* maigo-sagashi 迷子捜し

search party *n* sōsaku-tai 捜索隊

search warrant *n* sōsaku (rei-) jō 捜索(令)状, sashiosae 差(し)押さえ

search window *n* kensaku uindou 検索ウインドウ

searchlight *n* sāchi raito サーチライト, [BOOKISH] tanshōtō 探照灯

season 1. *n* kisetsu 季節; shíizun シーズン; jíki 時季; jísetsu 時節 2. *v* *(flavors it)* … ni aji o tsukemásu … (tsukéru, tsukéte) …に味を付けます（付ける, 付けて）

four seasons *n* shiki 四季

off-season *n* shiizun ofu シーズンオフ

season for traveling *n* ryokō shiizun 旅行シーズン

season ticket *n* teikí-ken 定期券

seasoning *n (food)* chō´mi 調味, aji 味; kagen 加減

seat *n* seki 席 (o-séki お席), zaseki 座席, shiito シート, koshi-káké 腰掛け; *(bottom, butt)* shirí 尻 (o-shiri お尻); *(taking a seat)* chakuseki 着席; **takes a ~** chakuseki shimásu (suru, shíte) 着席します（する, して）; **Are there seats (available)?** Suwaremásu ka? 座れますか?

seat belt *n* zaseki-béruto 座席ベルト; siíto-béruto シートベルト

seat number *n* zaseki-bángō 座席番号

secluded *adj* hotozato-hanareta 人里離れた, kakurisareta 隔離された

seclusion *n* kakuri 隔離

second 1. *adj* ni-banmé (no) 二番目（の）, futatsu-mé (no) 二つ目の; **the ~ day** futsuka-mé 二日目, *(of the month)* futsuka 二日 **2.** *n (of a minute)* -byō 秒; **one second** ichí-byō 一秒

second class *adj* ni-tō 二等; **~ class seat** nitō´-seki 二等席; **~ class ticket** nitō´ (seki)-ken 二等（席）券

second floor *n* ni-kai 二階 (o-níkai お二階)

second generation *n* ní-sei 二世

second helping *n* o-káwari おかわり

second opinion *n* sekando opinion セカンド・オピニオン, hoka no ishi no iken 他の医師の意見, betsu no ishi no shindan 別の医師の診断

second time *n* nido-mé 二度目, nikai-mé 二回目

secondary school *n* chūtō kōtō gakkō 中等高等学校

secondhand 1. *adj* chūko/chūburu (no) 中古（の）, furúi 古い **2.** *n (goods)* chūko-hin 中古品

secondhand book *n* huruhon 古本

secondhand car *n* chūko-sha 中古車

secondhand shop/ store *n* risaikuru shoppu リサイクル・ショップ

secondment *n* haichigae 配置換え, haken 派遣

secrecy *n* himitsu 秘密, [BOOKISH] kimitsu 機密

secrecy agreement *n* shuhi gimu keiyaku 守秘義務契約

secret 1. *n* himitsu 秘密, shiikuretto シークレット **2.** *n* **the secret** *(trick to it)* táne 種 **3.** *adj (confidential)* naisho (no) 内緒（の）

secret agent *n* himitsu kōsaku-in 秘密工作員

secretariat *n* jimu-kyoku 事務局

secretary *n* shóki 書記; *(private)* hishó 秘書

secretary of foreign affairs *n* gaimu chōkan 外務長官

secretion *n* bunpi 分泌

secretly *adv* kossori (to) こっそり（と）; himitsu ni/nide 秘密に/で

sect *n* shūha 宗派, ha 派, habatsu 派閥

section *n* bú 部; ká 課; sekushon セクション, …-ka …課; *(area)* chíkú 地区

section manager *n* ka-chō 課長

sector *n (area)* chíkú 地区; sekutā セクター

secure *adj* **1. is ~** chanto shite imásu (iru, ite) ちゃんとしています（いる, いて） **2. feels ~** anshin shimásu (suru, shíte) 安心します（する, して） **3. → get**

securely *adv* chanto ちゃんと; *(firmly)* shikkári しっかり

security *n (stock, bond)* shōken 証券; *(secure feeling)* anshin 安心

security deposit *n (for rental)* shikí-kin 敷金

sedan *n* sedan セダン

sedate *adj* ochitsuita 落ち着いた

sedation *n* chinsei 鎮静; chinsei sayō 鎮痛作用

sedative *n* chinsei-zai 鎮静剤; chintsū-zai 鎮痛剤

sedentary *adj* suwarigachi (no/na) 座りがち（の/な）

sediment *n* kásu かす・滓; ori おり・澱; chinden-butsu 沈殿物

sedition *n* sendō 扇動・せんどう

seduce v tarashi-komimásu (tarashi-komu, tarashi-konde) たらし込みます (たらし込む、たらし込んで)、yūwaku shimásu (suru, shíte) 誘惑します(する、して)

seducer n yūwakusha 誘惑者、(*men*) onna-tárashi 女たらし

seduction n yūwaku 誘惑

seductress n yūwakusha 誘惑者、(*women*) otoko-tárashi 男たらし

see v **1.** mimásu (míru, míte) 見ます(見る、見て)；[HONORIFIC] goran ni narimásu (náru, nátte) ご覧になります(なる、なって)；[HUMBLE] haiken shimásu (suru, shíte) 拝見します(する、して) **2.** (*meets a person*) ... ni aimásu (áu, átte) ...に会います(会う、会って)；[HUMBLE] o-me ni kakarimásu (kakáru, kakátte) お目にかかります(かかる、かかって) **3.** (*understands*) wakarimásu (wakáru, wakátte) 分かります(分かる、分かって)；*I see!* Naru-hodo! なるほど！ **4.** *~ one off* (mi-)okurimásu (okuru, okutte) (見)送ります(送る、送って)

seed n táne 種・タネ

seedling n náe 苗・ナエ

seedy adj **1.** tane ga ōi 種が多い **2.** misuborashiii みすぼらしい

seeing-eye dog n mōdō-ken 盲導犬

seek v **1.** busshoku shimásu (suru, shíte) 物色します(する、して) → **search (for)** **2.** → **aim at**

seem v (*like*) ... to miemásu (miéru, míete) ...と見えます(見える、見えて)、... (no) yō´desu ...(の)よう[様]です、... rashíi desu ...らしいです

seemingly adv (*outwardly*) mikake wa 見かけは、mikake-jō 見かけ上

seemly adj fusawashii ふさわしい、jōhin (na) 上品(な)

seep v shintō shimásu (suru, shíte) 浸透します(する、して)、shimidemásu (shimideru, shimidete) 染み出ます(染み出る、染み出て)、moremásu (moreru, morete) もれ[漏れ]ます(もれる、もれて)

seer n yogen-sha 預言者・予言者

seesaw n shiisō シーソー

see-through adj (*garment*) shiisurū no

(fuku) シースルーの(服)

segment n bubun 部分；segumento セグメント

segregate v bunri shimásu (suru, shite) 分離します(する、して)、hanashimasu (hanasu, hanashite) 離します(離す、離して)

seize v tsukamimásu (tsukámu, tsukánde) つかみ[掴み]ます(つかむ、つかんで)、toraemásu (toráeru, toráete) 捕らえます(捕らえる、捕らえて)、tsukamaemásu (tsukamaeru, tsukamaete) 捕まえます(捕まえる、捕まえて)；(*plunders*) ubaimásu (ubáu, ubátte) 奪います(奪う、奪って)；(*illegally takes over*) nottorimásu (nottóru, nottótte) 乗っ取ります(乗っ取る、乗っ取って)

seizure n **1.** (*illegal takeover*) nottori-jíken 乗っ取り事件 **2.** (*medical*) hossa 発作

seldom adv métta ni めった[滅多]に + [NEGATIVE]、hotóndo ほとんど・殆ど + [NEGATIVE]；(*infrequently*) tama ni たまに

select → **choose; selection** → **choice**

selection n sentaku 選択；serekushon セレクション

selective buying (*of stocks, ...*) busshoku-gai 物色買い

self n jibun 自分；ji-... 自...；onore 己；jíko 自己；hon-nin 本人

self-abandonment n sute-bachi 捨て鉢；jibō-jiki 自暴自棄

self-analysis n jiko bunseki 自己分析、deshabari 出しゃばり

self-assertion n jiko shuchō 自己主張

self-centered adj jíko chūshin-teki (na) 自己中心的(な)

self-confidence n jishin 自信

self-conscious；*feels ~* agarimásu (agaru, agatte) 上がり[あがり]ます(上がる、上がって)

self-defense n jiei 自衛、jiko bōei 自己防衛；(*weaponless*) ~ *art* goshin-hō 護身法 (*also* jū´dō 柔道、karate 空手、aikídō 合気道)

Self-Defense Forces n Jiei-tai 自衛隊

self-disgust, self-hatred n jiko ken'o 自己嫌悪

549

self-discipline *n* [BOOKISH] jiko tanren 自己鍛錬

self-employed *adj* jiei (no) 自営(の), jieigyō (no) 自営業(の)

self-esteem *n* jisonshin 自尊心

self-evident fact *n* jimei no jijitsu 自明の事実

self-pity *n* [BOOKISH] jiko renbin 自己憐憫

self-portrait *n* jiga zō 自画像

self-interested *n* jiko hon'i (no) 自己本位(の)

self-respect *n* [BOOKISH] jison-shin 自尊心

self-satisfaction *n* jiko manzoku 自己満足

self-service *adj* serufu sābisu (no) セルフサービス(の)

self-sufficiency *n* jikyū jisoku 自給自足

self-taught *adj* dokugaku (no) 独学(の)

selfish *adj* katte (na) 勝手(な), jibun-kátte/-gátte (na) 自分勝手(な), waga-mámá (na) わがまま・我が侭(な)

sell *v* **1.** *sells it* urimásu (uru, utte) 売ります(売る, 売って) **2.** *it sells (well)* (yóku) uremásu (ureru, urete) (良く)売れます(売れる, 売れて); hakemásu (hakéru, hákete) はけます(はける, はけて)

sell out *v* uri-kiremásu (uri-kiréru, uri-kírete) 売り切れます(売り切れる, 売り切れて)

sellout *n* uri-kire 売り切れ

sell retail *v* ko-uri shimásu (suru, shite) 小売りします(する, して)

sell wholesale *v* oroshi-uri shimásu (suru, shite) 卸売りします(する, して)

seller *n* uri-te 売り手; uri-nushi 売り主; (*dealer*) hanbai-nin 販売人

semen *n* sei eki 精液; ~ *test* sei eki kensa 精液検査

semester *n* gakki 学期

end of semester *n* gakki-matsu 学期末

semester final examination *n* kimatsu shiken 期末試験

semicircle *n* hanshū 半周

semicolon *n* semikoron セミコロン

semifinal *n* jun-kesshō 準決勝

seminar *n* zémi ゼミ, zeminā´ru ゼミナール, seminā セミナー, kōshūkai 講習会

seminary *n* shingakkō 神学校

senate *n* jōin 上院

senator *n* jōin giin 上院議員

send *v* okurimásu (okuru, okutte) 送ります(送る, 送って), yarimásu (yaru, yatte) やります(やる, やって), yosemásu (yoseru, yosete) 寄せます(寄せる, 寄せて); (*a telegram*) uchimásu (útsu, útte) 打ちます(打つ, 打って); (*a person*) ikasemásu (ikaseru, ikasete) 行かせます(行かせる, 行かせて)

send here yokoshimásu (yokósu, yokóshite) よこし[寄越し]ます(よこす, よこして)

sender *n* **1.** (*mail, etc.*) hassōnin 発送人, okurinushi 送り主 **2.** (*mail, e-mail, etc.*) sashidashinin 差出人, sōshin-sha 送信者

send-off *n* (*farewell*) sōbetsu 送別, ~ *party* sōbétsú-kai 送別会

senior *adj* (*older*) toshi-ue (no) 年上(の); (*colleague, fellow student*) senpai 先輩; (*4th-year student*) yonén-sei 四年生; ~ *essay* gakushi-rónbun 学士論文

senior citizen *n* toshiyóri 年寄り (o-toshiyori お年寄り), rōjin 老人, kōrei-sha 高齢者, kōrei no hito 高齢の人

senior high school *n* kōtō-gákkō 高等学校, kō-kō 高校; ~ *student* kōkō´-sei 高校生

sensation *n* (*feeling*) kimochi 気持ち・気持, kimí 気味; (*sense*) kankaku 感覚; (*excitement*) sensé´shon センセーション

sensational *adj* sensé´shonaru (na) センセーショナル(な), [BOOKISH] senjōteki (na) 扇情的(な)

sense *n* sénsu センス; *common* ~ jōshiki 常識; ~ *of honor* taimen 体面, [BOOKISH] renchí-shin 廉恥心; ~ *of obligation* girí 義理(o-giri お義理) → feel(ing) → meaning → significance → reason → consciousness

sense of humor *n* yūmoa no sensu ユーモアのセンス

senses; *come to one's ~* (*recovers consciousness*) ki ga tsukimásu (tsukú, tsúite) 気が付きます (付く, 付いて), me ga samemásu (saméru, sámete) 目が覚めます (覚める, 覚めて)

sensibility *n* kankaku 感覚

sensible *adj* gōri-teki (na) 合理的 (な), atarimae (no) 当り前 (の); *what is ~* dōri 道理

sensitive *adj* **1.** binkan (na) 敏感 (な) **2.** (*easily pained*) kizutsukiyasui 傷つきやすい, sensai (na) 繊細 (な), deri-kēto (na) デリケート (な) **3.** (*easily annoyed*) shinkei kabin (no) 神経過敏 (の) **4.** (*requiring caution*) chūi ga hitsuyō na 注意が必要な, chūi o haraubeki 注意を払うべき, shinchō o kisu 慎重を期す

sensual *adj* kannō-teki (na) 官能的 (な)

sentence *n* **1.** (*written*) bún(shō) 文(章), (*spoken*) kotó-ba・こと, kotoba 言葉 **2.** (*linguistic*) séntensu センテンス **3.** (*judicial verdict*) hanketsu 判決

sentiment *n* kanshō 感傷

sentimental *adj* senchiméntaru (na) センチメンタル (な), o-senchi (na) おせんち (な); kanshōteki na 感傷的 (の)

sentry *n* mihari 見張り, hoshō 歩哨

Seoul *n* Sóuru ソウル

separate **1.** *adj* (*different*) betsu (no) 別(の), barabara (ni) ばらばら(に) **2.** *v* (*separates them*) wakemásu (wakéru, wákete) 分けます(分ける, 分けて); (*gets them apart*) hedatemásu (hedatéru, hedátete) 隔てます(隔てる, 隔てて) **3.** *v* (*they separate*) wakaremásu (wakaréru, wakárete) 分かれ[別れ]ます(分かれ[別れ]る, 分かれ[別れ]て); (*gets distant*) hanaremásu (hanaréru, hanárete) 離れます(離れる, 離れて) **4.** *v separates it* (*from*) … o hanashimásu (hanásu, hanáshite) …を離します(離す, 離して)

separate bill *n* betsu-ryṓkin 別料金

separated; *is* (*lives*) *~ from* … to bekkyo shimásu (suru, shite) …と別居します(する, して)

separately *adv* wakárete 分かれて;

hanárete 離れて; *quite ~ from* … tówa betsu ni (shite) …とは別に (して)

separation *n* bun'ri 分離; bekkyo 別居

sepsis *n* (*medical*) haikesshō 敗血症

September *n* Ku-gatsú 九月・9月

septic *adj* (*medical*) haiketsu-sei (no) 敗血性 (の)

sequel *n* tsuzuki 続き, ren-zoku 連続

sequence *n* shiikuensu シークエンス, renzoku 連続, (*order*) júnjo 順序, zéngo 前後

in sequence *adv* jun (ni) 順 (に), junban (ni) 順番 (に)

serenade *n* serenādo セレナード, sayo-kyoku 小夜曲

serene *adj* odayaka (na) 穏やか・おだやか (な), shizuka (na) 静か (な)

sergeant *n* **1.** (*army*) gúnsō 軍曹 **2.** (*police*) junsa buchō 巡査部長

serial *n, adj* rensai (no) 連載 (の), renzoku (no) 連続の

serial killer *n* renzoku satsujin(-han) 連続殺人 (犯)

serial number *n* shiriaru nanbā シリアルナンバー; tōshi bangō 通し番号

serial port *n* shiriaru pōto シリアルポート

serialize *v* rensai shimásu (suru, shite) 連載します (する, して)

sericulture *n* yōsan 養蚕・ヨウサン

series *n* (hitó-)tsuzuki (ひと)続き; renzoku 連続; shiriizu シリーズ

drama series *n* renzoku dorama 連続ドラマ

TV series *n* renzoku terebi bangumi 連続テレビ番組

serious *adj* (*character*) majime (na) まじめ[真面目] (な); *He's ~.* 彼はまじめ[真面]です。; (*in earnest*) honki (no) 本気 (の); *I'm ~.* honki desu. 本気です。, (*not joking*) jōdán ja arimasén (nái) 冗談じゃありません (ない); (*heavy, grave*) omoi 重い, jūdai (na) 重大 (な), shinkoku (na) 深刻 (な); taihen (na) 大変 (な), tái-shita … 大した…; (*medical*) jūtoku (na) 重篤な

seriously *adv* majime (ni) まじめ[真面目] (に); honki (de) 本気 (で); hontō (ni) 本当 (に); jōdán de wa naku

551

冗談ではなく; [INFORMAL] maji (de) まじ(で); *takes it ~* … o honki ni shimásu (suru, shite) …を本気にします(する, して)

sermon *n* sekkyō 説教

serpent *n* **1.** (*snake*) hebi 蛇・ヘビ **2.** (*devil*) akuma 悪魔

serum *n* kessei 血清

servant *n* meshi-tsúkai 召し使い; shiyō-nin 使用人; yōmú-in 用務員, kózukai 小使い

serve 1. (*games*) sābu サーブ **2.** *v* (*a meal*) dashimásu (dásu, dáshite) 出します(出す, 出して); *meals are served* shokuji ga demásu (déru, déte) 食事が出ます(出る, 出て); *~ the saké* (o-)shaku o shimásu (suru, shite) (お)酌をします(する, して)

serve a purpose *v* yakúni tachimásu (tátsu, tátte) 役に立ちます(立つ, 立って), yaku-dachimásu (yaku-dátsu, yaku-dátte) 役立ちます(役立つ, 役立って)

serve the purpose *v* mokuteki ni kanaimásu (kanáu, kanátte) 目的に適います(かなう, かなって)

server *n* sābā サーバー

service *n* **1.** (*in restaurant, etc.*) sā´bisu サービス **2.** (*maintenance and repair*) afutāsābisu アフターサービス **3.** (*utility*) yakú 役 **4.** (*armed forces*) gúntai 軍隊 **5.** (*duty, work*) kínmu 勤務 **6.** (*games*) sābu サーブ

service area *n* sā´bisu eria サービスエリア

service charge *n* tesū´-ryō 手数料, sābisu-ryō サービス料

service industry *n* sābisu sangyō サービス産業

serviceman, service personnel *n* **1.** (*military*) gunjin 軍人 **2.** → repairman

spirit of good service *n* sābisu seishin サービス精神

service station → gas station

servicing *n* afutā-sā´bisu アフターサービス

… serving(s) … -nínmae …人前

serviette *n* (shokutaku yō) napukin (食卓用)ナプキン

servile *adj* iyashii いやしい・卑しい, hikutsu (na) 卑屈(な), dorei no yō (na) 奴隷のよう(な)

sesame *n* goma ごま・胡麻

session *n* **1.** sesshon セッション **2.** (*sitting of a court*) kaitei 開廷 **3.** (*assembly*) kai 会, kaigō 会合 **4.** (*meeting, conference*) kaigi 会議

set 1. *n* (*collection*) kumí 組, híto-kumi 一組; (*array*) soroi 揃い; *makes* (*up*) *a ~* soroimásu (soróu, sorótte) 揃います(揃う, 揃って), *makes into a ~* soroemásu (soroéru, soróete) 揃えます(揃える, 揃えて) **2.** *n* (*hair*) sétto セット **3.** *v sets* it (*puts it there*) okimásu (oku, oite) 置きます(置く, 置いて) **4.** → sit → settle → decide

set aside *v* atemásu (ateru, atete) 当てます(当てる, 当てて)

set free *v* hanashimásu (hanásu, hanáshite) 放します(放す, 放して)

set off/out *v* (*departs*) dekakemásu (dekakeru, dekakete) 出かけます(出かける, 出かけて)

set up *v* tatemásu (tatéru, tátete) 立てます(立てる, 立てて); (*provides*) mōkemásu (mōkéru, mō´kete) 設けます(設ける, 設けて); (*assembles*) kumi-tatemásu (kumi-tateru, kumi-tatete) 組み立てます(組み立てる, 組み立てて)

set back *n* zasetsu 挫折・ざせつ

set meal *n* teishoku 定食; *set series of chef's choices* kō´su (ryōri) コース(料理)

set price *n* teika 定価

setting *n* settingu セッティング, settei 設定

settle *v* (*decides it*) kimemásu (kimeru, kimete) 決めます(決める, 決めて), (*fixes*) sadamemásu (sadaméru, sadámete) 定めます(定める, 定めて); (*completes*) matomemásu (matomeru, matomete) まとめます(まとめる, まとめて); (*disposes of*) shímatsu shimásu (suru, shite) 始末します(する, して); (*solves, resolves*) kaiketsu shimásu (suru, shite) 解決します(する, して); (*gets relaxed/calm*) ochitsukimásu (ochitsuku, ochitsuite) 落ち着きます

552

(落ち着く, 落ち着いて); **~ down/in** osamarimásu (osamáru, osamátte) 収[治・納]まります(収[治・納]まる, 収[治・納]まって)

settled adj **1.** ittei (no) 一定(の) **2. gets ~** kimarimásu (kimaru, kimatte) 決まります(決まる, 決まって), sadamarimásu (sadamáru, sadamátte) 定まります(定まる, 定まって), matomarimásu (matomaru, matomatte) まとまります(まとまる, まとまって)

settlement n kimari 決まり; (solution) kaiketsu 解決

settling accounts n késsan 決算

setup n **1.** (organization) soshiki 組織 **2.** (arrangement) settoappu セットアップ, junbi 準備, settei 設定

seven n nána 七・7, shichí 七・7, nanátsu 七つ・7つ; sébun セブン

seven; seven days nanoka 七日・7日; **7 pieces** (small things) naná-ko 七個, **7 trees** (or long things) nanáhon 七本, **7 sheets** (flat things) naná-mai 七枚, **7 cats** (or small animals) naná-hiki 七匹; **7 cows** (or large aminals) naná-tō 七頭; **7 birds/rabbits** naná-wa 七羽; **7 cars** (or machines/vehicles) naná-dai 七台; **7 copies** (books/magazines) naná-satsu 七冊; **7 floors/stories** naná-kai 七階; **7 people** naná-nin 七人, naná-mei 七名; **7 fold** nana-bai 七倍; **7 degrees** naná-do 七度; **7 times** naná-dó 七度, naná-kái 七回, naná-hén 七遍; **7 o'clock** shichí-ji/naná-ji 七時; **7 hours** shichí-jíkan/naná-jíkan 七時間; **7 weeks** naná-shūkan 七週間; **7 months** naná-ká-getsu 七ヶ月; **7 years** shichí-nen/naná-nen 七年, nana-nénkan 七年間; **7 years old** nanátsu 七つ, naná-sai 七歳

seven hundred n naná-hyaku 七百・700

seventeen n jū-nána 十七・17, jūshichí 十七・17

seventeen-syllable poem n (Japanese traditional poem) senryū 川柳

seventh adj nana-banmé (no) 七番目(の), nana-tsu-mé (no) 七つ目(の); **the 7th day** nanoka-mé 七日目・7日目, (of the month) nanoka 七日・7日;

7th floor nana-kai 七階

seven thousand n nana-sén 七千・7,000

seventy n naná-jū 七十・70, shichi-jū 七十・70; **~ thousand** nana-mán 七万・70,000

several adj futatsú-mi(t)tsu (no) 二つ三つ(の), ní-san (no) 二三(の), jakkan (no) 若干(の); íkutsu ka (no) いくつか(の); sū-... 数... (**~ days** sū-jitsu 数日, **~ people** sū-nin 数人, **~ years** sū-nen 数年)

severally adv sorézore それぞれ, onóono 各々・おのおの

severe adj kibishíi 厳しい; kitsui きつい; (terrible) hidói ひどい・酷い; sibia シビア, (medical) jūdo (no) 重度(の)

sew v nuimásu (nū, nútte) 縫います(縫う, 縫って); **~ together/up** tsuzurimásu (tsuzuru, tsuzutte) 綴ります(綴る, 綴って)

sewage n gesui 下水, osui 汚水; **~ treatment plant** gesui shori-jō 下水処理場

sewer n gesui-kan 下水管

sewing n saihō 裁縫

sewing machine n míshin ミシン (how many nán-dai 何台)

sewing needle n núibari 縫い針

sewing set n saihō-dōgu 裁縫道具

sex n sei 性, sékkusu セックス; (the erotic) iró 色, éro エロ; **has ~** sékkusu o shimásu (suru, shite) セックスをします(する, して), [VULGAR] yarimásu (yaru, yatte) やります(やる, やって)

sexual adj sei-teki (na) 性的(な); **make (a) ~ advance(s)** kudokimasu (kudoku, kudoite) 口説きます(口説く, 口説いて)

sexual harassment n sekuhara セクハラ, sekusharu harasumento セクシャル・ハラスメント

shabby adj **1.** (worn) tsukaifurushita 使い古した **2.** (wearing worn clothes) boro (boro no fuku) o kita ぼろ(ぼろの服)を着た, boro (boro no fuku) o kiteiru ぼろ(ぼろの服)を着ている, (minari no) misuborashii 身なりのみすぼらしい **3.** (unworthy) somatsu (na) 粗末(な), o-somatsu (na) お粗末(な)

shack *n* hottate goya 掘っ立て小屋

shackle 1. *n* (*fetter*) sokubaku 束縛, ashi kase 足枷, kōsoku dōgu 拘束道具 **2.** *v* soku-baku shimás̱u (suru, shite) 束縛します(する, して), kōsoku shimás̱u (suru, shite) 拘束します(する, して), ashikase o kakemás̱u (kakeru, kakete) 足枷をかけます(かける, かけて)

shad *n* kohada こはだ

shade *n* káge 陰・かげ; (*of trees*) kíno káge 木の陰, kokage 木陰・木かげ; *window* ~ (mádo no) hiyoke (窓の)日よけ

shadow *n* káge 影, shadō シャドー, shadou シャドウ, (*from sunlight*) hi-kage 日影; (*of a person*) káge-bō´shi 影法師

shady *adj* (*questionable*) ayashii 怪しい, ikagawashíi いかがわしい

shaft *n* shafuto シャフト, e 柄

shaggy 1. *adj* mojamoja (no) もじゃもじゃ(の), kemukujara (no) 毛むくじゃら(の) **2.** *n* (*hairstyle*) shagii シャギー

shake 1. *v* (*shakes it*) furimás̱u (furu, futte) 振ります(振る, 振って); yusaburimás̱u (yusaburu, yusabutte) 揺さぶります(揺さぶる, 揺さぶって); *shakes hands* ákushu shimás̱u (suru, shíte) 握手します(する, して); ~ *out* haraimás̱u (haráu, harátte) 払います(払う, 払って) **2.** *v* (*it shakes*) furuemás̱u (furueru, furuete) 震えます(震える, 震えて), (*sways*) yuremás̱u (yureru, yurete) 揺れます(揺れる, 揺れて) **3.** *n* (*milkshake*) (miruku-)sḗ´ki (ミルク)セーキ, sheiku シェイク

shall 1. *Shall I/we do it?* Shimashō´ka. しましょうか. **2.** → **will**

shallow *adj* asai 浅い; *shallows* asase 浅瀬

sham *adj* mise-kake (no) 見せかけ(の)

shamble *n* yoromeita aruki よろめいた歩き

shame *n* hazukashíi (kotó) 恥ずかしい(こと), hají 恥; (*scandal*) ojoku 汚辱 *That's a* ~. Sore wa ikemasén ne. それはいけませんね.

shameful *adj* nasake-nái 情けない; hazukashíi 恥ずかしい; mittomo-nai みっともない

shameless *adj* zūzūshíi ずうずうしい・図々しい

shampoo 1. *n* shánpū シャンプー **2.** *v* kami o araimás̱u (araru, aratte) 髪を洗います(洗う, 洗って)

Shanghai *n* Shánhái シャンハイ・上海

shape *n* katachi 形, katá 型; (*figure*) súgata 姿, kakkō かっこう・格好・恰好; (*condition*) guai 具合

shapely *adj* kakkoíi かっこいい・カッコいい・格好[恰好]いい

shape-up *n* sheipu appu シェイプアップ

share 1. *n* (*portion*) toribún 取り分, wake-mae 分け前; (*allotment*) buntan 分担; *one's* ~ wari-ate 割り当て **2.** *v* → **divide** → **Dutch treat 3.** *v shares in, pays/does one's* ~ buntan shimás̱u (suru, shíte) 分担します(する, して)

shark *n* same サメ・鮫, fuka フカ・鱶, shāku シャーク

sharp *adj* surudói 鋭い, shāpu (na) シャープ(な); (*clever*) rikō (na) 利口(な); *gets* ~ (*pointed*) togarimás̱u (togaru, togátte) 尖り[とがり]ます(尖る, 尖って)

sharpen *v* (*pencil*) kezurimás̱u (kezuru, kezutte) 削ります(削る, 削って), togarashimás̱u (togarasu, togaráshite) 尖らし[とがらし]ます(尖らす, 尖らして); (*blade*) togimás̱u (tógu, tóide) 研ぎます(研ぐ, 研いで)

shave *v* hige o sorimás̱u (sóru, sótte) ひげを剃ります(剃る, 剃って)

shaver *n* (*electric*) denki-kámisori 電気かみそり

shaving cream *n* higesori-yō kuríimu ひげ剃り用クリーム

shawl *n* shōru ショール

she *pron* káno-jo 彼女, anó-hito あの人, anó-ko あの子 (*but use name, title, or role; often omitted*)

she-... (*animal*) ... no mesú ...の雌

sheaf *n* taba 束・たば

shear *n* ōbasami 大ばさみ・大鋏

sheath *n* sáya さや・鞘

shed *n* naya 納屋; (*storehouse*) mono-óki 物置; (*hut*) koya 小屋

sheep *n* h̲itsuji 羊・ヒツジ

sheet *n* (*of paper, glass, etc.*) (ichí)-

mai (一) 枚; (*bed sheet*) (beddo)
shíítsu (ベッド) シーツ, shikifu 敷布
sheet of paper *n* ichimai no kami
一枚の紙

shelf *n* tana 棚; *enclosed shelves*
to-dana 戸棚
book shelf *n* hon-dana 本棚, sho-dana
書棚

shell *n* kara 殻・カラ; (*of shellfish*)
kái 貝・カイ, kai-gara 貝殻・貝ガラ;
(*of tortoise etc.*) kōra 甲羅・コウラ;
eggshell tamago no kara 卵[玉子]の
殻; *bombshell* hōdan 砲弾

shellfish *n* kái 貝, …-gai …貝,
kōkaku-rui 甲殻類

shelter *n* sherutā シェルター, hinanjo
避難所

shepherd *n* hitsujikai 羊飼い

sherbet *n* shābetto シャーベット

sheriff *n* hoankan 保安官

sherry *n* sherii-shu シェリー酒

Shiba *n* Shíba 芝; *Shiba Park* Shiba-
Kō'en 芝公園

Shibuya *n* Shibuya 渋谷; *Shibuya
Station* Shibuyá-Eki 渋谷駅

shield 1. *n* táte 盾, shiirudo シールド
2. *v* (*protects*) hōgo shimásu (suru,
shite) 保護します(する, して);
(*covers*) ōimásu (ōu, ōtte) 覆い[おお
い]ます(覆う, 覆って)

shift 1. *v* (*it shifts*) utsurimásu (utsúru,
utsútte) 移ります(移る, 移って)
2. *v* (*shifts/changes it*) ten-jimásu (ten-jiru,
ten-jite) 転じます(転じる, 転じて)
3. *v* (*alternates*) kōtai shimásu (suru,
shite) 交替[交代]します(する, して)
4. *n* idō 移動 3. *n* henka 変化, shifuto
シフト
day shift *n* nikkin 日勤
night shift *n* yakin 夜勤
shift key *n* (*keyboard*) shifuto kii
シフトキー
shift system *n* shifuto-sei シフト制,
kōtai-sei 交代制

Shikoku *n* Shikóku 四国

shilling *n* shiringu シリング

Shimbashi *n* Shínbashi 新橋; *Shimbashi Station* Shinbashí-Eki 新橋駅

shimmer 1. *n* yurameki 揺らめき 2. *v*
yuramekimásu (yurameku, yurameite)
揺らめきます(揺らめく, 揺らめいて)

shin *n* suné すね・脛

shine 1. *n* (*gloss*) tsuya つや・ツヤ・
艶 2. *v* (*it shines*) hikarimásu (hikáru,
hikátte) 光ります(光る, 光って),
(*gleams*) kagayakimásu (kagayáku,
kagayáite) 輝きます(輝く, 輝いて);
(*the sun*) terimásu (téru, tétte) 照り
ます(照る, 照って); (*polishes it*)
migakimásu (migaku, migaite) 磨
きます(磨く, 磨いて) 3. *shines on
(illuminates*) …o terashimásu (terásu,
teráshite) …を照らします(照らす, 照
らして)

shingle *n* íta 板; *shingles a roof* íta de
yáne o fukimásu (fuku, fuite) 板で屋
根をふき[葺き]ます(ふく, ふいて)

shingles *n* (*herpes zoster*) (taijō-)
hō'shin (帯状)疱疹, herupesu ヘルペス

Shinjuku *n* Shinjuku 新宿; *Shinjuku
Station* Shinjukú-Eki 新宿駅

Shinto(ism) *n* Shíntō/Shíndō 神道;
Shinto music and dances kágura 神楽

Shinto shrine *n* jínja 神社; (o-)miya
(お)宮

shiny *adj* hikaru 光る, hikatte(i)
ru 光って(い)る, kagayaku 輝く,
kagayaite(i)ru 輝いて(い)る

ship 1. *n* fúne 船・舟, (*steamship*)
kisen 汽船, …-sen …船; (*how many*)
nán-seki 何隻, nán-sō 何艘(何艘) 2. *v*
(*loads/carries*) (fune ni) nosemásu
(noseru, nosete) (船に)載せます(載せ
る, 載せて)
ship building *n* zōsen 造船
ship's crew *n* sen'in 船員

shipwreck *n* nanpa 難破, sōnan 遭難
shipwrecked vessel *n* nanpa sen
難破船

shipyard *n* zōsen-jo 造船所

shirk *v* 1. okotarimásu (okotaru,
okotatte) 怠ります(怠る, 怠って),
namakemásu (namakeru, namakete)
怠けます(怠ける, 怠けて) 2. nogare-
másu (nogareru, nogarete) 逃れます
(逃れる, 逃れて), sakemásu (sakeru,
sakete) 避けます(避ける, 避けて),
[BOOKISH] kaihi shimásu (suru, shite)
回避します(する, して)
shirk one's job *v* shigoto o okotari-

másu (okotaru, okotatte) 仕事を怠り
ます(怠る, 怠って)

shirk payment *v* (shiharai o fumi-
taoshimásu (fumitaosu, fumitaoshite)
支払いを踏み倒します(踏み倒す, 踏
み倒して)

shirk responsibility *v* sekinin o nogare-
másu (nogareru, nogarete) 責任を逃れ
ます(逃れる, 逃れて), sekinin o kaihi
shimásu (suru, shite) 責任を回避しま
す(回避する, 回避して)

shirt *n* wai-shatsu Yシャツ; (*undershirt*)
shátsu シャツ; (*how many* nánmai 何枚)

shit → dung, feces → defecation →
defecate

shiver 1. *v* zotto shimásu (suru, shite)
ぞっとします(する, して), furuemásu
(furueru, furuete) 震えます(震える,
震えて), miburui (o) shimásu (suru,
shite) 身震い(を)します(する, して),
ononokimásu (ononoku, ononoite) お
ののき[慄き]ます(おののく, おの
のいて) **2.** *n with a* ~ zotto ぞっと,
samuke 寒け

shock *n* shókku ショック, [BOOKISH]
shōgeki 衝撃

shocking *adj* tonde-mo nai … とんで
もない…; shokkingu (na) …ショッキ
ング(な)…; tonda …とんだ…

shoe *n* kutsú 靴, (*outdoor shoes*) shita-
baki 下履き, (**1**: pair is-sóku 一足, **2**:
ní-soku 二足, **3**: sán-zoku/-soku 三足;
how many nán-zoku/-soku 何足)

shoe box *n* (*at entryway*) getabako
下駄箱

shoehorn *n* kutsu-bera 靴べら

shoelace *n* kutsú-himo 靴ひも[紐]

shoe-repair(er) *n* kutsu-náoshi 靴直し

shoeshine *n* kutsu-mígaki 靴磨き

shoe shop/store *n* kutsú-ya 靴屋

shoesole *n* kutsu no urá 靴の裏,
kutsu-zoko 靴底

shogunate *n* bákufu 幕府; bakufu-
jídai 幕府時代

shoot *v* **1.** uchimásu (útsu, útte) 撃ち
ます(撃つ, 撃って) **2.** (*arrow*) irimásu
(íru, itte) 射ります(射る, 射って)
3. (*shoot to death*) uchi-koroshimásu
(uchi-korosu, uchi-koroshite) 撃ち殺す
(撃ち殺す, 撃ち殺して) **4.** barashi-

másu (barásu, baráshite) ばらします
(ばらす, ばらして) **5.** (*film*) satsuei
shimásu (suru, shite) 撮影します(す
る, して)

shoot a dice *v* saikoro o furimásu
(furu, futte) サイコロを振ります(振
る, 振って)

shoot a film *v* eiga o satsuei shimásu
(suru, shite) 映画を撮影します(する,
して)

shoot for the stars *v* takanozomi o
shimásu (suru, shite) 高望みをします
(する, して),

shooting *n* shageki 射撃

shooting game *n* shūtingu gēmu
シューティング・ゲーム

shooting star *n* nagaré-boshi 流れ星

shop *n* (*store*) misé 店, uri-ba 売り場,
shō´ten 商店, shoppu ショップ; …-ya
…屋, …-ten …店; (**1**: ík-ken 一軒,
2: ní-ken 二軒, **3**: sán-gen 三軒; *how
many* nán-ken 何軒)

shop *v* (*does the shopping*; *buys*) kai-
mono shimásu (suru, shite) 買い物し
ます(する, して)

shop around for … *v* o busshoku
shimásu (suru, shite) …を物色します
(する, して)

shop clerk *n* ten'in 店員

shop curtain *n* noren のれん・暖簾

shopgirl *n* (joshi-)ten'in (女子)店員

shopkeeper *n* tenshu 店主; …-ya (san)
…屋(さん)

shoplift *v* kapparaimásu (kapparau,
kapparatte) かっぱらいます(かっぱら
う, かっぱらって), manbiki o shimásu
(suru, shite) 万引き[まんびき]をしま
す(する, して)

shoplifting, shoplifter *n* manbiki 万
引き

shopping *n* kaimono 買い物, shoppingu
ショッピング

shopping bag *n* shoppingu-bággu
ショッピングバッグ

shopping center *n* shoppingu-séntā
ショッピングセンター

shopping area, shop street(s) *n*
shōtén-gai 商店街

shop window *n* shō uindō ショー・
ウインドウ

shore n kishí 岸, [BOOKISH] kishíbe 岸辺; (seashore) kaigan 海岸, [BOOKISH] (seaside) umibe 海辺; [BOOKISH] (lakeshore) kogan 湖岸

short adj (not long) mijikái 短い; (not tall) (séga) hikúi (背が) 低い; (deficient) … ga tarimasén (tarinai) … が足りません(足りない)
in short adv tsúmari つまり, yōsuru ni 要するに

shortage n fusoku 不足, …-búsoku …不足
water shortage n mizu-búsoku 水不足

shortcake n shōto kēki ショートケーキ

shortchange v tsuri-sen o gomakashimásu (gomakásu, gomakáshite) 釣(り)銭をごまかします(ごまかす, ごまかして), kozeni o gomakashimásu (gomakásu, gomakáshite) 小銭をごまかします(ごまかす, ごまかして)

short circuit n (electric) (denki ga) shō'to (shimásu; suru, shite) ショート(します; する, して)

shortcoming n tánsho 短所, ketten 欠点

shortcut n 1. chiká-michi 近道 2. (computer) shōto katto ショートカット

shorten v 1. shortens it mijikáku shimásu (suru, shite) 短くします(する, して); chijimemásu (chijimeru, chijimete) 縮めます(縮める, 縮めて); herashimásu (herasu, herashite) 減らします(減らす, 減らして); (abbreviates) ryakushimásu (ryakúsu, ryakúshite) 略します(略す, 略して) 2. mijikáku narimásu (naru, natte) 短くなります(なる, なって); chijimárimásu (chijimaru, chijimatte) 縮まります(縮まる, 縮まって)

shorthand n sokki 速記

short-handed adj hitode ga tarinai 人手が足りない, hitode ga fusoku shiteiru 人手が不足している, hitode-busoku (no) 人手不足(の)

short hair n 1. mijikai kami 短い髪 2. (hair style) shōto katto ショートカット

shortly adv ma-mó-naku 間もなく, chikáku 近く

short-necked clam n asari アサリ・浅蜊

shortness n fusoku 不足
shortness of breath n (medical) ikigire 息切れ

shorts n 1. (outerwear) shōtopántsu ショートパンツ; tanpan 短パン 2. (undershorts) zubon-shita ズボン下

shortsighted adj (myopic) kinshi (no) 近視(の), kingan (no) 近眼(の); (not thinking ahead) tansaibō (na) 単細胞(な)

shortstop n (baseball) shō'to ショート

short story n tanpen shōsetsu 短編小説; shō'to sutōrii ショートストーリー

short-tempered adj tanki (no/na) 短気(の/な)

shortwave adj tanpa (no) 短波(の)

shot n 1. (fire) hassha 発射; happō 発砲 2. (for a goal) shūto シュート 3. (TV scene, film) katto カット
big shot n ōmono 大物; ōgosho 大御所
give it one's best shot v zenryoku o tsukushite (yatte) mimásu (miru, mite) 全力を尽くして[つくして](やって)みます(みる, みて)
Good shot! interj Naisu shotto! ナイスショット!
have a shot at v (tries) tameshite mimásu (tamesu, tameshite) 試してみます(試す, 試して)
long shot kanōsei no hikui 可能性の低い

shotgun n shotto-gan ショットガン; [BOOKISH] sandan-jū 散弾銃

should → **ought**

shoulder 1. n káta 肩 2. v (carries on shoulders) [INFORMAL] shoimásu (shou, shotte) しよいます(しょう, しょって), seoimásu (seou, seotte) 背負います(背負う, 背負って), hikiukemásu (hikiukeru, hikiukete) 引き受けます(引き受ける, 引き受けて)
over-the-shoulder adj katagoshi (no) 肩ごし・肩越し(の)
shoulder bag n shorudābaggu ショルダーバッグ
shoulder blade n kenkōkotsu 肩甲骨

shout 1. v (calls out) sakebimásu

(sakébu, sakénde) 叫びます(叫ぶ, 叫んで); (*chants*) tonaemásu (tonáeru, tonáete) 唱えます(唱える, 唱えて); (*yells*) donarimásu (donáru, donátte) どなり[怒鳴り]ます(どなる, どなって) **2.** *n* sakebi-goe 叫び声, ōgoe 大声

shove *n, v* tsuyoku oshimásu (osu, oshite) 強く押します(押す, 押して)

shovel *n* sháberu シャベル

show *n* **1.** (*display*) mié 見栄・ミエ **2.** (*an exhibit*) mise-mónó 見せ物, shō ショー **3.** → movie → play

show *v* **1.** (*displays it*) misemásu (miséru, mísete) 見せます(見せる, 見せて); [HUMBLE] o-me ni kakemásu (kakéru, kákete) お目にかけます(かける, かけて) **2.** (*reveals*) arawashimásu (arawásu, arawáshite) 表します(表す, 表して); (*indicates*) shimeshimásu (shimesu, shimeshite) 示します(示す, 示して) **3.** (*tells*) oshiemásu (oshieru, oshiete) 教えます(教える, 教えて)

show in *v* (*ushers*) tōshimásu (tō´su, tōshite) 通します(通す, 通して); annai shimásu (suru, shite) 案内します(する, して)

show off *v* jiman shimásu (suru, shite) 自慢します(する, して); misebirakashimásu (misebirakasu, mísebirakashite) 見せびらかします(見せびらかす, 見せびらかして); [BOOKISH] koji shimásu (suru, shite) 誇示します(する, して)

show up *v* arawaremásu (arawaréru, arawárete) 現れます(現れる, 現れて); (*comes*) miemásu (miéru, míete) 見えます(見える, 見えて)

Showa era *n* Shōwa jidai 昭和時代

showcase *n* shō kēsu ショー・ケース, tenji-yō kēsu 展示用ケース, [BOOKISH] chinretsu-dana 陳列棚

showdown *n* taiketsu 対決, dotanba 土壇場

shower 1. *n* (*bath*) sháwā シャワー; *rain ~* yūdachi 夕立(ち); *sudden ~* niwaka-áme にわか雨 **2.** *v* (*takes a shower*) sháwā o abimásu (abiru, abite) シャワーを浴びます(浴びる, 浴びて); *~ on* abisemásu (abiseru, abisete) 浴びせます(浴びせる, 浴びせて)

showing *n* (*movie*) jōei 上映

showroom *n* shō rūmu ショー・ルーム, tenji-shitsu 展示室, chinretsu-shitsu 陳列室

showy *adj* hanáyaka (na) 華やか(な), hadé (na) 派手(な)

shred *n* kirehashi 切れ端

shredder *n* shureddā シュレッダー

shrew *n* gamigami on'na がみがみ女

shrewd *adj* josai nai 如才ない

shrill *adj* kandakai 甲高い
　shrill voice *n* kiiroi koe 黄色い声, kandakai koe 甲高い声, kanakiri-goe 金切り声

shrimp *n* ebi エビ・海老; (*batterfried*) ebi-ten 海老天; (*fried in bread crumbs*) ebi-fúrai エビフライ; *giant ~* (*prawn*) kurumá-ebi 車えび・車海老・クルマエビ; *tiny ~* shiba ebi 芝エビ・芝海老; *mantis ~* sháko シャコ・蝦蛄

shrine *n* (*Shinto*) (o-)miya (お)宮; jínja 神社, (*large*) jingū´ 神宮

shrink *v* chijimimásu (chijimu, chijinde) 縮みます(縮む, 縮んで), chijimárimásu (chijimaru, chijimatte) 縮まります(縮まる, 縮まって), (*shortens, abridges*) tsuzumarimásu (tsuzumáru, tsuzumátte) つづまり[約まり]ます(つづまる, つづまって)

shrivel *v* chijimimásu (chijimu, chijinde) 縮みます(縮む, 縮んで), shioremásu (shioreru, shiorete) しおれます(しおれる, しおれて),

shrub *n* kanboku 灌木, yabu やぶ・藪

shudder *v* zotto shinmásu (suru, shite) ぞっと[ゾッと]します(する, して); *with a ~* zotto ぞっと・ゾッと

shuffle *v* mazemásu (mazéru, mazete) 混ぜます(混ぜる, 混ぜて); *~ the cards* toránpu o kiri-másu (kíru, kítté) トランプを切ります(切る, 切って)

shut *v* **1.** (*shuts it*) shimemásu (shiméru, shímete) 閉めます(閉める, 閉めて); (*a book, etc.*) tojimásu (tojíru, tójite) 閉じます(閉じる, 閉じて) **2.** (*it gets shut*) shimarimásu (shimáru, shimátte) 閉まります(閉まる, 閉まって); (*it puckers up*) tsubomarimásu (tsubomaru, tsubomatte) つぼまりま

す(つぼまる, つぼまって); **~ one's eyes** mé o tsuburimásu (tsuburu, tsubutte) 目をつぶり[瞑り]ます(つぶる, つぶって); **~ up** (not speak) damarimásu (damáru, damátte) 黙ります(黙る, 黙って)

shutter n (camera, etc.) shattā シャッター; (horizontal house or vertical storefront metal shutters) yoroi-do よろい[鎧]戸, (rain shutters) amádo 雨戸

shuttle bus n shatoru basu シャトルバス

shuttlecock n hane 羽根 → **battledore**

shy adj uchíki (na) 内気(な), shai (na) シャイ(な), hazukashíi 恥ずかしい; **acts ~** hanikamimásu (hanikámu, hanikánde) はにかみます(はにかむ, はにかんで), enryo shimásu (suru, shite) 遠慮します(する, して)

shyness n enryo 遠慮 (go-enryo ご遠慮)

Siberia n Shiberia シベリア

sibling n (brother) kyōdai 兄弟, (sister) shimai 姉妹

sick adj byōki (no) 病気(の); **gets ~ and tired** unzári shimásu (suru, shite) うんざりします(する, して) → **queasy**

sickly adj byōki-gachi (na) 病気がち(な)

sickness n byōki 病気

side n 1. yoko 横; -gawa 側 2. (beside, nearby) sóba そば・側・傍, (off to the side) hata 端 3. (of body) wakí わき・脇

both sides ryō-gawa 両側
that side achira-gawa あちら側
(the) left side hidari-gawa 左側
(the) right side migi-gawa 右側
the other side mukō-gawa 向こう側
this side (my/our side) kochira-gawa こちら側
one side … the other side ippó´… (mō) ippó 一方…(もう)一方; (party) senpō 先方
which side dochira-gawa どちら側
your side sochira-gawa そちら側

sideboard n shokki-tódana 食器戸棚

sideburns n momiage もみあげ

side dish n (to go with the rice) okazu おかず

side effect n fukusayō 副作用

side hill n san-puku 山腹

side job, sideline n arubáito アルバイト

sidestep v sakemásu (sakeru, sakete) 避けます(避ける, 避けて), [BOOKISH] kaihi shimásu (suru, shite) 回避します(する, して)

side street n yokochō 横丁

sidetracked; gets ~ dassen shimásu (suru, shite) 脱線します(する, して)

sidewalk n hodō 歩道

sideways, sidewise adj, adv yoko (no/ni) 横(の/に)

siege n hōi 包囲, hōi kōgeki 包囲攻撃

sieve, sifter n furui ふるい・篩, zarú ざる

sight n (scene) ari-sama ありさま・有り様, (scenery) késhiki 景色; (eyesight) shíryoku 視力; **sees the sights** kenbutsu shimásu (suru, shite) 見物します(する, して)

sightseeing n kenbutsu 見物, kankō 観光; **~ bus** kankō-básu 観光バス; **~ tour** kankō-tsuā 観光ツアー

sightseer n kankō´-kyaku 観光客

sign 1. n (symptom) shirushi しるし[徴], chōkō 徴候; (omen) zenchō 前兆 2. n (signboard) kanban 看板 3. n (marker) hyōshiki 標識 4. n (symbol) kigō 記号 5. v (writes one's name) shomei shimásu (suru, shite) 署名します(する, して)

sign language n (hand language) shuwa 手話

signs and symptoms n (medical) chōkō to shōjō 徴候と症状

signal n shingō 信号, aizu 合図, shigunaru シグナル

signature n shomei 署名, sain サイン

signboard n kanban 看板, taté-fuda 立て札

signer n shomei-sha 署名者

significance n ígi 意義

signpost n dōhyō 道標, dōro (annai) hyōshiki 道路(案内)標識

silencer n (gun) sairen-sā サイレンサー

silent; is ~ (not speak) damarimásu (damáru, damátte) 黙ります(黙る, 黙って)

silhouette *n* shiruetto シルエット

silicon *n* shirikon シリコン

silk *n* kínu 絹, shiruku シルク; *raw ~* kí-ito 生糸

silkworm *n* (o-)káiko (お)蚕・カイコ; *raising ~*, *silk farming* yōsan 養蚕

silky *adj* kínu no yō (na) 絹[きぬ]のような, yawarakai 柔らかい

sill *n* (*window/door*) *~* (mádo/to no) shíkii (窓/戸の)敷居

sillago *n* (*fish*) kisu キス・鱚

silly *adj* bakabakashii ばかばかしい, bakageteiru ばかげて[馬鹿げて]いる

silver **1.** *n* gín 銀, shirubā シルバー **2.** *adj* (*color*) gin-iro (no) 銀色(の)

similar *adj* onaji yō´(na) 同じような, hitoshíi 等しい, nita 似た, ruiji no 類似の

similarity *n* ruiji 類似

simile *n* tatóé 例え・たとえ, tatóí 例い・たとい

simple *adj* kantan (na) 簡単(な), tanjun (na) 単純(な), shínpuru (na) シンプル(な); (*easy*) wáke-nai わけない; (*plain*) assári shita あっさりした; (*frugal*) shísso (na) 質素(な); (*naive*) soboku (na) 素朴(な); (*tastefully restrained*) shibúi 渋い; *~* (*modest*) *tastes* wabi わび・佗び

simplehearted *adj* tanjun (na) 単純(な)

simple-minded *adj* tanjun (na) 単純(な); (o-)medetái (お)めでたい[目出度い]

simply *adv* **1.** kantan ni 簡単に; (*easily*) wáke-naku わけなく; assári (to) あっさり(と) **2.** (*merely*) táda ただ, ... ni sugimasén (sugínai) ...に過ぎません(過ぎない)

simultaneous *adj* dōji (no) 同時(の) simultaneous translation *n* dōjitsú´yaku 同時通訳

sin *n* tsúmi 罪; záiaku 罪悪

since **1.** *prep* ... kara ...から; (sono) áto/go (その)後・あと; *~ then* sono-go その後; (...) írai (...)以来 **2.** *conj* ... shite kara ...してから **3.** → because

sincere *adj* makoto (no) 誠(の), seijitsu (na) 誠実(な); (*heartfelt*) kokóro kara (no) 心から(の)

sincerity *n* seii 誠意, magokoro 真心

sing *v* utaimásu (utau, utatte) 歌います (歌う, 歌って)

singer *n* kashu 歌手, shingā シンガー

single **1.** *adj* (*for one person*) hitóri no 一人[独り]の **2.** *n* (*unmarried*) hitori-mónó 独り者, dokushin 独身

single (room) *n* shínguru シングル, shinguru-rū´mu シングルルーム

sink **1.** *n* (*in kitchen*) nagashi 流し **2.** *v* (*it sinks*) shizumimásu (shizumu, shizunde) 沈みます(沈む, 沈んで); (*sinks it*) shizumemásu (shizumeru, shizumete) 沈めます(沈める, 沈めて)

sip *v* suimásu (susū, susutte) 吸います (吸う, 吸って)

sir... ... sama ...様・さま, ... san ...さん

siren *n* (*sound*) sairen サイレン

sirloin *n* sāroin サーロイン

sirloin steak *n* sāroin-sutēki サーロインステーキ

sister *n* **1.** onna no kyō´dai 女の兄弟; (*older*) ane 姉, (o-)nē´-san (お)姉さん; (*younger*) imōtó 妹, (o-)imōto-san 妹さん **2.** (*nun*) sisutā シスター

sister-in-law *n* giríno ane/imōtó 義理の姉/妹 (*older/younger*)

sit *v* (*especially Japanese-style*) suwarimásu (suwaru, suwatte) 座ります(座る, 座って), (*on a cushion*) shikimásu (shiku, shiite) 敷きます (敷く, 敷いて); (*in chair*) (koshi-)kakemásu (kakéru, kákete) (腰)掛け ます(掛ける, 掛けて); *~ astride* ... ni matagarimásu (matagaru, matagátte) ... に跨がり[跨り]ます(跨がる, 跨がって)

site *n* (*building lot*) shíki-chi 敷地; genba 現場; basho 場所

sit-in (*strike*) *n* suwarikomi 座り込み

situation *n* jōtai 状態, jōkyō 状況, jítai 事態; (*circumstance*) ba(w)ai 場合; (*stand-point*) tachi-ba 立場; (*stage*) kurai 位; (*location*) íchi 位置

six *n* rokú 六・6, muttsú 六つ; shíkku-su シックス

six; *6 pieces* (*small things*) rók-ko 六個, *6 trees* (*or long things*) róp-pon 六本, *6 sheets* (*flat things*) rokú-mai 六枚; *6 cats* (*or small animals*) rop-píkí 六匹

6 cows (*or large aminals*) rokú-tō 六頭; *6 birds/rabbits* róp-pa 六羽; *6 cars* (*or machines/vehicles*) rokú-dai 六台; *6 copies* (*books/magazines*) rokú-satsu 六冊; *6 people* rokú-nin 六人, rokú-mei 六名; *6 floors/stories* rok-kai 六階; *6 fold* rokú-bai 六倍; *6 days* muika 六日・6日; *6 degrees* rokú-do 六度; *6 times* rokú-dó 六度, rok-kái 六回, rop-pén 六遍; *6 o'clock* rokú-ji 六時; rokú-jíkan 六時間; *6 days* muika 六日; *6 weeks* rokú-shūkan 六週間; *6 months* rokú-kágetsu 六ヶ月; *6 times* rokudo-mé 六度目, rokkai-mé 六回目; *6 years* rokúnen 六年, rokunén-kan 六年間; *6 years old* muttsú 六つ, rokú-sái 六歳

six hundred *n* rop-pyakú 六百・600

sixteen *n* jū-rokú 十六・16

sixth *adj* roku-banmé (no) 六番目 (の), muttsu-mé (no) 六つ目 (の); *the ~ day* muika-mé 六日目, (*of the month*) muika 六日

six thousand *n* roku-sén 六千・6,000

sixty *n* roku-jū´ 六十・60; *~ thousand* roku-mán 六万

size *n* ōkisa 大きさ, sáizu サイズ; (*model*) katá 型, …-gata …型

skate, skating 1. *n* sukē´to スケート, rōrā sukē´to ローラースケート 2. *v* sukē´to o shimásu (suru, shite) スケートをします(する, して); suberimásu (subéru, subétte) 滑ります (滑る, 滑って) ice skating *n* aisu sukēto アイススケート skateboard *n* sukēto bōdo スケートボード

sketch *n* shasei 写生, sukétchi スケッチ; shitae 下絵

skewer *n* yaki-gushi 焼き串

ski, skiing *n* sukíí (o shimásu; suru, shite) スキー(をします; する, して) figure skating *n* figyua sukēto フィギュアスケート ski resort *n* sukii-jō スキー場; sukii rizōto スキー・リゾート ski wear *n* sukii uea スキーウエア, sukii wea スキーウェア

skill *n* udemae 腕前; ginō 技能; sukiru スキル

skillful *adj* jōzú (na) じょうず[上手] (な) (o-jōzu おじょうず), umái うまい, takumi (na) 巧み(な); (*proficient*) tassha (na) 達者(な); (*nimble*) kíyō (na) 器用(な)

skim *v* (*grazes*) kasumemásu (kasumeru, kasumete) かすめ[掠め] ます(かすめる, かすめて); *~ off* kasume-torimásu (kasume-tóru, kasume-tótte) かすめ[掠め] 取ります(かすめ[掠め]取る, かすめ[掠め]取って)

skim milk *n* dasshí-nyū 脱脂乳

skin 1. *n* hifu 皮膚; (*of animal, potato, …*) kawá 皮 2. *v* (*pares/peels it*) mukimásu (muku, muite) むき[剥き] ます(むく, むいて), hagimásu (hagu, haide) はぎ[剥ぎ]ます(はぐ, はいで) human skin *n* (hito) hada (人)肌 skin cancer *n* (*medical*) hihu gan 皮膚がん・皮膚癌 skin care *n* sukin kea スキン・ケア

skinflint *n* kéchinbo(u) けちんぼ(う) ・けちん坊, kéchi けち

skip *v* (*leaves out*) nukashimásu (nukasu, nukashite) 抜かします(抜かす, 抜かして), tobashimásu (tobasu, tobashite) 飛ばします(飛ばす, 飛ばして)

skip school gakkō o saborimásu (sabóru, sabótte) 学校をさぼります (さぼる, さぼって), zuru-yásumi shimásu (suru, shite) ずる休みします (する, して)

skirt *n* sukā´to スカート

sky *n* sóra 空; (*heaven*) tén 天; (*blue, empty*) aozóra 青空

skydiving *n* sukai daibingu スカイ・ダイビング

skyscraper *n* kōsō-bíru 高層ビル

slack *adj* yuruí 緩い・弛い・ゆるい; *gets ~* taruminásu (tarumu, tarunde) たるみ[弛み]ます(たるむ, たるんで)

slacks *n* surákkusu スラックス, zubon ズボン

slander 1. *n* warú-kuchi/-guchi 悪口, [BOOKISH] hibō ひぼう・誹謗 2. *v* …o chūshō shimásu (suru, shite) …を中傷します(する, して)

slang *n* zokugo 俗語, surangu スラング

slant 1. *n* katamuki 傾き **1.** *v* (*leans*) katamukimásu (katamúku, katamúite) 傾きます(傾く, 傾いて)

slanting *adj* naname (no) 斜め(の), [BOOKISH] hasu (no) はす[斜](の)

slap *v* hatakimásu (hatáku, hatáite) はたき[叩き]ます(はたく, はたいて); hippatakimasu (hippataku, hippataite) 引っぱたきます(引っぱたく, 引っぱたいて); (*one's face*) … no kao o uchimásu (útsu, útte) …の顔を打ちます(打つ, 打って), … ni binta shimasu (suru, shite) ビンタします(する, して)

slash *n* surasshu スラッシュ; shasen 斜線, "/"

slave *n* dorei 奴隷; yakko やっこ・奴

sled *n* sóri そり・橇

sleep 1. *n* (*sleeping*) nemuri 眠り, ne 寝, suimin 睡眠; **not enough ~** ne-búsoku 寝不足 **2.** *v* (*sleeps*) nemurimásu (nemuru, nemutte) 眠ります(眠る, 眠って); yasumimásu (yasúmu, yasúnde) 休みます(休む, 休んで); (*goes to bed*) nemásu (neru, nete) 寝ます(寝る, 寝て); (*a leg, etc.*) **goes to ~** (*gets numb*) shibiremásu (shibiréru, shibírete) しびれ[痺れ]ます(しびれる, しびれて)

sleep soundly → sound asleep

sleeping bag *n* nebukuro 寝袋

sleeping car *n* shindái-sha 寝台車

sleeping pill *n* suimin-zai 睡眠剤, suimín-yaku 睡眠薬

sleepy *adj* nemui 眠い

sleet *n* mizore みぞれ

sleeve *n* (o-)sode (お)袖; (*end of kimono sleeve*) tamotó たもと・袂; **~ cord** tasuki たすき

slender *adj* hosói 細い

slice 1. *n* suraisu スライス **2.** *v* → cut; piece

sliced raw fish *n* sashimí 刺身 (o-sashi-mi お刺身)

slick *adj* subekkói すべっ[滑っ]こい

slide 1. *n* suberí-dai すべり台, (o-súberi お滑り) **2.** *v* suberimásu (subéru, subétte) 滑ります(滑る, 滑って)

slider *n* suraidā スライダー

sliding panel/door *n* **1.** (*translucent*) shōji 障子 **2.** (*opaque*) fusuma ふすま・襖

slight *adj* chótto shita … ちょっとした…

slip 1. *n* → slide **2.** **~ out of …** nuke-dashimásu (nuke-dásu, nuke-dashite) 抜け出します(抜け出す, 抜け出して)

slippers *n* suríppa スリッパ, uwabaki うわばき・上履き

slippery *adj* suberi yasui すべり[滑り]やすい; subekkói すべっ[滑っ]こい; **Slippery (Area)** "Surippu-jíko ō'shi" "スリップ事故多し"

slipshod *adj* zusan (na) ずさん[杜撰](な)

slogan *n* surō'gan スローガン, hyōgo 標語

slope *n* saká 坂

sloping road *n* saka-michi 坂道

sloppy *adj* zonzái (na) ぞんざい(な), zusan (na) ずさん[杜撰](な)

slot *n* kuchi 口, aná 穴

slot machine *n* (*vending machine*) (jidō-)hambái-ki (自動)販売機; (*gambling*) surotto mashiin スロットマシーン

slovenly *adj* zonzái (na) ぞんざい(な); darashinai だらしない; zusan (na) ずさん[杜撰](な)

slow *adj* osoi 遅い, surō' (na) スロー(な); (*sluggish*) norói のろい, yurúi 緩い; (*clock runs slow*) okurete imásu (iru, ite) 遅れています(いる, いて)

slow motion *n* (*film, etc.*) surō mōshon スローモーション

slowly *adv* yukkúri ゆっくり; (*tardily, late*) osoku 遅く

slug *n* (*coin*) tamá 玉

sluggish *adj* norói のろい

slum *n* suramu (-gai) スラム(街), [BOOKISH] hinmín-kutsu/-gai 貧民窟/街

sly *adj* zurúi ずるい; **~ dog/person** zurúi-yatsu ずるいやつ, tanuki タヌキ・狸

small *adj* (*little*) chiisái/chitchái 小さい/ちっちゃい, chíisa-na/chítcha-na …小さな/ちっちゃな…; ko-…小; (*fine*) komakái 細かい; (*small-scale*) sasáyaka (na) ささやか(な)

small boat *n* kobune 小舟

small change n komakái (o)-kane 細
かい(お)金, ko-zeni 小銭; o-tsuri お釣
り・おつり, tsuri-sen 釣り銭

smallpox n (*medical*) tennentō 天然痘・
てんねん痘

small restaurant n (*Japanese traditional*) koryōri-ya 小料理屋

small-size adj (*model*) kogata (no)
小型(の)

smart 1. adj (*intelligent*) atamá ga íi
頭がいい, rikō (na) 利口(な); (*stylish*)
sumá'to (na) スマート(な), iki (na) い
き[粋]な **2.** v (*it smarts*) shimimásu
(shimiru, shimite) 染みます(染みる、
染みて)

smartphone n (*multifunctional mobile
phone*) sumātofon スマートフォン

smash v **1.** (*breaks it*) kowashimásu
(kowásu, kowáshite) 壊します(壊す、
壊して), kudakimásu (kudáku, kudáite)
砕きます(砕く、砕いて); (*crushes it*)
tsubushimásu (tsubusu, tsubushite)
潰し[つぶし]ます(潰す、潰して) **2.**
(*it breaks*) kowaremásu (kowaréru,
kowárete) 壊れます(壊れる、壊れて),
kudakemásu (kudakéru, kudákete) 砕
けます(砕ける、砕いて); (*it crushes*)
tsuburemásu (tsubureru, tsuburete)
潰れ[つぶれ]ます(潰れる、潰れて)

smell 1. n (*odor*) niói におい[臭い・
匂い] **2.** v (*it smells*) nioimásu (nióu,
niótte) におい[臭い・匂い]ます(にお
う、におって), niói ga shimásu (suru
shite) におい[臭い・匂い]がします
(する、して) **3.** v (*smells it*) kagimásu
(kagu, kaide) 嗅ぎます(嗅ぐ、嗅いで)

smelly adj kusái 臭い・くさい

smile 1. v níkoniko shimásu (suru, shite)
にこにこします・ニコニコします(す
る、して); hohoemimásu (hohoému,
hohoénde) 微笑みます・ほほえみます
(微笑む、微笑んで) **2.** n (*smailing face*)
e-gao 笑顔; hohoemí 微笑み・ほほえ
み; [BOOKISH] bishō 微笑・びしょう

smoke 1. v (*tobacco*) tabako o
nomimásu (nómu, nónde) たばこを飲
み[呑み]ます(飲[呑]む、飲[呑]んで),
tabako o suimás̱u (sū, sutte) たばこを
吸います(吸う、吸って); kitsuen
shimásu (suru, shite) 喫煙します(す

る、して) **2.** v ibu-shimásu (ibusu,
ibushite) いぶし[燻し]ます(いぶす、
いぶして) **3.** n kemuri 煙・けむり

smoker n (*person who smokes*)
kitsuén-sha 喫煙者

smokestack n entotsu 煙突

smoking n kitsuen 喫煙
smoking corner n kin'en kōnā 喫煙コ
ーナー
smoking prohibited n kin'en 禁煙
nonsmoking seat n kin'en seki 禁煙席

smoky adj kemui 煙い・けむい,
kemutai 煙たい・けむたい

SMON n (*subacute myelo-optico
neuropathy*) súmon スモン, sumon-
byō スモン病

smooth 1. adj naméraka (na) 滑らか
・なめらか(な), sube sube shíta ,
(*flat*) taira (na) 平ら(な), (*slippery*)
subekkói 滑っこい・すべっこい; *not
~ arai* 粗い・あらい **2.** v narashimásu
(narásu, naráshite) ならし[均し]ます
(ならす、ならして); (*pats*) nademásu
(nadéru, nádete) なで[撫で]ます(なで
る、なでて)

smorgasbord n (*"Viking"*) báikingu
バイキング

smudge n yogore 汚れ・よごれ

smuggle v mitsuyu shimásu (suru,
shite) 密輸します(する、して)

snack n keishoku 軽食, karui monó/
tabemóno/shokuji 軽い物/食べ物/食
事; (*mid-afternoon*) o-sánji お三時,
o-yátsu おやつ

snack bar, snackshop n sunákku
スナック

snake n hébi 蛇・ヘビ

snap v **1.** (*it snaps*) hajikemásu
(hajikéru, hajíkete) はじけ[弾け]ます
(はじける、はじけて) **2.** (*snaps it*)
hajikimásu (hajíku, hajíite) はじき
[弾き]ます(はじく、はじいて)

snapping turtle n suppon すっぽん・
スッポン

sneakers n suniikā スニーカー,
zukkú-gutsu ズック靴

sneeze n, v kushámi (o shimásu; suru,
shite) くしゃみ(をします; する、して)

snivel n hana はな・洟・鼻, hana-
mizu 鼻水

snore *n, v* ibikí (o kakimásu; káku, káite) いびき・鼾 (をかきます; かく, かいて)

snoring *n* ibiki いびき・鼾; ~ *away* gū´gū ぐうぐう

snow *n* yukí (ga furimásu; fúru, fútté) 雪 (が降ります; 降る, 降って)

snowslide *n* yuki-nádare 雪なだれ, nadare なだれ・雪崩

snowstorm *n* fúbuki 吹雪・ふぶき

snow white *adj* masshíro (na) 真っ白・まっしろ (な)

so *adv* **1.** (*like that*) sō´ そう (sō そう + [VERB]), (*like this*) kō´ こう (kō こう + [VERB]). **2.** (*that much*) sonna ni そんなに, (*this much*) konna ni こんなに, **3.** (*and so*) … kara …から, …-te …て (…-kute …くて, … de…で); dá kara (sa) だから (さ)

so as to be [NOUN] ni に, [ADJECTIVE]-ku く; … yō ni …ように

so to speak *adv* iwaba いわば

soak *v* **1.** *soaks it* tsukemásu (tsukeru, tsukete) 漬けます (漬ける, 漬けて) **2.** *it soaks* tsukarimásu (tsukaru, tsukatte) 漬かります (漬かる, 漬かって) **3.** *it soaks in* shimimásu (shimiru, shimite) 染みます (染みる, 染みて)

so-and-so *n* **1.** dáredare だれだれ・誰々, dáresore だれそれ・誰それ; yátsu やつ・奴; (*scoundrel*) yarō 野郎 **2.** náninani なになに・何々

soap *n* sekken 石けん・石鹸, shabon シャボン, sōpu ソープ

soap bubble *n* shabon-dama シャボン玉

soap opera *n* hōmu-dorama ホームドラマ, mero dorama メロドラマ

sober *adj* (*in one's right mind*) shōki (no) 正気 (の); (*plain*) jimí (na) 地味 (な); (*undrunk*) shirafu (no) しらふ (の)

so-called *adj* iwayuru いわゆる

soccer *n* sákkā サッカー

soccer ball *n* sakkā bōru サッカーボール

soccer player *n* (*professional*) sakkā senshu サッカー選手

sociable *adj* aisó (aisó´) ga (/no) íi あいそ (う) [愛想] が (/の) いい, shakō-teki (na) 社交的 (な)

social *adj* shákai (no) 社会 (の); ~ *company* tsuki-ai 付き合い (o-tsukíai お付き合い), (*social friendly intercourse/relations*) kōsai 交際; ~ *standing* míbun 身分, shakai-teki chíi 社会的地位

social intercourse *n* shakō 社交

socialism *n* shakai-shúgi 社会主義

socialist *n* shakaishugí-sha 社会主義者

social science(s) *n* shakai-kágaku 社会科学

society *n* shákai 社会; (*association*) kyōkai 協会, (*scholarly*) gakkai 学会; …-kai …会

socket *n* sokétto ソケット; *two-way* ~ futamata-sokétto 二又ソケット

socks *n* kutsu-shita 靴下, (*anklets*) sókkusu ソックス, (*split-toe*) tábi たび・足袋; (**1:** pair is-sokú一足, **2:** ní-soku 二足, **3:** sán-zoku 三足; *how many* nán-zoku/-soku 何足)

soda water *n* tansán-sui 炭酸水; sōda ソーダ, sōdá-sui ソーダ水

soft *adj* yawarakái 柔らかい, sofuto (na) ソフト (な); ~ *ice cream* sofuto-kuríimu ソフトクリーム

software *n* sofutowéa ソフトウェア

soil 1. *n* (*earth*) tsuchí 土, tochi 土地; (*stain*) yogoré 汚れ **2.** *v* (*makes it dirty*) yogo-shimásu (yogosu, yogoshite) 汚します (汚す, 汚して); (*gets dirty*) yogore-másu (yogoreru, yogorete) 汚れます (汚れる, 汚れて)

sojourn *v* taizai (shimásu; suru, shite) 滞在します (する, して)

sold → **sell**; ~ *out* uri-kire (no) 売り切れ (の)

soldier *n* heishi 兵士, hei 兵, gunjin 軍人

sole 1. *n* (*fish*) shita-bírame 舌平目・シタビラメ **2.** *n* (*of foot*) ashi no urá 足の裏, (*of shoe*) kutsu no urá 靴の裏, kutsu-zoko 靴底 **3.** *adj* → **only** (*one*)

solicitude *n* omoi-yari 思いやり; *thanks to your* ~ okage-sama de お かげ [お蔭] さまで; *a visit of* ~ (o-) mimai (お) 見舞い

solid 1. *adj* (*firm*) katai 固い・硬い・堅い・かたい **2.** *n* (*a solid*) kotai 固体, rittai 立体

solid-color *adj* múji (no) 無地 (の)

solstice n *summer ~* geshi 夏至, *winter ~* tōji 冬至

solution n kaiketsu (saku) 解決(策)

solve v **1.** tokimásu (tóku, tóite) 解きます(解く, 解いて); *gets solved* tokemásu (tokéru, tókete) 解けます(解ける, 解けて) **2.** kaiketsu shimásu (suru, shite) 解決します(する, して)

Somalia n Somaria ソマリア

somber adj **1.** inki (na) 陰気(な) **2.** (*color*) kusunda くすんだ

some 1. adj (*pron*) (*a little*) sukoshi 少し (*but often omitted*); (*certain*) nánráka no … 何らかの… (*a certain amount*) íkura ka (no) いくらか・幾らか(の), (*a certain number*) íkutsu ka (no) いくつか・幾つか(の); tashō (no) 多少(の) **2.** pron (*particular*) áru …n da…; *~ people* áru hito ある人, … hítomo arimásu (áru, átte) …人もあります(ある, あって)

somebody → someone

someday adv izure いずれ, ítsu-ka いつか, [BOOKISH] ichijitsú 一日

somehow adv dō'ni ka どうにか; (*vaguely*) dō'no どうも; *~ or other* nán to ka shite 何とかして, (*necessarily*) dō-shitemo どうしても

someone pron dáre ka 誰か, (…) hito (…)人, *~ or other* dáredare だれだれ・誰々, dáresore だれそれ・誰それ

some other time izure いずれ

something pron náni ka 何か, (…) monó (…)物 something or other náninani なになに・何々 something the matter, something wrong n ijō 異常 something to drink n nomí-mono 飲み物 something to talk about n hanashí 話

sometime adj ítsu ka いつか; izure いずれ

sometimes adv tokidoki 時々, tokí ni 時に; (*occasionally*) tama ni たまに…; … (suru) kotó ga arimásu (áru, átte) … (する)事があります(ある, あって); *~ (intermittently) does/is* …-tári/ …-káttari/ … dáttari shimásu (suru, shite) …たり /…かったり/…だったりします(する, して)

somewhat adv sukóshi 少し, chótto ちょっと → **somehow**

somewhere adv doko ka どこか somewhere else yosó よそ somewhere or other dókodoko どこどこ, dókosoko どこそこ

son n musuko 息子; (*your son*) bótchan 坊ちゃん; *eldest* ~ chō'nan 長男

song n utá 歌, songu ソング

songwriter n sakushi-ka 作詞家

son-in-law n múko 婿(o-múko-san お婿さん)

soon adv ma-mó-naku 間もなく, mō (súgu) もう(すぐ), jiki ni じき[直]に as soon as … (suru) to (súgu) (する)と(すぐ), (shite) kara súgu (して)からすぐ; ([VERB]-i)-shídai (ni) ([VERB]い) 次第(に)

soot n súsu すす・煤

soothe v shizumemásu (shizumeru, shizumete) 静めます・鎮めます(静[鎮]める, 静[鎮]めて), nadamemásu (nadaméru, nadámete) なだめます(なだめる, なだめて)

sophisticated adj tokaiteki (na) 都会的(な), senrensareta 洗練された

sophomore n ninén-sei 二年生

sore 1. adj itái 痛い **2.** n (*a sore spot*) itái tokoró 痛い所, (*from shoe rubbing*) kutsu-zure 靴ずれ → **boil** → **wound**

sorry adj (*for you/him*) (o-)ki-no-dókúdesu (お)気の毒です Sorry! interj Sumimasén. すみません., Gomennasai. ごめんなさい.

sort n (*kind*) shúrui 種類, ís-shu 一種

so-so adj mā-mā まあまあ

soul n séishin 精神, támashii 魂・たましい; (*person*) hito 人, ningen 人間 soul mate n sōru meito ソールメイト

sound 1. n (*noise*) otó 音; ne 音 **2.** n (*audio*) onkyō 音響; saundo サウンド **3.** v *it sounds* narimásu (naru, natte) 鳴ります(鳴る, 鳴って), (*makes an animal sound*) nakimásu (naku, naite) 鳴きます(鳴く, 鳴いて) **4.** v *sounds it* narashimásu (narasu, narashite) 鳴らします(鳴らす, 鳴らして)

sound asleep adj gussúri ぐっすり, gūgū (nemutte imásu) ぐうぐう(眠っています)

sound effect n saundo efekuto サウンド・エフェクト; onkyō kōka 音響効果

sound out v (a person) dashin shimásu (suru, shíte) 打診します(する、して)

soundscape n saundo sukēpu サウンドスケープ; oto (no) fūkei 音(の)風景、onkei 音景

sound track n santora サントラ; saundo torakku サウンド・トラック

sound wave n onpa 音波

soup n (Western-style) sū´pu スープ、(Japanese broth and rich meat broths, etc.) shíru 汁、(o-)tsúyu (お)つゆ[汁]; (Japanese clear) sui-mono 吸い物; (Japanese bean-paste) mísoshíru みそ[味噌]汁; (sweet redbean-paste) (o-)shiruko お汁粉; (thick Western) potā´ju ポタージュ; (thin Western) konsome コンソメ

soup pan n sūpu nabe スープ鍋

soup plate n sūpu-zara スープ皿

soup stock n dashi だし・ダシ

sour 1. adj suppái すっぱい 2. v it sours kusarimásu (kusáru, kusátte) 腐ります(腐る、腐って)

source n moto もと・元; táne 種; okorí 起こり

south n minami 南, nan-... 南...; (the south) nanpō 南方, (the southern part) nánbu 南部

southeast n nantō 南東

southerly adj minami-yori (no kaze) 南寄り

southwest n nansei 南西

souvenir n (o-)miyage (お)みやげ[土産], miyage-mono みやげ[土産]物, kinen-hin 記念品

sow 1. v (seeds) makimásu (máku, máite) まき[蒔き]ます(まく、まいて) 2. n (female pig) mesubuta 雌豚・メスブタ

soy n daizu 大豆・ダイズ

soybean n daizu 大豆・ダイズ; fermented ~ nattō 納豆・ナットウ

soybean flour n kínako きなこ・黄な粉

soy sauce n (o-)shōyu (お)しょうゆ[醤油], (in sushi restaurant) murásaki 紫・ムラサキ

spa n supa スパ; onsen 温泉, tōji-ba 湯治場

space n 1. (available) ma 間; (between) aida 間; (interspace) kūkan 空間, sukima すき間, supēsu スペース; (outer space) úchū 宇宙; (room, leeway) yochi 余地 2. → blank

Spain n Supéin スペイン

span 1. n (term) kikan 期間, supan スパン 2. v (stretches over it) ... ni matagarimásu (matagáru, matagátte) ...に跨がり[またがり]ます(跨がる、跨がって)

Spaniard, Spanish n (person) Supeín-jín スペイン人

Spanish n (language) Supein-go スペイン語

Spanish paprika n tōgarashi 唐辛子

spare 1. adj (reserve) yóbi (no) 予備(の) 2. n (leeway, surplus) yoyū 余裕; ~ time hima ひま, yoka 余暇 3. → save

spark n híbana 火花

sparkle n kirameki きらめき・煌き, kagayaki 輝き

sparrow n suzume すずめ・雀

speak v hanashimásu (hanásu, hanáshite) 話します(話す、話して), iimásu (iu, itte) 言います(言う、言って)

speaker → loudspeaker

speaking ability n kaiwaryoku 会話力

speaking of ... ... wa ...は; ...no kotó/hanashí desu ga ...の事[こと]/話ですが

spear n yari 槍・ヤリ

special adj tokubetsu (no) 特別(の); supesharu (na) スペシャル(な), toku-... 特...; (peculiar) tokushu (no) 特殊(の); (favorite) tokui (na/no) 得意(な/の); (emergency) rinji (no) 臨時(の)

special class n tokubetsu kurasu 特別クラス; tokkyū 特級

special delivery n sokutatsu 速達

special express (train) n tokkyū 特急; special express ticket tokkyū´-ken 特急券

special feature/quality n tokushoku 特色, tokuchō 特徴・特長

special lunch n ranchi sā´bisu ランチ・サービス

special menu n supesharu menyū スペシャル・メニュー, tokubetsu menyū 特別メニュー

special offer *n* tokubetsu hōshi-hin 特別奉仕品

special price *n* tokubetsu kakaku 特別価格

specialist *n* senmon-ka 専門家; supesharisuto スペシャリスト; (*medical*) senmón-i 専門医

specialty *n* senmon 専門, (*forte*) tokui 得意, (*trick*) ohako おはこ・十八番

species …-rui …類; *a ~ of* … no ísshu …の一種

specific *adj* (*particular*) kore to iu これという; hakkiri to shita はっきりとした; gutaiteki (na) 具体的 (な)

spectator *n* kankyaku 観客

spectrum *n* supekutoru スペクトル

speculation *n* (*venture*) yamá やま, tōki 投機

speech *n* hanashí 話, kotobá 言葉, kuchi 口; (*public*) enzetsu 演説, kōen 講演, supiichi スピーチ

speed *n* háyasa 速さ, sókudo 速度, supíido スピード; (*hourly*) jísoku 時速

spell *v* (jí o) tsuzurimásu (tsuzuru, tsuzutte) (字を) 綴り [つづり] ます (綴る, 綴って)

spellbound; *is ~* uttóri shimásu (suru, shite) うっとりします (する, して)

spelling *n* tsuzuri 綴り, supéru スペル; (*written*) kaki-káta 書き方, (*letters*) jí 字

spend *v* tsukaimásu (tsukau, tsukatte) 使います (使う, 使って), (*pays*) dashimásu (dásu, dáshite) 出します (出す, 出して); (*uses time*) sugoshimásu (sugósu, sugóshite) 過ごします (過ごす, 過ごして); okurimásu (okuru, okutte) 送ります (送る, 送って)

spermatozoon *n* seishi 精子

sphere *n* kyū 球, kyūtai 球体

sphinx *n* sufinkusu スフィンクス

sphygmomanometer *n* ketsuatsukei 血圧計

spice *n* kō´(shin)ryō´ 香 (辛) 料, chōmi (-ryō) 調味 (料), supaisu スパイス

spice box *n* yakumi-ire 薬味入れ

spiced saké *n* (o-)tóso (お)とそ・屠蘇

spicy *adj* karai からい・辛い, supaishii スパイシー

spider *n* kúmo クモ・蜘蛛; *~ web* → cobweb

spill *v* (*it spills*) koboremásu (koboréru, kobórete) こぼれ [零れ] ます (こぼれる, こぼれて); (*spills it*) koboshimásu (kobósu, kobóshite) こぼし [零し] ます (こぼす, こぼして); tarashimásu (tarásu, taráshite) 垂らします (垂らす, 垂らして)

spinach *n* hōrénsō ほうれん草・ホウレンソウ; (*boiled and seasoned*) o-hitáshi おひたし・お浸し

spine *n* sebone 背骨

spinning *n* bōseki 紡績; *~ mill* bōseki-kō´jō 紡績工場

spiral *n* rasen 螺旋・らせん

spirit *n* séishin 精神, kokóro 心, támashii 魂, supiritto スピリット; kokoro-mochi 心持ち; ki 気

spit *n* (*skewer*) kushí 串, yakigushi 焼き串

spit **1.** *n* (*spittle*) tsúba ツバ・唾, tsubakí ツバキ・唾 **2.** *v* (*spits out*) (tsúba o) hakimásu (háku, háite) (つばを) 吐きます (吐く, 吐いて)

spite; *in ~ of* … (ná) no ni …(な) のに

splendid *adj* rippa (na) 立派 (な), suba-rashíi すばらしい・素晴らしい, suteki (na) すてき・素敵 (な), mígoto (na) 見事 (な), sakan (na) 盛ん (な), kékkō (na) 結構 (な)

splendidly *adv* rippa ni 立派に, suba-ráshiku すばらしく・素晴らしく

split *v* **1.** (*splits it*) sakimásu (sáku, sáite) 裂きます (裂く, 裂いて), warimásu (waru, watte) 割ります (割る, 割って) (*divides it*) wakemásu (wakéru, wákete) 分けます (分ける, 分けて) **2.** (*it splits*) sakemásu (sakéru, sákete) 裂けます (裂ける, 裂けて), waremásu (wareru, warete) 割れます (割れる, 割れて); (*it separates*) wakaremásu (wakaréru, wakárete) 別れます (別れる, 別れて)

splitting the bill *n* wari-kan 割り勘・ワリカン

split-toe socks *n* tábi たび・足袋

spoil *v* **1.** *spoils it* wáruku (damé ni) shimásu (suru, shite) 悪く (駄目にし) ます (する, して); itamemásu (itaméru,

itámete) 傷めます(傷める, 傷めて);
~ a person's mood kíbun o kowashi-másu (kowásu, kowáshite) 気分を壊します(壊す, 壊して), kíbun o gaishimásu (gaísu, gaíshite) 気分を害します(害す, 害して) **2. it gets spoiled** wáruku narimásu (náru, nátte) 悪くなります(なる, なって), itamimásu (itámu, itánde) 傷みます(傷む, 傷んで) **3. it spoils** (*sours*) kusarimásu (kusáru, kusátte) 腐ります(腐る, 腐って); (*rots*) itamimásu (itámu, itánde) 傷みます(傷む, 傷んで)

spoke → speak; spoken language kōgo 口語

sponge *n* kaimen 海綿, suponji スポンジ

sponge gourd *n* hechima ヘチマ・糸瓜

spongecake *n* kasutera カステラ; suponji kēki スポンジケーキ

spontaneously *adv* hitori-de ni 独りでに, onozukara 自ずから

spool *n* itomaki 糸巻き

spoon *n* supū´n スプーン, sájí さじ・匙; (**1:** íp-pon 一本, **2:** ní-hon 二本, **3:** sánbon 三本; *how many* nánbon 何本)

spoonful *n* (hitó)-saji (一)匙・(ひと)さじ; *how many spoonfuls* nán-saji 何匙, nan-hai 何杯

sport(s) *n* supó´tsu スポーツ, undō 運動; *Sports Day* (*2nd Monday of October*) Taiiku no hi 体育の日

spot *n*. ten 点; (*spotted*) madara (no) まだら[班](の), (*blot*) shimi 染み, (*with*) *spots* bótsubotsu ぽつぽつ・ボツボツ **2.** (*place*) basho 場所

sprain *v* (*an ankle*) (ashí o) kujikimásu (kujíku, kujíite) (足を)挫き[くじき]ます(挫く, 挫いて); *gets a sprained ankle* ashí ga kujikemásu (kujikéru, kujíkete) 足が挫け[くじけ]ます(挫ける, 挫けて)

spread *v* **1.** (*spreads it*) hirogemásu (hirogeru, hirogete) 広げます(広げる, 広げて), (*diffuses it*) hiromemásu (hiroméru, hirómete) 広めます(広める, 広めて); (*spreads it out*) nobashimásu (nobásu, nobáshite) 伸ばします(伸ばす, 伸ばして), nobemásu (nobéru, nobete) 伸べます(伸べる, 伸

べて); (*spreads it on*) harimásu (haru, hatte) 張ります(張る, 張って) **2.** (*it spreads*) hirogarimásu (hirogaru, hirogatte) 広がります(広がる, 広がって); (*it gets diffused*) hiromarimásu (hiromáru, hiromátte) 広まります(広まる, 広まって), fukyū shimásu (suru, shite) 普及します(する, して); (*it spreads out*) nobimásu (nobíru, nóbite) 伸びます(伸びる, 伸びて); (*it spreads on*) (batā o) nurimásu (núru, nútte) (バターを)塗ります(塗る, 塗って)

spread *n* shiki-mono 敷物

spring **1.** *n* (*season*) háru 春; (*device*) bane(-jíkake) ばね・バネ(仕掛け), (*of clock*) zenmai ぜんまい; *hot ~* onsen 温泉 **1.** *v springs forth* (*gushes*) wakimásu (waku, waite) わき[湧き]ます(わく, わいて) **3.** *v springs from* ... kara okorimásu (okóru, okótte) ...から起こります(起こる, 起こって)

spring → jump

springtime *n* háru 春

sprinkle; *sprinkles it* *v* furi-kakemásu (furi-kakéru, furi-kákete) 振りかけます(振りかける, 振りかけて)

sprout(s) → pepper sprout

spy *n* supai スパイ, [BOOKISH] kanbō 間諜

square *n* shikaku 四角; *adj* shikakú (no) 四角(の), shikakúi 四角い; kakú 角; (*plaza*) hiró-bá 広場

squared paper *n* genkō-yō´shi 原稿用紙

squash *v* tsuburemásu (tsubureru, tsuburete) つぶれ[潰れ]ます(つぶれる, つぶれて)

squat **1.** *n* sukuwatto スクワット **2.** *v* shagamimásu (shagamu, shagande) しゃがみます(しゃがむ, しゃがんで)

squeeze *adj* tsubushimásu (tsubusu, tsubushite) 潰し[つぶし]ます(潰す, 潰して); (*squeezes out*) shiborimásu (shibóru, shibótte) 絞ります(絞る, 絞って)

squid *n* ika イカ・烏賊

squilla *n* (*mantis shrimp*) sháko シャコ・蝦蛄

squirrel *n* rísu リス・栗鼠

Sri Lanka *n* Suriránka スリランカ

stab v (tsuki-)sashimásu (sásu, sáshite) (突き)刺します(刺す, 刺して)

stable 1. adj anteishita 安定した **2.** n uma-goya 馬小屋, kyūsha 厩舎

stadium n kyōgi-jō 競技場; **baseball ~** yakyū-jō 野球場, kyūjō 球場

stage n bútai 舞台; sutēji ステージ, (of a process) dankai 段階; **gets ~ fright** agarimásu (agaru, agatte) 上がります (上がる, 上がって)

stagger v yoro-mekimásu (yoro-méku, yoro-méite) よろめきます(よろめく, よろめいて)

staggered work hours n jisashúkkin 時差出勤

staggering adj yóroyoro (no) よろよろ(の), chidori-ashi (no) 千鳥足(の)

staging n (play, movie) enshutsu 演出

stain 1. n shimi 染み **2.** v (paints it) nurimásu (nuru, nutte) 塗ります(塗る, 塗って); (soils it) yogoshimásu (yogosu, yogoshíte) 汚します(汚す, 汚して), (gets soiled) yogoremásu (yogoreru, yogorete) 汚れます(汚れる, 汚れて)

stairs, stairway n kaidan 階段, (wooden) hashigo-dan はしご段

stake n (post) kúi 杭

stale adj (not fresh) furúi 古い

stalk n kuki 茎・クキ

stamp 1. n (postal) kitte 切手 (**how many** nánmai 何枚); **stamp album** kitte-chō 切手帳 **2.** n (seal) ín 印, (cancellation mark) keshi-in 消印 **3.** sutanpu スタンプ

stand 1. n (sales booth) uri-ba 売り場, baiten 売店, sutando スタンド; (food stall) yatai 屋台 **2.** v (stands up) tachimásu (tátsu, tátte) 立ちます(立つ, 立って); **stands it up** tatemásu (tatéru, tátete) 立てます(立てる, 立てて) **3.** **stands it** v (tolerates) gáman shimásu (suru, shite) 我慢します(する, して), koraemásu (koráéru, koráete) こらえます(こらえる, こらえて), taemásu (taéru, táete) 耐えます(耐える, 耐えて), shínbō shimásu (suru, shite) 辛抱します(する, して)

stand against (opposes) … ni taikō shimásu (suru, shite) …に対抗します (する, して)

stand firm ganbarimásu (ganbáru, ganbátte) がんばり[頑張り]ます(がんばる, がんばって)

stand out (prominently) medachimásu (medámáu, medátte) 目立ちます(目立つ, 目立って)

stand still tachi-domarimásu (tachi-domaru, tachi-domatte) 立ち止まります(立ち止まる, 立ち止まって)

standard 1. adj hyōjun (no) 標準(の); **~ Japanese** hyōjun-go 標準語 **2.** n meyasu 目安; kikaku 規格; kijun 基準

standardization n kikaku-ka 規格化; tōitsu 統一

standardize v tōitsu shimásu (suru, shite) 統一します(する, して); kikaku-ka shimásu (suru, shite) 規格化します(する, して)

standee n tachimi no kyaku 立ち見の客; **sees it as a ~** tachimi shimásu (suru, shite) 立ち見します(する, して)

standing room tachimí-seki 立ち見席

standpoint n tachi-ba 立場, kanten 観点

staple n (hochikisu no) hári (ホチキスの)針

stapler n hóchikisu ホチキス

star n hoshi 星; (symbol) hoshi-jírushi 星印; (actor) sutá´ スター, hanágata 花形

Hollywood star n hariuddo sutā ハリウッド・スター

star chart n seizu 星図

star sign n seiza 星座

starch n **1.** (laundry) norí のり・糊 **2.** (food) denpun でんぷん・澱粉; **potato ~** katakúriko 片栗粉 → **corncstarch**

No starch please. Norízukékinshı. 糊付け禁止。

stare v ~ (at) (… o) jíro-jiro mimásu (míru, míte) (…を)じろじろ見ます (見る, 見て); mi-tsumemásu (mi-tsumeru, mi-tsúmete) 見詰め[見つめ]ます(見詰める, 見詰めて), nagamemásu (nagaméru, nagámete) 眺めます(眺める, 眺めて)

start 1. n hajimari 始まり; shuppatsu 出発; **at (from) the ~** shoppana kara よっぱなから; **from the ~** hajime kara

始めから, hónrai 本来 **2.** v (it starts)
hajimarimásu (hajimaru, hajimatte)
始まります(始まる, 始まって); (sets
out) demásu (déru, déte) 出ます(出
る, 出て) **3.** v (starts it) hajimemásu
(hajimeru, hajimete) 始めます(始
める, 始めて); (starts doing it) shi-
hajimemásu (shi-hajiméru, shi-hají-
mete) し始めます(し始める, し始め
て); it starts to rain áme ga furi-haji-
memásu (furi-hajimaru, furi-hajimete)
雨が降り始めます(降り始める, 降り
始めて), áme ni narimásu (náru, nátte)
雨になります(なる, なって); **starts
the engine → engine 3. → startle**

starting n (a performance) kaien 開演

startle v bikkúri sasemásu (saseru,
sasete) びっくりさせます(させる, さ
せて); gets ~ bikkúri shimásu (suru,
shite) びっくりします(する, して)

start off/out v (departs) dekakemásu
(dekakeru, dekakete) 出かけます(出
かける, 出かけて)

starve v uemásu (uéru, úete) 飢えます
(飢える, 飢えて)

state **1.** n (of the U.S.) shū´ 州, ... -shū
...州; (status) bún 分; ~ of affairs
jōkyō 状況, jítai 事態 → condition →
nation **2.** v expressly states utaimásu
(utau, utatte) うたい[謳い]ます(うた
う, うたって) → say

static (noise) n zatsuon 雑音

station n **1.** (rail) éki 駅; (box lunches
sold at railroad stations) eki-ben 駅弁
2. → gas station

stationary n (not moving) ugokanai
動かない, henkanai 変化しない

stationery n (letter paper) binsen 便
箋; (writing supplies) bunbō´-gu 文房
具; (shop) bunbōgu-ya 文房具屋

stationmaster n ekichō 駅長; stationmaster's office ekichō-shitsu 駅長室

statistics n tōkei 統計

statue n zō 像, chōzō 彫像, (bronze)
dōzō 銅像

stature n (height) séi/sé 背・せ(い)

status n bún 分, (social, personal)
míbun 身分, (position) chíi 地位; the ~
quo genjō 現状

stay **1.** n (away from home) taizai 滞在

2. v taizai shimásu (suru, shite) 滞在
します(する, して) **3.** v imásu (iru, ite)
います(いる, いて), [DEFERENTIAL/
HUMBLE] orimásu (óru, ótte/orimáshite)
おります(おる, おって/おりまして),
[HONORIFIC] irasshaimásu (irassháru,
irasshátte/iráshite/irasshaimáshite) い
らっしゃいます(いらっしゃる, い
らっしゃって/いらして/いらっしゃ
いまして) = oide ni narimásu (náru,
nátte/narimáshite) おいでになります
(なる, なって/なりまして) **4.** v
todomarimásu (todomáru, todomátte)
とどまり[止まり・留まり]ます(と
どまる, とどまって); (overnight)
tomarimásu (tomaru, tomatte) 泊まり
ます(泊まる, 泊まって)

stay away v (from school, etc.)
yasumimásu (yasúmu, yasúnde) 休み
ます(休む, 休んで); (skips work)
saborimásu (sabóru, sabótte) サボりま
す(サボる, サボって)

stay up all night v tetsuya shimásu
(suru, shite) 徹夜します(する, して);
stay up late yofúkashi (o) shimásu
(suru, shite) 夜更し(を)します(する,
して)

steadily adv jitto じっと; zutto ずっと

steady adj katagi (na) 堅気(な), tega-
tai 手堅い; chakujitsu (na) 着実(な)

steak n sutēki ステーキ, (beef-steak)
biifutēki ビーフ・ステーキ

steal v nusumimásu (nusúmu, nusúnde)
盗みます(盗む, 盗んで), kapparaimásu
(kapparau, kapparatte) かっぱらいま
す(かっぱらう, かっぱらって)

stealth n (espionage) the art of ~ nínjutsu 忍術; a master of ~ nínja 忍者

steam **1.** n jō´ki 蒸気, yúge 湯気
2. v (steams food) fukashimásu
(fukásu, fukáshite) ふかします(ふか
す, ふかして), mushimásu (músu,
múshite) 蒸します(蒸す, 蒸して)

steam bath n mushiburo 蒸し風呂,
suchiimu basu スチーム・バス, sauna
サウナ

steamed bun n manjū´まんじゅう・
饅頭; (stuffed with bean jam) anman
あんまん, (ground pork) niku-man
肉まん

steamed custard n (*from broth and eggs*) chawan-mushi 茶碗蒸し
steamed fish cake n kamaboko かまぼこ・カマボコ
steamed foods n mushí-mono 蒸し物
steamship n kisen 汽船
steel n hagane 鋼・はがね, kōtetsu 鋼鉄, tetsu 鉄
steep adj (*precipitous*) kyū (na) 急(な), kewashíi 険しい
steering wheel n handoru ハンドル
stem n (*of plant*) kuki 茎
step 1. n (*stairs*) kaidan 階段, dan 段 2. n suteppu ステップ 3. v (*walk*) arukimásu (arúku, arúite) 歩きます(歩く, 歩いて) → **measure** → **stage** 4. v *steps into/on* fumi-komimásu (fumi-komu, fumi-kónde) 踏み込みます(踏み込む, 踏み込んで); *steps on the gas* ákuseru o fumimásu アクセルを踏みます
stepchild n mama-ko まま[継]子
stepfather n mama-chíchi まま[継]父
stepmother n mama-haha まま[継]母
steps → **stairs**
stereo adj (*phonic/scopic*) rittai-onkyō (no) 立体音響(の); suterео (onkyō) (no) ステレオ(音響)(の)
stereo n (*sound/player*) suterео ステレオ
sterilization n sakkin 殺菌
stew n shichū シチュー
steward n bōi ボーイ, kyū'ji 給仕, suchuwādo スチュワード
stewardess n suchuwā´desu スチュワーデス
stick 1. n (*club*) bō(-kkire) 棒(っ切れ); (*staff*) tsúe 杖 or (*cane*) sutékki ステッキ 2. n (*of gum, candy, etc.*) ichí-mai ...一枚, (*of yakitori, etc.*) íp-pon 一本 3. n (*lipstick*) kuchibeni 口紅 4. v (*it sticks to*) ... ni kuttsuki-másu (kuttsúku, kuttsúite) ...にくっつきます(くっつく, くっついて) 5. v (*sticks it on*) tsukemásu (tsukéru, tsukéte) 付けます(付ける, 付けて) (*pastes it on*) harimásu (haru, hatte) 貼ります(貼る, 貼って)
stickiness n nebarí 粘り
stick out (*sticks it out*) tsuki-dashimásu

(tsuki-dásu, tsuki-dáshite) 突き出します(突き出す, 突き出して) → **protrude**
sticky; *is* ~ nébaneba shimásu (suru, shite) ねばねばします(する, して)
stiff adj 1. → **hard** 2. (*shoulder*) *gets* ~ (katá ga) korimásu (kóru, kótte) 肩が凝ります(凝る, 凝って); ~ *shoulder*, *stiffness of shoulder* kata no kori 肩の凝り
still adv (*yet*) máda まだ; (*but*) (sore) démo (それ)でも; ~ *better* issō/náo íi 一層[いっそう]/尚[なお]いい; ~ *more* mótto もっと; náo 尚・なお; issō いっそう・一層
still image n seishi ga (-zō) 静止画(像)
still-life painting n seibutsu ga 静物画
still object n seibutsu 静物
still → **quiet**; *interj* **Stand still!** (Tatta mama) ugo-kánaide kudasai. (立ったまま)動かないで下さい., Jitto tatteite kudasai. じっと立っていて下さい.
stillness n seishi 静止
stimulate v unagashimásu (unagásu, unagáshite) 促します(促す, 促して)
stimulation n shigeki 刺激
sting 1. v sashimásu (sásu, sáshite) 刺します(刺す, 刺して) 2. n (*bee's sting*) hari 針
stingy adj kéchi (na) けち(な); ~ *person* kéchinbo けちんぼ, kéchinbō けちんぼう
stinking n kusái 臭い
stipulate v kitei shimásu (suru, shite) 規定します(する, して)
stipulation n kitei 規定 → **provision** → **condition**
stir v 1. *stirs it* kaki-mawashimásu (kaki-mawasu, kaki-mawashíte) かき回します(かき回す, かき回して) 2. *stirs up* (*fans, incites*) aorimásu (aóru, aótte) あおり[煽り]ます(あおる, あおって)
stock n 1. (*financial*) kabu 株; (*soup*) dashí だし・ダシ; (*on hand*) zaiko(-hin) 在庫(品), sutokku ストック; mochiawase (no) 持ち合わせ(の) 2. *has in* ~ (*on hand*) zaiko ga arimásu (aru, atte) 在庫があります(ある, あ

って）; mochi-awasemás̱u (mochi-awaseru, mochi-awasete) 持ち合わせます（持ち合わせる, 持ち合わせて）; motte imás̱u (iru, ite) 持っています（いる, いて）; oite imás̱u (iru, ite) 置いています（いる, いて）

stockings n kutsu-shita 靴下; (*1 pair* is-sokú 一足, **2:** ní-soku 二足, **3:** sán-zoku/-soku 三足; *how many pairs* nán-zoku/-soku 何足）

stomach n i-búkuro 胃袋, i 胃; (*strictly, belly*) o-naka おなか, hará 腹; *~ band* hará-maki 腹巻き; *~ and intestines* ichō 胃腸; *develops ~ trouble* o-naka o kowashimás̱u (kowáu, kowá-shi̱te) おなかを壊します（壊す, 壊して）

stomach cancer n (*medical*) i-gan 胃がん・胃癌

stone n ishí 石

stone lantern n tōrō 灯篭; ishi-dōrō 石灯籠

stop 1. v (*it comes to rest*) tomarimás̱u (tomaru, tomatte) 止まります（止まる, 止まって）, todomarimás̱u (todomáru, todomátte) とどまり［止まり・留まり］ます（とどまる, とどまって）→ **stand still**; (*it ceases*) yamimás̱u (yamu, yande) 止みます（止む, 止んで）**2.** v (*stops it*) tomemás̱u (tomeru, tomete) 止めます（止める, 止めて）, todomemás̱u (todoméru, todómete) とどめ［止め］ます（とどめる, とどめて）, yoshimás̱u (yósu, yóshi̱te) よします（よす, よして）; (*stops doing*) … o yamemás̱u (yameru, yamete) …を止めます（止める, 止めて）**3.** n (*halting place*) teiryū-jo 停留所; (*end*) owari 終わり

stop up fusagimás̱u (fusagu, fusaide) ふさぎます（ふさぐ, ふさいで）; *gets stopped up* fusa-garimás̱u (fusagáru, fusagátte) ふさがります（ふさがる, ふさがって）

stoppage of electricity (*power failure*) teiden 停電

stopper n (*cork*) kuchi 口; (*plug, cork*) sén 栓

store n (*shop*) misé 店; sutoa ストア

storeroom n (*storehouse*) kurá 倉・蔵

storm 1. n árashi 嵐, [BOOKISH] bōfū´

暴風 **2.** v (*rages*) abaremás̱u (abareru, abarete) 暴れます（暴れる, 暴れて）

story n **1.** hanashí 話, sutōrii ストーリー **2.** → **floor**

storyteller n hanashi-ka 噺家, sutōrii terā ストーリー・テラー

stove n sutō´bu ストーブ, (*kitchen*) kamado かまど・竈, kama かま・釜, rénji レンジ; (*portable cooking*) kónro コンロ

straddle v … ni matagarimás̱u (mata-gáru, matagátte) …に跨がり［またがり］ます（跨がる, 跨がって）

straight adj massúgu (na) まっすぐ・真っ直ぐ（な）

straight line n chokusen 直線

straighten v (*tidies it*) *~ it up* kata-zukemás̱u (katazukéru, katazúkete) 片付けます（片付ける, 片付けて）

strain 1. n (*tension*) kinchō 緊張 **2.** v (*forces*) múri ni shimás̱u (suru, shi̱te) 無理にします（する, して）; (*filters*) koshimás̱u (kosu, koshi̱te) こし［漉し］ます（こす, こして）, (*through cloth*) shiborimás̱u (shibóru, shibótte) 絞ります（絞る, 絞って）

strait(s) n kaikyō 海峡

strange adj hén (na) 変（な）, fushigi (na) 不思議（な）, kímyō (na) 奇妙（な）, okashíi おかしい; (*wondrous*) myō´ (na) 妙（な）; (*alien*) yosó (no) よそ（の）; (*unknown*) shiranai 知らない

stranger n (*unknown person*) shiranai hi̱tó 知らない人; (*outsider*) yosó no hi̱tó よその人, tanin 他人

strap n himo ひも・紐; (*to hang on to*) tsuri-kawa 吊り革; (*watch-band, etc.*) bando バンド

straw n wára わら・藁, mugiwara 麦わら［藁］; (*to drink with*) sutōrō ストロー

straw bag n tawará 俵・たわら

strawberry n ichigo イチゴ・苺

straw mat n (*thin floor mat*) gozá ござ・ゴザ

straw mushrooms n enokí-take/-dake エノキ茸・榎茸

straw raincoat n míno みの・蓑

straw sandals n zōri 草履・ゾウリ

stray 1. n (*child*) maigo ; (*animals*)

mayoi-inu (-neko) 迷い犬(猫) **2.** *adj*
michi ni mayotta 道に迷った, hagureta
はぐれた **3.** *v* (*digresses*) soremásu
(soréru, sórete) 逸れ[それ]ます(逸れ
る, 逸れて)

stream *n* nagaré 流れ; *in streams*
zorozoro ぞろぞろ

streamline *v* (*procedures, …*) gōri-ka
shimásu (suru, shite) 合理化します
(する, して)

street *n* michi 道, tōri 通り, shadō
車道, tsuji 辻; (*on*) *the street* gaitō (de)
街頭(で)

streetcar *n* romen densha 路面電車

street stall *n* yatai 屋台

strength *n* tsuyosa 強さ, (*power*)
chikará 力(o-chikara お力); (*real
strength*) jitsuryoku 実力; (*of
saturation*) kósa 濃さ

strengthen *v* **strengthens (it)** tsúyoku
shimásu (suru, shite) 強くします(す
る, して), katamemásu (katameru,
katamete) 固めます(固める, 固めて)

stretch 1. *v* (*stretches it*) nobashimásu
(nobásu, nobáshite) 伸ばします(伸ば
す, 伸ばして), (*it stretches*) nobimásu
(nobíru, nóbite) 伸びます(伸びる, 伸
びて), (*taut*) harimásu (haru, hatte)
張ります(張る, 張って) **2.** *n* nobi 伸
び, senobi 背伸び

stretch over (*extends over*) … ni
matagarimásu (matagáru, matagátte)
…に跨がり[またがり]ます(跨がる,
跨がって)

stretcher *n* tánka 担架

strew *v* chirashimásu (chirasu, chirashite) 散らします(散らす, 散らして)

stricken area *n* higái-chi 被害地

strict *adj* (*severe*) kibishíi 厳しい,
katai 固い・堅い, yakamashíi やかま
しい; (*precise*) genmitsu (na) 厳密
(な); genjū (na) 厳重(な)

stride *v* ~ *over* matagimásu (matágu,
matáide) 跨ぎ[またぎ]ます(跨ぐ, 跨
いで)

strife *n* arasoi 争い, [BOOKISH] sō´dō
騒動

strike 1. *n* (*job action*) sutó スト,
sutoraiki ストライキ; (*baseball*)
sutoráiku ストライク **2.** → hit

striking *adj* (*outstanding*) ichijirushíi
著しい

strikingly *adv* ichijirúshiku 著しく

string 1. *n* (*thread*) íto 糸; (*cord*) himo
ひも・紐; (*of violin or bow*) tsurú つ
る・弦 **2.** (*linked*) *in a ~* tsunagatte つ
ながって **3. strings up** *v* (*suspends*)
tsurimásu (tsuru, tsutte) 吊ります(吊
る, 吊って)

stripe *n* shimá しま・縞, sutoraipu
ストライプ

stripe pattern *n* shima-moyō 縞模様

striptease, strip show *n* sutoríppu ス
トリップ

strive *v* tsutomemásu (tsutoméru,
tsutómete) 努めます(努める, 努めて),
dóryoku shimásu (suru, shite) 努力し
ます(する, して), tsukushimásu (tsukúsu, tsukúshite) 尽くします(尽くす,
尽くして)

stroke 1. *n* (*sounds of bell*) (kane no)
hibiki (鐘の)響き **2.** *n* (*sports*) ichida
一打 **3.** *v* nademásu (nadéru, nádete)
なで[撫で]ます(なでる, なでて) **4.** *v*
(*strike*) uchimásu (utsu, utte) 打ちます
(打つ, 打って) **5.** *v* (*draw*) kakimásu
(kaku, kaite) 描きます(描く, 描いて)

stroke order *n* kakijun 書き順

stroll *v* sanpo (shimásu; suru, shite)
散歩します(する, して)

strong *adj* tsuyói 強い; (*coffee, etc.*)
kói 濃い; (*influential*) yūryoku (na)
有力(な)

strong point *n* (*merit*) chō´sho 長所

strong wind *n* ō-kaze 大風

structure *n* kōzō 構造, (*setup*) kumi-
tate 組み立て; (*system*) soshiki 組織

struggle 1. *n* (*contention*) arasoi 争い
2. *v* **struggles for** (*contends*) … o
arasoimásu (arasóu, arasótte) …を争
います(争う, 争って)

stucco *n* shíkkui しっくい・漆喰

stuck; gets ~ (*clogged*) tsumarimásu
(tsumáru, tsumátte) 詰まります(詰ま
る, 詰まって)

stuck-up *adj* (*affected*) kidotte imásu
気取っています, kidotta …気取った…

student *n* gakusei 学生, …-sei …生,
(*pupil*) séito 生徒; **~ between schools**
rōnin 浪人; **a ~ of the teacher's**

senséi no oshiego 先生の教え子; *the ~ of English* (*in general*) Eigo (no) gakushū´-sha 英語(の)の学習者

studio *n* (*private*) atorie アトリエ; (*public*) sutajio スタジオ
studio apartment *n* wan-rū´mu ワンルーム

studious person *n* benkyō-ka 勉強家
study **1.** *n* benkyō 勉強; gakushū 学習; *~ by observation, field ~* kengaku 見学 **2.** *n* (*room*) shosai 書斎 **3.** *v* (*studies it*) benkyō shimásu (suru, shite) 勉強します(する, して), manabimásu (manabu, manande) 学びます(学ぶ, 学んで), (*is tutored/taught*) osowarimásu (osowaru, osowatte) 教わります(教わる, 教わって); (*a basic subject*) gakushū shimásu (suru, shite) 学習します(する, して) **4.** *v* → **research** → **science**

stuff **1.** *n* (*thing*) monó 物 **2.** *v* (*crams*) tsumemásu (tsuméru, tsúmete) 詰めます(詰める, 詰めて)
stumble *v* tsuma-zukimásu (tsumazuku, tsumazuite) つまずき[躓き]ます(つまずく, つまずいて)
stump *n* (*tree*) kiri-kabu 切り株
stumped; *is* ~ mairimásu (máiru, máitte) 参ります(参る, 参って) → **perplexed**
stunt *n* kyokugéi 曲芸; *horseback stunts* kyokuba 曲馬
stupid *adj* báka (na) ばか・馬鹿(な)
sturdy *adj* jōbu (na) 丈夫(な)
style **1.** *n* fū´...-fū ...風; ...shiki/ ...-shiki ...式; *Japanese ~* Nihon-fū (no) 日本風(の) **2.** (*form*) tái 態
stylish *adj* sumá´to (na) スマート(な), iki (na) いき[粋](な), otsu (na) 乙(な)
styptic pencil *n* chi-dome 血止め; shiketsu-zai 止血剤
subject *n* (*topic*) mondai 問題, (*of conversation*) wadai 話題; táne 種; (*school*) kamoku 科目; (*grammar*) shúgo 主語
subjective *adj* shukan-teki (na) 主観的な; *subjectivity* *n* shukan 主観
submarine *n* sensui-kan 潜水艦
submissive *adj* súnao (na) すなお[素直](な)

subordinate *n* búka 部下, (*follower*) kó-bun 子分
subscribe *v* yoyaku shimásu (suru, shite) 予約します(する, して), mōshi-komimásu (mōshi-komu, mōshi-konde) 申し込みます(申し込む, 申し込んで)
subscription *n* yoyaku 予約
subsequently *adv* tsuide 次いで → **later** → **next**
substance *n* (*material*) busshitsu 物資
substantial *adj* **1.** (*concrete*) gutaiteki (na) 具体的(な) **2.** → **considerable**
substitute *n* kawari 代わり; daiyōhin 代用品
subtle *adj* wazuka (na) わずか(な), kasuka (na) 微か(な), (*delicate*) bimyō (na) 微妙(な)
subtract *v* hikimásu (hiku, hiite) 引きます(引く, 引いて)
suburb *n* kō´gai 郊外, shígai 市外, (*outskirts*) basue 場末; (*bedroom community*) beddotáun ベッドタウン
subway *n* chiká-tetsu 地下鉄
succeed *v* (*is successful*) seikō shimásu (suru, shite) 成功します(する, して); *~ to* (*takes over for*) uketsugimásu (uketsugu, uketsuide) 受け継ぎます(受け継ぐ, 受け継いで), tsugimásu (tsugu, tsuide) 継ぎます(継ぐ, 継いで); (*in a projection*) hiki-tsugimásu (hiki-tsúgu, hiki-tsúide) 引き継ぎます(引き継ぐ, 引き継いで); (*in a test*) ukárimásu (ukáru, ukátte) 受かります(受かる, 受かって)
success *n* seikō 成功, gōkaku 合格; *making a ~ out of life* shusse 出世
success story *n* seikō-dan 成功談; sakusesu sutōrii サクセス・ストーリー
successful *adj* umái うまい; umakuiku うまくいく; *is ~* → **succeed**
successfully *adv* umaku うまく
succession; *in ~* tsuide 次いで, tsuzuite 続いて; tsunagatte つながって; tsuzukete 続けて; *in rapid ~* zokuzoku ぞくぞく・続々
such *adj* sonna そんな, sono yō´na そのよう[様]な, sō yū そうゆう; (*like this*) konna こんな, kono yō´na このよう[様]な, kō yū こうゆう

such-and-such a place dókodoko どこどこ, dókosoko どこそこ

suck v suimásu (sū, sutte) 吸います (吸う, 吸って), shaburimásu (shaburu, shabutte) しゃぶります (しゃぶる, しゃぶって)

It sucks! saitē da 最低だ, hidoi ひどい

sucker n (dupe) kámo カモ・鴨

sudden adj (unexpected) totsuzen (no) 突然(の), níwaka にわか; (urgent) kyū (na) 急(な); ~ **shower** yūdachi 夕立, niwaka ame にわか雨

sudden illness n kyūbyō 急病

suddenly adv fui ni 不意に, totsuzen 突然, (unexpectedly) níwaka ni にわかに, (immediately) tachimachi (ni) たちまち(に); (urgently) kyū ni 急に; (with a rush) dotto どっと; (with a jerk/gulp) gutto ぐっと; (with a sudden start of surprise) hatto (shíte) はっと(して)

sue v uttaemásu (uttaeru, uttaete) 訴えます (訴える, 訴えて)

suffer v kurushimimásu (kurushímu, kurushínde) 苦しみます (苦しむ, 苦しんで), nayamimásu (nayámu, nayánde) 悩みます (悩む, 悩んで), wazuraimásu (wazurau, wazuratte) 煩います (煩う, 煩って); (incurs) kōmurimásu (kōmúru, kōmútte) 被ります (こうむり)ます (被る, 被って), ukemásu (ukéru, úkete) 受けます (受ける, 受けて)

suffer from … o wazuraimásu (wazurau, wazuratte) …を煩います(わずらい)ます(煩う, 煩って) → incur

suffering n kurushimi 苦しみ, (anguish) nayamí 悩み

suffice, sufficient v, adj tarimásu (tariru, tarite) 足ります (足りる, 足りて)

suffix n setsubi-go/-ji 接尾語/辞

sugar n satō´ 砂糖 (o-sató お砂糖)

suggest(ion) → **propose** (proposal) → **hint**

suicide n jisatsu 自殺

double suicide n shinjū 心中

suicidal wishes n jisatsu ganbō 自殺願望, [BOOKISH] kishi nenryo 希死念慮

suit 1. n yō-fuku 洋服 (o-yō fuku お洋服), fukú 服, (business) sebiro 背広, sū´tsu スーツ, (esp. woman's two-piece) tsūpíisu ツーピース;

(diving suit) sensui fuku 潜水服, daibingu sūtsu ダイビング・スーツ **2.** n (of playing cards) kumí 組 **3.** v (matches with) …ni aimásu (áu, átte) …に合います (合う, 合って); **suits one's taste** kuchi ni aimásu 口に合います **4.** v (is becoming to) …ni ni-aimásu (ni-áu, ni-átte) …に似合います (似合う, 似合って)

suitable adj fusawashíi ふさわしい, tekitō (na) 適当(な), tekigi (na) 適宜(な); (moderate) kakkō (na) 格好(な); **is ~** teki-shimásu (teki-súru, tekí-shite) 適します (適する, 適して); **the most ~** uttetsuke (no) うってつけ(の)

suitably adv fusawáshiku ふさわしく, tekitō ni 適当に

suitcase n kaban かばん・鞄, sūtsukē´su スーツケース; (luggage) (te-)nímotsu (手)荷物

sulk v fukuremásu (fukureru, fukurete) 膨れます (膨れる, 膨れて)

sullen face n butchō-zura 仏頂面

sultry adj (weather) mushi-atsúi 蒸し暑い; (behavior) jōnetsuteki (na) 情熱的(な); **gets ~** mushimásu (músu, múshite) 蒸します (蒸す, 蒸して)

sum 1. n gáku 額 **2. to ~ it up** yōsúru ni 要するに

sumac n (plant) háze はぜ・ハゼ

summarize v yōyaku shimásu (suru, shite) 要約します (する, して), tsumamimásu (tsumamu, tsumande) つまみます (つまむ, つまんで), tsuzumemásu (tsuzuméru, tsuzúmete) つづめ[約め]ます (つづめる, つづめて)

summary n taiyō 大要, yōyaku 要約, (gist) yō´shi 要旨; gaiyō 概要; **in ~** yōsúru ni 要するに

summer n natsú 夏; **~ gift** (o-)chūgen (お)中元; **~ period/term** káki 夏期; **~ school** kaki-kōshū 夏期講習; **~ solstice** geshi 夏至; **~ vacation/holidays** natsuyásumi 夏休み

summit n itadaki 頂, chōjō´ 頂上, mine 峰

summon v yobimásu (yobu, yonde) 呼びます (呼ぶ, 呼んで)

sumo → **wrestling, wrestler**

sun n táiyō 太陽, hi 日, o-ténto-sama

おてんとさま・お天道様, [BABY TAKI]
o-hi-sama お日様

sunbathing n (*enjoying the warmth of the sun*) hinata-bókko ひなた[日向]ぼっこ, (*sunbathing, tanning*) nikkōyoku 日光浴

sunburn n hiyake 日焼け

Sunday n Nichiyō´bi 日曜日

sundry adj zatta (na) 雑多(な); *sundries* zakka 雑貨

sunglass n sangurasu サングラス

sunny adj (*room, etc.*) hiatari ga íi 日当りがいい

sunrise n hinode 日の出

sunset n hinoiri 日の入り, nichibotsu 日没, (*time*) higure 日暮れ

sunshade n hiyoke 日よけ, hi-gasa 日傘

sunshine n hinata ひなた・日向, níkkō 日光, sanshain サンシャイン

super adj chō 超, sūpā スーパー

superman n sū´pāman スーパーマン, chōjin 超人

supernatural n chō shizen (no) 超自然(の)

supernatural power n chō nōryoku 超能力

superfluous adj yokei (na) 余計(な), (*surplus*) kajō (no) 過剰(の)

superintendent n kantoku 監督

superior 1. adj yūshū (na) 優秀(な); jōtō (no) 上等(の); ue (no) 上(の), meue (no) 目上(の) 2. adj erái 偉い; masatte iru 勝っている 3. n *a superior* menue no híto 目上の人

supermarket n sū´pā スーパー, sū´pā-mā´ketto スーパーマーケット

supervise v kantoku shimásu (suru, shite) 監督します(する, して)

supervisor n kantoku 監督, sū´pā-baizā スーパーバイザー, esu bui, esu vii SV

supper n ban-góhan 晩ご飯, yūshoku 夕食, yū-han 夕飯

supplement n hosoku 補足, zōho 増補; (*pills*) sapuriment サプリメント, sapuri サプリ; *food supplements* eiyōhojo-shokuhin 栄養補助食品

supplies n ...-yō´hin ...用品, (*necessities*) hitsuju-hin 必需品,

(*expendables*) shōmō-hin 消耗品

supply 1. v *supplies it* kyōkyū shimásu (suru, shite) 供給します(する, して); hokyū shimásu (suru, shite) 補給します(する, して) → **provide** → **give** → **sell** 2. *supply(ing)* n kyōkyū 供給; hokyū 補給

supply and demand n juyō to kyōkyū 需要と供給

support 1. n (*approval*) sansei 賛成, sandō 賛同; (*backing, help*) kōen 後援, bákku-appu バックアップ, ōen 応援; (*aid*) énjo 援助, sapōto サポート 2. v (*supports it*) ōen shimásu (suru, shite) 応援します(する, して); bákku-appu shimásu (suru, shite) バックアップします(する, して); (*props it*) sasaemásu (sasaeru, sasaete) 支えます(支える, 支えて); (*endorses*) shíji shimásu (suru, shite) 支持します(する, して)

supporter n (*football*) fan ファン; *athletic ~* (*jockstrap*) sapō´tā サポーター

suppose v ... to shimásu (suru, shite) ...とします(する, して); sō omoimásu (omou, omotte) そう思います(思う, 思って) → **think** → **imagine**

supposed adj katei (no) 仮定(の)

supposition n katei 仮定; (*conjecture*) suisoku 推測

suppress v appaku shimásu (suru, shite) 圧迫します(する, して)

suppression n appaku 圧迫

surcharge n tsuika-ryōkin 追加料金

sure adj táshika (na) 確か(な)
for sure adv kanarazu 必ず, táshika ni 確かに, zé-hi ぜひ・是非
makes sure v tashikamemásu (tashikaméru, tashikámete) 確かめます(確かめる, 確かめて); *to ~* nen no tamé (ni) 念のため(に)
to be sure adv móttómo もっとも → of course

surely adv kitto きっと

surf 1. n yoseru-nami 寄せる波 2. v sā´fin o shimásu (suru, shite) サーフィンをします(する, して); (*to surf the Internet*) netto sā´fin o shimásu (suru, shite) ネットサーフィンをします(する, して)

surface 1. n mén 面, hyōmén 表面; (*top*) uwabe うわべ・上辺; *entire ~* zenmen 全面 **2.** v (*becomes known*) barémasu (baréru, baréte) ばれます (ばれる、ばれて)

surfboard n sāfubōdo サーフボード, sāfínbōdo サーフィンボード

surf clam n (*geoduck*) mirú-gai みる貝・ミル貝

surfer, surfrider n sāfā サーファー

surfing, surfriding n nami-nori 波乗り, sā´fin サーフィン

surgeon n geká-i 外科医

surgery n (*surgical operation*) shújutsu 手術; (*as a medical specialty*) geka 外科

surmise 1. n suisoku 推測 **1.** v suisoku shimásu (suru, shite) 推測します(する、して)

surpass v sugure mas u (suguréru, sugúrete) 優れ[すぐれ]ます(優れる、優れて), nukimás u (nuku, nuite) 抜きます(抜く、抜いて), masarimás u (masaru, masatte) 勝ります(勝る、勝って)

surplus n yoyū 余裕; kajō (no) 過剰 (の)

surprised; gets ~ bikkúri shimás u (suru, shite) びっくりします(する、して), odorokimás u (odoróku, odoróite) 驚きます(驚く、驚いて)

surprising adj omoigakénai 思いがけない

surrender n, v kōfuku/kōsan (shimás u; suru, shite) 降伏/降参します(する、して)

surround v kakomimás u (kakomu, kakonde) 囲みます(囲む、囲んで); (*centers on*) megurimás u (meguru, megutte) 巡ります(巡る、巡って)

surrounding 1. adj the ~ … shūhen no … 周辺の…; **2.** adj (*centering on*) … o megutte …を巡って **3.** **surroundings** n shū´i 周囲

sushi n (o-)súshi (お)すし[寿司・鮨], sushí すし・寿司・鮨; *covered with fish tidbits* chirashi-zushi ちらし鮨; *in a bag of aburage (fried bean curd)* inarí-zushi いなりずし・稲荷鮨; *rolled in seaweed* norí-maki のり巻き; (*with cucumber*) kappa(-maki) かっぱ(巻き);

(*around tuna tidbit*) tekka(-maki) 鉄火(巻き); *hand-packed into small balls* nigirí-zushi にぎりずし[鮨]; *pressed with marinated fish in squarish molds* oshi-zushi 押しずし[鮨]

sushi bar n sushí-ya すし[寿司・鮨]屋 (o-sushiya [寿司・鮨]屋)

suspect 1. v utagaimás u (utagau, utagatte) 疑います(疑う、疑って) **2.** n yōgí-sha 容疑者

suspend v **1.** (*hangs it*) tsurimás u (tsuru, tsutte) 吊ります(吊る、吊って), burasagemás u (burasageru, burasagete) ぶら下げます(ぶら下げる、ぶら下げて) **2.** (*stops in the midst*) chūshi shimás u (suru, shite) 中止します(する、して)

suspenders n zubón-tsuri ズボンつり, sasupendā サスペンダー

suspense n sasupensu サスペンス suspense film n sasupensu eiga サスペンス映画

suspension n (*stoppage*) teishi 停止, (*abeyance*) chūshi 中止

suspicious adj fushigi (na) 不思議(な), ayashii 怪しい, ikagawashíi いかがわしい

sustain v (*incurs*) kōmurimás u (kōmúru, kōmútte) 被り[こうむり]ます(被る、被って)

sutra n (*Buddhist scripture*) o-kyō お経, kyōten 経典

swab n (*scrub*) tawashi たわし・タワシ, (*mop*) móppu モップ; (*cotton*) watá 綿, (*sponge*) suponji スポンジ; (*earpick*) mimikákí 耳かき

swagger v ibarimás u (ibáru, ibátte) 威張ります(威張る、威張って)

swallow 1. n (*the bird*) tsubame ツバメ・燕 **2.** v (*ingests*) nomi-komimás u (nomi-komu, nomi-konde) 飲み込みます(飲み込む、飲み込んで)

swamp n numá 沼

swan n hakuchō 白鳥・ハクチョウ

sway v **1.** (*it sways*) yuremás u (yureru, yurete) 揺れます(揺れる、揺れて) **2.** (*sways it*) yusuburimás u (yusuburu, yusubutte) 揺すぶります(揺すぶる、揺すぶって), yurimás u (yuru, yutte) 揺ります(揺る、揺って)

swear v **1.** (*vows*) chikaimásu (chikau, chikatte) 誓います(誓う, 誓って) **2.** (*reviles*) nonoshirimásu (nonoshíru, nonoshítte) ののしり[罵り]ます(ののしる, ののしって)

sweat n, v áse (ga demásu; déru, déte) 汗(が出ます; 出る, 出て)

sweater n sḗtā セーター (*how many*) nánmai 何枚

sweep v sṓji shimásu (suru, shite) 掃除します(する, して); hakimásu (háku, háite) 掃きます(掃く, 掃いて)

sweeper n sṓji-ki 掃除機

sweeping n sṓji shимásu (o-sṓji お掃除)

sweet adj amai 甘い
sweet and sour adj amazuppai 甘酸っぱい
sweet and sour pork n su-buta 酢豚・スブタ　sweet rice wine n mirin みりん・味醂
sweet roll with beanjam inside n anpan あんパン

sweetfish n (*river trout*) áyu アユ・鮎, ái あい

sweetheart n ii-hito いい人, koibito 恋人

sweet potato n satsuma-imo さつま[薩摩]芋・サツマイモ → **potato**

sweets n (*pastry, candy*) (o-)káshi (お)菓子

swell adj (*splendid*) suteki (na) すてき[素敵](な), (*terrific*) sugói すごい・凄い

swell v **~ (up)** haremásu (hareru, harete) 腫れ[はれ]ます(腫れる, 腫れて); fukuramimásu (fukuramu, fukurande) 膨らみ[ふくらみ]ます(膨らむ, 膨らんで); fukuremásu (fukureru, fukurete) 膨れ[ふくれ]ます(膨れる, 膨れて); [BOOKISH] bōchō shimásu (suru, shite) 膨脹します(する, して); ō´kiku narimásu (náru, nátte) 大きくなります(なる, なって) → **increase**

swelling n hare-mono 腫れ物; dekímóno できもの・出来物, o-déki おでき; (*bump*) kobú こぶ・瘤

swim 1. n (hitó-)oyogi (ひと)泳ぎ **2.** v oyogimásu (oyógu, oyóide) 泳ぎます(泳ぐ, 泳いで)
swim suit n mizu-gi 水着

swimming n oyogí 泳ぎ, suiei 水泳, suimingu スイミング; **~ pool** pū´ru プール

swimming meet n suiei taikai 水泳大会, suiei kyōgi kai 水泳競技会

swing 1. v (*it swings*) yuremásu (yureru, yurete) 揺れます(揺れる, 揺れて) **2.** v (*swings it*) yusuburimásu (yusuburu, yusubutte) 揺すぶります(揺すぶる, 揺すぶって), yurimásu (yuru, yutte) 揺ります(揺る, 揺って) **3.** n (*a swing*) búranko ぶらんこ **4. gets into the ~ of things** chōshi ni norimásu (noru, notte) 調子に乗ります(乗る, 乗って), chōshi ga demásu (déru, déte) 調子が出ます(出る, 出て)

swipe v kapparaimásu (kapparau, kapparatte) かっぱらいます(かっぱらう, かっぱらって); nusumimásu (nusúmu, nusúnde) 盗みます(盗む, 盗んで)

Swiss 1. adj Súisu no スイスの **2.** n (*person*) Suisú-jin スイス人

switch n suítchi スイッチ → **change** → **turn on/off**

Switzerland n Súisu スイス

sword n kataná 刀; (*double-edged*) kén/tsurugí 剣; yaiba やいば・刃

sword battle n chanbara ちゃんばら

swordfish n kájiki かじき・カジキ

sword-guard n tsúba つば・鍔

syllable n onsetsu 音節

symbol n shinboru シンボル, [BOOKISH] shōchō 象徴; (*mark*) kigō 記号
symbol of peace n heiwa no shōchō 平和の象徴, heiwa no shinboru 平和のシンボル

symmetry n tsuriai 釣り合い; taiō 対応

sympathize v **~ with** … ni dōjō shimásu (suru, shite) …に同情します(する, して); (*takes into consideration*) … o kumimásu (kumu, kunde) …を汲みます(汲む, 汲んで); sas-shimásu (sas-suru, sas-shite) 察します(察する, 察して)

sympathy n dōjō 同情, kyōkan 共感

symptom n (*sign*) shirushi しるし[徴]; shōjō 症状; (*unusual state*) ijō 異常

syndicate n shinjikēto シンジケート

syndrome *n* (*medical*) shōkōgun 症候群, shindorōmu シンドローム

synonym *n* dōi-go 同意語, dōgi-go 同義語

synthesis *n* sōgō 総合

synthesized *adj* (*composite*) sōgōteki (na) 総合的(な)

synthetic fiber *n* kagaku sen'i 化学繊維, kasen 化繊

syphilis *n* (*medical*) baidoku 梅毒

Syria *n* shiria シリア

syringe *n* (*for injections*) chūsháki 注射器; (*for water*) chūsúiki 注水器

syrup *n* shíróppu シロップ

system *n* soshiki 組織, séido 制度, taikei 体系, chitsujo 秩序, shisutemu システム

systematic *adj* kichōmen na きちょうめんな, kisoku-tadashii 規則正しい, tejundōri no 手順通りの (= **orderly**)

T

tab *n* tsumami つまみ; tábu タブ → **bill**

tabby *n* tora neko トラ猫

table *n* **1.** tēburu テーブル, táku 卓; (*dinner table*) shokutaku 食卓, (*low meal table*) (shoku)zen (食)膳(o-zen お膳, gó-zen ご膳) **2.** (*list*) hyō 表; (*inventory*) mokuroku 目録

multiplication table *n* kakezan hyō 掛け算表

tablecloth *n* tēburú-kake テーブル掛け; teburukurosu テーブルクロス

table d'hôte *n* (*meal of the house/day*) teishoku 定食

table knife *n* tēburu naifu テーブルナイフ, shokutaku-yō naifu 食卓用ナイフ

table lamp *n* denki sutando 電気スタンド

table of contents, TOC *n* mokuji 目次

table salt *n* shokúen 食塩, shokutakú-en 食卓塩

tablespoon *n* ō-saji 大さじ・大匙

table tennis *n* takkyū 卓球

tableware *n* shokki 食器

tablet *n* (*pill*) jōzai 錠剤, taburetto タブレット; (*note pad*) memo-chō メモ帳

taboo *n* tabū タブー; kinki 禁忌

taciturn *adj* mukuchi (na) 無口(な); [BOOKISH] kamoku (na) 寡黙(な)

tack *n* **1.** byō´ びょう・鋲; (*sewing*) shi-tsuke 仕付け **2.** *v tacks it on the wall …* o kabe ni byō´ de tomemásu (tomeru, tomete) …を壁にびょう[鋲]で留めます(留める, 留めて); (*with thread*) shi-tsukemásu (shi-tsukéru, shi-tsúkete) 仕付けます(仕付ける, 仕付けて)

tacking (*with thread*) *n* shi-tsuke 仕付け; ~ *thread* shitsuke-íto 仕付け糸

tackle *n* takkuru タックル

tact *n* **1.** kiten 機転, saiki 才気 **2.** kan-shoku 感触

tactful *adj* kiten no kiku 機転のきく

tactician *n* senjutsu-ka 戦術家

tactics *n* (*strategy*) senjutsu 戦術, sakusen 作戦

teddy bear *n* tedii bea テディベア

tadpole *n* otamajakushi オタマジャクシ

tag *n* fuda 札; (*baggage/package tag*) ní-fuda 荷札, tagu タグ

name tag *n* na fuda 名札

price tag *n* ne fuda 値札

tail *n* shippó しっぽ・尻尾, ó 尾; *the ~ end* びり, ketsu けつ・尻

tailor *n* shitate-ya 仕立屋, yōfuku-ya 洋服屋

Taisho era *n* Taishō jidai 大正時代

Taiwan *n* Taiwan 台湾; *a Taiwanese* Taiwán-jin 台湾人

Tajikistan *n* Tajikisutan タジキスタン

take *v* **1.** torimásu (tóru, tótte) 取ります(取る, 取って), totte/motte ikimásu (iku, itte) 取って/持って行きます(行く, 行って) **2.** hipparimásu (hippáru, hippátte) 引っ張ります(引っ張る, 引っ張って) **3.** (*requires*) yō-shimásu (yō-súru, yō´-shite) 要します(要する, 要して); (*requires time/money*) (jikan/kane ga) kakarimásu (kakáru, kakátte) (時間/金が) かかります(かかる, かかって) **4.** (*incurs*) ukemásu (ukéru, úkete) 受けます(受ける, 受けて); (*accepts; understands*) uke-torimásu

579

(uke-toru, uke-totte) 受け取ります (受け取る、受け取って); *takes it seriously* honki ni shimásu (suru, shíte) 本気にします(する、して); *takes one's blood pressure* ketsuatsu o hakarimásu (hakáru, hakátte) 血圧を計ります(計る、計って); *takes a bath* fúró ni hairimásu (hairu, háitte) 風呂に入ります(入る、入って); *takes a shower* sháwā o abimásu (abiru, abite) シャワーを浴びます(浴びる、浴びて); *takes medicine* kusuri o nomimásu (nómu, nónde) 薬を飲みます(飲む、飲んで); *takes a picture* shashin o torimásu (tóru, tótte) 写真を撮ります(撮る、撮って)、utsushimásu (utsusú, utsúshite) 写します(写す、写して)

take advantage of ... o riyō shimásu (suru, shíte) …を利用します(する、して); zu ni norimásu (noru, notte) 図に乗ります(乗る、乗って)

take away *v* totte ikimásu (iku, itte) 取って行きます(行く、行って); (*confiscates, deprives of*) tori-agemásu (tori-ageru, tori-agete) 取り上げます(取り上げる、取り上げて); (*clears from table*) sagemásu (sagéru, ságete) 下げます(下げる、下げて)

take aim *v* nerai o tsukemásu (tsukéru, tsukéte) 狙いをつけます(つける、つけて)

take apart *v* barashimásu (barásu, baráshite) ばらします(ばらす、ばらして)

take care of *v* **1.** (*handles*) ... o shóri shimásu (suru, shíte) …を処理します(する、して) **2.** (*takes care of a person*) ... no sewá o shimásu (suru, shíte) …の世話をします(する、して)、... no mendō´o mimásu (míru, míte) …の面倒をみます(みる、みて)

Take care (of yourself). *interj* O-daiji ni! お大事に!

take charge of ... *v* ... o hiki-ukemásu (hiki-ukéru, hiki-úkete) …を引き受けます(引き受ける、引き受けて)、tannin/tantō shimásu (suru, shíte) 担任/担当します(する、して)

take down *v* oroshimásu (orósu, oróshite) 下ろし[降ろし]ます(下ろす、下ろして)

take effect *v* (*is effective*) kikimásu (kíku, kiite) 効きます(効く、効いて)

take fright *v* kowagarimásu (kowagáru, kowagátte) 怖がり[こわがり]ます(怖がる、怖がって)

take in(to) *v* iremásu (ireru, irete) 入れます(入れる、入れて); *takes into consideration/account* kō´ryo ni iremásu (ireru, irete) 考慮に入れます(入れる、入れて)

take in trust *v* azukarimásu (azukáru, azukátte) 預かります(預かる、預って)

Take it easy. *interj* **1.** Go-yukkúri. ごゆっくり. **2.** → good-bye

take off *v* **1.** (*removes*) hazushimásu (hazusu, hazushíte) 外します(外す、外して); (*clothes, shoes, etc.*) nugimásu (núgu, núide), 脱ぎます(脱ぐ、脱いで) **2.** (*plane*) ririku shimásu (suru, shíte) 離陸します(する、して)

take-off *n* (*of a plane*) ririku 離陸

take offense *v* shaku ni sawarimásu (sawaru, sawatte) しゃく[癪]にさわり[障り]ます(さわる、さわって)

take over *v* hiki-tori/tsugimásu (hiki-tóru/tsúgu, hiki-tótte/tsuide) 引き取り/継ぎます(引き取る/継ぐ、引き取って/継いで); (*illegally seizes*) nottorimásu (nottóru, nottótte) 乗っ取ります(乗っ取る、乗っ取って)

takeover *n* (*illegal seizure*) nottori-jíken 乗っ取り事件

take pains *v* honé o orimásu (óru, ótte) 骨を折ります(折る、折って)

take refuge *v* hínan shimásu (suru, shíte) 避難します(する、して)

take responsibility for *v* (*responsibility for situation*) ... o hiki-ukemásu (hiki-ukéru, hiki-úkete) …を引き受けます(引き受ける、引き受けて)、... no sekinin o tori/oimásu (toru/ou, totte/otte) …の責任を取り/負います(取る/負う、取って/負って)

take revenge *v* fukushū shimásu (suru, shíte) 復讐します(する、して)

take time off *v* yasumimásu (yasúmu, yasúnde) 休みます(休む、休んで)

take up *v* tori-agemásu (tori-ageru, tori-agete) 取り上げます(取り上げる、取り上げて)

takeaway, takeout *n* (*food*) (o-) mochikaeri (お)持ち帰り

tale *n* (o-)hanashí (お)話, monogátari 物語

old **fairy tale** *n* yōsei monogatari 妖精物語, otogi-banashi おとぎ話

The Tale of the Bamboo-Cutter n Taketori monogatari 竹取物語

The Tale of Genji n Genji monogatari 源氏物語

talent *n* sainō 才能, sái 才; (*personality*) tarento タレント; **~ agency** *n* geinō purodakushon 芸能プロダクション

talented *adj* sainō (no) aru 才能 (の)ある

taleteller *n* (*liar*) usotsuki 嘘つき

talisman *n* (*of a shrine*) o-fuda お札, go-fu 護符, o-mamori お守り

talk 1. *n* hanashí 話; (*conference, discussion*) hanashi-ai 話し合い, (*consultation*) sōdan 相談 → **speech 2.** *v* (*speaks*) hanashimásu (hanásu, hanáshite) 話します (話す, 話して); **~ together** hanashi-aimásu (hanashi-au, hanashi-atte) 話し合います (話し合う, 話し合って)

talk back *v* kuchi-gotae o shimásu (suru, shite) 口答えをします (する, して)

talk big *v* (*boost*) hora o fukimásu (fuku, fuite) ほらを吹く

talk show *n* tōku shō トークショー, taidan bangumi 対談番組

talkative *adj* hanashizuki (na) 話し好き (な), oshaberi (na) おしゃべり・お喋り (な)

tall *adj* takái 高い; (*of body height*) sé ga takái 背が高い

tall story *n* (*unbelivable story*) hōra [法螺]

tambourine *n* tanbarin タンバリン

tame *v* **tames it** narashimásu (narásu, naráshite) 馴らします (馴らす, 馴らして), kainarashimásu (kainarásu, kainaráshite) 飼い慣らします (飼い慣らす, 飼い慣らして)

tan *n* hiyake 日焼け

tanned *adj* hiyakeshita 日焼けした

tandem *n* tandemu タンデム, futarinori-yō (no) jitensha/jidensha 二人乗り用(の)自転車

tangerine *n* (*Mandarin orange*) míkan みかん・蜜柑

tangible *adj* gutai-teki (na) 具体的(な)

tangle *n* (*entanglement*) motsure もつれ・縺れ

tangled *adj* (*complicated*) yayakoshíi/yaya(k)koshíi ややこしい/ややっこしい → **entangled**

tango *n* tango タンゴ

tank *n* tanku タンク

tank top *n* tanku toppu タンクトップ

tanka *n* tanka 短歌

tanker *n* tankā タンカー

tantalum *n* (*metal*) tantaru タンタル

Tanzania *n* Tanzania タンザニア

tap 1. *v* (*karuku*) tatakimásu (tataku, tataite) (軽く)たたき[叩き]ます (たたく, たたいて) **2.** *v* tōchō shimásu (suru, shite) 盗聴します (する, して) **3.** *n* jaguchi 蛇口 **4.** *n* (*tap-daicing*) tappu-dansu タップダンス

tap water *n* suidōsui 水道水

tape *n* tḗpu テープ; himo ひも・紐

adhesive tape *n* bansōkō 絆創膏sばんそうこう

adhesive cellophane tape *n* serohan tēpu セロハンテープ

gum tape *n* gamu tēpu ガムテープ

tape measure *n* makijaku 巻き尺, mejā メジャー

tape recorder *n* tēpu-rekō´dā テープレコーダー

tapestry *n* tapesutorii タペストリー

tapping *n* (*medical exam*) dashin 打診

tar *n* tāru タール

target *n* mato 的, taishō 対象; (*goal*) mokuhyō 目標, tāgetto ターゲット

tariff *n* kanzei 関税

tart *n* (*pie*) taruto タルト

tart pastry *n* taruto kiji タルト生地

tartan *n* tātan タータン

tartan check *n* tātan chekku タータンチェック

task *n* shigoto 仕事; tasuku タスク

task allocation *n* shigoto (no) haibun 仕事(の)配分; tasuku (no) haibun タスク(の)配分

Tasman Peninsula *n* (*Australia*) Tasuman hantō タスマン半島

tassel

tassel *n* fusa 房

taste **1.** *n* (*flavor*) aji 味, fūmi 風味; (*has flavor*) aji ga shimásu (suru, shite) 味がします(する, して) **2.** (*liking*) shúmi 趣味; tēsuto テースト, sensu センス. konomí 好み (o-konomi お好み); *simple* (*modest*) *tastes* wabi わび・侘び

bad taste *n* akushumi 悪趣味

bitter taste *n* nigai aji 苦い味, [BOOKISH] nigami 苦味

bitter taste of life *n* (jinsei no) nigai keiken (人生の) 苦い経験

good taste *n* yoi shumi 良い趣味, ii sensu いいセンス

sweet taste *n* amai aji 甘い味, [BOOKISH] kanmi 甘味

sour taste *n* suppai aji 酸っぱい味, [BOOKISH] sanmi 酸味

taste *v* (*tastes it*) ajiwaimásu (ajiwau, ajiwatte) 味わいます(味わう, 味わって), namemásu (naméru, námete) な め[舐め]ます(なめる, なめて); (*tries eating it*) tábete mimásu (míru, míte) 食べてみます(みる, みて)

tasty *adj* oishii おいしい・美味しい, umái うまい・旨い・美味い, bimi 美味

tatami *n* tatami タタミ・畳

tatami room *n* zashiki 座敷 (o-zashiki お座敷)

tattoo *n* ire-zumi 入れ墨・刺青

Taurus *n* (*star sign*) Oushi-za 牡牛座・おうし座

taught → teach; is taught osowari-másu (osowaru, osowatte) 教わります (教わる, 教わって)

taut; *stretched* ~ pin-to hatta ピンと張った

tavern *n* nomí-ya 飲み屋; izaka-ya 居酒屋

tax *n* zéi 税, zeikin 税金; *tax* (*revenue*) *stamp* shūnyū-ínshi 収入印紙

consumption tax *n* shōhi zei 消費税

corporation tax *n* hōjin zei 法人税

income tax *n* shotoku zei 所得税

national tax *n* koku zei 国税

residential tax *n* jūmin zei 住民税

regional taxation bureau *n* kokuzei-kyoku 国税局

sales tax *n* uriage zei 売上税

tax-free *adj* menzei (no) 免税(の); *tax-free goods* menzei-hin 免税品; *tax-free shop* menzei-ten 免税店

tax office *n* zeimusho 税務署

tax refund *n* zeikin (no) kanpu 税金 (の) 還付

withheld tax *n* gensen chōshū-zei 源泉徴収税

taxi *n* tákushii タクシー, ~ *stand/station* takushii nori-ba タクシー乗り場

TB *n* (hai-)kekkaku (肺) 結核, haibyō 肺病

tea *n* cha ほ; (*green*) ryoku-cha 緑茶, o-cha お茶, (*coarse*) bancha 番茶, (*bitter*) shibucha 渋茶, (*black*) kōcha 紅茶, tii ティー; (*powdered green, for tea ceremony*) matcha 抹茶; (*weak powdered*) usu-cha 薄茶, o-úsu お薄; *a cup of green* ~ [*sushi bar term*] agari 上がり; *makes* ~ o-cha o iremásu (ireru, irete) お茶を入れます(入れる, 入れて)

Japanese tea *n* nihon cha 日本茶

tea bag *n* tii baggu ティーバッグ

teacake *n* (o-)cha-gáshi (お) 茶菓子

tea canister/caddy *n* cha-ire 茶入れ; (*for tea ceremony*) natsume 棗・なつめ

tea ceremony *n* o-cha お茶, chano-yu 茶の湯, sadō 茶道; ~ *procedures* temae 点前 (o-témae お点前)

teacup *n* yunomí 湯飲み, yunomi-jáwan 湯飲み茶碗; (*also ricebowl*) chawan 茶碗 (o-cháwan お茶碗)

teakettle *n* yakan やかん, yuwákashi 湯沸し

teapot *n* do-bin どびん・土瓶, kyūsu 急須, cha-bin 茶瓶

tearoom *n* kissa-ten 喫茶店; (*for tea ceremony*) (o-)chashítsu (お) 茶室

tea scoop *n* (*for tea ceremony*) chashaku 茶杓

tea party *n* o-chakai お茶会

teaspoon *n* sájí さじ・匙, ko-saji 小さじ・小匙 cha-saji 茶さじ・茶匙, tii supūn ティースプーン

teatime *n* tii taimu ティータイム, o-cha no jikan お茶の時間

tea whisk *n* (*for tea ceremony*) chasen 茶筅

teach *v* oshiemásu (oshieru, oshiete) 教えます(教える, 教えて)

teacher *n* senséi 先生; (*school-teacher*) gakkō no senséi 学校の先生, (*instructor*) kyō´shi 教師

head teacher *n* kōchō (sensei) 校長 (先生)

teaching *n* kyōju 教授, oshie 教え; *classroom ~* júgyō 授業; *~ hours* jugyō-jíkan 授業時間

teaching materials *n* kyōzai 教材

team *n* chíimu チーム

team up (*with*) (… to) kumimásu (kúmu, kúnde) (…と)組みます(組む, 組んで)

teamwork *n* chiimu-wā´ku チームワーク, kyōdō sagyō 共同作業

tear *n* (*in eye*) námida 涙

burst into tears *v* watto nakidashimásu (nakidasu, nakidashite) わっと泣き出します(泣き出す, 泣き出して)

tear gland *n* ruisen 涙腺

tears of joy *n* ureshinamida 嬉し涙

tears of mortification *n* kuyashi-namida 悔し涙

tear *v* **1.** (*tears it*) sakimásu (sáku, sáite) 裂きます(裂く, 裂いて), yaburimásu (yabúru, yabútte) 破ります(破る, 破って); *tears into pieces* chigirimásu (chigiru, chigitte) 千切ります(千切る, 千切って) **2.** *v* (*it tears*) sakemásu (sakéru, sákete) 裂けます(裂ける, 裂けて), yaburemásu (yabúreru, yabúrete) 破れます(破れる, 破れて)

teardrop *n* namida no tsubu 涙の粒

teardrop-shaped (diamond) *n* namida-gata no (daiyamondo) 涙型の ダ(イヤモンド)

tearful *adj* namidagunda 涙ぐんだ

tearful eyes *n* namidagunda me 涙ぐんだ目

tearful farewell *n* namida no wakare 涙の別れ

tearful look *n* nakisō na kao 泣きそうな顔

tearful story *n* shimeppoi hanashi 湿っぽい話

tease *v* (*pokes fun at*) karakaimásu (karakáu, karakátte) からかいます(からかう, からかって); (*torments*) ijimemásu (ijimeru, ijimete) いじめ[苛め]ます(いじめる, いじめて)

technical *adj* senmon-teki (na) 専門

的(な); tekunikaru (na) テクニカル(な)

technical term *n* senmon-yōgo 専門用語; tekunikaru na yōgo テクニカルな用語

technician *n* gijutsu-ka 技術家

technique *n* gíjutsu 技術; waza 技; tekunikku テクニック

teenager *n* tiin eijā ティーンエイジャー; jūdai (no hito) 10代(の人); jūsan sai kara jūkyū sai 13歳から19歳

teens *n* (*teenager*) jūdai (no hito) 10代(の人); jūsan sai kara jūkyū sai 13歳から19歳

teeth → **tooth**

teething ring *n* osháburi おしゃぶり

Teheran *n* Teheran テヘラン

telecast *n* terebi hōsō テレビ放送

telecommunication *n* (denki) tsūshin (電気)通信

teleconference *n* denwa kaigi 電話会議; terebi kaigi テレビ会議

telegram *n* denpō (o uchimásu; útsu, útte) 電報(を打ちます; 打つ, 打って)

telephone 1. *n ~ call* denwa 電話 (o-dénwa お電話); *mobile ~, cell-phone* keitai denwa 携帯電話; *touch-tone ~* n pusshúhon プッシュホン

telephone book/directory *n* denwa-chō 電話帳

telephone booth *n* denwa-bókkusu 電話ボックス

telephone card *n* terehon kādo テレホンカード

telephone company *n* denwa-gaisha 電話会社

telephone line *n* denwa-sen 電話線

telephone number *n* denwa-bángō 電話番号

telephone operator *n* (denwa-)kōkán-shu (電話)交換手, (denwa) operētā (電話)オペレーター

telephone wire(s) *n* denwa-sen 電話線

2. telephones (*... ni*) denwa o kakemásu/shimasu (kakeru, kakete/suru, shite) (…に)電話をかけます(かける, かけて)/します(する, して)

teleport *v* tensō shimásu (suru, shite) 転送します(する, して)

teleportation *n* (*psychic powers, etc.*) terepōto テレポート

telescope *n* bōenkyō 望遠鏡
television *n* térebi テレビ, terebíjon テレビジョン
telex *n* terekkusu テレックス
tell *v* **1.** iimásu (iu/yū, itte/yutte) 言います(言う, 言って/ゆって); (*relates*) nobemásu (nobéru, nóbete) 述べます(述べる, 述べて); katarimásu (kataru, katatte) 語ります(語る, 語って) **2.** (*informs one of*) … no mimí ni iremásu (ireru, irete) …耳に入れます(入れる, 入れて); … ni kikasemásu (kikaseru, kikasete); …に聞かせます(聞かせる, 聞かせて), … ni tsugemásu (tsugeru, tsugete) …に告げます(告げる, 告げて) **3.** (*instructs*) oshiemásu (oshieru, oshiete) 教えます(教える, 教えて); *tells on* (*tattles*) ii-tsukemásu (ii-tsukéru, ii-tsukete) 言い付けます(言い付ける, 言い付けて)
teller *n* **1.** (*narrator*) hanashite 話し手; katarite 語り手 **2.** (*bank*) (ginkō no) suitō-gakari (銀行の)出納係
story teller *n* sutōrii terā ストーリー・テラー
telop *n* teroppu テロップ
temper **1.** *n* (*disposition*) ijí 意地; táchi たち・質, ténsei 天性, táido 態度 **2.** *v* (*forges metal*) kitaemásu (kitaeru, kitáete) 鍛えます(鍛える, 鍛えて)
be in a bad temper *v* kigen ga warui desu (warui, warukute) 機嫌が悪いです(悪い, 悪くて)
be in a good temper *v* kigen ga ii desu (ii, yokute) 機嫌がいいです(いい, 良くて)
hot temper, short temper *n* tanki 短気
lose one's temper *v* tanki o okoshimásu (okosu, okoshite) 短気を起こします(起こす, 起こして)
temperament *n* ténsei 天性; kishitsu 気質
temperature *n* óndo 温度; (*of body*) taion 体温; (*fever*) netsú 熱; (*air*) kion 気温; (*room air*) shitsuon 室温
temple *n* **1.** (*Asian*) terá 寺, o-tera お寺; …ji …寺 **2.** shinden 神殿; *temple of Jupiter* Yupiteru shinden ユピテル神殿 **3.** (*flat part on each side of the head*) komekami こめかみ

temple bell *n* tsurigane 釣り鐘
temple fair *n* énnichi 縁日
temple gate *n* sanmon 山門
tempo *n* tenpo テンポ, hayasa 速さ
temporal *adj* **1.** ichiji-teki (na) 一時的(な) **2.** sokutō-bu (no) 側頭部(の)
temporary *adj* rinji (no) 臨時(の), tōza (no) 当座(の); (*passing*) ichiji (no) 一時(の), ichiji-teki (na) 一時的(な); (*tentative*) kari (no) 仮(の), ka-… 仮…
temporary availability *n* ichiji-teki ni riyō kanō 一時的に利用可能, ichiji-teki ni nyūshu kanō 一時的に入手可能
temporary ceasefire *n* ichiji teisen 一時停戦
temporary expedient *n* ichiji shinogi 一時しのぎ, maniawase まにあわせ
temporary office *n* kari (no) jimusho 仮(の)事務所
temporary work *n* rinji (no) shigoto 臨時(の)仕事
tempt *v* sasoimásu (sasou, sasotte) 誘います(誘う, 誘って)
temptation *n* sasoi 誘い, yūwaku 誘惑
tempura *n* (*food fried in batter, especially shrimp*) tenpura てんぷら・天麩(婦)羅
tempura bowl *n* tendon 天丼
ten *n* jū´ 十・10, tó´ 十・10; *ten days* tōka 十日・10日
ten; *10 pieces* (*small things*) júk-ko 十個; *10 trees* (*long things*) júp-pon 十本; *10 sheets* (*flat things*) jū´-mai 十枚; *10 cats* (*or small animals*) júp-piki 十匹; *10 cows* (*or large aminals*) jút-tō 十頭; *10 birds/rabbits* júp-pa 十羽; *10 cars* (*or machines/vehicles*) jū´-dai 十台; *10 copies* (*books/magazines*) jus-satsu 十冊; *10 people* (*or persons*) jū´-nin 十人, jū´-mei 十名; *10 floors/stories* juk-kai 十階; *10 fold* jū´-bai 十倍; *10 degrees* jū´-do 十度; *10 times* jū´-dó 十度, juk-kái 十回, jup-pén 十遍; *10 o'clock* jū-ji 十時; *10 hours* jū-jíkan 十時間; *10 weeks* jús-shūkan 十週間; *10 months* júk-ká-getsu 十ヶ月; *10 years* jū´-nen 十年, jū´-nenkan 十年間; *10 years old* tō´ 十, jús-sai 十歳
tenacity *n* shūchaku 執着
tenant *n* (*of apartment, room*) magari-

nin 間借人, nyūkyō-sha 入居者,
tenanto テナント

tenant owner *n* tenanto no ōnā テナン
トのオーナー

tend (*to do/happen*) *v* yóku …
(shimásu) よく…(します); (shi-)yasúi
desu (し)やすいです

tendency *n* keikō 傾向

tender → gentle, soft → hurt

tenderness *n* nasake 情け (o-násake
お情け)

tendon *n* súji 筋
Achilles' tendon *n* akiresu ken アキレ
ス腱

tenement house *n* naga-ya 長屋

tennis *n* ténisu テニス
tennis court *n* tenisu kōto テニスコ
ート

tennis player *n* tenisu senshu テニス
選手, tenisu purēyā テニスプレーヤー

tennis racket *n* tenisu raketto テニスラ
ケット

tennis shoes *n* tenisu shūzu テニスシ
ューズ

tenor *n* ténā テナー, tenōru テノール

tense *v* (*taut*) hatte imásu (iru, ite)
張っています(いる, いて); (*strained*)
kinchō shite imásu (iru, ite) 緊張して
います(いる, いて); (*situation*)
kinpaku shimásu (suru, shite) 緊迫し
ます(する, して)

tension *n* kinchō 緊張; tenshon テン
ション

tent *n* ténto テント

tentative *adj* kari (no) 仮(の)

tenth *adj* jū-banmé (no) 十番目(の),
tō-mé (no) 十目(の); *the tenth day*
tōka-mé 十日目, (*of the month*) tōka
十日・10日; *tenth floor* juk-kai 十階

ten thousand *n* mán 万・10,000, ichi-
mán 一万・10,000

ten-thousandfold *adj* (ichi)manbai
(一)万倍

term *n* (*period*) kikán 期間, (*time limit*)
kígen 期限; (*of school*) gakki 学期;
(*technical word*) senmon-yōgo 専門用
語, yōgo 用語; (*stipulation*) jōken 条件

terminal *n* (*place*), terminus *n* shūten
終点; hatchaku-chi 発着地; tāminaru
ターミナル

terminology *n* senmon yōgo 専門用語

terms *n* (*between people*) náka 仲;
they are on good/bad ~ náka ga íi/
warúi desu 仲がいい/悪いです

terrace *n* terasu テラス

terrible *adj* (mono-)sugói (もの)すご
い・(物)凄い, taihen (na) 大変(な);
(*severe*) hidoi ひどい・酷い; (*frightening*)
osoroshíi 恐ろしい; (*shocking*) tonde-
mo nái とんでもない, tonda とんだ

terribly *adv* súgoku すごく・凄く,
mono-súgoku ものすごく・物凄く,
taihen 大変; hídoku ひどく・酷く;
osoróshiku 恐ろしく; (*extremely,
completely*) to(t)temo と(っ)ても;
(*unbearably*) yáke ni やけに

terrific *adj* sugói すごい・凄い, kowái
怖い

territorialism *n* nawabari arasoi 縄張
り争い

territory *n* ryō´do 領土, ryō´chi 領地,
teritorii テリトリー, nawabari 縄張り

terror *n* kyō´fu 恐怖
balance of terror *n* kyō´fu no kinkō
恐怖の均衡
holy terror *n* (*child*) itazurakko いた
ずらっ子, te ni amaru ko(domo) 手に
あまる子(供), te ni oenai ko(domo)
手に負えない子(供)
reign of terror *n* kyō´fu jidai 恐怖時代

terrorism *n* téro テロ

terrorist *n* terorisuto テロリスト

test *n* **1.** shikén 試験, tésuto テスト;
(*check of blood, etc.*) kénsa 検査 →
trial → experiment **2.** → try
achievement test *n* gakuryoku shiken
学力試験
blood test *n* ketsueki kensa 血液検査
DNA test *n* dii enu ei kantei DNA
鑑定
eye test *n* shiryoku kensa 視力検査
hearing test *n* **1.** (*checkup*) chōryoku
kensa 聴力検査 **2.** (*exam*) hiyaringu
tesuto ヒヤリング・テスト, hiyaringu
shiken ヒヤリング試験, kikitori
shiken 聞き取り試験
routine test *n* (*examination*) teiki
shiken 定期試験
test pilot *n* shaken sōjū-shi 試験操
縦士, shaken hikō-shi 試験飛行士,

shaken pairotto 試験パイロット

test tube *n* shiken-kan 試験管

testament *n* (*will*) yuigon 遺言; *the Old/New Testament* Kyū-/Shin-yaku 旧/新約

testicle(s) *n* kintamá 金玉, (*medical*) kōgan 睾丸

testifier *n* shōgen-sha 証言者

testify *v* shōgen shimásu (suru, shite) 証言します(する, して)

testimony *n* shōgen 証言

Texas *n* Tekisasu テキサス

text **1.** *n* bun 文, (*computer*) tekisuto テキスト **2.** *v* (mēru o) uchimás<u>u</u> (utsu, utte) (メール を)打ちます(打つ, 打って)

text book *n* tekisu<u>t</u>o テキスト, kyōká-sho 教科書

text file *n* tekisu<u>t</u>o fairu テキストファイル

textile *n* ori-mono 織物

textile industry *n* sen'i sangyō 繊維産業, bōseki kōgyō 紡績工業

texture *n* jí 地, ori-ji 織地; kimé きめ・肌理; (*touch*) tezawari 手触り・手ざわり, shitsukan 質感

...th *adj* ...-mé (no) ...目(の); *fifth* its<u>u</u>tsu-mé 五つ目

Thai *n* (*language*) Tai-go タイ語; (*person*) Tai-jin タイ人

Thailand *n* Tai タイ

than ... ... yóri ...より

thank *v* o-rei o iimás<u>u</u> (iu/yū, itte/yutte) お礼 を言います(言う/ゆう, 言って/ゆって)

Thank you. *interj* Arígatō gozaimás<u>u</u>. ありがとう[有り難う] ございます; Dō´mo. どうも; Sumimasén すみません; osóreirimás<u>u</u>. 恐れ入ります.

Thank you for everything you have done for me. *interj* Iroiro (to) o-sewa ni narimash<u>i</u>ta. いろいろ(と)お世話になりました.

Thank you for the hard work. *interj* Go-kúrō-sama (desh<u>i</u>ta). ご苦労さま(でした).

Thank you for the treat. *interj* Gochisō-sama (désh<u>i</u>ta). ご馳走[ごちそう]さま(でした). "*thank-you money*" (*to obtain rental*) rei-kin 礼金

Thank you in advance. *interj* Yoroshiku onegaishimasu. よろしくお願いします.

thank-you letter *n* o-rei no tegami お礼の手紙, sankyū retā サンキューレター; [BOOKISH] kansha-jō 感謝状, reijō 礼状

thanks *n* (*gratitude*) kansha (no kotobá) 感謝(の言葉); (o-)rei (お)礼; *~ to your solicitude* okagesama de お蔭さまで

thanksgiving *n* **1.** (*gratitude*) kansha 感謝 **2.** (*day*) kansha-sai 感謝祭

that *pron* **1.** (*one*) sore それ, soitsu そいつ, (*of two*) sochira/sotchí そちら/そっち; (*over there; obvious*) are あれ, (*of two*) achira/atchí あちら/あっち; *~ damn one* soitsu そいつ, aitsu あいつ, kyátsu きゃつ; *to ~ extent* sonna ni そんなに; anna ni あんなに **2.** *that ...* sono ... その...; ano ... あの...; (*said/thought that*) ... to ...と; (*which/who*) —not translated

that is to say *adv* sunáwachi すなわち・即ち

that kind of *adj* sono/ano yō na その/あのよう[様]な, sō/ā yū そう/ああゆう, sonna/anna そんな/あんな

that place *pron* **1.** soko そこ; sochira/sotchí そちら/そっち **2.** (*over there; obvious*) asoko あそこ, as<u>u</u>ko あすこ; achira/atchí あちら/あっち

that side *n* achira-gawa あちら側

that sort of → that kind of

That's right *interj* sō´ (desu) そう(です)

that time *adv*, *n* sono tókí その時, tō´ji 当時

that very day *adv*, *n* tōjitsu 当日

that way *n* (*like that*) sō´ yū (sō´ yū + [PARTICLE] or désu です); (*over there; obvious*) ā ああ (ā ああ + [PARTICLE] or désu です); (*that direction*) sochira/sotchí そちら/そっち, (*over there; obvious*) achira/atchí あちら/あっち

that... **1.** sono ...その...; (*over there; obvious*) ano ... あの...; *said/thought ~* ... (sono yō ni) itta/kangaeta, omotta (そのように)言った/考えた・思った **2.** [RELATIVE PRONOUN] = which..., who...

thatch 1. *n* káya かや・茅, (*straw*) wára ワラ・藁, (*grass*) kusá 草 **2.** *v* ***thatches a roof*** káya/wára/kusá de yáne o fukimásu (fuku, fuite) かや/わら/草で屋根をふきます(ふく、ふいて)

thaw *v* (*it thaws*) tokemásu (tokéru, tókete) 解(溶)けます(解(溶)ける/解(溶)けて); (*thaws it*) tokashimásu (tokásu, tokáshite) 解(溶)かします(解(溶)かす、解(溶)かして)

the *article* (*usually not translated*); ano … あの…, hon- ホン…

theater *n* (*building*) gekijṓ 劇場, za 座; (*drama*) engeki 演劇, (*play*) shibai 芝居, (*traditional*) kabuki 歌舞伎; ~ *people* engekí-jin 演劇人; *the Kabuki* ~ (*building*) Kabuki-za 歌舞伎座

theft *n* nusumí 盗み, tṓnan 盗難

them, they *pron* (*people*) anóhito-tachi あの人達, káre-ra 彼等 (*or name/title/role* + -tachi 達); (*things*) soré-ra それら

theme *n* (*topic*) tḗma テーマ, shudai 主題; (*composition*) sakubun 作文
theme park *n* tḗma pāku テーマパーク; yūenchi 遊園地
theme song *n* tḗma songu テーマソング; shudai-ka 主題歌

then *adv* (*at that time*) sono tókí その時, tṓji 当時; (*after that*) sore kara それから; (*in that case*) sore nára それなら; *and/well* ~ sá-te さて

theology *n* shingaku 神学

theoretic *adj* riron (no) 理論(の)

theoretical *adj* rironteki (na) 理論的(な), riron-jō (no) 理論上(の)

theory *n* riron 理論, rikutsu 理屈, seorii セオリー, …-ron …論

there *adv* soko (ni) そこ(に); (*over there*) asoko/asuko (ni) あそこ/あすこ(に)

therefore *adv* dákara (sa) だから(さ); (*accordingly*) shitagatte したがって・従って

there is/are … *adv* …ga arimásu (áru, átte) …があります(ある/あって), [DEFERENTIAL] gozaimásu (gozaimá-shite) ございます(ございまして); *there is/are no …* … ga (/wa) arimasén (nái, nákute) …が(/は)ありません(ない、なくて)

thermal *adj* netsu (no) 熱(の)
thermal conduction *n* netsu dendō 熱伝導
thermal conductivity *n* netsu dendō ritsu 熱伝導率
thermal energy *n* netsu enerugii 熱エネルギー

thermometer *n* ondo-kei 温度計; (*room*) kandán-kei 寒暖計; (*body*) taion-kei 体温計

thermos bottle *n* mahṓ-bin 魔法びん・魔法瓶

these *pron* … kono … この…; ~ (*ones*) koré-ra これら; ~ *damn ones* koitsú-ra こいつら

thesis *n* ronbun 論文, gakuirónbun 学位論文; *master's* ~ shūshi-rónbun 修士論文

they → them

thick *adj* atsui 厚い, buatsui 分厚い・部厚い, atsubottai 厚ぼったい; (*and round*) futói 太い; (*dense, close*) kói 濃い, mítsu (na) 密(な), missetsu (na) 密接(な); (*greasy*) kudói くどい

thicket *n* yabu やぶ・薮

thief *n* dorobō どろぼう・泥棒, [BOOKISH] zoku 賊, tōzoku 盗賊
sneak thief *n* koso-doro こそ泥; akisu 空き巣

thigh *n* mómo もも・股, futomomo 太股・太もも

thimble *n* yubi-nukí 指ぬき

thin 1. *adj* usui 薄い; (*and round*) hosói 細い **2.** *gets* ~ (*loses weight*) yasemásu (yaseru, yasete) やせ[痩せ]ます(やせる/やせて)

thing *n* monó 物, yátsu やつ・奴; (*fact, matter*) kotó 事; *things* monógoto 物事; *just the thing, adj* (*ideal*) motte-kói (no) もってこい(の)

think *v* (*that …*) (… to) omoimásu (omóu, omótte) (…と)思います(思う、思って), kangaemásu (kangáeru, kangáete) 考えます(考える、考えて); [DEFERENTIAL] zon-jimásu (zon-jiru, zon-jite) 存じます(存じる、存じて); [HUMBLE] zon-jiagemásu (zon-jíageru, zon-jiagéte) 存じあげます(あげる、あげて)

thinking *n* shikō 思考

thinking-over n hansei 反省

third adj sanbanmé (no) 三番目, mittsu-mé (no) 三つ目(の); **the ~ day** mikka-mé 三日目, (of the month) mikka 三日・3日; **~ or fourth** san-yo-banmé (no) 三、四番目(の)

third class adj san-tō (no) 三等(の)

third floor n san-gai 三階

third generation n sán-sei 三世

third time n sando-mé 三度目, sankai-mé 三回目

third-year student n sannén-sei 三年生

thirsty adj nódo ga kawaita のど[喉]が渇いた, nódo ga kawaite(i)ru のど[喉]が渇いて(い)る

thirteen n jū-san 十三・13

thirty n san-jū 三十・30

  thirty or forty n san-shi-jū 三、四十; **~ or forty thousand** san-yo(m)-man 三、四万

  thirty percent n sán-wari 三割, sanjup-pāsénto 三十パーセント・30%

this pron **1.** (one) kore これ, hon-...本...; (of two) kochira/kotchí こちら/こっち; **this damn one** koitsu こいつ; **to ~ extent** konna ni こんなに **2.** **this ... kono ...** この...

this afternoon adv, n kyō'no gógo 今日の午後

this evening adv, n kónban 今晩

this kind of adj kono yō'na このよう[様]な, kō yū こうゆう, konna こんな

this month adv, n kongetsu 今月

this morning adv, n késa 今朝; kyō'no ása 今日の朝

this much adv konna ni こんなに

this place pron koko ここ; kochira/kotchí こちら/こっち

this side n kochira-gawa こちら側; **this side of ...** no temae ...の手前

this sort of → this kind of

this time adv, n kóndo 今度, íma 今, kono tabí このたび[度]

this way n (like this) kō こう (+ [PARTICLE] or désu です); (this direction) kochira/kotchí こちら/こっち

this week adv, n konshū 今週

this year adv, n kotoshi 今年

thong n **1.** (kawa) himo (皮)紐[ひも] **2.** (on geta [下駄]) hanao 鼻緒

thorium n toriumu トリウム

thorn n togé トゲ・棘

thorny adj **1.** togé no ōi トゲ[棘]の多い **2.** ibara (no) イバラ・茨(の) **3.** yakkai (na) 厄介(な), muzukashii 難しい

thorny path n ibara no michi いばらの道, kon'nan na michi 困難な道

thorny problem n nandai 難題

thorough adj tettei-teki (na) 徹底的(な); (detailed) seimitsu (na) 精密(な)

thoroughbred n sarabureddo サラブレッド

thoroughfare n tsú'ro 通路, ōrai 往来

thoroughly adv tettei-teki ni 徹底的(に)

those → them

those ... pron sono ... その..., ano ... あの...; **those** (ones) soré-ra それら, aré-ra あれら; **~ damn ones** soitsú-ra そいつら, aitsú-ra あいつら; **~ present** shusséki-sha 出席者

those days n tō'ji 当時

though conj démo でも, kéredo (mo) けれど(も)

thought 1. n kangáe 考え, omói 思い, shikō 思考; shisō 思想; (fulness) shíryo 思慮 **2.** → think

thousand n sén 千・1,000, is-sén 一千・1,000; **a ~ yen** sen-en 千円・1,000円

thousandfold adj senbai (no) 千倍(の)

thread n íto 糸

threat n odoshi 脅し, [BOOKISH] kyōhaku 脅迫

threaten v odo(ka)shimásu (odo(ka)-su, odo(ka)shíte) 脅(か)します(脅(か)す, 脅(か)して)

threatening adj kyōhaku-teki (na) 脅迫的(な)

  threatening call n kyōhaku denwa 脅迫電話

  threatening e-mail n kyōhaku mēru 脅迫メール

  threatening letter n kyōhaku-jō 脅迫状

three n san 三・3, mittsú 三つ; san-...三 ..., mi-... 三...; surí スリー; (people) san-nín 三人, [BOOKISH] sánmei 三名

three; 3 pieces (*small things*) sán-ko 三個; **3 trees** (*or long things*) sánbon 三本; **3 sheets** (*flat things*) sánmai 三枚; **3 cats** (*or small animals*) sánbiki 三匹; **3 cows** (*or large aminals*) sán-tō 三頭; **3 birds/rabbits** sánba 三羽; **3 cars** (*or machines/vehicles*) sán-dai 三台; **3 copies** (*books/magazines*) sánsatsu 三冊; **3 floors/stories** san-gai 三階; **3 people** san-nín 三人, sán-mei 三名; **3 fold** sánbai 三倍; **3 degrees** sán-do 三度; **3 times** sán-dó 三度, sán-kái 三回, sánben 三遍; **3 o'clock** sán-ji 三時; **3 hours** sán-jíkan 三時間; **3 days** mikka 三日; **3 days from now** shiasátte しあさって・明々後日; **the first 3 days of the new year** sanganichi 三が日; **3 days ago** mikka máe 三日前; saki-ototói さきおととい・一昨々日; **3 weeks** sán-shūkan 三週間; **3 months** sán-ká-getsu 三ヶ月; **3 years** san-nen 三年, san-nen-kan 三年間; **3 years ago** san-nen máe 三年前, saki-otótoshi さきおととし・一作々年; **3 years old** mittsú 三つ, sán-sai 三歳

three-dimensional *adj* rittai (no) 立体の

three hundred *n* sánbyaku 三百・300

three nights ago *adv* mikka máe no ban/yoru 三日前の晩/夜; saki-ototói no ban/yoru さきおととい・一昨々日の晩/夜

three or four *n* san-shi- 三、四, *except for…* san-yo- 三、四; *3-4 hours* san-yo-jíkan 三、四時間, *3-4 o'clock* sán-ji ka yó-ji 三時か四時, *3-4 people* san-yo-nín 三、四人, *3-4 servings* san-yo-ninmae 三、四人前, *3-4 times* san-yon-kai 三、四回, *3-4 times as much* = sanbai ka yo(m)-bai 三倍か四倍, *3-4 yen* san-yó-en 三、四円, *3-4 days* san-yokka 三、四日, *3-4 hundred* san-shíhyaku 三、四百 = sánbyaku ka yónhyaku 三百か四百

three thousand *n* san-zén 三千・3,000

threshold *n* **1.** shíkii 敷居 **2.** (*threshold value*) ikichi 閾値

thrifty *adj* tsumashíi つましい・倹しい, ken'yaku (na) 倹約(な), komakái 細かい

thrill 1. *n* súriru スリル **2.** *adj* (*is thrilled*) waku-waku/zokuzoku shimásu (suru, shíte) わくわく/ぞくぞくします(する/して)

thrilling *adj* suriru o kanjisaseru スリルを感じさせる, waku-waku/zoku-zoku suru わくわく/ぞくぞくする

thrive *v* sakaemásu (sakáeru, sakáete) 栄えます(栄える/栄えて); uremásu (ureru, urete) 売れます(売れる/売れて)

throat *n* nódo のど・喉 [BOOKISH] inkō 咽喉

throb *v* dokidoki shimásu (suru, shíte) どきどき・ドキドキします(する/して)

throne *n* ōi 王位, ōza 王座

throng 1. *n* ōzéi 大勢, (*flock*) muré 群れ **2.** *they ~ together* *v* muragarimásu (muragáru, muragátte) 群がります(群がる/群がって)

through 1. *prep* **putting ~** …o tō'shite …を通して; **gets ~** tsū-jimásu (tsu-jiru, tsū-jite) 通じます(通じる, 通じて); **coming ~** …o tō'tte …を通って; (*via*) …o héte …を経て; …kéiyu (de/no) …経由(で/の) **2.** *prep* (*throughout*) …-jū …じゅう・中; …no aida-jū …の間じゅう[中]; **all the way ~** zutto ずっと **3.** (*by means of*) …o tsukatte …を使って **4.** (*extending through* …ni kákete …かけて **5.** *adv* (*is finished*) dekimashíta 出来ました, (shi)-te shimaimáshita (し)てしまいました

throughout *prep* (*the entire* [PLACE/TIME]) …-jū …じゅう・中; **~ the world** sekai-jū 世界中

throw *v* nagemásu (nagéru, nágete) 投げます(投げる, 投げて); **~ away** sutemásu (suteru, sutete) 捨てます(捨てる, 捨てて); **~ in extra** soemásu (soeru, soete) 添えます(添える/添えて); **~ into disorder** midashimásu (midásu, midáshite) 乱します(乱す, 乱して)

throwaway *adj* tsukaisute (no) 使い捨ての

throwaway chopsticks *n* wari-bashi 割りばし[箸]

throw up → vomit

thrush *n* tsugumi ツグミ

thrust *v* tsukimásu (tsuku, tsuite) 突き
ます(突く/突いて)
thrust stage *n* haridashi butai 張り出
し舞台
thumb *n* oya-yubi 親指
thumb drive *n* (*small computer
storage*) samu-doraibu サムドライブ
thumbprint *n* (*when used to stamp a
document*) boin 母印・拇印
thumbtack *n* gabyō 画びょう・画鋲
thunder *n* kaminári (ga narimásu;
naru, natte) 雷(が鳴ります; 鳴る, 鳴
って)
thunderstorm *n* ráiu 雷雨
Thursday *n* Mokuyō'bi 木曜日
thwart *v* habamimásu (habámu,
habánde) 阻みます(阻む, 阻んで)
Tibet *n* Chibetto チベット
tick *n* chekku チェック
tick mark *n* chekku māku チェックマ
ーク, re ten レ点
tick-tack *n* kachi kachi カチカチ
ticket *n* kippu 切符, chikétto チケッ
ト; …-ken …券; *just the ~* (*ideal*)
motte-kói (no) もってこい(の), (*most
suitable*) uttetsuke (no) うってつけ
(の); *admission* ~ nyōjō-ken 入場券
ticket agency *n* *theater* ~ pureigáido
プレイガイド ("*Play Guide*")
ticket book *n* (*for commuting*) kaisū´-
ken 回数券
ticket collecting *n* shūsatsu 集札
ticket examining *n* (*at wicket*)
kaisatsu 改札, (*aboard*) kensatsu 検札
ticket seller *n* kippú-uri 切符売り
ticket vending machine *n* kenbáiki
券売機
ticket wicket *n* kaisatsu-guchi 改札口
tickle *v* kusugurimásu (kusuguru,
kusugutte) くすぐります(くすぐる,
くすぐって)
ticklish *adj* kusugurttai くすぐったい;
(*dedicate*) kiwadói 際どい
tide *n* shió 潮; chōryū 潮流
tidy 1. *adj* kírei (na) きれい(な)
2. *tidies it up* *v* katazukemásu (katazukéru, katazúkete) 片付けます(片付
ける, 片付けて); *it gets* ~ katazuki-
másu (katazúku, katazúite) 片付きま
す(片付く, 片付いて)

tie 1. *v* musubimásu (musubu,
musunde) 結びます(結ぶ, 結んで);
(*fastens*) tsunagimásu (tsunagu, tsunaide)
つなぎます(つなぐ, つないで) **2.** *n*
(*necktie*) nékutai ネクタイ; (*game*)
hikiwake 引き分け
tie up (*binds*) shibarimásu (shibáru,
shibátte) 縛ります(縛る, 縛って)
tiff *n* mome-goto もめ事・揉め事
tiger *n* tora 虎・トラ; taigā タイガー
tight *adj* (*tight-fitting*) kitsui きつい;
(*hard*) katai 堅い; (*skimpy*) semái 狭い
→ **drunk**
tighten, tighten up on *v* shimemásu
(shiméru, shímete) 締めます(締める,
締めて)
tights *n* taitsu タイツ
tile 1. *n* (*roof*) kawara 瓦; *tile-roofed*
kawara-buki (no) 瓦ぶき・瓦葺き(の)
2. *n* (*floor, wall*) táiru タイル **3.** *v* *tiles
a roof* kawara de yáne o fukimásu
(fuku, fuite) 瓦で屋根をふき[葺き]ま
す(ふく, ふいて)
timber *n* zaimoku 材木
time 1. *n* tokí 時, … tókí …時, jikan
時間(o-jíkan お時間), jibun bun 時分;
(*specified*) jíkoku 時刻; (*season*) jíki
時期; (*opportunity*) jíki 時機, (*appropriate occasion*) jíki 時節; (*free*)
hima 暇, ma 間; (*taken up*) temá 手間
(o-téma お手間); (*interval, time while
…*) aida 間; *Do you have/know the
~?* Nán-ji ka wakarimásu ka. 何時か
分かりますか. **2.** *n* (*occasion*) tabí た
び・度, orí 折, sái 際, tokoró ところ;
(*period*) koro 頃; *at one* ~ kátsute か
って, kátte かって; *at the time of* … ni
sái-shite …に際して; *for the ~ being*
tōbun 当分, íma no tokoró wa 今の
ところは; *in* ~ yagate やがて; *is in
~* (*for* …) (… ni) ma ni aimásu (áu,
átte) (…に)間に合います(合う, 合っ
て); (*the trend of*) *the times* jisei 時勢
(go-jísei ご時世)
how many times *adv, n* nán-do 何度,
nán-kai 何回, nánben 何遍 (**1:** ip-pén
一遍, **2:** ni-hen 二遍, **3:** sánben 三遍);
~ *doubled* nanbai 何倍
in a short time *adv* mamonaku まもな
く, sugu (ni) すぐ(に)

in time *adv* (*eventually*) yagate やがて

on time *adv* jikandōri ni 時間通りに, teikoku ni 定刻に

this/next time *adv, n* kóndo 今度

what time *adv, n* nán-ji 何時

time and again *adv* nando mo (nando mo) 何度も(何度も), [BOOKISH] saisan saishi 再三再四

time deposit *n* teiki-yókin 定期預金

time difference, time-lag *n* jísa 時差

time killer *n* hima tsubushi (ni naru mono) 暇つぶし(になるもの), hima tsubushi (ni suru mono) 暇つぶし(にするもの)

time limit *n* taimu rimitto タイムリミット, seigen jikan 制限時間

time loan *n* teiki kashitsuke-kin 定期貸付金

time machine *n* taimu mashin タイムマシン

time management *n* jikan (no) kanri 時間(の)管理

time off *n* yasumí 休み

timepiece *n* tokei 時計

time schedule *n* jikoku-hyō 時刻表

timetable *n* jikoku-hyō 時刻表; (*school*) jikan-wari 時間割(り)

time travel *n* taimu toraberu タイムトラベル

timekeeper *n* (*person*) jikan kiroku-gakari 時間記録係

timely 1. *adj* taimurii (*na*) タイムリー(な) 2. *adj, adv* taimurii ni タイムリーに

timer *n* taimā タイマー

timid *adj* (*shy*) uchiki (na) 内気(な), (*cowardly*) okubyō (na) 臆病(な)

timid animal *n* okubyō na dōbutsu 臆病な動物

timid attitude *n* ozuozushita taido おずおずした態度

tin *n* buriki ブリキ, súzu スズ・錫

tin opener *n* kankiri 缶切り

tinhorn *n* hattari (ya) はったり(屋)

tinkle *n* chirin chirin (to iu oto) チリンチリン(という音)

tint *n* iroai 色合い

tiny *adj* totemo chiisana とても小さな, chippoke (na) ちっぽけ(な)

tiny tot *n* chibikko ちびっ子

tip 1. *n* (*money*) chíppu チップ, kokoro-zuke 心付け, chadai 茶代; (*point*) saki 先 2. *v it tips over* hikkuri-kaerimásu (hikkuri-káeru, hikkuri-káette) ひっくり返ります(ひっくり返る, ひっくり返って), *tips it over* hikkuri-kaeshimásu (hikkuri-káesu, hikkuri-káeshite) ひっくり返します(ひっくり返す, ひっくり返して)

tips *n* kotsu こつ・コツ, hiketsu 秘訣

tire *n* (*of wheel*) taiya タイヤ

tire chain *n* taiya chēn タイヤ・チェーン

tired; *gets ~* tsukaremásu (tsukaréru, tsukárete) 疲れます(疲れる, 疲れて), kutabiremásu (kutabiréru, kutabírete) くたびれます(くたびれる, くたびれて); *gets ~ of* ... ni akimásu (akíru, ákite) ...に飽きます(飽きる, 飽きて); *dead ~* ku (t) takúta く(っ)たくた; hetoheto へとへと

tireless *adj* tsukarenai 疲れない

tiresome *adj* akiakisaseru 飽き飽きさせる, taikutsu (na) 退屈な

tissue *n* tisshu-pē´pā ティッシュペーパー; hana-gami 鼻紙, chirigami ちり紙

Titan *n* Taitan タイタン

titanate *n* (*chemical*) chitan san'en チタン酸塩

title *n* (*of book , article, ...*) hyōdai 表題・標題, daimei 題名, midashi 見出し; (*job title*) katagaki 肩書; (*of anything, esp. movie, person, athlete*) táitoru タイトル; *title page* tobira 扉

end-title credit *n* kurejitto クレジット

end-title roll *n* endo rōru エンドロール

title catalogue *n* tosho mokuroku 図書目録

title match *n* taitoru matchi タイトルマッチ

to *prep* ... ni ...に, ... e ...へ

toad *n* hikigaeru ヒキガエル

toast 1. *n* tō´suto トースト; (*"bottoms up"*) kanpai 乾杯 2. *v* (*toasts it*) yaki-másu (yaku, yaite) 焼きます(焼く, 焼いて)

toaster *n* tō´sutā トースター

tobacco *n* tabako タバコ・煙草; ~ *shop* tabako-ya タバコ屋・煙草屋

today *n* kyō´ 今日; [BOOKISH] honjitsu 本日

toe *n* ashi no yubí 足の指; (*toe-tip*) tsumasaki つま先・爪先

Toei Line *n* (*bus*) Toei-basu 都営バス; (*subway*) Toei-chikatetsu 都営地下鉄; (*streetcar*) toden 都電

tofu *n* tōfu 豆腐

together *adv* issho ni いっしょ[一緒] に, tomo ni 共に

Togo *n* Tōgo トーゴ

toilet *n* tóire トイレ, tóirétto トイレット; keshō-shitsu 化粧室, teárai 手洗 (o-teárai お手洗), benjo 便所
 toilet paper *n* toiretto-pē´pā トイレットペーパー, kami 紙

token *n* (*sign, indication*) shirushi しるし・印・徴 (o-shirushi おしるし)

Tokyo *n* Tōkyō 東京; *Tokyo Station* Tōkyō´-Eki 東京駅; *the metropolis of Tokyo* Tōkyō´-to 東京都
 Tokyoite *n* Tōkyō´-jin 東京人; tomin 都民
 Tokyo Metro (Line) (*subway lines of Tokyo*) Tōkyō metoro 東京メトロ; Marunouchi-sen 丸の内線; Ginza-sen 銀座線; Hibiya-sen 日比谷線; Tōzai-sen 東西線; Chiyoda-sen 千代田線; Yūrakuchō-sen 有楽町線; Hanzōmon-sen 半蔵門線; Nanboku-sen 南北線; Fukutoshin-sen 副都心線
 Tokyo University *n* Tōkyō-Dáigaku 東京大学, Tō-dai 東大

told → **tell**

tolerate *v* gáman shimásu (suru, shite) 我慢します(する, して), taemásu (taeru, taete) 耐えます(耐える, 耐えて)

toll *n* tsūkō-ryō 通行料; (*telephone charge*) tsūwa-ryō 通話料
 toll-free *adj* tsūwa-ryō muryō (no) 通話料無料(の); furii daiyaru (no) フリーダイヤル(の)
 tollgate *n* ryōkin-jo 料金所

tomato *n* tomato トマト

tomb *n* (o-)haka (お)墓, boketsu 墓穴

tomboy *n* otenba おてんば・お転婆

tombstone *n* boseki 墓石, [BOOKISH] bohi 墓碑

tomcat *n* osu neko 雄猫・オスネコ

tomorrow *n* ashitá あした・明日, asú 明日; [BOOKISH] myō´nichi 明日
 tomorrow morning ashita no ása あした[明日]の朝; [BOOKISH] myōchō 明朝
 tomorrow night ashita no ban あした[明日]の晩; [BOOKISH] myō´ban 明晩

tone *n* (*sound*) neiro 音色, tōn トーン; (*coloring*) iro-ai 色合い; (*physical condition*) tai-chō 体調; (*voice*) kuchō 口調

tongs *n* (*for fire*) hí-bashi 火ばし[箸]; tongu トング

tongue *n* shitá 舌; *barbed/spiteful ~* doku-zetsu 毒舌
 ox tongue *n* gyūtan 牛タン

tonight *n* kónban 今晩; kón´ya 今夜
 tonight's guest *n* kónya no gesuto 今夜のゲスト

tonsil *n* hentō-sen 扁桃腺

too *adv* (*also*) ... mo ...も; (*overly*) anmari あんまり, amari あまり(に); ...-sugimásu (-sugíru, -súgite) ...すぎます(すぎる, すぎて)
 too bad zannen (na) 残念(な); (*in commiseration*) ikemasén (ikenai) いけません(いけない)
 too many ō-sugimásu (ō-sugíru, ō-súgite) 多すぎます(多すぎる, 多すぎて)
 is too much te ni amarimásu (amáru, amátte) 手に余ります(余る, 余って)

took → **take**

tool *n* dōgu 道具 (o-dōgu お道具), yō´gu 用具, utsuwa 器; tsūru ツール
 tool box *n* dōgu-bako 道具箱, yōgu-bako 用具箱

tooth *n* há 歯; *protruding (buck) ~* déppa 出っ歯
 toothache *n* ha-ita 歯痛; *has a ~* há ga itái 歯が痛い
 toothbrush *n* ha-búrashi 歯ブラシ
 toothpaste *n* neri-hamígaki 練り歯磨き; (*toothpowder*) hamígaki(-ko) 歯磨き(粉)
 toothpick *n* tsuma-yōji つまようじ・爪楊枝, yōji ようじ・楊枝

top 1. *n* ue 上; (*top side*) jōmen 上面, hyōmen 表面; (*highest part*) teppén てっぺん, (*summit*) chōjō´ 頂上 **2.** *n* *(toy)* kóma こま・独楽; ***top-spinning*** koma-máwashi こま[独楽]回し **3.** *adj (topmost, best)* saijō (no) 最上(の), saikō (no) 最高(の); toppu (no) トップ(の)

topaz *n* topāzu トパーズ

topcoat *n* ō´bā(kōto) オーバー(コート)

topflight *adj (elite)* ichiryū (no) 一流(の)

topic *n (of talk)* wadai 話題, topikku トピック; daimoku 題目, (hanashi no) táne (話の)種; *(problem)* mondai 問題

topmost *adj* saijō (no) 最上(の)

topping *n* toppingu トッピング

tops *adj (best)* saikō (no) 最高(の), saijō (no) 最上(の)

torch *n* táimatsu たいまつ・松明 → flashlight

tore, torn → tear

torment 1. *n (suffering)* nayamí 悩み; *(teasing)* ijime いじめ・苛め **2.** → tease

tornado *n* torunēdo トルネード, tatsumaki 竜巻

Toronto *n* Toronto トロント

torrential downpour *n* doshaburi 土砂降り; gō´u 豪雨

tortoise *n* káme 亀・カメ; **~ shell** bekkō べっこう・鼈甲

toss → throw

tot *n (tiny tot)* chibikko ちびっ子

total 1. *adj* zénbu (de/no) 全部(で/の); *(absolute)* zettai (no) 絶対(の) **2.** *n* zén(-) …全; tōtaru トータル, *(sum)* gōkei 合計, *(grand total)* sōkei 総計

totter *v* yoro-mekimásu (yoro-méku, yoro-méite) よろめきます(よろめく, よろめいて); ***tottering*** *adj* yóroyoro (to) よろよろと

touch *v* sawarimásu (sawaru, sawatte) 触ります(触る, 触って); … ni (téo) furemásu (fureru, furete) …に(手を)触れます(触れる, 触れて), …ni tsukimásu (tsukú, tsúite) …に付きます(付く, 付いて); atemásu (ateru, atete) 当てます(当てる, 当てて); *(comes in contact with)* ses-shimásu (se-suru, ses-shite) 接します(接する, 接して), sesshoku shimásu (suru, shite) 接触します(する, して); kandō sasemásu

(saseru, sasete) 感動させる(させる, させて); ***gets in ~ with*** … to renraku shimásu (suru, shite) …と連絡します(する, して), … to renraku o torimásu (toru, totte) …と連絡を取ります(取る, 取って); ***touches upon*** … ni furemásu (fureru, furete) …に触れます(触れる, 触れて), [BOOKISH] ni genkyū shimásu (suru, shite) …に言及します(する, して); ***out of ~ with*** … ni utói …に疎い

tough *adj* katai 固い・堅い → hard → strong

tough guy *n* tafu gai タフガイ

tour *n* ryokō (shimásu; suru, shite) 旅行(します; する, して); *(sight-seeing)* kankō 観光, tsúa ツアー; *(official, duty)* shutchō 出張

tourist *n* kankō´-kyaku 観光客; tsūrisuto ツーリスト

tourist lodge *n* minshuku 民宿

tournament *n* taikai 大会; shiai 試合; senshuken 選手権; tōnamento トーナメント

tow *v* hikimásu (hiku, hiite) 引[曳]きます(引[曳]く, 引[曳]いて)

toward *prep* … no hō´ e …の方へ; *(towards, confronting)* … ni tái-shite …に対して, … tái …対-

towel *n* te-nugui 手ぬぐい, táoru タオル, fukín 布きん・ふきん; **hand ~** (o-)tefukí (お)てふき, *(damp)* o-shíbori おしぼり

tower *n* tō´ 塔; tawā タワー

Tokyo Tower *n* Tōkyō tawā 東京タワー

town *n* machí 町, tokai 都会

town mayor *n* chō´chō 町長

tow truck *n* rékkā レッカー, rekkā´-sha レッカー車

toy *n* omócha おもちゃ・玩具

trace *n (clue)* tegákari 手掛かり, ate 当て; *(vestige)* konseki 痕跡, ato 跡

trace it back to sore o … ni sakano-borimásu (sakanobóru, sakanobótte) それを…にさかのぼり[遡り]ます(さかのぼる, さかのぼって)

tracing paper *n* torepe トレペ, torē-shingu-pē´pā トレーシングペーパー

track 1. *n (railtrack)* sénro 線路; *(for*

running) torakku トラック; (*remains*) ato 跡; ~ *number (six)* (roku)-bansen (六)番線; *what (number of)* ~ nanban-sen 何番線 2. *v* (*to go back and investigate*) ato o tsumemásu (tsukeru, tsurete) 跡を付けます(付ける、付けて)、(*to track an online the transaction of something*) suiseki shimásu (suru, shite) 追跡します(する、して)

tracking number *n* torakkingu nanbā トラッキングナンバー, tsuiseki bangō 追跡番号

tracks *n* ashi ato 足跡

tractable *adj* atsukaiyasui 扱いやすい

tractate *n* (*treatise*) ronbun 論文

tractile *adj* hikinobasukoto ga dekiru 引き伸ばすことができる

tractor *n* torakutā トラクター

trade 1. *n* (*international*) bōeki 貿易; (*business*) shō´bai 商売, (*commerce*) shō´gyō 商業; (*transaction*) tóri-hiki 取り引き 2. *v* tóri-hiki shimásu (suru, shite) 取り引きします(する、して); (*exchanges A for B*) A o B to kōkan shimásu (suru, shite) A を B と交換します(する、して)

trademark *n* shōhyō 商標; torēdo māku トレードマーク

trader *n* (*merchant*) shō´nin 商人; (*international*) bōékí-shō 貿易商; (*stock*) tōki-ka 投機家

tradition *n* dentō 伝統; (*legend*) den-setsu 伝説

traditional *adj* dentō-teki (na) 伝統的(な); (*accustomed*) imamade no 今までの, koremade no これまでの, [BOOKISH] jū´rai (no) 従来(の)

traditional agriculture *n* dentō nōgyō 伝統農業

traditional approach *n* jūrai no yarikata 従来のやり方

traditional arts *n* dentō geijutsu 伝統芸術

traditional event *n* dentō gyōji 伝統行事

traditional garment *n* dentō-teki na (i) fuku 伝統的な(衣)服

traditional lifestyle *n* dentō-teki na seikatsu yōshiki 伝統的な生活様式

traffic *n* kōtsū 交通; ōrai 往来

traffic accident *n* kōtsū jiko 交通事故

traffic circle *n* rō´tarii ロータリー

traffic jam *n* kōtsū-jū´tai 交通渋滞

traffic sign *n* (dōro) kōtsū hyō´shiki (道路)交通標識

traffic signal, traffic light *n* shingō-ki 信号機

tragedy *n* hígeki 悲劇

tragic *adj* hígeki-teki (na) 悲劇的(な); hísan (na) 悲惨(な); aénai あえない・敢えない; *tragically enough* aénaku mo あえなくも・敢えなくも

trailer *n* (*movie*) yokoku-hen 予告編、(eiga no) torērā (映画の)トレーラー

train 1. *n* densha 電車; ressha 列車; (*nonelectric/steam*) kishá 汽車; (*train numbers*) ...-gō´sha ...号車 2. *v* (*drills*) kúnren shimásu (suru, shite) 訓練します(する、して), (*practices*) renshū shimásu (suru, shite) 練習します(する、して); (*brings up children, disciplines*) shitsukemásu (shitsukéru, shitsúkete) しつけ[躾け]ます(しつける、しつけて)

bullet train *n* shinkansen 新幹線

local train *n* kakueki (densha) 各駅(電車)

night train *n* yakō ressha 夜行列車

rapid train *n* kaisoku (densha) 快速(電車)

train going downtown *n* kudari (densha) 下り(電車)

train going uptown *n* nobori (densha) 上り(電車)

train wreck *n* ressha-jíko 列車事故

trainee *n* kenshū-in 研修員, minarai 見習い

trainee doctor *n* kenshū-i 研修医

trainee teacher *n* kyōiku jisshū-sei 教育実習生

trainer *n* torēnā トレーナー

training *n* kúnren 訓練; (*practice*) renshū 練習; (*imparting discipline*) shitsuke しつけ・躾; (*in ascetic practices*) shugyō 修行

training course *n* kenshū kōsu 研修コース

training manual *n* kunren-yō manyuaru 訓練用マニュアル

training period n kenshū kikan 研修
期間

tram n rōmen densha 路面電車

trampoline n toranporin トランポリン

trance n toransu jōtai トランス状態;
in a trance muchū (no/de) 夢中 (の/
で)

tranquil adj nódoka (na) のどか・長
閑 (な)

transacting n (*dealing with*) shóri 処理

transaction n tori-atsukai 取扱い;
(*business*) torí-hiki 取り引き

transfer 1. v (*trains, etc.*) nori-kaemásu
(nori-káeru, nori-káete) 乗り換えます
(乗り換える, 乗り換えて); (*job*) tennin
(shimásu; suru, shite) 転任 (します, し
て), ten-jimásu (ten-jiru, ten-jite)
転じます(転じる, 転じて); (*transfers
it*) utsushimásu (utsúsu, utsúshite) 移し
ます(移す, 移して); furi-kaemásu
(furi-kaeru, furi-kaete) 振替えます(振
替える, 振替えて) 2. n idō 移動, nori-
kae 乗り換え

transformer n (*electric*) hen'átsu-ki
変圧器

transformer station n hendensho
変電所

transforming factor n (*biology*)
keishitsu tenkan inshi 形質転換因子

transmigrant n imin 移民, ijūsha
移住者

transmigration n 1. ijū 移住 2. (*metem-
psychosis*) rin'ne 輪廻. tensei 転生

transmigration of souls n rin'ne 輪廻

transmission n sōshin 送信, dentatsu
伝達, denpa 伝播

transit n tsukō 通行

transitive verb n tadō´shi 他動詞

transitory adj hakanái はかない

translate v yakushimásu (yakúsú,
yakúshite) 訳します(訳す, 訳して),
hon'yaku shimásu (suru, shite) 翻訳し
ます(する, して); (*Japanese into
English*) wayaku shimasu (suru, shite)
和訳します(する, して)

translate freely v iyaku shimásu (suru,
shite) 意訳します(する, して),

translate literally v chokuyaku
shimásu (suru, shite) 直訳します(す
る, して)

translation n hon'yaku 翻訳, yakú 訳

automatic translation n jidō hon'yaku
自動翻訳

English-Japanese translation n
einichi hon'yaku 英日翻訳, eibun
wayaku 英文和訳

Japanese-English translation n
nichiei hon'yaku 日英翻訳, wabun
eiyaku 和文英訳

machine translation n kikai hon'yaku
機械翻訳

translator n hon'yáku-sha 翻訳者, yakú-
sha 訳者

transmit v tsutaemásu (tsutaeru, tsutaete) 伝えます(伝える, 伝えて), tsūji-
másu (tsū-jiru, tsū-jite) 通じます(通じ
る, 通じて)

transmitted; *gets ~* tsutawarimásu
(tsutawaru, tsutawatte) 伝わります(伝
わる, 伝わって)

transom window (*opening*) ranma
欄間・らんま

transparent adj tōmei (na) 透明 (な)

transport(ation) n unsō 運送, unpan
運搬, yusō 輸送; (*traffic*) kōtsū 交通

trap 1. n wána わな・罠 2. v (*traps it*)
wána ni kakemásu (kakéru, kákete) わ
な[罠]にかけます(かける, かけて);
(*gets trapped*) wána ni kakarimásu
(kakáru, kakátte) わな[罠]にかかりま
す(かかる, かかって)

trash n (*scrap, junk*) kuzu くず・屑,
gomi ごみ

trash box n gomi-bako ごみ箱

travel n ryokō (shimásu; suru, shite)
旅行(します; する, して)

travel agency n ryokō dairiten 旅行
代理店

travel vendor n ryokō-gaisha 旅行
会社

traveler n ryokō´sha 旅行者, ryok(y)
aku 旅客, tsūrisuto ツーリスト

traveler's check n ryokōsha-yō
kogítte 旅行者用小切手; toraberāzu
chekku トラベラーズチェック

tray n (o-)bon (お)盆, torei トレイ,
(*dining tray, low meal table*) (o-)zen
(お)膳 (gó-zen ご膳) → ash tray

treachery n (*acts of treachery*) ura-giri
裏切り, haishin-kōi 背信行為

treasure *n* takará 宝 (o-takara お宝), takara-mono 宝物, [BOOKISH] zaihō 財宝

national treasure *n* kokuhō 国宝

treasure box *n* takará-bako 宝箱, tamate-bako 玉手箱

treasure hunt *n* takara sagashi 宝さがし

treasure island *n* takara-jima 宝島

treat 1. *n* gochisō (shimásu; suru, shite) ごちそう［ご馳走］（します; する、して） **2.** *v* (*pays the bill*) ogorimásu (ogoru, ogotte) おごります（おごる、おごって）; (*medically*) chiryō shimásu (suru, shite) 治療します（する、して） → **handle**

treatise *n* ronbun 論文, rón 論

treatment *n* téate 手当 (o-téate お手当); (*handling*) toriatsukai 取り扱い; (*reception*) taigū 待遇; (*medical*) chiryō 治療, ryōhō 療法

drug treatment *n* yakubutsu ryōhō 薬物療法

treaty *n* jōyaku 条約

tree *n* kí 木 (**1:** íp-pon 一本, **2:** ní-hon 二本, **3:** sánbon 三本; *how many* nánbon 何本); **trees** kígi 木々

tree-ears *n* (*an edible fungus*) kikúrage キクラゲ・木耳

trefoil leaves *n* mitsuba 三つ葉・ミツバ

tremble *v* furuemásu (furueru, furuete) 震えます（震える、震えて）, yuremásu (yureru, yurete) 揺れます（揺れる、揺れて）

tremor *n* yure 揺れ

trench coat *n* torenchi kōto トレンチコート

trend *n* (*tendency*) keikō 傾向, (*inclination*) katamuki 傾き, chōshi 調子; (*current*) chōryū 潮流; (*movement*) ugokí 動き; (*fashion*) ryūkō 流行; torendo トレンド

trendy *adj* torendii (na) トレンディ（な）, ryūkō (no) 流行（の）

trespass (*on*) *v* fumi-komimásu (fumi-kómu, fumi-kónde) 踏み込みます（踏み込む、踏み込んで）

trespassing; *No Trespassing.* "Tachiiri kinshi." 「立ち入り禁止。」

trial *n* (*legal*) sáiban 裁判; (*test*) shikén 試験, (*trying*) tameshí 試し, kokoromi 試み, toraiaru トライアル

trial version *n* taiken-ban 体験版; toraiaru-ban トライアル版

triangle *n* **1.** sánkaku 三角, sankaku-kei, sankakkei 三角形 **2.** (*instrument*) toraianguru トライアングル

love triangle *n* sankaku kankei 三角関係

tribe; *the tribe* (*group, gang*) *of …* …-zoku …族

trick *n* **1.** (*feat*) waza 業, géi 芸, torikku トリック, *one's favorite ~* ohako おはこ・十八番; (*move*) té 手; (*knack*) kotsú こつ・コツ, téguchi 手口; (*plot, scheme*) keiryaku 計略, hakarigoto 謀・はかりごと; *~ to it* (*the secret of it*) táne 種 **2.** → **cheat**

Trick or Treat. *interj* Okashi o kurenakya itazura suruzo. お菓子をくれなきゃ悪戯するぞ. , Okashi o kurenaito itazura suruyo. お菓子をくれないと悪戯するよ.

tricky *adj* zurúi ずるい, torikkii トリッキー, bimyō (na) 微妙（な）, (*difficult*) muzukashii 難しい

tricky politician *n* kōkatsu na seijika 狡猾な政治家

tricky question *n* kōmyō na shitsumon 巧妙な質問

tricycle *n* sanrín-sha 三輪車

trifling *adj* sásai (na) ささい［些細］（な）

trigger *n* hikigane 引き金, kikkake きっかけ

trigger finger *n* hitosashiyubi 人差し指

trigger-happy *adj* kōsen-teki (na) 好戦的（な）, (*critic*) arasagashi no sukina あら捜しの好きな

triggerman *n* koroshiya 殺し屋

trill *n* toriru トリル

trip *n* ryokō 旅行; *business trip* shutchō 出張

triple *n* sanbai 三倍; *adj* sanbai (no) 三倍（の）; toripuru トリプル

triple time *n* sanbyōshi 三拍子

trite *adj* heibon (na) 平凡（な）

trivial *adj* tsumaránai つまらない; chótto shita ちょっとした; sásai (na) ささい［些細］（な） → **unimportant**

trolley *n* torokko トロッコ
trombone *n* toronbōn トロンボーン
troops *n* (*army*) gúntai 軍隊, gún 軍; (*detachment*) bútai 部隊
trophy *n* torofii トロフィー
tropic(s) *n* nettai(-chíhō´) 熱帯(地方)
tropical *adj* nettai (no) 熱帯(の); toropikaru (na) トロピカル(な)
tropical fish *n* nettai-gyo 熱帯魚
tropical flora *n* nettai shokubutsu 熱帯植物
tropical fruits *n* toropikaru furūtsu トロピカルフルーツ
tropical island *n* nettai no shima 熱帯の島
tropical rainforest *n* nettai urin 熱帯雨林; ~ *climate* nettai urin kikō 熱帯雨林気候
tropical region *n* nettai chihō 熱帯地方
trouble *n* (*inconvenience*) tékazu 手数, tesū´ 手数 (o-tesū お手数); (*time taken up*) temá 手間 (o-téma お手間); (*nuisance*) (go-)méiwaku (ご)迷惑, (go-)mendō´ (ご)面倒, toraburu トラブル, (job) sewá 世話 (o-séwa お世話, o-sewa-sama お世話様); (*bother*) (go-)yákkai (ご)やっかい・厄介; (*difficulty*) kónnan 困難, komáru kotó 困ること; (*ailment*) wazurai 煩い, byōki 病気 → **worry**
goes to much trouble honé o orimásu (óru, ótte) 骨を折ります(折る, 折って)
is troubled by (*an ailment*), has trouble with … o wazuraimásu (wazuráu, wazuratte) …を煩います(煩う, 煩って)
troublemaker *n* toraburu mēkā トラブルメーカー; momegoto o okosu hito 揉め事を起こす人; gotagota o okosu hito ごたごたを起こす人
troublesome *adj* yaya(k)koshii ややこしい; méiwaku (na) 迷惑(な); yákkai (na) やっかい・厄介(な); mendō (na) 面倒(な); wazurawashii 煩わしい; hanzatsu (na) 煩雑(な)
trough shell *n* aoyagi あおやぎ・アオヤギ・青柳
trousers *n* zubón ズボン

trout *n* másu マス・鱒
truck *n* torákku トラック; (*3-wheeled*) ōto-sánrin オート三輪
truck driver *n* torákku (no) untenshu トラック(の)運転手
true *adj* honto/hontō (no) ほんと(う)/本当(の); *how* ~ naru-hodo なるほど・成る程
truly *adv* honto (hontō) ni ほんと(ほんとう)に・本当に, makoto ni 誠に, jitsúni 実に
trumpet *n* toranpétto トランペット, rappa ラッパ
trumpet-shell *n* hóra ほら・法螺, horá-gai ほら貝・法螺貝
trunk *n* (*of tree*) miki 幹; (*of elephant*) hana 鼻; (*baggage*; *car trunk*) toránku トランク
trunks *n* (*sports*) tanpan 短パン; (*swim*) suiei-pantsu 水泳パンツ; (*underwear*) torankusu トランクス, pantsu パンツ
trust 1. *n* tánomi 頼み, irai 依頼; shin'yō 信用, shinrai 信頼, ate 当て; anshin 安心 **2.** *v* (*trusts them*) shin'yō shimásu (suru, shite) 信用します(する, して), shin-jimásu (shin-jiru, shin-jite) 信じます(信じる, 信じて); *gives in* ~ azukemásu (azukéru, azúkete) 預けます(預ける, 預けて); *takes in* ~ azukarimásu (azukáru, azu-kátte) 預かります(預かる, 預かって)
truth *n* shinjitsu 真実, honto/hontō no kotó ほんと/ほんとう[本当]の事
try *v* **1.** (*attempt*) tameshimásu (tamésu, taméshite) 試します(試す, 試して); [BOOKISH] kokoromimásu (kokoromíru, kokorómite) 試みます(試みる, 試みて) **2.** (*doing*) (shi)-te mimásu (míru, míte) (し)てみます(みる, みて) **3.** (*to do*) (shi)-yō/(ya)-rō toshimásu (suru, shite) (し)よう/(や)ろうとします(する, して)
try hard(er) ganbarimásu (ganbáru, ganbátte) がんばり[頑張り]ます(がんばる, がんばって); dóryoku shimásu (suru, shite) 努力します(する, して)
trying *adj* (*hard to bear*) tsurai つらい・辛い
T-shirt *n* tii shatsu Tシャツ

Tsukuba n Tsukúba つくば・筑波;
Tsukuba University Tsukuba Dáigaku
筑波大学

tsunami n tsunami 津波

tub n óke 桶; (*basin*) tarai たらい;
(*bathtub*) yúbune 湯船; (*rice tub*)
o-hachi お鉢, o-hitsu おひつ・お櫃,
meshi-bitsu 飯びつ・飯櫃

tuba n chūba チューバ

tube n kúda 管, kán 管; (*flexible,
squeezable, inflatable*) chū´bu チューブ;
test ~ shikenkan 試験管; *TV ~*
buraunkan ブラウン管

tuberculosis n kekkaku (haikékkaku)
結核 (肺結核), haibyō 肺病; = *TB*

Tuesday n Kayō´bi 火曜日; *Tuesday-
Thursday* Kā-Moku 火木

tug; *tug at* hipparimásu (hippáru, hippátte) 引っ張ります (引っ張る, 引っ
張って)

tugboat n hiki-fune 引き船・曳き船;
tagu-bōto タグボート

tulip n chūrippu チューリップ

tumble v korogarimásu (korogaru,
korogatte) 転がります (転がる, 転が
って); taoremásu (taoréru, taórete) 倒
れます (倒れる, 倒れて), korobimásu
(korobu, koronde) 転びます (転ぶ,
転んで)

tummy n onaka おなか; (*baby talk*)
ponpon ポンポン

tumult n só´dō 騒動

tuna n maguro マグロ・鮪; (*fatty*) tóro
トロ, (*pink, medium-fat*) chū-toro 中ト
ロ, (*red, unfatty*) aka-mi 赤身; (*canned
tunafish*) tsúna ツナ; *tunafish sandwich* tsuna-sándo ツナサンド
fresh slices of raw tuna n maguro no
sashimi マグロ [鮪] の刺身

tundra n tsundora ツンドラ

tune n kyoku 曲; chōshi 調子; tōn
トーン, fushí 節

tuner 1. (*person*) chōritsu-shi 調律師
2. (*tool*) chūnā チューナー

tunnel n tonneru トンネル

turban shell, turbo n sázae サザエ・
栄螺; *turbo cooked in its shell* tsubo-
yaki つぼ焼き

turbot n karei カレイ・鰈

turf n shiba 芝, shibafu 芝生

turkey n shichimen-chō 七面鳥

Turkey n Tóruko トルコ

turn 1. n (*order*) junban 順番; (*spin*)
kaiten 回転; (*corner*) magarikado 曲
がり角 **2.** v (*changes directions*)
magarimásu (magaru, magatte) 曲がり
ます (曲がる, 曲がって); (*goes round*)
mawarimásu (mawaru, mawatte)
回ります (回る, 回って) **3.** v (*makes
it go round*) mawashimásu (mawasu,
mawashite) 回します (回す, 回して);
(*directs one's face/eyes/attention to*)
… ni mukemásu (mukeru, mukete) …
に向けます (向ける, 向けて)

turn aside (*diverts*) sorashimásu
(sorásu, soráshite) 逸らし [そらし] ま
す (逸らす, 逸らして)

turn back hiki-kaeshimásu (hiki-
káesu, hiki-káeshite) 引き返します (引
き返す, 引き返して)

turn inside out ura-gáeshimásu (ura-
gáesu, ura-gáeshite) 裏返します (裏返
す, 裏返して)

turn into 1. (*becomes*) ([NOUN] ni に,
[ADJECTIVE]-ku く) narimásu (náru, nátte)
なります (なる, なって) **2.** (*makes it
into*) ([NOUN] ni に, [ADJECTIVE]-ku く)
shimásu (suru, shite) します (する, して)

turn left/right sasetsu/usetsu shimásu
(suru, shite) 左折/右折します (する,
して)

turn loose nigashimásu (nigásu, nigáshite) 逃がします (逃がす, 逃がして)

turn off (*light, radio, etc.*) … o
keshimásu (kesu, keshite); を消します
(消す, 消して); *~ the ignition* suítchi
o kirimásu (kíru, kítté) スイッチを切
ります (切る, 切って)

turn on (*light, etc.*) … o tsukemásu
(tsukéru, tsukéte) …を付けます (付け
る, 付けて); *~ the ignition* suítchi o
iremásu (ireru, irete) スイッチを入れ
ます (入れる, 入れて)

turn over ura-gaeshimasu (ura-gaesu,
ura-gaeshite) 裏返します (裏返す, 裏
返して)

turn up (*it gets found*) mitsukari-másu
(mitsukaru, mitsukatte) 見付かります
(見付かる, 見付かって); *~ one's nose
at …* o hana de ashiraimásu (ashiráu,

ashirátte) ...を鼻であしらいます(あしらう、あしらって)

turning point n kawarime 変わり目, tenki 転機

turnip n kabu カブ・蕪, kabura カブラ・蕪

turtle n káme 亀・カメ; (snapping) suppon すっぽん・スッポン

turtleneck n tātoru nekku タートルネック

tusk n kiba 牙・キバ

tutelary deity n (guardian spirit) ujigami 氏神

tutor n kateikyō'shi 家庭教師, chūtā チューター

tutoring school n júku 塾

tuxedo n takishiido タキシード

TV n térebi テレビ

tweed n tsuiido ツイード

tweet 1. v (Internet) (tsuittā de) tsubuyaku (ツイッターで)つぶやく **2.** (bird) saezurimásu (saezuru, saezutte) さえずります(さえずる、さえずって) **3.** (bird) (kotori no) saezuri (小鳥の)さえずり

tweezers n pinsétto ピンセット

twelve n jū-ní 十二・12

twentieth adj nijū-banmé (no) 二十番目(の); **the ~ day** hatsukamé 二十日目, (of the month) hatsuka 二十日・20日

twenty n ní-jū 二十・20, futá-jū 二十; (20 years old) hátachi 二十歳・20歳, níjús-sai 二十歳・20歳

twenty thousand n ni-mán 二万・20,000, futa-mán 二万・20,000

twice adv (two times) ni-dó 二度, ni-kái 二回; (double) ni-bai 二倍

twilight n yūgata 夕方; tasogare たそがれ・黄昏

twin(-bed) room n tsúin ツイン, tsuinrū'mu ツインルーム

twin beds n tsuin-béddo ツインベッド

twine 1. n → string **2.** v (twists) yorimásu (yóru, yótte) より[縒り]ます(よる、よって)

twinkle 1. n kirameki きらめき・煌き **2.** v kirameki másu (kirameku, kirameite) きらめき[煌き]ます(きらめく、きらめいて), kagayakimásu (kagaya-

ku, kagayaite) 輝きます(輝く、輝いて)

twins n fútago 双子・ふたご

twist v nejirimásu (nejiru, nejítte) ねじります[捻り]ます(ねじる、ねじって), hinerimásu (hinéru, hinétte) ひねり[捻り]ます(ひねる、ひねって), yorimásu (yóru, yótte) よります(よる、よって); **gets twisted** (entangled) kojiremásu (kojiréru, kojírete) こじれ[拗れ]ます(こじれる、こじれて)

Twitter n (internet) tsuittā ツイッター

two n ní 二・2, futatsú 二つ・2つ; futa-... 二..., ni-... 二...; (people) futarí 二人, [BOOKISH] ní-mei 二名

two; 2 pieces (small things) ní-ko 二個, 2 trees (or long things) ní-hon 二本; 2 sheets (flat things) ní-mai 二枚; 2 fish/bugs/cats (or small animals) ní-hiki 二匹; 2 cows (or large aminals) ní-tō 二頭; 2 birds/rabbits ní-wa 二羽; 2 cars (or machines/vehicles) ní-dai 二台; 2 copies (books/magazines) ní-satsu 二冊; 2 people futa-rí ふたり・二人, ní-mei 二名; 2 floors/stories ni-kai 二階; 2 fold ni-bai 二倍; 2 degrees ní-do 二度; 2 times ni-dó 二度, ni-kái 二回, ni-hén 二遍; 2 o'clock ní-ji 二時; 2 hours ní-jíkan 二時間; 2 days futsuka 二日; 2 weeks ni-shūkan 二週間; 2 months ni-ká-getsu 二ヶ月; 2 years ní-nen 二年, ninén-kan 二年間; 2 years old futatsú 二つ, ní-sai 二歳

two hundred n ní-hyaku 二百・200, futá-hyaku 二百・200

two-piece woman's suit n tsū-píisu ツーピース

two thousand n ni-sén 二千・2,000, futa-sén 二千・2,000

two-way socket n futamata-sokétto 二又ソケット

two-way traffic n ryōmen-kōtsū 両面交通

two-year college (education) n tanki-dáigaku 短期大学, tan-dai 短大

type n táipu タイプ, (sort) shúrui 種類; (model) katá 型, ...-gata ...型; (print) katsuji 活字

different type n betsu no taipu 別のタイプ; chigau taipu 違うタイプ, [BOOKISH] kotonaru shurui 異なる種類

type (*write*) *n* táipu (shimásu; suru, shite) タイプ（します；する，して）
typewriter *n* taipuráitā タイプライター、táipu タイプ; (*how many* nán-dai 何台)
typhoon *n* taifū´ 台風
typhus *n* chifusu チフス

typical *adj* tenkei-teki (na) 典型的（な）, daihyō-teki (na) 代表的（な）; (*usual*) futsū (no) 普通（の）
typist *n* taipisuto タイピスト
tyrant *n* bōkun 暴君

U

Ueno *n* Ueno 上野; *Ueno Park* Ueno-Kō´en 上野公園; *Ueno Station* Uenó-Eki 上野駅
ugly *adj* (*look*) minikúi 醜い; mazúi まずい; *~ woman* búsu ぶす・ブス
uh *interj* ē-to ええと; *uh ... anō* あの う...; *uh-huh* n ん; *uh-uh, huh-uh* nn んん
UK *n* igirisu イギリス, eikoku 英国
ulcer *n* (*gastric*) i-káiyō 胃潰瘍・胃かいよう
ultimate 1. *n* kyūkyoku 究極 **2.** *adj* kyūkyoku no 究極の
ultimately *adv* saishū-teki ni 最終的に, kekkyoku 結局
ultimatum *n* saigo tsūchō 最後通牒, saishū tsūkoku 最終通告
ultrasound *n* **1.** chōonpa 超音波 **2.** (*ultrasound diagnosis*) chōonpa shindan 超音波診断
ultraviolet *n* shigaisen 紫外線, *adj* shigaisen (no) 紫外線の
umbrella *n* kása かさ・傘, amagása 雨傘; (*parasol*) hi-gása 日傘; (*oilpaper*) ban-gasa 番傘, kara-kása 唐傘; (*western-style*) kō´mori (-gása) こうもり・コウモリ（傘）, yō-gása 洋傘
umpire *n* shinpan(-in) 審判（員）
UN → United Nations
un- *prefix* fu- 不
unacceptable *adj* mitomerarenai 認められない
unaccountable *adj* setsumei dekinai 説明できない
unanimous *adj* manjō itchi (no/de) 満場一致（の/で）, zen'in itchi (no/de) 全員一致（の/で）
unanticipated *adj* omowánu ... 思わぬ

unapproachable *adj* chikayorigatai 近寄りがたい, chika-zukinikui 近づきにくい
unarmed *adj* hibusō (no) 非武装（の）
unassuming *adj* kidoranai 気取らない
unavoidable *adj* yamu-o-énai やむを得ない
unbalanced *adj* fuantei (na) 不安定（な）, katayotta (mono) 偏っている, baransu no warui バランスの悪い
unbeatable *adj* muteki (no) 無敵（の）
unbelievable *adj* shinjirarenai 信じられない
unbiased *adj* katayori no nai 偏りのない, sennyū-kan no nai 先入観のない
unbusy *adj* isogashikunai 忙しくない, hima (na) 暇（な）
unbutton *v ...* no botan o hazushimásu (hazusu, hazushite) ...のボタンを外します（外す，外して）; *comes unbuttoned* akimásu (aku, aite) 空きます（空く，空いて）, ... no botan ga hazuremásu (hazureru, hazurete) ...のボタンが外れます（外れる，外れて）
uncalled-for *adj* yokei (na) 余計（な）
uncanny *adj* sugói すごい・凄い; fushigi 不思議・ふしぎ
uncertain *adj* futei (no) 不定（の）; ayashii 怪しい・あやしい
unchaste *adj* futei (na) 不貞（な）
uncle *n* oji(-san) おじ[叔父, 伯父]（さん）
unclean *adj* fuketsu (na) 不潔（な）
uncomfortable *adj* kimochi ga warúi 気持ちが悪い; (*not feel at home*) igokochi ga warui 居心地が悪い; (*to wear*) kigokochi ga warui 着心地が悪い; (*constrained*) kyūkutsu (na) 窮屈（な）
uncommon *adj* mezurashíi 珍しい

unconcerned *adj* **1.** → calm **2.** ~ **with** ... ni mu-kánshin (na) ...に無関心(な)

unconditional *adj* mu-jṓ́ken (no) 無条件(の)

unconditionally *adv* mu-jṓken de 無条件で

unconnected *adj* ... to mukánkei (no) ...と無関係(の)

unconscious *adj* íshiki fumei (no) 意識不明(の); (*involuntary*) mu-íshiki (no/na) 無意識(の/な)

uncooked *adj* náma (no) 生(の)

uncork *v* (... no sén o) nukimásu (nuku, nuite) (...の栓を)抜きます(抜く, 抜いて); (... no kuchi o) akemásu (akeru, akete) (...の口を)空けます(空ける, 空けて)

uncover *v* bakuro shimásu (suru, shite) 曝露します(する, します)

uncultivated *adj* kyōyō no nai 教養のない; mukyōyō (no) 無教養(の); (*wild*) soya (na) 粗野(な)

undecided *adj* (*indefinite*) fútei (no) 不定(の)

under *prep, adv* ... no shitá (de/ni/no) ...の下(で/に/の); (*the tutelage of*) ... no motó (de) ...の下(で); ~ (*doing*) ...-chū (no) ...中(の)

undercut *v* **1.** (*cuts under*) shita o kirimásu (kiru, kitte) 下を切ります(切る, 切って) **2.** (*offers at a lower price*) yasune de urimásu (uru, utte) 安値で売ります(売る, 売って) **3.** (*golf*) andā katto shimásu (suru, shite) アンダーカットします(する, して)

underdog *n* makeinu 負け犬

underdone *adj* nama-yake (no) 生焼け(の)

underestimate *v* (*kids oneself about*) amaku mimásu (míru, míte) 甘く見ます(見る, 見て), (*person*) mikubirimásu (mikubiru, mikubitte) みくびります(みくびる, みくびって), kashōhyōka shimásu (suru, shite) 過小評価します(する, して)

undergo *v* (*experiences*) keiken shimásu (suru, shite) 経験します(する, して); ... mé ni aimásu (áu, átte) ...目に会います(会う, 会って)

undergraduate (*student*) *n* daigáku-sei 大学生

underground 1. *adj* chiká (no) 地下(の) **2.** → subway

underline *n, v* kasen (o hikimásu; hiku, hiite) 下線(を引きます; 引く, 引いて)

underneath 1. *n* shita 下 **2.** *prep, adv* shita ni 下に

underpants *n* zubon-shita ズボン下, pantsu パンツ

undershirt *n* shátsu シャツ

understand *v* (... ga) wakarimásu (wakáru, wakátte) (...が)分かります(分かる, 分かって); (... o) rikai shimásu (suru, shite) (...を)理解します(する, して)

understanding *n* rikai 理解, (*ability*) rikái-ryoku 理解力 → agreement

understood: *is ~* tsū-jimásu (tsū-jiru, tsū-jite) 通じます(通じる, 通じて)

undertake *v* (*plan, attempt, scheme*) kuwadatemásu (kuwadatéru, kuwadátete) 企てます(企てる, 企てて)

undertaker *n* (*funeral director*) sōgi-ya 葬儀屋

undertaking *n* shigoto 仕事; (*enterprise*) jígyō 事業, kuwada te 企て

undertone *n* kogoe 小声

undervalue *n* kashōhyōka shimásu (suru, shite) 過小評価します(する, して)

underwater 1. *adj* suichū (no) 水中(の) **2.** *adv* suichū de 水中で

underwear *n* shita-gi 下着, hadagí 肌着; (*underpants*) shitabaki 下穿き, pántsu パンツ, (*women's drawers*) zurṓsu ズロース, (*panties*) pántii パンティー

underworld *n* **1.** (*another world*) anoyo あの世 **2.** (*gang land*) ankoku-gai 暗黒街

undeserving *adj* (*Also; What a waste!*) mottai-nái もったいない

undisturbed *adj* sono mamá (de/no) そのまま(で/の)

undo *v* hazushimásu (hazusu, hazushite) 外します(外す, 外して); moto ni modoshimásu (modosu, modoshite) 元に戻します(戻す, 戻して); (*unties*) hodokimásu (hodóku, hodóite) ほどきます (ほどく、ほどいて), tokimásu (tóku, tóite) 解きます (解く、解いて)

undone; *comes* ~ tokemásu (tokéru, tókete) 解けてます (解ける、解けて); *leaves it undone* shinái de okimásu (oku, oite) しないでおきます (おく、おいて)

undoubtedly *adv* utagai náku 疑いなく, táshika ni 確かに, kitto きっと

undress *v* **1.** (*takes off one's clothes*) fuku o nugimásu (nugu, nuide) 服を脱ぎます (脱ぐ、脱いで) **2.** (*takes off someone's clothes*) fuku o nugasemásu (nugaseru, nugasete) 服を脱がせます (脱がせる、脱がせて)

unduly *adv* yatara ni やたらに

uneasiness *n* shinpai 心配

uneasy *adj* shinpai (na) 心配 (な), fuan (na) 不安 (な)

unemployed; ~ *person* shitsugyō-sha 失業者; ~ *samurai* rōnin 浪人

unemployment *n* shitsugyō 失業

uneven *adj* dekoboko (no) でこぼこ・凸凹 (の)

unexpected *adj* igai (na) 意外 (な), omoigakénai 思いがけない; (*sudden*) niwaka (no) にわか (の); (*but welcome*) mezurashíi 珍しい

unexpectedly *adv* igai ni 意外に, futo ふと, (*suddenly*) níwaka ni にわかに

unfair *adj* fu-kōhei, fu-kōhei (na) 不公平 (な); (*unjustified*) futō (na) 不当 (な); fea dewanai フェアではない

unfaithful *adj* (*to her husband*) futei (na) 不貞 (な)

unfasten *v* hazushimásu (hazusu, hazushite) 外します (外す、外して)

unfavorable *adj* fúri (na) 不利 (な); (*unlikable*) konomashikunái 好ましくない

unfazed (*by …*) **1.** *v* (…-témo) dō-ji-masén (dō-jinai, dō-jináide) (…ても) 動じません (動じない、動じないで) **2.** *adj* heiki (na) 平気 (な)

unfeeling *adj* hakujō (na) 薄情 (な)

unfixed *adj* futei (no) 不定 (の)

unfortunate *adj* (*unlucky*) fukō´ (na) 不幸 (な), fu-un (na) 不運 (な); (*regrettable, inopportune*) ainiku (na)

あいにく (な) → **pitiful**

unfortunately *adv* ainiku あいにく, zannen nagara/desuga 残念ながら/ですが, [BOOKISH] ikan nagara 遺憾ながら

unfriendly *adj* fushinsetsu (na) 不親切 (な), buaisō (na) 無愛想 (な), sokkenai そっけない

ungrateful *adj* on shirazu (na/no) 恩知らず (な/の), kansha shinai 感謝しない

unhandy *adj* fúben (na) 不便 (な)

unhappy *adj* (*unlucky*) fukó´ (na) 不幸 (な), (*gloomy*) inki (na) 陰気 (な), (*moody*) kigen ga warúi 機嫌が悪い, (*dissatisfied*) fuman (na) 不満 (な)

unhealthy *adj* **1.** fu-kenkō (na) 不健康 (な) **2.** (*bad for one's health*) karada ni warúi 体に悪い **3.** (*sickly*) byōki-gachi (na) 病気がち (な)

unhulled rice *n* momí もみ・籾

unification *n* tōitsu 統一

uniform 1. *n* seifuku 制服, yunifōmu ユニフォーム; (*military*) gunpuku 軍服; (*school*) gakuséi-fuku 学生服 **2.** *adj* (*the same*) byōdō (na) 平等 (な), taitō (no) 対等 (の) **3.** *v* (*equal*) soroemásu (soroéru, soroete) そろえます・揃えます (そろえる・揃えて)

unify *v* tōitsu shimásu (suru, shite) 統一します (する、して)

unimportant *adj* (*matter*) mondai ni naránai 問題にならない

unintentionally *adv* tsúi つい, ukkari うっかり, mu-ishiki ni 無意識に, itosezu ni 意図せずに

union *n* (*labor*) kumiai 組合, rōdōkúmiai 労働組合; (*alliance*) rengō 連合, renmei 連盟; (*joint*) kyōdō 共同, (*merger*) gappei 合併, gōdō 合同

unique *adj* yúitsu (no) 唯一 (の); yuniiku (na) ユニーク (な)

unit *n* tán'i 単位; (*military*) bútai 部隊

unite *v* (*they merge*) gappei/gōdō shimásu (suru, shite) 合併/合同します (する、して); (*combines dual functions as*) … o kanemásu (kanéru, kánete) …を兼ねます (兼ねる、兼ねて); (*partner*) kumimásu (kúmu, kúnde) 組みます (組む、組んで)

United Nations *n* Kokusai-Réngo 国際連合

United States *n* Amerika(-Gasshū´-koku) アメリカ(合衆国)

universe *n* úchū 宇宙; yunibāsu ユニバース

university *n* daigaku 大学; *at university* zaigaku(-chū) 在学(中)

unjustified *adj* fŭtō 不当(な)

unkind *adj* fu-shínsetsu (na) 不親切 (な) → **mean**

unknown *adj* fumei (no) 不明(の); shiranai 知らない

unless *conj* (shi)-nákereba (し)なければ, (shi)-nai to (し)ないと

unlikely *adj* ari-sō´mo nái ありそうもない; (shi)-sō mo nái (し)そうもない

unload *v* oroshimásu (orósu, oróshite) 降ろします(降ろす, 降ろして)

unlock *v* … no kagí o akemásu (akeru, akete) …の鍵を開けます(開ける, 開けて)

unlocked; comes ~ … (no kagí ga) akimásu (aku, aite) …(の鍵が)開きます(開く, 開いて)

unluckily *adv* ún-waruku 運悪く

unlucky *adj* ún ga warúi 運が悪い; (*fails to strike it lucky*) tsúite imasén (inai, inákute) ついていません(いない, いなくて)

unmarried *adj* hitori-mónó 独り者, dokushin 独身

unnatural *adj* fu-shízen (na) 不自然(な)

unnecessary, unneeded *adj* iranai いらない, muyō (na) 無用(な), fuyō (na) 不要(な); (*superfluous*) yokei (na) 余計(な)

unoccupied *adj* (*free of business*) hima (na) 暇(な)

unofficial *adj* hi-kō´shiki (no) 非公式(の)

unpack *v* nimotsu o hodokimásu (hodoku, hodoite) 荷物をほどきます(ほどく, ほどいて)

unperturbed *adj* heiki (na) 平気(な)

unpleasant *adj* iyá (na) 嫌(な); fuyúkai (na) 不愉快(な)

unpolished rice *n* génmai 玄米

unprofitable *adj* wari ga warúi 割が悪い, wari ni awanai 割に合わない

unqualified *adj* mushikaku (no) 無資格(の); (*unlimited*) mujōken (no) 無条件(の)

unreasonable *adj* múri (na) 無理(な); múcha (na) むちゃ[無茶](な); hidói ひどい

unrelated (*to …*) *adj* (… tó wa) mukánkei (no) (…とは)無関係(の)

unreliable *adj* ayashii 怪しい, deta-rame (na) でたらめ(な)

unreserved *adj* (*frank; rude*) buénryo (na) 無遠慮(な)

unreserved seat(s) *n* jiyū´-seki 自由席

unrest *n* sō´dō 騒動; fuan 不安; shinpai 心配

unsafe *adj* (*troubled*) bussō´ (na) 物騒(な)

unsavory rumors *n* tokaku no uwasa とかくのうわさ[噂]

unscrupulous *adj* akuratsu (na) 悪らつ(な)・悪辣(な)

unseemly, unsightly *adj* migurushíi 見苦しい

unsentimental *adj* dorai (na) ドライ(な)

unskillful *adj* hetá (na) へた[下手](な), mazúi まずい

unsociable *adj* bu-áisō (na) 無愛想(な)

unsophisticated *adj* sekenshirazu (na) 世間知らず(な); mújaki (na) 無邪気(な), soboku (na) 素朴(な)

unsuitable *adj* kakkō ga warúi かっこう・格好[恰好]が悪い

untangle *v* motsure o tokimásu (tóku, tóite) もつれを解きます(解く, 解いて), kaiketsu shimásu (suru, shite) 解決します(する, して)

untasty *adj* mazúi まずい

untidy *adj* kitanái 汚い; chirakatte(i)ru 散らかって(いる)

untie *v* tokimásu (tóku, tóite) 解きます(解く, 解いて), hodokimásu (hodóku, hodóite) ほどきます(ほどく, ほどいて)

until *prep* … máde …まで・迄; **~ now** ima-made 今まで[迄]

untouched *adj* sono mamá (de/no) そのまま(で/の)

unusual *adj* (*abnormal*) ijō (na) 異常(な); (*extreme*) hijō (na) 非常(な),

(*novel*) kawatta 変わった, mezurashí 珍しい

unusually *adv* mezuráshiku 珍しく; (*extremely*) hijō ni 非常に

unwell; *feeling ~* kimochi ga warúi 気持ちが悪い

unwilling (*to do*) *adj* (shi)-taku arimasén (nái, nákute) (し)たくありません(ない, なくて)

unzipped *adj comes ~* (chákku ga) akimásu (aku, aite) (チャックが)空きます(空く, 空いて); *to unzip a file* (*computer*) fairu o kaitō shimásu (suru, shite) ファイルを解凍します(する, して)

up *prep* (... no) úe e (...の)上へ; *up* (*higher by*) ¥100 hyakuén-daka 百円高 bring up *v* (*trains*) shitsukemásu (shitsukéru, shitsúkete) しつけ[躾け]ます(しつける, しつけて), (*rears*) sodatemásu (sodatéru, sodátete) 育てます(育てる, 育てて) get up *v* okimásu (okíru, ókite) 起きます(起きる, 起きて); (*gets one up*) okoshimásu (okósu, okóshite) 起こします(起こす, 起こして) go up *v* agarimásu (agaru, agatte) 上がります(上がる, 上がって), noborimásu (noboru, nobotte) 上り[昇り]ます(上[昇]る, 上[昇]って) make up for *v* oginaimásu (ogináu, oginátte) 補います(補う, 補って) up to now jū'rai 従来, ima-máde 今まで[迄] up-to-date *adj* (*modern*) géndai (no) 現代(の); (*latest*) saishin (no) 最新(の)

upbringing *n* shitsuke しつけ・躾; sodachí 育ち

update **1.** *n* kōshin 更新; saishin (-ban) 最新(版) **2.** *v* kōshin shimásu (suru, shite) 更新します(する, して), saishin (-ban) ni shimásu (suru, shite) 最新(版)にします(する, して), appudēto shimásu (suru, shite) アップデートします(する, して)

upfront money *n* atama-kin 頭金

upkeep *n* íji 維持; (*expense*) ijí-hi 維持費; (*care, repair*) te-iré 手入れ

upload *v* (*computer*) appurōdo shimásu (suru, shite) アップロードします(する, して)

upon → **on**

upper *adj* ue (no) 上(の)

upping the (*base*) **pay** bēsu-áppu ベースアップ, béa ベア

upright *adj* katai 堅い → **honest**

upright piano *n* appuraito piano アップライトピアノ

uprising *n* bōdō 暴動, hanran 反乱

upset **1.** *v* (*it overturns*) hikkuri-kaerimásu (hikkuri-káeru, hikkuri-káette) ひっくり返ります(ひっくり返る, ひっくり返って), (*overturns it*) hikkuri-kaeshimásu (hikkuri-káesu, hikkuri-káeshite) ひっくり返します(ひっくり返す, ひっくり返して) → **spill** **2.** *v* (*disturbs*) midashimásu (midásu, midáshite) 乱します(乱す, 乱して); (*is disturbed*) midaremásu (midaréru, midárete) 乱れます(乱れる, 乱れて), (*gets nervous*) dōyō shimásu (suru, shite) 動揺します(する, して); *has an ~ stomach* (o-naka no) guai ga warúi (おなかの)具合が悪い **3.** *n* (*stomach upset*) imotare 胃もたれ, muneyake 胸焼け

upsetting *adj* dōyō saseru 動揺させる

upshot *n* shímatsu しまつ・始末

upside *n* **1.** jōbu 上部, ue-no-hō 上のほう **2.** riten 利点

upside down *adv* sakasa(ma) (ni) 逆さ(ま)(に), abekobe (ni) あべこべ(に)

upstairs *adv* ni-kai 二階, o-níkai (de/ni, e, no) お二階(で/に, へ, の)

uptown (*Tokyo*) *n* yama-te 山手, yama-no-te 山の手

up until *adv* (...) ízen (...)以前

upwards of (...) íjō (...)以上

urban *adj* toshi (no) 都市(の); shínai (no) 市内(の)

urbanite *n* tokái-jin 都会人

urge *v* (*bustles up*) sekitatemásu (sekitateru, sekitatete) せき立て[急き立て]ます(せき立てる, せき立てて); susumemásu (susumeru, susumete) 勧めます(勧める, 勧めて); (*persuades*) unagashimásu (unagasu, unagáshite) 促します(促す, 促して)

urgency *n* shikyū 至急, kinkyū 緊急

urgent *adj* kyū (na) 急(な), kinkyū (na) 緊急(な), shikyu (no) 至急(の)

urgent business *n* kyūyō 急用

urgently *adv* kyū´ ni 急に, shikyū (ni) 至急(に)

urinal *n* (*place*) shōben-jo 小便所; (*thing*) shōben-ki 小便器, (*bedpan*) shibin しびん・し瓶

urinate *v* shōbén shimásu, shonben shimásu (suru, shite) 小便します(する, して), (*medical*) hainyō shimásu (suru, shite) 排尿します(する, して)

urine *n* shōbén, shonben 小便, (*medical*) nyō 尿, [BABY TALK] (o-)shikko (お)しっこ

urn *n* tsubo つぼ・壷

us *pron* watáshi-táchi わたしたち[私達], watakúshí-tachi [私達]; ware-ware われわれ・我々

U.S. *n* Amerika アメリカ, Beikoku 米国; Bei-... 米..., ...-Bei ...米

usable *adj* shiyō dekiru 使用できる, shiyō kanō (na) 使用可能(な), riyō dekiru 利用できる, riyō kanō (na) 利用可能(な)

usage *n* shiyō 使用, kanyō 慣用

use 1. *n* (*the use*) shiyō 使用; (*utilization*) riyō 利用; (*putting to use*) ōyō 応用 **2.** *n* (*for the use of*) ...-yō ...用 **3.** *n* (*service*) (go-)yō (ご)用, yakú 役 (o-yaku お役) **4.** *v* tsukaimásu (tsukau, tsukatte) 使います(使う, 使って), mochiimásu (mochiiru, mochiite) 用います(用いる, 用いて); (*makes use of*) riyō shimásu (suru, shite) 利用します(する, して)

used *adj* (*secondhand*) chūko (no) 中古(の), furúi 古い
used to (do) (shi)-ta monó/món desu (し)たもの/もんです; *gets ~* ... ni naremásu (naréru, nárete) ...に慣れます(慣れる, 慣れて)

useful *adj* yaku ni tatsu 役に立つ; yakudatsu 役立つ, yūyō (na) 有用 (な), chō´hō (na) 重宝(な); *is ~* yakú ni tachimásu (tátsu, tátte) 役に立ちます(役立つ, 役立って), yaku-dachimásu (yaku-dátsu, yaku-dátte) 役立ちます(役立つ, 役立って); chō´hō

shimásu (suru, shite) 重宝します (する, して)

useless *adj* **1.** (*wasteful*) muda (na) 無駄(な) **2.** (*of no use, unworthy*) muyō (no) 無用(の) **3.** (*unworthy of no value*) fuyō (no) 不用(の)

user *n* shiyō´-sha 使用者; riyō´-sha 利用者; (*computer*) yūza ユーザ, yūzā ユーザー

usher 1. *n* toritsugi 取り次ぎ; (*greeter*) annai-gákari 案内係, annai-nin 案内人 **2.** *v* (*ushers one*) annái shimásu (suru, shite) 案内します(する, して)

usual *adj* futsū (no) 普通(の), ítsumo (no) いつも(の), heijō (no) 平常(の), fúdan (no) 普段(の), tsūjō (no) 通常(の), tsúne (no) 常(の); *as usual* ítsumo no yō´ni いつものよう[様]に, aikawarazu 相変らず

usually *adv* (*normally*) futsū (wa) 普通(は), tsūjō (wa) 通常(は), (*mostly*) taitei (wa) たいてい・大抵(は), (*daily*) fúdan (wa) 普段(は), higoro (wa) 日頃(は), (*always*) ítsumo (wa) いつも(は)

utensil *n* utsuwa 器; ...-yōhin ...用品

utilities (*bills*) *n* kōkyō-ryō´kin 公共料金

utility *n* jitsuyō 実用

utilization *n* riyō 利用

utilize *v* riyō shimásu (suru, shite) 利用します(する, して)

utmost; *to the utmost* ákú-made (mo) あくまで(も); *does one's utmost* saizen o tsukushimásu (tsukúsu, tsu-kúshite) 最善を尽くします(尽くす, 尽くして)

utter → **speak, say;** *utter a curse* noroimásu (noróu, norótte) 呪います (呪う, 呪って)

utterly *adv* mattaku 全く, sukkári すっかり, zenzen 全然; *utterly exhausted* ku(t)takuta く(っ)たくた

U-turn *n* yūtā´n ユーターン・Uター ン; *makes a ~* yūtā´n shimásu (suru, shite) ユーターン・[Uターン]します (する, して)

V

vacant *adj* **1.** (*open*) aite imás̱u (iru, ite) 空いています(いる、いて) **2.** (*hollow*) utsuro (na) うつろ・虚ろ (な) **3.** ... aki-... 空き...; ~ *car* (*available taxi*) kū̱sha 空車; ~ *house* aki-ya 空き家; ~ *lot* aki-chi 空き地; ~ *room(s)* aki-ma 空き間, ~ *room/office* aki-shi̱tsu 空き室

vacate *v* akemás̱u (akeru, akete) 空けます(空ける、空けて)

vacation *n* yasumí 休み, kyūka 休暇, bakēshon バケーション

vacationer *n* gyōraku kyaku 行楽客

vaccination *n* wakuchin sesshu ワクチン接種, yobō sesshu 予防接種

vaccine *n* wakuchin ワクチン

vacuum *v* sōjiki o kakemás̱u (kakeru, kakete) 掃除機をかけます(かける、かけて)

vacuum bottle *n* mahō´bin 魔法瓶

vacuum cleaner *n* (denki) sōjíki (電気)掃除機

vagabond, vagrant *n* hōrōsha 放浪者; buraikan 無頼漢

vagina *n* chitsu 膣

vague *adj* aimai (na) あいまい(な)・曖昧(な); ii-kagen (na) いい加減(な)

vaguely *adv* aimai ni あいまいに・曖昧に; (*somehow*) dō´mo どうも

vain (*conceited*) *adj* unubore ga tsuyói うぬぼれが強い; in vain *adj, adv* munashii 空しい・虚しい・むなしい; muda (na/ni) 無駄(な/に)

Valentine's Day *n* barentain dē バレンタインデー

valiant *adj* yūkan (na) 勇敢(な)

valid *adj* yūkō (na) 有効(な)

valley *n* tani(-ma) 谷(間)

valuable *adj* taisetsu (na) 大切(な), kichō (na) 貴重(な) → **expensive**

valuables *n* kichō-hin 貴重品

value **1.** *n* káchi 価値, neuchi 値打ち **2.** *v* values (*cherishes*) *it* chōhō shir̠nás̱u (suru, shi̠te) 重宝します(する、して), chōhō-garimás̱u (chōhō-gáru, chōhō-gátte) 重宝がります(重宝がる、重宝がって)

valued *adj* chō´hō (na) 重宝(な) → **valuable**

valve *n* bén 弁

van *n* (*car*) raito ban ライトバン

vanilla *n* bánira バニラ

vanish *v* (*from sight*) miénaku narimás̱u (náru, nátte) 見えなくなります(なる、なって); (*from existence*) náku narimás̱u (náru, nátte) なくなります(なる、なって); (*gets extinguished*) kiemás̱u (kieru, kiete) 消えます(消える、消えて)

vanity *n* kyoei-shin 虚栄心, unubore うぬぼれ

vapor *n* kitai 気体 → **steam**

various *adj* iroiro (na/no) いろいろ [色々](な/の), ironna いろんな, samazama (na) 様々(な); ~ *places* tokorodókoro 所々

varnish *n* nísu ニス = wánisu (o nurimás̱u; nuru, nutte) ワニス(を塗ります; 塗る、塗って); nuri 塗り

vase *n* bin 瓶; (*for flowers*) kabin 花瓶, káki 花器

vast *adj* bakudai (na) 莫大(な)

vaudeville *adj* (*theater*) yose 寄席; engei(-jō) 演芸場

vegetable *n* yasai 野菜(o-yásai お野菜); (*greens*) aó-mono 青物, náppa 菜っ葉, ná 菜

vegetarian *n* bejitarian ベジタリアン; saishoku shugi-sha 菜食主義者; ~ *cuisine* shōjin-ryō´ri 精進料理

vehicle *n* nori-mono 乗り物, kuruma 車(o-kúruma お車), ...-sha ...車; (*how many*) nán-dai 何台)

vein *n* (*vena*) jōmyaku 静脈

veil *n* bēru ベール

velocity *n* sokudo 速度, hayasa 速さ, supiido スピード

velvet *n* birōdo ビロード, berubetto ベルベット

vending machine *n* hanbai-ki 販売機; *ticket* ~ kenbái-ki 券売機

vendor *n* uriko 売り子 → **seller, dealer**

venereal disease *n* seibyō 性病
Venezuela *n* benezuera ベネズエラ
vengeance *n* fukushū 復讐
ventilation *n* kanki 換気; **~ system**
kanki-sō´chi 換気装置
venture *n* bōken 冒険; tōkiteki jigyō
投機的事業; tōki 投機; (*speculation,
wild guess*) yamá やま・山
Venus *n* (*planet*) kinsei 金星
veranda *n* beranda ベランダ; engawa
縁側
verb *n* dōshi 動詞
verbal *adj* (*spoken*) kōtō (no) 口頭(の)
verbally *adv* kōtō (de) 口頭(で)
verification *n* shōmei 証明; kenshō
検証
verify *v* shōmei shimásu (suru, shite)
証明します(する, して)
vermifuge *n* mushi-kúdashi 虫下し
vermilion *n* shu(iro) 朱(色)
vernal equinox *n* shunbun 春分;
Vernal Equinox Day Shunbun no hí
春分の日
versatility *n* yūzū 融通; *is versatile*
yūzū ga kikimásu (kiku, kiite) 融通が
ききます(きく, きいて)
verse *n* shi 詩; (*17-syllable*) haiku 俳
句, hokku 発句; (*31-syllable*) wáka 和
歌, tánka 短歌; (*longer*) chō´ka 長歌
versus *prep* tai–… 対…
vertex *n* chōjō 頂上, chōten 頂点
vertical *adj* táte (no) 縦(の), suichoku
(no) 垂直(の)
vertically *adv* táte ni 縦に, suichoku
ni 垂直に
vertigo *n* memai めまい・眩い・目眩
very *adv* zúibun ずいぶん・随分, taihen
たいへん・大変, totemo とても, hijō
ni 非常に, táisō たいそう・大層, góku
ごく(極), amari (ni) あまり(に); *the ~ +* [NOUN] *=
the* [NOUN] *itself* … sono-monó…
そのもの
    at very beginning/first saisho (no/ni)
最初(の/に)
    very well (*satisfactory*) yoroshii よろ
しい; (*OK*) yóshi 良し
vest *n* chokki チョッキ; besuto ベスト
vestige *n* konseki 痕跡
vet *n* jū-i 獣医

veteran **1.** *n* taieki gunjin 退役軍人;
2. *adj* (*experienced*) beteran (no) ベテ
ラン(の)
veto **1.** *n* kyóhi 拒否 **2.** *v* (*rejects it*)
kyóhi shimásu (suru, shite) 拒否しま
す(する, して)
vexatious *adj* haradatashíi 腹立たしい
via … *prep* kéiyu (de); … o
tō´tte …を通って, … o héte …を経て
vibrate *v* shindō shimásu (suru, shite)
振動します(する, して)
vibration *n* shindō 振動; (*cell-phone,
etc.*) baiburēshon バイブレーション,
baibu バイブ
vibrato *n* (*music*) biburāto ビブラート
vice *n* warúi shūkan 悪い習慣, akushū
悪習
vice admiral *n* chū´jō 中将
vice-president *n* (*of company*) fuku-
sháchō 副社長; (*of nation*) fuku-
daitō´ryō 副大統領
vice versa *adv* hantai ni 反対に, gyaku
ni 逆に, gyaku mo onaji 逆も同じ,
gyaku mo dōyō 逆も同様
vicinity *n* fukín 付近, kínjo 近所,
chikáku 近く, … hen …辺
vicious *adj* warúi 悪い, hidói ひどい
victim *n* (*of sacrifice*) giséi-sha 犠牲者,
(*of injury*) higái-sha 被害者; *falls ~ to*
… no gisei ni narimásu (náru, nátte)
…犠牲になります(なる, なって)
victor *n* shōrí-sha 勝利者, yūshō-sha
優勝者
victory *n* shōri 勝利, yūshō 優勝; *wins
the ~* yūshō shimásu (suru, shite) 優勝
します(する, して)
video *n* *videotape* bidéotēpu ビデオ
テープ; **~ recorder** bideo ビデオ;
~ camera bidéo kamera ビデオカメラ
vie → compete
view **1.** *n* (*scenery*) nagamé 眺め; *in
view of* … ni teráshite …に照らして,
… o kángáete …を考えて **2.** *v* (*gazes
at*) nagamemásu (nagaméru, nagámete)
眺めます(眺める, 眺めて) **3.** →
**opinion → outlook → look →
standpoint**
viewpoint *n* kénchi 見地, mi-kátá
見方, tachi-ba 立場
vigilance *n* keikai 警戒

vigor *n* génki 元気, katsuryoku 活力

vigorous *adj* sakan (na) 盛ん（な）; sekkyoku-teki (na) 積極的（な）→ **energetic** → **healthy** → **strong**

villa *n* bessō′ 別荘

village *n* murá 村; ...-son ...村; sato 里

villain *n* warumono 悪者; akutō′ 悪党

vine *n* **1.** tsurú つる・蔓 **2.** (*grape tree*) budō no ki ブドウ[葡萄]の木

vinegar *n* sú 酢, o-su お酢

vineyard *n* budō-en 葡萄園・葡萄園

vintage 1. *n* bintēji ビンテージ **2.** *adj* gokujō (no) 極上（の）

vinyl *n* biníiru ビニール, bíniru ビニル

violate *v* (*breaks the law*) okashimásu (okasu, okashíte) 犯します（犯す, 犯して）; yaburimásu (yabúru, yabútte) 破ります（破る, 破って）; ... ni ihan shimásu (suru, shite) ...に違反します（する, して）, ... ni somukimásu (sumúku, somúite) ...に背きます（背く, 背いて）

violation *n* ihan 違反

violence *n* (*brute force*) bōryoku 暴力; domestic violence *n* katei-nai bōryoku 家庭内暴力, domesutikku baiorensu ドメスティック・バイオレンス

violent *adj* (*severe*) hageshíi 激しい・はげしい; (*unruly*) ranbō (na) 乱暴（な）; múri (na) 無理（な）

violet *n* sumire スミレ・菫

violin *n* baiorin バイオリン

virgin *n* (*female*) shójo 処女, bājin バージン, ki-músume 生娘; (*male*) dōtei 童貞

Virgo *n* (*star sign*) Otome-za 乙女座・おとめ座

virtue *n* bitoku 美徳, toku 徳

virus *n* bíirusu ビールス, uirusu ウイルス

visa *n* bíza ビザ, [BOOKISH] sashō 査証

visible *adj* (mé ni) mieru （目に）見える

vision *n* **1.** (*eyesight*) shíryoku 視力 **2.** (*dream*) kūsō 空想 **3.** (*foresight*) bijon ビジョン

visit 1. *v* hōmon shimásu (suru, shite) 訪問します（する, して）; tazunemásu (tazunéru, tazúnete) 訪ねます（訪ねる, 訪ねて）; [HUMBLE] ukagaimásu (ukagau, ukagatte) 伺います（伺う, 伺って）, mairimásu (máiru, máitte) 参ります（参る, 参って）**2.** *n* hōmon 訪問, (o-)asobi （お）遊び, (o-)ukagai （お）伺い; (*of solicitude*) (o-)mimai （お）見舞い; (*interview*) menkai 面会

visiting card *n* meishi 名刺

visitor *n* o-kyaku （お）客, o-kyaku-san/sámá お客さん/様; raikyaku 来客; (*solicitous*) mimái-kyaku 見舞い客; (*for interview*) menkai-nin 面会人

vitamin(s) *n* bitamin ビタミン; (*pills*) bitamin-zai ビタミン剤

vivid *adj* senmei (na) 鮮明（な）; azayaka (na) 鮮やか（な）; ikiiki to shita 生き生きとした

vividly *adv* senmei (ni) 鮮明（に）; azayaka (ni) 鮮やか（に）; ikiiki to 生き生きと

vixen *n* kuchi urusai onna 口うるさい女

vocabulary *n* kotobá 言葉, gói 語彙, tango 単語

vocal *adj* koe no 声の, ónsei (no) 音声（の）

vocalist *n* vōkaru ヴォーカル, bōkaru ボーカル, (*classical music*) seigaku-ka 声楽家

vocation *n* shokúgyō 職業

vocational *adj* shokugyō (no) 職業（の）, shokugyō-jō (no) 職業上（の）; vocational sickness *n* shokugyō-byō 職業病

vogue *n* ryūkō 流行

voice *n* kóe 声

voice mail *n* boisu mēru ボイスメール

voice-over *n* boisu ōbā ボイスオーバー, narētā no koe ナレーターの声

voiceprint *n* seimon 声紋

voice training *n* hassei renshū 発声練習, boisu torēningu ボイストレーニング

void → **invalid**

volcanic ash *n* kazánbai 火山灰

volcano *n* kázan 火山, borukēno ボルケーノ

volley *n* issei shageki 一斉射撃

volleyball *n* barēbō′ru バレーボール

volt *n* boruto ボルト

voltage *n* den′átsú 電圧; high-voltage cable *n* kōatsu-sen 高圧線

high-voltage current *n* kōatsu denryū
高圧電流

voltage converter *n* hen'átsú-ki
変圧機

volume *n* (*book*) hón 本, ...-bon ...本;
(*of a set*) (dái ...-) kan (第...)巻;
(*quantity*) ryō´ 裏

voluntarism *n* borantia seishin ボラン
ティア精神

voluntary *adj* mizukara 自ら;
(*optional*) zuii (no) 随意(の)

volunteer *n* borantia ボランティア

vomit 1. *n* hédo ヘど・反吐, (*medical*)
ōto 嘔吐, **2.** *v* modoshimásu (modósu,
modóshite) 戻す, 戻して)
3. *v* (hédo o) hakimásu (háku, háite)
(へどを)吐きます(吐く, 吐いて)

vote 1. *n* tōhyō 投票 **2.** *v* tōhyō shimásu

(suru, shite) 投票します

voter *n* tōhyō-sha 投票者, yūken-sha
有権者

vow → pledge

vowel *n* boin 母音, boon 母音

voyage *n* kōkai 航海; *makes a voyage*
kōkai shimásu (suru, shite) 航海します
(する, して)

Voyager *n* boijā ボイジャー

V-shaped *adj* bui-ji gata (no) V字形
(の), kusabi gata (no) くさび形(の)

V sign *n* bui sain Vサイン

vulgar *adj* gehín (na) 下品(な); iyashii
卑しい; (*mundane*) zoku (na) 俗(な)

vulgarities *n* gehín 下品; zoku 俗;
soya 粗野

vulture *n* kondoru コンドル; hage-
washi ハゲワシ; hagetaka ハゲタカ

W

wad *n* (chiisana) katamari (小さな)か
たまり

wadding *n* tsumemono 詰め物

waddle *v* yotayota/yochiyochi
arukimásu (aruku, aruite) よたよた/よ
ちよち歩きます(歩く, 歩いて)

wade *v* arúite ikimásu (iku, itte) 歩い
て行きます(行く, 行って), (*across*),
arúite watarimásu (wataru, watatte)
歩いて渡ります(渡る, 渡って)

wadge *n* (*lump, mass*) katamari 固まり

wafer *n* (*sweet*) uehāsu ウエハース

waffle *n* (*sweet*) waffuru ワッフル

wag *v* yuremásu (yureru, yurete) 揺れ
ます(揺れる, 揺れて), yureugokimásu
(yureugoku, yureugoíte) 揺れ動きます
(揺れ動く, 揺れ動いて), (*tail*) furimásu
(furu, fútte) 振ります(振る, 振って)

wage *n* chíngin 賃金, (*salary*) kyūryō
給料 → **salary**

waggish *adj* odoketa おどけた, hyōkin
(na) ひょうきん(な), itazura (na/no)
いたずら・悪戯(な/の)

Wagner *n* Wagunā ワグナー

wagon *n* **1.** ni basha 荷馬車 **2.** (*station
wagon*) sutēshon wagon ステーション
ワゴン; wagon-sha ワゴン車

wagtail *n* sekirei セキレイ

Wahabi, Wahhabi *n* Wahhābu-ha no
shinto ワッハーブ派の信徒

Waikiki *n* Waikiki ワイキキ

Wain *n* Hokuto shichisei 北斗七星

waist *n* koshi 腰 (= **loins**), uésuto
ウエスト; (*specifically*) koshi no
kubire 腰のくびれ, kubire くびれ

waist band *n* uesuto bando ウエスト
バンド, beruto ベルト

waistcoat *n* besuto ベスト, chokki
チョッキ

waist line *n* koshi no rain 腰のライン,
uesuto rain ウエストライン

waist pocket *n* waki poketto 脇ポケット

waiter *n* uéˆtā ウエーター; ueitā ウエ
イター; bˆoi(-san) ボーイ(さん) →
wait person

wait; *v* **~ for**... o machimásu (mátsu,
mátte) ...を待ちます(待つ, 待って)
Please wait a moment. *interj* Shōshō
omachikudasai. 少々お待ちください.
[INFORMAL] Chotto mattekudasai. ちょ
っと待ってください.
Please wait for a little while longer.
interj Mō shōshō omachikudasai. もう
少々お待ちください. [INFORMAL] Mō
chotto mattekudasai. もうちょっと待
ってください.

Please wait to be seated. *interj* (*restaurant*) Kakarinomono ga (o-seki ni) go-an'nai suru made omachikudasai. 係りの者が(お席に)ご案内するまでお待ちください.

waiting *n* taiki 待機

waiting for a long time *adj* machidō-shíi 待ち遠しい

waiting line *n* machi gyōretsu 待ち行列

waiting list *n* kyanseru machi risuto キャンセル待ちリスト, weitingu risuto ウェイティング・リスト

waiting room *n* machiái-shitsu 待合室

waiting time *n* machi jikan 待ち時間

wait person *n* kyū'ji 給仕; sekkyaku-gakari 接客係; kakari (no mono) 係(の者)

waitress *n* úē'toresu ウェートレス; ueitoresu ウエイトレス → **wait person**

wake up *v* méga samemásu (saméru, sámete) 目が覚めます(覚める, 覚めて), (*rises*) okimásu (okíru, ókite) 起きます(起きる, 起きて); (*wakes a person up*) ... o okoshimásu (okósu, okóshite) ...を起こします(起こす, 起こして)

Please wake me up. *interj* Okoshite kudasai. 起こしてください.

wake-up call *n* mōningu kōru モーニングコール

Wales *n* wēruzu ウェールズ, uēruzu ウエールズ

walk 1. *v* arukimásu (arúku, arúite) 歩きます(歩く, 歩いて), arúite iki-másu (iku, itte) 歩いて行きます(行く, 行って) **2.** *v* (*strolls*) sanpo (shimásu; suru, shite) 散歩(します; する, して); *goes for a* ~ sanpo ni ikimásu (iku, itte) 散歩に行きます(行く, 行って) **3.** *n* (*way*) hodō 歩道 **4.** *n* (*walking*) hokō 歩行

walkaway *n* rakushō 楽勝

walking *n* hokō 歩行, wōkingu ウォーキング

fire walking *n* hiwatari 火渡り

race walking *n* kyōho 競歩

walking shoes *n* wōkingu shūzu ウォーキングシューズ

walking stick *n* (*cane*) sutékki ステッキ, tsúe 杖

Walkman *n* Wōkuman ウォークマン

walkway *n* hodō 歩道

wall *n* (*of house*) kabe 壁; (*around courtyard, etc.*) hei 塀

wallet *n* saifu 財布・さいふ, gamaguchi がま口, (*billfold*) satsu-ire 札入れ

wallpaper *n* kabegami 壁紙

Wall Street *n* Wōru sutoriito ウォールストリート; Wōru-gai ウォール街

walnut *n* kurumi クルミ・胡桃

waltz *n* warutsu ワルツ

wander *v* (*walks around*) arukima-warimásu (arukimawaru, arukimawatte) 歩き回ります(歩き回る, 歩き回って), (*hangs round*) buratsukimásu (bura-tsuku, buratsuite) ぶらつきます(ぶらつく, ぶらついて), buraburashimásu (buraburasuru, buraburashite) ぶらぶらします(ぶらぶらする, ぶらぶらして), samayoimásu (samayou, sama-yótte) さまよい[彷徨い]ます(さまよう, さまよって)

want *v* **1.** ... ga irimásu (iru, itte) ...が要ります(要る, 要って), (*desires something*) hoshigarimásu (hoshigáru, hoshigátte) 欲しがります(欲しがる, 欲しがって); ... ga hoshíi desu ...が欲しいです; (*looks for, seeks to buy*) motomemásu (motoméru, motómete) 求めます(求める, 求めて) **2.** *wants to do* (*it*) (...ga) shi-tái desu (shi-tai, shi-tákute) (...が)したいです(したい, したくて), (... o) shi-tagarimásu (shi-tagaru, shi-tagátte) (...を)したがります(したがる, したがって); *wants to have* (*it*) *done* (*by...*) (...ni) ... o shite morai-tái desu (morai-tai, morai-tákute) (...に)...をしてもらいたいです(もらいたい, もらいたくて) **3.** → **need, poverty**

does as one wants *v* katte ni shimásu (suru, shite) 勝手にします(する, して)

wanted criminal *n* shimei-tehai(nin) 指名手配(人); *photograph of* ~ shi-mei-tehai sháshin 指名手配写真

war *n* sensō 戦争, rán 乱; *after/since the* ~ sengo (no) 戦後(の); (*after*) *the end of the* ~ shūsen(-go) 終戦(後);

before the ~ senzen (no) 戦前(の)；
during the ~ senji-chū 戦時中
a great war taisen 大戦；*world war*
sekai-táisen 世界大戦；*World War II*
Dái ní-ji Sekai-Táisen 第二次世界大戦
warbler; bush ~ n uguísu ウグイス・
鶯・鴬
ward n (city district) kú ku 区, …-ku …区
ward office n ku-yákusho 区役所
wardrobe n yōfuku dansu 洋服だんす,
ishō dansu 衣装だんす
ware n saiku 細工, (ceramic ware)
tō'ki 陶器, setomono 瀬戸物, …-yaki
…焼き
warehouse n sō'ko 倉庫, kurá 倉
warless adj sensō no nai 戦争のない
warlike adj kōsen-teki (na) 好戦的(な)
warm 1. v warms it up v ata-tamemásu
(ata-taméru, atatamete) あたため[温
め・暖め]ます(あたためる, あたため
て), nes-shimásu (nes-suru, nes-shíte)
熱します(熱する, 熱して)；*warms the
rice wine* (o-)kán o tsukemásu/shimásu
(お)燗をつけます/します **2.** v warms
up ata-tamárimásu (ata-tamáru, ata-
tamátte) あたたまり[温まり・暖まり]
ます(あたたまる, あたたまって)
3. adj atatakai/attakai あたたかい/あ
ったかい, (not cool) attakái 暖かい, (not cold)
温かい, (lukewarm liquids) nurúi ぬる
い, (dedicated) nesshin (na) 熱心(な)
warmhearted adj kokóro ga atatakái
心が温かい, atsui 厚い・篤い
warmheartedness n atsu-sa 厚さ・篤
さ; nínjō 人情
warmly adv ata-takáku あたたかく・
暖かく・温かく
warmth n (heat) atsu-sa 熱さ・暑さ
warn v keikoku shimásu (suru, shite)
警告します(する, して), chūi shimásu
(suru, shíte) 注意します(する, して)
warning n keikoku 警告, (alert) keihō
警報, (notice) kotowári 断り
warning label n keikoku hyōji 警告表
示, keikoku raberu 警告ラベル
warning message n keikoku messéji
警告メッセージ, keikoku tsūchi 警告
通知
warp 1. n sorí そり・反り **2.** v (it warps)
sorimásu (sóru, sótte) そり[反り]ます

(そる, そって)；(warps it) sorashimásu
(sorásu, soráshite) そらし[反らし]ま
す(そらす, そらして), yugamemásu
(yugameru, yugamete) 歪め[ゆがめ]
ます(歪める, 歪めて) **3.** gets warped
v (distorted) yugamimásu (yugamu,
yugande) 歪み[ゆがみ]ます(歪む, 歪
んで)；(crooked) kuruimásu (kurū',
kurútte) 狂います(狂う, 狂って) **4.**
n (vertical threads) tate-ito たて糸・
縦糸
warranty n hoshō(-sho) 保証(書)
warrior n **1.** senshi 戦士 **2.** (Japanese)
samurai 侍・サムライ, búshi 武士
warship n gunkan 軍艦
wartime n sénji(chū) 戦時(中), sensō
no toki 戦争の時
was v … déshita (… dátta) …でした
(…だった)；arimáshita (átta) ありま
した(あった)；imáshita (ita) いました
(いた) → is
wash 1. v araimásu (arau, aratte) 洗い
ます(洗う, 洗って)；(launders)
sentaku shimásu (suru, shíte) 洗濯しま
す(する, して) **2.** n the wash(ing) n
sentaku 洗濯, sentaku-mono 洗濯物
wash basin n senmén-ki 洗面器
wash towel n wosshu taoru ウォッシ
ュタオル
wash tub n sentaku tarai 洗濯たらい
washable adj sentaku (no) dekiru 洗濯
(の)できる, araeru 洗える
wash-and-wear adj wosshu ando wea
ウォッシュ・アンド・ウェア, airon
no iranai アイロンの要らない, airon
fuyō (no) アイロン不要(の)
washcloth n (hand towel) te-nugui 手
拭い, (dishcloth) fukín ふきん・布巾
washer n (washing machine) sentáku-
ki 洗濯機
washing machine → washer
Washington n Washínton ワシントン
washout n **1.** (big mistake) daishippai
大失敗 **2.** (a failure) shikkaku-sha
失格者
washroom n (o-)teárai (お)手洗い,
senmen-jo 洗面所
washstand n senmen dai 洗面台
wasn't v … ja/dewa arimásén deshita
(…ja nákatta) …じゃ/ではありませ

んでした(…じゃなかった); arimasén
deshita (nákatta) ありませんでした
(なかった); imasén deshita (inákatta)
いませんでした (いなかった) → **isn't**

wasp *n* hachi 蜂・ハチ, suzume-bachi
スズメバチ

waspish *n* suzume-bachi no yō (na)
スズメバチのよう(な), (*having a hot
temper*) okorippoi 怒りっぽい

waste 1. *n* (*trash*) kúzu くず・屑, kuzu-
mono くず物・屑物; (*extravagance*)
mudazukai 無駄遣い, rōhi 浪費 **2.**
v (*wastes it*) muda ni shimásu (suru,
shite) 無駄にします(する、して); (*is
extravagant with*) muda-zúkai shimásu
(suru, shite) 無駄使いします(する、し
て), rōhi shimásu (suru, shite) 浪費し
ます(する、して) **3.** *falls to ~* aremásu (areru, arete) 荒れます(荒れる、
荒れて)

waste away *v* shōmō shimásu (suru,
shite) 消耗します(する、して)

waste of effort *n* mudabone 無駄骨,
torō´ 徒労

waste of money *n* (o-)kane no mudazukai (お)金の無駄遣い, (o-)kane no
rōhi (お)金の浪費

waste of talent *n* takara no mochi-
gusare 宝の持ち腐れ

waste of time *n* jikan no muda 時間
の無駄

What a waste! *interj* Mottainai! もっ
たいない!

wastebasket *n* kuzú-kago くずかご

wasteful *adj* mottai-nái もったいない,
muda (na) 無駄(な)

wastepaper *n* kamikúzu 紙くず・紙
屑; *~ basket* kuzú-kago くずかご

wastewater *n* gesui 下水, osui 汚水,
haisui 排水

watch 1. *n* (*timepiece*) tokei 時計
2. *v* (*looks at/after*) mimásu (miru, mite)
見ます[見ます・観ます](みる、みて);
(*guards it*) … no bán o shimásu (suru,
shite) …の番をします(する、して)
3. *v* (*observes*) kansatsu shimásu (suru,
shite) 観察します(する、して)

night watch, night watchman yakei
(-in) 夜警(員), yakan keibiin 夜間警
備員, yo-máwari 夜回り

watch for neraimásu (nerau, neratte)
ねらい[狙い]ます(ねらう、ねらって);
~ a chance kikái o ukagaimásu (ukagau, ukagatte) 機会をうかがい[窺い]
ます(うかがう、うかがって)

watch out for (*guards against*) keikai
shimásu (suru, shite) 警戒します(す
る、して)

Watch out! Abunai! 危ない!

Watch your step! Ashi-mótó ni ki o
tsukéte! 足元に気を付けて!

watcher *n* (*nurse*) kango-nin 看護人;
(*observer*) kansatsu-sha 観察者;
(*researcher*) kenkyū-sha 研究者

fire-watcher *n* kasai keibiin 火災警備
員

watchful; keeps a ~ eye (*on the
situation*) (jōkyō o) ukagaimásu
(ukagau, ukagatte) (状況・情況を)う
かがいます(うかがう、うかがって)

watchman *n* bannín 番人, keibiin
警備員; (*gatekeeper*) mónban 門番 →
night watch, night watchman

watch tower *n* hinomi-yagura 火の見
やぐら[櫓]

watchword *n* (*motto*) mottō モットー;
hyōgo 標語; (*password*) aikotoba
合言葉

water *n* mizu 水; *hot ~* o-yu お湯, yú
湯; *drinking ~* nomí-mizu 飲み水,
o-híya お冷や・おひや

water gate *n* suimon 水門

waterfall *n* taki 滝・たき

water fowl *n* mizutori 水鳥・ミズトリ

waterfront *n* kashi 河岸

waterhole, watering hole *n* mizu
tamari 水溜り・水たまり

water imp *n* kappa かっぱ・河童

water level *n* suii 水位; suijun 水準

waterline *n* suii sen 水位線

water mill *n* suisha 水車

water pistol *n* mizu-déppō 水鉄砲

water pitcher *n* mizu-sáshi 水差し

waterpower *n* suiryoku 水力; *~ plant*
suiryoku hatsudensho 水力発電所

waterproof *adj* bōsui (no) 防水(の)

waterproofing *n* bōsui kakō 防水加工

waterscape *n* suikei-ga 水景画

water service → **waterworks**

watershed *n* bunkiten 分岐点

water-skiing *n* suijō sukii 水上スキー

waterworks *n* suidō 水道; **~ Bureau**
suidō´-kyoku 水道局; (*to cry, in order to get sympathy*) **turn on the ~** namida o nagasu 涙を流す

waterweed *n* mizukusa 水草

waterwheel *n* suisha 水車

watchmaker *n* tokei-ya 時計屋

watermelon *n* suika スイカ・西瓜

watt *n* watto ワット

wattage *n* watto-ryō ワット量

watt-hour *n* watto-ji ワット時

watt meter *n* denryoku-kei 電力計

wave **1.** *n* namí 波 **2.** *n* (*permanent*) páma パーマ **3.** *v* (*waves a hand*) té o furimásu (furu, futte) 手を振ります（振る、振って）

waveform *n* hakei 波形

wavelength *n* hachō 波長

wavelet *n* sazanami さざなみ

waver *n* yure 揺れ

wax *n* (*bee wax*) mitsurō ミツロウ・蜜蝋, rō´ロウ・蝋

waxwork *n* rō-zaiku 蝋細工・ろう細工, rō´ ningyō 蝋人形・ろう人形

way *n* michi 道; (*method*) shi-kata 仕方, shi-yō 仕様, yari-kata やり方; (*means*) shúdan 手段; (*manner*) tō´ri 通り, (*fashion*) fū´風, (*trick*) téguchi 手口
any way *adv* nanraka no hōhō (de) 何らか[なんらか]の方法で
all the way *adv* (*from far*) harubaru はるばる, tōi tokoro 遠いところ
by way of ... → via
by the way *adv, conj* **1.** (*incidentally*) sore wa sō´ to それはそうと, tokorode ところで, chinami ni ちなみに, tsuide ni ついでに, tokí ni 時に **2.** *adv* (*way of*) ... o tō´tte ... を通って; (*via*) ... keiyu (de/no) ... 経由(で/の)
gets in the way *v* (o-)jama ni nari-másu (náru, nátte) （お）じゃま[邪魔]になります（なる、なって）, (o-)jama o shimásu (suru, shíte) （お）じゃま[邪魔]をします（する、して）
get out of the way dokimásu (doku, doite) どき[退き]ます（どく、どいて）, nokimásu (noku, noite) のき[退き]ます（のく、のいて）
give way *v* yuzurimásu (yuzuru,

yuzutte) 譲ります（譲る、譲って）
make way *v* (*goes forward*) zenshin shimásu (suru, shite) 前進します（する、して）
in a way *adv* aru imi ある意味
No way! → no
on the way tochū (de) 途中（で）
one's way *adv* (*one's*) jikoryū de 自己流で, jibun no omou yarikata de 自分の思うやり方で
the way I am *v* arugamama no jibun あるがままの自分, arinomama no jibun ありのままの自分
way above... *adj* ...o haruka ni koeta ...をはるかに超えた
way ahead *adv* zutto saki (ni) ずっと先（に）
way back *adv* (*before*) zutto máe (ni) ずっと前（に）, zutto izen (ni) ずっと以前（に）, zutto mukashi (ni) ずっと昔（に）
way of ...ing [VERB INFINITIVE] + -kata ...方; **~ ...ing of saying/telling/putting it** ii-kata 言い方
wayside *n* michibata 道端; robō 路傍; gaitō 街頭
we *pron* watáshi-táchi わたしたち・私達, jibun-tachi 自分達, [BOOKISH] watakushí-tachi わたくしたち・私達; ware-ware われわれ・我々
weak *adj* **1.** yowái 弱い; fú-jiyū (na) 不自由（な）; (*coffee, etc.*) usui 薄い **2. grows ~** otoroe-másu (otoróéru, otoróete) 衰えます（衰える、衰えて）
weak point *n* (*shortcoming*) tánsho 短所; (*weakness*) yowami 弱み; jakuten 弱点, yowai tokoro 弱いところ
wealth *n* tómi 富, zaisan 財産, zái 財
wealthy → rich
weapon *n* heiki 兵器; buki 武器; kyōki 凶器
wear **1.** *n* fuku 服; irui 衣類 **2.** *v* (*on body*) kiteimásu (kiteiru, kite(i)te) 着ています（着ている、着て(いって）; [HONORIFIC] o-meshi ni narimásu (náru, nátte) お召しになります（なる、なって）; (*pants, footwear*) haiteimásu (haiteiru, haiteité) はいて[履いて]います（はいている、はいていて）, (*hat, headwear*) kabuttemásu (kabútteiru,

kabute(i)té かぶって[被って]います(かぶっている, かぶって(い)て), *(a pin, ornament, etc.)* tsuketeimásu (tsukéteiru, tsukéteite) 付けています(付けている, 付けていて), *(necktie, belt)* shimeteimásu (shiméteiru, shímeteite) 締めています(締めている, 締めていて), *(on hands, fingers)* hameteimásu (hameteiru, hameteite) はめています(はめている, はめていて)

weary 1. *adj* → **tired 2.** *v* **wearies** *(of …)* (…ni) akimásu (akíru, ákite) (…に)飽きます(飽きる, 飽きて)

weather *n* ténki 天気 (o-ténki お天気); kishō 気象; hiyori 日和
Nice weather, isn't it? *interj* Ii (o-)ténki desu ne. いい(お)天気ですね.

weather forecast *n* tenki-yóhō 天気予報

weather observatory/station *n* sokkō-jo 測候所; kishō-dai 気象台

weave *v* orimásu (óru, ótte) 織ります(織る, 織って)

weaver *n (person)* orite 織り手, *(machine)* hataori 機織り
the Festival of the Weaver Star Tanabata 七夕・たなばた *(7 July)*

web 1. → **cobweb, spiderweb 2.** → **Internet**

wedding *n* kekkon 結婚, wedingu ウェディング, *(ceremony)* kekkón-shiki 結婚式
wedding invitation *n* kekkonshiki (no) shōkai-jō 結婚式(の)紹介状
wedding party *n* kekkon shukuga-kai 結婚祝賀会, wedingu pātii ウェディングパーティ
wedding photo *n* kekkonshiki no shashin 結婚式の写真
wedding reception *n* kekkon hiróen 結婚披露宴

Wednesday *n* Suiyō´bi 水曜日, Suiyō´ 水曜

weed *n* kusá 草, zassō 雑草

week *n* shūkan 週間; shū´ 週, …-shū …週; *how many weeks* nan-shū´kan 何週間

week after next *n, adv* saraishū 再来週

week before last *n, adv* sensén-shū 先々週

weekend *n, adv* shūmatsu 週末
Have a nice weekend! *interj* Yoi shūmatsu o! 良い[よい]週末を!

weep *v* nakimásu (naku, naite) 泣きます(泣く, 泣いて); *(laments)* nagekimásu (nagéku, nagéite) 嘆きます(嘆く, 嘆いて)

weigh 1. *v it weighs …* (…) no omosa ga … arimásu (áru, átte) (…の)重さが…あります(ある, あって); *How much does it (do you) ~?* (…) no omosa ga dono-gurai arimásu ka (…の)重さがどの位ありますか **2.** *v weighs it* (…no) omosa o hakarimásu (hakáru, hakátte) (…の)重さを量ります(量る, 量って) **3.** *n* omosa 重さ, mekata 目方, jūryō 重量; *(of body)* taijū 体重; *(object)* omoshi 重し

weight-lifting *n* jūryō-age 重量挙げ, weito rifutingu ウェイトリフティング; *weight-lifter* jūryōage-sénshu 重量挙げ選手

weight/weighing scales *n* hakarí はかり・秤

weird *adj* ayashii 怪しい・あやしい, fushigi (na) 不思議・ふしぎ(な), sugói すごい・凄い; *(feeling)* kimí ga warúi 気味が悪い

welcome 1. *n (a welcome)* mukae 迎え, kangei 歓迎 **2.** *adj (it is welcome)* nozomashii 望ましい, arigatái ありがたい・有り難い **3.** *v (welcomes one)* … o mukaemásu (mukaeru, mukaete) …を迎えます(迎える, 迎えて), … o de-mukaemásu (de-mukaeru, de-mukaete) …を出迎えます(出迎える, 出迎えて)
Welcome! *interj* Yóku irasshaimáshita! よくいらっしゃいました!; Yō´koso! ようこそ!; Irasshaimáse! いらっしゃいませ!
You're welcome! *interj* Dō´ itashimáshite. どういたしまして.
Welcome back/home! *interj* O-kaeri nasái. お帰りなさい.

welfare *n* fukushi 福祉; *~ policy* fukushi-séisaku 福祉政策

well 1. *n (for water)* ído 井戸 **2.** *adj*

(*good, nice*) yóku よく・良く; (*healthy*) génki (na) 元気(な); (*splendid*) rippa (na/ni) 立派(な/に); **gets ~** naorimásu (naóru, naótte) 治り[直り]ます(治[直]る, 治[直]って) **3.** *adv* (*come on*) sā´ saあ; **~ now/then** (sore) dewa (それ)では, (sore) jā (それ)じゃあ, jā じゃあ, sáte さて; ē-to えーと; tokoró-de ところで; (*let me think*) sō´desu né そうですね; (*maybe*) mā まあ

very well (*satisfactory*) yoroshii よろしい

well versed in tsū-ji(tei)másu (tsū-ji(tei)ru, tsū-ji(tei)te) 通じ(てい)ます (通じ(ている, 通じ(ていて)

well-behaved *adj* otonashíi おとなしい・大人しい

well-known *adj* yūmei (na) 有名(な), chomei (na) 著明(な)

well-liked; **is ~** motemásu (motéru, mótete) もてます(もてる, もてて)

west *n* nishi 西, sei—... 西; (*the west*) seihō 西方, (*the western part*) séibu 西部, (*the Occident*) Séiyō 西洋, (*Europe and America*) O-Bei 欧米; **Western Japan** Kánsái 関西

West Indies *n* Nishi indo shotō 西インド諸島

westerly (*wind*) *adj* nishi-yori (no kaze) 西寄り(の風)

western 1. *adj* nishi (no) 西(の) **2.** *n* seibu-geki 西部劇

western paper *n* yōshi 洋紙

western style *n* (*Occidental*) Seiyō-fū 西洋風, yō-fū 洋風; yo-洋...; **~ building** yōkan 洋館; **~ room** yō-ma 洋間; **~ clothes** yō-fúku 洋服

wet 1. *adj* nureta ... ぬれた・濡れた (*moist*) shimetta 湿った, shimeppoi 湿っぽい **2.** *it gets ~* v nuremásu (nureru, nurete) 濡れます(濡れる, 濡れて) **3.** *makes it ~* v nurashimásu (nurasu, nurashíte) 濡らします(濡らす, 濡らして), (*dampens it*) shimeshi-másu (shimesu, shimeshíte) 湿します (湿す, 湿して)

whale *n* kujira クジラ・鯨

wharf *n* hato-ba 波止場

what *pron* náni 何 [nán 何 *before* t, d, n]; nán no ... 何の..., náni— 何...

what ... (*one/fact that*) ... (no) monó/ kotó...(の)物/事, ...no ...の

what color nani-iro 何色, dónna iró どんな色

what day (*of the week*) nan-yō´bi 何曜日; (*of the month*) nán-nichi 何日

whatever nan demo 何でも; **~ you like** nan demo sukina mono (o) 何でも好きな物(を), dore demo sukina mono (o) どれでも好きな物(を), nan demo hoshii mono (o) 何でも欲しい物(を), [BOOKISH] dore demo nozomu mono (o) どれでも望む物(を), náni (ga/o) ...-témo 何(が/を)...ても

what kind of dono yó´na どのよう[様]な, dō´yū どうゆう, dónna どんな

what language nani-go 何語

what month nán-gatsu 何月

what nationality naní-jin 何人, doko no kuni no hito どこの国の人, [HONORIFIC] dochira no (o-)kuni no kata どちらの(お)国の方

what part 1. (*where*) dóko どこ 2. (*thing*) dono bubun どの部分

what place dóko どこ; dóchira どちら, dótchi どっち

what's-his/her-name dáredare だれだれ・誰々, dáresore だれそれ・誰それ

what's-it(s-name) náninani 何々

what sort of → what kind of

what time nán-ji 何時

what university nani-dáigaku 何大学

what year nán-nen 何年

wheat *n* komúgi 小麦; múgi 麦・ムギ

wheedle *v* tarashi-komimásu (tarashi-komu, tarashi-konde) たらし込みます(たらし込む, たらし込んで)

wheel *n* wá 輪, sharin 車輪, hoiiru ホイール; (*steering wheel*) handoru ハンドル

wheelchair *n* kuruma isu 車いす

when *pron* ítsu いつ
about when itsugoro いつ頃
since when ítsu kara いつから
until when ítsu made いつまで
by when ítsu made ni いつまでに

when ... *adv* (*the time that* ...) ... (no) tokí...(の)時; (*where upon*) ... (suru)

to … （する）と，(shi)-tára … （し）た
ら，… (shi)-ta tókí… （し）た時；(and
then) (shi)-te （し）て，(shi)-tékara （し）
てから，(shi)-te sore kara （し）てそれ
から；(on the occasion of) … ni sái-
shite …に際して

where pron dóko どこ；[DEFERENTIAL]
dóchira どちら

**where … ** adv (the place that …) …
(no) tokoró… （の）所；(and there) …-te
soko (de/ni) …てそこ（で/に）

whereabouts n shozai 所在

whereupon 1. adv → when … **2.** …
tokoró ga …ところが

whether conj … ka dō´ka …かどうか

which pron (of two) dóchira/dótchi
no … どちら/どっちの…（or … no
dóchira/dótchi… のどちら/どっち）；
(of more than two) dóno … どの…（or
… no dóre …のどれ）

which damn (one) dóitsu どいつ

which 1. → that … **2.** (and that)
(soshite) sore (ga/wa) （そして）それ
（が/は）

while … conj (no) aida …（の）間；…
(shi)-nagara …（し）ながら；…-chu (ni)
…中（に）

(for) a while n shibáraku しばらく

a little while ago sakíhodo 先程，sákki
さっき

whip v múchi (de uchimásu; útsu, útte)
むち [鞭]（で打ちます；打つ，打って）

whipping cream n hoippu-kuríimu ホ
イップクリーム

whirlpool n uzú-maki 渦巻き，úzu 渦・
うず

whirlwind n sempū 旋風，tsumují-káze
つむじ風

whisky n uísúkíi ウイスキー，wísukii
ウィスキー；~ and water mizuwari
水割り

whisper 1. n (a whisper) kogoe 小声，
sasayaki ささやき・囁き **1.** v
(whispers it) sasayakimásu (sasayaku,
sasayaite) ささやき [囁き] ます（ささ
やく，ささやいて），mimiuchi shimásu
(suru, shite) 耳打ちします（する，
して）

whistle n fue 笛；(v) (with lips)
kuchibue (o fukimásu; fukú, fúite)

口笛（を吹きます，吹く，吹いて）；
(steam) kiteki 汽笛

white adj shirói 白い；shíro (no) 白
（の）；howáito (no) ホワイト（の）；
snow ~ masshíro (na) 真っ白（な）；the
~ of an egg shírómi 白身

whitebait n shirasu シラス・白子

who pron dáre 誰；[DEFERENTIAL] dónata
どなた，dóchira (sama) どちら（様）

who … 1. → that … **2.** (and he/she/
they) … (soshite) sonó-hito ga/wa …
（そして）その人が/は

whole adj zentai (no) 全体（の）；zén(-)
… zén全…；the ~ thing (all of it) zénbu
全部

one's whole life isshō 一生

wholesale adj óroshí (de) 卸し（で）；
selling ~ oroshi-uri 卸し売り

wholly adv zentai (teki) ni 全体（的）に

whore n baishun-fu 売春婦，jorō´ 女郎
→ prostitute

whorehouse n baishún-yado 売春宿

whose pron dáre no 誰の

whose … 1. → that … **2.** (and his/
her/ their) … (soshite) sonó-hito no …
（そして）その人の

why adv dō´shite どうして，náze なぜ，
dó´（どう）；that's ~ dákara (sá) だから
（さ）

wicker trunk n kō´ri 行李

wicket n kído 木戸；(ticket) kaisatsu-
guchi 改札口；(window) madó-guchi
窓口，…-guchi …口

wide 1. adj (haba ga) hirói （幅が）広い
2. adj hiroku 広く；widely adv hiroku
広く

widow n mibō´-jin 未亡人，yamome や
もめ，goke(-san) 後家（さん）

widower n otoko-yámome 男やもめ

width n hírosa 広さ，haba 幅；yoko 横；
yoko haba 横幅

wife n (your/his wife) óku-san/-sama
奥さん/様，fujin 夫人；(my wife) kánai
家内，sái/tsúma 妻，nyō´bo/nyō´bō
女房；wáifu ワイフ

wig n katsura かつら・鬘

wild adj **1.** wairudo ワイルド；
(disorderly) ranbō (na) 乱暴（な）；
(rough) arai 荒い；(roughneck) abare-
mono 暴れ者；(not cultivated) yasei no

616

野性の **2. gets ~** aremásu (areru, arete) 荒れます(荒れる, 荒れて)
wild duck n kámo カモ・鴨
wild goose n gán ガン・雁
wildlife n yasei dōbutsu 野生動物, yasei seibutsu 野生生物
wild person n abare-mono 暴れ者・あばれ者
will n (intention) íshi 意志, omói 思い; (testament) yuigon 遺言
will be ... ... désu (dá/nó/ná, dé, ní) ...です(だ/の/な, で, に)
will do shimásu (suru, shite) します(する, して)
willow n yanagi 柳; budding ~ aoyagi/ao-yánagi 青柳・アオヤナギ
win v (game/war) ... ni kachimásu (kátsu, kátte) ...に勝ちます(勝つ, 勝って); (prize) jushō shimásu (suru, shite) 受賞します(する, して), ... o (kachi) torimásu (tóru, tótte) ...を(勝ち)取ります(取る, 取って) → **victory**
wind 1. v magarimásu (magáru, magátte) 曲がります(曲がる, 曲がって) **2.** v ~ it (around/up) makimásu (maku, maite) 巻きます(巻く, 巻いて); (reel) kurimásu (kúru, kútté) 繰ります(繰る, 繰って) **3.** n (breeze) kaze 風; seasonal ~ 季節風; strong (heavy) ~ 強風
wind up (concludes it) shimemásu (shimeru, shimete) 締めます(締める, 締めて), keri o tsukemásu (tsukéru, tukéte) けりをつけます(つける, つけて); (ends up doing) (shi)-te shimaimásu (shimau, shimatte) (し)てしまいます(しまう, しまって)
against the wind sakaraimásu (sakaráu, sakarátte) 逆らいます(逆らう, 逆らって)
windbreaker n (jacket) uindo-burēkā ウインドブレーカー, jánpā ジャンパー
wind-chimes n fūrin 風鈴
window n mádo 窓; (opening, wicket) madó-guchi 窓口; transom ~ ranma 欄間
windowpane n mado-gárasu 窓ガラス
window screen n amido 網戸; bōchū-ami 防虫網, mushiyoké-ami 虫よけ網

windshield wiper n waípā ワイパー
windy adj kaze ga tsuyói 風が強い
wine n **1.** wáin ワイン, budō´shu ぶどう[葡萄・ブドウ]酒 **2.** → **rice wine, saké**
wine cup n (saké cup) sakazuki 杯 (o-sakazuki お杯), chóko ちょこ (o-chóko おちょこ)
wing n (of bird or plane) tsubasa 翼・つばさ; (of insect) hane 羽・羽根・翅; (of door/gate) tobira 扉・とびら
wink n ma-bátaki まばたき・瞬き, uínku/wínku (shimásu; suru, shite) ウインク/ウィンク(します; する, して)
winner n (victor) shōri-sha 勝利者, yūshō-sha 優勝者; (awardee) jushō´sha 受賞者
winter n fuyú 冬; ~ solstice tōji 冬至 winter vacation n fuyu yasumi 冬休み, [BOOKISH] tōki kyūka 冬期休暇
win-win relationship n win win no kankei ウィン・ウィンの関係; sōhō ga rieki o eru kankei 双方が利益を得る関係; sōhōga kachigumi ni naru kankei 双方が勝ち組になる関係
wipe v fukimásu (fuku, fuite) 拭きます(拭く, 拭いて); ~ away nuguimásu (nugú´, nugútte) 拭います(拭う, 拭いて)
wire n harigane 針金; (electric) densen 電線, (telephone line) denwa-sen 電話線 → **telegram**
wisdom n chié 知恵
wise adj kashikói 賢い, kenmei (na) 賢明(な)
wish n (o-)negai (お)願い, kibō 希望 my best wishes to ... (please send) ..., ni (dō´zo) yoroshiku ...に(どうぞ)よろしく[宜しく]
wish for ... ga hoshíi desu (hoshíi, hóshikute) ...が欲しいです(欲しい, 欲しくて)
wish that ... (it does) (shi)-tára íi desu (ga) (し)たらいいです(が); ~ (it had done) (shi)-tára yókatta desu (ga) (し)たら良かったです(が) or yókatta no ni (shi)-tára よかったのに(し)たら
wish to do (shi)-tái desu (shi-tai, shi-tákute) (し)たいです(したい, したくて)

wish to have it done (shi)-te morai-tái
desu (し)てもらいたいです
wisteria n fuji ふじ・藤
wit n yū´moa ユーモア, kíchi 機知,
witto ウィット
to wit sunáwachi すなわち・即ち
with prep ... to ...と, to issho ni ...と
一緒に; (by using) ... de ... で; (with
... attached/included) ... ga tsúita ...
が付いた, ...-tsuki (no) ...付き (の);
~ its being ... de ...で; ~ bath furo/
basu-tsuki (no) 風呂/バス付き (の); ~
difficulty yatto やっと; ~ forethought
mitōshite 見通して; ~ great delight
ō-yórokobi de 大喜びで; ~ meals
(included) shoku (ji)-tsuki (no) 食(事)
付き (の); ~ much devotion/effort
(but) sekkakú せっかく; ~ a shudder/
shiver zotto ぞっと
with respect to ... ni kákete wa ... に
かけては; ... ni kán-shite ... に関して
withdraw v 1. (leaves) hiki-agemásu
(hiki-agéru, hiki-ágete) 引き上げます
(上げる, 上げて), hiki-torimásu (hiki-
tóru, hiki-tótte) 引き取ります(引き取
る, 引き取って) 2. (takes out money)
(yokin/okane o) oroshimásu (orósu,
oróshite) (預金/お金を)下ろします
(下ろす, 下ろして); (yokin/okane
o) hiki-dashimásu (hiki-dasu, hiki-
dashite) (預金/お金を)引き出します
(引き出す, 引き出して)
wither v karemásu (kareru, karete)
枯れます(枯れる, 枯れて), naemásu
(naéru, náete) 萎え[なえ]ます(萎え
る, 萎えて)
within prep (...) ínai (...) 以内; ...-nai
...内; ... no náka (de/ni/no) ...の中
(で/に/の); ~ (time) ...-chu (ni) ...中
(に)
within the city shínai 市内
within the metropolis (of Tokyo) tónai
都内
within the office/company shánai (no)
社内 (の)
without prep (excluding) ... no hoka
ni ...のほか[他・外]に; (not having)
... ga nái ...がない, ... ga náku
(te) ...がなく (て), ... náshi ni ...な
しに; (omitting) ...-nuki (de/no) ...抜

き (で/の)
without exception (all) reigai náku 例
外なく, íssái いっさい・一切
without fail zé-hi 是非・ぜひ
without interruption (continuously)
taemanáku 絶え間なく, táezu 絶えず
without notice/permission mudan de
無断で
witness n (in court) shōnin 証人;
shōko 証拠
wolf 1. n ō´kami オオカミ・狼 2. v
(impose) tsukekomimásu (tsukekomu,
tsukekonde) つけ込みます(つけ込む,
つけ込んで)
woman n onná 女, onna no hǐtó/katá
女の人/方; josei 女性, jóshi 女子;
(lady) fujin 婦人; okámi おかみ・お
内儀
womanizer n onna-tárashi 女たらし
women's bath n onna-yu 女湯
women's college n joshi-dai(gaku)
女子大(学); ~ student joshi-dáisei 女
子大生
women's language (terms) joseigo 女
性語; onna kotoba 女ことば
womenswear n onna-mono 女物
wonder 1. v odorokimásu (odoróku,
odoróite) 驚きます(驚く, 驚いて); I
wonder ... ka shira ... かしら, ... ka
ne ...かね 2. n odoroki 驚き; fushigi
不思議; it is no ~ that ... ... no mo
múri wa arimasén (nái) ...のも無理は
ありません(ない)
wonderful adj subarashíi すばらしい
・素晴らしい, suteki (na) すてき・素
敵(な), sugói すごい・凄い; (delightful)
ureshíi うれしい; (wondrous) fushigi
(na) 不思議 (な), myō (na) 妙 (な)
won't do v shimasén (shinai, shináide)
しません(しない, しないで); it won't
do ikemasén (ikenai, ikenáide) いけま
せん(いけない, いけないで), damé-
desu (da/na, de, ni) だめです(だ/な,
で, に)
wood n kí 木, mokuzai 木材, (lumber)
zaimoku 材木 → firewood
woodblock print n mokuhan-ga 木版
画, hanga 版画
wooden adj 1. mokusei no 木製の
2. muhyōjō no 無表情の

wooden bucket *n* óke 桶

wooden shoes *n* getá げた・下駄

wooden stairs *n* hashigo-dan はしご段

woods *n (forest)* mori 森

woof *n (horizontal threads)* yokoito 横糸

wool *n* ū́ru ウール, ke 毛, keito 毛糸. yōmō 羊毛

woolen goods, woolens *n* keorimono 毛織物

word *n* **1.** kotobá 言葉・ことば, tango 単語; ...-go ...語; *(one's words/speech)* kuchi 口; *(written characters)* jí 字; *(compound word)* jukugo 熟語 **2.** *(news)* táyori 便り, shōsoku 消息

in other words *adv* sunáwachi すなわち・即ち, iikaeruto 言い換えると

word processor *n* wā-puro ワープロ

work **1.** *n* hataraki 働き; *(job)* shigoto 仕事 (o-shígoto お仕事); *(operations)* ságyō 作業; *place of ~* kinmú-saki 勤務先; shoku-ba 職場; *construction ~* kṓji 工事; *~ in progress* kōji-chū 工事中 **2.** *n a work (of literature or art)* sakuhin 作品 **3.** *n (workmanship)* saiku 細工 **4.** *v (does work)* shigoto o shimásu (suru, shíte) 仕事をします (する, して); *(labors)* hatarakimásu (hataraku, hataraite) 働きます (働く, 働いて); kínmu shimásu (suru, shíte) 勤務します (する, して); *(is employed at/by)* ... ni tsutóme imásu (iru, ite) ... に勤めています (いる, いて); *(hires oneself out for pay)* kasegimásu (kaségu, kaséide) 稼ぎます (稼ぐ, 稼いで); *~ as (a ...)* ... o tsutomemásu (tsutoméru, tsutómete) ... を務めます (務める, 務めて) **5.** *v (it works) (is effective)* kikimásu (kiku, kiite) 効きます (効く, 効いて) **6.** *v → study*

workaholic *n* wākahorikku ワーカホリック; hataraki-sugi (no hito) 働き過ぎ (の人); shigoto chūdoku (-sha) 仕事中毒 (者)

worker *n (laborer)* hiyatoi 日雇い; rodo-sha 労働者; *(workman)* koin 工員, shokko 職工; *(employee, staff)* shain 社員, shokuin 職員

workflow *n* sagyō no nagare 作業の流れ; wāku furō ワークフロー

working *n* hataraki 働き; *(duty, job)* tsutomé 勤め (o-tsutome お勤め); *(operating)* unten 運転, ságyō 作業; *~ hours* sagyō-jíkan 作業時間, kinmu-jíkan 勤務時間; *~ mom* wāking mazā ワーキング・マザー

world *n* sékái 世界; *(at large)* yo (no naka) 世 (の中), *(people)* séken 世間; *~ war* sekai-táisen 世界大戦

World Cup *n* Wārudo kappu ワールドカップ

worldwide *adj* sekai-teki (na) 世界的 (な), sekai-jū 世界中

worm *n* mushi 虫・ムシ; *~ remedy* mushi-kúdashi 虫下し

worry **1.** *n* shinpai 心配・しんぱい, ki-zúkái 気づかい・気遣い, wazurai わずらい・煩い **2.** *worries (about ...)* *v* (... o) shinpai shimásu (suru, shíte) (...を) 心配します (する, して), wazuraimásu (wazurau, wazuratte) 煩います [わずらい] ます (煩う, 煩って); ki-zukaimásu (ki-zukáu, ki-zukátte) 気づかい [気遣い] ます (気遣う, 気遣って); kokoró o itamemásu (itaméru, itámete) 心を痛めます (痛める, 痛めて) *Don't ~ about it.* Goshinpai náku. ご心配なく, Shinpai shinaide (kudasai). 心配しないで (ください).

worse *adj, adv* mótto warúi もっと悪い; otorimásu (otoru, ototte) 劣ります (劣る, 劣って); *is no ~ off even if ...* ...-témo motomoto désu ...てももともと [元々] です; *grow ~* akka shimásu (suru, shíte) 悪化します (する, して)

worsen *v (illness gets worse)* kojiremásu (kojiréru, kojírete) こじれます (こじれる, こじれて); akka shimásu (suru, shíte) 悪化します (する, して)

worship **1.** *n* sūhai 崇拝, *(service)* raihai 礼拝 **2.** *v* ogamimásu (ogámu, ogánde) 拝みます (拝む, 拝んで)

worst *adj* ichiban warúi 一番悪い; saiaku (no) 最悪 (の); *(lowest)* saitei (no) 最低 (の)

worth → value

worthless *adj* tsumaránai つまらない, yákuza (na) やくざ (な)

would → perhaps

would like → **want, wish**

wound 1. n (*injury*) kizu 傷, kegá けが・怪我 2. v (*gets wounded*) kizu-tsukimás<u>u</u> (kizu-ts<u>ú</u>kú, kizu-ts<u>ú</u>ite) 傷付きます(傷付く, 傷付いて), yararemás<u>u</u> (yarareru, yararete) やられます(やられる, やられて); (*injures*) kizu-ts<u>u</u>kemás<u>u</u> (kizu-ts<u>u</u>kéru, kizu-ts<u>u</u>kéte) 傷付けます(傷付ける, 傷付けて)

wound it → **wind it**

Wow! *interj* wā! わあ!

wrap v ts<u>u</u>tsumimás<u>u</u> (ts<u>u</u>tsúmu, ts<u>u</u>tsúnde) 包みます(包む, 包んで), hōsō shimás<u>u</u> (suru, sh<u>i</u>te) 包装します(する, して); (*something around it*) makimás<u>u</u> (maku, maite) 巻きます(巻く, 巻いて)

wrapper n (*traditional cloth*) furosh<u>i</u>ki ふろしき・風呂敷; (*package paper*) hōsōshi 包装紙

wrapping n rappingu ラッピング; hōsōshi 包装紙

wreath n (*lei*) hanawa 花輪; **~ shell** sázae サザエ・栄螺

wreck 1. n (*accident*) j<u>i</u>ko 事故, (*collision*) shōtotsu 衝突; (*ship wreck*) nanpa 難破, sōnan 遭難; (*train wreck*) ressha-j<u>i</u>ko 列車事故, sōnan 遭難; (*the wreckage*) zangai 残骸 2. v (*ruins it*) kowashimás<u>u</u> (kowásu, kowásh<u>i</u>te) 壊します(壊す, 壊して); **wrecks a car** kuruma o kowashimás<u>u</u> 車を壊します

wrecker n (*tow truck*) rékkā レッカー, rekkā´-sha レッカー車

wrench n rénchi レンチ, s<u>u</u>pána スパナ

wrestler n **sumo ~** sumō´-tóri 相撲取り, o-sumō-san お相撲さん; (*ranking*) seki-tóri 関取; (*champion*) ō´-zeki 大関; (*grand champion*) yokozuna 横綱

wrestler's belt n (*loincloth*) mawashi まわし・回し

wrestling n résuringu レスリング; (*professional*) puro-resu プロレス; (*Japanese*) sumō 相撲・すもう

wrestling ring n (*sumo*) dohyō 土俵

wrestling tournament n (*sumo*) basho 場所; **grand ~** ō-zúmō 大相撲

wretch n yátsu やつ・奴

wretched *adj* nasake-nái 情けない

wring (*out*) v shiborimás<u>u</u> (shibóru, shibótte) 絞ります(絞る, 絞って)

wrinkle 1. n shiwa しわ・皺 2. v (*it wrinkles*) shiwa ga dekimás<u>u</u> (dek<u>í</u>ru, dék<u>i</u>te) しわができます(できる, できて)

wrist n té-kubi 手首

wristwatch n ude-dókei 腕時計

write v kakimás<u>u</u> (káku, káite) 書きます(書く, 書いて); (*composes*) tsukuri-más<u>u</u> (ts<u>u</u>kúru, ts<u>u</u>kútte) 作ります(作る, 作って), tsuzurimás<u>u</u> (tsuzuru, tsuzutte) 綴ります(綴る, 綴って); (*publishes*) arawashimás<u>u</u> (arawásu, arawásh<u>i</u>te) 著します(著す, 著して)

writer n sakka 作家, chósha 著者; (*the author*) h<u>i</u>ssha 筆者

writing n (*written characters*) móji 文字, j<u>i</u> 字; shorui 書類; **~ a composition/theme** sakubun 作文

writing brush n fude 筆・ふで

writing paper n binsen 便せん・便箋

written explanation n setsumeisho 説明書

wrong 1. *adj* (*mistaken*) machigátta 間違った, (*is in error*) machigaemás<u>u</u> (machigáu, machigátte) 間違えます(間違う, 間違って); (*different*) chigat-ta 違った・ちがった; (*wrongful*) warúi 悪い; (*amiss*) (... no) guai ga warúi (...の)具合が悪い; **something ~** ijō 異常 2. n (*malfunction*) koshō 故障

wry *adj* shibúi 渋い, nigái 苦い; **~ face** shibúi/nigái kao 渋い/苦い・にがい顔

X

X *n* (*symbol "wrong"*) bátsu ばつ・バ
ツ, battén ばってん・罰点
Xanadu *n* tōgenkyō 桃源郷
Xavier *n* Zabieru ザビエル
x-axis *n* ekkusu jiku X軸
X box *n* ekkusu bokkusu エックスボッ
クス
xenophobia *n* (*hatred of foreign
people*) gaikoku-jin girai 外国人嫌い
xenophobic *adj* gaikoku girai (no) 外
国嫌い(の), (*hatred of foreign goods*)
hakuraihin girai (no) 舶来品嫌い(の),
(*hatred of foreign people*) gaikoku-jin
girai (no) 外国人嫌い(の)
Xerox *v* kopiishimasu (suru, shite)
コピーします(する, して)
Xian *n* shiian 西安・シーアン

Xmas *n* (*Christmas*) kurisumásu クリ
スマスプレゼント
Xmas cake *n* (*Christmas*) kurisumasu
kēki クリスマスケーキ
Xmas gift *n* (*Christmas*) kurisumasu
purezento クリスマスプレゼント
X-rating *n* seijin muke eiga shitei 成人
向き映画指定
xylitol *n* kishiritōru キシリトール
X-ray 1. *n* ekkūsu-sen X線, rentogen
(shashin) レントゲン(写真) **2.** *v*
ekkūsu-sen (de) kensa shimásu (suru,
shite) X線(で)検査します(する, し
て), rentogen (shashin) o torimásu
(toru, totte) レントゲン(写真)を撮り
ます(撮る, 撮って)

Y

yacht *n* **1.** (*sailboat*) yotto ヨット
2. (*motor cruiser*) kurūzā クルーザー
yahoo *interj* yahhō ヤッホー
Yahoo! *n* Yahū (kensaku enjin) ヤフー
(検索エンジン)
yak *n* (*animal*) yaku ヤク
yam *n* imó イモ・芋(o-imo お芋),
yamu imo ヤムイモ
Yankee *n* Yankii ヤンキー
yap *v* hoemásu (hoeru, hoete) 吠えます
(吠える, 吠えて)
yard *n* niwa 庭
yard goods *n* tanmono 反物
yard sale *n* garējisēru ガレージセール
(= *garage sale*)
yarn *n* íto 糸; (*for knitting*) ke-ito 毛糸
yawn 1. *n* akubi あくび[欠伸] **2.** *v*
akubi o shimásu (suru, shite) あくび
[欠伸]をします(する, して)
yeah *interj* ā ああ; un うん
year *n* toshí 年; nén 年, …-nen …
年; *years old* … -sai …歳; *1 year old*
hitótsu 一つ・ひとつ, *10 years old* tō
十・とお, *20 years old* hátachi/nijús-
sai 二十歳・はたち; *how many years
old* íkutsu いくつ・幾つ(o-ikutsu

おいくつ・お幾つ), nán-sai 何歳
year after next n sarainen 再来年
year before last n otótoshi おとと
し・一昨年 issakú-nen 一昨年
Zodiac Years n jūnishi 十二支
Year of the Boar n idoshi 亥年
Year of the Cock n toridoshi 酉年
Year of the Dog n inudoshi 戌年
Year of the Dragon n tatsudoshi 辰年
Year of the Horse n umadoshi 午年
Year of the Monkey n sarudoshi 申年
Year of the Ox n ushidoshi 丑年
Year of the Rabbit n udoshi 卯年
Year of the Rat n nedoshi 子年
Year of the Sheep n hitsujidoshi 未年
Year of the Snake n midoshi 巳年
Year of the Tiger n toradoshi 寅年
year-end *adj* kure (no) 暮れ(の), nen-
matsu (no) 年末(の); ~ *party* bōnén-
kai 忘年会; ~ *gift* (o-)seibo (お)歳暮
yearly 1. *adj* nén ichido (no) 年1度
(の), nen ikkai (no) 年1回(の) **2.** *adv*
nen (ni) ichido 年(に)1度, maitoshi
毎年, mainen 毎年(の)
yearn; ~ *for* akogaremásu (akogareru,
akogarete) あこがれ[憧れ]ます(あこ

621

がれる, あこがれて)
year period n néndo 年度
yeast n iisuto イースト
yell v wamekimásu (waméku, waméite) わめき[喚き]ます(わめく, わめいて), sakebimásu (sakébu, sakénde) 叫びます(叫ぶ, 叫んで) → **shout**
yellow 1. n kiiro 黄色 **2.** adj kiiroi 黄色い; kiiro (no) 黄色(の) **3.** adj (coward) okubyō (na) 臆病(な)
yellowtail n (fish) búri ブリ・鰤, (baby) inada いなだ・イナダ, (young) hamachi はまち・ハマチ
Yemen Arab Republic n Iemen arabu kyōwa-koku イエメン・アラブ共和国
yen n én 円, ...-en ...円
high value of the yen n en-daka 円高
low value of the yen n en-yasu 円安
yen basis n endate 円建て
yen credit n enshakkan 円借款
yes adv hái はい, ē´えぇ; sō´desu そうです; (or just say the verb) **Yes, I see./Yes, I will (comply).** Wakarimáshita. わかりました.
Yes and no. interj Dochiratomo iemasen. どちらとも言えません., Sā dōdeshō. さあどうでしょう.
Yes, sir/ma[d]am. interj Shōchi shimáshita. 承知しました
yes-man n iesu man イエスマン, gomasuri ゴマすり
yesterday n, adj, adv kinō´(no) きのう・昨日(の)
yet adv máda まだ, and ~ sore démo それでも, shiká-mo しかも → **but**
yew n ichii イチイ・櫟
yield 1. n (product; income) dekiagari 出来上がり **2.** v (gives in/up) yuzurimásu (yuzuru, yuzutte) 譲ります(譲る, 譲って) **3.** v (produces) sanshutsu shimásu (suru, shite) 産出します(する, して)
yin and yang n in yō 陰陽

YMCA n Wai emu shii ei YMCA, Kirisuto-kyō seinen-kai キリスト教青年会
yoga n yoga ヨガ
yogurt n yōguruto ヨーグルト
Yokohama n Yokohama 横浜; the port of ~ Yokohamá-kō 横浜港
yolk n (of egg) kimi 黄身
yonder adv achira あちら, atchí あっち
you pron anáta あなた, ánta あんた (but use name, title, or role whenever possible); sochira (sama) そちら(様); o-taku お宅, o-taku sama お宅様; (intimate) kimi 君; (condescending) omae お前・おまえ
you all miná-san みなさん・皆さん, anáta-tachi あなた達[たち], anata-gata あなた方
young 1. adj wakái 若い; very ~ osanái 幼い; ~ boy shōnen 少年, ~ girl shō´jo 少女; ~ novelist wakate-sákka 若手作家 **2.** the young → **youth**
younger adj toshi-shita (no) 年下(の); ~ brother otōtó 弟, (your) otōto-san 弟さん; ~ sister imōtó 妹, (your) (o-)imōto-san (お)妹さん
youngest adj ichiban wakái 一番若い, (toshi-)shita (no) (年)下(の)
young lady n ojō´-san お嬢さん; musume(-san) 娘(さん)
young man n seinen 青年
young person → **youth**
youngster n (young person) waka-mono 若者;
your(s) pron anáta-tachi/anata-gata no mono あなた達[たち]/あなた方の物
yourself, yourselves pron anáta-jishin あなた自身
youth n **1.** (period in life) wakasa 若さ **2.** (young person) wakamono 若者
youth hostel n yūsu-hósuteru ユースホステル

Z

Zaire *n* Zeiiru ザイール
Zambia *n* Zanbia ザンビア
zany *n* dōke-shi 道化師
zap *v* 1. (*shoots someone dead*) uchiko-roshimásu (uchikorosu, uchikoroshite) 撃ち殺します(撃ち殺す, 撃ち殺して)
2. (*defeats*) (uchi) makashimásu (makasu, makashite) (打ち)負かします(負かす, 負かして) 3. (*deletes*) sakujo shimásu (suru, shite) 削除します(する, して)
zapped 1. *adj* (*dead tired*) tsukareha-teta 疲れ果てた 2. *n* (*vigor*) genki 元気, katsuryoku 活力
zapper *n* (*remote control*) rimokon リモコン
zeal *n* (*enthusiasm*) netsui 熱意; netsujō 熱情; nesshin 熱心
zebra *n* shimauma シマウマ・縞馬
Zen *n* (*Buddhism*) Zén 禅
Zen Buddhist *n* Zen sō 禅僧
zero *n* réi 零, zéro ゼロ; (*written symbol*) maru 丸
zest *n* 1. (*enthusiasm*) netsui 熱意 2. (*interest*) tsuyoi kyōmi 強い興味 3. (*enjoyment*) yorokobi 喜び

Zeus *n* Zeusu ゼウス
ZIP, zip code *n* yūbinbángō 郵便番号
zipper *n* chákku チャック, jíppā ジッパー; fásunā ファスナー
zinc *n* aen 亜鉛
zodiac *n* (*horoscope*) jūnikyū-zu 十二宮図
　Zodiac Years *n* jūnishi 十二支 → year
zombie *n* (*person in a trance-like state*) zonbi ゾンビ
zone *n* chítai 地帯, kúiki 区域; zōn ゾーン; tái 帯, ...-tai ...帯
zoo *n* dōbutsu-en 動物園
zoology *n* dōbutsú-gaku 動物学
zoom *n* kakudai 拡大, (*camera*) zūmu ズーム
　zoom lens *n* (*camera*) zūmu-renzu ズームレンズ
Zoroastrianism *n* Zoroasutā-kyō ゾロアスター教
zucchini *n* (*vegetable*) zukkīni ズッキーニ
zygote *n* (*human egg*) setsukōshi 接合子
zzz *n, interj* gūgū グーグー, ぐうぐう

Samuel E. Martin is one of the leading authorities on Japanese and Korean and the author of numerous books including *A Reference Grammar of Japanese*, *A Reference Grammar of Korean*, *Essential Japanese*, *Basic Japanese Conversation Dictionary*, and *Easy Japanese*.

Sayaka Khan has a BSC (Biology, 2000) from Waseda University. She has worked as a translator and interpreter for companies in various industries, such as patent offices, science think tanks, pharmaceutical firms, film productions, game companies, etc. She has established a translation corporation with her husband, Afaque Khan.

Fred Perry has a BA (History, 1956) from Yale University as well as an MBA from St Sophia University, Tokyo (1984). He arrived in Japan in 1956, and continues to live there today. He has worked as a market researcher and consultant. Traveling throughout Japan as part of his job has provided the opportunity to learn about the local dialects spoken in different parts of the country.